Auditing

8th edition

David N. Ricchiute

Deloitte & Touche Professor of Accountancy
University of Notre Dame

THOMSON

SOUTH-WESTERN

Australia · Canada · Mexico · Singapore · Spain · United Kingdom · United States

THOMSON

SOUTH-WESTERN

Auditing, 8e

David N. Ricchiute

VP/Editorial Director:
Jack W. Calhoun

Publisher:
Rob Dewey

Acquisitions Editor:
Julie Moulton

Developmental Editor:
Carol Bennett

Marketing Manager:
Keith Chassé

Production Editor:
Amy McGuire

Manager of Technology, Editorial:
Vicky True

Sr. Technology Project Editor:
Sally Nieman

Manufacturing Coordinator:
Doug Wilke

Production House:
Cover to Cover Publishing, Inc.

Printer:
Quebecor World Versailles
Versailles, Kentucky

Art Director:
Tippy McIntosh

Internal Designer:
John Robb

Cover Designer:
Brenda Grannan
Grannan Graphic Design, Ltd.

Cover Image:
Collage by Grannan Graphic
   Design, Ltd.
Umbrella by Think Stock/Alamy

ASIA (including India)
Thomson Learning
5 Shenton Way
#01-01 UIC Building
Singapore 068808

CANADA
Thomson Nelson
1120 Birchmount Road
Toronto, Ontario
Canada M1K 5G4

AUSTRALIA/NEW ZEALAND
Thomson Learning Australia
102 Dodds Street
Southbank, Victoria 3006
Australia

UK/EUROPE/MIDDLE
EAST/AFRICA
Thomson Learning
High Holborn House
50-51 Bedford Road
London WC1R 4LR
United Kingdom

LATIN AMERICA
Thomson Learning
Seneca, 53
Colonia Polanco
11560 Mexico
D.F.Mexico

SPAIN (includes Portugal)
Thomson Paraninfo
Calle Magallanes, 25
28015 Madrid, Spain

Preface

To the Instructor

Audit practice and education have been affected dramatically by:

- A sea of change in *standard setting* and *professional governance*,
- An understanding that *earnings management* and *fraud* are central to most financial *restatements*, and
- A transition away from first-person delivery by classroom instructors only and toward third-person *discovery* by students both within and outside of the classroom.

Each has influenced the eighth edition. To incorporate changes in *standard setting* and *governance*, the eighth edition exposes students to the *Sarbanes-Oxley Act*, to auditor-independence rules, and to standards of the Public Company Accounting Oversight Board (PCAOB) and the Auditing Standards Board (ASB). For example, on *Sarbanes-Oxley*, the text introduces Sections 201, Services Outside the Scope of Practice of Auditors (Chapters 1 and 2); 301, Public Company Audit Committees (Chapter 7); 302, Corporate Responsibility for Financial Reports (Chapter 3); and 404, Management Assessment of Internal Control (Chapters 8, 10, and 12). On independence, the text explains the SEC's auditor-independence rules, the PCAOB's rules on inspection, and the AICPA's practice-monitoring system (Chapter 4). And on standards, the text addresses the roles of the PCAOB and the ASB (Chapters 1, 3, and 4), and important recent releases and pronouncements, including PCAOB *Auditing Standard No. 2*, "An Audit of Internal Control Over Financial Reporting Performed in Conjunction with an Audit of Financial Statements" (Chapters 8, 10, and 12); ASB *Statement on Auditing Standards No. 99*, "Consideration of Fraud in a Financial Statement Audit" (Chapter 7); and GAO *Government Auditing Standards, 2003 Revision* (Chapter 19).

To incorporate *earnings management* and *fraud*, the eighth edition revises Chapters 1, 2, 4, 6–8, and 10–17 to introduce a number of transactions and events that—with or without an auditor's complicity—lead to public-company restatements, to SEC Accounting and Auditing Enforcement Releases, or to protracted litigation. For example, among the companies discussed in the text are Adelphia Communications, AOL, Aurora Foods, Bausch & Lomb, Bristol Myers Squibb, ClearOne Communications, Enron, Genesco, Global Crossing, W.R. Grace, Microsoft, Microstrategy, Miniscribe, Rite Aid, Royal Ahold, Safety-Kleen, Sunbeam, Waste Management, WorldCom, and Xerox.

To encourage *discovery* learning, the eighth edition integrates academic research, offers audit-documentation review cases, and proposes research projects that expose students to databases, annual reports, and the professional literature. For example, the text explains what research reveals about time budget pressure, consulting fees, auditor-client disagreements, and management discretion in earnings manipulation. And a research project asks the question: Why wouldn't a client correct the circumstances that give rise to a qualified opinion? Auditing education today demands that educators expose students to real issues in real companies, and to draw where possible a convincing line between the issues auditors confront in practice and the understanding an informed student can bring to bear. The ever-expanding scope of issues auditors face in practice demands that students take responsibility for life-long, discovery learning.

To the Student

Auditing conveys experience about professional services for which most students will have little or no prior understanding—a limitation that places students' comprehension at risk. For example, a novel presents a similar hurdle, but the novelist's task is different, in part because much of his or her craft centers on narrative properties that set a story in motion by accessing scenes from a reader's existing memories. In auditing education, however, students typically have no scripted scenes about practice, since they've had little prior exposure to information systems, evidence, and the like, thereby providing few memories on which the learning experience might draw. But the limitation of no prior understanding also presents an opportunity: The student comes to the material with few biases or expectations that limit the boundaries of understanding, providing the textbook and the instructor with a unique opportunity to shape professional practice into insight and to make seemingly sterile professional tasks come to life. I urge you as a student to exploit the material presented in this text by allowing its chapters to awaken in you a curiosity about auditing and about how practitioners come to some of the complex decisions and judgment processes inherent in practice today.

Features

Fraud, Restatement, and Earnings Management

Over the past half-decade, an unprecedented number of public companies restated financial statements. For example, the GAO reports that of 8,494 companies listed on the New York Stock Exchange, NASDAQ, or the American Stock Exchange throughout the six-year period, 1997–2002, no less that 895 restated previously issued financial statements. Combined, the market capitalizations of the restated companies declined by $95.6 billion.[1] More surprising, the companies restating included some of the largest U.S. multinational corporations, among them Enron, Global Crossing, MicroStrategy, Rite Aid, Sunbeam, Waste Management, and Xerox. The recent literature on restatement offers an uncommon opportunity to introduce to students the issues that give rise to audit failure. The eighth edition integrates lessons from the restatement literature in Chapters 1, 2, 4, 6–8, and 10–17, illustrating with the following among other companies and issues:

Chapter 2: *Sunbeam* (restructuring reserves), *WorldCom* (capitalized period costs); Chapter 4: *Enron* (unconsolidated special-purpose entities); Chapter 7: *Xerox* (ex-

---

1   U.S. GAO, *Financial Statement Restatements: Trends, Market Impacts, Regulatory Responses, and Remaining Challenges.* Washington, D.C.: GAO, 2002.

cess reserves); Chapter 8: *Rite Aid* (internal control weaknesses); Chapter 10: *Rite Aid* (deduction management); Chapter 11: *Bausch & Lomb* (revenue recognition), *Bristol Myers Squibb* (revenue recognition), *Chambers Development* (capitalized landfill costs), *ClearOne Communications* (revenue recognition), *Genesco* (nonexistent shipments), *Global Crossing* (indefeasible rights of use), *IGI, Inc.* (sales cutoff manipulation), *Sunbeam* (channel stuffing and bill & hold), *MicroStrategy* (software revenue); Chapter 13: *AOL* (capitalized advertising costs), *Aurora Foods* (trade promotion fees, *Royal Ahold* (trade promotion fees); Chapter 13: *W.R. Grace* (excess reserves); Chapter 14: *Safety-Kleen* (capitalized payroll costs); Chapter 15: *Gerber Scientific* (final priced inventory), *Miniscribe* (nonexistent inventory transfers), *Rite Aid* (inventory shrink), *Waste Management* (depreciation); Chapter 16: *Citigroup* (round-trip energy transactions), *Conseco* (impaired securities), *Microsoft* (interest-rate fluctuations); Chapter 17: *Adelphia Communications* (related parties).

Also on earnings management, each of the chapters on substantive tests addresses questions that bear on an auditor's responsibility in selected key accounting issues. For example, what are management's incentives; how can those incentives be impounded into earnings management; and what are the legal and ethical implications in accounting for area development and franchise fees (Chapter 11), environmental liabilities (Chapter 13), post-retirement health care obligations (Chapter 14), impaired assets (Chapter 15), and financial instruments (Chapter 16)?

Real World Illustrations

To ground otherwise abstract issues in reality, the eighth edition offers examples of real world applications for a number of issues apart from fraud and restatement: Chapter 1: *Alyeska Pipeline Service Co.* (operational auditing), *HarperCollins* (information services consulting), *Intel* (Internet financial statements), *Waste Management* (consulting fees); Chapter 2: *Citizens Utilities* (materiality); *Delphi Automotive Systems, JPMorgan Chase, Sprint* (nonaudit fees); WorldCom (cost capitalization); Chapter 4: *PTL Club* (unethical business practices); Chapter 6: *SmarTalk Teleservices* (competence of audit evidence); Chapter 7: *Merck & Co.* (auditing in the pharmaceutical industry), *Chevron* (vision charts); Chapter 8: *Levi Strauss & Co., Lockheed Martin* (Internet technology), *Verizon* (home page management and global markets); Chapter 10: *Baltimore Orioles, Texas Rangers* (location and marketing services consulting); Chapter 11: *General Electric* (receivables); *Wal-Mart* (cash equivalents); *Union Carbide* (revenue recognition policies); *Taco Bell, Burger King* (area franchise fees); Chapter 12: *Bank of America* (purchase consulting services); *Camp Fire Girls & Boys, General Motors* (outsourced information services); Chapter 13: *AOL* (capitalized costs); *Coca-Cola* (payables and accruals); *Westinghouse, Columbia Gas System Inc.* (Superfund compliance costs); Chapter 14: *Safety-Kleen* (capitalized payroll); Chapter 15: *IBM, AT&T, Battle Mountain Gold Company* (impaired assets); Chapter 17: *American Bank Note Holographics* (management representation letters); Chapter 18: *Marriott, PepsiCo, Xerox* (health care provider quality); *Lucent Technologies* (letters for underwriters).

Audit Documentation Review

The center of gravity in an auditor's early career employment evaluations rests squarely on his or her performance in documenting audit evidence. To help equip students to *prepare* audit documentation, the eighth edition incorporates documentation *review* cases. The documents are realistic, replicate issues illustrated in the text, and are designed to lend insight into what reviewers are likely to look for. The cases appear in Chapters 6, 11, 13, 15, and 16, and include common early career audit areas, such as accounts receivable front summary schedules, receivables confirmations, intercompany and interbank transfers, bank reconciliations, accounts payable, accrued property taxes, physical inventory observations, fixed assets and accumulated depreciation, and marketable securities.

Client Strategies

Not unlike Ernst & Young's *Business Process Analysis* and KPMG's *Business Measurement Process*, the client strategy template introduced in Chapter 7 offers students a means to visualize audit clients not only from the level of financial transactions, but also from the vantage point of management's risks, the strategies management undertakes to overcome risk, and the transactions and events that are the product of management's strategies. For example, Chapter 7 explains how discount demands from managed care groups, patient copayments for prescription drugs, and physician incentives to prescribe generics—none of which are captured at the transaction level of a company—can translate into competitive pricing demands that compel financial analysts to predict at-risk growth strategies, and auditors to revise audit risk, for a research-based pharmaceutical company.

Research Projects

The eighth edition includes over forty end-of-chapter research projects linked to the professional literature, to publicly available data sources, and to annual reports of the student's/instructor's choice. The projects are intended as out-of-class, discovery-learning exercises that do not necessarily lend themselves to unambiguous solutions. For example, the research projects address issues such as becoming familiar with the profession's controversies, self-regulation, preparing client strategy templates, reporting on financial distress, unethical business practices, litigation against public accounting firms, tort reform, using the Internet to understand a client's industry, managing change in a selected industry, management discretion in earnings manipulation, internal controls in a selected industry, annual reports and the audit process, assurance services and retail electronic commerce, and internal auditing in selected industries.

Integration of Information Technology

Information technology pervades contemporary practice, largely because most all audit and assurance service clients are computerized. As a result, rather than address computers as a free-standing chapter, the eighth edition:

- Integrates information technology and internal control in Chapter 8, introducing systems such as local area networks, telecommunications, end-user computing, service bureaus, and Internet technology; and computer-assisted audit techniques such as base case system evaluation, test data, integrated test facilities, parallel simulation, audit hooks, audit modules, and transaction tagging.
- Introduces automated documentation, database management systems software, spreadsheet software, and text retrieval software in Chapter 8.
- Illustrates computer-assisted audit techniques in Chapters 10, 11, 12, 13, and 15.

Integration of Academic Research

The eighth edition incorporates the results of relevant academic research about, for example: Chapter 2: independence, audit risk, materiality; Chapter 3: auditor changes, predicting audit qualifications, financial distress, market reaction to bankruptcy filings; Chapter 6: heuristics and biases; Chapter 7: audit committee effectiveness, auditor-client disagreements, communication between predecessor and successor auditors, time budget pressure, analytical procedures, evidence planning, the review process; Chapter 10: revenue recognition, management incentives, share prices and management changes, predicting takeover targets, qualified opinions and share prices; Chapter 14: the choice of alternatives affecting health care obligations; Chapter 15: discretionary write-downs; Chapter 18: the voluntary purchase of quarterly reviews.

Risk and Evidence

The text, particularly Chapters 2, 6, and 7 and Parts III (Auditing the Revenue/ Receipt and the Expenditure/Disbursement Cycles) and IV (Auditing Other Cycles and Completing an Audit), explicitly incorporates the audit risk model from *SAS No. 47*, "Audit Risk and Materiality in Conducting an Audit," and the financial statement assertions from *SAS No. 31*, "Evidential Matter." The eighth edition devotes seven chapters to tests of controls and to substantive tests within four major transaction cycles: the revenue/receipt cycle (Chapters 10 and 11), the expenditure/disbursement cycle (Chapters 12, 13, and 14), the conversion cycle (Chapter 15), and the financing cycle (Chapter 16).

Professional Literature and Articles

The text provides extensive discussion of, and references to, the professional literature, including the Auditing Standards Board's *Statements on Auditing Standards* and *Statements on Standards for Attestation Services*; the Public Company Accounting Oversight Board's *Auditing Standards* and *Releases*; contemporary articles from magazines, journals, and newspapers like the *Journal of Accountancy*, *Auditing: A Journal of Practice & Theory*, *The Accounting Review*, *The Wall Street Journal*, *The New York Times*, *Accounting Today*, *Public Accounting Report*, *Business Week*, and *Fortune*, and important reports and monographs such as *Internal Control: Integrated Framework* (the COSO Report), and Mautz and Sharaf's *The Philosophy of Auditing*.

Edit/Update

All of the chapters have been edited for clarity of exposition and updated for, among other things:

- The *Sarbanes-Oxley Act* (Chapters 1, 2, 3, 7, 8, 10, and 12);
- ASB *Statement on Auditing Standards No. 99*, "Consideration of Fraud in a Financial Statement Audit" (Chapter 7);
- PCAOB *Auditing Standard No. 2*, "An Audit of Internal Control Over Financial Reporting Performed in Conjunction with a Financial Statement Audit" (Chapter 7);
- PCAOB *Auditing Standard No. 3*, "Audit Documentation" (Chapter 5);
- PCAOB rules on inspection (Chapter 4);
- SEC auditor-independence rules (Chapters 2, 4);

- SEC *Staff Accounting Bulletin No. 99*, "Materiality" (Chapter 2);
- SEC *Staff Accounting Bulletin No. 104*, "Revenue Recognition" (Chapter 11);
- AICPA Practice-Monitoring System (Chapter 4);
- AICPA Audit Practice Release *Audit Issues in Revenue Recognition* (Chapter 11);
- AICPA Audit Practice Release *Audit Sampling* (Chapter 9);
- Panel on Audit Effectiveness, *Report* (Chapters 2, 7, 8, 11, 17);
- GAO *Government Auditing Standards* (The "Yellow Book"), *2003 Revision* (Chapter 19); and
- Other recent PCAOB *Auditing Standards*, ASB *Statements on Auditing Standards*, and ARSC *Statements on Standards for Attestation Engagements* on, for example, attestation standards, information technology, audit adjustments, audit committee communications, management representations, establishing an understanding with clients, communications between predecessor and successor auditors, internal control, internal auditing, letters for underwriters, using specialists, compliance auditing, and compliance attestation.

Sampling (optional)

The eighth edition streamlines sampling into a single chapter that instructors may choose to cover or to omit. Also optional, instructors may selectively cover sampling in Chapters 10 through 13, which briefly illustrate audit sampling applications as follows:

Tests of controls:
- Chapter 10: Attributes estimation applied to billing.
- Chapter 12: Sequential sampling applied to cash disbursements.

Substantive tests:
- Chapter 11: PPS sampling applied to accounts receivable.
- Chapter 13: Nonstatistical sampling applied to accounts payable.

Organization

The eighth edition of *Auditing* is organized in five parts:

Part One: Responsibilities and Reporting

Chapters 1 through 5 introduce auditing and other assurance services, professional standards, reports, and a practitioner's responsibilities for ethical behavior and legal liability. Chapter 1, "An Introduction to Audit and Other Assurance Services," an overview of the public accounting profession, distinguishes among auditing, attestation, other assurance services, and consulting; introduces and motivates the demand for financial statement auditing; describes audit standard-setting; and introduces operational and compliance audits. Chapter 2, "Standards, Materiality, and Risk," introduces the profession's auditing and attestation standards in the context of independence, due care, evidence, and reporting and explains the roles of materiality and risk in a practitioner's interpretation of auditing standards. Chapter 3, "Audit Reports," introduces reports on assurance and attestation services, the standard audit report, the required circumstances and wording for modifications to a standard report, and reporting requirements for comparative financial statements and for financial statements prepared for use in a foreign country. Chapter 4, "Professional Ethics," considers questions of ethics through the AICPA's Code of Professional Conduct and the SEC's Auditor Independence Rules, discusses the collapse of Enron and Andersen, addresses the PCAOB's rules for inspections, the AICPA's Center for Public Company Audit Firms for firms that audit public companies, and the AICPA's peer review program for firms that audit nonpublic companies. Chapter 5, "Legal Liability," addresses the independent auditor's civil and criminal liability, describes an auditor's common law liability to clients and third parties, summarizes an auditor's liability under the *Securities Act of 1933* and the *Securities Exchange Act of 1934* and responsibility to detect and report illegal acts.

Part Two: The Audit Process and Internal Control

Chapters 6, 7, and 8 introduce evidence, the audit process, the consideration of internal control in a financial statement audit, and an audit of internal control under the *Sarbanes-Oxley Act*, Section 404 and PCAOB *Auditing Standard No. 2*. Chapter 6, "Evidence," addresses evidence and its relationship to financial statement assertions and procedures; cognitive biases that can interfere with interpreting evidence; the nature of tests of controls, substantive tests, and analytical procedures; and the purpose and content of audit documentation. Chapter 7, "The Audit Process and Detecting Fraud," introduces the major activities in the audit process—including the decision to accept an engagement, planning, interim and year-end audit work, and an auditor's responsibility to detect and report fraud. Chapter 8, "Internal Control," introduces the well-accepted framework developed by the Committee of Sponsoring Organizations (COSO) of the Treadway Commission, discusses an auditor's responsibility to consider internal control and to assess control risk, and integrates an auditor's responsibility in a public-company engagement to audit internal control over financial reporting under the *Sarbanes-Oxley Act*, SEC rules, and PCAOB standards.

Part Three: Auditing the Revenue/Receipt and the Expenditure/Disbursement Cycles

Chapter 9, "Audit Sampling," an optional chapter, introduces attribute estimation, sequential (stop-or-go) sampling, probability-proportional-to-size (PPS) sampling, and nonstatistical sampling. Chapters 10 through 13 introduce, discuss, and illustrate detailed tests of controls and substantive tests. Chapter 10, "Sales and Cash Receipts Transactions," and Chapter 11 "Accounts Receivable and Cash Balances," address the revenue/receipt cycle, sales and cash receipts transactions, accounts receivable, cash balances, and management discretion in revenue recognition. Chapter 12 "Purchases and Cash Disbursements Transactions," and Chapter 13, "Accounts Payable, Prepaids, and Accrued Liabilities," turn attention to purchases and cash disbursement transactions, accounts payable, prepaid expenses, accrued liabilities, and management discretion in accounting for environmental liabilities.

Part Four: Auditing Other Cycles and Completing an Audit

Chapters 14, 15, and 16 introduce tests of controls and substantive tests applicable, respectively, to personnel, payroll, and accounting for post-retirement health care; inventory, fixed assets, and accounting for impaired assets; and investments, debt, equity, and accounting for financial instruments. Chapter 17 completes the discussion of procedures, addressing a practitioner's considerable responsibilities when completing an engagement—for example, auditing accounting estimates, the review for subsequent events, communicating with the audit committee, inquiries of a client's legal counsel, management representation letters, and forming an opinion on financial statements.

Part Five: Other Assurance and Attestation Services, Compliance and Internal Auditing

Chapters 18 and 19 focus on engagements other than financial statement audits and two additional, and highly prominent, types of auditing in the United States. Chapter 18, "Other Assurance and Attestation Services," discusses examples of assurance services for the twenty-first century and a variety of contemporary attestation services, including reviews of financial statements, interim financial information, internal control, letters for underwriters, personal financial statements, financial forecasts and projections, and the application of accounting principles. Chapter 19, "Compliance Auditing and Internal Auditing," appears on the web http://ricchiute.swlearning.com) and introduces the governmental auditor's compliance audit under generally accepted government auditing standards, the GAO's "Yellow Book," and the *Single Audit Act*, and discusses the internal auditor's operational audit.

End-of-Chapter Materials

The end of each chapter includes:

- Key terms referenced to the chapter page on which the term is introduced and to a comprehensive Glossary at the end of the book.
- Extensive references to:
  - Authoritative literature (for example, PCAOB *Auditing Standards*, ASB *Statements on Auditing Standards*, SEC *Staff Accounting Bulletins*),
  - Professional reports (for example, *Panel on Audit Effectiveness: Report and Recommendations*),
  - Articles in research journals (for example, *The Accounting Review, Auditing: A Journal of Practice & Theory*), newspapers (for example, *The Wall Street Journal, The New York Times*), and business periodicals (for example, *BusinessWeek, Fortune*); and
  - Legislation (for example, the *Sarbanes-Oxley Act*, the *Private Securities Litigation Reform Act*).
- Review questions.
- Multiple choice questions.
- Problems and discussion cases.
- Research projects.

Supplemental Materials

Several teaching and learning aids are substantially revised or new to the eighth edition:

- **Solutions Manual**, 0-324-22631-4 (prepared by David N. Ricchiute, University of Notre Dame): The solutions manual contains error-checked solutions to all review questions, multiple choice questions, and problems and discussion cases.

- **Instructor's Resource Manual** (prepared by Barbara Muller, Arizona State University): Expanded for the eighth edition and located at the website (**http://ricchiute.swlearning.com**) and on the Instructor's Resource CD-ROM (0-324-22634-9), the instructor's manual includes a complete set of lecture notes for each chapter, sample syllabi, and transparency masters.
- **Test Bank**, 0-324-22630-6 (prepared by Jan Colbert, Western Kentucky University): Extensively revised and expanded for the eighth edition, the test bank offers multiple choice and short-answer questions and problems.
- **PowerPoint Presentations** (prepared by Gail Wright, Bryant College): Complete PowerPoint presentations for each chapter in the text appear at the website (**http://ricchiute.swlearning.com**) and on the Instructor's Resource CD-ROM (0-324-22634-9).
- **Instructor's Resource CD-ROM**, 0-324-22634-9: Includes on CD-ROM the Solutions Manual, Instructor's Resource Manual, Test Bank, ExamView Testing Software, and PowerPoint Presentations, enabling the instructor to customize the materials for his or her use.
- **ExamView Testing Software:** The software contains in electronic form all of the test bank questions and problems in an easy-to-use test-creation package that is compatible with Microsoft Windows. Instructors can select, add, or edit questions and problems and can administer online questions on the Internet or in local-area or wide-area networks.
- **Web Site** (**http://ricchiute.swlearning.com**): Designed for *Auditing*, eighth edition, the Web site includes online and downloadable instructor and student resources, online quizzes with automatic feedback, in-depth Internet cases, and PowerPoint lectures.

Acknowledgments

I gratefully acknowledge the following people for comments and suggestions:

Michael Akers
Marquette University

Joyce Allen
Xavier University

John Anderson
Virginia Polytechnic Institute and State University

Barbara Apostolou
Louisiana State University

Joseph Botana
Lakeland College

Edmund Boyle
University of Rhode Island

Freddie Choo
San Francisco State University

Jan Colbert
Western Kentucky University

Bill Coyle
Babson College

David Davidson
California State University at Long Beach

John Delaney
Southwestern University

Rajib Doogar
University of Illinois at Urbana-Champaign

Phillip Driscoll
Syracuse University

John Edwards
Louisiana Tech University

Keith Ehrenreich
California State University at Pomona

Robert Eskew
Purdue University

Rebecca Evans
University of Alaska, Anchorage

Dick Fremgen
University of Notre Dame

Linda Frye
Northwest Missouri State University

Stephen Goldberg
Purdue University

Jeremy Griffin
Borg Warner

Ron King
Washington University

David Kerr
Texas A&M University

Joyce Lambert
University of New Orleans

Mark Kovarik
PricewaterhouseCoopers LLP

Stanley Lewis
The University of Southern Mississippi

Donald Loster
University of California at Santa Barbara

D. Jordan Lowe
University of San Diego

David Middleton
Indiana Institute of Technology

Robert Minnear
Emory University

Fred Neumann
*University of Illinois at Urbana-
    Champaign*

Dave Nichols
University of Mississippi

Danny Pannese
Sacred Heart University

Marshall Pitman
The University of Texas at San Antonio

Mattie Porter
University of Houston-Clear Lake

Doug Prawitt
Brigham Young University

Sri Ramamoorti
Arthur Andersen LLP

John Rigsby
Mississippi State University

Michael Ruble
Western Washington University

Donna Rudderow
Franklin University

Brian Shapiro
University of Minnesota

Glen Sanderson
Illinois State University

Lisa Sedor
University of Notre Dame

Cindy Seipel
New Mexico State University

Glen Sumners
Louisiana State University

Susan Swanger
Western Carolina University

Rahmat Tavallali
Walsh University

Don Tidrick
Northern Illinois University

Manual A. Tipgos
Indiana University—Southeast

Edward R. Walker
McNeese State University

Dieter Weiss
Ferris State University

H. James Williams
Grand Valley State University

James Yardley
*Virginia Polytechnic Institute
    and State University*

In addition, I thank the verifiers for this edition: **Mike Metzcar**, *Indiana Wesleyan University*, and **Edward R. Walker**, *McNeese State University*.

David N. Ricchiute
University of Notre Dame

About the Author

David N. Ricchiute, Deloitte & Touche Professor of Accountancy, University of Notre Dame, has published articles in *The Accounting Review*, the *Journal of Accounting Research*, *Accounting Organizations & Society*, the *Journal of Applied Psychology*, *Organizational Behavior and Human Decision Processes*, the *Journal of Experimental Psychology*, *Issues in Accounting Education*, the *Journal of Accountancy*, and *The CPA Journal*, among others. Formerly on the audit staff of Price Waterhouse (now PricewaterhouseCoopers) and a visiting professor at the University of Michigan, Ann Arbor, he has served as Director of Research of the Audit Section of the American Accounting Association (AAA), on the editorial boards of accounting and auditing journals, as a professional and educational consultant to accounting firms, law firms, public companies, and state audit agencies throughout the country, and on committees of the AICPA and the AAA. His teaching awards include: *Outstanding Teacher of the Year*, College of Business Administration, University of Notre Dame.

Brief Contents

Contents

Attestation and Audit Services 3
The Demand for Financial Statement Audits; Financial Statements on the Internet; Financial Statement Audits and the Scientific Method of Inquiry

Audit Standard-Setting 9
The American Institute of Certified Public Accountants; The Securities and Exchange Commission; Prior Authoritative Bodies; The Auditing Standards Board and the Accounting and Review Services Committee; The Public Company Accounting Oversight Board and the Chief Auditor and Director of Professional Standards

Accounting, Auditing, and the Influence of Prominent Professional Organizations 12
The Financial Accounting Standards Board and the Governmental Accounting Standards Board; Professional Organizations

Other Audit Services 14
Operational Audits; Compliance Audits

Other Attestation Services 15

Consulting and Other Assurance Services 16
Consulting; Other Assurance Services

Values, Competencies, and Services 19

Summary 21

Audit and Attestation Standards 32
The AICPA Adopts and Revises Standards; Independence; Due Care; Evidence; Reporting

Risk 46
Attestation Risk and Audit Risk; Inherent Risk, Control Risk, and Detection Risk; Measuring Audit Risk and Detection Risk; Business Risk; Audit Risk and Auditor Failure

Part 1

Responsibilities and Reporting

1 Chapter

An Introduction to Audit and Other Assurance Services

Major topics discussed in this chapter are:

- The nature of audit and attestation services.
- The demand for financial statement audits.
- The audit standard-setting process.
- Organizations that influence accounting and auditing.
- Operational audits, compliance audits, and nonattest services.
- Other attestation services.
- Consulting and other assurance services.

Decision makers demand financial statement audits precisely because audits add value: Audits reduce information risk (the risk that information in financial statements is misstated materially), thereby reducing a company's cost of capital (the cost a company incurs for equity and debt). The link among financial statement audits, information risk, and the cost of capital is well understood in the financial community and, for that matter, well documented in the literature. For example, research on bank loan interest rates found that audited companies pay lower interest rates (on average, 25 basis points lower) and that the interest rate savings represent up to 50 percent of audit fees.[1]

However, events over the past several years have threatened investor confidence in auditor credibility. For example, an unprecedented number of public companies restated *audited* financial statements[2] and the U.S. Securities and Exchange Commission settled accounting fraud charges against individuals in several major companies, including Enron, WorldCom, and Adelphia Communications.[3] Regulators and Congress responded in kind. For example, in the most sweeping legislation on corporate governance since the Securities Acts of 1933 and

---

1   D. W. Blackwell, T. R. Noland, and D. B. Winters, "The Value of Auditor Assurance: Evidence from Loan Pricing," *Journal of Accounting Research* (Spring 1998), pp. 57–70.

2   See C. Bryan-Low, "Error-Driven Restatements Rose Again in 2003, But Pace Slowed," *The Wall Street Journal* (January 13, 2004), p. C3; and U.S. General Accounting Office, *Financial Statement Restatements; Trends, Market Impacts, Regulatory Responses, and Remaining Challenges* (GAO-03-138). Washington, D.C.: U.S. General Accounting Office, 2002.

3   SEC Accounting and Auditing Enforcement Release No. 1942, "SEC Settles Civil Fraud Charges Filed Against Andrew J. Fastow, Former Enron Chief Financial Officer" (January 14, 2004); SEC Accounting and Auditing Enforcement Release No. 1811, "The Honorable Jed Rakoff Approves Settlement of the SEC's Claim for a Civil Penalty Against WorldCom" (July 7, 2003); SEC Accounting and Auditing Enforcement Release No. 1664, "SEC v. Adelphia Communications Corp." (November 14, 2002).

1934, Congress in 2002 enacted the *Sarbanes-Oxley Act*, intended in part to restore investor confidence by redirecting the authority for audit standard-setting to an independent Public Company Accounting Oversight Board and by restricting the services an incumbent auditor can perform for a public company.

Clearly, the profession faces a difficult challenge. For example, in a speech at a National Conference on SEC Developments, Donald Nicolaisen, SEC Chief Accountant, said accountants who "fail to recognize that our profession is changing, and that each individual and firm must embrace a culture that champions the interests of investors, should not be surprised if they become the focus of disciplinary action."[4] However, the profession has been challenged before—for example, the unprecedented McKesson Robbins fraud of the 1930s, Equity Funding and the Moss and Metcalf committee congressional investigations in the 1970s, the savings and loan industry debacle and Dingell Committee hearings of the 1980s[5]— and is positioned to face the challenges of today. One could have picked no more interesting time to study auditing, in part because controversy has brought about sweeping change, the effects of which are uncertain.

This chapter explains the intuition underlying audit services. The chapter begins by introducing financial statement audits, the dominant assurance service that practicing auditors offer today. In turn, the chapter motivates the demand for financial statement audits, and describes audit standard-setting and the organizations that influence practice. The chapter concludes by introducing operational and compliance audits, other attestation services, and consulting and other assurance services.

Attestation and Audit Services

Assurance services are *three-party contracts* in which an assurer reports on (or improves) the *quality of information*. As Figure 1-1 illustrates, some assurance services are called *attestations*, and some attestations are called *audits*. Attestation and audit service are offered commonly today by professional service providers traditionally called *public accounting firms*. Most firms are organized as limited liability partnerships (LLPs), which limit the extent of a partner's liability for claims against the firm to his or her investment in the firm, although litigants can make claims against a partner's personal assets for liability linked to his or her own actions. The professional staffs of public accounting firms include **certified public accountants (CPAs)** and professionals with expertise in areas as diverse as actuarial science, organizational design, government regulation, information processing, employee benefits, and human resource management. The four largest firms, called the Big Four, are Deloitte & Touche LLP, Ernst & Young LLP, KPMG LLP, and PricewaterhouseCoopers LLP. Other international firms include BDO Seidman LLP and Grant Thornton LLP. Prominent regional firms, some with

---

4   K. Rankin, "SEC's Nicolaisen: Embrace a Culture of Investor Protection," *Accounting Today* (January 26–February 8, 2004), pp. 5, 33.

5   J. McCarten, "The Greatest Accountant in the World," *The New Yorker* (December 16, 1939), pp. 86–95; AICPA, *Report of the Special Committee on Equity Funding*. New York: AICPA, 1975; U.S. House of Representatives, *Federal Regulation and Regulatory Reform (Moss Committee Report)*. Washington, D.C.: U.S. Government Printing Office, 1976; U.S. Senate, *The Accounting Establishment (Metcalf Committee Report)*. Washington, D.C.: U.S. Government Printing Office, 1976; N. N. Minnow, "Accountants' Liability and the Litigation Explosion," *Journal of Accountancy* (September 1984), pp. 70–86; J. Gerth, "The Savings Debacle: How Safeguards Failed—A Blend of Tragedy and Farce," *The New York Times* (July 3, 1990), p. D1; U.S. House of Representatives, *SEC and Corporate Audits: Part I (Dingell Committee Hearings)*, 1985.

FIGURE 1-1:
Audit, Attestation, and Other Assurance Services

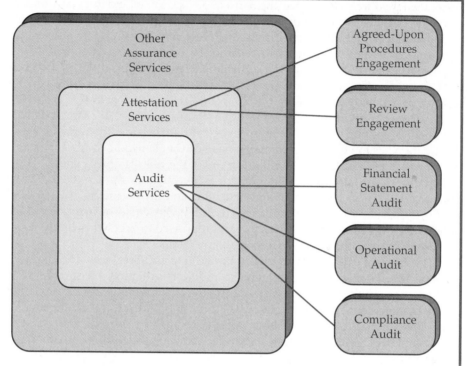

Agreed-upon procedures engagement: An attestation service in which the independent accountant is engaged to report on an item using procedures the contracting parties agree to.

Review engagement: An attestation service in which the independent accountant performs analytical procedures, makes inquiries of client personnel, and issues a report that provides limited (sometimes called negative) assurance, using language that states the accountant is "not aware of any material modifications that should be made to the financial statements in order for them to be in conformity with GAAP."

Financial statement audit: An audit in which the certified public accountant determines whether financial statements present fairly, in all material respects, financial position, results of operations, and cash flows in accordance with GAAP.

Operational audit: An audit performed by an entity's internal auditors (or by independent auditors) to assess the efficiency and effectiveness of management's operating procedures.

Compliance audit: An audit designed to assess whether a not-for-profit entity's financial statements are presented fairly in accordance with GAAP and whether the entity has complied with applicable laws and regulations.

international affiliations, include BKD LLP, Crowe Chizek LLP, Moss Adams LLP, and Plante & Moran LLP.

    Attestation services are a type of assurance service in which an attestor (an independent accountant) offers assurance about subject matter (for example, compliance with debt covenants) that is the responsibility of another party (for example, a manufacturer). Two attestation services are quite common in practice (Figure 1-1): agreed-upon procedures engagements and review engagements. In an **agreed-upon procedures engagement**, the attestor is engaged to report on an item using procedures the contracting parties agree to. For example, the Federal Depository Insurance Corporation (FDIC) *Improvement Act of 1991* requires that independent accountants perform agreed-upon procedures that test an insured depository institution's compliance with the FDIC's "safety and soundness" laws and regulations, which relate primarily to loans made to insiders and to dividend requirements. The agreed-upon procedures are similar in all FDIC engagements and were developed jointly by the AICPA and the American Bankers Association. Other common attestation services include debt covenant compliance, financial forecasts and projections, descriptions of accounting information systems, inventory quantities and locations, and contract costs.[6]

In a **review engagement**, a common attestation service for financial statements, a public accounting firm gives limited assurance about whether an entity's financial statements conform with generally accepted accounting principles (GAAP). Review services are usually purchased by small, privately owned companies whose creditors are willing to rely on limited assurances, rather than to demand that a business purchase a more expensive financial statement audit. In practice, public accounting firms offer two types of attestation services for financial statements: a *review*, which provides limited (sometimes called "negative") assurance, and a financial statement *audit* (discussed in detail next), which provides positive assurance. The difference in the level of assurance accountants give in reviews and in financial statement audits corresponds to the difference in the amount of effort required to perform each service. (Incidentally, accounting firms also perform a financial statement service, mostly for small companies, that offers no assurance at all: a *compilation* of financial statements, which merely compiles financial information into proper form.) In a **financial statement audit** performed by a certified public accountant, the auditor assures management's written financial statement assertions. For example, in the financial statement disclosure "Inventory . . . . $2,000,000," management makes no less than five assertions: inventory physically exists, includes all products on hand, is represented by rights of ownership, is stated at the lower-of-cost-or-market, and is classified properly as a current asset.

The Demand for Financial Statement Audits

To illustrate why **audit services** are demanded, consider the case of The Coca-Cola Company, the world's largest manufacturer, marketer, and distributor of nonalcoholic beverage concentrates and syrups. In 2003 alone, Coca-Cola received approximately $3.0 billion and $150 million, respectively, from the issuance of debt and equity. Does it weigh on you that Coca-Cola had compelling incentives to overstate their financial position (for example, by overstating assets or net income), thereby biasing investors' decisions to participate in either offering? A competent investor likely would not have participated in Coca-Cola's offerings absent a written assurance (called an *audit report*) from an independent party (an **independent auditor**) that the assertions embodied within Coca-Cola's financial statements are reliable. An audit provides Coca-Cola with a singularly valuable service: Lacking an audit, Coca-Cola's cost of obtaining capital would have been much higher, since investors would have demanded compensation (for example,

---

6   K. S. Brackney and G. L. Helms, "A Survey of Attestation Practices," *Auditing: A Journal of Practice & Theory* (Fall 1996), pp. 85–98.

a lower stock price) for *information risk*, the risk that Coca-Cola's financial information was misstated.

In addition to investors, Coca-Cola's financial statement disclosures reveal other parties who have a need, and therefore have established a demand, for an audit. Examples include employee pension and restricted stock option award plan participants; post-retirement benefit plan participants; dividend and cash investment plan participants; and Coca-Cola Enterprises, the world's largest soft-drink bottler. Other parties not named in the financial statements include labor unions, suppliers, stock exchanges, regulatory agencies (for example, the SEC), and tax authorities (for example, the IRS, state sales tax agencies), all of which are at risk if Coca-Cola's financial statements are misstated. Internal users, such as management, financial officers, and sales executives, also rely on audit reports.

None of the parties who demand an audit are positioned to obtain private information about a company from anyone other than the company's management, placing them at a comparative disadvantage when negotiating contracts with the company. As a result, all of these parties are at risk if management manipulates private information into misleading financial statements. For example, assume that Citigroup loaned Coca-Cola $100 million and stipulated that the five-year loan would be payable immediately if Coca-Cola's current ratio (current assets/current liabilities) fell below one-to-one (called a *debt covenant*). Because the incentives of Coca-Cola's management (for example, profit sharing, growth in shareholder wealth) differ from those of Citigroup (for example, loan repayment, protection of principal), management has incentives to misstate the financial statements for their self-interest. For example, at the end of the loan period's first year, management could deliberately understate current liabilities, thereby inflating the current ratio and masking the debt-covenant violation.

To minimize the risk of materially misstated financial statements, users demand that an unbiased monitor (an independent auditor) report on whether the assertions embodied within management's financial statements are reliable. In the United States (and in some foreign countries), audits are not only demanded by users but they are required by law as a prerequisite for listing on a stock exchange. The *Securities Exchange Act of 1934*, which regulates the trading of securities, requires that a publicly traded company file Form 10-K annually with the Securities and Exchange Commission. Apart from nonfinancial information about the company, management, and the directors, Form 10-K also includes an independent auditor's report and audited financial statements. Companies that fail to file Form 10-K can be delisted from the stock exchange on which shares are traded, effectively precluding the company from obtaining capital in regulated U.S. markets.

Financial statements are audited by independent auditors, but the statements are the representations and responsibility of management, not the auditor. An independent auditor is responsible for expressing an opinion on management's financial statements, but management is responsible for the assertions embodied within the financial statements. For example, management, not the auditor, is responsible that all recorded assets and liabilities exist, that all recorded transactions occurred, that no transactions are omitted, that assets are the rights and liabilities are the obligations of the entity, that all disclosed amounts are appropriate, and that the financial statements are properly classified and disclosed.

Even though auditors audit management's financial statements, management, ironically, is not the auditor's client. The client in the audit of a public company is the board of directors, the body elected by shareholders to protect their interests. Although this has never been unclear, a decade ago the Public Oversight Board (until *Sarbanes-Oxley*, an independent monitor of the public's confidence in the audit process) made clear the relationship among auditors, management, and the board of directors:

. . . it is essential for the auditing profession to bring greater clarity to the issue of who is their client. The board of directors, as the representative of the shareholders, should be the client, not corporate management. Corporate boards . . . should make this clear to auditors.[7]

Financial Statements on the Internet

Traditionally, companies have printed annual financial statements and audit reports in Annual Reports to Shareholders that are hard bound and self-contained. More recently, some companies have posted financial statements and audit reports on the Internet with hyperlinks to sites that offer information extraneous to the audited financial statements. For example, in a footnote explaining a company's revenue recognition policies, management may have embedded a link to continuously updated promotional information about product performance and quality. The hyperlink causes a problem: How can the reader be made aware that the auditor's report applies to the financial statements but not to information accessed by the link? In practice, some companies have overcome the problem with annual report page headings (for example, "Annual Report"), with dedicated Web page warnings (for example, "You are leaving the financial statements"), and with print defaults that print the financial statements without either the hyperlinks or the hyperlinked text.

Other companies use headings to alert readers that hyperlinked material is unaudited. For example, Intel's consolidated financial statements (**http://www. intel.com**) include a footnote that introduces unaudited quarterly financial information this way:

Intel

Supplement information (unaudited)

Quarterly information for the two years ended December 25, 2004 is presented in "Financial information by quarter (unaudited)."

The form of management's financial statements—hard copy or electronic—has no bearing on a financial statement audit but can cause confusion about the extent of an auditor's responsibilities.

Financial Statement Audits and the Scientific Method of Inquiry

Some years ago, the American Accounting Association's Committee on Basic Auditing Concepts drafted a definition of auditing that offers some insight into the audit process:

Auditing is a systematic process of objectively obtaining and evaluating evidence regarding assertions about economic actions and events to ascertain the degree of correspondence

---

7 Public Oversight Board, *Directors, Management, and Auditors: Allies in Protecting Shareholder Interests.* Stamford, CT: POB, 1995, p. 4.

between those assertions and established criteria and communicating the results to interested users.[8]

The definition implies that auditing involves both an investigation and a report. *Investigation* means gathering and evaluating evidence as a basis for *reporting* an opinion about whether management's financial statement assertions correspond in all material respects with GAAP. The opinion conveyed in an audit report may indicate that the financial statements present fairly financial position, results of operations, and cash flows in conformity with GAAP; that the statements present fairly *except for* a matter revealed in the report; or that the statements are not presented fairly. Alternatively, the auditor may not report an opinion at all, for example, if sufficient evidence cannot be obtained to support or refute management's assertions.

The audit process begins when an entity engages an independent auditor and ends when the auditor issues an audit report. A similar process—the *scientific method of inquiry*—occurs when a scientist confronts a research problem. Like the audit process, the scientific method of inquiry is a framework for reaching reasoned, defendable conclusions. Cohen and Nagel, in *An Introduction to Logic and Scientific Method*, capture the essence of the scientific method:

Scientific method . . . is the persistent application of logic as the common feature of all reasoned knowledge . . . but in essence scientific method is simply the pursuit of truth as determined by logical considerations.[9]

If the words *scientific method* were replaced by *auditing*, Cohen and Nagel would capture the essence of auditing as well.

To illustrate the similarities between the scientific method of inquiry and a financial statement audit, Figure 1-2 equates each step in the scientific method to the steps in the audit process. As the illustration implies, auditing can be thought of as a special application of the scientific method of inquiry.

FIGURE 1-2: *Auditing and the Scientific Method of Inquiry*

Scientific Method	Financial Statement Audit
Observe a problem.	A client requests an opinion on whether financial statements present fairly in all material respects financial position, results of operations, and cash flows.
Formulate a hypothesis.	Financial statements present fairly in all material respects.
Gather evidence.	Assess risk, design audit procedures.
Evaluate evidence and conclude.	Evaluate the evidence gathered and conclude whether the evidence supports, refutes, or is inconclusive that the financial statements are presented fairly.

8   Committee on Basic Auditing Concepts, "A Statement of Basic Auditing Concepts," *The Accounting Review,* supplement to vol. 47 (1972), p. 18.

9   M. R. Cohen and E. Nagel, *An Introduction to Logic and Scientific Method*. New York: Harcourt, Brace, and Company, 1934, p. 192.

Audit Standard-Setting

Several organizations and authoritative bodies influence audit practice today, including (1) the American Institute of Certified Public Accountants, the national trade association of CPAs; (2) the Securities and Exchange Commission, a federal agency empowered to protect securities traders; (3) the Auditing Standards Board, a senior technical body of the AICPA designated to issue authoritative pronouncements for nonpublic company audit and attestation services; (4) the Accounting and Review Services Committee, another senior technical body of the AICPA designated to issue authoritative pronouncements for nonpublic company accounting and review services; and (5) the Public Company Accounting Oversight Board, empowered in 2003 by the *Sarbanes-Oxley Act of 2002* to issue authoritative pronouncements for public company audit and attestation services.

The American Institute of Certified Public Accountants

The **American Institute of Certified Public Accountants (AICPA)** is a professional trade association with over 400,000 members. Although all voting members are CPAs, not all offer audit services. For example, some hold positions in industry or government (as CEOs, CFOs, controllers, financial officers, and internal auditors); others teach in colleges and universities; and still others serve in the executive and legislative branches of federal, state, and local governments. Since organizing in the late nineteenth century, the AICPA has had a marked influence on accounting and auditing thought. For example, the Institute issues pronouncements about nonpublic company accounting, auditing, attestation, professional ethics, management advisory, and tax services. Studies done by or for the AICPA have resulted in publications such as Audit and Accounting Guides, Auditing Procedures Studies, and Auditing Research Monographs, none of which are binding on members, but all of which are available to the audits of nonpublic companies. The AICPA publishes a monthly periodical, the *Journal of Accountancy*, a leading professional publication devoted to current developments in accounting and auditing.

The Securities and Exchange Commission

Created by Congress in 1934, the **Securities and Exchange Commission (SEC)** consists of five presidentially appointed commissioners who, in conjunction with 3,100 staff in four divisions and 18 offices, regulate the registration and exchange of securities under the *Securities Act of 1933* and the *Securities Exchange Act of 1934*. The SEC is not empowered to issue authoritative auditing pronouncements per se, but does issue publications that govern publicly traded corporations in periodic filings to the SEC, including *Form 10-K*, the annual financial report; *Form 10-Q*, the quarterly financial report; and *Form 8-K*, a form filed when significant events occur, such as the sale of a subsidiary or a change in auditors. Currently, the SEC issues two types of releases that affect the independent auditors of public companies: *Financial Reporting Releases*, which announce accounting and auditing matters of general interest; and *Accounting and Auditing Enforcement Releases*, which announce accounting and auditing matters related to the SEC's enforcement activities. The SEC also issues *Staff Accounting Bulletins*, interpretations that guide practitioners when applying SEC regulations. For example, *Staff Accounting Bulletin No. 99*, "Materiality," discussed in Chapter 2, expresses the SEC's view that relying exclusively on numerical thresholds to assess materiality is wholly inappropriate.

Prior Authoritative Bodies

As illustrated in Figure 1-3, since the 1930s five succeeding standard-setting bodies have been empowered to issue authoritative guidelines for audit, attestation, and accounting services. In 1939, the AICPA appointed the **Committee on Auditing Procedure (CAP)** to ". . . examine into auditing procedure . . . in light of recent public discussions"—the "public discussions" referring to McKesson & Robbins' $19 million overstatement of inventory and accounts receivable in the mid-1930s. Although common today, McKesson & Robbins' auditors did not test the existence of recorded inventory or accounts receivable. In May 1939, the CAP issued a report, "Extensions of Auditing Procedure," which recommended physical inventory observations (Chapter 15) and accounts receivable confirmations (Chapter 11) as accepted audit practice. The report became the first of 54 **Statements on Auditing Procedure (SAP)** the CAP issued from 1939 to 1972.

FIGURE 1-3: *Standard-Setting Bodies*

Body	Tenure	Pronouncement
Nonpublic Companies		
Committee on Auditing Procedure (CAP)	1939–1972	Statements on Auditing Procedure (SAP)
Auditing Standards Executive Committee (AudSEC)	1972–1978	Statements on Auditing Standards (SAS)
Auditing Standards Board (ASB)	1978–present	Statements on Auditing Standards (SAS)
Accounting and Review Services Committee (ARSC)	1978–present	Statements on Standards for Accounting and Review Services (SSARS)
Public Companies		
Public Company Accounting Oversight Board (PCAOB)	2003–present	Auditing Standards

In 1972, the name of the committee was changed to the **Auditing Standards Executive Committee (AudSEC)**, and the CAP's 54 SAPs were codified into *Statement on Auditing Standards (SAS) No. 1*. The title change from Statements on Auditing *Procedure* to **Statements on Auditing Standards (SAS)** suggested that the statements would interpret standards rather than merely promulgate procedures, underscoring AudSEC's role as a standard-setting body. From 1972 to 1978, AudSEC issued SAS Nos. 2 through 23, covering issues such as reports on audited financial statements, related-party transactions, the auditor's responsibility for detecting fraud, and illegal acts by clients.

The Auditing Standards Board and the Accounting and Review Services Committee

In 1978, the AICPA's independent Commission on Auditors' Responsibilities (the Cohen Commission) issued a 195-page report about the responsibilities of independent auditors. Section 10, "The Process of Establishing Auditing Standards," offered several criticisms of AudSEC, among them that SASs were typically published long after a controversial project first reached AudSEC's technical agenda and that most SASs were oriented toward audits of public companies to the exclusion of nonpublic companies, the major challenge of many smaller accounting firms.

As a partial response to these criticisms, the AICPA disbanded AudSEC and appointed two senior technical committees: the **Auditing Standards Board (ASB)**, a 15-member body designated to issue SASs and **Statements on Standards for Attestation Engagements (SSAE)**; and the **Accounting and Review Services Committee (ARSC)**, a 15-member body designated to issue **Statements on Standards for Accounting and Review Services (SSARS)** about unaudited financial information for nonpublic entities. The individual pronouncements of both bodies are numbered sequentially when issued, and the provisions of all pronouncements are codified within code sections of the *AICPA Professional Standards*. For example, SASs are codified within the AICPA's *Codification of Auditing Standards*.[10] Today, the pronouncements of the Auditing Standards Board and the Accounting and Review Services Committee apply to engagements for nonpublic companies. Audit and attestation standards in engagements for public companies are the authority of the Public Company Accounting Oversight Board, introduced next.

The Public Company Accounting Oversight Board and the Chief Auditor and Director of Professional Standards

Until 2003, the Auditing Standards Board was *the* most influential body issuing standards for public and nonpublic company audit and attestation services. However, owing to the *Sarbanes-Oxley Act*, the SEC usurped the Auditing Standards Board's standard-setting authority for *public-company* audit and attestation services, assigning the responsibility to the five-member **Public Company Accounting Oversight Board (PCAOB)**, a private-sector nonprofit organization chaired by William J. McDonough, former president and CEO of the Federal Reserve Bank of New York. A private-sector nonprofit corporation, the PCAOB was "created by the Sarbanes-Oxley Act to oversee the auditors of public companies in order to protect the interests of investors and further the public interest in the preparation of informative, fair, and independent audit reports."[11] The Board operates out of five offices (Atlanta, Dallas, New York City, San Francisco, and Washington D.C.) and employs Chief Auditor and Director of Professional Standards Douglas R. Carmichael, a former accounting professor at Baruch College (City University of New York). Unlike the Auditing Standards Board, which has no enforcement authority, the PCAOB confirmed at a public hearing in July 2003, its obligation

---

10 References in this book to sections and paragraphs of the AICPA's *Codification* are made parenthetically after the sentence or passages referenced, with "Section" abbreviated Sec.

11 See the PCAOB Web site at **http://www.pcaobus.org/**.

to fine, censure, suspend, or bar from practice registered firms that violate the *Sarbanes-Oxley Act*.[12]

Under the *Act*, the PCAOB had the authority to adopt some or all of the Auditing Standards Board's SASs and SSAEs or, in contrast, to establish new standards. In April 2003, the PCAOB, through Release No. 2003-006, announced the establishment of **Interim Professional Practice Standards**, which adopted temporarily the Auditing Standards Board's SASs and SSAEs under the title **Interim Professional Auditing Standards** (existing Statements on Auditing Standards) and **Interim Attestation Standards** (existing Statements on Standards for Attestation Engagements). Going forward, the PCAOB would review each interim standard to judge whether the standard will be made permanent, repealed, or modified. In December 2003, the PCAOB issued the first standard to supersede a provision of the Interim Professional Auditing Standards: *Auditing Standard No. 1*, "References in Auditors' Reports to the Standards of the PCAOB." *Auditing Standard No. 1* directs the independent auditor of a public company to state in an audit report (Chapter 3) that the engagement was conducted in accordance "with the standards of the Public Company Accounting Oversight Board (United States)."

The PCAOB's decision to issue **auditing standards**, rather than adopt the Auditing Standards Board's standards, marks the first time in history that practitioners have dealt with two sets of audit and attestation standards for nongovernmental engagements, one for nonpublic companies and one for public companies (see Figure 1-3). For example, under *Auditing Standard No. 1*, the audit report of a public company refers to "the standards of the Public Company Accounting Oversight Board (US)" but, consistent with *Statement on Auditing Standards No. 95*, "Generally Accepted Auditing Standards," the audit report of a nonpublic company refers to "U.S. generally accepted auditing standards." Going forward, the differences in standards will likely bear more directly on the nature of the procedures a practitioner applies to public and nonpublic audits.

Accounting, Auditing, and the Influence of Prominent Professional Organizations

Largely because auditing is studied in "accounting" curricula and practiced by public "accountants," auditing is often viewed as a subdivision of accounting. However, accounting and auditing are related because auditors are accountants first, not because auditing is accounting first. Mautz and Sharaf comment:

Auditing is analytic, not constructive; it is critical, investigative, concerned with the basis for accounting measurements and assertions. Auditing emphasizes proof, the support for financial statements and data. Thus auditing has its principal roots, not in accounting which it reviews, but in logic on which it leans heavily for ideas and methods.[13]

Accounting and auditing contemplate different bodies of knowledge. However, a facility with audit method is not wholly sufficient to render an auditor competent. Because an auditor audits financial statements, he or she must also be famil-

---

12 J. Burns, "Accounting Panel Provides Insights Into Its Workings," *The Wall Street Journal* (July 29, 2003), p. A2.

13 R. K. Mautz and H. A. Sharaf, *The Philosophy of Auditing*. Sarasota, FL: American Accounting Association, 1961, p. 14.

iar with GAAP. As a result, the organizations that influence accounting also influence auditing. Prominent among them are the Financial Accounting Standards Board, the Governmental Accounting Standards Board, and several professional organizations.

The Financial Accounting Standards Board and the Governmental Accounting Standards Board

The Financial Accounting Standards Board (FASB) and the Governmental Accounting Standards Board (GASB) are independent standard-setting bodies that issue authoritative *Statements of Financial Accounting Standards* for nongovernmental entities and *Statements of Governmental Accounting Standards* for governmental entities, respectively. For example, the FASB has issued statements on leases and pensions for nongovernmental entities such as public companies, and the GASB also has issued statements on leases and pensions, though for governmental entities such as state agencies. Except in rare circumstances, an independent auditor is precluded from expressing an opinion that financial statements are presented in conformity with GAAP if the statements contain a material departure from accounting principles promulgated by the FASB or GASB (Chapter 3). Auditors who are unfamiliar with FASB and GASB statements risk violating GAAP.

Professional Organizations

Professional organizations that influence audit standards and practice include the Institute of Internal Auditors (IIA), the Institute of Management Accountants (IMA), the American Accounting Association (AAA), and the International Federation of Accountants (IFAC). The Institute of Internal Auditors (IIA) is a voluntary membership organization for internal auditors. The Institute conducts and sponsors research and continuing professional education programs, sponsors the Certified Internal Auditor (CIA) examination, and publishes a bimonthly journal, *The Internal Auditor*.

The Institute of Management Accountants (IMA), an organization composed primarily of management accountants, also conducts and sponsors research and continuing education programs. The IMA publishes a monthly journal, *Management Accounting*, and sponsors the Certificate in Management Accounting (CMA) examination. Among its many and varied publications, the IMA issues position papers on a variety of accounting and reporting topics. Although these papers are not binding on accountants, they do influence accounting thought.

The American Accounting Association (AAA) is an organization of accounting educators. In addition to its journals—among them, *The Accounting Review, Accounting Horizons,* and *Auditing: A Journal of Practice & Theory*—the AAA also publishes research monographs and committee reports, including the *Report of the Committee on Basic Auditing Concepts*, from which a definition of auditing was introduced earlier in this chapter.

The International Federation of Accountants (IFAC) is a global federation of accountants that serves over 2.5 million accountants in over 150 member organizations and over 110 countries, including the AICPA and IMA in the United States. In January 2004, the IFAC's International Auditing and Assurance Board issued "Assurance Engagements Other Than Audits or Review of Historical Financial Information," becoming the first standard-setting body to address assurance services other than auditing and attestation. Although not binding on

U.S. accountants, the standard develops principles and procedures for assurance engagements.

Other Audit Services

In addition to financial statement audits, other audit services include *operational audits* and *compliance audits*.

Operational Audits

An **operational audit** (Figure 1-1) assesses the efficiency and effectiveness of management's operations, rather than the fair presentation of management's financial statements. Operational audits focus on information systems and operating procedures, not on recorded dollar amounts or reported financial information, and can address an entity's entire scope of operations or selected procedures. For example, the board of directors of BP, a major oil and gas company, assigned the company's **internal auditors** to appraise policies the company's upstream extraction division and downstream refining division use to negotiate crude oil transfer prices between divisions.

Unlike independent auditors in public accounting firms, internal auditors are employed by a single entity and vary in number depending on the entity's size and sophistication. For example, a middle-market company might employ just one internal auditor to perform relatively routine tasks. In contrast, General Electric, a company with total assets exceeding $600 billion, employs a vice president, audit staff to supervise hundreds of internal auditors who perform challenging operational audits around the globe in operating segments such as aircraft engines, appliances, industrial products and systems, plastics, power systems, and the NBC television network. To be effective, internal auditors should report to the highest levels of the organization, preferably to the audit committee of the board of directors, thereby maintaining independence from the personnel reviewed and allowing freedom from coercion when reporting.

Operational audits are not always performed by internal auditors. For example, built in the 1970s, the Trans Alaska pipeline had been criticized by whistleblowers and congressional investigators for alleged repeated violations of environmental and safety regulations. In response, the U.S. Interior Department's Bureau of Land Management engaged a Kansas-based engineering consultant to audit the pipeline's operator, Alyeska Pipeline Service Co., a consortium owned at the time by Atlantic Richfield, Exxon, and British Petroleum.[14] The operational audit, the first in the pipeline's history, focused on Alyeska's information processing system, management's performance, and alleged violations of air pollution standards and electrical codes.

Compliance Audits

A **compliance audit** (Figure 1-1) is similar in part to a financial statement audit, but is performed most often in governmental entities such as state governmental agencies, municipalities, and school districts, and in commercial entities such as contractors that comply with federal requirements. Like a financial statement

---

14 C. McCoy, "Trouble-shooter Heading Team Sent to Audit Alyeska Pipeline Practices," *The Wall Street Journal* (August 30, 1993), p. B3.

audit, a compliance audit can be designed to determine whether an entity's financial statements are presented fairly in accordance with GAAP. Unlike a financial statement audit, however, a compliance audit also can be designed to determine whether the entity has complied with applicable laws and regulations that may have a material effect on financial statements (hence the name "compliance" audit). For example, many state governmental agencies, such as Departments of Human Services or Departments of Motor Vehicles, receive direct grants from the federal government that impose requirements on how a grantee disburses grant funds. A compliance audit for the recipient agency would focus not only on whether the agency's financial statements conform with GAAP, but also on whether the agency complied with the federal government's restrictions on disbursing grant funds.

Compliance audits are conducted either by independent auditors or by **governmental auditors**, of which there are several types, including state auditors and U.S. General Accounting Office (GAO) auditors. Each of the 50 states maintains a state audit department, which may report to the elected legislature or to the governor's office (or both), depending on the state's constitution. Generally, state auditors perform compliance audits of state agencies and local governmental units within the state. For example, the Office of the Auditor General in New York performs a compliance audit of New York City, although the city's port authority (for example, LaGuardia and Kennedy airports) is audited by a public accounting firm. In contrast, GAO auditors, headed by the Comptroller General of the United States, report solely to Congress about the results of compliance audits of federal departments and agencies and about special audit engagements assigned by Congress. For example, in two highly publicized reports issued in the 1980s, each entitled *CPA Audit Quality*, the GAO, on special assignment by a House subcommittee, reported an alarming number of substandard governmental audits that small public accounting firms had performed.

Other Attestation Services

Although lending institutions commonly engage practitioners to perform FDIC safety-and-soundness attestations, other companies engage practitioners for far less common agreed-upon procedures, including the reliability of software specifications and insurance claims, and representations about market feasibility and shopping mall shelf space. Consider these two examples, one for Wilson Sporting Goods and another for Kaplan, Inc. First, Wilson Sporting Goods Co., a unit of Finland's Amer Group, introduced the Wilson Ultra golf ball and asserted in writing that the Ultra outdistances the competition by an average of 5.7 yards per drive. To justify the claim, Wilson engaged PricewaterhouseCoopers to attest to Wilson's assertion about the yards by which amateurs' Ultra drives outdistance the competition.

Second, in written agreements with college applicants, Kaplan, Inc., a test preparation firm, asserted that prior Kaplan-prepared applicants improved their College Entrance Examination Board (CEEB) Scholastic Assessment Test (SAT) scores by 115 points over their most recent SAT (or Preliminary SAT) scores. Kaplan guaranteed that Kaplan applicants who failed to improve their scores by 115 points could repeat the test preparation course free. To lend credibility to the claim, Kaplan engaged PricewaterhouseCoopers to attest to Kaplan's written assertion about the test performance of prior Kaplan-trained applicants. Kaplan appealed to college applicants with a written assertion backed by the reputation of a major firm. Although both Wilson Sporting Goods and Kaplan, Inc., are the clients *and* are responsible for a *written* assertion, sometimes the client is *not* the responsible party and the subject matter is *not* a written assertion. For example, prior to an acquisition, an acquiring company (the client) might engage a practitioner to report on a target company's (the responsible party) compliance with laws and regulations for which the target has not offered a written assertion. Notice the distinction between the two examples: In the former, the client (Wilson, Kaplan) is the responsible party, and the responsible party has made a written assertion; in the latter, the client is not the responsible party and the responsible party (the target company) has not made a written assertion.

To capture additional market share, Wilson Sporting Goods and Kaplan, Inc., respectively, supplied PricewaterhouseCoopers' attestations to attract market share. However, in some cases, companies supply attestations in order to recapture lost market share. Consider two examples. First, in the 1990s, two 35-year-olds paid to access a database that a dating service asserted in writing would include the names of 100, like-aged, Los Angeles-area professionals. They paid, accessed the database, found few, and sued. Owing to demand from other potential clients, the dating service hired a firm in southern California to attest that management's service assertions were reliable. Second, a retired steelworker invested in a cash management fund that offered exceptional investment returns. The actual five-year rate of return having been half the range of rates asserted, the retiree's investment underperformed, and he sued. The *Public Accounting Report*, a bimonthly newsletter, reported that 21 of the 26 largest U.S. investment companies have hired accounting firms to attest that assertions about rate of return are reliably consistent with performance presentation standards sanctioned by the Association for Investment Management and Research. In both examples, a party (a dating service, a cash management fund) made a written assertion (names, rate of return) that another party (two purchasers, a retired steelworker) relied on to his or her detriment. Both the dating service and the cash management fund attempted to regain market share by leveraging off of the accounting profession's reputation for independence.

Consulting and Other Assurance Services

In the 1990s, observers criticized financial statement audits as a remnant of a long-past industrial age.[15] Some argued that traditional financial statements issued well after the close of a fiscal year are untimely and, therefore, lack incremental value, driving investors to rely instead on alternate forms of financial and nonfinancial information, such as analysts' forecasts and time-to-market, respectively. In response, the profession expanded the scope of services toward value-added consulting and assurance services other than attestations and audits.

Consulting

Most **consulting services** are *two-party contracts* in which a consultant recommends *uses for information*. Consultants include international, multiservice firms

---

15 See, for example, W. Davidow, "Why Profits Don't Matter," *Forbes* (April 8, 1996), p. 24; R. K. Elliott, "The Third Wave Breaks on the Shores of Accounting," *Accounting Horizons* (September 1994), pp. 106–124; P. F. Drucker, "We Need to Measure, Not Count," *The Wall Street Journal* (July 17, 1993), p. B6.

such as Booze-Allen & Hamilton, A.T. Kearney, McKinsey & Company, Mercer Consulting, Towers Perrin, and smaller boutique firms devoted to niche markets. For example, in the 1990s, the Summit Group, an information services consulting firm with principal offices in the Midwest, entered into a long-term, two-party contract with HarperCollins, a publishing house, to recommend nationwide textbook distribution routes that would minimize transportation costs. HarperCollins' information processing system captures all the data relevant to textbook distribution. However, owing to constraints on expertise and time, HarperCollins chose to outsource the textbook distribution plan rather than to hire additional planning staff. The Summit Group's task was to recommend how HarperCollins could minimize costs given information HarperCollins provided about warehouse locations, inventory quantities, delivery deadlines, available transportation modes, and shipment destinations. Like other consulting projects, the Summit Group recommended how HarperCollins could *use* information, but lent no assurances about the *quality* of the information from which the recommendations were made. For example, unknown to HarperCollins, the inventory quantities may have been incorrect. Consulting projects typically focus on the use of information, not on the quality of the information used.

Public accounting firms have traditionally offered a variety of consulting services. Examples include business valuation, financial planning, litigation support, information system design and processing, financial forecasts and projections, actuarial services, tax compliance and planning, and feasibility studies for new product development and for business combinations and joint ventures. Over the years, some of these services had been criticized by the SEC, which argued that the handsome fees generated from consulting could motivate auditors to compromise their objectivity when auditing the entity's financial statements. For example, in 2000, two years after Waste Management, Inc., had restated financial statements for the years 1992 through 1997, *The Wall Street Journal* reported that the SEC was investigating whether consulting fees paid by Waste Management may have compromised the independence of their independent auditor. The *Journal* reported that from 1991 to 1997 Waste Management paid its incumbent auditor $10 million in audit fees but five times more, about $50 million, in consulting fees.[16] Two years later, the stakes got higher: The press reported that Enron in 2000 paid Arthur Andersen $25 million in audit fees and $27 million in consulting fees[17] and that Andersen had disposed of a "significant but undisclosed number" of Enron documents,[18] creating for the profession a crisis of confidence.[19] Following the U.S. Justice Department's indictment of Andersen on charges of obstruction of justice,[20] and conviction in a jury trial, Congress, acting in part on the presumption that consulting may compromise auditor independence, enacted in 2002 the *Sarbanes-Oxley Act*. Among other things, the Act limits the consulting services

---

16 "SEC Probes Arthur Andersen's Auditing Work for Waste Management," *The Wall Street Journal* (August 25, 2000), p. B1.

17 See, for example, J. Hirsh, "Enron Audit Fees Raise Some Brows," *The Los Angeles Times* (January 23, 2002), p. A1; J. Weil, "Double Enron Role Played by Andersen Raises Questions," *The Wall Street Journal* (December 14, 2001), p. A4.

18 See, for example, K. Eichenwald and F. Norris, "Enron's Auditor Says It Destroyed Documents," *The New York Times* (January 11, 2002), p. 1; J. Weil et al., "Audit Nightmare: Arthur Andersen Says It Disposed of Documents that Related to Enron," *The Wall Street Journal* (January 11, 2002), p. A1.

19 J. Kahn, "One Plus One Makes What? The Accounting Profession Had a Credibility Problem Before Enron, Now It Has a Crisis," *Time* (February 1, 2002), p. 67.

20 K. Eichenwald, "Andersen Charged with Obstruction in Enron Inquiry," *The New York Times* (March 15, 2002), p. 1.

an auditor can provide to public companies (Chapter 2, Figure 2-2). For example, Section 201, Services Outside the Scope of Practice of Auditors, prohibits auditors from providing at least nine nonaudit services, including the design and implementation of financial information systems. No restrictions are placed on the consulting services a practitioner supplies to nonpublic companies or to public companies the practitioner does not audit.

Other Assurance Services

In contrast, whereas consulting services recommend uses for information, assurance services, as noted earlier, report on (or improve) the *quality of information.* Assurers include public accounting firms, consulting firms, and independent nonprofit institutions, among others. For example, Consumers Union has long performed independent tests of consumer products, such as home appliances, and reported product quality ratings in *Consumer Reports,* a monthly periodical devoted exclusively to product comparisons. Home appliance manufacturers, such as Whirlpool and KitchenAid, provide product performance information in promotional pamphlets and advertising copy, but the information may be unreliable since manufacturers have incentives to misrepresent quality. Consumers Union receives revenue from *Consumer Reports* subscribers, but accepts no advertising or other fees from product manufacturers. Consumers value the product performance assurances published in *Consumer Reports* because Consumers Union receives no revenue from—and therefore is independent of—product manufacturers.

Over the years, some public accounting firms have been rather aggressive in offering assurance services. For example, PricewaterhouseCoopers has long assured the Academy Awards balloting; Crowe Chizek assured a drug-monitoring program to an athletic oversight authority; and several firms in the late 1990s began assuring Web-based business-to-consumer assertions, such as Web site claims about business practices and transaction integrity (Chapter 18). However, unlike Consumers Union, the public accounting profession had not fully exploited its reputation for independence, integrity, and objectivity in the market for value-added assurance services. In response, the American Institute of Certified Public Accountants (AICPA) established a Special Committee on Assurance Services, chaired by Robert K. Elliott (the Elliott Committee), a KPMG partner, to develop a strategic plan for the profession's further penetration into the market.

In addressing market opportunities, the Committee speculated that in the future the consumers of information—rather than the providers—will have the power to decide the content of the information they'll consume. For example, although newspaper editors once held exclusive domain over the news reported to readers, a reader today can access online news services that report what the reader demands. Interestingly, information technology can access the economic information that consumers demand. For example, although investors once relied passively on information reported by management in financial statements, investors today actively demand information not reported traditionally in financial statements, such as social and ecological awareness, market share and back order data, and management's decisions to invest in politically repressed countries. The profession's task is to predict the information that decision makers will demand and to design assurance services that will improve the quality of the information demanded—that is, value-added assurance services, although marketed to nonpublic companies and to public companies a practitioner does not audit.

The profession's entry into the assurance services market is not without barriers. For example, the marketplace views CPAs as the preferred provider for financial statement services, but may be less willing to equate a CPA's core competencies with, say, a major consulting firm for services unrelated to financial statements. For this among other reasons, some observers have been suspicious of the profession's move into the assurance services market. The New York State Society of CPAs sponsored a symposium that addressed the work of the Elliott Committee. Some of the panelists supported the Committee's work, but others were less forgiving.[21] What's clear is that there is a demand for assurance services. For example, witness the well-respected work of Consumers Union. What's unclear is whether the market necessarily views the public accounting profession as the first-stop supplier of assurance services in quite the same way that the financial community views the profession as *the* supplier of auditing services. A close read of the *Sarbanes-Oxley Act of 2002* suggests Congress believes that the independent auditors of public companies should be the preferred providers of financial statement audits, only. In the post-*Sarbanes-Oxley* era, the market is not likely to embrace assurance services with anything near the enthusiasm that the profession did in the 1990s.

Values, Competencies, and Services

Begun as a grassroots effort involving the AICPA and practicing CPAs, among others, the AICPA produced a forward-looking report, *CPA Vision Project: 2011 and Beyond* (**http://www. aicpa.org/vision/index.htm**), which contemplates a constantly evolving service mix that positions CPAs further up the "knowledge value chain"—for example, services that focus less on compliance and more on value. For example, the compilation of financial statements, a traditional compliance service, arguably offers a client less value than, say, risk assessment or performance benchmarking because, unlike compiled financial statements, knowledge about business risk and competitive benchmarking equip clients with intuition that can translate into business strategies. The Institute's vision, stated in only two sentences, demands that CPAs view themselves as enablers armed with two strategic assets: insight and integrity:

AICPA Vision Statement:

CPAs are the trusted professionals who enable people and organizations to shape their future. Combining insight with integrity, CPAs deliver value by communicating the total picture with clarity and objectivity, translating complex information into critical knowledge, anticipating and creating opportunities, and designing pathways that transform vision into reality.

The vision statement is consistent with value-added assurance services, in part because the project contemplates values and competencies that improve an assurer's ability to judge the quality of information assured. Figure 1-4 summarizes the vision project's core values, competencies, and services, and can be interpreted by students as a fairly succinct statement of what the profession will expect from them.

---

21 R. Telberg, "CPAs Cautioned on Assurance Services," *Accounting Today* (January 22–February 11, 1996), p. 34.

FIGURE 1-4: *Values, Competencies, and Services*

Core Values

Continuing Education and Lifelong Learning CPAs believe in continuing education beyond certification and believe it is important to continuously acquire new skills and knowledge.

Competence CPAs are able to perform high quality work in a capable, efficient, and appropriate manner.

Integrity CPAs conduct themselves with honesty and professional ethics.

Attuned to Broad Business Issues CPAs are in tune with the overall realities of the business environment.

Objectivity CPAs are able to deal with information free of distortions, personal bias or conflicts of interest.

Core Competencies

Communications and Leadership Skills Able to give and exchange information within meaningful context and with appropriate delivery and interpersonal skills. Able to influence, inspire, and motivate others to achieve results.

Strategic and Critical Thinking Skills Able to link data, knowledge, and insight together to provide quality advice for strategic decision-making.

Focus on the Customer, Client and Market Able to anticipate and meet the changing needs of clients, employers, customers, and markets better than competitors.

Interpretation of Converging Information Able to interpret and provide a broader context using financial and nonfinancial information.

Technologically Adept Able to utilize and leverage technology in ways that add value to clients, customers, and employers.

Core Services

Assurance and Information Integrity Provide a variety of services that improve and assure the quality of information, or its context, for business decision-making.

Management Consulting and Performance Management Provide advice and insight on the financial and nonfinancial performance of an organization's operational and strategic processes through broad business knowledge and judgment.

Technology Services Provide services that leverage technology to improve objectives and decision-making including business application processes, system integrity, knowledge management, system security, and integration of new business processes and practices.

Financial Planning Provide a variety of services to organizations and individuals that interpret and add value by utilizing a wide range of financial information. These include everything from tax planning and financial statement analysis to structuring investment portfolios and complex financial transactions.

International Services Provide services to support and facilitate commerce in the global market.

Source: AICPA, *CPA Vision Project: 2011 and Beyond* (**http://www.aicpa.org**).

SUMMARY

Performed by certified public accountants, financial statement audits are the primary assurance service that public accounting firms offer today. Audits reduce the risk that information in financial statements is misstated materially, thereby reducing the cost a company incurs to issue and service equity and debt. Other audit services include operational audits and compliance services, and other attestation services include agreed-upon procedures and financial statement reviews. Although the Public Company Accounting Oversight Board issues standards for the audits of public companies, and the Auditing Standards Board issues standards for the audits of nonpublic companies, a number of professional organizations influence the practice of auditing. Prominent among them are the Securities and Exchange Commission, the American Institute of CPAs, the Accounting and Review Services Committee, the Financial Accounting Standards Board, the Governmental Accounting Standards Board, the Institute of Internal Auditors, the Institute of Management Accountants, and the American Accounting Association.

Investors have long demanded timely information that captures management's capacity to innovate and the value of information. In response, the profession in the 1990s offered a variety of consulting and other assurance services that some believe threatened an auditor's independence. Coincidentally, an unprecedented number of public companies restated financial statements and the SEC settled several controversial accounting fraud cases, prompting Congress to enact the *Sarbanes-Oxley Act of 2002*, which precluded public accounting firms from offering most types of consulting and other assurance services. The profession is entrusted with a major responsibility: auditing the financial statements of companies that compete for capital in domestic and global markets. The volume, value, and complexity of the transactions that transform into financial statements forecast well for career opportunities in auditing.

KEY TERMS

Accounting and Review Services Committee (ARSC) 11
Agreed-upon procedures engagement 5
American Institute of Certified Public Accountants (AICPA) 9
Assurance services 3
Attestation services 4
Audit services 5
Auditing standards 12
Auditing Standards Board (ASB) 11
Auditing Standards Executive Committee (AudSEC) 10
Certified public accountants (CPAs) 3
Committee on Auditing Procedure (CAP) 10
Compliance audit 14
Consulting services 16
Financial statement audit 5
Governmental auditors 15
Independent auditor 5

Interim Attestation Standards 12
Interim Professional Auditing Standards 12
Interim Professional Practice Standards 12
Internal auditors 14
Operational audit 14
Public Company Accounting Oversight Board (PCAOB) 11
Review engagement 5
Securities and Exchange Commission (SEC) 9
Statements on Auditing Procedure (SAP) 10
Statements on Auditing Standards (SAS) 10
Statements on Standards for Accounting and Review Services (SSARS) 11
Statements on Standards for Attestation Engagements (SSAE) 11

REFERENCES

Public Company Accounting Oversight Board Releases:

PCAOB Release No. 2003-005, "Statement Regarding the Establishment of Auditing and Other Professional Auditing Standards."

PCAOB Release No. 2003-006, "Establishment of Interim Professional Auditing Standards."

PCAOB Release No. 2003-009, "Compliance with Auditing and Related Professional Practice Standards."

Professional Standards:

Auditing Standard No. 1, "References in Auditors' Reports to the Standards of the PCAOB" (PCAOB Release No. 2003-025).

AICPA, *Codification of Auditing Standards*. New York: AICPA, Appendix A.

SSAE No. 10, "Attestation Standards: Revision and Recodification."

Legislation:

Sarbanes-Oxley Act. 2002. H.R. 3763.

Professional Reports:

AICPA, *Interim Report on Special Committee on Assurance Services* (the Elliott Committee). New York: AICPA, 1995.

AICPA, *Report of the Special Committee on Financial Reporting* (the Jenkins Committee), *Improving Business Reporting: A Customer Focus: Meeting the Information Needs of Investors and Creditors*. New York: AICPA, 1994.

National Commission on Fraudulent Financial Reporting (the Treadway Commission), *Report of the National Commission on Fraudulent Financial Reporting*, 1987.

Public Oversight Board, *Panel on Audit Effectiveness: Report and Recommendations*. Stamford, CT: POB, 2000.

SEC Practice Section Professional Issues Task Force, *Practice Alert 97-1, Financial Statements on the Internet*. New York: AICPA, updated through 1999.

Articles, Books:

Blackwell, D. W., T. R. Noland, and D. B. Winters, "The Value of Auditor Assurance: Evidence from Loan Pricing," *Journal of Accounting Research* (Spring 1998), pp. 57–70.

Brackney, K. S., and G. L. Helms, "A Survey of Attestation Practices," *Auditing: A Journal of Practice & Theory* (Fall 1996), pp. 85–98.

Carey, J. L., *The Rise of the Accounting Profession from Technician to Professional*. New York: American Institute of Certified Public Accountants, 1969.

Couston, H., L. M. Leinicke, W. M. Rexroad, and J. A. Ostrosky, "Sarbanes-Oxley: What It Means to the Marketplace," *Journal of Accountancy* (February 2004), pp. 43–47.

Dennis, A., "Taking Account: Key Dates for the Profession," *Journal of Accountancy* (October 2000), pp. 97–105.

Elliott, R. K., "Who Are We As A Profession—and What Must We Become?" *Journal of Accountancy* (February 2000), pp. 81–84.

Elliott, R. K., "Twenty-First Century Assurance," *Auditing: A Journal of Practice & Theory* (March 2002), pp. 139–146.

Harrington, C., "The New Accounting Environment," *Journal of Accountancy* (August 2003), pp. 28–33.

Mancino, J. M., and C.E. Landes, "A New Look at the Attestation Standards," *Journal of Accountancy* (July 2001), pp. 41–45.

Mautz, R. K., and H. A. Sharaf, *The Philosophy of Auditing*. Sarasota, FL: American Accounting Association, 1961.

McConnell, D. K., Jr., and G. Y. Banks, "How Sarbanes-Oxley Will Change the Audit Process," *Journal of Accountancy* (September 2003), pp. 49–55.

Niemotko, K. "Restoring Public Trust: An Interview with SEC Commissioner Harvey J. Goldschmid," *The CPA Journal* (October 2003), pp. 13–15.

Roy, R. H., and J. H. MacNeil, *Horizons for a Profession*. New York: American Institute of Certified Public Accountants, 1967.

Tie, R., "The Profession's Roots," *Journal of Accountancy* (November 2003), pp. 57–59.

Zarowin S., "Facing the Future," *Journal of Accountancy* (April 2001), pp. 26–31.

Zeff, S. A., "How the U.S. Accounting Profession Got Where It Is Today: Part I," *Accounting Horizons* (September 2003), pp. 189–205.

Zeff, S. A., "How the U.S. Accounting Profession Got Where It Is Today: Part II," *Accounting Horizons* (December 2003), pp. 267–286.

QUESTIONS

1. Why is there a need for financial statement audits?
2. What is a limited liability partnership?
3. What is the scientific method of inquiry, and how does it relate to auditing?
4. What are attestation services?
5. Prepare a representative list of users of financial statements.
6. What are Staff Accounting Bulletins?
7. What are the Committee on Auditing Procedure, the Auditing Standards Executive Committee, and the Auditing Standards Board?
8. Distinguish between consulting and assurance services.
9. When is an assurance service an attestation?
10. Identify the major types of audits performed in the United States today.
11. What services are generally provided to clients by public accounting firms?
12. Why has Congress criticized nonattest services?
13. What does management assert in the disclosure, "Trade receivables . . . $1,200,000."
14. What roles are served by the AICPA's two current standard-setting bodies for auditing and for accounting and review services?
15. How are auditing and accounting related?

MULTIPLE CHOICE QUESTIONS

1. Financial statement audits:
    a. Confirm that financial statement assertions are accurate.
    b. Lend credibility to the financial statements.
    c. Confirm that financial statements are presented fairly.
    d. Assure that fraud has been detected.

2. Financial statement audits:
    a. Reduce the cost of capital.
    b. Report on compliance with laws and regulations.
    c. Assess management's efficiency and effectiveness.
    d. Overlook information risk.

3. Which of the following best describes why an independent auditor reports on financial statements?

   a. Independent auditors are likely to detect fraud.
   b. Competing interests may exist between management and the users of the statements.
   c. Misstated account balances are generally corrected by an independent audit.
   d. Ineffective internal controls may exist.   (AICPA Adapted)

4. The audited financial statements of a public company are the representations and responsibility of:

   a. The board of directors.
   b. Management.
   c. The independent auditor.
   d. The Public Company Accounting Oversight Board.

5. The client in an audit of a public company's financial statements is:

   a. Management.
   b. Employees.
   c. Shareholders.
   d. The public.

6. Financial statements and audit reports posted on the Internet pose a risk that readers will:

   a. Fail to read the statements and reports entirely.
   b. Misinterpret the responsibilities of management.
   c. Fail to open hyperlinks.
   d. Presume incorrectly that the auditor's report extends to hyperlinks.

7. Gathering evidence in a scientific experiment is most similar in an audit to:

   a. Planning an engagement.
   b. Hypothesizing that financial statements are presented fairly.
   c. Assessing risk and designing audit procedures.
   d. Evaluating whether financial statements are presented fairly.

8. Most public accounting firms are organized as:

   a. Proprietorships.
   b. Partnerships.
   c. Limited liability partnerships.
   d. Corporations.

9. A manufacturer has engaged a public accounting firm to issue a report on the accuracy of product quality specifications included in trade sales agreements. This is an example of a (an):

   a. Financial statement audit.
   b. Attestation service.
   c. Compliance audit.
   d. Operational audit.

10. Review engagements are often purchased by:

    a. Small, owner-managed companies.
    b. Mid-market public companies.
    c. Large public companies.
    d. Government agencies.

11. A public accounting firm's primary role in performing nonattest services is to:

    a. Hedge against declines in the firm's audit practice.
    b. Establish the firm as a consultant.
    c. Provide advice valuable to a client's effectiveness.
    d. Acclimate staff members to the client's business and industry.

12. Which of the following types of audits is designed to determine whether a governmental entity's procurement practices are sound?

    a. A financial statement audit
    b. An operational audit
    c. A program audit
    d. A compliance audit

13. Which of the following authoritative bodies issues pronouncements relevant to attestation service engagements for nonpublic companies?

    a. Accounting and Review Services Committee
    b. Auditing Standards Board
    c. Public Company Accounting Oversight Board
    d. AICPA

14. Which of the following authoritative bodies issues pronouncements relevant to audit service engagements for public companies?

    a. Accounting and Review Services Committee
    b. Auditing Standards Board
    c. Public Company Accounting Oversight Board
    d. Securities and Exchange Commission

15. The role of the Auditing Standards Board is to:

    a. Define accepted auditing procedures applicable in practice.
    b. Develop auditing standards for new *Statements of Financial* (or *Governmental*) *Accounting Standards* issued by the Financial (or Governmental) Accounting Standards Board.
    c. Promulgate auditing standards and procedures.
    d. Lobby Congress on matters related to audit practice.

16. The role of the Public Company Accounting Oversight Board is to:

    a. Revise pronouncements of the Auditing Standards Board for use by auditors of public companies.
    b. Monitor operational and compliance audits for public companies.
    c. Regulate the exchange of securities under federal securities laws.
    d. Oversee the audits of public companies that are subject to federal securities laws.

17. *Statements on Auditing Standards (SASs)* differ from *Auditing Standards* in that:

    a. Once superseded by the PCAOB, individual *SASs* no longer apply to the audits of nonpublic entities.
    b. Until superseded by the PCAOB, individual *SASs* apply to the audits of public entities.
    c. *SASs* apply to operational audits and *Auditing Standards* apply to compliance audits.
    d. *SASs* are issued by the PCAOB and *Auditing Standards* are issued by the Auditing Standards Board.

18. Unlike consulting services, assurance services:

    a. Make recommendations to management.
    b. Report on how to use information.
    c. Report on the quality of information.
    d. Are two-party contracts.

19. In the cases of both Waste Management and Enron, the press was critical that auditors:

    a. Ignored existing audit standards.
    b. Failed to plan the audit engagements properly.
    c. Overlooked suspicions of earnings management reported in the press.
    d. Received significant consulting fees relative to audit fees.

20. The core competencies of certified public accountants include:

    a. Assurance and information integrity.
    b. Objectivity.
    c. Strategic and critical thinking skills.
    d. Lifelong learning.

PROBLEMS AND DISCUSSION CASES

1-1 *Is There Value to an Audit?*

The Carter Wright Corporation entered into a consulting contract with Accenture to outsource Carter Wright's information processing to Accenture. The $3.5 million, multiyear contract would include the cost of computer upgrades to IBM workstations and of Microsoft Windows dedicated software designed by Accenture. One year ago, Accenture received an ISO 9000 quality control report from the McKinsey Group.

Required: You are the engagement partner for Carter Wright's financial statement audit. Carter Wright's board of directors has asked that you explain the value added to Carter Wright by your firm's audit. Discuss.

1-2 *Identifying Types of Audits*

Within the chapter, three different types of audits were identified:

- Financial statement audit
- Operational audit
- Compliance audit

Each type of audit is designed for a particular purpose and is selected depending on the specific objectives of report users.

Required: For each of the following circumstances, indicate the type of audit required.

1. Management is interested in whether the purchasing department operates economically.
2. The state legislature is concerned that the requirements of a federal grant may have been violated.
3. A commercial bank will not approve a working capital loan without a report on whether the company's financial statements are presented fairly.
4. A state agency is not eligible for federal grants lacking a report on whether the agency's financial statements are presented fairly.
5. Management is interested in whether controls over highly sensitive inventory are reasonable and adequate.

6. Management is required to obtain a report indicating whether the objectives of a direct grant have been achieved.

1-3 *The Market for Audit Services*

During the past several decades, auditing has gained a considerable amount of attention both within the financial community and within academic curricula. For example, independent audits are now performed commonly for all publicly traded and for many privately owned corporations. Further, not only do undergraduate accounting curricula typically include an introductory auditing course, but many colleges and universities also offer advanced undergraduate and graduate auditing courses. There appears to be an established need for auditing.

Required: Explain why each of the following institutions needs auditing services.
1. Publicly owned corporations
2. Privately owned corporations
3. State and local governmental agencies
4. Partnerships

✓ 1-4 *Comparing Auditing to the Sciences*

One of your classmates, Kristin Lea, a chemistry major, is puzzled about what an auditor does. She says to you, "My only impression about auditors comes from Bob Cratchit, Tiny Tim's father, in Charles Dickens' A Christmas Carol. It sure seems to me as though there's little science in an auditor's work!"

Required: Explain the role of an auditor using terms that would be familiar to a chemistry major.

✓ 1-5 *Misconceptions About Auditing*

The following two statements are representative of attitudes and opinions sometimes encountered by independent auditors:

a. Today's audit consists of test checking, a dangerous policy since test checking depends on the auditor's judgment, which may be defective. An audit can be relied on only if every transaction is audited.
b. An audit is essentially unproductive and contributes to neither the gross national product nor the general well-being of society. Rather than create, the auditor merely checks what someone else has done.

Required: Evaluate the previous statements, indicating:
1. Areas of agreement with the statement, if any.
2. Areas of misconception, incompleteness, or fallacious reasoning included in the statement, if any.

1-6 *Why an Audit?*

Feiler, the sole owner of a small hardware business, has been told that the business should have financial statements reported on by an independent certified public accountant. Having some bookkeeping experience, Feiler has personally prepared the company's financial statements and does not understand why the statements should be audited by a CPA. Feiler discussed the matter with Farber, a CPA, and asked Farber to explain why an audit is considered important.

Required:
1. Describe the objectives of a financial statement audit.
2. Identify 10 ways in which a financial statement audit may be beneficial to Feiler.

(AICPA Adapted)

✓ **1-7** *Why Appoint an Outside Auditor?*

Marc David is an employee-stockholder of the Lexington Corporation. Because he has extensive accounting experience, Marc proposes to the other stockholders that he, rather than a public accounting firm, be appointed independent auditor for Lexington Corporation. Marc argues that because of his ownership in the company, the other owners' interests would be served best by his appointment. At a meeting of stockholders, Marc states, "I'd be much better for the job. For one thing, I can do the work and, for another, it won't cost us a small fortune."

Required: Indicate the deficiencies in Marc David's arguments. Be specific.

✓ **1-8** *Audit Standard-Setting*

Appointment in 1939 of the AICPA's Committee on Auditing Procedure, the first authoritative audit standard-setting body in the United States was a response to public sector demands that the private sector ". . . examine into auditing procedure and other related questions in light of recent public discussions." The "public discussions" related in part to the McKesson & Robbins, Inc., $19 million overstatement of inventory and accounts receivable. McKesson & Robbins' auditors neither observed physical inventory on hand nor confirmed accounts receivable balances with debtors. In 1939, the Committee on Auditing Procedure responded with *Statement on Auditing Procedure No. 1*, which recommended physical inventory observation and accounts receivable confirmation, both of which have since become common practice.

Required: Do these beginnings, a response to a highly publicized fraud, have any implications for audit standard-setting today which, for nonpublic companies, is essentially the same with the Auditing Standards Board as it was in 1939 with the Committee on Auditing Procedure?

✓ **1-9** *The Public Company Accounting Oversight Board and the Auditing Standards Board*

The Public Company Accounting Oversight Board was established by the SEC under the authority of the *Sarbanes-Oxley Act of 2002* to "oversee the auditors of public companies in order to protect the interests of investors and further the public interest in the preparation of informative, fair, and independent audit reports." In 2003, the Board issued *Auditing Standard No. 1*, "References in Auditors' Reports to the Standards of the PCAOB." In contrast, the Auditing Standards Board was established by AICPA Council under the authority of AICPA Bylaws to "be responsible for the promulgation of auditing standards and procedures to be observed by members of the AICPA in accordance with the Institute's rules of conduct." Since 1978, the Board has issued over 100 *Statements on Auditing Standards*.

Required:
1. Discuss the implications of two audit standard-setting bodies.
2. What bearing do the Auditing Standards Board's *Statements on Auditing Standards* have on the audits of public and nonpublic companies?

1-10 *Proposing Assurance Services*

To compete with manufacturers like Cray Research, the Singer Corporation, a manufacturer of mid-range supercomputers, makes oral claims of product superiority to engineers and scientists, its targeted end users. Some of the claims amount to little more than puffery, "the best . . . , the most . . . ," but others relate to performance and to market share. Two that are particularly important to Fred Singer, the corporation's chief operating officer, are:

- Average post-purchase user support time is 75 hours per end user.
- Three hundred fifty satisfied customers.

During the financial statement audit, Laurie Feldman, engagement partner, discovers that the performance and market share claims will be made in an upcoming advertising campaign and included in sales contracts. Feldman decides to propose an assurance service to Fred Singer.

Required:
1. What argument could Feldman make to justify that the proposed assurance service will add value to Singer Corporation's product performance and market share claims?
2. Is the proposed assurance service an attestation? Why or why not?
3. Use your imagination to explain what evidence Feldman would gather to test Singer's claims.

1-11 *Assurance Services and Reported SAT Scores*

The Wall Street Journal reported that the National Association of College Admissions Counselors, a professional organization for admission officers and high school guidance counselors, had threatened sanctions against colleges that allegedly misrepresented SAT scores to bias college rankings, among them *U.S. News & World Report's* annual ranking of the top colleges in America (S. Stecklow, "Universities Face Trouble for Enhancing Guide Data," October 10, 1995, pp. B1, B11). The article reported that, "Some concerned academic leaders, meanwhile, are calling for accountant-certified disclosure statements to help verify . . . test scores . . ."

Required:
1. What type of professional service does the quote in the article likely refer to?
2. Do you think the service represents an important assurance market for the public accounting profession? Why or why not?

> **Internet problems and discussion cases are available at http://ricchiute.swlearning.com**

RESEARCH PROJECTS

1. Audit Standard-Setting

Two different bodies issue authoritative auditing pronouncements in the United States—one in the public sector, the full-time Public Company Accounting Oversight Board (PCAOB), which has issued standards since 2004 for the audits of public companies; and a second in the private sector, the part-time Auditing Standards Board (ASB), which has issued standards since 1978. Each of the two boards are empowered by different authorities, financed by different means, driven by largely different technical agendas, and distinguished by decidedly different responsibilities for enforcement. For example, the ASB has no enforcement authority, but Section 105 of the *Sarbanes-Oxley Act of 2002* grants the PCAOB broad authority to establish by rule fair procedures to investigate public accounting firms registered to audit public companies. In September 2003, the Board adopted Release No. 2003-015, "Rules on Investigations and Adjudications."

Required: Using online sources (PCAOB: **http://www.pcaobus.org**; AICPA: **http://www.aicpa.org**), compare the Public Company Accounting Oversight Board and the Auditing Standards Board on these dimensions:

1. Authority (on what authority is each board empowered?).
2. Financing (how is each board financed?).
3. Membership (who comprises each board?).

4. Agenda (describe key issues on each board's current agenda).
5. Pronouncements (compare each board's most recent pronouncements on form, tone, and requirements).

2. Financial Statement Restatements

Much of the controversy surrounding financial statement auditing was driven by the unprecedented number of public companies that restated previously issued financial statements that had been audited by major public accounting firms. For example, among the companies that restated were 3COM, Adelphia Communications, Alcoa, AOL, Aurora Foods, Avon Products, Bausch & Lomb, Best Buy, Boise Cascade, Boston Chicken, Boston Scientific, Calpine, Campbell Soup, Cendant, Clorox, ConAgra Foods, Corel, CVS, Dean Foods, Del Monte Foods, Dollar General, DuPont, Enron, Federal-Mogul, Food Lion, Gateway, Genentech, Genesco, Guess?, Golden Bear Golf, Harrah's Entertainment, Hewlett-Packard, Host Marriott, Icon Office, J.C. Penney, Kmart, Krispy Kreme, Kroger, Land's End, Lucent Technologies, McDonald's, MicroStrategy, Monsanto, MSB Financial, National Steel, North Face, Pennzoil-Quaker State, Phar-Mor, PG&E, Phillips Petroleum, Rayovac, Raytheon, Reader's Digest, Rite Aid, Saucony, Schlotzsky's, Sony, Sunbeam, SunTrust Banks, Texas Instruments, Toro, Tyco, Urban Outfitters, Waste Management, Williams-Sonoma, WR Grace, Xerox, and Yahoo! What's striking is the breadth of industries represented and that most of the companies are rather well known.

Required: For any one of the restating companies previously listed (or another of your choosing):
1. Access from **http://www.sec.gov** the company's restated financial statements. The restatement could appear in annual reports or in quarterly reports to the SEC on Form 10-K/A or on Form 10-Q/A, respectively.
2. Using disclosures within the restated financial statement, draft a report that summarizes:
   - The issues that gave rise to the restatement, and
   - The generally accepted accounting principles the company violated.

3. Will Financial Statements Become Obsolete?

In the 1990s, the financial press began to question the information content of traditional historical cost balance sheets. For example, Peter Drucker commented that:

Balance sheets were designed to show what a business would be worth if it was liquidated today . . . What managements need, however, are balance sheets that relate the enterprise's current condition to its future wealth-producing capacity . . . Financial accounting, balance sheets, profit-and-loss statements, allocations of costs, etc., are an X-ray of the enterprise's skeleton. But much as the diseases we most commonly die from—heart disease, cancer, Parkinson's—do not show up in a skeletal X-ray, a loss of market standing or a failure to innovate do not register in the accountant's figures until the damage has been done. (P. F. Drucker, "We Need to Measure, Not Count," *The Wall Street Journal*, July 17, 1993, p. B6. See also P. F. Drucker, Post-Capitalist Society. New York: HarperCollins, 1992.)

And William Davidow, writing in Forbes, said:

Double-entry bookkeeping, developed by Luca Pacioli in 1494, lets businesses keep track of changes in their assets. But this system, still in use today, deals primarily with tangible assets such as cash, inventory, accounts receivable, factory plants and equipment. It ignores intangible assets: goodwill, employee knowledge, quality of management, customer relationships, information infrastructure, trade secrets, patents, etc. (W. Davidow, "Why Profits Don't Matter," *Forbes*, April 8, 1996, p. 24.)

In response to claims that financial statements may no longer be relevant, the AICPA established a Special Committee on Financial Reporting, chaired by Edmund Jenkins (the Jenkins Committee), to recommend improvements in business reporting. Following three years of deliberations, the Committee released a series of recommendations, among them that businesses report forward-looking information (AICPA, *Report of the Special Committee on Financial Reporting* (the Jenkins Committee), *Improving Business Reporting: A Customer Focus: Meeting the Information Needs of Investors and Creditors*, 1994). However, the recommendations have received mixed reviews. For example, Dennis Beresford, former FASB chair, stated, "It is going to be a very important document for us, a real stimulus for changes and improvement in financial reporting over the next 5 to 10 years." In contrast, Frank Borelli, the Financial Executive Institute's CFO Advisory chair, thought otherwise, stating, ". . . the committee's recommendations can be viewed as very self-serving. It looks as if they are trying to generate more services, which equates to more revenue."

Required: Select an annual report from the SEC's EDGAR system (**http://www.sec.gov**), from a public company's home page, or from a library, and prepare a report that:

1. Documents and criticizes the key recommendations of the Jenkins Committee report.
2. Explains how the Jenkins Committee's recommendations would bear on the annual report you selected.
3. Explains nonfinancial disclosures you think would improve the annual report given the company's industry (for example, the identity and stability of foreign, crude oil, supply sources in the oil and gas industry).

4. Developing a Case Study in Assurance Services

The AICPA Special Committee on Assurance Services (the Elliott Committee) proposed a series of assurance service opportunities including assurances on risk assessment, systems reliability, entity performance, electronic commerce, health care, and geriatric care. At least two of the proposed services have been rolled out and supported by the AICPA: WebTrust (electronic commerce) and ElderCare. Clearly there are obstacles to proposing new services, among them the provisions of the *Sarbanes-Oxley Act* for public companies and persuading clients that the profession's market permissions extend to services unrelated to historical cost financial statements.

Required:
1. Identify an assurance service that interests you—for example, a service from the AICPA's Web site (**http://www.aicpa.org**), from an accounting firm's Web site, or a service you've experienced, heard about, or imagined.
2. Draft a discussion case (and class discussion points, that is, a solution) that could be presented to, and discussed with, the class. The case should capture, for example:
   - the scope and objectives of the service.
   - the core competencies required to deliver the service.
   - potential demand.
   - a company or industry that might value the service.
   - evidence gathering and measurement.
   - evaluation criteria.
   - deliverables.

Issues in Accounting Education, a publication of the American Accounting Association, publishes Instructional Cases that offer a useful guide for how discussion cases can be structured.

Interactive quizzes are available as a student learning resource at http://ricchiute.swlearning.com

2 Chapter

Standards, Materiality, and Risk

Major topics discussed in this chapter are:

- Audit and attestation standards.
- Concepts that underlie financial statement auditing: independence, due care, evidence, and reporting.
- Audit risk.
- Materiality in a financial statement audit.

Just as constitutional law is based on interpretations of a single document, the U.S. Constitution, so too are audit services. Generally accepted auditing standards are to audit services what the Constitution is to constitutional law, and the standards guide questions about training, independence, due care, supervision, evidence, reporting, and control. This chapter focuses on standards, materiality, and audit risk. The chapter begins by introducing the profession's eleven attestation standards and ten generally accepted auditing standards in the context of four concepts crucial to the profession's reputation: independence, due care, evidence, and reporting. In turn, the chapter addresses materiality and risk, two issues that weigh heavily on a practitioner's interpretation of standards.

Audit and Attestation Standards

The AICPA Adopts and Revises Standards

In 1941, the SEC issued *Accounting Series Release No. 21*, which required in part that an auditor report whether an audit engagement had been conducted in accordance with generally accepted standards. But no written standards existed at the time. In response, the AICPA's Committee on Auditing Procedure began deliberating on a series of standards for auditing. Interrupted by World War II, the Committee did not finalize the nine original standards until 1947 in *Tentative Statement of Auditing Standards: Their Generally Accepted Significance and Scope*. The nine standards were approved by AICPA member vote in 1948, and a tenth was adopted from *Statement on Auditing Procedure No. 23* and approved in 1949. The ten **generally accepted auditing standards (GAAS)**, presented in Figure 2-1, right column, are classified as **general standards**, **standards of field work**, and **standards of reporting**.

Throughout the 1970s, practitioners criticized GAAS, complaining that the standards were not sufficiently specific. In contrast, others argued that the standards were not sufficiently robust, especially to apply to the ever-expanding scope

FIGURE 2-1: *Attestation Standards and Auditing Standards*

Attestation Standards	*Auditing Standards*

General Standards

1. The engagement shall be performed by a practitioner or practitioners having **adequate technical training and proficiency** in the attest function.

    1. The audit is to be performed by a person or persons having **adequate technical training and proficiency** as an auditor.

2. The engagement shall be performed by a practitioner or practitioners having **adequate knowledge** in the subject matter of the assertion.

3. The practitioner shall perform an engagement only if he or she has reason to believe that the following two conditions exist:
   - The **assertion is capable of evaluation against reasonable criteria** that either have been established by a recognized body or are stated in the presentation of the assertion in a sufficiently clear and comprehensive manner for a knowledgeable reader to be able to understand them.
   - The assertion is **capable of reasonably consistent estimation or measurement** using such criteria.

4. In all matters relating to the engagement, an **independence** in mental attitude shall be maintained by the practitioner or practitioners.

    2. In all matters relating to the assignment, an **independence** in mental attitude is to be maintained by the auditor or auditors.

5. **Due professional care** shall be exercised in the performance of the engagement.

    3. **Due professional care** is to be exercised in the performance of the audit and the preparation of the report.

Standards of Field Work

1. The work shall be adequately **planned** and assistants, if any, shall be properly **supervised**.

    1. The work is to be adequately **planned** and assistants, if any, are to be properly **supervised**.

    2. A sufficient understanding of **internal control** is to be obtained to plan the audit and to determine the nature, timing, and extent of tests to be performed.

2. Sufficient **evidence** shall be obtained to provide a reasonable basis for the conclusion that is expressed in the report.

    3. Sufficient competent **evidential matter** is to be obtained through inspection, observation, inquiries, and confirmations to afford a reasonable basis for an opinion regarding the financial statements under audit.

(continues)

FIGURE 2-1 *(continued)*

Attestation Standards	*Auditing Standards*

Standards of Reporting

1. The report shall identify the **assertion** being reported on and state the character of the engagement.

2. The report shall state the practitioner's conclusion about whether the assertion is presented in conformity with the **established or stated criteria** against which it was measured.

   1. The report shall state whether the financial statements are presented in accordance with **generally accepted accounting principles**.

3. The report shall state all of the practitioner's **significant reservations** about the engagement and the presentation of the assertion.

   2. The report shall identify those circumstances in which such **principles have not been consistently observed** in the current period in relation to the preceding period.

   3. Informative **disclosures** in the financial statements are to be regarded as reasonably adequate unless otherwise stated in the report.

   4. The report shall either contain an expression of **opinion** regarding the financial statements taken as a whole, or an assertion to the effect that an overall opinion cannot be expressed. When an overall opinion cannot be expressed, the reasons therefore should be stated. In all cases where an auditor's name is associated with financial statements, the report should contain a clear-cut indication of the character of the auditor's work, if any, and the degree of responsibility the auditor is taking.

4. The report on an engagement to evaluate an assertion that has been prepared in conformity with agreed-upon criteria or an engagement to apply agreed-upon procedures should contain a **statement limiting its use** to the parties who have agreed upon such criteria or procedures.

of services that lie outside of financial statements. Despite the criticisms, GAAS were not revised until the mid-1980s when the profession was urged to reconsider the standards by several opinion leaders, among them Robert K. Elliott, a former KPMG partner and AICPA chair.[1] The Auditing Standards Board and the Accounting and Review Services Committee responded jointly in 1986 with *Statement on Standards for Attestation Engagements (SSAE No. 1)*, "Attestation Standards."[2] Like GAAS, the eleven **attestation standards**, presented in Figure 2-1, left column, are classified as general standards, standards of field work, and standards of reporting. The attestation standards are broader than GAAS, since they provide guidance for a broader range of services. Rather than supersede any of the auditing standards, the attestation standards serve as an umbrella over the entire range of attest services. GAAS apply exclusively to one attestation service: financial statement audits.

The Public Company Accounting Oversight Board: Standards for Public Company Engagements

At the turn of the century, an unprecedented number of public companies restated financial statements. For example, the GAO reports that of 8,494 companies listed on the New York Stock Exchanges, NASDAQ, or the American Stock Exchange throughout the six-year period 1997 through 2002, no less that 895 (9.95 percent) restated financial statements and the restatements reduced the market capitalizations of the restated companies by a total of $95.6 billion.[3] The previously issued financial statements had been audited, raising questions about audit quality and about the adequacy of generally accepted auditing standards. In response, Congress, through Section 103 of the *Sarbanes-Oxley Act of 2002*, empowered the Public Company Accounting Oversight Board (PCAOB, Chapter 1) to adopt existing generally accepted auditing standards in whole or in part or, in contrast, to develop new standards for audits of public companies. Owing in part to highly publicized audit failures and restatements, the PCAOB in 2003, through Release No. 2003-006, "Establishment of Interim Professional Auditing Standards," announced the establishment of Interim Professional Practice Standards for public company engagements, temporarily adopting *generally accepted auditing standards* under the title Interim Professional Auditing Standards and *attestation standards* under the title Interim Attestation Standards.

In December 2003, the PCAOB issued the first standard to supersede a provision of the Interim Professional Auditing Standards: *Auditing Standard No. 1*, "References in Auditors' Reports to the Standards of the PCAOB." *Auditing Standard No. 1* directs the independent auditor of a public company to state in an audit report (Chapter 3) that the engagement was conducted in accordance "with the standards of the Public Company Accounting Oversight Board (United States)." Today, the Auditing Standards Board sanctions standards for engagements serving nonpublic companies, and the PCAOB, through the Chief Auditor and Director of Professional Standards (Chapter 1), sanctions professional standards for

---

1   P. D. Jacobson and R. K. Elliott, "GAAS: Reconsidering the 'Ten Commandments'," *Journal of Accountancy* (May 1984), pp. 77–88.

2   In January 1989, the *Statements on Standards for Attestation Engagements (SSAEs)* entitled, "Attestation Standards" (AT 100), "Financial Forecasts and Projections" (AT 200), and "Reporting on Pro Forma Financial Information" (AT 300) were codified in SSAE No. 1, "Attestation Standards."

3   U.S. GAO, *Financial Statement Restatements: Trends, Market Impacts, Regulatory Responses, and Remaining Challenges.* Washington, D.C. U.S. Government Printing Office: 2002.

engagements serving public companies. However, note carefully that auditors of nonpublic companies are not precluded from conducting audits in accordance with standards the PCAOB sanctions. In fact, auditors, in consultation with nonpublic clients, may judge PCAOB standards preferable in some cases—for example, if a nonpublic client contemplates going public in the future.

Although the term "auditing standards" had been used loosely over the years, practitioners generally referred to GAAS as the standards of audit practice and to the Auditing Standards Board's *Statements on Auditing Standards* as interpretations of GAAS. However, the Auditing Standards Board issued *SAS No. 95*, "Generally Accepted Auditing Standards," in 2001 and *SAS No. 98*, "Omnibus SAS," in 2002, which clarify the term by distinguishing between *auditing standards* and *interpretive publications*. *Standards* refers both to GAAS and to *SASs*, and *interpretive publications* refers to "recommendations on the application of SASs" the Auditing Standards Board issues formally under the title "Interpretations," to appendixes of the SASs, to auditing guidance within AICPA Audit & Accounting Guides, and to AICPA auditing Statements of Position. For example, *SAS No. 59* captures the standards for considering an audit client's ability to continue as a going concern, and AU Sec. 341A.02 interprets *SAS No. 59*. No auditing publications other than GAAS, *SASs*, and Interpretations are authoritative—not articles in professional magazines, such as the *Journal of Accountancy*; not published guidebooks; and not textbooks.

Neither the attestation standards nor GAAS offers step-by-step procedures (for example, would you feel comfortable approaching your very first engagement armed with nothing more than the declarative sentences in Figure 2-1?). Nor were they intended to. Standards are the guidelines from which procedures are derived, the measures of quality against which completed engagements are judged. Because they are guidelines, the standards rarely change over time. For example, since enactment, none of the attestation standards and only two of the GAAS have been revised significantly.[4] Procedures, in contrast, are detailed methods or techniques that change as technology changes. For example, wide area networks (WANs) require different auditing procedures than stand-alone desktop computers. Procedures are the means by which standards are fulfilled. Much like engineering or economics, attestations and audits are grounded in several well-pitched concepts. Four concepts underlie both the attestation standards and GAAS: *independence* and *due care* (which underlie the general standards), *evidence* (the standards of field work), and *reporting* (the standards of reporting).

Independence

Independence *in fact* is a state of mind—an attitude of impartiality—that underlies both an attestation standard (Figure 2-1, 4th general standard) and a GAAS (2nd general standard). In practice, independence is powerfully important to the profession's reputation as a trusted player in the market for audit services. The financial community values the reports of certified public accountants precisely because CPAs are perceived as having no vested financial or personal interest in the outcome of the engagement. However, because a practitioner's "state of mind" cannot be observed in quite the same way that a behavior—say, a head nod—can

---

4   The second field work standard and the second reporting standard (Figure 2-1, right column) were revised in 1988 by *SAS Nos. 55* and *58*, respectively.

be observed, the profession has relied on independence _in appearance_. That is, to demonstrate independence in fact, practitioners remain free of any overt interest in a client that would damage the appearance of independence. For example, an auditor who owns an interest in a business he or she audits might well be intellectually honest when auditing the business but would not appear independent to a bank loan officer, since the auditor has a financial interest in the bank's lending decision.

Consulting and the SEC's Engagement-Team Independence Rules of 2000

In a May 2000 speech, "Renewing the Covenant with Investors," former SEC Chairman Arthur Levitt, Jr., argued that audit firms compromise independence by accepting consulting fees from audit clients:

> . . . _consulting and other services may shorten the distance between the auditor and management. Independence—if not in fact, then certainly in appearance—becomes a more elusive proposition. . . . More than a hundred years ago, it was said, "A public accountant acknowledges no master but the public." But, when auditors engage in extensive services for an audit client truly unrelated to the audit, they must now also serve another master—management. In this dual role, the auditor, who guards the integrity of the numbers, now both oversees and answers to management._[5]

In the same speech, Levitt asked that the SEC staff propose new independence rules "to deal with the conflicts created by the profession's ever-expanding menu of services."

In July 2000, the SEC proposed sweeping changes to independence rules that had been intact since the 1930s. Among other things, the proposed rules would have banned firms from providing information technology (IT) and internal audit services to SEC audit clients.[6] With some exceptions, the proposed rules would have restricted firms to offering only one service to public companies: financial statement audits. Testimony on the proposed rules, made in Fall 2000 before Congress, was both pointed and split. For example, John D. Hawke, comptroller of the Treasury, supported the proposed rules: "In an ideal world, the external auditor should be free from any extraneous influences and motivations."

In contrast to their united stance denouncing similar calls for independence reform in the 1970s and 1980s, the Big Four firms and the AICPA broke into two separate camps in the 1990s: PricewaterhouseCoopers and Ernst & Young, both of whom had announced plans to spin off their consulting practices, generally supported the proposed rules. However, Deloitte & Touche, KPMG, and the AICPA argued that the SEC's proposed rules would prohibit firms from undertaking lucrative consulting engagements, thereby stifling the revenue growth that firms had enjoyed in the 1990s.[7] For example, Arthur Levitt estimated in 2000 that profession-wide auditing revenues had grown by 9 percent per year since 1993 but that consulting revenues had grown by a staggering 27 percent per year.[8] Influenced in part by a September 21, 2000, compromise proposal submitted by Ernst

---

5   Arthur Levitt, Jr., "Renewing the Covenant with Investors." Remarks by the SEC Chairman. New York University Center for Law and Business, May 10, 2000.

6   K. Rankin, "Levitt Strikes Back," _Accounting Today_ (July 10–23, 2000), pp. 1, 58.

7   "Independence Rules Split Big Five," _Public Accounting Report_ (July 31, 2000), p. 2.

8   Arthur Levitt, Jr., "Renewing the Covenant with Investors." Remarks by the SEC Chairman. New York University Center for Law and Business, May 10, 2000.

& Young and PricewaterhouseCoopers, the SEC issued final rules in November 2000 that stepped back significantly from the rules proposed in July 2000.[9] The final rules mandated an engagement team (rather than a firm-wide) model of independence, emphasized independence in appearance, softened the SEC's proposed rules for information technology and internal audit consulting, and required that public companies disclose in proxy statements their incumbent auditor's audit and nonaudit fees, among other things.

Disclosure of aggregate fees was a centerpiece of the SEC's final rules, since the disclosure allowed users to judge for themselves whether nonaudit service fees compromise an auditor's independence in appearance. To investigate, *The Wall Street Journal* studied disclosures made by 307 of the Standard & Poor's 500 companies. The study found that all of the 307 companies paid their incumbent auditor a nonaudit fee, and that nonaudit fees totaled three times more than audit fees: $2.65 billion in nonaudit fees and $909 million in audit fees.[10] For example, Sprint paid Ernst & Young $63.8 million and $2.5 million, Delphi Automotive Systems paid Deloitte & Touche $62.3 million and $3.9 million, and JPMorgan Chase paid PricewaterhouseCoopers $84.2 million and $21.3 million, respectively, in nonaudit and audit fees. *The Wall Street Journal* reported that Lynn Turner, then SEC chief accountant, expected that nonaudit fees would approximate 25 to 40 percent of audit fees and that the magnitude of nonaudit fees would raise difficult issues for auditors. However, although research on the effect of nonaudit fees on auditor independence is mixed, some found evidence that nonaudit fees may not affect independence. For example, Defond et al. found no association between nonaudit service fees and independence impairment, and speculated that "incentives, such as reputation loss and litigation costs, promote auditor independence and outweigh the economic dependency created by higher fees."[11]

The Sarbanes-Oxley Act of 2002 and the SEC's Independence Rules of 2003

> earnings management

Coincident with the debate over nonaudit services, the press in 2001 and 2002 reported that a number of public companies had harnessed accounting rules to manage earnings.[12] For example, Enron and Krispy Kreme reportedly used off-balance sheet financing to obscure long-term debt,[13] Global Crossing swapped underwater cable rights to enhance revenue,[14] and IBM netted the gain on an asset sale against overhead expenses.[15] On grounds of compromising independence,

---

9   M. McNamee, "A Compromise from the Crusader," *Business Week* (November 13, 2000), pp. 196–197; M. Schroeder, "Tougher Curbs on Auditors Likely at SEC," *The Wall Street Journal* (November 14, 2000), p. C1; R. I. Miller, "The SEC's Final Rule on Auditor Independence Generally Reflects Negotiated Compromise," *The CPA Letter* (January 2001), p. 1.

10 J. Weil and J. Tannenbaum, "Big Companies Pay Audit Firms More for Other Services," *The Wall Street Journal* (April 10, 2001), pp. C1–C2.

11 M. L. Defond, K. Raghunandan, and K. R. Subramanyam, "Do Non-Audit Service Fees Impair Auditor Independence? Evidence from Going Concern Audit Opinions," *Journal of Accounting Research* (September 2002), pp. 1247–1274.

12 See, for example, D. Henry, "The Numbers Game," *Business Week* (May 14, 2001), p. 100; S. Liesman, "Deciphering the Black Box—Many Accounting Practices, Not Just Enron's, Are Hard to Penetrate," *The Wall Street Journal* (January 23, 2002), p. C1; A. Serwer, "Dirty Rotten Numbers," *Fortune* (February 18, 2002), p. 74; K. Brown, "Creative Accounting: How to Buff a Company," *The Wall Street Journal* (February 2, 2002), p. C1.

13 S. Lubove and E. MacDonald, "Enron is Hardly Alone When it Comes to Creative Off-Balance Sheet Accounting," *Forbes Magazine* (February 18, 2002), p. 56.

14 D. Berman and D. Solomon, "Optical Illusion? Accounting Questions Swirl Around Pioneer in the Telecom World," *The Wall Street Journal* (February 13, 2002), p. A1.

15 "IBM's Accounting Questioned," *The Washington Post* (February 15, 2002), p. E2.

the reports also implicated auditors, since the financial statements of the companies had all been audited. Erosion of faith in auditor independence prompted the
SEC to conduct hearings in Washington, D.C. and New York, and prompted Congress in 2002 to enact the *Sarbanes-Oxley Act*. Among other things, the Act establishes the Public Company Accounting Oversight Board (Chapter 1), addresses accountability for corporate and criminal fraud, and amends Section 10A of the   ➤ fraud
Securities Exchange Act of 1934 to limit the consulting services an auditor can provide to public companies. The Act limits consulting services in two ways. First,
Section 201, Services Outside the Scope of Practice of Auditors, reproduced in part
in Figure 2-2, prohibits nine services, including the design and implementation of
financial information systems, which had long been lucrative for accounting
firms. Second, although the Act permits an incumbent auditor to provide services
other than those in Figure 2-2, including tax, Section 201 requires that the audit
committee of the audit client's board of directors approve the services in advance.

FIGURE 2-2: *Sarbanes-Oxley, Section 201, Services*
Outside the Scope of Practice of Auditors (in part)

(g) **Prohibited Activities**—Except as provided in subsection (h), it shall be unlawful
for a registered public accounting firm that performs for any issuer any audit . . . to
provide to that issuer . . . any nonaudit service, including—

  (1) bookkeeping or other services related to the accounting records or financial
      statements of the audit client;
  (2) financial information systems design and implementation;
  (3) appraisal or valuation services, fairness opinions, or contribution-in-kind
      reports;
  (4) actuarial services;
  (5) internal audit outsourcing services;
  (6) management functions or human resources;
  (7) broker or dealer, investment adviser, or investment banking services;
  (8) legal services and expert services unrelated to the audit; and
  (9) any other service that the Board determines, by regulation, is impermissible.

(h) **Preapproval Required for Nonaudit Services**—A registered public accounting
firm may engage in any nonaudit service, including tax services, that is not described
in any of paragraphs (1) through (9) of subsection (g) for an audit client, only if the activity is approved in advance by the audit committee of the issuer, in accordance with
subsection (i).

Under the authority of Section 208 of the Sarbanes-Oxley Act, the SEC in January 2003 announced further regulations on auditor independence. The regulations speak to issues that had long been controversial, among them the rotation of
auditors, client's employing former auditors, and audit partner compensation
plans. For example, the regulations:

  ● Require that an engagement partner rotate after no more than five or seven
    consecutive years, depending on the partner's involvement in the audit;
  ● Establish rules that an accounting firm would not be independent of a client
    that employs one of the client's former auditors within the one-year period
    preceding the audit;

- Establish rules that an auditor is not independent of a client if he or she earned compensation based on selling to the client a service other than an audit, review, or other attest service; and
- Require that an auditor report certain matters, including "critical" accounting policies, to the client's audit committee.

The SEC's rules and the *Sarbanes-Oxley Act* apply to public companies an auditor audits, not to public companies an accountant does *not* audit (and not to nonpublic companies).

In the wake of the SEC's rules and *Sarbanes-Oxley*, the consulting operations of many public accounting firms were denied access to a major source of business: the firm's audit clients. For example, since the turn of the century, three of the Big Four firms spun-off parts of their consulting practices: CapGemini acquired Ernst & Young Consulting, IBM acquired PwC Consulting, and KPMG Consulting went public. Among the Big Four, only Deloitte & Touche Consulting remains.

Independence Issues in Other Assurance Services

As practitioners embark on new assurance services, *assurance* independence will likely raise questions quite apart from those raised by *audit* or *attest* independence, since, in some assurance services, the assurer is also the asserter! For example, compare PricewaterhouseCoopers' audit service for BP to its assurance service for the Academy of Motion Picture Arts and Sciences. In the audit service, BP management is the asserter (that is, the preparer of financial statements) and PricewaterhouseCoopers is the attestor. However, in the assurance service, PricewaterhouseCoopers is both asserter and attestor, raising a unique set of questions not otherwise raised by audit services. For example, can assurers be independent of themselves? Can a public accounting firm reasonably claim independence if an audit client, say Paramount Pictures, has a movie nominated for Best Picture? These questions beg for independence in which a practitioner has no interest in an outcome—for instance, an assurance report—other than the reliability of the outcome.

Due Care

Due care underlies two issues within the attestation standards and GAAS: <u>care when delivering professional services</u> (Figure 2-1: 1st, 2nd, 3rd, and 5th general attestation standards; 3rd general GAAS), <u>and training</u> (1st general attestation standard; 1st general GAAS).

Think of a work by a gifted artist or a performance by a talented actor. That work, that performance, *that* is due professional care. The following quote, on the same topic, is from *Cooley on Torts*.

Every man who offers his service to another and is employed assumes the duty to exercise in the employment such skill as he possesses with reasonable care and diligence. In all these employments where peculiar skill is prerequisite, if one offers his service, he is understood as holding himself out to the public as possessing the degree of skill commonly possessed by others in the same employment, and, if his pretensions are unfounded, he commits a species of fraud upon every man who employs him in reliance on his public profession.

No other quote so clearly captures the essence of due care. In short, a practitioner is responsible to exercise reasonable care—and to be <u>intellectually honest about</u>

possessing requisite skills—or risk committing an inexcusable fraud upon all who rely on his or her work.

WorldCom

Failure to exercise due care—either knowingly and recklessly, or unknowingly and unintentionally—has given rise to allegations that equate due care to the auditor's Achilles' heel. In 2002, WorldCom, then the second largest long-distance carrier in the United States, announced an intent to restate financial statements for each of the five quarters ended March 31, 2002. Rather than charge to income fees WorldCom paid to access other telecommunications providers' networks, World-Com had capitalized the costs in amounts sufficient to report earnings consistent with analysts' expectations. Capitalizing the costs violated **generally accepted accounting principles (GAAP)**. On June 26, 2002, one day after WorldCom's announcement, the SEC filed a complaint in U.S. District Court, charging that World-Com had inflated income and had violated federal antifraud provisions of the federal securities laws.[16] In his opinion on the monetary settlement phrase of the case, Judge Jed Rakoff characterized WorldCom as "perhaps the largest accounting fraud in history, with the company's income overstated by an estimated $11 billion, its balance sheet overstated by over $75 billion, and losses to shareholders estimated at as much as $200 billion."[17]

➤ fraud
➤ restatement

Neither the judge's opinion nor the SEC's complaint charged WorldCom's auditor. Although the auditor issued a statement that WorldCom's chief financial officer had not disclosed to them the accounting practices in question,[18] documents accompanying an internal WorldCom report showed that senior finance executives had notified the auditor of improperly shifted expenses two years prior, suggesting "the first evidence that (the auditor) had reason to question (the CFO) about his treatment of fees paid to other communications companies for use of their networks. . . ."[19] On the public's right to expect that a fraud of this magnitude should have been detected, despite a cover up, Lynn Turner, former SEC chief accountant, said, "I think when you cross that three, $4 billion threshold, as we have on WorldCom, there's no question that even if there's management fraud involved, the public expects, and I think rightfully so, for the auditors to detect that."[20] What Turner is speaking to is due professional care.

The Prudent Practitioner

Clearly, practitioners are not expected to be infallible. Like physicians, attorneys, and other responsible professionals, providers of audit services are subject to human error. However, also like other professionals, providers are entrusted with the responsibility to perform their duties with the degree of care expected of the *prudent practitioner*. In the legal profession, the notion of a "reasonable person" is often applied by the courts to determine the extent and limits of an individual's

---

16 *SEC Accounting and Auditing Release No. 1585*, "SEC Charges WorldCom with $3.8 Billion Fraud," June 26, 2002.

17 Opinion and Order, *SEC v. WorldCom, Inc.*, United States District Court, Southern District of New York, July 7, 2003 (02 Civ. 49-63).

18 S. Romero and A. Berenson, "WorldCom Says It Hid Expenses, Inflating Cash Flow $3.8 Billion," *The New York Times* (June 26, 2002), p. A1.

19 K. Eichenwald, "Auditing Woes at WorldCom Were Noted Two Years Ago," *The New York Times Abstracts* (July 15, 2002), p. 1.

20 National Public Radio, Morning Edition (June 27, 2002).

responsibility. The "prudent practitioner" serves a similar purpose in auditing and, like the "reasonable person," is subject to judgment and interpretation. Mautz and Sharaf offer some interpretation:[21]

The prudent practitioner will:

- Take steps to *foresee unreasonable risk or harm to others*.
- Attend to any employee, department, transaction, or resource that experience or history suggests may carry *extra risk*.
- Consider any *unusual circumstances* or relationships when planning and performing the engagement.
- Recognize *unfamiliar situations* and take precautions.
- Take all appropriate steps to *resolve doubt* or unanswered questions about matters material to his or her report.
- *Keep abreast of developments* in his or her area of competence.
- *Review the work of assistants* with the full understanding of the importance of the task.

Mautz and Sharaf's interpretation provides a framework for understanding the nature of professional care.

A practitioner comes to appreciate due care through formal preprofessional education (for example, baccalaureate or graduate degrees), continuing professional education (for example, AICPA seminars), and properly supervised, on-the-job experience. Education and experience complement each other, are part of an attitude of lifelong learning, and are the basis for a practitioner to develop what he or she sells: *professional judgment*. Underscoring the importance of professional judgment in auditing, the *Codification of Auditing Standards* includes over 100 references to the need for professional judgment in practice. For example, the Codification states:

- *The auditor should obtain a level of knowledge of the entity's business that will enable him . . . to obtain an understanding of the events, transactions, and practices that, in his judgment, may have a significant effect on the financial statements.*
- *The auditor should plan the audit so that audit risk will be limited to a low level that is, in his professional judgment, appropriate for issuing an opinion on the financial statements.*
- *The assessment of possible error as of the balance sheet date should be based on the auditor's judgment of the state of the particular account(s) as of that date.*

As the number of references to judgment suggests, the hallmark of audit services is neither the responsibilities addressed in Chapters 3 through 6 nor the methods in Chapters 7 through 16. Rather, the hallmark is the sequence of complex professional judgments that constitute decision making. Much as physicians are compensated for judgments about identifiable symptoms, probable cause, and likely diagnosis, audit service providers are compensated for complex professional judgments about the collection, interpretation, and reporting of evidence.

The Panel on Audit Effectiveness

In an often quoted September 28, 1998, speech, "The Numbers Game," SEC Chairman Arthur Levitt, Jr., called for the Public Oversight Board (until *Sarbanes-Oxley*,

---

21 Adapted from R. K. Mautz and H. A. Sharaf, *The Philosophy of Auditing*. Sarasota, FL: American Accounting Association, 1961, pp. 135–138.

an independent monitor of the public's confidence in the audit process) to investigate the relationship between due care in financial statement audits and reported accounting failures:

I don't think it should surprise anyone here that recent headlines of accounting failures have led some people to question the thoroughness of audits. . . . I have just proposed that the Public Oversight Board form a group of all the major constituencies to review the way audits are performed and assess the impact of recent trends on the public interest.[22]

In response, the Public Oversight Board appointed an 8-member panel, which reviewed the audits of 126 SEC registrants in 28 offices of the 8 largest firms, read the firms' audit policies, and solicited the views of opinion leaders through interviews, questionnaires, research, and public hearings. Testifying in a public hearing before the Panel, Levitt made clear his concerns about due care and the management of audit firms:

I fear that the audit process, long rooted in independence and forged through professionalism, may be diminished—perhaps even sacrificed in the name of more financial and commercial opportunities. In recent years, the amount of revenue generated by accounting firms in areas of business other than traditional auditing services has increased exponentially. Some firms—perhaps preferring to distance themselves from the roots that have given them such opportunities—prefer to think of themselves as multi-disciplinary organizations.[23]

In an August 2000 report, the Panel concluded that its "in-depth reviews of audits were favorable and did not support the view that audits are being conducted in an ineffective manner." However, the Panel also concluded that they were "concerned that the auditing profession has not kept pace with a rapidly changing environment, and that the profession needs to address vigorously the issue of fraudulent financial reporting, including fraud in the form of illegitimate earnings management."[24] For example, the Panel suggested that auditors modify their traditional "neutral concept of professional skepticism" to presume that a dishonest management may falsify documents or withhold valid documents. The Panel's suggestion is a lesson of WorldCom.

Evidence   → *Conclusions*

Evidence, the basis for decisions in all attestation and audit engagements, contemplates three issues: evidential matter (Figure 2-1: 2nd field work attestation standard; 3rd field work GAAS), planning and supervision (1st field work attestation standard; 1st field work GAAS), and internal control (2nd field work GAAS).

The nature and measurement of evidence varies depending on whether a practitioner is performing an attestation engagement or an audit engagement. For example, consider PricewaterhouseCoopers' attestation engagement for Wilson Sporting Goods' Ultra golf ball, asserted by Wilson to outdistance the competition by 5.7 yards per drive. In this case, the *nature* of the evidence is a sample of drives observed by PricewaterhouseCoopers' professionals, and the *measurement* scale is

---

22 Arthur Levitt, Jr., "The 'Numbers Game'," speech at New York University Center for Law and Business, September 28, 1998.

23 Arthur Levitt, Jr., Remarks to the Panel on Audit Effectiveness of the Public Oversight Board. New York, October 7, 1999.

24 The Panel on Audit Effectiveness, *Report and Recommendations*, Stamford, CT: 2000, p. ix.

yards per drive. Compare that evidence to PricewaterhouseCoopers' audit engagement for Wilson Sporting Goods, in particular management's assertion that the Ultra golf ball inventory exists and is valued properly. In this case, the *nature* of the evidence is stacked cartons of golf balls PricewaterhouseCoopers' professionals observed, and the *measurement* scale is GAAP.

The professional literature has been far more forthcoming about the nature of evidence in audit engagements than in attestation engagements. For example, *Statement on Auditing Standards No. 31*, "Evidential Matter" (AU Sec. 330), describes **audit evidence** as the underlying accounting data and all related corroborating information available to an auditor. *Underlying accounting data* includes journals, ledgers, reconciliations, and accounting manuals. *Corroborating information* includes receiving reports, invoices, contracts, and representations from third parties, such as confirmations of receivables balances with debtors (Chapter 11).

Audit decision making is based on sufficient, competent evidential matter. *Sufficiency* refers to the quantity of audit evidence obtained, although it does not mean "the more, the better." Audit decisions must be reached within a reasonable length of time and at reasonable cost, requiring that an auditor balance the cost of obtaining additional evidence with the usefulness of the evidence obtained. In contrast, *competence* refers to the validity and relevance of evidence, both of which depend heavily on whether the evidence is obtained from independent sources, obtained directly by the auditor, or processed through reliable information systems. For example, several well-established presumptions about evidence follow.

- Evidence obtained by an auditor from independent sources (for example, banks, debtors) is more reliable than evidence obtained from management.
- Evidence obtained directly by an auditor through physical examination, observation, computation, and inspection is more persuasive than evidence obtained indirectly from management.
- Reliable evidence is more likely to be produced by effective, rather than by ineffective, systems of internal control.

Independent auditors would much prefer to obtain entirely convincing, rather than merely persuasive, audit evidence. However, because the cost of obtaining evidence should not exceed the usefulness of the evidence obtained, audit evidence is often persuasive rather than wholly convincing. But this is quite acceptable in audit practice, since an audit is designed to provide reasonable, not absolute, assurance about management's assertions in financial statements. The nature, types, and documentation of evidence are discussed more fully in Chapter 6.

Audit engagements should be planned by competent professional staff, and the work of all assistants assigned to the engagement should be supervised. Due care demands no less. For example, an independent auditor should be appointed before (or soon after) an entity's fiscal year begins, because early appointment allows ample time to plan and to consider completing some audit field work before the balance sheet date. An auditor can accept an audit engagement near or after the balance sheet date, but should alert management that the engagement cannot be completed unless all relevant audit evidence can be accessed. For example, if appointed after the close of a prospective client's fiscal year, the auditor may have difficulty obtaining persuasive evidence that recorded inventory existed at the balance sheet date.

Statement on Auditing Standards No. 22, "Planning and Supervision" (AU Sec. 311), describes *planning* as the process of developing objectives and an overall strategy. The extent of an audit plan depends on the size and complexity of the entity, and the practitioner's knowledge of and experience with the entity's business. Planning considerations include the nature of the business and the industry in which the entity operates, the entity's organizational design, operating policies, preliminary estimates of materiality (discussed later in this chapter), and financial statement disclosures likely to require correcting. Above all, an auditor is best prepared to complete an audit when thoroughly familiar with the client as well as the client's business and industry—that is, an audit should not be conducted in a vacuum. *Supervision* is the process of directing the efforts of assistants toward the objectives of the engagement, and determining whether the objectives are achieved. All work performed by assistants should be thoroughly reviewed, and their conclusions should be consistent with the opinion communicated in an audit report. Procedures also should be established to determine how to resolve differences of opinion among staff members about accounting and auditing issues.

Auditors often plan to conduct some auditing procedures—for example, tests of controls and analytical procedures—at interim dates prior to the balance sheet date. One purpose of interim audit work is to determine the risk that an entity's internal controls may fail to detect or prevent material misstatements in the financial statements. In fact, when controls are found to be effective, year-end work may consist mainly of analytical procedures—such as comparison of current with prior-year account balances—and less extensive detailed tests, assuming controls remain effective. Emphasis on tests of controls and analytical procedures is more appropriate for accounts with large numbers of transactions, and emphasis on detailed testing is more appropriate for accounts with few transactions. Extensive, time-consuming tests of controls for accounts with only a small number of transactions is inefficient, since less audit time is consumed by simply testing all or most of the transactions directly.

An entity's **internal controls** represent the policies and procedures that the board of directors and management have implemented to provide themselves with reasonable assurance that their objectives will be achieved. Although the attestation standards do not address internal control explicitly, attestation engagements about internal control are common. For example, Deloitte & Touche attested for years to an assertion the management of a West Coast client makes about the adequacy of stock transfer and shareholder servicing controls as defined by Rule 17Ad-13(a)(3) of the *Securities Exchange Act of 1934*. In contrast, GAAS are explicit about internal control. The second standard of field work requires that an auditor obtain an understanding of an entity's internal controls to help in planning the audit and in designing audit tests. The standard also points implicitly to an important inverse relationship between the effectiveness of an entity's internal controls and the extent of audit procedures required: As the effectiveness of an entity's internal controls increases, the amount of evidence necessary to reach an opinion on the financial statements should decrease, since effective controls can reduce the risk of materially misstated financial statements.

Reporting

Practitioners issue reports in all attestation and audit engagements. Most attestation reports conclude whether management's written assertion is presented in conformity with established or stated criteria, and audit reports conclude whether management's financial statements are presented in accordance with GAAP. For example, Deloitte & Touche's *attestation report* for the stock transfer and share-holder servicing controls introduced earlier read, in part, as follows:

In our opinion, management's assertion that, during the year ended, the Company maintained an effective internal control structure, including appropriate segregation of responsibilities and duties, over the transfer agent and shareholder servicing functions . . . and that no material inadequacies existed as defined by Rule 17Ad-13(a)(3) of the Securities Exchange Act of 1934, is fairly stated, in all material respects, based upon criteria established by Rule 17Ad-13(a)(3) of the Securities Exchange Act of 1934.

Consistent with the attestation standards of reporting (Figure 2-1, left column), the report identifies management's assertion ("*. . . maintained an effective . . .*") and the established criteria against which the assertion was measured (*Rule 17 Ad-13(a)(3)*).

Deloitte & Touche's *audit report* for the same company reads, in part, as follows:

In our opinion, the financial statements referred to above present fairly, in all material respects, the financial position of the company . . . , and the results of its operations and its cash flows . . . , in conformity with generally accepted accounting principles.

Consistent with the GAAS of reporting (Figure 2-1, right column), the report states that the financial statements comply with GAAP ("*. . . in conformity with . . .*") and expresses an opinion ("*present fairly*"), but reports neither that the accounting principles were applied inconsistently nor that the disclosures were inadequate, because apparently they were not. Reporting is discussed extensively in Chapter 3.

Risk

In the attestation and audit reports previously illustrated, Deloitte & Touche used the terms *opinion* and *material*. The attestation report reads, "In our *opinion* . . . no *material* inadequacies," and the audit report reads, "In our *opinion* . . . in all *material* respects." The phrases imply to readers that the reports are statements of opinion, rather than statements of fact, and therefore that Deloitte & Touche may have unknowingly failed to modify the attestation report for material undetected inadequacies in internal control, or the audit report for material undetected misstatements in financial statements. That is, despite performing the engagements in accordance with attestation standards and with auditing standards, respectively, there is a risk that management's assertions about their internal controls and about their financial statements may contain *material* omissions or misstatements. For example, in the attestation engagement, there may be inappropriate commingling of responsibilities that, if known, would have driven the SEC to sanction management for violations of *Rule 17Ad-13(a)(3)*, and in the audit engagement there may be omitted disclosures that, if known, would have driven an investor to divest an equity investment. Practitioners attempt to hold risk to a relatively low level, but no practitioner can eliminate all risk completely, in part because attestation and audit engagements are designed to provide reasonable, not absolute, assurance.

Attestation Risk and Audit Risk

In an attestation engagement, **attestation risk** is the probability that an attestor may unknowingly fail to modify a written conclusion about an assertion that is materially misstated. For example, in Deloitte & Touche's attestation engagement, the firm sustains a risk that the attestation report fails to capture undetected material misstatements in management's assertions about stock transfer and shareholder servicing controls. In contrast, in a financial statement audit, **audit risk** is the probability that an auditor may unknowingly fail to modify an opinion on financial statements that are materially misstated. For example, in the audit engagement for the same client, Deloitte & Touche sustains a risk that the audit report fails to capture undetected material misstatements in management's assertions about the financial statements. Practitioners plan engagements so that attestation risk or audit risk—whether assessed quantitatively (for example, 5 or 10 percent) or qualitatively (for example, high, moderate, or low)—will be limited to a level that is low enough to issue a report confidently, without undue risk that management's assertions are materially misstated.

The professional literature about risk and materiality is not well developed for attestation services, but is quite rich for financial statement audits. For decades, most audits were driven largely by prescribed sets of audit procedures that varied little across engagements, apart from minor changes for industry differences: so-called *procedures-driven* audits. The logic of a procedures-driven audit was to cast a wide net, and to enjoy efficiencies on an engagement from year to year by learning to perform procedures more quickly. Procedures-driven audits gave way in the 1990s to *risk-driven* audits—that is, audits in which the auditor allocates disproportionately more effort to the assertions, accounts, and disclosures that he or she judges the most risky, since low-risk accounts or disclosures are not likely misstated and, therefore, not worthy of significant effort. However, the transition to risk-driven audits is not without critics. For example, some observers point to high-profile audit failures and argue that risk-driven audits may have more to do with controlling audit cost than with improving audit effectiveness.[25] Today, effective risk management is at the center of gravity both in financial statement audits and in attestation engagements.

Inherent Risk, Control Risk, and Detection Risk

In a financial statement audit, audit risk for any one individual account, such as Accounts Receivable or Inventory, consists of the:

- *Inherent* and *control risks* that the account contains errors that could be material when combined with errors in other accounts, and
- *Detection risk* that the auditor will not detect material errors.

Inherent, control, and detection risk are introduced next, followed by how they translate into audit risk.

Inherent risk is the susceptibility of an account balance to error that could be material, assuming there are no related internal controls. For example, technological developments in the telecommunications industry could render some replacement parts inventory obsolete, thereby increasing the inherent risk that the

---

25 J. Weil, "Behind the Wave of Corporate Fraud: A Change in How Auditors Work," *The Wall Street Journal* (March 25, 2004), pp. A1, A14.

carrying value of inventory is overstated. Some accounts are inherently more risky than others because of their very nature, rather than observable outside influences such as changes in technology. For example, liquid assets such as cash and marketable securities are far more susceptible to theft, and therefore are inherently more risky, than nonliquid assets such as coal or timber. Auditors can do little to influence inherent risk. Rather, the task is to assess inherent risk completely by considering the client's business and industry (for example, a technologically driven industry?), management's predisposition to manage earnings (does GAAP in the industry offer income-enhancing accounting alternatives?), and insights obtained from prior engagements (prior-year inventory pricing errors?).

Control risk is the likelihood that error could occur and not be prevented or detected by internal controls. The more effective the internal controls are, the less control risk sustained by the auditor. In practice, auditors sometimes combine inherent and control risk, and sometimes assess the two risks separately. However, regardless of whether the risks are assessed separately or in combination, the auditor should have a basis for judging risk. For example, as a basis for assessing control risk, an auditor could use evidence gathered when documenting an entity's internal controls. And, as a basis for assessing inherent risk for high-tech inventory, an auditor could use a specially designed technological obsolescence questionnaire. Like inherent risk, auditors can do little to influence control risk. Instead, auditors attempt to manage inherent and control risk by controlling detection risk, the one risk that auditors *can* influence.

Detection risk is the likelihood that error could occur and not be detected by the auditor's procedures. In practice, detection risk arises partly because auditors do not normally test all of the transactions comprising an account balance, and partly because of other uncertainties that may arise even when testing all transactions, such as poor judgment. Inherent and control risk are inversely related to detection risk; that is, the higher a client's assessed levels of inherent and control risks, the less detection risk an auditor can accept. For example, if a client's controls over precious metals are inadequate, an auditor would be willing to accept only a very low detection risk, since (1) precious metals are highly susceptible to theft, indicating high inherent risk; and (2) controls are inadequate, indicating high control risk. In this case, an auditor would require particularly effective audit procedures to minimize detection risk.

Measuring Audit Risk and Detection Risk

In practice, auditors often express audit risk in words (for example, high, medium, or low) rather than numbers, primarily because inherent, control, and detection risk are often difficult to judge with precision. However, assuming they can be quantified for a given audit client, an auditor could measure audit risk for particular accounts according to an expression implied in *SAS No. 47*, "Audit Risk and Materiality in Conducting an Audit":[26]

$$AR = IR \times CR \times DR$$

---

26 See W. S. Waller, "Auditors' Assessments of Inherent and Control Risk in Field Settings," *The Accounting Review* (October 1993), pp. 783–803 for a review of *a priori* analyses of the audit risk model's assumptions and of auditor's risk assessments in experimental settings, and for an empirical test of the statistical association between control and inherent risk in practice.

where: AR = Audit risk for an account
$\quad\quad IR$ = Inherent risk
$\quad\quad CR$ = Control risk
$\quad\quad DR$ = Detection risk

In practice auditors more commonly preset audit risk at a level acceptable to the firm, evaluate the magnitude of control and inherent risk for an individual account, and then solve for an *acceptable level of detection risk* using the following, a rearrangement of the previous expression.

$$DR = \frac{AR}{IR \times CR}$$

In short, because detection risk can be controlled by the auditor's procedures, detection risk is treated as the dependent variable (the variable on the left side of the equal sign). To illustrate, assume that an auditor wishes to hold audit risk to 2 percent for precious metals inventory and estimates from evidence obtained in prior engagements that inherent risk is 50 percent and control risk is 40 percent. The acceptable level of detection risk for inventory would be:

$$DR = \frac{0.02}{0.50 \times 0.40}$$

$$= 0.10$$

Two observations are apparent about how to interpret an acceptable level of detection risk, in this case 10 percent: First, an auditor would use the acceptable level of detection risk to plan the *amount* of evidence he or she need gather to hold audit risk for inventory to 2 percent. The auditor's task is to gather enough evidence to feel confident that the likelihood of material undetected inventory errors does not exceed 10 percent.

Second, the acceptable level of detection risk is inversely related to the *amount* of audit evidence the auditor would plan to gather. That is, as the acceptable level of detection risk goes up, the amount of evidence gathered goes down, and vice versa. For example, if audit risk for inventory in this illustration were preset at 4 percent (rather than 2 percent), detection risk would go up to 20 percent (rather than 10 percent) and the auditor would require *less* evidence to hold audit risk for inventory to 4 percent than he or she would require to hold audit risk to 2 percent. Why? Because:

$1 - DR$ = *Level of confidence*

Level of confidence is the likelihood that the audit procedures did not fail. To illustrate, 20 percent detection risk translates to an 80 percent level of confidence that audit procedures did not fail; 10 percent detection risk translates to 90 percent confidence. An auditor would require *less* evidence to be 80 percent confident than to be 90 percent confident. Of course, the reliability of numerical measures of detection risk, such as 10 and 20 percent, is directly dependent on the accuracy of an auditor's assessments of control, inherent, and audit risk.

Business Risk

Some practitioners believe that audit risk, the likelihood of unknowingly failing to modify an opinion on materially misstated financial statements, is not unrelated to **business risk**, the probability that a practitioner may incur damages despite issuing an appropriate report. For example, an auditor may face litigation brought by the shareholders of a bankrupt audit client even though the audit report raised substantial doubt about the entity's ability to continue as a going concern (discussed in Chapter 3). Public accounting firms vary in how they respond to business risk. Some firms argue that the level of assurance provided in a financial statement audit does not vary across engagements and therefore do not alter audit risk (or the amount of evidence gathered) in engagements for which business risk is greater than a relatively low level. In contrast, other firms argue that audit risk and business risk are inextricably related. These firms alter audit risk when factors such as those listed in Figure 2-3 suggest that business risk is greater than a relatively low level. For example, if an entity has recurring losses and negative cash flows, and prior unrelated civil convictions reveal that management may lack integrity, some auditors may be predisposed to (1) set audit risk at a level lower than would be necessary in the absence of business risk, (2) decrease the acceptable level of detection risk, (3) increase the amount of evidence gathered and evaluated, or (4) drop the client. In fact, in a move unparalleled just one decade prior, the Big Five public accounting firms in the mid-1990s dropped no less than 245 publicly traded companies, culling from their client lists companies for which audit fees did not justify the risk of future litigation.[27]

FIGURE 2-3: *Factors Affecting Business Risk*

- Management is aggressive about financial reporting and disclosure.
- Management integrity or reputation is suspicious.
- Management faces conflicts of interest and regulatory problems.
- Management turnover is high.
- The entity operates in an industry that is new and unstable or mature and stagnant.
- The entity has recurring losses and negative cash flows.
- Significant debt or credit is denied or at risk.
- Material transactions are planned with related parties.
- Shares are traded publicly.
- Significant litigation is threatened or pending.
- Pending legislation challenges existing or planned markets.
- The entity has not been audited previously.

Audit Risk and Auditor Failure

The public expects that auditors specify risk with the intent to detect material error and the resolve to propose that management correct the errors detected. However, in a number of recent cases, the SEC exposed evidence counter-witness to the public's expectations. Consider, for example, the SEC's investigations of, and enforcement releases about, the officers and auditors of Sunbeam, a manufacturer of household appliances and outdoor products sold under brand names that included Oster, Coleman, and Signature Brands.

Owing to lagging sales and declining share price, Sunbeam in June 1996 hired as CEO Albert J. Dunlap, a seasoned executive credited with having turned

---

27 E. MacDonald, "More Accounting Firms are Dumping Risky Clients," *The Wall Street Journal* (April 25, 1997), p. B1.

around Crown-Zellerbach and Scott Paper.[28] Consistent with prior Dunlap turn-arounds, the market expected that he would restructure the company by slashing the number of employees and manufacturing plants, and dropping or reengineering nonperforming products. Dunlap did and Sunbeam's share price responded (Figure 2-4). However, during a period from the last quarter of 1996 to June 1998, "... senior management created the illusion of a successful restructuring of Sunbeam in order to inflate its stock price and thus improve its value as an acquisition target."[29] Management allegedly created the illusion with two among other means of manipulating earnings: an inflated restructuring accrual in the fourth quarter of 1996 and bill and hold sales in the fourth quarter of 1997.

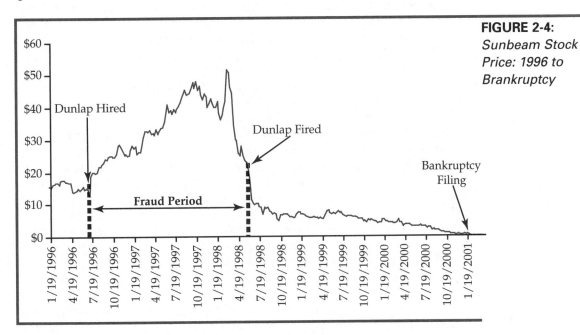

FIGURE 2-4:
*Sunbeam Stock
Price: 1996 to
Brankruptcy*

Restructuring accruals represent actual costs management reasonably expects to pay next period for plant closings and employee severance, among other things. In turn, although uncommon, bill and hold sales contemplate that the buyer, not the seller, request that the seller bill now but hold inventory for delivery later, and that the buyer, not the seller, have a substantial business reason for structuring the sale as bill and hold. On Sunbeam senior management's use of restructuring and bill and hold, the SEC concluded that:

... senior management created $35 million in improper restructuring reserves ... as part of a year-end 1996 restructuring, which were reversed into income the following year. Also in 1997, Sunbeam's management engaged in ... improper "bill and hold" sales. ... At year-end 1997, at least $62 million of Sunbeam's reported income of $189 million came from accounting fraud.[30]

---

28 J.A. Byrne, *Chainsaw: The Notorious Career of Al Dunlap in the Era of Profit at Any Price*. New York: Harper-Business, 1999.
29 *SEC Accounting and Auditing Enforcement Release No. 1393*, In the Matter of Sunbeam Corporation (May 15, 2001).
30 Ibid.

Described by the SEC as a "massive financial fraud,"[31] management's accounting for restructuring accruals and for bill and hold sales among other things drove Sunbeam's stock price from about $15 when Dunlap was hired, to a peak of over $50 in winter 1998, and back to about $15 when Dunlap was fired. Burdened by $2 billion in long-term debt and a deteriorating stock price, Sunbeam in early 2001 filed for bankruptcy protection[32] and, following reorganization, emerged in December 2002 as American Household, Inc.[33]

Didn't the auditors audit the restructuring charge and detect bill and hold sales? In direct contradiction to the public's expectations, the SEC concluded on the restructuring charge that the Sunbeam engagement partner ". . . identified these components of Sunbeam's restructuring reserves as not in compliance with GAAP and proposed that the Company reverse the improper accounting entries. (He) proposed adjustments for these entries, which management rejected, and (he) passed on the proposed adjustments after incorrectly applying a materiality analysis."[34] And on the bill and hold sales, the SEC concluded that the engagement partner ". . . failed to ensure that the . . . audit team performed procedures adequate to verify that the Company's bill and hold sales complied with GAAP . . ."[35] Sunbeam restated 1996 and 1997 earnings.

In May 2001, the audit firm, without admitting either fault or liability, settled a securities class action suit for $110 million, one of the largest settlements an accounting firm had paid to that date. Although uncommon, documented audit failures like Sunbeam cast a revealing eye on the otherwise unthinkable practice of failing to perform procedures that would reduce audit risk to a relatively low level. For example, in Sunbeam, the SEC noted that the engagement partner ". . . identified a number of audit risks . . . and should have known these items could have a material impact on the financial statements, [but] he failed to perform sufficient audit procedures to determine whether the financial statements were in conformity with GAAP."[36] Although Sunbeam was dominated by a senior management that had a disproportionate influence on reported earnings, the auditors were apparently willing to ignore evidence that suggested an unacceptably high audit risk. The SEC's investigation and enforcement releases suggest that, in the case of Sunbeam, the issue wasn't so much audit failure as it was *auditor* failure.

Materiality

The question, "What is material in what situations?" never really has been resolved with certainty, although there is consensus from SEC regulations, the courts, and the authoritative literature about what the term **materiality** means.

---

31 SEC Press Release, "SEC Sues Former CEO, CFO and Other Top Officers of Sunbeam Corporation in Massive Financial Fraud," Washington, D.C., May 15, 2001.

32 N. Harris, "Sunbeam Files for Chapter 11 Protection," *The Wall Street Journal* (February 7, 2001), p. B4.

33 "Sunbeam Corp.: Reorganization Plan Confirmed, Change of Name is in the Works," *The Wall Street Journal* (November 26, 2002).

34 *SEC Accounting and Auditing Enforcement Release No. 1706*, In the Matter of Phillip E. Harlow, CPA (January 27, 2003).

35 Ibid.

36 *SEC Accounting and Auditing Enforcement Release No. 1706*, In the Matter of Phillip E. Harlow, CPA (January 27, 2003).

For example, the Securities and Exchange Commission defines materiality in *Rule 1-02 of Regulation S-X*:

The term material, when used to qualify a requirement for the furnishing of information as to any subject, limits the information required to those matters about which an average prudent investor ought reasonably to be informed.

Several court cases also have defined materiality. For example, in *Escott v. BarChris Construction Corp.*, the court defined a material fact as:

. . . a fact that if it had been correctly stated or disclosed would have deterred or tended to deter the average prudent investor from purchasing the securities in question.[37]

Similarly, the court in *SEC v. Texas Gulf Sulphur Co.* stated:

The basic test of materiality . . . is whether a reasonable man would have attached importance . . . in determining his choice of action in the transaction in question.[38]

And the FASB defined materiality as:

. . . the magnitude of an omission or misstatement of accounting information that, in the judgment of a reasonable person relying on the information, would have been changed or influenced by the omission or misstatement.[39]

Clearly, there is general agreement among the SEC, the courts, and the FASB that a transaction, event, or disclosure is material if it would affect a decision made by an average prudent investor, a reasonable person, or the like. However, although appealing on a conceptual level, these definitions provide little guidance about how to make materiality decisions in practice. The following addresses materiality decisions in practice by discussing when an auditor makes materiality decisions in financial statement audits, how an auditor arrives at an overall preliminary estimate of materiality for an entire set of financial statements taken as a whole, and how an auditor might allocate the overall estimate to individual financial statement components.

Materiality Decisions in Practice

As explained in *Statement on Auditing Standards No. 47*, "Audit Risk and Materiality in Conducting an Audit" (AU Sec. 312), there is an inverse relationship between audit risk and materiality. For example, the risk that a financial statement account, say, Accounts Receivable, could be misstated by a rather large amount (say, $1 million) might be quite low, but the risk that the account could be misstated by an extremely small amount (say, $100) might be quite high. Holding other things constant, either a decrease in the allowable level of audit risk or a decrease in the amount of error deemed material would cause the auditor to do one or more of the following: select more effective audit procedures, perform auditing procedures closer to the balance sheet date, or increase the extent of the procedures applied. For example, if an auditor suspected that a kitchen equipment

---

37 *Escott et al. v. BarChris Construction Corp.*, 283 F. Supp. 681 (S.D.N.Y., 1966).
38 *SEC v. Texas Gulf Sulphur Co.*, 401 F. 2d 849 (C.A. 2nd, 1968).
39 *Statement of Financial Accounting Standards No. 2*, "Qualitative Characteristics of Accounting Information," Stamford, CT: FASB, 1980, par. 132.

manufacturer had offered extended payment terms to prompt retailers to accelerate expected Q1 2007 orders into Q4 2006 (say, 6-month terms for orders shipped by December 31, but 1-month terms otherwise), the auditor would likely proceed as follows: First, the auditor might decrease the allowable level of audit risk (say, from 5 percent in the prior engagement to 1 percent in the current engagement), since extended payment terms increase the likelihood that the orders may either be returned or unpaid, thereby potentially overstating 2006 earnings. Second, the auditor might increase over the prior-year engagement the number of sales contracts he or she read completely to assess the extent of extended-term December 31 receivables.

During a financial statement audit, an auditor considers materiality at least twice: once while planning the engagement, and again after all audit procedures have been completed. When planning an engagement, the auditor determines a *preliminary estimate of materiality* for the entire set of financial statements taken as a whole (although the preliminary estimate can be revised during the engagement—for example, for conditions not known when planning, such as a newly implemented product line). The preliminary estimate is the maximum amount by which a set of financial statements could be misstated and still not cause the auditor to believe that the decisions of reasonable users would be affected. For example, if a preliminary estimate is $200,000, then combined misstatements of less than $200,000 for all accounts would be considered immaterial. The purpose of determining a preliminary estimate of materiality is to help the auditor plan the extent of audit evidence to accumulate during the engagement. For example, if the preliminary estimate were revised downward to $150,000, then the extent of audit procedures would increase, since the auditor would need to examine more evidence in order to find smaller misstatements.

Audit effort →

Toward the end of an engagement, after all audit evidence has been gathered and evaluated, an auditor again considers materiality by comparing the combined misstatement for all accounts with the preliminary (or revised) estimate for the entire set of financial statements taken as a whole. If the combined misstatement exceeds the preliminary estimate, then the financial statements would be misstated materially, and the auditor could either perform additional audit procedures or request that management adjust the misstated accounts. Of course, if additional procedures are not performed and the client refuses to adjust the misstated accounts, then the auditor would issue either a "qualified" or an "adverse" opinion, as discussed in Chapter 3.

Determining a preliminary estimate of materiality is a crucial step in the audit process because it affects both the extent of audit procedures performed and, ultimately, whether combined misstatement is likely to affect users' decisions. But how do auditors determine a preliminary estimate?

Preliminary Estimates of Materiality

Statement on Auditing Standards No. 22, "Planning and Supervision" (AU Sec. 311), states that an auditor should consider a preliminary estimate of materiality when planning an audit engagement. The preliminary estimate need not necessarily be quantified, but many practitioners find quantification useful for assuring that all professional staff assigned to the engagement view materiality similarly. For example, if the preliminary judgment were determined by the audit partner to be high, rather than stated numerically, not all members of the staff may interpret "high" materiality alike. In practice, auditors sometimes determine a preliminary estimate of materiality using decision aids and predetermined materiality criteria, as discussed next.

The Relationship Among Audit Risk, Materiality, and Audit Effort

Over the years, practicing auditors have designed and implemented various decision aids, not to supplant professional judgment but to guide decision making. For example, Figure 2-5 illustrates a decision aid the AICPA has published to guide auditors' preliminary estimates of materiality for commercial companies. The decision aid requires that an auditor first determine the larger of estimated revenues or assets and then calculate a preliminary estimate of materiality. For example, if a client's estimated revenues are $22,500,000 and estimated assets are $15,750,000, then the preliminary estimate of materiality would be:

$85,500 + ([$22,500,000 − $10,000,000] × 0.00461) = $143,125

FIGURE 2-5: *A Materiality Decision Aid*

Larger of Total Revenues or Total Assets is: Over	*But Not Over*	*Planning Materiality is*	+	*Factor*	×	*Excess Over*
$ 0	$ 30 thousand	$ 0	+	0.059300	×	$ 0
$ 30 thousand	$ 100 thousand	$ 1,780	+	0.031200	×	$ 30 thousand
$ 100 thousand	$ 300 thousand	$ 3,960	+	0.021500	×	$ 100 thousand
$ 300 thousand	$ 1 million	$ 8,260	+	0.014500	×	$ 300 thousand
$ 1 million	$ 3 million	$ 18,400	+	0.009950	×	$ 1 million
$ 3 million	$ 10 million	$ 38,300	+	0.006740	×	$ 3 million
$ 10 million	$ 30 million	$ 85,500	+	0.004610	×	$ 10 million
$ 30 million	$ 100 million	$ 178,000	+	0.003120	×	$ 30 million
$ 100 million	$ 300 million	$ 396,000	+	0.002150	×	$ 100 million
$ 300 million	$ 1 billion	$ 826,000	+	0.001450	×	$ 300 million
$ 1 billion	$ 3 billion	$ 1,840,000	+	0.000995	×	$ 1 billion
$ 3 billion	$ 10 billion	$ 3,830,000	+	0.000674	×	$ 3 billion
$ 10 billion	$ 30 billion	$ 8,550,000	+	0.000461	×	$ 10 billion
$ 30 billion	$ 100 billion	$17,800,000	+	0.000312	×	$ 30 billion
$ 100 billion	$ 300 billion	$39,600,000	+	0.000215	×	$ 100 billion
$ 300 billion	$	$82,600,000	+	0.000148	×	$ 300 billion

Source: AICPA, *Audit Sampling*, New York: AICPA, 1999, Table C.1.

However, this estimate is merely input—a baseline estimate—that would be revised based on the auditor's assessment of audit risk. If the auditor judged risk on the engagement to be relatively low, then the preliminary estimate could be higher, and the amount of audit effort required would be lower. Likewise, if the auditor judged audit risk to be relatively high, then the preliminary estimate would be lower, and the amount of audit effort required would be higher. That is, there is an inverse relationship between audit risk and materiality, and an inverse relationship between materiality and audit effort (measured in audit hours). For example, consider the preliminary estimate, $143,125, and assume the auditor had planned to perform the audit in 2,000 hours. If audit risk were judged to be low, then the auditor could raise the preliminary estimate, say, to $175,000. Now, because the preliminary estimate of materiality is higher, the auditor need not expend effort to detect aggregate misstatements below $175,000, and can therefore reduce budgeted audit hours to, say, 1,800 hours. This illustration reveals an important insight about the relationship between audit risk and audit effort: As risk goes down, audit effort goes down.

Quantitative Materiality Criteria

Figure 2-6, Panel A, summarizes, and the following discusses, three quantitative materiality criteria that research reveals some auditors used in practice:[40]

FIGURE 2-6: *Quantitative and Qualitative Materiality Criteria*

Panel A: Quantitative Criteria
Effect on:
- Net income
- Total revenue
- Total assets

Panel B: Qualitative Criteria
Whether a misstatement:
- Affects compliance with loan covenants or other contractual requirements
- Masks a change in earnings or other trends
- Conceals an unlawful transaction, such as a violation of the *FCPA*
- Prompts undue expectations about the future
- Hides a failure to meet analysts' consensus expectations
- Arises from an item capable of precise measurement or from an estimate
- Affects management's compensation

Effect on Net Income

By far, the most common quantitative materiality criterion used by practicing auditors has been the *percentage effect on net income.* For example, a study of 181 equity-for-debt swap transactions among 149 different companies supported the conventional wisdom that auditors view effect on net income as a primary factor when judging materiality.[41] Although practicing auditors differ about precisely what percentage is likely material, the AICPA's Auditing Practice Release, *Audit Sampling*, states that "A common rule of thumb for materiality is 5 percent to 10 percent of pretax net income." In contrast, research reveals two things. First, the

---

40 Studies include S. M. Woolsey, "Materiality Survey," *Journal of Accountancy* (September 1973), pp. 91–92; J. R. Boatsman and J. C. Robertson, "Policy-Capturing on Selected Materiality Judgments," *The Accounting Review* (April 1974), pp. 342–352; J. W. Pattillo, *The Concept of Materiality in Financial Reporting.* New York: Financial Executives Research Foundation, 1976; S. Moriarity and F. Baton, "Modeling the Materiality Judgments of Audit Partners," *Journal of Accounting Research* (Autumn 1976), pp. 320–341; M. Firth, "Consensus Views and Judgment Models in Materiality Decisions," *Accounting, Organizations and Society* (Vol. 4, No. 4, 1979), pp. 283–295; J. L. Krogstad, R. T. Ettenson, and J. Shanteau, "Context and Experience in Auditors' Materiality Judgments," *Auditing: A Journal of Practice & Theory* (1984), pp. 54–74; B. W. Carpenter and M. W. Dirsmith, "Early Debt Extinguishment Transactions and Auditor Materiality Judgments," *Accounting, Organizations and Society* (1992), pp. 709–740.
41 E. G. Chewning, Jr., S. W. Wheeler, and K. C. Chan, "Evidence on Auditor and Investor Materiality Thresholds Resulting from Equity-for-Debt Swaps," *Auditing: A Journal of Practice & Theory* (Spring 1998), pp. 39–53.

average investor's threshold for materiality is between 0.1 percent and 0.2 percent of pretax income,[42] an amount considerably lower than "5 percent to 10 percent." Second, rather than a percentage of a base, materiality appears to increase at a decreasing rate with client size, and to increase with a client's rate of return on assets.[43]

SEC *Staff Accounting Bulletin No. 99*, "Materiality," urges auditors to avoid relying on quantitative rules of thumb as anything other than an initial step in judging materiality:

The use of a percentage as a numerical threshold, such as 5%, may provide the basis for a preliminary assumption that . . . a particular item . . . is unlikely to be material. . . . The staff has no objection to such a "rule of thumb" as an initial step is assessing materiality. But quantifying, in percentage terms, the magnitude of a misstatement in only the beginning of an analysis of materiality; it cannot appropriately be used as a substitute for a full analysis of all relevant considerations.[44]

Furthermore, the courts overlook consensus thresholds in auditor liability cases, ruling instead that materiality must be judged based on the facts of the case. For example, referring to a 1976 research study published by the Financial Executives Research Foundation,[45] the FASB's *Statement of Financial Accounting Concepts (SFAC) No. 2*, "Qualitative Characteristics of Accounting Information," comments that the study's "principal conclusion was that a 'rule of thumb' of 5–10 percent of net income is widely used as a general materiality criterion." However, in 1996, the court declined in *In re Westinghouse Securities Litigation*[46] to adopt the criteria cited in *SFAC No. 2*. What the courts have done instead is to rule on what is *imma*terial (called by the courts "de minimis"). For example, the court ruled that a 0.54 percent change in net income was immaterial *In re Westinghouse Securities Litigation*, and that a 0.2 percent effect on earnings was immaterial *In re Burlington Coat Factory Securities Litigation*.[47]

Although used commonly in practice, effect on net income has drawbacks. For one, income is not always stable from year to year, suggesting that materiality thresholds based on net income alone could vary widely from year to year. For another, net income is subject to manipulation, in particular when accounting policies provide management with discretion. Management discretion in manipulating income, and the auditor's course of action, is discussed in later chapters for several important accounting issues, including revenue recognition (Chapter 11), environmental liabilities (Chapter 13), impaired assets (Chapter 15), and financial instruments (Chapter 16).

Effect on Total Revenues and Total Assets

For these and other reasons, both the *percentage effect on total revenues* and the *percentage effect on total assets* also are important quantitative criteria, particularly when used in conjunction with net income. For example, if a large, publicly traded

---

42 S-Y Cho, R. L. Hagerman, S. Nabar, and E. R. Patterson, "Measuring Stockholder Materiality," *Accounting Horizons* (Supplement 2003), pp. 63–76.

43 H. Blokdijk, F. Drieenhuizen, D. A. Simunic, and M. T. Stein, "Factors Affecting Auditors' Assessments of Planning Materiality," *Auditing: A Journal of Practice & Theory* (September 2003), pp. 297–307.

44 *SEC Staff Accounting Bulletin No. 99*, "Materiality," 1999.

45 J. W. Pattillo, *The Concept of Materiality in Financial Reporting*. New York: Financial Executives Research Foundation, 1976.

46 *In re Westinghouse Securities Litigation*, 90 F. 3d 696, 714n. 14, 3rd Cir. (1996).

47 *In re Burlington Coat Factory Securities Litigation*, 114 F. 3d 1410, 1427 3rd Cir. (1997).

company were to report net income of $2,000,000 in one year and $1,000 in the following year, with total assets approximating $20,000,000 in both years, an auditor certainly wouldn't conclude in the latter year that 10 percent of net income, or $100, is material. Rather, the auditor would focus on total revenues and total assets. Unlike net income, total revenue and total assets are usually more stable and highly correlated.

Qualitative Factors: The SEC's Staff Accounting Bulletin No. 99

Interestingly, the effect of a quantitatively *immaterial* GAAP violation on net income has important implications in capital markets. For example, management's failure to meet analyst's earnings expectations by an amount as small as a penny has had an extraordinary impact on share prices. In a 1998 letter to Thomas Ray, AICPA director of audit and attest services, Lynn Turner, then SEC chief accountant, commented on intentional immaterial GAAP violations:

The high earnings multiples on which stocks are assessed and traded in today's markets have heightened the importance of reported earnings. Familiar measures of materiality, for example, 5% of pre-tax income, may not be adequate in a marketplace with price/earnings multiples of 40, where missing the market's expectation of earnings per share by a penny can have significant consequences. The SEC staff believes that auditors must assess the qualitative factors important in determining whether information would be considered material to investors. The use of quantitative factors alone is not sufficient. Percentage tests, such as one based upon the relationship of the item in question to earnings figures, often are not conclusive, sometimes not relevant.

Consistent with the Turner's comments, the SEC's *Staff Accounting Bulletin No. 99,* "Materiality," reaffirmed several long-standing conventions sometimes overlooked in practice, among them that:

- Auditors should not rely solely on quantitative materiality criteria,
- Auditors should judge the materiality of detected misstatements both individually and in the aggregate, and
- Intentional, but immaterial, misstatements are inappropriate and may be unlawful.

All three conventions bear on factors that can render an otherwise quantitatively immaterial misstatement to be material qualitatively, because they go to the heart of the U.S. Supreme Court's conclusion in *TSC Industries v. Northway, Inc.*: A fact is material if there is "a substantial likelihood that the . . . fact would have been viewed by the reasonable investor as having significantly altered the 'total mix' of information made available."[48] In short, relying solely on quantitative criteria, or ignoring the materiality either of aggregate or of intentional misstatements, deprives an investor of the "total mix" of information relevant to his or her investment decision.

Figure 2-6, Panel B, lists several qualitative materiality criteria adapted from *SAB No. 99*. Four examples follow.

---

48 *TSC Industries v. Northway, Inc.*, 426 U.S. 438, 449 (1976).

Loan Covenant Compliance

One common example of a qualitatively material item is a quantitatively immaterial adjustment to working capital that, if recorded, would *affect compliance with loan covenants*. To illustrate, assume that a client held a $1 million long-term bank loan that carried a debt covenant: The loan would become immediately due and payable if the current ratio went below 3 to 2. Toward the end of the engagement, a staff member proposes a $5,000 adjusting journal entry to reclassify credit balances in receivables to Accounts Payable (debit Accounts Receivable, credit Accounts Payable) that, although quantitatively immaterial, reduces the current ratio to just below 3 to 2. In this case, although $5,000 is immaterial, violation of the debt covenant would require that the $1 million long-term debt be classified as a current liability, and the reclassification is more likely to be material.

Masking an Earnings Trend Change

A second qualitative factor, *masking a change in an earnings trend*, is sometimes interpreted by auditors as a materiality criterion, even when the percentage effect on net income, total revenues, and total assets appears quantitatively immaterial. To illustrate, assume that in four consecutive years a company's earnings per share had been $2.50, $2.75, $3.03, and $3.33, respectively—an approximate increase of 10 percent per year. An otherwise quantitatively immaterial audit adjustment that altered the 10 percent trend negatively might be considered material because of the potential effect on financial statement users. A commercial loan officer, for example, might consider the reversal to be the "tip of the iceberg," the beginning of a long-term downward trend. That is, the loan officer might be concerned that financial position may deteriorate over the loan repayment period, thereby reducing the likelihood of repayment. The loan officer might not necessarily deny the loan, but might require a marginally higher interest rate to compensate the bank for increased risk.

Concealing an Unlawful Transaction

A third factor is more subtle: a quantitatively immaterial illegal payment that *conceals an unlawful transaction*, such as a violation of the *Foreign Corrupt Practices Act* (FCPA). For example, assume an entity made two immaterial $5,000 payments to a foreign political official, ostensibly to secure favorable treatment in upcoming contract negotiations. In this case, disclosing the payments may be necessary for at least two reasons. First, the *FCPA* carries rather severe fines ($1 million per payment) that may result in material contingent liabilities if the Justice Department or the SEC were to prosecute. Second, financial statement users may be influenced by the fact that management is apparently predisposed to making questionable or illegal payments.

Prompting Undue Expectations

A Second Circuit Court of Appeals case, *Ganino v. Citizens Utilities Co.* (2000), illustrates a fourth qualitative factor, *prompting an undue expectation about the future.* Plaintiffs' alleged that Citizens Utilities reported $10.1 million received in 1995 as 1996 income, thereby affecting first- and second-quarter 1996 after-tax net income by 17.7 and 11.9 percent, respectively. Although the lower court considered the effects of the misstatement on annual reports only, the Second Circuit focused on a May 1996 press release in which management touted first quarter income as a predictor of full-year results and claimed the company "was well on its way toward a 52nd consecutive year of increased revenues, net income and earnings per share."[49] Reversing the lower court decision, the Second Circuit ruled that there is no bright line numerical test to arrive at materiality decisions, since numerical tests overlook context. Rather, the court relied on the provisions in the SEC's *SAB No. 99* that, although lacking the force of law, "was thoroughly reasoned and consistent with existing law"[50] in observing that an otherwise quantitatively immaterial misstatement can be material qualitatively.

Allocating Preliminary Estimates of Materiality

Although an auditor's opinion relates to an entire set of financial statements taken as a whole, an audit is actually conducted piece by piece, on individual financial statement assertions and accounts, one assertion and account at a time. As a result, some firms allocate the preliminary estimate of materiality among accounts as a planning tool for the staff members assigned to audit the accounts. In practice, most auditors who allocate the preliminary estimate to individual accounts choose to allocate to the balance sheet, rather than to the income statement accounts, because usually there are fewer balance sheet than income statement accounts, and most income statement errors also affect the balance sheet.

There are several approaches to allocating the preliminary estimate of materiality to individual accounts, among them allocations based on:

- The relative magnitude of financial statement accounts.
- The relative variability of financial statement accounts.
- Professional judgment.

Relative Magnitude

One method is to allocate the preliminary estimate based on the relative dollar balances in each balance sheet account. However, the allocation ignores accounts that will not be audited, such as Retained Earnings, and accounts that will be audited 100 percent, such as Contingent Liabilities. A simplified model follows:[51]

$$
\begin{array}{l}
\text{Preliminary} \\
\text{estimate of} \\
\text{materiality for} \\
\text{an individual} \\
\text{balance sheet} \\
\text{account}
\end{array}
=
\begin{array}{l}
\text{Preliminary} \\
\text{estimate of} \\
\text{materiality for} \\
\text{all accounts}
\end{array}
\sqrt{\frac{\text{Amount of balance sheet account}}{\begin{array}{c}\text{Sum of all balance sheet accounts,} \\ \text{less accounts not audited and} \\ \text{accounts audited 100 percent}\end{array}}}
$$

Other, more comprehensive, models can be developed to allocate materiality more efficiently, although the cost to develop a more comprehensive model may exceed

---

49 *Ganino v. Citizens Utilities Co.* (22493 2d Cir. 2000).
50 Ibid.
51 G. R. Zuber, R. K. Elliott, W. R. Kinney, Jr., and J. J. Leisenring, "Using Materiality in Audit Planning," *Journal of Accountancy* (March 1983), p. 50.

the benefits, given particularly that the model should be used to generate "initial," not final, allocations. That is, rather than blindly accept each allocation, an auditor should consider other factors affecting each account audited. For example, some balance sheet accounts, such as Cash, process relatively large volumes of transactions but do not normally carry dollar balances representative of the volume of transactions processed. Thus, regardless of which model is applied, the allocation of materiality to Cash is apt to be adjusted.

Relative Variability

Relative magnitude focuses on the dollar balance of each account, thereby presuming that there's more information in the size of an account than in the relative number of transactions processed in the account. To compensate, some auditors allocate materiality on the basis of a measure of the *variability* of the transactions processed in the balance sheet accounts—for example, the standard deviation of transactions processed—reasoning that as variability rises, so does an auditor's uncertainty and, therefore, audit risk. For example, if two balance sheet accounts, such as Receivables and Payables, each had recorded book values of $1 million, then relative magnitude would yield identical materiality allocations. However, if the standard deviation was $150 for receivables and $950 for payables, an auditor would likely conclude that Payables transactions were less homogeneous than Receivables transactions, and therefore might desire a lower materiality allocation for Payables.

Professional Judgment

Many auditors use subjective professional judgment, only, to assess materiality for each financial statement account and then compare the sum of all materiality assessments to the overall preliminary estimate of materiality, revising as necessary. The essential difference between relative magnitude and relative variability on one hand, and professional judgment only on the other, is this: The former uses decision aids and the latter does not.

Materiality in Auditing and in Accounting

Although accountants and auditors both use similar criteria to evaluate materiality, their ultimate thresholds often differ. In general, auditors have a higher threshold of materiality than do the accountants employed by the entity audited. For example, a $20,000 understatement of advertising expense is more apt to be material to the entity's controller than to the independent auditor. The controller may be more concerned because a division manager's annual bonus is based on net income, or the advertising department's expenditures for the period are about to exceed amounts budgeted. In contrast, an auditor may be less concerned because the decisions of users, such as creditors or shareholders, are not likely to be affected. Regardless of how an auditor makes materiality decisions, what matters most is that materiality is crucial to many, if not most, audit practice decisions and, therefore, to an auditor's compliance with auditing standards.

SUMMARY

First developed in the 1940s, the AICPA's ten generally accepted auditing standards still stand today as the guidelines, the measures of quality, for contemporary audit practice in the United States. But generally accepted auditing standards are applicable to only one type of attestation engagement: independent financial statement audits. For other attest engagements, practitioners are guided by attestation standards, developed jointly in 1986 by the Auditing Standards Board and by the Accounting and Review Services Committee.

Materiality and risk affect applications both of attestation standards and of generally accepted auditing standards because they bear heavily on a practitioner's judgments about evidence and on the responsibility a practitioner assumes for the conclusions he or she reports. The truth is that a practitioner has neither the time nor the resources to examine all of the evidence that bears on management's assertions. Only the most material and risky transactions and events command the practitioner's attention.

KEY TERMS

Attestation risk 47
Attestation standards 35
Audit evidence 44
Audit risk 47
Business risk 49
Control risk 48
Detection risk 48
Generally accepted accounting principles (GAAP) 41

Generally accepted auditing standards (GAAS) 32
General standards 32
Inherent risk 47
Internal controls 45
Materiality 52
Standards of field work 32
Standards of reporting 32

REFERENCES

Public Company Accounting Oversight Board Releases:

PCAOB Release No. 2003-005, "Statement Regarding the Establishment of Auditing and Other Professional Auditing Standards."

PCAOB Release No. 2003-006, "Establishment of Interim Professional Auditing Standards."

PCAOB Release No. 2003-009, "Compliance with Auditing and Related Professional Practice Standards."

Professional Standards:

AICPA, *Codification of Auditing Standards.* New York: AICPA (AU Sec. 150, 201, 210, 220, 230, 311, 312, 325, 326, 411, 431, 504).

SAS No. 22, "Planning and Supervision" (AU Sec. 311).

SAS No. 26, "Association with Financial Statements" (AU Sec. 504).

SAS No. 31, "Evidential Matter" (AU Sec. 326).

SAS No. 32, "Adequacy of Disclosure in Financial Statements" (AU Sec. 431).

SAS No. 47, "Audit Risk and Materiality in Conducting an Audit" (AU Sec. 312).

SAS No. 60, "Communication of Internal Control Structure Related Matters Noted in an Audit" (AU Sec. 325).

SAS No. 69, "The Meaning of 'Present Fairly in Conformity with Generally Accepted Accounting Principles' in the Independent Auditor's Report" (AU Sec. 411).

SAS No. 95, "Generally Accepted Auditing Standards" (AU Sec. 150).

SEC Staff Accounting Bulletin No. 99, "Materiality," 1999.

Professional Reports and Speeches:

AICPA, *The Expectation Gap Standards: Proceedings of the Expectation Gap Roundtable,* May 11–12, 1992, Charleston, SC. New York: AICPA, 1993.

AICPA, Auditing Practice Release, *Audit Sampling.* New York: AICPA, 1999.

Levitt, A. "The 'Numbers Game'," speech at the New York University Center for Law and Business, September 28, 1998.

Levitt, A. Remarks by the SEC Chairman to the Panel on Audit Effectiveness. New York University Center for Law and Business, October 7, 1999.

Levitt, A. "Renewing the Covenant with Investors." Remarks by the SEC Chairman. New York University Center for Law and Business, May 10, 2000.

Public Oversight Board. *Panel on Audit Effectiveness: Report and Recommendations.* Stamford, CT: POB, 2000.

Articles, Books:

Banhan, R., "Period of Adjustment," *Journal of Accountancy* (February 2003), pp. 43–48.

Blokdijk, H., F. Drieenhuizen, D. A. Simunic, and M. T. Stein, "Factors Affecting Auditors' Assessments of Planning Materiality," *Auditing: A Journal of Practice & Theory* (September 2003), pp. 297–307.

Caswell, B., and C. Allen, "The Engagement Team Approach to Independence," *Journal of Accountancy* (February 2001), pp. 57–63.

Chewning, E. G., Jr., S. W. Wheeler, and K. C. Chan, "Evidence on Auditor and Investor Materiality Thresholds Resulting from Equity-for-Debt Swaps," *Auditing: A Journal of Practice & Theory* (Spring 1998), pp. 39–53.

Cho, S-Y, R. L. Hagerman, S. Nabar, and E. R. Patterson, "Measuring Stockholder Materiality," *Accounting Horizons* (Supplement 2003), pp. 63–76.

Defond, M. L., K. Raghunandan, and K. R. Subramanyam, "Do Non-Audit Service Fees Impair Auditor Independence? Evidence from Going Concern Audit Opinions," *Journal of Accounting Research* (September 2002), pp. 1247–1274.

Frankel, R. M., M. F. Johnson, and K. K. Nelson, "The Relation Between Auditors' Fees for Nonaudit Services and Earnings Management," *The Accounting Review* (Supplement 2002), pp. 71–105.

Gist, W. E., and T. Shastri, "Revisiting Materiality," *The CPA Journal* (November 2003), pp. 23–26.

Jacobson, P. D., and R. K. Elliott, "GAAS: Reconsidering the 'Ten Commandments'," *Journal of Accountancy* (May 1984), pp. 77–88.

Mautz, R. K., and H. A. Sharaf, *The Philosophy of Auditing.* Sarasota, FL: American Accounting Association, 1961.

McGrath, S., A. Siegel, T. W. Dunfee, A. S. Glazer, and H. R. Jaenicke, "A Framework for Auditor Independence," *Journal of Accountancy* (January 2001), pp. 39–42.

Schandl, C. W., *Theory of Auditing: Evaluation, Investigation, and Judgment.* Houston: Scholars Book Co., 1978.

Schroeder, M., and J. Weil, "SEC's Auditor Rules Could Pose a Dilemma for Big Client Firms," *The Wall Street Journal* (November 16, 2000), p. C1.

Tuttle, B., M. Coller, and R. D. Plumlee, "The Effect of Misstatements on Decisions of Financial Statement Users: An Experimental Investigation of Auditor Materiality Thresholds," *Auditing: A Journal of Practice & Theory* (March 2002), pp. 11–27.

QUESTIONS

1. What does the AICPA mean by the term "standards"?
2. Briefly trace the historical development of attestation standards and generally accepted auditing standards.
3. What is the difference between auditing standards and interpretive publications?
4. Explain some of the key provisions of the SEC's 2003 independence rules.
5. Distinguish between engagement team and firm-wide independence.
6. What precautions can be expected of a prudent practitioner?
7. Explain how WorldCom misstated earnings in 2001 and 2002.
8. What does the profession mean by audit evidence?
9. What does *sufficient*, competent evidential matter mean?
10. Distinguish a procedures-driven from a risk-driven audit.
11. Explain how Sunbeam manipulated earnings in 1996 and 1997.
12. Distinguish audit risk from business risk.
13. When during an engagement does an auditor consider materiality?
14. What is the significance of *TSC Industries v. Northway, Inc.*?
15. Identify and describe the quantitative criteria often used by practicing auditors when making materiality decisions.
16. Identify and describe qualitative criteria practitioners use to judge materiality.
17. What approaches are available for allocating a preliminary estimate of materiality to individual financial statement accounts?
18. Identify and describe the three component risks underlying audit risk for a financial statement account.
19. What is the significance of *SAB No. 99*, "Materiality"?
20. Why might an auditor and management have different thresholds for materiality?

MULTIPLE CHOICE QUESTIONS

1. Attestation standards were developed jointly by:
   a. The SEC and the Auditing Standards Board.
   b. The Auditing Standards Board and the Accounting and Review Services Committee.
   c. The Auditing Standards Board and the Public Company Accounting Oversight Board.
   d. The AICPA and the Public Accounting Oversight Board.

2. A practitioner should comply with applicable attestation standards:
   a. On every attestation engagement, without exception.
   b. On every attestation engagement, except financial statement audits.
   c. On consulting engagements.
   d. On all engagements that involve financial statements.

3. Which of the following best describes the purpose of attestation standards and of auditing standards?
   a. Measures of quality for attestation and audit engagements
   b. Methods to discharge professional responsibilities in attestation and audit engagements
   c. Rules that represent the public's expectations on attestation and audit engagements
   d. Objectives used to select evidence for attestation and audit engagements

4. Through the *Sarbanes-Oxley Act*, Congress empowered the Public Company Accounting Oversight Board (PCAOB) to:

   a. Adopt regulations of the Public Oversight Board.
   b. Require that audit reports refer to "the standards of the PCAOB."
   c. Adopt existing, or develop new, auditing standards.
   d. Require that auditors comply with generally accepted auditing standards.

5. In audits of nonpublic companies, "standards" refers to:

   a. Generally accepted auditing standards.
   b. Generally accepted auditing standards and interpretive publications.
   c. Statements on Auditing Standards.
   d. Statements on Auditing Standards and Statements on Standards for Attestation Engagements.

6. Independence in fact:

   a. Is a prerequisite for independence in appearance.
   b. Is expected of consultants.
   c. Is a state of mind.
   d. Contemplates auditor rotation.

7. Engagement-team independence:

   a. Minimizes risk.
   b. Modernizes the rules of independence.
   c. Defends against liability.
   d. Achieves compliance with the standards of field work.

8. Of the following services, which could an incumbent auditor perform for a public company without violating the *Sarbanes-Oxley Act*?

   a. Installation of an enterprise resource planning system
   b. Design of a general ledger accounting system
   c. Draft a line of questions for an upcoming deposition
   d. Due diligence on a pending asset acquisition approved in advance by the audit committee

9. Which of the following best describes due care?

   a. Tact in avoiding legal liability
   b. Requisite skill and diligence
   c. Reasonable infallibility
   d. Freedom from undue influence

10. What is the focus of the standards of field work for audit engagements?

    a. Guidelines for training, proficiency, and due care
    b. Guidelines for the content of the practitioner's report
    c. Guidelines for planning and for gathering evidence
    d. Guidelines for maintaining an independence in mental attitude

11. The validity of evidence depends ultimately on the:

    a. Attestation standards and GAAS.
    b. Availability of subordinate evidence.
    c. Relevance of the evidence.
    d. Practitioner's professional judgment.

12. Audit evidence does not include:

    a. Audit reference manuals.
    b. Underlying accounting data.
    c. Interview notes.
    d. Corroborating information.

13. In any financial statement audit, an auditor sustains a risk that:

    a. Management's assertions contain material omissions or misstatements.
    b. Criteria against which to measure management's assertions are not established.
    c. Materiality thresholds exceed reported account balances.
    d. Investors may fail to understand the audit report.

14. Auditors plan engagements so that audit risk will be:

    a. Consistent with the risk associated with the auditor's portfolio of engagements.
    b. Limited to a relatively low level.
    c. Captured in the auditor's fee.
    d. Acceptable to the SEC.

15. The susceptibility of an account balance to error that could be material, assuming there are no related controls, is called:

    a. Compensation risk.
    b. Control risk.
    c. Detection risk.
    d. Inherent risk.

16. The level of confidence an auditor achieves on an audit engagement is:

    a. Related to detection risk.
    b. Equivalent to detection risk.
    c. One hundred percent.
    d. Set at a level lower than would be necessary absent business risk.

17. An item is material to a company's financial statements if the item:

    a. Exceeds one percent of reported income.
    b. Causes the company to miss analysts' earnings expectation.
    c. Alters the total mix of information significantly.
    d. Reflects a new class of transactions.

18. Which of the following may be assessed nonquantitatively?

	Inherent Risk	Control Risk	Detection Risk
a.	Yes	Yes	No
b.	Yes	No	Yes
c.	No	Yes	Yes
d.	Yes	Yes	Yes

    (AICPA Adapted)

19. Materiality is:

    a. Addressed within a practitioner's attestation and audit reports.
    b. Expressed in terms of dollars.
    c. Measured using guidelines established by the AICPA.
    d. Not applicable to attestation engagements.

20. Assurance service engagements, other than audits and attestations:

    a. Do not require independence.
    b. Require application of all attestation standards and GAAS.
    c. Are performed currently without professional standards.
    d. Do not require evidence.

PROBLEMS AND DISCUSSION CASES

2-1 *Comparing Attestation Standards and GAAS*

The AICPA's attestation standards and GAAS are classified as general standards, standards of field work, and standards of reporting, and are closely aligned with four concepts: independence, due care, evidence, and reporting. As illustrated in Figure 2-1, some of the standards match almost identically, and others are unmatched—that is, they address entirely different issues. For example, the first general standard of the attestation standards matches the first general GAAS (adequate technical training and proficiency), but the second GAAS of field work (internal control) has no match among the attestation standards.

Required: For each unmatched attestation standard and GAAS in Figure 2-1, explain why you think the Auditing Standards Board and the Accounting and Review Services Committee did not draft a matching standard.

2-2 *GAAS: Obsolescence or Endurance?*

Interrupted by World War II, the Committee on Auditing Procedure, forebear to today's Auditing Standards Board, responded in the late 1940s to the SEC's 1941 call for auditing standards. The first nine standards were approved by AICPA member vote in 1948, a tenth was adopted by member vote in 1949, and few changes have been made to the standards since.

Required: You are the engagement partner for the financial statement audit of a publicly traded software producer. The CFO has asked how your profession's standards—presumably, the profession's measures of quality for a financial statement audit—could possibly be responsive to a client today, given that the standards were produced half a century ago. Discuss.

2-3 *Standards versus Procedures*

Generally accepted auditing standards are an auditor's guidelines for selecting and designing detailed audit procedures. In practice, an auditor typically applies selected procedures to determine whether an entity's financial statements are presented in accordance with generally accepted accounting principles. Thus, generally accepted auditing standards, audit procedures, and generally accepted accounting principles are fundamentally related to one another in a financial statement audit.

Required:
1. What is the difference between: (a) generally accepted auditing standards and (b) auditing procedures?
2. Why is it important that an auditor's report state whether an entity's financial statements are presented "in conformity with generally accepted accounting principles"?

2-4 *Training and Proficiency*

Although not yet engaged, Andrea Farell, a local CPA, has been approached by management to audit the financial statements of The Whitely Corporation, a relatively new, nonpublic company that processes accounting data in a local area network (LAN). Not having been exposed to LANs previously, Farell enrolls in a professional development course that provides hands-on exposure to:

- Data processing.
- Tests of controls and achieving compliance with generally accepted auditing standards.
- System documentation.
- Auditing problems peculiar to LANs.

Farell completes the rather extensive course and is impressed both with the quality of instruction and with the depth and extent of coverage.

Required:
1. The first general standard of GAAS requires that an auditor have adequate technical training and proficiency. Has Farell complied with the standard? Discuss.
2. Why is training in computers necessary before Farell can accept the Whitely engagement? Discuss.

2-5 *Independence*

The second general standard of GAAS states: "*In all matters relating to the assignment, an independence in mental attitude is to be maintained by the auditor or auditors.*" In addition to Rule 101 of the AICPA's Code of Professional Conduct (Chapter 4) and selected Securities and Exchange Commission releases, the second general standard is the profession's primary guideline relating to independence.

Required: Discuss the importance of, and difficulties in achieving, independence in mental attitude.

2-6 *Professional Qualifications and the Scope Paragraph*

A public accounting firm, Rodgers and Burge, performed an audit of Lexington Manufacturing Company's December 31, 2007, financial statements. The scope paragraph of the unqualified report reads as follows:

We conducted our audits in accordance with generally accepted auditing standards. Those standards require that we plan and perform the audit to obtain reasonable assurance about whether the financial statements are free of material misstatement. An audit includes examining, on a test basis, evidence supporting the amounts and disclosures in the financial statements. An audit also includes assessing the accounting principles used and significant estimates made by management, as well as evaluating the overall financial statement presentation. We believe that our audits provide a reasonable basis for our opinion.

Required: What does the scope paragraph imply about (1) the professional qualifications of Rodgers and Burge and the quality of their work and (2) the conduct of their audit work?

2-7 *Accepting an Engagement*

You are the managing partner of Berke & Co., LLP. On February 2, 2008, you receive a letter from the president of Barbizon, Inc., requesting the following: "We have made arrangements with Farmers Loan and Trust to borrow $125,000 to finance the purchase of new equipment. The bank has asked us to submit audited financial statements for the fiscal year ended December 31, 2007. Barbizon has not been audited previously and requests that you perform the audit."

Required:
1. Can you accept the engagement? Explain.
2. Assuming you accept the engagement, what can be done about confirming December 31, 2007, accounts receivable balances with debtors and observing December 31,

2007, physical inventory quantities, two auditing procedures that you would have conducted if the engagement were accepted prior to December 31?

2-8 *Evidence*

The third generally accepted standard of field work requires that the auditor obtain sufficient competent evidential matter to afford a reasonable basis for an opinion on the financial statements audited. In considering what constitutes sufficient competent evidential matter, *SAS No. 31*, "Audit Evidence," distinguishes between underlying accounting data and corroborating information available to the auditor.

> Required:
> 1. Discuss the nature of the evidence an auditor should gather in terms of underlying accounting data and corroborating information, and the methods by which an auditor tests or gathers evidential matter.
> 2. Discuss briefly the meaning of competence in relation to audit evidence, and state the general presumptions that can be made about the validity of evidential matter.
>
> (AICPA Adapted)

2-9 *Standards of Field Work*

You have been assigned by your firm to complete the audit of the financial statements of Carter Manufacturing Corporation. The senior associate and an inexperienced assistant who began the engagement were hospitalized because of an accident. The engagement is about one-half completed. Your auditor's report must be delivered in three weeks, an agreement made when your firm accepted the engagement. You estimate that by utilizing the client's staff you can complete the engagement in five weeks. Your firm cannot assign an assistant to you.

The documents show the status of work on the audit as follows:

a. Completed: cash, plant assets, depreciation, mortgage payable, and stockholders' equity.
b. Completed except as noted below: inventories, accounts payable, tests of purchase transactions, and payrolls.
c. Nothing done: trade accounts receivable, inventory receiving cutoff and price testing, accrued expenses payable, unrecorded liability test, tests of sales transactions, payroll deductions test and observation of payroll check distribution, other expenses, analytical procedures, vouching of December purchase transactions, auditor's report, consideration of internal control, letter on control structure deficiencies, minutes, preparation of tax returns, procedural recommendations for management, subsequent events, supervision, and review.

Your review discloses that the assistant's audit documentation is incomplete and was not reviewed by the senior accountant. For example, the inventory documents present incomplete notations, incomplete explanations, and no cross-referencing.

> Required:
> 1. List the field work standards that have been violated by the senior associate who preceded you on the assignment. Explain why you feel the standards you list have been violated.
> 2. In planning your work to complete the engagement, you should scan the documents, schedule certain work as soon as possible, and identify work that may be postponed until after the report is issued to the client.
>   a. List the areas on which you should plan to work first—say, in your first week of work—and explain why each item deserves early attention.
>   b. State which work you believe could be postponed until after the report is issued to the client, and give reasons why the work may be postponed.
>
> (AICPA Adapted)

2-10 *Standards of Reporting*

You are engaged to audit the financial statements of Rapid, Inc., and Slow Corporation, a recently acquired subsidiary. In acquiring Slow Corporation during 2008, Rapid, Inc., exchanged a large number of shares of its common stock for 90 percent of the outstanding common stock of Slow Corporation in a transaction accounted for as a purchase. Rapid, Inc., is now preparing the annual report to shareholders and proposes to include in the report combined financial statements for the year ended December 31, 2008, with a footnote describing the transaction. Rapid, Inc., also proposes to include in the 2008 report their prior year annual report (2007), including a five-year financial summary and your unqualified opinion.

Required:
1. Discuss the objectives or purposes of the standard of reporting that requires the auditor's report to identify circumstances in which generally accepted accounting principles have not been applied consistently.
2. Briefly discuss whether Rapid, Inc.'s, proposed presentation of financial statements in the 2008 annual report would affect comparability.

(AICPA Adapted)

2-11 *The Effect of Reporting Standards on Audit Reports*

Leer, CPA, has discussed various reporting considerations with two audit clients. The two clients asked how the following situations would affect the audit report.

a. A client has a loan agreement that restricts the amount of cash dividends that can be paid and requires the maintenance of a predetermined current ratio. The client complies with the terms of the agreement, and it is not likely that there will be a violation in the foreseeable future. The client believes there is no need to mention the restriction in the financial statements because it may mislead the readers.

b. During the year, a client correctly accounted for the acquisition of a majority-owned domestic subsidiary but did not properly present the minority interest in retained earnings or net income of the subsidiary in the consolidated financial statements. The client agrees with Leer that the minority interest presented in the consolidated financial statements is materially misstated, but takes the position that the minority shareholders of the subsidiary should look to that subsidiary's financial statements for information concerning their interest.

Required: Each of these situations relates to one of the four generally accepted standards of reporting. Identify and describe the applicable reporting standard in each situation, and discuss how the situation relates to the standard and to Leer's report.

(AICPA Adapted)

2-12 *Failure to Comply with GAAS*

Smith, the owner of a small company, engaged Holmes, a CPA, to perform a financial statement audit. Smith told Holmes that an audit was to be completed in time to submit audited financial statements to a bank as part of a loan application. Holmes immediately accepted the engagement and agreed to provide an auditor's report within three weeks. Smith agreed to pay Holmes a fixed fee plus a bonus if the loan was granted.

Holmes hired two accounting students to perform the audit and spent several hours telling them exactly what to do. Holmes told the students not to spend time reviewing the controls but instead to concentrate on proving the mathematical accuracy of the accounts and summarizing the data in accounting records that support Smith's financial statements. The students followed Holmes's instructions and after two weeks gave Holmes the financial statements, which did not include footnotes. Holmes reviewed the statements and prepared an unqualified auditor's report. The report, however, did not refer to generally accepted accounting principles.

Required: Briefly describe each of the generally accepted auditing standards and indicate how Holmes's actions resulted in a failure to comply with each standard.

(AICPA Adapted)

2-13 *Audit Risk*

Audit risk, the probability that an auditor may unknowingly fail to modify his or her opinion on materially misstated financial statements, occurs on all audit engagements, partly because auditors usually do not test all transactions underlying an account balance and partly because of other uncertainties, such as inadequate planning and supervision.

Required:
1. Briefly describe inherent risk, control risk, and detection risk, the three component risks underlying audit risk for individual financial statement accounts.
2. Why are some financial statement accounts inherently more risky than others?
3. Explain why detection risk bears an inverse relationship to inherent and control risk.
4. Assuming inherent, control, and detection risks are judged by an auditor to be 0.75, 0.50, and 0.25, respectively, for Trade Accounts Receivable, what is audit risk for the account?
5. In regard to requirement 4, assume inherent risk is revised downward to 0.50.
   a. What is audit risk?
   b. In comparison with requirement 4, how will the new audit risk level affect the auditor's revised estimate of materiality for Trade Accounts Receivable?

2-14 *Standards for an Assurance Services Engagement*

Paul Dietz, CEO of the St. Joseph Medical Center, a 200-bed hospital in northwest Indiana, has approached you, a partner in Dirksen & Co., a public accounting firm. The Medical Center's board of directors has approved a strategy to market arthroscopic surgery in alliance with Hankin Orthopedic Surgery and Sports Medicine, a group of sports medicine doctors in Gary, Indiana. Management plans a print and radio advertising campaign to compete with two major suppliers of arthroscopic surgery in the Chicago area: Northwestern Medical Facility and the University of Chicago Hospital. Although known in medical circles for pioneering research and state-of-the-art surgical procedures, the Hankin group is not well known by the general public. Dietz proposes to you that an independent panel of American Medical Association members drawn from the editorial boards of leading research journals be commissioned by the Medical Center to design measures of quality for arthroscopic surgery from which Dirksen & Co. would measure the Hankin group's quality. Dirksen & Co. would be asked to compile "scores" using the independent panel's measures of quality, and would be identified as "a public accounting firm" in print and radio ads. In discussing the proposed assurance service with your partners, one asks, "What standards would you propose we apply on this engagement?"

Required:
1. Is the proposed service an assurance service other than an attestation?
2. In advising the Medical Center, do you see a problem with the assurance service as proposed by Dietz?
3. Respond to your partner's question: What standards would you propose to apply?

2-15 *Effect of Audit Risk on Materiality*

In planning a December 31, 2008, year-end audit, you note that for the 2007 engagement your firm's assessment of audit risk was high, and the preliminary estimate of materiality, $1,200,000, was allocated to balance sheet accounts based on the standard deviation of recorded transactions within each unaudited account. Owing to the design of a new accounting information system and improved control procedures—both supervised by your firm's management consulting division—you judge that, unlike 2007, the risk in 2008 that material errors could occur and not be prevented by the internal controls is now well below the maximum.

Required:
1. In comparison to 2007, will the 2008 preliminary estimate of materiality likely be higher or lower? Discuss.
2. What is the purpose of the preliminary estimate of materiality? Discuss.

2-16 *Materiality*

The concept of materiality is important to the audit of financial statements and to an auditor's expression of an opinion on the statements.

Required: Discuss the following:
1. How is materiality (and immateriality) related to the proper presentation of financial statements?
2. In what ways will materiality affect the auditor in:
   a. Developing an audit program?
   b. Performing auditing procedures?
3. What factors and measures should the auditor consider in assessing the materiality of an exception to financial statement presentation?
4. How will the materiality of an auditor's exceptions to the financial statements influence the type of opinion expressed?

(AICPA Adapted)

2-17 *Calculating and Allocating a Preliminary Estimate of Materiality*

Richard Yates, CPA, is auditing the Levitan Corporation's financial statements for the year ended December 31, 2008. In prior years, Levitan's financial statements were audited by other auditors. Levitan's unaudited accounts receivable, inventory, and plant assets are $2,500,000, $7,750,000, and $15,000,000, respectively, and all other assets total $12,750,000. Total current liabilities are $9,900,000, and net income is expected to be $4,500,000 on $35,000,000 of total revenues. Levitan Corporation is publicly traded.

Because Yates has not previously audited Levitan, he decides to audit all of the balance sheet accounts and to audit accounts payable, recorded at $3,000,000, 100 percent, since controls are not reliable and the balance represents a small number of individual accounts.

Required:
1. Determine a preliminary estimate of materiality for Levitan Corporation's financial statements taken as a whole.
2. What portion of the preliminary estimate of materiality should be allocated to accounts receivable, inventory, and plant assets, assuming Yates uses the relative magnitude approach to determine the allocation?

2-18 *Materiality*

During the course of an audit engagement, an independent auditor gives serious consideration to the concept of materiality, a concept that is inherent in the work of the independent auditor and is important for planning, preparing, and modifying audit programs. The concept of materiality underlies the application of all the generally accepted auditing standards, particularly the standards of field work and reporting.

Required:
1. Briefly describe what is meant by the independent auditor's concept of materiality.
2. What are some common financial statement relationships and other considerations used by the auditor in judging materiality?
3. Describe how the planning and execution of an audit program might be affected by the independent auditor's concept of materiality.

Internet problems and discussion cases are available at http://ricchiute.swlearning.com

RESEARCH PROJECTS

1. MD&A and Risk

SEC *Regulation S-K*, Item 303, "Management Discussion and Analysis of Financial Position and Results of Operations," requires that management discuss and analyze liquidity, capital resources, and the results of operations in annual reports (*Form 10-K*), and material changes in financial position and in results of operations in quarterly reports (*Form 10-Q*). Although generally accepted accounting principles standardize across companies the accounting for like-kind transactions, *Regulation S-K* does not standardize what management discusses and analyzes.

To encourage more diagnostic MD&A, the SEC in December 2003 published Release No. 33-8350, "Commission Guidance Regarding Management's Discussion and Analysis of Financial Condition and Results of Operations," an interpretation of Item 303. For example, the Release encourages avoiding unnecessary duplication with disclosures that appear in financial statements, an executive-level overview that provides context for the remainder of the discussion, eliminating immaterial information that does not promote understanding, and key nonfinancial performance indicators. For example, on nonfinancial performance indicators, most of the major competitors in the consumer foods industries report volume data, but some in somewhat different forms—Campbell Foods, General Mills, Kellogg, and Kraft Foods all report unit-volume growth rates in percentages, but only Kraft Foods reports volume in units (pounds).

Interestingly, a number of issues that bear on a company's risk profile are disclosed typically in MD&A, including conflicts of interest and regulatory problems, key turnover, recurring losses and negative cash flows, significant debt requirements, related-party transactions, significant pending litigation, and challenges in existing or planned markets.

Required: Select a *Form 10-K* from the SEC's EDGAR system (**http://www.sec.gov**), from a public company's home page, or from a library:
1. Read carefully MD&A, and
2. Draft a report that links and discusses disclosures in the MD&A to issues insightful about risk. For example, discussion about significant litigation, often included in MD&A, can represent a significant unplanned drain on cash flow in the form, for example, of defense and settlement costs.

2. Materiality and Audit Risk

An office of one Big Four firm determines a preliminary estimate of materiality this way: An audit partner:

1. Judges overall materiality for the financial statements taken as a whole to be an amount falling within a range of 5 percent (lower limit) to 8 percent (upper limit) of net income, and
2. Instructs staff to document any proposed adjusting journals entries (PAJEs) that equal or exceed an amount falling within the range of 10 percent of the lower materiality limit to 20 percent of the upper materiality limit.

For example, assuming net income is $85 million, then:

		Lower limit	*Upper limit*
● Overall materiality	=	$0.05 \times \$85$ million	$0.08 \times \$85$ million
	=	$4.25 million	$6.80 million
● PAJE	=	$0.10 \times \$4.25$ million	$0.20 \times \$6.80$ million
	=	$0.425 million	$1.36 million

The partner's selection of overall materiality and a PAJE threshold falls toward the lower limit on higher risk engagements and the upper limit on lower risk engagements, since materiality and audit risk are inversely related.

Required: Select an annual report from the SEC's EDGAR system (**http://www.sec.gov**), from a public company's home page, or from a library, and prepare a report that:
1. Calculates a range (lower and upper limits) for overall materiality and for a PAJE threshold, and
2. Uses information captured within the annual report and other services (for example, analysts' reports, Factiva, the company's home page, etc.) to identify risks and, thereby, to judge whether overall materiality and the PAJE threshold should, in your judgment, fall toward the lower limits (high risk) or upper limits (low risk) calculated in requirement 1.

3. Violations of GAAS: The SEC's Accounting and Auditing Enforcement Releases

The SEC's Division of Enforcement investigates violations of federal securities laws by investors, broker-dealers, lawyers, and accountants, among others. Based on the Division's recommendations, the Commission may initiate administrative proceedings or seek court-ordered injunctions. In most years, the Commission initiates in excess of 250 administrative proceedings and in excess of 170 federal court injunctions.

Injunctions and proceedings that involve violations of Regulation S-X, the SEC's principal accounting requirements, are published in SEC Accounting and Auditing Enforcement Releases (AAER). AAERs often involve auditor violations of generally accepted auditing standards. For example, in one AAER, the SEC ordered a CPA to cease and desist violations of securities laws and denied the CPA the privilege of practicing before the SEC. On violations of GAAS, the AAER read in part as follows:

Failure to Exercise Due Professional Care

An auditor must exercise due professional care in performing an audit and preparing the audit report. . . . (auditor) failed to exercise due professional care in the performance of his audits of (the company's) financial statements by (1) opining that these financial statements were prepared in conformity with GAAP, and audited in accordance with GAAS, when, in fact, they were not; (2) inadequately planning the audits; (3) failing to obtain sufficient competent evidential matter; and (4) improperly issuing unqualified audit reports. Due care also imposes a responsibility upon the auditor to observe the standards of field work and reporting prescribed by GAAS. In addition, an auditor should exercise due care in planning, performing, and evaluating the results of audit procedures, and maintain a level of professional skepticism sufficient to reasonably assure that material errors and irregularities will be detected. During the course of his audits of (the company's) financial statements, (the auditor) failed to exercise due care and to maintain a healthy degree of skepticism by ignoring facts and GAAP accounting pronouncements which contradicted (the company's) accounting for certain transactions. For example, (the auditor) ignored the family relationships, the sharing of office space and expenses and other "red flags". . .

Required: Select an Accounting and Auditing Enforcement Release from the SEC's online database (**http://www.sec.gov**) and prepare a report that:
1. Identifies which of the AICPA's ten GAAS the auditor violated.
2. Explains in detail the accounting, auditing, or disclosure issue that gave rise to each violation.

4. Programming, Investigative, and Reporting Independence

The concept of independence relates both to the *actual* independence of individual practitioners (practitioner independence) and to the *apparent* independence of all practitioners collectively (profession independence). Mautz and Sharaf (*The Philosophy of Auditing*. Sarasota, FL: American Accounting Association, 1961, p. 206) describe *practitioner independence* as a state of mind that pervades a practitioner's approach to attestations and audits and identify three dimensions of practitioner independence that can minimize potential threats to impartiality:

- *Programming independence:* Freedom from control or undue influence when selecting and applying procedures.
- *Investigative independence:* Access to all relevant information, and freedom from control or undue influence when selecting information to investigate.
- *Reporting independence:* Freedom from control or undue influence when reporting information revealed by the engagement, or when making recommendations or expressing opinions.

Clearly, practitioner independence demands that professional judgment neither be subordinated to nor influenced by stakeholders, including management, employees, or the board of directors. In contrast, *profession independence* is a perception held by the public about all practitioners collectively. To the extent that the public perceives that the profession lacks independence, the perceived independence of otherwise impartial practitioners may be at risk. Thus, public perceptions of profession independence have a direct impact on the reputation—and indeed the livelihood—of individual practitioners, and have been a major preoccupation of the public accounting profession for years.

Required: Select an article from the press (for example, *Business Week, The Wall Street Journal, The New York Times*) that describes independence issues raised about an audit firm. For example, the press reported that the SEC settled charges against a firm whose partners had purchased equity securities of audit clients and that the SEC issued a cease-and-desist order against a firm for affiliating with a corporate turnaround specialist who had served one of the firm's audit clients. From the text of the article, draft a report that:

1. Describes how the audit firm's alleged behavior bears on each of Mautz and Sharaf's three dimensions of practitioner independence, and
2. Explains whether you think that the firm's alleged behavior bears on profession independence.

Interactive quizzes are available as a student learning resource at
http://ricchiute.swlearning.com

3 Chapter

Audit Reports

Major topics discussed in this chapter are:

- Reports on audited financial statements.
- Unqualified, qualified, and adverse opinions, and disclaimers of opinion.
- Explanatory paragraphs and modifications to audit reports.
- Reports on updated opinions and on financial statements prepared for use in foreign countries.
- Reports on attestation services and on other assurance services.

This chapter introduces carefully phrased written reports that explain a practitioner's findings. The chapter begins by introducing standard audit reports in the United States (Procter & Gamble), Japan (Hitachi Zosen Corporation), and Germany (Daimler-Benz) and illustrating circumstances for which an auditor would modify a standard report, among them circumstances that affected reports issued for Sprint, GenCorp, Whirlpool, and Kmart. For example, what special reporting problems arise when management's financial statements depart materially from generally accepted accounting principles, or when an auditor doubts an entity's ability to continue as a going concern? In turn, the chapter discusses reports on comparative financial statements (Sony Corporation) and on financial statements used in a foreign country (Kubota Corporation). The chapter concludes by introducing and illustrating reports on attestation services (equivalent subscribers to a cable TV stock purchase agreement) and on other assurance services (Consumers Union).

Reports on Financial Statement Audits

An **audit report** is a letter communicating what was audited, management's and the auditor's responsibilities, what an audit entails, and the auditor's opinion. Most financial statement audits result in a three-paragraph **standard audit report**. The report uses standard language stating that, in the auditor's opinion, management's financial statements present fairly, in all material respects, financial position, results of operations, and cash flows in conformity with generally accepted accounting principles (GAAP). The language was first standardized in a 1934 pamphlet, "Audits of Corporate Reports," by George O. May, Price Waterhouse (today's PwC) senior partner and chair of the American Institute of Accountants' (today's AICPA) Committee on Cooperation with Stock Exchanges. In 1949, following adoption of the ten generally accepted auditing standards (GAAS,

Chapter 2), the AICPA revised the language to incorporate an explicit reference to standards.

Although the standard report remained essentially unchanged from 1949 to 1988, it was not without critics, among them Congress, the SEC, and the Commission on Auditors' Responsibilities, all of whom concluded the language was ambiguous, confusing, and a poor portrayal of the responsibilities assumed by an independent auditor. Partly in response to hearings conducted by the House Subcommittee on Oversight and Investigations in the 1980s, the Auditing Standards Board in 1988 reconsidered and revised the language of a standard audit report in *Statement on Auditing Standards No. 58*, "Reports on Audited Financial Statements" (AU Sec. 508). The following introduces today's standard report.

Unqualified Opinion

A standard audit report gives an **unqualified opinion**, which means it is the independent auditor's opinion that management's financial statements present fairly in all material respects the financial position, results of operations, and cash flows in conformity with GAAP. To issue an unqualified opinion for a public company the auditor must comply with auditing standards issued by the Public Company Accounting Oversight Board (PCAOB); to issue an unqualified opinion for a nonpublic company, the auditor must comply with GAAS. A departure from auditing standards or GAAS (or from GAAP) would preclude an unqualified opinion.

An unqualified opinion pertains only to an entity's financial statements, not to the quality of the entity as an investment or credit risk. For example, a company experiencing a net loss and negative cash flows might prove a poor investment or credit risk, but if an audit reveals that the financial statements conform with GAAP, the auditor would issue an unqualified opinion. Figure 3-1 illustrates Deloitte & Touche's three-paragraph, unqualified opinion for the Procter & Gamble Company, and Figure 3-2 lists the report's basic elements.

Title and Management's Responsibility

The title "Independent Auditor's Report" is included largely to distinguish an auditor's report on the financial statements from management's accompanying financial statements. For years, companies have acknowledged management's responsibility for financial statements in statements of responsibility that often appeared on the same page as, or the page facing, the auditor's report in an annual report to shareholders. The statements typically declared that management took responsibility for the financial statements, that the statements were prepared in accordance with GAAP, and that the company had developed and maintains internal controls.

However, the *Sarbanes-Oxley Act of 2002* raised the bar for management's responsibility statement. Under Section 302, Corporate Responsibility for Financial Reports, *both* the chief executive officer and the chief financial officer *certify* that:

- They *reviewed the entire annual (or quarterly) report* (not just the financial statements),
- The report *does not contain any untrue statement of a material fact or omit a material fact,*
- The *financial statements present fairly in all material respects the financial condition and results of operations,*

FIGURE 3-1: *Financial Statement Audit Report*

Independent Auditor's Report

To the Board of Directors and Shareholders of
The Procter & Gamble Company

We have audited the accompanying consolidated balance sheets of The Procter & Gamble Company and subsidiaries as of June 30, 2004 and 2003, and the related consolidated statements of earnings, retained earnings, and cash flows for each of the three years in the period ended June 30, 2004. These financial statements are the responsibility of the companies' management. Our responsibility is to express an opinion on these financial statements based on our audits.

We conducted our audits in accordance with the standards of the Public Company Accounting Oversight Board (United States). Those standards require that we plan and perform the audits to obtain reasonable assurance about whether the financial statements are free of material misstatement. An audit includes examining, on a test basis, evidence supporting the amounts and disclosures in the financial statements. An audit also includes assessing the accounting principles used and significant estimates made by management, as well as evaluating the overall financial statement presentation. We believe that our audits provide a reasonable basis for our opinion.

In our opinion, the financial statements referred to above present fairly, in all material respects, the financial position of the companies at June 30, 2004 and 2003, and the results of their operations and their cash flows for each of the three years in the period ended June 30, 2004, in conformity with accounting principles generally accepted in the United States of America.

Deloitte & Touche
July 31, 2005

- They are *responsible for establishing and maintaining, and have evaluated the effectiveness of, internal controls,*
- They have *identified to the auditors* all *significant deficiencies* in the design or operation of internal controls and any *fraud*, whether material, that involves management or others with a significant role in internal controls.

Figure 3-3 on page 80 illustrates the Section 302 certification signed by Procter & Gamble's CEO; the CFO's certification is identical. The requirements of the *Sarbanes-Oxley Act*, Section 302, a response to the fraudulent financial reporting discussed in Chapter 1, renders moot the defense that perpetrators offered repeatedly: "None of those things are my responsibility; that's why I hire accountants and auditors."

Addressee

An auditor's report for a corporation is commonly addressed to the shareholders, to the board of directors, or to both, as in the Procter & Gamble report (Figure 3-1). Management is rarely included among the addressees, thereby underscoring the auditor's independence from management. A report for an unincorporated entity may be addressed to the partners, the general partners, or the proprietor; a report for a governmental entity may be addressed to the taxpayers or to an oversight body such as a city council or town board.

FIGURE 3-2: *Elements of a Standard Audit Report*

Opening
- A title that includes the word "independent"
- The addressees

Introductory Paragraph
- A statement that the financial statements were audited
- A statement that the financial statements are management's responsibility, and that the auditor's responsibility is to express an opinion

Scope Paragraph
- A statement that the audit was conducted in accordance with U.S. generally accepted auditing standards
- A statement that generally accepted auditing standards require planning and performing the audit to obtain reasonable assurance about whether the financial statements are free of material misstatement
- A statement that the audit includes (1) examining evidence on a test basis, (2) evaluating the accounting principles and significant estimates used by management, and (3) evaluating the overall financial statement presentation

Opinion Paragraph
- A statement of opinion on whether the financial statements present fairly in all material respects the financial position, results of operations, and cash flows in conformity with U.S. generally accepted accounting principles

Closing
- The firm's signature
- The date of the auditor's report

Occasionally, an auditor is engaged by one entity to audit the financial statements of another entity (for example, when a company contemplates purchasing the audited company), in which case the auditor's report is generally addressed to the potential purchaser rather than to the entity whose statements were audited. Parties named as addressees do not necessarily enjoy exclusive legal rights against an auditor in the event of an audit failure, since other third parties, such as creditors, also may have a legal claim against the auditor (Chapter 5), even though they are not named as addressees in the auditor's report.

Introductory Paragraph

The **introductory paragraph** identifies the financial statements audited (typically the balance sheet and statements of earnings, retained earnings, and cash flows), and indicates that the statements are management's, not the auditor's, responsibility. The independent auditor is responsible only for expressing an opinion on the statements, not for the assertions within the statements. Thus, apart from identifying the statements audited, the role of the introductory paragraph is to differentiate management's responsibility (for the financial statements) from the auditor's responsibility (to express an *opinion* on management's financial statements). Although auditors customarily report on two years for nonpublic companies, note that The Procter & Gamble Company report applies to three years, an SEC requirement for public companies.

FIGURE 3-3: *Management's Sarbanes-Oxley, Section 302, Certification*

I, (chief executive officer), certify that:

(1) I have reviewed this annual report on Form 10-K of The Procter & Gamble Company;

(2) Based on my knowledge, this report does not contain any untrue statement of a material fact or omit to state a material fact necessary to make the statements made, in light of the circumstances under which such statements were made, not misleading with respect to the period covered by this report;

(3) Based on my knowledge, the financial statements, and other financial information included in this report, fairly present in all material respects the financial condition, results of operations and cash flows of the registrant as of, and for, the periods presented in this report;

(4) The registrant's other certifying officer(s) and I are responsible for establishing and maintaining disclosure controls and procedures (as defined in Exchange Act Rules 13a-15(e) and 15d-15(e)) for the registrant and have:

   (a) Designed such disclosure controls and procedures, or caused such disclosure controls and procedures to be designed under our supervision, to ensure that material information relating to the registrant, including its consolidated subsidiaries, is made known to us by others within those entities, particularly during the period in which this report is being prepared;

   (b) Evaluated the effectiveness of the registrant's disclosure controls and procedures and presented in this report our conclusions about the effectiveness of the disclosure controls and procedures, as of the end of the period covered by this report based on such evaluation; and

   (c) Disclosed in this report any change in the registrant's internal control over financial reporting that occurred during the registrant's fourth fiscal quarter (the registrant's fourth fiscal quarter in the case of an annual report) that has materially affected, or is reasonably likely to materially affect, the registrant's internal control over financial reporting; and

(5) The registrant's other certifying officer(s) and I have disclosed, based on our most recent evaluation of internal control over financial reporting, to the registrant's auditors and the audit committee of the registrant's board of directors (or persons performing the equivalent functions):

   (a) All significant deficiencies and material weaknesses in the design or operation of internal control over financial reporting which are reasonably likely to adversely affect the registrant's ability to record, process, summarize and report financial information; and

   (b) Any fraud, whether or not material, that involves management or other employees who have a significant role in the registrant's internal control over financial reporting.

Chairman of the Board, President and Chief Executive

Scope Paragraph

Because Procter & Gamble is a public company, the **scope paragraph** states that the engagement complied with "the standards of the Public Company Accounting Oversight Board (United States)"—a requirement of the PCAOB's *Auditing Standard No. 1*, "References in Auditors' Reports to the Standards of the PCAOB." For nonpublic companies, the paragraph states that the engagement complied with "generally accepted auditing standards in the United States," a requirement of the

Auditing Standards Board's *Statement on Auditing Standards No. 93*, "Omnibus SAS–2000."

In turn, the paragraph describes briefly what an audit entails. The description uses several critical terms: reasonable assurance, free of material misstatement, and test basis, although *reasonable assurance* is the glue that holds all three together. Recall from Chapter 2 (Figure 2-1) that the third standard of field work states that an auditor should obtain "sufficient competent evidential matter . . . to afford a *reasonable basis* for an opinion. . . ." Because an audit need provide only a reasonable (rather than an absolute) basis for an opinion, the scope paragraph implies that the auditor may overlook immaterial misstatements and test samples, rather than the entire population of transactions and events underlying the financial statements.

A standard scope paragraph can be used when, for nonpublic company audits, the auditor complies with each of the general and field work standards, suggesting that the paragraph can be interpreted as follows:

Compliance with General Standards

The auditor:

- Was *adequately trained and proficient*,
- Maintained an *independence* in mental attitude, and
- Exercised *due professional care* when performing the audit and preparing the report.

Compliance with Field Work Standards

The auditor:

- *Planned* the engagement and *supervised* assistants,
- Obtained an *understanding of internal control* sufficient to plan the audit and to determine the nature, timing, and extent of audit tests, and
- Obtained *sufficient competent evidential matter* to afford a reasonable basis for an opinion on the financial statements.

Each statement must be true, without qualification, for an auditor to use the wording of a standard scope paragraph. If not, the scope paragraph is modified. Examples of departures from the wording of a standard scope paragraph are presented later in the chapter.

Opinion Paragraph

The opinion paragraph appears after the scope paragraph. Like the unqualified opinion illustrated for The Procter & Gamble Company (Figure 3-1), the **opinion paragraph** states that the financial statements present fairly, in all material respects, the entity's financial position, results of operations, and cash flows in conformity with U.S. GAAP. When one or more prior-period financial statements are presented with current-period statements, both the introductory and opinion paragraphs include a reference to all prior periods. For example, the Procter & Gamble report draws attention to the 2003 financial statements even though 2004 is the current year audited. The terms "audit report" and "audit opinion" are sometimes used interchangeably, but "report" refers to the entire three paragraphs (and to the title, signature, and date) and "opinion" refers to the opinion paragraph only.

Just as the wording of a standard scope paragraph implies compliance with the general and field work standards, the wording of a standard opinion paragraph implies compliance with all four reporting standards. Thus, a standard opinion paragraph can be interpreted as follows:

Compliance with Reporting Standards

- The financial statements are *presented in accordance with U.S. GAAP.*
- Accounting principles are applied *consistently.*
- Informative *disclosures* are reasonably adequate.
- The *opinion* applies to the financial statements taken as a whole.

Each of these statements must be true, without qualification, for an auditor to use the wording of a standard opinion paragraph. However, when an opinion is based partly on the report of another auditor (for example, when one firm audits a parent company and another audits a subsidiary) or when an auditor emphasizes a matter within the report, an explanatory paragraph may be added to the standard report without distorting or detracting from the meaning of an unqualified opinion. These and other examples of departures from the wording of a standard opinion paragraph are presented later in the chapter.

Prior to the mid-1970s, auditors sometimes issued *piecemeal opinions*: reports that gave an opinion on selected accounts, but disclaimed an opinion on the financial statements taken as a whole. Piecemeal opinions were issued, for example, when scope limitations precluded auditing some accounts, such as Inventory or Accounts Receivable. However, piecemeal opinions overlook the fact that many accounts are related (for example, the debit sides of Receivables and Cash and the credit side of Sales all figure in a credit sale transaction), and none are wholly independent. As a result, *SAS No. 58*, "Reports on Audited Financial Statements" (AU Sec. 508), reiterated a long-standing prohibition against issuing piecemeal opinions under any circumstances. However, *SAS No. 58* does not prohibit auditors from issuing an opinion on an individual financial statement, such as a balance sheet or an income statement.

Signature

An audit report is signed by the engagement partner, but in the name of his or her firm. For example, the engagement partner signed "Deloitte & Touche" in The Procter & Gamble Company report, not his or her own name.

Report Date

Under *SAS No. 98*, "Omnibus SAS–2002," an auditor dates an audit report as of the *completion of field work.* For example, in Figure 3-1, the Procter & Gamble report is dated July 31, 2004, because field work for the June 30, 2004, engagement was completed on July 31. Deloitte & Touche likely completed other work in their own offices after July 31 (for example, assembling audit documentation, drafting a report) and may not have issued the report until later. Nevertheless, the report is dated July 31, because the date of the completion of field work is the last date on which the firm is responsible for detecting *subsequent events* (Chapter 17)—material events occurring between July 1, 2004, and July 31, 2004, that would require disclosure in the June 30 financial statements.

On occasion, a material subsequent event may occur, and come to an auditor's attention, after the last day of field work but before the report is released—for example, August 15, 2004, in the case of Procter & Gamble. If the financial statements are revised to disclose a subsequent event, the auditor has two alternatives for dating the report:

- *Dual date:* July 31, 2004, except for Note X, August 15, 2004
- *Event date:*August 15, 2004

Dual dating extends an auditor's responsibility beyond the last day of field work (from July 31 to August 15), but only for the event disclosed. In contrast, dating as of the subsequent event (August 15) extends the auditor's responsibility to *all* events occurring on or before August 15, even those unknown to the auditor.

Unqualified Opinions in Other Countries

Cultural differences in foreign countries create barriers to U.S. entrepreneurship overseas. For example, although bribes are common in some countries, the U.S. *Foreign Corrupt Practices Act (FCPA)* prohibits U.S. companies from unlawfully influencing foreign governments, thereby placing U.S. companies at a disadvantage in competing for foreign business and some foreign countries at a disadvantage in attracting U.S. capital. Likewise, cultural differences have driven different accounting standards, and different audit reports, across countries. For example, like U.S. auditors, Japanese auditors are guided by private sector standards, but German auditors are guided largely by commercial law.

Figure 3-4 shows the standard unqualified audit report issued by a Japanese firm and by a German firm. The Ashi & Co. report for the Hitachi Zosen Corporation refers to generally accepted auditing standards and to generally accepted accounting principles, and renders an opinion that, like the U.S. report, uses the term "present fairly." In contrast, the KPMG Deutsche report for Daimler also refers to generally accepted accounting principles, but consistent with a European Union directive on company accounts, uses the term "true and fair view," rather than "present fairly." Interestingly, prior to World War II, Japan's audit reports were more like German reports, but since the war, they are now more like U.S. reports. Some differences across countries are real (for example, the *FCPA*) and others imagined (for example, present fairly versus true and fair), but all point to a need for harmonization, given that the capital markets are now largely global. To that end, the SEC has worked with the FASB, with the International Federation of Accountants, and with the International Organization of Securities Commissioners to harmonize accounting standards and auditing standards.

Other Types of Opinions

In an audit engagement, an unqualified opinion can be issued only if the audit has complied with PCAOB standards (public company audit) or with GAAS (nonpublic) and the financial statements comply with GAAP. Departures from PCAOB standards, GAAS, and/or GAAP in an audit engagement require that an auditor issue either a qualified or an adverse opinion, or disclaim an opinion. Each is described briefly here and illustrated in the next section of the chapter. Figure 3-5 summarizes the meaning of unqualified (previously discussed), qualified, and adverse opinions, and disclaimers of opinion.

Qualified Opinion

A **qualified opinion** means that *except for* the effects of a matter, management's financial statements present fairly in all material respects financial position, results of operations, and cash flows in conformity with GAAP. Only the term *except for*

FIGURE 3-4: *Standard Audit Reports in Foreign Countries*

Japan

Hitachi Zosen Corporation
Ashi & Co, CPAs

We have examined the accompanying consolidated balance sheets of Hitachi Zosen Corporation and its consolidated subsidiaries at 31st March, 2003 and 2004, and the related consolidated statements of income and shareholders' equity for the years then ended, all expressed in Japanese yen. Our examinations were made in accordance with generally accepted auditing standards in Japan and, accordingly, included such tests of the accounting records and such other auditing procedures as we considered necessary in the circumstances.

In our opinion, the accompanying consolidated financial statements mentioned above, expressed in yen, present fairly the financial position of Hitachi Zosen Corporation and its consolidated subsidiaries at 31st March, 2003 and 2004, and the results of their operations for the years then ended, in conformity with generally accepted accounting principles in Japan applied on a consistent basis.

We have also reviewed the translation of the financial statements mentioned into U.S. dollars on the basis described in Note 1. In our opinion, such statements have been properly translated on such basis.

Germany

Daimler-Benz
KPMG Deutsche Treuhand-Gesellschaft

We rendered an unqualified opinion on the consolidated financial statements and the business review report in accordance with Section 322 HGB (German Commercial Code). The translation of our opinion reads as follows:

"The consolidated financial statements, which we have audited in accordance with professional standards, comply with the legal provisions. With due regard to the generally accepted accounting principles, the consolidated financial statements give a true and fair view of the assets, liabilities, financial position and results of operations of the Daimler-Benz group. The business review report, which summarizes the state of affairs of Daimler-Benz Aktiengesellschaft and that of the group, is consistent with the financial statements of Daimler-Benz Aktiengesellschaft and the consolidated financial statements."

or some variation—such as *except*, *exception*, or *with the exception of*—may be used to qualify an opinion. Qualified opinions are issued when:

- Financial statements depart materially from GAAP,
- Management is unable to justify a material change in accounting principles, or
- The scope of an audit is limited materially.

Adverse Opinion

An **adverse opinion** means management's financial statements *do not* present fairly in all material respects the financial position, results of operations, and cash flows in conformity with GAAP. Adverse opinions are issued when:

- Financial statements depart materially from GAAP, or

FIGURE 3-5: *Types of Opinions*

Opinion	Interpretation
Unqualified	Management's assertions (in an attestation) or financial statements (in an audit) are presented fairly in all material respects . . .
Qualified	Except for the effects of a matter, the assertion or financial statements are presented fairly . . .
Adverse	The assertion or financial statements do not present fairly . . .
Disclaimer of opinion	The attestor or auditor does not express an opinion . . .

- Management is unable to justify an accounting change, and
- The effect of the departure or change is so highly material that a qualified opinion is unwarranted.

Disclaimer of Opinion

A **disclaimer of opinion** means an auditor does not express an opinion on the financial statements. Generally, disclaimers are issued when:

- The effects of a scope limitation are so highly material that the auditor does not have a reasonable basis to reach an opinion, or
- The auditor is not independent of management.

Note carefully the difference between a disclaimer of opinion and an adverse opinion: An auditor disclaims when evidence is insufficient to reach an opinion—for example, when a client limits the scope of an audit—and issues an adverse opinion when evidence is sufficient to conclude the financial statements are highly materially misstated.

Explanatory Paragraphs and Modifications to Standard Reports

Auditors in the United States add an explanatory paragraph, or otherwise modify the wording of standard reports, for the circumstances listed in Figure 3-6. For many of the circumstances, the type of opinion required depends on whether the effect of the circumstance is material or highly material. Figure 3-7 summarizes the report modifications required for each of the circumstances listed in Figure 3-6. Each circumstance is discussed and illustrated in the following sections.

Opinion Based Partly on the Report of Another Auditor

In practice, the audit of a geographically diverse company may necessitate that an auditor rely partly on the report of another auditor. For example, an East Coast, local public accounting firm might rely on a West Coast firm to report on the financial statements of a wholly owned, West Coast subsidiary. Relying on another firm's report does not necessarily preclude an auditor from issuing an unqualified opinion for the combined statements, although it could if the other firm's opinion were qualified, adverse, or a disclaimer.

FIGURE 3-6: *Modifications to Standard Reports*

- *Another Auditor:* The auditor's opinion is based in part on the report of another auditor.
- *Emphasize a Matter:* The auditor wishes to emphasize a matter about the financial statements.
- *Departure from GAAP:* The financial statements are affected by a departure from generally accepted accounting principles.
- *Inconsistency:* Accounting principles have not been applied consistently.
- *Scope Limitation:* The scope of the audit is affected by conditions that preclude applying one or more necessary auditing procedures.
- *Going Concern:* The auditor has substantial doubt about an entity's ability to continue as a going concern.
- *Lack of Independence:* The auditor is not independent of the entity.

FIGURE 3-7: *Modifications to the Wording of Standard Reports*

Circumstance	Material	Highly Material	Paragraph(s) Modified	Explanatory Paragraph
Opinion based partly on another auditor	Unqualified	Unqualified	Introductory/ Opinion	No
Emphasize a matter	Unqualified	Unqualified	—	Yes
Departure from GAAP	Qualified	Adverse	Opinion	Yes
Inconsistency: Management justifies	Unqualified	Unqualified	—	Yes
Management does not justify	Qualified	Adverse	Opinion	Yes
Scope limitation	Qualified	—	Scope/ Opinion	Yes
	—	Disclaimer	Introductory/ Opinion (Omit scope)	Yes
Going concern	Unqualified	Unqualified	—	Yes
Lack of independence	Disclaimer	Disclaimer	Omit introductory, Scope, Opinion	Yes

When an opinion is based partly on the report of another auditor, the auditors must decide who is the **principal auditor**, considering factors such as (AU Sec 543):

- The *materiality* of the financial statements audited by each auditor,
- The extent of each auditor's *knowledge of the overall financial statements*, and
- The significance of the financial statements audited in relation to the *combined entity taken as a whole*.

The principal auditor is responsible for reporting on the combined financial statements, but must decide whether to refer in his or her report to the other auditor's work, although most do. When no reference is made to another auditor's work, the principal auditor takes full responsibility. However, if the principal auditor shares responsibility, his or her audit report refers to the other auditor's work (though not typically to the other auditor's name) and clearly indicates the division of responsibility by disclosing the statements and/or the assets and revenues audited by the other auditor.

For example, Ernst & Young, principal auditor of Sprint Corporation, a worldwide provider of domestic and international long-distance and local telecommunications services, shared responsibility with another firm that audited Sprint Spectrum Holding Company, a partnership in which Sprint holds a 40 percent interest. Ernst & Young issued an unqualified opinion on the consolidated financial statements taken as a whole, but shared responsibility in the introductory and opinion paragraphs.

Sprint Corporation
Ernst & Young

(Introductory Paragraph)
. . . Our responsibility is to express an opinion on these financial statements . . . based on our audits. The 1997 financial statements and financial statement schedule of Sprint Spectrum Holding Company, L.P., a partnership in which Sprint has a 40% interest, have been audited by other auditors whose report has been furnished to us; insofar as our opinion on the 1997 consolidated financial statements relates to data included for Sprint Spectrum Holding Company, L.P., it is based solely on their report. In the consolidated financial statements, Sprint's equity in Sprint Spectrum Holding Company, L.P. is stated at $749 million at December 31, 1997, and Sprint's equity in the net loss of Sprint Spectrum Holding Company, L.P. is stated at $625 million for the year then ended . . .

(Opinion Paragraph)
In our opinion, based on our audits and the report of the other auditors, the consolidated financial statements present fairly, in all material respects, the consolidated financial position of Sprint . . .

Emphasis on a Matter

An auditor may emphasize a matter and still issue an unqualified opinion. For example, as noted in Chapter 1, an unprecedented number of public companies in the past few years have restated previously audited financial statements, necessitating that an independent auditor—often, the incumbent auditor—audit, and issue an opinion on, the restated financial statements. In 2002, Ernst & Young audited the restated financial statements of GenCorp, the successor to General Tire

& Rubber, an automotive and chemical products manufacturer. Ernst & Young emphasized the matter in an explanatory paragraph to the 2001 audit report, but made no changes to the standard introductory, scope, or opinion paragraphs.

GenCorp Inc.
Ernst & Young
(Explanatory Paragraph)
The accompanying consolidated financial statements for the years ended November 30, 2000 and 1999 have been restated as discussed in Note 2.

The paragraph recites the *fact* that the financial statements have been restated but, rather than explain why, refers to management's explanation in Note 2 to the financial statements. As is common, the note explains that management became aware of potential accounting issues and notified both the audit committee and Ernst & Young, and that the audit committee engaged outside counsel (and consultants) to investigate.

Note 2 (in part)
In January 2002, the Company became aware of certain potential accounting issues at two of its GDX Automotive manufacturing plants in North America. The Company promptly notified both its Audit Committee and its independent accountants. Under the direction and oversight of the Audit Committee and with the assistance of outside legal advisors and accounting consultants, the Company conducted an inquiry into these and related accounting issues as well as a more complete evaluation of accounting practices and internal control processes throughout the Company. As a result of this process, due primarily to activities at one GDX Automotive manufacturing plant, the Company is, by means of this filing, restating its previously issued financial statements for the years ended November 30, 2000 and November 30, 1999.

Departure from GAAP

When management's financial statements depart materially from an accounting principle promulgated in an official pronouncement, such as an FASB or GASB statement, Rule 202 of the AICPA's *Code of Professional Conduct* (Chapter 4) prohibits an unqualified opinion, unless the auditor can demonstrate that, owing to rare and unusual circumstances, complying with the pronouncement would actually cause the financial statements to be misleading—for example, when a long-standing pronouncement is applied to a new industry. In those circumstances, which are both rare (with a capital *R*) and unusual (capital *U*), the auditor issues an unqualified opinion and explains the departure, the approximate effects on the financial statements, and why compliance with the pronouncement would necessarily mislead readers. In practice, departures from GAAP arise typically when disclosures are inadequate or when management applies accounting principles inappropriately and, depending on materiality, result in a qualified or an adverse opinion.

Qualified Opinion

A material departure from GAAP requires an explanatory paragraph to disclose the misstatement and a modified opinion paragraph, but no change to the introductory or scope paragraphs. To illustrate, consider Andersen's report for the

Union Bank, which, rather than record goodwill as an asset (to be amortized), charged goodwill to shareholders' equity.

Union Bank
Andersen
(Explanatory Paragraph)
As discussed in Note 2 to the financial statements, the Bank has charged goodwill to shareholders' equity. GAAP require that goodwill be recorded as an asset and amortized to expense over future periods.

(Opinion Paragraph)
In our opinion, except for the effects of the accounting treatment for goodwill as discussed in the preceding paragraph, the financial statements referred to above present fairly . . .

Research has reported several interesting findings about qualified opinions. First, companies that receive qualified opinions switch audit firms more frequently than companies that don't, but not necessarily to firms with a history of issuing proportionately fewer qualified opinions.[1] Second, in some cases, publicly available financial data (such as ratios) and market data (such as stock prices) can predict which companies will receive qualified opinions for the first time.[2] Third, a study in Australia revealed that qualified opinions were associated with delays in the issuance of annual reports—the more serious the qualification, the longer the delay.[3]

Adverse Opinion

A departure from GAAP may be so highly material as to require an adverse opinion that includes one or more explanatory paragraphs. To illustrate, assume that a company carries property, plant, and equipment at appraisal values, rather than historical costs.

(Explanatory Paragraphs)
As discussed in Note C to the financial statements, the Company carries property, plant, and equipment at appraisal values, and provides depreciation on the basis of such values. Generally accepted accounting principles require that property, plant, and equipment be stated at an amount not in excess of cost, reduced by depreciation, and that deferred income taxes be provided.

Because of the departure from generally accepted accounting principles identified above, as of December 31, 2007 and 2006, inventories have been increased $_____ and $_____ by inclusion in manufacturing overhead of depreciation in excess of that based on cost; property, plant, and equipment, less accumulated depreciation, is carried at $_____ and $_____ in excess of an amount based on the cost to the Company; and deferred income taxes of $_____ and $_____ have not been recorded; resulting in an increase of $_____ and $_____ in retained

---

1   C. Chow and S. Rice, "Qualified Audit Opinions and Auditor Switching," *The Accounting Review* (April 1982), pp. 326–335.
2   N. Dopuch, R. Holthausen, and R. Leftwich, "Predicting Audit Qualifications with Financial and Market Variables," *The Accounting Review* (July 1987), pp. 431–454.
3   G. Whittred, "Audit Qualification and the Timeliness of Corporate Annual Reports," *The Accounting Review* (October 1980), pp. 563–577.

earnings and in appraisal surplus of $_____ and $_____, respectively. For the years ended December 31, 2007 and 2006, cost of goods sold has been increased $_____ and $_____, respectively, because of the effects of depreciation accounting and deferred income taxes of $_____ and $_____ have not been provided, resulting in an increase in net income of $_____ and $_____, respectively.

(Opinion Paragraph)

In our opinion, because of the effects of the matter discussed in the preceding paragraphs, the financial statements referred to above do not present fairly . . .

Inconsistency

An unqualified opinion is appropriate if a newly adopted accounting principle is generally accepted *and* management justifies the change, although auditors add an explanatory paragraph to draw attention to the newly adopted principle. For example, Ernst & Young reported in an explanatory paragraph that Whirlpool, like many other companies, had changed its method of accounting for goodwill in 2002 and its method of accounting for derivatives in 2001—changes that were driven, respectively, by the company's adopting *Statement of Financial Accounting Standards No. 142*, "Goodwill and Other Intangible Assets," and *Statement of Financial Accounting Standards No. 133*, "Accounting for Derivative Instruments and Hedging Activities." Ernst & Young mentioned both changes because their opinion relates to 2002 and to 2001. The explanatory paragraph appeared after the opinion paragraph, largely because the matter explained did not drive a qualification and therefore was not prefatory to the opinion paragraph.

Whirlpool Corporation
Ernst & Young

(Explanatory Paragraph)

As discussed in Note 3 to the consolidated financial statements, the Company changed its method of accounting for goodwill and other intangibles. As discussed in Note 1 to the consolidated financial statements, in 2001 the Company changed its method of accounting for derivative instruments and hedging activities.

✳ Explanatory paragraphs are used in practice for other types of inconsistencies. For example, under *SAS No. 88, Part 2*, "Reporting on Consistency," a change in reporting entity that *is not* driven by a transaction—for example, a city that deletes a water district from the city's financial statements solely to obscure a recurring deficit fund balance—would demand an explanatory paragraph. In contrast, a change in reporting entity that *is* driven by a transaction—for example, a business combination—would not require an explanatory paragraph.

However, a qualified or an adverse opinion is required if a *newly adopted accounting principle is not generally accepted*, if the accounting for the effect of the change *departs from GAAP*, or if management has *not sufficiently justified the reason for the change*. The opinion issued—qualified or adverse—depends on the materiality of the effect of the change.

Qualified Opinion

An opinion qualified for inconsistency requires an explanatory paragraph and a modified opinion paragraph, but no change to the introductory or scope paragraphs. For example, the Public Service Company of Indiana, Inc., accounted for revenues and pensions inconsistently. Andersen's modified opinion paragraph follows:

Public Service Company of Indiana, Inc.
Andersen

(Opinion Paragraph)

... present fairly the financial position, results of operations, changes in common stock equity and cash flows ... in conformity with generally accepted accounting principles which, except for the effects of accounting for revenues and for pension costs, as more fully discussed in Note 4 and Note 10, respectively, were applied on a consistent basis.

Interestingly, research has found that stock price behavior does not differ significantly between companies that do and do not receive audit opinions qualified for inconsistency, suggesting that, although required, qualifications for inconsistency may not carry significant information to the capital markets.[4]

Adverse Opinion

Inconsistency may have such a highly material effect on an entity's financial statements that an adverse opinion is required. The adverse opinion requires no reference in the introductory or scope paragraphs, an explanatory paragraph that discloses all substantive reasons for the opinion and the principal effects of the change, and an adverse opinion paragraph.

Continuing the Public Service Company example, assume the inconsistent accounting for revenues and pensions is so material to the financial statements that Andersen issues an adverse opinion. Although the explanatory paragraph (not illustrated) would not change, an adverse opinion paragraph would be presented, as illustrated earlier for departures from GAAP.

Scope Limitation

The scope of a financial statement audit is limited when conditions preclude an auditor from gathering evidence. Limitations may result from client-imposed restrictions, missing documents, inadequate record keeping, or when an auditor is engaged after the balance sheet date. For example, a client may prevent an auditor from mailing receivables confirmations (Chapter 11), arguing that customers misinterpret confirmations as past-due notices. Material scope limitations that prevent an auditor from applying one or more necessary auditing procedures ordinarily result in a qualified opinion or a disclaimer of opinion.

Qualified Opinion

Opinions qualified for scope limitations require no change to the introductory paragraph, a modified scope paragraph, an explanatory paragraph, and a modified opinion paragraph. To illustrate, consider the report Wilson, Haig & Co. issued for Advanced Monitoring Systems Inc., a company that had not provided

---

4 H. F. Mittlestaedt, P. Regier, E. Chewning, and K. Pany, "Do Consistency Modifications Provide Information to Equity Markets?" *Auditing: A Journal of Practice & Theory* (Spring 1992), pp. 83–98.

evidence relating to a material contingent liability. Modified scope and opinion paragraphs, and an explanatory paragraph, follow:

Advanced Monitoring Systems Inc.
Wilson, Haig & Co.

(Scope Paragraph)

Except as discussed in the following paragraph, we conducted our audit . . .

(Explanatory Paragraph)

We were unable to obtain evidential matter supporting the Company's representations regarding the contingent liability as discussed in Note 8 to the consolidated financial statements.

(Opinion Paragraph)

In our opinion, except for the effects of such adjustments, if any, as might have been determined to be necessary had a response from the Company's legal counsel been obtained, the consolidated financial statements referred to above present fairly . . .

Disclaimer of Opinion

A scope limitation may be so highly material as to require a disclaimer of opinion. Disclaimers for scope limitations require a modified introductory paragraph, omission of the standard scope paragraph, an explanatory paragraph explaining why the audit did not comply with GAAP, and a paragraph explaining that the scope of the audit was not sufficient to warrant an opinion. For example, consider Andersen's explanatory and closing paragraphs for Sunshine Jr. Stores, a Florida company that filed for bankruptcy.

Sunshine Jr. Stores
Andersen

(Explanatory Paragraph)

The Company did not give effect to all adjustments to the carrying value of assets and classification of liabilities that might be necessary as a consequence of bankruptcy proceedings.

(Closing Paragraph)

Because of the possible material effect of the matters discussed in the preceding paragraphs, we are unable to express, and we do not express, an opinion on the financial statements referred to above. Our audits were made for the purpose of forming an opinion on the basic financial statements taken as a whole.

Going Concern

The opinion paragraph of a standard audit report acknowledges GAAP, and one of the principles specific to GAAP is that financial statements be prepared assuming an entity is a going concern. But the going concern assumption is sometimes unwarranted for financially distressed companies that are unable to continue meeting obligations without disposing of assets or restructuring debt. As a result, *Statement on Auditing Standards No. 59*, "The Auditor's Consideration of an Entity's Ability to Continue as a Going Concern" (AU Sec. 341), requires that an auditor evaluate on every audit whether there is substantial doubt about an entity's ability to continue as a going concern. The evaluation is made for a reasonable period of time into the future, not to exceed one year beyond the date of the financial statements, and is based on the results of audit procedures performed normally, not on procedures designed to reveal financial distress. For example, inquiry of an entity's lawyer about litigation, claims, and assessments (Chapter 16) may reveal that a client has lost a judgment for substantial uninsured claims that, in the aggregate, raise serious questions about the going concern assumption. Other evidence gathered in the normal course of an audit may raise doubts as well—for example, recurring operating losses, working capital deficiencies, loan defaults, denial of credit from suppliers, work stoppages, loss of key management, and loss of principal customers or suppliers.

When evidence raises substantial doubt about continued existence, the auditor considers management's plans to alleviate the problem and whether the plans can be implemented. For example, if management plans to raise resources by disposing of some assets, the auditor should consider the apparent marketability of the assets, possible effects on operations, and whether there are restrictions on disposing the assets, such as loan covenants or encumbrances. After considering management's plans and other evidence, an auditor may conclude that he or she does not have substantial doubt about the entity's ability to continue as a going concern. In that case, the auditor considers the need to disclose in the financial statements the principal conditions that gave rise to doubt, but would not modify the standard audit report. However, if substantial doubt remains, the auditor considers the recoverability and classification of recorded assets and the amounts and classification of liabilities, and modifies the report by adding an explanatory paragraph after the opinion paragraph. (The opinion paragraph is not modified since an unqualified opinion remains appropriate.) To illustrate, consider PricewaterhouseCoopers' report for Kmart Corporation, which on January 22, 2002, filed a voluntary petition for reorganization under Chapter 11 of the federal bankruptcy laws. PricewaterhouseCoopers' explanatory paragraph follows:

Kmart Corporation
PricewaterhouseCoopers

(Explanatory Paragraph)

The accompanying consolidated financial statements have been prepared assuming that Kmart Corporation will continue as a going concern, which contemplates continuity of Kmart's operations and realization of its assets and payments of its liabilities in the ordinary course of business. As more fully described in the notes to the consolidated financial statements, on January 22, 2002, Kmart Corporation filed a voluntary petition for reorganization under Chapter 11 of the United States Bankruptcy Code. The uncertainties inherent in the bankruptcy process and Kmart's recurring losses from operations raise substantial doubt about Kmart Corporation's ability to continue as a going concern. Kmart Corporation is currently operating its business as a Debtor-in-Possession under the jurisdiction of the Bankruptcy Court, and continuation of Kmart as a going concern is contingent upon, among other things, the confirmation of a Plan of Reorganization, Kmart's ability to comply with all debt covenants under the existing debtor-in-possession financing agreement, and Kmart Corporation's ability to generate sufficient cash from operations and obtain financing sources to meet its future obligations. If no reorganization plan is approved, it is possible that Kmart's assets may be liquidated. The consolidated financial statements do not include any adjustments to

> reflect the possible future effects on the recoverability and classification of assets or the amount and classification of liabilities that may result from the outcome of these uncertainties.

The reorganization that PricewaterhouseCoopers refers to was approved, and Kmart emerged from bankruptcy in 2003.

Although a report modified for substantial doubt is *not* a prediction of bankruptcy, research suggests the modification may reduce some of the surprise in bankruptcy filings. For example, research reveals that modifications may increase investors' expected probability of financial failure,[5] may be useful in predicting bankruptcy (although, as stated above, bankruptcy prediction is not the intent of a modification),[6] and may be somewhat useful in predicting bankruptcy resolution.[7] Further, reports modified for substantial doubt may also be useful in explaining stock market reaction to bankruptcy filings. For example, a study reports that bankrupt companies that had received substantial doubt modifications experienced lower share price declines than bankrupt companies that had not.[8]

The generalizeability of the results of the research cited above to the reports issued today under *SAS No. 59* is not clear, because much of the research studied audit reports issued prior to the effective date of *SAS No. 59*, which altered the language of going concern reports. However, one study examined audit reports issued both before and after *SAS No. 59*, and found that auditors were more likely to issue modified reports *after SAS No. 59* than they were before,[9] suggesting that the Auditing Standards Board had responded to what motivated *SAS No. 59*: the financial community's call for early warnings of impending financial doom.

Lack of Independence

Statement on Auditing Standards No. 26, "Association with Financial Statements" (AU Sec. 504), requires a disclaimer of opinion when an auditor lacks independence, even if the audit has been completed and an opinion formulated. Lacking independence, an auditor's opinion would not be credible to users. The following explanatory paragraph (the report's only paragraph) disclaims an opinion.

> **(Explanatory Paragraph)**
> We are not independent with respect to the Trailways Company, and the accompanying balance sheet . . . , and the related statements of income, retained earnings, and cash flows for the year then ended were not audited by us. Accordingly, we do not express an opinion on them.

Note that the paragraph declares that the auditor is not independent, but does not explain why and does not reveal any auditing procedures that may have been per-

5   J. Campbell and J. Mutchler, "The 'Expectations Gap' and Going-Concern Uncertainties," *Accounting Horizons* (March 1988), pp. 42–49.

6   W. Hopwood, J. McKeown, and J. Mutchler, "A Reexamination of Auditor Versus Model Accuracy Within the Context of the Going-Concern Opinion Decision," *Contemporary Accounting Research* (Spring 1994), pp. 409–432; W. Hopwood, J. McKeown, and J. Mutchler, "A Test of the Incremental Explanatory Power of Opinions," *The Accounting Review* (January 1989), pp. 28–48.

7   D. Kennedy and W. Shaw, "Evaluating Financial Distress Resolution Using Prior Audit Opinions," *Contemporary Accounting Research* (Fall 1991), pp. 97–114.

8   K. Chen and B. Church, "Going Concern Opinions and the Market's Reaction to Bankruptcy Filings," *The Accounting Review* (January 1996), pp. 117–128.

9   K. Raghunandan and D. Rama, "Audit Reports for Companies in Financial Distress: Before and After SAS No. 59," *Auditing: A Journal of Practice & Theory* (Spring 1995), pp. 50–63.

formed. To do either might lead the reader to the false impression that the auditor is expressing limited assurance.

Reporting on Comparative Financial Statements

As illustrated in the Procter & Gamble report (Figure 3-1) and implied throughout this chapter, audit reports normally cover two or more fiscal years. In fact, auditing standards require no less, since the language of the fourth standard of reporting (Figure 2-1)—". . . expression of opinion regarding the financial statements, *taken as a whole*"—applies not only to the financial statements of the current period, but also to those of one or more of the prior periods presented. However, reporting on comparative periods raises the problem of having different opinions in compared years and the corresponding problem of updating a previously issued opinion. Each problem is discussed next.

Report with Differing Opinions

Because circumstances may change from period to period, an auditor could issue different opinions for two different years in a single report. For example, Grant Thornton issued an unqualified opinion for the J.M. Peters Company's 1991 (and 1990) financial statements. However, owing to uncertainties about the company's ability to continue as a going concern and about the ultimate realizations from the sale of real estate projects, Grant Thornton disclaimed an opinion for 1992. Notice three things particularly about the report. First, the scope (second) paragraph refers only to the years 1991 and 1990, for which opinions are expressed, but not to 1992, for which one is not. Second, paragraphs five and six disclose separately both of the reasons for disclaiming in 1992. And third, notice by nothing more than the sheer length of the report that, although unusual in practice, audit reports can be quite complex.

J.M. Peters Company, Inc.
Grant Thornton

We have audited the accompanying consolidated balance sheets of J.M. Peters Company, Inc., and subsidiaries (the "Company") as of February 29, 1992 and February 28, 1991, and the related consolidated statements of operations, stockholders' equity (deficit) and cash flows for the years ended February 29, 1992 and February 28, 1991 and 1990. These financial statements are the responsibility of the Company's management. Our responsibility is to express an opinion on these financial statements based on our audits.

We conducted our audits in accordance with generally accepted auditing standards. Those standards require that we plan and perform the audit to obtain reasonable assurance about whether the financial statements are free of material misstatement. An audit includes examining, on a test basis, evidence supporting the amounts and disclosures in the financial statements. An audit also includes assessing the accounting principles used and significant estimates made by management, as well as evaluating the overall financial statement presentation. We believe that our audits of the 1991 and 1990 consolidated financial statements provide a reasonable basis for our opinion.

In our opinion, the 1991 and 1990 consolidated financial statements referred to above present fairly, in all material respects, the consolidated financial position of the Company as of February 28, 1991 and 1990, and the results of its operations and its cash flows for the years then ended, in conformity with generally accepted accounting principles.

As discussed in Note 14, subsequent to year end the Company entered into a mutual release with its parent regarding $60.7 million in certain tax sharing claims.

The consolidated financial statements have been prepared assuming that the Company will continue as a going concern. As discussed in Note 2, the carrying values of the Company's real estate projects are dependent upon future economic, market and financing conditions which may cause the ultimate realizations to be materially different from amounts presently estimated. The current state of the financial markets, caused in part by the current regulatory environment, coupled with the Company's 1992 and 1991 operating losses, and the insolvency of its parent have adversely affected the liquidity of the Company. Furthermore, the Company is in default under most of its financing agreements at February 29, 1992, all of which raises substantial doubt as to the Company's ability to achieve estimated net realizable values and to continue as a going concern. Management's plans concerning these matters are described in Note 2. The consolidated financial statements do not include any adjustments to reflect the possible future effects on the recoverability of assets and amounts of liabilities that would be necessary should the Company be unable to continue as a going concern.

As discussed in Note 1, the Company carries its real estate projects at the lower of cost or net realizable value assuming completion of development and disposition in accordance with management's current plans and intentions. Net realizable value is substantially greater than fair market value. As further discussed in Note 2, the Company's parent is engaged in active negotiations for the sale of its 85.8% interest in and loans made to the Company. Due to the potential change in the Company's ownership, coupled with the uncertainties discussed in the preceding paragraph, management may change its development and disposition plans of its real estate projects. Therefore, ultimate realizations from the sales of the Company's real estate projects may be substantially less than current carrying amounts.

Because of the potential material uncertainties discussed in the preceding two paragraphs, we are unable to and do not express an opinion on the consolidated financial statements as of February 29, 1992 and for the year then ended.

Report with an Updated Opinion Different from a Previous Opinion

Auditors sometimes become aware of circumstances or events that affect the financial statements reported on in a prior year. For example, resolution in the current year of a matter that caused a qualified opinion in a prior year may result in an updated opinion for the prior year within the current report. In addition to an updated opinion paragraph, the report also includes an explanatory paragraph disclosing the date of the prior report, the type of opinion expressed, the circumstances that caused a different opinion in the prior year, and the fact that the auditor's updated opinion for the prior year is now different. For example, the following, from PricewaterhouseCoopers' report for Sony Corporation, illustrates an explanatory paragraph for a prior-year departure from GAAP, updated in the current year.

Sony Corporation
PricewaterhouseCoopers

(Explanatory Paragraph)

In our report dated May 21, 1992, we expressed a qualified opinion that the company's consolidated financial statements for the years ended March 31, 1991 and 1992 did not disclose segment information concerning operations in different industries, and foreign operations and export sales, which was required by accounting principles generally accepted in the United States. As described in Note 18 to the accompanying consolidated financial statements, the company has disclosed . . . segment information for the years ended March 31, 1991 and 1992 in conformity with accounting principles generally accepted in the United States of America. Accordingly, our opinion on the consolidated financial statements for the years ended March 31, 1991 and 1992, as presented herein is different from that expressed in our previous report.

Reporting on Financial Statements Prepared for Use in Foreign Countries

U.S. corporations ordinarily prepare financial statements in conformity with accounting principles generally accepted in the United States, and auditors therefore audit the statements in accordance with the U.S. auditing standards. However, as a result of foreign investment in U.S. companies, it has become increasingly common for auditors to audit financial statements that are both prepared in conformity with accounting principles generally accepted in another country and intended for use outside the United States. For example, the financial statements of a U.S. domestic corporation may be prepared for inclusion in the consolidated statements of a non-U.S. parent or, in contrast, they may be used to raise capital in another country. *SAS No. 51*, "Reporting on Financial Statements Prepared for Use in Other Countries" (AU Sec. 534), describes an auditor's obligation under U.S. and foreign auditing standards, and prescribes audit reports for use outside and within the United States.

General and Field Work Standards

Even when auditing the financial statements of a U.S. corporation that are prepared in conformity with the accounting principles of another country, an auditor complies with U.S. general and field work standards. However, audit procedures may be modified because the assertions embodied in financial statements prepared to conform with foreign accounting principles may differ significantly from those embodied in statements prepared to conform with U.S. accounting principles. For example, some foreign countries require that certain assets be revalued to adjust for the effects of inflation, and other countries neither require nor permit recognizing deferred taxes and related-party transactions. As a result, when reporting on financial statements prepared for use in other countries, an auditor should be familiar with the accounting principles accepted in the other country and, if necessary, consult with foreign accountants.

Statements Used Outside the United States Only

When reporting on financial statements intended for use outside the United States *only*, the auditor identifies the statements audited, refers to a note that describes the basis of financial statement presentation, states that the audit was made in accordance with U.S. auditing standards, and includes a paragraph expressing an opinion on whether the statements are presented fairly in conformity with the basis described. The following illustrates Deloitte Touche Tohmatsu's report for Kubota Corporation.

Kubota Corporation
Deloitte Touche Tohmatsu

(Introductory Paragraph)

... years in the period ended ... , all expressed in Japanese yen, ... as described in Note 10, have been prepared on the basis of accounting generally accepted in Japan. These financial statements are the responsibility of the Company's management. Our responsibility is to express an opinion on these financial statements based on our audits.

(Scope Paragraph)

We conducted our audits in accordance with auditing standards generally accepted in the United States and Japan. Those standards require that we plan and perform the audit to obtain reasonable assurance about whether the financial statements are free of material misstatement. An audit includes examining, on a test basis, evidence supporting the amounts and disclosures in the financial statements. An audit also includes assessing the accounting principles used and significant estimates made by management, as well as evaluating the overall financial statement presentation. We believe that our audits provide a reasonable basis for our opinion.

(Opinion Paragraph)

In our opinion, the financial statements ... present fairly, in all material respects ... in conformity with accounting principles generally accepted in Japan.

An auditor also may use the standard report format of another country, but only if the format would be used by auditors in the other country in similar circumstances, and the auditor understands—and is in a position to make—the attestations contained in the report.

Statements Used in the United States

If an auditor reports on financial statements prepared in accordance with accounting principles accepted in another country, and those statements will have more than limited distribution in the United States, he or she uses the standard audit report illustrated earlier in this chapter, modified for departures from U.S. accounting principles. In addition, the auditor may include a separate paragraph in the report to express an opinion on whether the financial statements are presented in conformity with accounting principles generally accepted in the other country.

Reports on Attestation Services

An **attestation report** is a letter communicating management's and the attestor's responsibilities, the attestor's opinion and, if written, management's assertion(s). Most attestation engagements result in a three-paragraph report that uses relatively standard language drawn from the *Codification of Statements on Standards for Attestation Engagements.*

Unqualified Opinion

An *unqualified opinion* in an attestation report means it is the independent attestor's opinion that management's assertions are presented fairly in all material respects in conformity with some established criteria. Figure 3-8, adapted from a Big Four firm's attestation report, illustrates a report in an agreed-upon procedures engagement for a private cable television company organized as a limited partnership. The intuition underlying the engagement is that a cable television company's stock purchase agreement entitles three parties—Aspenarger, Hardigan, and Petrie—to purchase shares in a limited partnership at a price derived from the number of equivalent basic subscribers. Aspen Telecommunication's management has engaged a public accounting firm, Cheever & Yates, to attest to management's written assertion about the number of equivalent basic subscribers.

FIGURE 3-8: *An Attestation Report*

Report of the Independent Accountants
To the Partners of
Aspen Telecommunications Company

We have examined the accompanying schedule of number of equivalent subscribers (the Schedule) of Aspen Telecommunications Company, Limited Partnership, as of August 31, 2007, pursuant to Section 1.3(a) of the Stock Purchase Agreement by and among Richard Aspenarger, Charles Hardigan, and Joseph Petrie dated February 12, 2007, and amended by the First Amendment dated August 31, 2007 (the Agreement). Our examination was made in accordance with attestation standards established by the American Institute of Certified Public Accountants and, accordingly, included such procedures as we considered necessary in the circumstances. The Schedule and the assertions on which it is based are the responsibility of Aspen Telecommunications Company management. Our responsibility is to express an opinion on the Schedule based on our examination.

In our opinion, the Schedule presents, in all material respects, the number of equivalent subscribers of Aspen Telecommunications Company as of August 31, 2007 computed in accordance with the measurement criteria set forth in Note 2 to the Schedule.

This report is intended solely for the information and use of the partners of Aspen Communications Company and should not be used for any other purpose.

Cheever & Yates, LLP
September 17, 2007

The *title*, "Report of the Independent Accountants," distinguishes the attestor's report from management's schedule of the number of equivalent subscribers. The *addressee*, the partners of Aspen Telecommunications, is the party that hired Cheever & Yates and to whom the *closing paragraph* limits distribution of the report. The *introductory* (first) *paragraph* identifies the assertion attested to (the number of equivalent basic subscribers), and indicates both that the assertion is management's responsibility and that the attestor is responsible only for an opinion on the assertion, not for the assertion. The *opinion* (second) *paragraph* explicitly conveys an unqualified opinion that the schedule presents, in all material respects, the number of basic equivalent subscribers. The engagement partner signs the firm's name (Cheever & Yates), not his or her own name, and dates the report as of the *last day of field work*, the date that the firm completed work in

Aspen's office. Implicitly, the introductory, opinion, and closing paragraphs in an unqualified opinion convey to the reader that all eleven attestation standards (Chapter 2, Figure 2-1) were followed without exception.

Other Types of Opinion

In an attestation engagement, an unqualified opinion can be issued only if the engagement has complied with the attestation standards and management's assertion complies with established criteria, such as the stock purchase agreement in the Aspen Telecommunications engagement. However, departures from either the attestation standards or the established criteria require that the attestor issue a qualified opinion, an adverse opinion, or disclaim an opinion. As summarized in Figure 3-5 (both for attestation engagements and for audit engagements), a *qualified opinion* means that *except for* the effects of a matter, management's assertions are presented fairly in all material respects. An *adverse opinion*, in contrast, means that management's assertions are *not* presented fairly. A *disclaimer of opinion* means that the attestor or auditor does not express an opinion, usually because there is insufficient evidence. All three types of opinion were illustrated above for audit engagements, but the intuition underlying each is transferable to attestation engagements as well.

Reports on Other Assurance Services

Audit and attestation reports have been guided by standards of reporting since 1949 and 1986 (Chapter 2), respectively. However, assurance services have no generally accepted standards of reporting for at least two reasons. First, the profession does not have a long history of delivering assurance services. But a second reason is more telling: Many assurance services have not traditionally required reports. For example, consider the time-honored assurance services offered by some firms for achievement award balloting, such as the movie industry's Oscars, the New York theater's Tony Awards, and some national book awards. In these and other cases, the assurer (the public accounting firm) is also the asserter and, by tradition, there is no report apart from winners' names inscribed within envelopes. For example, on Oscar night, celebrities open envelopes on stage and announce the winners to an audience that includes the board of the Academy of Motion Pictures Arts and Sciences. In all audit and attestation engagements, the asserter—for example, management—is aware of the assertion long before a public accounting firm issues a report.

In contrast, another assurance provider, Consumers Union (Chapter 1), has been serving and reporting to the public since 1936. Consumers Union's *Buying Guides* and *Consumer Reports* each carry language that captures three concepts introduced in Chapter 2 as important to audit and attestation standards: *independence* from product manufacturers, *due care* in rating the products tested, and *evidence* used to test and rate products. Figure 3-9 contains assurance report excerpts that illustrate these concepts.

Consumers Union establishes *independence* from product manufacturers by accepting no advertising or sample products, and by purchasing all products tested. To achieve *due care*, products are tested at Consumers Union's National Research and Testing Center in Yonkers, New York, under laboratory conditions controlled to assure that procedures are alike for all products tested. There is a reasonable presumption that *evidence* is competent because the products tested are the prod-

FIGURE 3-9: *Excerpts from an Assurance Report*

Report to Readers

Consumers Union derives its income solely from the sale of CONSUMER REPORTS and other publications. In addition, expenses of occasional public service efforts may be met, in part, by nonrestrictive, noncommercial contributions, grants, and fees. Consumers Union accepts no advertising or product samples and is not beholden in any way to any commercial interest. Its Ratings and reports are solely for the use of the readers of its publications. Neither the Ratings, nor the reports, nor any Consumers Union publications, including this book, may be used in advertising or for any commercial purpose. Consumers Union will take all steps open to it to prevent such uses of its material, its name, or the name of CONSUMER REPORTS.

Independence Statements

CONSUMER REPORTS magazine is published monthly by Consumers Union, a nonprofit independent testing organization serving consumers. We are a comprehensive source for unbiased advice about products and services. Since 1936, our mission has been to test products, inform the public, and protect consumers.

We buy all the products we test.

We test products under controlled laboratory conditions.

We survey our millions of readers to bring you information on services and on the reliability of autos and major products.

We report on issues of consumer concern, bringing you information on matters that affect your health, money, and well-being.

We accept no ads from companies. Our income is derived from the sale of CONSUMER REPORTS and other services and from nonrestrictive, noncommercial contributions, grants, and fees. The ads in CONSUMER REPORTS and the BUYING GUIDE are for our other services, which share the same aims. We don't permit use of reports or Ratings for any commercial purpose. If that happens, we take whatever steps are open to us. Reproductions of CONSUMER REPORTS is forbidden without prior written permission (and never for commercial purposes).

ucts bought and because the measurement rules (rating scales) are not influenced by product manufacturers. Consumers Union does not operate under the general, field work, and reporting standards prescribed by an authoritative body in quite the same way that certified public accountants operate under standards prescribed by the Public Company Accounting Oversight Board and the AICPA's Auditing Standards Board and Accounting and Review Services Committee. However, the concepts of independence, due care, and evidence are evident in the work of Consumers Union, and ought to be in the assurance services of public accounting firms as well.

SUMMARY

Owing to a rich history in audit and attestation engagements, the profession uses common reports for both types of engagements, and the reports include several common components: a title that includes the word *independent*; an addressee; a signature in the firm's name; a date; and a series of paragraphs that explain what was audited or attested to, management's and the auditor's or the attestor's responsibility, the standards the auditor or attestor complied with, and an opinion. Audit and attestation reports express any one of four types of opinions: unqualified (the assertion that financial statements are *presented fairly*), qualified (presented fairly *except for*), adverse (are *not* presented fairly), or disclaimer ("We *do not express an opinion . . .*"). The type of opinion expressed depends on the circumstances and on materiality. Although the profession has not developed standards for assurance engagements, the concepts that underlie auditing and attestation standards—independence, due care, evidence, and reporting—are generally applicable to assurance engagements (although reporting sometimes is not: for example, achievement award balloting) and offer some insights into the role of assurance reports. For example, three of the concepts are apparent in reports issued by Consumers Union.

KEY TERMS

Adverse opinion 84
Attestation report 98
Audit report 76
Disclaimer of opinion 85
Introductory paragraph 79
Opinion paragraph 81

Principal auditor 87
Qualified opinion 83
Scope paragraph 80
Standard audit report 76
Unqualified opinion 77

REFERENCES

Professional Standards:

Auditing Standard No. 1, "References in Auditors' Reports to the Standards of the PCAOB," (PCAOB Release No. 2003-025).

AICPA, *Codification of Auditing Standards*. New York: AICPA (AU Sec. 341, 410, 411, 420, 431, 504, 508, 530, 543, 544).

SAS No. 26, "Association with Financial Statements" (AU Sec. 504).

SAS No. 58, "Reports on Audited Financial Statements" (AU Sec. 508).

SAS No. 59, "The Auditor's Consideration of an Entity's Ability to Continue as a Going Concern" (AU Sec. 341).

SAS No. 79, "Reporting on Uncertainties" (AU Sec 508).

SAS No. 88, "Service Organizations and Reporting on Consistency."

SAS No. 93, "Omnibus SAS–2000."

SAS No. 98, "Omnibus SAS–2002."

Codification of Statements on Standards for Attestation Engagements. New York: AICPA.

Professional Report:

Public Oversight Board, *Panel on Audit Effectiveness: Report and Recommendations*. Stamford, CT: POB, 2000.

Articles:

Chen, K. C. W., and B. K. Church, "Going Concern Opinions and the Market's Reaction to Bankruptcy Filings," *The Accounting Review* (January 1996), pp. 117–128.

Geiger, M. A., "SAS No. 58: Did the ASB Really Listen?" *Journal of Accountancy* (December 1988), pp. 55–57.

Miller, J. R., S. A. Reed, and R. H. Strawser, "Bank Loan Officers' Perceptions of the New Audit Report," *Accounting Horizons* (March 1993), pp. 39–52.

Raghunandan, K., and D. V. Rama, "Audit Reports for Companies in Financial Distress: Before and After SAS No. 59," *Auditing: A Journal of Practice & Theory* (Fall 1995), pp. 50–63.

QUESTIONS

1. Explain the significance of the audit report date.
2. What is meant by dual dating an audit report?
3. On what should an auditor base his or her opinion about compliance with GAAP?
4. Under what conditions is a qualified audit opinion issued ordinarily?
5. Under what conditions is an adverse audit opinion issued ordinarily?
6. How does a standard audit report differ from a report that, owing to a scope limitation, disclaims an opinion?
7. Departures from GAAP may result in either a qualified or an adverse opinion, depending on materiality. How does an auditor judge materiality?
8. What type of opinions might an auditor issue if a newly adopted accounting principle is not generally accepted? Why?
9. What is a *Sarbanes-Oxley* Section 302 certification?
10. What is included in the introductory paragraph of a standard audit report?
11. What is included in the scope paragraph of a standard audit report?
12. What is included in the opinion paragraph of a standard audit report?
13. On what basis do auditors judge the identity of the principle auditor?
14. Over what period into the future does an auditor decide the ability of an entity to continue as a going concern?
15. How does an auditor proceed when evidence suggests an entity may not continue in existence as a going concern?
16. What would an auditor include in a current year report if he or she resolved in the current year a matter that caused a qualified opinion in the prior year?
17. Why would a U.S. auditor be engaged to report on financial statements for use in another country?
18. What is an attestation report?
19. What message does an attestation report convey to readers?
20. What does the language in Consumers Union's *Buying Guides* and *Consumer Reports* have in common with reports issued by public accounting firms?

MULTIPLE CHOICE QUESTIONS

1. In most all financial statement audits, independent auditors deliver a (an):
   a. Unqualified opinion.
   b. Qualified opinion.
   c. Adverse opinion.
   d. Standard audit report.

2. In all financial statements produced to the SEC, the chief executive and chief financial officers are required to certify in writing that they:
   a. Approved appointment of the independent auditor.
   b. Reported to the audit committee any material fraud.
   c. Evaluated disclosure controls and procedures.
   d. Approved the company's policy on ethics.

3. An independent auditor's report on the financial statements of a public company would likely include a statement that the:

   a. Auditor was appointed by the audit committee of the board of directors.
   b. Audit was conducted in accordance with the standards of the Public Company Accounting Oversight Board.
   c. Auditor did or did not detect fraud.
   d. Audit was conducted in accordance with generally accepted auditing standards.

4. Which of the following circumstances would most likely require a disclaimer of opinion?

   a. Management has denied the auditor access to evidence bearing on trade accounts receivable.
   b. Management's accounting for revenue recognition violates SEC *Staff Accounting Bulletin No. 104*, "Revenue Recognition."
   c. The auditor detected an employee scheme that diverted funds to an off-shore company.
   d. The auditor disagrees with a change management implemented for long-term construction contract accounting.

5. A report issued by a public accounting firm uses the language, "*In our opinion, the schedule presents, in all material respects . . .*" The firm's report is likely:

   a. A standard audit report.
   b. A qualified audit report.
   c. An attestation report.
   d. A qualified attestation report.

6. Does an auditor make the following representations explicitly or implicitly in an unqualified audit report?

	Consistent Application of Accounting Principles	Examined Evidence on a Test Basis
a.	Implicitly	Explicitly
b.	Implicitly	Implicitly
c.	Explicitly	Explicitly
d.	Explicitly	Implicitly

   (AICPA Adapted)

7. Does an accountant make the following representations explicitly or implicitly in an unqualified attestation report?

	Assertion is Capable of Evaluation Against Reasonable Criteria	Assertions are Management's Responsibility
a.	Explicitly	Explicitly
b.	Implicitly	Implicitly
c.	Implicitly	Explicitly
d.	Explicitly	Implicitly

8. Which of the following is likely a scope limitation?

   a. The auditor is reporting on the balance sheet only.
   b. A subsidiary's financial statements are audited by another auditor.
   c. Sufficient evidence is not available.
   d. The auditor is engaged after the balance sheet date.

9. A departure from GAAP is disclosed in a note to the financial statements. The auditor should:

   a. Issue an unqualified opinion, but emphasize the matter in an explanatory paragraph.
   b. Issue an unqualified opinion with no explanatory paragraph, because the departure from GAAP is disclosed.
   c. Issue a qualified opinion.
   d. Disclaim an opinion.

10. The opinion paragraph to a qualified opinion could include the expression:

    a. "With the exception . . ."
    b. "When read in conjunction to note 10 to the financial statements . . ."
    c. "With the foregoing explanation . . ."
    d. "Subject to the departure from generally accepted accounting principles . . ."

11. Management's financial statements disclose uncertainties about future events that are not susceptible to reasonable estimation. The auditor should issue:

    a. An unqualified opinion.
    b. A qualified opinion.
    c. An adverse opinion.
    d. A disclaimer of opinion.

12. A manufacturer has violated FASB *EITF 01-09*, "Accounting for Consideration Given by a Vendor to a Customer." The independent auditor will decide between issuing:

    a. An unqualified opinion or a qualified opinion.
    b. A qualified opinion or an adverse opinion.
    c. An adverse opinion or a disclaimer of opinion.
    d. A qualified opinion or a disclaimer of opinion.

13. In an adverse opinion issued because a client violated GAAP, the auditor's opinion paragraph would refer to:

    a. An explanatory paragraph.
    b. The accounting principle the client violated.
    c. The scope paragraph.
    d. An inconsistency in the application of accounting principles.

14. An audit report is typically dated as of:

    a. The date of the assertion or financial statements.
    b. The date the report is delivered.
    c. The last date on which a subsequent event occurs.
    d. The last day of field work.

15. An explanatory paragraph reads as follows:

    The Company has adopted the first-in, first-out method of determining inventory costs, whereas it previously used the last-in, first-out method. Although use of the first-in, first-out method is in conformity with generally accepted accounting principles, in our opinion the Company has not provided reasonable justification for seeking a change as required by Opinion No. 20 of the Accounting Principles Board.

    The paragraph likely appears in:

    a. An unqualified opinion.
    b. An unqualified opinion that emphasized the matter.
    c. A qualified opinion.
    d. A disclaimer of opinion.

16. An explanatory paragraph reads as follows:

    On October 15, 2007, the Company emerged from bankruptcy. As discussed in the notes to the financial statements, the Company accounted for the reorganization using "fresh start accounting" and, as a result, the post-reorganization financial statements are not comparable to the pre-reorganization financial statements.

    The paragraph likely is intended to:

    a. Qualify an opinion.
    b. Emphasize a matter.
    c. Report an inconsistency.
    d. Indicate a departure from generally accepted accounting principles.

17. A note to a public company's audited financial statements reads as follows:

    As of January 1, the Company adopted Statement of Financial Accounting Standards No. 142, "Goodwill and Other Intangible Assets." As a result of adopting SFAS No. 142, goodwill is no longer amortized, and intangible assets are to be tested at least annually for impairment. Goodwill amortization of $50 million is included in depreciation and amortization.

    The auditor's report will likely include:

    a. An unqualified opinion.
    b. An unqualified opinion and an explanatory paragraph.
    c. A qualified opinion.
    d. An explanatory paragraph, depending on materiality.

18. An introductory paragraph reads in part as follows:

    We have audited the accompanying balance sheet of Hastings Company and subsidiaries as of December 31, 2007, and the related consolidated statements of operations, shareholders' equity, and cash flows for the year then ended. . . . The accompanying 2006 and 2005 consolidated financial statements were audited by other auditors who have ceased operations. Those auditors expressed an unqualified opinion on those consolidated financial statements. . . .

    For the year ended December 31, 2007, the auditor's report likely expresses:

    a. An unqualified opinion.
    b. A unqualified opinion that emphasizes the matter.
    c. A qualified opinion.
    d. No opinion on the 2006 financial statements.

19. The last day of audit field work is January 21, 2007, for the audit of ExPro Inc., which will include the following footnote in December 31, 2006, financial statements:

    Note 9

    On November 20, 2004, the United States Bankruptcy Court for the Northern District of Illinois issued an Order that approved the claims of Boylston LLC against the Company. The First National Bank, as agent for the lenders under Boylston's $800 million Senior Secured Credit Agreement, filed four lawsuits against ExPro. On March 4, 2007, the Company reached a settlement agreement with First National, pursuant to which all four of the cases, including ExPro's counterclaim, were dismissed without prejudice. ExPro released to First National its claim to the $370 million that was previously paid into an escrow account in April 2006.

    Which of the following is the most appropriate date for the auditor's report?

    a. January 21, 2007.
    b. January 21, 2007, except for Note 9, March 4, 2007.
    c. March 4, 2007.
    d. December 31, 2006.

20. Resolution in 2007 of a material departure from GAAP that drove a qualified opinion in 2006 would likely cause an independent auditor in 2007 to:
    a. Reissue the 2006 audit report with an unqualified opinion.
    b. Include in the 2007 audit report an unqualified opinion on 2006 and an explanatory paragraph.
    c. Include in the 2007 audit report an unqualified opinion for 2006 but not an explanatory paragraph.
    d. Include in the 2007 audit report a qualified opinion for 2006.

PROBLEMS AND DISCUSSION CASES

3-1 *Interpreting an Audit Report*

Below is Deloitte & Touche's January 30, 2003, audit report for The Dow Chemical Company:

To the Stockholders and Board of Directors
of The Dow Chemical Company:

We have audited the accompanying consolidated balance sheets of The Dow Chemical Company and its subsidiaries as of December 31, 2002 and 2001, and the related consolidated statements of income, stockholders' equity, comprehensive income and cash flows for each of the three years in the period ended December 31, 2002. These financial statements are the responsibility of the Company's management. Our responsibility is to express an opinion on the financial statements based on our audits. The consolidated financial statements give retroactive effect to the merger of The Dow Chemical Company and Union Carbide Corporation, which has been accounted for as a pooling of interests as described in Note C to the consolidated financial statements. We did not audit the statements of income, stockholders' equity and cash flows of Union Carbide Corporation for the period ended December 31, 2000, which consolidated statements reflect total revenues of $6,550 million. Those consolidated statements were audited by other auditors whose report has been furnished to us, and our opinion, insofar as it relates to the amounts included for Union Carbide Corporation for 2000, is based solely on the report of such other auditors.

We conducted our audits in accordance with auditing standards generally accepted in the United States of America. Those standards require that we plan and perform the audit to obtain reasonable assurance about whether the financial statements are free of material misstatement. An audit includes examining, on a test basis, evidence supporting the amounts and disclosures in the financial statements. An audit also includes assessing the accounting principles used and significant estimates made by management, as well as evaluating the overall financial statement presentation. We believe that our audits and the report of the other auditors provide a reasonable basis for our opinion.

In our opinion, based on our audits and the report of the other auditors, the consolidated financial statements referred to above present fairly, in all material respects, the financial position of The Dow Chemical Company and its subsidiaries at December 31, 2002 and 2001, and the results of their operations and their cash flows for each of the three years in the period ended December 31, 2002, in conformity with accounting principles generally accepted in the United States of America.

As discussed in Notes A and H to the consolidated financial statements, effective January 1, 2001, The Dow Chemical Company changed its method of accounting for derivative instruments and hedging activities to conform to Statement of Financial Accounting Standards No. 133.

As discussed in Notes A and F to the consolidated financial statements, effective January 1, 2002, The Dow Chemical Company changed its method of accounting for goodwill to conform to Statements of Financial Accounting Standards Nos. 141 and 142.

Deloitte & Touche LLP
Midland, Michigan

January 30, 2003

Required:
1. What type of opinion did Deloitte & Touche issue?
2. Using Figure 3-6 as a guide, explain how the report departs from the wording of a standard report.

✳ (3-2) *Identifying Audit Opinions and Circumstances for Departure*

The following are excerpted sentences and phrases from audit reports issued by independent public accounting firms.

a.
(Scope Paragraph)
Except as described in the following paragraph . . .

(Explanatory Paragraph)
Because of insufficient records we were not able to examine sufficient evidence in support of dividend income received from a short-term investment and we were unable to satisfy ourselves as to the dividend income by means of other procedures.

(Opinion Paragraph)
In our opinion, except for the effect of the matter described in the preceding paragraph, the financial statements referred to above present fairly . . .

b.
(Explanatory Paragraph)
The accompanying financial statements have been prepared assuming that the Company will continue as a going concern. As discussed in Note 11 to the financial statements, under existing circumstances there is substantial doubt as to the ability of the company to continue as a going concern.

c.
(Explanatory Paragraph)
As explained in Note 12 to the financial statements, certain adjustments have been made to the financial statements to conform to generally accepted accounting principles. These adjustments have not been recorded in the books.

d.
(Explanatory Paragraph)
As disclosed in Note 8 to the financial statements, the company has adopted the first-in, first-out method of determining inventory costs, whereas it previously used the last-in, first-out method. Although use of the first-in, first-out method is in conformity with generally accepted accounting principles, in our opinion the company has not provided reasonable justification for seeking a change as required by Opinion 20 of the Accounting Principles Board.

(Opinion Paragraph)
In our opinion, except for the change in accounting principles discussed in the preceding paragraph, the financial statements referred to above present fairly . . .

Required: For each report, identify the type of opinion (for example, "qualified") and the circumstance for departing from the standard wording of an unqualified opinion (for example, "departure from GAAP").

(3-3) *Modifications to an Audit Report*

Christine Burke has completed field work for the Willingham Corporation engagement, a December 31, 2008, year-end audit, and is now deciding whether to modify her report. Following are two unrelated situations that arose during the engagement.

- In September 2008, a lawsuit was filed against Willingham requesting that the court order Willingham to install pollution control equipment at an aged production plant. Willingham's attorney has informed Burke that the outcome of the litigation cannot be predicted, and management has informed Burke that pollution control equipment is far too costly and that the plant will close if the litigation is lost. In addition, management told Burke that the production plant and equipment had only minimal resale values, and that lost production could not be recovered at other plants.

- During 2008, Willingham paid 20 percent of its assets to purchase a franchise granting the exclusive right to produce and sell a newly patented product in the New England states, although there has been no appreciable production or sales of the product anywhere in the United States to date. Neither the franchiser nor any U.S. franchisee has conducted market research about the product.

Required: For each of the two situations, discuss the issues Burke should consider (not the type of report Burke should issue). Consider each situation separately, thoroughly, and under the assumption that each is disclosed in notes to the financial statements.

(AICPA Adapted)

3-4 *Audit Report Deficiencies*

Timothy Ross completed field work on September 23, 2008, and issued the following report to the directors of The Rancho Corporation:

To the Directors of The Rancho Corporation:

We have audited the balance sheet of The Rancho Corporation as of July 31, 2008 and the related statements of income and retained earnings. In accordance with your instructions, a complete audit was conducted.

We conducted our audit in accordance with generally accepted auditing standards. An audit includes examining, on a test basis, evidence supporting the amounts and disclosures in the financial statements. We believe that our audit was appropriate in the circumstances.

In many respects, this was an unusual year for The Rancho Corporation. The weakening of the economy in the early part of the year and the strike of plant employees in the summer of 2008 led to a decline in sales and net income. After making several tests of sales records, nothing came to our attention that would indicate that sales have not been properly recorded.

In our opinion, with the explanation given above and the exception of some minor errors that are considered immaterial, the aforementioned financial statements present fairly, in all material respects, the financial position of The Rancho Corporation at July 31, 2008, and the results of its operations for the year then ended, in conformity with pronouncements of the Financial Accounting Standards Board.

Timothy Ross, CPA
September 23, 2008

Required: List and explain deficiencies and omissions in Ross's report. Do not discuss the type of opinion (unqualified, qualified, adverse, or disclaimer). Organize your answer by paragraph (introductory, scope, explanatory, and opinion).

(AICPA Adapted)

3-5 *Audit Report Deficiencies*

The following proposed audit report was drafted by an associate at the completion of an engagement and submitted to the engagement partner for review. The partner reviewed the associate's audit documentation thoroughly, and concluded that a scope limitation relating to inventory was sufficiently material to warrant a qualified opinion.

To Carl Corporation Controller:

We have audited the accompanying financial statements of Carl Corporation as of December 31, 2008. These financial statements are the responsibility of the Company's management. Our responsibility is to express an opinion on these financial statements based on our audit.

We conducted our audit in accordance with generally accepted auditing standards. Those standards require that we plan and perform the audit to obtain reasonable assurance about whether the financial statements are free of material misstatement. An audit includes examining, on a test basis, evidence supporting the amounts and disclosures in the financial statements. An audit also includes assessing the accounting principles used and significant estimates made by management, as well as evaluating the overall financial statement presentation. We believe that our audit provides a reasonable basis for our opinion.

On January 15, 2008, the company issued debentures in the amount of $1,000,000 for the purpose of financing plant expansion. As indicated in Note 6 to the financial statements, the debenture agreement restricts the payment of future cash dividends to earnings after December 31, 2007.

The company's unconsolidated foreign subsidiary did not close down production during the year audited for physical inventory purposes and took no physical inventory during the year. We made extensive tests of book inventory figures for accuracy of calculation and reasonableness of pricing. We did not make physical tests of inventory quantities. Because of this, we are unable to express an unqualified opinion on the financial statements taken as a whole. However, except for the scope limitation regarding inventory, in our opinion the accompanying balance sheet presents the financial position of Carl Corporation at December 31, 2008, subject to the effect of the inventory on the carrying value of the investment. The accompanying statements of income and of retained earnings present the incomes and expenses and the results of transactions affecting retained earnings in accordance with generally accepted accounting principles.

December 31, 2008
Pate & Co., LLP

> **Required:** Identify the deficiencies in the accountant's proposed report.
> (AICPA Adapted)

3-6 *Audit Report Deficiencies*

The following audit report was drafted by an associate and submitted to the engagement partner in the accounting firm of Better & Best, LLP.

To the Audit Committee of American Widgets, Inc.:

We have audited the consolidated balance sheets of American Widgets, Inc., and subsidiaries as of December 31, 2008 and 2007, and the related consolidated statements of income, retained earnings, and cash flows for the years then ended. These financial statements are the responsibility of the Company's management. Our responsibility is to express an opinion on these financial statements based on our audit. Other auditors examined the financial statements of certain subsidiaries and have furnished us with reports thereon containing no exceptions. Our opinion expressed herein, insofar as it relates to the amounts included for those subsidiaries, is based solely upon the reports of the other auditors.

As discussed in Note 4 to the financial statements, on January 8, 2006, the company halted the production of certain medical equipment as a result of inquiries by the Food and Drug Administration, which raised questions as to the adequacy of some of the Company's sterilization equipment and related procedures. Management is not in a position to evaluate the effect of this production halt and the ensuing litigation, which may have an adverse effect on the financial position of American Widgets, Inc.

As fully discussed in Note 7 to the financial statements, in 2008 the Company extended the use of the last-in, first-out (LIFO) method of accounting to include all inventories. In examining inventories, we engaged Dr. Irwin Same (Nobel Prize winner, 1997) to test check the technical requirements and specifications of certain items of equipment manufactured by the Company.

In our opinion, except for the effects, if any, on the financial statements of the ultimate resolution of the matter discussed in the second preceding paragraph, the financial statements referred to above present fairly, in all material respects, the financial position of American Widgets, Inc., as of December 31, 2008, and the results of operations and its cash flows for the year then ended in conformity with generally accepted accounting principles.

To be signed by

Better & Best, LLP

March 1, 2006, except for Note 4 as to which the date is January 8, 2006

> **Required:** Identify the deficiencies in the accountant's proposed report.
>
> (AICPA Adapted)

3-7 *Drafting an Audit Report*

On January 15, 2008, Marc David, CPA, was engaged to audit Kristin Manufacturing Company's December 31, 2007, financial statements. Kristin had taken a physical inventory on December 31, 2007; the carrying value of the final priced inventory was $275,400 ($263,000 in 2006), which represented approximately 10 percent of total assets. David was unable to satisfy himself as to inventory quantities through other auditing procedures because of the condition of Kristin's inventory records.

> **Required:** Draft an audit report assuming no other circumstances require departure from a standard audit report.

3-8 *Drafting an Opinion Paragraph*

Sturdy Corporation owns and operates a large office building in a desirable section of New York City's financial district. For many years the management of Sturdy Corporation has (a) written-up building accounts to appraisal values and (b) accounted for depreciation expense on the basis of appraised values. Wyley, the successor auditor, was engaged to audit Sturdy's financial statements for the year ended December 31, 2008. After completing the audit, Wyley concluded that, consistent with prior years, an adverse opinion would have to be issued because of the materiality of the apparent departure from historical cost.

> **Required:**
> 1. Describe in detail what Wyley should include in an explanatory paragraph.
> 2. Draft the opinion paragraph.
>
> (AICPA Adapted)

3-9 *Drafting an Audit Report*

On March 17, 2008, Ross, Sandler & Co., LLP, completed an audit of The Fairfax Corporation's December 31, 2007, financial statements. The firm issued an unqualified opinion. Because of a scope limitation arising from the inability to observe the January 1, 2006, physical inventory, the predecessor auditors, Smith, Ellis & Co., issued a report that contained an unqualified opinion on the December 31, 2006, balance sheet and a qualified opinion on the statements of income, retained earnings, and cash flows for the year then ended. The management of The Fairfax Corporation will present comparative (2007 and 2006) financial statements in their annual report.

> **Required:** Prepare an audit report assuming the March 1, 2007, report of Smith, Ellis & Co. is not presented.
>
> (AICPA Adapted)

3-10 *Drafting an Audit Report*

On March 15, 2008, you completed the audit of Excelsior Corporation's December 31, 2007, financial statements, the second year you've supervised the engagement. The following information came to your attention during the engagement.

a. Excelsior is presenting comparative financial statements.

b. Excelsior does not wish to present a statement of cash flows for either year.

c. During 2007, Excelsior changed its method of accounting for long-term construction contracts, reported the effect of the change in the current year's financial statements, and restated the prior year's statements. You are satisfied with Excelsior's justification for making the change, which is disclosed in Note 12.

d. Although unable to confirm accounts receivable, you used alternate procedures to satisfy yourself that receivables are presented fairly.

e. Excelsior Corporation is the defendant in a litigation, the outcome of which is highly uncertain. If the case is settled in favor of the plaintiff, Excelsior will be required to pay a substantial amount of cash, which might require the sale of some plant assets. The litigation and the possible effects are disclosed in Note 11.

f. Excelsior issued debentures on January 31, 2007, in the amount of $10,000,000. The funds obtained from the issuance were used to finance the expansion of plant facilities. The debenture agreement restricts the payment of future cash dividends to earnings after December 31, 2010. Excelsior declined to disclose this data in the notes to the financial statements.

Required: Draft an audit report.   (AICPA Adapted)

3-11 *The Repercussions of Substantial Doubt*

An article entitled, "American Gaming Says Its Chairman Resigns; Audit Raises Questions" reported that the board chairman of a public company had resigned, and that the company faced financial difficulties. On the matter of financial difficulties, the article stated, in part, ". . . the company said an independent audit by Deloitte & Touche found that American Gaming's problems—including recurring losses, negative working capital, defaults under debt agreements and uncertainty relating to the liquidation of subsidiaries—'raise substantial doubt about the ability of the company to continue as a going concern.'" The article made no link between the chairman's resignation and the auditor's opinion, but did appropriately link American Gaming's financial position to the opinion.

At a meeting between Christine Schutt, an engagement partner assigned to audit a middle-market building materials company, and the company's chief executive officer (CEO), Schutt reveals that she has substantial doubt about the company's ability to continue as a going concern and that she may have to add an explanatory paragraph to the audit report. The CEO says, "I understand your dilemma. You've explained that to me. But what you don't understand is that no supplier will give me credit, even for a week, if you claim you have substantial doubt. What's more, a statement like 'substantial doubt' won't work. If you'll say in your report that you have doubt, I'll buy that, and my creditors may too. But, if you insist on substantial doubt, I'll find another auditor."

Required:

1. Do you think Schutt can overlook the word substantial? Discuss.
2. What is the dilemma the CEO explained to Schutt? Discuss.

3-12 *Other Information in Annual Reports*

The annual reports for public companies typically include information that is not part of management's financial statements and, therefore, that is not captured in a financial statement audit. Examples include the chief executive officer's letter to shareholders, nonfinancial information about product lines, and summaries of significant financial results over a five- or ten-year period. Under *Statement on Auditing Standards No. 8*, "Other Information in Documents Containing Audited Financial Statements" (AU Sec. 550), an auditor is not obligated to corroborate, but should read, the other information to determine whether the information (or the way the information is presented) is inconsistent with the financial statements. For example, if the income statement reports earnings per share (EPS) of $5.25, the CEO's letter should not report a higher EPS. The auditor should revise the audit report, withhold the report, or withdraw from the engagement if the client refuses to revise an inconsistency.

Required: Explain the role of *SAS No. 8*, given that an audit reports on management's financial statement assertions and that *SAS No. 8* addresses information outside of the financial statements.

3-13 *Opinion Based Partly on the Report of Another Auditor*

Lando Corporation controls two wholly owned domestic subsidiaries. Michaels, CPA, the principal auditor, has been engaged to audit the financial statements of Lando and one of the subsidiaries. Thomas, CPA, the other auditor, has audited the financial statements of the other subsidiary, an entity whose operations are material to the consolidated financial statements.

Michaels' audit work is sufficient to justify Michaels serving as the principal auditor. Michaels has not yet decided to make reference to Thomas, the other auditor.

Required: What are the reporting requirements if Michaels decides to name Thomas and make reference to the audit work Thomas did? (AICPA Adapted)

3-14 *Financial Statement Deficiencies and Omissions*

The Maumee Corporation's August 31, 2008, financial statements are presented below.

Required: List deficiencies and omissions in the statements and discuss the probable effect of each deficiency or omission individually on the auditor's report. Assume that The Maumee Corporation is unwilling either to change the financial statements or to make additional disclosures. (AICPA Adapted)

The Maumee Corporation
Balance Sheet
August 31, 2008
(in Thousands of Dollars)

Assets		
Cash		$ 103
Marketable securities,		
at cost that approximates market value		54
Trade accounts receivable (net of $65,000		
allowance for doubtful accounts)		917
Inventories, at cost		775
Property, plant, and equipment	$3,200	
Less accumulated depreciation	1,475	1,725
Prepayments and other assets		125
Total assets		$3,699
Liabilities and Stockholders' Equity		
Accounts payable	$ 221	
Accrued taxes	62	
Bank loans and long-term debt	1,580	
Total liabilities		$1,863
Capital stock, $10 par value (authorized 50,000		
shares, issued and outstanding 42,400 shares)	$ 424	
Paid-in capital in excess of par value	366	
Retained earnings	1,046	
Total stockholders' equity		1,836
Total liabilities and stockholders' equity		$3,699

The Maumee Corporation
Statement of Income and Retained Earnings
For the Year Ended August 31, 2008
(in Thousands of Dollars)

Product sales (net of $850,000 sales returns and allowances)		$10,700
Cost of goods sold		8,700
Gross profit on sales		$ 2,000
Operating expenses:		
Selling expenses	$1,500	
General and administrative expense	940	2,440
Operating loss		$ (440)
Interest expense		150
Net loss		$ (590)
Retained earnings, September 1, 2007		1,700
		$ 1,110
Dividends:		
Cash—$1 per share	$ 40	
Stock—6% of shares outstanding	24	64
Retained earnings, August 31, 2008		$ 1,046

3-15 The Intuition Underlying an Attestation Report

On January 27, 2008, Sandeen & Walsh LLP issued the following attestation report:

Independent Accountant's Report

As required by Article VI, Section 7(a)(4) of the Supplemental Unemployment Benefit Plan (the Plan) between North American Motors Corp. (the Company) and International Union, United Automobile, Aerospace and Agricultural Implement Workers of America and its affiliated Local Unions as designated (collectively, the Union), we have examined the following special purpose statements:

1. The amounts of maximum funding of the fund and credit unit cancellation base for the months of January to December 2007, inclusive,
2. The amounts by which the Company contribution to the Union was reduced for benefits paid and amounts of net Company contributions for the months of January to December 2007,
3. The number of hours for which employees received pay and the number of such hours with respect to which the Company shall not have made contributions to the fund and the amount of Company contributions at the applicable rate for each hour for the months of January to December 2007, inclusive, and
4. The number and amount of Automatic Short-Week Benefits paid to employees and the amount of such benefits used to reduce contributions for the months of January to December 2007, inclusive.

These special purpose statements are the responsibility of the Company's management. Our responsibility is to express an opinion on these statements based on our examination.

The accompanying statements have been prepared for the purpose of complying with the provisions of Article VI, Sections 7(a)(1) and (a)(2) of the Plan.

In our opinion, the above-mentioned statements present fairly, in all material respects, the information stated therein for the months of January to December 2007, inclusive, in accordance with the provisions of Article VI, Sections 7(a)(1) and (a)(2) of the Plan.

This report is intended solely for the information and use of the Board of Directors of the Company and the Union, and should not be used for any other purpose.

Required: Discuss the economic motive—the intuition—underlying the report.

3-16 *The Economic Motive and Apparent Risk in an Attestation Engagement*

The following is an independent accountant's attestation report.

Independent Accountant's Report

Crownhill Super Computers, Inc.
4500 Columbus Way
Springfield, IL 62703

We have examined the accompanying schedule computing the average post-purchase end-user support time supplied by Crownhill Super Computers, Inc., (the Schedule) to major purchasers for the period November 1, 2007 to October 31, 2008. Our examination was made in accordance with attestation standards established by the American Institute of Certified Public Accountants and, accordingly, included such procedures as we considered necessary in the circumstances. Our responsibility is to express an opinion on the Schedule.

In our opinion, the Schedule presents, in all material respects, the average post-purchase end-user support time supplied by Crownhill Super Computers, Inc., to major purchasers for the period November 1, 2007 to October 31, 2008.

This report is intended solely for the information and use of the management of Crownhill Super Computers, Inc., and should not be used for any other purpose.

Hemphill & Noyes, LLP

> **Required:**
> 1. Discuss the intuition—the economic motive—underlying the engagement.
> 2. What risks do you see accruing to Hemphill & Noyes from the wording of the report?

Internet problems and discussion cases are available at http://ricchiute.swlearning.com

RESEARCH PROJECTS

1. Why Wouldn't a Client Correct the Circumstance That Gave Rise to a Qualified Opinion?

In the overwhelming majority of cases, independent auditors issue unqualified, rather than qualified, opinions for their publicly traded clients since it is unusual (though not rare):

- For a client's financial statements to depart materially from GAAP,
- For a client to fail to justify an accounting change, or
- For a client to impose scope limitations on the auditor.

These are the three circumstances in Figure 3-7 for which an auditor would issue a qualified opinion.

Before issuing a qualified opinion, an auditor will first alert the client of an impending qualification, largely because in each of the three circumstances listed the issue that gives rise to a qualification is not only correctable by the client but if corrected would result in an unqualified opinion. For example, to avoid a qualified opinion, the client in most cases could simply comply with GAAP, avoid the unjustified accounting change, or lift the limitation on the scope of the engagement.

Required: Using LEXIS-NEXIS, the SEC's EDGAR file (http://www.sec.gov), the AICPA's *Accounting Trends and Techniques*, or copies of annual reports in a library, search for an example of one of the three circumstances requiring a qualified opinion. Draft a report that:

1. Explains the issue that gave rise to the circumstance (use both the explanatory paragraph and the footnote, if any, in the annual report),
2. Compares the language used in the independent auditor's report to the language illustrated in the chapter, and
3. Gives your impressions of the likely tension that transpired between the client and the auditor in resolving that a qualified opinion was required. For example, why would the client decide that it was in its best interests to accept a qualified opinion rather than to correct the financial statements?

2. Reporting on Financial Distress

Over the years, a substantial amount of literature has been devoted to financial distress, and in particular to the independent auditor's decision to modify a report for substantial doubt about the ability of an entity to continue as a going concern. The literature appears within the popular financial press (such as *The Wall Street Journal, Business Week, Harvard Business Review*), the professional accounting and auditing literature (such as *Journal of Accountancy, The CPA Journal, Financial Analysts Journal*), and the academic research literature (such as *Auditing: A Journal of Practice & Theory, The Accounting Review, Journal of Accounting Research*). For example, numerous articles in the financial press report financial distress coincident with an auditor's report that raises substantial doubt, articles in the professional literature report how auditors consider substantial doubt, and articles in the academic literature link stock price reaction to auditors' reports of substantial doubt.

Required: Select three articles about financial distress and the auditor's substantial doubt decision, one each from the financial press, the professional literature, and the academic literature. Draft a report that:
1. Summarizes the key issues in each article.
2. Identifies key issues common to all three articles. For example, is there a question posed in one article that is answered in part in another article?

3. The Language Auditors Use in Explanatory Paragraphs

The language of a three-paragraph unqualified audit report is standardized in *SAS No. 58*, "Reports on Audited Financial Statements." All audit firms use the same language. However, although *SAS No. 58* offers guidance for, and a number of examples of, reports that depart from the standard wording of an unqualified opinion, an auditor has the latitude to draft language that fits the circumstances at hand, largely because the many circumstances that could give rise to an explanatory paragraph couldn't possibly be predicted by a Statement on Auditing Standards. In practice, auditors place considerable care in the selection of language. In fact, large firms commonly approve drafts of reports at the highest levels of the firm.

Required: Using LEXIS-NEXIS, the SEC's EDGAR file (**http://www.sec.gov**), the AICPA's *Accounting Trends and Techniques*, or copies of annual reports in a library, search for three examples of audit reports modified for the same general purpose. Draft a report that compares the language used in each report and reasons why you believe the language was chosen.

4. Examples of Audit Reports

Within the chapter, illustrations were offered for each of the following issues and types of audit reports, among others:

Issue	Type of Report	Company	Auditor
Another auditor	Unqualified	Sprint Corporation	Ernst & Young
Emphasis on a matter	Unqualified	GenCorp	Ernst & Young
Departure from GAAP	Qualified	Union Bank	Andersen
Inconsistency	Unqualified	Whirlpool	Ernst & Young
	Qualified	Public Service Company of Indiana	Andersen
Scope limitation	Qualified	Advanced Monitoring Systems	Wilson, Haig & Co.
	Disclaimer	Sunshine Jr. Stores	Andersen
Going concern	Unqualified	Kmart	PwC

Required: Using LEXIS-NEXIS, the SEC's EDGAR file (**http://www.sec.gov**), or copies of annual reports in a library, search for one example of each of the types of audit reports listed and illustrated in the chapter. Draft a report that compares the language used in each audit report.

Interactive quizzes are available as a student learning resource at http://ricchiute.swlearning.com

4 Chapter

Professional Ethics

Major topics discussed in this chapter are:

- General and professional ethics, and the collapse of Enron and Andersen.
- The AICPA Code of Professional Conduct.
- The AICPA Rules of Conduct and SEC Auditor Independence Rules.
- Ethics enforcement.
- The PCAOB's rules for inspecting firms and the AICPA's practice-monitoring system.

Although most of the issues faced in practice are largely technical in nature, certified public accountants also confront ethical questions related to their threefold responsibility to the public, to clients, and to their colleagues in practice. Interestingly, many ethical questions derive from the unique contractual relationship between practitioners and clients. For example, unlike lawyers who report directly to and act as advocates for their clients, practitioners performing audit services report mostly to external users and act as independent attestors about—not advocates for—assertions made by their clients. In fact, the profession's well-established obligation for independence, integrity, and objectivity is partly why audit services have value, and why the financial community is predisposed to trust practitioners. In short, the profession is in a position of trust, the AICPA Code of Professional Conduct is the emblem of that trust, and the Public Company Accounting Oversight Board's (PCAOB) rules for inspections and the AICPA's practice-monitoring programs are the means by which the emblem is affirmed.

However, although the Rules of Conduct within the AICPA Code of Professional Conduct are explicit, some of the temptations faced in practice have little to do with the rules and everything to do with the utility function of the practitioners who break the rules. For example, the engagement partner for the audit of the PTL Club, a religious broadcast network, certainly knew that—Rules 102 (Integrity and Objectivity) and 501 (Acts Discreditable) aside—maintaining a secret check register to finance management's excessive lifestyle (including a Palm Springs ranch house, a Florida condominium, luxury automobiles, and an unrecorded executive payroll) was both unethical and illegal, given particularly that his firm, the now defunct Leventhal & Horwath, would suffer immeasurably following indictment as a codefendant in a $750 million class action suit filed by PTL contributors. Some of the rules introduced in this chapter, among them Rule 302 on contingent fees, will likely be news to you. Others, though, will be nothing other than entirely obvious.

This chapter considers questions of ethics through the AICPA Code of Professional Conduct and the SEC's Auditor Independence Rules—both of which are the standards of behavior for practitioners performing audit and attestation services[1]—and through means of ethical reasoning well established in the business and accounting ethics literatures. The chapter begins by introducing general and professional ethics, and discussing the collapse of Enron and Andersen. Next, the Principles, Rules, Interpretations, and Rulings of the AICPA Code of Professional Conduct are discussed, and the Code's Rules of Conduct and the SEC's Independence Rules are interpreted. In turn, the chapter addresses quality control in public accounting firms and the profession's means for monitoring quality control: the PCAOB's rules for inspections and the AICPA's Center for Public Company Audit Firms for firms that audit public companies and the AICPA's peer review program for firms that audit nonpublic companies.

General Ethics, Professional Ethics, and the Collapse of Enron and Andersen

General ethics, the study of ideal conduct and behavior, is one of several fields of study in philosophy—others include aesthetics (the study of ideal form or beauty), logic (the study of ideal method in thought and research), metaphysics (the study of ultimate reality), and politics (the study of ideal social organization). As Mautz and Sharaf point out, questions of professional ethics—whether in law, medicine, or auditing—apply general ethics to the choices and consequences embedded within a particular profession:

Ethical behavior in auditing or in any other activity is no more than a special application of the general notion of ethical conduct devised by philosophers. . . . Ethical Conduct in auditing draws its justification and basic nature from the general theory of ethics.[2]

However, unlike general ethics, professional codes of ethics do not, and cannot, require ideal standards of behavior, since minimum standards—the standard imposed by professional codes—can be enforced on practitioners and ideal standards cannot. But by mandating a minimum standard, professional codes of ethics risk encouraging mediocrity. And it is precisely for this reason that the reputation of a profession, particularly public accounting (a profession for which a practitioner's work product is observable but his or her work is not), rests squarely on each practitioner's willingness to reach for a standard of conduct well beyond his or her code: a standard worthy of the trust entrusted to that practitioner by the public, by clients, and by the profession that will bear the burden of adverse reputation effects. In fact, many of the audit failures attributed by some to a failing of ethics turn on behavior that the accountants in the cases may have thought complied with their standard of professional ethics, but that observers judged below *their* expectations of general ethics. Take, for example, the case of Enron and Arthur Andersen.

---

1 The Association of Government Accountants and Institute of Internal Auditors each have a code of ethics.
2 R. K. Mautz and H. A. Sharaf, *The Philosophy of Auditing*. Sarasota, FL: American Accounting Association, 1961, p. 232.

Enron and Andersen

Accounting issues raised in the Enron case were complicated, many, uncommon, and varied—among them, charging as a deduction from shareholders' equity notes received for common stock, and reporting at inflated values broadband assets and content-service businesses. But none captured the financial community's attention quite like the treatment of off-the-books partnerships as unconsolidated special-purpose entities (SPEs). Treating the partnerships as SPEs offered this advantage: Management could load debt onto the SPEs and, equally important, record gains on sales to the SPEs. The alternative, apparently unacceptable to management, would consolidate the partnerships in Enron's financial statements and eliminate the gains in consolidation. For example, one SPE, called JEDI (for Joint Energy Development Investments), a joint venture between Enron and the California Public Employee Retirement System (CalPERS), incurred debt on Enron's behalf (thereby allowing Enron to maintain an inflated debt rating), and engaged in sales transactions with Enron (thereby inflating Enron's earnings). In short, SPEs allowed Enron to off-load debt *and* to inflate earnings. When CalPERS liquidated its interest in JEDI, Enron reimagined JEDI as Chewco, which borrowed $11.4 million from Barclays Bank, $6.6 million of which was guaranteed by Enron, leaving only $4.8 million "at risk," an amount that fell below the 3 percent-of-the-investment-at-risk rule imposed at the time by *SFAS No. 125* (now superseded).[3]

Since less than 3 percent of the investment was at risk, GAAP required that Enron consolidate Chewco. Enron didn't consolidate Chewco, and Andersen didn't issue a qualified opinion.

Documents made public by the House Committee on Energy and Commerce investigating Enron revealed that individuals within both Enron and Andersen had raised red flags about SPEs, among other things. For example, a vice president of corporate development, in an unsigned memo to Enron's chairman, wrote:

I am incredibly nervous that we will implode in a wave of accounting scandals. My eight years of Enron work history will be worth nothing on my resume, the business world will consider the past successes as nothing but an elaborate accounting hoax.[4]

And a partner in Andersen's Professional Standards Group wrote in an email:

I have not spoken to the Practice Director. I do not know if he knows how much we cannot support this. Where do we go from here? This is a big item and the team apparently does not want to go back to the client on this.[5]

It's tempting to rush to judgment. After all, we know in hindsight that people within both Enron and Andersen had reason to believe that Enron's financial position and results of operations were misstated and, more to the point, that both Enron and Andersen collapsed (Chapter 1). However, we also know that summa-

---

3   See W. C. Powers, Jr., R. S. Troubh, and H. S. Winokur, Jr., *Report of Investigation by the Special Investigative Committee of the Board of Directors of Enron (Powers Report)*. 2002; M. A. Hiltzik and J. Leeds, "Enron Kept Crucial Information from Auditors, Memo Discloses," *Los Angeles Times* (February 7, 2002), p. C1; P. Behr, "How Chewco Brought Down an Empire," *The Washington Post* (February 4, 2002), p. A1.

4   "Text of Letter to Enron's Chairman After Departure of Chief Executive," *The New York Times* (January 16, 2002), p. A6.

5   *Tauzin, Greenwood Release Internal Andersen Memos*, April 2, 2002 (**http://energycommerce.house.gov/107/News/04022002_527.htm**). Documents at **http://energycommerce.house.gov/107/pubs/EnronDocumentsApril2.pdf**.

rizing Enron in a mere few sentences overlooks the millions upon millions of documents Enron and Andersen produced to regulators, legislators, and litigants and overlooks the larger issue for practitioners going forward: How do auditors—how do people—come to judgments about ethics? Figure 4-1 summarizes five means of ethical reasoning commonly included in books on business ethics and accounting ethics.[6]

FIGURE 4-1: *Ethical Reasoning*

Opinion
Ethical reasoning is purely a matter of personal opinion, absent self-interest; ethical judgment is neither rational nor objective—there is no right or wrong, no moral or immoral, except relative to one's culture or society: "What do I think?" (called by ethicists *ethical relativism*)

Self-interest
Ethical reasoning is subordinated to unrestrained self-interest "What's in it for me?" (*psychological egoism*)

Consequence
Ethical reasoning is guided by which outcome delivers the greatest (least) good (consequence) to the largest number: "What's in it for everyone?" (*utilitarianism*)

Duty
Ethical reasoning is guided by duties and obligations: "What is my duty?" (*deontological ethics*)

Character
Ethical reasoning is guided by character and virtue; not what I should do (decision and actions), but who I should be (character and virtue): "How will this reflect on me?" (*virtue ethics*)

The means of ethical reasoning in Figure 4-1 essentially distill to different ways of approaching choice. The first, *opinion*, denies that there is a right or a wrong choice, or that people make rational or ethical judgments. Rather, the question is, my self-interest aside, "what do I think?" For example, what do you think about Enron's accounting for SPEs and Andersen's compliance in the wake of red flags raised in rebuttal? In contrast, each of the next three means listed in Figure 4-1 frames ethical reasoning as decisions and actions from different points of view. *Self-interest* centers reasoning on the interests of the decision maker *only*—"What's in it for me?" For example, a number of reports attribute Andersen's behavior to individual partners' self-interest in increasing their compensation by cross-selling consulting to audit clients.[7] *Consequence* guides choice toward the decision or outcome that delivers the greatest good, or the least consequence, to the largest number of constituents, thereby broadening the question to "what's in it for everyone?" For example, arguably, nothing was in it for the investors and retirees who had invested heavily in Enron, a company that had once ranked seventh on the

---

6   See, for example, J. Desjardins, *An Introduction to Business Ethics*. New York: McGraw Hill, 2003; and R. F. Duska and B. S. Duska, *Accounting Ethics*. Malden, MA: Blackwell Publishing, 2003.

7   See, for example, K. Brown and J. Weil, "Questioning the Books: How Andersen's Embrace of Consulting Altered the Culture of the Auditing Firm," *The Wall Street Journal* (March 12, 2002), p. C1.

Fortune 500 list. In turn, *duty* centers reasoning not on consequence or self-interest, but on duties and obligations, recasting the question to "what is my duty?" For example, what was Andersen's duty under the AICPA's Code of Professional Conduct? Finally, rather than decisions and actions, *character* focuses on character and virtue—not what should I do, but "How will this reflect on me?" For example, as is common in audit failures, today most observers have less to say about the actions than they do about the character of the people close to the Enron debacle and to the Andersen collapse.

Figure 4-1 offers a way to think about ethics. The idea isn't so much which of the five means of ethical reasoning is best; ethicists have debated the issue for centuries. Rather, the idea is to gather a fulsome set of evidence and to arrive at ethical choices with a clear understanding that the issues are complex and that there are a variety of ways to reason about the issues.

Changes in Professional Ethics

Actually, criticisms of accounting ethics is not at all new. Prior to the mid-1980s, some observers criticized the AICPA's then existing Code of Professional Ethics, arguing that the Code did not adequately encompass the profession's expanding scope of attestation and assurance services. Responding to the criticism, the AICPA appointed a Special Committee on Standards of Professional Conduct, chaired by George D. Anderson, a former AICPA chair, to evaluate the relevance of the Code to the profession's commitment to professionalism, quality, and the public interest. The committee recommended unprecedented reform: a mandatory quality assurance review (QAR) program, and a new code that would apply to *all* professional services (rather than to auditing alone) and to *all* AICPA members (rather than to members in public practice alone). In 1988, 92 percent of the voting AICPA members approved a new QAR program and a new Code of Professional Conduct.

Similarly, at the turn of the century, the SEC criticized public accounting firms for providing increasingly more nonaudit services to audit clients. For example, Arthur Levitt, then SEC chair, argued in May 2000 that "consulting and other services may shorten the distance between the auditor and management"[8] (see Chapter 2) and the SEC concluded in November 2000 that "the trend of available data suggests a rapid increase in the provision of non-audit services to audit clients—in 1999, 4.6% of Big Five SEC audit clients paid MAS fees in excess of audit fees, an increase of over 200% in two years."[9] Consistent with the SEC's conclusion, an independent Panel on Audit Effectiveness found that, for Big Five SEC audit clients, "the ratio of accounting and auditing revenues to consulting revenues dropped from approximately 6 to 1 in 1990 to 1.5 to 1 in 1999."[10] The SEC issued new rules in 2000 that revised the Commission's rules for nonaudit services and for financial, employment, and family relationships between auditors and clients, and new rules again in 2003 that marked the Commission's requirements to the intent of the *Sarbanes-Oxley Act* for nonaudit services, conflicts of interest in em-

8   Arthur Levitt, Jr., "Renewing the Covenant with Investors." Speech at New York University Center for Law and Business, May 10, 2000.

9   SEC, *Revision of the Commission's Auditor Independence Requirements.* Washington, D.C.: U.S. Government Printing Office, November 21, 2000.

10   Public Oversight Board, *Panel on Audit Effectiveness: Report and Recommendations.* Stamford, CT: POB, 2000, p. 112.

ployment relationships, partner rotation, audit committees, partner compensation, and expanded disclosure about fees.

The AICPA Code of Professional Conduct applies to all services offered by AICPA members including, ironically, a contemporary service not at all common when the Code was developed in 1988: an "ethics audit." Although discussed for years, public accounting firms have only recently begun to offer services that report on management's performance in monitoring the risk of unethical behavior company-wide. For example, packaged as "ethics process management," KPMG offers a service related to risks that bear on corporate ethics—among them, harassment, environmental contamination, antitrust infractions, improper foreign payments, fraudulent financial reporting, and discrimination. KPMG's service offers management an "ethics vulnerability risk assessment"—not an ethics scorecard, but an assessment of where management may be at risk for violating express or implied assertions about ethics. For example, based on focus-group interviews with key management (with questions such as "what is your policy about employees receiving gifts?") and with employees (with questions such as "how often have you declined a supplier's gift?"), the firm identifies gaps where management's standards of employee behavior are unclear to employees.

Smaller firms also have tapped the market for ethics audits. For example, one shareholder in Vain, Hen & Co., a full-service firm in Casabas, California, earned a certificate in ethics training at Marina Del Rey's Josephone Institute of Ethics, affiliated with a licensed clinical social worker and investigative reporters, and developed a market niche by delivering ethics audits to mid-size companies, lecturing at trade conferences, and advertising in publications such as *Business Week*. Although ethics management services are becoming popular, some observers are critical. For example, *The Wall Street Journal* reported, albeit sardonically, "Think about it: Companies trying to mitigate a sentence before a crime has been committed, or found out. What more evidence did anyone need that corporate America knew it had an ethics problem and—more to the point—that it was willing to pay good money to ameliorate it?"[11]

AICPA Code of Professional Conduct

The **AICPA Code of Professional Conduct** consists of *Principles* and *Rules of Conduct*. In addition, the executive committee of the AICPA's professional ethics division issues *Interpretations* of, and *Ethics Rulings* about, the Rules of Conduct.

Principles

Collectively, the six **Principles of the Code of Professional Conduct**, listed and explained in Figure 4-2, express responsibilities for all AICPA members to the public, to their clients, and to their colleagues in the profession. The principles demand an uncompromising commitment to the public interest and to the highest standards of self-discipline, even at the expense of personal gain. Like general ethics, the Principles of the Code of Professional Conduct are not enforceable. Rather, they provide a framework for the Rules of Conduct, which, like the rules of conduct in other professions, are minimum standards and therefore *are* enforceable on AICPA members.

---

11 "This Auditing Team Wants to Create a Moral Organization," *The Wall Street Journal* (January 19, 1996), p. B5.

FIGURE 4-2: *Principles of Professional Conduct*

Responsibilities
In carrying out their responsibilities as professionals, members should exercise sensitive professional and moral judgment in all their activities.

The Public Interest
Members should accept the obligation to act in a way that will serve the public interest, honor the public trust, and demonstrate commitment to professionalism.

Integrity
To maintain and broaden public confidence, members should perform all professional responsibilities with the highest sense of integrity.

Objectivity and Independence
A member should maintain objectivity and be free of conflicts of interest in discharging professional responsibilities. A member in public practice should be independent in fact and appearance when providing auditing and other attestation services.

Due Care
A member should observe the profession's technical and ethical standards, strive continually to improve competence and the quality of services, and discharge professional responsibility to the best of the member's ability.

Scope and Nature of Services
A member in public practice should observe the Code of Professional Conduct in determining the scope and nature of services to be provided.

Rules of Conduct

The **Rules of Conduct**, discussed in detail later, govern the performance of all AICPA members—including those in public practice, industry, government, and education—in five general areas: independence, integrity, and objectivity; professional standards; responsibilities to clients; responsibilities to colleagues; and other responsibilities and practices. Figure 4-3 lists the eleven Rules of Conduct,

FIGURE 4-3: *AICPA Rules of Conduct and Interpretations*

Rule of Conduct	Related Interpretations
101 Independence	• Employment or Association with Attest Clients • Performance of Other Services • Honorary Directorships and Trusteeships of Not-for-Profit Organizations • Loans from Financial Institution Clients • The Effect of Litigation on Independence • The Effect on Independence of Financial Interests in Nonclients Having Investor or Investee Relationships with a Member's Client • The Effect on Independence of Relationships with Entities Included in Governmental Financial Statements • Independence and Cooperative Arrangement with Clients

FIGURE 4-3 *(continued)*

Rule of Conduct	Related Interpretations
	• Extended Audit Services • The Effect of Alternative Practice Structures on Independence
102 Integrity and Objectivity	• Knowing Misrepresentations in the Preparation of Financial Statements or Records • Conflicts of Interest • Obligations of a Member to an Employer's External Accountant • Subordination of Judgment by a Member • Application of Rule 102 to Members Performing Educational Services • Professional Services Involving Client Advocacy
201 General Standards	• Competence
202 Compliance with Standards	
203 Accounting Principles	• Departure from Established Accounting Principles • Status of FASB and GASB Interpretations • Responsibility of Employees for the Preparation of Financial Statements in Conformity with GAAP
301 Confidential Client Information	• Confidential Information and the Purchase, Sale, or Merger of a Practice
302 Contingent Fees	• Contingent Fees in Tax Matters
501 Acts Discreditable	• Retention of Clients' Records • Discrimination and Harassment in Employment Practices • Negligence in the Preparation of Financial Statements or Records • Failure to Follow Requirements of Governmental Bodies, Commissions, or Other Regulatory Agencies in Performing Attest or Similar Services • Solicitation or Disclosure of CPA Exam Questions and Answers • Failure to File Tax Return or Pay Tax Liability
502 Advertising and Other Forms of Solicitation	• False, Misleading or Deceptive Acts in Advertising or Solicitation
503 Commissions and Referral Fees	
505 Form of Practice and Name	• Application of Rule 505 to Alternative Practice Structures • Application of Rules of Conduct to Members Who Operate a Separate Business

all of which are introduced and interpreted in the next section of the chapter. The Rules are to professional conduct what generally accepted auditing standards are to audit engagements and what attestation standards are to attest engagements: guidelines for behavior and measures of quality against which behavior is judged.

Because the Rules of Conduct are enforceable upon AICPA members, new or revised Rules require member approval by formal ballot before becoming effective. Proposals to amend the Rules may be made by the professional ethics division, by the Institute's board of directors, by any 30 members of the AICPA Council, in writing by any 200 or more AICPA members, or by petition of 5 percent of the members. For example, in response to the profession's expanding scope of attest and assurance services, the AICPA proposed and the membership approved substantial amendments to the Institute's Rules of Conduct in 1988.

Interpretations and Ethics Rulings

Interpretations of the Rules of Conduct are issued by the executive committee of the Institute's professional ethics division and are intended to interpret both the scope and the applicability of the Rules of Conduct. Figure 4-3 illustrates major interpretations issued to date. Prior to adoption, all proposed Interpretations are first exposed to state societies (or associations) of CPAs, state boards of accountancy, and others for comment. **Ethics Rulings** also are issued by the ethics division's executive committee after exposure to state societies and boards of accountancy, among others. The Rulings summarize the applicability of Rules of Conduct and Interpretations to detailed fact situations, many of which are drawn from practice. AICPA members must justify departures from the Rules of Conduct, Interpretations, and Ethics Rulings.

Rules of Conduct

Section 7 of the AICPA bylaws provides the authority for the Code of Professional Conduct in general and for the Rules of Conduct in particular. The Rules apply to all professional services rendered by AICPA members, except where the rule obviously indicates otherwise. For example, independence, the subject of Rule 101, applies to audit, attest, and assurance services, but not to consulting. Following a hearing for allegedly violating any provision of the Rules, an ethics trial board may expel or suspend an offending AICPA member (for not more than two years) or impose a lesser sanction, such as a letter of admonishment. Of course, an AICPA member cannot engage a nonmember to carry out violations on his or her behalf, since acts carried out in a member's behalf are deemed to have been performed by the member. Each Rule is discussed in the sections that follow.

Independence, Integrity, Objectivity and the SEC's Auditor Independence Rules

Independence, integrity, and objectivity are the cornerstones of the profession. But they are also unobservable: You can't observe a practitioner's independence from a client any more than you can a practitioner's objectivity when he or she evaluates evidence. Owing to its importance, independence over the years has been the subject of more Interpretations and Rulings than any other Rule of Conduct, and at the turn of the century was the subject of lengthy congressional hearings and new rules now applied in public company audits.

Rule 101—Independence

A member in public practice shall be independent in the performance of professional services as required by standards promulgated by bodies designated by Council.

Rule 101 applies to all practicing CPAs performing financial statement audits and other attest services, such as review engagements and reports on prospective financial statements (Chapter 18). The AICPA's professional ethics division has issued a number of interpretations of Rule 101, all of which lend insight into issues that may detract from independence "in fact" or from independence "in appearance," both of which were introduced in Chapter 2. For example, when management commences or expresses an intent to commence legal action against an auditor—say, for example, for failing to detect fraud—the auditor and client are suddenly placed in adversary positions, thereby raising questions about the client's candor and about the auditor's objectivity, self-interest, and independence. An AICPA Interpretation cites four instances in which litigation would impair auditor independence:

- Litigation by management alleging deficiencies in audit work,
- Litigation by the auditor alleging management fraud or deceit,
- An expressed intent by management to commence litigation alleging deficiencies in audit work, and
- Litigation unrelated to audit work but material nevertheless either to the firm's or to the client's financial statements (for example, disputes about bills for services or the outcome of tax or consulting services).

The Interpretation is clear and, for that matter, largely uncontroversial. But, what about issues that *are* controversial? An illustration follows.

The SEC's Auditor Independence Rules

Considerable controversy surfaced in the late 1990s about revisions to the SEC's auditor independence rules (which apply to all practicing CPAs auditing *public* companies.) For example, in a November 30, 1998, letter to AICPA SEC Public Section Executive Committee Chair Michael Conway, Lynn Turner, then SEC chief accountant, wrote that the SEC questioned whether public accounting firms had monitored properly problems such as auditors who own stock in audit clients— an investment that clearly compromises independence in appearance, since the auditor presumably has a vested interest in the outcome of the audit.[12] Turner's claim was not unfounded: Two years later, in January 2000, the SEC settled charges against PricewaterhouseCoopers (PwC) in which, over a two-year period involving 2,159 clients, 1,885 PwC professionals had a total of 8,064 infractions.[13] In the fall of 2000, the SEC held public hearings, issued proposed rules that splintered the then Big Five firms (see Chapter 2), and in November 2000 issued compromise independence rules that, as discussed in Chapter 2, mandated an engagement team (rather than firm-wide) model of independence and emphasized independence in appearance.

---

12 Public Oversight Board, "Message from the Board: Auditor Independence," *Annual Report 1999*, Stamford, CT: POB, 1999, p. 5.
13 Ibid.

However, following enactment of the *Sarbanes-Oxley Act of 2002*, the SEC was charged with the responsibility of fulfilling the mandate of the Act's Title II, Auditor Independence. The Act restricts a registered public accounting firm from supplying nine nonaudit services to audit clients (Chapter 2, Figure 2-2), but doesn't restrict tax services specifically. The question was whether the SEC would restrict explicitly what the *Sarbanes-Oxley Act* had not. On January 22, 2003, the Commission voted to allow firms to supply tax services to audit clients, although not without preapproval by a board of directors' audit committee. Reaction to the vote was mixed. On one hand, AICPA Chair William Ezzell said, "The final rule is consistent with the intent and spirit of the Sarbanes act itself," but, on the other, an industry consultant said, "If the interpretation allows for independent auditors to now market tax avoidance strategies, clearly the SEC has taken a couple of steps backwards from Sarbanes-Oxley's original intent."[14]

The SEC's Auditor Independence Rules are summarized in Figure 4-4. Among other things, the rules require that the *lead and review partners rotate* off of an engagement after five consecutive engagements, that the *audit committee preapprove all audit and nonaudit services* an auditor provides (see also, Chapter 2, Figure 2-2) unless nonaudit fees are less than 5 percent of total fees, and that an accounting firm is not independent of an audit client if any audit *partner received compensation* based on the partner securing with the client billable work for other than audit, review, and attest services. On *expanded disclosure*, public companies report fees for each of four types of services: audit, audit related, tax, and all other. The SEC rules provide also that independence is impaired if at any time during the period cov-

FIGURE 4-4: *SEC Auditor Independence Rules*

Scope of Services Auditor Provides
An accounting firm is prohibited from performing nonaudit services made unlawful by *Sarbanes-Oxley* (Chapter 2, Figure 2-2).

Conflicts of Interest in Employment Relationships
An accounting firm is not independent of a client that employs one of the client's former auditors within the one year period preceding the audit.

Partner Rotation
A lead (coordinating) partner and a review (concurring) partner rotate off of an engagement after five consecutive years.

Audit Committee
Audit committees pre-approve audit services and permitted nonaudit services, unless nonaudit service fees are less than 5 percent of total fees.

Partner Compensation
An accounting firm is not independent of an audit client if any audit partner is compensated for securing with the client billable work for services other than audit or attestation.

Expanded Disclosure
Public companies disclose audit fees and fees for an explanation of audit-related, tax, and all other services.

---

14 T. Miller-Segarra, "SEC Hands Accountants a Big Win," *Accounting Today* (February 10–23, 2003), pp. 1, 30.

ered by an engagement the *auditor is employed by an audit client*. In short, during the engagement period, an auditor cannot be employed by an audit firm and by the client concurrently, or by the audit firm and then by the client thereafter.

In January 2003, the SEC announced rules governing clients hiring auditors assigned formerly to the client's audit: An accounting firm is not independent of a client that employs one of the client's former auditors within the one-year period preceding the audit (Figure 4-4). The rule recognizes that the appearance of a firm's independence may be impaired if, for example, a client hires as CFO a former engagement partner, since investors may judge that the distance between the former engagement partner and his or her firm is far too close. Like most of the rules, the employment relationships rule has subtleties. For example, consider the implications for dual-career families. The rule does not *always* prohibit a firm from auditing companies that employ an immediate family member of assigned audit staff. The prohibition is less restrictive: An auditor is not independent if his or her spouse is employed by an audit client and has more than minimal influence over accounting records, financial statements, or persons who prepare financial statements. For example, an engagement partner would not be independent if his or her spouse was an audit client's chief financial officer (CFO), but would be independent if the spouse was employed as a marketing executive with no influence over accounting records or financial personnel.

Clearly, the *Sarbanes-Oxley Act* and the SEC's January 2003 Auditor Independence Rules address with force the SEC's long-held position that nonaudit services may influence audits inappropriately, that some nonaudit services may impair independence inherently, and that nonaudit services may affect investor confidence. However, the SEC prohibits several other issues not necessarily apparent in either the January 2003 Rules (Figure 4-4) or *Sarbanes-Oxley* (Figure 2-2: Services Outside the Scope of Practice). For example, independence is impaired if an accountant prepares an audit client's financial statements, operates or supervises an audit client's information system, or supplies to an audit client services requiring that he or she be admitted to practice before U.S. courts. Note, though, that some of the services the SEC prohibits in the United States are allowed in foreign countries and encouraged by some foreign companies. For example, consider legal services offered by accounting firms: Although banned by the American Bar Association, state courts, and the SEC, so-called "multidisciplinary practices" (MDP) that provide both accounting and legal services are common in Europe and, owing to cost efficiencies, are demanded by some European clients. For example, New Venturetec, a Swiss venture capital company, cut ties with a Swiss law firm, engaged KPMG's European MDP, and estimated cost savings of 20 percent ($60,000) in legal, tax, and audit fees when the company began trading on the Swiss Stock Exchange.[15] Interestingly, in 2001, the largest employer of lawyers in the world was not a law firm—it was Arthur Andersen, which employed over 3,500 lawyers worldwide.

Financial Relationships

Can a practitioner be independent of an audit client with which he or she has a financial interest? Clearly, a CPA might well be intellectually honest in claiming

---

15 M. A. Jacobs, "Accounting Firms Covet Forbidden Fruit–Piece of U.S. Legal Market," *The Wall Street Journal* (May 31, 2000), p. C1.

independence in fact, but all parties who rely on his or her report have a legitimate claim that the practitioner lacks the appearance of independence, since he or she would have a vested interest in the outcome of the engagement. For example, although the CPA may be unbiased in attesting to the financial position, results of operations, and cash flows of the business he or she owns, a bank loan officer would likely suspect that the CPA's report lacks credibility, since the CPA has a vested interest in the loan decision.

Under the AICPA's Code of Professional Conduct, the appearance of independence is impaired if, for example, the practitioner has:

- A *direct* financial interest (for example, owns stock) or *material indirect* financial interest (for example, immediate family owns stock) in a client,
- A *joint, closely held business investment* with the client that is material to the practitioner's (or his or her firm's) net worth,
- Any *loan* to or from the client (other than automobile loans or leases, credit card and cash advance balances less than $5,000 in the aggregate, loans on the cash surrender value of insurance policies, and loans collateralized by cash deposits) or any individual who owned 10 percent or more of a client's equity securities, or
- Alone, or in with his or her family, an *investment* that exceeds 5 percent of a client's equity securities.

Although unrelated to financial interest, independence also is impaired if a practitioner (or a firm) acts as a promoter, underwriter, voting trustee, director, or officer for a client, or in any other capacity equivalent either to management or to employment, or is a trustee for any pension or profit-sharing trust.

Under the SEC's Auditor Independence Rules, an accountant is not independent of an audit client if, at any point during the engagement period, he or she has a direct financial interest or a material indirect financial interest in an audit client, such as an investment, an uncollateralized loan, or a demand deposit that exceeds amounts insured, for example, by the Federal Deposit Insurance Corporation. However, be careful when interpreting the breadth of the rule. Traditionally, the SEC had prohibited most anyone in public accounting firms from owning shares in a client of the firm, even if the audit was performed by an out-of-state office. Today, the SEC substantially limits the circle of people prohibited from maintaining a financial relationship in an audit client: The prohibition extends only to **covered persons** (for example, the engagement team, a partner or manager who provides the client at least 10 hours of nonaudit services, and any partner employed in the lead engagement partner's office) and "immediate family members" (for example, a spouse, spousal equivalent, or dependent).

Business Relationships

The AICPA Code of Professional Conduct offers little explicit guidance on business relationships with clients. However, the SEC's rules are more forthcoming: Independence is impaired if at any time during the period covered by the engagement the accountant has a direct or material indirect business relationship with an audit client, or with decision-making persons associated with the audit client, such as an officer, director, or substantial stockholder. For example, although the affiliation is now dissolved, KPMG in the mid-1990s affiliated with KPMG BayMark, a firm that specialized in corporate turnarounds. KPMG made a $100,000 loan to Edward Olsen, one of four BayMark owners and president of Porta Systems, a KPMG 1996 audit client run by KPMG BayMark. An administrative judge ruled that KPMG was not independent, but that the firm had made a good faith effort to comply with the SEC's independence rules, since the engagement team had no knowledge of the loan. However, in January 2001, the SEC took issue with the judge's ruling, claiming that KPMG had "failed to undertake any reasonable inquiry that necessarily would have led them to discover clear impairments of independence."[16] KPMG was neither fined nor subjected to additional reporting requirements, although the SEC issued a cease-and-desist order prohibiting the firm from further arrangements similar to Porta and BayMark.

Honorary Directorships

The AICPA's Code of Professional Conduct includes a number of interpretations and rulings that are not covered directly by the SEC's Rules. Consider, for example, honorary directorships. Accountants are often asked to serve as honorary directors for not-for-profit charitable organizations, a topic the SEC rule does not address. Can an accountant serve both as an honorary director and as an auditor without violating the appearance of independence? For example, wouldn't a major philanthropic organization have cause for alarm if a grant application from a local arts commission reports that a partner in a public accounting firm serves both as an honorary director and as independent auditor for the commission? Doesn't the partner's joint appointment pose a conflict of interests? Under the Code of Professional Conduct, independence is not impaired as long as the accountant's position is purely honorary and does require that he or she vote or otherwise participate in management activities.

Nonattest Independence Rules

Both Rule 101 and the SEC's Auditor Independence Rules relate to attest services: services in which an auditor issues a written conclusion about a client's written assertions—in this case, reports on audited financial statements. In June 2003, the AICPA's professional ethics executive committee adopted Interpretation 101-3, Performance of Nonattest Services, which presents three general requirements for nonattest services, such as business risk consulting, bookkeeping, and executive and employee search. The rules specify that an accountant:

- May not perform management functions or make management's decisions,
- Must be satisfied that management is willing and able to perform all management functions the engagement may require, and
- Must document certain aspects of the engagement, such as the client's agreement to oversee the service.

The rules go to independence in this sense: nonattest services should be performed to help management make decisions for themselves. For example, the rules contemplate that the client will assign to a competent employee responsibility to oversee the accountant's services, set the scope of the service, and accept responsibility for the results of the service.

---

16 F. Norris, "SEC Faults KPMG's Conduct in an Audit," *The New York Times* (January 20, 2001), p. 2.

Rule 102—Integrity and Objectivity

In the performance of any professional service, a member shall maintain objectivity and integrity, shall be free of conflicts of interest, and shall not knowingly misrepresent facts or subordinate his or her judgment to others.

Rule 102 requires that in performing *any* professional service, not just financial statement auditing, an AICPA member remain objective (that is, impartial with respect to the client) and perform the service with integrity (that is, an attitude of uprightness, honesty, and sincerity). For example, an auditor would lack both objectivity and integrity if he or she knowingly allowed a client to overstate the carrying value of obsolete inventory. In fact, an Interpretation issued under Rule 102 specifically states that an accountant who knowingly makes—or directs another to make—false or misleading entries in an entity's records or financial statements (for example, proposes an inappropriate income-enhancing journal entry), or signs—or permits another to sign—a false or misleading document (for example, an audit or a review report) is considered to have knowingly misrepresented facts in violation of Rule 102.

In practice, situations can unfold unexpectedly that raise suspicions of a conflict of interest. For example, a client may appeal to a municipal board of tax appeals that includes as a member the client's auditor, or a plaintiff may ask that a client's auditor perform litigation support services in an action against the client. Either of these two examples creates a conflict of interest in which the auditor would have to decide which client to serve: the board of tax appeals or the client; the plaintiff or the client. Rule 102 does not preclude an auditor from switching affiliations, but would preclude serving both affiliations.

As noted earlier, auditors are independent attestors, not advocates for their audit clients. However, a public accountant could act as an advocate for tax or consulting clients without violating Rule 102. For example, an accountant could research exhaustively the Internal Revenue Code, a commercial tax service, and relevant court cases to support a deduction on a client's tax return. If the deduction has substantial authoritative support, the accountant could justifiably sign the tax return as preparer without infringing on Rule 102. But if the accountant's research does not support the deduction, then signing the return as preparer would lack both objectivity and integrity, since the accountant would have subordinated his or her judgment to the client.

General and Technical Standards

The general and technical standards of the Rules of Conduct relate to an AICPA member's professional obligation to be competent and to be aware of, and comply with, the profession's published, authoritative standards.

Rule 201—General Standards

A member shall comply with the following standards and with any interpretations thereof by bodies designated by Council.

A. *Professional Competence.* Undertake only those professional services that the member or the member's firm can reasonably expect to be completed with professional competence.

B. *Due Professional Care.* Exercise due professional care in the performance of professional services.

C. *Planning and Supervision.* Adequately plan and supervise the performance of professional services.
D. *Sufficient Relevant Data.* Obtain sufficient relevant data to afford a reasonable basis for conclusions or recommendations in relation to any professional services performed.

Rule 201A explicitly precludes a member from accepting engagements beyond the scope of his or her competence—competence being the technical qualifications of the practitioner, the ability to supervise and evaluate the work of subordinates, his or her knowledge and understanding of applicable standards, and sound professional judgment. However, Rule 201 does not preclude members from improving their competence (for example, through research, consultation with other practitioners, and continuing professional education) in order to offer new services. For example, seasoned auditors commonly consult industry publications and seek continuing professional education before proposing on engagements in industries they had not serviced previously.

Rules 201B, C, and D relate to issues also addressed in generally accepted auditing standards, specifically the third general standard (201B) and the first (201C) and third (201D) standards of field work (see Chapter 2, Figure 2-1, right column). The Code of Professional Conduct reinforces the importance of these three standards to financial statement auditing, although all three rules apply equally to other professional services performed by AICPA members in public practice and to members not in public practice.

In practice, auditors and clients sometimes disagree about the type of audit opinion required, the interpretation of accounting principles, or the need for financial statement disclosure, among other things. When there are disagreements, some clients will engage competing accounting firms to advise them on the disputed matters, thereby raising questions about Rule 201D, sufficient relevant data, since the responding firm is likely to have only a subset of the evidence available to the incumbent auditor. The Code of Professional Conduct does not preclude an accountant from providing advice to nonclients, but *Statement on Auditing Standards No. 50*, "Reports on the Application of Accounting Principles," recognizes that questions from nonclients are often prompted by disagreements and that the accountant should first consult with the incumbent accountant before providing advice. In short, advice should not be given without first considering all of the facts and both sides of the issue. Reporting on the application of accounting principles is illustrated in Chapter 18.

Rule 202—Compliance with Standards

A member who performs auditing, review, compilation, management advisory, tax, or other professional services shall comply with standards promulgated by bodies designated by Council.

Rule 202 requires that AICPA members comply with all professional standards relevant to the service rendered. In audit and attestation engagements, respectively, generally accepted auditing standards (and all *Statements on Auditing Standards*) and attestation standards (and all *Statements on Standards for Attestation Engagements*) are the "standards promulgated by bodies designated by Council." Apart from audit and attestation services, other professional services also have standards. For example, for compilation engagements and financial forecast and projection engagements, the standards of professional practice are included in *Statements on Standards for Accounting and Review Services* and *Standards for Forecasts and Projections*, respectively, both of which are discussed in Chapter 18. Violating an auditing standard, an attestation standard, or the standards for any other professional service in turn violates the Code of Professional Conduct.

> ### Rule 203—Accounting Principles
> A member shall not (1) express an opinion or state affirmatively that the financial statements or other financial data of any entity are presented in conformity with generally accepted accounting principles or (2) state that he or she is not aware of any such material modifications that should be made to such statements or data in order for them to be in conformity with generally accepted accounting principles, if such statements or data contain any departure from an accounting principle promulgated by bodies designated by Council to establish such principles that has a material effect on the statements or data taken as a whole. If, however, the statements or data contain such a departure and the member can demonstrate that due to unusual circumstances the financial statements or data would otherwise have been misleading, the member can comply with the rule by describing the departure, its approximate effects, if practicable, and the reasons why compliance with the principle would result in a misleading statement.

Rule 203 relates to all engagements for which financial statements or other financial data are reported on by an AICPA member. Thus the rule applies to financial statement audits and to special engagements for which an accountant reports on GAAP, such as reports on a comprehensive basis of accounting other than GAAP (for example, cash basis statements) or reports on specified elements of a financial statement (for example, gross sales), both of which are introduced in Chapter 18.

Clearly, departures from FASB *Statements of Financial Accounting Standards*, GASB *Statements of Governmental Accounting Standards*, *Opinions of the Accounting Principles Board*, and *Accounting Research Bulletins* are prohibited under Rule 203. However, how does an auditor judge GAAP under Rule 203 when the pronouncements of more than one authoritative body differ? For example, FASB *Statement of Financial Accounting Standards (SFAS) No. 52*, "Foreign Currency Translation," requires that exchange-rate losses be expensed in all circumstances. However, the International Accounting Standards Committee's *International Accounting Standard (IAS) No. 21*, "The Effects of Changes in Foreign Exchange Rates," permits two methods of accounting for exchange rate losses, one of which is consistent with *SFAS No. 52* (expense) and the other of which allows an international company to add the loss to the cost of the asset purchased—two different pronouncements and two different treatments that could have a material effect on reported earnings. To address competing standards, the Auditing Standards Board issued *SAS No. 69*, "The Meaning of 'Present Fairly in Conformity with GAAS,'" which establishes the Rule 203 GAAP hierarchy reproduced in Figure 4-5 for nongovernmental entities (such as corporations and not-for-profit organizations) and for governmental entities (such as state and local governmental agencies). In Figure 4-5, higher ordered categories of GAAP overrule lower ordered categories. For example, in the exchange rate loss example, *SFAS No. 52*, a "Category A" GAAP in Figure 4-5, would overrule *IAS No. 21*, an "Other" category GAAP.

A strong presumption is made that adherence to the accounting principles contained in authoritative pronouncements, like *Statements of Financial Accounting*

FIGURE 4-5: *Rule 203 GAAP Hierarchy*

Category	Nongovernmental Entities	Governmental Entities
A	FASB Statements of Financial Accounting Standards and Interpretations, APB Opinions, and AICPA Accounting Research Bulletins	GASB Statements and Interpretations, AICPA and FASB pronouncements that GASB makes applicable to state and local governments
B	FASB Technical Bulletins, AICPA Industry Audit and Accounting Guides, and AICPA Statements of Position	GASB Technical Bulletins, and AICPA Industry Audit and Accounting Guides, and AICPA Statements of Position that GASB makes applicable to state and local governments
C	AICPA Accounting Standards Executive Committee Practice Bulletins	AICPA Accounting Standards Executive Committee Practice Bulletins that GASB makes applicable to state and local governments
D	AICPA accounting interpretations, FASB implementation guides, and practices widely recognized and prevalent either generally or in an industry	GASB implementation guides, and practices widely recognized and prevalent either generally or in an industry
Other	For example, FASB Statements of Financial Accounting Concepts; AICPA Issues Papers; International Accounting Standards; GASB statements; interpretations, and technical bulletins; pronouncements of other professional associations or regulatory agencies; Technical Information Service Inquiries; AICPA Technical Practice Aids; and textbooks, handbooks, and articles	For example, GASB Concept Statements, Categories A–D for nongovernmental entities; AICPA Issues Papers; International Accounting Standards; pronouncements of other professional associations or regulatory agencies; Technical Information Service Inquiries; AICPA Technical Practice Aids; and textbooks, handbooks, and articles

Source: *SAS No. 69*, "The Meaning of 'Present Fairly in Conformity with GAAP' in the Independent Auditor's Report."

Standards, would in nearly all instances result in financial statements that are not misleading. However, in rare and unusual circumstances, such as new legislation or a creative business transaction, an accountant may believe that the literal interpretation and application of an accounting pronouncement would result in misleading financial statements. An Interpretation of Rule 203 recognizes that, because it is difficult for authoritative bodies to anticipate all of the circumstances to which accounting principles might apply, the proper accounting treatment for a transaction or event may deviate from the requirements of an official pronouncement. Applications of the Interpretation in practice, though, are quite rare, since the operative word in the Interpretation is "unusual."

Responsibilities to Clients

In serving the public, a practitioner is obligated to be independent and to perform the engagement with integrity and objectivity. However, an AICPA member also has an obligation to be fair to (although not compromised by) his or her client's interests as well.

Rule 301—Confidential Client Information

A member in public practice shall not disclose any confidential client information without the specific consent of the client.

This rule shall not be construed (1) to relieve a member of his or her professional obligations under rules 202 and 203, (2) to affect in any way the member's obligation to comply with a validly issued and enforceable subpoena or summons, (3) to prohibit review of a member's professional practice under AICPA or state CPA society authorization, or (4) to preclude a member from initiating a complaint with or responding to any inquiry made by a recognized investigative or disciplinary body.

Members of a recognized investigative or disciplinary body and professional practice reviewers shall not use to their own advantage or disclose any member's confidential client information that comes to their attention in carrying out their official responsibilities. However, this prohibition shall not restrict the exchange of information with a recognized investigative or disciplinary body or affect, in any way, compliance with a validly issued and enforceable subpoena or summons.

In the course of an engagement, a practitioner typically encounters confidential information. Common examples include product development, salaries, forthcoming earnings releases, production technologies, and product cost information. Disclosing confidential information without a client's consent is prohibited because disclosure could be detrimental to a client's competitive position. The purpose of Rule 301 is to encourage a client to provide confidential information freely without threat that the information will be released unnecessarily. However, the rule does not act as a shield against legitimate claims for a practitioner's knowledge or work product. For example, the rule does *not* relieve him or her from complying with a validly issued subpoena or summons, from complying with laws and government regulations, from disclosing information under the PCAOB's rules for inspections or the AICPA's practice-monitoring programs, or from responding to an inquiry by the AICPA's professional ethics division.

Information obtained in a professional services engagement is "confidential," but is the information "privileged" in the same way, say, that information communicated between physicians and patients and between attorneys and clients is privileged? The question is important for this reason: Confidential communications can be subpoenaed by a court of law but privileged communications cannot. Information communicated between a CPA and client is confidential but not privileged under common law, partly because accounting is a much younger profession than medicine and law, but mostly because auditors are independent attestors, not advocates for their clients. However, information communicated between a CPA and client *is* privileged under the statutes of some states.

Rule 302—Contingent Fees

A member in public practice shall not:
(1) Perform for a contingent fee any professional service for, or receive such a fee from, a client for whom the member or member's firm performs: (a) an audit or review of a financial statement; or (b) a compilation of a financial statement when the member expects, or reasonably might expect that a third party will use the financial statement and the member's compilation report does not dis-

> close a lack of independence; or (c) an examination of prospective financial information; or
>
> (2) Prepare an original or amended tax return for a tax refund for a contingent fee for any client.

Rule 302 prohibits fee arrangements with audit and attest clients whereby no fee is paid unless a particular outcome is attained (for example, an unqualified audit opinion) or the fee is contingent upon a particular outcome (for example, 10 percent of reported net income), the intent being to remove AICPA members from potentially compromising conflicts. However, the rule allows a contingent fee in two broad areas. For one, a fee may be dependent on the complexity of an engagement. For example, a member may charge more per hour of audit work for a complex multinational oil- and gas-producing company than for a local retail gas station that sells refined oil and gas products. And for another, the rule allows a number of contingent fee arrangements for tax services other than preparing a return. For example, an accountant could charge a contingent fee for representing a client in a proceeding before a state or federal revenue agent, for filing an amended return that claims a refund based on a tax issue for which another taxpayer is proceeding in a test case, or for filing an amended return claiming a refund in an amount greater than the threshold for review by the Joint Committee on Internal Revenue Taxation.

Prior to the 1990s, the AICPA had prohibited contingent fee arrangements with *nonattest* clients. However, in a 1987 letter to the National Association of State Boards of Accountancy (NASBA), the Federal Trade Commission (FTC) questioned the prohibition against contingent fees, claiming that contingent fees would link an accountant's fees to the results of his or her work, not to the hours worked, thereby potentially lowering the cost and raising the quality of accounting services. The FTC claimed that contingent fees were in restraint of trade. But what about the potential for conflicts of interest, the motivation for Rule 302? Since the conflict pertains largely to attest engagements, such as audits or reviews, the AICPA agreed to prohibit contingent fees for attestation services (a proposal made originally by the FTC in a 1988 consent order to the AICPA), and for original and amended tax returns filed for a refund. Note, though, that some states do not allow contingent fees under any circumstances.

The SEC's Auditor Independence Rules, discussed earlier under Rule 101, also include a "contingent fee" provision, although, apart from one issue, the provision is consistent with the AICPA's Rule 302. The one issue addresses a fee arrangement common among investment bankers and becoming more common among CPAs: value-added fees that bill based on the value a service adds for a client rather than the number of hours worked, the profession's traditional means for billing. The SEC's rule allows value-added fees, although, cognizant of potential abuses, the commission warns that SEC staff "will look closely to determine whether a fee labeled 'value added' is in fact an impermissible contingent fee."[17]

Responsibilities to Colleagues

Every practicing accountant owes to every other practicing accountant an express obligation to remain competent and to participate intellectually in the profession by contributing to professional organizations (such as AICPA and state societies)

---

17 SEC, *Revision of the Commission's Auditor Independence Requirements.* Washington, D.C.: U.S. Government Printing Office, November 21, 2000.

and by cooperating in the profession's self-regulation (for example, ethics enforcement, quality control, and quality review). Self-regulation also requires that a member testify as a fact witness in proceedings brought against another practitioner—for example, in a judicial proceeding or ethics division inquiry. In professional practice, an accountant is obligated to follow and, in the case of acting as a fact witness, to uphold the Code of Professional Conduct.

Although not an interpretation of the Rules of Conduct, *Statement on Auditing Standards No. 84,* "Communication Between Predecessor and Successor Auditors" (AU Sec. 315), addresses responsibilities to colleagues when a client changes auditors. The statement defines a **successor auditor** as one who has accepted an engagement or been invited to submit a proposal, and places the burden on the successor to initiate communication with the **predecessor auditor** (the auditor being replaced). The predecessor, however, must first obtain the client's permission before responding. Under Rule 301, introduced earlier, a predecessor auditor may not disclose confidential client information without a client's permission.

Clearly, a practicing accountant must be competitive to develop a viable client base, and a natural by-product of competition is that some members will gain new clients and others will lose clients. Shifts in client bases, however, are healthy for the profession, since competition creates incentives for accountants to produce their services more efficiently. But competition should not be so intense that the interests of the profession as a whole are undermined. Rather, accountants should be competitive in providing quality professional services, yet responsible to avoid unscrupulous means for attracting potential clients.

Prior to the 1990s, there were two Rules of Conduct on responsibilities to colleagues, but both were deleted by AICPA member vote.

Other Responsibilities and Practices

Rule 501 covers acts not covered specifically by other Rules of Conduct.

> ### Rule 501—Acts Discreditable
> A member shall not commit an act discreditable to the profession.

Although the term "discreditable" is not defined, three Interpretations of Rule 501 lend insight. Audit documents are the accountant's property and need not be surrendered to the client. However, in some instances accountants prepare documents that contain information not included or recorded within the client's books and records, such as listings of cash receipts/disbursements and depreciation schedules. For example, one Interpretation of Rule 501 recognizes that some documents actually constitute part of the client's records, and should therefore be made available to the client upon request, even if the client disputes the auditor's fee. Examples of documents considered part of a client's records include:

- Adjusting, closing, combining, and consolidating entries an auditor proposes,
- Information contained normally in journals and in general or subsidiary ledgers, and
- Tax and depreciation carry forward information.

Any documents an accountant develops that do not change a client's records, or are not in themselves part of the records a client ordinarily maintains, are not generally the client's property.

Other interpretations of Rule 501 contemplate violations that bear more literally on the language of the rule's title: acts discreditable. For example, one Interpretation provides that discrimination based on race, color, sex, age, or national origin in hiring, promotion, salary, or other employment practices constitutes an act discreditable to the profession that violates Rule 501. And another concludes that an accountant who solicits or knowingly discloses questions or solutions to CPA Examinations held on or after May 1996, the date the exam became undisclosed, commits an act discreditable that violates Rule 501.

Rule 502—Advertising and Other Forms of Solicitation

A member in public practice shall not seek to obtain clients by advertising or other forms of solicitation in a manner that is false, misleading, or deceptive. Solicitation by the use of coercion, overreaching, or harassing conduct is prohibited.

For over 50 years accountants were prohibited from advertising. However, in 1976, the Institute's professional ethics division became aware that state attorneys general, the Justice Department, and the FTC were beginning to advise several professional groups to repeal prohibitions against advertising. In 1977 the U.S. Supreme Court ruled 5 to 4 in *Bates v. State Bar of Arizona* (97 S. Ct. 2691) that the Arizona Bar, a state agency, could not deprive attorneys of their First Amendment (free speech) rights. In response, the AICPA put to member vote a proposal to modify the language of Rule 502, and members in 1988 voted overwhelmingly to adopt the current language of Rule 502.

Under Rule 502, false, misleading, or deceptive advertising is prohibited. For example, an Interpretation of Rule 502 identifies four instances of advertising that are deceptive and therefore not in the public interest: advertising that creates false expectations of favorable results; implies an ability to influence any court or regulatory body; states a service will be performed for a stated fee, estimated fee, or fee range likely to increase substantially; or makes any other representation that would likely cause a reasonable person to misunderstand or to be deceived.

Rule 503—Commissions and Referral Fees

A. *Prohibited Commissions.* A member in public practice shall not for a commission recommend or refer to a client any product or service, or for a commission recommend or refer any product or service to be supplied by a client, or receive a commission, when the member or the member's firm also performs for that client:
   (a) an audit or review of a financial statement; or
   (b) a compilation of a financial statement when the member expects, or reasonably might expect, that a third party will use the financial statement and the member's compilation does not disclose a lack of independence; or
   (c) an examination of prospective financial information.

This prohibition applies during the period in which the member is engaged to perform any of the services listed above and the period covered by any historical financial statements involved in such listed services.

B. *Disclosure of Permitted Commissions.* A member in public practice who is not prohibited by this rule from performing services for or receiving a commission and who is paid or expects to be paid a commission shall disclose that fact to any person or entity to whom the member recommends or refers a product or service to which the commission relates.

C. *Referral Fees.* Any member who accepts a referral fee for recommending or referring any service of a CPA to any person or entity or who pays a referral fee to obtain a client shall disclose such acceptance or payment to the client.

Owing to the potential for conflicts of interest, Rule 503 prohibits a member from receiving or paying commissions for referring services, or for recommending products, to clients for whom the member provides attestation services, such as financial statement audits or reviews. For example, if a practitioner recommends software to an audit client, the practitioner may not collect a commission either from the client for providing advice or from the software vendor for recommending the product. Rule 302 does not prohibit commissions or referral fees for products or services recommended to a nonattest client—for example, a commission paid by a software vendor to a practitioner who recommended software to his or her consulting client—although the practitioner must disclose the commission or fee to the client.

Prior to the 1990s, commissions and referral fees were prohibited for all clients, attest and nonattest. However, the FTC, in the same letter to the National Association of State Boards of Accountancy (NASBA) referred to earlier for contingent fees, criticized Rule 503's prohibition of commissions, arguing that permitting commissions would allow consumers an option for "one-stop financial shopping" and thereby encourage competition in the market for financial services. As with contingent fees, the AICPA agreed to prohibit commissions and referral fees for attest clients only. Note that, like contingent fees, some states do not allow commissions under any circumstances.

Occasionally, an accounting firm will advise a client that, although the firm has begun work on an engagement, the firm realizes now that, under the first general standard of the AICPA's generally accepted auditing standards, or the first and second attestation standards (Chapter 2), they are not proficient to complete the engagement. Typically, the firm would then refer a successor firm. Rule 503 does not prohibit either the successor firm or the client from paying the referring practitioner for work completed on the engagement to date. In addition, Rule 503 does not prohibit firms from compensating staff for practice development (that is, engaging new clients), since securing new clients does not by itself create a conflict of interest.

Rule 505—Form of Practice and Name

A member may practice public accounting only in the form of organization permitted by state law or regulation whose characteristics conform to resolutions of Council.

A member shall not practice public accounting under a firm name that is misleading. Names of one or more past partners or shareholders may be included in the firm name of a successor partnership or corporation.

A firm may not designate itself as "Members of the American Institute of Certified Public Accountants" unless all of its partners or shareholders are members of the Institute.

A firm of certified public accountants may organize in any form permitted by state law, which in all states includes sole proprietorship (that is, a self-employed CPA), partnership, professional corporation, and limited liability corporation.

In a *partnership*, each partner is jointly and severally liable for the partnership's debts, obligations, and wrongful acts and, under a legal concept known as "vicarious liability," each partner's personal assets are at risk regardless of the extent of their investment in the partnership or involvement in the debt, obligation, or act. A *professional corporation* represents a corporation in form, but a partnership in substance. Unlike traditional corporations, professional corporations do not provide relief from vicarious liability in some states; rather, each shareholder in the firm is jointly and severally liable in litigation brought against the firm in those states.

Prior to 1992, Rule 505 permitted only the proprietorship, partnership, or professional corporation forms of organization. But, responding to a litigation explosion in the 1980s (Chapter 5) and to the rights afforded other practicing professionals (among them, members of the American Bar Association and the American Medical Association), AICPA members voted resoundingly in 1991 to permit CPA firms to organize in any manner permitted by state law, including a **limited liability partnership (LLP)**, introduced briefly in Chapter 1. An LLP provides a CPA firm with the benefits of taxation as a partnership, thereby avoiding double taxation (that is, corporate taxes to the professional corporation and individual taxes to the shareholders), and with limited liability, thereby providing relief from vicarious liability. For example, an individual partner's liability extends to his or her investment in the firm, except that a litigant can make claims against a partner's personal assets for liability linked to his or her own actions. In short, LLPs limit to their investment in the firm the liability of partners or shareholders who are not themselves involved in a negligent act done in a firm's name. Some form of LLP is available in all states.

The name of a public accounting firm can indicate a specialization, provided that the firm name or specialization is not misleading. For example, the firm name, "Raymond Carver, CPA, Tax Specialist," is acceptable, but "O'Hara and Shaw, CPAs" is *un*acceptable if one of the two is not a CPA. In this context, Rule 505 is consistent with Rule 502 on advertising: Only firm names or specializations that are false, misleading, or deceptive are prohibited. Also, all firm partners or shareholders must be AICPA members in order for the firm to carry the designation "Members of the AICPA."

Monitoring Public Accounting Firms

The value of an audit or attestation report rests squarely on a practitioner's impartiality—his or her freedom from the influences that management or others may exert. But given that a practitioner's judgment processes and his or her work product—called *audit documentation*—are not matters of public record, how do we know that practitioners comply with auditing and attestation standards? Who audits the auditors?

Until 2003, much like medicine and law, the accounting profession was completely self-regulated through the AICPA's Quality Review Division in general, and through pronouncements of the Institute's Quality Review Executive Committee in particular. Today, however, the regulation of public accounting firms is achieved through three means:

- All firms — **Quality control**, the internal policies and procedures a firm designs to assure consistent performance and achievement across engagements
- Firms that audit public companies — PCAOB rules for inspections and AICPA Center for Public Company Audit Firms

- Firms that do not audit   AICPA peer review program
  public companies

In short, quality control is expected of all firms, but is monitored differently, depending on whether a firm audits public companies.

Quality control depends in turn on the quality of each of the firm's completed engagements: A whole is equal to the sum of its parts. Since auditing and attestation standards are the measures of quality in an audit or attestation engagement, it follows that the quality of a firm's practice is dependent on the application of standards to each engagement. Quality control is the vehicle public accounting firms use to assure that standards are followed on each engagement and, as a result, that the firm maintains a quality practice. Firms establish quality control policies to provide reasonable assurance that they comply with standards on each *individual engagement*, and compliance across engagements bears on the quality of a firm's *practice as a whole*.

Each public accounting firm is obligated to maintain a comprehensive and suitably designed quality control system, encompassing the firm's organizational structure and internal policies and procedures. The extent of a firm's system of quality control will depend on its size and organizational structure, the degree of operating autonomy vested in administrative personnel and practice offices, the nature of the practice, and the cost and expected benefits of the system. For example, a Big Four firm will have a far more extensive system than a single-office local firm. However, despite the extent of a firm's system, the firm should have policies and procedures that address each of the elements of quality control identified in Figure 4-6: independence, integrity, and objectivity; personnel management; client acceptance and continuance; engagement performance; and monitoring. For example, to operationalize these elements, a firm might require that all staff disclose audit clients in which they own securities, designate one senior professional to assign staff to engagements, outsource background checks of proposed clients' management, designate a consulting partner for each industry the firm serves, and assign an assessment director to document the firm's quality control compliance.

The PCAOB's rules for inspection and the AICPA's practice-monitoring program are introduced next.

The PCAOB's Rules for Inspecting Registered Firms

In 2003, under the authority of the *Sarbanes-Oxley Act*, Section 104, Inspections of Public Accounting Firms, the PCAOB, through Release 2003-019, "Inspection of Registered Public Accounting Firms," announced rules to inspect accounting firms registered to practice before the board. Inspections contemplate a thorough review of a firm's compliance with the *Sarbanes-Oxley Act*, with rules of the PCAOB, and with rules and regulations of the SEC. In general, the inspection process includes a review of documentation for audit and review engagements various offices of the firm completed, an evaluation of the firm's system of quality control, and tests of the quality control system the board thinks appropriate.

The board imposes two types of inspections:

- Regular inspections   Imposed annually on firms that, in the prior year, audited more than 100 public companies, and
- Special inspections   Imposed once in three years on firms that, during one of the three prior years, audited at least one but no more than 100 public companies.

FIGURE 4-6: *Elements and Examples of Quality Control Policies*

Independence, Integrity, and Objectivity
Establish policies to provide reasonable assurance that all staff are independent of attest clients to the extent required by the AICPA Code of Professional Conduct.

Example:
Require that all staff identify attest clients in which they own securities.

Personnel Management
Establish policies for hiring, advancement, assigning personnel to engagements, and professional development.

Example:
Designate a staff member to assign personnel to engagements. Base assignments on engagement needs and on staff career development.

Acceptance and Continuance of Clients
Establish policies to preclude accepting or continuing services for managements that lack integrity.

Example:
Outsource background checks for all proposed clients' management.

Engagement Performance
Establish policies for planning, performing, supervising, reviewing, documenting, and communicating the results of each engagement.

Example:
Assign staff to review planning memos, audit documents, and reports, and designate a consulting partner for each industry the firm serves.

Monitoring
Establish policies for monitoring compliance with the firm's quality control policies and procedures.

Example:
Assign an assessment director to document quality control compliance.

Section 104 makes clear that the PCAOB's threefold responsibility in an inspection, whether regular or special, is to inspect for violations of the *Act* and of rules of the PCAOB and the SEC; report violations to the SEC and to state regulatory agencies; and, in the case of a violation, either begin a further (and formal) investigation or impose disciplinary action.

The AICPA's Practice-Monitoring Program (Peer Review)

The AICPA in the 1970s established the profession's first **peer review** system, categorizing member firms into those that audited public companies (called at the time, SEC Practice Section firms) and those that did not (called the Private Companies Practice Section firms). However, with the advent of the PCAOB's rules for inspections, the system dissolved in 2003 and was replaced in 2004 with a practice-monitoring program that consists of two sections:

- Center for Public Company Audit Firms peer review program (called Center PRP), and
- AICPA peer review program (AICPA PRP).

Firms enrolled in the Center PRP are all those registered with, and inspected by, the PCAOB. Center PRP firms submit to a PCAOB inspection, not to an AICPA peer review. However, enrolled firms do submit to a review the Center conducts on segments of the firm's practice the PCAOB does not inspect, thereby allowing the firm to comply with state licensing and AICPA membership requirements.

In contrast, firms enrolled in the AICPA PRP submit to a peer review performed by another public accounting firm, by a state CPA society, by the AICPA, or by a regional association of firms. A peer review is an independent outside review of a firm's quality control performed by practitioners not otherwise employed by the firm reviewed. In general, a peer review team is charged to:

- Study and evaluate the firm's system of quality control,
- Examine the firm's compliance with its quality control procedures, and
- Examine the firm's documentation for quality control compliance.

Review teams report their findings to the reviewed firm. Deficiencies in quality control policies or in compliance with program requirements can result in fines, suspensions, expulsion from membership, or other actions against the reviewed firm. However, under *SAS No. 98*, "Omnibus SAS–2002," deficiencies in quality control, or instances of noncompliance, "do not, in and of themselves, indicate that a particular audit engagement was not performed in accordance with generally accepted auditing standards."

The AICPA's practice-monitoring program for participating firms is both educational and remedial, encouraging self-regulation and self-discipline within the profession by imposing practice requirements for all firms. In addition to establishing and maintaining a program of peer review for firms, the AICPA practice-monitoring programs are intended to improve the quality of each firm's services to clients by sanctioning practice requirements and disciplinary action.

Joint Ethics Enforcement

Three organizations enforce ethical conduct among CPAs: the AICPA, state societies of CPAs (both of which are voluntary membership organizations), and the state boards of accountancy (which are state regulatory agencies). The AICPA enforces the AICPA Code of Professional Conduct and state societies enforce state codes. After a timely investigation and a hearing (usually within 15 months), each organization can suspend or expel a violator and can publicize ethics violations. However, because the state boards of accountancy are empowered to regulate the practice of public accounting within their own states, and therefore can revoke a CPA's license to practice, state boards are the most powerful of the three organizations, since a CPA can practice regardless of membership in the AICPA or a state society but cannot practice without a license.

In practice, CPAs generally belong both to the AICPA and to a state society: two organizations, each with separate (but largely consistent) codes of conduct. How does the profession handle enforcement, given particularly that a violation of one code is likely a violation of the other and investigations of both would be largely redundant? To standardize enforcement and disciplinary proceedings across the states, the AICPA and virtually all of the state societies cooperate in a joint ethics enforcement program (JEEP) that permits a single investigation and, if warranted, a single settlement agreement or a Joint Trial Board hearing. However, the program doesn't *require* a single investigation. Rather, the AICPA's ethics division and state society ethics committees sometimes act independently and sometimes refer a case to the Joint Trial Board. For example, charges that involve more than one state, potential litigation, or profession-wide concerns are generally investigated by the AICPA's professional ethics division, and others are investigated by the state society ethics committee. Cases reach the Joint Trial Board if:

- Both the AICPA and the state society concur on their findings, yet do not issue a joint administrative reprimand, or
- Either the AICPA or the state society takes action individually.

Following a disciplinary hearing, the National Joint Trial Board may acquit, censure, suspend (up to two years), or expel a member, or issue a judgment requiring that the member participate in continuing professional education. Cases involving litigation are placed in a suspense file until the dispute is completed or settled. Although members have a right to a hearing, AICPA bylaws revoke a member's right in some well-specified instances. For example, the right to a hearing is revoked, and a CPA's membership suspended or terminated automatically, when he or she is convicted of a crime punishable by more than one year in prison, fails to file an income tax return, or willfully files for a client a false or fraudulent tax return.

SUMMARY

General ethics relate to ideal conduct, choice, and the consequences of choice and are the basis for codes of ethics in the professions. The AICPA Code of Professional Conduct consists of two sections, Principles and Rules of Conduct, and also includes Interpretations and Ethics Rulings. Six principles underlie the Code: responsibilities; the public interest; integrity; objectivity and independence; due care; and the scope and nature of services. The Rules of Conduct relate to independence, integrity, and objectivity; general and technical standards; responsibilities to clients and colleagues; and other responsibilities. Like Interpretations and Ethics Rulings, the Rules of Conduct are enforceable by the AICPA upon members. Interpretations are intended to interpret the scope and applicability of specific Rules of Conduct, and Ethics Rulings are intended to summarize the applicability of Rules and Interpretations to specific fact situations. Interpretations and Ethics Rulings are issued by the AICPA's professional ethics division.

Enforcement of the AICPA and individual state society codes had been relatively ineffective prior to the 1990s. As a result, the AICPA and the states developed a joint ethics enforcement system with the National Joint Trial Board. The system allows the AICPA and the state societies to act either independently or jointly to review complaints and to reprimand ethics violators although, under the *Sarbanes-Oxley Act*, auditors of public companies are inspected by the PCAOB. Today, the monitoring of public accounting firms is achieved by the PCAOB's rules for inspecting registered firms and by the AICPA's practice-monitoring program.

KEY TERMS

AICPA Code of Professional Conduct 123
Covered persons 130
Ethics Rulings 126
Interpretations of the Rules of Conduct 126
Limited liability partnership (LLP) 141
Peer (quality) review 143

Predecessor auditor 138
Principles of the Code of Professional Conduct 123
Quality control 141
Rules of Conduct 124
Successor auditor 138

REFERENCES

Public Company Accounting Oversight Board and SEC Releases:

PCAOB Release No. 2003-019, "Inspection of Registered Accounting Firms."

SEC, *Revision of the Commission's Auditor Independence Requirements*, Washington, D.C.: U.S. Government Printing Office, November 2000.

SEC, *Auditor Independence Rules*, Washington, D.C.: U.S. Government Printing Office, January 2003.

Professional Standards:

AICPA Professional Standards, Vol. 2. New York: AICPA.

SAS No. 50, "Reports on the Application of Accounting Principles" (AU Sec. 625).

SAS No. 69, "The Meaning of 'Present Fairly in Conformity with GAAP' in the Independent Auditor's Report" (AU Sec. 411).

SAS No. 84, "Communication Between Predecessor and Successor Auditors" (AU Sec. 315).

SAS No. 98, "Omnibus SAS–2002."

SQCS No. 2, "System of Quality Control for a CPA Firm's Accounting and Auditing Practice."

SQCS No. 3, "Monitoring a CPA Firm's Accounting and Auditing Practice."

Professional Reports:

President's Council on Integrity and Efficiency. *Study of Disciplinary Processes of State Boards of Accountancy*, 1988.

Public Oversight Board, "Auditor Independence," Chapter 5, *Panel on Audit Effectiveness: Report and Recommendations*. Stamford, CT: POB, 2000.

Public Oversight Board, *Annual Report 1999*. Stamford, CT: POB, 1999.

Articles, Books:

Allen, C. R., "AICPA Issues Nonattest Services Independence Rules," *Journal of Accountancy* (December 2003), pp. 81–83.

Duska, R. F., and B. S. Duska, *Accounting Ethics*. Malden, MA: Blackwell Publishing, 2003.

Jenkins, J. G., "A Declaration of Independence," *Journal of Accountancy* (May 1999), pp. 31–33.

Mautz, R. K., and H. A. Sharaf. *The Philosophy of Auditing*. Sarasota, FL: American Accounting Association, 1961.

McGrath, S., A. Siegel, T. W. Dunfee, A. S. Glazer, and H. R. Jaenicke, "A Framework for Auditor Independence," *Journal of Accountancy* (January 2001), pp. 39–42.

Morales, A. M., and E. D. Almer, "Independence and Public Perception: Why We Need to Care," *Journal of Accountancy* (April 2001), pp. 69–70.

Myers, R., "Ensuring Ethical Effectiveness," *Journal of Accountancy* (February 2003), pp. 28–33.

Velasquez, M., *Business Ethics: Concepts and Cases*, 5th. ed. Englewood Cliffs, NJ: Prentice Hall, 2002.

QUESTIONS

1. What are general ethics, and how do they relate to professional ethics?
2. Explain five means of ethical reasoning.
3. Identify and briefly describe the four components of the AICPA Code of Professional Conduct.
4. Relate the Principles of Professional Conduct, ideal conduct, and trust. Be specific.
5. Discuss the applicability of the AICPA Rules of Conduct.
6. Identify at least four examples of situations in which an AICPA member would not be deemed independent.
7. May an AICPA member serve as an attorney for an audit client? Explain.
8. What is the purpose of the general and technical standards of the AICPA Code of Professional Conduct?
9. Does Rule 301, "Confidential Client Information," preclude AICPA members who serve on AICPA ethics division subcommittees and members of state society ethics committees from exchanging confidential client information that is central to an ethics investigation? Explain.
10. Who should initiate communication between predecessor and successor auditors when there is a change in auditors? Explain. What impact does Rule 301, "Confidential Client Information," have on communication between predecessor and successor auditors?
11. Rule 502, "Advertising and Other Forms of Solicitation," precludes a member from advertising in a manner that is false, misleading, or deceptive. What is meant by "false, misleading, or deceptive" advertising?
12. When referring a client to another CPA, can an AICPA member accept a referral fee from the CPA if (a) the amount is clearly immaterial, and (b) it merely covers the AICPA member's costs (that is, time and expenses) of referring? Explain.
13. What is peer review?
14. Briefly explain the AICPA's quality review program for public accounting firms.
15. Explain how quality control, attestation standards, and generally accepted auditing standards are related.
16. Who monitors firms that audit public companies?
17. What is the Public Company Accounting Oversight Board's responsibility in an inspection of a registered public accounting firm?
18. What is a review team's responsibility in a peer review?
19. Explain the AICPA's practice-monitoring programs.
20. What is the joint ethics enforcement program?

MULTIPLE CHOICE QUESTIONS

1. General ethics is the study of:
   a. Ideal method in thought.
   b. Ultimate reality.
   c. Ideal conduct.
   d. Ideal social organization.

2. An individual who guides a decision by asking "how will this reflect on me?" is behaving consistent with which of the following means of ethical reasoning?
   a. Self-interest.
   b. Consequence.
   c. Duty.
   d. Character.

3. Professional codes of ethics:

    a. Are uncommon in professions other than public accounting.
    b. Mandate ideal standards of behavior.
    c. Are enforceable if based in standards of ideal behavior.
    d. Mandate minimum standards of behavior.

4. The Principles of the Code of Professional Conduct:

    a. Promulgate ethics rules for the practice of public accounting.
    b. Are monitored by the PCAOB.
    c. Are not enforceable on AICPA members.
    d. Require that a firm document quality control compliance.

5. Interpretations of the Rules of Conduct:

    a. Reply to fact situations practitioners submit.
    b. Can be rescinded by any 30 members of AICPA Council.
    c. Interpret the Principles of the Code of Professional Conduct.
    d. Are enforceable.

6. The SEC's auditor-independence rules:

    a. Mirror the *Sarbanes-Oxley Act*.
    b. Restrict accountants from performing tax services for public company audit clients.
    c. Relate to nonaudit services only.
    d. Apply to the audit of public and nonpublic companies.

7. A practitioner can perform accounting and auditing services for a privately owned client assuming that:

    a. The practitioner takes responsibility for management's assertions.
    b. The practitioner has a financial interest in management's assertions.
    c. The practitioner is independent of assertions about management's information system.
    d. The practitioner is certain the conflict of interest is immaterial to the firm and to the client.

8. According to the profession's Rules of Conduct, an auditor would be considered independent in which of the following instances?

    a. The auditor's checking account is held at a client financial institution.
    b. The auditor, an attorney, serves as the client's general counsel.
    c. An employee of the auditor serves as the unpaid treasurer of a charitable organization that is an audit client.
    d. The client owes the auditor fees for two consecutive years.

    (AICPA Adapted)

9. The Rules of Conduct would most likely be violated if an auditor:

    a. Owns a building and leases floor space to an attestation client.
    b. Has an insured account with a brokerage firm audit client.
    c. Is engaged by an audit client to identify potential acquisitions.
    d. Screens candidates for an audit client's vacant controllership.

    (AICPA Adapted)

10. Objectivity refers to a practitioner's ability to:

    a. Remain impartial.
    b. Identify assertions that are appropriate.

   c. Be unyielding in all disputes.

   d. Choose independently between accounting principles and auditing standards.

11. Absent a client's consent, a practitioner is precluded from disclosing confidential client information to:

   a. The National Joint Trial Board.

   b. A state board of accountancy.

   c. The board of directors of an audit client's investee.

   d. An AICPA ethics committee.

12. Which of the following fee arrangements would violate the AICPA Code of Professional Conduct?

   a. A fee based on the approval of a bank loan.

   b. A fee based on the outcome of a bankruptcy proceeding.

   c. A per-hour fee that includes out-of-pocket expenses.

   d. A fee based on the complexity of the engagement.

13. Which of the following would an auditor *not* be required to make available to a client?

   a. Entries that eliminate profit on intercompany sales

   b. A document that replicates the cash disbursements journal

   c. A spreadsheet that summarizes detailed staff billing records

   d. A schedule documenting interperiod income tax allocation

14. Which of the following published in a promotional brochure would likely violate the AICPA Rules of Conduct?

   a. Names and addresses, telephone numbers, numbers of partners, office hours, foreign language competence, and date the firm was established

   b. Services offered and fees for such services, including hourly rates and fixed fees

   c. Educational and professional attainments, including date and place of certification, schools attended, dates of graduation, degrees received, and memberships in professional associations

   d. Names, addresses, and telephone numbers of the firm's clients, including the number of years served   (AICPA Adapted)

15. Which of the following acts by a CPA who is not in public practice would most likely be considered a violation of the profession's Code of Professional Conduct?

   a. Using the designation "CPA" on a report accompanying financial statements intended for external use without disclosing that the CPA is employed by the company issuing the statements

   b. Distributing business cards indicating "CPA" and the CPA's title and employer

   c. Corresponding on the CPA's employer's letterhead, which contains the CPA's designation and employment status

   d. Compiling the CPA's employer's financial statements and making reference to the CPA's lack of independence

16. Quality control policies for the acceptance and continuance of clients are established to:

   a. Enable the auditor to report on management's integrity.

   b. Comply with standards established by regulatory bodies.

   c. Minimize the likelihood of associating with managements that lack integrity.

   d. Reduce exposure to litigation from failing to detect fraud.

         (AICPA Adapted)

17. Accounting firms that audit more than 100 public companies in any given year are subject the next year to:

    a. Regular inspection.
    b. Special inspection.
    c. A Center for Public Companies peer review.
    d. An AICPA peer review.

18. Under the *Sarbanes-Oxley Act*, the PCAOB is responsible to:

    a. Inspect for violations of PCAOB rules.
    b. Monitor compliance with generally accepted auditing standards.
    c. Expel violators of the *Act* from the AICPA.
    d. Oversee the AICPA's practice-monitoring programs.

19. Which of the following is not a responsibility of a peer review team?

    a. Study and evaluate the firm's system of quality control.
    b. Examine the firm's compliance with its quality control procedures.
    c. Examine compliance with PCAOB's rules for inspections.
    d. Examine the firm's documentation for quality control compliance.

20. Which of the following organizations have a responsibility in the enforcement of ethical behavior by accountants?

    a. The SEC and the PCAOB
    b. The PCAOB and the AICPA
    c. The AICPA and the Joint Trial Board
    d. The Joint Trial Board and the SEC

PROBLEMS AND DISCUSSION CASES

4-1 *Means of Ethical Reasoning*

In a foreshadowing one of the issues that would come to bear on the *Sarbanes-Oxley Act*, the Panel on Audit Effectiveness, a special panel created by the now disbanded Public Oversight Board, made this statement in 2000:

The growth in equity values over the past decade has introduced extreme pressures on management to achieve earnings, revenue, or other targets. These pressures are exacerbated by the unforgiving nature of the equity markets as securities valuations are drastically adjusted downward whenever companies fail to meet 'street' expectations. Pressures are further magnified because management's compensation often is based in large part on achieving earnings or other financial goals of stock-price increases. These pressures on management, in turn, translate into pressures on how auditors conduct audits and in their relationship with audit clients (Public Oversight Board, "Auditor Independence," Chapter 5, *Panel on Audit Effectiveness: Report and Recommendations*. Stamford, CT: POB, 2000, pp. 2–3.)

Required: Imagine yourself as a partner in a public accounting firm confronted with a chief executive officer and a chief financial officer bent on meeting analysts' consensus earnings expectations and on achieving incentive-compensation thresholds that are tied to earnings. Although many auditors faced with the same pressures have not been complicit, the press reports that a number of auditors have. Evaluate this situation using each one of three means of ethical reasoning: self-interest, consequence, and duty.

4-2 *Rationale for Code of Professional Conduct*

In the 1980s, the financial press raised the public consciousness by publicizing a series of audit failures and financial failures, most notably in the banking and government securities industries. The profession responded in 1988 with a new Code of Professional Conduct that captured the expanding scope of assurance services and imposed on practitioners a rigorous code for professional behavior.

Required: Discuss why the profession requires a code of professional conduct. Why have a code at all?

4-3 *The SEC's Auditor Independence Rules*

Like the AICPA, the SEC has issued auditor independence rules that address a broad range of issues. Consider each of the following situations, all of which relate to Summit Holdings, Inc., a publicly traded financial institution audited by the Boston, Massachusetts, office of Hastings & Ford LLP, a firm with principal offices in Baltimore, Boston, New York, Philadelphia, and Providence.

a. An audit partner in Providence, Rhode Island, owns 1,000 shares of Summit class A common stock. Six years ago, while an audit senior, the partner observed Summit investments held in a Rhode Island bank and charged 40 hours to the audit engagement.

b. The spouse of a manager assigned to the Summit engagement holds 100 shares of Summit class A common stock in an investment portfolio contained in a trust that includes controlling interests in two Fortune 1000 companies.

c. A Boston office audit senior unassigned to the Summit engagement owns Summit preferred stock.

d. The lead engagement partner's spouse is employed as an accounting clerk responsible to perform monthly bank reconciliations for both the general and payroll accounts maintained by each of the company's nine branch offices.

e. A former partner in Hastings & Ford's Baltimore office, now Summit's controller, receives from the firm a monthly retirement benefit tied to the partner's capital account on the date of retirement and to the consumer price index.

f. An audit partner in the Boston office purchases stock tracking software and periodic updates from Summit.

g. In a cost-cutting move, Summit management proposes to eliminate a number of accounting personnel and to have Hastings & Ford design and maintain the company's financial information system.

h. Summit management proposes that Hastings & Ford interview, and advise the company about the competence of, applicants for a new financial position, assistant controller, who will report to the controller and be responsible for maintaining general ledger control accounts.

Required: Discuss whether, in your judgment, each situation raises an independence issue.

4-4 *The AICPA's Code of Professional Conduct*

The AICPA's Code of Professional Conduct provides members with principles and rules about their responsibilities to the public, to clients, and to their colleagues in practice. The Code applies to all AICPA members, including those in public practice, industry, government, and education. Consider each of the following situations, all of which relate to the audit of, and preparation of tax returns for, Tillinghast, Inc., a privately owned manufacturer audited by the Portland, Oregon, office of Baker & Kilmartin LLP, a firm with principal offices in Boise, Portland, and Seattle.

a. Tillinghast plans a deduction under Internal Revenue Code Section 162 for expenses related to forgiving a $100,000 loan to the company's chief executive officer, who holds 10,000 shares of Tillinghast class A common stock. The lead engagement partner believes that the expenses should be treated as a dividend. Management believes that the expenses are immaterial to the financial statements, which report $4.5 million in total assets and $5 million in total sales.

b. Although the lead engagement partner relies on FASB *Technical Bulletin No. 79-4* to include Tillinghast's Puerto Rican subsidiary's losses within domestic operations, management produces an article in an accounting handbook to argue that the subsidiary is foreign and, therefore, that the losses can be excluded from domestic operations when the company reports domestic earnings.

c. Baker & Kilmartin is contemplating a merger with Blass Ecton LLP, a larger West Coast firm that, as part of the negotiations, will review the permanent files, tax files, and audit documentation for Baker & Kilmartin's largest clients, among them Tillinghast, which is developing new product technologies documented in the permanent file. Upon learning about the merger, Tillinghast management comments that, although Baker & Kilmartin, the incumbent audit firm, is precluded from disclosing confidential information, Blass Ecton is not.

d. Rather than go public, Tillinghast management plans to seek either a publicly traded acquirer or, failing that, a private placement of debt management plans for expansion. Tillinghast's chief executive and chief financial officers propose that Baker & Kilmartin participate in Tillinghast's due diligence work for the acquisition and that the firm's audit fees be based in part on a negotiated amount and in part on whether an acquisition occurs.

e. A tax partner has withheld the completed tax return of a board member and major shareholder who refuses to pay the partner's bill.

Required: Discuss whether, in your judgment, each situation raises issues relevant to the AICPA's Code of Professional Conduct.

4-5 *Violations of Rule 101, Independence?*

Practitioners repeatedly face situations that call for an immediate response: Is this a violation of the Code of Professional Conduct? The following situations, all related to independence, are posed to a member of the AICPA.

a. A practitioner is performing an attestation service for a privately owned corporation that includes the practitioner's cousin as a minority shareholder.

b. A commercial bank in which a practitioner carries two automobile loans has approached the practitioner to perform a financial statement audit.

c. A privately owned company that has outsourced its information processing system to a public accounting firm approaches the firm for a financial statement review engagement.

d. Although unrelated to the audit, an audit client has initiated litigation against a public accounting firm that is immaterial to the firm but material to the client's financial statements.

e. A practitioner has been engaged to compile the financial statements of a company owned partly by his children.

Required: Discuss whether, in your judgment, each situation violates Rule 101 of the Code of Professional Conduct or whether the situation is inconclusive.

4-6 *Independence*

An auditor must not only be independent in fact, but also must appear independent in fact.

Required:
1. Explain the concept of "independence" as it applies to third-party reliance on management's assertions.
2. a. What determines whether a practitioner is independent in fact?
   b. What determines whether a practitioner appears to be independent?
3. Explain how a practitioner may be independent in fact but not appear to be independent.

4. Would a practitioner be considered independent for an audit of the financial statements of a:
   a. Church for which he or she is serving as treasurer without compensation? Explain.
   b. Civic club for which the auditor's spouse is serving as treasurer-bookkeeper and the practitioner does not receive a fee for the audit? Explain.

   (AICPA Adapted)

4-7 *Independence*

The attribute of independence traditionally has been associated with the CPA's function of auditing and expressing opinions on financial statements.

Required:
1. What is meant by "independence" as applied to the CPA's function of auditing and expressing opinions on financial statements? Explain.
2. CPAs have imposed upon themselves certain rules of professional conduct that induce their members to remain independent and to strengthen public confidence in their independence. Which of the rules of professional conduct are concerned with the CPA's independence? Explain.
3. The Wallydrag Company is indebted to a CPA for unpaid fees and has offered to issue to the CPA unsecured interest-bearing notes. Would acceptance of these notes have any bearing upon the CPA's independence from the Wallydrag Company? Discuss.
4. The Rocky Hill Corporation was formed on October 1, 2005, and its fiscal year will end on September 30, 2006. A CPA has audited, and issued an unqualified opinion on, the corporation's opening balance sheet. A month after submitting the report, the CPA is offered the position of secretary of Rocky Hill because of the need for a complete set of officers and for convenience in signing various documents. The CPA will have no financial interest in the company through stock ownership or otherwise, will receive no salary, will not keep the books, and will have no influence on its financial matters other than occasional advice on income tax matters and similar advice normally given a client by the CPA.
   a. Assume that the CPA accepts the offer but plans to resign the position before beginning the annual audit and to again assume the office after issuing an opinion on the statements. Is the CPA independent? Discuss.
   b. Assume that the CPA accepts the offer on a temporary basis until the corporation has gotten under way and can employ a secretary, but in any event would permanently resign the position before conducting the annual audit. Is the CPA independent? Discuss.

   (AICPA Adapted)

4-8 *Rule 101 Independence*

Ruth Shafer, CPA, is auditing the financial statements of Nelson Company. Her son, age 16, owns 100 shares of the 50,000 shares of Nelson Company common stock outstanding at the balance sheet date.

Required: Discuss the effect, if any, the son's stock ownership would have on the auditor's opinion.

4-9 *Independence and Consulting*

Your audit client, Nuesel Corporation, a private company, requests that you conduct a feasibility study to advise management of the best way for the corporation to utilize computer equipment and which computer, if any, best meets the corporation's needs. You are technically competent in this area and accept the engagement. Upon completion of your study, the corporation accepts your suggestions and installs the computer and related equipment that you recommended.

Required:
1. Discuss the effect that accepting this management services engagement would have on your independence in expressing an opinion on the financial statements of the Nuesel Corporation.
2. Data Print, Inc., a local printer of data processing forms, customarily offers a commission for recommending Data Print as a supplier. The client is aware of, and suggests you accept, the commission. Would accepting the commission with the client's approval be proper? Discuss.   (AICPA Adapted)

4-10 *Independence and a Retired Audit Partner*

Benjamin Leon, a retired partner of your public accounting firm, has just been appointed to the board of directors of Palmer Corporation, a private company your firm audits. Leon is also a member of your firm's income tax committee, which meets monthly to discuss income tax problems of the partnership's clients. The partnership pays Leon $500 for each committee meeting he attends and a monthly retirement benefit of $10,000.

Required: Discuss the effect of Leon's appointment to the board of directors of Palmer Corporation on your firm's independence in expressing an opinion on the Palmer Corporation's financial statements.   (AICPA Adapted)

4-11 *Independence and Nonaudit Services*

Audrey Campbell, CPA, has audited the financial statements of the Grimm Company for several years. Grimm's president has now asked Campbell to install an inventory control system for the company.

Required: Discuss the factors that Campbell should consider in determining whether to accept this engagement.   (AICPA Adapted)

4-12 *Competence to Perform Professional Services*

Charles Adams, CPA, has practiced public accounting for several years but feels uncomfortable with computers. As a result, he contemplates hiring an additional professional staff member who specializes in systems analysis and computers.

Required: Must Adams be personally able to perform all of the services that the specialist can perform in order to supervise the new hire? Explain.

4-13 *Compliance with Standards*

Paulette Martin, CPA, has been approached by a staff associate about the applicability of the AICPA Rules of Conduct to unaudited financial statements. The associate notes that Rule 202, "Compliance with Standards," does not permit an AICPA member's name to be associated with financial statements in a manner that would imply the member is acting as an independent public accountant unless he or she has complied with the applicable standards. The associate then asks: "Since generally accepted auditing standards appear to relate to audited and not to unaudited financial statements, does Rule 202 effectively prohibit an AICPA member from being associated with unaudited financial statements?"

Required: Is the assistant's interpretation of Rule 202 correct? Explain.

4-14 *Internal Use Statements*

Donald Bowie, CPA, is the assistant controller for Aberdeen Industries, a highly diversified conglomerate operating in the United States and abroad. Bowie has been asked by Aberdeen's corporate controller to perform audits and to express an opinion on several of Aberdeen's more significant holdings. The opinions are for distribution to, and use by, Aberdeen's officials only.

Required: Is Bowie in violation of the AICPA Code of Professional Conduct if he conducts the audits and issues an internal use opinion? Explain.

4-15 *Confidential Client Information*

Doris Sweeny, CPA, is engaged by the local municipal government to conduct periodic personal property tax audits of companies operating within the municipality. The property tax relates to business inventories, equipment, and machinery; thus Sweeny will examine accounts and records related to sales, purchases, and gross profit percentages, among other things.

Ashton Manufacturing Company, a local producer of tool and die equipment, resents the fact that Sweeny is conducting the property tax audits because she also provides audit services to several competing tool and die manufacturing companies. Ashton fears that Sweeny, while conducting the property tax audit, may encounter trade secrets beneficial to some of her audit clients. As a result, Ashton approaches the ethics division of the AICPA arguing that it is unethical for Sweeny to conduct its property tax audit.

Required: Does Sweeny violate the AICPA Code of Professional Conduct by conducting a property tax audit of Ashton, a tool and die equipment manufacturer, and by providing audit services to competing companies within the same industry? Explain.

4-16 *Confidential Client Information*

Judy Hanlon, CPA, is engaged to prepare the federal income tax return for Guild Corporation for the year ended December 31, 2005, Hanlon's first engagement of any kind for Guild Corporation. In preparing the 2007 return, Hanlon finds an error on the 2006 return: Accumulated depreciation brought forward from 2005 to 2006 was understated and, therefore, the 2005 base for declining balance depreciation was overstated, causing the 2006 depreciation to be overstated significantly.

Hanlon reports the error to Guild's controller, the officer responsible for tax returns. The controller says: "Let the revenue agent find the error," and further instructs Hanlon to carry forward the material overstatement of the depreciable base to the 2007 depreciation computation. The controller notes that this error also had been made in the financial records for 2006 and 2007 and offers to furnish Hanlon with a letter assuming full responsibility for this treatment.

Required:
1. Evaluate Hanlon's action in this situation.
2. Discuss the additional action that Hanlon should now undertake.

(AICPA Adapted)

4-17 *Contingent Fees*

Certified public accountants often serve as expert witnesses in damage suits involving accounting and auditing matters. For example, accountants acting as expert witnesses could be asked to testify about appropriate auditing procedures or applicable accounting principles in given nonroutine circumstances.

Required: When acting as an expert witness in a damage suit, may a CPA receive compensation based on the amount awarded a plaintiff?

4-18 *Advertising*

Each of the following situations relates to Rule 502, "Advertising and Other Forms of Solicitation":
a. A trade association engages a CPA to analyze specific problems affecting members of the association. The results of the CPA's analysis will bear the CPA's name, be reproduced by the association, and be distributed to association members.

Required: Does Rule 502 prohibit distribution of results of the CPA's analysis? Explain.

b. A CPA is engaged by the local chapter of a national accounting association to conduct a continuing education course for its members. The CPA is identified in promotional material distributed by the association.

Required: What responsibility does the CPA have for information included within the promotional material? Explain.

c. A CPA is retained by a stock brokerage client to prepare a booklet on the tax aspects of security transactions. The client bears all printing costs and compensates the CPA for time expended on the project. A legend on the cover of the booklet states that it was prepared by the CPA. Booklets are mailed to the brokerage client's customers with end-of-month statements.

Required: Is there any objection to this practice? Explain.

4-19 *Form of Practice and Name*

Several CPAs within the firm of Harding & Co. specialize in professional services related to client acquisitions and mergers. The policy committee of Harding & Co. decides to form a separate partnership to perform acquisition and merger services. Harding & Co. believes that the separate partnership can indicate a specialization on its business stationery because the acquisition and merger partnership will not practice public accounting, per se.

Required: May the separate partnership indicate a specialization on business stationery? Explain.

4-20 *Commissions*

A CPA in public practice wishes to be a representative of a computer company that services tax practitioners. The CPA will utilize contacts with professional tax practitioners to introduce and promote use of the service. The CPA will receive a fee from the computer tax service for each tax return processed for a practitioner who was referred by the CPA.

Required: Does this arrangement violate Rule 503, "Commissions"? Explain.

4-21 *Nonaudit Services*

Tom Jencks, CPA, conducts a public accounting practice. This year, Jencks and Raymond Curtis, a non-CPA, organized Electro-Data Corporation to specialize in computerized bookkeeping services. Jencks and Curtis each supplied 50 percent of Electro-Data's capital, and each holds 50 percent of the capital stock. Curtis is the salaried general manager of Electro-Data. Jencks is affiliated with the corporation only as a stockholder; he receives no salary and does not participate in day-to-day management. However, he has transferred all of his bookkeeping accounts to the corporation and recommends its services whenever possible.

Required: Organizing your presentation around Jencks' involvement with Electro-Data Corporation, discuss the propriety of a CPA's:
1. Participation in an enterprise offering computerized bookkeeping services.
2. Transfer of bookkeeping accounts to a service company.
3. Recommendation of a particular bookkeeping service company.

(AICPA Adapted)

4-22 *Elected Office*

A CPA in public practice is considering running for the elected office of state controller. Principal functions of the state controller include maintaining control over all state fund accounts, administering disbursements, and allocating revenue among county and local governments. The CPA intends to continue practicing public accounting if elected.

Required: Can the CPA practice public accounting and serve as state controller? Explain.

4-23 *Form of Practice and Name*

Your CPA firm decides to form a partnership with Faye Reitz, a non-CPA management consultant, which would result in a "mixed partnership" of a CPA and a non-CPA.

Required: Under what circumstances, if any, would it be ethically proper for a CPA to form a mixed partnership? Discuss. (AICPA Adapted)

4-24 *Form of Practice and Name*

Although not partners, two CPAs share an office, maintain joint bank accounts, and work together on each other's engagements. As a result, they decide to have a joint letterhead showing both names, their address, and the designation "Certified Public Accountants."

Required: Is the joint letterhead (including the address and the designation "Certified Public Accountants") proper? Explain.

4-25 *Dual Professional Services*

Frank Gilbert and Gloria Aponte formed a corporation called Financial Services, Inc., each taking 50 percent of the authorized common stock. Gilbert is a CPA and a member of the American Institute of CPAs; Aponte is a CPCU (Chartered Property Casualty Underwriter). The corporation performs auditing and tax services under Gilbert's direction and insurance services under Aponte's supervision. The opening of the corporation's office was announced by a three-inch, two-column "card" in the local newspaper.

One of the corporation's first audit clients was Grandtime Company. Grandtime had total assets of $600,000 and total liabilities of $270,000. In the course of his audit, Gilbert found that Grandtime's building with a book value of $240,000 was pledged as security for a 10-year note in the amount of $200,000. The client's statements did not mention that the building was pledged as security for the note. However, since the failure to disclose the lien did not affect either the value of the assets or the amount of the liabilities, and since his audit was satisfactory in all other respects, Gilbert issued an unqualified opinion on Grandtime's financial statements. About two months after the date of his opinion, Gilbert learned that an insurance company was planning to loan Grandtime $150,000 in the form of a first-mortgage note on the building. Realizing that the insurance company was unaware of the existing lien on the building, Gilbert had Aponte notify the insurance company of the fact that Grandtime's building was pledged as security for the note. Shortly after these events took place, Gilbert was charged with a violation of professional ethics.

Required: Identify and discuss the ethical implications of those acts by Gilbert that were in violation of the AICPA Code of Professional Conduct.

(AICPA Adapted)

4-26 *Accepting an Engagement*

Lakeview Development Corporation was formed on January 2, 2005, to develop a vacation-recreation area on land purchased the same day by the corporation for $100,000. The corporation also purchased for $40,000 an adjacent tract of land that the corporation plans to subdivide into 50 building lots. When the area is developed, the lots are expected to sell for $10,000 each.

The corporation borrowed a substantial portion of its funds from a bank and gave a mortgage on the land. A mortgage covenant requires that the corporation furnish quarterly financial statements.

The quarterly financial statements prepared at March 31 and June 30 by the corporation's bookkeeper were unacceptable to the bank officials. The corporation's president now offers you the engagement of preparing unaudited quarterly financial statements. Because of limited funds, your fee would be paid in Lakeview Development Corporation common stock rather than in cash. The stock would be repurchased by the corporation when funds become available. You would not receive enough stock to be a major stockholder.

Required:

1. Discuss the ethical implications of accepting the engagement and the reporting requirements that are applicable if you should accept the engagement.
2. Assume that you accept the engagement to prepare the September 30, 2005, statements. What disclosures, if any, would you make of your prospective ownership of corporation stock in the quarterly financial statements?
3. The president insists that you present the 50 building lots at their expected sale price of $500,000 in the September 30 unaudited statements as was done in prior statements. The write-up was credited to Contributed Capital. How would you respond to the president's request?
4. The corporation elected to close its fiscal year September 30 and you are requested to prepare the corporation's federal income tax return. Discuss the implication of signing the return and the disclosure of your stock ownership in Lakeview Corporation (disregard the write-up of the land).
5. Assume that you accept the engagement to prepare the tax return. In the course of collecting information for the preparation of the return you find that the corporation's president paid the entire cost of a family vacation from corporate funds and listed the expense as travel and entertainment. You ascertain that the corporation's board of directors would not consider the cost of the vacation as either additional compensation or a gift to the president if the facts were known. What disclosure would you make in (a) the tax return and (b) the financial statements?
6. After accepting your unaudited September 30 financial statements, the bank notified the corporation that the December 31 financial statements must be accompanied by a CPA's opinion. You were asked to conduct the audit and told that your fee would be paid in cash. Discuss the ethical implications of accepting the engagement.

(AICPA Adapted)

4-27 *Quality Control*

In response to the AICPA's practice-monitoring program for individual public accounting firms, many firms have drafted quality control documents that describe policies and procedures designed to provide reasonable assurance that the firm is complying with attestation standards and generally accepted auditing standards on all engagements. Following is a selected list of policies and procedures taken from a public accounting firm's quality control document.

a. As a participant in the AICPA peer review program, the firm is subject to and cooperates in peer reviews. The firm's Audit Monitoring Committee is responsible for scheduling periodic audit documentation reviews for completed engagements and for ensuring that all professional personnel are made aware of the knowledge gained by the reviews.
b. The firm is not to express an opinion in an attestation or audit engagement if professional staff serve as executor, trustee, officer, or director of the organization. Other appointments to these positions in either client or nonclient organizations must be in agreement with the AICPA Code of Professional Conduct.
c. Situations occur or questions arise that require certain technical accounting or auditing knowledge, or specialized industry knowledge that may not exist within the engagement team. In these cases, the engagement partner or others associated with the engagement shall consult with the Partner for Technical Services or other designated personnel to obtain the assistance needed or to otherwise resolve the issue.
d. The following factors are considered by the Scheduling Partner in achieving a balance of the personnel elements of the engagement: staffing requirements, personnel skills, individual development, and staff utilization during the job.
e. At the annual partners meeting, the Administrative Partner assures that no partner has any loan from a client other than those specifically permitted by professional ethics.

f. On each engagement, adequate review is to be performed at all organizational levels, as appropriate, considering the training, ability, and experience of the personnel assigned and the complexity of the engagement.

g. Each year, all professional staff are responsible for developing a personal plan that includes goals for participating in on-the-job training through challenging and diversified assignments, formal programs prepared and conducted by the firm and by professional organizations, individual development through self-study and other activities, and participation in and service to professional, community, and public and/or private organizations and activities.

h. The personal attributes sought in entry-level professional staff include but are not limited to the following: motivation, professional potential, language skills, demonstrated involvement, and leadership.

i. Personnel are periodically evaluated and are advised formally of their progress. Staff personnel files are maintained for each professional staff member and contain written evaluations of performance.

j. The reputation of a company's directors, officers, and principal shareholders or owners is of great importance. The firm seeks to minimize the likelihood of associating with a client whose management lacks integrity and a fair degree of stability over time. In addition, the nature of the business, its sources of financing and financial need, its internal controls, and the purpose for and nature of the audit or attestation engagement are all considerations in evaluating the relative risk of our professional liability in serving the company.

Required:
1. Explain the relationship between quality control and peer review for a public accounting firm.
2. For each of the policies and procedures listed, indicate the element of quality control the firm addressed.

Internet problems and discussion cases are available at http://ricchiute.swlearning.com

RESEARCH PROJECTS

1. Ethics and the SEC's Accounting and Auditing Enforcement Releases

SEC Accounting and Auditing Enforcement Releases often go to issues that relate to the ethical behavior of accountants and auditors. For example, a recent release reads in part as follows:

Partner of accounting firm engaged in improper professional conduct in recklessly failing (1) to plan and supervise two annual audits of an investment company; (2) to maintain an appropriate attitude of professional skepticism regarding management representations; and (3) to obtain sufficient competent evidential matter to support statements in the auditors' reports for the two annual audits.

The excerpt points to several violations of the AICPA's Code of Professional Conduct. For example, the failure to plan and supervise the audit violates Rule 202, Compliance with Standards, and the failure to maintain an attitude of professional skepticism, violates Rule 102, Integrity and Objectivity.

Required: Select an SEC Accounting and Auditing Enforcement Release (**http://www.sec.gov**) and draft a report that maps the SEC's conclusions to the rules within the AICPA Code of Professional Conduct and the SEC's Auditor Independence Rules.

2. Unethical Business Practices

The financial press often reports business practices that raise ethical issues. For example, consider a single issue confronting all major oil and gas exploration companies: Although double-hull oil tankers are less likely to spill crude oil in transit, single-hull tankers are far less costly. Interestingly, this issue affects several interested stakeholders (for example, wildlife, shareholders), raises questions of alternative courses of action (for example, accruals for environmental liabilities), and poses considerable practical constraints to the stakeholders (for example, cost of double hulls versus benefits of preserving environment).

Required: Select an article or series of articles from the recent press (such as *Business Week*, *The Wall Street Journal*, *The New York Times*) about a business problem you think raises ethical issues and draft a report that addresses:

1. Each of the following questions (developed in M. Velasquez, *Business Ethics: Concepts and Cases*, 5th. ed. Englewood Cliffs, NJ: Prentice Hall, 2002).
   - What are the relevant facts?
   - What are the ethical issues?
   - Who are the primary stakeholders?
   - What are the possible alternatives?
   - What are the ethics of the alternatives?
   - What are the practical constraints?
   - What actions should be taken?
2. Each of the following means of ethical reasoning (Figure 4-1):
   - Opinion
   - Self-interest
   - Consequence
   - Duty
   - Character

3. Something's Wrong, Something's Amiss

Ethical issues are faced in all professions, including those for which there is a presumption that ethics drives the profession, such as the financial aid professionals in colleges and universities. For example, to attract students to less popular majors, the financial aid office of a prominent East Coast university, one long-distinguished by a number of premed majors, awarded less aid to admitted premeds than to humanities majors in order to attract underrepresented majors to campus. Referring to an admitted premed, an article in *The Wall Street Journal* (S. Stecklow, "Expensive Lesson: Colleges Manipulate Financial Aid Offers, Shortchanging Many," April 1, 1996) reported, "And so in an experiment last spring, it quietly offered fatter financial-aid grants to incoming humanities majors than to most of their premed counterparts. While Peter is getting $14,000 a year, he might have snared about $3,000 more if he planned to major in, say, art history." An unethical practice? The article mentions "ethical concerns" and "ethical questions" and, for that matter, so does Peter's mother: "What you're telling the kid is, lie to get into college." No profession, no industry, is immune from the potential for unethical behavior.

Required: Select two articles from the recent press (such as *Business Week*, *The Wall Street Journal*, *The New York Times*) about problems you think raise ethical issues and draft a report that describes the issues. Discuss how you think the perpetrators could have satisfied their objective by a means you think ethical.

Interactive quizzes are available as a student learning resource at
http://ricchiute.swlearning.com

Chapter 5

Legal Liability

Major topics discussed in this chapter are:

- The issues underlying legal liability to clients and to third parties.
- An auditor's common law liability to foreseen third parties under the Restatement of Torts and under the New York Court of Appeals decisions in *Ultramares* and *Credit Alliance*.
- The scope of an auditor's involvement with the Securities Acts.
- An auditor's statutory liability to securities purchasers and sellers under the Securities Acts, and securities litigation reform.
- An auditor's liability for criminal offenses.
- An auditor's responsibility to detect and report illegal acts.
- Precautions to minimize the risk of legal liability.

More lawsuits have been filed against auditors in the last fifteen years than in the entire history of the profession, and two issues help explain why. First, under the doctrine of **joint-and-several liability**, a plaintiff in an action against an auditor could, until recently, recover potentially all damages from the auditor alone, even though the auditor's report may have contributed only partially to the plaintiff's loss—a bankrupt client, for example, having contributed the balance. Second, unlike a physician or a lawyer, an auditor has little control over who uses his or her work product, and therefore may be liable to parties who are not in **privity** (parties in a contractual relationship with the auditor). Through the efforts of the Coalition to Eliminate Abusive Securities Suits (CEASS), the profession helped introduce and pass the *Private Securities Litigation Reform Act of 1995*, legislation that reduces joint-and-several liability to **proportionate liability** (defendants liable only for their share of responsibility), except for defendants who knowingly engage in fraud. Litigation reform and restoration of the privity doctrine have provided some relief for the profession, although both were long in coming, partly because the public is reluctant to erase long-standing traditions of liability that evolved primarily to protect the public.

This chapter addresses the independent auditor's civil and criminal liability, beginning with a review of the basic questions that underscore most liability cases. Next, the chapter describes an auditor's common law liability to clients and third parties, introduces the *Securities Act of 1933* and the *Securities Exchange Act of 1934*, and summarizes an auditor's statutory liability to securities purchasers and sellers under the 1933 and 1934 acts. In turn, the chapter discusses criminal liability and an auditor's responsibility to detect and report illegal acts. The chapter concludes by addressing an auditor's role in minimizing the risk of legal liability.

A word of caution: Be careful when transporting the contents of this chapter into practice. The generalizations drawn within the chapter are based on constantly evolving standards of liability, and in some instances represent majority rather than unanimous views. Generalizations are helpful in education, particularly in attempting to cope with the complex legal issues confronting practitioners today, but judgments in real-world lawsuits against auditors are based on the facts and legal issues at hand and on legal precedent in the jurisdiction trying the case, not on generalizations.

An Overview of Civil Liability Under Common and Statutory Law

In civil liability cases against auditors, four questions underscore the issues at stake: Under what source of law is the plaintiff suing? Who is the plaintiff? What is the auditor's potential liability? And which party—plaintiff or defendant—has the burden of proving what? The answers to these questions are outlined in Figure 5-1 and explained in the following sections.

Source of Law

A plaintiff may bring action against an auditor under common law or statutory law. The source of **common law** is the written opinions of prior courts within a

FIGURE 5-1: *Summary of Issues in Auditor Civil Liability Cases*

Source of Law
- Common law
- Statutory law (federal):
  - Securities Act of 1933
  - Securities Exchange Act of 1934

Plaintiff
- Under common law:
  - Client
  - Third-party primary beneficiaries
  - Foreseen third parties
  - Foreseeable third parties
- Under Securities Act of 1933:
  - Initial purchasers of securities
- Under Securities Exchange Act of 1934:
  - Subsequent purchasers or sellers of securities

Auditor's Potential Liability, Common and Statutory Law
- Ordinary negligence
- Gross negligence
- Fraud

Burden of Proof on Either Plaintiff or Defendant
- Damage or loss
- Misstated financial statements or erroneous advice
- Reliance on financial statements or advice
- Deficient auditor conduct

state (called legal *precedent*), each state having its own common law. Common law is based in the doctrine of *stare decisis*—that is, handing down precedent-setting principles of law to succeeding cases. Lower courts in a state are bound by the precedent of the state's highest court, but the highest court is not bound by its own prior opinions and may borrow precedent from other states.

In contrast, **statutory law** refers to written statutes established by Congress at the federal level and by state legislatures at the state level. Federal (and state) courts are bound by federal (state) statutes, unless the statute violates the U.S. (state) constitution. At the federal level, the primary focus of this chapter, the *Securities Act of 1933* (usually Section 11) and the *Securities Exchange Act of 1934* [usually Section 10(b), SEC Rule 10b-5, or Section 18], both administered by the SEC, are the two most prominent statutes affecting an auditor's legal liability.

Identity of Plaintiff

Plaintiffs in a civil proceeding against auditors vary depending on whether the action is brought under common law or statutory law.

Common Law

Under common law, an action may be initiated against an auditor by a client or by third parties. A client may bring action against an auditor for breach of contract or for tort. Clients may sue for **breach of contract** because clients are parties (they are *in privity*) to an express or implied contract for audit services. Suits for breach of contract usually allege that an auditor violated either auditing standards or the auditor-client confidential relationship. A **tort** is a wrongful act, other than breach of contract, that results in injury to another person. Suits in tort usually allege negligence, gross negligence, or fraud.

Common law recognizes two major classes of third parties who may bring action against an auditor: primary beneficiaries and foreseen third parties. **Primary beneficiaries** are identified specifically to auditors as the beneficiaries of audit services—the auditor would not have been engaged were it not for the primary beneficiary. For example, many closely held, nonpublic companies engage auditors primarily because a third-party creditor, such as a specifically named commercial bank, requires audited financial statements as part of a credit application. In these cases, clients engage independent auditors to perform a financial statement audit for the third-party creditor's primary benefit.

Foreseen third parties are not identified specifically as benefactors of audit services, although their general identity and specific purpose for relying on an audit report are known to the auditor. For example, if a client intended to use audited financial statements to secure a loan from an unnamed creditor, the party that extended credit to the client would be a foreseen third party. Whereas common law actions by clients may be brought for breach of contract or for tort, actions by primary and foreseen third parties are usually brought under tort law.

Closely related to foreseen third parties are other **foreseeable third parties**, parties who have a reasonable need to rely on an entity's financial statements but, because they're the furthest removed from a contractual agreement for audit services, generally endure the least favorable position in auditor liability cases. Examples of foreseeable third parties include bondholders, shareholders, and some creditors. Over the years, the rights of foreseeable third parties against auditors have depended largely on the affirmation, erosion, and later reaffirmation of the privity doctrine, although auditor liability to foreseeable parties is imposed in only two states today, Mississippi and Wisconsin.

Statutory Law

Under federal securities law, third parties may bring action against auditors for violating either of the Securities Acts, among other federal statutes. A plaintiff in an action under the *Securities Act of 1933* may be any person purchasing securities identified within a registration statement, which usually includes both (1) a prospectus describing the entity and the securities offered and (2) other detailed information such as balance sheets and statements of earnings. In contrast, a plaintiff in an action under the *Securities Exchange Act of 1934* may be any person purchasing or selling publicly traded securities.

Potential Liability

> fraud

Under either common or statutory law, an auditor may be liable for ordinary negligence, gross negligence, or fraud. **Ordinary negligence** means a lack of reasonable care when performing services, such as a departure from one of the auditing standards introduced in Chapter 2. When used alone, the term "negligence" is generally understood to mean ordinary negligence. **Gross negligence**, in contrast, is a lack of even minimum care when performing services, such as a reckless departure from generally accepted auditing standards. **Fraud** is an intentional misstatement or omission of a material fact (or a theft) that results in another party being deceived and then injured, the operative word being "intentional." In a precedent-setting 1931 case, *Ultramares Corp. v. Touche*, the New York Court of Appeals noted that gross negligence could be so great as to constitute constructive (as opposed to actual) fraud. Constructive fraud lacks intent, an essential condition in actual fraud, but the result of both constructive and actual fraud is identical: Another party is deceived and then injured. The court's use of constructive fraud has been confirmed many times over the years, including cases involving small firms.[1]

Ordinary negligence imposes a higher degree of responsibility on an auditor than gross negligence, and gross negligence a higher degree than fraud for this reason: A "departure" from generally accepted auditing standards (the operational definition of ordinary negligence) is less burdensome for a plaintiff to prove than a "reckless departure" (gross negligence), and reckless departure is less burdensome to prove than an "intent" to deceive and injure (fraud).

Burden of Proof

The extent of an independent auditor's liability under either common or statutory law rests on four essential points. The plaintiff or the independent auditor (defendant) may have the burden of proving or disproving that:

- The plaintiff sustained a damage or loss,
- The audited financial statements were materially misstated,
- The plaintiff relied on the financial statements, and/or
- The auditor's conduct was deficient.

---

1 See, for example, *Barger v. McCoy, Hillard and Parks*, North Carolina Court of Appeals, 1995.

The burden of proving the first point, *damage or loss*, always falls on the plaintiff. The amount of damage or loss may be represented a number of ways. For example, in a securities class action suit, damages might be calculated as the difference between the "price line" paid by class-member plaintiffs and the "true value line" of traded securities determined by removing the effect of a fraud on the market from inflated share prices.

The second point, *misstated financial statements*, is the basis for a plaintiff to claim damage or loss—that is, what the plaintiff alleges to be the cause of the damage or loss. Like damage or loss, the plaintiff always has the burden of proving that audited financial statements are misstated materially.

Reliance on financial statements, the third point, entails two separate but related issues: Did the plaintiff actually rely on the statements to reach a decision? And did reliance on the statements actually lead to the damage or loss? The burden of proving reliance falls on the plaintiff under both common law and the *Securities Exchange Act of 1934*. However, under the *Securities Act of 1933*, the plaintiff does not have to prove reliance. Rather, the defendant—the auditor—has the burden of proving that a plaintiff's damage or loss did not result from relying on the financial statements.

The fourth point, an *auditor's conduct*, represents the degree of due professional care exercised when performing audit or other attest services. The standard of conduct owed to a plaintiff depends on an auditor's knowledge of a plaintiff's existence and identity, and the plaintiff's reason for relying on the financial statements. For example, in comparison with some third parties, a client's existence, identity, and reason for relying on financial statements are more clearly known to an auditor. Thus, an auditor's expected level of conduct is higher for clients than for some third parties. Under the *Securities Act of 1933* and Section 18 of the *Securities Exchange Act of 1934*, an auditor has the burden of proving that a reasonable investigation was made and, therefore, that his or her level of conduct was adequate (called the "due diligence" defense). In contrast, the plaintiff suing an auditor has the burden of proving deficient auditor conduct under common law and Section 10(b) of the *Securities Exchange Act of 1934*.

Common Law Liability

Under common law, an auditor may be liable to the party contracting for audit services (the client) and to third parties who, although not party to a contract, nevertheless use the auditor's work product. As explained above, third parties may be classified as primary beneficiaries, who are treated much like clients under common law, foreseen third parties, and foreseeable third parties. The following discusses an auditor's potential liability to clients and third parties.

Liability to Clients

An auditor's common law liability to clients is based on the contractual relationship between an auditor and a client, and on the auditor's status as an independent contractor. A contractual relationship results because an auditor and a client enter into an express written agreement for audit services (an "engagement letter," Chapter 7). The auditor's status as an independent contractor, rather than an agent or employee, results because an auditor's tasks are not controlled by the client. A client may initiate a common law civil action when an auditor is alleged to have failed in carrying out the duties of an audit services contract. For example, a client may take action against an auditor when the client sustains a loss from relying on materially misstated financial statements or when the auditor fails to discover a fraud, such as a cash embezzlement.

The auditor's common law liability to clients is traceable to the first recorded legal action brought against an auditor, an 1887 case in England: *Leeds Estate, Building and Investment Co. v. Shepherd*. Leeds, a lending institution, sued the auditor for breach of duty, winning primarily on grounds that the auditor was wrongful in not inquiring into a balance sheet's "substantial accuracy." Similar to the Leeds case, an auditor's common law liability to clients today is for ordinary negligence, although clients may bring action for gross negligence if they believe the auditor departed recklessly from auditing standards, or for fraud if they believe the auditor intended to deceive and injure. To recover damages, a client has the burden of proving a damage or loss, misstated financial statements, reliance on the financial statements, and deficient auditor conduct.

➤ fraud

An auditor's liability to clients also extends to parties who acquire a client's rights by subrogation (substitution). For example, if a bonding company reimburses a client for an employee's embezzlement, the bonding company succeeds to the client's right to sue the auditor for failing to detect the embezzlement. A 1940 case, *Maryland Casualty Co. v. Jonathon Cook*, illustrates. Over a period of seven years, the Flint, Michigan, city treasurer embezzled monies from municipal funds. Jonathon Cook & Company accepted the 1932 audit engagement that was to be based on procedures included within an audit services contract. The procedures would have been sufficient to uncover the embezzlement, but Cook essentially ignored them. As a result, Maryland Casualty, which carried a surety bond on the treasurer, reimbursed the city of Flint and initiated action against Cook. The court found in favor of Maryland Casualty, ruling that the engagement should have been conducted in accordance with the terms of the contract.

➤ fraud

Liability to Primary Beneficiaries

English common law, forebear of U.S. legal precedent, traditionally held that only parties in privity to a contract may enforce the contract. However, in the mid-nineteenth century, U.S. courts began to equate primary beneficiaries with clients. For example, in an 1859 case, *Lawrence v. Fox*, the court effectively ruled that privity was not essential for primary beneficiaries to sue, assuming that contractual duties were limited to third parties rather than to clients. Some six decades later, however, in *Glanzer v. Shepard*, the court firmly established a primary beneficiary's right to sue for damages even though contractual duties extended only between the parties to the contract. Although *Glanzer v. Shepard* did not involve an auditor, the case is generally recognized as an important influence on an auditor's legal liability to primary beneficiaries. Today, primary beneficiaries typically enjoy a status similar to clients. An auditor is liable to primary beneficiaries for lack of reasonable care (ordinary negligence), and primary beneficiaries have the burden of proving damage or loss, misstated financial statements, reliance on the financial statements, and deficient auditor conduct.

Liability to Foreseen Third Parties

Some third parties are identified only tangentially to an auditor (for example, commercial bank lenders or an unsolicited telephone call from a holding company) and others are not specifically identified at all (for example, present or potential shareholders). Yet their general identities and purposes for relying on audited financial statements can be reasonably foreseen (for example, loans, takeovers, investments). In practice, independent auditors can be held liable to third parties who, although not parties to an audit services contract, nevertheless allege to have suffered losses from unpaid commercial loans, unprofitable takeovers, or poor investment decisions, among other things. However, the basis of law varies across jurisdictions. A majority of jurisdictions rely on the *Restatement of Torts,* and a minority rely on the privity doctrine established in *Ultramares v. Touche* and on the three-point linkage test established in *Credit Alliance v. Arthur Andersen.* The following discusses an auditor's common law liability to foreseen third parties in the *Restatement of Torts* jurisdictions and in the privity or *Credit Alliance* jurisdictions. Figure 5-2 summarizes the discussion.

The Restatement of Torts Jurisdictions

In a majority of states,[2] generally called the "Restatement of Torts Jurisdictions," the courts have adopted Section 552 of the *Restatement of Torts,* a multivolume compendium of tort law written by legal scholars. The *Restatement* provides that:

One who, in the course of his . . . profession . . . provides false information for the guidance of others . . . is subject to liability for pecuniary loss caused by their justifiable reliance upon the information, if he fails to exercise reasonable care or competence in obtaining or communicating the information.

The *Restatement* establishes an auditor's liability to a narrow class of third parties the auditor could reasonably have foreseen. However, because the language in the *Restatement* is broad, courts have interpreted the *Restatement* differently. Today, the *Restatement* jurisdictions fall into two camps: The majority of courts in the *Restatement* jurisdictions *do not* require the auditor to have known that a third-party plaintiff would rely on the auditor's report, and a minority of courts in the *Restatement* jurisdictions *do.*

Majority View The majority view holds, in general, that an auditor is liable to a third-party foreseen plaintiff if he or she:

1. Knew the recipient of the report would use the report to influence the plaintiff, or
2. Intended to influence the plaintiff.

Either but not both conditions must hold, although most cases brought against auditors relate to the first. *Rusch Factors, Inc. v. Levin* (1968) illustrates an auditor's liability when he or she knew the recipient of audited financial statements would influence a plaintiff. Levin audited financial statements his client used to support a loan application to Rusch Factors. The statements erroneously showed the company to be solvent. Rusch Factors relied on the financial statements, granted the loan, and the borrower went into receivership. The Rhode Island court held that

---

2   *Restatement of Torts* states include Alaska, Arizona, California, Colorado, Florida, Georgia, Hawaii, Iowa, Kentucky, Louisiana, Maine, Massachusetts, Minnesota, Missouri, New Hampshire, New Mexico, North Carolina, North Dakota, Ohio, Pennsylvania, Rhode Island, South Carolina, Tennessee, Texas, Washington, and West Virginia. See D. Y. Causey, Jr., *Duties and Liabilities of Public Accountants,* 7th ed. Starkville, MI: Accountant's Press, 2001.

FIGURE 5-2: *Common Law Liability to Foreseen Beneficiaries*

Restatement of Torts Jurisdictions	Privity or Credit Alliance Jurisdictions
Permits foreseen third parties to recover.	*Permits foreseen third parties in privity to recover.*
Majority View	**Minority View**
Key Distinguishing Feature	
Does not require knowledge of plaintiff's reliance.	Requires knowledge of plaintiff's reliance.	Requires knowledge of plaintiff's reliance and linkage between auditor and plaintiff.
Liability		
Auditor liable if:	Auditor liable if:	Auditor liable if:
1. Knew recipient would use report to influence plaintiff, or	1. Knew recipient would use report to influence plaintiff, or	1. Knew report would be used for a specific purpose,
2. Intended to influence plaintiff.	2. Intended to influence plaintiff, and	2. Knew plaintiff would rely, and
	3. Knew plaintiff would rely.	3. Evidence links auditor to plaintiff.
Key Case		
Rusch Factors v. Levin (1968)	*Second National Bank of Warren v. Demshar* (1997)	*Ultramares v. Touche* (1931)
Marcus Brothers Textiles v. Price Waterhouse (1999)		*Credit Alliance Corp. v. Arthur Andersen* (1985)

Levin knew the company would use the financial statements to influence Rusch Factor's loan decision: ". . . an accountant should be liable in negligence for careless financial misrepresentations relied upon by actually foreseen and limited classes of persons . . . the defendant knew that his certification was to be used for, and had as its very aim and purpose, the reliance of potential financiers of the Rhode Island corporation."

A more recent case, *Marcus Brothers Textiles v. Price Waterhouse* (1999), a North Carolina Supreme Court decision, affirms *Rusch Factors*. Marcus Brothers Textiles sold woven textile products to Piece Goods Shops, a North Carolina retailer Price Waterhouse audited from 1989 to 1992. From December 30, 1992 to April 5, 1993, Marcus relied on Piece Goods' 1992 and 1991 financial statements and on Price Waterhouse's unqualified opinion to extend $288 thousand in credit to Piece Goods, which filed for bankruptcy on April 19. Marcus Brothers offered three pieces of evidence to support the claim that Price Waterhouse knew Piece Goods (the recipient of the report) would use the financial statements and unqualified opinion to influence Marcus Brothers' (the plaintiff) decision to grant Piece Goods credit, including a Price Waterhouse memo stating that vendors (such as Marcus) were accustomed to receiving a creditor's (such as Piece Good's) financial statements. The court found that Price Waterhouse knew Piece Goods regularly provided financial statements to a limited number of major trade creditors, including Marcus.

Minority View In contrast, the courts in a minority of Restatement of Torts jurisdictions rely on 1 or 2, above, but add a subtle third requirement that the auditor:

3. Knew the plaintiff would rely on the report.

For example, not only did the auditor know that the *recipient* of the report would influence the plaintiff (1 above) but, in addition, the auditor knew that the *plaintiff* would rely on the report as well. *Second National Bank of Warren v. Demshar* (1997), an Ohio Court of Appeals case illustrates:

Beidler-Taylor Roofing hired Demshar, a CPA, in May 1993 to review (not audit) the 1993 financial statements of Beidler-Taylor, which between January and May 1994 had completely exhausted a $250,000 line of credit granted by Second National Bank of Warren, Ohio. In March 1994, Demshar gave Beidler-Taylor's December 31, 1993, financial statements and a standard review report (Chapter 18) to Second National Bank. The report disclaimed an opinion on the financial statements. In May 1994, Second National reaffirmed and increased Beidler-Taylor's line of credit by $50,000. In the fall of 1994, Beidler-Taylor defaulted on the obligation and filed for bankruptcy. In August 1995, Second National filed suit against Demshar, claiming to have relied on Demshar's March 1994 report when the bank increased the line of credit in May. The court ruled that Demshar did not owe a duty of care to Second National Bank because the bank failed to produce evidence that Demshar had foreseen, or should have foreseen, that Second National would rely on the report.

The Privity or *Credit Alliance* Jurisdictions

In jurisdictions that do not follow the *Restatement of Torts*, generally called the "Privity or *Credit Alliance* Jurisdictions" (or the "New York Rule" states), the courts rely on the privity doctrine established originally in *Ultramares v. Touche*

(1931) and on a three-point "linkage" test (a test of whether evidence "linked" the auditor to the third-party plaintiff) established in *Credit Alliance v. Arthur Andersen* (1985). Like the minority of the *Restatement of Torts* jurisdictions, the *Credit Alliance* jurisdictions require the auditor to have known that a third-party plaintiff would rely on the auditor's report (that is, privity). However, the *Credit Alliance* jurisdictions add this: Evidence such as meetings or memoranda must link the auditor to the plaintiff (that is, the linkage test). Compared to the *Restatement of Torts*, the New York Rule is a more conservative interpretation of auditor culpability. For example, commenting on the difference between the *Restatement* and the New York Rule, the Supreme Court of Tennessee, a *Restatement* jurisdiction, said ". . . the *Restatement* is more generous than New York's 'near privity' rule . . . the *Restatement* contemplates identification of a narrow group, not necessarily the specific membership within that group."[3]

> fraud

The Privity Doctrine: *Ultramares* *Ultramares Corp. v. Touche* (1931), a landmark New York Court of Appeals case, established that auditors are liable to third parties for fraud—intentional misstatements, omissions, or theft—but they are *not* liable to unidentified third parties for negligence, since they are not parties to a contract. Relying on financial statements audited by Touche, Ultramares Corporation made loans to Fred Stern & Co., a rubber importer that in reality was insolvent. Stern was unable to repay the loans and subsequently declared bankruptcy. The court ruled that accountants are liable for negligence only to those parties in privity—that is, to clients and to those third parties whom the accountant knows will rely on the financial statements, such as primary beneficiaries.

The Linkage Test: *Credit Alliance* Several cases decided in the early 1980s served to erode the privity doctrine in some states. However, a 1985 New York Court of Appeals case, *Credit Alliance v. Arthur Andersen & Co.*, strongly reaffirmed the privity doctrine in *Ultramares*, and stands today as key precedent in jurisdictions that have not adopted the *Restatement of Torts*. Credit Alliance, a finance company, loaned large sums of money to L. B. Smith, Inc., a heavy equipment lessor and audit client of Andersen. L. B. Smith subsequently went bankrupt and was unable to repay approximately $9 million. Credit Alliance prevailed, arguing it was in privity since L. B. Smith had used the audited financial statements to solicit financing. The court acknowledged that other courts throughout the nation had moved away from *Ultramares*, but reaffirmed preexisting New York law by ruling that negligence suits against auditors require privity or a relationship "so close as to approach that of privity." The court's opinion established a three-point test of the "linkage" between the auditor and third party, ruling that in the absence of a contract an accountant is liable to a third party only if:

1. The accountant knew the audited financial statements would be used for a specific purpose,
2. The accountant knew a specific third party would rely on the statements, and
3. Evidence linking the accountant with the plaintiff third party shows the accountant understood the statements would be relied on by the plaintiff.

---

3   *Bethlehem Steel Corporation v. Ernst & Whinney* 822 S.W. 2nd 592 (Tenn. 1991).

Three years later, the New York Court of Appeals in *William Iselin and Co., Inc. v. Mann Judd Landau* (1988) extended the linkage test to review engagements (Chapter 18) as well.

Osborne, Security Pacific, Cherry,* and *Parrot Cases decided in the last decade reaffirmed both the privity concept established in *Ultramares* and the linkage test in *Credit Alliance*. Several prominent cases illustrate: *Bily v. Arthur Young & Co.* (1993) involved the extraordinary rise and fall of Osborne Computer Corporation, manufacturer in 1981 of the first portable personal computer. The plaintiffs, venture capitalists who had invested heavily in a private offering of securities just months before Osborne filed for bankruptcy in September 1993, sued Arthur Young, alleging errors in the 1992 audited financial statements on which they claimed to have relied. The court reversed a series of rulings by the state's appellate courts, holding that "an auditor owes no general duty of care regarding the conduct of an audit to persons other than the client." The court reasoned in part that, "If . . . third parties are simply permitted to recover from the auditor for mistakes in the client's financial statements, the auditor becomes, in effect, an insurer of not only the financial statements, but of bad loans and investments in general." All other plaintiffs, among them foreseen third parties, may recover only if they can demonstrate the auditor intended to deceive and injure—that is, fraud.

➤ fraud

In *Security Pacific v. Peat Marwick* (1993), the New York Court of Appeals reasserted the three-point linkage test from *Credit Alliance*, holding that a single telephone call between a Security Pacific vice president and a Peat Marwick audit partner was insufficient to establish a relationship sufficiently approaching privity. Consequently, the court ruled that Peat Marwick's work product benefited the client primarily and others only incidentally. Consistent with the *Security Pacific* case, the same Court in *Cherry v. Joseph S. Herbert & Co.* (1995), a case about a solvency opinion, ruled that the linkage test in *Credit Alliance* was established by meetings among parties before a transaction occurs, a firm's knowledge of why a client required an opinion, and a firm's oral assurances of solvency.

Quoting from opinions in prior cases, the New York Court of Appeals in *Harold Todd Parrot v. Coopers & Lybrand*, a case decided in 2000, explained why the Court, unlike the *Restatement of Torts*, requires both privity and the three-point linkage test:

We have reiterated time and again that "before a party may recover in tort for pecuniary loss sustained as a result of another's negligent misrepresentations there must be a showing that there was either actual privity of contract between the parties or a relationship so close as to approach that of privity." . . . *We have explained that our decision to circumscribe liability in this area by privity of contract or its equivalent rests on "concern for the indeterminate nature of the risk," and that "such a requirement is necessary in order to provide fair and manageable bounds to what otherwise could prove to be limitless liability."*

Today, eight states follow privity and *Credit Alliance*: Connecticut, Idaho, Indiana, Maryland, Montana, Nebraska, New York, and Virginia.[4]

---

4 D. Y. Causey, Jr., *Duties and Liabilities of Public Accountants*, 7th ed., Starkville, MI: Accountant's Press, 2001.

Liability to Foreseeable Third Parties

In *H. Rosenblum, Inc. v. Adler* (1983), the court strayed from the privity concept established in *Ultramares*, ruling that accountants can be held liable not only to clients and primary beneficiaries, but also to foreseeable third parties who suffer a loss from relying on materially misstated financial statements. Liability to foreseeable third parties is the most liberal interpretation of auditor culpability, since the auditor is liable to any reasonable user of financial statements, which translates to an almost unlimited class of plaintiffs. The *Rosenblum* decision was followed by similar decisions, such as *Touche Ross v. Commercial Union Insurance Co.* (Mississippi, 1987) and *Citizens State Bank v. Timm, Schmidt & Co.* (Wisconsin, 1983). For example, in *Citizens State Bank*, the court held an accounting firm liable for foreseeable injuries, even though the firm had no intention of influencing the bank and no knowledge the client would use the report to influence the bank. Today, only Mississippi and Wisconsin impose liability to foreseeable third parties,[5] although to differing degrees: Mississippi requires that the plaintiff receive the auditor's report directly from the entity audited, and Wisconsin imposes liability regardless of the auditor's knowledge.

The Securities Acts

This section discusses the independent auditor's role in the two most prominent federal statutes affecting audit practice—the *Securities Act of 1933* and the *Securities Exchange Act of 1934*—and introduces the sections of each act that affect an auditor's liability. Thereafter, an auditor's statutory liability under the two acts is addressed in detail.

By 1933, most states had adopted so-called "blue-sky" laws to regulate the exchange of debt and equity securities. Although adequate for intrastate exchanges, the blue-sky laws were less effective in regulating interstate exchanges. As a result, the Securities Acts were enacted and the SEC was created. An auditor's potential legal liability under the Securities Acts derives from an attempt by Congress to hold accountants and other professionals, such as lawyers and underwriters, more accountable to third parties than they would be under common law.

Created under the *Securities Exchange Act of 1934*, the **Securities and Exchange Commission (SEC)** was charged to administer both the 1934 Act and the *Securities Act of 1933*, which had been administered by the Federal Trade Commission. The SEC, headquartered in Washington, D.C., consists of five appointed commissioners (one of whom is designated chairman), a number of administrative divisions or offices (one of which is the Office of the Chief Accountant), and nine regional branches throughout the United States. Today, in addition to the Securities Acts, the Commission administers a number of acts, including the *Public Utility Holding Company Act of 1935*, the *Trust Indenture Act of 1939*, the *Investment Company Act of 1940*, the *Investment Advisors Act of 1940*, the *Securities Investor Protection Act of 1970*, portions of the *Foreign Corrupt Practices Act of 1977*, the *Insider Trading Sanctions Act of 1984*, the *Securities Fraud Enforcement Act of 1988*, and the *Private Securities Litigation Reform Act of 1995*.

---

5 Ibid.

The Securities Act of 1933

The **Securities Act of 1933**, sometimes referred to as the "truth in securities" law, regulates the initial public offering (IPO) and sale of securities. The Act prohibits fraudulent misrepresentations in IPOs and requires that an entity first file a registration statement, including a prospectus, with the Commission before offering securities for sale publicly.

The Registration Process

A **registration statement** is filed on a prescribed form, usually Form S-1, and reports information that includes:

- An entity's nature, history, and capital structure,
- Descriptions of the securities offered and the underwriting arrangements,
- Officers' and directors' salaries and security holdings,
- Estimated net proceeds from the offering and their intended use, and
- Detailed financial information.

Rather than "fill in the blank" questionnaires, registration forms require extensive narrative responses, and the completion process is both time-consuming and demanding. Once filed, a registration statement is examined by an SEC Division of Corporation Finance review team that consists of an accountant, an attorney, and a financial analyst. Following review, the SEC either accepts the registration statement or issues a letter of comment requesting revisions. If the statement is not revised, the SEC can accept the original filing (rarely done), issue a refusal order that does not halt the registration process (sometimes done), or issue a stop order that halts the registration process. In practice, these alternatives are not often used, since most registrants respond promptly and properly to letters of comment.

The Independent Auditor

An auditor's liability under the *Securities Act of 1933* derives from his or her involvement in the registration process. For example, in a typical registration, an auditor will audit the registrant's financial statements, read the registration statement for material inconsistencies with the financial statements, review events from the date of the audited financial statements to the registration statement's effective date, and issue a letter for underwriters, called a "comfort letter." The comfort letter addresses selected representations appearing in the registration statement and is prepared in accordance with *Statement on Auditing Standards Nos. 72*, "Letters for Underwriters and Certain Other Requesting Parties" and *76*, "Amendments to SAS No. 72" (Chapter 18).

Most suits against auditors under the *Securities Act of 1933* are brought under Section 11. The statutory basis for an auditor's liability is contained in Section 11(a), which states in part:

Section 11(a)

In case any part of the registration statement, when such part became effective, contained an untrue statement of a material fact or omitted to state a material fact required to be stated therein or necessary to make the statements therein not misleading, any person acquiring such security . . . may sue . . . every accountant . . . who has with his consent been named as having prepared or certified any part of the registration statement . . .

In general, Section 11 is intended to protect potential investors by imposing liability on anyone who makes untrue statements or omits material facts in connection with a registration statement.

The Securities Exchange Act of 1934

Whereas the 1933 Act regulates the initial public offering and sale of securities, the **Securities Exchange Act of 1934** regulates the trading of securities offered and sold. Under the 1934 Act, an entity must register securities with and report to the SEC if there are 500 or more shareholders and if assets exceed $10 million. In general, the Act's purpose is to promote adequate and accurate disclosure of material facts on a continuing basis.

The Registration and Periodic Reporting Process

Companies subject to the 1934 Act must register classes of traded securities and report selected information periodically. Of the registration forms available, Form 10-K, an annual financial statement, is used most commonly. Form 10-K is filed by every company for which another form is not specified, and those that file Form 10-K also file Form 10-Q, a quarterly financial report. Companies that file registration forms other than Form 10-K are required to use specially designated forms for periodic reporting. However, all entities, regardless of the registration form filed, are required to file Form 8-K, a notice of significant current events affecting the company which, in the case of a change in auditors, must be filed within three business days after the change. Through these various reports, the 1934 Act effectively provides continuous disclosure to interested parties.

The Independent Auditor

An auditor's liability under the *Securities Exchange Act of 1934* derives typically from his or her involvement with Forms 10-K and 10-Q. Most suits brought against auditors under the 1934 Act relate to either Section 10(b) or Section 18.

> **Section 10(b)**
>
> It shall be unlawful for any person, directly or indirectly, by the use of any means or instrumentality of interstate commerce or of the mails, or of any facility of any national securities exchange . . . (b) to use or employ, in connection with the purchase or sale of any security registered on a national securities exchange or any security not so registered, any manipulative or deceptive device or contrivance in contravention of such rules and regulations as the Commission may prescribe as necessary or appropriate in the public interest or for the protection of investors.

Under Section 10(b) the SEC issued Rule 10b-5, "Employment of Manipulative and Deceptive Devices," which states:

> **Rule 10b-5**
>
> It shall be unlawful for any person, directly or indirectly, by the use of any means or instrumentality of interstate commerce, or of the mails, or of any facility of any national securities exchange, (a) to employ any device, scheme, or artifice to defraud, (b) to make any untrue statement of a material fact or to omit to state a material fact necessary in order to make the statements made, in the light of the cir-

cumstances under which they were made, not misleading, or (c) to engage in any act, practice, or course of business which operates or would operate as a fraud or deceit upon any person, in connection with the purchase or sale of any security.

Section 10(b) and Rule 10b-5 are antifraud provisions that protect the purchasers and sellers of securities from manipulation and deception by an auditor or any other person. In contrast, Section 18 of the 1934 Act is a disclosure provision that states in part:

Section 18
Any person who shall make or cause to be made any statement in any application, report, or document filed . . . which . . . was . . . false or misleading with respect to any material fact, shall be liable to any person (not knowing that such statement was false or misleading) who, in reliance upon such statement, shall have purchased or sold a security at a price which was affected by such statement, for damages caused by such reliance, unless the person sued shall prove that he acted in good faith and had no knowledge that such statement was false or misleading.

Section 18 protects purchasers and sellers from false and misleading statements.

Liability Under the Securities Acts

An auditor may be liable to securities purchasers under the *Securities Act of 1933*, Section 11, for his or her involvement in the registration process, and to securities purchasers and sellers under the *Securities Exchange Act of 1934*, Sections 10(b) and 18, for involvement with a Form 10-K or 10-Q. Figure 5-3 summarizes an auditor's minimum basis for potential liability (ordinary negligence, gross negligence, or fraud) to all classes of plaintiffs, and which party (the plaintiff or the defendant auditor) has the burden of proving which points under statutory law. An auditor's liability under each relevant section follows.

Liability: 1933 Act, Section 11

Under Section 11 of the 1933 Act, an auditor may be held liable to any party who purchases securities in an initial public offering and who alleges a material false or misleading statement within the registration statement. Figure 5-3 summarizes an auditor's statutory liability to securities purchasers under Section 11. An auditor is liable for lack of reasonable care (ordinary negligence) and also sustains the burden for proving either:

- The purchaser's damages or losses resulted from relying on information other than the registration statement, or
- The auditor acted in good faith.

The latter, referred to as the "due diligence" defense, is typically the defense chosen, since proving reliance on other information can be quite difficult. The plaintiff (purchaser), on the other hand, sustains the burden of proving damage or loss and that the financial statements are misstated.

Escott v. BarChris Construction Corp. illustrates an auditor's liability under Section 11. BarChris, which constructed recreational bowling centers, filed an S-1 registration statement on March 30, 1961. Peat Marwick had previously audited

➤ fraud

FIGURE 5-3: *Liability Under Statutory Law*

Plaintiff	Minimum Basis for Potential Auditor Liability	Burden of Proof	
		Upon Plaintiff	*Upon Defendant*
Under 1933 Act Section 11: Security purchaser	Ordinary negligence	Damage or loss Financial statements misstated or erroneous advice	Lack of reliance or auditor conduct not deficient (due diligence)
Under 1934 Act Section 10(b), Rule 10b-5: Security purchaser or seller	Gross negligence or fraud	Damage or loss Financial statements misstated or erroneous advice Reliance Auditor conduct deficient	
Under 1934 Act Section 18: Security purchaser or seller	Gross negligence	Damage or loss Financial statements misstated or erroneous advice Reliance	Auditor conduct not deficient (due diligence)

BarChris's December 31, 1960, financial statements, but a comfort letter (sometimes called an "S-1 review") was required, covering the period from the most recent balance sheet date to the registration statement's effective date. Most of the S-1 review was performed by a senior accountant who was not yet a CPA, was inexperienced in the construction industry, and was supervising his first engagement as a senior accountant. He and his assistants failed to discover material transactions and events occurring in the subsequent period. On October 29, 1962, after registered debentures (unsecured bonds) were offered and sold, BarChris filed for bankruptcy. Purchasers of the debentures subsequently filed suit against Peat Marwick, among others, alleging the registration statement contained false and misleading information. The court ruled for the purchasers, rejecting the auditors' due diligence defense:

There had been a material change for the worse in BarChris's financial position. That change was sufficiently serious so that the failure to disclose it made the 1960 figures misleading. (The senior) did not discover it. As far as results were concerned, his S-1 review was useless. Accountants should not be held to a standard higher than that recognized in their profession. I do not do so here. (The senior's) review did not come up to that standard. He did not take some of the steps which Peat Marwick's written program prescribed.

He did not spend an adequate amount of time on a task of this magnitude. Most important of all, he was too easily satisfied with glib answers to his inquiries. . . . The burden of proof is on Peat Marwick. I find that the burden has not been satisfied. I conclude that Peat Marwick has not established its due diligence defense.

The court's opinion not only reaffirmed an auditor's potential liability for ordinary negligence under the 1933 Act, but also prompted *Statement on Auditing Procedure No. 47*, "Subsequent Events" (AU Sec. 560), discussed in Chapter 17.

Liability: 1934 Act, Section 10(b), Rule 10b-5

An auditor's liability under Section 10(b) is quite broad: A plaintiff (purchaser or seller) may sue for *any* alleged false statement, whether the statement is filed with the SEC or not. Thus, even though, as explained in the following paragraphs, an auditor is not liable for ordinary negligence, there is significant exposure to liability under Section 10(b), since any form of statement may result in liability. Figure 5-3 summarizes an auditor's statutory liability to security purchasers and sellers under Section 10(b) and Rule 10b-5. In contrast with Section 11 of the 1933 Act, an auditor is liable under the 1934 Act for lack of minimum care (gross negligence), not lack of reasonable care (ordinary negligence). The plaintiff purchaser or seller has the burden of proving damage or loss, that financial statements are misstated, reliance on the statements, and deficient auditor conduct.

The courts have been inconsistent on the issue of negligent conduct under Section 10(b) and Rule 10b-5. Although *Ernst & Ernst v. Hochfelder* (1976), a landmark U.S. Supreme Court case, helped to resolve some issues, the court chose not to address all of the issues. Ernst & Ernst were auditors for the First Securities Company of Chicago from 1946 through 1967. In 1968, Leston B. Nay, president and 92 percent stockholder of First Securities, left a suicide note stating that First Securities was bankrupt and describing his embezzlement from several escrow accounts. Nay perpetrated the embezzlement by inducing customers to invest in nonexistent high-yield accounts. Customers were instructed to make checks payable to Nay, who, through his "mail rule," restricted employees from opening mail addressed to him, even during his absence. Nay diverted the proceeds to his own use, and the accounts were neither known nor available to Ernst & Ernst. Following Nay's suicide disclosure, investors sued Ernst & Ernst, claiming the firm was negligent in not discovering the mail rule. The investors reasoned that once discovered, the rule would have prevented a proper audit, prompting disclosure of the rule to the SEC and exposure of the embezzlement. Ernst & Ernst noted that the mail rule had no bearing on First Securities' internal controls, which were claimed to be adequate otherwise. On the other hand, the plaintiff produced three expert witnesses, all of whom agreed the mail rule reflected a significant inadequacy in internal control.

The U.S. Supreme Court ruled in favor of Ernst & Ernst, concluding that, for Ernst & Ernst to be held liable under Section 10(b) and Rule 10b-5, the plaintiff had to prove "scienter": the *intent* to deceive, manipulate, or defraud. As a result of the *Hochfelder* decision, accountants are not liable under Section 10(b) and Rule 10b-5 in the absence of scienter, thus eliminating ordinary negligence as a basis for liability. However, the Court left open the question of whether gross negligence can satisfy the scienter requirement:

In certain areas of the law recklessness is considered to be a form of intentional conduct for purposes of imposing liability for some act. We need not address here the question whether,

> fraud

in some circumstances, reckless behavior is sufficient for civil liability under 10(b) and 10b-5.

Since the *Hochfelder* decision, liability has been imposed on accountants in some cases under Section 10(b) and Rule 10b-5 for reckless or willful misconduct. For example, in *McLean v. Alexander*, the U.S. District Court of Delaware held the accountant liable for recklessness, characterizing his conduct as "far more than mere negligence" but less than "a preconceived actual intent to defraud."

In both the *Hochfelder* and the *McLean* cases, the accountants were sued as "aiders and abettors," but not as "direct participants" with management in securities fraud, a far more egregious allegation. A case decided in 1994 drew attention to the distinction. Heralded at first as a major victory for the profession, the U.S. Supreme Court swept aside decades of lower court precedents, ruling in *Central Bank of Denver v. First Interstate Bank of Denver* (1994) that accountants and other professionals could be sued in securities fraud cases as direct participants, not merely as aiders and abettors. However, the decision does not diminish the SEC's power, since ". . . the number of lawsuits that would be dismissed after the ruling was far less certain than the fact that aggressive plaintiffs' attorneys would redouble efforts to charge accountants not as mere abettors but as participating co-conspirators."[6] The issue of accountants' liability under Section 10(b) and Rule 10b-5 in the absence of intent remains unsettled. However, *McLean*, among other decisions subsequent to *Hochfelder*, suggests that accountants are potentially liable for reckless misconduct (gross negligence).

Liability: 1934 Act, Section 18

An auditor's legal liability is narrower under Section 18 than under Section 10(b). A Section 18 action may be taken only for alleged false statements filed with the SEC, while a Section 10(b) action may be based on any alleged false statements, even those not filed. Figure 5-3 summarizes an auditor's statutory liability to securities purchasers and sellers under Section 18. As under Section 10(b), an auditor is liable under Section 18 for lack of minimum care (gross negligence). The plaintiff purchaser or seller has the burden of proving damage or loss, that financial statements are misstated, and reliance on the statements. In contrast with Section 10(b), an auditor must prove due diligence—that he or she acted in good faith and without knowledge that the statements were false or misleading.

Securities Litigation Reform

Although many lawsuits against accountants have merit, many others do not. For example, aggressive litigators commonly file or threaten lawsuits, hoping that accounting firms will settle out of court rather than risk the fate of an unsympathetic jury or an uninformed press. In legislation intended to reduce the number of frivolous class action suits, Congress passed the *Private Securities Litigation Reform Act of 1995*. The Act imposes hefty sanctions against attorneys who rely on legally frivolous or factually impertinent arguments, but retains joint-and-several liability on parties who knowingly perpetrate a fraud. However, in an extraordinary departure from U.S. custom, the Act imposes *proportionate liability* on peripheral, less culpable defendants, although with some exceptions: All defendants are jointly-

---

6   R. Telberg, "Top Court's Ruling Rocks Profession," *Accounting Today* (May 2, 1994), p. 46.

and-severally liable to investors who lose more than 10 percent of total net worths valued below $200,000, and proportionately liable defendants are further liable for up to 50 percent of proportionate liability to cover judgments against insolvent codefendants.

The Act was received as a welcome sign of relief to many practitioners. For example, the *Journal of Accountancy* said, ". . . under the new law, a defendant who is found only to have acted recklessly, but who did not knowingly commit fraud, would be responsible for only a proportionate amount of the damages."[7] However, a report released by the National Economic Research Association found both that the proportion of federal class action suits against accountants has not declined since enactment of the *Litigation Reform Act* and that more plaintiffs are suing accountants in state court, where tort reform has been slow in coming.[8] On the proportion of suits against accountants, Joseph Grundfest and Michael Perino, both of Stanford Law School, testified before the Senate Committee on Banking, Housing, and Urban Affairs that 150 securities class action suits were filed in the first year following enactment of the *Litigation Reform Act*, and estimated that 163 suits would have been filed absent the Act.[9] On the danger of plaintiffs suing in state court, Congress in 1998 passed the *Securities Litigation Uniform Standards Act*, making federal courts the only venue for most securities class action suits involving 50 or more parties. Summarizing securities litigation in the wake of the Act, Grundfest and Perino testified to more suits alleging accounting fraud, larger alleged market capitalization (shares outstanding × share price) declines (before enactment: 19 percent; after enactment: 31 percent), continued disproportionately high numbers of suits against technology companies, significant declines in the number of institutional investors acting as lead plaintiff, and the increased dominance of one single law firm as plaintiff's class action counsel (before enactment: 31 percent appearance ratio; after enactment: 59 percent nationwide and 83 percent in California).

Criminal Liability

An auditor can be held criminally liable under several federal statutes, including the *Securities Act of 1933* (Section 24), the *Securities Exchange Act of 1934* [Section 32(a)], the *Federal False Statements Statute*, the *Federal Mail Fraud Statute*, and the *Racketeer Influenced and Corrupt Organizations Act*. Section 24 of the 1933 Act holds an auditor criminally liable for willfully making a false statement or omitting a material fact in connection with a registration statement. Section 32(a) of the 1934 Act also holds an auditor criminally liable for willfully making a false or misleading statement in reports filed under the Act. Criminal penalties against individuals under either section may include fines or not more than five years imprisonment, or both. Under the *Federal False Statements Statute*, criminal liability can result from any issue within a federal department's or agency's jurisdiction; and under the *Federal Mail Fraud Statute*, from any mailing or conspiracy to mail false financial statements. The *Racketeer Influenced and Corrupt Organizations Act*,

7 "Securities Litigation Reform Bill is Now Law," *Journal of Accountancy* (February 1996), p. 14.
8 "Tort Reform, Short Reform," *The Public Accounting Report* (November 15, 1996), pp. 1, 5.
9 Joint Written Testimony of J. A. Grundfest and M. A. Perino, Subcommittee on Securities of the Senate Committee on Banking, Housing, and Urban Affairs, Federal Document Clearing House Inc., July 24, 1997.

discussed more fully later, is a federal criminal statute that includes a civil provision that can be imposed on independent auditors.

Continental Vending

> fraud

Over the years there have been only a few criminal liability cases involving auditors, the overwhelming majority of cases having been for civil liability. A particularly prominent criminal liability case involving auditors was decided in 1969, *United States v. Simon*, popularly known as the "Continental Vending" case, and involved both Section 32(a) of the 1934 Act and the *Federal Mail Fraud Statute*.

Harold Roth was president of Continental Vending and owner of about 25 percent of both Continental and its affiliate, Valley Commercial Corporation. From 1958 to 1962, Continental loaned over $3 million to Roth through Valley Commercial, whose operations were supervised by Roth. Because Roth could not repay Valley, Valley could not repay Continental. Thus, Roth pledged collateral, about 80 percent of which was Continental stock. Although the receivable from Valley was recorded by Continental, it was not collectible because Roth was unable to pay Valley, and the market value of Roth's collateral was less than the amount owed. Bankruptcy followed, and the government sued the auditors, alleging that a footnote in Continental's September 30, 1962, financial statements did not adequately disclose that Roth ultimately received money loaned by Continental to Valley and that Roth's collateral consisted largely of Continental securities.

The auditors argued that they had followed generally accepted accounting principles and thus were free of criminal liability. However, the court ruled in the government's favor, stating that improper activities should be disclosed. In part, the court said:

But it simply cannot be true that an accountant is under no duty to disclose what he knows when he has reason to believe that, to a material extent, a corporation is being operated not to carry out its business in the interests of all the stockholders but for the private benefit of its president.

Further, regarding an auditor's obligations, the court said:

Generally accepted accounting principles instruct an accountant what to do in the usual case when he has no reason to doubt that the affairs of the corporation are being honestly conducted. Once he has reason to believe that this basic assumption is false, an entirely different situation confronts him.

Thus the court effectively ruled that compliance with accepted standards—due diligence—is not a wholly sufficient defense in criminal cases. The auditors were convicted of willfully making a false or misleading statement and for using the mails to distribute false and misleading financial statements, although they received a presidential pardon.

Racketeer Influenced and Corrupt Organizations Act

Passed originally as part of the *Organized Crime Control Act of 1970*, the **Racketeer Influenced and Corrupt Organizations (RICO) Act** was intended to curtail the movement of organized crime into legitimate business. Although RICO is a federal criminal statute, a last-minute change by Congress added a civil provision that has been used widely against legitimate businesses and professionals, including independent accountants.

Rather than define the nebulous term "organized crime," Congress listed acts typically associated with organized crimes, such as murder, arson, and extortion, and other acts such as mail fraud, wire fraud, and fraud in the sale of securities, all of which were growing in prominence in the late 1960s. Although targeted toward organized crime, RICO has greatly impacted the profession because the Act is broadly worded, defines a "pattern of racketeering activity" as two or more convictions (civil or criminal) within a 10-year period, and contains a provision that permits private parties, such as shareholders, to bring civil suits that include treble damages and attorneys' fees. As Virginia Congressman Frederick C. Boucher said, ". . . the result of combining this broadly worded statute with the unfettered use made of it by private parties has been an explosion of RICO treble-damage claims in cases against people Congress never intended to be victimized by this powerful weapon."[10] Among those individuals who may be victimized are professionals, such as certified public accountants, who are not even remotely connected with organized crime.

In 1985, the U.S. Supreme Court, in a 5 to 4 decision (*Sedima v. Imrex Company*), ruled that RICO's civil provisions could be applied to virtually any commercial dispute, which effectively increased the potential exposure of professional accountants, since suits against auditors typically involve a commercial dispute. However, the Court also noted that RICO has been applied legally to defendants not intended by Congress, and that any correction of the Act's defects must lie with Congress. For example, in an op-ed piece in *The Wall Street Journal*, U.S. Supreme Court Chief Justice William H. Renquist stated, "The legislative history of the RICO Act strongly suggests that Congress never intended it to be used in ordinary disputes divorced from the influences of organized crime. . . . I think the time has arrived for Congress to enact amendments to civil RICO to limit its scope to the sort of wrongs that are connected to organized crime. . . ."[11]

Consistent with Chief Justice Renquist's statement, the U.S. Supreme Court in 1993 upheld (7 to 2) an appeals court ruling in *Reves v. Arthur Young* that an independent audit does not meet RICO's criteria for involvement in the management ➤ fraud of a corrupt organization and therefore that auditors cannot be sued under RICO. But the decision was narrow, providing no relief for auditors who participate directly with management to perpetrate a fraud. The Court's ruling is a significant victory for the profession, since the AICPA, among others in the financial community, had been working with Congress since 1985 to enact changes in RICO, among them proposed legislation that would reduce treble damages to single damages and exclude securities cases from RICO's reach.

Illegal Acts by Clients

An auditor's responsibility for detecting client errors and fraud (Chapter 7) has long been a major preoccupation of regulatory agencies, the financial markets, the financial press, and professional accounting organizations such as the AICPA. In contrast, an auditor's responsibility for illegal acts by clients gained widespread prominence only within the last three decades. Prior to the 1970s, conventional

---

10 F. C. Boucher, "Why Civil RICO Must Be Reformed," *Journal of Accountancy* (December 1985), p. 103.
11 W. H. Renquist, "Get RICO Cases Out of My Courtroom," *The Wall Street Journal* (May 19, 1989), p. B2.

wisdom held that material illegal corporate payments, such as bribes to influence political officials, were virtually nonexistent. But in a dramatic turn of events, a 1976 SEC-sponsored voluntary compliance program disclosed that over 250 U.S. corporations had made questionable or illegal payments both in the United States and abroad. Congress responded in 1977 by enacting the *Foreign Corrupt Practices Act*, discussed later in the chapter, and the AICPA issued a Statement on Auditing Standards (*SAS No. 17*). In 1988, the Auditing Standards Board issued *Statement on Auditing Standards No. 54*, "Illegal Acts by Clients" (AU Sec. 317), which defines **illegal acts** as violations of laws or governmental regulations, and provides guidance in three general areas:

- An auditor's responsibility for detecting and disclosing illegal acts.
- The audit procedures an auditor should consider both in the apparent absence of illegal acts and when illegal acts are possible.
- How an auditor should respond to detected illegal acts.

Responsibility

Two important issues underscore an auditor's responsibility for illegal acts: dependence on legal judgment and the proximity of a questionable act to the financial statements. *Dependence on legal judgment* simply means that determining the illegality of specific acts is normally beyond the scope of an independent auditor's professional competence. Auditors are proficient in accounting and auditing, not the law. True, an auditor's experience and understanding of a client's industry may provide a basis for recognizing some illegal acts—for example, violations of federal tax or securities laws—but determining legality should generally be left to attorneys and to due process of the law.

The likelihood of detecting an illegal act depends on the *proximity of the act* to recorded transactions and events. The further removed an illegal act is from the transactions and events normally reflected in financial statements, the less likely an auditor is to become aware of the act. For example, although violations of federal tax laws are likely to be detected during an audit, violations of other laws and regulations, such as the *Occupational Safety and Health Act*, are beyond the scope of an audit and therefore are far less likely to be detected. Even if they are detected, an auditor considers these laws from the perspective of their relation to audit objectives, not from the perspective of legality. Not surprisingly, many of the questionable or illegal payments disclosed through the SEC's voluntary compliance program were made through off-the-books accounts and therefore were not susceptible to reasonable investigation by auditors.

An auditor's responsibility to detect and report misstatements resulting from illegal acts that have a *direct and material* effect on financial statement amounts is identical to that for fraud: to assess the risk that they may cause materially misstated financial statements and to consider the assessment in designing audit procedures. Examples of illegal acts that have a direct and material effect include violations of federal tax laws or government grant contracts. Regarding illegal acts that have a material but *indirect* effect on the financial statements—that is, those acts that are removed from the transactions and events reflected in financial statements—the auditor should be aware that they may have occurred, although an audit provides no assurance that they will be detected. Examples of material but indirect illegal acts include violations of antitrust and equal employment laws.

Auditing Procedures

A financial statement audit normally does not include procedures designed specifically to detect illegal acts. However, some audit procedures that are motivated by audit objectives unrelated to illegal acts could lend insight into violations of the law. For example, reading the minutes of the board of directors' meetings, a procedure not motivated by its potential to reveal illegal acts, may provide the auditor's first evidence of an impending investigation by the Environmental Protection Agency, which may require disclosure of fines and penalties as a contingent liability. When there is no reason to believe that illegal acts exist, the auditor should make inquiries of management about the entity's compliance with laws and regulations and, where applicable, also inquire about management's policies for preventing illegal acts, such as the issuance of policy directives internally. No other audit procedures are necessary in the absence of evidence suggesting that illegal acts may exist.

When an auditor becomes aware of information concerning a possible illegal act, he or she should obtain (1) an understanding of the circumstances of the act—for example, by making inquiries of management above those involved—and (2) enough evidence to judge the effect of the act on the financial statements. If evidence provided by management doesn't convince the auditor that an illegal act has not occurred, the auditor should consult with the entity's legal counsel and consider other procedures. For example, the auditor might consider confirming significant information with intermediaries, such as bankers and lawyers, or with other parties to the transaction.

Responding to Detected Illegal Acts

When an illegal act has occurred or is likely to occur, an auditor should consider the effect of the act on the financial statements and on the audit report, including an evaluation of the materiality of the act. As discussed in Chapter 2, materiality in accounting and auditing is a matter of professional judgment, and this is no less the case when applied to illegal acts. For example, in the past, several high-ranking corporate officials dismissed their company's questionable payments as immaterial and therefore of little consequence to financial information users. Although specific acts alone may be immaterial in amount, two other factors, namely contingent monetary effects and loss contingencies, may render an act material. **Contingent monetary effects** include fines, penalties, and damages that, in some circumstances, such as violations of the *Foreign Corrupt Practices Act* (discussed in the next section), may be quite substantial. Loss contingencies, such as the threat of expropriation of assets, enforced discontinuance of foreign operations, or possible litigation, are frequently more substantial than either contingent monetary effects or, for example, an illegal payment itself. Thus when considering the materiality of an illegal act, an auditor should consider contingent monetary effects and loss contingencies, not just the dollar amount of the payment itself.

Under *SAS No. 54*, illegal acts should be reported to the audit committee of the board of directors or to others with equivalent authority, such as the federal agencies that monitor direct federal grants to local governments and to nonprofit organizations such as local community theaters. However, an auditor's responsibility for illegal acts detected in public companies is more forthcoming: The "Auditor Disclosure of Corporate Fraud" provision of the *Private Securities Litigation Reform*

Act of 1995 requires that auditors report possible illegal acts to management and to the audit committee and, if neither takes remedial action, the provision requires that the auditor notify the full board of directors in writing and that the entity forward the report to the SEC within one business day. Disclosure to other parties is not ordinarily the auditor's responsibility, although there is a duty to notify a successor auditor and there may be a duty to respond to a subpoena. If management does not disclose a direct and material illegal act properly in the financial statements, the auditor should express a qualified or an adverse opinion since, as explained in Chapter 3, failure to disclose is a departure from generally accepted accounting principles. If prevented by management from obtaining evidence, the auditor should disclaim an opinion on the financial statements.

The Foreign Corrupt Practices Act

The **Foreign Corrupt Practices Act (FCPA)** evolved primarily from investigations by the Office of the Watergate Special Prosecutor and an SEC voluntary disclosure program, both of which provided evidence of significant illegal acts perpetrated by U.S. multinational companies overseas. The intent of Congress in legislating the Act was to respond directly as critics of corporate governance and responsibility through legislation that would require corporations to implement internal controls sufficient to detect illegal payments and to enable accurate financial statements. The Act includes two provisions, one related to unlawful influence (bribes), and another to record keeping and internal control.

Unlawful Influence

The unlawful influence provision of the Act makes it illegal for any U.S. domestic company or foreign SEC-registrant company to influence foreign governments, officials, political parties, or political candidates through payments or gifts. For example, it would be unlawful for a U.S. importer to protect domestic market share by bribing a foreign political official to influence legislation that would increase the foreign country's export tariff. However, the Act does not prohibit so-called "grease" or "facilitating" payments companies may make, for example, to ministerial or clerical government employees to expedite the processing of shipments through customs. A company convicted of a bribe, whether willful or not, can be fined up to $1,000,000. An officer, director, or stockholder of a convicted company can be fined up to $10,000 and/or imprisoned for up to five years, although bribes must be willful. Fines imposed on individuals may not be paid by an employer.

Record Keeping and Internal Control

The record-keeping and internal control provision of the Act requires that the management of a public company implement internal controls sufficient to provide reasonable assurances that (1) transactions are executed in accordance with management's authorization, (2) transactions are recorded as necessary, and (3) access to assets is permitted only to employees management authorizes. Because the Act amends Section 13(b) of the *Securities Exchange Act of 1934*, the provision is administered and enforced by the SEC. A company violating the record-keeping and internal control provision of the Act can be fined up to $10,000. An officer, director, or stockholder of a violating company can be fined up to $10,000 and/or imprisoned up to five years. Again, fines imposed on individuals may not be paid by an employer.

Coping with Potential Liability

How does an auditor cope with the inevitable risk of litigation, a risk sustained on virtually any portfolio of audit engagements? The following describes several precautions practitioners take to minimize the risk of potential litigation.

Arbitration or Mediation

In a move intended to minimize litigation costs, BDO Seidman and Ernst & Young were first in the profession to include language in engagement letters urging clients for all professional services to waive the right to a jury trial, opting instead for alternative dispute resolution—mediation or arbitration—to resolve disputes.[12] For example, Ernst & Young engagement letters called first for discussions with an impartial mediator agreed to by each party or assigned by the American Arbitration Association (AAA), followed 90 days thereafter by binding arbitration using procedures in the AAA's *Arbitration Rules for Professional Accounting and Related Services Disputes*. Unlike jury trials, arbitration does not award punitive damages, does not incur court costs or excessive legal fees, and does not lack for timely resolutions. Today, it's quite common for accountants to call for alternative dispute resolution in engagement letters.

Practice Development

If you think public accounting firms don't "fire" clients, think again. To avoid risk, firms have been declining engagements regularly at least since the mid-1990s. For example, over a decade ago *Business Week* reported that one accounting firm discontinued auditing a West Coast bank, another declined to audit about sixty companies considering initial public offerings, and that several major firms refused to audit small banks and thrift institutions at all.[13] And *The Wall Street Journal* reported that the Big Five public accounting firms dropped 245 publicly traded clients in the mid-1990s.[14] Although firms once tripped over themselves to develop new business, practice development has taken a new twist in recent years. For example, all major firms now employ personnel whose primary function is to investigate the backgrounds of new clients and their managements, and some use independent investigative firms such as Securatis Group, successor to Pinkertons, a security services firm with roots in the 1800s.

What's clear is that unlimited growth in client lists does not necessarily yield a successful audit practice and may lead to legal action, rendering increased audit fees trivial when compared to the damages sometimes awarded to clients and other third parties. Practice development should not flourish at the expense of quality. Rather, new clients should be scrutinized carefully for integrity, and

---

12 B. Goodman, "E&Y Enacts Mediation Policy to Cut Courtroom Expenses," *Accounting Today* (May 6–19, 1996), pp. 5, 49.

13 K. Holland and L. Light, "Big Six are Firing Clients," *Business Week* (March 1, 1993), pp. 76–77.

14 E. MacDonald, "More Accounting Firms are Dumping Risky Clients," *The Wall Street Journal* (April 25, 1997), p. B1.

assigned audit staff should be alert to undue risk of fraudulent financial reporting. The watchword today is professional skepticism.

Engagement Letters

Both *Maryland Casualty Co. v. Jonathon Cook* (above) and *1136 Tenants' Corp. v. Max Rothenberg & Co.* (Chapter 7), illustrate the importance of engagement letters. Among other things, engagement letters provide an explicit agreement of the professional services expected by a client and intended by the auditor, and serve to eliminate, or at least minimize, misunderstandings between the auditor and client about the scope of the engagement, thereby eliminating potential legal liability for services neither contracted for nor performed. Engagement letters, discussed more fully in Chapter 7, should be prepared for every professional engagement performed by an independent accountant, audit or otherwise. If a potential client refuses to sign an engagement letter, the practitioner should strongly consider refusing the engagement.

Auditing Standards and Quality Control

The Public Company Accounting Oversight Board's auditing standards and the AICPA's generally accepted auditing standards are the profession's guidelines for performing audit engagements and measures of quality for evaluating completed engagements. Nevertheless, some courts have ruled that auditors should reach for a higher standard of care, particularly in cases alleging criminal liability, as illustrated earlier in *United States v. Simon* (Continental Vending). Although it is not clear whether the courts will in the future require a higher standard of care than imposed by auditing standards, it is clear the courts will never accept a lower standard.

As explained in Chapter 4, quality control includes the internal policies and procedures that a firm establishes to regulate itself, and peer review is the process through which firms "audit" the quality control procedures of other firms. Of the two, quality control plays a more important role in minimizing potential legal liability, because it defines a standard of care that is applied to each of the firm's professional engagements, a "measuring stick" designed to minimize substandard performance on individual engagements. The stronger a firm's system of quality control, the less likely a substandard engagement.

Professional Liability Insurance

Owing to large settlements involving the large national firms, malpractice insurance rates skyrocketed for all firms, and insurance companies became increasingly reluctant to underwrite professional liability insurance for independent accountants. For example, insurance premium increases of 200 to 400 percent in one year were not uncommon, and the number of insurance companies offering liability insurance to small and medium-size firms dropped from almost a dozen in the 1980s to a small handful a decade later. Even Lloyd's of London, the major insurer of the international firms at the time, threatened to drop coverage unless awards against accountants were restrained. In short, the soaring malpractice suits once associated primarily with the medical profession had spread to public accounting.

In response to the high costs and diminishing sources of accountants' liability insurance, the AICPA established a special committee to consider the nature and extent of accountants' liability in general, and potential remedies to the explosion in liability suits in particular. In the 1990s, liability insurance rates became more reasonable, largely because of the influence of the AICPA. But among the profession's more far-reaching proposals has been a movement to seek legislation limiting the liability of independent accountants in individual cases, a proposal that is not without precedent. For example, the *Atomic Energy Act of 1954* limits liability for nuclear accidents to $650 million and, not unrelated, the liability of accountants in some foreign countries is limited by statute.

Countersuits

Interestingly, there is precedent for public accounting firms to countersue clients who, by perpetrating unscrupulous schemes to "cook the books," fraudulently induce unknowing auditors to issue unqualified opinions. In a 1992 precedent-setting development, Manor Care Inc., a Maryland company that acquired Cenco Inc. in 1981, agreed to settle a 14-year-old counterclaim filed by BDO Seidman in the case of *Cenco, Inc. v. Seidman & Seidman*. The settlement occurred just days before a jury trial was to begin in Illinois state court. Responding to the decision, Dan Goldwasser, an attorney and consultant to the New York State Society of CPAs, said, "it's likely that we're going to see more countersuits of this nature filed by accounting firms. The firms can no longer passively accept the risk of liability exposure when there has been clear evidence of fraud on the part of an audit client's management."[15]

➤ fraud

Limited Liability Partnerships (LLPs)

Partnerships in some countries, among them the German GmbH (*Gesellschaft mit beschrankter Haftung*) and Latin American *limitada* companies, exempt partners from personal liability beyond their respective investments in the company. As discussed in Chapter 4, Rule 505 of the Code of Professional Conduct allows a CPA firm to organize in any manner permitted by state law, and in all states, as in Germany and Latin America, limited liability partnerships (LLPs) restrict the extent of a partner's liability to his or her investment in the partnership (or involvement in an obligation or illegal act). The first LLP legislation was enacted in Wyoming in 1977. Since then, all the states have responded and, as discussed in Chapter 1, so too have most public accounting firms.

SUMMARY

In any civil liability case involving auditors, several issues are relevant, including the source of law (common or statutory); the identity of the plaintiff; potential liability; and who sustains the burden of proving damage or loss, that financial statements are misstated, reliance on financial statements, and deficient auditor conduct. Under common law, an independent auditor may be liable to clients,

15 L. Berton, "BDO Seidman Wins Fraud Settlement in Countersuit Against an Audit Client," *The Wall Street Journal* (November 11, 1992), p. 7.

primary beneficiaries, and foreseen third parties. Under Section 11 of the *Securities Act of 1933*, an auditor may be liable to purchasers of securities; under Sections 10(b) and 18 of the *Securities Exchange Act of 1934*, an auditor may be liable to purchasers of securities, sellers, or both.

An independent auditor's criminal liability extends from several federal (and state) statutes, the most prominent being Section 24 of the 1933 Act, Section 32(a) of the 1934 Act, and the *Federal False Statements* and *Mail Fraud Statutes*. In addition, auditors may be held liable under the *Racketeer Influenced and Corrupt Organizations Act*. Few cases have been decided regarding an auditor's criminal liability, but criminal penalties have been and may continue to be levied.

Professional standards govern an auditor's responsibility for illegal acts: An auditor is responsible to assess the risk that they may cause materially misstated financial statements and to consider the assessment in designing audit procedures. Even though determining illegality is beyond the scope of an auditor's expertise, he or she should have a reasonable basis for identifying potentially improper acts, although the likelihood of detection depends on the proximity of the act to the transactions and events underlying an entity's financial statements. The *Foreign Corrupt Practices Act* makes it unlawful for companies to influence foreign governments or officials through gifts or payments, and requires that SEC registrants comply with record-keeping and internal control requirements.

Given today's legal environment, auditors should take precautions to minimize potential legal exposure, such as requiring mediation or arbitration, limiting practice development, preparing engagement letters for all professional engagements, adhering to generally accepted auditing standards and promoting quality control, documenting all audit decisions and conclusions, maintaining adequate professional liability insurance, filing countersuits, and organizing as a limited liability company. Even with these precautions, though, the risk of litigation is large.

Practitioners have offered attestation services since the 1980s, and other assurance services somewhat more recently. However, case law for these services is quite limited compared to case law for auditing, a professional service with a rich tradition extending back to the Industrial Revolution. For example, this chapter cites precedent-setting auditing cases from five of the last six decades, and two from the nineteenth century. But generalizations about liability in attestation and assurance services are problematic, except for one: Although both services, like auditing, are generally three-party contracts, the third-party plaintiff in attestation and assurance engagements is less likely to be a *class* of litigants and the plaintiff is more likely to prevail in suits brought for *breach of contract* than in suits demanding the excessive punitive damages sometimes brought against auditors in tort.

KEY TERMS

Breach of contract 163
Common law 162
Contingent monetary effects 183
Foreign Corrupt Practices Act (FCPA) 184
Foreseeable third parties 163
Foreseen third parties 163
Fraud 164
Gross negligence 164

Illegal acts 182
Joint-and-several liability 161
Ordinary negligence 164
Primary beneficiaries 163
Privity 161
Proportionate liability 161
Racketeer Influenced and Corrupt
 Organizations (RICO) Act 180

REFERENCES

Baliga, W., "New York Clarifies Privity Requirements," and "Third Party Reliance on Audit Curtailed," *Journal of Accountancy* (January 1993), p. 17.

Causey, D. Y., Jr., *Duties and Liabilities of Public Accountants*, 7th ed. Starkville, MI: Accountant's Press, 2001.

Fisch, J. E., "The Scope of Private Securities Litigation: In Search of Liability Standards for Secondary Defendants," *Columbia Law Review* (June 1999).

Goldwasser, D. L., "Policy Considerations in Accountants' Liability to Third Parties for Negligence," *Journal of Accounting, Auditing & Finance* (Summer 1988), pp. 185–212.

Miller, R. I., and M. R. Young, "Financial Reporting and Risk Management in the 21st Century," *Fordham Law Review*, 1999.

Sweeney, P., "Five Tips to Steer Clear of the Courthouse," *Journal of Accountancy* (July 2002), pp. 34–38.

Wynne, M. M., "Primary Liability Amongst Secondary Actors: Why the Second Circuit's 'Bright Line' Standard Should Prevail," *Saint Louis University Law Journal* (Fall 2000).

QUESTIONS

1. Discuss the two issues that help explain the litigation explosion against independent auditors.
2. Identify the major issues involved in a civil action against an independent auditor.
3. Distinguish between ordinary negligence, gross negligence, and fraud.
4. In general, what elements must be proved by various parties to a legal liability case involving auditors?
5. What is the auditor's common law liability to clients? What is the minimum basis for liability?
6. What lesson is learned from *Maryland Casualty Co. v. Jonathon Cook*?
7. Briefly describe the facts in *Ultramares Corp. v. Touche* and cite the significance of the case.
8. Explain how primary beneficiaries differ from foreseen third parties. Give examples.
9. What is the significance to the profession of *Bily v. Arthur Young & Co.*, a 1993 California Supreme Court case?
10. Describe an auditor's alternative defenses under Section 11 of the *Securities Act of 1933*.
11. What lessons does *Escott v. BarChris Construction Corp.* offer about an inexperienced audit staff?
12. How does the burden of proof under Section 18 of the *Securities Exchange Act of 1934* differ from that under Section 10(b) and Rule 10b-5?
13. What is the significance of *United States v. Simon* to an independent auditor?
14. Identify several precautions an auditor might take to avoid litigation.
15. How should an independent auditor proceed if the effect of an illegal act on financial statements is not susceptible to reasonable investigation?
16. What is the purpose of the record-keeping and internal control provisions of the *Foreign Corrupt Practices Act*?
17. What are "grease" or "facilitating" payments, and how are they treated in the *Foreign Corrupt Practices Act*?

18. What penalties may be imposed on an entity, officers, directors, or stockholders for violating the *Foreign Corrupt Practices Act*?
19. How can practice development help to limit an accounting firm's potential legal liability?
20. Explain the role of countersuits in auditor liability cases.

MULTIPLE CHOICE QUESTIONS

1. Which of the following most compromises an auditor's position in legal liability?

   a. Privity
   b. Joint-and-several liability
   c. Proportionate liability
   d. Common law

2. Which of the following would most likely be a primary beneficiary?

   a. A shareholder
   b. A commercial bank
   c. An employee
   d. A supplier

3. Foreseen third parties are typically:

   a. In the least favorable position in auditor liability cases.
   b. Known by name to an auditor before an engagement begins.
   c. Not known by name to an auditor before an engagement begins.
   d. Creditors.

4. Auditor liability to foreseeable third parties is more of a threat in:

   a. Massachusetts.
   b. New York.
   c. Texas.
   d. Wisconsin.

5. A 1940 case, *Maryland Casualty Co. v. Jonathon Cook*, illustrates that:

   a. Auditors are responsible to detect material embezzlements.
   b. Auditors are culpable to clients who carry surety bonds on employees.
   c. Auditors are liable to parties who acquire a client's rights by subrogation.
   d. Auditors' liability under common law is dependent on the terms of the audit services contract.

6. The *Osborne, Security Pacific, and Cherry* cases:

   a. Overlook fraudulent inducement.
   b. Reaffirm the privity doctrine.
   c. Held that a phone call is insufficient to establish linkage.
   d. Establish law in privileged communications.

7. Reaffirmed in the 1980s and 1990s, the privity doctrine, first established in *Ultramares Corp. v. Touche* (1931), now requires a three-point linkage test established in a New York Court of Appeals case, *Credit Alliance v. Arthur Andersen & Co.* Among other things, the linkage test requires that:

   a. The accountant knew a specific third party would rely on the statements.
   b. Evidence links the accountant with the client.
   c. The accountant knew why the client required an opinion.
   d. The accountant provided an oral assurance of the client's solvency.

Questions 8 and 9 each relate to the following:

Gilmore, Inc., a privately owned manufacturer of jewelry, was audited by Balch & Ferris, CPAs. Relying on Gilmore's financial statements, Evergreen Commercial Credit Corp., a lending institution, granted Gilmore a long-term loan. Gilmore's statements were materially misstated, and Gilmore then went bankrupt. Evergreen Commercial Credit is suing Balch & Ferris for negligence in the audit.

8. Among other things, Evergreen must show:

   a. Misstated financial statements.
   b. Scienter.
   c. Compliance with truth-in-lending laws.
   d. Gross negligence.

9. In this case, Evergreen is most likely a:

   a. Foreseeable third party.
   b. Foreseen third party.
   c. Primary beneficiary.
   d. Client.

10. Alsap Corporation's April 2007, $35 million initial public offering included Singer & Revine's unqualified opinion on Alsap's December 31, 2006, audited financial statements. Owing to material misstatements related to inventory and receivables, securities purchasers sued Singer & Revine, who likely can avoid liability if:

    a. Singer & Revine can demonstrate due diligence.
    b. Singer & Revine's engagement letter called for mediation and arbitration.
    c. Alsap management caused the misstatements.
    d. Some of the purchasers did not rely on the audited financial statements.

11. An auditor may be held liable under the *Securities Act of 1933* for materially false or misleading financial statements if the security purchaser:

    a. Can establish reliance on the registration statement.
    b. Can establish gross negligence.
    c. Brings suit within four years after the security is offered to the public.
    d. Can establish that the financial statements were misstated.   (AICPA Adapted)

12. Which of the following correctly portrays the scope of Section 10(b) of the *Securities Exchange Act of 1934*?

    a. Section 10(b) protects shareholders of securities listed on a national stock exchange.
    b. Section 10(b) applies exclusively to securities registered under the *Securities Exchange Act of 1934*.
    c. Securities registered under the *Securities Act of 1933* are exempt from Section 10(b).
    d. Section 10(b) applies to purchases as well as sales of registered securities.

13. A client sues Jane Corning, an independent accountant, for negligence, alleging that because she failed to apply generally accepted auditing standards, she failed to discover large thefts of marketable securities. Under these circumstances:

    a. Corning is not bound by generally accepted auditing standards unless she is a member of the AICPA.
    b. Corning is negligent if she failed to apply generally accepted auditing standards.
    c. Generally accepted auditing standards apply to financial statements taken as a whole, not to audits of individual accounts.
    d. If Corning failed to apply generally accepted auditing standards, she would likely have committed a fraud.

14. Accountants' liability to third parties under common law:

    a. Has not changed substantially over the years.
    b. Is identical to accountants' liability under the *Securities Act of 1933*.
    c. Is identical to accountants' liability under the *Securities Exchange Act of 1934*.
    d. Is not uniform across all jurisdictions.

15. Columbus, Inc., a publicly traded corporation, is audited by Corrente & Corrente, CPAs. Because of inaccurate disclosures and serious losses from trading Columbus's securities, Columbus shareholders are suing Corrente & Corrente. In this case, the auditor's defense is:

    a. The financial statements were not misleading despite the inaccurate disclosures.
    b. Their conduct was not deficient under generally accepted auditing standards.
    c. Lack of privity.
    d. Lack of reliance.

16. Lincoln purchased Tally Corporation securities in a public offering subject to the *Securities Act of 1933*. Rosemere & Co., CPAs, issued an unqualified opinion on Tally Corporation's most recent statements (which were included in Tally's registration statement) and a comfort letter that revealed no material exceptions. Rosemere & Co. is being sued by Lincoln for alleged misstatements within the registration statement. To prevail, Lincoln must prove:

    a. Damages, reliance, and scienter.
    b. Damages, material misstatements, and reliance.
    c. Damages and material misstatements.
    d. Material misstatements and reliance.

17. If an auditor is certain an illegal act has a material effect on financial statements and the client agrees to adjust the statements accordingly, the auditor should:

    a. Withdraw from the engagement.
    b. Disclaim an opinion on the financial statements taken as a whole.
    c. Issue a qualified opinion.
    d. Issue an unqualified opinion.

18. An auditor's responsibility for illegal acts by clients:

    a. Depends on any contingent monetary effects and loss contingencies resulting from the act.
    b. Requires that he or she assess the risk of material misstatement of the financial statements due to illegal acts.
    c. Does not relate to direct, material illegal acts.
    d. Is unrelated to the proximity of the act to the financial statements.

19. The *Foreign Corrupt Practices Act* requires that:

    a. Auditors of publicly held companies report all illegal payments to the SEC.
    b. Publicly held companies establish audit committees consisting only of outside directors.
    c. U.S. firms doing business abroad report publicly all significant payments made to non-U.S. citizens.
    d. Publicly held companies devise and maintain an adequate system of internal control.

20. The arguments offered by third parties in litigation against a practitioner for an assurance service are likely to involve:

   a. Joint-and-several liability.
   b. Privity of contract.
   c. Reliance on advice.
   d. Due diligence.

PROBLEMS AND DISCUSSION CASES

5-1 *Common Law Liability and the Linkage Test*

Reno Poli, chief executive officer of Lincoln Avenue Bank, phoned Valerie Valentine, an audit partner in Tally & Rosemere LLP and the engagement partner for Bloomfield Plating Company, an electrolyte plating company serving the costume jewelry industry in southeastern New England. Poli told Valentine that he'd be forwarding a memorandum of understanding to Charles Bloomfield, the owner-manager of Bloomfield Plating, outlining the bank's understanding that a $300,000 working capital loan to Bloomfield Plating was conditional on Tally & Rosemere's issuing an unqualified opinion on Bloomfield's financial statements. Valentine told Poli that, although she had taken over the engagement from a recently retired partner, she planned to offer the same quality service that Tally & Rosemere had for the past nine years. Tally & Rosemere issued an unqualified opinion, Lincoln granted the loan to Bloomfield, and, owing to a cash embezzlement scheme perpetrated by Charles Bloomfield, the company defaulted on the loan. Lincoln Avenue Bank sued Tally & Rosemere. In a pretrial meeting, attorneys representing Lincoln Bank argued that Poli had satisfied the linkage test in *Credit Alliance v. Arthur Andersen & Co.* by having notified Valentine orally—and Bloomfield in writing—that the loan was conditional on the firm's audit.

> **Required:**
> 1. Explain Lincoln's motive in arguing that the linkage test had been established.
> 2. Will Lincoln prevail? Discuss the merits of Lincoln's argument.

5-2 *Common Law Liability to a Third Party*

Milady's Fashions, Inc., a Rhode Island discount retailer of women's apparel, has an excessively large inventory on hand and is in urgent need of additional cash. The company is bordering on bankruptcy (especially if the inventory has to be liquidated by sale to other stores rather than to the public), and about 15 percent of the inventory is resalable only at a discount drastically below cost. Faced with this financial crisis, Milady's approached several suppliers, one of which, Brent Brothers Apparel, Inc., was willing to loan Milady's $300,000 under certain conditions. First, Milady's was to submit audited financial statements for the express purpose of revealing the company's financial condition. Milady's engagement letter with Penting & Dunn LLP stated explicitly that the loan decision would be based on the financial statements. Second, Brent Brothers insisted on a secured position in all the unsecured inventory, accounts receivable, and other related personal property. In response, a security agreement was drawn and a financing statement was filed and recorded.

In preparing the financial statements, Milady's valued the inventory at cost, which was approximately $100,000 over current fair market value, and did not disclose two secured creditors to whom substantial amounts were owed and who took priority over Brent Brothers' security interests. Penting & Dunn issued an unqualified opinion, believing Milady's financial statements were presented fairly in all material respects. Six months later, Milady's filed for bankruptcy. Brent Brothers received $125,000 as its share in bankruptcy and is suing Penting & Dunn for the loss of $175,000. Penting & Dunn deny liability, claiming lack of privity and lack of negligence.

> **Required:** Is Brent Brothers entitled to recover from Penting & Dunn? Why or why not?

5-3 *Common Law Liability to Foreseen Third Parties Under the Restatement of Torts*

Claiming to have relied on an unqualified opinion and December 31, 2007, audited financial statements Sterling & Timm LLP issued for Ocean Technologies, Inc., Ashton Finance Company has sued Sterling & Timm to recover $2.3 million in losses from unpaid loans Ashton made to Ocean, a Florida company. Ashton claims the financial statements failed to report that, on or about October 31, 2007, the Internal Revenue Service had filed against Ocean a $147,700 federal tax lien for nonpayment of corporate taxes, and that, as of April 24, 2008, Ocean had failed to remit $120,000 in past-due first quarter 2008 payroll tax payments. In response, Sterling & Timm claims Ashton failed to establish that Ashton was one of a "limited group of persons" for whose benefit Sterling & Timm had supplied a report on audited financial statements or that Sterling & Timm knew Ocean intended to supply the report to Ashton.

During the engagement, Sterling & Timm's audit team dealt primarily with Thomas Dufrane, president, and Angela Servanti, controller. Servanti states in an affidavit that, when Sterling & Timm was retained, "I provided the firm with a list of contracts that Ocean had entered into or expected to enter into and that required the issuance of payments. I also told them that audited financial statements were needed in order for Ocean to obtain loans to make the payments." Sterling & Timm's audit planning memo reads in part: "The client has requested we work with them to complete the audit as quickly as possible as they need the audited financial statements for additional financing negotiations." In a deposition, Arthur Jaworski, a Sterling & Timm engagement partner, testifies, "Servanti's affidavit and the planning memo only go to show that Ashton was merely one of a whole myriad of foreseeable users rather than a limited group. Ashton was never named."

Following up on a conversation between Dufrane and Jaworski, Dufrane sent Jaworski a letter on January 6, 2006, which reads in part as follows:

I have heard rumors that our audited financial statements would not be complete and available to us until March 31, 2008. In all of the conversations we have had with you and others in your organization, I think that you all realized the importance of our obtaining an audited statement as soon as possible. Some of the reasons causing this urgency are as follows: . . . Our banking limit is set at a $450,000 line of credit and we cannot expect any other consideration until the 2007 audited statement is complete.

Required: The case will be tried in a *Restatement of Torts* jurisdiction. Is Ashton Finance entitled to recover from Sterling & Timm? Why or why not?

5-4 *Common Law Liability to Foreseen Third Parties Under Privity and Credit Alliance*

Claiming to have relied on an unqualified opinion and December 31, 2007, audited financial statements Hasting & Ford LLP issued for Jasper Manufacturing, Dual Manufacturing has sued Hasting & Ford to recover $1.5 million Dual paid to purchase the assets of Jasper, a Connecticut company. Dual claims that several letters to Jasper made clear Dual's concern that the carrying value of some of Jasper's tangible assets were uncertain. For example, a December 5, 2007, letter from Raphael Jeter, Dual president, to Lisa Gotshal, Jasper's president, read in part as follows:

The purchase price will be based in part on the carrying value of inventory and fixed assets. However, as you told us, the financial statements you submitted to us are unaudited. We await 2007 audited financial statements, which you told us will be forthcoming by the end of February.

Dual claims the engagement team was told repeatedly that, owing to Dual's inability to fulfill customer orders, the company was actively seeking either to acquire a company or to acquire assets. In response, Hasting & Ford claims that Dual produced no evidence to prove that Dual was in privity and, therefore, that Hasting & Ford owed Dual no duty.

Required: The case will be tried in a *Credit Alliance* jurisdiction. Is Dual Manufacturing entitled to recover from Hasting & Ford? Why or why not?

5-5 *Initial Public Offerings and Securities Act of 1933*

Baldoni & Literick LLP issued an unqualified opinion on the September 30, 2007, financial statements of Service Paper Company, a publicly owned paper products company. Owing both to an increasing market share and to limited capacity, Service Paper filed a registration statement for an initial public offering of class B common shares under the *Securities Act of 1933*, and engaged Baldoni & Literick to issue a comfort letter for the period between October 1, 2007 and December 15, 2007, the effective date of the registration statement. Following sale of the securities, Service Paper revealed that sales and receivables from transactions arising after October 1 were overstated materially, trading in the securities was suspended, and Baldoni & Literick was named as a defendant in a class action suit, which alleged that the firm intentionally disregarded, or failed to exercise reasonable care to discover, material facts that occurred subsequent to October 15, 2007, the date of the audit report.

Required: Discuss Baldoni & Literick's liability for events that occurred between the date of the auditor's report and the effective date of the public offering.

5-6 *Liability Under Section 10(b) and Rule 10b-5*

Gordon & Groton, CPAs, were the auditors of Jordan & Company, a brokerage firm and member of several national and international stock exchanges. Gordon & Groton audited and reported on the financial statements of Jordan, which were filed with the Securities and Exchange Commission.

Several of Jordan's customers were swindled by a fraudulent scheme perpetrated by Jordan's president, who owned 90 percent of the voting stock of the company. The facts established that Gordon & Groton were negligent, but not reckless nor grossly negligent, in conducting the audit, and neither participated in, nor knew of, the fraudulent scheme.

The customers are suing Gordon & Groton under the antifraud provisions of Section 10(b) and Rule 10b-5 of the *Securities Exchange Act of 1934* for aiding and abetting the president's fraudulent scheme. The customers' suit for fraud is grounded on the auditors' failure to conduct a proper audit under generally accepted auditing standards and, therefore, on failure to discover the fraudulent scheme.

Required: Discuss the issues and the probable outcome of the case.

(AICPA Adapted)

5-7 *Statutory Liability and the Private Securities Litigation Reform Act*

Andrew Christie, a recently hired entry-level associate in Fallon & Goff LLP, was assigned to audit the receivables at Edgemere Company, a publicly traded manufacturer of roofing materials. Owing to errors in entering credit sales in late June, the last month of the fiscal year, the reported earnings, credit sales, and customer receivables balances were materially misstated, though unintentionally. A class action suit attributes significant stock price declines to public announcements of the errors. Fallon & Goff's audit program for receivables called for analytical procedures and for the confirmation of receivables balances with debtors, but neither Christie nor the working paper review process detected the need to follow up on unusual fluctuations in the receivables balance or in the number of days' sales in receivables. Plaintiffs in a class action suit do not suggest fraud by Fallon & Goff, but do allege gross negligence. Fallon & Goff recognizes their culpability but argues that the firm should share responsibility under the *Private Securities Litigation Reform Act*. In a separate action, a small investor claims Fallon & Goff is jointly-and-severally liable under the same Act.

Required:
1. To recover, what must the plaintiffs show in the class action suit?
2. Discuss both Fallon & Goff's and the small investor's claims about the *Private Securities Litigation Reform Act*.

5-8 *Gross Negligence and Criminal Liability*

Cragsmore & Company LLP was engaged to audit the financial statements of Marlowe Manufacturing, Inc., a publicly traded corporation. Prior to preparing the audit report, Susan Cragsmore, a partner, and Fred Willmore, a senior associate, reviewed the notes disclosed within the financial statements. One note reported the terms, costs, and obligations of a lease between Marlowe and Acme Leasing Company. Willmore suggested that the footnote read: "The Acme Leasing Company is owned by persons who have a 35 percent interest in the capital stock and who are officers of Marlowe Manufacturing, Inc.," although on Cragsmore's recommendation the note was revised by substituting "minority shareholders" for "persons who have a 35 percent interest in the capital stock and who are officers."

The audit report and financial statements were forwarded to Marlowe Manufacturing for review. The officers-shareholders of Marlowe, who also owned Acme Leasing, objected to the revised wording and insisted that the footnote be changed to describe the relationship between Acme and Marlowe as an affiliation. Cragsmore agreed and issued an unqualified opinion that appears both within Marlowe's annual report to shareholders and within Form 10-K to the SEC. The audit working papers included drafts of the wording of the footnote. Thereafter, Marlowe suffered a substantial, uninsured fire loss and was forced into bankruptcy. The failure of Marlowe to carry any fire insurance coverage was not reported in the financial statements.

Attorneys representing Cragsmore & Company reveal in a private meeting with Susan Cragsmore that the plaintiffs may have grounds to allege fraud or gross negligence and, since the footnote was included within Form 10-K, the plaintiffs' attorneys may even have grounds to argue criminal liability.

Required: Discuss the grounds on which the plaintiffs could allege fraud, gross negligence, and criminal liability against Cragsmore & Company.

(AICPA Adapted)

5-9 *Legal Liability and Employee Fraud*

Jackson, an early career associate in Harrison & Weeks LLP, began but did not finish the audit of inventory in Bosco Corporation, a manufacturer and marketer of expensive watches. During the audit, Jackson resigned from Harrison & Weeks and the firm assigned Davidson, an entry-level staff member, to complete Jackson's work. Due to the staff change and to busy-season time pressure, the firm did not audit inventory adequately. Had appropriate procedures been used, Jackson and Davidson would likely have discovered that watches worth more than $20,000 were missing, all stolen by a sales clerk. The clerk stole $75,000 in watches before the thefts were discovered six months after Harrison & Weeks completed the audit.

Required: Discuss the legal problems that Harrison & Weeks will likely face.

(AICPA Adapted)

5-10 *Reporting Illegal Acts to Third Parties*

The partner in charge of your firm is concerned that associates may not be aware of current professional standards about communicating illegal acts to parties other than management and the board of directors, given particularly that the standards have changed in the 1970s, the 1980s, and again in the 1990s.

Required: Draft a memorandum for distribution to all staff members about procedures for reporting illegal acts. Be specific.

5-11 *A Controller Engaged in Fraud*

Winston & Mall LLP was engaged to audit the financial statements of Fast Cargo Company, a retailer. The auditors tested a sample of 100 disbursement transactions, all of which were to be supported by purchase orders, receiving reports, and invoices. However, tests revealed several instances where purchases had been recorded and paid, although a receiving report had not been filed. These exceptions were noted in working papers prepared by Martin, a staff associate. Mall, the partner in charge of the engagement, called these exceptions to the attention of Harris, Fast Cargo's CFO, who promised to locate and file the receiving reports. Mall accepted this explanation, did nothing further to investigate, and issued an unqualified opinion on Fast Cargo's financial statements.

Unknown either to Mall or to Martin, Harris, the controller, was engaged in a fraud: Merchandise was diverted to a private warehouse where Harris leased space and the invoices were sent to Fast Cargo for payment. The scheme was discovered, and a preliminary estimate indicates that the loss to Fast Cargo will exceed $50,000.

Required:
1. Discuss Winston & Mall's liability, if any.
2. What additional steps, if any, should Mall have taken? Explain.

(AICPA Adapted)

5-12 *An Unpaid Bank Loan and Undetected Fraud*

Martinson, Brinks & Sutherland LLP audited the financial statements of Masco Corporation, a medium-size wholesaler that leased warehouse facilities. Masco sought bank financing for the leases, assuring the bank that the leasehold improvements would result in efficiencies and therefore a more profitable operation. On the basis of these assurances, the bank granted Masco a line of credit.

The loan agreement required annual audited financial statements. Masco submitted 2007 audited financial statements to the bank, which disclosed net income of $75,000, leasehold improvements of $250,000, and net worth of $350,000. Relying on the audited statements, the bank loaned Masco $200,000. The audit report accompanying the financial statements disclaimed an opinion because the cost of the leasehold improvements could not be determined from the company's records. An excerpt of the audit report that addresses leasehold improvements follows:

Additions to fixed assets in 2006 were found to include principally warehouse improvements. Practically all of this work was done by company employees and the cost of materials and overhead was paid by Masco. Unfortunately, fully completed, detailed cost records were not kept of these leasehold improvements, and no exact determination could be made as to the actual cost of said improvements. The total amount capitalized is set forth in Note 4.

In late 2007 Masco went out of business, and the claimed leasehold improvements were discovered to be totally fictitious. The labor expenses charged as leasehold improvements actually proved to be operating expenses, none of the materials costs had been recorded, and the auditors had not investigated whether the leasehold improvements existed. Had the $250,000 not been capitalized, the income statement would have reflected a substantial loss from operations and net worth would have decreased correspondingly.

The bank sustained a loss on the $200,000 loan to Masco and now seeks to recover damages from Martinson, Brinks & Sutherland, alleging the firm was negligent.

Required:
1. Will the disclaimer of opinion absolve Martinson, Brinks & Sutherland from responsibility for not detecting the fraud?
2. Are partners who did not take part in the audit liable?

(AICPA Adapted)

5-13 *Monitoring Compliance with the FCPA*

The *Foreign Corrupt Practices Act* can seriously impact the business operations of many corporations, especially Securities and Exchange Commission registrants who are subject both to the unlawful influence and to the record-keeping and internal control provisions of the Act. Assume you are the manager of internal auditing for a publicly traded multinational corporation that manufactures and distributes aluminum alloy products throughout the world. The corporation's chief executive officer requests that you draft a plan for complying with the *Foreign Corrupt Practices Act.*

Required: Draft a plan for complying with the FCPA. The plan should emphasize a strategy for encouraging and monitoring compliance with the Act, rather than detailed procedures for complying with specific provisions of the Act.

Internet problems and discussion cases are available at http://ricchiute.swlearning.com

RESEARCH PROJECTS

1. Auditor Liability and the Securities Class Action Clearinghouse

Compiled by Stanford University Law School, the Securities Class Action Clearinghouse archives complaints, briefs, filings, and other information about the prosecution, defense, and settlement of federal class action securities fraud cases since enactment of the *Private Securities Litigation Reform Act.* The archive includes reports on interesting aggregate data, such as year-in-review summaries of filings and settlements; charts reporting the number of class action complaints by year and by quarter; and a listing of the most active court, sued sector (such as services), and sued industry (such as technology). The archive also includes detailed information about individual cases, stored by company name. For example, for each company, the archive includes a summary, a listing of plaintiff attorneys hyperlinked to their Web sites, the complaint, and a link to court filings powered by Google™.

Required: Access the original or amended complaints for two auditor liability cases from the vast inventory of litigations archived at the Securities Class Action Clearinghouse (**http://securities.stanford.edu/**). Draft a report that (1) briefs the accounting and auditing issues the complaint raises in each case and (2) compares and contrasts the allegations plaintiffs make against the independent auditors. For example, which of the individual allegations about violations of generally accepted accounting principles and violations of auditing standards are similar and which are dissimilar?

2. Litigation Against Accounting Firms and Current Reform

The financial press has been, and continues to be, replete with references to legal liability cases—and to large monetary judgments—against public accounting firms under both common law and federal securities law. Coincident with these cases, over 300 professional service firms, trade associations, accountants, and corporations formed the Coalition to Eliminate Abusive Securities Suits (CEASS) that sought and won the *Private Securities Litigation Reform Act of 1995,* which adopted proportionate liability to replace joint-and-several liability, adopted a modified loser-pays-the-winner's-court-costs provision, and eliminated the payment of bounties to professional plaintiffs in class action suits.

Required: Using recent articles from the business and accounting press (for example, *The Wall Street Journal, The New York Times, Accounting Today*), LEXIS, or Factiva:

1. Select an article (or, preferably, a series of articles) related to litigation against a public accounting firm and outline the case according to the summary of issues appearing in Figure 5-1 and discussed in the chapter:
   a. What is the source of law?
   b. Who is the plaintiff?
   c. What is the auditor's potential liability?
   d. Who has the burden of proving what?

2. Would the outcome of the case likely have been any different had the *Private Securities Litigation Reform Act* applied to your case?

3. Tort Reform

The *Private Securities Litigation Reform Act of 1995* and the U.S. Supreme Court's decision in *Central Bank of Denver v. First Interstate Bank of Denver* represent major victories in the profession's deliberate stance against unmerited legal liability for public accounting firms. The Act imposes only proportionate liability on peripheral defendants and, although debatable, the Court's decision reduces the securities liability of aiders or abettors. However, one major effort has been less successful: tort reform. In legislation introduced at the state level, a number of stakeholders, including some state societies of CPAs, have introduced tort reform legislation. For example, Arizona Senate Bill 1383 attempted to conform Arizona securities laws to federal laws, and California Bill 1862 attempted to limit punitive awards to no more than three times compensatory damages. Other industries have sought tort reform as well, including liability limits in the automobile industry and contingency fee limits in the legal profession.

Required: Identify tort reform legislation in the accounting profession or other industries for your state or others. Sources include a state representative or senator, and an article that briefly identifies state initiatives, such as, "Accountants Resume Tort Reform Quest at State Level," *Public Accounting Report* (February 29, 1996), pp. 2, 7. Draft a report that:
1. Identifies the stakeholders supporting and opposing the legislation, and discusses each stakeholder's interests.
2. Describes the major provisions of the legislation.
3. Lists the status of the legislation.

Interactive quizzes are available as a student learning resource at
http://ricchiute.swlearning.com

Part 2

The Audit Process and Internal Control

Chapter 6

Evidence

Major topics discussed in this chapter are:

- The acquisition and evaluation of audit evidence.
- Financial statement assertions, audit objectives, and audit procedures.
- Tests of controls, substantive tests of details, analytical procedures, and nonfinancial measures.
- The purpose, content, and form of audit documentation.

A CPA's advantage in the market for audit services is a grasp of the ways of evaluating evidence. However, the purpose of evaluating evidence is not to confirm management's assertions. Rather, the purpose is to afford a reasonable basis to conclude objectively *whether* management's assertions are confirmed. While subtle, this distinction is crucial to understanding the role that *independent* auditors serve. Acquiring, evaluating, and documenting objective evidence is the common thread across all audit engagements and the subject of this chapter. The chapter begins by introducing how practitioners acquire evidence in audit engagements. In turn, the chapter relates financial statement assertions to audit objectives and to audit procedures, and introduces the use of audit procedures as tests of controls, substantive tests of details, and analytical procedures. Finally, the chapter describes and illustrates audit documentation, the work product that auditors use to memorialize the evidence they acquire and the conclusions they reach.

Audit Evidence

Both the second attestation standard of field work and the third auditing standard of field work (Chapter 2, Figure 2-1) address evidence, although the professional literature (for example, *SAS No. 31*) is far more insightful about *audit* evidence. For example, the third GAAS of field work, reproduced below, is interpreted in *Statement on Auditing Standards No. 31*, "Evidential Matter" (AU Sec. 326) and *SAS No. 80*, "Amendment to SAS No. 31."

Sufficient competent evidential matter is to be obtained through inspection, observation, inquiries, and confirmations to afford a reasonable basis for an opinion regarding the financial statements under audit.

Sufficient refers to the quantity of evidence an auditor acquires to test management's financial statement assertions, and *competent* refers to the relevance, validity, and reliability of the evidence acquired. For example, in a typical financial statement audit, an independent auditor must judge *how much* (sufficiency) and *what kinds* (competence) of evidence he or she need acquire to conclude whether the sales transactions management recorded actually occurred during the period ending on the balance sheet date.

Evidential matter consists of the accounting data that underlies management's financial statements and the corroborating information that supports the accounting data. *Underlying accounting data* includes records of original entry (for example, journals), general and subsidiary ledgers, data files, and spreadsheets that capture the details summarized in financial statements. *Corroborating information* includes checks, records of electronic fund transfers, invoices, contracts, minutes of meetings, and other documents; written representations from vendors, attorneys, banks, and other third parties; and information obtained by questioning management or by observing a client's employees at work.

In some entities, some accounting data and corroborating information are available in electronic form only, such as electronic data interchange (EDI) or image processing systems. In *electronic data interchange* systems, paper source documents do not exist; customers and suppliers link electronically to transact purchases, sales, shipping, billing, cash receipts, and cash disbursements. In *image processing systems*, paper source documents exist, but are scanned into electronic images and, in some systems, discarded thereafter. As noted in *SAS No. 80*, "Amendment to SAS No. 31, 'Evidential Matter,'" information systems like EDI and image processing may produce electronic evidence that adds two extra hurdles for the auditor. First, the auditor should determine the time period that evidence will be available, since evidence may not be retrievable if files are changed and backup files are not maintained. Second, the auditor should be aware that irretrievable electronic evidence makes more problematic the practicality of relying exclusively on substantive tests (introduced in this chapter) to reduce detection risk to an acceptably low level.

Because audits need to be completed in reasonable time and at reasonable cost, auditors cannot examine evidence for every transaction or event relevant to management's assertions. Rather, auditors more often test samples of transactions, reach conclusions about the samples, and then generalize the results to the accounting populations from which the samples were drawn. For example, an auditor might examine purchase orders, receiving reports, and invoices supporting 100 randomly selected accounts payable and conclude from these results that assertions about the entire population of 5,000 payables are reliable. Because audit conclusions are drawn from testing some, rather than all, of the evidence underlying an accounting population, aggregate audit evidence is often *persuasive*, rather than wholly *convincing*, and an auditor's strategy is to gather the most persuasive evidence available.

Misspecifying the Competence and Sufficiency of Audit Evidence

➤ restatement

Three items above—the terms "competence" and "sufficiency" in the third standard of field work and the reference to "samples"—all conspire to raise an important point about audit evidence: Lax decisions about the *relevance* and the *amount* of evidence an auditor acquires can affect directly the linkage between audit risk and audit evidence and the merit of a previously issued audit report. Take, for example, the case of SmarTalk Teleservices, Inc., a publicly traded provider of prepaid telephone cards and wireless services that restated financial statements for the fiscal year ended December 31, 1997, and the first two quarters of 1998. In

1997, SmarTalk recorded a $25 million restructuring charge to exit in 1998 some of the operations of six prepaid phone card companies SmarTalk acquired. The charge and related reserve included anticipated costs for contract termination fees, asset write-downs, and employee severance benefits. However, to establish a restructuring reserve, FASB *Emerging Issues Task Force (EITF) No. 94-3*, "Liability Recognition for Certain Employee Termination Benefits and Other Costs to Exit an Activity," requires that management first establish an exit plan that identifies, for example, how and when management will dispose of the activities exited. Not only did management lack a plan, but management charged against the restructuring reserve over $1 million in executive travel, entertainment, telephone, and moving expenses, among other things, all of which the SEC concluded were operating expenses, rather than exit costs.

Following an offer of settlement, the SEC in an Accounting and Auditing Enforcement Release cited a 1997 risk-assessment document in which the auditors identified potential risk factors that included management's excessive interest in using unusually aggressive accounting practices to maintain share price and earnings trends. In the SEC's view, knowledge of these risks and of management's failure to produce an exit plan should have prompted the auditor to probe more deeply into the restructuring charge. On the competence and sufficiency of audit evidence, and the appropriateness of the auditor's unqualified opinion, the SEC cited findings that the auditor neither admitted nor denied. The auditor:

failed to obtain sufficient, competent evidence . . . in support of SmarTalk's accounting for its establishment of each component of the restructuring reserve and its charging 1997 expenses against the restructuring reserve that purportedly had been established for anticipated 1998 expenses [and] *failed to render an accurate audit report when they stated that SmarTalk's financial statements had been prepared in conformity with GAAP and the audit had been performed in accordance with GAAS. In fact, the financial statements were not in conformity with GAAP, and the audit was not performed in accordance with GAAS.*[1]

The case of SmarTalk, one of a number that point to the same conclusion, raises a timely insight into the relationship among audit risk (Chapter 2), reporting (Chapter 3), and evidence (this chapter): There is no substitute for professional skepticism when mapping management's assertions to the auditor's objectives, and the objectives to the procedures the auditor selects to control audit risk, all of which are discussed next.

Relating Assertions and Objectives

Much of an auditor's work consists of acquiring and evaluating evidence about the explicit and implicit assertions embodied in financial statements. That is, the auditor's role is to test the assertions underlying financial statement disclosures, not merely to test the account balances disclosed. For example, in the disclosure, "Inventory . . . $2,000,000," management makes no less than five **financial statement assertions**:

- Inventory physically exists,
- Inventory includes all products on hand,

---

1   SEC Accounting and Auditing Enforcement Release No. 1787, "In the Matter of Pricewaterhouse-Coopers, LLP" (May 22, 2003).

- The entity has legal title or similar rights of ownership,
- Inventory is stated properly at the lower of cost or market, and
- Inventory is classified properly as a current asset.

Since the financial statements are management's responsibility, the assertions are management's representations and can be categorized broadly as in Figure 6-1. From the assertions contained within management's financial statements, an auditor develops *audit objectives*, which may vary from one engagement to another depending on an entity's business and on the accounting practices unique to its industry. The following explains each financial statement assertion and illustrates some related audit objectives.

FIGURE 6-1: *Financial Statement Assertions*

Existence or Occurrence
All recorded assets, liabilities, and equities exist, and all recorded transactions occurred.

Completeness
All transactions and accounts that should be presented in the financial statements are presented.

Rights and Obligations
Assets are the rights, and liabilities are the obligations, of the entity.

Valuation or Allocation
Assets, liabilities, equities, revenues, and expenses are included in the financial statements at appropriate amounts; revenues, costs, and expenses are allocated to the proper accounting periods.

Presentation and Disclosure
Financial statement components are properly classified, described, and disclosed.

Existence or Occurrence

In financial statements presented in conformity with generally accepted accounting principles (GAAP), management asserts that all assets, liabilities, and equities disclosed in the financial statements actually existed at the balance sheet date, and that all recorded transactions actually occurred during the period ending on the balance sheet date. The auditor's objective is to test whether the assertion is appropriate. For example, in auditing inventory, an auditor's objective is to test whether inventory physically existed at the balance sheet date, whether recorded inventory purchases actually occurred, and whether sales transactions in the income statement represent the exchange of goods or services for cash or other consideration.

Completeness

In the occurrence assertion, management asserts that all *recorded* transactions actually *occurred*, but in completeness management asserts the opposite: All transactions that *occurred* during the period were *recorded*. Compared to other financial statement assertions, completeness is often the most challenging, since the auditor's task is to detect unrecorded transactions. In auditing inventory, for example, the auditor's objective is to test whether all purchases of goods and services are recorded, and in auditing payables the objective is to test whether all obligations are included as liabilities in the financial statements.

Rights and Obligations

Assertions about rights and obligations mean that the entity has property rights to all recorded assets, and that all liabilities represent obligations at the balance sheet date. In auditing plant assets, for example, an auditor's objective is to test whether the entity has title to land, equipment, and buildings, and in auditing long-term debt the objective is to test whether the entity has a bona fide obligation to debt holders. Note that the rights assertion does not necessarily mean the entity legally "owns" the asset, since not all assets on the balance sheet are owned by the entity—for example, a capital lease in the hands of a lessee.

Valuation or Allocation

The valuation assertion means that the recorded value of all assets, liabilities, equities, revenues, and expenses are carried in the financial statements at appropriate amounts. Closely related, allocation means that revenues, costs, and expenses are allocated to the proper accounting periods. An auditor's objective in testing valuation or allocation varies depending on the account audited. For example, in auditing inventory, the auditor's objective is to test whether inventories are valued at the lower of cost or market in accordance with the cost flow assumption (for example, FIFO, LIFO) adopted, thereby affecting both the valuation of inventory at the end of the period and the allocation of costs to the appropriate periods.

Presentation and Disclosure

In the presentation and disclosure assertion, management represents that all financial statement components are classified properly (for example, current versus noncurrent), described adequately (for example, "Net income from operations," not "Profit"), and disclosed in a manner that reflects GAAP for the entity's industry. For example, although depreciation is common in manufacturing companies, GAAP for state and local governmental entities preclude recording depreciation in any fund other than an enterprise fund. The auditor's objective is to assure that the financial statements and related notes reveal the substance, not just the form, of recorded transactions.

Relating Objectives and Procedures

To achieve audit objectives, and thereby address each financial statement assertion for each material account, an auditor selects **audit procedures** to acquire sufficient, competent evidential matter. The selection of audit procedures is based on the objectives, the quantity and types of evidence available, materiality, and the assessed level of audit risk. Evidence acquired from a single audit procedure may address one or more objectives, or more than one procedure may be needed to acquire evidence for a single objective. For example, in the audit of accounts receivable, confirmations provide evidence about the existence, rights, and valuation assertions, but both confirmations and tests of bad debts are used to address the rights assertion. Figure 6-2 lists the most common audit procedures used by auditors to gather evidence, and the following sections explain.

FIGURE 6-2: *Audit Procedures*

Observation
Physically examine a tangible asset, or develop impressions.

Documentation
Examine documents and records.

Confirmation
Obtain written statements from third parties.

Mechanical Tests of Data
Recompute amounts, or trace transactions through an information system.

Comparisons
Develop and analyze trends and relationships among data.

Inquiries
Obtain oral or written statements from management.

Observation

An auditor can acquire direct evidence about the existence of assets, such as inventory and plant assets, by physically observing the asset on the client's premises. Observation also provides information about the condition of tangible assets, an important determinant in addressing the valuation assertion. For example, an auditor may observe obsolete or damaged inventory during a physical inventory observation, and propose that management reduce the carrying value of inventory to its net realizable value. Observation, often a source of valuable impressions and insights, extends not only to tangible assets, but also to a client's accounting procedures. For example, observing client personnel perform tasks may be useful to an auditor's assessment of control risk, particularly in determining whether authorized employees actually perform their assigned duties.

Documentation

Documents used in auditing include internal evidence such as purchase orders, receiving reports, and sales invoices, and external evidence such as contracts, bank statements, and letters. The form of the documents may be electronic or paper. By inspecting documents and records, an auditor can determine whether recorded transactions are adequately supported and properly authorized. In applying this procedure, sometimes called *vouching*, an auditor selects recorded transactions and then examines the documents supporting the transactions selected. For example, an auditor could examine electronic transfers to vouch recorded cash disbursements, or contracts to support recorded liabilities.

Confirmation

The existence and valuation of some account balances can be substantiated by requesting confirmation in the form of letters or affidavits from independent third parties. In short, confirmations produce documents that represent evidence. For example, an auditor might confirm receivable and payable balances with debtors and creditors, respectively, confirm securities and other negotiable instruments held by independent custodians, confirm bank balances with banks and other depositories, or confirm the terms of a lease agreement with a lessor.

Mechanical Tests of Data

An auditor can verify the mathematical accuracy of underlying accounting data by *recomputing* calculations management performed originally. For example, an auditor might total—some say "foot"—the columns in a receipts journal, or recalculate depreciation expense, prepaid insurance, or accrued vacation pay. *Tracing,* another type of mechanical test, means following a transaction through the accounting system—for example, from source document to journal to subsidiary and general ledgers—and is used primarily to determine whether transactions are properly recorded and classified.

Comparisons

Auditors often compare current disclosures with similar disclosures from prior accounting periods to reveal trends, or with other disclosures in the current period to establish informative relationships. For example, a significant increase in current advertising expense (in the absence of either a new product launch or a major advertising campaign) may suggest that management has inadvertently misclassified expenses as advertising and therefore that the auditor may need to extend testing. Analyses of trends and relationships can be particularly useful in identifying areas requiring further audit work and are discussed later in the chapter as *analytical procedures*.

Inquiries

Evidence obtained from documentation, confirmation, and mechanical tests is often more persuasive than written and oral information the auditor obtains from inquiries posed to management. Although management's responses can be insightful, particularly in generating "leads," the auditor should consider the respondent's incentives to misdirect the auditor—called, sometimes, *source credibility*. For example, a credit manager—an employee whose job depends on customers paying the debts he or she approved—has incentives to misdirect an auditor who believes the allowance for bad debts may be understated. Oral responses should be corroborated through other procedures, among them documentation, confirmation, and mechanical tests.

Tests of Controls, Substantive Tests, and Audit Risk

Depending on an auditor's objectives, the procedures in Figure 6-2—observation, documentation, confirmation, mechanical tests, comparisons, and inquiries—can be used to perform tests of controls or substantive tests. **Tests of controls** are audit procedures that assess the ability of management's internal controls to prevent or detect material misstatements. In turn, **substantive tests** are audit procedures that detect material misstatements or that identify disclosures likely to contain material misstatements.

Tests of Controls and Control Risk

Procedures used as tests of controls address questions such as:

- How are management's internal controls applied?
- Are controls applied consistently?
- By whom are the controls applied?

Evidence acquired from procedures used as tests of controls helps an auditor reach a conclusion about the *assessed level of control risk*, which is the auditor's assessment of the effectiveness of management's internal controls to prevent or detect material misstatements. An auditor uses the assessed level of control risk to determine an *acceptable level of detection risk*. Recall from Chapter 2 that as the assessed level of control risk increases, the acceptable level of detection risk decreases. Tests of controls are introduced here, but are illustrated and discussed in detail in Chapters 10, 12, 14, 15, and 16.

Most of the control activities that audit clients use in practice can be classified into one of two categories: controls that create documentation—that is, leave an "audit trail"—and controls that do not. The distinction between the two is essential to understanding which procedures from Figure 6-2 to apply as tests of controls. For example, consider two fairly common controls:

- *Credit approval*: Sales orders are approved and initialed by the credit manager before goods are shipped.
- *Bank reconciliations*: Monthly bank reconciliations are prepared by an employee not otherwise involved in approving or recording cash transactions.

The first control, credit approval, is an example of a control that *creates documentation*: the credit manager's approval initials on the face of a sales order. Credit approval is also an example of what auditors call a "prevention control," since approval occurs before a credit sale transaction is executed and is intended to help prevent uncollectible receivables. To test control activities that create documentation, auditors often rely on the audit procedures of documentation (for example, inspect sales orders for approval initials), inquiry (for example, ask how the credit approval process is performed: credit checks, payment history, outstanding balance?), and observation (for example, observe the credit approval process).

In contrast, the second control, a bank reconciliation an independent employee prepares, creates a document (the reconciliation), but the documentation does not provide evidence about whether the preparer is independent of the cash function (who actually prepared the reconciliation?). Bank reconciliations are also an example of a "detection control," since the reconciliation occurs after cash transactions have been executed and is intended to detect misapplied cash. For bank reconciliations, as well as other control activities that rely on segregation of duties (for example, cash and ticket collection at a movie theater), an auditor would likely rely on the audit procedures of inquiry (for example, ask how—out of the view of cash-processing employees?—and when—monthly?—the reconciliation is performed), and observation (that is, observe who prepares the reconciliation).

Substantive Tests and Detection Risk

After considering inherent risk and control risk, an auditor performs substantive tests to hold detection risk to an acceptable level. Substantive tests provide evidence about monetary misstatements. However, the *extent* of substantive testing—that is, how much testing is done—depends on the acceptable level of detection risk, which depends on the assessed level of control risk, which depends in turn on the results of tests of controls. For example, if tests of controls indicate that the two controls identified above—credit approval and bank reconciliations—are operating as planned, then related substantive tests can be reduced, although not eliminated, because control risk is low.

The linkage between tests of controls and substantive tests is crucial, since each offers evidence useful in controlling audit risk: Tests of controls offer evidence about control risk, and substantive tests offer evidence about detection risk. To exploit the relationship among each type of test and audit risk, auditors often perform **dual-purpose tests**, which are intended to provide evidence both about control risk and about likely monetary error. For example, when recomputing the mathematical extensions on sales invoices (for example, quantity × unit price), an auditor is actually performing both a test of controls and a substantive test of details—a test of controls in the sense that the auditor is determining whether client personnel are extending sales invoices properly, and a substantive test in the sense that the auditor is determining whether monetary error exists.

Substantive tests can be classified either as *tests of details* of transactions and balances or as *analytical procedures*. Substantive **tests of details** are intended to detect material misstatement in financial statement accounts. For example, to test whether recorded receivables exist at the balance sheet date, an auditor could confirm balances directly with customers and perform other tests to determine whether sales and receivables transactions are recorded in the proper accounting period. Auditors use tests of details to test any of management's five financial statement assertions.

Tests of controls and tests of details differ in one critical respect: Tests of controls provide evidence about whether misstatement is *likely* (a means to assess control risk), and substantive tests of details provide evidence about whether misstatement actually *exists* (a means to control detection risk). For example, if a test of controls indicates that a control procedure is not reliable, and therefore that control risk is high, then the auditor concludes that material misstatement at the balance sheet date is likely. Therefore, substantive tests of details must be extended to control detection risk. But if tests of details reveal material monetary error, then the auditor concludes that misstatement actually exists and that further tests should be conducted or the financial statements adjusted. Examples of substantive tests of details are discussed and illustrated in Chapters 11 and 13 through 16.

Analytical Procedures

The procedures, called "comparisons" above, commonly are referred to in practice as **analytical procedures** and defined in *Statement on Auditing Standards No. 56*, "Analytical Procedures" (AU Sec. 329), as evaluations of financial information made by a study of plausible relationships among both financial and nonfinancial data.

Presumptions

Analytical procedures are based on the presumption that plausible relationships may reasonably be expected to exist among data for two reasons. First, in double-entry accounting, *each recorded transaction affects two or more financial statement accounts*. For example, a debit to Accounts Receivable requires a corresponding credit to another account, often Sales, thereby relating the two accounts to each other. If gross sales for a company decrease from one period to the next by 50 percent, an auditor might reasonably expect a substantial decrease in accounts receivable as well. Second, *nonfinancial drivers are correlated with recorded account balances*. For example, declining market share translates to declining sales. If market share declines from one period to the next by 8 percent, an auditor might reasonably expect sales to decline. If accounts receivable did not decrease by a substantial amount in the first example, or if sales did not decline in the second example, then the auditor would make inquiries of management and/or perform additional tests of details to determine whether monetary misstatement exists in recorded gross sales, recorded receivables, or both. Thus analytical procedures are not necessarily intended to isolate monetary misstatement, as might, for example, a test of details. Rather, analytical procedures identify accounts that are likely to contain monetary misstatement.

Comparing Analytical Procedures to Tests of Details

Analytical procedures differ from substantive tests of details in two ways that are not altogether obvious. First, whereas tests of details can be used to test any of management's five financial statement assertions, analytical procedures offer little insight about either the existence assertion or the rights and obligations assertion. For example, the existence of inventory can be tested best by in-person, on-site observation. Second, whereas tests of details allow an auditor to draw conclusions about aggregated data (say, for example, about an account balance), analytical procedures allow the auditor to test aggregated data to reach conclusions about detail. In fact, conclusions from aggregated data are sometimes more persuasive. For example, testing the details of recorded payroll—for example, individual employee time summaries—to explain a 5 percent increase in total payroll expense is likely to be less informative than mapping the increase to a 3 percent increase in employee wages and a 2 percent increase in the number of people employed.

Well-designed analytical procedures can offer an efficient alternative to tests of details, particularly in low-risk accounts. For example, rather than expend audit hours to test individual write-offs in a low-risk credit sales system, an auditor could test the Allowance for Uncollectible Accounts by comparing management's estimate to an independent estimate based on prior-year actual and current-year sales volume, write-offs, product mix, and payment history. In practice, auditors use analytical procedures as the primary, or the only, test of an account balance when, like in the Allowance for Uncollectible Accounts example, the evidence generated by the procedures is sufficiently persuasive to cause the auditor to believe that the benefit of gathering additional evidence is not worth the cost. In fact, analytical procedures sometimes offer the only effective means to test an account balance. For example, assuming that a middle-market client does not have an elaborate inventory costing system, thereby precluding either tests of controls or tests of details, an auditor could estimate overhead in inventory from direct labor hour records, such as employee time records and production spreadsheets.

Types of Analytical Procedures

SAS No. 56 requires that analytical procedures be applied to some extent during an engagement's planning stage and final review stage, and recommends they be used as substantive tests during the engagement, each for the following purpose:

	Purpose
• Planning	To direct attention to likely misstatements.
• Year-end substantive tests	To support (misstatement unlikely) or refute (misstatement likely) financial statement account balances.
• Year-end overall review	To review the reasonableness of financial statement account balances.

In practice, auditors use a number of different types of analytical procedures, including the following:

- Trend analysis.
- Ratio analysis.
- Modeling.

Trend Analysis In trend analysis, an auditor compares financial and nonfinancial data to prior periods, to management's budgets, to operating data, or to industry data. Comparison to *prior periods* is often done for two periods, the current year versus the prior year, since audited financial statements will display current- and prior-year balances. However, comparison over periods of three to five years can be more informative, particularly in industries like airplane manufacturing, where product development is lengthy and expensive, and new product launch can spell operating success or failure. Significant changes in a business can distort the comparison of financial data, even in multiyear comparisons. For example, current-year operating revenue could decline from employee strikes, industry declines, price-level changes, production modifications, or the sale or abandonment of a line of business. When distortions are prevalent, auditors compare periods using common-size financial statements that display financial information as percentages rather than numbers, thereby offering a basis to compare accounts across periods independent of widespread changes in revenue.

Comparison to *budgets* offers the auditor a baseline comparison between actual results and management's best estimate of year-end operating results, particularly when the budgetary process captures industry conditions. However, budgets can be uninformative to an auditor if prior-period budgets did not map to prior-period results, or if management uses budgets to motivate employee performance. For example, management may budget unrealistic sales goals to motivate commissioned salespersons, knowing full well that the goal is unattainable. Comparison to *operating data* leverages off of well-known, reliable relationships between financial and nonfinancial data. For example, Accrued Vacation Expense may be tied to hours worked and Rent Revenue may be tied to the square footage of leased floor space. Nonfinancial data may be more reliable when maintained by personnel independent of accounting, as is typically the case for applied labor hours and for units purchased and sold.

Industry data provides evidence of how aggregated, industry-wide data is affected by conditions in the industry, such as declining demand and constrained profit margins. For example, an increase in a client's accounts receivable balance is less likely to suggest a collection problem if a significant increase is apparent in the industry. Called "benchmarking," and discussed in Chapter 7 as a tool to assess risk, comparison to industry data is powerful because, unlike budgets or operating data, industry data is completely independent of a client's control. However, industry data can be misleading for two reasons. First, competing companies may vary by the number, variety, and quality of products; by the identity and loyalty of customer bases; by the prevalence of influential institutional investors; and by management's ability to innovate. Second, a company operating in more than one line of business may not be comparable to readily available industry data, particularly when management is preoccupied with innovation in another business. Many practitioners have found that industry comparisons are most informative in specialized industries for which regulators, associations, and public interest groups follow the industry closely and industry-specific data is available, such as banking, insurance, utilities, and pharmaceuticals.

Ratio Analysis Whereas trend analysis compares one point estimate over time—for example, current- and prior-year net sales—ratio analysis compares combined point estimates over time—for example, current- and prior-year net sales divided by total assets. Ratios are informative because they can reveal conditions that are obscured by comparing account balances only. For example, while no change in sales from the prior to the current year carries no information about a company, a decline in sales divided by total assets for the same company could signal that management's decision to invest in assets has not translated to increased revenue. In practice, auditors rely on four categories of ratios:

- Activity ratios.
- Profitability ratios.
- Liquidity ratios.
- Solvency ratios.

Figure 6-3 lists and interprets examples of each category of ratios.

Activity ratios measure management's effectiveness in managing available resources, among them total assets, inventory, and receivables. Take, for example, inventory turnover (Figure 6-3: Cost of Sales/Average Inventory), a measure of inventory management in general, and the number of times inventory was replaced during the year in particular. An increase in inventory turnover suggests that management has managed inventory balances effectively: Inventory moves quickly, thereby minimizing the costs of carrying excessive inventory. In contrast, a decrease in inventory turnover indicates that inventory is moving more slowly, which could suggest that inventory is excessive in quantity, slow moving, or, worse still, obsolete. However, auditors are cautious about leaping to conclusions from activity ratios. For example, a decline in inventory turnover could simply reflect seasonal sales patterns, such as inventory stockpiling in anticipation of the holiday buying season.

Profitability ratios measure management's effectiveness in turning a profit on their investment in assets and on shareholders' investments in the company, and can be more comprehensive than income statements. For example, return on equity (Figure 6-3: Operating Income Before Interest and Taxes/Average Shareholders' Equity), a measure of net return on the equity invested by shareholders, reveals in one ratio management's ability to manage collectively the company's operating sales, debt service, and tax liability. Management in public companies takes far more than a benign interest in profitability ratios, since financial analysts typically report the ratios in periodic investment reports that recommend companies to investors.

Liquidity ratios compare short-term assets to short-term liabilities, and measure management's ability to meet current obligations. However, the current ratio or the quick ratio, two primary liquidity ratios (Figure 6-3), can be deceiving, since increases in either does not necessarily mean that income from operations drove cash flow. For example, although short-term assets includes cash, the medium through which management pays current obligations, an increase in income could be captured in uncollected receivables that have not yet generated the cash to liquidate current obligations. *Solvency ratios*, in contrast, measure management's long-term financial dexterity in one of two ways: effectiveness in managing borrowed funds or in generating income on borrowed funds. For example, times interest earned (Figure 6-3: Income Before Interest and Taxes/Interest Expense) measures management's ability to service interest obligations from operating earnings.

FIGURE 6-3: *Common Financial Ratios*

Ratio	Numerator	Denominator	Interpretation
Activity Ratios			
Asset Turnover	Net Sales	Total Assets	Capital intensity: Number of times assets converted in sales
Inventory Turnover	Cost of Sales	Average Inventory	Inventory management: Number of times inventory turned over
Number of Days' Supply in Inventory	360 Days	Inventory Turnover	Inventory management: Average age of inventory
Accounts Receivable Turnover	Net Sales	Average Accounts Receivable	Credit effectiveness: Number of times credit sales turned over
Number of Days' Sales in Receivables	360 Days	Accounts Receivable Turnover	Credit effectiveness: Average age of credit sales
Profitability Ratios			
Return on Assets	Operating Income Before Interest and Taxes	Average Total Assets	Asset management: Net return on investment in assets
Return on Equity	Operating Income Before Interest and Taxes	Average Shareholders' Equity	Equity management: Net return on equity invested
Operating Margin	Operating Income Before Interest and Taxes	Net Sales	Operating profitability: Net return on operations
Liquidity Ratios			
Current Ratio	Current Assets	Current Liabilities	Working capital management: Adequacy of current assets to cover current liabilities
Quick Ratio	Cash, Marketable Securities, and Receivables	Current Liabilities	Working capital management: Adequacy of liquid assets to cover current liabilities
Solvency Ratios			
Debt-to-Equity Ratio	Long-Term Debt	Shareholders' Equity	Debt management: Operations financed by debt
Times Interest Earned	Income Before Interest and Taxes	Interest Expense	Interest management: Number of times operations earn interest obligations
Asset Leverage	Total Assets	Shareholders' Equity	Equity management: Assets financed by shareholders

Modeling Modeling applies statistical techniques, often regression analysis, to calculate expected values from financial and nonfinancial data. For example, a hospital's expected room revenue (called the "dependent variable" in regression analysis) could be predicted from occupancy rates, available capacity, regional disease and injury data, and room rate charges (the "independent variables"), providing a benchmark against which to compare recorded room revenue. Trend and ratio analysis are easy to use and informative, but modeling has two important advantages. First, modeling usually correlates nonfinancial, operating information (for example, occupancy rates) with related financial information (for example, recorded room revenue), thereby exploiting by design the relationship between nonfinancial information and financial information. Second, research reveals that modeling tends to outperform trend and ratio analysis, in part because modeling incorporates more data and produces more precise estimates. For example, while trends and ratios usually compare two financial numbers, the room revenue example correlates more numbers, both financial and nonfinancial.

Documenting Analytical Procedures

Responding to a recommendation of the Panel on Audit Effectiveness (Chapter 2), *SAS No. 96*, "Audit Documentation," imposes on an auditor three documentation requirements when he or she uses analytical procedures as substantive tests. First, the auditor documents the benchmark expectation against which he or she compared the analytical procedures. For example, an auditor analyzing days' sales in receivables might judge 30 days a benchmark for a client that sells product on 30 days' credit. Second and third, respectively, the auditor should document the results of the analytical procedure, and the auditing procedures performed in the wake of a significant unexpected difference. For example, in the illustration, the auditor might document that actual days' sales in receivables was 50; that, compared to 30 days, 50 days raised the risk that recorded receivables may not be fully collectible; and that he or she performed in response additional tests of the collectibility of receivables (Chapter 10).

Judgment in Analytical Procedures

Mistakes in the application of analytical procedures can lead an unsuspecting auditor to ill-informed judgments. Consider these mistakes:

- Overreliance on unaudited numbers
- Disregard for unchanging account balances
- Overreliance on management's explanations

A client's *unaudited account balances* are not usually the most productive starting point in analytical procedures. For example, in trend analysis, an auditor might compare current unaudited sales to prior-year actual sales, note no significant difference, and conclude from the comparison that there is no reason to expect that sales are either understated or overstated. However, the conclusion to *disregard unchanging balances* could be inappropriate. For example, in a mature or declining industry, the management of a laggard competitor may have incentives to equate sales to prior-year actual sales and thereby stave off a deteriorating stock price. To overcome the risk of overrelying on unaudited balances, auditors do three things. First, they consider industry-specific economic conditions (for example, is the industry declining?). Second, they weigh a client's competitive position within the industry (for example, is the client a laggard?). Third, and most important, auditors compare prior-year actual balances with an independent expectation—say, for example, an expectation from regression analysis—rather than an unaudited balance. An independent expectation that incorporates both nonfinancial and financial data is far more reliable than unaudited financial data, and more likely to reveal an unexpected fluctuation. To investigate an unexpected fluctuation, auditors first seek an *explanation from management*. However, an auditor should not view management's explanation as corroborating evidence for the fluctuation. Rather, the auditor evaluates management's explanation for reasonableness, includes reasonable explanations among the set of potential alternative explanations, and seeks evidence to reach closure.

Nonfinancial Measures

The financial community has traditionally based a company's performance on well-established financial measures (many of which are illustrated in Figure 6-3) that are calculated from information in financial statements. For example, profitability might be measured by return on assets, liquidity by the current ratio, and solvency by the debt-to-equity ratio. Although informative, financial measures tell a story about the results of actions management has taken already. In contrast, nonfinancial operational measures, such as time-to-market and defect rates, tell a story about the drivers of future financial performance. Stated another way, operational measures are *lead* measures and financial measures are *lags*. The point of an independent auditor using nonfinancial measures is not to undermine the importance of financial measures. Rather, an auditor uses nonfinancial operational measures to offer insights about audit risk. For example, on-time delivery can be a leading indicator of eroding market share, an outcome that might raise an auditor's professional skepticism about recorded sales close to the balance sheet date. The following introduces nonfinancial measures about *today* that are often correlated with—and leading predictors of—financial measures reached *tomorrow*. The measures address three perspectives about a company: the customer, internal business, and internal learning perspectives.[2]

Customer Perspective

A company's customer perspective focuses on *who* (not what) delivers a company's revenue: *customers* (not products or services). It asks, simply: *How do we look to our customers?* In practice, this question might translate in some companies to the following issues, all of which relate to the company's goals of customer satisfaction and brand loyalty:

Issue	*Example Measure*
• Time	On-time delivery
• Quality	Customer complaints
• Performance/service	Comment cards
• Cost	Low-cost provider

---

2 This discussion is adapted from the literature on balanced scorecards. See, for example, R. S. Kaplan and D. P. Norton, "The Balanced Scorecard: Measures That Drive Performance," *Harvard Business Review* (January–February 1992), pp. 71–79; R. S. Kaplan and D. P. Norton, "Putting the Balanced Scorecard to Work," *Harvard Business Review* (September–October 1993), pp. 134–147; R. S. Kaplan and D. P. Norton, *The Balanced Scorecard*. Boston: Harvard Business School Press, 1996.

Not all of these examples necessarily apply in all industries. For example, lead time in the delivery of existing products is less telling in the pharmaceutical industry since, absent unusual production delays, retailers are unlikely to experience serious stockouts. A pharmaceutical company might measure satisfaction by patient surveys and physician focus groups, and loyalty by tracking physicians' repeat referrals, both for individual products within a product line and for other product lines. For example, pharmaceutical companies often sponsor physician focus groups at meetings of the American Medical Association, the intent being to gather anecdotal evidence about patient risks and recovery.

Underscoring the importance of customer perspective, Mercer Management, a growth strategy and business design group within the Mercer Consulting Group, studied why the share prices of 100 companies within the Fortune 1000 lost more than 25 percent in a single month during the decade-long bull market of the 1990s. Mercer found that unexpected declines in customer demand drove 24 percent of share price reaction, far outweighing 5 other drivers commonly associated with share price declines: competitive pressure (12%), cost overruns (11%), troublesome acquisitions (7%), accounting irregularities (7%), and ineffective management (7%). Explaining the results, a Mercer principal observed, "It used to be that if you developed a superior product or cost advantage you could ride it for five years or a decade. Increasingly, competitive advantages last you only 36 or 24 months. It is like milk: It starts going bad the second you get it."[3] How a company reacts to changing patterns of customer demand is no less important than product superiority and cost advantage, offering a leading indicator of future earnings growth.

Internal Business Perspective

A company's internal business perspective answers a key question about the processes management uses to achieve customer satisfaction: *What processes do we excel at?* In some companies, this question might translate to:

Issue	*Example Measure*
• Product development	First to market
• Quality	Defect rates
• Productivity	Mark to standard production time
• Core competencies	Certifications

The internal business perspective might address quality, product development, production efficiency, and environmental sensitivity by defect rates, time-to-market, capacity utilization, and waste recovery, respectively. Interestingly, the internal business perspective is enriched in some industries by strategic alliances that allow partnering companies to leverage their best features into comparative advantages that are otherwise unavailable to the individual companies. For example, an alliance in the pharmaceutical industry between Merck and DuPont allowed DuPont to leverage its patented radiopharmaceutical imaging agents with Merck's cross-border market permissions.

---

3   D. Henry, "Street Talk," *USA Today* (March 11, 1999), p. 3B.

Internal Learning Perspective

A company's internal learning perspective answers a key question about improving business processes (and indirectly about improving customer satisfaction and brand loyalty): *How do we learn and improve?* Continued learning repositions a company's comparative advantage in the marketplace for ideas, offering opportunities to launch new products, improve operating efficiencies, penetrate new markets, and create more value for customers. For many companies, internal learning means:

Issue	*Example Measure*
● Improved performance	Benchmark to best practices
● Innovation	New product development

For most any company, each of these would bear on internal learning, as would two issues that focus on employees: *safety* and *satisfaction*, measured, for example, by compensation claims, lost time, and injury rates, and by interviews, surveys, and focus groups, respectively. However, internal learning often requires acts of creative thinking that far exceed time-honored measures and conventional wisdom. For example, had you asked focus groups in the 1960s how to improve audit efficiency, you would likely have heard calls for a handheld adding machine, not the laptop computer.

Audit Risk

To help assess audit risk, practitioners import financial measures into the analytical procedures described earlier as trend analysis, ratio analysis, and modeling. For example, declining returns on investment and equity, and declining current and quick ratios, are negative trends that could prompt senior executives to accelerate the recognition of revenue. Owing to the power of operational measures in forecasting financial measures, some practicing auditors also leverage off of customer, internal business, and internal learning measures to help identify areas in which the auditor ought to increase his or her professional skepticism about the likelihood of misstatements and financial distress. In many cases, nonfinancial operational measures offer insights about risk before traditional financial measures offer the same insights. For example, significant increases in the defect rates of products manufactured for credit sale could raise an auditor's professional skepticism about customers' willingness to pay—and, therefore, a client's ability to collect—receivables recorded near the balance sheet date.

Figure 6-4 lists several nonfinancial measures that might raise an auditor's professional skepticism. Declining sales volume sometimes can be traced to declining *on-time delivery rates*, to increasing *customer complaints*, to increasing *defect rates*, or to *customer comment cards* returned increasingly with troublesome remarks. For example, some manufacturers depend on timely deliveries to minimize carrying costs in a just-in-time inventory system. An audit client that repeatedly fails to deliver on-time risks order cancellations, thereby threatening demand, reputation, and market share. In some industries, such as retail automobile sales, consumers believe that quality differentiation drives product pricing—for example, a high-end luxury sedan and a low-end coupe will transport you reliably to work, but consumers are willing to pay more for a luxury car. However, failure to be the *low-cost provider* is problematic in other industries, such as

FIGURE 6-4: *The Customer, Internal Business, and Internal Learning Perspectives and Reasons for Professional Skepticism*

Perspective	*Issue*	*Measures That Might Raise Professional Skepticism*
Customer	Time	Declining on-time delivery rates
	Quality	Increasing customer complaints
	Performance	Customer comment cards returned increasingly more often with product complaints
	Cost	Failure to be the low-cost provider
Internal Business	Development	Failure to be first to market
	Quality	Increasing defect rates
	Productivity	Unfavorable price or quantity variances
	Core competencies	Employees fail certification exams
Internal Learning	Improved performance	Poor performance against industry best practices
	Innovation	Lagging product development

over-the-counter antihistamines. Consumers who believe that quality is roughly constant across brands will reward the low-cost provider, and threaten sales for audit clients that cannot compete on price.

Failure to be the *first to market* can be problematic in some industries and catastrophic in others. For example, although Chrysler Corporation was first to market a line of minivans in the 1970s, General Motors and Ford recovered market share thereafter by introducing attractive lines of competing vehicles. However, although diminished by the *Drug Price Competition and Patent Term Restoration Act*, a pharmaceutical company that introduces a new, high-demand drug in a therapeutic class exercises a preemptive strike against all competitors. In both industries, automotive and pharmaceutical, the company that is first to market simultaneously signals to the market which competitors have lagged in product development and therefore have sacrificed to competitors the first-mover's advantage.

Unfavorable *price and quantity variances* and employee failure in *certification exams* are central to a company's competitive edge, since one threatens efficiency and the other belies the company's knowledge base. For example, management's capacity to innovate depends on new ideas from creative employees. Decades ago, the A.T. Cross pen and the Ford Taurus each succeeded because of employee-driven design ideas. Although certifications such as a professional engineer are not necessarily emblematic of creativity, failure on certification exams suggests to the auditor a failure to demonstrate minimum professional standards, thereby raising questions about a company's ability to attract (or retain) market share through innovation.

Each of these measures signals performance about an individual company over time, usually a number of quarters or years. In short, the basis for comparison is the company's past performance. However, measures of a company's performance can be even more informative when compared against *industry best practices*. Poor performance against industry rivals on financial and nonfinancial measures can signal a company's comparative disadvantage, raising an auditor's professional skepticism about management's motivation to stretch the limits of discretion when applying accounting principles.

Cognitive Biases in Evaluating Evidence

Accountants are limited in the same way that decision makers in all complex decision settings are limited: Our capacity to process information cognitively is limited, and our well-intentioned decision strategies are sometimes biased. For example, practitioners who cast decisions into likelihood assessments—for example, the likelihood of fraud, misstatement, or financial distress—risk overlooking the laws of probability and relying instead on simplifying rules of thumb, called *heuristics*, that bias decision making unnecessarily.[4] Three heuristics have troubled auditors: representativeness, availability, and anchoring-and-adjustment.

Representativeness occurs when decision makers evaluate the likelihood of, say, item *b* belonging to class *A* by judging how much item *b* resembles other items from class *A*, rather than by the laws of probability. The question is not, "How representative is item *b* of items in class *A*?" but rather, "What is the *probability* that item *b* came from class *A*?" For example, research has found that auditors overstate the likelihood that management perpetrated a fraud by overweighting the similarity between a manager's psychological profile and the profile of admitted perpetrators, and by underweighting the fact that not one of one hundred managers described in the study had been involved in fraud previously.[5]

Availability occurs when decision makers evaluate the likelihood of an outcome by the ease with which similar instances come to mind, particularly when the outcome is rare and sensational, such as a plane crash, high-rise fire, or coal mine collapse. For example, an unsuspecting auditor may judge that infrequent, but highly publicized, illegal hazardous waste disposal occurs disproportionately more often than the profession's collected experience would predict.

Anchoring-and-adjustment occurs when decision makers assess the likelihood of an outcome by making initial, and sometimes biased, likelihood estimates (an anchor) and then adjusting the likelihood, though insufficiently, when presented with new information. For example, in practice, auditors often consult prior-year audit documentation when planning the current engagement, but may fail to revise the current audit plan sufficiently for changed circumstances, such as management turnover, outsourced transaction processing, or newly implemented

---

4   For a review, see J. F. Smith and T. Kida, "Heuristics and Biases: Expertise and Task Realism in Auditing," *Psychological Bulletin* (Vol. 109, No. 3, 1991), pp. 472–489.
5   See, for example, E. J. Joyce and G. C. Biddle, "Are Auditors' Judgments Sufficiently Regressive?" *Journal of Accounting Research* (Autumn 1981), pp. 323–349.

controls. Although mixed, the results of prior research suggest that auditor behavior is generally consistent with the anchoring-and-adjustment heuristic.[6]

Apart from heuristics, other biases can plague practitioners when evaluating evidence, among them overrelying on the source of written or oral evidence (*source credibility*), seeking evidence that confirms a prior belief (*confirmatory bias*), underestimating sampling error in small samples (*insensitivity to sample size*), and overlooking prior information (*base rate neglect*). Because many decisions in practice are complex, time-constrained, and made under conditions of uncertainty, practitioners sometimes adopt decision rules that are fraught with the potential for bias. The task of the well-informed practitioner is to evaluate evidence with full respect for the pitfalls of bias, and with the resolve to bear witness only to what the evidence reveals. Due care (Chapter 2) demands no less.

**AUDIT
DOCUMENTATION
REVIEW**

Audit Documentation

The Auditing Standards Board (ASB) in 2002 and the Public Company Accounting Oversight Board (PCAOB) in 2004 each produced a standard for audit documentation although, for one thing, the standards are compatible and, for another, the PCAOB's standard does not replace the ASB's documentation requirements. Under either standard, **audit documentation**[7] is an auditor's principal record of the evidence obtained and of the nature, timing, and extent of auditing procedures applied; and the principal support for the auditor's conclusions and report. Rather than a mere by-product, audit documentation is an integral part of an audit that not only memorializes compliance with the field work standards (Chapter 2) but actually serves to facilitate the planning, performance, and supervision of the engagement. For example, documentation compiled for an engagement this year will help in planning the engagement next year.

ASB Standard

The ASB's standard for nonpublic audits appears in *SAS No. 96*, "Audit Documentation" (AU Sec 339). Consistent with the standards of field work, audit documentation should show that the auditor:

- Planned the work and properly supervised assistants.
- Obtained an understanding of internal control sufficient to plan the audit and to determine the nature, timing, and extent of tests performed.
- Obtained sufficient, competent evidential matter.

Auditors prepare and maintain audit documentation on all engagements, although the form and content of the documentation will vary depending on the circumstances. In practice, an individual document may take virtually any form, including, for example, a spreadsheet or a manual ("pencil and paper") schedule documenting the calculation of carrying value, a memorandum tax staff prepared

---

6   See, for example, E. J. Joyce and G. C. Biddle, "Anchoring and Adjustment in Probabilistic Inference in Auditing," *Journal of Accounting Research* (January 1982), pp. 55–69; and W. R. Kinney and W. C. Uecker, "Mitigating the Consequences of Anchoring in Auditor Judgments," *The Accounting Review* (January 1982), pp. 55–69.

7   Throughout, this text uses more often the term "audit documentation," coined in *SAS No. 96*, "Audit Documentation," than the traditional term "working papers," although the terms are used interchangeably in practice.

for the treatment of a complicated tax allocation problem, or a schedule extracting significant matters from a client's board of directors meeting. In short, any evidence bearing on management's assertions could potentially be presented as a document.

The nature and extent of audit documentation vary from engagement to engagement. For example, documentation for a public company audit is likely to be far more voluminous than documentation for a nonpublic company review engagement. The auditor's judgment about the nature and extent of audit documentation for a particular engagement would depend on an auditor's judgment about the:

- Risk that an assertion (for example, inventory exists), account (for example, Inventory), or class of transactions (for example, purchases) is misstated.
- Extent of judgment an auditor invests in performing audit work and in evaluating evidence.
- Nature of the procedures an auditor applies.
- Significance of the evidence obtained to the assertion tested.
- Nature and extent of assertions tested.
- Need to document a conclusion, or the basis for the conclusion, that is not readily determinable otherwise from the documentation.

Critical to the informativeness of audit documentation is the auditor's judgment about which of his or her findings is significant enough to memorialize. How does an auditor judge which findings are significant? In general, an auditor's judgment is guided by the relevance of the finding to his or her opinion on the financial statement taken as a whole. However, more specifically, _SAS No. 96_ offers an incomplete list of significant findings or issues:

- The selection, application, and consistency of accounting principles that relate to complex or unusual transactions and estimates or uncertainties
- Evidence indicating that the financial statements could be misstated materially or that auditing procedures should be modified significantly
- Difficulty in applying auditing procedures the auditor considered necessary
- Potential modifications of the auditor's report

Over the years, peer reviewers (Chapter 4) have observed considerable inconsistency in what auditors do and do not include in audit documentation. To mitigate some of the inconsistency, _SAS No. 96_ requires that audit documentation include copies (or abstracts) of significant contracts or agreements that support major transactions (for example, leases), and replicable summaries of tests of controls and substantive tests that were performed by inspecting documents or confirmations (for example, a list of credit receivable balances confirmed). Under _SAS No. 96_, documentation should be retained for a period of time that is consistent with the auditor's needs and with applicable laws and regulations.

PCAOB Standard

The PCAOB's standard for public company audits appears in _Auditing Standard No. 3_, "Audit Documentation," although, as discussed in Chapter 2, PCAOB standards may be used for nonpublic company audits as well. In contrast to _SAS No. 96_, the PCAOB standard adopts the "reviewability standard" from the U.S. General Accounting Office's (GAO) generally accepted _governmental_ auditing

PCAOB

standards (GAGAS)[8] and the "rebuttable presumption" standard from the California Business and Professions Code. The **reviewability standard** means that an audit engagement's documentation should be sufficient to enable an experienced auditor—particularly one not assigned to an engagement—to understand _who_ performed _what_ work _when_, and _why_ the work lead to the significant judgments and conclusions documented. How else could the PCAOB inspect a registered accounting firm's compliance with the _Sarbanes-Oxley Act_ or with PCAOB and SEC rules (Chapter 4)? In turn, **rebuttable presumption** means that, absent documentation showing the audit work was performed—say, for example, procedures to test inventory carrying value—there is a presumption that the work was _not_ performed, although an auditor could rebut the presumption with persuasive evidence. The reviewability standard and rebuttable presumption translate to this: audit documentation should stand on its own; there should be no need at all for oral or written explanations.

The standard is clear that an auditor must document significant findings (for example, previously unreported environmental liabilities), the actions taken to address the findings, and the basis for the conclusions the auditor reaches. The PCAOB included in the standard each of the examples of significant findings in _SAS No. 96_ (above), and added:

- **Adjusting entries**—journal entries the auditor proposes to conform management's financial statements to generally accepted accounting principles.
- Issues identified during a quarterly review of financial statements.
- Disagreements about conclusions among members of the audit team.
- Changes in audit risk.

The standard imposes a responsibility to identify all significant findings in an engagement completion memorandum that is cross-referenced to supporting documentation and is sufficiently specific for an experienced auditor—for example, a reviewer—to understand the findings completely.

Although _SAS No. 96_ is vague about the retention of audit documentation (a period of time consistent with the auditor's needs and with law), the PCAOB standard is specific about completion, retention, and subsequent changes: Audit documentation must be completed within 45 days after the auditor's report is released, and retained for 7 years by the office that issued the report. If, after completion, documentation is changed, the changes must be dated and the original documentation retained.

Audit Documentation Files

Audit documentation remains in the custody, and is the property, of the auditor. In fact, some state statutes designate the auditor as the owner of audit documentation, although the auditor's property rights are subject to the limitations of AICPA _Rule of Conduct 301_, confidential client information (Chapter 4), which prohibits disclosure without management's consent.

Although automation can blur the line between files compiled for an engagement, some information for an audit engagement traditionally has been maintained separately from the audit documentation, since the information is of continuing interest year after year or relates directly to the preparation of tax returns.

---

8   U.S. General Accounting Office, _Government Auditing Standards: Standards for Audit of Governmental Organizations, Programs, Activities and Functions._ Washington, D.C.: U.S. Government Printing Office, 2003.

Although groupings and classifications of information vary somewhat among firms, the following types of files are representative of the files maintained for a client other than an audit documentation file:

- Correspondence file
- Permanent file
- Tax file

Correspondence File

The correspondence file, sometimes called the administrative file, contains all correspondence to, from, or on behalf of a client and is especially useful for planning an audit. For example, early in an engagement, a client may have communicated with the auditor about an accounting or reporting issue, such as a change in accounting for postretirement benefits. Correspondence related to the issue is included in the correspondence file, signaling to the audit staff that the current engagement should consider the issue.

Permanent File

The permanent file contains information of continuing interest and relevance to an engagement. For example, the file might include a client's background and history, organization charts, articles of incorporation, bylaws, a charter, bond indenture agreements, contracts, articles from the financial press, and flowcharts. Permanent files are consulted and updated as needed, and should be reviewed by all audit team members unfamiliar with the client.

Tax File

The tax file contains information relevant to a client's past, current, and future income and property tax obligations, and serves as a basis for preparing current-year returns or for performing other tax services, such as representing the client in an IRS audit. For example, the file might include prior-year state and federal income tax returns, tax-related correspondence, research and rulings, and schedules of significant temporary differences between pretax accounting (book) income and taxable income. All relevant tax information arising during an engagement is included in the tax file.

Content and Arrangement of Audit Documentation

Although content varies from engagement to engagement, audit documentation ordinarily includes evidence that:

- Work was adequately planned, supervised, and reviewed (consistent with the first field work standard),
- Internal control was considered as a basis for planning substantive tests (second field work standard) and, in a public company audit, for concluding on management's assessment of internal control over financial reporting, and
- Sufficient competent evidential matter was obtained (third standard of field work).

In practice, the physical form of audit documentation varies considerably. For example, some firms capture most audit documentation in databases (for example,

Lotus Notes), some bind printed documents, and others arrange loose, unbound documents within file folders. The physical form of completed audit documentation is inconsequential, although the arrangement should be logical and documents should be indexed, referenced, and accessible.

Figure 6-5 depicts a common arrangement for audit documentation. A *draft of financial statements* is presented first, followed by an *engagement letter* (Chapter 7) and a *preliminary audit planning memorandum* (Chapter 7). The *working trial balance* is the source for preparing a draft of the audited financial statements. All dollar amounts within the working trial balance are referenced to detailed schedules within the audit documentation. Adjusting and reclassification entries, an auditor's "correcting" journal entries, are presented next. Adjusting entries conform management's financial statements to GAAP, generally affect reported net income, and therefore are given to the client to record. In contrast, **reclassification entries** are made within the auditor's audit documentation to reclassify accounts for presentation in the financial statements but are not recorded in the client's books.

FIGURE 6-5:

Arrangement of Audit Working Papers

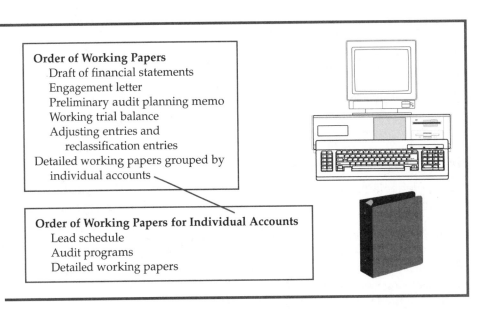

Order of Working Papers
Draft of financial statements
Engagement letter
Preliminary audit planning memo
Working trial balance
Adjusting entries and
reclassification entries
Detailed working papers grouped by
individual accounts

Order of Working Papers for Individual Accounts
Lead schedule
Audit programs
Detailed working papers

Detailed audit documents are subdivided and grouped by individual financial statement accounts, which in turn often are filed in balance sheet order—that is, the order of appearance in the financial statements. Hence, the Cash account documents might appear first, followed by Marketable Securities, Accounts Receivable, and so on. However, research reveals that balance sheet order may actually increase the cognitive effort required to complete audit tasks that rely on evidence compiled throughout the audit documents, and that the increased effort interferes with decision tasks, such as the auditor's going concern decision (Chapter 3).[9] To avoid increased cognitive effort, some firms store going concern evidence in databases and then access the evidence with systems software that displays the evidence in an order that reduces cognitive effort (for example, causal

---

9 D. N. Ricchiute, "Working-Paper Order Effects and Auditors' Going-Concern Decisions," *The Accounting Review* (January 1992), pp. 46–58.

order) rather than in balance sheet order. In more traditional systems, audit documentation for each asset, liability, and equity account may begin with a *lead schedule* summarizing the account's unaudited balance, adjusting and reclassification entries, and the final audited balance. The lead schedule also includes the auditor's conclusion about whether the account is fairly stated, and these conclusions are the basis for an auditor's opinion on the financial statements taken as a whole.

Audit programs are listings of detailed procedures applied to specific financial statement accounts or activities, and under *SAS No. 77* should be prepared in writing on every audit. Usually a separate program is prepared for each significant account or activity audited. For example, separate programs may exist for marketable securities, for postretirement health care, and so on. As depicted in Figure 6-5, programs typically follow the related lead schedules, although programs for specific activities, such as a review for subsequent events, might be filed elsewhere (for example, following adjusting and reclassification entries). A portion of a sample audit program appears in Figure 6-6. Three observations about the sample program follow:

- The program steps (audit procedures) are explicit and detailed.
- A reference is provided to other documents that contain detailed audit work.
- The staff member initials the program step when completed, thereby taking responsibility for the work done.

FIGURE 6-6: *Sample Audit Program*

Program Steps (Uncollectible Receivables)	Document Reference	Performed By
•		
•		
7. Obtain prior year-end balance from general ledger.	B6	KLR
8. Review accounts written off during the year.	B7	KLR
9. Calculate provision for uncollectible accounts.	B10	KLR
•		
•		

Detailed audit documents usually are presented after the audit programs, offer evidence that audit program steps are complete, and represent the bulk of an audit documentation file. Figure 6-7 illustrates a typical detailed audit document in the form of a schedule. The significance of Figure 6-7 is not in the schedule itself, but in the following items, which are common to most audit documents:

- Indexes
- References
- Preparer and reviewer initials
- Dates
- Tick marks and explanations

FIGURE 6-7:

Sample Document

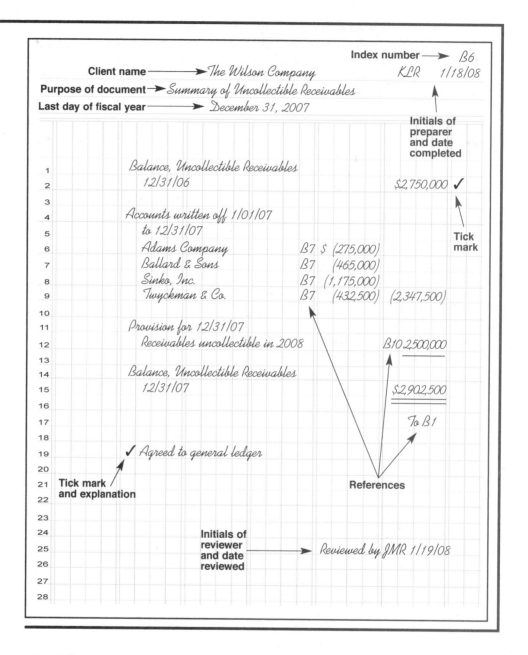

The *index* serves the same purpose as the page number of a book. However, audit documents are numbered sequentially within account groups with page numbers preceded by an account code. For example, the alphanumeric index *B6* in Figure 6-7 indicates the sixth page of the accounts receivable documents. Account groups within the documents could be identified as follows: Single letters (*A, B, C,* etc.) = asset accounts; double letters (*AA, BB, CC,* etc.) = liability and equity accounts; numerals (*10, 20, 30,* etc.) = revenue and expense accounts. For example, *10-1* might represent the schedule for sales revenue accounts.

References are a means to transfer information within the audit documentation. For example, in Figure 6-7, the $275,000 written off for Adams Company is referenced *from* document *B7*, and the $2,902,500 total uncollectible receivables is referenced *to B1*, the Accounts Receivable lead schedule. Indexing and referencing provide a road map through audit documentation. A reviewer should be able to follow his or her way through an entire set of properly indexed and referenced audit documentation without difficulty.

Initials of preparers and reviewers of audit documentation are included to affix responsibility for the work performed, allowing a supervisor in charge of the engagement to direct specific inquiries about work performed to the individuals responsible. The preparer and reviewer also should indicate the *dates of completion and review*, respectively. The completion date for a document indicates the last day on which related audit work was performed. Thus, transactions and events from this date to the audit report date should be reviewed the last day of field work. Another date appearing on each document is the entity's fiscal year end. The *year-end date* identifies the year under audit, distinguishing the document from similar papers prepared in other years.

Unless self-explanatory, all information or data contained in audit documentation should be referenced from another schedule or "tick marked" and explained. *Tick marks* are symbols (asterisks, etc.) used on audit documents. An example of a tick mark and related explanation appears in Figure 6-7.

Automated Documentation

For generations, audit documentation had been prepared manually, stored, and used as a single-copy record of audit evidence. However, with the advent of personal computers, auditors now prepare and store most or virtually all audit documentation on computers, using *spreadsheets*, *database management systems*, and the *Internet*.

Spreadsheets

Spreadsheet software—such as Microsoft's *Excel*, and Lotus *Notes*—is the most common application used in practice today. Spreadsheets are easy to use, easily modified across engagements, and, for that matter, are expected by clients. Auditors use spreadsheets for analytical procedures (such as ratio analysis and modeling), data import and export across files, graphing and sorting, financial statement automation, and all of the engagement applications listed in Figure 6-8.

Many public accounting firms have developed proprietary spreadsheet software that provides standard tabular formats for selected schedules, thereby requiring that staff merely input data for the current engagement and manipulate the data as necessary. For example, in years past, a common but tedious year-end audit activity often assigned to entry-level staff was the preparation of a *working trial balance* for all general ledger accounts and *lead schedules* for each individual balance sheet account. Preparing the trial balance and lead schedules manually was not only time-consuming, but could result in math errors, particularly when the auditor posted adjusting journal entries through the lead schedules to the working trial balance. However, with the advent of spreadsheets in the 1980s, each task was accomplished in significantly less time, and posting was accomplished with a macro.

Database Management (DBM) Systems

DBM systems—such as Microsoft's *Access*, and Borland's *dBASE*—are particularly powerful for *relational structuring* across files—that is, combining two or more files

FIGURE 6-8: *Spreadsheet Applications in Auditing*

Cash
- Preparing cash lead sheets
- Preparing bank reconciliations or proofs of cash

Receivables
- Calculating estimated bad debt expense
- Calculating turnover statistics
- Preparing confirmation requests
- Preparing aging summaries

Inventory
- Calculating LIFO indexes, layers, and final balances
- Calculating turnover statistics
- Tracing inventory test counts to perpetual records
- Analyzing variances

Fixed Assets
- Calculating depreciation
- Computing capitalized interest
- Computing sale-leaseback gain deferral

Investments
- Determining portfolio valuation at the lower of cost or market
- Obtaining market prices at year end from public data sources

Liabilities
- Calculating warranty reserves
- Determining debt covenant compliance
- Preparing loan amortization schedules

Income Taxes
- Analyzing permanent and timing differences
- Reconciling pretax accounting and taxable income
- Computing deferred taxes
- Calculating effective tax rates

Equity
- Computing earnings per share
- Computing stock splits and preferred stock dividends
- Analyzing treasury stock

Engagement Administration
- Controlling confirmations sent and responses received
- Controlling correspondence
- Monitoring time charged to engagements
- Controlling and monitoring client-prepared schedules
- Assigning staff to engagements

to perform an application with a single query. For example, an auditor might relate data in an accounts receivable file and a cash receipts file to monitor collection of past-due accounts. Auditors use DBM software for a variety of other applications, including advanced analytical procedures, receivables confirmation requests, sampling, engagement administration tasks (such as staff scheduling and time and expense control), and global data.

DBM software can be advantageous in both small and large engagements. However, there are additional advantages for large multinational clients, since the auditor acquires evidence from locations around the globe rather than from a single, centrally located accounting department. For example, the physical inventory observations (Chapter 15) for several international retail stores, including Sears and Wal-Mart, now are accomplished on linked spreadsheets prepared in various stores and warehouses around the world and then are linked to a centrally located office of the firm conducting the audit, usually the office in charge of the multinational engagement. Since the schedules are preformatted, all inventory data are in a common form, allowing easy manipulation and efficient reconciliation with the client's final priced inventory.

The Internet

Many practitioners today use the Internet to retrieve professional pronouncements, such as FASB standards (**http://www.fasb.org**) and PCAOB releases (**http://www.pcaobus.org**); to access text-retrieval sites, such as LEXIS-NEXIS and the SEC's EDGAR database; and to acquire audit planning information useful to understanding a client's business and industry. For example, consider the case of a practitioner with a new client in the pharmaceutical industry. Using a readily available portal, such as Microsoft's *Explorer* or Netscape's *Communicator*, a practitioner could link from the search term "pharmaceutical industry" to a menu of directories including *Business*, to the business subdirectory *Companies*, to the *Health* industry, to the *Pharmaceuticals* subindustry, and finally to publication services such as *World Pharma Web* (an archived pharmaceutical news and company profile service) and to the home pages of major competitors such as Bristol-Myers Squibb, Eli Lilly, Merck, and Pfizer, among others. Alternatively, the practitioner could access the home page of competitors directly, such as Merck (**http://www.merck.com**), to access a company overview, annual report, or product information, among other things.

Access to Audit Documentation

Although audit documentation can be subpoenaed (Chapter 5), prior to the 1980s no precedent existed for government agencies to access an auditor's documentation. However, following nine years of judicial proceedings, the U.S. Supreme Court ruled in *United States v. Arthur Young & Co. et al.* that an auditor's tax accrual documents—evidence used to determine a client's current and deferred tax liability—*are* relevant to an Internal Revenue Service (IRS) tax audit, and therefore are *not* protected from disclosure under the theory of accountant-client privileged communications provided by law in some states. Other cases have addressed the issue, but the Arthur Young case is particularly noteworthy because it caused considerable concern within the profession and was the first case to reach the U.S. Supreme Court.

The case first received attention in 1975 when the IRS, in an audit of Amerada Hess Corporation's 1972–1974 tax returns, detected questionable payments of $7,830. As a result of the questionable payments, what had been a routine tax audit became a criminal investigation. The IRS issued an administrative summons seeking the tax accrual documents prepared by Arthur Young. Amerada Hess, however, instructed Young not to comply with the summons, prompting the IRS to seek enforcement in U.S. District Court. The court ruled in favor of the IRS, arguing that the tax accrual documents were relevant to the IRS audit and that the accountant-client privilege did not protect the papers. On appeal, the U.S. Court of Appeals agreed the tax accrual documents were relevant to the IRS audit, but held that the public interest and the integrity of the securities markets were best served by protecting a client's confidential communications from public scrutiny.

The dispute ended on further appeal when the U.S. Supreme Court ruled that tax accrual documents (1) are relevant to an IRS audit within the meaning of *Internal Revenue Code (IRC) Section 7602*, and (2) are not protected from disclosure under *IRC Section 7602*. In general, the Court reasoned that an IRS summons should be judged by the *potential relevance* of tax accrual documents to an IRS tax audit, not by the relevance standards typically used in judging the admissibility of evidence in court. Interestingly, the profession reacted to the Court's opinion with some alarm, since the ruling could discourage some audit clients from communicating openly with auditors about tax matters and, correspondingly, may alter how auditors prepare and maintain audit documentation, particularly documentation that may be subjected to public scrutiny through the courts.

SUMMARY

No competent practitioner would consider issuing any of the reports introduced in Chapter 3 without the evidence to back what they're reporting. Auditors use the procedures of observation, documentation, confirmation, mechanical tests of data, comparison, and inquiry as tests of controls, substantive tests of details, and analytical procedures to evaluate evidence about five financial statement assertions: existence or occurrence, rights and obligations, valuation or allocation, completeness, and presentation and disclosure. Procedures are the means to accomplish audit tests, and the tests access evidence about management's assertions. Audit documentation, the practitioner's means for organizing and cataloging the evidence obtained, provides the principal support for an auditor's conclusions about management's assertions and for his or her opinion on the financial statements taken as a whole.

KEY TERMS

Adjusting entries 222
Analytical procedures 209
Audit documentation 220
Audit procedures 205
Audit programs 225
Completeness 204
Dual-purpose tests 209
Evidential matter 202
Existence or occurrence 204
Financial statement assertions 203

Presentation and disclosure 205
Reclassification entries 224
Rebuttable presumption 222
Reviewability standard 222
Rights and obligations 205
Substantive tests 207
Tests of controls 207
Tests of details 209
Valuation or allocation 205

REFERENCES

Professional Standards:

Auditing Standard No. 3, "Audit Documentation."

AICPA, *Codification of Auditing Standards*. New York: AICPA.

SAS No. 31, "Evidential Matter" (AU Sec. 326).

SAS No. 56, "Analytical Procedures" (AU Sec. 329).

SAS No. 77, "Amendments to SAS No. 22, 'Planning and Supervision,' No. 59, 'The Auditor's Consideration of an Entity's Ability to Continue as a Going Concern,' and No. 62, 'Special Reports.'"

SAS No. 80, "Amendment to SAS No. 31, 'Evidential Matter'" (AU Sec. 326).

SAS No. 96, "Audit Documentation" (AU Sec. 339).

Professional Reports:

Public Oversight Board, *Panel on Audit Effectiveness: Report and Recommendations*. Stamford, CT: POB, 2000.

Articles, Books:

Gibson, K. M., and S. M. McEachern, "The Once and Future Auditors," *Journal of Accountancy* (February 1998), pp. 63–66.

Glover, S. M., J. Jambalvo, and J. Kennedy, "Analytical Procedures and Audit-Planning Decisions," *Auditing: A Journal of Practice & Theory* (Fall 2000), pp. 27–45.

Mautz, R. K., and H. A. Sharaf, *The Philosophy of Auditing*, Chapter 5, "Evidence." Sarasota, FL: American Accounting Association, 1961.

Sheriff, R., "The Audit from the Inside," *Journal of Accountancy* (January 1998), pp. 49–51.

Whittington, R., and G. Fischbach, "The New Audit Documentation Requirements," *Journal of Accountancy* (April 2002), pp. 53–59.

QUESTIONS

1. Explain the terms *sufficient*, *competent*, and *evidential matter* as used in the third standard of field work.
2. An auditor attempts to obtain the most persuasive evidence available. What general criteria can an auditor apply to evaluate the competence of evidence?
3. Identify and briefly explain management's financial statement assertions, and explain the relationship among assertions, audit objectives, and audit procedures.
4. What are tests of controls?
5. What are substantive tests of details?
6. What are analytical procedures?
7. Identify mistakes that are common to analytical procedures.
8. How can nonfinancial measures be helpful in a financial statement audit?
9. What are heuristics, and why do they matter to auditors?
10. What is the reviewability standard?
11. What is a rebuttable presumption?
12. In the audit of a nonpublic company, how does an auditor judge whether a finding or issue is significant?
13. Identify and briefly describe the major files auditors typically maintain separately from audit documentation.
14. Explain the major functions of audit documentation.
15. Describe a typical arrangement of audit documentation.
16. Distinguish between adjusting and reclassification journal entries.

17. Compare the documentation retention standards for public and for nonpublic company audits.
18. Distinguish between indexing and references in audit documentation.
19. What is database management software?
20. How does *United States v. Arthur Young & Co. et al.*, a tax case, bear on auditing?

MULTIPLE CHOICE QUESTIONS

1. Which of the following statements about the competence of evidence is always true?
   a. Evidence gathered by an auditor from third parties is reliable.
   b. Accounting data developed when control risk is low is more relevant than data developed when control risk is high.
   c. Oral representations made by management are not valid evidence.
   d. To be competent, evidence must be both valid and relevant.

2. The case of SmarTalk Teleservices, Inc., illustrates the relationship between:
   a. Exit plans and accounting for restructuring costs.
   b. Audit risk and audit evidence.
   c. Offers of settlement and SEC Accounting and Auditing Enforcement Releases.
   d. Sufficient evidential matter and generally accepted auditing standards.

3. Management's assertions relate to an auditor's objectives because:
   a. The financial statements are management's responsibility.
   b. Management asserts that all assets, liabilities, and equities actually exist.
   c. An auditor's objective is to reach conclusions about management's assertions.
   d. An audit opinion is dependent on an auditor's objectives.

4. Management asserts that all transactions that occurred were recorded. This is the assertion of:
   a. Completeness.
   b. Existence.
   c. Rights.
   d. Occurrence.

5. A practitioner uses audit procedures to:
   a. Decide the types and quantity of evidence to gather.
   b. Design tests of controls and substantive tests of details.
   c. Gather sufficient, competent evidence.
   d. Satisfy PCAOB standards.

6. Examining receiving reports as evidence of the date and quantity a client received inventory is an example of the procedure of:
   a. Observation.
   b. Documentation.
   c. Confirmation.
   d. Comparison.

7. Tests of controls are:
   a. Intended to detect material misstatements in financial statement accounts.
   b. Concerned with how internal control policies or procedures are applied.
   c. Evaluations of financial information made by a study of plausible relationships among both financial and nonfinancial data.
   d. Procedures that lend hindsight to amounts and information disclosed in financial statements as of the balance sheet date.

8. Sales orders a credit manager approves before goods are shipped is an example of a:

   a. Test of controls.
   b. Financial statement assertion.
   c. Documentation.
   d. Control that leaves an audit trail.

9. One of the linkages between tests of controls and substantive tests is:

   a. Analytical procedures.
   b. Assertions.
   c. Risk.
   d. Timing.

10. Analytical procedures are:

    a. Intended to detect material misstatements in financial statement accounts.
    b. Concerned with how internal control policies or procedures are applied.
    c. Evaluations of financial information made by a study of plausible relationships among both financial and nonfinancial data.
    d. Procedures that lend hindsight to amounts and information disclosed in financial statements as of the balance sheet date.

11. When applying analytical procedures, an auditor could develop an independent expectation of an account balance to compare to:

    a. Management's unaudited balance.
    b. Management's unaudited balance adjusted for trends in the industry.
    c. The prior-year audited balance.
    d. The prior-year audited balance adjusted for trends in the industry.

12. Trend analysis:

    a. Supports or refutes a financial statement account balance.
    b. Compares point estimates over time.
    c. Applies statistics to calculate expected values.
    d. Is an example of an analytical procedure.

13. Which of the following would not likely result in a mistake in judgment common to analytical procedures?

    a. An accounts receivable clerk's spreadsheet of balances due by month
    b. A recorded account balance that did not vary significantly from the prior period
    c. Comparing an account balance to an amount a statistical procedure predicted
    d. Relying on a credit manager's explanation for an overdue account

14. Audit programs should:

    a. Summarize the nature, timing, and extent of audit procedures applied.
    b. Be prepared for all financial statement accounts.
    c. Be prepared by audit partners.
    d. Be prepared in writing.

15. On a balanced scorecard, benchmarks to best practices are measures common to the:

    a. Financial perspective.
    b. Customer perspective.
    c. Internal business perspective.
    d. Internal learning perspective.

16. In 2005 and 2006, an auditor found that approximately 4 percent of processed sales invoices were not mathematically accurate. In late 2006, the client implemented a control requiring that all sales invoices be extended by two independent employees. When planning the 2007 engagement, the auditor estimated a 4 percent error rate for processed sales orders. This is an example of which heuristic?

    a. Availability
    b. Anchoring-and-adjustment
    c. Representativeness
    d. Base rate neglect

17. The documentation an auditor prepares in a financial statement audit is:

    a. Owned by the auditor.
    b. Owned by the audit client.
    c. The principal support for audit conclusions.
    d. Retained in the auditor's office until a change in auditors.

18. The Auditing Standards Board's *SAS No. 96*, "Audit Documentation":

    a. Replicates the Public Company Accounting Oversight Board's standard.
    b. Includes adjusting entries as an example of a significant finding.
    c. Includes among audit documentation abstracts of contracts or agreements.
    d. Requires that audit documentation be completed within a specified period of time.

19. The most common computer application in audit practice is:

    a. Internet access.
    b. Spreadsheet software.
    c. Trial balance preparation.
    d. Time and expense reports.

20. The quantity of audit documentation compiled on an engagement would be affected most by:

    a. Management's integrity.
    b. Control risk.
    c. A new engagement.
    d. The auditor's experience.

PROBLEMS AND DISCUSSION CASES

6-1 *Audit Evidence*

In a financial statement audit, an independent auditor must judge the validity of audit evidence obtained.

   Required: Assume you have assessed a low level of control risk.
1. In the course of an audit, the auditor asks many questions of client officers and employees.
    a. Describe the factors an auditor should consider in evaluating oral evidence provided by officers and employees.
    b. Discuss the validity and limitations of oral evidence.
2. An auditor's tests may include recomputation of various balance sheet and operating ratios for comparison with prior years and industry averages. Discuss the validity and limitations of ratio analysis.

3. An auditor is observing the physical inventory of a manufacturing company's finished goods, which consists of expensive, highly complex equipment. Discuss the validity and limitations of the audit evidence provided by observation.

(AICPA Adapted)

6-2 *Financial Statement Assertions*

Much of an auditor's work during a financial statement audit consists of obtaining and evaluating evidence about the assertions embodied within an entity's financial statements. Following are several tasks or questions considered by an auditor.

1. Observe client personnel count inventory quantities.
2. Include the following statement within the management representation letter: "There are no material transactions that have not been properly recorded in the accounting records underlying the financial statements."
3. For a sample of product lines, trace prices used in the final priced inventory to recent invoice prices.
4. Do the financial statements include separate captions for raw materials, work in process, and finished goods inventory?
5. Confirm inventory held in public warehouses.

Required: For each of the tasks or questions, discuss the dominant financial statement assertion addressed.

6-3 *Identifying Audit Procedures*

Auditors frequently refer to the terms *standards* and *procedures*. Auditing standards relate to the measures of quality achieved in an engagement, and auditing procedures to the methods or techniques used by the auditor to gather evidence.

Required: Identify and discuss procedures an auditor typically uses in a financial statement audit.

6-4 *Underlying Accounting Data and Corroborating Information*

The third generally accepted standard of field work requires that an auditor obtain sufficient competent evidential matter to afford a reasonable basis for an opinion regarding the financial statements audited. In considering what constitutes sufficient competent evidential matter, a distinction is often made between underlying accounting data and corroborating information available to the auditor.

Required: Discuss underlying accounting data, corroborating information available to the auditor, and the methods by which the auditor gathers competent evidential matter.

6-5 *Audit Procedures*

The purpose of all auditing procedures is to gather sufficient competent evidence for an auditor to form an opinion on an entity's financial statements taken as a whole.

Required: Identify and describe the auditing procedures used most commonly in audit practice.

(AICPA Adapted)

6-6 *Analytical Procedures*

Analytical procedures consist of evaluations of financial information made by a study of plausible relationships among both financial and nonfinancial data. These procedures range from simple comparisons to complex models involving many relationships, and involve comparing recorded amounts, or ratios developed from recorded amounts, to expectations the auditor develops.

Required:

1. Describe the broad purposes of analytical procedures.
2. Identify the sources of information from which an auditor develops expectations.

(AICPA Adapted)

6-7 *Applying Analytical Procedures*

You are planning the audit of MediCorp, Inc., a publicly traded company that develops and markets products used in the prevention and treatment of infectious diseases. MediCorp markets two products—CytoMed, used in the prevention of bronchiolitis, and RespiMed, used in the treatment of pneumonia—and has eight new product candidates in various stages of development. One industry analyst is quoted as saying, "R2V, the code name of the company's breakthrough drug to treat RSV disease, the leading cause of bronchiolitis and pneumonia in certain high-risk children, has performed well in clinical trials." The following annual data is available:

Average Accounts Receivable	$ 5.6	million
Average Inventory	6.1	million
Average Total Assets	110.6	million
Cost of Sales	19.7	million
Current Assets	132.8	million
Current Liabilities	19.5	million
Interest Expense	2.2	million
Net Sales	25.9	million
Operating Income (Loss)	(26.1)	million

All credit sales terms are 30 days. Although not included in average inventory, MediCorp management plans to carry R2V in inventory at $0.8 million.

Required:

1. Calculate and interpret activity, profitability, liquidity, and solvency ratios that will be useful in planning the audit.
2. Do you agree with management's plans to carry R2V in inventory?

6-8 *The Customer Perspective at Waste Management*
(http://www.wastemanagement.com)

Waste Management, Inc., a Houston-based waste disposal company, provides integrated solid waste services to commercial, industrial, municipal, and residential customers. Services in the United States include solid waste collection, resource recovery, on-site integrated hazardous waste management, disposal in over 130 sanitary landfill facilities, curbside recycling to over 8 million households, and 220,000 commercial and industrial recycling centers. Waste Management, Inc., a New York Stock Exchange Company, is the largest waste disposal company in the world.

Required: Access the Web site of Waste Management, Inc. Identify and discuss relevant metrics to measure the customer perspective for two of Waste Management's broad customer groups: municipal landfills and residential customers.

6-9 *The Internal Business Perspective of the Cleveland Clinic*
(http://www.clevelandclinic.org)

Half of the children born in the United States suffer from pneumonia, bronchiolitis, or croup within one year of birth. The symptoms of these diseases are treatable for most children, but can be life threatening for children with heart, lung, or immune system complications. In the late 1990s, the Learner Research Institute of The Cleveland Clinic, a major teaching and research hospital, announced that scientists had cloned the virus that causes these diseases, an encouraging development that prompted Amiya Banerjee, a molecular biologist at Lerner, to comment that, "This is a breakthrough . . . some fine tuning could produce a unique virus that might be used as a vaccine."

Required: Access the Web site of The Cleveland Clinic, other research institutes, or research-based pharmaceutical companies to identify and discuss internal business measures for the Lerner Research Institute's progress in investigating the virus.

6-10 *The Internal Learning Perspective of Ford Motor Company* (http://www.ford.com)

The Ford Motor Company operates in two principal lines of business: automotive (the design, assembly, and sale of cars and trucks) and financial services (financing, leasing, and insurance). In the late 1990s, Ford announced an aggressive plan to develop advanced technologies that improve vehicle fuel efficiency and achieve cleaner emissions. For example, compared to comparable vehicles that require more than 2,000 pounds of steel, the design of the Ford P2000 requires only 500 pounds of steel. Ford reports that the P2000 achieves over 60 miles to the gallon and is environmentally friendly.

Required: The Ford Motor Company is designing performance measures for the internal learning perspective of the company's lightweight technologies initiative. Using online and other public sources of information, suggest researchable design opportunities to manufacture lighter passenger cars. For example, Ford could investigate the use of aluminum and other lightweight materials such as carbon fiber and magnesium.

6-11 *The Purpose of Audit Programs*

The first generally accepted standard of field work requires, in part, that "the work is to be adequately planned," and an audit program is one tool auditors use to plan audit work.

Required: What is an audit program, and what purposes would it serve?

6-12 *Cognitive Heuristics*

Andrew Mills, an entry-level staff member with less than six months professional experience, is assigned to audit the cash accounts of Drexel Industries, a long-standing audit client of Rollins, Hunterfield, and Dodge, LLP. Dodge, the engagement partner, tells Mills, "Drexel is a rather low-risk client. In fact, in all the years I've been associated with Drexel, I don't recall any serious problems, particularly in cash—controls are tight and management is trustworthy. Tell you what, I've got to be away for a few days. I haven't been out to Drexel or even talked with management in months, but why don't you look at last year's papers, and run with it." Following Dodge's advice, Mills copies last year's audit program and follows the procedures explicitly.

Upon returning, Dodge calls Mills and asks, "How did it go?" Mills says, "Fine—things seemed so clean, I only had to talk with management once, and that was just to locate the cash records."

Required: Which, if any, of the cognitive heuristics may apply here? Explain.

6-13 *Cognitive Heuristics*

Alpine Roofing Company, an audit client of Marques, CPA, manufactures two products: tar shingles and aluminum gutters. In examining Alpine's Reserve for Warranty Guarantees as of December 31, 2007—that is, the estimated liability for warranty repairs and allowances resulting from 2007 sales—Marques reviews internal quality control and engineering reports and learns the following:

- Alpine processes approximately 75 sales orders per business day for tar shingles and 25 orders per day for aluminum gutters.
- Warranty repairs and allowances are claimed on about 20 percent of the recorded sales orders for shingles and on 10 percent of the sales for gutters, both of which are of concern to management.

Because sales were unusually high in October and more than 25 percent warranty claims for either product could prove damaging to Alpine's reputation, management asks

Marques which product, shingles or gutters, is more likely to have more than 25 percent warranty claims resulting from October sales. Marques concludes that tar shingles are more likely to have more than 25 percent claims because shingle sales outperformed gutter sales 3 to 1 in October, just as in the daily estimates.

Required:

1. Which of the cognitive heuristics—representativeness, availability, or anchoring—may have caused bias in Marques' response? Explain.
2. Is Marques correct? Why or why not?

6-14 *Cognitive Heuristics*

From data available in the public press, a public accounting firm estimates that undetected management fraud may occur in 20 out of every 1,000 large, publicly traded companies and in 80 out of every 1,000 small, privately owned companies. But because the data may not be wholly reliable, the firm's executive committee decides to poll its regular and small business audit partners at the annual partners' meeting. Regular partners will be surveyed about publicly traded companies, and small business partners will be surveyed about privately owned companies. The survey results will be used to redesign the firm's audit planning checklist, which, in the executive committee's view, does not adequately address the firm's responsibility to detect and report management fraud.

At the annual partners' meeting, all regular audit partners are given a questionnaire that asks the following two questions:

- From your experience, do you believe that the incidence of management fraud in large public companies is:
  a. *More* than 20 out of every 1,000 companies?
  b. *Less* than 20 out of every 1,000 companies?
- What is your estimate of the percentage of large public companies involved in management fraud?

Small business partners were asked the same questions for private companies:

- From your experience, do you believe that the incidence of management fraud in small private companies is:
  a. *More* than 80 out of every 1,000 companies?
  b. *Less* than 80 out of every 1,000 companies?
- What is your estimate of the percentage of small private companies involved in management fraud?

Compiled responses from each partner group indicated the incidence of management fraud was estimated to be 0.025 (2.5 percent) for large, public companies and 0.18 (18 percent) for small, private companies.

Required:

1. For the survey described, which of the cognitive heuristics—representativeness, availability, or anchoring—could bias the responding partners? Discuss.
2. From the results indicated, have either or both of the partner groups apparently been biased by the heuristic(s) you identified in requirement 1? Explain.
3. How could the firm have avoided any suspicion that heuristics might bias the survey results?

AUDIT DOCUMENTATION REVIEW

6-15 *Audit Documentation Standards*

In 2004, two years after the Auditing Standards Board (ASB) issued *SAS No. 96*, "Audit Documentation," the Public Company Accounting Oversight Board (PCAOB) issued a standard that incremented the documentation requirements for public company audits. In a September 2003 PCAOB Round Table, held in Washington, D.C. to solicit the views of opinion leaders about audit documentation, William J. McDonough, PCAOB chair, said, "We view the auditor's work papers as a integral part of a quality audit. That is, work papers document not only the nature, timing, and extent of the work, but also the professional judgments made by members of a well-trained audit engagement team."

   Required:
   1. Explain the requirements in the PCAOB's standard that are incremental to the ASB's standard.
   2. Referring to Chairman McDonough's remark, how does compliance with the PCAOB's standard on audit documentation bear witness to an auditor's professional judgments?

6-16 *Audit Documentation Review*

Adam Fionte, an entry-level staff member in a public accounting firm, prepared the following document, the lead sheet, for J&K Sales Co., Inc., for December 31, 2007, trade accounts receivable:

AUDIT
DOCUMENTATION
REVIEW

B

	Accounts Receivable			
	Adjusted Balance 12/31/06	*Balance Per Bks. 12/31/07*	*Adjs./ Reclass Dr <Cr>*	*Adjusted Balance 12/31/07*
Accounts Rec.: Trade				
Regular Customers	$450,000	$657,985		$657,985 c
Special Discount				
Customers	105,000	135,760	(9,500)	126,260 c
Allowance for Doubtful				
Accounts	(35,000)	(65,000)		(65,000)c
	$520,000	$728,745	$(9,500)	$719,245 c
	f	f	f	f

c Crosscast/AF
f Footed/AF

   Required: Discuss the deficiencies in this document.

6-17 *Audit Documentation Review*

The following documents an auditor's test for *kiting*, an intentional irregularity that conceals cash shortages by transferring funds from one bank (or company) to another, recording the receipt on or before the balance sheet date, and recording the disbursement after the balance sheet date.

AUDIT
DOCUMENTATION
REVIEW

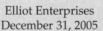
Elliot Enterprises   A9
December 31, 2005

				Disbursement Date		Receipt Date	
Ck No.	Transferred From	To	Amount	Per Books	Per Bank	Per Books	Per Bank
Interbank Transfers							
1021	Society Bank	St. Joe Bank *A5*	5,500	12/30#	01/02	12/30@	01/02&
1246	St. Joe Bank	Trust Corp. *A6*	15,000	12/31#	01/02	12/31@	01/02&
1524	Society Bank	Union Bank	7,500	12/31#	01/02	12/31@	01/02&
Intercompany Transfers							
4678	Westco (Subsidiary)	Elliot *A8*	25,000	01/01#	01/02	12/31@	01/02&

& Agreed to bank statement/RC
# Agreed to cash disbursement records/RC
@ Agreed to cash receipts records/RC

   Required: Discuss the deficiencies in this document.

**AUDIT
DOCUMENTATION
REVIEW**

6-18 *The Purpose and Content of Audit Documentation*

Preparing audit documentation is an integral part of a financial statement audit.

Required:

1. a.   What are the purposes or functions of audit documentation?
   b.   What records may be included in audit documentation?
2. What factors affect the auditor's judgment about the type and content of documentation appropriate for a particular engagement?
3. Discuss the relationship between audit documents and each of the standards of field work.
4. You are instructing an inexperienced associate whose first auditing assignment is to audit an account. An analysis of the account has been prepared by the client for inclusion in audit documentation. Prepare a list of the information and notations that the staff member should include in the account analysis to provide an adequate document as evidence of work accomplished. (Do not include a description of auditing procedures applicable to the account.)

(AICPA Adapted)

Internet problems and discussion cases are available at http://ricchiute.swlearning.com

RESEARCH PROJECTS

1. Analytical Procedures and Reengineered Audit Processes

In a letter to the AICPA director of audit and attest standards, former SEC Chief Accountant Lynn Turner criticized large audit firms for reengineering audit approaches that:

- Focus more on risk assessment through analytical procedures than on substantive tests of details, and
- Assign the assessment to inexperienced staff.

The letter reads in part as follows:

The recent combination of changes in the audit process and high profile financial frauds have raised questions about the efficacy of the audit process. For example, auditors have changed their audit procedures to use a risk assessment model that places increased reliance on analytical procedures, while decreasing the use of substantive audit procedures, such as confirmations with debtors and detailed testing of transactions, account balances, and the activity in those accounts. This restructuring of the audit process has come at a time when the press has reported several frauds involving materially and in some cases hugely misstated financial statements that appear to have gone undetected by auditors.

Use of this audit process involves substantial ongoing assessments of operations and associated risks, and how those risks might impact the reported results. The SEC staff is concerned that many of the individuals performing audit work today may lack the practical business experience necessary to perform these high level assessments, which may have significant detrimental effects on the quality of audits.

However, research published in journals such as *The Accounting Review*, the *Journal of Accounting Research*, *Contemporary Accounting Research*, and *Accounting Organizations & Society* reveals that analytical procedures can be an effective means for predicting financial statement error and for focusing an auditor's attention to risky accounts and disclosures

Required: Using articles published in the journals mentioned above, among others, draft a memorandum that contradicts the SEC's position.

2. What Research Reveals About Audit Documentation

Research published in accounting journals such as *The Accounting Review*, the *Journal of Accounting Research*, *Contemporary Accounting Research*, and *Accounting Organizations & Society*, and in experimental psychology journals such as *Organizational Behavior and Human Decision Processes* and the *Journal of Experimental Psychology*, offers a number of insights about audit documentation, including the following:

- Audit managers detect conceptual errors more accurately than audit seniors, and audit seniors detect mechanical errors more accurately than audit managers.
- Audit documentation reviewers detect more errors in evidence documented by preparers with whom they are familiar than in evidence documented by preparers with whom they are unfamiliar.
- Audit partner's decisions are affected by the order in which evidence is documented.

Dozens of articles about audit documentation have been published in these journals.

Required: Search the research journals mentioned above for articles about audit documentation. For any two articles, draft a report that explains both the key insight offered by the research and your recommendation for how auditors can leverage off of the insight to improve audit effectiveness.

3. Using the Internet to Understand a Client's Industry

An auditor has a wealth of readily accessible data to help understand a client's business and industry, particularly for industries not served previously by the auditor. What once had been done with newspapers, magazines, and hardbound volumes can now be done instantaneously using an Internet search that accesses links to and about a variety of industries such as aerospace, agriculture, apparel, entertainment, real estate, telecommunications, or transportation.

Required: Select an industry that interests you. Prepare a report that:
1. Identifies and summarizes key news issues that would bear on an auditor engaged in the industry. For example, news that foreign crude oil exploration slowdowns had driven artificial price supports could affect an oil and gas refining client's oil supplies. Or, news of rising interest rates could affect a construction client's new housing starts.
2. For three companies in the industry:
   a. Summarize each company's major products, and explain how the news you identify could bear on the companies' results of operations.
   b. Summarize each company's most recent reported financial results, and explain whether the news you identify is good or bad for the companies' results of operations.

**Interactive quizzes are available as a student learning resource at
http://ricchiute.swlearning.com**

7 Chapter

The Audit Process and Detecting Fraud

Major topics discussed in this chapter are:

- The audit process, including client strategies, the decision to accept an engagement, establishing an understanding with management, planning, and interim and year-end audit work.
- The auditor's responsibility to detect and report fraud.

Chapter 6 introduced the means to acquire, evaluate, and document evidence. However, the evidence an auditor chooses to acquire depends in part on a client's industry, since industry-specific risks drive client-specific strategies to cope with risk. For example, in the retail apparel industry, J. Crew's market share depends on clothing lines that appeal to target consumers, and in the pharmaceutical industry, Pfizer's survival depends on a pipeline of breakthrough drugs. The two industries differ, risk-coping strategies differ, and, correspondingly, a practitioner's evidence-acquisition decisions depend on how a client's strategies bear on risk. This chapter explains the steps in the audit process, including how auditors come to understand what drives a business *before* designing an audit and how auditors endow an audit plan to detect material fraud.

The chapter begins by summarizing the audit process, including the steps an auditor undertakes to achieve the standards and control the risks introduced in Chapter 2, and to issue the reports illustrated in Chapter 3. For example, the chapter introduces a client strategy template, a tool to summarize a client's industry, business, and strategies, and to assess audit risk. The template is similar in approach to the tools firms use commonly in practice today, among them Ernst & Young's *Business Process Analysis* and KPMG's *Business Measurement Process*. To add both context and reality, part of the discussion emphasizes one industry (pharmaceuticals) and one Dow Jones Industrial company (Merck & Co., Inc.). An Appendix introduces the assurance process in a performance-measurement benchmarking service, including planning, selecting relevant performance measures, collecting evidence, and displaying evidence in vision charts and reliability indices.

The Audit Process

A financial statement audit proceeds from planning, to analysis, to integration in the form of a report. Figure 7-1 lists the major steps in the audit process, includ-

FIGURE 7-1: *The Audit Process*

Approximate Dates	Activity
March	Communicate with the audit committee.
	Decide whether to accept or continue the engagement.
	Establish an understanding with the client.
	Establish an understanding of the client's strategies and characteristics of the business.
April–May	Consider the risk of misstatements arising from fraud.
	First-quarter planning (Figure 7-8).
July–August	Consider potential adverse influences, threats to the business, and audit risk.
	Second-quarter planning (Figure 7-8).
September–November	Interim audit work (Figure 7-10).
December–February	Year-end audit work (Figure 7-11).
	Subsequent events.
Last day of field work	Management representation and legal letters.
	Reports.

ing representative dates, assuming a December 31 fiscal year end, and either a continuing or initial engagement accepted early in the year. In practice, the audit process may vary somewhat from engagement to engagement, depending on an entity's industry and size, among other things. However, most financial statement audits are similar both in logic and in breadth—similar in logic because they resemble the scientific method of inquiry (Chapter 1), and similar in breadth because they are all driven by the same set of guidelines: auditing standards. The following discusses each step in the audit process, although the discussion is weighted this way: the steps before interim and year-end work (for example, communicating with the audit committee, establishing an understanding with the client, and audit planning) are discussed in detail, and interim and year-end work are discussed briefly as an introduction to Chapters 8 through 17, which discuss and illustrate those issues completely.

Communicate with the Audit Committee

Auditors commonly propose audit service engagements to the **audit committee** of a potential (or continuing) client's board of directors. Thereafter, as discussed in Chapter 1, the board of directors, with the audit committee serving as intermediary—not management—is the audit client.

Although not common until the 1970s, audit committees were first encouraged as early as 1940 in SEC *Accounting Series Release No. 19*, which recommended that registrants establish committees composed of nonofficer board members; again in the AICPA's 1967 *Statement on Audit Committees of Boards of Directors*; and then again in the SEC's 1972 *Accounting Series Release No. 123*, "Standing Audit Committees Composed of Outside Directors." However, the first authoritative mandate for audit committees came in 1978 when the New York Stock Exchange required that all listed companies appoint audit committees consisting of outside directors only. Since then, the role and responsibilities of audit committees have changed dramatically, largely because of a Blue Ribbon Committee on Audit Committees, the SEC's Rules on Audit Committees, and the *Sarbanes-Oxley Act of 2002*.

Blue Ribbon Committee on Audit Committees

Research in the 1990s offered two findings about the resolve and effect of audit committees. One study reported that effective audit committees require a strong organizational mandate—for example, through a written charter and recognition by management and the independent auditor.[1] Another showed that audit committees reduce the frequency of shareholder lawsuits alleging management fraud, quarterly earnings restatements, SEC enforcement actions, illegal acts, and auditor turnover when management disagrees with an accounting principle.[2] However, in the late 1990s, the SEC criticized audit committees. For example, in a well-publicized 1998 speech at New York University's Center for Law and Business, "The Numbers Game," Arthur Levitt, then SEC chairman, said, "Sadly, stories abound of audit committees whose members lack expertise in the basic principles of financial reporting as well as the mandate to ask probing questions."

Levitt offered an initiative on audit committee effectiveness: an announcement that the New York Stock Exchange and the National Association of Securities Dealers would sponsor an 11-member Blue Ribbon Committee on Improving the Effectiveness of Corporate Audit Committees. In 1999, the committee made ten recommendations, among them that:

- Audit committees be required not only to monitor whether a public company's financial statements comply with GAAP, but also whether management uses "the best accounting principles."
- Committee members not have any family or other financial ties to the company.
- The committee report to shareholders.

Responding to the Blue Ribbon Committee's recommendations, the Auditing Standards Board in 2000 issued *SAS No. 89*, "Audit Committee Communications," which requires that an auditor discuss with the audit committee "the quality, not just the acceptability" of management's accounting principles and earnings. The discussions should be open and frank and should include matters such as:

- The consistency of management's accounting principles, and
- The clarity and completeness of management's financial statements.

Consistent with language in FASB *Statement of Financial Concepts No. 2*, "Qualitative Characteristics of Accounting Information," the auditor's discussion with the audit committee should include items that have a significant impact on the "representational faithfulness, verifiability, and neutrality of accounting information" included in financial statements. Stated another way, disclosures should offer the reader a transparent view of the transactions and events that underlie the financial statements. For example, in an effort to meet analysts' expectations for reported operating earnings, some companies have netted nonoperating gains

1   L. P. Kalbers and T. J. Fogarty, "Audit Committee Effectiveness: An Empirical Investigation of the Contribution of Power," *Auditing: A Journal of Practice & Theory* (Spring 1993), pp. 24–49.
2   D. A. McMullen, "Audit Committee Performance: An Investigation of the Consequences Associated with Audit Committees," *Auditing: A Journal of Practice & Theory* (Spring 1996), pp. 87–103.

against exposures such as environmental liabilities (*Dr* Nonoperating Gains, *Cr* Environmental Liabilities), thereby avoiding the recognition of environmental expenses, overstating operating earnings, and masking the nonoperating gain as operating. Netting is neither representationally faithful to the company's environmental exposures nor, for that matter, altogether transparent.

The SEC's Audit Committee Rules and Sarbanes-Oxley

In response to the Blue Ribbon Committee's recommendations, the SEC, effective in 2000, issued *Final Rule: Audit Committee Disclosure*, which broadened the responsibilities of audit committees. For example, although reviews by independent accountants of a public company's quarterly financial statements (*Form 10-Q*) were voluntary prior to 2000, the rule now mandates quarterly reviews (Chapter 18), in part because accountants' reviews will "reduce the likelihood of restatements or other year-end adjustments and enhance the reliability of financial information." The rule also requires that audit committees include in proxy statements a report to shareholders explaining whether the audit committee:

- Discussed with management the audited financial statements.
- Discussed with the auditors estimates and uncertainties, unusual transactions, newly adopted accounting principles, and auditor independence.

Consistent with the SEC's Rules, the *Sarbanes-Oxley Act*, Section 301, "Public Company Audit Committees," prohibits a company from trading publicly absent an audit committee, and requires that all committee members be independent—meaning, for example, that no members may receive consulting fees from, or be otherwise affiliated with, the company. Audit committees generally meet repeatedly throughout a year; serve as intermediaries between the auditor and the full board of directors; and, under Section 301, are responsible for an auditor's appointment, compensation, and oversight (including resolving differences of opinion between the auditor and management). Other typical responsibilities include:

- The scope and timing of the audit,
- Internal control,
- Internal audit,
- Accounting changes,
- The results of the audit,
- Disclosures within management's financial statements, and
- The quality of reported earnings.

Audit committees are common today, even in nonpublic companies. For example, audit committees are required for Federal Deposit Insurance Corporation (FDIC) insured depository institutions, and many governmental entities, such as municipalities, town boards, and port authorities.

Decide Whether to Accept or Continue the Engagement

Considering Risk

Public accounting firms establish policies and procedures for deciding whether to accept (or continue) an engagement, thereby minimizing the likelihood of associating with an untrustworthy or an unduly risky client. For example, large firms exercise considerable caution in deciding whether to audit a risky client, although the responsibility for the decision varies across firms. In some firms, the decision is made by individual partners, in others by office-managing or regional partners, and in others by national office partners.[3] Examples documenting *why* public accounting firms decline on individual engagements is not observable publicly. However, research shows that firms are less likely to accept clients that appear risky[4] although, in some instances, firms may invoke risk management strategies, such as assigning specialists to mitigate the risk.[5]

Public accounting firms use a variety of sources in deciding whether to accept or continue an engagement. For example, when considering a new client, an auditor could:

- Evaluate the firm's ability to service the proposed client properly.
- Review the proposed client's financial statements.
- Inquire of third parties, such as bankers and lawyers, about a proposed client's reputation.
- Investigate enforcement filings, such as SEC Accounting and Auditing Enforcement Releases.
- Review for bankruptcy filings.
- Investigate the background of key management.

For upstart companies whose management is not known in the community, some firms outsource background investigations to specialist firms, such as Securatis Group (Chapter 5).

On new engagements, a firm also should consider whether the predecessor auditor's resignation or replacement was linked to a disagreement between the predecessor and management about accounting principles. For example, the resignation may have been precipitated by disagreements over the income statement, such as revenue recognition and channel stuffing (Chapter 11), or over the balance sheet, such as impaired assets (Chapter 15) or restructuring reserves (Chapter 6). Interestingly, research reveals some commonality among companies for which a disagreement drove an auditor change: Compared to clients that changed auditors for reasons unrelated to a disagreement (for example, an intent to take the company public), the clients have relatively poorer earnings performance, more debt, fewer current assets, and poorer stock price performance.[6]

Communicating with Predecessor Auditors

When a new engagement involves replacing a predecessor auditor, the successor should communicate with the predecessor before accepting the engagement. In fact, when more than one potential successor proposes on a new engagement, the successor typically accepts the engagement conditional on communicating with

---

3   H. F. Huss and F. A. Jacobs, "Risk Containment: Exploring Auditor Decisions in the Engagement Process," *Auditing: A Journal of Practice & Theory* (Fall 1991), pp. 16–32.

4   See, for example, K. M. Johnstone, "Client Acceptance Decisions: Simultaneous Effects of Client Business Risk, Audit Risk, Auditor Business Risk, and Risk Adaptation," *Auditing: A Journal of Practice & Theory* (Spring 2000), pp. 1–25.

5   K. M. Johnstone and J. C. Bedard, "Risk Management in Client Acceptance Decisions," *The Accounting Review* (October 2003), pp. 1003–1025.

6   D. S. Dhaliwal, J. W. Schatzberg, and M. A. Trombley, "An Analysis of the Economic Factors Related to Auditor-Client Disagreements Preceding Auditor Changes," *Auditing: A Journal of Practice & Theory* (Fall 1993), pp. 22–38.

the predecessor, since the communication may reveal circumstances unacceptable to the successor. For example, the predecessor may reveal to the successor that management lacks integrity. *Statement on Auditing Standards (SAS) No. 84*, "Communications Between Predecessor and Successor Auditors," places the initiative for communication on the successor auditor. Since Rule 301 of the Code of Professional Conduct precludes an auditor from disclosing confidential information without a client's permission (Chapter 4), the successor asks the prospective client to authorize the predecessor to respond fully to the successor's inquiries. If the prospective client refuses, or limits the information a predecessor may disclose, the successor determines the reason for refusal and the impact on the decision to accept the engagement.

Under *SAS No. 84*, the successor makes specific and reasonable inquiries that bear on his or her decision to accept the engagement. For example, the successor may make inquiries about management's integrity, disagreements with management, and the reason management is changing auditors. In response, the predecessor auditor should reply fully and promptly, although the predecessor may alert the successor that his or her response is limited due to circumstances such as pending or threatened litigation. Surprisingly, research reveals that, despite the responsibility to communicate with predecessors, some successor auditors do not. For example, one study found that fully one-fourth of 550 successor auditors did not communicate with predecessors (and that the extent of noncommunication was higher in smaller firms),[7] and another found that a startling three-fourths of 151 successors did not communicate.[8] Unless asked by the successor, the predecessor is under no obligation to communicate information to the successor auditor, even if the predecessor is aware of facts that would bear on the successor's decision to accept the new engagement, such as repeated violations of authoritative accounting pronouncements.

Establish an Understanding with the Client

After a decision is made to accept (or continue) an engagement, *SAS No. 83* (and *SSAE No. 7*), "Establishing an Understanding with the Client," requires that the practitioner establish an understanding with his or her client about the objective and limitations of the engagement and management's responsibilities. For example, the objective of a financial statement audit is to express an opinion about whether management's financial statements present fairly, in all material respects, the financial position, results of operations, and cash flows in conformity with GAAP. However, consider the objective of a financial statement service other than an audit. For example, the objective of an agreed-upon procedures engagement to issue a report about a bank's compliance with the Federal Depository Insurance Corporation's (FDIC) "safety and soundness" regulations (Chapter 1) is quite different from the objective of a financial statement audit, driving an important limitation in the engagement: The bank, among other parties such as the FDIC, can rely on the practitioner's report for no purpose other than assurance about the bank's compliance with the FDIC regulations, not, for example, about management's compliance with GAAP.

---

7   J. C. Lambert, S. J. Lambert III, and T. G. Calderon, "Communication Between Successor and Predecessor Auditors," *Auditing: A Journal of Practice & Theory* (Spring 1991), pp. 97–109.
8   G. W. Glezen and M. B. Elser, "The Auditor Change Process," *Journal of Accountancy* (June 1996), pp. 73–77.

In a financial statement audit, management is responsible for:

- The financial statements,
- Establishing and maintaining effective internal control over financial reporting,
- Assuring compliance with applicable laws and regulations,
- Making all financial records and information available to the auditor, and
- Providing the auditor with a letter confirming representations management made during the engagement.

Depending on arrangements negotiated between the auditor and the client, management's responsibilities also might include, for example, compiling spreadsheets and retrieving evidence for the auditor.

Engagement Letters

SAS No. 84, "Communications Between Predecessor and Successor Auditors," requires that an auditor document his or her understanding, preferably through a written communication called an **engagement letter**. The engagement letter is drafted by the auditor for the chief executive officer's signature and, as illustrated in Figure 7-2, is a written agreement between the auditor and the client that serves to minimize misunderstandings, alert the client to the purpose of the engagement and role of the auditor, and help minimize legal liability for services neither contracted nor performed. Engagement letters are recommended, though not required, by *SAS No. 84*. However, practitioners have every reason to prepare an engagement letter for every professional engagement, since the risk of misunderstanding can, and sometimes does, result in serious legal judgments against the independent auditor. For example, consider *1136 Tenants' Corp. v. Max Rothenberg & Co.*, a prominent and precedent-setting case regarding engagement letters. 1136 Tenants' Corporation, an apartment cooperative, engaged Max Rothenberg & Co., without an engagement letter, to conduct nonaudit accounting services. Rothenberg provided services from 1963 to 1965, when it was discovered that a former manager had absconded with funds from the corporation. 1136 Tenants sued Max Rothenberg, arguing that an audit should have been performed. In defense, Rothenberg unsuccessfully argued that an audit was not agreed to. The professional fees for the engagement amounted to only $600 per year, but Rothenberg was ordered to pay $230,000 in damages. Engagement letters have been common ever since.

Although *1136 Tenants'* suggested that engagement letters could limit an accountant's liability to services included in the letter, *Congregation of the Passion, Holy Cross Province v. Touche Ross & Co.*, an Illinois Supreme Court case, suggests otherwise. The Congregation, a Roman Catholic religious order, engaged Touche Ross to prepare unaudited financial statements in 1973. Beginning in 1976, the Congregation entrusted full responsibility for a $2 million investment portfolio to an investment advisor who entered into a leveraged arbitrage strategy that exposed the Congregation to losses far beyond the amount invested. The Congregation was fully informed by transaction confirmations from securities dealers, but sued Touche Ross in federal court for securities laws violations and then in Illinois state court for breach of contract and negligence. Federal charges were dismissed but the Illinois Supreme Court ruled in favor of the Congregation, arguing that an accountant's duty to clients is defined both by the engagement letter and by *extracontractual* responsibilities, suggesting that an engagement letter is necessary but not always sufficient to define the limits of an accountant's responsibility to clients. The majority opinion did not define "extracontractual" responsibilities,

⤚ fraud

FIGURE 7-2: *Engagement Letter*

Cheever & Yates, LLP
Suite 2600
650 Madison Avenue
New York, NY 10022

March 24, 2007

Mr. Raymond Carver, President
The Wilson Company
15 Artubus Drive
Stony Brook, NY 11790

Dear Mr. Carver:

This will confirm our understanding of the arrangements for our audit of the financial statements of The Wilson Company for the year ended December 31, 2007.

We will audit the company's balance sheet at December 31, 2007, and the related statements of income, retained earnings, and cash flows for the year then ended for the purpose of expressing an opinion on them. Our audit will be made in accordance with generally accepted auditing standards. Our procedures will include tests of documentary evidence supporting the transactions recorded in the accounts, tests of the physical existence of inventories, and direct confirmation of receivables and certain other assets and liabilities by correspondence with selected customers, creditors, legal counsel, and banks. At the conclusion of our audit, we will request certain written representations from management about the financial statements and related matters.

Management is responsible for the fair presentation of financial statements in conformity with generally accepted accounting principles and for the development, implementation, and maintenance of adequate internal controls.

Management is responsible for adjusting the financial statements to correct material misstatements and for affirming to the auditor in the representation letter that the effects of any uncorrected misstatements aggregated by the auditor during the current engagement and pertaining to the latest period presented are immaterial, both individually and in the aggregate, to the financial statements taken as a whole.

Although we may consult with you about accounting principles, management is responsible for their selection and application. Our engagement is subject to the risk that material errors, frauds, or illegal acts, if they exist, will not be detected. However, we will inform you of any such matters that come to our attention.

We will review the company's federal and state income tax returns for the fiscal year ended December 31, 2007. These returns, we understand, will be prepared by the controller. Further, we will be available during the year to consult with you on the tax effects of any proposed transactions or contemplated change in business policies.

Our fee for these services will be at our regular per diem rates, plus travel and other out-of-pocket costs. Invoices will be rendered monthly and are payable on presentation.

We are pleased to have this opportunity to serve you.

If this letter expresses your understanding, please sign the enclosed copy where indicated and return it to us.

Sincerely,

_____
Cheever & Yates, LLP

Arrangements accepted:

_____   _____
President   Date
The Wilson Company

prompting a dissenting justice to write, "What are these extracontractual duties? If these duties cannot be articulated in a contract, how is it that the client is able to articulate that they have been breached in a complaint?"[9] The boundary of an accountant's extracontractual responsibilities remains an open question.

Proposed Adjusting Journal Entries

Prior to completing a financial statement audit, an auditor proposes to management what are often called *proposed adjusting journal entries*—adjusting journal entries that, if recorded, would conform management's financial statements to GAAP. However, in the 1990s, the chairman and the chief accountant of the SEC each expressed concerns that some auditors had "waived" known potential misstatements on the grounds of immateriality.[10] Although appropriate in some circumstances (for example, when a misstatement is immaterial, unintentional, and unlikely to affect the decisions of users), waiving adjusting journal entries runs the risk that management could invoke the waiver as prima facie evidence that alleged misstatements weren't material misstatements at all, an argument that runs counter to the third paragraph in the engagement letter illustrated in Figure 7-2: Management (not the auditor) is responsible for the fair presentation of financial statements in conformity with GAAP.

To emphasize management's responsibility for the fair presentation of financial statements, the Auditing Standards Board issued *SAS No. 88*, "Audit Adjustments," which imposes the three responsibilities outlined in Figure 7-3. First, in the planning stage of an engagement, management's engagement letter includes a statement that management understands their responsibility to record material proposed adjusting journal entries and to confirm in a representation letter at the end of the engagement that unrecorded adjusting journal entries are immaterial, both individually and in the aggregate. (The engagement letter in Figure 7-2 illustrates relevant language in the fourth paragraph.) Second, at year end, management is responsible to confirm in a representation letter the responsibility represented in the engagement letter: The proposed but unrecorded adjusting journal entries summarized in the letter are immaterial, both individually and in the aggregate. And third, at year end, the auditor informs the audit committee about management's representation, usually at a regularly scheduled audit committee meeting.

Establish an Understanding of the Client's Strategies and Business

In practice, much of what an auditor does during an engagement—stated another way, much of what you'd see if you observed an auditor in the field—is preoccupied with acquiring, evaluating, and documenting evidence about transactions that bear on management's financial statement assertions. However, to think that an auditor ventures no further than financial transactions wholly overlooks the range of relevant evidence that auditors seek, such as:

- Management's *risks*,
- The *strategies* management undertakes to overcome risk, and
- The *transactions and events* that are the product of management's strategies.

---

9   D. Crawford, D. Franz, R. A. Zimmerman, and P. R. Fink, "Exposure to the Extracontractual," *Journal of Accountancy* (December 1995), pp. 90–91.

10 Public Oversight Board, *Panel on Audit Effectiveness: Report and Recommendations*. Stamford, CT: POB, 2000, pp. 55–56.

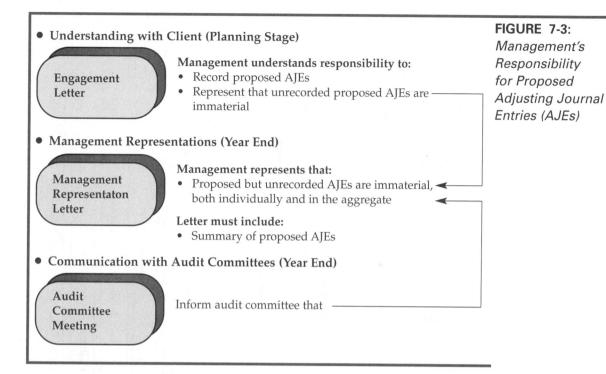

FIGURE 7-3:
Management's Responsibility for Proposed Adjusting Journal Entries (AJEs)

Transactions alone don't drive a business. Rather, management's mission, strategies, and capacity to innovate drive the transactions that a business enters into. In short, the unit of analysis in a financial statement audit is not necessarily transactions. Transactions alone are far too narrow to capture the complex web of truths that preoccupy management—for example, truths about market share, competition, backorders, stockouts, patent infringements, product development, and the market's acceptance of the products developed. An auditor's line of vision is pitched to the risks management endures and the strategies management enacts to overcome risk.

One way an auditor can document management's strategies is a **client strategy template**, illustrated in Figure 7-4 for Merck. Compiled during the planning stage of an engagement, the template summarizes the following client strategies and characteristics:

Strategies
- Growth strategy
- Financial goals and operating priorities

Characteristics of the Business
- Major business units
- Markets
- Products
- Customers
- Competitors
- Strategic alliances and joint ventures
- Potential adverse influences

The following introduces the pharmaceutical industry and illustrates a client strategy template for Merck.

FIGURE 7-4: *Client Strategy Template: Merck & Co., Inc.*

Strategies

Growth Strategy: Demonstrate the value of medicines to patients, payers, and providers. Discover new medicines through breakthrough research.

Financial Goals and Operating Priorities: Remain in the top quartile of leading health care companies. Maximize revenue growth. Preserve the profitability of core pharmaceutical business through continuous improvements in productivity and organizational effectiveness. Achieve the full potential of managed pharmaceutical care.

Characteristics of the Business

Major Business Units: The Americas, Europe/Middle East/Africa, Asia Pacific, Merck-Medco Managed Care, Vaccines

Markets: Elevated cholesterol, Hypertension/heart failure, Anti-ulcerants, Antibiotics, Ophthalmologicals, Vaccines/Biologicals, Human immunodeficiency virus (HIV), Osteoperosis, Animal health/crop protection

Products: Cozaar (high blood pressure), Zocor (elevated cholesterol), Fosamax (postmenopausal osteoporosis), Proscar (symptomatic benign prostate enlargement), Pepcid (ulcers and gastroesophageal reflux disease), Mefoxin (antibiotic), Primaxin (antibiotic), Dolobid (arthritis and pain), Indocin (arthritis), Chibroxin (conjunctivitis), Timoptic (glaucoma), Singulair (asthma), Pneumovax 23 (adult pneumonia), Recombivax HB (hepatitis B), Ivermectin (animal parasites), Thiabendazole (crop fungal infestation), Maxalt (migraine headaches)

Customers: End users (human, animal), Health care providers, Insurance companies, Center for Disease Control

Competitors: American Home Products, Bayer, Bristol-Myers Squibb, Eli Lilly, GlaxoSmithKline, Pfizer, Pharmacia, Schering-Plough

Strategic Alliances/Joint Ventures: Astra, DuPont, Johnson & Johnson, Chugai, Pasteur Merieux, Merial

Potential Adverse Influences: Managed care, Generics, Declining exclusivity periods, Federal Drug Administration, Patent expiration, Market acceptance and demand, Global and domestic politics, Interest rates, Currency fluctuations, Knowledge transmission

The Industry

The Pharmaceutical Research and Manufacturers of America (PhRMA) Foundation reports that pharmaceutical companies spend $30 billion annually on research and development (R&D), that only 1 in 5,000 screened compounds achieve U.S. Food and Drug Administration (FDA) approval, and that only 3 in 10 produce revenues that exceed R&D costs. The cost to discover and develop a new drug averages $800 million, an amount more than three times the cost of a Boeing 747 jumbo jet. Equally daunting, the time span from research to market ranges roughly from ten to fifteen years. For example, Merck's Pepcid AC, a nonprescription stomach acid controller, received FDA approval for U.S. distribution in 1995, 32 years after industry research had begun on a competing drug, GlaxoSmithKline's Tagamet, the first prescription drug to exceed $1 billion in sales.

Complicating the relationship between risk and return, the U.S. market for health care services has witnessed unprecedented change in the way that care is delivered and providers are compensated. Today 4 out of 5 employed Americans are covered by managed care organizations (MCOs) that deploy a number of cost-containment strategies targeted specifically to prescription drugs. For example, about 90 percent of the people enrolled in MCOs are constrained in drug purchases by what the industry calls "formularies," a list of prescription drugs that an MCO approves for coverage. Managed care organizations work tirelessly to reduce health care costs, driving a friction unwelcome to pharmaceutical companies: downward pressure on revenues.

Pharmaceutical companies once recouped research and development costs by monopolizing product sales, since patent laws forbid competition by rival companies. However, the *Drug Price Competition and Patent Term Restoration Act* of 1984 enabled rivals to seek approval quickly for generic copies, thereby reducing a brand-name drug's "exclusivity period," the time that a newly introduced drug stands alone in a therapeutic class. For example, although prescription Tagamet enjoyed exclusivity for six years, Invirase, the first in a class of antiviral protease inhibitors, was exclusive for only three months. Declining exclusivity periods reduce significantly the profitable life span of a new drug and, like managed care organizations, threaten the profitability of research-based pharmaceutical companies.

Business Units, Markets, Products, and Customers

As outlined in Figure 7-4, Merck operates in five autonomous business units to serve health care providers, insurance companies, and consumers worldwide. In most years, the company manages roughly 50 development-stage product candidates and FDA-approved products.

Merck's mission, "developing innovations and solutions that improve the quality of life," translates into two strategies for growth (Figure 7-4):

- Demonstrate the value of medicines to patients, payers, and providers.
- Discover new medicines through breakthrough research.

Merck has enjoyed exceptional sales on four drugs in decidedly different product-cycle stages: Zocor, an established cholesterol drug; Cozaar, a high blood pressure drug; Fosamax, a bone deterioration deterrent; and Singulair, the company's asthma drug. However, despite an acknowledged commitment to state-of-the-art research, Merck has suffered setbacks. For example, Merck stunned the industry with news that the company had begun large-scale human testing on an experimental antidepressant that targeted a mysterious brain chemical called "substance P." The drug was expected to dominate the $7 billion antidepressant market, but Merck reported one year later that tests on several hundred patients had produced similar results among patients that had received the drug and patients that had received a placebo. The news was disappointing, in part because it added pressure to other development-stage drugs.

News about patent expirations, among them Zocor, and threats to new product development prompted warnings about Merck's growth strategy. For example, one investment house remarked that Merck's early stage drug pipeline was "well below the number of pipeline drugs at Merck's largest competitors. An optimist would simply assume that Merck is disclosing fewer products or taking only higher-quality products into the clinic, but we find it difficult to judge."[11]

Financial Goal and Operating Priorities

Merck reports one financial goal and three operating priorities (Figure 7-4):

- Remain in the top quartile of leading health care companies.
- Maximize revenue growth.
- Preserve the profitability of core pharmaceutical business.
- Achieve the full potential of managed pharmaceutical care.

Evidence over the past half decade shows that the company more than accomplished the goal of remaining in the top quartile of leading health care companies, and achieved both revenue growth and profitability in core pharmaceutical products. For example, Merck repeatedly enjoyed over 15 percent annual earnings per share growth (compared to average negative returns for the industry at large), revenues that represented approximately 15 percent of all pharmaceutical revenues, a spin-off of Medco Managed Care that improved relationships with other managed care companies, and a restructuring plan scheduled to produce significant annual cost savings. The consensus view among some observers is that Merck can remain in the top quartile, continue revenue growth, and preserve core profits. For example, one major investment house estimates sales and income growth approximating 10 and 6 percent, respectively, through the end of the decade.

Competitors and Strategic Alliances

Merck faces competition from a number of high-profile rivals, including Bayer, Bristol-Myers Squibb, Eli Lilly, GlaxoSmithKline, Pfizer, Schering-Plough, and Wyeth. Keen competition among rival companies does, on balance, constrain profit for those rivals that lose the first-mover's race to market. On the other hand, consumers benefit through lower cost medicines that could linger in development absent competition. For example, in the past several years the FDA approved medicines affecting more than 200 million people, including:

- The first medicine to treat Crohn's disease, a chronic and debilitating gastrointestinal disorder.
- The first new tuberculosis drug in 25 years.

---

11 "No Major Zetia-Zocor Push; Hunkering Down," Merrill Lynch, December 10, 2003.

- The first in a class of drugs for Parkinson's disease, a progressive neurological disorder affecting 1.5 million Americans.

In the same period, pharmaceutical companies developed over 300 new medicines, helping to reduce deaths from heart disease, cancer, infection, and AIDS.

To overcome long lead time to market and low risk/return ratios, Merck, among other pharmaceutical companies, has entered into strategic alliances to bypass research and to share risk. For example, Merck entered into a strategic alliance with AstraZeneca to develop and market Astra products in the United States, thereby allowing Merck to bypass developing the products and Astra to penetrate U.S. markets. Merck entered into alliances with DuPont for radiopharmaceutical imaging agents and with Johnson & Johnson for nonprescription medicines, the intent of both alliances being to share risk. Strategic alliances are, for want of a better term, "leverage assets" that complement Merck's core business by offering revenue sources not otherwise available.

The information in Merck's client strategy template (Figure 7-4) approaches the company at a level far removed from the transactions summarized in Merck's financial statements, thereby offering insights into potential adverse influences, threats to the business, and risks that are not otherwise apparent from recorded transactions alone. These issues are discussed below as part of audit planning.

Planning

Nothing in an orderly, well-done audit could be that way without planning, although the extent of planning depends on the auditor's understanding and experience with the client's strategies, business, size, and complexity. For example, more planning would be required on a new engagement for a large client in an industry the auditor had not served previously.

Consider the Risk of Misstatements Arising From Fraud

The scope paragraph of a standard audit report (Chapter 3), states that an auditor obtains ". . . reasonable assurance about whether the financial statements are free of material *misstatement*." In practice, misstatements occur most often because of errors client personnel may make unintentionally when recording, classifying, and summarizing transactions and events. But sometimes misstatement is intentional. Two examples: First, in *Cedars of Lebanon Hospital Corp. v. Touche Ross* (1982), management and the board of directors brought suit against Touche Ross (legacy to today's Deloitte & Touche) for failing to detect an embezzlement perpetrated by the hospital's administrator. A Circuit Court of Dade County, Florida, not only found for Touche Ross, but also awarded the firm legal and accounting fees and punitive damages. And second, in *Cenco, Inc. v. Seidman & Seidman* (1982), new management at Cenco, a Chicago medical products firm, sued Seidman for failing to uncover a $25 million inventory fraud perpetrated by Cenco's former management. In a three-judge decision, the U.S. Court of Appeals for the Seventh Circuit upheld a lower federal court, ruling that Seidman was not negligent for failing to uncover the fraud, since "auditors aren't detectives hired to ferret out fraud," and the fraud was quite difficult to detect because former management turned the company "into an engine of theft against outsiders." In both cases, the auditors were not found legally liable for failing to detect fraud. Rather, the courts

➤ fraud

concluded that an audit designed to obtain reasonable assurance about material misstatements does not impose a legal obligation to detect cleverly concealed fraud.

➤ fraud

Fraud Controversy and Reform Coincident with hearings conducted by the House Subcommittee on Oversight and Investigations, the AICPA and the Institute of Internal Auditors, among others, reached agreement in 1985 to form an independent National Commission on Fraudulent Financial Reporting, chaired by James C. Treadway, Jr., a former SEC commissioner. Over a two-year existence, the Treadway Commission considered the extent to which management fraud undermines the integrity of financial reporting, the extent to which fraud can be prevented, the role of independent auditors in detecting management fraud, and whether changes in auditing standards were necessary. Although the Commission appreciated that an auditor cannot be held responsible for detecting all frauds (for example, the Cedars of Lebanon and Cenco cases), particularly those involving a carefully concealed forgery or collusion, they recommended that auditors be held responsible to assess the likelihood of fraud in *every* audit, to design tests that would provide reasonable assurance of detection, and to be professionally skeptical of management, rather than assume unilaterally that management has integrity. *SAS No. 53*, "The Auditor's Responsibility To Detect and Report Errors and Irregularities," issued in 1988, responded to all three recommendations.

Over the next half-decade, the actions of the Public Oversight Board (POB)—a predecessor to the Public Company Accounting Oversight Board (Chapter 1)—and of Congress made plain the profession's need to again address fraud. For example, the POB recommended strongly in a 1993 report, *In the Public Interest*, that auditors exercise more professional skepticism. And Congress, in a provision of *The Private Securities Litigation Reform Act of 1995*, required that auditors report fraud to management and to the audit committee and, failing immediate reaction, report in writing to the full board of directors and to the SEC within one business day. In response, the Auditing Standards Board in 1997 issued *SAS No. 82*. However, in a marked change from years prior, financial frauds were alleged or revealed from 1998 to 2002 for an unprecedented number of well-known companies, including Enron, Rite Aid, Sunbeam, Waste Management, WorldCom and Xerox. For example, in April 2002, Xerox announced a settlement in principal with the SEC that required restatement of 1997–2002 financial statements, principally for the recognition of expenses and adjustments in the timing and allocation of revenue from bundled leases.[12] In October 2002, the Auditing Standards Board replaced *SAS No. 82* with *SAS No. 99*, "Consideration of Fraud in a Financial Statement Audit." *SAS No. 99* differs considerably from prior pronouncements. For example, rather than consider fraud during the planning stage of an engagement primarily, "The new standard aims to have the auditor's consideration of fraud seamlessly blended into the audit process and continually updated until the audit's completion."[13]

---

12 U.S. GAO, *Financial Statement Restatements: Trends, Market Impacts, Regulatory Responses, and Remaining Challenges.* Washington, D.C.: U.S. Government Printing Office, 2002.

13 M. Ramos, "Auditors' Responsibility for Fraud Detection," *Journal of Accountancy* (January 2003), p. 28.

An Auditor's Responsibility for Fraud Errors are unintentional misstatements or omissions in financial statements. Examples include mistakes in gathering or processing accounting data, mistakes in applying accounting principles, and incorrect accounting estimates, such as allowances for uncollectible receivables, that arise from oversight or misinterpretation of facts. **Fraud**, in contrast, arises from fraudulent financial reporting and from misappropriation of assets:

> fraud

Fraudulent financial reporting	*An intentional misstatement or omission of an amount or disclosure in financial statements.*
	Examples include the manipulation, falsification, or alteration of records or documents; the misrepresentation or omission of transactions or events; and the intentional misapplication of an accounting principle.
Misappropriation of assets	*A theft of assets.*
	Examples include embezzling cash, stealing inventory, or causing payment for services not received.

Fraudulent financial reporting and misappropriation of assets differ in this way: The former is usually committed by management to deceive financial statement users, whereas the latter is usually committed by employees and deceives management.

As indicated by the definitions and examples, *intent* is the primary difference between an error and a fraud. In practice, however, intent is often difficult to measure. For example, an unreasonably low estimate of the allowance for uncollectible accounts receivable could result from an unintentional bias, which would constitute an error, or from an intentional attempt to misstate the financial statements, a fraud. An auditor's responsibility for detecting errors and fraud is identical because both misstate the financial statements. However, distinguishing between the two in practice is important nevertheless, because fraud is intentional and, as a result, raises concerns about management's integrity.

In a financial statement audit, an auditor is responsible to obtain reasonable assurance about whether the financial statements are free of material misstatement, and whether any misstatement is caused by unintentional error or intentional fraud. However, fraud may occur on any audit, even those for which the unsuspecting auditor has no reason to believe it may. For example, Touche Ross did not suspect that an administrator had embezzled from Cedars of Lebanon Hospital and Seidman did not suspect inventory mismanagement at Cenco. As a result, under *SAS No. 99*, generally accepted auditing standards require that an auditor:

Exercise professional skepticism, discuss among audit staff the risk of fraud causing material misstatement, obtain information needed to identify risk, identify risks that may cause material misstatement, assess the risks, respond to the assessment, and evaluate audit evidence.

Figure 7-5 summarizes the discussion that follows.

FIGURE 7-5: *An Auditor's Responsibility for Fraud*

Exercise professional skepticism
Conduct an engagement with the resolve that, despite an expectation that management is honest, material misstatement due to fraud is possible.

Discuss among audit staff throughout the engagement
the risk of fraud causing material misstatement
Exchange ideas about managements' or employees' *incentives* and *opportunities* to commit, and *rationalizations* they might impose to justify, fraud.

Obtain information to identify the risk of fraud
Inquire of management (have employees made allegations?); probe the results of analytical procedures (are sales higher but cash flows down?); and consider incentives, opportunities, and rationalizations that bear on the risk of material misstatement due to fraud. (See Figure 7-7).

Identify risks that may cause material misstatement
Consider the *type* (fraudulent financial reporting, or misappropriation of assets?), *significance* (potentially lead to material misstatement?), *likelihood* (likely to lead to material misstatement?), and *pervasiveness* (affect an assertion only, or the financial statements as a whole?) of fraud.

Assess the risks identified
Evaluate whether management's programs (a code of ethics?) or controls (cash receipts remitted to a lockbox?) mitigate the risk of material misstatement due to fraud. Presume that improper revenue recognition is a fraud risk, and that management can override programs and controls.

Respond to the assessment
Alter the nature (replace analytical procedures with substantive tests of details?), timing (observe inventory on unexpected dates?), and extent (confirm orally written confirmations received from customers?) of auditing procedures to reduce the risk of fraud.

Evaluate audit evidence
Consider discrepancies in accounting records (transactions unsupported or unauthorized?), conflicting or missing evidence (documents missing?), and problematic relationships between the auditor and management (management impose undue time pressures?).

Professional Skepticism An auditor should not presume without reason that management is dishonest, since a presumption of dishonesty in all cases would be contrary to the accumulated experience of practicing auditors. In fact, in considering the risk of material misstatements from errors and fraud, honesty is not necessarily the point. Rather, an auditor should conduct an engagement with the resolve that material misstatement due to fraud *is* possible since, for example, personal financial pressures may compel otherwise honest managers to overstate earnings, thereby maintaining artificially the value of stock options that soon will vest. Professional skepticism should be exercised both at the planning stage of an engagement and while performing audit procedures and gathering evidence. If an auditor concludes during the planning stage that there is significant risk of material misstatement, audit strategy would be redirected by assigning sufficiently ex-

perienced audit staff and by altering the nature, timing, and extent of audit procedures. The "nature" of procedures might be altered by obtaining more evidence
from independent sources, "timing" might be altered by performing tests at or
near the balance sheet date, and "extent" might be altered by increasing sample
size or performing more extensive analytical procedures. However, auditors often
confront troublesome scenarios while performing audit procedures that had not
been foreseen during the planning stage of the engagement, among them discrepancies in accounting records and conflicting (or missing) evidence. But, how
often? What does the evidence reveal about the incidence of fraud in practice?

The Incidence of Fraud in Practice Continuing a tradition from 1994 and 1998,
KPMG published a survey of 450 executives in industry and government that assessed the incidence of fraud in 2003 and benchmarked against the 1994 and 1998   ➤ fraud
surveys. The survey reported that 75 percent of the responding organizations experienced an instance of fraud (13 percentage points more than the 1998 survey),
that employee fraud was the most common (for example, check fraud, expense account abuse, merchandise returns), and that fraudulent financial reporting (for example, improper revenue recognition, misstated assets) and medical/insurance
fraud (for example, false claims) were the most costly. However, the survey also
reported a significant increase in organizations implementing antifraud measures,
both reactive (for example, immediate investigation, employee dismissal, legal action) and preemptive (for example, controls, compliance audits, background
checks). The three most common means for detecting fraud were internal control,
internal audit, and employee whistleblowers. KPMG concluded from the survey
"Organizations are reporting a rise in fraud, responding with expanded fraud
measures both reactive and preemptive, and planning further actions for the
future."[14]

Fraud Screens Can financial statement information offer clues about whether a
company committed fraud? Research has isolated several financial ratios that correctly identified about half of a sample of companies in which fraud was discov-   ➤ fraud
ered,[15] three of which focus on the balance sheet: asset quality, total-accruals to
total-assets, and days' sales in receivables. The ratios compare for a client two successive years of financial data to help an auditor judge whether, all other things
being equal, there is reason to increment his or her professional skepticism about
the risk of fraud.

The *asset-quality* ratio isolates the change in the proportion of noncurrent assets for which future benefits are likely less certain—that is, has the proportion of
less tangible assets increased? For example, to increase earnings, management
might capitalize expenses as intangible assets, such as goodwill or deferred costs,
two assets for which the future benefits are comparatively less certain than tangible assets, like plant and equipment. An increase in the asset-quality ratio would

---

14 KPMG, *Fraud Survey 2003.* New York: KPMG, 2003.
15 M.D. Beneish, "The Detection of Earnings Manipulation," *Financial Analysts Journal* (September/
    October 1999), pp. 24–36. Discussions of the ratios appear both in professional accounting journals
    (J. T. Wells, "Irrational Ratios," *Journal of Accountancy* (August 2001), pp. 23–26) and in practice guides
    (C. R. Lundelius, Jr., *Financial Reporting Fraud: A Practical Guide to Detection and Internal Control.* New
    York: AICPA, 2003).

suggest that, compared to the prior period, current-period balances in less-certain benefit noncurrent assets have increased. The ratio measures the change in noncurrent assets other than net fixed assets, and appears in Figure 7-6, Panel A, for

FIGURE 7-6: *Screens on Asset-Quality, Total-Accruals to Total-Assets, and Accounts Receivable Turnover*

	Carter Rice, Inc.		Storrs & Bement Co.	
Selected Financial Data (000 omitted)	2006	2005	2006	2005
Cash	$ 1,975	$ 64	$ 620	$ 485
Accounts receivable	1,310	664	612	472
Current assets	3,437	1,408	1,356	1,290
Working capital	2,310	801	1,339	598
Land, buildings and equipment, net	2,764	1,501	1,405	1,295
Accumulated depreciation	1,854	1,678	768	720
Total assets	16,540	5,091	4,574	4,141
Current taxes payable	146	301	292	125
Current portion of long-term debt	248	349	312	245
Sales	7,949	5,450	5,173	4,435

Panel A: Asset Quality

$$\frac{1 - \left(\dfrac{\text{Current assets}_t + \text{Net fixed assets}_t}{\text{Total Assets}_t} \right)}{1 - \left(\dfrac{\text{Current assets}_{t-1} + \text{Net fixed assets}_{t-1}}{\text{Total Assets}_{t-1}} \right)} = \qquad 1.45 \qquad 1.05$$

where:
$t \quad = 2006$
$t - 1 = 2005$

Panel B: Total Accruals to Total Assets

$$\frac{\begin{array}{l} \text{Working capital}_{t-(t-1)} \\ -\text{Cash}_{t-(t-1)} \\ -\text{Current taxes payable}_{t-(t-1)} \\ -\text{Current portion of long term debt}_{t-(t-1)} \\ -\text{Accumulated depreciation and amortization}_{t-(t-1)} \end{array}}{\text{Total Assets}_t} = \quad 0.04 \qquad 0.07$$

where:
$t \quad = 2006$
$t - 1 = 2005$

Panel C: Accounts Receivable Turnover

$$\frac{\text{Accounts Receivable}_t / \text{Sales}_t}{\text{Accounts Receivable}_{t-1} / \text{Sales}_{t-1}} = \qquad 1.35 \qquad 1.03$$

where:
$t \quad = 2006$
$t - 1 = 2005$

two companies: Carter Rice, Inc., 1.45, and Storrs & Bement, Co., 1.05. Research showed that the mean asset-quality ratio for the sample of nonfraud companies was 1.039 and for the sample of fraud companies was 1.254.[16] This suggests that Carter Rice's asset-quality ratio is behaving more like the fraud companies and Storrs & Bement's more like the nonfraud companies. However, this does not mean that Carter Rice is a fraud company (or, for that matter, that Storrs & Bement is not), since there are a number of alternative explanations that could explain the ratio. For example, the dramatic increase in total assets for Carter Rice (2006: $16,540,000; 2005: $5,091,000) could have been driven by acquiring another company.

The *total-accruals to total-assets* ratio isolates the proportion of working capital that has shifted from cash to receivables and inventory—that is, has the proportion of working capital *net of cash* relative to total assets increased? For example, to increase earnings, management might reverse a restructuring accrual (*Dr* Accrual, *Cr* Expense), thereby creating income that did not produce cash. To refine the ratio, the current portion of taxes and long-term debt are deducted to reduce measurement variation from company to company, and depreciation and amortization are deducted as a proxy for capital expenditures. An increase in the total-accruals to total-assets ratio would suggest that, relative to total assets, cash is declining, signaling a motive to commit fraud. The ratio appears in Figure 7-6, Panel B, for Carter Rice, 0.04, and for Storrs & Bement, 0.07. Research showed that the mean total-accrual to total-assets ratio for the sample of nonfraud companies was 0.018 and for the sample of fraud companies was 0.031.[17] This suggests that each company's ratio is behaving more like the nonfraud companies.

The *accounts receivable to sales* ratio isolates the change in the proportion of receivables to sales—that is, has the proportion of uncollected receivables increased? A significant increase could signal potentially uncollectible receivables or an acceleration in the recognition of revenue. For example, to induce otherwise reluctant customers to buy product, management might offer a guaranteed right of return and recognize revenue immediately, despite *Statement of Financial Accounting Standards No. 48,* "Revenue Recognition When a Right of Return Exists," which requires that revenue be deferred. The ratio appears in Figure 7-6, Panel C, for Carter Rice, 1.35, and for Storrs & Bement, 1.03. Research showed that the mean change in receivable turnover for the sample of nonfraud companies was 1.031 and for the sample of fraud companies was 1.465.[18] This suggests that, like for asset quality, Carter Rice is behaving more like the fraud companies, and Storrs & Bement more like the nonfraud companies. However, rather than fraud, an alternative explanation could be that Carter Rice changed credit terms.

In this case, the auditor for Carter Rice would likely plan tests that reduced to a relatively low level the risk that noncurrent assets other than fixed assets (asset-quality ratio) and that receivables and sales (receivables to sales ratio) are materially misstated. However, these three among other ratios are not necessarily prescriptive, and should not be relied on unrealistically. For example, recall that the research on fraud screens did not predict 100 percent of the fraud companies. Rather, the ratios offer examples of cost-effective screens that many firms

---

16 M. D. Beneish, "The Detection of Earnings Manipulation," *Financial Analysts Journal* (September/October 1999), pp. 24–36.

17 Ibid.

18 Ibid.

impound into proprietary algorithms that capture risk in complex ways that three simple ratios cannot.[19]

Discussion Among Audit Staff: Identifying and Assessing Fraud Risk To assess the risk that fraudulent financial reporting or the misappropriation of assets may cause material misstatements, *SAS No. 99* introduces to the auditing literature a new responsibility: First while planning—and then throughout—the engagement, *all* members of an engagement team should meet to exchange ideas about what some practitioners call the "fraud triangle":

> ➤ fraud

- Managements' or employees' *incentives or pressures* to commit fraud,
- Managements' or employees' *opportunities* to commit fraud, and
- *Rationalizations* management or employees may impose for having committed fraud.

SAS No. 99 describes the meetings as an "exchange of ideas or 'brainstorming' among the audit team members . . . about how and where they believe the entity's financial statements might be susceptible to material misstatement due to fraud, how management could perpetrate and conceal fraudulent financial reporting, and how assets of the entity could be misappropriated." In short, the meetings should center on questions like "What pressures have been brought to bear on management?" "What opportunities exist for management to perpetrate a fraud?" And "How might a manager rationalize fraud?"

Adopted from *SAS No. 99*, Figure 7-7 offers some structure to how an audit team would think through the fraud triangle. For example, an audit team might reasonably expect that the management of a publicly traded consumer products manufacturer has *incentives* to report earnings fraudulently if, say, the CEO is committed to achieving analysts' earnings forecasts. The team may suspect an *opportunity* to commit fraud if, despite the sales department's policy to maintain margins, the CEO has the ability to structure bill-and-hold sales for out-of-season products (for example, outdoor grills in late December) at prices retailers can't ignore. In turn, the team may judge that the CEO's public preoccupation with growing shareholder value translates to a *rationalization* the CEO might think plausible.

Figure 7-7 offers a reasonable approximation of some of the incentives, opportunities, and rationalizations that an auditor might consider. However, *SAS No. 99* describes two conditions that auditors *must* consider: Improper revenue recognition,[20] and management override of existing programs and controls. Both appear in the previous consumer products example: The bill-and-hold transactions bear on revenue recognition and the CEO has overridden the sales department's policy. In this case, the audit team would conclude that the fraud that might be committed is fraudulent financial reporting (Figure 7-5: *type*), that the fraud could lead to material misstatement (*significance*), and that the fraud could affect the financial statements taken as a whole (*pervasiveness*). The audit team would likely assess inherent risk for sales transactions at the maximum, assess allowable detection risk

---

19 See, for example, T. Bell, J. C. Bedard, K. M. Johnstone, and E. F. Smith, "KRisk[SM]: A Computerized Decision Aid for Client Acceptance and Continuance Risk Assessments," *Auditing: A Journal of Practice & Theory* (September 2002), pp. 97–113.

20 Chapter 11 discusses improper revenue recognition in detail in the context of criteria in SEC *Staff Accounting Bulletin No. 104*, "Revenue Recognition" (see Figure 11-14 for a summary) and common means perpetrators use to manipulate earnings (Figure 11-15).

FIGURE 7-7: *Examples of Factors Affecting the Risk of Fraud*

Risk of Fraudulent Financial Reporting

Incentives/Pressures
Financial stability or profitability threatened by economic, industry, or entity operating conditions:
- Competition, market saturation, or declining margins
- Vulnerability to rapid changes in technology, product obsolescence, or interest rates
- Significant declines in customer demand
- Operating losses that increase the threat of bankruptcy or hostile takeover
- Negative cash flows despite earnings and earnings growth
- Rapid growth or unusual profitability compared to competitors

Excessive pressure to meet the requirements or expectations of third parties:
- Unduly aggressive or unrealistic profitability or trend expectations
- Need to obtain additional debt or equity financing to stay competitive
- Marginal ability to meet listing requirements or debt repayment or covenant requirements
- Adverse effects of reporting poor financial results on pending transactions

Management or the board of directors' finances are threatened by the entity's financial position:
- Significant financial interests in the entity
- Significant portions of compensation is contingent on achieving aggressive targets
- Personal guarantees of debts of the entity

Excessive pressure to meet financial targets the board of directors or management set.

Opportunities
Opportunities to engage in fraudulent financial reporting:
- Significant related-party transactions
- Ability to dictate terms to suppliers or customers
- Assets, liabilities, revenues, or expenses dependent on estimates
- Significant, unusual, or highly complex transactions, especially those close to period end
- Significant bank accounts or subsidiary or branch operations in tax-haven jurisdictions

Ineffective monitoring of management:
- Management dominated by one person or a small group
- Ineffective board or audit committee oversight over financial reporting and internal control

Complex or unstable organizational structure:
- Difficulty identifying the organization or individuals that have a controlling interest in the entity
- Overly complex organizational structure involving unusual legal entities or lines of authority
- High turnover of senior management, counsel, or board members

Internal control is deficient:
- Inadequate monitoring of controls
- High employee turnover or ineffective accounting, internal audit, or information technology staff
- Ineffective accounting and information systems

FIGURE 7-7 *(continued)*

Attitudes/Rationalizations

Ineffective implementation or enforcement of values or ethical standards by management:
- Management's preoccupation with shareholder value and the selection of accounting principles
- History of violations of securities laws
- Excessive interest by management in stock price or earnings trend
- Management commits to achieve aggressive or unrealistic forecasts
- Management justifies questionable accounting on the basis of immateriality
- The relationship between management and the auditor is strained by disputes on accounting, reporting or audit scope or by restrictions that limit the auditor's access to people or information

Risk of Misappropriation of Assets

Incentives/Pressures

Misappropriation of assets motivated by relationships between management and employees:
- Known or anticipated future employee layoffs
- Recent or anticipated changes to employee compensation or benefit plans
- Promotions, compensation, or other rewards inconsistent with expectations

Opportunities

Opportunities to misappropriate assets:
- Large amounts of cash on hand or processed
- Inventory items that are small in size, valuable, or in demand
- Easily convertible assets, such as bearer bonds, diamonds, or computer chips
- Fixed assets that are small in size, marketable, or lack observable identification of ownership

Inadequate internal control over assets:
- Inadequate segregation of duties or independent checks
- Inadequate management oversight of employees responsible for assets
- Inadequate screening of job applicants who will have access to assets
- Inadequate system of transaction authorization and approval
- Inadequate physical safeguards over cash, investments, inventory, or fixed assets
- Lack of complete and timely asset reconciliations
- Lack of timely documentation of transactions, such as credits for merchandise returns

Attitudes/Rationalizations

Attitudes or behavior of employees with access to assets:
- Disregard for the need to monitor or to reduce the risk of asset misappropriations
- Overriding existing controls that protect assets or failing to correct known control deficiencies
- Behavior consistent with displeasure toward management's treatment of an employee
- Changes in behavior or lifestyle that may indicate assets have been misappropriated

at a relatively low level, expand the extent of planned audit procedures, and encourage more than the usual level of professional skepticism.

Although seemingly benign, transactions recorded incompletely could be symptomatic of fraudulent financial reporting (notice that the language is *could be*, not *is*). For example, management could inappropriately fail to record the companion cost-of-sales entry to a recorded sales entry, thereby enabling a 100 percent profit margin on the sale and overstating earnings by the historical cost of the product sold. In turn, management could postpone recording the cost-of-sales entry until after the balance sheet date, thereby recording the sales and cost-of-sales entries properly, albeit in the wrong period. Other symptoms include unsupported balances (for example, lack of documentation to support a recorded sales transaction), unauthorized transactions (for example, earnings-enhancing price terms on land purchases from a related party), misclassified accounting entries (for example, repair expenses charged to the assets repaired rather than to period expenses), or last-minute adjustments that affect reported earnings significantly (for example, reversal of a previously recorded accrued expense).

There is a presumption in practice that audit evidence is both valid and reliable, absent a reason to suspect otherwise. Sometimes, however, there *is* reason to suspect otherwise, such as vague, inconsistent, or implausible responses from management about unusual fluctuations in account balances. For example, imagine that, in response to a question about significant declines in gold inventory, the management of a major manufacturer of college rings says, "Students just aren't buying rings these days." The response is at once both vague and unverifiable. Who can say for sure what college students are thinking? However, consider this response: "We've lost market share." Now the response is both diagnostic and verifiable: diagnostic because the auditor has a plausible hypothesis (that is, it's reasonable that management would reduce gold inventory, since orders are declining and gold is used in the manufacture of rings), and verifiable because the auditor can review sales contracts to calibrate the loss of market share. Other suspicions include the consistent unavailability of original documents, unusual discrepancies between recorded balances and confirmation replies, and recorded assets that cannot be located.

Despite the profession's heightened awareness of fraud, a properly planned and executed audit may still fail to detect a cleverly concealed fraud, particularly one involving forgery or collusion among employees or management. For example, auditors are neither trained nor expected under generally accepted auditing standards to judge the authenticity of forged documents. An auditor is not an insurer and an audit report is not a guarantee, because an audit opinion and audit procedures are based on the concept of reasonable, not absolute, assurance. Nevertheless, an auditor should exercise both due care and professional skepticism to provide reasonable assurance that material errors and fraud will be detected.

First-Quarter Planning

Initial first-quarter planning, usually performed soon after the first quarter of an audit client's fiscal year, is intended to identify early the important accounting, auditing, or reporting issues that are apparent from financial or nonfinancial sources. An auditor's typical first-quarter planning activities, summarized in Figure 7-8, begin with reviews of prior-year audit work and current-year first-quarter financial information.

Review of Prior-Year Audit Work and First-Quarter Financial Results The *review of prior-year audit work* is designed to assess potentially risky audit areas, identify areas scheduled for emphasis during the engagement, and consider improvements for the current year. For example, an unusually large number of adjusting journal entries and unexpectedly high actual hours in the audit of receivables last

FIGURE 7-8: *Audit Planning*

Approximate Dates	Activity
April–May	First-quarter planning
	Review prior-year audit work.
	Review first-quarter financial results.
	Prepare preliminary audit time budget.
July–August	Second-quarter planning
	Review second-quarter financial results.
	Prepare final audit time budget.
	Perform analytical procedures.
	Prepare preliminary audit planning memorandum.
	Coordinate with assigned staff.
	Coordinate with client.
	Prepare interim audit programs.

year may prompt the auditor this year to reallocate budgeted audit hours from a low-risk account to receivables. The *review of first-quarter financial results* is similarly motivated: The auditor attempts to isolate unexpected fluctuations or inconsistencies from prior-year statements that may signal potentially risky audit areas this year. For example, an intensive January advertising campaign followed by poor first-quarter sales may have implications for the valuation assertion, since the carrying value of inventory may exceed net realizable value. The review of first-quarter results also includes newspaper and magazine accounts that offer insights about product lines that support expected earnings. For example, a *Wall Street Journal* account about Merck's first-quarter results revealed that "Fosamax, the company's osteoporosis therapy, had sales of $44 million, surpassing [an analyst's] estimate," and that "Zocor and another of Merck's cholesterol-lowering drugs together command about 40% of the worldwide market." Both pieces of information are helpful to the auditor's understanding of Merck's business and to the company's competitive standing in the industry.

Prepare Preliminary Audit Time Budget As part of first-quarter planning, an auditor also prepares a *preliminary audit time budget*, an estimate of total planned audit time by staff level and audit activity. For example, a preliminary time budget for cash, marketable securities, and receivables might appear in part as follows:

Partial Preliminary Time Budget

Total		Estimated Hours		Estimated Hours by Staff Level		
Audit Area	Interim	Year End	Assistant	Senior	Manager	Partner
Cash	40	(35)	36 (31)	2 (2)	1 (1)	1 (1)
Marketable Securities	20	(15)	17 (12)	1 (1)	1 (1)	1 (1)
Accounts Receivable	40	(30)	34 (25)	4 (3)	1 (1)	1 (1)

Audit time budgets should be realistic to the risks expected but respectful of the experience of assigned staff, since tight audit budgets can affect audit quality. For example, a considerable amount of research literature has addressed tight time budgets and the propensity for audit staff to shirk. One study in three offices of two firms revealed that time pressure drove over one-half of 152 responding staff auditors to sign off audit program steps prematurely, to reduce audit effort below levels they considered appropriate, to overlook researching an accounting principle, to review client documents superficially, and to accept weak oral explanations from management.[21] Although the study did not address the cause of shirking, the effect is clear: an absence of due care that seriously undermines audit quality.

Consider Potential Adverse Influences, Threats to the Business, and Audit Risk

Research-based pharmaceutical companies endure pressure from stakeholders, among other external influences, much of which is beyond the companies' control. Stakeholders include managed care groups and elected legislatures that exert pressure for cost containment, stockholders who demand share value, physicians and consumers who judge the acceptance of new medicines, and employers burdened with the rising costs of employee and retiree health care costs. For example, General Motors, the largest private purchaser of health care in the United States, spends annually over $1 billion on prescription drugs, $37 million alone on Merck's Zocor, a cholesterol prescription drug.[22] Other influences include legislation, interest rates, the transmission of proprietary knowledge to competitors, and competition from generic suppliers. However, the key question facing Merck and its auditors is how industry-wide adverse influences, among other matters specific to a company, add threats to the business and risk to the auditor.

Merck is quite large: The company enjoys annual revenues in excess of $30 billion and a market capitalization over $100 billion. Size offers advantages, including accessibility to financing and the reach of an abundant salesforce. However, size also raises the bar, since earnings growth depends crucially on trumping the competition with sought-after breakthrough products that drive widespread demand. Small markets and limited demand do not pay off for large companies. For Merck, like other large pharmaceutical companies, one key question is, "Who can do for cancer today what Jonas Salk did for polio?" This one observation is at the core of two threats to Merck's strategies, goals, and priorities:

- At-risk growth strategy.
- Competitive pricing.

Figure 7-9 summarizes evidence bearing on both threats.

Evidence in the press suggests that Merck's *growth strategy may be at risk*. For example, as illustrated in Figure 7-9, a report in the Dow Jones News Service warns that growth is threatened by patent expirations, and an analyst from Deutsche Bank Securities believes that growth may depend on merger. Patent expiration is a constant threat in the industry, and merger between drug companies

---

21 T. Kelly and L. Margheim, "The Impact of Time Budget Pressure, Personality, and Leadership Variables on Dysfunctional Auditor Behavior," *Auditing: A Journal of Practice & Theory* (Spring 1990), pp. 21–42.
22 "GM's War on Drug Costs," *Newsweek* (February 26, 2001), pp. 46–48.

FIGURE 7-9: *Threats to Client Strategies*

Threat	Evidence
At-risk growth strategy	Deutsche Bank Securities analyst's report:
	Company may need to ". . . consider a significant merger to boost its growth prospects."
Competitive pricing	Dow Jones News:
	". . . there is concern in the market about its future growth . . . because the company faces a number of upcoming patent expirations."
	Discount demands from managed care groups.
	Federal and state legislative proposals to reduce health care costs.
	Increased patient copayments for prescription drugs.
	Physician incentives to prescribe generics.
	Employer pressures to curb increases in health care costs.

is not uncommon, having accelerated when Glaxo Wellcome merged with SmithKline-Beecham, creating the world's largest pharmaceutical company. In turn, there is abundant evidence that stakeholders are exerting considerable pressure on Merck to *contain costs and price competitively* and others are seeking low-cost alternatives, all of which could serve to constrain Merck's profitability. For example, managed care groups and employers are demanding discounts and curbs to health care cost increases, federal and state legislatures are drafting proposals to reduce health care costs, physicians have incentives to prescribe lower cost generics, and patients in some health care plans are required to make out-of-pocket, unreimbursed copayments for prescription drugs.

Judging the predictive ability of any of these claims is not the auditor's concern, and seeking contradictory information is not necessarily the auditor's responsibility. Rather, the auditor considers the reliability of the source of each attributed claim and the reasonableness of each unattributed claim. For example, absent evidence to the contrary, an auditor would have no reason to believe that reputable securities companies and a well-known news service have incentives to make prejudicial claims about a company's growth strategy. And, on the face of it, although unattributed to any particular source, the claims about competitive pricing appear eminently reasonable. Who among us can offer evidence contradicting the claim that health care costs are rising? In this case, an auditor would have every reason to believe that the information *is* reliable and, therefore, would have a due diligence obligation to impound the information into his or her assessment of risk. Specifically, an at-risk growth strategy and a competitive pricing strategy would bear on the company's ability to produce sustainable profits and, in the extreme, on the auditor's professional skepticism about management motivation to engage in fraudulent financial reporting.

Growth strategies and pricing practices could bear explicitly on an auditor's assessment of risk. Two examples: First, an unrealistic earnings growth target could motivate management to manipulate earnings, thereby increasing the risk of fraudulent financial reporting. Second, an auditor's motivation to probe a company's ability to continue as a going concern beyond what's required by *SAS No. 59* (Chapter 3) depends in part on his or her professional skepticism about financial distress, which could go unprovoked if the auditor were unaware of a reputable securities analyst's resolve about a growth strategy at risk. Interestingly, motivated by the insights often included in analysts' reports, some firms partner with investment companies to factor analysts' reports into the firms' assessments of risk and financial distress for publicly traded audit clients. Analysts synthesize large volumes of data, offer reasoned predictions for high-end stakeholders, and have insights that auditors have no reason to ignore.

Second-Quarter Planning

First-quarter planning focuses on preliminary evaluations—first pass, first thoughts—based on the auditor's general understanding of a client's business, industry, and other relevant factors. However, the informativeness of first-quarter planning is constrained, particularly in cyclical companies, since only one-fourth of the fiscal year has transpired.

Review Second-Quarter Results, Finalize Budget, and Perform Analytical Procedures Second-quarter planning, also summarized in Figure 7-8, is usually performed in the month following the end of the second fiscal quarter, and begins with updates to the results of first-quarter planning by *reviewing second-quarter financial results* and *finalizing the audit time budget*. During second-quarter planning, the auditor also *performs analytical procedures* that are used to assist in planning the nature, timing, and extent of anticipated auditing procedures and in drafting the preliminary audit planning memorandum. For example, consistent with *SAS No. 56*, "Analytical Procedures," an auditor might compare on-time delivery rates, price (and quantity) variances, capacity utilization, and selected financial ratios between the first and second quarters and between the prior- and current-year's second quarters. Planning-stage analytical procedures typically focus on improving the auditor's understanding of the entity's transactions and on identifying risky audit areas, and vary in sophistication from firm to firm depending on the engagement. For example, some auditors use simple comparisons and ratios of account balances between the current and prior year(s), and investigate those accounts that deviate from expectations beyond a significant threshold, called by some an "investigation threshold." However, the economic significance of a threshold is difficult to interpret unaided (that is, how large need a threshold be to reveal a deviation worth testing?), prompting some auditors to use statistical decision aids that optimize audit effectiveness by predicting and overlooking unproductive thresholds.[23]

Prepare Preliminary Planning Memorandum The auditor then prepares a *preliminary audit planning memorandum*, an overview of planned audit activity by staff level that includes the final audit time budget.

---

23 For example, see R. M. Harper, Jr., J. R. Strawser, and K. Tang, "Establishing Investigation Thresholds for Preliminary Analytical Review," *Auditing: A Journal of Practice & Theory* (Fall 1990), pp. 115–133.

Typically, the planning memorandum describes in general terms the audit approach intended for each audit area. For example, the memorandum might state the following for a client's income tax-related transactions and accounts:

Income Taxes

At interim, a tax department representative will complete a checklist designed to identify tax-planning and disclosure problems. The tax department representative will prepare a memorandum of findings for distribution to and discussion with the audit partner, manager, and if necessary, the client. At year end, the audit staff will review the client's calculation of accumulated income tax prepayments, deferred income taxes, and income tax expense, consulting the tax department when necessary. A tax department representative will review year-end audit documentation and prepare a memorandum on the adequacy of related tax accounts. The audit supervisor will reach a conclusion as to whether all tax accounts are fairly stated at the balance sheet date.

The planning memorandum includes similar paragraphs for each audit area and is distributed to each professional staff member assigned to the engagement.

Coordinate with Assigned Staff and with the Client After completing and approving the planning memorandum, an auditor schedules available staff members for the audit and plans a meeting to *coordinate with professional staff assigned to the engagement*. The purpose of the meeting is to introduce each staff member to the engagement and discuss the planned audit approach. Since the meeting is ideally held in advance of field work, assigned staff should have sufficient time to prepare for the engagement—for example, by reviewing the planning memorandum, the correspondence and permanent files, and prior-year documents. The auditor needs also to *coordinate with the client* about the scheduled audit dates and anticipated client assistance in preparing schedules, retrieving documents, and providing administrative help.

Prepare Interim Audit Programs The final second-quarter planning activity involves drafting *interim audit programs* for tests of controls. Illustrated in Chapter 6 (Figure 6-6), an audit program is a detailed list of procedures to be performed for a particular aspect of an engagement. Individually, each audit program helps an auditor to estimate the time required for a particular audit area, to determine staff requirements, and to schedule audit work. Collectively, all of the programs prepared for an engagement assist in maintaining control as the audit progresses. For initial engagements, interim audit programs are not usually prepared until the client's internal controls have been reviewed and documented, since the auditor has no prior information about the controls. However, in continuing engagements, interim audit programs can be drafted in advance of field work, since the auditor has prior knowledge of the client's controls and prior information about the results of previous assessments of control risk. Of course, if necessary, the programs may be revised when actually used, although the reasons for revision should be justified (for example, unreliable information during second-quarter planning, information system changes).

Importantly, audit planning does not end with second-quarter planning. In fact, planning continues throughout an engagement, since a plan is subject to revision as more current information becomes available.

Interim Audit Work

Figure 7-10 summarizes an auditor's typical interim audit activities.

FIGURE 7-10: *Interim Audit Work*

Approximate Dates	Activity
September–October	Obtain an understanding of internal controls.
	Perform tests of controls.
	Assess control risk.
November	Prepare preliminary year-end audit programs.

Understand Internal Control, Perform Tests of Controls, and Assess Control Risk

The objective of interim work is to assess control risk (and inherent risk), thereby lending insight into the level of year-end detection risk necessary to hold audit risk to a relatively low level. For example, assume an auditor's combined assessment of control and inherent risk is 30 percent and that he or she wishes to hold audit risk to 6 percent. The audit risk model, introduced in Chapter 2, is:

$$AR = IR \times CR \times DR$$

where: AR = Audit risk for an account
IR = Inherent risk
CR = Control risk
DR = Detection risk

Rearranging the audit risk model reveals that the acceptable level of detection risk would be 20 percent, calculated as follows:

$$DR = \frac{AR}{IR \times CR}$$

$$= \frac{0.06}{0.30}$$

$$= 0.20$$

As discussed more fully in Chapter 8, a thorough assessment of control risk usually requires that an auditor perform two tasks. First, the auditor *obtains an understanding of an entity's internal controls* by documenting the controls through questionnaires, flowcharts, and narrative memoranda. An auditor uses his or her understanding to help predict the types of misstatements that may occur in an entity's financial statement assertions. For example, poor controls over the receipt and shipment of goods could drive a company to record purchase or sales transactions in the wrong accounting period at year end, called a "cutoff" problem, thereby affecting the occurrence or the completeness assertions. Second, after obtaining an understanding, the auditor *performs tests of controls*, often the most time-consuming part of interim work, focusing on the misstatements that could occur and the procedures management used to control against misstatements. For example, tests of controls over purchase and sales transactions would give the auditor insight into the risk of misstatements related to the occurrence or completeness assertions. That is, tests of controls lend insight about whether poor controls identified when documenting internal control are likely to cause material misstatements. Next, the auditor *assesses control risk* from his or her understanding of internal control and from the results of tests of controls. The assessment may be quantitative (for example, 30 percent) or qualitative (for example, medium).

Prepare Preliminary Year-End Audit Programs

The final interim audit activity involves drafting *preliminary year-end audit programs*. Year-end programs are heavily dependent upon the engagement's objectives, risky audit areas, audit areas to be emphasized, and most important, results of the auditor's assessment of control risk. Thus, year-end audit programs cannot be drafted during the planning stages of an audit, since a critical determinant of year-end detection risk—control risk—is not yet known.

Interim audit work is discussed and illustrated in detail in Chapters 8, 10, 12, 14, 15, and 16.

Year-End Audit Work

Figure 7-11 summarizes an auditor's typical year-end audit activities. Consistent with the third standard of field work, the objective of year-end audit work is to obtain sufficient competent evidential matter to afford a reasonable basis for an opinion on management's financial statements.

FIGURE 7-11: *Year-End Audit Activities*

Approximate Dates	Activity
December	Coordinate with client.
	Finalize year-end audit programs.
January–February	Perform substantive tests and analytical procedures.
	Evaluate audit test results: material errors and fraud.
	Perform subsequent events review.
	Obtain representation letters.
	Review audit documentation.
	Draft and sign reports.

Coordinate with the Client

Because the fiscal year for many companies corresponds with the calendar year, December 31 year-end audit engagements typically impose significant staff-assignment and time-pressure constraints for public accounting firms. Many audits need be completed at the same time. As a result, firms carefully *coordinate with the client* before beginning audit work, focusing particularly on dates that are critical to the client. For example, for public companies, when does management expect to announce earnings publicly? The auditor should meet with the client, usually well before year end, to confirm audit dates, finalize a list of audit documents the client will prepare, and arrange for banks to mail statements directly to the auditor. Coordination is much more critical at year end than at interim, since year-end work must be completed early enough to afford a timely audit report. For example, audit work for public companies must be completed in sufficient time to allow timely filing of Form 10-K to the SEC. Interim audit work, in contrast, can be conducted at almost any time during the year under audit, although, independent of interim work, an auditor is responsible to review financial statements included in a client's first-, second-, and third-quarter Forms 10-Q to comply with the SEC's *Audit Committee Disclosure* rules.

Finalize Year-End Audit Programs, and Perform Substantive Tests and Analytical Procedures

Prior to performing year-end audit procedures, the auditor should *finalize year-end audit programs* prepared initially at interim. The auditor reviews and evaluates any significant system changes or other circumstances occurring since interim and updates the audit programs. Finally, an auditor undertakes the most time-consuming year-end audit activity: *performing year-end substantive tests* that include tests of details and analytical procedures. The purpose of substantive tests is to detect material misstatements that had not been prevented or detected by the entity's internal controls. The nature, timing, and extent of substantive tests map to the assessed level of detection risk and will vary depending on the client's industry. For example, a study of 368 adjusting journal entries for 171 engagements in six different industries found that, compared to companies in nonregulated industries (such as manufacturing, merchandising), companies in regulated industries (such as banks, insurance companies) have fewer total financial statement errors. However, the errors are more likely to be nonroutine (for example, judgments about uncollectible accounts) than routine (for example, miscalculations) and more likely to be detected using internal evidence (such as documentation) than external evidence (such as confirmations).[24]

Evaluate Audit Test Results: Material Errors and Fraud

Material errors detected by applying audit procedures should be corrected through adjusting journal entries. Material fraud, in contrast, has additional implications because fraud is intentional. If an auditor detects fraud, but has determined also that the effect on the financial statements could not be material (for example, if there have been misappropriations of small amounts of cash from a small imprest fund), the auditor should:

➤ fraud

- Refer the matter to an appropriate level of management that is at least one level above those involved, and
- Be satisfied that, given the position of the likely perpetrator, the fraud has no implications for other aspects of the audit or that those implications have been adequately considered.

---

24 M. Maletta and A. Wright, "Audit Evidence Planning: An Examination of Industry Error Characteristics," *Auditing: A Journal of Practice & Theory* (Spring 1996), pp. 71–86.

However, if the auditor detects a material fraud or has been unable to evaluate materiality, he or she should:

- Consider the implications for other aspects of the audit,
- Discuss the matter and the approach to further investigation with an appropriate level of management that is at least one level above those involved,
- Attempt to obtain evidence to determine whether in fact material fraud exists and if so, the effect, and
- If appropriate, suggest that the client consult with legal counsel about questions of law.

If an auditor concludes that an entity's financial statements are affected materially by fraud, he or she should insist that the statements be revised. If management agrees, the statements would be revised by management, and the auditor should issue an unqualified opinion. But if management refuses, the auditor should express a qualified or an adverse opinion because, as discussed in Chapter 3, the financial statements will have departed from GAAP. In turn, if the auditor is precluded from applying necessary audit procedures or is unable to reach a conclusion about materiality, he or she should issue a qualified opinion or disclaim an opinion on the basis of a scope limitation, as explained in Chapter 3. Further, the auditor should report his or her findings to the board of directors' audit committee. Disclosing fraud to parties other than senior management and the audit committee is not ordinarily part of an auditor's responsibility but may be necessary in some circumstances, such as disclosure in response to a court-ordered subpoena, an auditor change (SEC Form 8-K), an inquiry from a successor auditor, or a federal funding agency.

Year-end audit work is discussed and illustrated in detail in Chapters 11, 13, 14, 15, and 16.

Subsequent Events

An audit report is usually dated as of the last day of field work—for example, February 14, 2007, for a December 31, 2006, fiscal year end. For public companies, the last day of field work usually coincides with the date that management releases earnings to the public. Although the audit report and audit work relate to the period January 1 through December 31, 2006, the auditor is also responsible for transactions and events occurring between January 1 and February 14, 2007, called the "subsequent period," that have an effect on the December 31, 2006, financial statements. For example, if an auditor learns on January 21, 2007, that a customer of an audit client is unable to pay a debt that arose in 2006, adjustment of the December 31, 2006, account receivable may be necessary depending on the circumstances. An auditor is responsible for, and must plan to search for, subsequent events, as discussed more fully in Chapter 17.

Management and Legal Representations

During the course of an audit, management and other parties make many representations to an auditor, both oral and written. For example, management represents that all material transactions have been recorded in the accounting records and that the entity has title to all owned assets. *SAS No. 85,* "Client Representations," requires that an auditor obtain written representations from management in the form of a *management representation letter*. The representations an auditor obtains from management depend on the circumstances of the engagement but, at a minimum, management is required to represent that the financial statements are presented fairly in conformity with GAAP. Auditors also request written representations from other parties, such as *legal letters* from a client's lawyer, as required by *SAS No. 12*, "Inquiry of a Client's Lawyer Concerning Litigation, Claims, and Assessments." Management representation letters and legal letters are discussed more fully in Chapter 17.

Audit Documentation Review

In practice, supervisory staff typically review the audit work performed by subordinate staff. For example, in an audit of a commercial bank, an audit senior might review an audit staff member's loan-loss reserve documents and, thereafter, an audit manager might review both the staff member's work and the senior's conclusions. Not surprisingly, research has found that the review process reduces the variance in judgments between supervisory and subordinate staff, and increases the accuracy of the documents.[25]

In some firms, some engagement partners believe that seniors and managers may vary in their capability to detect errors made by subordinate staff, and therefore review all (or most of the) audit documentation on or about the last day of field work. Consistent with this practice, research suggests that audit managers may be more accurate than seniors in detecting conceptual errors (for example, an undocumented audit procedure), and that audit seniors may be more accurate than managers at detecting mechanical errors (for example, disagreement between an account balance in audit documentation and a financial statement balance).[26] However, other firms and partners forgo the detailed review of documents, preferring instead to rely on one of three other approaches: review by interview, review by presentation, or an overriding review. In *review by interview*, the engagement partner interviews assigned staff about the work accomplished and, based on the discussions and his or her experience, reviews detailed documents as necessary. For example, an audit partner might interview a staff member about detailed work on loan-loss reserves and then review in part evidence bearing on the valuation of real property pledged as collateral. In *review by presentation*, assigned staff present their approach and findings, often to the entire audit team rather than to the engagement partner only, thereby encouraging interaction and exposing less experienced staff to challenging audit issues. In an *overriding review*, an engagement partner reviews selected detailed documents that the partner judges most critical to his or her opinion on the financial statements. Regardless of the approach—detailed review, review by interview, review by presentation, or overriding review—the purpose of the partner's review is to judge compliance with auditing standards and with the firm's quality control and performance standards.

Reports

As discussed more fully in Chapters 3 and 8, respectively, auditors conclude the audit process by preparing and issuing an audit report and, for public companies, a report on internal control. The audit report expresses the auditor's opinion on

---

25 K. T. Trotman, "The Review Process and the Accuracy of Auditor Judgments," *Journal of Accounting Research* (Autumn 1985), pp. 740–752; K. T. Trotman and P. W. Yetton, "The Effect of the Review Process on Auditor Judgments," *Journal of Accounting Research* (Spring 1985), pp. 256–267.

26 R. J. Ramsey, "Senior/Manager Differences in Audit Workpaper Performance," *Journal of Accounting Research* (Spring 1994), pp. 127–135.

the financial statements, and for a public company, the report on internal control expresses the auditor's opinion on management's assessment of internal control over financial reporting. The auditor's opinion on financial statements and opinion on internal control should be documented clearly in the audit documentation and communicated on a timely basis. The audit report, required by the fourth standard of reporting, is dated generally as of the last day of field work. The report on internal control is required by *Auditing Standard No. 2*, "An Audit of Internal Control Over Financial Reporting," and is discussed in Chapter 8.

SUMMARY

The audit process is logical, systematic, and designed to gather and evaluate evidence. The process begins with communication between auditors and the audit committee, a decision to accept or continue an engagement, and preparation of an engagement letter. An auditor then proceeds to establish an understanding with the client and about the client's strategies, and conducts planning activities over the next few months. Interim audit work, designed to assess control risk, begins after the planning stages, though usually well before year end. Year-end audit work, designed to control detection risk through substantive tests of account balances and disclosures, begins near the end of the fiscal year and includes a review for subsequent events. Obtaining representation letters and preparing reports is the final activity of the audit process.

The assurance process, similar in nature to an audit, includes establishing an understanding of management's strategies, identifying comparison groups and performance measures, collecting and displaying evidence, and integrating the evidence into a deliverable. An application of the assurance process to business performance measurement and benchmarking is introduced next in an Appendix.

APPENDIX: THE ASSURANCE SERVICE PROCESS

Although both audit services and assurance services improve the quality of information, each service defines quality differently. In auditing, quality means the *reliability* of reported financial information relative to GAAP, and in assurance services quality means *relevance*. For example, an assurance service that assesses the relevance of Merck's operational measures might benchmark Merck to best practices in research-based pharmaceutical companies and in leading companies from other industries. In short, the service would benchmark Merck on a set of measures that are most relevant to Merck alone, not on a common set of measures that are generally accepted for all U.S. companies, such as GAAP in a financial statement audit. This section illustrates the assurance service process using one means of performance measurement,[27] benchmarking.

---

27 Other performance measurement services offered by public accounting firms include, for example, international quality standards such as ISO 9000 (the International Organization for Standardization's standards for product quality) and ISO 14000 (standards for environmental management systems).

Benchmarking

Benchmarking is one of a number of tools that underlie the principles of *total quality management (TQM)*, an approach to process management that holds quality as management's most important pursuit. The Xerox Corporation, a pioneer in performance measurement, defines **benchmarking** as the "process of measuring our products, services and practices against our toughest competitors or those companies known as leaders."[28] Benchmarking allows Xerox to address three questions that bear on the company's strengths and weaknesses:

Key Question	Type of Benchmarking
• How do we compare within the industry?	Competitive
• How do our divisions/departments compare?	Internal
• How do we compare outside the industry?	Functional

Interestingly, functional benchmarking has offered Xerox insights for improvement that were otherwise unavailable from competitive benchmarking in the office products industry. For example, although a manufacturer and supplier of office equipment, Xerox benchmarks product distribution against L.L.Bean, a retail clothing and outdoor equipment supplier long recognized for a distribution system that is efficient, reliable, and cost effective.

Benchmarking has been used in some companies to measure performance, but in other companies to rethink the organization. For example, many organizations benchmark in-house, among them BP Amoco, Chevron, Compaq Computer, Deere, Lucent Technologies, Shell International, the State of Texas, and the U.S. Treasury Department. However, others elect to outsource the service in much the same way that some companies outsource internal auditing. Outsourced performance measurement and benchmarking are important potential service offerings for CPAs that the AICPA's Special Committee on Assurance Services (the Elliott Committee) encouraged in the late 1990s and the AICPA's Special Committee on Financial Reporting (the Jenkins Committee) recommended in the mid-1990s. For example, the Jenkins Committee concluded that "Business reporting must . . . focus on factors that create longer term value, including non-financial measures indicating how key business processes are performing."[29]

Figure 7-12 lists the major steps, activities, and methods a practitioner uses to assess the relevance of benchmarking measures. Of course, the assurance process will vary somewhat depending on the nature of the service offered. For example, an electronic commerce assurance service (Chapter 18) will likely focus less on the collection of evidence and more on integration.

Planning

Done well, benchmarking services can add significant value. For example, a study conducted by the American Productivity & Quality Center's *International Benchmarking Clearinghouse* reported that more than 30 organizations realized an average $76 million payback in the first year of benchmarking and that the most

---

28 R. C. Camp, *Business Process Benchmarking: Finding and Implementing the Best Practices.* Milwaukee, WI: Quality Press, 1995.

29 AICPA, Report of the *Special Committee on Financial Reporting*, "Improving Business Reporting: A Customer Focus: Meeting the Information Needs of Investors and Creditors," 1994, p. 5.

FIGURE 7-12: *The Assurance Process:*
An Application to Performance Benchmarking

Step	Activity	Method
Planning	Establish an understanding of the client's strategies and characteristics of the business.	Client strategy template
	Identify the client's mission and goals.	Interviews
Analysis	Identify comparison group and performance measures.	Literature search Interviews
	Collect evidence.	Original Sources: Face-to-face and phone interviews Surveys Focus groups Archived Sources: Service organizations Periodicals Online databases Commercial archival and search services Archived client and industry data
	Display evidence.	Balanced scorecards Vision charts Descriptive statistics Histograms and bar charts Pareto charts Scatter diagrams Cause and effect diagrams Graphs
Deliverable	Integration	Communicate report. Suggest action plan.

experienced benchmarkers averaged $189 million. However, research[30] also confirms that the service can add value only if senior management adopts an attitude shared by companies such as Xerox, Motorola, and Chrysler:

- A mandate to integrate performance measures into an *action plan,* and
- A commitment to a *culture of continuous improvement.*

Absent management's resolve to embrace this mandate and commitment up front, benchmarking services are unlikely to be rewarding either to the client or to the CPA.

---

30 *Organizing and Managing Benchmarking Final Report,* International Benchmarking Clearinghouse, American Productivity & Quality Center, 1995.

Establish an Understanding of the Client's Business and Industry

Assurance services demand that practitioners think of a client on two levels: First, to fully understand a client's *business and industry*, practitioners invest sufficient effort to document—and to hold in memory—the level of detail presented earlier in the chapter for Merck. A tall order to hold in memory that level of detail, but management will expect nothing less. In fact, management will expect more, since one purpose of the engagement is to bring to bear a means for the company to gauge performance and to transform past performance into an action plan of continuous improvement.

Second, to fully appreciate *management's style*, practitioners focus on a client's leadership, strategic objectives, economic constraints, organizational structure, goals, and sources of value. For example:

Does management view	*Or*	*As the principle*
Articulation of vision	Command and control	Form of leadership?
Continuous improvement	Consistency	Strategic objective?
Creativity	Capital	Economic constraint?
Self-organizing teams	Hierarchies	Organizational structure?
Synthesis of minds	Divisions of labor	Means to accomplish goals?
Information and knowledge	Land and materials	Sources of value?

Companies whose management favors the left-most captions are the companies most likely to benefit from benchmarking.

Identify the Client's Mission and Goals

In a performance measurement assurance service, a CPA interviews senior management to understand the company's mission and goals. For example, consider the mission statement for Chevron, a publicly held, worldwide producer of oil and chemical products:

We are an international company providing energy and chemical products vital to the growth of the world's economies. Our mission is to create superior value for our stockholders, our customers and our employees.

The mission statement identifies three major audiences and translates for the company into six explicit goals: delighted customers, public favorability, competitive operating advantage, superior financial performance, superior stockholder return, and committed team. For Chevron, the objective is to identify comparison groups and performance measures that converge on each goal.

Analysis

Identify Comparison Groups and Performance Measures

Practitioners identify comparison groups and performance measures through literature searches and interviews with management. Literature searches include service organization publications and other periodicals that focus wholly or in part on quality and performance measurement. Relevant service organizations include the American Productivity & Quality Center (APQC), the American Society for Quality Control, the Association for Quality and Participation, and the

American Management Association. For example, the APQC offers a number of hardcopy and online publications (http://www.apqc.org) on benchmarking, including best-practices white papers for senior management, practice papers covering individual member companies (such as Sprint, North American Coal), and a subscription-based international benchmarking clearinghouse. Relevant periodicals include *Quality Progress, Target, National Productivity Review*, the *Journal on Quality Improvement (JQI)* and, to a lesser extent, *BusinessWeek* and the *Harvard Business Review*. For example, *JQI* publishes benchmarking articles on health care units, such as inpatient surgical care, outpatient emergency care, and health care maintenance education.

Driven in part by technology, consumers have replaced producers as the principle source of economic authority in the twenty-first century. For example, customer satisfaction is one of only three principles in total quality management (the others being employee involvement and continuous improvement). A CPA interviews management to understand how customers (not managers) define quality and to identify relevant performance measures that mimic customer satisfaction. Although evidence of quality may vary across products, services, and customer demographics, several dimensions of quality are common, among them:

Dimension	*Example Question*
• Expectations	Does the product conform to expected life?
• Value	Does the product perform at a level commensurate with price?
• Support	Is product-support service commensurate with warranty claims?
• Impressions	Is the product presented and packaged well?

For these questions, customer satisfaction might be measured as obsolescence rates, failure rates, and support time or with customer surveys, comment cards, and focus groups.

Collect Evidence

The collection of evidence in an assurance service engagement is similar to the collection of audit evidence in at least two ways: First, evidence may be obtained from testimony (for example, surveys), intuitively (for example, product comparisons), from accepted assumptions (for example, product safety varies inversely with injury rates), from perceptual experience (for example, quality ratings), and from practical results (for example, product warranty claims). Second, as discussed in Chapter 4, evidence consists of underlying data (such as product quality ratings) and corroborating information (such as defect rates). However, evidence collection in assurance services differs markedly from audit evidence in one critical way: While auditors are armed with generally accepted criteria for measurement and reporting—that is, GAAP—assurers are not. For example, there are no generally accepted criteria for measuring a company's value-creating activities in a performance measurement engagement. Rather, CPAs rely on their understanding of the client's business and their information-search skills to identify relevant performance measures.

Although CPAs have no generally accepted measurement criteria for benchmarking services, the literature does include guidelines for judging the mix of financial and nonfinancial measures appropriate for a company. For example,

Lynch and Cross, in *Measure Up! Yardsticks for Continuous Improvement*, a popular book on continuous improvement and performance measurement, propose a method to translate strategic goals into performance measures across a variety of core business processes, such as new product development and distribution channels. A practitioner's search for measures also includes both original and archived sources. *Original sources* include face-to-face and telephone interviews, surveys, and focus groups. For example, a well-designed, sharply focused survey could offer useful insights into why loyal customers may value a product and why potential customers may not. *Archived sources* include service organization Web sites and publications, online databases, commercial search services, and archived client and industry data. For example, APQC's *International Benchmarking Clearinghouse*, introduced earlier, offers a benchmarking database for a number of industries and companies worldwide.

Display Evidence

Unlike financial statements, benchmarked performance measures have no generally accepted form of display. A CPA could display measures in a number of ways, including descriptive statistics and vision charts, among others.

Descriptive Statistics The Midwest Benchmarking Alliance Group, an emergency medicine benchmarking consortium, consists of nine member hospitals that meet quarterly to address cost containment and service improvement. The Group offers several measures that illustrate descriptive statistics relevant to emergency care benchmarking:

Dimension	*Example Measure*
● Clinical protocols	Post-treatment recovery time.
● Productivity	Time physicians/nurses spend in each phase of a treatment protocol (for example, diagnosis, treatment delivery).
● Patient satisfaction	Patients rate response time.
● Patient discharge	Time patients spend in each phase of discharge (for example, physician clearance, administrative clearance).
● Operational issues	Throughput cycle time.

To be useful, a measure need be relevant and, like the measures above, worthy of an entity's effort to achieve.

Vision Charts Similar to balanced scorecards, which offer financial and nonfinancial measures across four drivers—an entity's financial, customer, internal business, and internal learning activities[31]—*vision charts* offer measures across a different set of drivers: the goals that map to management's mission. Figure 7-13, a vision chart for Chevron, includes measures for each of the company's six goals

---

31 See, for example: R. S. Kaplan and D. P. Norton, "The Balanced Scorecard: Measures That Drive Performance," *Harvard Business Review* (January–February 1992), pp. 71–79; R. S. Kaplan and D. P. Norton, "Putting the Balanced Scorecard to Work," *Harvard Business Review* (September–October 1993), pp. 134–147; and R. S. Kaplan and D. P. Norton, *The Balanced Scorecard*. Boston: Harvard Business School Press, 1996.

FIGURE 7-13: *Chevron's Vision Chart*

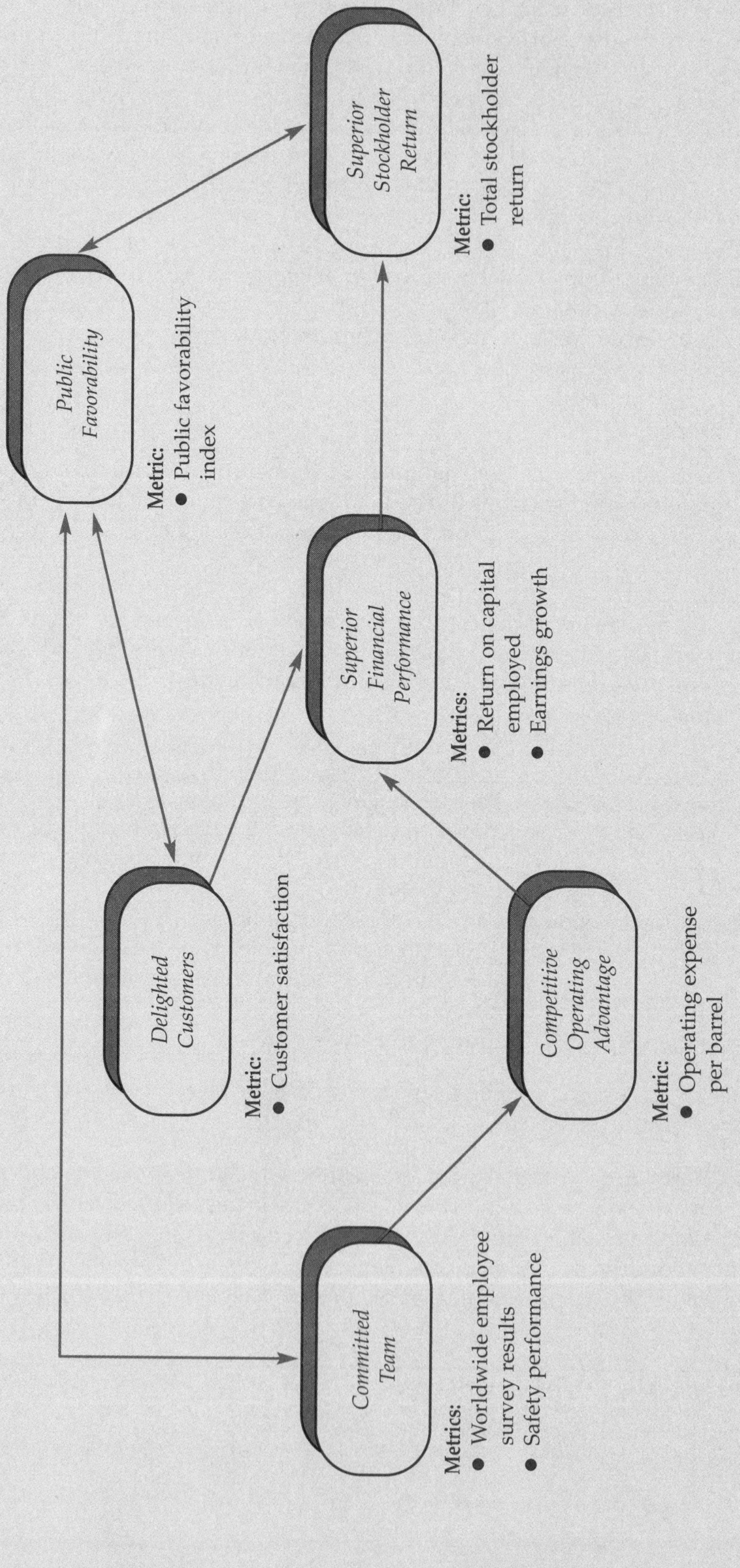

Source: K. Derr, "The Chevron Way to a Strong Board," *Directors & Boards* (Fall 1998), p. 31.

listed earlier. For example, the two metrics for *committed team* are worldwide employee survey results and safety performance. The choice between a balanced scorecard and a vision chart can be simple. For example, does management view the driver of the company to be the four generic activities common to a balanced scorecard or the goals that management has set for the company? However, balanced scorecards have an advantage: The four drivers in a balanced scorecard are well accepted in the financial community, thereby allowing for comparability with other companies that use a balanced scorecard. In contrast, vision charts are driven by goals that may not be wholly comparable across companies. For example, the *financial perspective* in a balanced scorecard is comparable to the *superior financial performance* and *superior stockholder return* goals in Chevron's vision chart (Figure 7-13). But Chevron's measure of *public favorability* (the "public favorability index") does not have a readily comparable metric in a balanced scorecard, making direct benchmarking between two companies problematic.

Other Displays In practice, CPAs use a variety of other means to arrange evidence in performance measurement engagements. Two examples: *Reliability indices* measure the probability that merchandise will operate properly as a product of the reliability of each subsystem within the product. For example, consider an electric garage door opener with three subsystems:

Subsystem	# of Defects per 100	Reliability	Failure Rates
Motor housing	4	0.96	0.04
Battery-operated remote unit	2	0.98	0.02
Aluminum track assembly	1	0.99	0.01
	7		

In this case, the reliability of the garage door opener is:

$$r_g = (r_1)(r_2)\dots(r_n)$$
$$= (0.96)(0.98)(0.99)$$
$$= 0.93$$

Reliability indices are rather useful in benchmarking, since they offer a means to compare one dimension of quality—reliability—across products within a company's product line (for example, low-end versus high-end garage door openers) and within products across competitors (for example, high end versus high end).

Pareto charts, another means to benchmark product quality, leverage off of Pareto's 80-20 rule. In the garage door opener illustration, the rule translates to this: 80 percent of the operation of the opener is likely attributed to only 20 percent of the electrical and mechanical tasks that the opener completes on each trial. Many more tasks are at work, but Pareto's rule predicts that product failures will result from only 20 percent of the tasks. A Pareto chart depicts the defect rate and the cumulative defect percentage across subsystems.

Deliverable

In an assurance service to assess the relevance of benchmarking measures, the deliverable is an open-ended, nonstandardized report to senior management and the board of directors. The report could conclude whether management's performance measures are relevant to the company's mission and goals, and whether management's information systems offer reliable measures. Alternatively, senior management could engage the CPA as a consultant to perform any of the following, among other related services:

- Design relevant performance measures.
- Design and implement a performance measurement system.
- Advise management how to improve the performance measures or the performance measurement system.

The steps listed in Figure 7-12 would likely apply to any of these services, although the deliverable may vary. For example, as a value enhancement to financial statement audits, Ernst & Young offers selected audit clients an industry analysis and benchmarking scorecard, called a business intelligence memo (BIM), as part of a financial statement audit.

Quality measurement is at once both well regarded and well rewarded within the financial community. For example, in 1987 Congress enacted the prestigious Malcolm Baldridge National Quality Award, named for a former secretary of commerce long a proponent of product and service quality. Each year a maximum of two awards are made in three categories (large manufacturers, large service providers, and small manufacturers and service providers), and recipients have included IBM, Federal Express, Merrill Lynch, and Motorola. Interestingly, "... *benchmarking* and competitive comparisons are the management concepts with the single greatest influence . . . in a Baldridge assessment" (emphasis supplied).[32] CPAs have long held the core competencies necessary to perform performance measurement services, largely because the service requires roughly the same skill set and mimics the same process used in the profession's core service, financial statement auditing.

KEY TERMS

Audit committee 243	Engagement letter 248
Benchmarking 277	Error 257
Client strategy template 251	Fraud 257

REFERENCES

Professional Standards:

AICPA, *Codification of Auditing Standards*. New York: AICPA.

SAS No. 11, "Using the Work of a Specialist" (AU Sec. 336).

SAS No. 12, "Inquiry of a Client's Lawyer Concerning Litigation, Claims, and Assessments" (AU Sec. 337).

SAS No. 22, "Planning and Supervision" (AU Sec. 311).

SAS No. 31, "Evidential Matter" (AU Sec. 326).

SAS No. 45, "Substantive Tests Prior to the Balance Sheet Date" (AU Sec. 313).

SAS No. 45, "Related Parties" (AU Sec. 334).

SAS No. 54, "Illegal Acts by Clients" (AU Sec. 317).

---

32 C. Bogan and M. J. English, *Benchmarking for Best Practices*. New York: McGraw Hill, 1995, p. 30.

SAS No. 56, "Analytical Procedures" (AU Sec. 329).

SAS No. 60, "The Communication of Internal Control Structure Related Matters Noted in an Audit" (AU Sec. 325).

SAS No. 61, "Communication with Audit Committees" (AU Sec. 380).

SAS No. 77, "Amendments to *SAS No. 22*, 'Planning and Supervision,' *No. 59*, 'The Auditor's Consideration of an Entity's Ability to Continue as a Going Concern,' and *No. 62*, 'Special Reports.'"

SAS No. 80, "Amendment to *SAS No. 31*, 'Evidential Matter'" (AU Sec. 326).

SAS No. 83 (and *SSARS No. 7*), "Establishing an Understanding with the Client" (AU Sec. 310.05-07).

SAS No. 84, "Communications Between Predecessor and Successor Auditors" (AU Sec. 315).

SAS No. 85, "Management Representations" (AU Sec. 333).

SAS No. 88, "Audit Adjustments" (AU Sec. 310).

SAS No. 89, "Audit Committee Communications" (AU Sec. 380).

SAS No. 93, "Omnibus Statement on Auditing Standards" (AU Sec. 315).

SAS No. 96, "Audit Documentation."

SAS No. 99, "Consideration of Fraud in a Financial Statement Audit" (AU Sec. 316).

Professional Reports and Speeches:

Beasley, M. S., J. V. Carcello, and D. R. Hermanson, *Fraudulent Financial Reporting: 1987–1997 An Analysis of U.S. Public Companies*, Research Commissioned by the Committee of Sponsoring Organizations of the Treadway Commission, 1999.

Blue Ribbon Committee on Improving the Effectiveness of Corporate Audit Committees, *Report and Recommendations*. New York Stock Exchange and the National Association of Securities Dealers, 1999.

KPMG, *Fraud Survey 2003*. New York: KPMG, 2003

Levitt, A. "The Numbers Game." Remarks by the SEC Chairman, New York University Center for Law and Business, September 28, 1998.

National Commission on Fraudulent Financial Reporting, *Report*, Chapter 3 (National Commission on Fraudulent Financial Reporting, 1987).

Public Oversight Board, Panel on Audit Effectiveness, *Report and Recommendations*, Stamford, CT: 2000.

Articles, Books:

Albrecht, W. S., and C. C. Albrecht, "Root Out Financial Deception," *Journal of Accountancy* (April 2002), pp. 30–34.

Bean, J. W., Jr., "The Audit Committee's Road Map," *Journal of Accountancy* (January 1999), pp. 47–54.

Beasley, Mark S., J. V. Carcello, and D. R. Hermanson, "Top 10 Audit Deficiencies," *Journal of Accountancy* (April 2001), pp. 63–66.

Beek, C. M., W. M. Rexroad, L. M. Leinick, and J. A. Ostrosky, "The CPA as Sleuth: Working the Fraud Beat," *Journal of Accountancy* (April 1999), pp. 20–23.

Beneish, M. D., "The Detection of Earnings Manipulation," *Financial Analysts Journal* (September/October 1999), pp. 24–36.

Bogan, C. E., and M. J. English, *Benchmarking for Best Practices*. New York: McGraw-Hill, 1995.

Davia, H. R., P. C. Coggins, J. C. Wideman, and J. T. Kastanin, *Accountant's Guide to Fraud Detection and Control*, 2nd edition. New York: John Wiley & Sons, Inc., 2000.

DeZoort, F. T., D. R. Hermanson, and R. W. Houston, "Audit Committee Member Support for Proposed Audit Adjustments: A Source Credibility Perspective," *Auditing: A Journal of Practice & Theory* (September 2003), pp. 189–205.

Erickson, M., B. W. Mayhew, and W. L. Felix, Jr., "Why Do Audits Fail? Evidence from Lincoln Savings and Loan," *Journal of Accounting Research* (Spring 2000), pp. 165–194.

Glover, S. M., D. F. Prawitt, J. J. Schultz, Jr., and M. F. Zimbelman, "A Test of Changes in Auditors' Fraud-Related Planning Judgments Since the Issuance of SAS No. 82," *Auditing: A Journal of Practice & Theory* (September 2003), pp. 237–251.

Hall, J. J., "How to Spot Fraud," *Journal of Accountancy* (October 1996), pp. 85–88.

Heiman-Hoffman, V. B., K. P. Morgon, and J. P. Patton, "The Warning Signs of Fraudulent Financial Reporting," *Journal of Accountancy* (October 1996), pp. 75–78.

Johnstone, K. M., and J. C. Bedard, "Risk Management in Client Acceptance Decisions," *The Accounting Review* (October 2003), pp. 1003–1025.

Lundelius, C. R., Jr., *Financial Reporting Fraud: A Practical Guide to Detection and Internal Control.* New York: AICPA, 2003.

Lynch, R. L. and K. F. Cross, *Measure Up! Yardsticks for Continuous Improvement*, New York, NY: Blackwell Publishers, 1995.

McConnell, D. K., Jr., and G. Y. Banks, "Expanded Guidance for Auditor Fraud Detection Responsibilities," *The CPA Journal* (July 2003).

Nelson, M. W., J. A. Elliott, and R. L. Tarpley, "Evidence From Auditors About Managers' and Auditors' Earnings Management Decision," *The Accounting Horizons* (Supplement 2002), pp. 175–202.

Nelson, M. W., J. A. Elliott, and R. L. Tarpley, "How are Earnings Managed? Examples from Auditors," *Accounting Horizons* (Supplement 2003), pp. 17–35.

Ramos, M., "Auditors' Responsibility for Fraud Detection," *Journal of Accountancy* (January 2003), pp. 28–36.

Ramos, M., *Fraud Detection in a GAAS Audit: SAS No. 99 Implementation Guide.* New York: AICPA, 2003.

Sheriff, R., "The Audit from the Inside," *Journal of Accountancy* (January 1998), pp. 49–51.

Wells, J. T., "Irrational Ratios," *Journal of Accountancy* (August 2001), pp. 23–26.

Wells, J. T., "Occupational Fraud: The Audit as Deterrent," *Journal of Accountancy* (April 2002), pp. 24–28.

Zacharias, C., "New Rules, New Responsibilities," *Journal of Accountancy* (August 2000), pp. 53–55.

QUESTIONS

1. What strategies and business characteristics are included in a client strategy template, and how can the template be used in practice?
2. Explain the nature and purpose of an audit committee.
3. Briefly describe an auditor's decision process when deciding to accept or continue an engagement.
4. What are the purposes of an engagement letter?
5. Why does an auditor obtain an understanding of a client's business and industry before beginning an audit engagement?
6. What is the purpose and typical contents of a preliminary audit planning memorandum?
7. Distinguish between client errors and fraud.
8. Distinguish between fraudulent financial reporting and a misappropriation of assets.
9. What topics would auditors discuss at a brainstorming session to identify and assess fraud risk?
10. What should an auditor do if he or she decides that an audit client's financial statements are affected materially by fraud?
11. In light of material undetected errors or fraud, what inherent risk does an auditor sustain by not auditing all of an entity's transactions and events during a financial statement audit? How do current auditing standards deal with that risk?
12. What is the objective of the interim phase of an audit engagement?
13. Why is coordination with the client prior to beginning year-end audit work especially important?
14. Subsequent events occur after the last day of a client's fiscal year and on or before the report date. Why would an auditor be concerned about transactions and events subsequent to the period reported on?

15. From whom does an auditor obtain written representations at the end of an audit? As of what date are the representations made?
16. Apart from a detailed document-by-document review, how else might an audit partner review audit documentation?
17. How is quality defined in an audit service and in an assurance service?
18. What questions can benchmarking potentially address that historical financial statements alone cannot?
19. What does a reliability index measure?
20. What is a Pareto chart?

MULTIPLE CHOICE QUESTIONS

1. Audit committees were first required for public companies by:
   a. SEC's 1972 *Accounting Series Release No. 123*, "Standing Audit Committees Composed of Outside Directors."
   b. A 1978 New York Stock Exchange mandate.
   c. The 1999 Blue Ribbon Committee on Improving the Effectiveness of Corporate Audit Committees.
   d. The *Sarbanes-Oxley Act of 2002.*

2. A public company's audit committee should consist of:
   a. Representatives of management, shareholders, suppliers, and customers.
   b. The audit partner, chief financial officer, legal counsel, and at least one outsider.
   c. Representatives of the major equity interests (bonds, preferred stock, common stock).
   d. Board members who are not officers or employees.   (AICPA Adapted)

3. The SEC's *Final Rule: Audit Committee Disclosure,* issued in 2002, requires that audit committees include in proxy statements a report to shareholders explaining whether the audit committee:
   a. Approved the auditor's fees.
   b. Reviewed the auditors' documentation.
   c. Delivered to management the audited financial statements.
   d. Discussed with management the audited financial statements.

4. Communication with a predecessor auditor is initiated by:
   a. Management.
   b. The successor auditor.
   c. The audit committee of the board of directors.
   d. The chair of the board of directors.

5. Management is not responsible for:
   a. The audited financial statements.
   b. Preparing spreadsheets for the auditor.
   c. The auditors' report.
   d. Compliance with laws and regulations.

6. In the pharmaceutical industry:
   a. The cost to develop a prescription drug is less than the cost of a 747 jumbo jet.
   b. Managed care organizations insure less than 75 percent of U.S. employees.
   c. The *Drug Price Competition and Patent Term Restoration Act* has reduced the exclusivity period of brand-name drugs.
   d. Research reveals that formularies reduce patients' use of hospital emergency rooms.

7. Merck & Co., Inc., a research-based pharmaceutical company:

   a. Dominates the market for generic substitutes.
   b. Offers a full line of prosthetic replacement limbs.
   c. Shares risk through strategic alliances.
   d. Relies only on clinical trials from company-sponsored research.

8. Among other things, client strategy templates address:

   a. The relevance of management's growth strategy and financial and operating goals.
   b. The reliability of management's strategic alliances and joint ventures.
   c. The auditor's assessment of audit risk.
   d. The assurer's assessment of management's performance measures.

9. An independent auditor has been approached to perform an audit. Research suggests that the auditor may fail to:

   a. Distinguish between a regulated and nonregulated industry.
   b. Coordinate audit dates with the client.
   c. Initiate discussion with the predecessor auditor.
   d. Establish investigation thresholds for analytical procedures.

10. To avoid misunderstandings between a practitioner and client, engagement arrangements are written in:

    a. A legal letter.
    b. An engagement letter.
    c. A client representation letter.
    d. A letter on reportable conditions.

11. Which of the following procedures would an auditor most likely perform when planning an audit?

    a. Review prior-year audit documents.
    b. Inquire about potential litigation, claims, and assessments.
    c. Obtain a representation letter from management.
    d. Determine whether internal controls are applied as prescribed.

    (AICPA Adapted)

12. Evidence shows that:

    a. Auditors may accept a risky client when specialists can mitigate the risk.
    b. Fraudulent financial reporting is the most common fraud.
    c. Audit partners sign-off audit program steps prematurely.
    d. Companies in regulated industries have comparatively more financial statement errors.

13. Which of the following is an example of a misappropriation of assets?

    a. An altered document
    b. An unrecorded transaction
    c. Unauthorized credit card use
    d. Misapplication of an accounting principle

14. Which of the following would auditors most likely discuss in a brainstorming session to identify and assess fraud risk?

    a. Pressures on client employees
    b. Audit time budgets
    c. The audit committee's awareness of fraud
    d. Former auditors employed by the client

15. Which of the following, if material, would be a fraud?

    a. Errors in the application of accounting principles.
    b. Clerical errors in accounting data underlying the financial statements.
    c. Misinterpretation of facts that existed when the financial statements were prepared.
    d. Misappropriation of an asset or groups of assets.

16. Which of the following is an inappropriate reaction to a material fraud detected in a publicly traded company?

    a. Report the matter to the SEC.
    b. Discuss the matter with the audit committee of the board of directors.
    c. Obtain further evidence.
    d. Suggest that the client consult with legal counsel about questions of law.

17. Which of the following statements best describes an auditor's responsibility to detect fraud?

    a. The auditor is responsible for failing to detect fraud when the failure clearly results from not performing audit procedures described in the engagement letter.
    b. The auditor must extend auditing procedures to search actively for fraud.
    c. The auditor must assess the risk that material fraud may exist.
    d. The auditor is responsible for failing to detect fraud only when an unqualified opinion is issued.

18. An increase in a company's asset-quality ratio could suggest that:

    a. The market value of assets is increasing.
    b. Working capital has shifted from receivables and inventory to cash.
    c. Assets with less certain benefits are increasing.
    d. The proportion of collectible receivables is increasing.

19. A purpose of reviewing first-quarter financial results during audit planning is to:

    a. Identify unexpected fluctuations occurring in account balances since the prior-year financial statements.
    b. Become familiar with accounts likely to appear in the financial statements.
    c. Plan evidence to be gathered in auditing accounts that are new to the first-quarter financial statements.
    d. Assess first-quarter financial position, results of operations, and cash flows.

20. Compared to a financial statement audit, an assurance service on the relevance of performance measures:

    a. Leverages off of benchmarking.
    b. Leverages off of a different skill set.
    c. Ignores measures of financial performance.
    d. Delivers an open-ended report.

PROBLEMS AND DISCUSSION CASES

7-1 *Client Strategy Template: EMC Corp.* **(http://www.emc.com)**

EMC Corp., the world's leading supplier of intelligent enterprise storage and retrieval technology, has pioneered two breakthrough developments in stand-alone digital storage. In the 1980s, when many companies stored data in large dedicated hard drives, the company essentially strapped together dozens of small, off-the-shelf disk drives into closet-size storage boxes, an innovation that stored more data more quickly. In the 1990s, the company again redefined the storage industry by introducing open systems storage that linked together two otherwise incompatible systems: mainframe computers and operating system networks, such as Microsoft Windows. EMC holds over 30 percent of the stand-alone storage market, and IBM holds 20 percent.

Required: Using online and other public sources of information, prepare a client strategy template for EMC Corp. that summarizes the company's mission and the characteristics of the business.

7-2 *Client Strategy Template: Exxon Corporation* **(http://www.exxon.com)**

Headquartered in Houston, the Exxon Corporation enjoys earnings approaching $5 billion, a return on equity exceeding 20 percent, proven reserves over 1 billion gallons, and a market capitalization of $175 million—the fifth largest among U.S. multinational corporations and largest by far among major integrated oil companies. The company conducts upstream exploration and/or production in 30 countries worldwide and global downstream business in over 75 countries.

Required: Using online and other public sources of information, prepare a client strategy template for Exxon that summarizes the company's financial goals and operating strategies and the characteristics of the business.

7-3 *Client Strategy Template: The Gillette Company* **(http://www.gillette.com)**

The Gillette Company, a Boston-based global manufacturer and marketer of consumer products, has a $50 billion market capitalization, among the 50 largest in the United States. Annual sales exceed $10 billion and an estimated 1.2 billion people use Gillette products daily. Products launched in the last five years of the 1990s represent almost half of the company's sales, and most of that came from well-recognized products that led all rivals in volume, among them the Gillette Mach 3 shaving systems launched in 1998.

Required: Using online and other public sources of information, prepare a client strategy template for The Gillette Company that summarizes the company's mission statement, values, and characteristics of the business.

7-4 *Client Strategy Template: The Coca-Cola Company* **(http://www.coca-cola.com)**

Homework

Coca-Cola, the world's largest manufacturer, distributor, and marketer of soft drink concentrates and syrups, has a market capitalization over $100 billion. Rather than produce finished soft drinks, Coca-Cola distributes roughly one-third of the concentrate and syrup to fountain retailers and wholesalers, and two-thirds to authorized bottling and canning operations that either combine the syrup with carbonated water or combine the concentrate with sweetener, water, and carbonated water to produce finished soft drinks. The company employs 30,000 people worldwide, and realizes approximately 70 percent of worldwide earnings from sources outside of the United States.

Required: Using online and other public sources of information, prepare a client strategy template for Coca-Cola that summarizes the company's mission and the characteristics of the business.

7-5 *Nonfinancial Measures and Professional Skepticism*

Stable & Platt, Co., Inc., manufactures and markets low-priced lines of consumer products in three main business segments: soap, detergent, and household cleaning agents. All three product lines are sold in highly competitive, price-sensitive markets, whose participants include industry leaders such as Procter & Gamble and Dow Chemical. A small company, S&P has succeeded with a strategy that forgoes research in favor of developing low-cost competitors to market-dominant products developed by industry leaders. For example, S&P marketed products within two years after Procter & Gamble introduced Comet (1956), the first scouring cleanser, and Dawn (1972), the first effective grease-cutting liquid. Not unlike generic alternatives to brand-name pharmaceuticals, S&P's products capture the most price-sensitive consumers in a high-demand market, offering a return that is small by Procter & Gamble standards but large by S&P standards.

While planning S&P's 2007 financial statement audit, you compile nonfinancial measures. You learn that compared to the prior year, retailer-returned cases increased from 340 to 495, cases shipped increased from 17,000 to 17,900, and no brand-name manufacturer had introduced a high-demand product. Although privately owned, S&P anticipates an initial public offering of equity securities, and employs approximately 1,000 people in one midwestern plant.

Required: Discuss how S&P's strategy and performance would raise your professional skepticism about sales, receivables, inventory, and management's plan to offer securities publicly.

7-6 *Audit Planning*

In late spring of 2007, you are appointed the in-charge auditor of your firm's recurring annual audit of a major client, the Lancer Company. You are given the engagement letter for the audit covering the calendar year ending December 31, 2007, and a list of personnel assigned to the engagement. Your responsibility is to plan and supervise field work for the engagement.

Required: Discuss the sources you should consult in preparing and planning the Lancer Company engagement, the type of information you would seek, the preliminary plans and preparations you would make for field work, and the agenda you would plan for a preliminary meeting with staff assigned to the engagement.

(AICPA Adapted)

7-7 *Responding to the Warning Signs of Fraudulent Financial Reporting*

You are auditing Balforoni Waste, Inc., a publicly traded, solid waste disposal company that dominates the household and commercial hauling markets in the upper Midwest. In conversations with management following an analysts' conference-call meeting, management makes clear that, despite pricing pressures from local municipalities, unlikely success in renewing the permit on a major dump site, significant environmental remediation on closed landfills, and competition from national haulers, the company is committed to meeting a consensus annual earnings estimate of $1.10 per share, an amount that exceeds the prior year's actual earnings by $0.08 per share. Consistent with their commitment, management reminds you that an industrial-cleaning subsidiary will be sold at a gain and that a new landfill is under construction in Michigan.

Management's incentive compensation is contingent both on earnings and on Balforoni's December 31 stock price. For example, over the five years you have audited Balforoni, both the chief executive officer and the chief financial officer have earned about one-third of their compensation from salary and about two-thirds from incentives. You have no reason to expect that management necessarily has a disregard either for ethics or for the representational faithfulness that shareholders expect from financial statements. However, you learn that, in a study published in the October 1999 *Journal of Accountancy*, Heiman-Hoffman, Morgon, and Patton report that, of the warning signs of fraudulent financial reporting listed now in *SAS No. 99*, "Consideration of Fraud in a Financial Statement Audit" (most of which are reproduced in Figure 7-5), practicing auditors ranked the following two as the third and eighth most important:

- Management places undue emphasis on meeting earnings projections or other quantitative targets.
- A substantial portion of management compensation depends on meeting quantified targets.

Required:
1. How do analysts' expectations affect share prices?
2. How could Balforoni management enhance reported earnings?

7-8 *Fraud Detection Responsibility and Reporting*

Several years ago, Dale Holden organized Holden Restaurants. Holden started with one small restaurant, but over time the restaurant became quite popular due largely to the quality of the food and service, an attractive yet modest atmosphere, and reasonable prices.

Success with his first restaurant encouraged Holden to open at least one new restaurant in each of the last five years, resulting today in eight successful restaurants located in metropolitan areas throughout the state. Owing to recent rapid expansion of the business, Holden has hired a controller and supporting staff to manage the individual restaurants, allowing Holden to focus attention on the aggregate operations and to plan future expansion.

Holden has applied to a bank for additional financing to open another restaurant this year. For the first time ever, the bank asked him to provide financial statements audited by an independent auditor. The bank assured Holden that the audited statements were not required because they doubted his integrity or thought him to be a poor credit risk. Rather, bank policy required all businesses over a certain size to supply audited statements with loan applications, and Holden's business had long since reached that size.

Holden was not surprised by the bank's requirement. He had ruled out an audit previously because he trusts his controller's integrity and wanted to avoid the fee associated with an initial audit as long as possible. However, his absence from everyday hands-on operations now makes an audit advisable since, trust aside, he also believes an additional benefit of the audit will be the probable detection of any fraud that may have occurred at his restaurants.

To fulfill the bank's request for audited financial statements, Dale Holden has hired Hill & Associates, LLP.

Required:
1. Discuss Hill & Associates' responsibilities to detect fraud in a financial statement audit.
2. What effect, if any, would the detection of fraud by Hill & Associates have on their opinion on the financial statements?

7-9 *Using Ratios as Fraud Screens*

On the following page are comparative consolidated balance sheets for Putnam, Inc., a manufacturer and supplier of bottling equipment.

Putnam, Inc.
Consolidated Balance Sheets (in millions)

Assets	2007	2006
Current Assets:		
Cash and cash equivalents	$ 222	$ 277
Accounts receivable, less allowance of $67 in 2007 and $42 in 2006	922	823
Inventories	378	331
Prepaid expenses and other current assets	215	117
Total current assets	$ 1,737	$1,548
Property, plant and equipment, net of accumulated depreciation of $1,935 in 2007 and $1,170 in 2006	3,308	2,543
Intangible assets, net	4,687	3,684
Investment in debt defeasance trust	170	—
Other assets	125	82
Total assets	$10,027	$7,857

	2007	2006
Liabilities and Shareholders' Equity		
Current Liabilities:		
Accounts payable	$ 936	$ 834
Taxes payable	243	170
Short-term borrowings	69	77
Total current liabilities	$ 1,248	$1,081
Long-term debt	4,523	3,285
Other liabilities	819	550
Deferred income taxes	1,265	1,021
Minority interest	348	319
Total liabilities	$ 8,203	$6,256
Shareholders' Equity:		
Common stock, par value $0.01 per share		
authorized 900 shares, issued 310 shares	$ 3	$ 3
Additional paid-in capital	1,750	1,739
Retained earnings	1,066	649
Accumulated other comprehensive loss	(468)	(370)
Treasury stock: 30 shares and 29 shares in 2007		
and 2006, respectively, at cost	(527)	(420)
Total shareholders' equity	$ 1,824	$1,601
Total liabilities and shareholders' equity	$10,027	$7,857

Net sales in 2007 and 2006 were $9,216 and $8,443, respectively.

Required:
1. Calculate for Putnam, Inc., the asset-quality, total-accruals to total-assets, and accounts receivable turnover ratios.
2. Interpret the ratios.

7-10 *Using Ratios as Fraud Screens*

Following are comparative consolidated balance sheets for SeaCrest, Inc., a manufacturer and supplier of household products:

SeaCrest, Inc.
Consolidated Balance Sheets (in millions)

	2007	2006
Assets		
Current assets:		
Cash and cash equivalents	$ 52,378	$ 11,526
Receivables, net	335,550	213,438
Inventories	216,180	162,252
Net assets of discontinued operations and other assets		
held for sale	—	102,847
Deferred income taxes	36,706	93,689
Prepaid expenses and other current assets	17,191	40,411
Total current assets	$ 658,005	$ 624,163
Property, plant and equipment, net	240,897	220,088
Trademarks and trade names, net of accumulated depreciation of $104,774 in 2007 and $136,254 in 2006	194,372	200,262
Other assets	27,010	28,196
	$1,120,284	$1,072,709

	2007	2006
Liabilities and Shareholders' Equity		
Current liabilities:		
Short-term debt and current portion of long-term debt	$ 668	$ 921
Accounts payable	105,580	107,319
Restructuring accrual	10,938	63,834
Taxes payable	52,844	(21,942)
Other current liabilities	28,069	121,451
Total current liabilities	$ 198,099	$ 271,583
Long-term debt	194,580	201,115
Other long-term liabilities	141,109	152,451
Deferred income taxes	54,559	52,308
Total liabilities	$ 588,347	$ 677,457
Shareholders' equity:		
Common stock (issued 89,984,425 and 88,441,479 shares)	$ 900	$ 884
Paid-in capital	483,384	447,948
Retained earnings	141,134	35,118
Other	(30,436)	(25,310)
	$ 594,982	$ 458,640
Treasury stock, at cost (4,454,394 and 4,478,814 shares)	(63,045)	(63,388)
Total shareholders' equity	$ 531,937	$ 395,252
	$1,120,284	$1,072,709

Net sales in 2007 and 2006 were $1,168,182 and $984,236, respectively.

Required:
1. Calculate for SeaCrest, Inc., the asset-quality, total-accruals to total-assets, and accounts receivable turnover ratios.
2. Interpret the ratios.

7-11 *A Client Resents a Search for Fraud*

Several months prior to beginning an audit engagement of the Taunton Manufacturing Company, you point out to Taunton's CFO, Marsha Wade, that as part of your responsibilities, you will design the audit to provide reasonable assurance of detecting any material errors or fraud that may exist. Wade, somewhat alarmed by your statement, responds that all of her employees are trustworthy and, therefore, refuses to pay any portion of the audit fee relating to a search for fraud. Further, she states her understanding that auditors are not responsible for detecting fraud, assuming generally accepted auditing standards are followed.

Required: Respond to each of the controller's statements.

7-12 *Predecessor and Successor Auditors*

The audit committee of the board of directors of Unicorn Corp. asked Tish & Field, LLP, to audit Unicorn's financial statements. Tish & Field explained the need to make an inquiry of the predecessor auditor and requested permission to do so. Unicorn's management agreed and authorized the predecessor auditor to respond fully to Tish & Field's inquiries.

After communicating with the predecessor auditor, Tish & Field drafted an engagement letter that was mailed to the audit committee of Unicorn's board of directors. The engagement letter described arrangements concerning the involvement of the predecessor auditor and other matters.

Required:

1. What information should Tish & Field have obtained during their inquiry of the predecessor auditor prior to accepting the engagement?
2. Describe what other matters Tish & Field would likely have included in the engagement letter.

(AICPA Adapted)

7-13 *Audit Committees*

The financial community has long recognized the importance of—and has endorsed forming—audit committees. For example, audit committees were first encouraged by the Securities and Exchange Commission in the 1940s, and first mandated by the New York Stock Exchange in the 1970s. Today audit committees are required by the SEC's *Final Rule: Audit Committee Disclosure* for all public companies, and independent auditors have become increasingly more involved with audit committees.

Required:

1. What is an audit committee?
2. Identify the reasons why audit committees have been formed and are used currently.
3. What are the functions of an audit committee?

7-14 *The Decision to Accept an Engagement*

Jones is approached by a prospective client who wishes to engage him to perform an audit that in prior years was performed by another auditor.

Required: Discuss the procedures Jones should follow in accepting or declining the engagement.

(AICPA Adapted)

7-15 *Using Specialists*

Tom Majors, an entry-level staff auditor, has been assigned to observe the physical inventory of the Lewiston Chemical Company, a processor and distributor of three different industrial chemicals.

Upon arriving at Lewiston's manufacturing plant, Majors learns that there are 15 above-ground cylindrical-shaped storage tanks, each 50 feet tall, and three rectangular underground storage tanks. Above-ground tanks are connected in lots of five. Underground pipes stretch over two miles in length and can be accessed at each tank and at access ports throughout the plant.

In addition to the tanks and pipes, there is a shipping/receiving depot. Three separate pipelines run to the depot, allowing immediate access for receiving and shipping. Tank trucks deliver and ship chemicals to and from the depot.

Required:

1. What audit problems does Majors face when observing Lewiston's chemical inventory?
2. What specialists should Majors consider engaging to assist in the physical inventory observation? For example, which specialists are uniquely positioned for what potential audit problems?

7-16 *Is Share Price Influenced by Waiving Audit Adjustments?*

An engagement partner distributes a spreadsheet detailing six proposed audit adjustments to the audit committee of Abadon Industries, a publicly traded manufacturer of automotive parts and accessories. The adjustments involve two issues: understated accruals and accelerated revenue recognition from fourth-quarter channel stuffing achieved by offering deep end-of-quarter discounts to U.S. automobile manufacturers. The partner tells the committee that the adjustments would decrease after-tax earnings by $1 million (one-half cent per share), that management believes the adjustments are immaterial to the financial statements individually and in the aggregate, and that both the partner and the firm's national office agree. Earnings reported in the audited financial statements meet analysts' consensus expectation, both for the fourth quarter and for the year. Abadon has not missed consensus earnings expectations since going public seven years ago.

Required: Has Abadon management overstated net income by waiving the audit adjustments and, therefore, influenced share price?

7-17 *Is Share Price Influenced by Netting Passed Adjustments Against Unexpected Gains?*

One year after Beldon Company management waived audit adjustments aggregating $1.5 million, management unexpectedly realizes $1.5 million in gains on the disposition of assets used to produce products sold in noncore markets. Beldon's CFO, recalling the audit partners' spirited defense of prior-year proposed (but passed) audit adjustments, nets the $1.5 million unexpected gains against the audit firm's prior-year audit adjustments. Management does not disclose the netting in Beldon's financial statements.

Required: Given that the adjustments were judged immaterial in the prior year, does netting current unexpected gains against prior-year adjustments warrant disclosure in the current year?

7-18 *Performance Measurement Benchmarking at The Boeing Company* (http://www.boeing.com)

The Boeing Company, one of the world's leading aerospace companies, operates in two principal industries: commercial aircraft (for example, jet transport aircraft) and information, space, and defense systems (for example, military aircraft, missile systems, rocket engines, satellite-launching vehicles). In 1996, the Department of Defense awarded Boeing a 51-month contract to proceed with the Joint Strike Fighter (JSF) Concept Demonstration Program, the culmination of a two-decade-old Department of Defense initiative to restore Boeing as a manufacturer of fighter aircrafts.

Boeing's strategy was to exploit design and production protocols from the Boeing 777, the B-2 bomber, and the F-22 air-dominance fighter in the development of an affordable fighter aircraft that is responsive to what are called "variants" in the industry: design variations that render the aircraft accessible to more than one branch of service. For example, the Air Force may require air-to-ground strike capability, and the Navy may require high-range, carrier-to-air capability. In 1999, on news that Boeing had successfully completed a formal review by the Department of Defense, Frank Statkus, Boeing vice president and JSF general manager, said, "We clearly demonstrated to our customer that we are on schedule, on cost, and very much on track with manufacture and assembly of our JSF concept demonstration aircraft."

Required: Using online and other public sources of information, construct for Boeing's Joint Strike Fighter aircraft areas of performance testing relevant to each of the following four questions:

1. How do we look to the financial markets?
2. How do we look to our customers?
3. What processes do we excel at?
4. How do we learn and improve?

For example, unlike commercial aircraft, performance testing for fighter aircraft requires testing at high angles of attack.

Internet problems and discussion cases are available at http://ricchiute.swlearning.com

RESEARCH PROJECTS

1. Client Strategy Templates and Large-Cap Public Companies

Visualizing engagement risks and engagement strategies for a complex, large-cap client demands that public accounting firms understand intimately the nexus of relationships that drive a client's financial, customer, internal, and organizational learning goals. Understanding a client at the transactions level only can satisfy an assurer's attest objectives minimally, but also can undermine his or her capacity to serve the client fully. In response, the Big Four and other firms have developed templates to summarize their clients' strategies, offering the firm a comparative advantage in assessing audit risk.

Required:
1. Select a large-cap, publicly traded company in an industry that interests you—for example, airlines, financial services, health care, manufacturing, pharmaceuticals, telecommunications.
2. Using Internet (and other publicly available) sources—such as the company's home page, EDGAR (**http://www.sec.gov**), and Hoover's Online (**http://www.hoovers. com**)—prepare a PowerPoint slide that, similar to the client strategy template illustrated in the text, identifies major business units, markets, products, customers, competitors, strategic alliances/joint ventures, and potential adverse influences.

2. Research and Audit Practice

Throughout this chapter numerous references are made to audit research that lends insight into audit practice. For example, we learn from research that cognitive biases and document order affect audit decision-making, that successor auditors sometimes fail to initiate communication with predecessor auditors, and that companies in regulated industries may have fewer financial statement errors than companies in nonregulated industries. Research in auditing appears in a variety of journals, including *Auditing: A Journal of Practice & Theory (A:AJP&T)*, *The Accounting Review (AR)*, and the *Journal of Accounting Research (JAR)*. Although the research methods described in articles appearing in these journals can be inaccessible to some nonresearchers, the abstracts, introductions, and conclusions are intended to be accessible to all interested readers.

Required: Select one of the steps in the audit process listed in Figures 7-1, 7-8, 7-10, and 7-11. For the step selected, locate at least two related articles from *A:AJP&T*, *AR*, and/or *JAR*, and prepare a report that summarizes how the articles add to your understanding of the audit process.

3. Client Strategy Templates, Risks, and Assurance Service Opportunities

Select a company from the following list.

Abercrombie & Fitch (apparel retailer), AFLAC Inc. (insurance, life and health), Baxter International Inc. (medical supplies), Best Buy, Inc. (specialty retailer), Biogen (biotechnology), BP (oil), Browning Ferris Industries (waste disposal), Charles Schwab (securities brokers), Cigna (insurance, full line), Citigroup (banking), Cox Communication (broadcasting), CVS Corp. (drug-based retailer), Deere & Co. (heavy machinery), Dell Computer (computers), Walt Disney (entertainment), Dow Chemical (chemicals), The Gap (apparel retailers), General Motors (auto manufacturer), Georgia-Pacific (forest products), Goodyear Tire & Rubber (tires and rubber), Hasbro (toys), Home Depot (home repair), Humana (health care provider), Immunex (biotechnology), Illinois Central Corp. (railroads), International Paper Company (paper products), Johnson Controls (auto parts and equipment), Kroger (food retailers and wholesalers), Marriott International (lodging), McDonald's (restaurants), McGraw-Hill (publishing), Merrill Lynch (financial services), MGM Grand (casinos), Microsoft Corp. (software), Morrison Knudsen (heavy construction), Motorola (communication technology), Nike (footwear), Nextel Communications (mobile communications systems), Owens-Illinois (containers and packaging), PepsiCo (soft drinks), Philip Morris (tobacco), Royal Caribbean Cruises Ltd. (recreational services), Sprint Corporation (long-distance telephone systems), Sun America (insurance, life and health), Sunbeam Corporation (home furnishings), Sun Microsystems (computers), US Airways Group (airline), USX-US Steel Group (steel), Walgreen Co. (drug-based retailer), Wal-Mart Stores (retailer), Xerox Corporation (office equipment), Yahoo! (Internet service provider).

Required:

1. Using Internet (and other publicly available) sources—such as the company's home page, EDGAR (**http://www.sec.gov**), Hoover's Online (**http://www.hoovers. com**)—construct for the company, and discuss, a client strategy template.
2. Identify and discuss actual or potential threats to the company's strategies.
3. Identify for the company (and discuss) audit risk and assurance service opportunities.

Present your findings in a professional service proposal to the executive team of the company you've selected. Demonstrate understanding and insight that transcends the trivial and the obvious, makes clear to the executive team that you've digested its strategies fully, and wins the executive team's confidence that you should be hired. Be specific and be complete.

Interactive quizzes are available as a student learning resource at
http://ricchiute.swlearning.com

Chapter 8

Internal Control

Major topics discussed in this chapter are:

- The *COSO Report's* framework for evaluating internal control, including the control environment, risk assessment, control activities, information and communication, and monitoring.
- The consideration of internal control and assessment of control risk in a financial statement audit.
- An audit of internal control over financial reporting mandated by the *Sarbanes-Oxley Act*, the SEC's rule on management reports on internal control, and the PCAOB's standards.
- Assurance services related to information systems.

This chapter addresses an auditor's responsibility to consider and, under the *Sarbanes-Oxley Act*, to audit internal control in a financial statement audit. On *considering* internal control, the chapter addresses questions central to an auditor's planning: What is the assessed level of control risk and, correspondingly, is the assessed level sufficiently low to allow an auditor to relax the nature, timing, and extent of substantive tests? On *auditing* internal control, the chapter focuses on the *Sarbanes-Oxley Act*, on the SEC's rules for complying with the Act, and on the Public Company Accounting Oversight Board's (PCAOB) standard for complying with the SEC's rules.

The chapter begins with an introduction to internal control using the well-accepted framework developed by the Committee of Sponsoring Organizations (COSO) of the Treadway Commission. Next, the chapter discusses an auditor's responsibility to consider internal control and to assess control risk under the second standard of field work, and integrates into the discussion an auditor's responsibility in a public-company engagement to audit internal control over financial reporting under the *Sarbanes-Oxley Act* (Section 404), SEC rules (*Management's Reports on Internal Control Over Financial Reporting*), and PCAOB standards (PCAOB *Auditing Standard No. 2*, "An Audit of Internal Control Over Financial Reporting"). The chapter concludes with examples of assurance services related to information services.

The COSO Framework

Following three years of extensive study, the Committee of Sponsoring Organizations (COSO) of the Commission on Fraudulent Financial Reporting (the

Treadway Commission) issued in 1992 a four-volume document, *Internal Control: Integrated Framework*, commonly referred to as the *COSO Report*. The *Report* provided a framework against which companies could assess their internal controls and, for the first time ever, established a common definition of internal control that serves the needs of a variety of groups, including directors, management, internal auditors, independent accountants, legislators, and regulators, rather than fragmented definitions that serve the needs of only one group, as had been the case in the past. No prior document on internal control had been so far-reaching in scope, not even *Statement on Auditing Standards No. 55*, "Consideration of the Internal Control Structure in a Financial Statement Audit," since it served but one group: independent auditors. Widely used by public companies today, the COSO framework offers an insightful springboard from which to define internal control and to understand the components of internal control: the control environment, risk assessment, control activities, information and communication systems support, and monitoring.

The *COSO Report* defines **internal control** as:

a process, effected by an entity's board of directors, management, and other personnel, designed to provide reasonable assurance regarding the achievement of objectives in the following categories:

- *Effectiveness and efficiency of operations.*
- *Reliability of financial reporting.*
- *Compliance with applicable laws and regulations.*[1]

The definition embodies four key concepts. First, internal control is a *process* (not a single event) integrated within (not added onto) another process: the process management uses to plan, to execute transactions and events, and to monitor results. An auditor considers internal control in every financial statement audit, but establishing and maintaining control is management's, not the independent auditor's, responsibility. Second, internal control is accomplished by *people* at every level of an organization, including the board of directors, management, and employees. As a result, the effectiveness of internal control can be diminished by the inherent limitations of people. For example, even the most logically designed and carefully implemented controls may be undermined by employee errors, by management's intentional acts to circumvent the controls, by mistakes in judgment, and by misunderstandings. Third, rather than an end in itself, internal control is a means to achieve an entity's *objectives*, most of which generally fall within three categories:

	Example
• Operations objectives	Market share, return on investment, product or service diversification
• Financial reporting objectives	Production of reliable financial statements
• Compliance objectives	Compliance with laws and regulations

Fourth, internal controls can be expected to provide *reasonable, but not absolute, assurance* that objectives will be accomplished, since the benefits expected from

---

1   Committee of Sponsoring Organizations of the Treadway Commission (COSO). *Internal Control: Integrated Framework*. Framework. New York: COSO, 1992, p. 9.

some controls (for example, reduced risk of employee petty theft) may not be worth the cost of implementation.

The SEC and the PCAOB: Control Over Financial Reporting

Enabled by Section 404, "Management Assessment of Internal Controls," of the *Sarbanes-Oxley Act of 2002,* the SEC issued in 2003 *Final Rule: Management's Reports on Internal Control Over Financial Reporting,* which included a definition of a subset of a company's internal control—internal control over financial reporting—that the PCAOB adopted in *Auditing Standard No. 2,* "An Audit of Internal Control Over Financial Reporting Performed in Conjunction with an Audit of Financial Statements." The SEC's definition is important because Section 404 makes management responsible to certify in each Form 10-K that internal control over *financial reporting*—not over all internal controls—is effective. In the same Form 10-K, the incumbent auditor is responsible to issue an opinion (unqualified, qualified, adverse, or disclaimer of opinion: Chapter 3) on management's certification. The SEC's (and the PCAOB's) definition of **internal control over financial reporting** is:

A process designed by, or under the supervision of, the . . . principal executive and principal financial officers . . . to provide reasonable assurance regarding the reliability of financial reporting and the preparation of financial statements for external purposes in accordance with generally accepted accounting principles and includes those policies and procedures that:

- *Pertain to the maintenance of records that in reasonable detail accurately and fairly reflect the transactions and dispositions of the assets;*
- *Provide reasonable assurance that transactions are recorded as necessary to permit preparation of financial statements in accordance with generally accepted accounting principles, and that receipts and expenditures . . . are being made only in accordance with authorizations of management and directors; and*
- *Provide reasonable assurance regarding prevention or timely detection of unauthorized acquisition, use or disposition of the registrant's assets that could have a material effect on the financial statements.*[2]

The difference between the two definitions is this: The COSO definition includes the *reliability of financial reporting* as one of three means to achieve management's objectives (the other two being operations and compliance), and the SEC's definition adds clarity about three details that bear on financial reporting: reasonably detailed *records;* fairly stated *financial statements, cash* receipts and disbursements; and the prevention and detection of *misappropriated assets.* In short, the SEC's definition fits under the umbrella of the COSO definition. Management is responsible to design, implement, and monitor internal controls over the processes that bring to bear a company's operations objectives, financial reporting objectives, and compliance objectives and to certify in writing annually the effectiveness of one category: internal control over financial reporting.

---

2   SEC, *Final Rule: Management Reports on Internal Control Over Financial Reporting and Certification of Disclosure in Exchange Act Period Reports.* Washington, D.C.: SEC, 2003.

Components of Internal Control

In addition to defining internal control, the *COSO Report* also identifies five inter-related components of internal control that should be integrated within management's process:

- Control environment
- Risk assessment
- Control activities
- Information and communication systems support
- Monitoring

Control Environment

A company's **control environment** represents management's and the board of directors' attitude (that is, what's the "tone at the top"?), awareness (for example, do they know how cash is controlled?), and actions (for example, does management implement internal auditors' recommendations?) about internal control. The control environment captures the importance of control in management's operating style. For example, an active audit committee, a competent internal audit department, current information technology, and direct management control over the authority delegated to employees would all suggest that management is committed to effective internal control.

In practice, though, auditors sometimes underweight the significance of management's attitude, awareness, and actions. For example, although the Panel on Audit Effectiveness found that auditors in 126 SEC engagements had assessed the control environment, the Panel also found that "on nearly 17 percent of the reviewed engagements the audit would have been improved by more thoughtful analysis and in-depth auditor knowledge of the entity's control environment."[3] In a well-designed and executed audit, the auditor's objective in considering the control environment is to obtain an understanding of management's and the board of directors' attitude, awareness, and actions concerning:

	Example
• Integrity and ethical values	Do codes of conduct describe acceptable business practice, conflicts of interest, and standards of ethical behavior?
• Commitment and competence	Are employees committed to quality?
• Board of directors or audit committee	Is the board independent of management?
• Management's philosophy and operating style	What is management's attitude toward manipulated or falsified records?
• Organizational structure	Does information flow to the appropriate levels of management?
• Assignment of authority and responsibility	Are the responsibilities of key managers defined?
• Human resource policies and practices	Are there policies for hiring, training, promoting, and compensating employees?

---

3   The Panel on Audit Effectiveness, *Report and Recommendations*. Stamford, CT: Public Oversight Board, 2000, p. 29.

For some entities, an auditor may have additional concerns, such as a not-for-profit organization's need to comply with laws and regulations governing direct federal grants. For others, like a small owner-managed service company, there may be a strong sense of integrity and ethical values even though there is no written code of conduct.

Risk Assessment

Every entity faces risks, both external, such as technological developments and changing customer demands, and internal, such as employee pilferage and computer down time. Management's task is to identify the risks that affect their operations, financial reporting, and compliance objectives and to take the action necessary to manage them. For example, an entity might confront the following risks solely as a result of managing change.

	Example
• Changed operating environment	Divestiture in the telecommunications industry
• New personnel	A new senior executive may not fully understand the entity's culture
• New information systems	Unusually tight time constraints in redesigning systems software
• Rapid growth	Capacity constraints may lead to excessive back orders
• New technology	Just-in-time inventory may lead to production delays
• New products or services	Unfamiliar services may impose unfamiliar risks
• Corporate restructuring	A leveraged buyout may be accompanied by staff reductions and inadequate supervision
• Foreign operations	The control environment in a foreign subsidiary may be driven by local customs and culture

Although these risks are important to management, they are less problematic to an auditor, whose primary concern is audit risk. However, management's response to managing change can influence the auditor's consideration of an entity's ability to continue as a going concern.

Control Activities

Control activities (also called **control procedures**) are those policies and procedures in addition to the control environment and the information system that management establishes to provide reasonable assurance that objectives are achieved. The independent auditor's objective is to understand an entity's control activities sufficiently to plan the audit.

In practice, control activities take various forms, but generally fall into two categories: controls that prevent and controls that detect. *Preventive controls* are intended to prevent a misstatement. For example, daily "flash" reports, a control activity a parts distributor's regional managers might perform and forward to the national sales manager, serve both to accrue sales commissions properly (an operations objective) and to record sales properly (a financial reporting objective). In contrast, *detective controls* are intended to detect misstatements that have occurred already, and sometimes serve as a check on a preventive control. For example, to check the accuracy of the daily "flash" reports, management might implement a control that compares quantities relieved from inventory to quantities shipped to parts-supply retailers.

Generally, control activities are established over (1) authorization and execution of transactions, (2) segregation of duties, (3) the design and use of documents and records, and (4) access to assets and records.

Transaction Authorization   All transactions should be authorized by responsible personnel acting within the scope of their prescribed authority and responsibility. Without a formal system of transaction authorization, any employee could commit resources without regard to the company's objectives.

The type of authorization, specific or general, required for a transaction (or series of related transactions) depends on the nature, scope, and frequency of occurrence. *Specific authorization* means authorization is required each time the transaction is proposed and is typically used for unusual, material, or infrequent projects. For example, specific authorization might be required for plant expansion, purchases or sales of subsidiaries, or capital asset purchases in excess of a designated amount. In contrast, *general authorization* means the company has policies and procedures that personnel should follow to determine if a proposed transaction or project is authorized in general. For example, a company may have authorized pricing and credit sale policies, and personnel may complete transactions meeting these prescribed policies without first obtaining specific authorization. General authorization avoids the inefficiencies of specifically reauthorizing routine transactions. No proposed transaction should be executed without first having either general or specific authorization.

Authorization is not the same as approval. *Authorization* means authority has been given to acquire or expend resources. *Approval*, in contrast, means the conditions for authorization have been met and resources may therefore be acquired or expended. For example, an employee might approve payment of a vendor's invoice for materials acquired to anchor on the floor a capital asset acquisition the board of directors authorized specifically. Transaction authorization usually precedes approval, although they may occur simultaneously.

Segregation of Duties   No set of policies and procedures can prevent **collusion**, a fraud perpetrated by two or more employees, each of whom is necessary to complete the scheme. For example, even if different employees authorize, execute, and record cash payments, no information system could prevent them from conspiring to transact a fraudulent payment and sharing the misappropriated funds. As a result, preventing collusion is not usually an objective of a system of internal control. The best alternative is the segregation of responsibilities to prevent any one employee, acting alone, from committing and concealing frauds. Optimum **segregation of duties** exists when collusion is necessary to circumvent controls.

To achieve optimum segregation of responsibilities, a company's management, custodial, accounting, and monitoring functions should be performed by different employees. That is, the following responsibilities would be separated:

- Transaction authorization   (a management function)
- Transaction execution   (a custodial function)

- Transaction recording   (an accounting function)
- Independent checks on performance   (monitoring functions)

If any one employee is responsible for all four functions, his or her opportunities to misappropriate assets are nearly limitless. If any one employee is responsible for three or two functions, his or her opportunities diminish progressively but do not vanish. Optimum segregation of duties suggests that no employee be responsible for any more than one function because:

- Restricting employee responsibility to one function means at least four different employees are required to authorize, execute, record, and check a transaction. Thus, a system of checks and balances reevaluates the validity of a transaction four separate times. If two, three, or four functions are performed by a single employee, the system of checks and balances becomes progressively weaker.
- The more employees a transaction requires to complete, the more employees necessary to commit and conceal frauds, and it is reasonable to assume that employees are less apt to attempt collusion as the number of employees required to commit fraud increases. In cases of fraud, there is no safety in numbers since, as the number of perpetrators increases, the risk of exposure increases.

Design and Use of Documents, Screens, and Records To obtain accurate and reliable accounting data, transactions must be recorded promptly in the proper accounting periods and dollar amounts, and classified properly in subsidiary and control accounts. Satisfying these requirements, however, depends on documents (such as a receiving report), screens (such as a purchase order template), and accounting records that accurately reflect all executed transactions. Documents and records are evidence of executed transactions and collectively represent the **audit trail** that auditors often rely on when tracing transactions through an accounting system.

However, computers can remove or otherwise obscure audit trails, since many documents and records are not printed for archiving. For example, many companies use online time clocks that allow employees to punch in and out with plastic identification cards, and rely on the system to automatically accumulate and transfer hours worked to payroll. Because all payroll information is stored within the system's files (for example, SAP, Oracle, a proprietary system), employee time cards—source documents common to manual payroll systems—are not used, thereby eliminating a segment of the audit trail. With audit trails eliminated or distorted, auditors are unable to trace the flow of transactions explicitly from source documents to journal entries and to general ledger postings. As a result, rather than focus on audit trails, auditors often focus on management's controls over the system by testing whether the controls are designed properly and operating effectively.

The design of documents, screens, and accounting records can have considerable impact on how efficiently an accounting system operates, and therefore on how efficiently an audit can be performed. For example, documents, screens, and records should be:

- Designed for multiple use,
- Numbered consecutively for identification, and
- Clear and relatively easy to complete.

The transaction-recording process and the accounting records should be described clearly and unambiguously in a posted *procedures manual*. The purpose of the procedures manual is to encourage consistent use and completion of prescribed accounting records and documents and to provide a ready reference for newly hired personnel. A procedures manual is also an important reference for auditors attempting to determine how management intends an entity's control activities to operate.

Access to Assets and Records Only authorized personnel should have access to assets and records. Several means can be used to limit access, including protection devices, online recording, and access codes. *Protection devices* restrict unauthorized personnel from gaining direct access to assets. For example, locked storerooms could restrict access to parts inventories, and fireproof vaults to expense vouchers. *Online recording* limits access to assets and records by limiting the number of employees involved in recording and posting transactions. For example, online cash registers record cash sales both within the cash register and in off-site files, creating multiple records of a single transaction and yet requiring only one employee. *Access codes,* such as employee identification and personal identification numbers (PIN), restrict access to data that could be used to alter records or to misappropriate assets.

Information and Communication Systems Support

To operate efficiently, an entity needs to identify, capture, and communicate both external and internal information in a form and time frame that enables employees to discharge their assigned responsibilities. External information includes market share, regulatory requirements, and customer complaints. Internal information, the source of most audit evidence, includes the **accounting system**, which consists of the methods and records management establishes to record and report transactions and events and to maintain accountability for assets and liabilities. To be effective, an accounting system should (1) include methods and records that will identify all valid transactions; (2) record transactions in the proper accounting period; and (3) describe transactions on a timely basis and in sufficient detail to permit proper classification, to measure the transaction properly, and to present summarized transactions and related disclosures accurately in the financial statements. The auditor's objective in considering an entity's accounting system is to obtain an understanding of:

- Major classes of transactions,
- How transactions are initiated,
- The records, documents, and accounts used in the processing and reporting of transactions,
- The processing of transactions, and
- Financial reporting procedures.

The central activity of most businesses typically involves a series of related functions, all of which the accounting system must capture. Although sometimes complex, these functions can be described in general as follows:

Capital funds are received from debt and equity security holders (creditors and owners) and either held for use in operations or invested; funds for operations are used to acquire resources (goods and services) from vendors and employees in exchange for obligations to pay; resources are used in operations or held or transformed and distributed to outsiders in exchange for promises of future payments; outsiders pay for resources distributed to them; and obligations to vendors and employees are paid.

Figure 8-1 categorizes these functions into four groups of transactions called **transaction cycles**, the means through which an accounting system processes transactions: (1) financing, (2) expenditure/disbursement, (3) conversion, and (4) revenue/receipt.[4] The number of cycles will vary from industry to industry and from company to company, since business functions themselves vary across industries and companies. Thus, these four cycles are representative, not definitive, although they include most of a manufacturing, merchandising, or service company's business functions. In fact, if sufficiently significant to a particular entity, any one function could represent a separate cycle.

FIGURE 8-1: *Relating Business Functions and Transaction Cycles*

Business Functions	
• Capital funds are received from investors and creditors. • Capital funds are held for use in operations or invested.	Financing
• Resources (goods and services) are acquired from vendors and employees in exchange for obligations to pay. • Obligations to vendors and employees are paid.	Expenditure/ Disbursement
• Resources are used, held, or transformed.	Conversion
• Resources are distributed to outsiders in exchange for promises of future commitments. • Outsiders pay for resources distributed to them.	Revenue/ Receipt

Focusing on transaction cycles does not mean that individual financial statement accounts are ignored. Rather, it means an auditor focuses on processes (cycles) in order to understand end results (accounts). Financial statement accounts essentially translate to storage bins in which processed transactions are recorded, classified, and summarized. In fact, the dollar balances within some accounts actually result from transactions processed through more than one cycle. For example, debits to Cash result from cash received from customers, a function of the revenue/receipt cycle, and from creditors and investors, a function of the financing cycle. Credits to Cash result from cash disbursements, a function of the expenditure/disbursement cycle. Thus, the dollar balance in Cash reflects the net result

---

4   An external financial reporting cycle is also common and relates to complying with generally accepted accounting principles, gathering and summarizing information for financial statements and other historical financial reports, and preparing and reviewing financial statements. The cycle is not addressed in this chapter, since it does not relate directly to the processing of transactions.

of transactions processed through three cycles. Accounts are much more meaningful to an auditor if he or she understands the processes (cycles) relating to accounts and their dollar balances. Figure 8-2 illustrates the financial statement accounts that are generally captured within each cycle, and also lists the chapters in this book devoted to each cycle.

FIGURE 8-2: *Relating Business Transaction Cycles and Financial Statement Accounts*

Cycles	Financial Statement Accounts	Text Chapters
Revenue/ Receipt	Sales Receivables Cash Receipts Cash	10, 11
Expenditure/ Disbursement	Purchases Payables Personnel and Payroll Cash Disbursements	12, 13, 14
Conversion	Inventory Costs of Sales Fixed Assets	15
Financing	Investments Long-Term Debt Capital Stock	16

Monitoring

To assure quality, internal controls should be monitored—through continuing or periodic evaluations, or both—and discrepancies resolved by management at least one level above those responsible. The reliability of an accounting system can be evaluated by comparing recorded assets with actual assets continually or periodically. For example, recorded quantities in perpetual inventory records can be compared with actual quantities in stock either continually in an online system (for example, after every transaction) or periodically through a physical inventory count (for example, annually). To maximize effectiveness, monitoring should take advantage of the element of surprise, be performed by personnel independent of the functions tested, and result in appropriate corrective action. The element of surprise encourages employees to execute and record transactions accurately, since their work may be audited at any time. Of course, monitoring would be much less effective if performed by employees responsible for the functions tested, since the results would lack objectivity. Thus, periodic monitoring should be performed by personnel independent of the functions tested.

➢ fraud
➢ restatement

Restatement, Fraud, and Internal Control

One might expect intuitively that the role of substantive tests in a financial statement audit dominates the role of tests of controls—after all, substantive tests iso late actual monetary error and tests of controls isolate likely error. However, the full gravity of internal control, both to management and to an auditor, becomes apparent in restatements and in related SEC enforcement proceedings. Consider, for example, the case of Rite Aid Corporation, the nation's third largest drugstore chain.

On June 30, 1999, days after Rite Aid filed restated financial statements for the fiscal years ended 1997 and 1998, KPMG, in a letter dated June 24 to the audit committee of the board of directors, described a number of material weaknesses in internal control that were insufficient to allow management "to accumulate and reconcile information necessary to properly record and analyze transactions on a timely basis."[5] Owing to the seriousness of the weaknesses, KPMG apparently also announced to the committee that the firm would not issue quarterly review reports (Chapter 18) until the weaknesses were resolved and, equally important, was not willing to rely on representations Rite Aid's chief financial officer made to KPMG, although members of the committee deny that KPMG made the announcements. On November 11, KPMG resigned and withdrew its audit report.

The SEC initiated a formal investigation into Rite Aid's accounting for related-party transactions, under accrued stock appreciation rights, undisclosed markdowns, and so-called vendor "up-charges" (discussed in Chapter 10), among other things. However, the SEC also added traction to the importance of internal control in an Accounting and Auditing Enforcement Release that alleged fraud and found that Rite Aid had violated the reporting, books and records, and internal control provisions of the *Securities Exchange Act of 1934*:

Section 13(b)(2)(B) of the Exchange Act requires issuers to devise and maintain a system of internal accounting controls sufficient to provide reasonable assurances that transactions are recorded as necessary to permit preparation of financial statements in conformity with generally accepted accounting principles and to maintain the accountability of assets . . . Rite Aid's system of internal accounting controls was not designed to provide reasonable assurances that transactions were recorded as necessary to permit preparation of financial statements in conformity with GAAP or to maintain the accountability of assets. Rite Aid's system of internal accounting controls failed to prevent, and indeed facilitated, the improper accounting practices described in detail above . . .[6]

The lesson learned is that internal control is hardly benign. Rather than a matter of efficiency and convenience, internal control in public companies is a matter of law.

Assessing Control Risk & Auditing Internal Control Over Financial Reporting

Responsibility

In the audit of any entity—whether a public or nonpublic company, a government agency, or a nonprofit organization—an independent auditor considers internal control to *assess control risk* (Chapter 2). However, in the audit of a public company,

---

5   U.S. General Accounting Office, *Financial Statement Restatements: Trends, Market Impacts, Regulatory Responses, and Remaining Challenges* (GAO-03-138), Washington, D.C.: U.S. General Accounting Office, 2002, p. 188.

6   Accounting and Auditing Enforcement Release No. 1579, *In the Matter of Rite Aid Corporation*, June 21, 2003.

the auditor considers internal control not only to assess control risk but, also, to *audit internal control over financial reporting,* a responsibility that derives from the *Sarbanes-Oxley Act,* Section 404, "Management Assessment of Internal Control." Under Section 404, management is obligated annually to assess in writing the effectiveness of internal control over financial reporting. The auditor, guided by PCAOB *Auditing Standard No. 2,* "An Audit of Internal Control Over Financial Reporting Performed in Conjunction with an Audit of Financial Statements," is obligated to *audit* internal control over financial reporting to this end: The auditor must form an opinion on whether management's assessment of the effectiveness of internal control over financial reporting is fairly stated in all material respects and issue an unqualified, qualified, or adverse opinion or to disclaim an opinion (Chapter 3), assuming the auditor finds no basis in fact to withdraw from the engagement (discussed later).

Owing to the *Sarbanes-Oxley Act,* Section 404, Form 10-K, the annual report of a public company, includes two reports on internal control over financial reporting—one in which:

- Management (a) acknowledges responsibility to establish and maintain internal controls over financial reporting, and (b) assesses the effectiveness of internal control over financial reporting (called a "404 certification");

and another, in which:

- The independent auditor reports on management's assessment.

Therefore, in the audit of a public company, an auditor considers internal control to *assess control risk* and to *audit internal controls over financial reporting,* and issues two reports, one on the *financial statements* (Chapter 3) and one on *internal control over financial reporting* (although the reports may be combined). Auditors have similar reporting obligations in other audits. For example, in the audit of a non-public company, the auditor reports on the consideration of internal control over financial reporting under *SAS No. 60,* "Communication of Internal Control Related Matters Noted in an Audit," which includes requirements similar to the PCAOB's *Auditing Standard No. 2.*

The following discussion integrates the auditor's assessment of control risk and the auditor's audit of internal control over financial reporting.

Overview

An auditor's assessment of control risk, and formation of an opinion on the effectiveness of internal control over financial reporting, unfolds generally in three phases. Figure 8-3 partitions the phases into tasks related to *assessing control risk* (left column), and *auditing internal control over financial reporting* (right column). Collectively, the tasks translate to these phases:

1. *Obtain an understanding* of how management has designed policies and procedures for the control environment, risk assessment, the control activities, information and communication, and monitoring for operations, financial reporting, and compliance with laws and regulations.
2. *Assess control risk* for financial statement assertions related to the account balances and transaction classes, and *evaluate* the design and operating effectiveness of *internal controls over financial reporting.*
3. *Determine* the nature, timing, and extent of *substantive tests,* and form an *opinion on internal control over financial reporting.*

FIGURE 8-3: *Assessing Control Risk and Auditing Internal Control Over Financial Reporting*

Assessing Control Risk	*Auditing Internal Control Over Financial Reporting*
• *Obtain an understanding* of the design of controls over the control environment, risk assessment, the control activities, information and communication, and monitoring for *operations*, financial reporting, and *compliance with laws and regulations*.	• *Obtain an understanding* of the design of controls over the control environment, risk assessment, the control activities, information and communication, and monitoring for *financial reporting*.
• *Assess control risk* for financial statement assertions related to the account balances and transaction classes.	• *Evaluate* the design and operating effectiveness of *internal controls over financial reporting*.
• *Determine* the nature, timing, and extent of *substantive tests*.	• Form an *opinion on internal control over financial reporting*.

Figure 8-4 illustrates and the following discusses the three phases for the assessment of control risk and for auditing internal control over financial reporting. However, the level of understanding an auditor should obtain varies from engagement to engagement depending on the complexity and sophistication of an entity's operations and accounting system (for example, a publicly traded versus an owner-managed company), the auditor's previous experience with the entity (for example, an initial versus a continuing engagement), the assessed level of inherent risk, the auditor's understanding of the entity's industry, and the materiality of transactions processed through the internal controls.

Obtain an Understanding of Internal Control

In every financial statement audit, an auditor obtains an understanding of internal control sufficient to plan the audit, even for audits of small owner-managed businesses that employ only a few accounting employees. As the Panel on Audit Effectiveness pointed out, "Obtaining an understanding of internal control does not require the auditor to reach any conclusions about the *effectiveness* of internal control"[7] (emphasis added). Rather, an understanding of internal control allows an auditor to identify the types of material misstatements that could occur in the financial statements, to consider factors that affect the risk of material misstatements, to design substantive tests of account balances and transaction classes that are processed by the internal controls, and to reach a conclusion on management's assessment of the effectiveness of internal control over financial reporting.

An auditor begins by reviewing prior-year audit documentation and client procedures manuals, making inquiries of management, and observing client personnel to obtain a general understanding of the control environment, management's assessment of the risks they face, the control activities, the flow of information and communication throughout the accounting system, and how management monitors internal controls. An understanding of the control environment,

---

7   The Panel on Audit Effectiveness, *Report and Recommendations*. Stamford, CT: Public Oversight Board, 2000, p. 25.

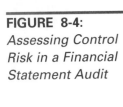

FIGURE 8-4:

Assessing Control Risk in a Financial Statement Audit

Obtain an under-standing of inter-nal control

Determine an as-sessed level of con-trol risk and evaluate internal control over financial reporting

Plan the nature, tim-ing, and extent of substantive tests and form an opinion on internal control over financial reporting

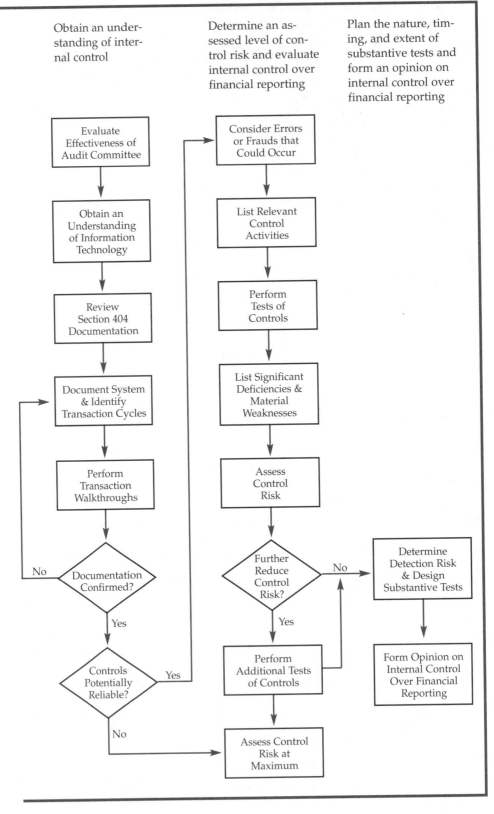

risk assessment, and control activities provides the auditor with a general knowledge of the entity's organizational structure, of methods used to communicate responsibility and authority, and of methods management uses to supervise the system. In turn, an understanding of the flow of information and monitoring provides the auditor with a general knowledge of the various classes of transactions and the methods by which each significant class of transactions is authorized, executed, initially recorded, and subsequently processed. First, though, the auditor evaluates the effectiveness of the audit committee.

Evaluate the Audit Committee's Effectiveness

The audit committee of the board of directors is an essential element of an entity's control environment, the full embodiment of the tone at the top, since the committee is the final (if not the only) authority over financial reporting the chief executive and chief financial officers approve. For example, investigations prompted by whistleblowers at a host of major companies, including General Mills and Kmart, were done by major law firms engaged by the audit committees, not by management. In the *Sarbanes-Oxley* era, an effective audit committee challenges the chief executive and financial officers over financial reporting, seeks the advice and consent of the independent auditor, and engages independent counsel when, like in the case of a whistleblower, an investigation independent of the auditor makes sense. The tone set by an audit committee helps set the tone at the top.

To assess the effectiveness of an audit committee, the auditor evaluates a number of factors that bear on independence, resolve, and diligence. For example, the auditor would evaluate the:

- Nomination (for example, a search firm nominee? the CEO's friend?) and independence (for example, a related party?) of each committee member.
- Clarity of the committee's responsibilities and level of management's cooperation.
- Committee's involvement with the independent auditor and with internal audit.
- Time the committee devotes to committee responsibilities in general, and to internal control in particular.

To be competent, the *Sarbanes-Oxley Act*, Section 407, "Disclosure of Audit Committee Financial Expert," requires that an audit committee include at least one financial expert, the requirements for which focus largely on relevant experience. For example, to qualify as a financial expert, a person needs to have an understanding of generally accepted accounting principles; experience preparing or auditing financial statements; experience accounting for estimates, accruals, and reserves; experience with internal control; and an understanding of audit committees. To be independent and to fulfill the committee's due diligence obligations under the *Sarbanes-Oxley Act*, Section 301, "Public Company Audit Committees," no individual committee member may accept from the company any consulting, advisory, or other fees, and the full committee must establish procedures to receive anonymously and investigate rigorously complaints employees file about financial reporting.

Obtain an Understanding of Information Technology

Years ago, most all audit clients used roughly the same manual accounting information system. Forms differed, details differed, but most clients posted handwritten journal entries through paper-and-pencil ledgers, trial balances, and financial statements. The similarity was striking. In practice today, however, businesses rely heavily on alternative information systems that differ markedly in technology. For example, whereas a small drug store may use information technology as part of a free-standing system to accomplish selected tasks, such as billings or payroll, a large pharmaceutical company may use information technology in a complex enterprise resource system that encompasses financial reporting, operations, and compliance with laws and regulations. Information technology offers significant benefits that bear on the effectiveness and efficiency of internal control, such as consistently applying management-imposed criteria for routine but large-dollar-volume purchases; easing the analysis of complex data; and enhancing the timeliness, availability, and accuracy of financial and nonfinancial information. However, information technology also poses risks, such as potential losses of information and unauthorized access (or changes) to sensitive information.

Underscoring the need to understand alternative technologies, the Panel on Audit Effectiveness observed, "an increasing need for auditors to have a higher level of technology skills and for more effective participation in audits by information technology specialists."[8] *All* independent auditors have a professional obligation to understand the technology a client deploys, partly to plan and execute the audit and partly to know when to engage specialists. The following introduces several information systems that practitioners confront commonly in practice, discusses developments in information software, and explains how information technology affects control risk.

Personal Computers Although they vary in physical form—for example, desktops, laptops, notebooks—personal computers (PCs) are a powerful, affordable, and cost-effective information processing alternative for entities that might otherwise be constrained by manual processing. Many small entities—among them retail pharmacies, town boards, and local real estate brokerage firms—handle all of their data processing needs with a single, stand-alone, desktop PC that may include, for example, a high-speed coprocessor, a modem or wi-fi hookup, and a laser printer. In short, not much more than a student might have.

Local Area Networks (LANs) To increase processing capability economically, personal computers can be linked to **local area networks (LANs)** that access files and software from a central file server and direct print jobs from a central print server. LANs increase an entity's processing power-to-cost ratio because each linked personal computer—called a workstation—shares application software, data files, and peripherals such as optical scanners and printers. LANs are common in entities where data files, software, and peripherals are accessed by a number of end users physically located within a single building or adjacent buildings. However, networks need not be restricted to local areas. For example, many large, multinational companies link local area networks to *wide area networks* (WANs) that allow access across LANs and through password-protected on-line databases.

---

8   The Panel on Audit Effectiveness, *Report and Recommendations*. Stamford, CT: Public Oversight Board, 2000, p. 29.

Database Management Systems Database management (DBM) systems are integrated collections of stored data—a database that is interrelated by means of relationships among data, not by the location of bits of stored data. Among the advantages of database systems is that they avoid unnecessary redundancy in data files. For example, in a college or university, data about a student—such as name, student identification number, address, and telephone number—could be included in several files, among them current semester registration files, tuition files, financial aid files, residence deposit files, vehicle registration files, and library circulation files. A database management system eliminates redundancy by storing relevant data in a single record, which authorized end users can then access with software.

End-User Computing In most PC, LAN, or database management systems, end users access software that is purchased or written by management. However, some entities also use **end-user computing**, in which management authorizes end users to develop task-specific application software. For example, in a mid-size bank served by a local area network, a commercial loan officer might write software to analyze loan-loss risk for the local recreational vehicle industry. End-user computing demands that management implement controls over end-user access to data files that lie beyond the end user's responsibility and authority.

Telecommunications Many entities use **telecommunications** to transmit alphanumeric, voice, video, facsimile, and other data by wire, fiber optics, satellites, or laser. Telecommunications applications offer access to markets, information, and transactions not otherwise accessible by other information systems. A variety of telecommunications links are used commonly, including *electronic data interchange (EDI)* systems that link trading partners (purchasers and sellers) without using paper and without incurring handling costs, *point of sale (POS)* systems in the retail industry that link customers to price and order-entry information, *electronic funds transfer (EFT)* systems in the banking industry, and commercial online databases that offer access to financial news, market price quotations, and credit ratings.

Service Bureaus Service bureaus provide computer services to entities wishing either to supplement limited internal computer capabilities or to outsource processing to outside vendors. For example, a construction contractor might outsource payroll and billing to a service bureau, but process accounts payable in-house. In local area networks and end-user computing, computers are owned or leased by the client and physically housed on-site. However, the use of service bureaus creates an additional problem for auditors: Because an audit client's accounting data are processed through the service bureau's computer, the service bureau's internal controls are part of the client's internal controls. To alleviate the logistical problem of many auditors descending on a single service bureau to consider internal control, large service bureaus commonly engage one independent auditor to report on the service bureau's internal controls, and the auditors of the bureau's customers rely on that report. *Statement on Auditing Standards No. 70,* "Reports on the Processing of Transactions by Service Organizations," provides guidance on preparing and using reports on service bureaus.

Internet Technology Of the information systems discussed, local area networks (LANs) have had the most impact on businesses and therefore on practitioners. However, there is ample reason to believe that LANs, among other information systems, may one day be as obsolete as the 80-column IBM cards of the 1960s. What is at work is the proliferation of technologies designed to service the Internet. For example, PCs and LANs rely on application software that is generally stored within the PC or on file servers. However, the Internet offers a commonly used alternative: import on-demand shared application software using high-speed high-bandwidth lines. Some companies have leveraged the technology into *intra*nets, linking coworkers in applications and communications around the globe. For example, although common today, over a decade ago, Levi Strauss & Co. was among the first to link approximately 10,000 employees worldwide, and Lockheed Martin, an aerospace company, and Merrill Lynch, a brokerage firm, were among the first companies to install intranets.[9] Although technological change is difficult to predict, that there *will be* change is not. The practitioner's task is to stay ahead of the technology curve.

Software for Information Systems Computer software, particularly operating software and application software, controls how computers are used. **Operating software** is a group of computer programs that monitor and control all input, processing, and output operations. For example, many personal computers are operated by Microsoft Windows. In contrast, **application software** interacts with operating software to perform specific tasks, such as processing customer orders, making airline reservations, scanning product codes at grocery checkout counters, or word processing.

Since the 1950s, computer software has matured through several generations of languages. The first generation, called *machine languages*, consisted of simple strings of binary digits (*0s* and *1s* used to represent negative and positive electrical charges). Interestingly, the only language computers understand even today is machine language, although programmers now write software in higher generation languages that translate commands into machine language. The second generation, *assembly languages*, originated in the 1950s and consisted of symbolic codes translated by assemblers into machine-readable form. Developed in the 1960s, third-generation *procedural languages* were designed to meet application requirements in specific professions—for example, FORTRAN (for "formula translation") in the sciences and COBOL (for "common business oriented language") in business. A number of computer applications used today were written using third-generation languages.

Fourth-generation languages (sometimes called *4GLs*) focus not on *how* a task ought to be performed (the role of first-, second-, and third-generation languages), but on *what is to be done*, and they create at least one distinct advantage for the programmer: significantly fewer lines of code than earlier languages, often as few as one-tenth the number of lines. Today, 4GLs are user-friendly, easy to learn, easy to debug, and readily accessible by nonprofessionals. A fifth generation of computer languages draws from stored knowledge bases (like tax laws or accounting rules) and accomplishes intelligent tasks (that is, artificial intelligence). While it is

---

9   S. Zarowin, "The New Computer," *Journal of Accountancy* (March 1996), pp. 51–52.

not altogether necessary for an auditor to understand computer languages, it is helpful to have a general understanding of developments that affect the processing of accounting information, since they have implications for an entity's internal controls.

Review "Section 404 Documentation"

Under the SEC's *Final Rule: Management's Reports on Internal Control Over Financial Reporting*, management is obligated—they *must*—accept responsibility for the effectiveness of internal control. Management must evaluate effectiveness objectively and thoroughly, support the evaluation with documentation, and prepare a written assessment as of the end of the fiscal year that maps to the documentation. If the auditor judges that management has not accepted responsibility, he or she must communicate to the board of directors (and management) in writing that an audit of internal control over financial reporting cannot be completed satisfactorily and that the auditor must disclaim an opinion.

Management's documentation—called, in practice, the "404 documentation" (after the *Sarbanes-Oxley Act*, Section 404)—memorializes management's process for assessing the effectiveness of internal control over financial reporting. Obtaining an understanding of management's assessment process contemplates that the auditor review the Section 404 documentation and arrange the review around a number of questions—among them, did management:

- Document and test controls over initiating, recording, processing, and reporting significant accounts and assertions, the selection and application of accounting principles, fraud prevention, accounting estimates, unusual transactions, and end-of-period adjusting entries?
- Evaluate the effectiveness of controls and the likelihood of failure and misstatement?
- Communicate findings fully to the auditor?
- Reach an assessment that the documentation supports?

The form of management's documentation varies in practice—there is no generally accepted template. For example, one Fortune 100 company's proprietary Section 404 documentation includes PowerPoint slides listing management's assessment process, an inventory of direct responsibilities across organizational levels for individual financial statement assertions, exhaustive flowcharts, detailed narrative descriptions, extensive tests of documents and procedures, key control descriptors, and fulsome explanations of control gaps and deficiencies. An audit of management's assessment of internal control over financial reporting demands that management's Section 404 documentation be insightful, rigorous, probative, and complete. If the documentation is inadequate—for example, if the documentation lacks adequate testing, or fails to support management's assessment—the auditor is obligated to communicate in writing to the audit committee and management that he or she cannot complete the audit of internal control and, therefore, will disclaim an opinion on internal control over financial reporting.

Document System and Identify Transaction Cycles

To document an entity's internal controls, an auditor relies on discussions with client personnel and reviews accounting records, employee procedures manuals, and documentation the client prepares. For example, an auditor might interview the chief financial officer, internal auditors, and employees responsible for particular accounting functions (for example, the manager of accounts receivable and his or her employees); review organization charts and transaction documentation (for example, purchase orders, receiving reports, and vendor invoices); and consult the client's procedures manuals to confirm the procedures discussed or observed. The documentation need pertain specifically to controls that monitor operations, financial reporting, and compliance with laws and regulations, not necessarily every control management has implemented. For example, the documentation should serve the auditor's needs, which are to understand the flow of transactions, identify where in the flow that misstatements could occur (what errors or frauds could occur), and identify the controls that management has implemented (what control activities could prevent or detect the errors or frauds).

In practice today, auditors document an entity's internal controls using, for example, narrative memoranda, flowcharts, and questionnaires. A **narrative memorandum** is a written description of a particular phase or phases of an accounting system. Figure 8-5 illustrates a narrative description for a company's cash collections on credit sales. Although useful for describing uncomplicated systems, narratives may be inappropriate when a system is complex or revised frequently. A **flowchart** consists of interrelated symbols that diagram the flow of transactions and events through a system. Flowcharts are powerful in the sense that they can capture the complexity of a system succinctly, allowing the auditor to focus sharply on key controls within the system. On the other hand, using flowcharts can be an overreaction when a system is routine, as, for example, in a small owner-managed company. Figure 8-6 flowcharts the system described in narrative form in Figure 8-5. Note, though, that in practice an auditor would not use both a narrative description and a flowchart to document the same system or class of transactions; rather, one or the other would be used.

FIGURE 8-5: *Narrative Description of Accounting System*

The Wilson Company
Memorandum: Cash Collections on Credit Sales
December 31, 2007

Two departments are involved in the cash collection function: the Mail Room and Cash Receipts. In the Mail Room, envelopes containing remittance advices and the customers' checks are opened. Each check is restrictively endorsed, and a mail room employee prepares two copies of a list of the day's receipts. Copy 1 of the list of receipts and all remittance advices are forwarded to Accounts Receivable for posting; Copy 2 and all checks are forwarded to Cash Receipts.

In Cash Receipts, Copy 2 of the list of receipts and the checks are used to prepare a bank deposit slip and two copies of a cash summary sheet, and to update cash records. Checks and the deposit slip are hand carried to the First National Bank for deposit, and Copy 1 of the cash summary is forwarded to Accounts Receivable and General Accounting for recording. Copy 2 of the cash summary and Copy 2 of the list of receipts are filed in Cash Receipts.

BLK 9/30/07

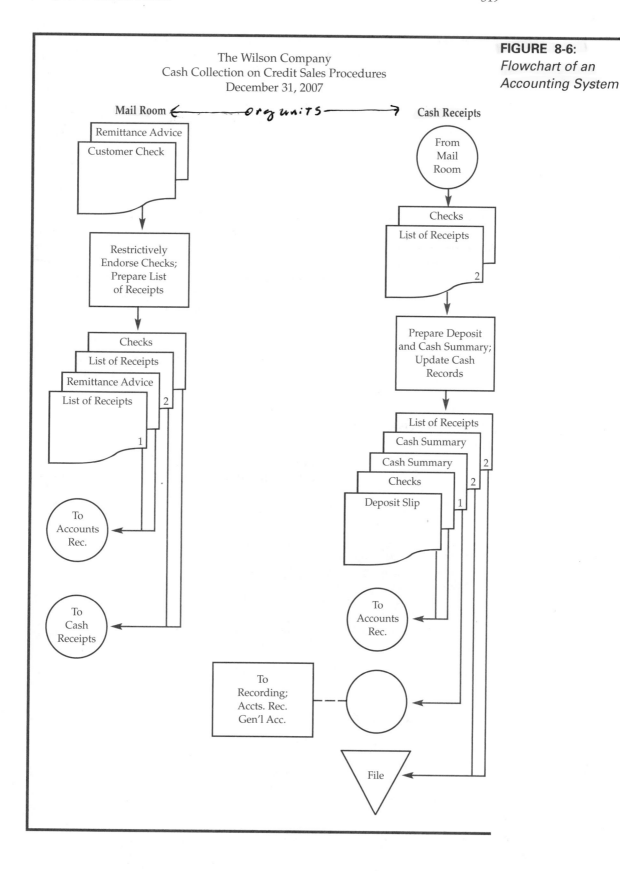

The Wilson Company
Cash Collection on Credit Sales Procedures
December 31, 2007

Mail Room ←———— *org units* ————→ Cash Receipts

FIGURE 8-6:
Flowchart of an Accounting System

An internal control **questionnaire** consists of a series of questions designed to detect control deficiencies. Questionnaires require *Yes, No,* or *Not Applicable (N/A)* responses: *Yes* responses suggest satisfactory control conditions, and *No* responses signal potential significant deficiencies that could lead to errors, frauds, or illegal acts. Figure 8-7 illustrates an internal control questionnaire related to the cash collection procedures described in narrative form in Figure 8-5 and flowcharted in Figure 8-6. Note that the internal control questionnaire in Figure 8-7 indicates one *No* response and therefore suggests one potential deficiency: that "cash collection employees are not bonded," which means that the company is not insured against losses from employees who misappropriate cash receipts. Questionnaires can be adapted to almost any system, since they usually contain questions about many conceivable potential deficiencies, thereby increasing the likelihood of detection. On the other hand, questionnaires can result in unreliable documentation, since client employees may respond inaccurately to questions asked by the auditor. This may occur particularly when an employee attempts to provide the expected answer or responds to questions that should be directed to other employees. To avoid inaccurate responses, an auditor should attempt to verify responses with supervisory personnel and with the entity's procedures manual.

Of course, an auditor could use any combination of narratives, flowcharts, and/or questionnaires to document an entity's internal controls, thereby maximizing the advantages of each. For example, an auditor might decide to flowchart

FIGURE 8-7: *Questionnaire*

The Wilson Company
Cash Collection on Credit Sales
December 31, 2007

Question	Answer: Yes, No, or N/A	Remarks	Performed by
1. Are mail receipts opened by personnel independent of shipping, billing, sales invoice processing, and recording?	yes		BLK
2. Are checks restrictively endorsed immediately upon opening the mail?	yes		
3. Are lists of receipts prepared when all mail receipts are opened?	yes		
4. Are checks forwarded promptly to personnel responsible for preparing bank deposits?	yes		
5. Are checks deposited daily?	yes		
6. Are cash summaries prepared and forwarded to recording?	yes		
7. Are all employees who handle cash adequately bonded?	no	cash collection employees are not bonded	

the major aspects of an entity's accounting system and use narratives to describe less important operations.

Because the number and nature of transaction cycles varies from industry to industry and from company to company, an auditor must identify each client's major classes of transactions and the cycles that process them: transaction cycles. Identifying cycles involves five steps:

1. Review account components for homogeneity.
2. Identify representative cycles.
3. Flowchart each cycle, supplementing with narratives and questionnaires as necessary.
4. Trace one or a few representative transactions through each cycle (a transaction walkthrough).
5. Revise flowcharts if necessary.

Every financial statement account has two components: a debit side and a credit side. *Reviewing account components for homogeneity* involves examining the normal business function associated with each major account component. *Transaction cycles are then identified* by components with similar business functions. For example, Accounts Receivable is debited and Sales is credited when resources are distributed to outsiders in exchange for promises of future payments. Likewise, Cash is debited and Accounts Receivable is credited when outsiders pay for resources distributed to them. Because resource distribution and outsiders' payments are both functions of the revenue/receipt cycle, debits to Cash, credits to Sales, and debits and credits to Accounts Receivable are homogeneous account components related to the revenue/receipt cycle, as the following example illustrates:

Revenue/Receipt Cycle

Account	Related Account Component	
	Dr.	Cr.
Cash	x	
Sales		x
Accounts Receivable	x	x

The process of reviewing account components is continued until all major cycles are identified. As noted earlier, a particular business function may be significant enough to represent a cycle by itself; others may justify grouping into one cycle, as in the preceding illustration.

After all major cycles are identified, each can be *flowcharted*, supplementing with narratives and questionnaires as necessary. The flowcharts are pictures of the cycles, and can be invaluable to an auditor in attempting to understand the logic and complexities of an entity's accounting system and control activities. Flowcharts are often far superior to narratives and questionnaires exclusively, since the information for an entire control structure is compressed into so few cycles.

Perform Transaction Walkthroughs

After documenting a client's system—including the review of management's "404 documentation"—the auditor performs transaction walkthroughs. In walkthroughs, the auditor traces a wide range of transactions, both common and uncommon, drawn from each transaction cycle through the entire system—that is, from authorization, to execution, to recording, and to summarization in the financial statements. Walkthroughs, described in *Auditing Standard No. 2* as "required procedures," offer evidence that confirms the auditor's understanding of internal control and, equally important, focuses the auditor's attention on controls that are missing. If transaction walkthroughs isolate differences from the auditor's understanding, or from the client's or the auditor's documentation, the reason for the differences should be resolved and the documentation revised if necessary.

Walking through a "wide range" of transactions contemplates not only high-volume transactions that occur repeatedly throughout the period—say, for example, sales transactions—but also, equally important, end-of-period transactions. For example, in the consumer foods industry, manufacturers and suppliers like Kraft Foods and Frito-Lay have long engaged in a practice called *trade promotion*, which essentially translates to payments suppliers make to distributors and retailers to promote product on the shelves—for example, newspaper coupons and end-isle displays. However, the SEC has accused several suppliers of inducing distributors and retailers at quarter end with unusually high trade promotions, thereby inducing incremental end-of-quarter shipments that overload distributors and retailers with low-cost inventory, but spike the manufacturers' earnings to meet analysts' expectations.[10] During transaction walkthroughs auditors are obligated to understand controls over end-of-period financial reporting, particularly for transactions that increment earnings. For example, on trade promotion in the consumer foods industry, the auditor could investigate controls that enable salespersons to authorize trade promotion and controls over returns in the weeks following the end of the quarter.

Identify Controls That Are Potentially Reliable

From information gathered by documenting the system, an auditor evaluates whether the entity's control activities can be relied on in assessing control risk below the maximum. If an entity's control activities are not suitably designed to justify reliance, the auditor would not perform tests of controls and therefore would discontinue considering the internal controls, assess control risk at the maximum level, and plan an audit approach that relies heavily on substantive tests. However, relying on substantive tests exclusively can be problematic for at least two reasons: First, in companies that process evidence electronically through *electronic data interchange (EDI)* or *image processing systems*, the auditor may not be able to reduce detection risk to an acceptable level by substantive tests alone, since there is a risk that evidence may be altered. Rather, the auditor could perform tests of controls to support an assessed level of control risk, for example, for the completeness or occurrence assertions only. Second, lacking reason to justify reliance raises serious doubt that management could conclude, under the *Sarbanes-Oxley Act*, Section 404, that internal control over financial reporting is effective.

Assuming that control activities are suitably designed and potentially reliable in assessing control risk below the maximum, and that management could con-

---

10 S. Ellison and S. Kilman, "SEC Expands Food Industry Probe: Kraft, Dean, and Frito-Lay Could Face Civil Lawsuit in Revenue-Inflation Case," *The Wall Street Journal* (March 16, 2003), p. A3. `

clude reasonably that internal control over financial reporting is effective, the auditor would continue to consider internal control as follows.

Assess Control Risk

Control risk, introduced in Chapter 2, is the risk that a material misstatement could occur in the financial statements and not be prevented or detected on a timely basis by the entity's internal controls. The auditor's role is to assess control risk for relevant assertions related to each significant account balance or transaction class, but the auditor need not assess every assertion for every account balance or transaction class, since some assertions may not be significant for a particular account. For example, the rights and obligations assertions may not be relevant for an entity's investment in an unconsolidated subsidiary.

To determine an assessed level of control risk, the auditor:

- Considers the *errors or frauds that could occur* and that could result in misstatements in the financial statements,
- Identifies relevant *control activities* designed to prevent or detect the errors or frauds, and
- Performs *tests of controls* on the control activities that may prevent or detect the errors or frauds.

Consider Errors or Frauds That Could Occur and Relevant Control Activities

For each major transaction cycle, an auditor considers the errors or frauds that could occur and then identifies control activities that could serve either to prevent or to detect the errors or frauds. In view of the concept of reasonable assurance, introduced earlier, an auditor must have a general understanding of how employees could make errors or intentionally commit and conceal frauds. The risk of undetected errors or frauds can be affected by a number of situations that need exist only occasionally to result in material misstatements, such as:

- Transactions are not authorized.
- Transactions are approved but do not conform to what is authorized.
- Tangible assets, blank forms, accounting records, or passwords are exposed to unauthorized access.
- Tangible assets written off are exposed to unauthorized use or disposal.
- Accounting policies are not formally authorized and documented, or financial presentations do not conform to authorized policies.

Any of these situations can present opportunities for intentional frauds and therefore should be considered by an auditor when evaluating control effectiveness. However, to commit and conceal a fraud, an employee needs access both to assets and to records: Access to assets is needed to commit a fraud, and access to records is needed for concealment.

After considering the types of errors or frauds that could occur, the auditor next considers control activities that management has implemented to detect or prevent the errors or frauds. For example, an auditor might identify the following potential error or fraud and related control activities for cash receipts transactions.

Example of an Error or Fraud That Could Occur	*Examples of Controls Designed to Prevent or Detect the Error or Fraud*
• Cash receipts on credit sales could be lost or diverted, potentially resulting in overstated receivables and unrecorded cash.	• Establish the cash receipts function in a centralized location. • Require daily reconciliation of cash receipts records with bank deposit slips. • Prepare list of cash receipts in the mail room. • Establish periodic procedures for reconciling cash records with bank statements.

The auditor would then apply tests of controls to each relevant control activity in order to assess control risk for the financial statement assertions related to account balances or transaction classes that may contain the identified errors or frauds.

Perform Tests of Controls

In a financial statement audit, **tests of controls** consist of audit procedures directed toward testing the effectiveness of the design or the operation of an internal control policy or procedure. Tests of controls directed toward the *design* of a policy or procedure address one issue:

- Whether the policy or procedure is suitably designed to prevent or detect material misstatements in specific financial statement assertions.

Tests of controls over the *design* of a policy or procedure include inquiring of client personnel, inspecting documents and reports, and observing employees performing the policy or procedure. For example, to control cash admission receipts in a movie theater, a client may require that one employee receive cash and dispense tickets and another employee collect ticket stubs as patrons enter the theater. To assure that the control is operating as designed, the auditor might attend a movie unannounced, observing the cash and ticket collection functions firsthand.

In contrast, tests of controls directed toward the *operation* of a policy or procedure address three questions:

- Were the necessary control activities performed?
- How were they performed?
- By whom were they performed?

Like tests directed toward the design of a policy or procedure, tests directed toward their operation include inquiries, inspection of documents and reports, and observation, but they also include the auditor reperforming procedures the client performed previously. For example, to determine whether cash receipts are recorded and deposited promptly, an auditor might perform the tests of controls illustrated in Figure 8-8, which require both inspection of documentation and reperformance.

Ideally, tests of controls should be applied to transactions and detailed records that were executed and prepared throughout the entire fiscal year under audit. However, by tradition, auditors often had performed tests of controls at interim, such as September or October for a December 31 year-end engagement, thereby

FIGURE 8-8: *Tests of Controls*

The Wilson Company
Cash Collection and Deposits
December 31, 2007

Program Step   *Performed by*

Collections

1. On a surprise basis, take control of the bank deposit (deposit slip and checks) just before delivery by client personnel to the bank.
2. Compare the total dollar amount of the checks to the total recorded on the deposit slip.
3. Compare the checks (in the deposit package) to details in the cash receipts records and the accounts receivable subsidiary records (for example, customer names and amounts), and determine whether the lapse of time between cash receipt and deposit is reasonable.

Deposits

4. For sample deposits:
   a. Compare the entries in the cash receipts journal with the deposits listed on the monthly statement to determine whether all cash receipts are deposited promptly.
   b. Determine whether cash receipts not listed on the bank statement are listed as deposits in transit in the bank reconciliation and are included with the deposits in the subsequent month's bank statement.
5. Trace the totals in the cash receipts journal to postings in the general ledger.
6. Document any weaknesses or discrepancies.

raising the question of whether additional tests are necessary for the remaining period. In deciding whether to perform tests of controls for the remaining period, an auditor considers:

- The results of tests of controls that were performed at interim.
- Management's responses to inquiries about the remaining period.
- The length of the remaining period.
- The nature and amount of the transactions or balances involved.
- Evidence of the control activities within the remaining period that may be obtained from substantive tests performed by the auditor, by the internal auditors, or by both.

Although these considerations continue to have some basis in fact today, under PCAOB *Auditing Standards No. 2*, an auditor's opinion on internal control over financial reporting is "as of" the last day of the fiscal year, thereby compromising the tradition of completing tests of controls at interim. For example, for a fiscal year ended December 31, the management of a fresh fruit supplier, as a means to assure the accuracy of year-end gross profit, may implement a control that monitors the cost of early January product returns unknown at December 31. The control doesn't operate until *after* December 31, necessitating that the auditor apply tests of controls after December 31, since the language in the auditor's opinion on internal control would demand no less. Owing to their responsibility to issue an opinion "as of" the last day of the fiscal year, auditors perform some tests of controls after year end (the example above), and vary from year to year the timing (and the nature and extent) of tests of controls.

When performing tests of controls, an auditor may find differences between what was expected and what actually occurred. For example, a vendor's invoice may have been paid without the accounts payable manager's initials of approval. Such differences are appropriately called *exceptions*, *deviations*, or *occurrences*, rather than errors, because an exception does not necessarily mean that an error had been made in the accounting records. For example, the fact that a vendor's invoice lacks approving initials does not necessarily mean that the invoice should not have been paid.

Auditors rarely examine *all* of the transactions and detailed records related to the controls tested. Rather, the auditors more often select samples from the population of all available transactions or records for the period. Audit sampling in tests of controls is discussed in Chapter 9.

Computer-Assisted Tests of Controls In fully automated computer systems, the nature of an auditor's tests of controls depends on whether audit evidence generated by the computer is:

- External to the computer, and therefore directly observable, or
- Internal to the computer, and therefore not directly observable.

Tests of controls involving *external, directly observable audit evidence* usually take the form of (1) inquiries, (2) observation, and (3) inspection of documents. Figure 8-9 illustrates tests of computer controls when audit evidence can be observed directly by the auditor. For example, the first general control listed in Figure 8-9 is "Segregate computer department and users," and the tests listed for this control include corroborative inquiries of computer personnel, management, and operating employees; observation of actual operations; and inspection of documentary evidence such as management reports and organization charts.

In contrast, tests of controls involving *internal, unobservable audit evidence* require that an auditor use the computer to obtain a reasonable degree of assurance that controls are operating as planned. Figure 8-10 on page 331 lists several computer-assisted tests of controls (called *computer-assisted audit techniques: CAAT*), any one of which can be used alone or in conjunction with others. Each one approaches tests of controls from a different perspective, though all are designed to provide a basis for determining whether prescribed controls are complied with and operating as planned. Several computer-assisted tests of controls are used commonly as *historical* audit techniques—that is, "cross-sectional" tests that audit computer controls at a point in time. Historical techniques include test data, base case system evaluation, integrated test data, and parallel simulation. Several other computer-assisted tests of controls are used commonly as *continuous* audit techniques—that is, "time series" tests that audit computer controls throughout a period. Continuous techniques include embedded audit modules, systems control audit review files, audit hooks, and transaction tagging.

Test Data An entity's computer system normally uses the client's software to process the client's data on the client's computer—client personnel control all phases

FIGURE 8-9: *Tests of Computer Controls* *observable audit evidence*

Controls	Tests of Controls
General Controls	
Organization and Operation Controls:	
• Segregate computer department and users.	• Make inquiries of personnel and review organization charts and job descriptions for evidence of proper segregation of duties. • Observe actual operations and note the degree of management supervision being exercised. • Discuss with management and operating employees the extent and effectiveness of management supervision. • Review available management reports, studies, or evaluations concerning the operations of the data processing system.
• Provide general authorization over the execution of transactions.	• Review the reconciliation of control totals maintained outside the computer department with the results of computer processing. • Examine available evidence indicating the reconciliations take place in the normal course of operations. • Review preprocessing, processing, and postprocessing controls to determine if they provide for processing in accordance with management's authorization.
• Segregate functions within the computer department.	• Observe computer operations to determine that systems analysts and programmers do not have unrestricted access to hardware, files, or programs. • Review procedures for granting access to programs and data. • Observe the operation of the control group to determine whether it is independent of the systems and programming and processing groups.
Systems Development and Documentation Controls:	
• Participation by user department, accounting personnel, and internal auditors in system design.	• Interview representatives of user departments for evidence of the level of their participation in systems design. • Review appropriate documents and related approvals for evidence that user departments adequately understand input and processing requirements, control requirements, and system output.

(continues)

FIGURE 8-9 *(continued)*

Controls	Tests of Controls
	• Review the extent of internal auditors' involvement in systems design and review their related work papers. • Interview users and computer department personnel about the extent of their involvement in systems design and implementation.
• Review and approval of system specifications.	• Review the computer department's guidelines for systems design. • Review design specifications, seeking written evidence of approval. • Interview management, users, and computer personnel to determine what approval procedures are used.
• Joint system testing by user department and computer personnel.	• Review testing and modification standards, test data, and resulting output for adequacy. • Interview user and computer department personnel to determine test procedures used during implementation. • Process independently prepared test data.
• Final approval over new applications.	• Review evidence of the approval of significant computer accounting applications. • Interview management, users, and computer department personnel involved in the approval process, inquiring about their understanding of the system.
• Control over master file and transaction file conversion.	• Review the computer department's procedures for reconciling files. • Observe conversion procedures and controls. • Test conversions by tracing detailed records from original to updated files and vice versa.
• Approval of computer program changes.	• Interview systems, programming, and processing personnel to determine the procedures for controlling program changes. • Review documentation in support of program changes to determine if changes are properly approved. • Review the results of tests made to verify system changes.

FIGURE 8-9 *(continued)*

Controls	Tests of Controls
• Formal procedures to create and maintain documentation.	• Review documentation standards for adequacy. • Review selected documentation for compliance with prescribed documentation standards.
Hardware Controls: • Controls built into computers by manufacturers.	• Review the computer manufacturer's literature or other sources to determine the available hardware control capabilities. • Review and evaluate available hardware controls. • Determine the potential misstatements that may result from ignored control features.
Access Controls: • Limit access to computer hardware, software, data files, and software support documentation to authorized personnel.	• Review procedures for collecting and analyzing hardware utilization data. • Review selected available hardware utilization logs. • On a test basis, compare hardware utilization logs and processing schedules. • Review procedures for controlling access to programs, data files, and program support documentation. • Review the librarian's method of controlling unauthorized access to programs, data files, and support documentation.
Data and Procedural Controls: • Written procedures and authorization manuals.	• Review procedures manuals, determining whether they provide operators with an understanding of processing requirements. • Observe operations on a test basis, determining whether prescribed procedures are followed.
• Control groups.	• Review the control group's organizational function. • Interview users, computer department personnel, and control group personnel about control group activities. • Review procedures for distributing output to determine that only authorized users receive output. • Review control group working papers and reports to determine the extent and quality of the work.

(continues)

FIGURE 8-9 *(continued)*

Controls	Tests of Controls
of **Application Controls**	

Controls	Tests of Controls
Input Controls:	
• Input authorization and approval.	• Obtain or prepare a list of input transaction sources along with required authorizations. • On a test basis, examine evidence that transactions were properly authorized. • Investigate significant authorization exceptions.
• Code verification.	• Review procedures for verifying identification codes. • On a test basis, trace identification codes to supporting source documents to assure that codes are accurate.
• Data conversion control.	• Review the procedures and techniques for controlling data conversion. • Observe the performance of verification procedures and the processing and disposition of exception listings. • Trace batch totals to control logs on a test basis. • Use a test deck (test data) to test the operations of specific controls.
• Data movement control.	• Review the adequacy of data movement controls. • On a test basis, trace a representative group of transactions through the system from initiation to completion. • Test the reconciliation of key department-to-department or run-to-run totals, reconciling any differences.
• Occurrence correction.	• Review and/or observe the adequacy of procedures for resolving occurrences. • Determine if any occurrences remain unresolved for an unreasonable period of time. • Test representative occurrences for resolution.
Processing Controls:	
• Control totals.	• Review the procedures for generating and reconciling control totals. • Observe the reconciliation process. • Trace control totals to related input totals.
• File labels.	• Review the adequacy of file controls.

FIGURE 8-9 *(continued)*

Controls	Tests of Controls
	• Determine how selected occurrences were resolved.
• Limit (reasonableness) tests.	• Review program support documentation for available limit tests. • Review representative output for evidence that limit tests are applied. • Use auditor-prepared test data to test the accuracy of limit tests.
Output Controls: • Control totals comparisons.	• Review the procedures for comparison. • Observe personnel making comparisons.
• Output distribution.	• Review procedures for controlling output distribution. • Observe output distribution. • Test the distribution of selected output, determining whether recipients are properly authorized.

of processing. However, **test data** shifts control over processing to the auditor by utilizing the client's software to process auditor-prepared test data that includes both valid transactions and invalid transactions. For example, invalid transactions may include unauthorized purchases or sales, transactions with missing data, or transactions for which control totals are wrong. If embedded controls are functioning properly, the client's software should detect all the exceptions planted in the auditor's test data; if not, errors or control overrides are possible, suggesting control risk is at the maximum. However, despite an auditor's proficiency and imagination in designing test data, the approach is totally ineffective if a client does not use the software tested! As a result, an auditor should run test data on a

FIGURE 8-10: *Computer-Assisted Tests of Controls*   *unobservable audit evidence*

Historical Audit Techniques
- Test data
- Base case system evaluation (BCSE)
- Integrated test data (integrated test facility)
- Parallel simulation

Continuous Audit Techniques
- Embedded audit modules
- Systems control audit review files (SCARFs)
- Audit hooks
- Transaction tagging

surprise basis, if possible, thereby increasing the likelihood of testing software that the client actually uses.

Base Case System Evaluation and Integrated Test Data A special type of test data, **base case system evaluation (BCSE)**, develops test data that purports to test every possible condition that an auditor expects a client's software will confront. BCSE can provide an auditor with much more assurance than test data alone, but is time-consuming (and expensive) to develop and therefore cost effective only in rather large computer systems for which an auditor can rely on internal auditors to develop the base case. Yet another type of test data, **integrated test data** (sometimes called an *integrated test facility: ITF*) improves on test data by providing a vehicle for testing whether a client actually uses the software that the auditor tests. Unlike test data, which is run independent of client data, an ITF integrates fictitious data with actual client data without management's knowledge, allowing the auditor to compare the client's output with the results expected by the auditor. Because management is unaware of integrated test data, fictitious data must be removed from the client's records by journal entry or by program commands prior to compiling financial reports. When processed throughout the year, integrated test data provides assurance that the software tested is actually used to compile financial reports.

Parallel Simulation Roughly the opposite of test data, **parallel simulation** shifts control over computer software—rather than data—to the auditor. Thus, in parallel simulation, an auditor prepares software to process the client's data on the client's or the auditor's computer. If an entity's controls have been operating effectively, the client's software should generate the same exceptions as the auditor's software. The potential for control override is suggested when a client's software fails to detect exceptions detected by the auditor's software. Importantly, parallel simulation provides auditors with independence from client computer personnel in that software is prepared by the auditor rather than the client. However, much like test data, parallel simulation provides no assurance that the client's software is actually used throughout the entire year to process all data. Thus, parallel simulation should be performed on a surprise basis (or throughout the year) if possible.

Embedded Audit Modules and Systems Control Audit Review Files **Embedded audit modules** differ from integrated test data (ITD) in that ITD actually integrates fictitious data with the client's data, whereas audit modules are used to select client data for subsequent testing and analysis. For example, an auditor could place an accounts receivable confirmation module within an entity's monthly billing program. When desired, the audit module would be activated by the auditor, used to select customer accounts for confirmation, and commanded to print the confirmation. Embedded audit modules are sometimes used to create what are called **systems control audit review files (SCARFs)**, logs that collect transaction information for review subsequently by the auditor.

Audit Hooks and Transaction Tagging In general, **audit hooks** are "exits" in an entity's software that allow an auditor to insert commands for audit processing. That is, at appropriate points in the client's software, audit hooks allow an auditor to modify the software by inserting specific commands to accumulate totals or otherwise manipulate data for audit purposes. Of course, the use of audit hooks depends on whether an entity's software includes appropriate exit points, which are often built into software packages written by software vendors. Auditors sometimes use audit hooks to accomplish **transaction tagging**, in which a transaction record is "tagged" and then traced through critical control points in the information system.

In practice, auditors apply both the manual tests of controls illustrated in Figure 8-8 and the computer-assisted tests of controls listed in Figure 8-10. However, the objective of both manual and computer-assisted tests of controls is to help the auditor assess control risk and, applied properly, both are equally powerful.

Control Risk and Information Technology

Information technology has improved exponentially the reliability of processed transactions. For example, management can reasonably expect that all transactions processed by computer are processed alike. However, as illustrated by the examples in Figure 8-11, information technology also can affect control risk in ways that manually processed transactions cannot. Computers eliminate human processing errors, such as computational mistakes, thereby eliminating the likelihood of random error attributed for example to employee fatigue. Computers also increase the likelihood of systematic error attributed to unintentional software error, such as lines of code that mistakenly import obsolete unit prices. To assess risk attributed to systematic error, auditors may focus attention on software that processes repetitive, but potentially material, transactions.

FIGURE 8-11: *Risks in Information Technology*

Systematic Error	Computers eliminate human error (for example, human processing errors), but systematically process software errors unintentionally.
Audit Trails	Computers distort or eliminate paper source documents and records that otherwise provide a trail of evidence supporting recorded transactions.
Remote Access	Computers can be accessed from remote sites with unauthorized passwords.
Data Loss	Computer information can be destroyed instantaneously by an unprotected virus, sabotage, or power loss.

Traditional definitions of a "document"—say, for example, "a written piece of paper that furnishes evidence"—have been challenged as more and more entities resort to electronic document management (EDM) systems that create, process, and store evidence electronically. EDM systems reduce the cost of creating evidence (for example, paper costs decline) and storing evidence (for example, filing costs decline). However, as discussed earlier in the chapter, EDM also obscures or eliminates the audit trail, since source documents and records are unavailable to support recorded transactions. To assess the risk attributed to eliminated audit trails, auditors may coordinate with management to access live transactions from remote sites throughout the year audited. Although an advantage to the auditor, remote access can influence control risk, since perpetrators with unauthorized access to passwords and user IDs could alter or eliminate files and software.

Although not necessarily peculiar to information technology, computer information can be lost or destroyed instantaneously by an unprotected virus, loss of power, vandalism, or fraud. To control the risk of *data loss*, many companies have implemented disaster recovery plans ranging from quick-fix off-site storage sites to fully functional alternate processing facilities.

Identify Significant Deficiencies and Material Weaknesses in Internal Control

Largely through tests of controls—but also through observation, inquiries, confirmation, and comparisons done *throughout* an engagement—an auditor becomes aware of **internal control deficiencies**. Deficiencies are controls that do not allow management or employees to prevent or detect misstatements in the normal course of business. In practice, internal control deficiencies appear either in the design or in the operation of a control. A deficiency in *design* occurs when a control has not been implemented. For example, lacking a control to prevent salespersons from offering unauthorized side agreements (say, granting rights to wholesalers to return unsold product), management risks violating FASB *Statement of Financial Accounting Standards No. 48*, "Revenue Recognition When a Right of Return Exists," which would require that revenue be deferred until wholesalers sell products at retail. In contrast, a deficiency in *operation* occurs when a control has been designed but, owing for example to lax implementation, is not effective. For example, management may have implemented a control that requires sales terms be approved in advance by a manager who fails to comply consistently.

Internal control deficiencies are at the center of gravity in an audit of internal control over financial reporting, since the deficiencies may be significant, and significant deficiencies may be weaknesses in internal control. The auditor's task is to judge whether an internal control deficiency is a significant deficiency, and then to judge whether the significant deficiency is a material weakness according to this script: A **significant deficiency** is a deficiency that, alone or in combination with other deficiencies, adversely affects the ability to initiate, record, process, or report reliably in accordance with generally accepted accounting principles and, more to the point, is *more than remotely likely* to cause a *more than inconsequential misstatement* that will not be prevented or detected. Worse, a **material weakness in internal control** over financial reporting is a significant deficiency that, alone or in combination with other deficiencies, is *more than remotely likely* to cause *a material misstatement* that will not be prevented or detected. In short, both significant deficiencies and material weaknesses are associated with misstatements, but in different orders of magnitude: A significant deficiency is more than remotely likely to cause a more than inconsequential misstatement, and a material weakness is more than remotely likely to cause a material misstatement.

To illustrate the distinction between a significant deficiency and a material weakness, assume tests of controls reveal that, for a sample of 40 cash disbursements, 8 failed to have the approval initials of the accounts payable manager before payment, a control activity implemented by management to assure that only approved invoices are paid. Clearly, a significant deficiency. But, a material weakness? In this case, assume management has implemented a compensating control, which provides that the chief operating officer's manual signature appear beneath the chief executive officer's facsimile signature on all checks exceeding $5,000. If for all 8 deviations the manual signature appears on the check and the auditor concludes all 8 are bona fide disbursements, then the significant deficiency would not be a material weakness since, although significant, the evidence suggests that the deficiency is less than remotely likely to cause a material misstatement.

Assessing Control Risk: Further Considerations

The task of assessing control risk involves a judgment about whether to assess control risk at the maximum (in quantitative terms, 100 percent) or below the maximum for relevant financial statement assertions. An auditor assesses control risk from his or her understanding of the internal controls in general, and from evidence obtained by tests of controls in particular. The assessment is at the level of control risk for financial statement *assertions* related to the account balances and transaction classes the internal controls processed, not at the level of financial statement accounts. For example, do assets exist, have transactions occurred, are assets and liabilities valued properly? If control risk is low—that is, the controls can be expected to prevent or detect aggregate errors in excess of the auditor's planned materiality—then the auditor may restrict the extent of substantive tests of account balances, although not below a level sufficient to reduce audit risk to an amount the auditor judges appropriate for issuing an opinion on financial statements.

Audit documentation supporting the assessed level of control risk will vary depending on whether the risk is assessed at the maximum or below. When control risk is assessed at the maximum, the auditor needs only to document the assessment—for example, "control risk for the rights and obligations assertion related to receivables is assessed at the maximum"—but not the basis for the assessment. However, when control risk is assessed below the maximum, the auditor does not need to document the specific level below maximum (for example, slightly below maximum, moderate, low), but he or she should document the basis for the assessment, such as the documented results of relevant tests of control. Generally, the lower the level of control risk an auditor desires, the more assurance he or she will require from evidence obtained in tests of controls.

The auditor assesses control risk for financial statement assertions related to the account balances and transaction classes that the internal controls process, and tests and evaluates the design and operating effectiveness of controls over financial reporting. If control risk is low—that is, the controls can be expected to prevent or detect aggregate errors in excess of the auditor's planned materiality—then the auditor may restrict the extent of substantive tests of account balances, although not below a level sufficient to reduce audit risk to an amount the auditor judges appropriate for issuing an opinion on financial statements. Finally, the auditor determines an acceptable detection risk to plan substantive tests of account balances and forms an opinion on internal control over financial reporting. The auditor's *consideration* of internal control under the second of field work and *audit* of internal control over financial reporting under PCAOB *Auditing Standard No. 2* is not a substitute for substantive tests of details. Rather, tests of controls and substantive tests complement each other.

Reducing Control Risk Further

On occasion, an auditor may want to reduce further the assessed level of control risk—that is, below the level indicated by completed tests of controls—in order to reduce even further the extent of substantive tests to be applied to year-end account balances. In such cases, additional tests of controls are necessary. However, the additional tests would be performed only if the auditor believes evidential matter is available to support a further reduction and if the expected effort to perform additional tests is likely to result in less audit effort for substantive tests.

Plan the Nature, Timing, and Extent of Substantive Tests and Form Opinion on Internal Control Over Financial Reporting

Determine Detection Risk and Design Substantive Tests

After considering the assessed level of control risk (and inherent risk) for financial statement assertions, the auditor next determines the nature, timing, and extent of substantive tests necessary to *restrict detection risk to an acceptable level*. As explained in Chapter 2, control risk and detection risk are inversely related: As the assessed level of control risk *increases*, the acceptable level of detection risk *decreases*. Correspondingly, in planning substantive tests an auditor would perform *more* persuasive tests, perform tests at the *balance sheet date* rather than at interim dates, and would test *more* extensively. In contrast, as the assessed level of control risk *decreases*, the acceptable level of detection risk *increases*. Correspondingly, in planning substantive tests an auditor would perform *less* persuasive tests, perform tests at the *interim dates* rather than at the balance sheet date, and would test *less* extensively. Figure 8-12 depicts the relationship between detection risk and the nature, timing, and extent of substantive tests. However, regardless of how low the assessed level of control risk, the acceptable level of detection risk could never be so high as to preclude the need for any substantive tests at all. The auditor always performs some substantive tests—for example, analytical procedures—for all significant account balances and transactions.

Forming an Opinion and Reporting on Internal Control Over Financial Reporting

For decades, the profession argued the advisability of *mandatory* public reporting on internal control. In the 1970s and 1980s, the main players in the debate were the

FIGURE 8-12: *Relationship of Detection Risk to the Nature, Timing, and Extent of Substantive Tests*

Effect of Detection Risk	*Acceptable Level of Detection Risk*	
	Lower	*Higher*
Nature of substantive tests	Should use more persuasive tests (for example, confirmations from independent parties)	Could use less persuasive tests (for example, rely on documentation within the entity)
Timing of substantive tests	Perform tests at balance sheet date	Perform tests at interim dates
Extent of substantive tests	Test more extensively (for example, increase sample size)	Test less extensively (for example, decrease sample size)

SEC (which favored mandatory reports) and the AICPA (which didn't).[11] And in the 1990s, two new players weighed in: the Commission on Fraudulent Financial Reporting (the Treadway Commission) and the U.S. General Accounting Office, whose pointed disagreement appeared in an exchange of letters published in the *Journal of Accountancy*.[12] In fact, through 2003, only the *FDIC Improvement Act of 1991*, a response to the savings and loan debacle of the 1980s, required public reports—from federally insured banks and thrifts with assets exceeding $150 million. Only about one in four public companies reported voluntarily otherwise. However, effective 2004, the *Sarbanes-Oxley Act of 2002* put the debate to bed for public companies.

To form an opinion on management's assessment of internal control over financial reporting, the auditor evaluates reports issued by internal auditors, significant deficiencies, and the results of tests of controls *and* substantive tests of details, since the opinion will be dated as of the last day of field work and cover a period through the last day of the fiscal year. The auditor's opinion hinges on whether he or she judges that a significant deficiency, alone or in combination with others, constitutes a material weakness in internal control. If the auditor detects no material weaknesses (and the scope of the auditor's work has not been limited), he or she issues an unqualified opinion. Figure 8-13 illustrates the language of an unqualified opinion. Notice that the report:

- Acknowledges in the *introductory paragraph* that the effectiveness of internal control is marked to criteria established in the *COSO Report*, that management is responsible for assessing the effectiveness of internal control over financial reporting, and that the auditor expresses an opinion on management's assessment.
- Explains in the *definition paragraph* that internal control over financial reporting is a process and that internal control pertains to the maintenance of records and reasonable assurances that the financial statements comply with generally accepted accounting principles and that unauthorized transactions are prevented.
- Explains in the *scope paragraph* that the audit was conducted in accordance with standards established by the PCAOB.
- Warns in the *inherent limitations* paragraph that internal control over financial reporting may not prevent or detect misstatements, may not be effective in future periods, and may deteriorate.
- Offers in the *opinion paragraph* an opinion that management's assessment that the company maintained effective internal control over financial reporting as of the last day of the fiscal year is fairly stated, in all material respects, based on criteria established, in this case, the *COSO* report.

However, what if there are one or more material weaknesses in internal control over financial reporting? Section 404 (a) of the *Sarbanes-Oxley Act* provides that "Management is not permitted to conclude that . . . internal control over financial reporting is effective if there are one or more material weaknesses. . . ." One

---

11 L. M. Savoie and D. N. Ricchiute, "Reports by Management: Voluntary or Mandatory?" *Journal of Accountancy* (May 1981), pp. 84–94.

12 "The COSO Report: Challenge and Counterchallenge," *Journal of Accountancy* (February 1993), pp. 10–18, reprints two pointed letters exchanged by the GAO, which favored public reporting, and COSO, which did not. The letters bear directly on the debate in the 1990s.

FIGURE 8-13: *Unqualified Opinion on Management's Assessment of the Effectiveness on Internal Control Over Financial Reporting*

Cheever & Yates, LLP
Suite 2600
650 Madison Avenue
New York, NY 10022

March 24, 2008

Audit Committee
Board of Directors
The Wilson Company
15 Artubus Drive
Stony Brook, NY 11790

(Introductory paragraph)
We have audited management's assessment, included in the accompanying Report of the Chief Executive and Financial Officers on the Effectiveness of Internal Control Over Financial Reporting, that The Wilson Company maintained effective internal control over financial reporting as of December 31, 2007, based on criteria established in Internal Control—Integrated Framework issued by the Committee of Sponsoring Organizations of the Treadway Commission (COSO). The Wilson Company's management is responsible for its assessment about the effectiveness of internal control over financial reporting. Our responsibility is to express an opinion on management's assessment based on our audit.

(Definition paragraph)
A company's internal control over financial reporting is a process designed to provide reasonable assurance regarding the reliability of financial reporting and the preparation of financial statements for external purposes in accordance with generally accepted accounting principles. A company's internal control over financial reporting includes those policies and procedures that (1) pertain to the maintenance of records that in reasonable detail accurately and fairly reflect the transactions and dispositions of the assets of the company; (2) provide reasonable assurance that transactions are recorded as necessary to permit preparation of financial statements in accordance with generally accepted accounting principles, and that receipts and expenditures of the company are being made only in accordance with authorizations of management and directors of the company; and (3) provide reasonable assurance regarding prevention or timely detection of unauthorized acquisition, use, or disposition of the company's assets that could have a material effect on the financial statements.

(Scope paragraph)
We conducted our audit in accordance with auditing and related professional practice standards established by the Public Company Accounting Oversight Board. Those standards require that we plan and perform our audit to obtain reasonable assurance about whether effective internal control over financial reporting was maintained in all material respects. Our audit included obtaining an understanding of internal control over financial reporting, testing and evaluating the design and operating effectiveness of internal control, and performing such other procedures as we considered necessary in the circumstances. We believe that our audit provides a reasonable basis for our opinion.

(Inherent limitations paragraph)
Because of its inherent limitations, internal control over financial reporting may not prevent or detect misstatements. Also, projections of any evaluation of effectiveness to future periods are subject to the risk that controls may become inadequate because of

FIGURE 8-13 *(continued)*

changes in conditions, or that the degree of compliance with the policies or procedures may deteriorate.

(Opinion paragraph)
In our opinion, management's assessment that The Wilson Company maintained effective internal control over financial reporting as of December 31, 2007, is fairly stated, in all material respects, based on criteria established in Internal Control—Integrated Framework issued by the Committee of Sponsoring Organizations of the Treadway Commission.

Cheever & Yates, LLP

material weakness, whether detected by management or by the auditor, would drive management to assess internal control over financial reporting is *in*effective, and the auditor to issue an unqualified opinion on management's assessment. In contrast, if in the face of a material weakness, management nevertheless assesses internal control over financial reporting as effective, the auditor would issue an adverse opinion.

A scope limitation imposed by the *client* would cause the auditor to withdraw from the engagement or to disclaim an opinion. In contrast, a scope limitation imposed by the *circumstances* would cause the auditor to withdraw or disclaim, but also may cause the auditor to issue a qualified opinion, depending on the auditor's judgment of the importance of the procedures he or she omitted. For example, an auditor faced with insufficient evidence caused by the unavailability of evidence erased inadvertently from a computer might reasonably issue a qualified opinion. Like an auditor's opinion on management's financial statements, the auditor's opinion on internal control over financial reporting for public companies is included in *Form 10-K*.

Other Assurance Services

Information systems have long been the most important consulting market served by public accounting firms, although never more than in the past decade as a result of developments in **information technology**, including networks, telecommunications, and late-generation programming languages. Interestingly, developments in information technology also have led to new markets for assurance services, several of which firms have entered already. Services offered independently by Verizon Wireless, Deloitte & Touche, and PricewaterhouseCoopers help illustrate.

In the late 1990s, Verizon Wireless marketed a full suite of Internet services designed both for businesses and for consumers.[13] The services include high-speed links to global markets, home page management, and one-button access to search portals. Coincident with Verizon's service, Deloitte & Touche and software developer Gradient Technologies partnered to offer *secure password access* by client

---

13 J. Sandberg, "Bell Atlantic Enters the Internet Arena, Planning Links for Business, Consumers," *The Wall Street Journal* (April 11, 1996), p. B5.

network servers to the Internet,[14] and PricewaterhouseCoopers performed a *privacy audit* for Firefly Network, a Cambridge, Massachusetts, firm that uses intelligent-agent software to profile and shield the privacy of Internet users.[15]

PricewaterhouseCoopers' privacy audit is part of the firm's Internet Assurance Services practice, a line of business that includes data security assurances for companies that trade on the Internet. For example, Narrowline, a Web-based advertising brokerage, links Internet advertising-media suppliers with media buyers to facilitate low-cost purchases of electronic advertising. Narrowline contracted with PricewaterhouseCoopers to perform quarterly assurance services about Narrowline's electronic architecture, thereby adding credibility to the company's control activities over data security, confidentiality, and accountability to suppliers and buyers.[16] The services offered by Verizon, Deloitte & Touche, and PricewaterhouseCoopers point to a growing market for assurance services related to the *security* of information transmitted over the Internet through telecommunications channels that are exposed both to surveillance and to piracy.

The profession's presence in assurance markets is not independent of developments in information technology. For example, a decade ago the AICPA Future Issues Committee observed, "Given the technological developments and our increasing information-based society, CPAs will become more involved with information technology. In order to remain competitive in such an environment, firms will have to acquire access to technological developments. . . . The demands for information management must be met to ensure the profession's continued relevance."[17] Interestingly, the profession's rich history, with information systems in general, and with internal control in particular, offers ample reason to be optimistic about the profession's continued presence. For example, in 1997, the AICPA Special Committee on Assurance Services (the Elliott Committee) suggested several new services that the profession may have a comparative advantage in offering, among them electronic commerce assurance (Chapter 18). However, the *Sarbanes-Oxley Act* restricts auditors from supplying nonaudit services to public companies, a topic that was addressed in Chapter 2.

SUMMARY

Management views internal control rather broadly, its interest being to implement policies and procedures that channel resources toward meeting operations, financial, and compliance objectives. The independent auditor's view of internal control is somewhat narrower, since his or her interest is to issue reports on only a part of the company's interests: management's financial statements and management's assessment of internal control over financial reporting. By necessity, the auditor is concerned with those policies and procedures that affect the assertions embodied within the entity's financial statements (Chapter 6)—the policies and

14 "D&T Pushes Internet/Intranet Security Services," *Public Accounting Report* (March 31, 1996), p. 3.
15 "Coopers & Lybrand Searches for Net Profit,'" *Public Accounting Report* (October 31, 1996), p. 2.
16 "C&L's Net Practice Snares Assurance Client," *Public Accounting Report* (December 15, 1996), p. 3.
17 AICPA Future Issues Committee, *Strategic Thrusts for the Future*, second edition, New York, NY: AICPA, May 1991.

procedures related to management's assertions about existence or occurrence, completeness, rights and obligations, valuation or allocation, and presentation and disclosure.

The design, implementation, and monitoring of internal control—including the control environment, risk assessment, control activities, information and communication, and monitoring—are the responsibilities of management, not the independent auditor. The auditor's responsibility is to obtain an understanding of the internal controls sufficient to plan the audit; to determine the nature, timing, and extent of tests to be performed; and to reach an opinion on management's assessment of internal control over financial reporting. However, significant deficiencies and material weaknesses in internal control should be communicated to the audit committee. Reporting on a public company's internal controls is governed by the *Sarbanes-Oxley Act*, Section 404, "Management Assessment on Internal Controls," regulated by the SEC's *Management's Reports on Internal Control Over Financial Reporting*," and guided by the PCAOB's *Auditing Standard No. 2*, "An Audit of Internal Control Over Financial Reporting Performed in Conjunction with a Financial Statement Audit."

Developments in information technology—among them networks, telecommunications, and later-generation computer languages—have opened new markets for consulting, assurance, and attestation services, and have refocused an auditor's consideration of internal control in a financial statement audit. In turn, developments in our understanding of internal control, in particular COSO's four-volume *Internal Control: Integrated Framework*, have altered the way that management and the independent auditor consider internal control.

KEY TERMS

Accounting system 306
Application software 316
Audit hooks 332
Audit trail 305
Base case system evaluation (BCSE) 332
Collusion 304
Control activities (procedures) 303
Control environment 302
Database management (DBM) systems 315
Embedded audit modules 332
End-user computing 315
Flowchart 318
Information technology 339
Integrated test data 332
Internal control 300
Internal control deficiency 334

Internal control over financial reporting 301
Local area networks (LANs) 314
Material weakness in internal control 334
Narrative memorandum 318
Operating software 316
Parallel simulation 332
Questionnaire 320
Segregation of duties 304
Significant deficiency 334
Systems control audit review files (SCARFs) 332
Telecommunications 315
Test data 331
Tests of controls 324
Transaction cycles 307
Transaction tagging 333

REFERENCES

Professional Standards:

PCAOB Auditing Standard No. 2, "An Audit of Internal Control Over Financial Reporting Performed in Conjunction with a Financial Statement Audit."

AICPA, *Codification of Auditing Standards*. New York: AICPA.

SAS No. 55, "Consideration of the Internal Control Structure in a Financial Statement Audit" (AU Sec. 319).

SAS No. 60, "Communication of Internal Control Related Matters Noted in an Audit" (AU Sec. 325).

SAS No. 70, "Reports on the Processing of Transactions by Service Organizations" (AU Sec. 324).

SAS No. 78, "Consideration of the Internal Control in a Financial Statement Audit: An Amendment to SAS No. 55."

SAS No. 87, "Restricting the Use of an Auditor's Report" (AU Sec. 532).

SAS No. 94, "The Effect of Information Technology on the Auditor's Consideration of Internal Control in a Financial Statement Audit" (AU Sec. 319).

SSAE No. 2, "Reporting on an Entity's Internal Control Structure Over Financial Reporting."

SSAE No. 6, "Reporting on an Entity's Internal Control Over Financial Reporting. An Amendment to SSAE No. 2."

Professional Reports:

AICPA, *Auditing Procedure Study: Audit Implications of Electronic Document Management*. New York: AICPA, 1997.

Committee of Sponsoring Organizations of the Treadway Commission (COSO), *Internal Control: Integrated Framework*. Evaluation Tools. New York: COSO, 1992.

Committee of Sponsoring Organizations of the Treadway Commission (COSO), *Internal Control: Integrated Framework*. Executive Summary. New York: COSO, 1992.

Committee of Sponsoring Organizations of the Treadway Commission (COSO), *Internal Control: Integrated Framework*. Framework. New York: COSO, 1992.

Committee of Sponsoring Organizations of the Treadway Commission (COSO), *Internal Control: Integrated Framework*. Reporting to External Parties. New York: COSO, 1992.

Public Oversight Board, *Panel on Audit Effectiveness: Report and Recommendations*. Stamford, CT: POB, 2000.

Articles, Books:

Cashell, J. D., "The Effects of SAS No. 55 on Audits of Small Businesses," *Accounting Horizons* (September 1995), pp. 11–25.

Couston, H., L. M. Leinicke, W. M. Rexroad, and J. A. Ostrosky, "Sarbanes-Oxley: What it Means to the Marketplace," *Journal of Accountancy* (February 2004), pp. 43–47.

Helms, G. L., and J. Mancino, "The Electronic Auditor," *Journal of Accountancy* (April 1998), pp. 45–48.

Monk, H. L., Jr., and K. W. Tatum, "Applying SAS No. 55 in Audits of Small Businesses," *Journal of Accountancy* (November 1988), pp. 40–56.

Musaji, Y., *Auditing and Security*. New York: John Wiley & Sons, Inc., 2001.

Tempkin, R. H., and A. J. Winters, "SAS No. 55: The Auditor's New Responsibility for Internal Control," *Journal of Accountancy* (May 1988), pp. 86–98.

Willis, D. M., and S. S. Lightle, "Management Reports on Internal Controls," *Journal of Accountancy* (October 2000), pp. 57—64.

QUESTIONS

1. What advantages do local area networks (LANs) offer over individual personal computers?
2. What advantage does Internet technology offer over local area networks (LANs)?
3. What are the key concepts embodied within the *COSO Report's* definition of internal control?

4. Identify the components of internal control that are integrated within the management process.
5. Briefly explain the components of internal control.
6. Briefly explain management's responsibility for internal control.
7. Why is a formal system of transaction authorization necessary?
8. Which functions must be separated in order to achieve optimum segregation of duties? Why?
9. Briefly explain the concept of reasonable assurance.
10. What is an auditor's objective when obtaining an understanding of an entity's information system?
11. Explain each of the two reports the *Sarbanes-Oxley Act* requires in a public company's Form 10-K on internal control over financial reporting.
12. Identify and indicate the major components of each phase of an auditor's consideration of internal control.
13. What methods can an auditor use to document internal control?
14. What is the purpose of transaction walkthroughs?
15. What key issues do tests of controls address?
16. Briefly describe the process of identifying transaction cycles.
17. How does an auditor determine an assessed level of control risk?
18. In your own words, briefly define what is meant by a "material weakness in internal control."
19. Explain the effect of the inverse relationship between the assessed level of control risk and the acceptable level of detection risk on the nature, timing, and extent of substantive tests.
20. Explain what an auditor communicates to readers in a report on management's assessment of internal control over financial reporting.

MULTIPLE CHOICE QUESTIONS

1. An integrated services digital network is a high-speed line that can be used to:
   a. Access software from a service bureau.
   b. Access software from the Internet.
   c. Enhance the processing capability of local area networks (LANs).
   d. Encourage end-user computing.

2. Information systems that access software from file servers and direct print jobs from print servers are called:
   a. Local area networks (LANs).
   b. Telecommunications channels.
   c. Intranets.
   d. Service bureaus.

3. Matching invoices to receiving reports before preparing a check is an example of:
   a. A preventive control.
   b. A detective control.
   c. An authorization control.
   d. A disbursement control.

4. Which of the following is most closely associated with an entity's control environment?
   a. Assignment of authority and responsibility
   b. The decision to restructure
   c. Controlling unfamiliar risks
   d. The design of documents and records

5. A public accounting firm has issued a report that refers to criteria established in *Internal Control: Integrated Framework* issued by the Committee of Sponsoring Organizations (COSO) of the Treadway Commission. The report likely relates to:

   a. A consulting engagement.
   b. An assurance engagement.
   c. A special engagement.
   d. An audit engagement.

6. As part of a periodic planning exercise, a company discovers that an eastern European political dispute may interfere with supply sources. This is an example of:

   a. Control environment.
   b. Risk assessment.
   c. Control activities.
   d. Monitoring.

7. Internal control should provide reasonable (but not necessarily absolute) assurance, which means that:

   a. Internal control is management's, not the auditor's, responsibility.
   b. An attestation engagement about management's internal control assertions may not necessarily detect all reportable conditions.
   c. The cost of control activities should not exceed the benefits.
   d. There is always a risk that reportable conditions may result in material misstatements.

8. Documents should be:

   a. Prepared in multiple copies.
   b. Explained in a procedures manual.
   c. Included within an audit trail.
   d. Easy to complete.

9. Which of the following statements is an example of an inherent limitation of internal control?

   a. The effectiveness of control activities depends on segregation of duties.
   b. Procedures are designed to assure that transactions are executed as management authorizes.
   c. Errors may arise from mistakes in judgment.
   d. Computers process large numbers of transactions.

10. An auditor considers internal control to:

    a. Determine whether assets are safeguarded.
    b. Suggest improvements in internal control.
    c. Plan audit procedures.
    d. Express an opinion.

11. After obtaining an understanding of internal control, an auditor may assess control risk at the maximum for some assertions because the auditor:

    a. Believes internal control activities are unlikely to be effective.
    b. Determines that internal control is not well documented.
    c. Performs tests of controls to restrict detection risk to an acceptable level.
    d. Identifies control activities that are likely to prevent material misstatements.

    (AICPA Adapted)

12. In an audit of a public company, the auditor's responsibility for internal control does not include:

    a. Considering the effectiveness of the audit committee.
    b. Implementing financial reporting controls.
    c. Assessing control risk.
    d. Issuing an opinion on internal control over financial reporting.

13. After obtaining an understanding of internal control and assessing control risk, an auditor may next:

    a. Perform tests of controls to verify management's assertions that are embodied in the financial statements.
    b. Consider whether to reduce the assessed level of control risk further.
    c. Discontinue searching for reportable conditions.
    d. Evaluate whether control activities can detect material misstatements.

14. The primary purpose of performing tests of controls is to provide reasonable assurance that:

    a. Internal control is effective.
    b. The accounting system is documented accurately.
    c. Transactions are recorded at the amounts executed.
    d. All control activities leave visible evidence.   (AICPA Adapted)

15. Which of the following statements is not true about test data?

    a. Test data should consist only of conditions that interest the auditor.
    b. Only one transaction of each type need be tested.
    c. Test data must consist of all possible valid and invalid conditions.
    d. Test data are processed by the client's software under the auditor's control.

16. Processing data through the use of simulated files provides an auditor with information about the effectiveness of control activities. One of the computer-assisted audit techniques that uses this approach is:

    a. Test data.
    b. Parallel simulation.
    c. Base case system evaluation.
    d. Audit hooks.

17. General controls relate to all computer activities and application controls relate to specific tasks. General controls include:

    a. Controls designed to assure that all data submitted for processing has been properly authorized.
    b. Controls that relate to the correction and resubmission of data that were initially incorrect.
    c. Controls for documenting and approving software and changes to software.
    d. Controls designed to assure the accuracy of the processing results.

18. Which of the following computer-assisted audit techniques allows fictitious and real transactions to be processed together without client personnel being aware of the testing process?

    a. Parallel simulation
    b. Integrated test data
    c. Audit hooks
    d. Audit modules

19. As the assessed level of control risk decreases:

    a. The assessed level of inherent risk increases.
    b. The extent of substantive tests of details decreases.
    c. The acceptable level of detection risk increases.
    d. The assessed level of audit risk decreases.

20. An auditor has detected one material weakness in internal control over financial reporting. The auditor's report would carry a(an):

    a. Unqualified opinion.
    b. Qualified opinion.
    c. Adverse opinion.
    d. Disclaimer of opinion.

PROBLEMS AND DISCUSSION CASES

8-1 *Internal Control Objectives*

An entity's internal controls should be designed to achieve a variety of objectives. Assume that an entity wishes to accomplish the following four control objectives:

1. Transactions should be executed in accordance with management's authorization.
2. Transactions should be recorded as necessary to permit preparation of financial statements in conformity with generally accepted accounting principles and maintain accountability for assets.
3. Access to assets should be permitted only in accordance with management's authorization.
4. The recorded accountability for assets should be compared with the existing assets at reasonable intervals, and appropriate action taken for any differences.

To achieve these objectives, management could institute a number of control activities, including the following:

a. Unused, blank checks are stored in locked safes.
b. A bank reconciliation is prepared monthly by personnel independent of the cash function.
c. Credit approval is required for all new customers and for all credit purchases over $10,000.
d. Accounts receivable postings are made from a listing of remittances prepared daily.
e. Perpetual inventory records are updated daily from manufacturing reports.
f. A physical inventory observation is performed monthly.
g. All capital asset acquisitions are reviewed by the board of directors.
h. Only authorized personnel are allowed to enter manufacturing sites.

   Required: For each of the control activities a through h, indicate which objective (1 through 4) is achieved.

8-2 *Controlling Against Concealed Fraud*

An auditor must have a general understanding of how employees could make errors or intentionally commit and conceal fraud. Otherwise, the auditor would be unable to recognize potential deficiencies in internal control and, more importantly, less likely to detect misstatements that are material to the financial statements. Consider the following cases.

Case A

Checks from customers are received by the company's receptionist who stamps each check received with a restrictive endorsement and prepares a list of all funds received and the name of each corresponding customer.

Case B

A company has three accounts payable clerks, each of whom prepare vouchers for payment. Supporting documents, such as receiving reports and bills of lading, are attached to each voucher as backup for the payment request. The vouchers and support are then forwarded to the company's controller for approval and check signing.

Case C

A company maintains a petty cash fund to pay for small, miscellaneous items such as office supplies or postage. The fund is maintained at $500. Whenever funds are disbursed, a signed request form is filed with the remaining cash. One office clerk is designated as the fund's custodian, who makes all withdrawals and reimbursements.

Required: Evaluate each of the cases independently. For each case discuss:
1. How an employee could attempt concealment.
2. What control(s) should be present to prevent concealment.

8-3 *Identifying Business Functions and Transactions Cycles*

You have been assigned to the audit of F&S Savings and Loan Association. In preparing for the audit, you learn the following about F&S.

Total assets approximate $400 million. F&S has a main office downtown, and 13 branch offices throughout the city. Four hundred people are employed by F&S, with a total payroll of $6 million.

F&S derives revenue from two principle sources, the major source being interest and fee income from loans. According to its articles of incorporation, F&S is restricted to making loans only to consumers for purposes such as home mortgages, auto loans, and other personal loans; that is, it cannot make loans to commercial enterprises. The second revenue source is income from investments. F&S invests funds in short-term instruments, such as government securities and certificates of deposit, in order to have a ready source of available funds. Interest earned on investments may or may not be material to earnings, depending on the amount of funds invested during a period.

F&S has two major expenses: administrative costs, such as payroll, building maintenance, utilities, and taxes; and interest paid to depositors. The dollar magnitude of these interest payments varies considerably, depending on current market rates of interest.

Required: Using Figure 8-1 as a guide, identify the major business functions and related transaction cycles for F&S Savings and Loan Association.

8-4 *Objectives and Limitations of Internal Control*

An auditor who has been engaged to audit the financial statements of Ajax Inc. is ready to begin considering Ajax's internal controls.

Required:
1. What are the objectives of internal control?
2. What are the reasonable assurances that internal control provides?
3. What are the inherent limitations of internal control?   (AICPA Adapted)

8-5 *Limitations of, and Communications About, Internal Control*

Apart from assessing control risk, an auditor's consideration of internal control lends insight into inherent limitations and significant deficiencies that ought to be communicated to management under *SAS No. 60*, "Internal Control Structure Related Matters Noted in an Audit."

Required:
1. Describe the inherent limitations an auditor should recognize when considering the potential effectiveness of internal control.
2. Under generally accepted auditing standards, what is the auditor's obligation to communicate significant deficiencies detected while considering internal control?

8-6 *The Auditor's Consideration of Internal Control*

The Committee of Sponsoring Organizations (COSO) *Internal Control: Integrated Framework* defines internal control as a process, effected by an entity's board of directors, management, and other personnel, designed to provide reasonable assurance regarding the achievement of objectives in the following categories: effectiveness and efficiency of operations, reliability of financial reporting, and compliance with applicable laws and regulations.

Required:
1. What is the purpose of the auditor's consideration of a public company's internal controls over financial reporting?
2. What are the objectives of a preliminary evaluation of internal control?
3. How is the auditor's understanding of internal control documented? Discuss the advantages of each type of documentation.
4. What is the purpose of tests of controls?
5. If an auditor is satisfied after considering internal control that no significant deficiencies exist, is it necessary to perform substantive tests of details?

8-7 *The Auditor's Consideration of Internal Control*

Jim Harrison, CPA, is preparing a seminar on internal control for his entry-level professional staff. His predominant concern is to present the staff with an overview of critical issues confronted during an auditor's consideration of internal control under the second standard of field work.

Required: To aid in developing the seminar's materials, Harrison asks you to respond to the following questions:
1. Why and how does an auditor consider internal control?
2. How does an auditor document internal control?
3. How does an auditor identify an entity's relevant transaction cycles?
4. What is the purpose of a transaction walkthrough?
5. After obtaining an understanding, how would an auditor proceed if control activities were not suitably designed to justify reliance?
6. What is the purpose of tests of controls, and what general questions do tests of controls attempt to answer?
7. In tests of controls, what is the difference between an "exception" and an "error"?
8. How does an auditor evaluate internal control from having obtained an understanding of the system and performed tests of controls?

8-8 *Why Do Tests of Controls?*

An in-charge auditor is drafting interim tests of controls for American Optical Company, a nonpublic December 31 year-end optics manufacturer located in Southbridge, Massachusetts. Tests will be performed in mid-September, engage three staff for two weeks each, and, assuming the audit team's tolerable rates of deviation exceed the estimated population rates of deviation, will likely drive the engagement partner to assess control risk below the maximum.

Required: Why bother? Why not simply perform substantive tests of financial statement account balances and disclosures at year end? After all, the firm's opinion will say everything about the financial statements, and nothing about control risk. Discuss.

8-9 *Identifying Weaknesses in Internal Control*

The town of Bullet Park operates a public parking lot near the railroad station for the benefit of town residents. The guard on duty issues annual prenumbered parking stickers to residents who submit an application form and show evidence of residency. The sticker is affixed to the auto and allows the resident to park anywhere in the lot for twelve hours if eight quarters are placed in the parking meter. Applications are maintained in the guard office at the lot. The guard checks to see that only residents are using the lot and that no resident has parked without paying the required meter fee.

Once a week the guard on duty, who has a master key for all meters, takes the coins from the meters and places them in a locked steel box. The guard delivers the box to the town storage building, where the box is opened and the coins are counted by a storage department clerk. The clerk records the total cash counted on a "Weekly Cash Report," which is sent to the town accounting department. The storage department clerk puts the cash in a safe, and on the following day the cash is picked up by the town's treasurer, who recounts the cash, prepares the bank deposit slip, and delivers the deposit to the bank. The deposit slip, authenticated by the bank teller, is sent to the accounting department where it is filed with the "Weekly Cash Report."

Required: Describe deficiencies in the existing system and recommend one or more improvements for each of the deficiencies to strengthen control activities over the parking lot cash receipts.

8-10 *Communicating Deficiencies in Internal Control*

As part of your audit of Call Camper Company, a public company, you are responsible to issue an opinion on internal control over financial reporting. Your document includes management's Section 404 documentation, a completed internal control questionnaire, flowcharts, and spreadsheets summarizing the results of tests of controls. Your tests of controls and substantive tests identify a number of significant deficiencies in internal control; for some of these, corrective action by management is not practical.

Required: Discuss the form and content of the report and the reasons for the report. Do not write a report.

8-11 *Defending a Material Weakness*

Several days prior to completing field work at Ansonia Wire & Cable Co., the engagement partner, Colleen Kelly, discusses with Ansonia's CFO, Alan Rothstein, significant deficiencies that her audit staff detected while considering internal control and that she plans to include within the firm's letter communicating reportable conditions to the board of directors. Kelly reveals five significant deficiencies and explains to Rothstein that one, *approval initials on the face of invoices prior to payment*, is—and will be communicated in the firm's letter as—a material weakness in internal control. Rothstein, visibly upset, argues that the significant deficiency is not a material weakness.

Required: Discuss each of the following:
1. What is Kelly's argument?
2. Why would she care?
3. What is Rothstein's argument?
4. Why would he care?

8-12 *An Auditor's Responsibility to Report on Management's Assessment of Internal Control Over Financial Reporting*

Owing to the *Sarbanes-Oxley Act*, Section 404, "Management Assessment of Internal Controls," auditors are required to issue a report on management's assessment of internal control over financial reporting. Public reporting on internal control had been debated for decades by stakeholders that included the AICPA; the national trade association of certified public accountants; and the SEC, the U.S. government's monitor of integrity in the securities market, but came to fruition as part of Congressional reaction to accounting manipulations reported at the turn of the century.

Required:
1. The following statement in the chapter characterizes the decades-old positions of the SEC and the AICPA on mandatory public reporting on internal control: "the main players in the debate were the SEC (which favored mandatory reports) and the

AICPA (which didn't)." Why do you think the SEC did, and the AICPA did not, favor public reporting on internal control?

2. Explain the conditions under which an auditor would issue an unqualified opinion, qualified opinion, adverse opinion, and disclaimer of opinion on management's assessment of internal control over financial reporting.

8-13 *Deficiencies in Preventive and Detective Controls Documented in Section 404 Documentation*

Management of Sagamore, Inc., a publicly traded automotive parts manufacturer and distributor, has prepared Section 404 documentation for internal controls over the company's financial reporting. The documentation includes detailed flowcharts that identify critical control points linked by reference number to a spreadsheet of deficiencies. The list follows:

a. The payables department is not reviewing all supporting documentation from sales representatives when approving payments for two of the company's ten major chain retailers.

b. There is no signature to validate that authorized managers have reviewed and verified price changes.

c. There is no control in place requiring that accounts receivable personnel review and approve the area district managers' weekly sales-clearing report.

d. There are no records indicating that month-end workman's compensation accruals are approved.

e. The same person who enters changes into the parts-price file also reviews the monthly price activity report.

f. There is no control to review the price list after a price change.

Required: For each of the deficiencies listed, identify whether the deficiency likely would not allow management to *prevent* or to *detect* a misstatement.

8-14 *Significant Deficiencies and Material Weaknesses in Internal Control*

During the course of a financial statement audit, an auditor may become aware of matters relating to the client's internal controls that may be of interest to the client's audit committee or to individuals with an equivalent level of authority and responsibility, such as the board of directors; the board of trustees; or the owner of a middle-market, owner-managed enterprise. Some of these matters may be significant deficiencies and others may be material weaknesses.

Required:
1. What is meant by the terms "significant deficiencies" and "material weaknesses"?
2. What are the auditor's responsibilities to identify and report these matters?

(AICPA Adapted)

8-15 *Internal Control and Computer Systems*

Shannon Bracken, CPA, is considering internal control for the Rumford Company, a December 31 year-end company. Rumford's purchasing, billing, receivables, payables, and job-order cost accounting systems are fully computerized.

Required: Respond to each of the following:
1. Provide an overview of an auditor's consideration of internal control in a computerized system.
2. What is the purpose of an auditor's preliminary review of a computer system?
3. What is the purpose of tests of prescribed computer controls, and what specific questions are addressed by tests of controls?

8-16 *Conversion to Computer Information Systems*

When a company converts from a manual to a computer accounting system, many records and documents become unnecessary and therefore are not prepared. With the audit trail eliminated or distorted, the auditor must focus on controls over computer applications. Consider the following brief description of a manual cash disbursements system:

Purchase invoices are received in the accounting department from the various departments that have purchased goods and services. The accounts payable clerk matches the purchase invoices with supporting documents such as purchase orders, receiving reports, and inventory records. The clerk then prepares a voucher to record a liability for the amount of the purchase. Another clerk schedules the payments due to assure that all discounts for early payment are earned. Five days before the due date, the clerk prepares the documentation and the check, which are submitted to the controller for review and approval.

Required:
1. List and explain areas that could be automated.
2. What controls should be present in the proposed automated system?

8-17 Tests of Controls in Computer Information Systems

During your preliminary review of an entity's computer system, you note the following:

a. Purchase orders initiated by line personnel within the manufacturing plant may be authorized and executed by computer department personnel.
b. Software and data files are maintained in an unlocked filing cabinet in the information systems department. User department personnel are not denied access to the information systems department.
c. Transactions initiated by user departments are usually, but not always, processed, thereby requiring manual processing thereafter.
d. Line personnel sometimes receive weekly paychecks for amounts in excess of normal weekly pay. Overtime is not uncommon, particularly in peak production periods.
e. Transaction files may not be fully posted to updated master files.

Required: For each of the observations, indicate the specific general or application control violated and the test(s) most likely to detect errors.

8-18 Controls in Computer Information Systems

When auditing a computer information system, the independent auditor should have a general familiarity with the effects of using a computer on the various characteristics of control and on the auditor's consideration of internal controls. The independent auditor must be aware of those control activities that are commonly referred to as general controls and those commonly referred to as application controls. General controls relate to all computer activities and application controls relate to specific accounting tasks.

Required:
1. What are the general controls that should exist in computer information systems?
2. What are the purposes of each of the following categories of application controls?
   a. Input controls.
   b. Processing controls.
   c. Output controls.

(AICPA Adapted)

8-19 Controls in Computer Information Systems

Linder Company is completing the implementation of a new computerized inventory control and purchase order system. Linder's controller wants the controls that are incorporated into the software of the new system to be reviewed and evaluated in order to ensure that all necessary controls are included and function properly. The controller respects and has confidence in the department's work and evaluation procedures, but would like a separate appraisal of the control activities by the internal audit department. Hopefully, a review would reveal any deficiencies in control activities and lead to immediate correction before the system is online. The internal audit department carefully reviews controls when evaluating a new system.

Required: Identify the types of controls that should be incorporated in the new software.   (AICPA Adapted)

Internet problems and discussion cases are available at http://ricchiute.swlearning.com

RESEARCH PROJECTS

1. Managing Change in Selected Industries

Of the four volumes in the *COSO Report*, one (Committee of Sponsoring Organizations of the Treadway Commission (COSO), *Internal Control: Integrated Framework*. Evaluation Tools. New York: COSO, 1992) provides blank evaluation forms (called "evaluation tools") against which entities can assess each of their five components of internal control: control environment, risk assessment, control activities, information and communication, and monitoring. Pages 131–203 of the volume provide sample filled-in forms for a hypothetical medium-size aerospace parts manufacturer, including an overall internal control evaluation (pages 201–203) and an overall conclusion (page 203).

Unrelated to the *COSO Report*, the AICPA publishes AICPA *Audit & Accounting Guides*, reprinted as of May 1 each year, in a variety of industries, among them:

- Airlines
- Banks
- Casinos
- Colleges and universities
- Construction contractors
- Finance companies
- Investment companies
- Property and liability insurance companies
- Providers of health care services
- State and local governmental units

Required: Few risks are more crucial to an entity's long-term survival than its ability to adapt to change. For any industry you choose, use the blank and filled-in evaluation tools on pages 25–27 and 162–165 of the *COSO Report* (all of which relate to managing change within the risk assessment component of internal control), the related AICPA *Audit & Accounting Guide* for the industry you choose, and articles in business periodicals (such as *BusinessWeek, Forbes*) and newspapers (such as *The Wall Street Journal, Barron's*) to identify and briefly describe risks in the industry that relate specifically to managing change.

2. Reporting on Internal Control: Public Companies

The profession has argued for decades about the advisability of mandatory reporting on internal control by public companies and by governmental entities. In the 1970s and 1980s, the main players in the debate were the Commission on Auditors' Responsibilities (the Cohen Commission), the AICPA, and the SEC, among others, and their arguments were chronicled in L. M. Savoie and D. N. Ricchiute, "Reports by Management: Voluntary or Mandatory?" *Journal of Accountancy* (May 1981), pp. 84–94. More recently, in addition to the AICPA and the SEC, new players, most supportive of mandatory reporting, have entered the debate, including the Commission on Fraudulent Financial Reporting (the Treadway Commission), the Committee of Sponsoring Organizations (COSO) of the Treadway Commission, the U.S. General Accounting Office, and the Federal Deposit Insurance Corporation (FDIC), which, through the FDIC Improvement Act, requires public reporting for large federally insured banks and thrifts. "The COSO Report: Challenge and Counterchallenge," *Journal of Accountancy* (February 1993), pp. 10–18, reprints two pointed letters exchanged by COSO and the GAO, some of which bears directly on the debate in the 1990s. Prior to the *Sarbanes-Oxley Act of 2002*, Section 404, about one in four public companies and three in five Fortune 500 companies voluntarily reported on internal control.

   Required: Select a *Form 10-K* for a period ended prior to November 15, 2004 (the effective date of Section 404), that includes a report by management on internal control, and a *Form 10-K* for a period ended after November 15, 2004, that includes management's assessment of internal control over financial reporting, and draft a report that:
   1. Compares the two reports.
   2. Argues either for or against public reporting on internal control.

3. Reporting on Internal Control: Nonpublic Companies

For nonpublic companies, an auditor reports significant deficiencies to the board of directors' audit committee or, lacking an audit committee (for example, in small nonpublic companies), to individuals with equivalent authority and responsibility. Following is an illustrative written report for a nonpublic company that reports the significant deficiency illustrated by the questionnaire in Figure 8-7: "Employees who handle cash are not bonded."

In planning and performing our audit of the financial statements of (the company) for the year ended (date), we considered its internal control over financial reporting in order to determine our auditing procedures for the purpose of expressing our opinion on the financial statements and not to provide assurance on internal control. Our consideration of internal control would not necessarily disclose all deficiencies in internal control that might be significant deficiencies or material weaknesses. However, we noted certain deficiencies involving internal control that we consider to be significant deficiencies under standards established by the American Institute of Certified Public Accountants. A significant deficiency is an internal control deficiency that could adversely affect the entity's ability to initiate, record, process, and report financial data consistent with the assertions of management in the financial statements.

   We noted one significant deficiency: Employees who handle cash are not bonded.

   A material weakness is a significant deficiency in one or more of the internal control components that alone or in the aggregate precludes the entity's internal control from reducing to an appropriately low level the risk that material misstatements in the financial statements will not be prevented or detected on a timely basis. We believe that the significant deficiencies described above are not a material weakness.

   This report is intended solely for the information and use of the audit committee, management, and others in the company and is not intended to be and should not be used by anyone other than these specified parties

The report is an example of what the profession calls a "restricted use"—as opposed to a "general use"— report, which are reports intended for specified parties (such as the audit committee of the board of directors in the illustration). For example, note in the illustration that the closing sentence makes clear that the report is restricted, thereby alerting unintended audiences that, apart from the audit committee, the auditor is not responsible to parties who rely on the report.

Required: Select a *Form 10-K* that includes the chief executive and chief financial officers' Section 404 assessment of internal control over financial reporting and draft a report that compares the language in the report with the language in the previous nonpublic report.

**Interactive quizzes are available as a student learning resource at
http://ricchiute.swlearning.com**

Part 3

Auditing the Revenue/ Receipt and the Expenditure/ Disbursement Cycles

Chapter 9

Audit Sampling

Major topics discussed in this chapter are:

- The use of sampling in audit engagements.
- The role of sampling and nonsampling risk, the risks of assessing control risk too high or too low, and the risks of incorrect rejection and incorrect acceptance.
- The distinction between statistical and nonstatistical sampling.
- Audit sampling techniques to accomplish tests of controls and substantive tests of details: attribute estimation, sequential (stop-or-go) sampling, probability-proportional-to-size (PPS) sampling.

There is neither sufficient time nor, given the laws of probability, sufficient reason to test all of the transactions underlying an entity's account balances or classes of transactions. As a result, many if not most of the conclusions auditors reach about controls, balances, and classes of transactions are based on testing samples rather than entire populations. This chapter introduces audit sampling plans auditors use to test internal controls and account balances. The chapter begins by introducing the nature of audit sampling, discussing risk, and explaining the difference between statistical and nonstatistical sampling. Thereafter, the chapter introduces frequently used audit sampling techniques: *attribute estimation*, *sequential (stop-or-go) sampling*, *probability-proportional-to-size (PPS) sampling*, and *nonstatistical sampling*.

Sampling in Auditing

Auditors have long used sampling, largely as a means to draw conclusions about high-volume audit populations, such as receivables and sales transactions. For example, attributes estimation, illustrated in the chapter, was first used in the 1960s by accounting firms such as PricewaterhouseCoopers, which applied a sampling plan developed with Herbert Arkin, a statistician at the City College of New York. Today, practitioners also use attributes estimation in audits of internal control over financial reporting (Chapter 8), since the auditor's interest in a financial statement audit and in an audit of internal control over financial reporting is similar: Are management's assertions about control procedures reliable?

In practice, sampling is generally used when an entity's controls leave a trail of observable evidence, such as approval initials on the face of a vendor's invoice, and when the controls do not depend primarily on adequate segregation of duties, which is observable but generally not documented. Sampling can still be used when evidence is observable but not documented, although the sampling plan would require that observations be planned early in the engagement. For example, if an auditor wishes to observe cash collection at a theater, he or she would select the days for observation early in the engagement to allow each day in the period audited an equal chance of being selected for observation.

Audit Populations and Sampling Plans

Simply stated, **sampling** means that the auditor examines less than 100 percent of the items that constitute a population. In many cases, a sample can be sufficiently representative of a population to warrant reasonably reliable conclusions without testing the entire population. For example, a randomly selected sample of 100 sales invoices drawn from a population of 10,000 sales invoices can be audited in about 1 percent (100/10,000) of the time it would take to audit the entire population and, owing to the laws of probability, can yield fairly reliable conclusions. A **population** may consist of all the items within a class of transactions, such as all credit sales processed during the year, or all the transactions constituting an account balance, such as Accounts Receivable. A **sampling plan**—the procedures used to test a sample—aids the auditor in forming conclusions about one or more characteristics of either a particular class of transactions or a particular account balance. For example, the sample of 100 sales invoices could offer conclusions about credit-approval controls and about recorded sales and receivables balances. In any sampling plan, however, the characteristic of interest depends on whether the auditor uses sampling to help perform tests of controls or substantive tests.

Sampling in Tests of Controls

As introduced in Chapter 6, and discussed more fully in Chapter 8, tests of controls are designed to obtain evidence about whether an entity is complying with the controls that management prescribes. In sampling for tests of controls, the auditor identifies what are called **attributes**, the characteristics of a control (for example, unit prices and quantities on an invoice), and **deviations**, the absence of attributes. An **attributes sampling plan** is used most commonly to test an entity's *rate of deviation* (also called *rate of occurrence*) from a prescribed control procedure. For example, an auditor might use an attributes sampling plan to test controls over disbursement processing, billing systems, payroll and personnel systems, inventory pricing, and depreciation, among other things.

Sampling in Substantive Tests

In contrast, substantive tests, also introduced in Chapter 6, are designed to obtain evidence about whether monetary error exists within a class of transactions or an account balance, and the auditor's characteristic of interest is called a *variable*. A **variables sampling plan** is most commonly used to test whether recorded account balances are fairly stated. For example, an auditor might use a variables sampling plan to test recorded dollar amounts for receivables, inventory, payroll expense, and fixed asset additions, among other things. In summary, attributes sampling is generally used to reach a conclusion about a rate of deviation, and variables sampling is generally used to reach a conclusion about a population dollar amount. This chapter is devoted to attributes sampling and to variables sampling.

Sampling and Audit Risk

Sampling and audit risk are well established in audit practice and implicitly recognized in the third standard of field work, which states in part that ". . . evidential matter is to be obtained . . . to afford *a reasonable basis* for an opinion" (emphasis provided). If an "absolute" basis were necessary to form an opinion, then auditors would have to examine entire populations rather than samples, thereby rendering financial statement audits far too costly. Furthermore, audit risk cannot be totally eliminated by 100 percent testing, because risks not related to sampling, such as human error, would still exist. But what risks are sustained by an auditor in a typical financial statement audit, and how does sampling, despite its advantages, actually add to those risks? The following discussion focuses on the components of audit risk, which are summarized in Figure 9-1.

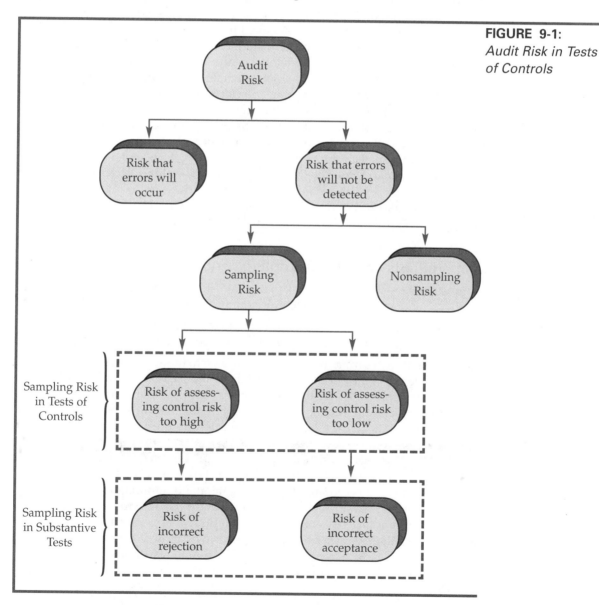

FIGURE 9-1:
Audit Risk in Tests of Controls

Components of Audit Risk

In Chapter 2, audit risk was defined as the likelihood that an auditor may unknowingly fail to modify his or her opinion on materially misstated financial statements. Audit risk is a combination of two components:

- The risk that material errors[1] *will occur* in the process by which financial statements are developed (the combination of control risk and inherent risk in Chapter 2).
- The risk that any material errors that occur *will not be detected* by the auditor (detection risk in Chapter 2).

The first component, the risk that errors will occur, can be classified further into control risk and inherent risk, both of which were introduced in Chapter 2. Control risk is the risk that errors could occur, but would not be prevented or detected by the entity's internal controls. For example, control risk would be higher in a company that does not maintain effective physical control over blank checks. Inherent risk is the susceptibility of an account balance to errors that could be material and that are not monitored by related control procedures. For example, inherent risk is often higher for liquid assets, such as cash, than for nonliquid assets, such as property, plant, and equipment. Because neither control risk nor inherent risk is directly controllable by an auditor, the risk that material errors will occur— the first component of audit risk—is not directly controllable by the auditor.

The second component of audit risk, the risk that material errors will not be detected, is called detection risk, defined in Chapter 2 as the risk that errors could occur, but would not be detected by the auditor's procedures. Detection risk is directly controllable by the auditor through substantive tests of details and other substantive audit procedures. For example, if both control risk and inherent risk are high, an auditor could reduce allowable detection risk by increasing sample size.

Sampling Risk and Nonsampling Risk

As illustrated in Figure 9-1, the risk that material errors may occur and remain undetected is influenced by two categories of uncertainties:

- Sampling risk: Uncertainties related to sampling.
- Nonsampling risk: Uncertainties unrelated to sampling.

Sampling risk arises from the fact that, unknown to the auditor, a sample may not be representative of the population tested. For example, a sample of sales invoices may contain disproportionately more or fewer control deviations than exist in the population of sales transactions, suggesting that the auditor's conclusions about recorded sales may be different if all of the sales invoices are tested. Since sampling risk can be reduced simply by increasing sample size, sampling risk varies inversely with sample size: the larger the sample size, the smaller the sampling risk. Why? Because, if sample size was increased to include all the items in a population, there would be no sampling and therefore no sampling risk.

Nonsampling risk includes all aspects of audit risk not due to sampling. For example, nonsampling risk could result from human error, such as failing to detect pricing mistakes or overlooking shipments to fictitious customers. Several factors can serve to reduce nonsampling risk, including staff training and supervision, and encouraging effective audit documentation review.

---

1   Throughout this chapter, the term "errors" is intended to include fraud.

Risks of Assessing Control Risk Too High or Too Low

As illustrated in Figure 9-1, two aspects of sampling risk are critical in tests of controls:

- Risk of assessing control risk too high.
- Risk of assessing control risk too low.

The **risk of assessing control risk too high** is the risk that a sample deviation rate supports assessing control risk at the maximum when, unknown to the auditor, the true deviation rate in the population would lead the auditor to assess control risk below the maximum. For example, assessing control risk too high would occur if an auditor estimated a 5 percent rate of deviation but was willing to tolerate only 3 percent, and the true but unknown population rate of deviation was really just 2 percent. In this example, the auditor would probably conclude that the control is not effective, since the sample deviation rate (5 percent) exceeds the tolerable deviation rate (3 percent). Therefore, he or she would assess a higher level of control risk in determining the nature, timing, and extent of substantive tests. But, unknown to the auditor, he or she would actually be *assessing control risk too high* because the true population deviation rate (2 percent) is less than the tolerable rate (3 percent).

The **risk of assessing control risk too low** is the opposite of assessing control risk too high: It is the risk that a sample supports assessing control risk below the maximum when, unknown to the auditor, the true deviation rate in the population supports assessing control risk at the maximum. For example, assessing control risk too low would occur if an auditor estimated a 4 percent rate of deviation but was willing to tolerate as much as 6 percent, and the true but unknown population rate was really 7 percent. In this example, the auditor would conclude that the control is effective. Therefore, he or she would assess a lower level of control risk in determining the nature, timing, and extent of substantive tests, because the sample indicated fewer deviations (4 percent) than the auditor was willing to tolerate (6 percent). However, unknown to the auditor, he or she would actually be *assessing control risk too low* since the true population rate (7 percent) exceeds the tolerable rate (6 percent).

Assessing control risk too high is *inefficient*: When an auditor concludes that control risk is high, he or she ordinarily sets a lower acceptable detection risk and expands the scope of substantive tests to compensate for the perceived control deficiency. If the expanded scope of substantive tests is unjustified, the audit will be less efficient since more substantive tests will be performed than necessary. Assessing control risk too low, in contrast, is *ineffective*, because the scope of substantive tests will be restricted under the erroneous assumption that the control is effective and control risk is low. Thus, the substantive tests may be ineffective in detecting material misstatements.

Risks of Incorrect Rejection or Incorrect Acceptance

As illustrated in Figure 9-1, two aspects of audit risk are critical in substantive tests of account balances:

- Risk of incorrect rejection
- Risk of incorrect acceptance

The **risk of incorrect rejection** is the risk that an audit sample will support concluding that a recorded account balance is materially misstated when, unknown to the auditor, the account is fairly stated. For example, owing to sampling risk, an auditor could select a sample that contains disproportionately *more* error than the population contains. Like the risk of assessing control risk too high in attributes sampling, the risk of incorrect rejection weighs on the *efficiency* of an audit, because an auditor would ordinarily reverse an erroneous conclusion that an account balance is misstated after he or she considers additional evidence or performs additional audit procedures. For example, an auditor would reverse an initial conclusion that Cost of Goods Sold is misstated if a subsequent physical inventory observation and inventory price testing revealed that Inventory was not misstated, and other procedures also revealed that Accounts Receivable and Sales were not misstated.

The **risk of incorrect acceptance**, in contrast, is the risk that an auditor's sample supports concluding that a recorded account balance is fairly stated when, unknown to the auditor, the account is materially misstated. For example, again owing to sampling risk, an auditor could select a sample that contains disproportionately *less* error than the population contains. Like the risk of assessing control risk too low in attributes sampling, the risk of incorrect acceptance bears on audit *effectiveness*. However, incorrect acceptance is far more consequential to the auditor for this reason: Incorrectly accepting a materially misstated account balance as fairly stated could cause the unwary auditor to issue an unqualified opinion on financial statements that depart materially from GAAP. In short, audit ineffectiveness translates to audit failure.

When designing a statistical sampling plan, an auditor considers the risks of assessing control risk too high and too low, and the risks of incorrect rejection and incorrect acceptance. Risk can't be eliminated, but it can be controlled as illustrated in the sampling plans introduced later in the chapter.

Statistical and Nonstatistical Sampling

Statistical sampling plans apply the laws of probability to aid an auditor in designing an efficient sample, in measuring the sufficiency of evidence obtained, and in evaluating the sample results. In contrast, **nonstatistical sampling plans** rely exclusively on judgment to determine sample size and to evaluate sample results. A properly designed nonstatistical sampling application can produce results that are just as effective as the results produced from a properly designed statistical sampling application. However, there is one crucial difference between statistical and nonstatistical sampling: Statistical sampling plans allow an auditor to *measure sampling risk* quantitatively; nonstatistical sampling plans do not.

The choice between a statistical and a nonstatistical sampling plan is based primarily on the auditor's assessment of the relative costs and benefits. For example, an auditor might use nonstatistical sampling if the cost of selecting a statistical random sample is too high. However, an auditor might consider the cost justifiable if the related controls were critical, and a measure of sampling risk is therefore essential. Note that the choice between a statistical and a nonstatistical sampling plan is made independent of the selection of audit procedures, since audit sampling, whether statistical or nonstatistical, is merely a means to accomplish audit procedures.

In practice, sampling is generally used when an entity's controls leave a trail of observable evidence, such as approval initials on the face of a vendor's invoice, and when the controls do not depend primarily on adequate segregation of duties, which is observable but generally not documented. Sampling can still be used when evidence is observable but not documented, although the sampling plan would require that observations be planned early in the engagement. In some instances, audit sampling is inappropriate, and the auditor must therefore test the entire population. For example, an auditor may be unwilling to accept any sampling risk for contingent liabilities and therefore would test the entire population. Sampling is also inappropriate in tests of control procedures that depend primarily on segregation of duties or that otherwise provide no audit trail. Audit evidence for these types of controls is gathered through observation and inquiry.

The following illustrates two commonly used attributes sampling techniques: attribute estimation sampling and sequential (stop-or-go) sampling.

Attributes Estimation Sampling in Tests of Controls

Attributes estimation sampling, a statistical sampling plan for tests of controls, is appropriate when an auditor wishes to estimate a true but unknown population rate of deviation. To illustrate, assume a first-year audit engagement is being planned for Chandler Wire & Cable Company, a large supplier of synthetic conductor cable for U.S. and foreign electronics manufacturers.

Determine the Objectives, Attributes, and Deviation Conditions

Although Chandler has long been respected for high-quality products, discussions with Chandler personnel reveal to the auditor that quality control may have deteriorated recently, a contention supported by an excessively large number of returns. The auditor's objective in this case is to determine whether control procedures for sales returns can be relied on during substantive tests of details.

Discussion with the predecessor auditor revealed that tests of sales returns in prior years had indicated relatively high deviation rates. Based on this information and interviews with client personnel, the auditor designs the following tests of controls for sales returns, all of which are explained more fully in Chapter 10.

Step	Tests of Controls
1.	Obtain a random sample of credit memoranda from files in the Customer Order department.
2.	Test unit pricing and extensions on sampled credit memoranda.
3.	Trace details of sampled credit memoranda to: a. Receiving reports. b. Perpetual inventory records. c. Entries in Inventory and Cost of Goods Sold. d. Entries in Sales Returns and in the accounts receivable subsidiary ledger and general ledger.
4.	Review the credit register (a listing of credit memoranda) for unusual items such as credits for very large amounts or an unusually large number of credits for the same customer, and investigate.
5.	Document test results.

The auditor is now confronted with a very real and recurring question in auditing: Can any of these procedures be accomplished with statistical or nonstatistical sampling, thereby potentially saving audit time and cost? In this case, nonstatistical sampling is likely *in*appropriate, because the auditor has prior knowledge of potential problems and therefore needs an estimate of sampling risk. Statistical sampling can be useful, particularly since the population of credit memoranda is assumed to be too large to justify testing the entire population. But which of the tests of controls can be accomplished statistically?

Steps 4 and 5 of the tests of controls cannot be accomplished with statistical sampling: Step 4 requires reviewing the entire population of credit register entries for attributes not clearly defined as either existing or not existing (a requirement of attribute estimation), and Step 5 does not involve testing. Steps 1, 2, and 3, however, involve attributes that can be defined clearly as either existing or not existing, and the attributes can be found on an unambiguous **sampling unit** (sometimes called a "logical unit"): credit memoranda. For example, the credit memoranda are either recorded properly in perpetual inventory records (Step 3b) or they are not; there are no uncertainties about outcome. Thus, Steps 1, 2, and 3 can be accomplished with attribute estimation.

Steps 1, 2, and 3 require one sampling unit and five attributes, as follows:

Sampling unit:
Credit memoranda

Attributes of interest:
1. Unit pricing and extensions on the credit memorandum are accurate.
2. Quantity and other data on the credit memorandum agree with the receiving report.
3. Quantity and other data on the credit memorandum agree with perpetual inventory records.
4. Journal entry is properly recorded as a debit to Inventory and a credit to Cost of Goods Sold.
5. Journal entry is properly recorded as a debit to Sales Returns and a credit to Accounts Receivable.

For each attribute, the deviation condition would be defined as the absence of the attribute. For example, for the first attribute, the deviation condition would be defined as "Unit pricing and extensions on the credit memorandum are *not* accurate."

Define the Population

In attributes sampling, a *population* consists of all items constituting a class of transactions. Because sample results can be projected only to the population from which the sample is selected, the defined population must be appropriate for the auditor's objectives. In this case, the population would be defined as all credit memoranda issued from the first day of the fiscal year, January 1, through the date that tests are performed. Assume that Chandler's balance sheet date is December 31, that interim testing of sales returns is planned as of October 20, and that the first sequentially numbered credit memorandum issued on January 2 was No. 4329 and the last credit memorandum issued on October 20 was No. 5948. From this information, the population would be represented by all credit memoranda numbered 4329 through 5948. The sampling unit in this case would be individual credit memoranda.

Determine Sample Size

In order to determine sample size for an attributes sampling plan, an auditor must first consider:

- Acceptable risk of assessing control risk too low,
- Tolerable rate of deviation, and
- Expected population deviation rate.

Acceptable Risk of Assessing Control Risk Too Low

Although an auditor is concerned with the risks of assessing control risk too high and too low, attributes sampling plans usually quantify the risk of assessing control risk too low only, since assessing risk too low relates to an audit's effectiveness—that is, to the likelihood of issuing an inappropriate audit report. The risk of assessing control risk too high, on the other hand, relates to efficiency only.

Auditors sometimes refer to their reliability or confidence levels when applying attributes sampling. *Reliability* or *confidence level* is actually the complement of the risk of assessing control risk too low (that is, one minus the risk). For example, for a 5 percent risk of assessing control risk too low, the reliability level would be 95 percent (that is, 1.00 – 0.05). Therefore, specifying an acceptable risk of assessing control risk too low depends largely on the degree of confidence an auditor desires. Because there is an inverse relationship between sample size and the risk of assessing control risk too low (for example, as the acceptable risk decreases, sample size increases), sample sizes are larger when an auditor specifies a lower acceptable risk of assessing control risk too low and smaller for higher acceptable risks. In most engagements, auditors vary the risk for individual controls, assigning a lower acceptable risk to controls deemed critical.

Tolerable Rate of Deviation

A **tolerable rate of deviation** (sometimes called a tolerable rate of occurrence) is the maximum population rate of deviation from a control procedure that an auditor will tolerate without modifying the assessed level of control risk. Specifying a tolerable rate of deviation is a matter of professional judgment and depends primarily on the auditor's assessment of control risk when planning the nature, timing, and extent of substantive tests. In general, a lower tolerable rate is appropriate when an auditor assesses a lower control risk.

Expected Population Deviation Rate

The expected population deviation rate can be estimated from either the prior-year results of testing the identical control or from a pilot sample. The prior-year sample deviation rate can be used only if the related control and client personnel have not changed since the prior-year sampling plan was applied. If there have been changes, the prior-year results would not be applicable, since the rate of deviation would not reflect current conditions. When prior-year results are either nonexistent or inapplicable, an auditor can estimate the expected population deviation rate from a *pilot sample* drawn from the population of interest. Pilot sample items can be used as part of the audit sample, and typically are. For example, if 40 items are examined in a pilot sample and the audit sample size is 100, only 60 additional sample items need to be selected and examined, since 40 had been examined in the pilot sample.

If an auditor judges that the expected population deviation rate equals or exceeds the tolerable rate, then the auditor expects to find more deviations than he or she is willing to tolerate, leading to the conclusion that the control is not effective. Under these conditions, the auditor would assess a higher control risk and, correspondingly, require extensive substantive tests to restrict detection risk to a relatively low level.

Sample Size

The auditor's acceptable risk of assessing control risk too low, tolerable rate of deviation, and expected population deviation rate appear in Figure 9-2 for each of the five attributes of interest. (Note that the sample size, number of deviations, sample results, and audit conclusion are also displayed on the completed Figure 9-2, but are discussed later.) For example, for the first attribute, *accurate unit pricing and extensions on credit memoranda*, the auditor is willing to accept a 5 percent risk of assessing control risk too low, which, as discussed earlier, corresponds to 95 percent reliability, the auditor's planned level of confidence. The tolerable and expected rates of deviation for attribute 1 are 0.04 and 0.0075, respectively, indicating that the auditor expects a 0.0075 deviation rate but is willing to tolerate 4 percent, more than four times the rate of deviation expected.

Sample size for each attribute is determined from Figures 9-3 or 9-4. Figure 9-3, used when the acceptable risk of assessing control risk too low is 5 percent, is appropriate for attributes 1, 2, 4, and 5. Figure 9-4, used when the acceptable risk is 10 percent, is appropriate for attribute 3. Required sample size for each attribute is indicated in Figure 9-2. For example, for attribute 1, required sample size per Figure 9-3 is 117, the intersection of the column associated with a 4 percent tolerable rate of deviation and the row associated with a 0.75 percent expected population deviation rate. Note that in Figure 9-2, the auditor has rounded sample size up to 125 items (to accommodate the sample evaluation tables on pages 371–372).

Effect on Sample Size of Risk and Population Size

Increasing or decreasing any of the sample size parameters (that is, acceptable risk of assessing control risk too low, tolerable rate of deviation, and expected population deviation rate) will have an impact on required sample size. Figure 9-5 (page 368) illustrates the effect on sample size of changes in any one parameter; the effect of changes in more than one would depend on the magnitude and direction (increase or decrease) of each change. However, population size has little effect on sample size, particularly for populations over 5,000 items. For example, the following table illustrates that for a 5 percent acceptable risk of assessing control risk too low, 5 percent tolerable deviation rate, and 1 percent expected population deviation rate, sample size is identical (93) for population sizes ranging from 5,000 to 100,000—increasing the population twenty times (100,000/5,000) has no bearing on population size.

Population Size	Required Sample Size
50	45
100	64
500	87
1,000	90
2,000	92
5,000	93
100,000	93

FIGURE 9-2: *Audit Documentation of Sample Results*

B12
DM
10/21/2007

Chandler Wire and Cable Co.
Attribute Estimation Worksheet—Sales Returns
December 31, 2007

Attribute	1 Acceptable Risk of Assessing Control Risk Too Low	2 Tolerable Rate of Deviation	3 Expected Population Deviation Rate	4 Sample Size Table	4 Sample Size Used	5 Number of Deviations	6 Sample Deviation Rate	Maxim Population Deviation Rate
1. Unit pricing and extensions on the credit memo are accurate.	.05	.04	.0075	117	125	1*	.008	.038
2. Quantity and other data on credit memo agrees with the receiving reports.	.05	.05	.015	124	125	2*	.016	.05
3. Quantity and description on credit memo agree with perpetual inventory.	.10	.08	.02	48	50	1*	.02	.076
4. Entry properly recorded as debit to Inventory and credit to Cost of Goods Sold.	.05	.05	.01	93	100	0	0	.03
5. Entry properly recorded as debit to Sales Returns and credit to Accounts Receivable.	.05	.05	.01	93	100	0	0	.03

*See analysis of deviations at B13.

Audit Conclusion

Based on procedures performed, the tolerable rate of deviation equals or exceeds the maximum population deviation rate for all five attributes tested; therefore, controls over sales returns are considered effective in preventing or detecting misstatements. Control risk for assertions related to sales returns is set below the maximum.

FIGURE 9-3: *Statistical Sample Sizes for Tests of Controls, 5 Percent Risk of Assessing Control Risk Too Low*

Expected Population Deviation Rate	Tolerable Rate										
	2%	3%	4%	5%	6%	7%	8%	9%	10%	15%	20%
0.00%	149	99	74	59	49	42	36	32	29	19	14
0.25	236	157	117	93	78	66	58	51	46	30	22
0.50	*	157	117	93	78	66	58	51	46	30	22
0.75	*	208	117	93	78	66	58	51	46	30	22
1.00	*	*	156	93	78	66	58	51	46	30	22
1.25	*	*	156	124	78	66	58	51	46	30	22
1.50	*	*	192	124	103	66	58	51	46	30	22
1.75	*	*	227	153	103	88	77	51	46	30	22
2.00	*	*	*	181	127	88	77	68	46	30	22
2.25	*	*	*	208	127	109	77	68	61	30	22
2.50	*	*	*	*	150	109	77	68	61	30	22
2.75	*	*	*	*	173	129	95	68	61	30	22
3.00	*	*	*	*	195	148	95	84	61	30	22
3.25	*	*	*	*	*	167	112	84	61	30	22
3.50	*	*	*	*	*	185	112	84	76	40	22
3.75	*	*	*	*	*	*	129	100	76	40	22
4.00	*	*	*	*	*	*	146	100	89	40	22
5.00	*	*	*	*	*	*	*	158	116	40	30
6.00	*	*	*	*	*	*	*	*	179	50	30
7.00	*	*	*	*	*	*	*	*	*	68	37

*Sample size is too large to be cost-effective for most audit applications.

Source: AICPA, *Auditing Practice Release: Audit Sampling.* New York: AICPA, 2001, p. 85.

Perform the Sampling Plan

If an audit sample is selected at *random*—that is, if each sampling unit is given an equal chance of being selected—the auditor can apply the laws of probability to determine the likelihood that the sample is representative of the population from which it was drawn. A sample can be evaluated in terms of probability only if the sample is selected randomly and thus free from sampling bias. If each item in a population is not given an equal chance of selection, the sample would be biased toward the population items with the greater chance of selection. Some common methods of selecting a sample are:

- Random-number sampling.
- Systematic sampling.

FIGURE 9-4: *Statistical Sample Sizes for Tests of Controls, 10 Percent Risk of Assessing Control Risk Too Low*

Expected Population Deviation Rate	Tolerable Rate										
	2%	3%	4%	5%	6%	7%	8%	9%	10%	15%	20%
0.00%	114	76	57	45	38	32	28	25	22	15	11
0.25	194	129	96	77	64	55	48	42	38	25	18
0.50	194	129	96	77	64	55	48	42	38	25	18
0.75	265	129	96	77	64	55	48	42	38	25	18
1.00	*	176	96	77	64	55	48	42	38	25	18
1.25	*	221	132	77	64	55	48	42	38	25	18
1.50	*	*	132	105	64	55	48	42	38	25	18
1.75	*	*	166	105	88	55	48	42	38	25	18
2.00	*	*	198	132	88	75	48	42	38	25	18
2.25	*	*	*	132	88	75	65	58	38	25	18
2.50	*	*	*	158	110	75	65	58	38	25	18
2.75	*	*	*	209	132	94	65	58	52	25	18
3.00	*	*	*	*	132	94	65	58	52	25	18
3.25	*	*	*	*	153	113	82	58	52	25	18
3.50	*	*	*	*	194	113	82	73	52	25	18
3.75	*	*	*	*	*	131	98	73	52	25	18
4.00	*	*	*	*	*	149	98	73	65	25	18
5.00	*	*	*	*	*	*	160	115	78	34	18
6.00	*	*	*	*	*	*	*	182	116	43	25
7.00	*	*	*	*	*	*	*	*	199	52	25

*Sample size is too large to be cost-effective for most audit applications.

Source: AICPA, *Auditing Practice Release: Audit Sampling.* New York: AICPA, 2001, p. 86.

- Block sampling.
- Haphazard sampling.
- Stratified sampling.

Random-Number Sampling

Random-number sampling uses computer-generated random numbers to select sampling units from a population. For example, to select on October 21 a sample of credit memos sequentially numbered from 4329 (the first credit memo used on January 2) through 5948 (the last memo used on October 20), an auditor would specify that the random-number generator display four-digit numbers within the range 4329 through 5948. If the sampling units are not numbered consecutively,

FIGURE 9-5: *The Effect on Sample Size of Increasing or Decreasing Parameters: Attributes Sampling*

Parameter	Direction of Change	Effect on Sample Size Increase	Effect on Sample Size Decrease
Acceptable risk of assessing control risk too low	Increase		X
	Decrease	X	
Tolerable rate of deviation	Increase		X
	Decrease	X	
Expected population deviation rate	Increase	X	
	Decrease		X

the auditor could establish correspondence between the population items and random digits by assigning numbers to each sampling unit. Random-number sampling is appropriate both for statistical sampling and for nonstatistical sampling.

Systematic Sampling

Systematic sampling involves selecting every *n*th item from a population of sequentially ordered items. Systematic sampling eliminates the need to establish correspondence between population items and random numbers, and therefore is useful when population items lack identification numbers. The number of sequential items to skip when selecting a sample systematically is determined by dividing population size by sample size. Continuing points may be changed periodically to minimize any potential starting-point bias. Systematic selection is useful for nonstatistical sampling, and can be useful for statistical sampling if the starting point is selected at random.

Block Sampling

A block sample is a group of items arranged contiguously within a larger grouping of sampling units. For example, a block sample could consist of all credit memos processed on January 21, May 24, September 28, and November 13. In this case, if 50 credit memos had been processed on these four days, then the sample would consist of 4 items, not 75, since the sampling unit is expressed in time—that is, in days—not transactions. Generally, so few blocks of sample items are insufficient to justify generalizing sample results to the population, suggesting that block sampling often results in excessively high sampling risk. Although a block sample could be designed with enough blocks to minimize sampling risk, testing large numbers of blocks is likely to be inefficient. Auditors generally don't use block sampling for either statistical or nonstatistical sampling, absent considerable care in controlling sampling risk.

Haphazard Sampling

A haphazard sample consists of sampling units selected without special reason, but also without conscious bias. For example, a haphazard sample could consist of 50 items selected simply by pulling credit memos from a file cabinet drawer. Like block sampling, haphazard sampling may fail to select samples that are wholly representative of the population tested. Haphazard sampling is inappropriate for statistical sampling but may be useful for nonstatistical sampling.

Stratified Sampling

Stratified sampling involves subdividing populations into homogeneous subgroups or strata, and selecting (and evaluating) separate samples for each subgroup. The samples may be selected by random numbers, systematically, in blocks, or haphazardly. Stratified sampling is based on the assumption that items in some population strata are more similar to each other than to any other items in the population. For example, individual credit memos of less than $100 are apt to be more similar to each other than to credit memos over $100,000. When compared, subgroups are apt to have strikingly dissimilar characteristics, such as different credit terms and different potential for material errors or for fraud. Thus, each group represents a stratum, and the variability of sampling units in each stratum is apt to be less than the variability of all population items together.

In practice, auditors usually select more sampling units than required, thereby providing replacements for voided items and for documents that cannot be located. For example, an auditor might select 75 sampling units even though required sample size is 65, and then use the remaining 10 in the order selected if needed. Voided items generally should not be considered deviations. However, missing items would ordinarily be considered deviations, since the auditor would have no basis to conclude that the controls were operating as prescribed by management.

The auditor for Chandler selects random-number sampling because the sequential four-digit credit memorandum numbers correspond readily to random-number tables. However, because sample size varies for the attributes tested—that is, 50 for attribute 3, 100 for attributes 4 and 5, and 125 for attributes 1 and 2—an initial sample of 50 can be selected for all attributes, an additional 50 for attributes 1, 2, 4, and 5, and another 25 for attributes 1 and 2.

Following selection, the auditor examines the sampling units and documents any observed deviations for each attribute. Figure 9-2 indicates that one deviation was observed for attribute 1, two for attribute 2, and one for attribute 3; none were observed for attributes 4 and 5. Figure 9-6 is the auditor's analysis of each individual deviation. Note particularly the auditor's judgment expressed in Figure 9-6 about the effect of each deviation on substantive tests of details: In each case, no additional audit work—none beyond the substantive tests necessary to control detection risk to the level planned—was considered necessary for the reasons cited.

Evaluate the Sample Results

The results of the attribute estimation sampling plan are tabulated in the last two columns of Figure 9-2. The auditor calculates for each attribute, a **sample deviation rate**—the auditor's estimate of the true but unknown population deviation rate—by dividing the number of deviations by sample size. For example, for attribute 1, the sample deviation rate is approximately 0.008 (1 deviation divided by 125 sampling units).

The maximum population deviation rate for each attribute is determined from Figures 9-7 and 9-8. Figure 9-7 (page 371), used when the risk of assessing control risk too low is 5 percent, is appropriate for attributes 1, 2, 4, and 5. Figure 9-8 (page 372), used when the risk is 10 percent, is appropriate for attribute 3. The maximum

FIGURE 9-6: *Audit Documentation of Deviations Observed in a Sample*

B13
DM
10/21/2007

Chandler Wire and Cable Co.
Analysis of Deviations: Sales Returns and Allowances
December 31, 2007

Attribute	Number of Deviations	Nature of Deviation	Effect on Substantive Detailed Testing
1	1	Cr. Memo #4823: $1,269. Although unit prices were correct, the extensions were incorrect, resulting in a $59 understatement.	No additional audit work is considered necessary at year end because (1) the resulting error is immaterial and (2) the maximum population deviation rate (.038) is less than the tolerable rate (.04).
2	2	Cr. memo #4934: $2,528; Cr. memo #4687: $1,729. In both cases, the description of returned inventory is inaccurate.	No additional audit work is considered necessary at year end because (1) both credit memos were recorded properly, despite the inaccurate descriptions and (2) the maximum population deviation rate (.05) is equal to the tolerable rate (.05).
3	1	Cr. memo #4731: $5,421. The quantity recorded within perpetual records was inaccurate.	No additional audit work is considered necessary at year end because (1) journal entries were properly recorded for this credit memo (attributes 4 and 5) and (2) the maximum population deviation rate (.076) is less than the tolerable rate (.08).

population deviation rate for each attribute is indicated in Figure 9-2. For example, for attribute 1, the maximum population deviation rate from Figure 9-7 is 0.038, the intersection of the column associated with one deviation and the row associated with a sample size of 125. In statistical terms, the auditor's conclusion for attribute 1 could be expressed as follows:

Based on procedures applied, the estimated population deviation rate is 0.008, and there is a 95 percent probability (that is, 1–5 percent risk of assessing control risk too low) that the true but unknown population rate of deviation is less than or equal to 0.038.

A similar conclusion is reached for each of the other attributes tested.

FIGURE 9-7: *Statistical Sample Results Evaluation Table for Tests of Controls, Maximum Population Deviation Rates at 5 Percent of Assessing Control Risk Too Low*

Sample Rate	Actual Number of Deviations Found										
	0	1	2	3	4	5	6	7	8	9	10
25	11.3	17.6	*	*	*	*	*	*	*	*	*
30	9.5	14.9	19.6	*	*	*	*	*	*	*	*
35	8.3	12.9	17.0	*	*	*	*	*	*	*	*
40	7.3	11.4	15.0	18.3	*	*	*	*	*	*	*
45	6.5	10.2	13.4	16.4	19.2	*	*	*	*	*	*
50	5.9	9.2	12.1	14.8	17.4	19.9	*	*	*	*	*
55	5.4	8.4	11.1	13.5	15.9	18.2	*	*	*	*	*
60	4.9	7.7	10.2	12.5	14.7	16.8	18.8	*	*	*	*
65	4.6	7.1	9.4	11.5	13.6	15.5	17.4	19.3	*	*	*
70	4.2	6.6	8.8	10.8	12.6	14.5	16.3	18.0	19.7	*	*
75	4.0	6.2	8.2	10.1	11.8	13.6	15.2	16.9	18.5	20.0	*
80	3.7	5.8	7.7	9.5	11.1	12.7	14.3	15.9	17.4	18.9	*
90	3.3	5.2	6.9	8.4	9.9	11.4	12.8	14.2	15.5	16.8	18.2
100	3.0	4.7	6.2	7.6	9.0	10.3	11.5	12.8	14.0	15.2	16.4
125	2.4	3.8	5.0	6.1	7.2	8.3	9.3	10.3	11.3	12.3	13.2
150	2.0	3.2	4.2	5.1	6.0	6.9	7.8	8.6	9.5	10.3	11.1
200	1.5	2.4	3.2	3.9	4.6	5.2	5.9	6.5	7.2	7.8	8.4

*Over 20 percent.

Note: This table presents maximum population deviation rates as percentages. This table assumes a large population.

Source: AICPA, *Auditing Practice Release: Audit Sampling.* New York: AICPA, 2001, p. 87.

Based on the statistical conclusions, the auditor formulates an audit conclusion for the entire set of attributes tested (or for individual attributes, in the case of mixed results). Because the tolerable rate is greater than or equal to the maximum population deviation rate for all five attributes (see Figure 9-2) and no other qualitative evidence exists to the contrary (for example, intentional fraud), the audit conclusion would be that the control is effective in preventing or detecting material misstatements. The auditor's conclusion for Chandler Wire & Cable Company appears in Figure 9-2.

Other Considerations

Three observations about the results achieved and documented in Figure 9-2: First, the auditor's conclusions relate only to the period for which credit memoranda

FIGURE 9-8: *Statistical Sample Results Evaluation Table for Tests of Controls, Maximum Population Deviation Rates at 10 Percent of Assessing Control Risk Too Low*

Sample Rate	Actual Number of Deviations Found										
	0	1	2	3	4	5	6	7	8	9	10
20	10.9	18.1	*	*	*	*	*	*	*	*	*
25	8.8	14.7	19.9	*	*	*	*	*	*	*	*
30	7.4	12.4	16.8	*	*	*	*	*	*	*	*
35	6.4	10.7	14.5	18.1	*	*	*	*	*	*	*
40	5.6	9.4	12.8	16.0	19.0	*	*	*	*	*	*
45	5.0	8.4	11.4	14.3	17.0	19.7	*	*	*	*	*
50	4.6	7.6	10.3	12.9	15.4	17.8	*	*	*	*	*
55	4.1	6.9	9.4	11.8	14.1	16.3	18.4	*	*	*	*
60	3.8	6.4	8.7	10.8	12.9	15.0	16.9	18.9	*	*	*
70	3.3	5.5	7.5	9.3	11.1	12.9	14.6	16.3	17.9	19.6	*
80	2.9	4.8	6.6	8.2	9.8	11.3	12.8	14.3	15.8	17.2	18.6
90	2.6	4.3	5.9	7.3	8.7	10.1	11.5	12.8	14.1	15.4	16.6
100	2.3	3.9	5.3	6.6	7.9	9.1	10.3	11.5	12.7	13.9	15.0
120	2.0	3.3	4.4	5.5	6.6	7.6	8.7	9.7	10.7	11.6	12.6
160	1.5	2.5	3.3	4.2	5.0	5.8	6.5	7.3	8.0	8.8	9.5
200	1.2	2.0	2.7	3.4	4.0	4.6	5.3	5.9	6.5	7.1	7.6

*Over 20 percent.

Note: This table presents maximum population deviation rates as percentages. This table assumes a large population.

Source: AICPA, *Auditing Practice Release: Audit Sampling.* New York: AICPA, 2001, p. 88.

were available for testing, January 1 through October 20. Thus, the conclusions do not apply to the period October 21 through December 31, in the absence of additional testing. Second, recall that the prior auditor experienced relatively high deviation rates for tests of sales returns. However, the results in Figure 9-2 indicate otherwise for the current year, illustrating the very real phenomenon of changing audit conditions from year to year.

Third, note that for attribute 2 in Figure 9-2 the maximum population deviation rate, 0.05, is equal to the tolerable rate. Because the maximum population rate and tolerable rate are equal, the auditor might consider the control questionable. On the other hand, the control attribute itself—credit memo quantity and other data agree with receiving reports—may not be sufficiently critical to warrant assessing control risk at the maximum, since there may be compensating controls and existing evidence that credit memoranda are recorded properly in the accounts. The auditor's decision, the assessed level of control risk, would be based on weighing these two points of view and is an example of the types of trade-offs considered by auditors in practice. In this case, it's likely the auditor would assess control risk for sales returns below the maximum.

In Chapter 10, attribute estimation is illustrated for tests of controls applied to the billing function of a supplier of handheld power tools.

Sequential (Stop-or-Go) Sampling

Audit sampling can be accomplished with either a fixed or a sequential sampling plan. In a *fixed sampling plan*, such as attribute estimation, the auditor tests a single sample. However, in **sequential sampling**, the plan is performed in several steps. Following each step, an auditor decides whether to stop testing or to go on to the next step, thus accounting for why the plan is sometimes called *stop-or-go sampling*.

Sequential sampling can be used as an alternative to attribute estimation when an auditor expects zero or very few deviations within an audit population. For example, for a continuing audit engagement, an auditor might decide to use sequential sampling if the prior year's attribute estimation sampling plans yielded very low maximum population deviation rates, the prior year's observed deviations did not result in material misstatements, and there was no reason to expect that deviations in the current year would result in material misstatements. For this set of circumstances, an auditor could possibly minimize sample size by using sequential sampling, thereby minimizing audit time and improving audit efficiency.

Assuming that the objectives, attributes, deviation conditions, and population are defined properly and that the sample selection method is chosen, an auditor would proceed as follows.

Determine Sample Size

Determining sample size in sequential sampling requires that an auditor first specify the desired reliability and the tolerable rate of deviation. As noted earlier, *desired reliability* is the complement of the risk of assessing control risk too low, which was needed to determine sample size in attribute estimation. As a result, desired reliability is also a matter of professional judgment and may be deduced from an auditor's acceptable risk of assessing control risk too low. That is, if an auditor intended to assess control risk below the maximum and therefore decided on a rather low risk of assessing control risk too low, such as 2 percent, then desired reliability would be 98 percent (that is, 1.00 − 0.02). Note that because there is an inverse relationship between sample size and the risk of assessing control risk too low, there is a direct relationship between desired reliability and sample size: Sample size is larger when an auditor specifies a higher desired reliability. In general, a higher desired reliability is appropriate when an auditor believes the internal controls may be effective, resulting in a lower control risk; a lower reliability level is appropriate otherwise.

As in attribute estimation, the *tolerable rate of deviation* is the maximum rate an auditor is willing to accept in the sample without deciding a control is ineffective. A lower tolerable rate of deviation is appropriate when an auditor plans to assess control risk low. Unlike attribute estimation, sequential sampling does not require an estimate of the expected population deviation rate, because sequential sampling is applied only when an auditor expects zero or very few deviations.

In sequential sampling, sample size can be determined from standard tables such as Figure 9-9, which also is used to evaluate results. Figure 9-9 is appropriate for populations over 2,000 items and is used as follows:

- Locate the column associated with the tolerable rate of deviation (the percentages in the table) and row associated with zero errors.
- Beginning with the smallest sample size (that is, 50 at the extreme top left column of the table) and continuing for increasingly higher sample sizes, review the column and row (zero deviations) intersections until you locate the sample size that achieves at least the desired level of reliability.

For example, assume:

- Desired reliability = 0.95
- Tolerable rate of deviation = 0.05

In Figure 9-9, the smallest sample size that achieves at least 95 percent reliability for zero expected deviations is 70.

Note that for a smaller sample size of 50, the intersection of 5 percent tolerable rate of deviation and zero expected deviations results in a reliability level of 92.31 percent, which is clearly below the desired reliability level of 95 percent. However, for a sample size of 70, the intersection of 5 percent tolerable rate and zero expected deviations results in a reliability level of 97.24 percent, a level that is acceptable—that is, at least 95 percent for this example.

Perform the Sampling Plan and Evaluate Results

Sampling units are selected using, for example, random-number sampling or systematic sampling, as in attribute estimation. After examining the sampling units included within the initial sample selection, an auditor then decides from the sample results whether to stop or to go on with the sampling plan. The decision to stop or go depends primarily on how many deviations are observed. If no deviations are observed, the auditor can conclude that the actual population deviation rate is within the predetermined tolerable rate, and therefore may stop the sampling plan. For the preceding example, no observed deviations would yield a conclusion as follows:

Based on procedures applied, there is a 97.24 percent probability that the actual population deviation rate is less than 0.05.

However, if one or more deviations are observed within the original sample, the auditor could decide to increase sample size in an attempt to seek additional deviation-free sampling units and reevaluate the sample accordingly. In this situation, Figure 9-9 would be used in essentially the same way as in determining initial sample size.

In Chapter 12, sequential sampling is illustrated for tests of controls applied to the cash disbursements of a medium-size manufacturer of paper products.

Nonstatistical Sampling in Tests of Controls

Even though nonstatistical sampling plans do not measure sampling risk, they can provide results as effective as statistical plans, and often are chosen by auditors when the costs of generating statistical samples exceed the benefits. Generally, the steps in a nonstatistical sampling plan are the same as those in a statistical plan,

FIGURE 9-9: Sequential Sampling: Table for Determining Sample Size and Evaluating Sample Results

Sample Size Examined	No. of Deviations Found	Probability That Deviation is Less Than:														
		1%	2%	3%	4%	5%	6%	7%	8%	9%	10%	12%	14%	16%	18%	20%
50	0	39.50	63.58	78.19	87.01	92.31	95.47	97.34	98.45	99.10	99.49	99.83	99.95	99.98	100.00	100.00
	1	8.94	26.42	44.47	59.95	72.06	81.00	87.35	91.73	94.68	96.62	98.69	99.52	99.83	99.94	99.98
	2	1.38	7.84	18.92	32.33	45.95	58.38	68.92	77.40	83.95	88.83	94.87	97.79	99.10	99.65	99.87
	3	0.16	1.78	6.28	13.91	23.96	35.27	46.73	57.47	66.97	74.97	86.55	93.30	96.88	98.64	99.43
	4	0.02	0.32	1.68	4.90	10.36	17.94	27.10	37.11	47.23	56.88	73.21	84.72	91.92	96.01	98.15
	5		0.05	0.37	1.44	3.78	7.76	13.51	20.81	29.28	38.39	56.47	71.86	83.23	90.71	95.20
	6		0.01	0.07	0.36	1.18	2.89	5.83	10.19	15.96	22.98	39.35	56.16	70.81	81.99	89.66
70	0	50.52	75.69	88.14	94.26	97.24	98.69	99.38	99.71	99.86	99.94	99.99	100.00	100.00	100.00	100.00
	1	15.53	40.96	62.47	77.51	87.03	92.81	96.10	97.93	98.92	99.45	99.86	99.97	99.99	100.00	100.00
	2	3.34	16.50	35.08	53.44	68.63	79.87	87.59	92.60	95.72	97.58	99.28	99.80	99.95	99.99	100.00
	3	0.54	5.19	15.87	30.71	46.61	61.15	73.07	82.10	88.53	92.88	97.48	99.19	99.76	99.93	99.98
	4	0.07	1.32	5.93	14.85	27.21	41.13	54.77	66.80	76.61	84.12	93.36	97.51	99.16	99.74	99.92
	5		0.28	1.86	6.12	13.72	24.27	36.58	49.24	61.06	71.28	85.94	93.92	97.64	99.17	99.73
	6		0.05	0.50	2.18	6.04	12.61	21.75	32.70	44.40	55.82	74.98	87.57	94.50	97.81	99.20
	7			0.12	0.68	2.34	5.80	11.54	19.54	29.33	40.12	61.33	78.13	89.04	95.08	98.00
	8			0.02	0.19	0.80	2.38	5.49	10.54	17.59	26.37	46.66	66.03	80.85	90.36	95.63
	9				0.05	0.25	0.88	2.36	5.14	9.60	15.86	32.88	52.46	70.10	83.23	91.55
100	0	63.40	86.74	95.25	98.31	99.41	99.80	99.93	99.98	99.99	100.00	100.00	100.00	100.00	100.00	100.00
	1	26.42	59.67	80.54	91.28	96.29	98.48	99.40	99.77	99.91	99.97	100.00	100.00	100.00	100.00	100.00
	2	7.94	32.33	58.02	76.79	88.17	94.34	97.42	98.87	99.52	99.81	99.97	100.00	100.00	100.00	100.00
	3	1.84	14.10	35.28	57.05	74.22	85.70	92.56	96.33	98.27	99.22	99.86	99.98	100.00	100.00	100.00
	4	0.34	5.08	18.22	37.11	56.40	72.32	83.68	90.97	95.26	97.63	99.47	99.90	99.98	100.00	100.00
	5	0.05	1.55	8.08	21.16	38.40	55.93	70.86	82.01	89.55	94.24	98.48	99.66	99.93	99.99	100.00
	6	0.01	0.41	3.12	10.64	23.40	39.37	55.57	69.68	80.60	88.28	96.33	99.03	99.78	99.96	99.99

(continues)

FIGURE 9-9 *(continued)*

Size Sample Examined	No. of Deviations Found	Probability That Deviation is Less Than:																		
		1%	2%	3%	4%	5%	6%	7%	8%	9%	10%	12%	14%	16%	18%	20%
100	7		0.09	1.06	4.75	12.80	25.17	40.12	55.29	68.72	79.40	92.39	97.67	99.39	99.86	99.97
	8		0.02	0.32	1.90	6.31	14.63	26.60	40.74	55.06	67.91	86.14	95.08	98.53	99.62	99.91
	9			0.09	0.68	2.82	7.75	16.20	27.80	41.25	54.87	77.44	90.78	96.84	99.08	99.77
	10			0.02	0.22	1.15	3.76	9.08	17.57	20.82	46.68	66.63	84.40	93.93	98.00	94.43
	11				0.07	0.43	1.68	4.69	10.29	18.76	29.70	54.58	75.91	89.39	96.05	98.74
	12				0.02	0.15	0.69	2.24	5.59	11.38	19.82	42.39	65.66	82.97	92.89	97.47
	13					0.05	0.26	0.99	2.82	6.45	12.39	31.14	54.36	74.69	88.19	95.31
	14					0.01	0.09	0.41	1.33	3.41	7.26	21.60	42.94	64.90	81.77	91.96
	15						0.03	0.16	0.59	1.69	3.99	14.15	32.27	54.20	73.70	87.15

although the auditor's judgment is guided not by statistical theory, but by experience and by prior knowledge and current information about the client. The following addresses some considerations in nonstatistical sampling not specifically covered earlier in the chapter.

Determine Sample Size

An auditor considers exactly the same parameters when determining nonstatistical sample size as when calculating statistical sample size: the risk of assessing control risk too low, the tolerable rate of deviation, and the expected population deviation rate. However, in nonstatistical sampling, the parameters may be expressed in relative terms, such as low, medium, high, etc., rather than in quantitative terms. When determining sample size in nonstatistical sampling, the auditor should consider the impact on sample size of increasing or decreasing the acceptable risk of assessing control risk too low and the tolerable and expected rates of deviation, as illustrated earlier in Figure 9-3. For example, an auditor could justifiably consider decreasing sample size if his or her tolerable rate of deviation increased.

Alternatively, in a nonstatistical sampling plan the auditor could subjectively quantify each population parameter and then use standard tables (for example, Figure 9-3 or 9-4) to determine sample size. Calculated sample size could then either be used or altered judgmentally to reflect the auditor's reconsideration of each parameter in Figure 9-3 and sampling risk.

As in statistical sampling, sampling units can be selected using random-number sampling or systematic sampling, either of which could achieve randomness, thereby improving the likelihood of selecting representative sample items. Two other selection methods are available: block sampling and haphazard sampling, both of which require extreme care by the auditor, as discussed earlier.

Evaluating Sample Results

Because nonstatistical sampling plans do not yield an estimate of sampling risk, the auditor must determine judgmentally whether the difference between his or her tolerable rate of deviation and the estimated population deviation rate is an adequate allowance for sampling risk. For example, assume that an auditor will tolerate 8 percent deviations and observes 3 deviations in a sample of 50. In this case, the estimated population rate of deviation is the sample deviation rate of 6 percent (3/50). Since the tolerable rate of deviation is 8 percent, then the auditor would be faced with the decision of whether 2 percent (8 percent tolerable rate minus 6 percent estimated population rate) is an adequate allowance for sampling risk.

Variables Sampling in Substantive Tests of Details

Sampling plans applied to substantive tests of details are designed either to:

- Estimate an account balance that is not recorded within an entity's accounts, called dollar-value estimation, or
- Test the reasonableness of a recorded account balance, called hypothesis testing.

Although a substantive test, *dollar-value estimation* is not actually an auditing procedure, since its purpose is to create an account balance rather than to audit a recorded account balance. For example, an auditor might suggest dollar-value estimation to management as a means to convert a FIFO inventory to LIFO for purposes of financial reporting. *Hypothesis testing*, however, is an auditing procedure, since its purpose is to evaluate, not create, an account balance. For example, as part of a financial statement audit, an auditor might use sampling to test whether recorded accounts receivable are fairly stated at the balance sheet date. The variables sampling plan introduced in this section is used for hypothesis testing, not dollar-value estimation. In general, an auditor's objectives in hypothesis testing are to determine whether a recorded account balance is fairly stated or materially misstated. Once an objective is stated, the auditor identifies the *characteristic of interest*. For example, if an auditor's objective is to determine whether an account is fairly stated, the characteristic might be defined as monetary error—that is, the monetary differences between recorded and audited dollar amounts.

Audit sampling is not used to accomplish all of an auditor's planned substantive tests of details, only those for which the auditor believes sampling is appropriate. For example, an auditor would not use sampling to accomplish the procedures of inquiry and observation, such as interviewing management and observing cash-handling procedures, or to accomplish analytical procedures, such as comparing current-period financial statement accounts with prior-period balances. However, when sampling is appropriate—for example, when a large number of transactions are captured within a single account—auditors generally choose from among probability-proportional-to-size sampling, which uses attributes sampling theory to evaluate results; nonstatistical sampling, which relaxes the assumptions of classical statistical theory; or a classical variables sampling technique such as difference estimation (Appendix), which relies on normal distribution theory to evaluate audit samples. In practice, auditors first decide between statistical and nonstatistical sampling. If statistical sampling is chosen, the auditor then decides between probability-proportional-to-size sampling and classical variables sampling.

The choice between a statistical and a nonstatistical sampling plan is generally based on whether the auditor requires a quantitative estimate of sampling risk (which, as explained earlier, can only be accomplished with statistical sampling) and the relative costs and effectiveness of each plan in the circumstances. In turn, the choice between PPS sampling and classical variables sampling is based on the relative advantages and disadvantages of each plan, several of which are listed in Figure 9-10. For example, probability-proportional-to-size sampling automatically stratifies an audit population because, as explained in the following section, sampling units are selected in proportion to their dollar amount. However, in classical variables sampling, auditors attempt to control sample size by *stratifying* a highly variable audit population into strata (for example, accounts over or under $20,000, accounts over or under 90 days), thereby minimizing variability within strata and eliminating variability between strata.

Probability-Proportional-to-Size Sampling

Probability-proportional-to-size (PPS) sampling[2] expresses results in dollars but is derived from attributes sampling theory. Although appropriate when one

---

2   Variations of PPS sampling include dollar-unit sampling, cumulative monetary amount sampling, and combined attributes variables sampling.

FIGURE 9-10: *Relative Advantages and Disadvantages of Probability-Proportional-to-Size (PPS) Sampling and Classical Variables Sampling*

Probability-Proportional-to-Size (PPS) Sampling

Advantages:

- PPS sampling automatically results in a stratified sample because items are selected in proportion to their dollar amounts.
- If no errors are expected, PPS sampling usually results in a smaller sample size than classical variables sampling.
- A PPS sample can be designed more easily and sample selection can begin before the complete population is available.

Disadvantages:

- If a PPS sample includes understatement errors, evaluation of the sample will require special design considerations.
- When errors are found, PPS evaluation may overstate the allowance for sampling risk.
- PPS sampling generally includes an assumption that the audited amount of a sampling unit should not be less than zero or greater than the recorded amount.

Classical Variables Sampling

Advantages:

- If there are many individual differences between recorded and audited amounts in the population, classical variables sampling may result in a smaller sample size.
- Selection of zero or negative balances within a sample generally does not require special sample design considerations.
- If necessary, expanding classical variables samples may be easier than expanding probability-proportional-to-size samples.

Disadvantages:

- Classical variables sampling is more complex than probability-proportional-to-size sampling.
- To determine sample size, the auditor must have an estimate of the population standard deviation.
- Normal distribution theory, the basis underlying classical variables sampling, may not be appropriate when the sample size is not large and there are either very large items or very large differences between recorded and audited amounts in the population.

or a few population errors are expected, PPS sampling is best applied when no errors are expected. Why? Because when many errors are expected, required sample size may be much higher for PPS sampling than for difference estimation (Appendix).

In PPS sampling, the auditor's strategy is to randomly select individual dollars from a population and then to audit the balances, transactions, or documents—called *logical units*—that include the dollars selected. Each dollar in the population has an equal chance of being selected, but the likelihood of selecting any one logical unit for testing is directly proportional to its size, thereby accounting for the name "probability-proportional-to-size." For example, if a company's trade accounts receivable balance is $1,750,000, then the population size is 1,750,000 and an individual customer account with a balance of $87,500 has a 5 percent ($87,500/$1,750,000) chance of being selected for testing. For this reason, PPS sampling has two important properties. First, PPS sampling automatically stratifies audit populations by monetary value, since larger dollar value balances or transactions have a higher probability of being selected. Second, overstatements are more likely to be detected than understatements, since larger dollar value accounts have a higher probability of being selected. As a result, PPS sampling is most appropriate when an auditor judges there is a risk of material overstatements, since understated accounts have less chance of being selected for testing.

Define the Population

In PPS sampling, the population represents the class of transactions or account balance that an auditor intends to test. In practice, the population could vary markedly from engagement to engagement, depending on the circumstances. For example, in testing trade accounts receivable, the audit population could consist of:

- Customer debit balances only, or
- All customer balances, including debit balances, credit balances, and zero balances.

Negative balances in a population, such as credit balances in accounts receivable, usually require special consideration because they may contain properties not present in positive balances. For example, credit balances in accounts receivable may indicate overpayments or progress payments on revolving accounts. Auditors often exclude negative balances from the sample selection process, electing instead to test them separately. In addition, zero balances are often treated separately, since they have no chance of being selected in a PPS sampling plan otherwise. In this illustration, assume that an auditor's objective is to determine whether The Wilson Company's trade accounts receivable are overstated materially. The population is defined as all customer accounts with debit balances, and the recorded book value of these accounts is $1,750,000.

Determine Sample Size

PPS sample size requires that an auditor determine:

- A reliability factor for overstatement errors.
- Tolerable error.
- Anticipated error and an expansion factor.

Reliability Factor for Overstatement Errors

The reliability factor for overstatement errors can be determined from tables after first specifying:

- The expected number of overstatement errors, and
- The risk of incorrect acceptance.

In PPS sampling, the risk of incorrect acceptance is incorporated into the sampling plan explicitly through the reliability factor for overstatement errors. However, the risk of incorrect rejection is not incorporated explicitly. Since PPS sampling is most appropriate when no errors are expected, zero is the appropriate estimate for the *expected number of overstatement errors* (even when a small number of errors are expected). In PPS sampling, the *risk of incorrect acceptance* represents an auditor's assessment of the risk that book value is not materially overstated when, in fact, material monetary overstatement exists.

Figure 9-11 can be used to determine a reliability factor at various risks of incorrect acceptance and for various numbers of overstatement errors. The reliability factor appears where the identified column and row intersect. For example, if the auditor's risk of incorrect acceptance for The Wilson Company's trade accounts receivable balance is 15 percent, the reliability factor would be 1.90, the intersection of the column associated with a 15 percent risk of incorrect acceptance and the row associated with zero expected overstatement errors.

FIGURE 9-11: *PPS Sampling: Reliability Factors for Overstatement Errors*

Number of Over-statement Errors	Risk of Incorrect Acceptance								
	1%	5%	10%	15%	20%	25%	30%	37%	50%
0	4.61	3.00	2.31	1.90	1.61	1.39	1.21	1.00	.70
1	6.64	4.75	3.89	3.38	3.00	2.70	2.44	2.14	1.68
2	8.41	6.30	5.33	4.72	4.28	3.93	3.62	3.25	2.68
3	10.05	7.76	6.69	6.02	5.52	5.11	4.77	4.34	3.68
4	11.61	9.16	8.00	7.27	6.73	6.28	5.90	5.43	4.68
5	13.11	10.52	9.28	8.50	7.91	7.43	7.01	6.49	5.68
6	14.57	11.85	10.54	9.71	9.08	8.56	8.12	7.56	6.67
7	16.00	13.15	11.78	10.90	10.24	9.69	9.21	8.63	7.67
8	17.41	14.44	13.00	12.08	11.38	10.81	10.31	9.68	8.67
9	18.79	15.71	14.21	13.25	12.52	11.92	11.39	10.74	9.67
10	20.15	16.97	15.41	14.42	13.66	13.02	12.47	11.79	10.67
11	21.49	18.21	16.60	15.57	14.78	14.13	13.55	12.84	11.67
12	22.83	19.45	17.79	16.72	15.90	15.22	14.63	13.89	12.67
13	24.14	20.67	18.96	17.86	17.02	16.32	15.70	14.93	13.67
14	25.45	21.89	20.13	19.00	18.13	17.40	16.77	15.97	14.67
15	26.75	23.10	21.30	20.13	19.24	18.49	17.84	17.02	15.67
16	28.03	24.31	22.46	21.26	20.34	19.58	18.90	18.06	16.67
17	29.31	25.50	23.61	22.39	21.44	20.66	19.97	19.10	17.67
18	30.59	26.70	24.76	23.51	22.54	21.74	21.03	20.14	18.67
19	31.85	27.88	25.91	24.63	23.64	22.81	22.09	21.18	19.67
20	33.11	29.07	27.05	25.74	24.73	23.89	23.15	22.22	20.67

Source: AICPA, *Auditing Practice Release: Audit Sampling.* New York: AICPA, 2001, p. 97.

Tolerable Error, Anticipated Error, and Expansion Factor

Tolerable error in PPS sampling is closely related to an auditor's planned level of materiality, since it represents the maximum monetary error that may exist in an account balance without causing the financial statements to be misstated materially. Assume the auditor judges tolerable error to be $43,750 in the trade accounts receivable illustration for The Wilson Company.

As noted earlier, PPS sampling is best applied when no errors are expected, since sample size may be too high otherwise. However, if some errors are expected, the dollar value of anticipated error is explicitly incorporated into the sample size formula. For the Wilson case, assume anticipated error is $9,000, determined from the auditor's prior experience with the client.

An expansion factor for expected errors is based on the auditor's risk of incorrect acceptance and is determined from Figure 9-12. For the Wilson illustration, the risk of incorrect acceptance is 15 percent, and the expansion factor from Figure 9-12 is 1.4. The expansion factor is multiplied by anticipated error and, as illustrated next, the result is subtracted from the denominator in the sample size formula, thereby serving to increase sample size. If no errors are anticipated in the sample, anticipated error and the expansion factor are not used.

FIGURE 9-12: *PPS Sampling: Expansion Factors for Expected Errors*

	Risk of Incorrect Acceptance								
	1%	5%	10%	15%	20%	25%	30%	37%	50%
Factor	1.9	1.6	1.5	1.4	1.3	1.25	1.2	1.15	1.10

Source: AICPA, *Auditing Practice Release: Audit Sampling.* New York: AICPA, 2001, p. 98.

Sample Size

Sample size for a PPS sampling plan is calculated as follows:

$$n = \frac{RF \times B}{TE - (AE \times EF)}$$

where:

RF = Reliability factor for overstatement errors
B = Recorded book value
TE = Tolerable error
AE = Anticipated error
EF = Expansion factor

To illustrate, sample size in the accounts receivable application for The Wilson Company would be:

$$n = \frac{1.90 \times \$1,750,000}{\$43,750 - (\$9,000 \times 1.4)}$$

$$= 107 \text{ (rounded)}$$

Determine the Method of Sample Selection

In PPS sampling, logical units—the documents, transactions, or accounts tested—may be selected using random-number sampling or systematic sampling. Assume the auditor in The Wilson Company example uses systematic sampling.

To facilitate sample selection, all population items are arrayed in a spreadsheet, a cumulative listing of logical units is displayed, and logical units are then selected from the cumulative listing. For example, in the Wilson accounts receivable illustration, sample size is 107 and population size is 1,750,000. As a result, the *sampling interval* is 16,355 (1,750,000/107) and, following a randomly selected start, every 16,355th dollar from the cumulative balance is selected and the related customer account tested. Assuming a random start at the 5,000th cumulative dollar, the following customer accounts would be selected.

Customer No.	Book Value	Cumulative Dollars	Dollar Selected
1001	$ 6,500	1 – 6,500	5,000
1002	18,945	6,501 – 25,445	21,355
1003	2,210	25,446 – 27,655	
1004	12,500	27,656 – 40,155	37,710
1005	3,200	40,156 – 43,355	
	•		
	$1,750,000		

In this illustration, customer number 1001 would be selected for testing because 5,000, the random start, falls within the cumulative dollars 1 and 6,500; customer 1002 is selected because 21,355 (5,000 + 16,355, the sampling interval) falls within the cumulative dollars 6,501 and 25,445; and customer 1004 is selected because 37,710 [5,000 + (16,355 × 2)] falls within the cumulative balance 27,656 and 40,155. The selection process continues until all logical units—in this case customer accounts—are identified.

Evaluate the Sample

To evaluate the results of a PPS sample, an auditor estimates the *upper error limit*, which is the sum of the projected error in the sample and the allowance for sampling risk. However, the procedure for evaluating results depends on whether overstatement errors are found in the sample.

No Errors in the Sample

If no errors are found in the sample, then the projected population error is zero, and the allowance for sampling risk is no more than tolerable error. Stated another way, when no errors are found in the sample, the upper error limit is less than or equal to tolerable error. The auditor can therefore conclude that the recorded book value in the population is not overstated by more than tolerable error at the specified risk of incorrect acceptance. For example, if no errors are found in the trade accounts receivable illustration for The Wilson Company, then the auditor could conclude that:

The recorded book value of the population, $1,750,000, is not overstated by more than $43,750 (tolerable error) with a 15 percent risk of incorrect acceptance.

Errors Found in the Sample

If overstatement errors are found (that is, if the recorded book value exceeds the audited value), the auditor calculates the projected population error and the allowance for sampling risk and sums the two to arrive at an estimate of the upper error limit. Understatement errors, in contrast, require special consideration, in part because PPS sampling is designed primarily for overstatements.[3]

---

3 When an auditor judges that understatement errors may be significant, he or she should consider a separate test designed specifically to detect understatements. For example, see D. M. Roberts, *Statistical Auditing*. New York: AICPA, 1978, p. 124.

The *projected population error* is calculated differently depending on whether logical units containing errors, such as the customer balances in the Wilson illustration, are recorded at amounts:

- Less than the sampling interval, or
- Greater than or equal to the sampling interval.

The calculation is done separately for each logical unit containing error in this way: For each logical unit recorded at less than the sampling interval, the error in the logical unit is projected to the population in the same proportion that the overstatement percentage, called a *tainting percentage*, bears to the sampling interval. For each logical unit recorded at an amount greater than or equal to the sampling interval, the projected error equals the overstatement error found. To illustrate, assume that overstatement errors are found in three customer receivable balances, the logical unit in The Wilson Company illustration. The projected error is calculated as follows:

	(a)	*(b)*	*(c)*	*(d)* Tainting	*(e)*	*(f)* Projected
Error Number	*Book Value*	*Audited Value*	*Difference (a) − (b)*	*Percentage (c) ÷ (a)*	*Sample Interval*	*Error (d) × (e)*
Logical units recorded at less than sampling interval:						
1	$12,000	$ 9,000	$3,000	.25	$16,355	$4,089
2	10,000	9,500	500	.05	16,355	818
						$4,907
Logical unit greater than or equal to sampling interval:						
3	29,000	25,500	3,500	—	—	3,500
	$51,000	$44,000	$7,000			$8,407

The *allowance for sampling risk* requires two separate calculations: basic precision and an incremental allowance for sampling risk. *Basic precision* is determined by multiplying the sampling interval by the reliability factor in Figure 9-11 associated with the auditor's risk of incorrect acceptance for zero errors. For example, in the Wilson illustration, basic precision is:

Sampling interval	$16,355
RF, reliability factor for 0.15 risk of incorrect acceptance	× 1.90
Basic precision	$31,075 (rounded)

The *incremental allowance* is determined from the projected error for each logical unit recorded at less than the sampling interval—for example, error numbers 1 and 2 in the Wilson illustration—and the actual error for each logical unit greater than (or equal to) the sampling interval.

One approach to calculating the incremental allowance for logical units less than the sampling interval is to:

- Rank the logical units containing errors in order of tainting percentage, and
- Multiply the projected error for each logical unit by the incremental change in reliability factor at a specified risk of incorrect acceptance.

This approach is illustrated for The Wilson Company accounts receivable example as follows (note that for error number 3, recorded in an amount greater than the sampling interval, the projected error is the actual error detected):

Error Number	Projected Error	Incremental Change in Reliability Factor			Projected Error × Increment
		No. of Errors	*Reliability Factor*	*Increment*	
Logical units recorded at less than sampling interval:					
		0	1.90		
1	$4,089	1	3.38	1.48	$ 6,052
2	818	2	4.72	1.34	1,096
	$4,907				$ 7,148
Logical unit greater than or equal to sampling interval:					
3	$3,500	—	—	—	3,500
					$10,648

Thus, in the Wilson illustration, the allowance for sampling risk is:

Basic precision	$31,075
Incremental allowance	10,648
Allowance for sampling risk	$41,723

From these results, the auditor would conclude that:

There is a 15 percent risk (that is, the risk of incorrect acceptance) that the recorded book value, $1,750,000, is overstated by $41,723 or more.

If the upper error limit is less than tolerable error, the results support the conclusion that the recorded book value in the population is not overstated by more than tolerable error at the specified risk of incorrect acceptance. For example, in the Wilson case, the upper error limit, $41,723, is less than tolerable error, $43,750. Therefore, the auditor can conclude that recorded book value, $1,750,000, is not overstated by more than $43,750 with a 15 percent risk of incorrect acceptance.

However, if the upper error limit exceeds tolerable error, recorded book value may be overstated. If this occurs, an auditor could (1) examine additional logical units from the population; (2) perform additional substantive tests directed toward the same audit objective; and, following these two steps, (3) have the client correct the errors found, reduce the upper error limit accordingly, and compare the revised upper error limit with tolerable error. However, recall that these alternatives are unlikely in well-planned applications, since an auditor's baseline expectation when applying PPS sampling is that there are no errors in the population.

Nonstatistical Sampling in Substantive Tests of Details

There are two general approaches to audit sampling, statistical and nonstatistical, and either can provide sufficient, competent evidential matter when applied properly. In short, a properly designed and executed nonstatistical sampling plan can be just as effective as a properly designed statistical sampling plan. Generally, auditors select a nonstatistical sampling plan when:

- There is no apparent need to quantify sampling risk.

- The cost of designing individual samples to meet statistical sampling requirements exceeds the benefits.
- The cost to select sampling units randomly exceeds the expected benefits.

Following is an example of a nonstatistical sampling plan. The discussion focuses on how an auditor determines sample size and evaluates the sample results. Note carefully, though, that the discussion addresses only one example of a nonstatistical sampling plan, since a number of different plans are applied in practice.[4]

Determine Sample Size

In a nonstatistical sampling plan, an auditor first determines the following:

- The degree of audit assurance desired
- An appropriate assurance factor
- An estimated tolerable error

The Degree of Audit Assurance Desired and Assurance Factor

The degree of audit assurance desired is assessed judgmentally based on the auditor's assessment of the effectiveness of internal control (that is, control risk) and on other procedures. For example, the degree of audit assurance could be assessed as follows:

Degree of Audit Assurance	*Effectiveness of Internal Control and Other Procedures*
Substantial	Little or none
Moderate	Some
Little	Considerable

The degree of audit assurance is determined after the auditor obtains an understanding of internal control.

From the desired degree of audit assurance, the auditor next chooses a numerical factor based on the frequency and amount of errors expected in the population. For example, the assurance factor could be chosen as follows:

	Assurance Factor	
Audit Assurance Desired	*Little Error Expected*	*Some Error Expected*
Substantial	6	12
Moderate	4	8
Little	2	2

These numerical assurance factors are illustrative only.

Estimated Tolerable Error and Key-Dollar Items

As in statistical sampling, tolerable error is the auditor's assessment of the maximum monetary error that may exist without causing the financial statements to be misstated materially. *Key-dollar items,* in contrast, are the items an auditor plans to test 100 percent. For example, assuming tolerable error of $8,000, the key-dollar

---

4   See for example, AICPA, *Auditing Practice Release: Audit Sampling,* Chapter 5. New York: AICPA, 2001.

items would, at a minimum, include all population items of $8,000 or more, because a misstated item of at least $8,000 would alone consume the auditor's tolerable error for the entire account balance. As a result, the key-dollar items would be at least $8,000, and probably less.

Once an assurance factor is chosen and tolerable error and key-dollar items are estimated, preliminary sample size could be calculated as follows:

$$n = \left(\frac{B - KD}{TE}\right) \times AF$$

where:

B = Recorded account balance
KD = Sum of key-dollar items
TE = Tolerable error
AF = Assurance factor

To illustrate, assume the recorded account balance is $150,000, 12 key-dollar items sum to $70,000, tolerable error is $8,000, and the auditor desires moderate assurance and expects little error (that is, assurance factor = 4). From these data, preliminary sample size would be 52, represented by 12 key-dollar items and 40 sampling units calculated from the previous formula:

$$n = \left(\frac{\$150,000 - \$70,000}{\$8,000}\right) \times 4$$

$$= 40$$

Alternatively, the auditor could use tables rather than a formula to determine sample size.

Unlike statistical sample sizes, preliminary nonstatistical sample sizes do not represent the minimum number of items necessary to achieve an auditor's acceptable risks of incorrect rejection and incorrect acceptance. Rather, the nonstatistical sample size is preliminary and may be lowered or raised judgmentally based on factors such as those listed in Figure 9-13. For example, a lower sample size may be appropriate if the auditor decides to increase tolerable error or expects smaller and less frequent errors. As in nonstatistical sampling for attributes, an auditor can select the 40 sampling units with random-number sampling or systematic sampling, or select judgmentally with block or haphazard sampling.

FIGURE 9-13: *Factors Affecting Nonstatistical Sample Size*

| | Conditions Leading to | |
| | Smaller Sample Size | Larger Sample Size |
Factors		
Measure or tolerable error	Larger	Smaller
Expected size and frequency of misstatements	Smaller misstatements or less frequency	Larger misstatements or more frequency
Reliance on internal control	More	Less
Reliance on other substantive tests	More	Less

Evaluate the Sample Results

An auditor completes the nonstatistical sampling plan by determining *known error* (the misstatement observed within the sampling units tested) and by projecting *likely error* (the auditor's estimate of total population misstatement). For example, for the preceding data, assume that for the 12 key-dollar items, two overstatement errors are observed totaling $6,000, and for the 40 sampling units, 5 overstatement errors are observed totaling $1,000. Thus, known error is $7,000. Assume population size is 500 items. Likely error can be estimated by adding the $6,000 overstatement error for the key-dollar items to the error projected for the 40 sampling units:

Key-dollar error   = $ 6,000

Sampling units:

$$\frac{\$1,000}{\left(\dfrac{40}{(500-12)}\right)} = \underline{12,195}$$

Total projected error $\underline{\$18,195}$

Projected error for the 40 sampling units is estimated by dividing known error, $1,000, by the ratio of the number of sampling units to population size less the number of key-dollar items. In this case, likely error is $18,195, and the auditor has three alternative courses of action: (1) propose an audit adjustment, (2) perform additional substantive tests, or (3) request that the client revalue the entire population. In Chapter 13, nonstatistical sampling is applied to the accounts payable of a wholesaler of college and high school supplies.

SUMMARY

Audit sampling, whether statistical or nonstatistical, involves testing less than 100 percent of the items that compose an audit population and is intended to aid an auditor in reaching cost-effective conclusions about audit populations. Attributes sampling plans focus on rates of deviation from prescribed internal controls and are used to accomplish tests of controls. However, attributes sampling does entail some risk, partly because the auditor is not certain that a sample is wholly representative of the population from which the sampling units were drawn. Therefore, the auditor is not certain whether he or she is likely to assess control risk too high, which would affect the efficiency of the audit, or too low, which would affect the effectiveness of the audit.

Attributes sampling plans may be either statistical or nonstatistical, and either approach can provide reliable results if designed properly. A properly designed statistical or nonstatistical sampling plan should consider the auditor's objectives; properly defined attributes, deviation conditions, and populations; a defendable method of sample selection; a rational means of determining sample size; and justifiable procedures for performing the sampling plan and evaluating the results. Two generally accepted statistical sampling plans are attribute estimation and sequential (stop-or-go) sampling, both of which were illustrated in detail in the chapter.

Variables sampling plans focus on population monetary balances rather than rates of deviation. PPS sampling, used commonly in practice today, applies concepts from attributes sampling to reach conclusions about dollar amounts. The name "probability-proportional-to-size" derives from the fact that each sampling unit's likelihood of being selected for testing is directly proportional to its size. For this reason, PPS sampling automatically stratifies an audit population. As an alternative to classical variables sampling and PPS sampling, an auditor could choose a nonstatistical sampling plan and probably would if there were no apparent need to quantify sampling risk or if the cost of designing and selecting statistical samples exceeded the benefits of quantifying sampling risk. Difference estimation, introduced next in an Appendix, is a long-established statistical sampling plan for variables that can be applied when each population item has a recorded value, total recorded value is known and corresponds to the sum of all population items, and differences between audited and recorded values are not too rare.

APPENDIX: DIFFERENCE ESTIMATION—A CASE STUDY

Difference estimation and a competing plan, **ratio estimation**, are two similar classical variables sampling techniques that may be appropriate when the audit objective is to estimate a population's true but unknown monetary balance. Difference estimation focuses on the monetary difference between a sampling unit's audited and recorded book values. In contrast, ratio estimation focuses on the ratio between a sampling unit's audited and book values. Except for their focus on differences and ratios, respectively, the two plans are identical in approach.

Three conditions must exist before either difference or ratio estimation can be applied:

- Each population item must have a recorded book value (for example, perpetual, rather than periodic, inventory).
- Total population book value must be known (for example, a recorded general ledger book value) and must correspond to the sum of all individual population items.
- Expected differences between audited and recorded book values must not be too rare.

The first and second conditions are related, and result because recorded book values are required in order to calculate either differences or ratios between audited and recorded book values. The third condition, that differences must not be too rare, results because sample size would be too large otherwise. If differences are rare, a relatively large number of sampling units would be required in order to observe representative population differences. Ordinarily, about 30 sample differences are sufficient to assure a reasonable estimate of the true but unknown population monetary balance.

When the three necessary conditions exist, an auditor may choose either difference or ratio estimation, although one method may be more efficient than the other depending on the relationship between differences and recorded book values. In general, ratio estimation is more appropriate when the differences are nearly proportional to book values—that is, when the absolute amounts of the differences tend to increase as book values increase. Difference estimation, on the other hand, is more appropriate when there is little or no relationship between the absolute amounts of the differences and the book values. When differences are somewhat proportional but there is no strong tendency toward either proportionality or nonproportionality, ratio and difference estimation will yield similar results.

In difference estimation, the strategy is to estimate the amount of monetary misstatement in the population, called the difference estimate, from misstatement observed in the sample, and then to calculate an estimated audited value for the population by netting the difference estimate with the recorded account balance. To determine a difference estimate, the auditor sums all sample differences between recorded and audited values to yield a net sample difference, divides the net sample difference by sample size, and then multiplies the result by population size. The difference estimate is then added to the recorded account balance if there is a net understatement (or subtracted if there is a net overstatement) to yield the estimated audited value. In turn, the auditor estimates an allowance for sampling risk. The following example illustrates difference estimation.

Define the Population

Assume an auditor is applying difference estimation to The Wilson Company's trade accounts payable. Each payable has a recorded book value, the sum of all recorded payables agrees with the general ledger balance, and differences between audited and recorded book values are not rare. The auditor has selected difference rather than ratio estimation because past experience indicates that differences are not proportional to recorded book value, and therefore that there is no discernible relationship between the absolute amounts of differences and the recorded book values. The audit population consists of 4,100 individual payable accounts, each one of which represents a sampling unit. Recorded book value for all payables is $3,350,000.

Determine Sample Size

Sample size requires estimates of the variation within the population, the estimated population standard deviation, an acceptable risk of incorrect rejection, an acceptable risk of incorrect acceptance, and tolerable error. Each can be determined as follows.

Estimated Population Standard Deviation

A pilot sample can be used to estimate a population standard deviation from the following formula:

$$S = \sqrt{\sum_{i=1}^{n} \frac{d_i^2 - n(\bar{d})^2}{n-1}}$$

where:

S = Estimated population standard deviation
d = Difference between audited value (a_i) and book value (b_i) of the ith item
n = Sample size
$\bar{d}$ = Average difference between audited and book value for all pilot sample items.

In this case, assume that the sum of all squared differences in the pilot sample, d_i^2, is $765,000; the pilot sample size, n, is 50; and the average difference in the pilot sample, $\bar{d}$, is \$10. From these facts, the estimated population standard deviation would be:

$$S = \sqrt{\left[\$765,000 - 50(10)^2 \right] \div 49}$$

$$= \$125 \text{ (rounded)}$$

Risk and Tolerable Error

Sample size calculations also require that the auditor specify the acceptable risk of incorrect rejection, the acceptable risk of incorrect acceptance, and tolerable error. From these parameters the auditor calculates the *desired allowance for sampling risk* (sometimes called desired precision), which is the auditor's allowance for the risk that the sample selected may contain disproportionately more or less monetary misstatement than exists within the population as a whole. The allowance for sampling risk is calculated as follows:

$$A = R \times TE$$

where:

A = Desired allowance for sampling risk
R = Ratio of desired allowance for sampling risk to tolerable error
TE = Tolerable error

The ratio of desired allowance for sampling risk to tolerable error (R) is determined from Figure 9-14. For example, assume the auditor specifies the following:

- Acceptable risk of incorrect rejection   =   0.10
- Acceptable risk of incorrect acceptance   =   0.05
- Tolerable error   =   \$170,000

From Figure 9-14, the ratio of desired allowance for sampling risk to tolerable error is 0.500, the intersection of the column associated with a 10 percent risk of incorrect rejection and the row associated with a 5 percent risk of incorrect acceptance. Desired allowance for sampling risk is then calculated as follows:

$$A = 0.500 \times \$170,000$$

$$= \$85,000$$

Sample Size

Audit sample size can be determined by the following formula designed to generate the minimum number of observations required, given population size and estimated variability, the acceptable risk of incorrect rejection, and the desired allowance for sampling risk:

$$n = \left(\frac{S \times U \times N}{A} \right)^2$$

where:

S = Estimated population standard deviation
U = Acceptable risk of incorrect rejection
N = Population size
A = Desired allowance for sampling risk
n = Sample size

FIGURE 9-14: *Ratio of Desired Allowance for Sampling Risk to Tolerable Error*

Risk of Incorrect Acceptance	Risk of Incorrect Rejection			
	.20	.10	.05	.01
.01	.355	.413	.457	.525
.025	.395	.456	.500	.568
.05	.437	.500	.543	.609
.075	.471	.532	.576	.641
.10	.500	.561	.605	.668
.15	.511	.612	.653	.712
.20	.603	.661	.700	.753
.25	.653	.708	.742	.791
.30	.707	.756	.787	.829
.35	.766	.808	.834	.868
.40	.831	.863	.883	.908
.45	.907	.926	.937	.952
.50	1.000	1.000	1.000	1.000

Source: AICPA, *Auditing Practice Release: Audit Sampling.* New York: AICPA, 2001, p. 99.

U, the standard normal deviate for the desired risk of incorrect rejection, is determined from Figure 9-15, a table of commonly used risk levels. In this case, the risk of incorrect rejection is 0.10, and from Figure 9-15, the standard normal deviate is 1.65. The risk levels in Figure 9-15 vary from 0.01 to 0.30, the typical range of risk levels accepted by most practicing auditors. Note from the table that as the risk of incorrect rejection increases—for example, from 0.01 to 0.05—the standard normal deviate decreases (from 2.58 to 1.96) and, because U is in the numerator of the sample size formula, sample size decreases as well.

Based on the information for The Wilson Company, sample size would be:

$$n = \left(\frac{\$125 \times 1.65 \times 4,100}{\$85,000}\right)^2$$

$$= 99 \text{ (rounded)}$$

FIGURE 9-15: *Standard Normal Deviate for Selected Risks of Incorrect Rejection*

Risk of Incorrect Rejection	U, Standard Normal Deviate
.01	2.58
.05	1.96
.10	1.65
.15	1.44
.20	1.28
.25	1.15
.30	1.04

Determine the Method of Sample Selection, Perform the Sampling Plan, and Evaluate the Sample Results

Continuing the illustration, the auditor examines evidence supporting each of the 99 sampled payable accounts. An audited value is determined for each account, differences between audited and recorded book values are documented, and the following summary calculations are made:

$\hat{D}$ = The total projected monetary difference between the population value and the recorded account balance

$\hat{X}$ = The estimated population value

A' = The achieved allowance for sampling risk

In difference estimation, the total projected monetary difference between the population value and the recorded account balance is calculated as follows:

$$\hat{D} = N\bar{d}$$

where:

N = Population size

$\bar{d}$ = Average difference, calculated by dividing the sum of the differences by sample size

To illustrate the evaluation of sample results for a difference estimation sampling plan, partial sample data for The Wilson Company are presented in Figure 9-16. Book and audited values are shown for the first through the tenth sample items and for the 99th item, and totals are presented for all sample items. As shown in Figure 9-16, total book value for the 99 accounts examined is $74,416, and total audited value for these accounts is $76,000, yielding a net understatement difference of $1,584.

FIGURE 9-16: *The Wilson Company: Sample Data—Trade Accounts Payable*

Sample Item	Book Value (b_i)	Audited Value (a_i)	Difference ($d_i = a_i - b_i$)
1	$ 1,550	$ 1,550	$ 0
2	1,700	1,741	40
3	930	930	0
4	520	907	387
5	841	841	0
6	1,335	1,225	−110
7	655	655	0
8	185	185	0
9	420	420	0
10	310	320	10
•	•	•	•
•	•	•	•
•	•	•	•
99	489	312	−177
	$74,416	$76,000	$−1,584

The average difference is $16 ($1,584 ÷ 99), and the population size (N) is 4,100. Thus, the total projected monetary difference is:

$$\hat{D} = 4{,}100 \times \$16$$

$$= \$65{,}600$$

The estimated population value ($\hat{X}$), sometimes referred to as the point estimate, is calculated by adding the total projected difference to the recorded account balance (B):

$$\hat{X} = \hat{D} + B$$

$$= \$65{,}600 + \$3{,}350{,}000$$

$$= \$3{,}415{,}600$$

To determine the achieved allowance for sampling risk (A'), the auditor first calculates the sample standard deviation from the formula used earlier to calculate the pilot sample standard deviation. Assume that for the 99 sampling units examined, the sample standard deviation is $120. The achieved allowance for sampling risk is calculated as follows:

$$A' = \frac{S \times U \times N}{\sqrt{n}} \sqrt{1 - \frac{n}{N}}$$

$$A' = \frac{\$120 \times 1.65 \times 4{,}100}{\sqrt{99}} \sqrt{1 - \frac{99}{4{,}100}}$$

$$= \$80{,}772 \text{ (rounded)}$$

A *precision interval*, determined from the estimated population value and achieved allowance for sampling risk, follows:

$$\text{Precision interval} = \hat{X} \pm A'$$

$$= \$3{,}415{,}600 \pm \$80{,}772$$

$$= \$3{,}334{,}828 \text{ to } \$3{,}496{,}372$$

From the sample results, the auditor would conclude:

Based on procedures applied, the estimated population value is $3,415,600, and there is a 95 percent probability (1 – risk of incorrect acceptance) that the true but unknown population value is included in the precision interval, $3,334,828 to $3,496,372. Conversely, there is a 5 percent risk that the true but unknown population value falls outside the precision interval.

In this case, the sample results support the conclusion that trade accounts payable for The Wilson Company are not materially misstated, since the precision interval ($3,334,828 to $3,496,372) includes the recorded account balance ($3,350,000), and the achieved allowance for sampling risk ($80,772) does not exceed the desired allowance ($85,000). Therefore, the auditor would accept the recorded account balance. However, what if the recorded account balance fell outside the precision interval and/or the achieved allowance for sampling risk exceeded the desired allowance for sampling risk? These conditions are discussed next.

Adjusting Recorded Account Balances in Classical Variables Sampling

In the illustration above, recorded account balances were accepted as fairly stated because (1) the precision interval included the recorded account balance and (2) the desired allowance for sampling risk exceeded the achieved allowance for sampling risk. But what if these two conditions were not met? Each situation is discussed separately next.

Recorded Account Balance Falls Outside Precision Interval

A recorded account balance falling outside the precision interval could still be accepted as fairly stated if tolerable error exceeds the difference between (1) the recorded account balance and (2) the farthest end of the precision interval. For example, assume that the recorded account balance is $1,020,000, tolerable error is $125,000, estimated population value is $950,000, and the achieved allowance for sampling risk is $50,000, yielding a precision interval from $900,000 to $1,000,000, as illustrated in Figure 9-17.

FIGURE 9-17: *Recorded Account Balance Falls Outside Precision Interval*

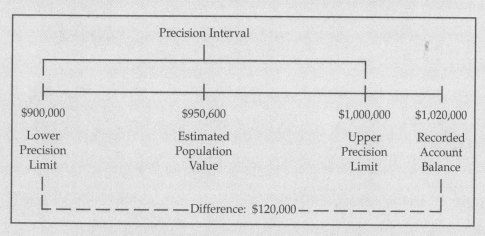

From Figure 9-17 the difference between the recorded account balance ($1,020,000) and the farthest end of the precision interval (in this case, the lower precision limit, $900,000) is $120,000, which is less than the auditor's tolerable error ($125,000). As a result, the recorded account balance is accepted as fairly stated, since the amount of error the auditor is willing to tolerate (tolerable error) exceeds the maximum likely error in the population. Incidentally, this situation typically occurs when the auditor's tolerable error greatly exceeds the achieved allowance for sampling risk, as in the illustration (that is, tolerable error = $125,000; achieved allowance for sampling risk = $50,000).

In contrast, if tolerable error does not exceed the maximum likely error, an auditor could (1) increase sample size and reevaluate for all sampling units, (2) request that the client revalue the population, or (3) propose an audit adjustment, as illustrated next.

Achieved Allowance for Sampling Risk Exceeds Desired Allowance

If the achieved allowance for sampling risk (A') exceeds the desired allowance for sampling risk (A), the risk of incorrect acceptance becomes greater, because the precision interval, $\hat{X} \pm A'$, is larger than $\hat{X} \pm A$. Thus, for the larger $\hat{X} \pm A'$, there is a greater probability of accepting a materially misstated account balance—that is, the risk of incorrect acceptance. The alternatives available to the auditor are the same as those identified in the preceding illustration (increase sample size, request that the client revalue the population, or propose an audit adjustment).

Altering the facts from the previous illustration, assume tolerable error is $60,000, and the desired allowance for sampling risk is $40,000. In this case, the recorded account balance could not be accepted as fairly stated, absent additional substantive tests, because (1) the recorded account balance ($1,020,000) falls outside the precision interval ($900,000 to $1,000,000), (2) the achieved allowance for sampling risk ($50,000) exceeds the desired allowance for sampling risk ($40,000), and (3) tolerable error ($60,000) does not exceed the difference between the recorded account balance ($1,020,000) and the lower precision limit ($900,000). As a result, an audit adjustment could be proposed. The adjusted book value would be $960,000, the lower precision limit ($900,000) plus tolerable error ($60,000), and the proposed audit adjustment would be $60,000, computed by subtracting the adjusted book balance from the recorded balance.

KEY TERMS

Attribute 356	Risk of incorrect acceptance 360
Attributes estimation sampling 361	Risk of incorrect rejection 359
Attributes sampling plan 356	Ratio estimation 389
Deviation 356	Sample deviation rate 369
Difference estimation 389	Sampling 356
Nonsampling risk 358	Sampling plan 356
Nonstatistical sampling plans 360	Sampling risk 358
Population 356	Sampling unit 362
Probability-proportional-to-size (PPS) sampling 378	Sequential (stop-or-go) sampling 373
Risk of assessing control risk too high 359	Statistical sampling plans 360
Risk of assessing control risk too low 359	Tolerable rate of deviation 363
	Variables sampling plan 356

REFERENCES

Professional Standards:

AICPA, *Codification of Auditing Standards*. New York: AICPA (AU Sec. 312, 319, 350).

SAS No. 39, "Audit Sampling" (AU Sec. 350).

SAS No. 47, "Audit Risk and Materiality in Conducting an Audit" (AU Sec. 312).

SAS No. 55, "Consideration of the Internal Control Structure in a Financial Statement Audit" (AU Sec. 319).

SAS No. 78, "Consideration of Internal Control in a Financial Statement Audit: An Amendment to SAS No. 55" (AU Sec. 319).

Professional Report:

AICPA, *Auditing Practice Release: Audit Sampling*. New York: AICPA, 2001.

QUESTIONS

1. What is meant by the term *audit sampling*?
2. Distinguish between sampling for attributes and sampling for variables.
3. What is the purpose of attributes sampling in tests of controls?
4. Describe the nature and components of audit risk.
5. What is nonsampling risk and how can it be controlled?
6. Identify the sampling risks inherent in sampling for attributes.
7. Compare and contrast nonstatistical and statistical audit sampling plans.
8. Why is it important that audit populations be defined properly?
9. How can an auditor achieve randomness when selecting a statistical sample?
10. What is the purpose of stratifying an audit population?
11. Identify the three parameters necessary to determine sample size in attribute estimation sampling plans.
12. Describe the alternative available to an auditor when an attributes sampling plan suggests that a control is not effective.
13. When is attribute estimation appropriate?
14. When is sequential sampling appropriate?
15. Identify and briefly describe two aspects of audit risk that are critical in an auditor's substantive tests of account balances.
16. Explain the difference between *dollar-value estimation* and *hypothesis testing* in audit sampling. Which of the two is more common in auditing?
17. Define what is meant by an *audit population*. What is the importance of an auditor's *characteristic of interest* when defining an audit population?
18. What is a *sampling unit*?
19. Identify the relative advantages and disadvantages of classical variables sampling.
20. Identify the relative advantages and disadvantages of probability-proportional-to-size sampling.
21. Define *tolerable error*.
22. Briefly describe the auditor's strategy when applying probability-proportional-to-size sampling.
23. Why is probability-proportional-to-size sampling most appropriate when an auditor desires testing for material overstatements?
24. Under what conditions would an auditor choose a nonstatistical sampling plan in substantive tests of details?

Appendix

25. Identify three conditions that must exist before difference estimation can be applied.
26. Under what condition is difference estimation more appropriate than ratio estimation?
27. Assume an auditor sets acceptable risks of incorrect rejection and incorrect acceptance at 0.10 and 0.05, respectively, applies difference estimation, and obtains the following results: estimated population value, $250,000; achieved allowance for sampling risk, $32,500. Draft the auditor's conclusion.

MULTIPLE CHOICE QUESTIONS

1. Tests of controls provide reasonable assurance that controls are applied as prescribed. A sampling method that is useful when testing controls is:

    a. Nonstatistical sampling.
    b. Attribute estimation.
    c. Random sampling.
    d. Stratified random sampling.

2. Statistical sampling:

   a. Measures quantitatively the risk of testing only part of an audit population.
   b. Allows the same degree of confidence as nonstatistical sampling but with substantially less work.
   c. Allows the auditor to replace some judgments with quantitative measures.
   d. Measures the reliability of misstatements.

3. Assessing control risk too high is the risk that the sample:

   a. Does not support tolerable error for some or all of management's assertions.
   b. Contains proportionately more deviations from prescribed control procedures than actually exist in the population as a whole.
   c. Contains monetary misstatements that could be material to the financial statements when aggregated with misstatements in other account balances or classes of transactions.
   d. Contains proportionately fewer deviations from prescribed control procedures than actually exist in the population as a whole.

4. Which of the following statements is correct?

   a. The expected population deviation rate has little or no effect on sample size.
   b. As the population size doubles, the sample size also should double.
   c. For a given tolerable rate, a larger sample size should be selected as the expected population deviation rate decreases.
   d. The population size has little or no effect on sample size except for very small populations.

   (AICPA Adapted)

5. When sampling for attributes, which of the following would decrease sample size?

	Risk of Assessing Control Risk Too Low	Tolerable Rate	Expected Population Deviation Rate
a.	Increase	Decrease	Increase
b.	Decrease	Increase	Decrease
c.	Increase	Increase	Decrease
d.	Increase	Increase	Increase

6. An auditor is performing an attribute estimation sampling plan. Assuming 0.05 acceptable risk of assessing control risk too low, 0.04 tolerable rate of deviation, and 0.01 expected population deviation rate, what is the required sample size?

   a. 156
   b. 96
   c. 93
   d. Not determinable from the facts given

7. An auditor is performing an attribute estimation sampling plan. The risk of assessing control risk is 0.05 and sample size is 80. Assuming one deviation is detected, what is the auditor's estimate of the maximum population deviation rate?

   a. 0.037
   b. 0.048
   c. 0.058
   d. Not determinable from the facts given

8. An auditor is performing a sequential (stop-or-go) sampling plan. Assuming 0.95 desired reliability and 0.04 tolerable rate of deviation, what is the auditor's initial sample size?

   a. 50
   b. 70
   c. 100
   d. Not determinable from the facts given

9. Which of the following sampling plans varies sample size?

   a. Attribute estimation
   b. Sequential sampling
   c. Systematic sampling
   d. Stratified sampling

10. Which of the following statements is true about nonstatistical sampling in tests of controls?

    a. Nonstatistical sampling plans provide a quantitative measure of sampling risk.
    b. The auditor's judgment in nonstatistical sampling is guided by classical statistical sampling concepts.
    c. The calculated nonstatistical sample should never be altered judgmentally.
    d. The auditor considers the same parameters when determining a nonstatistical sample size as when determining a statistical sample size.

11. Which of the following is necessary to determine sample size?

    a. Population size
    b. Expected population deviation rate
    c. Estimated population monetary error
    d. Risk

12. Which of the following statements is an advantage of classical variables sampling?

    a. If no errors are expected, variables sampling will result in a smaller sample size than probability-proportional-to-size sampling.
    b. A variables sampling plan can begin before the completed population is available.
    c. Variables sampling may result in a smaller sample size than probability-proportional-to-size sampling if there are many differences between recorded and audited amounts.
    d. Variables sampling does not require recorded values for individual sampling units.

13. Which of the following situations would increase sample size: a decrease in:

    a. Risk of incorrect rejection?
    b. Estimated population standard deviation?
    c. Expected frequency of errors?
    d. Tolerable error?

14. The risk of incorrect acceptance relates to the:

    a. Effectiveness of the audit.
    b. Efficiency of the audit.
    c. Preliminary estimate of materiality.
    d. Allowable risk of tolerable error.

                                                                    (AICPA Adapted)

15. Sample results support the conclusion that a recorded account balance is materially misstated, but unknown to the auditor, the account is not misstated, suggesting the risk of:

    a. Incorrect rejection.
    b. Incorrect acceptance.
    c. Assessing control risk too high.
    d. Assessing control risk too low.

16. Probability-proportional-to-size sampling will likely result in selecting a sample with characteristics roughly equivalent to:

    a. A classical variables sampling plan stratified by dollar amount.
    b. Difference estimation.
    c. Ratio estimation.
    d. Nonstatistical sampling.

17. In probability-proportional-to-size sampling, each invoice:

    a. Has an equal probability of being selected.
    b. Can be represented by no more than one dollar unit.
    c. Has an unknown probability of being selected.
    d. Has a probability proportional to its dollar value of being selected.

18. Which of the following is improper when using probability-proportional-to-size sampling?

    a. Combining negative and positive dollar error items
    b. Using a sample selection technique in which the same account balance could be selected more than once
    c. Selecting a random starting point and then sampling every nth dollar unit
    d. Defining the sampling unit as an individual dollar and not as an individual account balance

19. In a probability-proportional-to-size sampling plan with a $10,000 sampling interval, an auditor discovered that a selected account receivable with a recorded amount of $5,000 had an audited amount of $2,000. The projected error for the sample is:

    a. $3,000.
    b. $4,000.
    c. $6,000.
    d. $8,000.

20. A nonstatistical sampling plan can:

    a. Overstate the estimate of sampling risk.
    b. Misdirect an auditor to unreliable sampling units.
    c. Replicate the results of a statistical sampling plan.
    d. Understate the degree of audit assurance desired.

Appendix

21. In a difference estimation sampling plan for a population of 1,500 items, an auditor found total recorded and audited value for a sample of 100 items to be $120,000 and $126,000, respectively. What is the total projected monetary difference for the population?

    a. $6,000
    b. $90,000
    c. $126,000
    d. Indeterminate

PROBLEMS AND DISCUSSION CASES

9-1 *Sampling and Audit Risk*

Auditors do not often have the luxury of testing 100 percent of the transactions and events underlying account balances or classes of transactions. More often they rely on samples, thereby reducing audit costs but also creating a risk that the samples selected will not be representative of the population.

Required:
1. What risks does an auditor sustain solely as a result of sampling?
2. Explain how an inefficient audit can increase audit risk.

9-2 *Sampling and Audit Judgment*

The use of statistical sampling in a financial statement audit does not eliminate the need for professional judgment.

Required: Identify and explain four areas where judgment may be exercised by an auditor in planning a statistical sample.

(AICPA Adapted)

9-3 *Methods of Sample Selection*

A sample of 80 accounts payable vouchers is to be selected from a population of 3,200. The vouchers are numbered consecutively from 1 to 3,200 and are listed in a computer spreadsheet file.

Required: Describe the techniques for selecting a random sample of vouchers for review.

(AICPA Adapted)

9-4 *Selecting Sampling Plans*

Within the chapter, two alternative statistical sampling plans were introduced and illustrated for use when conducting tests of controls under the second standard of field work: attribute estimation and sequential sampling. Neither of the two statistical sampling plans is necessarily appropriate for all tests. Rather, each is appropriate for particular audit circumstances; blindly applying a sampling plan to inappropriate populations can lead to audit inefficiencies and, in some cases, ineffectiveness.

Required:
1. Explain the circumstances under which attribute estimation and sequential sampling are appropriate.
2. Explain the circumstances under which an auditor might justifiably decide to switch to attribute estimation after sequential sampling already has begun.

9-5 *Attributes Sampling*

Sampling for attributes is often used to allow an auditor to reach a conclusion concerning the rate of occurrence in a population. A common use in auditing is to test the rate of deviation from a prescribed control procedure in order to assess control risk.

Required:
1. When an auditor samples for attributes, identify the factors that should influence the auditor's judgment about the (a) acceptable risk of assessing control risk too low, (b) tolerable deviation rate, and (c) expected population deviation rate.
2. State the effect on sample size of an increase in each of the following factors, assuming all other factors are held constant: (a) acceptable risk of assessing control risk too low, (b) tolerable deviation rate, and (c) expected population deviation rate.
3. Evaluate the sample results of a test for attributes if authorizations are found to be missing on 7 check requests out of a sample of 100 tested. The population consists of

2,500 check requests, the tolerable deviation rate is 8 percent, and the acceptable risk of assessing control risk too low is, itself, low.

4. How may the use of statistical sampling assist the auditor in evaluating the sample results in requirement 3?

9-6 *Attribute Estimation*

Assume that your audit objective is to estimate a true but unknown population rate of deviation. The risk of assessing control risk too low is 0.05, maximum tolerable rate of deviation is 0.07, and the expected population deviation rate is 0.0325.

Required:
1. Determine sample size.
2. What would be your statistical conclusion if four deviations are observed?
3. How would the sample results be interpreted in forming an audit conclusion?

9-7 *Attribute Estimation*

Walter Cole has decided to use statistical, rather than nonstatistical, sampling to test a client's control over purchase transactions. Specifically, Cole is testing whether vendor invoices are properly approved for payment as evidenced by the initials of authorized personnel on the face of the invoice. Cole estimates that a sample size of more than 80 could prove uneconomical, since he simply does not have sufficient budgeted audit hours to examine more than 80 documents. In addition, Cole believes that the expected population rate of deviation lies between 2 and 5 percent, and his tolerable rate of deviation cannot exceed 8 percent.

Required:
1. Given the parameters established by Cole, indicate the combination of tolerable and expected population rates of deviation that will achieve a sample size of 80 or less, assuming a 10 percent risk of assessing control risk too low.
2. Can Cole justifiably alter the tolerable rate of deviation for the express purpose of limiting sample size? Why or why not?

9-8 *Using Statistical Sampling to Achieve Audit Program Steps*

Robin Hamilton, a first-year associate, is reviewing the following selected audit procedures scheduled for use during the consideration of Windham Incorporated's internal controls.

Step	Tests of Controls
1.	Review evidence of internal controls for:
	a. Reconciliation of daily sales summaries with sales journal totals by General Accounting personnel.
	b. Periodic reconciliation of accounts receivable trial balances with general ledger control balances.
2.	Scan sales journal for unusual transactions or <u>unusually</u> large amounts and follow up on any such items identified.
3.	Examine <u>shipping documents</u> to determine whether the document:
	a. Is accompanied by a sales order bearing Credit and Inventory Control authorization.
	b. Agrees with a sales order as to description of goods, quantity, and destination.
4.	Trace details of <u>sales invoices</u> to entries in the sales journal and accounts receivable subsidiary ledger.

Required:
1. Indicate which of the procedures could be accomplished with statistical sampling. Assume attribute estimation is to be used.
2. Identify the <u>sampling unit</u> you would use for each test of controls accomplished with statistical sampling.

9-9 Attributes Estimation

Assume you are considering controls over a client's purchasing activities, and estimate the following for acceptable risk of assessing control risk (CR) too low, tolerable rate of deviation, and expected population deviation rate.

Attribute	Risk of CR Too Low	Tolerable Rate	Expected Rate
1. Voucher package (for example, purchase requisition, purchase order, receiving report, and invoice) is canceled after payment is made.	.05	.07	.01
2. Purchase is properly authorized.	.05	.05	.015
3. Details on purchase requisition, purchase order, receiving report, and invoice agree.	.05	.06	.0125
4. Purchase order in voucher package agrees with copy filed in Purchasing department.	.10	.07	.035
5. Canceled checks contain appropriate signatures and endorsements.	.05	.08	.02
6. Details on voucher package agree with canceled check (for example, check number, date, payee, and amount).	.05	.08	.03

The sampling results for each attribute follow.

Attribute	Number of Deviations
1	2
2	2
3	1
4	4
5	2
6	2

Required:

1. Using Figure 9-2 as a guide, prepare a work sheet documenting the attribute estimation sampling results. The work sheet should indicate required sample size determined (and sample size used, if different), estimated population deviation rate, and maximum population deviation rate.
2. Write a statistical conclusion and an audit conclusion for each attribute.

9-10 Attribute Estimation

You are planning interim tests of credit approval procedures for a December 31 year-end client, a manufacturer of name-brand children's toys. The attribute of interest is the credit manager's approval initials on the face of customer sales orders, and the population consists of all prenumbered sales orders issued through September 30, the date of the interim audit tests.

Required:

1. What is the sampling unit?
2. Assume your desired reliability is 95 percent and that the expected population deviation rate is .75 percent. Select a tolerable deviation rate between 4 and 10 percent, and indicate the sample size you would actually use for your tests.

3. What is the maximum population deviation rate if you detect one deviation in the sample?
4. Do the results for your sample indicate you can rely on the credit approval procedures to reduce control risk below the maximum? Why?
5. Upon returning for the year-end phase of the engagement but before performing audit procedures, the audit manager asks your opinion about the effectiveness of credit approval procedures during the holiday buying season. Respond.

9-11 Sequential (Stop-or-Go) Sampling

From prior audits of Bristol Inc. and recent discussions with management, an auditor believes that sales invoices agree in detail with related shipping documents, with very few exceptions. Therefore, zero or very few deviations are expected, and sequential sampling is selected as the statistical sampling plan. The auditor defines each relevant line item on the sales invoice as a separate sampling unit. Following are the auditor's desired reliability and tolerable rates of deviation for each attribute.

Attribute	Desired Reliability	Tolerable Rate of Deviation	Dev
1. Customer name	.90	.04	0
2. Description	.90	.05	0
3. Quantity	.95	.06	1
4. Unit price	.95	.05	1
5. Extensions	.95	.05	1

No deviations were observed for attributes 1 and 2, and one deviation was observed for attributes 3, 4, and 5, though not on the same sales invoices.

Required:
1. Determine initial sample size for each attribute.
2. How can the sales invoices be selected if sample size varies from attribute to attribute?
3. For each attribute, indicate whether to stop or go, and why.

9-12 Nonstatistical Sampling

Statistical sampling is not a panacea and is not necessarily appropriate for all tests of controls; nonstatistical sampling is often applied by practicing auditors, and for good reason.

Required:
1. Describe three conditions under which nonstatistical sampling would probably be inappropriate.
2. What sample selection techniques are available in nonstatistical sampling? Do they differ from those used in statistical sampling? Why?

9-13 Sample Selection and Evaluation

You are auditing the financial statements of Elite Corporation, a continuing audit client, for the year ended December 31, 2007. Unlike prior years, you decide to use a statistical sampling plan to test the effectiveness of the company's controls over sales invoices, all of which are sequentially numbered. In prior years, you selected one representative two-week period during the year and tested all of the invoices issued during that period.

Required:
1. Explain the procedures you would use to determine sample size.
2. Once sample size has been determined, how would you select the individual invoices to be included in the sample? Explain.
3. Compared with the selection procedure used in prior years, would the use of statistical sampling improve the audit of sales invoices? Discuss.

4. Assume that the company issued 50,000 sales invoices during the year and that you specified an acceptable risk of assessing control risk too low of 5 percent and a tolerable rate of 5 percent. Does this mean that the auditor would be willing to conclude a control is effective if errors are found on no more than 4 sales invoices out of every 95 invoices examined (that is, a sample deviation rate of 0.0421)? Discuss.

(AICPA Adapted)

9-14 *The Risks of Incorrect Rejection and Incorrect Acceptance*

The risks of incorrect rejection and incorrect acceptance are related but involve two entirely different outcomes: Incorrect rejection means the risk of concluding that recorded book value is materially misstated when material monetary error does not exist, and incorrect acceptance means the risk of concluding that recorded book value is not materially misstated when in fact material monetary error does exist. Importantly, difference estimation requires an estimate of the risks of incorrect rejection and incorrect acceptance, and probability-proportional-to-size sampling requires an estimate of the risk of incorrect acceptance.

Required:
1. Explain why the risks of incorrect rejection and incorrect acceptance are competing risks. Why, for example, does increasing the risk of incorrect acceptance necessarily decrease the risk of incorrect rejection?
2. How can an auditor systematically reduce both the risk of incorrect rejection and the risk of incorrect acceptance simultaneously?

9-15 *Circumstances Under Which Probability-Proportional-to-Size May Not Be Cost Effective*

In 1999, the Auditing Standards Board's Audit Sampling task force issued *Auditing Practice Release, Audit Sampling* (New York), which offers practical guidance about complying with *SAS No. 39*, "Audit Sampling," the profession's interpretation of generally accepted auditing standards when an auditor uses statistical and nonstatistical sampling in a financial statement audit. The *Release* identifies several circumstances under which probability-proportional-to-size "might not be the most cost-effective approach:"

- Inventory test counts and price tests when an auditor expects a significant number of understatements and overstatements.
- An application for which the auditor's objective is to estimate the dollar value of an account balance.
- Conversion of inventory from first in, first out to last in, first out.

Identifying these circumstances is a timely caution to practitioners that other approaches might be more cost effective.

Required:
1. Explain what you believe the task force means by a "cost-effective" audit sampling plan.
2. For each of the three circumstances, explain why probability-proportional-to-size sampling might not be cost effective.

9-16 *Sample Size in Probability-Proportional-to-Size Sampling*

One of the features of PPS sampling is that, under some circumstances, the plan usually results in a smaller sample size than classical variables sampling. For example, assuming population size of 4,100, acceptable risk of incorrect acceptance and rejection of 0.05 and 0.10, respectively, tolerable error of $170,000, and estimated population standard deviation of $125, difference estimation, a variables sampling plan introduced in the Appendix to the chapter, would require a sample size of roughly 100. If no errors are expected, PPS sampling would require a smaller sample size.

Required: Explain why PPS sampling usually results in a smaller sample size than classical variables sampling when no errors are expected.

9-17 *Applying Probability-Proportional-to-Size Sampling*

An auditor expects no errors in an audit population but is concerned about potential monetary overstatement and, therefore, elects to use PPS sampling. Recorded book value is $1,200,000, maximum tolerable overstatement is $67,500, and the risk of incorrect acceptance is preset at 15 percent.

After sample size is determined and sampling units are selected and examined, the following differences are noted:

Invoice No.	Recorded Value	Audited Value
1826	$15,000	$12,000
2041	$16,000	$15,050

Required:
1. Calculate sample size.
2. Calculate the allowance for sampling risk.
3. Reach a conclusion.

9-18 *Applying Probability-Proportional-to-Size Sampling*

Assume your audit objective is to estimate the upper error limit for an audit population and, therefore, you select PPS sampling. From prior-year working papers and evidence accumulated during the consideration of internal control, you concluded that errors are expected and that the risk of incorrect acceptance is 0.10.

The following information is also known.

- Recorded book value $1,000,000
- Maximum tolerable overstatement $100,000
- Anticipated error $15,000

After testing logical units, three differences are observed as follows:

Recorded Value	Audited Value	Difference
$20,000	$18,000	$2,000
$15,000	$14,250	$750
$40,000	$38,000	$2,000

Required: From this information, determine:
1. The reliability factor for overstatement errors.
2. The expansion factor.
3. Sample size.
4. The sampling interval.
5. Basic precision.
6. The incremental allowance.
7. The allowance for sampling risk (the upper error limit).
8. The audit conclusion.

9-19 *Applying Nonstatistical Sampling*

An auditor has no apparent need to quantify sampling risk and, therefore, uses a nonstatistical sampling plan for inventory price testing. From prior experience with the client and current information about internal control, the auditor expects some pricing errors but also desires moderate assurance that the pricing of physical goods is fairly accurate. The auditor presets tolerable error at $12,000 and decides to test the 15 highest dollar items, totaling $50,000, which represents 40 percent of total recorded book value, $125,000.

After determining sample size and selecting and examining the sampling units, the auditor compiles the following results:

	Number of Errors	Total Error
Key-dollar items	3	$5,000 overstatement
Sampled items	5	$1,500 overstatement

Population size is 600.

Required:
1. Determine an appropriate assurance factor.
2. Determine sample size.
3. Calculate likely error from the results.
4. Is recorded book value acceptable to the auditor? Why or why not?

9-20 *Applying Nonstatistical Sampling*

You are auditing the Tyco Corporation, a Midwest wholesaler of office supplies. Because tests revealed that controls over payables were not likely to produce aggregate error in excess of tolerable error, you assess control risk below the maximum. However, tests did reveal delays up to 72 hours in recording disbursements, thereby suggesting potential year-end cutoff problems that could result in overstated payables and overstated cash at December 31, the balance sheet date. You conclude that controls over payables are effective, but that delays in recording disbursements could drive overstated payables and cash balances at the balance sheet date. Although Tyco's cash disbursements volume is high, payables represent only 4 percent of total liabilities.

From this information, you decide to confirm a sample of accounts payable balances, since year-end balances could be overstated and, in this case, you believe confirmations would be less costly than extensive cutoff tests. You decide to use a nonstatistical sampling plan because there is no apparent reason to quantify audit risk.

At December 31, the audit population consists of 235 vendor accounts, totaling $350,000. The accounts payable trial balance, the source for selecting accounts for confirmation, is clerically accurate and agrees in total with the general ledger. Each vendor account represents a sampling unit. You decide to set tolerable error, the maximum monetary error that may exist without causing the financial statements to be misleading, at $30,000, which is over 8 percent of Tyco's recorded book value. The engagement partner sets the amount of key-dollar items at $6,500. You find that 15 of the 235 account balances in the population are $6,500 or more, and in total sum to $175,000.

Confirmations and other audit procedures reveal $3,815 of known error, $1,625 from the key-dollar items and $2,190 from the randomly selected items.

Required:
1. Determine an appropriate assurance factor.
2. Determine sample size.
3. Calculate likely error from the results.
4. Is recorded book value acceptable to the auditor? Why or why not?

9-21 *Nonstatistical versus Statistical Sampling*

An auditor is selecting from among alternative variables sampling plans for accounts receivable and gathers the following information. The client, a Midwestern manufacturer of high-technology electrical components, had been audited previously by a local public accounting firm. In five prior engagements, the predecessor auditors had issued unqualified opinions, except for last year when they issued a qualified opinion because of departures from generally accepted accounting principles. The client maintains subsidiary records for each individual customer account, and supporting documents are filed within the Accounts Receivable department. A review of selected sections of the predecessor auditor's working papers indicates that differences between recorded and audited values for individual customer accounts tended to increase as recorded book value increased.

Required:
1. Is nonstatistical sampling appropriate in this case? Explain.
2. Explain why probability-proportional-to-size sampling may be appropriate or inappropriate in this case.

Appendix

9-22 *Difference Estimation*

Because there is no discernible relationship between the absolute amount of differences (that is, audited value versus recorded book value) and recorded book value for 50 preliminary sample items, an auditor decides to use difference estimation in the audit of accounts receivable. The following data are known.

- Population size   2,500
- Estimated population standard deviation $20
- Acceptable risk of incorrect rejection   .05
- Desired allowance for sampling risk $10,000

After sample size is calculated and the sampling units selected and examined, the following summary data are available.

- Total recorded value for all sampling units $65,220
- Total audited value for all sampling units $64,970
- Net difference (that is, between recorded and
  audited amounts) for all sampling units $250
- Squared differences for all sampling units $215,000
- Estimated population standard deviation $48.53

Required: Assume difference estimation is applied and total recorded book value is $500,000. Determine:

1. Sample size.
2. Total projected monetary difference.
3. Estimated population value.
4. Achieved allowance for sampling risk.
5. Precision interval.

9-23 *Difference Estimation*

The following information is available for 50 sample items.

	Sample Item	Book Value	Audited Value
Subtotals, nondifference items	—	$55,265	$55,265
Difference items	5	670	720
	11	1,265	1,165
	18	1,980	1,800
	24	895	1,030
	29	725	912
	34	230	215
	38	415	490
		$61,445	$61,597

Population size is 2,100 items, recorded book value is $1,235,000, the risk of incorrect rejection is 0.10, the risk of incorrect acceptance is 0.05, and the sample standard deviation is $46.

Required: Formulate a conclusion for the data assuming difference estimation is used. Show all work supporting your conclusion.

9-24 *Difference Estimation*

Following are data for four different audit populations to which variables sampling will be applied.

	Population			
	1	*2*	*3*	*4*
Acceptable risk of incorrect rejection	.10	.05	.05	.01
Acceptable risk of incorrect acceptance	.20	.10	.25	.05
Population size	2,500	3,000	2,750	2,100
Estimated population standard deviation	$20	$12	$10	$15
Tolerable error	$8,750	$6,200	$7,000	$9,000

Required: Calculate sample size for each population. Assume sampling without replacement and do not ignore the finite population factor.

9-25 *Adjusting Recorded Account Balances*

When completing a variables sampling plan, an auditor's evaluation is based on the relationship between and among a number of factors, including recorded account balance, estimated total population value, tolerable error, the desired allowance for sampling risk, and the achieved allowance for sampling risk. The following table contains data for these factors.

	Case			
	1	*2*	*3*	*4*
Recorded account balance	$260,000	$255,000	$217,000	$238,000
Estimated population value	$235,000	$235,000	$223,000	$220,000
Tolerable error	$20,000	$37,500	$18,000	$32,000
Desired allowance for sampling risk	$12,000	$18,000	$10,000	$22,000
Achieved allowance for sampling risk	$15,000	$15,000	$12,000	$20,000

Required: For each case, indicate whether the recorded account balance can be accepted as fairly stated or not accepted and why. If an account balance is not accepted as fairly stated, determine the proper adjusted book value.

Internet problems and discussion cases are available at http://ricchiute.swlearning.com

RESEARCH PROJECTS

1. Sampling Risk, Reasonable Assurance, and Audit Risk: Who But Us Understands?

Translating *sampling risk* and *audit risk* into layman terms is rather straightforward: Sampling risk translates loosely to "the risk that what you're looking for is not where you're looking," and audit risk to "the risk of issuing an inappropriate opinion." But reconciling those risks with the concept of *reasonable* (rather than absolute) *assurance* is somewhat trickier when the audience is an aggrieved financial statement user. How do you explain to a commercial lender swindled in a high-profile embezzlement scheme that you were looking somewhere else, that your opinion was wrong but, because no audit guarantees absolute assurance, you're not culpable? Remember, this lender was swindled.

Required: Select an article that reports fraud in a corporate or governmental entity from the business or accounting press (for example, *The Wall Street Journal*, *Accounting Today*, *Public Accounting Report*, *BusinessWeek*, *The New York Times*) or from an automated newspaper research service like LEXIS-NEXIS or Factiva, and draft a report about:

1. How attributes estimation or sequential sampling might have signaled the fraud.
2. Arguments that might explain the relationship among sampling risk, audit risk, and reasonable assurance to the defrauded parties.

2. Attributes Sampling and the Professional Literature

Although the attributes sampling plans introduced in this chapter are accurate portrayals of plans applied in practice, they are by necessity generic. Over the years, professional journals such as the *Journal of Accountancy*, a monthly journal published by the American Institute of CPAs, have published articles offering advice about potential practical problems under titles such as "Audit Sampling: Dealing with the Problems" and "Attributes Sampling: A Local Firm's Experience." These articles not only provide timely cautions about audit sampling applications but also lend insight into the practical problems faced by auditors in practice.

Required: Select an article about attributes sampling from one of the following (or other) professional accounting journals.

- *The CPA Journal*
- *Journal of Accountancy*
- *Management Accounting*
- *The Practical Accountant*
- A state society of CPAs journal, such as *The Ohio CPA*, *The Michigan CPA*, etc.

For the article selected, draft a report that addresses each of the following:

1. Summarize the article in your own words.
2. What recommendations does the article offer to practitioners?
3. Do you believe that the article addresses the efficiency or the effectiveness (or both) of audit sampling?

3. Classical Variables Sampling and PPS Sampling

Applied widely first in the 1960s and 1970s, the use of statistical sampling initially was motivated largely by questions raised in legal liability cases involving public accounting firms, among them: Why did the firm not become aware of embezzlement schemes that, when made public thereafter (often by the perpetrators themselves, for example, *Ernst & Ernst v. Hochfelder*, Chapter 5), led to an audit client's financial collapse? In response, several major public accounting firms consulted with statisticians to develop sampling plans that would document not only the strategy used to examine the account balance or class of transactions audited but that also would provide a defense for why specific transactions were selected for testing and others were not (for example, random sampling).

However, in recent years some auditors have become more cautious about applying classical variables and probability-proportional-to-size sampling in practice, partly because some sampling plans may result in excessive sample sizes in some circumstances and partly because research suggests caution before blindly overrelying on the sampling results obtained from some sampling applications. For example, D. W. Wright, "Augmenting a Sample Selected with Probabilities Proportional to Size," *Auditing: A Journal of Practice & Theory* (Spring 1991), cautions auditors that augmented (that is, supplemental) samples obtained with systematic monetary-unit skip-intervals will tend to include sampling units that over- (under-) represent the smaller (larger) population items.

Required: Select an article about classical variables or probability-proportional-to-size sampling from one of the following journals:
- *Auditing: A Journal of Practice & Theory*
- *The Accounting Review*
- *Journal of Accounting Research*

For the article selected, draft a report that answers each of the following questions.

1. What is the researcher's motivation for the study—that is, why is the study important? (Note: the motivation for a study is typically communicated in the opening sections of a journal article.)
2. Summarize the article in your own words.
3. What, if any, are the implications of the article for audit practice—that is, should auditors think differently about audit sampling as a result of the article?

4. Applying Probability-Proportional-to-Size Sampling in Practice

Owing to economical sample sizes and ease of application, probability-proportional-to-size (PPS) sampling has become the most widely used statistical sampling plan in practice today, even by local practitioners, some of whom had been reluctant to apply the more cumbersome classical variables sampling plans. Applications in practice range from inventory valuation in single-site retail stores to elaborate receivables confirmation plans for user fees, property taxes, and gaming receipts in state government.

Required: Select an *AICPA Audit & Accounting Guide* for an industry (for example, airlines, banks, casinos, colleges and universities, construction contractors, finance companies, investment companies, property and liability insurance companies, providers of health care services, state and local governmental units). Draft a PPS sampling plan that could be applied to a financial statement account the guide leads you to believe is characteristic of the industry, such as third-party reimbursements in the health care industry or frequent-flier liabilities in the airline industry.

**Interactive quizzes are available as a student learning resource at
http://ricchiute.swlearning.com**

10 Chapter

Sales and Cash Receipts Transactions

Major topics discussed in this chapter are:

- **The nature of the revenue/receipt cycle, including the flow of information through customer order, credit, inventory control, shipping, billing, recording, and cash collection.**
- **An auditor's assessment of control risk and audit of internal control over financial reporting for sales and cash receipts transactions.**
- **The integration of computer auditing, sampling, and tests of controls within the revenue/receipt cycle.**
- **Assurance and consulting services related to revenue recognition.**

Designing an audit is a creative process in which a practitioner impounds professional responsibilities (Chapters 1–5) and available technology (Chapters 6–9) into his or her judgments about the nature, timing, and extent of the procedures to be applied. This chapter—and the next six—introduce the procedures typically applied in a financial statement audit, focusing sharply on how an auditor performs tests of controls and substantive tests within the four transaction cycles introduced in Chapter 8 (Figure 8-1): the revenue/receipt, expenditure/disbursement, conversion, and financing cycles. Each chapter is one in a series of interrelated segments in a financial statement audit.

This chapter and Chapter 11 focus on auditing the revenue/receipt cycle. Tests of controls are introduced here, and substantive tests are introduced in Chapter 11. The chapter begins by introducing the nature of the revenue/receipt cycle and representative internal controls over the customer order, credit, inventory control, shipping, billing, recording, and cash collection functions. In turn, the chapter discusses an auditor's consideration of internal control and uses deduction management in the consumer products industry to illustrate how an auditor forms a preliminary opinion on internal control over financial reporting under the *Sarbanes-Oxley Act* (Section 404) and PCAOB *Auditing Standard No. 2*, "An Audit of Internal Control Over Financial Reporting." Next, the chapter presents a case illustration that integrates material introduced in Chapter 8 (information systems), Chapter 9 (sampling), and this chapter. Finally, the chapter offers examples of assurance and consulting services related to revenue recognition.

The Revenue/Receipt Cycle

The **revenue/receipt cycle** encompasses both the sale of goods or services to customers ("revenue" in the cycle's title) and the collection of cash ("receipt"). The cycle is related to each of the other three transaction cycles, since it:

- Receives resources and information provided by the financing and conversion cycles, and
- Provides resources and information to the expenditure/disbursement cycle.

For example, the revenue/receipt cycle might receive cash from the proceeds of a public offering of securities through the financing cycle, receive inventory produced by the conversion cycle to sell to customers, and provide cash to pay for raw materials purchased through the expenditure/disbursement cycle.

Figure 10-1 summarizes the scope of the revenue/receipt cycle, listing the primary business functions and activities, journal entries, and forms common to the cycle. Two major business functions are associated with the cycle:

- Resources (goods or services) are sold to customers in exchange for promises of future payment.
- Cash is collected from customers.

FIGURE 10-1: *The Scope of the Revenue/Receipt Cycle*

Business Functions	Common Activities	Common Entries	Common Forms
• Resources are sold to customers in exchange for promises for future payments • Cash is collected from customers for resources sold to them	• Customer orders (order entry) • Credit approval • Inventory control • Shipping • Billing • Recording • Cash collection (and deposits) • Sales returns	• Sales • Sales discounts • Sales returns and allowances • Cash receipts • Allowance for uncollectible accounts • Write-off of specific uncollectible accounts	• Customer order • Sales order • Shipping document • Sales invoice • Customer remittance advice

The cycle begins when a customer order is received by fax, mail, email, telephone, or electronic data integration (EDI), and a decision is made to grant or deny credit. If credit is granted, the ordered goods are shipped, the sale is recorded, and the customer is billed. In turn, the customer remits either cash (for example, a check) or digital cash in accordance with the terms of sale.

Throughout the revenue/receipt cycle, journal entries are made for sales, including discounts, returns and allowances, cash receipts, allowances for potentially uncollectible accounts, and write-offs of accounts that won't be collected. Paper or electronic documents affecting the revenue/receipt cycle include:

- **Customer order**: A request from a customer to purchase goods.
- **Sales order**: Identifies goods ordered by a customer, including relevant information about price, quantity, payment terms, etc.

- **Shipping document**: Identifies goods shipped, and represents a contract between the seller and carrier (for example, a trucking company); a shipping document is often in the form of a **bill of lading**, a Uniform Commercial Code document used by common carriers.
- **Sales invoice**: Identifies goods sold and represents formal notice to a customer about the amount and terms of payment (often called the *bill*).
- **Customer remittance advice**: Accompanies a sales invoice but is intended to be returned with a customer's payment (remittance); a returned remittance advice indicates the purpose of a cash payment, facilitating handling and recording.

Documents used throughout the revenue/receipt cycle are necessary to authorize, execute, and record a transaction. The documents form an audit trail and are an important source of audit evidence, although the form of the trail varies depending on whether the documents are electronic or paper. For example, in systems that process information electronically only, the audit trail consists of computer screens and images, and access to the screens is restricted by user IDs and passwords. In systems that process paper, the audit trail consists of paper documents filed within departments, and access to the documents is restricted by restricting access to the department.

Revenue/receipt cycle activities and controls vary from one entity to another and are influenced by several factors, including the nature of an entity's industry (such as manufacturing, service, financial, government), the entity's size and organizational structure, and the extent to which accounting information is processed by computer. However, the activities of most businesses that sell goods are similar to those identified in Figure 10-1, although the activities would be modified somewhat for service companies. Credit sales activities and controls are explained next for each of the following functions (cash collection is discussed separately later):

- Customer order
- Credit
- Inventory control
- Shipping
- Billing
- Recording

Credit Sales

Figure 10-2 flowcharts representative credit sales activities and common documents. In turn, Figure 10-3 summarizes the credit sales activities flowcharted in Figure 10-2. The following explains each major activity and related documents.

When a customer order is received by phone, fax, electronic transmission, or mail, a *sales order* is prepared by an employee in the Customer Order department. A sales order describes the goods ordered, including catalog or stock numbers, prices, quantities, and payment terms. Copies of sales orders are typically sent to customers in the same form the customer order was received, and are distributed to the Credit, Shipping, and Billing departments, as indicated in Figure 10-2. A copy of the sales order is retained by the Customer Order department until notice is received from Shipping that ordered goods have been shipped.

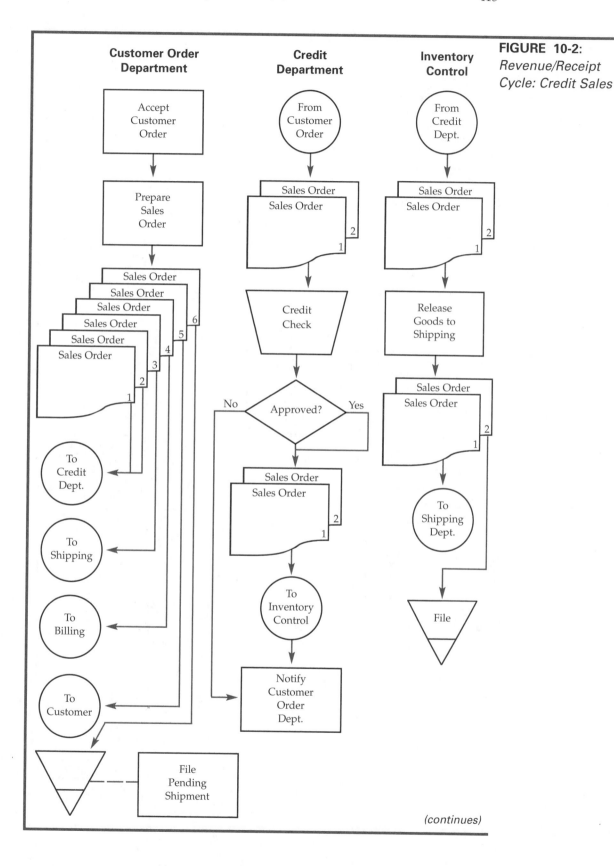

FIGURE 10-2:
Revenue/Receipt Cycle: Credit Sales

(continues)

FIGURE 10-2
(continued)

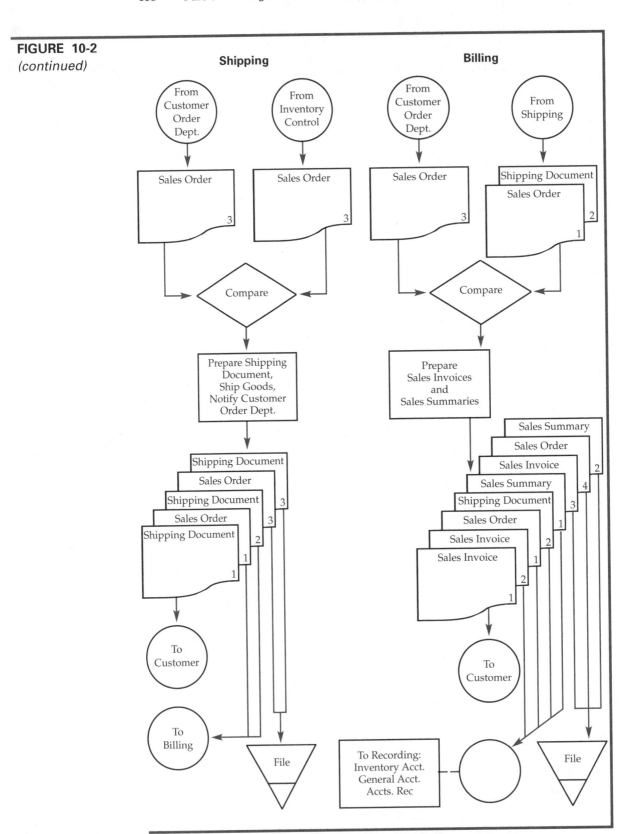

FIGURE 10-3: *Summary of Credit Sales Activities*

Customer Order Department
- Accept customer order.
- Prepare sales order, distribute copies, and retain copy in unfilled order file.

Credit Department
- Review sales order and investigate customer credit information.
- Initial copy of sales order if credit is approved and forward the order to Inventory Control. If credit is denied, notify the Customer Order department.

Inventory Control
- Review sales order.
- Initial copy of sales order to authorize the release of goods from the warehouse.
- Forward goods and a copy of the sales order to Shipping, and retain a file copy of the sales order.

Shipping
- Compare sales order from Inventory Control with sales order from Customer Order.
- Examine goods from warehouse and compare with sales orders.
- Prepare goods for shipment and complete shipping documents.
- Release goods to carrier and obtain receipt.
- Notify Customer Order department that goods have been shipped.
- Forward copy of sales order and shipping documents to Billing; retain file copy of sales order and shipping documents.

Billing
- Compare documents from Shipping with sales order from Customer Order.
- Prepare sales invoice, send copy to customer and to Inventory Accounting along with copy of sales order and shipping documents, and retain file copy.
- Prepare daily sales summary, send copy to General Accounting, and retain file copy.

Recording
- Inventory Accounting: Enter cost information on sales invoice, update inventory records, and forward sales invoice and related documents to General Accounting.
- General Accounting: Record sale and forward sales invoice and related documents to Accounts Receivable.
- Accounts Receivable: Post sale to customer's account and file sales invoice and related documents.

Before a credit sale is executed, a customer's credit is first reviewed and approved by Credit department personnel to minimize the likelihood of shipping goods to high-risk customers. Approved sales orders are forwarded to Inventory Control (whose role is addressed more fully in Chapter 15), where the goods are released for shipment. Goods transferred from Inventory Control to Shipping are accompanied by a copy of the sales order bearing the approval of an inventory control employee authorized to release goods from inventory.

Shipping personnel compare the goods received from Inventory with what is listed on the sales order, and prepare *shipping documents*. When goods are shipped, Shipping personnel obtain a receipt for the goods from the common carrier (for example, a trucking company). Receipts often take the form of a *Uniform Commercial Code (UCC) bill of lading*, which describes the goods shipped and represents a contract between the seller and the carrier. Shipping notifies Customer Order that the goods have been shipped, and Customer Order updates the unfilled order file.

After shipment, a copy of the shipping documents and a copy of the sales order approved by Credit and Inventory Control are sent to Billing. Billing personnel compare shipping documents and sales orders and prepare sales invoices, which are faxed, mailed, emailed, or transferred by EDI to customers, and distributed to Inventory Accounting, General Accounting, and Accounts Receivable for recording. A sales invoice describes the goods sold, and the customer's copy (his or her "bill") notifies the customer of the amount due and the terms of payment. Some companies prepare a *remittance advice* to accompany each customer's sales invoice. A remittance advice is intended to be returned with a customer's payment (his or her remittance) and facilitates the company's handling and recording of cash receipts.

Copies of sales invoices prepared by Billing personnel, as well as sales orders and shipping documents, are sent to Inventory Accounting. Billing personnel also prepare *daily sales summaries*, which are sent to General Accounting. Inventory Accounting personnel determine the cost of the goods described in each sales invoice and update inventory records accordingly. The cost information also is recorded on the sales invoice, which is then sent to General Accounting where sales are recorded in the sales journal and posted to the general ledger. Daily totals of sales journal entries are compared with daily sales summaries prepared by Billing. Finally, the sales invoices are routed from General Accounting to Accounts Receivable, where sales are posted to individual customer accounts in the accounts receivable subsidiary records.

The documents processed through the revenue/receipt cycle provide evidence that transactions are properly authorized, executed, and recorded. Note that a document is prepared by each execution function: sales orders by Customer Order, shipping documents by Shipping, and sales invoices by Billing. Authorization functions do not generate documents; rather, they approve documents initiated elsewhere. Recording functions neither prepare nor approve documents; instead, they transfer information from documents to accounting records.

All documents should be prenumbered consecutively and, if paper, missing forms should be accounted for. Copies of documents should be distributed to appropriate functional areas. Multiple documentation provides important crosschecks that minimize the potential for errors or fraud.

Cash Collection

The revenue/receipt cycle is completed for a transaction when cash is collected for the goods or services sold. Collection from customers and activities related to uncollected accounts are illustrated in Figure 10-4 and discussed in the following sections.

The Cash Collection Process

Assuming cash remittances are received by mail, incoming checks are listed immediately and endorsed restrictively (for example, "for deposit to First National Bank account number . . .") by Mail Room personnel. One copy of the list of incoming checks (and returned remittance advices, if applicable) is forwarded to Accounts Receivable for posting to individual customer accounts. All incoming customer checks and another copy of the list of checks are forwarded to the Cash

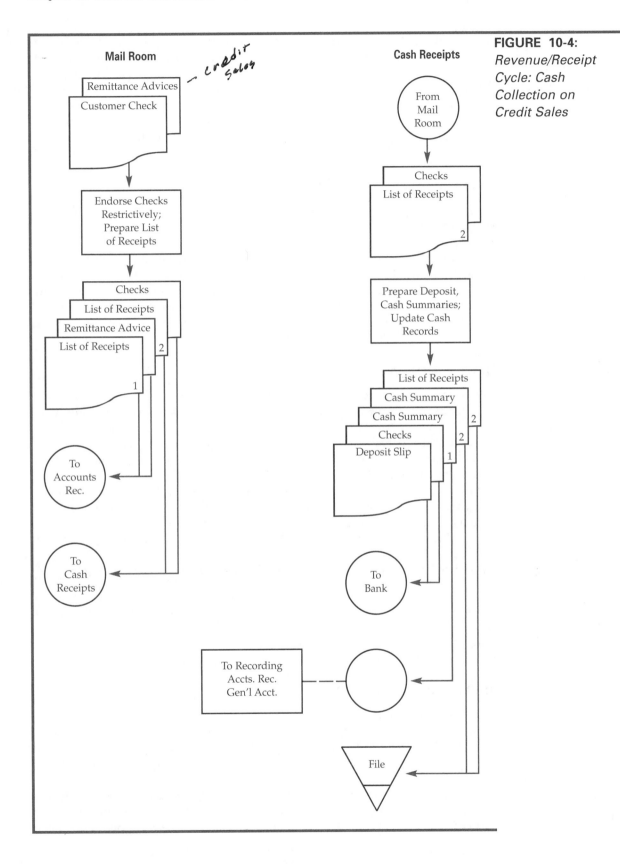

Mail Room

~ Credit Sales

Remittance Advices

Customer Check

Endorse Checks Restrictively; Prepare List of Receipts

Checks

List of Receipts

Remittance Advice

List of Receipts

2

1

To Accounts Rec.

To Cash Receipts

Cash Receipts

From Mail Room

Checks

List of Receipts

2

Prepare Deposit, Cash Summaries; Update Cash Records

List of Receipts

Cash Summary

Cash Summary

Checks

Deposit Slip

2

2

1

To Bank

To Recording Accts. Rec. Gen'l Acct.

File

FIGURE 10-4:
Revenue/Receipt Cycle: Cash Collection on Credit Sales

Receipts department, where a daily bank deposit is assembled, cash summaries are prepared, and cash records are updated. Separate lists of totals are forwarded to General Accounting for recording in the cash receipts journal and posting to the general ledger.

In all but rather small entities, personnel involved in cash collection are segregated from Accounts Receivable, General Accounting, and Billing, since combining cash collection with any of these other three functions provides opportunities to misappropriate cash.

Sales Returns and Allowances

Customer requests for adjustments on returned goods should be reviewed by personnel independent of cash collection and recording—for example, by Customer Order personnel and, if appropriate, by the salesperson or regional sales manager who services the account. An approved request is documented as a **credit memorandum**, copies of which are forwarded to Accounts Receivable for posting and to Inventory Control. Control totals are forwarded to General Accounting for recording and posting. Returned goods are handled through the Receiving department and returned to the warehouse along with a **receiving report**. Inventory Control personnel match the receiving report with a copy of the credit memorandum.

Uncollected Accounts

Accounts Receivable personnel should review individual customer accounts periodically as a check against unauthorized credit limits and prepare monthly accounts receivable trial balances (that is, summaries of unpaid balances) for reconciliation with general ledger control accounts. In addition, accounts receivable balances are aged periodically and reviewed by personnel independent of the Credit department.

Delinquent accounts should be reviewed periodically by personnel who report to the treasurer and are independent of recording functions. When an individual customer account is judged uncollectible, written authorization to write off the account is sent to Accounts Receivable and to General Accounting.

Internal Control Objectives and Potential Errors or Frauds

The following discussion, summarized in Figure 10-5, identifies control objectives, describes examples of errors or frauds that may arise if an objective is not achieved, and offers examples of control activities designed to prevent or detect errors or frauds in the revenue/receipt cycle. The control objectives relate generally to transaction authorization, execution, and recording and access to assets.

Transaction Authorization

Before accepting a customer's sales order, the customer's credit should be approved. Otherwise, shipments could be made to poor credit risk customers, potentially resulting in uncollectible receivables. Most companies perform a credit check for all new customers and prepare (and periodically update) authorized customer lists, indicating maximum credit limits for each customer.

In addition to authorizing credit limits, management should establish unit prices and sales terms that are consistent with the company's revenue objectives and cash flow needs. Prices also should be set so that no customers are treated

FIGURE 10-5: *Revenue/Receipt Cycle: Control Objectives, Potential Errors or Frauds, and Control Activities*

Clients →

Control Objectives	Types of Errors or Frauds That Could Occur If Objective Is Not Met	Control Activities Designed to Prevent or Detect Errors or Frauds
Transaction Authorization		
• Customers' credit should be approved prior to shipping goods.	Shipments could be made to unauthorized parties, potentially resulting in uncollectible accounts receivable. *Revenue os AR - os*	Perform a credit check for all new customers. Prepare and periodically update lists of authorized customers, indicating a maximum credit limit for each customer.
• Unit prices and sales terms should be established for all products or services.	Orders could be accepted at unauthorized prices or unfavorable sales terms, potentially resulting in reduced revenues or inadequate cash flows.	Maintain updated lists of authorized prices and sales terms. Establish procedures for reviewing and approving prices and sales terms before shipment.
• Sales-related deductions and adjustments should be made in accordance with management's authorization.	Unauthorized deductions or adjustments could be granted to undeserving customers, potentially resulting in uncollectible receivables. Otherwise collectible accounts receivable could be written off, potentially resulting in failure to realize the service potential of an asset.	Establish written criteria and policies for granting sales deductions and adjustments. Prenumber and control credit memoranda or other related forms.
Transaction Execution		
• Approved orders should be shipped in accordance with customer specifications and on a timely basis.	Shipments could be delivered to the wrong party, potentially resulting in uncollectible accounts receivable. Shipments could be delivered too late, potentially resulting in returned goods and canceled sales. Incorrect shipments could be delivered, potentially resulting in returned goods and canceled sales.	Verify that ordered products are in stock, and therefore can be shipped on a timely basis. Limit access to shipping documents to authorized personnel. Document policies and procedures for scheduling shipments.

(continues)

FIGURE 10-5 (*continued*)

Control Objectives	Types of Errors or Frauds That Could Occur If Objective Is Not Met	Control Activities Designed to Prevent or Detect Errors or Frauds
• All shipments should be followed by prompt billing.	Shipments could go unbilled, potentially resulting in loss of revenue. Shipments could be billed late, resulting in delayed cash payments from customers.	Prenumber bills of lading and assure that related billings are made on a periodic (e.g., daily) basis. Establish procedures for prompt reporting and investigation of shipments not billed (and billings not shipped). Require prompt delivery of bills of lading (and related sales orders) to the Billing department.
Recording • Sales, cash receipts, and related transactions should be recorded at the correct amounts, in the proper period, and should be properly classified.	General ledger account balances may be inaccurate, potentially resulting in misstated financial statements.	Total input documents (e.g., number of documents, dollar amounts) and reconcile appropriate journals and ledgers. Establish processing and recording procedures. Compare actual and planned (e.g., forecasted, budgeted) results, and analyze variances.
• Billings, collections, and related adjustment transactions (e.g., returns and allowances) should be posted accurately to individual customer accounts.	Summaries of detailed records may not agree with control accounts, potentially resulting in adjusting journal entries prompted by inaccurate information. Transactions may be posted to improper customer accounts, potentially resulting in improper billings.	Reconcile totals of individual customer accounts with control totals. Promptly investigate correspondence from customers. Reconcile input totals with processed and output totals. Review customer statements for accuracy and follow up on discrepancies. *(continues)*

FIGURE 10-5 *(continued)*

Control Objectives	Types of Errors or Frauds That Could Occur If Objective Is Not Met	Control Activities Designed to Prevent or Detect Errors or Frauds
• Recorded accounts receivable balances (and related transactions) should fairly reflect underlying transactions and events.	Accounts may include errors or frauds, potentially resulting in materially misstated financial statements. Management decisions may be based on erroneous data, potentially resulting in improper decisions.	Periodically substantiate and evaluate recorded account balances. Reconcile subsidiary ledgers with general ledger control accounts. Establish policy and procedures manuals, organization charts, and supporting documentation (e.g., compare selected customer balances with underlying documents). Follow up promptly on customer complaints.
Access to Assets • Access to cash and cash-related records should be restricted to personnel authorized by management.	Cash receipts on credit sales could be lost or diverted, potentially resulting in overstated accounts receivable and unrecorded cash. Cash receipts on noncredit sales could be unreported, potentially resulting in unrecorded cash. Cash shortages could go undetected, potentially resulting in lost cash and overstated cash balances.	Establish the cash receipts function in a centralized location. Require daily reconciliation of cash receipts records with bank deposit slips. Prenumber and control cash remittance advices. Prepare separate lists of incoming cash receipts in the mailroom. Separate responsibility for handling and recording cash. Establish periodic procedures for reconciling cash records with bank statements. Establish physical barriers over cash and unused checks.

(continues)

FIGURE 10-5 *(continued)*

Control Objectives	Types of Errors or Frauds That Could Occur If Objective Is Not Met	Control Activities Designed to Prevent or Detect Errors or Frauds
• Access to shipping, billing, inventory control, and accounting records should be restricted to personnel authorized by management.	Records or assets may be misused, potentially resulting in misappropriated assets.	Maintain insurance and fidelity bonds for personnel handling cash. Maintain listings—and signature samples—of authorized signatories. Inform the bank that no checks payable to the company are to be cashed (i.e., deposited only). Restrictively endorse checks received from customers. Segregate responsibilities for authorization, execution, and recording functions. Prenumber and control custody of forms and documents.

unfairly, since differential pricing could result in dissatisfaction among customers not offered favorable terms and could even lead to violations of federal antitrust laws. Management can remove the risk of differential pricing by updating price and sales terms lists periodically and by establishing procedures for reviewing and approving sales transactions before shipment.

Following shipment and delivery, customers may request allowances or adjustments for damaged, defective, or unwanted goods. All sales-related allowances and adjustments should be made only in accordance with policies and practices authorized by management. Management should establish written policies for sales-related deductions and adjustments. Forms, such as credit memoranda, should be numbered and controlled.

Transaction Execution

Once customer orders are approved, goods should be shipped on a timely basis. Delayed or incorrect shipments not only tie up resources (for example, delay cash collection) but result in returned goods, canceled orders, or uncollectible receivables. To encourage timely and accurate shipments, management should establish policies for scheduling prompt shipment and for verifying that ordered products are in stock.

Following shipment, customers should be billed promptly, thereby avoiding losses arising either from unbilled shipments or from delayed cash collections. To avoid unbilled shipments, management should require prenumbered shipping documents, periodically assuring that all sequentially numbered documents result in timely billing. Management also should establish procedures to investigate unbilled shipments promptly.

Recording

All sales, cash receipts, and related transactions should be recorded at the correct amounts, in the proper period, and be classified properly within the accounts. Obviously, inaccurate recording can result in misstated account balances and financial statements. Management can control the recording function by establishing written procedures, reconciling control totals (e.g., tracing the number and dollar amount of input documents to summarized output) and periodically comparing actual results with budgets, if available.

Proper recording within general ledger control accounts, though, does not necessarily mean that billing, collection, and returns and allowances will be posted accurately to individual customer accounts. As a result, even if general ledger control accounts are accurate, summaries of detailed records may not agree with the control accounts, potentially resulting in improper billings or adjusting journal entries prompted by insufficient or inaccurate information. Several procedures are available to control inaccurate postings, among them promptly investigating customer complaints and reconciling customer account balances to control accounts.

Related to the accurate recording and posting of sales, billings, and receipts, management also should establish procedures to assure that recorded receivables balances fairly reflect the underlying transactions and events they represent. Otherwise, billings and management decisions may be based on improper data or, equally distressing, recorded receivables may reflect material errors or frauds. To control the recording of receivables, management could periodically substantiate and evaluate individual customer balances and reconcile supporting detailed ledgers to the general ledger.

Access to Assets

Within the revenue/receipt cycle, management attempts to safeguard assets by restricting access to cash and cash-related records, thereby controlling against loss or diversion and, correspondingly, against misstated cash balances. Restricting access is critical throughout a business organization, but particularly for cash because, unlike most types of inventory and plant assets, cash is liquid and therefore highly susceptible to theft or diversion. Normally, the cash receipts function is maintained in a centralized location that is off-limits to unauthorized personnel. As further controls over authorized personnel, however, management could establish procedures to prenumber and control remittance advices, prepare separate lists of incoming mail receipts, and periodically reconcile cash receipts records to deposit slips and bank statements.

Management also should limit physical access within Shipping, Billing, and Inventory Control, primarily to avoid the misappropriation of assets between or among related departments. For example, Shipping personnel could be restricted from Inventory Control, thereby minimizing opportunities for unauthorized shipments. In many companies, however, access is not restricted, although employees are restricted from performing job functions outside of their own departments.

Assessing Control Risk and Auditing Internal Control Over Financial Reporting

As explained in Chapter 6, an auditor's consideration of an entity's internal controls involves obtaining an understanding of the controls, performing tests of controls, and assessing control risk. The following discussion focuses on an auditor's consideration of revenue/receipt cycle controls.

Obtain an Understanding

An auditor's objective when considering internal control is to obtain an understanding of a client's prescribed policies and procedures sufficient to plan the audit and, in the case of a public company, to audit internal control over financial reporting. Apart from evaluating the audit committee's effectiveness and obtaining an understanding of information technology and reviewing *Sarbanes-Oxley*, Section 404, documentation (Chapter 8), obtaining an understanding of the system includes:

1. Performing a *review of Section 404* or other *documentation,*
2. *Documenting* the system,
3. Performing *transaction walkthroughs,* and

Determining whether existing control activities are potentially reliable in assessing *control risk* below the maximum.

Review *Sarbanes-Oxley* Section 404 or Other Documentation

An auditor begins for a public company by reviewing the *Sarbanes-Oxley* Section 404 documentation management prepared to memorialize the process for assessing the effectiveness of internal control over financial reporting. The auditor develops a general understanding of the control environment; the control activities; and how the entity identifies, captures, communicates, and monitors external and internal information in a form and time frame that enables employees to discharge their assigned responsibilities. How is this done? The auditor reviews the client's documentation and interviews employees in the Customer Order, Credit, Inventory Control, Shipping, Billing, and Cash Receipts departments—the departments introduced earlier and illustrated in Figures 10-2 and 10-4. In a public company, the Section 404 documentation typically adds considerable detail for each of the columns depicted in Figures 10-2 and 10-4. For example, Figure 10-4, Cash Collection on Credit Sales, presumes that checks from customers are in amounts that agree to the customers' invoices. In practice, checks do not always agree to invoices because customers take deductions, some of which are authorized and some of which are not. For example, a check that a manufacturer receives from a retail department store may reflect a deduction the manufacturer authorized for product advertising or for in-store displays, called in the industry "trade promotion" or "trade spending." To distinguish between, and account properly for, authorized and unauthorized deductions, management's Section 404 documentation might appear as illustrated in Figure 10-6, which abbreviates what most large public companies would document. Notice that the documentation includes a flowchart of the procedures, a brief explanation of the deduction-management process, and a list of controls management implemented over financial reporting.

A nonpublic entity's management may not have assessed the effectiveness of internal control over financial reporting and, therefore not have documented internal control in any way near the detail that a public company would to comply with *Sarbanes-Oxley*. For a nonpublic entity, the auditor performs a preliminary review to determine whether further consideration of internal control is likely to justify assessing control risk below the maximum, thereby allowing the auditor to relax detection risk and therefore to reduce the extent of substantive tests on sales, accounts receivable, and cash, three financial statement accounts affected by the revenue/receipt cycle. If the preliminary review reveals that management's control activities are inadequate to justify assessing control risk below the maximum, then the auditor's documentation of the system would be limited to a memorandum in the working papers describing the reasons for deciding not to consider internal control further. However, if the control activities appear potentially adequate, the auditor would continue by documenting the system.

System Documentation

Auditors typically document an entity's internal controls with flowcharts, questionnaires, and/or written narratives. Flowcharts generally provide concise, informative, and unambiguous descriptions of internal controls and are used when an entity's system is complex and processes large volumes of transactions. Although flowcharts vary in physical layout, the format used in Figures 10-2 and 10-4 is particularly useful to an auditor, since the activities are grouped by department, thereby clearly indicating responsibilities and providing the auditor with a basis for judging whether segregation of duties is adequate.

Questionnaires, in contrast, are designed to detect control deficiencies and, as explained in Chapter 8, typically require one of three responses for each question: *yes*, *no*, or *N/A* (not applicable). *No* responses indicate potential deficiencies. Figure 10-7 illustrates a questionnaire for the customer order, credit, shipping, billing and recording, and cash receipts functions within the revenue/receipt cycle.

FIGURE 10-6:
Sarbanes-Oxley
*Section 404
Documentation:
Deduction
Management*

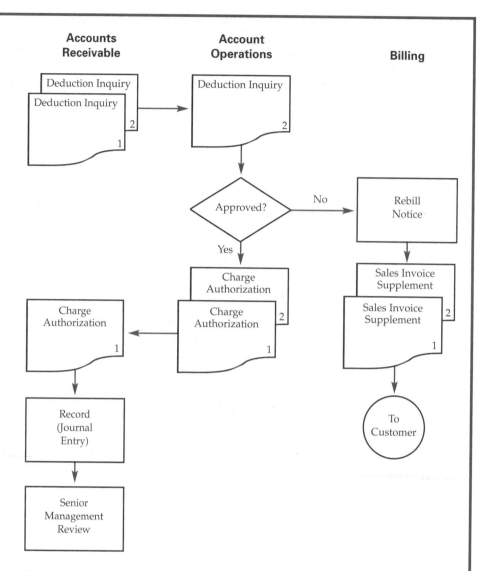

Deduction Management Process

Customer remittances may reflect both authorized and unauthorized deductions for reasons including customer-paid promotions (for example, print advertising, in-store displays), quantity shortages (for example, quantity received is less than quantity ordered and billed), and close-to-expiration dated donations (for example, homeless shelters, food pantries). Accounts Receivable transmits a deduction inquiry to Account Operations, which prepares and transmits a charge authorization to Accounts Receivable for authorized deductions (customer accounts are relieved) and a rebill notice to Billing (customers are rebilled for the amount of the unauthorized deduction).

Controls

- Accounts Receivable monitors deductions.
- Account Operations approves deduction inquiries.
- Senior management reviews entries to relieve customer balances (approved deductions) and to rebill customers (unapproved deductions).

FIGURE 10-7: *Questionnaire: Credit Sales and Cash Collection*

Prepared by_____

Date_____

Question	Answer: Yes, No, or N/A	Remarks

Customer Order

1. Are policies and procedures for accepting and approving customer orders clearly defined?
2. Are prenumbered sales orders prepared for all approved customer orders?
3. Is current information regarding prices, policies on discounts, sales taxes, freight, warranties, and returned goods available and communicated to Customer Order personnel?
4. Are copies of sales orders forwarded to Credit, Shipping, and Billing?

Credit

1. Are policies for approving credit established and clearly communicated to Credit personnel?
2. Is credit investigated before approval?
3. Are Credit personnel independent of Billing, Cash Collection, and Accounting personnel?
4. Is information about past-due accounts communicated to Credit personnel?

Shipping

1. Are goods shipped only in accordance with approved sales orders?
2. Are shipping documents prepared for all shipments?
3. Is access to Inventory Control restricted so that goods are released only in accordance with approved sales orders?
4. Are quantities of shipped goods verified either by double-counting or by independent counts (e.g., by the shipping company)?
5. Are shipping documents reviewed and compared with billings to assure that all shipped goods are billed?
6. Are Shipping personnel independent of billing, cash collection, and recording?

Billing and Recording

1. Are prenumbered sales invoices prepared for all shipped goods?
2. Are sales invoices matched with approved sales orders and shipping documents, and are they checked for clerical accuracy?
3. Are prenumbered credit memos matched with receiving reports, and are they recorded promptly?
4. Is the accounts receivable subsidiary ledger reconciled periodically with the general ledger?
5. Are monthly statements reviewed and mailed by personnel independent of Accounts Receivable and Cash Receipts?

(continues)

FIGURE 10-7 *(continued)*

Question	Answer: Yes, No, or N/A	Remarks
6. Is an aged schedule of accounts receivable prepared monthly by personnel independent of Billing and Cash Receipts?		
7. Does the credit manager review receivables balances and the aged analysis, and does he or she investigate past-due accounts?		
8. Is billing performed by personnel independent of Credit and Cash Receipts?		
Cash Collection		
1. Are mail receipts opened by personnel independent of Shipping, Billing, and Accounting?		
2. Are checks endorsed restrictively immediately upon opening the mail?		
3. Are lists of receipts prepared when mail is opened?		
4. Are checks forwarded promptly to personnel responsible for preparing bank deposits?		
5. Are checks deposited daily?		
6. Are cash summaries prepared and forwarded to Accounting?		
7. Are all employees who handle cash bonded adequately?		

Written *narratives* describe in prose one or more phases of management's controls. Because the controls described in narratives are more difficult to envision than those cast in flowcharts, narratives are used most often for phases that are not complex or do not process material transactions, such as petty cash. In practice, auditors use all three means of documentation. For example, in considering revenue/receipt cycle controls, an auditor might document the system as follows:

- *Flowchart* selling activities from customer order acceptance through recording of the sale and related receivable.
- Document cash collection activities with a *questionnaire*.
- Prepare a *narrative* description of activities related to sales returns and allowances and write-offs of uncollectible accounts.

Regardless of the form of documentation, employee responsibilities and document flow should be identified clearly.

An auditor obtains information about a system through inquiries of management and employees, by observing employees perform tasks, and by reviewing written policies and procedures in the entity's procedures manuals, if any. In the case of a continuing engagement, an auditor should review prior-year documentation and determine whether it accurately reflects current conditions. Prior documentation can be relied on only if there have been no changes in assigned responsibilities and prescribed procedures.

Transaction Walkthroughs

An auditor tests his or her understanding of a system, and complies with responsibilities the PCAOB imposed for public company audits (Chapter 8), by performing transaction walkthroughs. For example, an auditor could trace sales transactions from acceptance of customers' orders to receipt of the customers' cash payments. If tracing transactions reveals deviations from the system the auditor documented, the reasons for the differences should be determined and the documentation revised if necessary.

Identification of Control Activities

Once an auditor understands an entity's internal controls and determines that the controls are potentially reliable in assessing control risk below the maximum, he or she continues as follows:

- Identify the system's *control objectives*. The first column of Figure 10-5 identifies control objectives for credit sales and cash receipts transactions.
- Consider the *potential errors or frauds* that might result if specific control objectives are not achieved. The second column of Figure 10-5 identifies examples of potential errors or frauds.
- Determine what *control activities* management uses to prevent or detect potentially material errors or frauds. The third column of Figure 10-5 identifies examples of control activities.
- Design *tests of controls*.

Only those control activities relevant to management's <u>financial statement assertions</u> are subjected to tests of controls, which are discussed next.

Tests of Controls: Credit Sales and Cash Collections

Sales, receivables, and cash receipts usually represent a large volume of transactions for most entities, suggesting that if control risk is at the maximum and acceptable detection risk is at the minimum, the extent of substantive tests of details at year end is likely to be extensive. With this and their responsibility for public companies to report on management's assessment of internal control in mind, auditors usually expend considerable effort when testing controls over the revenue/receipt cycle, because evidence from tests of controls that suggests control risk is below the maximum would justify assessing acceptable detection risk above the minimum and, therefore, reduce the extent of substantive tests of account balances at year end. But first, tests of controls are necessary in order to provide a reasonable degree of assurance that employees comply with management's control activities and that the procedures operate as management planned. Tests of an entity's sales activities usually focus on whether sales are properly authorized, executed, and recorded. In turn, tests of cash collection activities focus on whether cash receipts are recorded and deposited promptly. And tests of controls over returns, allowances, and uncollectible accounts focus on proper authorization and recording.

Some representative tests of controls follow for the shipping, billing, recording, and cash collection (and deposit) functions illustrated in Figures 10-2 and 10-4, and for sales returns and allowances and uncollectible accounts. For each function, the discussion briefly introduces an auditor's major risks, lists a series of representative tests of controls, and then describes the purpose of each test listed. The tests of controls are derived from the second column of Figure 10-5—that is, the auditor first considers what <u>errors or frauds are possible</u> and then designs tests to determine whether the related control activities are effective. At this point, the discussion introduces the purpose and role of a variety of tests used in testing controls of the revenue/receipt cycle. Later, the chapter describes further how an auditor documents some of the tests.

Shipping

Weaknesses in Shipping department controls present two major risks for errors or frauds: Goods may be shipped without authorization (for example, to fictitious or related parties), or shipped goods may not be billed and recorded at all. Thus, tests of controls for Shipping are intended to determine whether shipments are made only in accordance with approved sales orders and whether shipments have been billed and recorded properly. Following are some illustrative tests for Shipping.

Tests of Controls: Shipping

1. Randomly select a sample of shipping documents from Shipping department files.
2. Examine each shipping document to determine whether the document:
   a. Is accompanied by a sales order bearing Credit and Inventory Control authorization.
   b. Agrees with the sales order as to description of goods, quantity, destination, etc.
3. Trace details of sampled shipping documents to copies of shipping documents and their related sales invoices in Billing department files.
4. Trace details of the related sales invoices (for example, customer name, extended dollar amount) to entries in the sales journal and accounts receivable subsidiary ledger.
5. Trace sales invoices to inventory records in Inventory Accounting.

As suggested by Step 1 of the tests of controls, shipping documents are the primary source from which the remaining tests of shipping are performed. That is, all further tests of shipping derive from information contained on the shipping documents. The tests are intended to determine whether shipped goods are for bona fide sales and whether shipments are recorded and billed properly.

In Step 2a, the auditor tests two issues: First, by comparing shipping documents with their related sales orders, the auditor is testing whether shipments are properly authorized and, therefore, whether goods may have been shipped without authorization for an employee's or management's benefit. Second, by comparing shipping documents with Inventory Control authorization on the sales order, the auditor is testing whether goods were actually transferred from the warehouse to Shipping. In Step 2b, the auditor tests whether clerical, mathematical, or other errors have been made in transcribing information from sales orders to shipping documents. Step 3 is designed to determine that shipments are billed, and that the bills reflect the quantities shipped.

While Steps 2 and 3 address transaction authorization and execution, Steps 4 and 5 focus on the recording of transactions. Step 4 tests whether the sales invoices related to sampled shipments are accurate and recorded properly in the sales journal and receivables ledger. Step 5 is intended to determine whether Inventory records reflect the transfer of goods to Shipping.

Billing

The preceding tests of controls address whether shipments are billed properly. The following tests, in contrast, focus on whether billed goods have been shipped and whether bills (that is, sales invoices) are accurate and have been prepared properly and recorded.

Tests of Controls: Billing
1. Randomly select a sample of sales invoices from Billing department files.
2. For each sampled invoice, verify unit prices and clerical accuracy.
3. Trace details of sampled sales invoices to shipping documents.
4. Trace details of sampled sales invoices to entries in the sales journal and accounts receivable subsidiary ledger.
5. Trace sales invoices to inventory records in Inventory Accounting.

Just as shipping documents are the primary source documents for tests of shipping, sales invoices are the primary source for tests of billing. Step 2 requires that an auditor compare unit prices and sales terms on sales invoices with lists of authorized prices and sales terms. Thus, Step 2 tests whether goods are billed at appropriate prices and terms.

In Step 3, the auditor traces sales invoices to shipping documents and, therefore, focuses on whether the goods listed on sales invoices were actually shipped. Step 3 is analogous to Step 3 of the shipping tests: The shipping test addressed whether all shipments were billed, and the billing test addresses whether recorded sales are shipped.

Step 4 turns attention to the recording function, testing whether sales invoices are properly recorded in the sales journal and the accounts receivable subsidiary ledger. Step 5, also a test of recording, tests whether inventory records accurately reflect transfers of goods—that is, for every sales entry, there should be a corresponding cost of sales entry.

Recording

The tests described for shipping and billing included tracing the details of shipping documents to sales invoices and sales invoices to accounting records, the purpose being to verify that the sampled transactions were recorded. Following are additional tests related specifically to the recording function.

Tests of Controls: Recording
1. Review evidence of internal procedures for:
   a. Reconciliation of daily sales summaries with sales journal totals by General Accounting personnel.
   b. Periodic reconciliation of accounts receivable trial balances with general ledger control balances.
2. Scan the sales journal for unusual transactions or unusually large amounts.
3. Verify the clerical accuracy of the sales journal for selected periods and trace totals to postings in the general ledger.

The objective of all three tests for recording is to determine whether details are summarized, periodically reconciled, and, most important, accurately posted to sales journals, to the accounts receivable ledger, and finally to the general ledger. Steps 1a and 1b are not tests per se, but rather are intended to determine whether management has implemented procedures to reconcile sales summaries with sales journals (Step 1a) and accounts receivable subsidiary records with the general ledger (Step 1b). In short, sales summaries should agree with sales journals, and accounts receivable subsidiary records should agree with the general ledger. If all sales are made on credit, the sales journal also should agree with accounts receivable records.

In Step 2, the auditor scans the sales journal for unusual transactions. For example, large sales to related parties, such as sales to, or for the indirect benefit of, officers, directors, or shareholders, may require special disclosure as discussed in Chapter 17. Step 3 tests the mathematical accuracy of the sales journal and traces totals to postings in the general ledger—that is, from details to the control accounts.

Cash Collection

An entity's cash collection activities are particularly susceptible to frauds, since receipts in the form of checks are easily convertible into cash or easily deposited into improper accounts—only a forged endorsement is necessary. Representative tests of controls over cash collections and deposits follow.

Tests of Controls: Cash Collection and Deposits

Cash Collection:

1. On a surprise basis, take control of bank deposits (deposit slip and checks) just prior to delivery by client personnel to the bank.
2. Compare the total dollar amount of checks to the total recorded on the deposit slip.
3. Compare checks to details in cash receipts records and the accounts receivable subsidiary ledger (for example, customer names, amounts) and determine that the lapse of time between cash receipt and deposit is reasonable.

Deposits:

4. For an interim month (or months):
   a. Compare entries in the cash receipts journal with deposits listed on the monthly bank statement.
   b. Determine that cash receipts not listed on the bank statement are listed as deposits in transit in the bank reconciliation and are included with deposits in the subsequent month's bank statement.
5. Trace totals in the cash receipts journal to postings in the general ledger.

Steps 1 through 3 are designed to detect misappropriation of cash receipts and, in particular, **lapping**, a fraud that conceals cash shortages by delaying the recording of cash collections. Lapping simultaneously involves both execution (cash collection) and recording (accounts receivable) functions and, therefore, is most likely to occur when one employee is responsible both for cash collections and for receivables.

To accomplish lapping, an employee responsible for cash collections and accounts receivable simply retains a customer's payment for his or her personal use, and covers the shortage with a payment from a second customer; the first customer's receivable balance is credited when the second customer's check is received. In turn, the second customer's receivable balance is credited when a third customer's check is received, and so on. The lapping procedure may cease when the perpetrating employee replaces the cash shortage, may continue indefinitely, or may multiply in scope as a result of additional cash misappropriations.

Absent *lock box* systems (customers remit checks directly to a bank) or *digital cash* (customers remit electronically), segregation of cash collection and accounts receivable is the best control against lapping. Mandatory vacations for all employees is a second, though less effective, control. However, even if collections and accounts receivable are segregated, an auditor should still test for lapping, in the event that two or more employees are in collusion. Steps 1 through 3 address lapping by determining whether a customer's check is both deposited and recorded promptly. Of course, the tests should be performed on a surprise basis to minimize the likelihood of an employee (or employees) temporarily correcting a cash shortage in anticipation of an audit.

Steps 4 and 5 address whether recorded cash collections are deposited in total and promptly. Step 4a traces entries from the cash receipts journal to deposits listed on bank statements, thereby testing whether recorded receipts are deposited. Step 4b relates to cash received and deposited too late to appear on the next bank statement; the receipts are traced to a bank reconciliation (deposits in transit) and to subsequent bank statements when available. Step 5 traces cash receipts totals to the general ledger in order to assure that detailed records agree in total with the control accounts.

Sales Returns and Allowances

An auditor's tests of controls for sales returns and allowances focus on whether credit memoranda are approved and recorded properly. Selected tests follow.

Tests of Controls: Sales Returns and Allowances

1. Obtain a random sample of credit memoranda from the files of the issuing department (for example, Customer Order).
2. Trace details of sampled credit memoranda to:
   a. Receiving reports,
   b. Perpetual inventory records, and
   c. Entries in the accounts receivable subsidiary ledger and general ledger.
3. Review the credit register (or other listing of approved credit memoranda) for unusual items, such as credits for very large amounts or an unusually large number of credits for the same customer, and investigate.

In Step 1, credit memoranda, the primary source document for tests of sales returns and allowances, are obtained from the issuing department, often the Customer Order department. Step 2 addresses whether goods were actually returned by tracing credit memoranda details to receiving reports and to entries in perpetual inventory and accounts receivable records; this step also traces totals from accounts receivable to the general ledger, thereby testing the accuracy of postings. Step 3 is designed to detect unusual credits. For example, credits for very large amounts could signal excessive returns in the future as well, suggesting that material receivables may not be collectible.

Uncollectible Accounts

An auditor's tests of controls over uncollectible accounts focus on whether write-offs are properly authorized and recorded. Some representative tests follow.

Tests of Controls: Uncollectible Accounts

1. Select a sample of write-off entries.
2. Trace each entry to the related write-off authorization memo; examine the memo for appropriate authorization and compare the authorized amount with the recorded amount.
3. Trace each entry to a posting in the general ledger.
4. Review all write-off entries for unusual items, such as very large amounts or multiple write-offs for the same customer, and investigate.

Tests of controls over uncollectible accounts start from recorded write-off entries, rather than from a source document as in the tests of controls discussed previously. In Step 2, the auditor tests whether write-offs are authorized, usually by examining write-off authorization memoranda and related correspondence between the company and a customer. Step 3 traces write-off entries to the general ledger, thereby testing controls over posting. Assuming write-offs are sampled rather than tested 100 percent, Step 4 reviews write-off entries for unusual items, such as multiple write-offs for one customer, which could suggest an error or fraud, because orders generally should not be accepted for previously uncollectible accounts.

Assess Control Risk

To complete the consideration of internal control within the revenue/receipt cycle, an auditor reviews system documentation and the results of tests of controls, and he or she determines whether existing controls are effective and can be relied on to:

1. Assess control risk below the maximum,
2. Assess detection risk above the minimum, and therefore
3. Restrict substantive tests of sales, receivables, and cash.

If existing controls are not effective, control risk is set at the maximum, detection risk at the minimum, and the auditor plans expanded substantive tests.

In practice, auditors assess control risk for the financial statement *assertions* embodied in a transaction cycle's related account balances, transaction classes, and financial statement disclosures—that is, the five assertions introduced in Chapter 6: existence or occurrence, completeness, rights and obligations, valuation or allocation, and presentation and disclosure. To illustrate, consider the first objective for transaction authorization in Figure 10-5:

Objective:
Customers' credit should be approved prior to shipping goods.

The corresponding control activity (third column) for that objective is:

Control activity:
Perform a credit check for all new customers.

Step 2a of the tests of controls for shipping tests whether the control activity from Figure 10-5 is operating effectively:

Test of control:
Examine each shipping document to determine whether the document is accompanied by a sales order bearing Credit and Inventory Control authorization.

Assume the auditor performs the test and discovers that most of the accompanying sales orders *do not* bear Credit department authorization. In this case, the auditor would conclude that control risk for the assertion *valuation* is at the maximum. Why? Because failure to check and approve credit before the sale may serve to overstate the net realizable value—that is, the balance sheet valuation—of trade accounts receivable, because the entity may be granting credit to poor credit risk customers. Thus, in assessing control risk, the auditor must link the results of a test of controls to its related financial statement assertion. Substantive tests applicable to revenue/receipt cycle accounts are introduced in Chapter 11.

Form a Preliminary Opinion on Management's Assessment of Internal Control Over Financial Reporting

Under the *Sarbanes-Oxley Act* (Section 404) and PCAOB *Auditing Standard No. 2,* "An Audit of Internal Control Over Financial Reporting," an auditor of a public company is obligated to form an opinion on management's assessment of internal control over financial reporting as of the end of the company's fiscal year (Chapter 8). The opinion is based on factors such as the reports of internal auditors; tests of controls performed during and, in some cases, after the end of the fiscal year; and substantive tests performed later in an entity's fiscal year. Tests of controls performed at interim, particularly those focused on financial reporting, are an important piece of the puzzle, since they are the basis for forming a preliminary opinion that will be updated through tests of controls and substantive tests performed later. The tests of controls illustrated above relate to financial reporting, and the tests and the controls are fairly common in practice. Consider, however, some tests an auditor might perform for controls over the deduction management process illustrated at Figure 10-6.

To control against retailers taking deductions without authorization, the system illustrated at Figure 10-6 involves three departments: Accounts Receivable, Account Operations, and Billing. Accounts Receivable detects deductions by comparing a customer's check with the customer's balance: A discrepancy triggers Accounts Receivable to initiate a deduction inquiry to Account Operations, the department that would have authorized the deduction. If Account Operations had previously authorized the deduction, the customer's deduction is approved, and Accounts Receivable is notified. If not, the deduction is disapproved, and Billing is notified to rebill. The auditor's tests translate to three critical questions:

- Does Accounts Receivable monitor deductions?
- Does Account Operations approve deduction inquiries?
- Does senior management review decisions made by Accounts Receivable and Account Operations?

Representative tests follow.

Tests of Controls: Deduction Management

1. From postings to Accounts Receivable and cash receipts, select a sample of entries for which customers took deductions.
2. Trace each entry in the sample to a deduction inquiry; examine notation indicating Account Operations' approval or disapproval.
   a. Trace approved inquiries to charge authorizations and to entries in Accounts Receivable.
   b. Trace disapproved inquiries to rebill notices, and to supplemental sales invoice.
3. Inspect for evidence of senior management review.

In Step 1, the auditor seeks the set of transactions for which customers took deductions, since initiating the tests from the set of deduction inquiries would overlook deductions that Accounts Receivable overlooked. Thereafter, deduction inquiries are the primary source documents for testing deduction management. In Step 2, the auditor traces each deduction inquiry either to an approved charge authorization (and to an entry in Accounts Receivable relieving the customer's balance) or to a rebill notice (and to a supplemental invoice that rebills the customer for the amount of the unauthorized deduction). Finally, in Step 3, the auditor seeks evidence that senior management has reviewed the approved and the disapproved inquiries—for example, a manager's notation on the deduction inquiries or a summary memo.

> fraud
> restatement
> earnings management

In many companies, deduction management plays an important role in controlling financial reporting, since customers have incentives to reduce costs by most any means available, particularly well after sales prices have been negotiated and goods received. For example, one such customer was Rite Aid Corporation, the drugstore chain introduced in Chapter 8 in the context of internal control. To overstate reported income, Rite Aid took unauthorized deductions from vendors that did not require retailers to return damaged or outdated product. Rite Aid destroyed product, inflated the value of the product destroyed, and deducted from future payments to vendors amounts equal to the inflated value. In effect, Rite Aid's income was overstated by the amount that deductions were inflated. The SEC explains:

Rite Aid systematically inflated deductions it took against amounts owed to vendors for damaged and outdated products ("D&Os"). For those vendors that did not require Rite Aid to return D&Os to them ("deduct vendors"), Rite Aid had the product destroyed and reported to the deduct vendors the quantity and dollar value of the destroyed product. Rite Aid then deducted the dollar value of destroyed product from a future remittance to the vendor. Rite Aid improperly inflated the quantities and dollar value of D&Os reported to the deduct vendors through a practice known within Rite Aid as the vendor "up-charge." The vendors did not agree to or know about the up-charge. The effect of this practice was to overstate Rite Aid's reported net income.[1]

Vendor "up-charges" overstated Rite Aid's 1998 and 1999 pretax income by $8 million and $28 million, respectively.

Evidence that the deduction management process is ineffective—for example, if Step 1 reveals that deductions are not always inquired, or Step 3 shows that senior management does not review—would cause the auditor to invoke the judgment process introduced in Chapter 8. Does the ineffectiveness translate to a control that does not allow management to prevent or detect misstatements in the normal course of business (a deficiency)? If so, is the ineffectiveness more than remotely likely to cause a more than inconsequential misstatement (significant deficiency) or, worse, a *material* misstatement (material weakness in internal control)? Recall from Chapter 8 that one material weakness in internal control that is not corrected completely by the last day of the fiscal year would cause the auditor to reach an adverse opinion about management's internal controls over financial reporting. Material weaknesses detected at interim offer management the opportunity to implement corrective action, illustrating an advantage of interim tests of controls.

---

1   *SEC Accounting and Auditing Enforcement Release No. 1579, In the Matter of Rite Aid Corporation,* June 21, 2003.

Computer Auditing and Sampling Applied to Tests of Controls Over Billing

To illustrate material introduced in this chapter and, equally important, to integrate with material presented on information technology (Chapter 8) and audit sampling (Chapter 9), assume a continuing audit engagement for a December 31 year-end client, the Letts Corporation, a medium-size supplier of handheld power tools. The objective in this case is to determine whether Letts' controls over billing are effective.

Computer System: Billing, Data Entry, and Computer Processing

Early this year, Letts computerized the billing function, resulting in the billing, data entry, and computer processing system partially flowcharted in Figure 10-8. As shown in Figure 10-8, the Billing department's activities are similar to those illustrated in Figure 10-2. Orders are entered and the data is sorted, compared with the price and sales terms master file, and merged with the accounts receivable master file to yield:

1. An updated accounts receivable master file,
2. Sales invoices,
3. Sales summaries, and
4. An exception report.

Consideration of Internal Control

The auditor's understanding of the system, tests of controls, and evaluation of Letts Corporation's billing function follow.

Understanding the System

Because Letts' billing system has not been reviewed previously, the auditor decides to document the system by flowcharting and by using a questionnaire. The flowchart appears in Figure 10-8, and a transaction walkthrough indicates that the flowchart is accurate. The questionnaire consists of the eight billing and recording questions from the questionnaire shown in Figure 10-7. Questions 4 and 5 received "*No*" responses, indicating the following deficiencies:

- The accounts receivable subsidiary ledger is not reconciled periodically with the general ledger.
- Monthly statements and bills are not reviewed by personnel independent of Accounts Receivable.

Despite these weaknesses, the auditor decides to continue considering internal control because Billing processes large volumes of transactions and the deficiencies relate to manual output controls only, not to computer processing controls.

Tests of Controls

Because of the deficiencies, the auditor elects a twofold strategy for testing controls: First, test data (explained in Chapter 8) will be used to test the effectiveness of computer controls over data entry and computer processing. Second, sampling will be used to test transactions processed during the year. In short, test data will

FIGURE 10-8: *Letts Corporation: Flowchart of Billing, Data Entry, and Computer Processing*

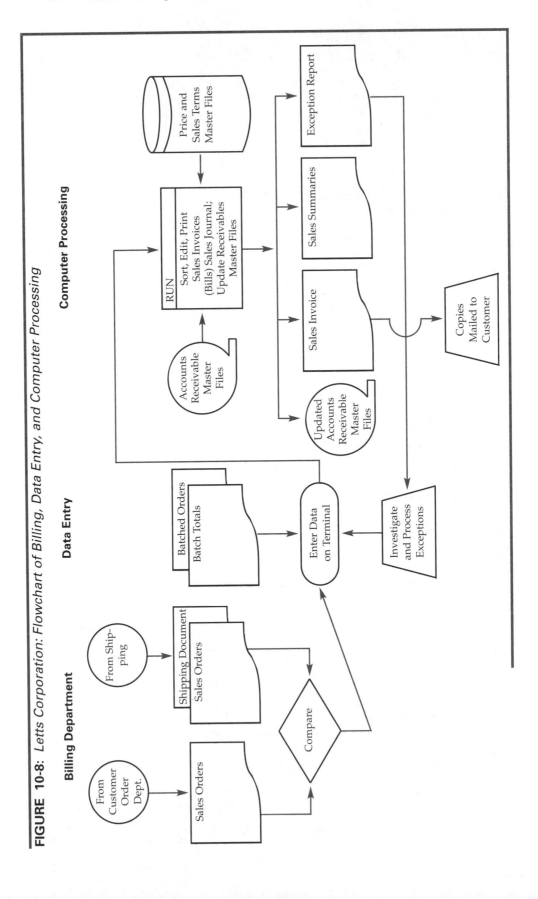

focus on the effectiveness of controls when the system processes error-packed, auditor-prepared test data, and the sampling plan will focus on live data previously processed by the system.

The auditor prepares a file of test data that is planted with errors intended to test the following input and processing controls.

Controls	Planted Errors
Input Controls	
Code verification	False user identification codes.
Data entry controls	Inaccurate control totals.
Processing Controls	
Control totals	Processed records do not agree with record counts.
Limit test	Transactions exceed the authorized maximum dollar amount.

The test data are processed on Letts' computer under the auditor's supervision, and no exceptions are found.

Given the deficiencies noted per the questionnaire, two types of errors or frauds could occur. The first appears at the sixth objective of Figure 10-5 (middle column) and the second appears at the seventh objective:

Potential errors or frauds:

- *General ledger account balances may be inaccurate, potentially resulting in misstated financial statements.*
- *Transactions may be posted to improper customer accounts, potentially resulting in improper billings.*

After considering these potential errors or frauds, the auditor decides to focus tests of controls on the posting of sales information from detailed records to control accounts and, therefore, drafts the following tests, all of which were explained earlier in the chapter.

Steps	Tests of Billing Controls
1.	Randomly select a sample of sales invoices from Billing department files.
2.	For each sampled sales invoice, verify unit prices and clerical accuracy.
3.	Trace details of sampled sales invoices to shipping documents (bills of lading).
4.	Trace details of sampled sales invoices to entries in the sales journal and accounts receivable subsidiary ledger.
5.	Trace sales invoices to inventory records in Inventory Accounting.

As discussed in Chapter 9, the auditor next determines whether these steps can be accomplished by sampling and, in turn, whether to use statistical or nonstatistical sampling. In this case, Steps 2 through 5 can be accomplished with sampling. In addition, the auditor decides to sample statistically, because the billing system has not been tested previously (a newly implemented system) and, therefore, the auditor desires a quantified estimate of sampling risk. Because the auditor has no reason to expect low deviation rates, attribute estimation rather than sequential (stop-or-go) sampling is chosen as the statistical sampling plan. The results of the attribute estimation sampling plan are summarized in Figure 10-9, an attribute estimation spreadsheet, and Figure 10-10, an analysis of deviations.

FIGURE 10-9: *Attribute Estimation Spreadsheet*

Letts Corporation
Attribute Estimation Spreadsheet—Billing
December 31, 2007

B15
KR
11/20/07

Attribute	1 Risk of Assessing CR Too Low	2 Tolerable Rate	3 Expected Rate	4 Sample Size Table*	4 Sample Size Used	5 Number of Deviations	5 Sample Rate	6 Maximum Population Deviation Rate***
1. Unit pricing and extensions on the sales invoice are accurate.	.05	.05	.01	93	100	1**	.01	.047
2. Details on the sales invoice agree with bill of lading.	.05	.04	.005	117	125	1**	.008	.038
3. Details on the sales invoice tie to sales journal and accounts receivable postings.	.05	.05	.0125	124	125	0	0	.024
4. Details on the sales invoice tie to inventory records.	.05	.07	.01	66	70	0	0	.042

*See Figure 9-3.
**See analysis of deviation at B16.
***See Figure 9-7.

Conclusion
Based on procedures performed, the tolerable rate of deviation exceeds the maximum population deviation rate for all four attributes tested.

FIGURE 10-10: *Analysis of Deviations*

Letts Corporation   B16
Analysis of Deviation—Billing   KR
December 31, 2007   11/20/07

Attribute	Number of Deviations	Nature of Deviations	Effect on Substantive Tests of Details
1	1	Sales Invoice #12267, August 23, $10,657; unit prices did not reflect August 22 price increase.	No additional audit work is necessary because (1) the price and sales terms master file disk was updated on August 23, and (2) the maximum population deviation rate (.047) is less than the tolerable rate (.05).
2	1	Sales Invoice #17631, November 15, $7,650; shipping documents indicate 170 units were shipped, but the sales invoice bills for only 165 units.	No additional audit work is necessary because (1) the client's November 15 exception report noted the difference and customer was rebilled, and (2) the maximum population deviation rate (.038) is less than the tolerable rate (.04).

Assessing Control Risk

The auditor's assessment of control risk for Letts Corporation's controls over billing would be based on the following quantitative and qualitative factors:

- No exceptions were noted when test data were run with client-prepared programs.
- The tolerable rate of deviation exceeded the maximum population deviation rate for all four billing-related attributes tested (Figure 10-9).
- The internal control questionnaire revealed two deficiencies in internal control.

In this case, the auditor's decision would likely be to assess control risk below the maximum for assertions related to controls over billing, since test data and audit sampling indicate that the two deficiencies are not likely to produce aggregate error in excess of tolerable error.

Other Assurance and Consulting Services

Accountants have long been testing internal control and designing accounting information systems, particularly in transaction cycles, which, like the revenue/receipt cycle, leverage heavily in information technology to process large volumes of transactions. In practice, information system assurance services include both *system assurance* (for example, does the system provide reliable, relevant output information?) and *data assurance* (for example, is input data reliable, relevant?).

For example, consider information system assurance services for retailers who, like industry leaders Wal-Mart and Kmart, use proprietary *point-of-sale (POS)* systems rather than generic *electronic data integration* systems to transact electronic commerce. Practitioners offer system and data assurances both to the retailer and to their customers about, for example, the POS system's price, order entry, customer identification, document protection, and digital cash remittance security features. In fact, the nonpublic retailers' incumbent auditors are particularly well suited for these engagements, since knowledge acquired on the financial statement audit spills over to the assurance engagement, and vice versa.

Prior to enactment in 2002 of the *Sarbanes-Oxley Act*, knowledge spillovers, technological savvy, and, in particular, an existing client base had proven particularly fortuitous for the Big Four firms in partnering with worldwide technology leaders. For example, in the 1970s, 1980s, and 1990s the consulting practices of the Big Four public accounting firms installed the majority of the customized information systems their audit and nonaudit clients implemented. All four firms partnered with German-based SAP AG to install a full suite of SAP prepackaged, client-server application software to clients seeking company-wide, technological reengineering. The relationship was one of the most productive in the profession's history. For example, by the mid-1990s, worldwide SAP consulting fees and worldwide Big Four SAP consulting personnel were estimated at $3 billion and 8,900, respectively.[2] However, owing to the *Act's* Section 201, "Services Outside the Scope of Practice of Auditors" (Chapter 2), auditors can provide information-systems consulting to public companies they do not audit and to any nonpublic company, even those they audit.

The profession has routinely offered consulting services in the revenue/receipt cycle, most notably the design of automated billing and collection systems. However, some firms have offered revenue-related consulting services that are neither routine nor associated typically with the public accounting profession. For example, a firm in Chattanooga, Tennessee, consults with professional athletic teams—among them, the Baltimore Orioles, Texas Rangers, San Diego Padres, and St. Louis Cardinals—to determine whether stadiums are located optimally and operated economically to maximize home game revenue. Location, real estate, demographic, and marketing services account for about 5 percent of the firm's gross annual billings, up 5 times from 5 years prior. The profession also offers consulting services that benefit both the providers and users of information processed through the revenue/receipt cycle. For example, a West Coast firm consults with record companies and musicians about royalty revenues earned for the use of music written and recorded under contract.

SUMMARY

The revenue/receipt cycle encompasses an entity's selling and collection activities and involves two major business functions: the distribution of resources to outsiders and the subsequent collection for resources distributed. Internal activities typically associated with the selling or distribution function include customer

---

2 "Big Six IT Practices Tap SAP Success," *Public Accounting Report* (April 30, 1996), pp. 1, 4.

order, credit, inventory control, shipping, billing, and recording. Basic documentation associated with selling activities, including sales orders, shipping documents, and sales invoices, provides both a basis for recording sales transactions and an audit trail. Effective control over selling activities requires proper transaction authorization, execution, and recording, and appropriate segregation of duties.

An auditor tests controls within the revenue/receipt cycle after documenting the system and identifying control activities to be relied on. The results of tests of controls are used to assess control risk, which is crucial in assessing allowable detection risk, the basis for judging the extent of year-end substantive tests of details. Tests of controls also bear on an auditor's opinion of management's assessment of internal control over financial reporting. Substantive tests of accounts receivable, sales, and cash balances are performed to satisfy the audit objectives of existence or occurrence, rights, valuation, completeness, and presentation or disclosure, and are discussed in Chapter 11.

KEY TERMS

Bill of lading 414	Receiving report 420
Credit memorandum 420	Revenue/receipt cycle 413
Customer order 413	Sales invoice 414
Customer remittance advice 414	Sales order 413
Lapping 434	Shipping document 414

REFERENCES

Professional Standards:

PCAOB *Auditing Standard No.2,* "An Audit of Internal Control Over Financial Reporting."
AICPA, *Codification of Auditing Standards.* New York: AICPA.

Books:

Committee of Sponsoring Organizations of the Treadway Commission (COSO), *Internal Control: Integrated Framework.* Evaluation Tools. New York: COSO, 1992.

Committee of Sponsoring Organizations of the Treadway Commission (COSO), *Internal Control: Integrated Framework.* Executive Summary. New York: COSO, 1992.

Committee of Sponsoring Organizations of the Treadway Commission (COSO), *Internal Control: Integrated Framework.* Framework. New York: COSO, 1992.

Committee of Sponsoring Organizations of the Treadway Commission (COSO), *Internal Control: Integrated Framework.* Reporting to External Parties. New York: COSO, 1992.

QUESTIONS

1. What are the major business functions and activities common to the revenue/receipt cycle?
2. How does a transaction cycle create an audit trail?
3. Describe the major documents associated with the revenue/receipt cycle.
4. Explain why the billing function should be segregated from granting credit, cash collection, and accounting.
5. What potential errors or frauds could occur if customer credit is not approved by authorized personnel? Identify controls that management could implement to assure that a customer is creditworthy.

6. How can management assure that all shipped goods are billed?
7. Accurate recording within general ledger control accounts does not necessarily mean that billing, collection, and adjustment transactions will be posted accurately to individual customer accounts. What controls can management implement to mitigate the likelihood of inaccurate postings to individual customer accounts?
8. In most circumstances, management is more concerned with restricting employee access to cash than restricting access to inventory. But shouldn't management be more concerned with inventory, since inventory is usually more material to the financial statements than cash? Explain.
9. Why does an auditor test controls?
10. What is the primary focus of the tests of controls performed on an entity's selling and cash receipts activities?
11. What is lapping?
12. Identify the two major errors or frauds that could result from weaknesses in shipping controls.
13. What is the primary source document from which most shipping-related tests of controls evolve?
14. In performing tests of controls, why would an auditor compare shipping documents with approved sales orders?
15. What is the focus of an auditor's tests of billing, and how do the tests complement tests of shipping controls?
16. What is the primary source document for an auditor's tests of billing?
17. If a credit memorandum was issued for returned goods, how might an auditor determine whether the goods were actually returned?
18. How does an auditor evaluate the effectiveness and reliability of a client's control activities over revenue/receipt cycle activities?
19. What is an auditor's likely course of action if tests of controls reveal that management's control activities are inadequate?
20. What is deduction management?

MULTIPLE CHOICE QUESTIONS

1. Which of the following business functions is associated with the revenue/receipt cycle?
   a. Obligations are paid to vendors and employees.
   b. Resources are distributed to outsiders in exchange for promises of future payments.
   c. Resources are used, held, or transformed.
   d. Capital funds are received from investors and creditors.

2. A document that describes products delivered to a customer and notifies the customer about the amount and terms of payment is called a:
   a. Receiving report.
   b. Shipping document.
   c. Sales invoice.
   d. Remittance advice.

3. Following the release of goods, Inventory Control would forward an approved sales order to:
   a. Billing.
   b. Shipping.
   c. Credit department.
   d. Customer Order department

4. Before preparing a shipping document, Shipping would:

    a. Access credit approval from the Credit department.
    b. Compare a sales order to the sales summary.
    c. Access approval from Inventory Control.
    d. Compare sales orders processed by Customer Order and Inventory Control.

5. Which of the following departments would prepare a sales invoice?

    a. Customer Order
    b. Credit
    c. Shipping
    d. Billing

6. From what source documents would a company prepare a bank deposit?

    a. Checks and a list of checks received
    b. Checks and remittance advices
    c. A list of checks received and remittance advices
    d. Remittance advices and a deposit slip

7. How could management control against unbilled shipments?

    a. Reconcile customer accounts to control totals.
    b. Deliver promptly shipping documents to the Billing department.
    c. Review customer statements monthly.
    d. Establish written criteria for shipping and billing.

8. Verifying that ordered goods are in stock would likely serve the objective of:

    a. Authorization.
    b. Execution.
    c. Recording.
    d. Access to assets.

9. Which of the following documents would likely be sent to a customer?

    a. Sales order
    b. Credit approval
    c. Shipping document
    d. Sales summary

10. A Shipping department would not likely:

    a. Compare shipped goods with a sales order.
    b. Prepare a sales order.
    c. Notify Customer Order that goods were shipped.
    d. Prepare shipping documents.

11. A bill of lading provides evidence of:

    a. Goods ordered.
    b. Goods shipped.
    c. Goods returned.
    d. The weight of goods shipped.

12. To test whether sales have been recorded, a sample should be drawn from a file of:

    a. Purchase orders.
    b. Sales orders.
    c. Sales invoices.
    d. Bills of lading.

13. Tracing copies of sales invoices to shipping documents provides evidence that:
    a. Shipments were recorded as receivables.
    b. Billed sales were shipped.
    c. Debits to Accounts Receivable were for sales shipped.
    d. Shipments were billed.

14. Tracing shipping documents to sales invoices provides evidence that:
    a. Shipments were billed.
    b. Shipments were recorded as sales.
    c. Recorded sales were shipped.
    d. Invoiced sales were shipped.

15. Which of the following control activities could prevent or detect errors or frauds arising from shipments made to unauthorized parties?
    a. Document policies and procedures for scheduling shipments.
    b. Establish procedures for reviewing and approving prices and sales terms before sale.
    c. Prenumber bills of lading and assure that related billings are made on a periodic basis.
    d. Prepare and periodically update lists of authorized customers.

16. Which of the following control activities would most likely assure that access to shipping, billing, inventory control, and accounting records is restricted to personnel authorized by management?
    a. Segregate responsibilities for authorization, execution, and recording, and prenumber and control custody of documents.
    b. Establish the cash receipts function in a centralized location and require daily reconciliation of cash receipts records with deposit slips.
    c. Establish policy and procedures manuals, organization charts, and supporting documentation.
    d. Periodically substantiate and evaluate recorded account balances.

17. An entity has implemented a control activity that requires authorized personnel to reconcile the total of individual customer accounts receivable with control totals. This control relates to which of the following control objectives?
    a. Sales, cash receipts, and related transactions should be recorded in the correct amounts, in the proper period, and should be properly classified.
    b. Recorded accounts receivable balances should reflect underlying transactions and events.
    c. Billings, collections, and related adjustments transactions should be posted accurately to individual customer accounts.
    d. Access to cash and cash-related records should be restricted to personnel management authorizes.

18. A purpose of tests of controls for shipping is to determine whether:
    a. Billed goods are shipped.
    b. Shipments are made in accordance with approved sales and orders.
    c. Sales orders are properly recorded.
    d. Shipping personnel route goods to related parties.

19. A purpose of tests of controls for billing is to determine whether:
    a. Billed goods have been shipped.
    b. Sales orders agree with shipping documents.
    c. Sales orders have been approved by Credit department personnel.
    d. Billing personnel process returned goods properly.

20. What sequence of steps does an auditor undertake when identifying control activities that are potentially reliable in assessing control risk below the maximum?

    a. Consider the errors or frauds that might occur, determine control activities, identify control objectives, and design tests of controls.

    b. Determine control activities, design tests of controls, consider the errors or frauds that might occur, and identify control objectives.

    c. Identify control objectives, consider the errors or frauds that might occur, determine control activities, and design tests of controls.

    d. Design tests of controls, determine control activities, consider the errors or frauds that might occur, and identify control objectives.

PROBLEMS AND DISCUSSION CASES

10-1 *Tests of Controls and Credit Sales*

Within the revenue/receipt cycle, several documents typically are used to create an accounting system and, correspondingly, an audit trail for credit sales and cash collections. Among these documents are sales orders, shipping documents, and sales invoices.

    Required:

    1. Explain how approved sales orders can be used to test credit sales for understatements.

    2. Explain how shipping documents can be used to test whether all sales transactions that should be recorded are actually recorded.

    3. Explain how an auditor can use sales invoices to test whether billed sales were actually shipped.

10-2 *Controls Over Credit Sales and Cash Collections*

Assume you are considering an entity's internal controls over credit sales and cash collection. System documentation was accomplished through a questionnaire and written narratives and, in conjunction with a transaction walkthrough, revealed the following potential weaknesses in internal control, some of which, depending on their severity, could prompt you to set control risk at the maximum.

    a. New customers are not approved before ordered goods are shipped.

    b. Sales prices vary from customer to customer.

    c. No approval is required for returned goods from customers.

    d. Subsidiary accounts receivable records do not always agree with the general ledger control account.

    e. Blank checks are left unprotected in an unlocked safe.

    Required: For each potential weakness, indicate a control or controls that management could implement to reduce the likelihood of errors or frauds.

10-3 *Errors, Fraud, and Control Activities*

During your audit of Lish and Company's financial statements, you become aware of the following controls or procedures Lish implemented over credit sales and cash collections.

    a. Sales terms are approved by supervisory personnel before shipment.

    b. All credit memoranda are prenumbered sequentially and controlled.

    c. Shipping documents are prenumbered sequentially and controlled.

    d. Copies of shipping documents are hand-carried to the Billing department within one hour after shipment.

    e. Sales invoices are compared with sales journals and with customers' individual subsidiary records.

f. In contrast to prior years, noncredit (cash) sales are handled in one centralized location, rather than throughout all departments.

g. Unused checks are prenumbered and locked in a fireproof vault accessible only to the treasurer, who is one of two endorsers on customers' checks.

Required: For each control or procedure, indicate (1) a potential error or fraud that might circumvent the control or procedure and (2) the internal control objective that is served by the control or procedure.

10-4 *Interpreting a Systems Flowchart*

A partially completed flowchart for the Bottom Manufacturing Corporation's credit sales is presented on the following page. When a customer's order is received, a six-part sales order is prepared and copies are distributed as shown:

Copy No. 1:	Billing copy	to	Billing department
Copy No. 2:	Shipping copy	to	Shipping department
Copy No. 3:	Credit copy	to	Credit department
Copy No. 4:	Stock request copy	to	Inventory Control
Copy No. 5:	Customer copy	to	Customer
Copy No. 6:	Sales order copy	filed	Customer Order department

When a sales order copy reaches a department, control activities and documents are required. Some of the procedures and documents are identified on the flowchart. Others are labeled with letters *a* to *r*.

Required: List the unidentified procedures or documents that are labeled *c* to *r* in the flowchart. Procedures for the letters *a* and *b* follow:

Flowchart Letter	Procedure or Document
a.	Prepare six-part sales order.
b.	File by order number.

(AICPA Adapted)

10-5 *Designing Software to Extract Receivables Data*

You are auditing trade accounts receivable for Winston-McCabe Company, a farm-equipment retailer doing business in three Midwestern cities. All accounting, shipping, billing, and receivables records are maintained on a local area network (LAN). You are particularly interested in the validity, accuracy, and age of the receivables. Winston-McCabe has a programmer available to develop software for extracting data from the receivables files.

Required: Discuss procedures you want the software to perform, including any reports, schedules, and lists you expect.

10-6 *Identifying Weaknesses and Recommending Improvements*

The Art Appreciation Society operates a museum for the benefit of the community. During hours when the museum is open to the public, two clerks are positioned at the entrance and collect a $5 admission fee from each nonmember patron. Members of the Art Appreciation Society are permitted to enter free of charge on presentation of their membership cards.

At the end of each day, one of the clerks delivers the proceeds to the treasurer. The treasurer counts the cash in the presence of the clerk and places the cash in a safe. Each Friday afternoon the treasurer and one of the clerks deliver all cash held in the safe to the bank and receive a deposit slip that drives a weekly entry in the cash receipts records.

The board of directors of the Art Appreciation Society has identified a need to improve the system of internal control over cash admission fees. The board has determined that the cost of installing turnstiles or sales booths or otherwise altering the physical layout of the

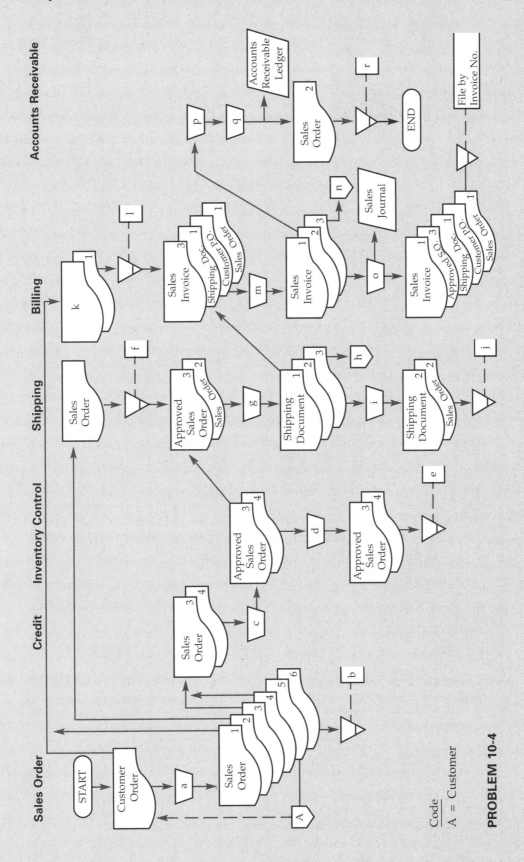

PROBLEM 10-4

Code
A = Customer

museum will greatly exceed the potential benefits. However, the board agrees that controls over the sale of admission tickets needs improvement.

You have been asked by the board of directors to review internal control over cash admission fees and provide suggestions for improvement.

Required: Indicate weaknesses in the existing system of internal control over cash admission fees and recommend one improvement for each weakness. For example:

Weakness	Recommendation
1. There is no basis for establishing the number of paying patrons.	Prenumbered admission tickets should be issued upon payment of the admission fee.

10-7 *Identifying Potential Frauds and Recommending Procedures to Improve Control*

You are auditing the Alaska branch of Far Distributing Co., a branch that has substantial annual sales, all of which are billed and collected locally. During your preliminary review of internal control, you discover the following procedures for handling cash receipts:

- Cash collections on over-the-counter and COD sales are received by the cashier from the customer or from the delivery service. Upon receiving cash, the cashier stamps the sales ticket "paid" and files a copy. The only record of COD sales is a copy of the sales ticket, which is given to the cashier to hold until cash is received from the delivery service.

- Mail is opened by the credit manager's secretary, and remittances are given to the credit manager for review. The credit manager then places the remittances in a tray on the cashier's desk. At the time of the daily deposit—called "deposit cutoff time"—the cashier delivers the checks and currency to the assistant credit manager, who prepares remittance lists and the bank deposit, and carries the deposit to the bank. The assistant credit manager also posts remittances to customer accounts receivable files and verifies allowable cash discounts.

- You learn that the credit manager obtains approval to write off uncollectible accounts from the executive office of Far Distributing Co., located in Chicago, and that as of the end of the fiscal year some remittances that were received on various days during the last month are retained in the credit manager's custody.

Required:
1. Describe the frauds that might occur under the procedures now in effect for handling cash collections and remittances.
2. What procedures would you recommend to improve control over cash collections and remittances?

(AICPA Adapted)

10-8 *Recommending Improvements to Internal Control*

You are auditing the financial statements of Fashionation, Inc., a retail clothing store, and have prepared the following narrative description for cash sales procedures.

All sales are for cash; no credit cards are accepted. Each individual sale is rung by the sales clerk on a cash register that ejects a sales slip. The sales slip is given to the customer, and a copy of the sales slip is made by the cash register on a continuous tape locked inside the machine. At the end of the day, the sales clerk presses a total key and the machine prints the total sales for the day on the continuous tape. The clerk then unlocks the cash register, removes the day's tape, makes an entry in the cash receipts book, counts the cash in the drawer, retains a change fund of $100, and turns the rest of the cash over to the cashier. The sales clerk then files the cash register tape and is ready for the next day.

Required: From the narrative description of Fashionation's cash sales procedures, discuss specific recommendations to improve controls over cash.

10-9 *Designing Controls Over Cash Receipts and Warehousing*

Trapan Retailing, Inc., has decided to diversify operations by selling through vending machines. Trapan plans to purchase 312 vending machines that will be placed in 78 different locations within one city, and to rent a warehouse to store merchandise. Trapan plans to vend canned beverages only.

Management has hired an inventory control clerk to oversee the warehousing functions and two truck drivers who will periodically fill the machines with merchandise and deposit cash collected at a designated bank. Drivers will be required to report to the warehouse daily.

Required: What procedures will control the cash receipts and warehousing functions?

(AICPA Adapted)

10-10 *Drafting Tests of Controls From an Internal Control Questionnaire*

Following are selected questions from internal control questionnaires about a company's customer order, credit, shipping, billing, and cash receipts functions. A *yes* response to any question would indicate a potential strength, and a *no* response a potential weakness of the system.

a. Are sales orders prepared for all approved customer orders?
b. Are copies of sales orders forwarded to the Credit, Shipping, and Billing departments?
c. Is credit investigated before the customer is approved?
d. Are goods shipped only in accordance with approved sales orders?
e. Are shipping documents reviewed and compared with billings to assure that all shipped goods are billed?
f. Are all credit memos prenumbered, matched with approved sales orders and shipping documents, and checked for clerical accuracy?
g. Is the accounts receivable subsidiary ledger reconciled periodically with the general ledger?
h. Are mail receipts opened by personnel independent of Shipping, Billing, Sales Invoice Processing, and Recording?

Required: Assume that inquiries indicate the answer is *yes* to each question. For each question, draft a test you believe would provide persuasive evidence that controls are reliable.

10-11 *Cash Receipts Controls and Designing Audit Procedures*

You are the in-charge accountant auditing the financial statements of Gutzler Company for the year ending December 31, 2007. In late October 2007, you, with the help of Gutzler's controller, complete an internal control questionnaire and prepare a memorandum describing Gutzler's accounting procedures. Your comments about cash receipts follow.

All cash receipts are sent directly to the accounts receivable clerk with no processing by the Mail department. The accounts receivable clerk keeps the cash receipts journal, prepares the bank deposit slip in duplicate, posts from the deposit slip to the subsidiary accounts receivable records, and mails the deposit to the bank.

The controller receives the validated deposit slips directly (unopened) from the bank and also receives the monthly bank statement directly (unopened) from the bank and prepares a reconciliation.

At the end of each month, the accounts receivable clerk sends the monthly totals of the cash receipts journal to the accounting clerk for posting to the general ledger.

Each month, the accounting clerk makes an entry to record the total debits to Cash from the cash receipts journal. In addition, the general ledger clerk on occasion makes debit entries in the general ledger cash account from sources other than the cash receipts journal, for example, funds borrowed from the bank.

You also performed the following procedures on cash receipts:

a. Totaled and cross-totaled all columns in the cash receipts journal.
b. Traced postings from the cash receipts journal to the general ledger.
c. Examined remittance advices and related correspondence to support entries in the cash receipts journal.

Required: Considering Gutzler's control over cash receipts and the audit procedures performed already, list and give reasons for all other auditing procedures that should be performed to obtain audit evidence for cash receipts. (Do not discuss cash disbursements and cash balances.) Assume adequate controls exist to assure that all sales transactions are recorded.

(AICPA Adapted)

10-12 *Detecting Delays in the Posting of Receivables: Lapping*

During the year, Strang Corporation began to encounter cash flow difficulties, and a cursory review by management revealed collection problems. Strang's management engaged Stanley, CPA, to perform a special review. Stanley studied the billing and collection functions of the revenue/receipt cycle and noted the following:

The accounting department employs one bookkeeper who receives and opens all incoming mail. The bookkeeper is also responsible for depositing receipts, filing remittance advices daily, recording receipts in the cash receipts journal, and posting receipts in the individual customer accounts and the general ledger accounts. There are no cash sales. The bookkeeper prepares and controls the mailing of monthly statements to customers.

The concentration of duties entrusted to the bookkeeper and the collection problems cause Stanley to suspect a systematic delay in the posting of customers' remittances (lapping of accounts receivable). Stanley was surprised to find that no customers complained about receiving erroneous monthly statements.

Required: Identify procedures Stanley could perform to determine whether lapping exists. Do not discuss deficiencies in internal control.

(AICPA Adapted)

10-13 *Sales Returns and Fraud*

Within the revenue/receipt cycle, controls must be implemented not only for sales and shipments, but also for sales returns and allowances. Otherwise, sales could be overstated and the financial statements significantly misstated.

Required:
1. Draft and explain the journal entry an employee could make to commit a fraud with sales returns and allowances.
2. In tests of controls over credit memoranda, how can an auditor test whether goods related to sales returns and allowances were actually returned?

10-14 *Control Objectives in Data Entry*

The president of I&M Electric, a large regional utility, has asked that you perform a special engagement unrelated to the financial statement audit: Audit the customer payment system but with emphasis on data entry and data transmission at local branch offices. Customers may send their payments to the central office or may pay in person at any of the company's 25 branch locations. When a customer pays a utility bill at a branch office, an employee enters the payment immediately into the branch payment system via a workstation that is connected online to the company's main office. I&M divides the branch office collection procedures into three categories: data entry, data transmission, and data processing.

Required: List data entry control objectives and briefly describe control techniques to accomplish each objective.

10-15 *Steps in an Audit Sampling Plan*

Barry Hannah, CPA, plans to use attribute estimation to help assess control risk for the Oxford Company's control activities over credit sales transactions. Hannah has begun to outline main steps in the sampling plan:

a. State the objectives of the test (for example, to test the reliability of controls over sales).
b. Define the population (and the period covered by the test).
c. Define the sampling unit (for example, sales invoices).

Required:
1. What are the remaining steps Hannah should include in the statistical test of sales invoices?
2. How does statistical sampling help the auditor?

10-16 *Attribute Estimation and Tests of Shipping Controls*

Galway Kinnell plans to apply an attribute estimation sampling plan to the shipping controls used by the Raffel & Olds Corporation, a December 31, 2007, year-end printing company in New York. Based on a planning meeting with Jack Gilbert, engagement partner, Kinnell assesses the following risks of assessing control risk too low and expected population deviation rates for each of five tests of controls.

Test of Control	Risk of Assessing Control Risk Too Low	Expected Population Deviation Rate
1. Examine each shipping document to determine whether the document:		
a. Is accompanied by a sales order bearing Credit and Inventory Control authorization, and	.06	.0125
b. Agrees with the sales order as to description of goods, quantity, destination, etc.	.04	.0075
2. Trace details of sampled shipping documents to copies of shipping documents and their related sales invoices in Billing department files.	.05	.0125
3. Trace details of the related sales invoices to entries in the sales journal and accounts receivable subsidiary ledger.	.07	.015
4. Trace sales invoices to inventory records in Inventory Accounting.	.07	.015

The tolerable rate of deviation is .05 for all five tests. Kinnell performs the sampling plan on September 15 and finds one deviation each for tests No. 1b (although shipping document #0167, May 21, $21,450 reads 1,200 units, the sales order reads 1,050 units) and No. 4 (although sales invoice #21261, July 12, reads $19,725, the inventory records reflect $19,275).

Required: Prepare audit working papers to document the attribute estimation sampling plan and the analysis of deviations.

Internet problems and discussion cases are available at http://ricchiute.swlearning.com

RESEARCH PROJECT

Internal Control and Transaction Cycles in Selected Industries

Auditors facing engagements within a given industry—say, for example, airline companies or commercial banks—face clients with largely similar control environments, risk assessment profiles, control activities, information and communication needs, and monitoring requirements. In short, in all but the very smallest owner-managed companies, systems of internal control are likely to be similar among clients competing within the same industry and quite different for clients operating in dissimilar industries.

Required:
- Select an AICPA *Audit & Accounting Guide* for the industry of your choice (for example, the AICPA publishes guides for airlines, banks, casinos, colleges and universities, construction contractors, finance companies, investment companies, property and liability insurance companies, and providers of health care services, among others), and
- Using the annual report file in an online research service (for example, LEXIS-NEXIS, the SEC's EDGAR [**http://www.sec.gov**]) or copies of annual reports in a library, select an annual report for an entity in the same industry.

Draft a report that:

1. Describes the major control considerations identified in the *Audit & Accounting Guide*.
2. Identifies the financial statement accounts likely processed by the entity's revenue/receipt, expenditure/disbursement, financing, and (if a manufacturer) conversion cycles. (Use the selected entity's financial statements, including footnotes, and other disclosures in the annual report to address this question.)

Interactive quizzes are available as a student learning resource at http://ricchiute.swlearning.com

Chapter 11

Accounts Receivable and Cash Balances

Major topics discussed in this chapter are:

- The relationship between financial statement assertions and audit procedures in the audit of receivables and cash balances.
- The relationship among audit risk; client strategies; and the nature, timing, and extent of substantive tests.
- Substantive tests applicable to assertions about sales, accounts receivable, and cash balances.
- Revenue recognition and earnings manipulation related to channel stuffing, telecom revenue, landfill costs, and software sales.
- Audit sampling in substantive tests of accounts receivable.
- Computer-assisted audit techniques applicable to accounts receivable.

Based on the assessed levels of control and inherent risk for assertions within the **revenue/receipt cycle**, an auditor determines acceptable levels of detection risk and then designs substantive tests for the major financial statement accounts processed by the cycle: sales, accounts receivable, and cash. This chapter focuses on substantive tests of details for these accounts. The chapter begins by discussing how each of the financial statement assertions introduced in Chapter 6—existence or occurrence, completeness, rights and obligations, valuation or allocation, and presentation and disclosure—is tested for audits of sales, accounts receivable, and cash, and how audit risk and client strategies bear on the nature, timing, and extent of an auditor's substantive tests. In turn, the chapter relates the assertions to substantive tests for these accounts and then describes and illustrates each test. Thereafter, the chapter introduces common means to overstate revenue; explains revenue recognition problems related to channel stuffing and telecom revenue; and addresses audit, legal, and ethical questions that arise when the timing of revenue recognition is subject to management's discretion. The chapter concludes by illustrating how audit sampling, introduced in Chapter 9, can be used in substantive tests of receivables balances, and by discussing computer-assisted audit procedures applicable to accounts receivable.

Financial Statement Assertions, Objectives, and Audit Procedures

As explained in Chapter 6, much of an auditor's work during a financial statement audit consists of obtaining and evaluating evidence about the assertions embodied within an entity's financial statements. For example, management asserts that recorded receivables and cash balances:

- Exist,
- Include all transactions that should be presented,
- Represent rights of the entity,
- Are valued appropriately, and
- Are presented and disclosed properly within the financial statements.

Each financial statement assertion translates to an audit objective for which auditors design procedures to obtain evidence. For example, management's assertion that cash and receivables exist creates a corresponding audit objective to determine whether each asset actually does exist, and auditors generally use confirmation procedures to test their existence. Hence, financial statement assertions are synonymous with audit objectives. But, specifically, what procedures do practicing auditors commonly use to address which financial statement assertions? The following relates each financial statement assertion to audit procedures that practitioners commonly use to audit revenue/receipt cycle accounts. The assertions and procedures are summarized in Figure 11-1.

FIGURE 11-1: *Relating Financial Statement Assertions and Audit Procedures: Sales, Receivables, and Cash Balances*

	Audit Procedures		
Assertions	*Sales*	*Receivables*	*Cash Balances*
Existence or occurrence	Test cutoff.	Confirm with debtors. Test cutoff.	Confirm with banks. Test cutoff.
Completeness	Perform analytical procedures. Test cutoff.	Perform analytical procedures. Test cutoff.	Test cutoff. Examine bank reconciliations or proofs of cash. Examine inter-company and interbank transfers.
Rights and obligations		Confirm with debtors. Review collectibility.	Confirm with banks.
Valuation or allocation	Perform analytical procedures.	Confirm with debtors. Review collectibility. Verify accuracy of aged trial balance.	Confirm with banks. Verify mathematical accuracy of recorded cash balances. Test cutoff.
Presentation and disclosure	Compare statement presentation and disclosures with those required by GAAP.	Compare statement presentation and disclosures with those required by GAAP.	Compare statement presentation and disclosures with those required by GAAP.

Existence or Occurrence

Within the revenue/receipt cycle, the existence or occurrence assertion addresses whether all recorded sales, receivables, and cash balances actually exist and whether all recorded transactions actually occurred. Existence is normally tested by physical observation or confirmation with outside parties. In practice, the existence of receivables is often tested by confirming balances with debtors (customers), the existence of cash on deposit is tested by confirming bank balances with banks, and the existence of cash on hand can be observed physically and counted. In addition, auditors use cutoff testing to determine whether recorded sales transactions and related receivables and cash transactions are recorded in the proper period.

Completeness

The completeness assertion addresses whether all receivables, sales, and cash transactions that should be presented in the financial statements actually are presented. Generally, completeness is tested by examining documentation and by applying analytical procedures, such as making comparisons among related accounts. For sales and receivables, completeness is tested by performing analytical procedures, which helps determine whether recorded receivables and sales balances are reasonable at the balance sheet date, and by testing cutoff, which determines whether transactions are recorded in the proper accounting period. Auditors typically test completeness for cash balances by examining cutoff bank statements to assure that all receipts and disbursements are recorded in the proper period, and by examining bank reconciliations (or proofs of cash) and records of intercompany and interbank transfers.

Rights and Obligations

Within the revenue/receipt cycle, the rights and obligations assertion addresses whether an entity has property rights—for example, claims against third parties—for recorded receivables and cash balances. That is, does the company have legally binding claims against customers for receivables balances and against commercial banks and other depositories for recorded cash balances? Generally, an auditor tests rights by examining documentation and through confirmations and inquiries. Rights to receivables are typically tested by confirming balances with debtors and by reviewing the collectibility of confirmed and unconfirmed customer balances. In turn, rights to cash are tested primarily by confirming balances and deposit terms (for example, demand deposits and compensating balances) with banks.

Valuation or Allocation

The valuation assertion addresses whether receivables, sales, and cash balances are reported in the financial statements at appropriate amounts. That is, are they valued in accordance with generally accepted accounting principles (GAAP)? In general, auditors test valuation by examining documentation; confirming, observing, performing mechanical tests; and making inquiries. More specifically, the carrying value of receivables is tested by confirming balances with debtors and reviewing collectibility—both of which also address rights and obligations—and by verifying the accuracy of management's aged trial balance. Recorded values for cash are tested by confirming balances with banks, by verifying the mathematical accuracy of recorded cash balances, and by examining the details within cutoff bank statements.

Presentation and Disclosure

The presentation and disclosure assertion addresses whether recorded transactions and balances are properly classified, described, and disclosed in the financial statements. Generally, auditors address this assertion by comparing an entity's financial statement presentation and disclosures with those required by GAAP. Presentation and disclosure guidelines, such as the AICPA's annually updated *Accounting and Audit Manual* and proprietary audit-firm databases, are often used by practicing auditors to address this assertion.

Audit Risk: Client Strategies, Threats to the Business, and Substantive Tests in the Revenue/Receipt Cycle

As explained in Chapter 7, an auditor completes interim audit work by drafting preliminary year-end audit programs—that is, by planning substantive audit procedures, the *nature*, *timing*, and *extent* of which are based on:

- *Detection risk (DR)*, the likelihood that error could occur and not be detected by audit procedures, which is based in turn on the auditor's interim assessments of two other risks:
- *Control risk (CR)*, the likelihood that material error could occur and not be detected by internal control, and
- *Inherent risk (IR)*, the susceptibility of an account balance to material error for which there is no related internal control.

In Chapter 7 much was made of the role of client strategies in the assessment of audit risk. For example, discussion in Chapter 7 about Merck's client strategy template (summarized in Figure 7-4, page 252) suggested two threats to the company's business (Figure 7-9, page 268). First, consistent with the threat that Merck's *growth strategy may be at risk*, a Deutsche Bank Securities analyst commented that the Company may need to ". . . consider a significant merger to boost its growth prospects," and a Dow Jones News Service Report commented that ". . . there is concern in the market about its future growth . . . because the company faces a number of upcoming patent expirations." Second, consistent with the claim that *competitive pricing may threaten future earnings*, Chapter 7 offered evidence that managed care groups are demanding discounts, federal and state legislatures are proposing reductions in health care costs, patient co-payments are increasing for prescription drugs, physicians are facing incentives to prescribe generic drugs, and employers are pressuring providers to curb increases in health care costs. Both threats would raise an auditor's professional skepticism in this way: Since growth and pricing affect reported earnings, management has incentives to manipulate earnings in the wake of constricted market share and constrained pricing, and an auditor has reason to design audit procedures that will offer persuasive evidence bearing on reported earnings.

The audit programs illustrated in this chapter assume that an auditor has assessed control risk and inherent risk for the assertions of *existence, completeness, rights,* and *valuation* at the maximum for two reasons: First, assume that tests of controls over shipping, billing, and cash deposits (Chapter 10) reveal that internal control deficiencies are likely to produce aggregate error in excess of tolerable error for the following control procedures:

- *Shipping:* Shipping documents are accompanied by a sales order bearing credit and inventory control authorization.
- *Billing:* Sales invoices are agreed to shipping documents.
- *Deposits:* Deposits are compared with entries in the cash receipts journal.

Second, assume that, owing to an at-risk growth strategy and competitive pricing, the auditor is skeptical about management's incentives to enhance reported earnings.

As a result, to hold audit risk to a *minimum*, the auditor assesses the acceptable level of detection risk at the minimum. That is, from Chapter 2:

$$DR = \frac{AR}{IR \times CR}$$

$$Minimum = \frac{Minimum}{Maximum \times Maximum}$$

Assessing acceptable detection risk at the minimum bears directly on the nature, timing, and extent of planned substantive tests as follows:

- *Nature:* Use more persuasive procedures (for example, receivables confirmations).
- *Timing:* Perform procedures at the balance sheet date (that is, rather than an interim date).
- *Extent:* Test more extensively (for example, increase sample sizes).

Prior to performing substantive tests at year end, auditors review and evaluate any significant changes that might have occurred since assessing control and inherent risk at interim and revise the year-end audit programs as necessary. For example, if internal controls over shipping, billing, and cash deposits have changed since interim, an auditor could perform additional tests of controls; reevaluate control and inherent risk; reassess detection risk; and rethink the nature, timing, and extent of substantive tests.

In substantive tests of revenue/receipt cycle accounts, an auditor obtains and evaluates evidence about transactions and events that bear on an entity's sales and collection activities. However, an auditor does not blindly apply the same audit procedures on every engagement, largely because both audit risk and materiality vary from engagement to engagement. In an effort to make clear the intuition underlying an auditor's role in substantive tests of revenue/receipt cycle accounts, the following discussion proceeds through two categories of audit problems. First, tests for receivables (and sales) and cash balances, respectively, are introduced in representative audit programs that assume control and inherent risk are at the maximum, and that are keyed to and discussed in the context of the financial statement assertions presented earlier: existence or occurrence, completeness, rights and obligations, valuation or allocation, and presentation and disclosure. Second, the discussion then focuses on problems an auditor confronts when, unlike typical sales transactions for which revenue is recognized at the point of sale, the recognition of revenue is less certain, such as channel stuffing, telecom revenue, and accounting for area franchise fees.

Accounts Receivable and Sales

Figure 11-2 illustrates a program of representative year-end substantive tests for accounts receivable and sales. The tests are explained in the context of the financial statement assertions that the tests address and, as illustrated above, assume maximum levels of control and inherent risks and a minimum level of acceptable detection risk. Again, not all of these procedures would necessarily be performed in every audit, since risk varies from engagement to engagement. For example, if control risk is assessed below the maximum, detection risk would be assessed above the minimum and, therefore, the auditor would plan less extensive substantive tests.

FIGURE 11-2: *Substantive Tests: Accounts Receivable and Sales*

Assertions	Procedures

Valuation	1. Verify mathematical accuracy of accounts receivable.
	  a. Obtain an accounts receivable aged trial balance from Accounts Receivable department personnel.
	  b. Foot (add columns) and cross-foot (add column totals across) the trial balance.
	  c. Compare total accounts receivable per the trial balance to accounts receivable in the general ledger.

Existence Rights Valuation	2. Confirm year-end accounts and notes receivable balances with debtors.
Existence or occurrence Completeness	3. Test cutoff to determine whether sales and receivables are recorded in the proper accounting period.
Valuation Rights	4. Review the collectibility of receivables, and determine the adequacy of the allowance for doubtful accounts.
Existence or occurrence Completeness Valuation	5. Perform analytical procedures to determine whether recorded sales and receivables balances appear reasonable.

Presentation and
  disclosure
	6. Review financial statements to determine whether:
	  a. Accounts and notes receivable and sales are properly classified and described.
	  b. Disclosures are adequate.

Verify Mathematical Accuracy

The financial statement assertion of valuation is addressed in part by recomputing the mathematical accuracy of amounts recorded in the client's general ledger. For example, to accomplish tests of mathematical accuracy, an auditor could import a client's aged trial balance into a spreadsheet file, such as the Microsoft Excel screen illustrated in Figure 11-3, and write commands to foot [for example, =SUM(H010:H598)] and cross-foot [for example, =SUM(C598:H598)] the trial balance and to compare and reconcile the trial balance total with the client's recorded general ledger balance.

FIGURE 11-3: *Accounts Receivable Aged Trial Balance*

(Schedule prepared by client)

The Wilson Company
Accounts Receivable Aged Trial Balance
December 31, 2007

Account Number	Customer Name	Balance Dec. 31, 2007	0-30 Days	31-60 Days	61-90 Days	Over 90 Days
0103	Andrie Supplies	$ 6,319.07	$ 6,319.07			
0107	Alpine Roofing	1,754.00	1,754.00			
0108	Atwells, Inc.	5,629.83	5,629.83			
0110	Bennington & Co.	10,743.76		$10,243.76	$ 500.00	
0112	Blakely & Schuster	8,250.00	7,250.00	1,000.00		
0115	Burns & Alec	1,805.00				$1,805.00
		•	•	•	•	•
		•	•	•	•	•
		•	•	•	•	•
0960	Van Allen Sales	2,500.00	1,500.00		1,250.00	
0961	Victor Company, Inc.	16,000.00	16,000.00			
0967	Webster Corporation	1,724.30	1,724.30			
0968	Wellington & Shine	6,225.40	6,225.40			
0971	Yellowstone Stores	5,280.50	5,280.50			
0974	Zelanie & Aveno	17,250.00	17,250.00			
		$232,228.57	$190,922.50	$21,222.42	$14,462.15	$5,621.50

The mathematical accuracy of a client's aged trial balance is crucial, since the trial balance also is used as the basic source for other receivables tests included in Figure 11-2. For example, the aged trial balance is typically used to select individual customer balances for confirmation, discussed next in the chapter, and to identify credit balances that should be reclassified to accounts payable under GAAP.

Confirm Receivables Balances

Confirming receivables balances with debtors—that is, asking a customer in writing whether a recorded receivable is the responding entity's account payable—is a powerful audit procedure because confirmations address simultaneously no less than three financial statement assertions:[1]

- Existence: Do recorded receivables exist at the balance sheet date?
- Rights: Do recorded receivables represent rights the audited entity holds over debtors (for example, have the receivables been assigned or sold)?
- Valuation: Are receivables reported at appropriate amounts?

There is a presumption in the profession that an auditor bears the burden of justifying his or her opinion on an entity's financial statements when receivables are not confirmed. Given the information content of confirmations, under what circumstances might an auditor judge that confirmations are unnecessary? *Statement on Auditing Standards No. 67*, "The Confirmation Process," lists three cases in which failing to confirm receivables is justifiable: (1) when receivables are immaterial to the financial statements, (2) when confirmations would likely be ineffective (for example, the federal government does not respond to receivables confirmations), or (3) when audit risk is acceptably low. Receivables balances are usually confirmed as of the balance sheet date, although it is appropriate to confirm receivables at interim when an auditor is satisfied that internal control is effective (and, therefore, that control risk is below the maximum) and when the balances in receivables and sales accounts can be reconciled from the interim confirmation date (say, October 31) to the balance sheet date (say, December 31).

Confirming receivables balances requires that an auditor communicate in writing with customers in what are called positive or negative confirmation requests. **Positive confirmations** ordinarily request that a customer review the account balance listed on the confirmation and respond to the auditor directly about whether the balance is correct or incorrect, as illustrated in Figure 11-4. However, *SAS No. 99*, "Consideration of Fraud in a Financial Statement Audit," imposes a responsibility on auditors to presume a risk of material misstatement due to fraud in the recognition of revenue and, in response, to consider confirming with customers terms not ordinarily included in positive confirmations. For example, an auditor might confirm delivery and payment terms, rights to return product, and the absence of kickbacks or side-agreements. In contrast, **negative confirmations** request that a debtor respond to the auditor only if the balance in an attached statement is *incorrect*, as illustrated in Figure 11-5. For positive or negative confirmations inadvertently returned by fax rather than by mail, the auditor should call the respondent, confirm what the faxed confirmation reveals, and, for a sample of the faxed confirmations, request that the customer mail the original confirmation,

---

1   Apart from these assertions, confirmations of accounts receivable also are used to test for lapping, a fraud introduced in Chapter 10.

FIGURE 11-4: *Positive Accounts Receivable Confirmation*

THE WILSON COMPANY
15 Artubus Drive
Stony Brook, NY 11970

January 4, 2008

Wellington & Shine
6540 Lincolnway Road
Los Angeles, CA 90041

Please confirm the correctness of your December 31, 2007 account balance of $6,225.40 directly to our auditors:

Cheever & Yates, LLP

who are auditing our financial statements. This is not a request for payment.

An envelope addressed to our auditors is enclosed.

                                        Maxine Kuman
                                        Controller

☐ The above balance is correct.

☐ The above balance is incorrect as noted below.

By:_____

Date:_____

FIGURE 11-5: *Negative Accounts Receivable Confirmation*

Please examine the attached statement. If the statement disagrees with your records, respond directly to our auditors:

Cheever & Yates, LLP

who are auditing our financial statements. An envelope addressed to our auditors is enclosed.

THIS IS NOT A REQUEST FOR PAYMENT

thereby allowing the auditor to compare the return post mark to the customer's address. If the customer has discarded the original confirmation, the auditor could mail a new one.

In general, positive confirmations are appropriate when individual account balances are relatively large or when substantial numbers of inaccuracies or frauds are expected. Negative confirmations are generally appropriate when internal control is adequate, balances are small, and the auditor has no reason to believe that debtors will not return the confirmation request. In practice, auditors often use both types of confirmations for a particular engagement—for example, positive requests could be used for larger account balances, and negative requests for smaller balances. Regardless of the type of confirmation used, the request should be mailed in the auditor's, not the client's, envelope—that is, an envelope that includes the auditor's return address—to assure that envelopes "returned to sender" by the Postal Service are mailed to the auditor, not the client, thereby precluding the client from tampering with the confirmation and allowing the auditor to test whether the customer actually exists. Likewise, the return self-addressed envelope included with the confirmation mailing (and referred to on the confirmation form—see Figures 11-4 and 11-5) also should be addressed to the auditor, not the client.

When positive confirmations are used, an auditor should mail second (and perhaps even third) requests to nonrespondents, attempting to maximize the number of responses. If a statistical sampling plan is used to select and evaluate the confirmations, a poor response rate could affect sampling risk, requiring that an auditor alter or abandon the sampling plan. However, despite the efforts expended to maximize response rates, a number of customers invariably will fail to respond, thereby requiring alternative audit procedures for those accounts. In the absence of a returned confirmation, an auditor could examine other evidence, such as:

- Subsequent cash collections to determine whether the customer has paid,
- Shipping documents to determine whether goods were shipped to the customer, and
- Sales invoices to determine whether the customer was billed.

Notes receivable confirmation requests are similar in substance to positive accounts receivable requests, although negative notes receivable confirmations are not used commonly in practice.

Leveraging off of *SAS No. 67*, one Big Four accounting firm has significantly reduced the extent of receivables confirmations for *low risk* clients that agree to allow the firm online access to automated collections records. The firm uses software to monitor customer collection data, to compile collection profiles (for example, days' sales in receivables, percentage of receivables per aging category), and to confirm only those balances, if any, that appear unusual, such as erratic payment trends on past-due accounts. The firm's strategy is based on this logic: Although confirmations address no less than three assertions (existence, rights, valuation), they are also relatively expensive, since preparing and following up on confirmations is rather labor intensive. Hence, the firm balances audit evidence with audit effort in the face of audit risk.

Test Cutoff

Auditors acquire additional evidence of existence, and initial evidence of completeness, through *cutoff* tests that address whether sales transactions are recorded in the same period that title to the goods passed to the customer. Cutoff could be inaccurate if, for example, a December 31, 2006, year-end client inadvertently or intentionally recorded a $100,000 January 2, 2007, sales transaction as a 2006 sale: 2006 sales and receivables would be overstated by $100,000. To test cutoff, auditors examine a sample of sales entries recorded at or near the balance sheet date. For example, assuming a December 31, 2006, year end, an auditor might examine a sample of sales transactions recorded for a reasonable period around December 31—say, all recorded sales ≥ $50,000 from December 25 through January 5. For each sampled sale, the auditor obtains the related shipping documents and notes the shipping terms—*FOB* (free-on-board) *shipping point* versus *FOB destination*—to determine when title passed and therefore whether the sampled sales entry was recorded in the proper period. Sales should be reflected in the current year, 2006, if shipping terms were:

- *FOB shipping point* and the goods were shipped on or before December 31, 2006, or
- *FOB destination* and the goods were received by the customer on or before December 31.

However, assume that, owing to a client strategy template (Chapter 7), which revealed both an at-risk growth strategy and competitive pricing, an auditor's professional skepticism about earnings manipulation may drive him or her to increase the scope of sales cutoff tests, say, to all recorded sales ≥ $25,000 for the period December 20 to January 10.

Cutoff testing goes to the timing of revenue recognition and sometimes offers evidence of earnings manipulation. For example, consider the case of IGI, Inc., a diversified producer and marketer of animal health products, including veterinary pharmaceuticals and poultry vaccines. Although company policy required that revenue be recognized when products were shipped, management routinely recorded sales prior to shipment. Without admitting or denying guilt, IGI, Inc., consented in 2002 to an Order Instituting Public Administrative Proceedings in which the SEC reported that:

> ➤ fraud
> ➤ restatement
> ➤ earnings management

At or around the end of each quarter, the former President directed his subordinates to hold IGI's books open and to backdate invoices and shipping documents. This caused IGI to record out-of-period sales and to overstate its revenue and net income at the end of each quarter.[2]

Owing to cutoff errors alone, IGI, Inc., misstated assets, revenue, and earnings in each of the two years 1995 and 1996 and the first three quarters of 1997.

Review Collectibility of Receivables

Despite management's policies and procedures for reviewing and approving customer requests for credit, the entity cannot eliminate completely the risk that some accounts will not be paid. As a result, the valuation or carrying value of receivables is usually less than the sum of all outstanding balances. An auditor evaluates the carrying value of receivables by reviewing their collectibility, and by determining the adequacy of an entity's allowance for uncollectible accounts. For example, an auditor might obtain evidence of collectibility by examining an accounts receivable aged trial balance, by discussions with Credit department

---

2 *SEC Accounting and Auditing Enforcement Release No. 1520, In the Matter of IGI, Inc.* March 12, 2002.

personnel, by reviewing post-balance-sheet-date collections, by reviewing available correspondence with delinquent debtors, and by examining credit ratings with recognized bureaus such as Dun & Bradstreet, Inc.

Perform Analytical Procedures

In general, the role of analytical procedures is to direct an auditor's attention to accounts or balances that appear unusual or unreasonable, and therefore that may require additional substantive tests of details in order to reduce audit risk to an acceptably low level. Thus, within the revenue/receipt cycle, analytical procedures can be used to identify accounts that appear to be either:

- Reasonable: That is, accounts appear to be behaving as expected, and therefore do not require additional testing, and
- Unreasonable (or unusual): That is, accounts do *not* appear to be behaving as expected, and therefore require additional testing beyond the extent of procedures planned.

Figure 11-6 presents in detail the intuition and potential explanations for several key analytical procedures, and lists several other procedures used commonly in practice. For example, consider the number of days' sales in receivables and accounts receivable turnover. If the number of days' sales in receivables was at or around 30 days and receivables therefore turned over 12 times (360 days/30 days) for four successive years, this would suggest that sales, receivables, and collection activity were behaving similarly for the four-year period and would not signal the need for additional substantive tests of details. However, if the number of days' sales were at or around 30 days for the three preceding years and 45 days for the current year (turnover = 360/45 = 8 times), then this unexpected variation could indicate any one or more of the following potential explanations:

- Collection problems: Management could be extending credit more liberally than in prior years to increase sales.
- Overstated sales.
- Understated accounts receivable.

No one of the preceding analytical procedures necessarily will detect material misstatements. Rather, the procedures will direct the auditor's attention to accounts or balances requiring additional inquiries or substantive tests of details.

Review Financial Statement Presentation and Disclosure

The audit program in Figure 11-2 concludes with the auditor's review of financial statement presentation and disclosure of revenue/receipt cycle accounts. An auditor should determine whether the accounts, notes, and other receivables and related sales accounts are classified, described, and disclosed in accordance with GAAP.

Accounts and notes receivable usually are classified as current or noncurrent assets, depending on the terms of payment, and carried at net realizable value—that is, net of an allowance for uncollectible accounts, unearned discounts, interest, and finance charges. Some large companies disclose separately in a footnote to the financial statements the portion of current receivables attributable to customers and the portion attributable to associated companies. For example, General Electric discloses in a footnote current receivables for nine categories of business segments (including, aircraft engines, Power Systems, and the NBC television

FIGURE 11-6: *Analytical Procedures for Accounts Receivable and Sales*

Analytical Procedure	Intuition/Comparisons	Potential Explanations
Receivables Turnover: $$\frac{\text{Credit sales}}{\text{Average accounts receivable}}$$	Computes the number of times receivables turn over during the year. Compare to prior years and to industry data. Compare to payables turnover. Compare to inventory turnover.	*Increases* Fast collections Overstated sales Understated receivables *Decreases* Slow collections Understated sales Overstated receivables
Number of days' sales in receivables: $$\frac{360\text{ days}}{\text{Receivables turnover}}$$	Computes the number of days that receivables are outstanding. Compare to prior years and to industry data. Compare to credit sales terms.	*Increases* Slow collections Understated sales Overstated receivables *Decreases* Fast collections Overstated sales Understated receivables
Compare: Accounts receivable balance to Prior-year receivables balance + Credit sales – Cash receipts – Write-offs	Reconstructs the ending receivables balance from three sources: the prior-year balance, and additions to (credit sales) and deletions from (cash receipts, write-offs) the prior-year balance.	*Accounts Receivable Balance >* Overstated receivables Understated credit sales Overstated cash receipts Overstated write-offs

(continues)

FIGURE 11-6 *(continued)*

Analytical Procedure	Intuition/Comparisons	Potential Explanations
		Accounts Receivable Balance Understated receivables Overstated credit sales Understated cash receipts Understated write-offs
Compare: Sales to Market share × Industry sales	Estimates sales from industry data.	*Sales* > Overstated sales *Sales* < Understated sales
Compare: Actual receivables write-offs to Provision for uncollectible receivables	Relates actual year 1 write-offs in year 2 to year 1 provisions for receivables expected to have been written off.	*Actual Write-offs* > Overstated bad debt expense Understated allowance for doubtful accounts *Actual Write-offs* < Understated bad debt expense Overstated allowance for doubtful accounts

Other analytical procedures

Compare product-line sales and gross margin percentages by month and by year to identify potential overstatements or understatements of sales.

Compare receivables aging categories (for example, 0–30 days, 31–60 days, 61–90 days, etc.) and uncollectible accounts as percentages of accounts receivable for a series of years to test the reasonableness of the allowance for uncollectible accounts.

Compare actual bad debt write-offs with recorded bad debt expense for prior years to test the reasonableness of the provision for bad debts in the current year. Compare the ratio of the provision for bad debts to total receivables to the ratio for prior years to test the reasonableness of the provision for bad debts in the current year.

Compare both the average balance and the largest individual balances to prior years to test the reasonableness of the allowance for uncollectible accounts.

network), distinguishes customer from associated company receivables, and reveals the company's largest customer this way:

General Electric

Receivables balances at December 31, 2003 and 2002, before allowance for losses, included $6,746 million and $6,269 million, respectively, from sales of goods and services to customers, and $226 million and $304 million, respectively, from transactions with associated companies. Current receivables of $444 million at year-end 2003 and $344 million at year-end 2002 arose from sales, principally of aircraft engine goods and services, on open account to various agencies of the U.S. government, which is our largest single customer. About 4% of our sales of goods and services were to the U.S. government in 2003, 2002, and 2001.

Trade notes and accounts receivable should be segregated from nontrade receivables, such as employee or officer receivables. All material information should be disclosed in the financial statements or in the notes to the financial statements. Disclosures should include, for example, information about pledged or assigned receivables.

Cash Balances

Figure 11-7 presents a program of representative year-end substantive tests for cash balances. Each procedure is tied to related financial statement assertions and discussed in the following sections.

FIGURE 11-7: *Substantive Tests: Cash Balances*

Assertions	Procedures
Existence, Rights Valuation	1. Confirm year-end cash balances with all banks and other depositories.

Valuation	2. Verify mathematical accuracy of recorded cash balances.
	   a. Foot cash journals.
	   b. Trace totals to the general ledger and to year-end bank reconciliations prepared by the client.
	   c. Test cash on hand as necessary.

Existence
Completeness
Valuation
	3. Test cutoff.
	   a. Obtain cutoff bank statements directly from banks.
	      (1) Verify accuracy of cutoff bank statements.
	      (2) Examine information (e.g., dates and amounts) on cutoff bank statements and trace to reconciling items in year-end bank reconciliation and to entries in cash journals.
	      (3) Consider necessity of preparing a proof of cash.
	   b. Reconcile recorded cash balances with returned bank confirmations.
	   c. Examine intercompany and interbank transfers near year end.

Presentation and
disclosure
	4. Review financial statements to determine whether:
	   a. Cash balances are properly classified and described.
	   b. Disclosures are adequate.

Confirm Cash Balances

Cash deposited in banks (for example, checking accounts and certificates of deposit) and in other depositories (for example, money market funds) is confirmed by auditors in much the same manner as accounts receivable. However, unlike receivables, an auditor confirms all, rather than a sample, of the cash accounts using a standard form the AICPA, the American Bankers Association, and the Bank Administration Institute approved in 1990. All cash accounts are confirmed with banks because, as illustrated in Figure 11-8, the standard confirmation also requests information about whether the client was directly liable to the financial institution for loans (question 2). For example, note in Figure 11-8 that the First National Bank discloses not only a $175,517.10 cash balance (question 1), but also a long-term loan of $150,000 (question 2), a disclosure that is crucial to the audit of the entity's liabilities, as discussed in Chapter 14.

Verify Mathematical Accuracy

To test the mathematical accuracy of recorded cash balances, and therefore to address in part the valuation of cash balances, an auditor recomputes totals in the cash journals and in client-prepared bank reconciliations (such as the reconciliation illustrated in Figure 11-9). The auditor then traces the cash journal totals to postings in the general ledger and to the bank reconciliation caption "balance per books" (Figure 11-9, note f).

Even though often immaterial in relation to the financial statements taken as a whole, cash on hand, sometimes called "petty cash," is tested on some audit engagements, primarily because cash is highly susceptible to misappropriation. To test cash on hand, an auditor counts the cash fund in the presence of the fund custodian and examines undeposited cash receipts and paid vouchers that reconcile cash on hand to the imprest balance. For example, if cash on hand is imprest at $500 and $175 is on hand, undeposited receipts and paid vouchers should total $325.

Test Cutoff

Like tests of sales cutoff, tests of cash cutoff address the existence and completeness assertions, and question whether recorded transactions, in this case receipts and disbursements, are recorded in the proper accounting period. The tests reconcile internal documents created by the client, such as:

- Cash journals,
- The general ledger, and
- Bank reconciliations

with external documents created by banks, such as:

- Year-end bank statements,
- Cutoff bank statements, and
- Returned bank confirmations.

Item 3a of the audit program in Figure 11-7 requires that the auditor obtain cutoff statements directly from the bank (or banks) for each bank account. Unlike typical month-end bank statements, **cutoff bank statements** do not represent a full month's transactions. Rather, they represent transactions (cleared checks, deposits, and miscellaneous debits and credits) for a short period after year end (for

FIGURE 11-8: *Bank Confirmation*

STANDARD FORM TO CONFIRM ACCOUNT *A6*
BALANCE INFORMATION WITH FINANCIAL INSTITUTIONS

The Wilson Company

CUSTOMER NAME

Financial **First National Bank**
Institution's
Name and
Address

We have provided to our accountants the following information as of the close of business on **Dec. 31, 2007**, regarding our deposit and loan balances. Please confirm the accuracy of the information noting any exceptions to the information provided. If the balances have been left blank, please complete this form by furnishing the balances in the appropriate space below.* Although we do not request nor expect you to conduct a comprehensive, detailed search of your records, if during the process of completing this confirmation, additional information about other deposit and loan accounts we may have with you comes to your attention, please include such information below. Please use the enclosed envelope to return the form directly to our accountants.

1. At the close of business on the date listed above, our records indicated the following deposit balance(s):

ACCOUNT NAME	ACCOUNT NO.	INTEREST RATE	BALANCE*
General Account	**158-6798-321**	**None**	**$175,517.10** *A5*

2. We were directly liable to the financial institution for loans at the close of business on the date listed above as follows:

ACCOUNT NO./ DESCRIPTION	BALANCE*	DATE DUE	INTEREST RATE	DATE THROUGH WHICH INTEREST IS PAID	DESCRIPTION OF COLLATERAL
158-6799-322	**$150,000** *BB10*	**6/10/09**	**9.5**	**12/1/07**	**Warehouse**

Maxine Kuman **Controller**

_____   **December 31, 2007**
(Customer's Authorized Signature)   (Date)

The information presented above by the customer is in agreement with our records. Although we have not conducted a comprehensive, detailed search of our records, no other deposit or loan accounts have come to our attention except as noted below.

Anne Sexton

_____   **January 7, 2008**
(Financial Institution Authorized Signature)   (Date)

Manager
_____
(Title)

EXCEPTIONS AND/OR COMMENTS
None

Please return this form directly to our accountants: **Cheever & Yates, LLP**
Certified Public Accountants

*Ordinarily, balances are intentionally left blank if they are not available at the time the form is prepared.

D451 5061

Approved 1990 by American Bankers Association, American Institute of Certified Public Accountants, and Bank Administration Institute. Additional forms available from: AICPA–Order Department, P.O. Box 1003, NY, NY 10106-1003

FIGURE 11-9: *Bank Reconciliation*

(Schedule prepared by client)   A5

                                                                  SC 1/18/08

The Wilson Company
Bank Reconciliation: Peoples Bank—Acct. 1001
December 31, 2007

Balance per bank, 12-31-07		$17,551,710[b]
Add: Deposits in transit, 12-31-07	$1,578,143[c]	
Check drawn by Martin Davis Co. charged to Marc David, Inc., by bank in error	275,000[d]	1,853,143
Deduct outstanding checks:		
No. 5775 12-24	$1,431,000[e]	
No. 5776 12-26	156,050[e]	
No. 5779 12-26	181,021[e]	
No. 5780 12-27	2,169,540[e]	
No. 5781 12-29	1,589,176[e]	
No. 5785 12-30	1,191,240[e]	
Adjusted bank balance, 12-31-07		(6,718,027)
		$12,686,826
		a
Balance per books, 12-31-07		$13,241,386[f]
Deduct: December bank service charge	$ 28,500[b]	
Check from Apex Services, Inc., deposited 12-15 returned for insufficient funds, 12-18	526,060[b]	(554,560)
Adjusted book balance, 12-31-07		$12,686,826
		a

a Footed.
b Agreed to 12-31-07 bank statement.
c Agreed to cutoff bank statement and to cash receipts journal.
d Agreed to cutoff bank statement.
e Agreed to cutoff bank statement and to cash disbursements journal.
f Agreed to general ledger.

example, seven to ten days) and are used by auditors to verify reconciling items appearing on year-end bank reconciliations prepared by the client. For example, December 31 year-end bank reconciliations usually include deposits in transit and outstanding checks that could not otherwise be verified until January bank statements are received in early February. Cutoff bank statements are requested in a cover letter attached to the standard bank confirmation request and, like receivables confirmations, are sent directly to the auditor by the bank, thereby providing the auditor with persuasive external evidence received directly from third parties rather than external evidence received, held, and potentially altered by a client. (When the auditor is finished testing the cutoff bank statement, it is given to the client and a statement for the remaining days in the month is forwarded by the bank directly to the client at month's end.)

If returned by the bank, individual canceled checks, deposit slips, and debit/credit memoranda accompanying each cutoff bank statement should be compared with listings printed on the statement. Each item on the cutoff statement should then be traced to the client-prepared, year-end bank reconciliation and to cash journals. Dates of entries in cash journals and clearings on bank statements should be examined to verify that receipts and disbursements near year end are recorded in the proper period, thereby providing insight into two prominent misstatements:

- Delays in recording cash disbursements to present an overstated cash position on the balance sheet, and
- Checks written and recorded as disbursements prior to year end, but not mailed until after the balance sheet date to understate liabilities.

Copies of client-prepared bank reconciliations are typically included in audit documentation as evidence of tests of cutoff. Figure 11-9 presents an illustrative year-end bank reconciliation with appropriate indexes, tick marks, and explanations. Note that the reconciliation adjusts both the bank and the book balances, yielding a true cash balance at a particular date.

Internal auditors typically prepare a form of reconciliation called a *proof of cash* at one or more times during the year to verify the reliability of monthly bank reconciliations. However, if the client lacks an internal audit department or if discrepancies are observed in client-prepared year-end bank reconciliations, the independent auditor may decide to prepare a proof of cash for one or more periods. Routine monthly bank reconciliations, audited in item 3b Figure 11-7 (and illustrated in Figure 11-9), focus on cash balances, while a proof of cash focuses both on balances and on transactions. Figure 11-10 depicts a four-column proof of cash for two successive months, November and December, 2007. Like the bank reconciliation in Figure 11-9, the proof of cash adjusts both the bank and book balances, yielding a true cash balance, although for two successive months rather than one particular date.

Item 3c from Figure 11-7, cutoff tests applicable when an entity engages in intercompany transactions or maintains more than one bank account, are illustrated in Figure 11-11. *Intercompany cash transfers* at or near year end should be tested to determine whether they are recorded properly as both a receipt by one entity and a disbursement by another in the same accounting period; if not, cash balances for the consolidated group of entities could be misstated. For example, if a subsidiary records a $10,000 cash receipt from a parent on December 31, but the parent defers recording the disbursement until January 1, consolidated December 31 financial statements would overstate cash by $10,000, because the related receipt and disbursement are recorded in different accounting periods. Intercompany transfers can be tested by reviewing all transfers between related entities for a period, for example, five days before and after year end; corresponding receipt and disbursement entries should accompany each transfer and should be recorded in the same accounting period.

Interbank transfers, similar in nature to intercompany transfers, also can be tested by examining transactions near the year-end date. For each transfer of funds between banks, a receipt and corresponding disbursement should be recorded in the same period; otherwise, cash will be misstated on the balance sheet. While tests of interbank transfers may reveal understatements of cash (that is, a disbursement recorded on or before year end and the corresponding receipt recorded after year end), the tests are designed primarily to detect cash overstatements. For example, concealment of a cash shortage could be attempted by transferring funds

FIGURE 11-10: *Proof of Cash*

(Schedule prepared by client)

A10
FM 1/15/08

The Wilson Company
Proof of Cash: Old Stone Bank—Acct. 101
December 31, 2007

	11/30/07	December Receipts	Disbursements	12/31/07
Balance per bank	$ 8,576,110[b]	$41,954,430[b]	$ (41,694,175)[b]	$ 8,836,365[b]
Deposits in transit: 11/30	2,462,590[c]	(2,462,590)		
12/31		2,170,050[d]		2,170,050
Outstanding checks: 11/30	(3,156,129)[e]		2,876,582	(279,547)
12/31			(1,933,212)[f]	(1,933,212)
Adjusted bank balance:	$ 7,882,571	$41,661,890	$ (40,750,805)	$ 8,793,656[b]
	a	a	a	a
Balance per books 11/30	$ 7,905,571[g]	$41,661,890[h]	$ (40,748,805)[i]	$ 8,818,656[g]
Bank service charge: 12/31	(23,000)[j]		23,000	
			(25,000)[b]	(25,000)
Adjusted book balance	$ 7,882,571	$41,661,890	$ (40,750,805)	$ 8,793,656
	a	a	a	a

a Footed.
b Agreed to December bank statement.
c Agreed to December bank statement and cash receipts journal.
d Agreed to cutoff bank statement and to cash receipts journal.
e Agreed to December bank statement and to cash disbursements journal.
f Agreed to cutoff bank statement and cash disbursements journal.
g Agreed to general ledger.
h Agreed to cash receipts journal.
i Agreed to cash disbursements journal.
j Agreed to November bank statement.

FIGURE 11-11: *Interbank and Intercompany Transfers*

A9
KC 1/21/08

The Wilson Company
Schedule of Interbank and Intercompany Transfers
December 31, 2007

Check No.	From	To	Amount	Disbursement Date Per Books	Per Bank	Receipt Date Per Books	Per Bank
Interbank Transfers							
6721	First Nat'l Bk	Union Trust	$25,000[a]	12/30[b]	1/2[c]	12/30[d]	1/2[c]
6741	First Nat'l Bk	Peoples Bk	35,500[a]	12/31[b]	1/3[c]	12/31[d]	1/2[c]
6743	First Nat'l Bk General Account	First Nat'l Bk Payroll Account	75,000[a]	12/31[b]	1/2[c]	12/31[d]	1/2[c]
Intercompany Transfers							
6742	Wilson (Union Trust)	Westco (subsidiary)	25,000[a]	12/31[b]	1/2[c]	12/31[d]	1/2[e]

a Agreed check number, payee, payor, and amount to cash disbursements journal.
b Per cash disbursements journal.
c Agreed to Wilson cutoff bank statement.
d Per cash receipts journal.
e Agreed to Westco cutoff bank statement.

from one bank account to another and recording the receipt on or before year end and the disbursement after year end. Overstating cash through interbank transfers is called **kiting**.

Review Financial Statement Presentation and Disclosure

The audit program in Figure 11-7 concludes with a review of financial statement presentation and disclosure. An auditor should determine whether cash balances are classified, described, and disclosed in accordance with GAAP.

Amounts presented as cash and cash equivalents in the current assets section of a balance sheet should represent cash on hand, unrestricted deposits, and investments with rather short-term maturities, usually three months or less. For example, Wal-Mart's 2003 annual report discloses cash and cash equivalents of $2.8 billion and in Note 1, Summary of Significant Accounting Policies, explains the maturity terms of cash equivalents:

Wal-Mart

The Company considers investments with a maturity of three months or less when purchased to be cash equivalents.

In addition to three-month maturity, General Electric's 2003 Summary of Significant Accounting Policies footnote discloses a second hurdle for including securities as cash equivalents: Securities must not be designated as available for sales and classified as investments:

General Electric

Debt securities with original maturities of three months or less are included in cash equivalents unless designated as available for sale and classified as investment securities.

Special-purpose funds, such as cash set aside for plant expansion, should be reported separately from cash. Balances subject to withdrawal restrictions, such as compensating balances and certificates of deposit, should be reported as separate components of cash or described and disclosed in the balance sheet or in notes to the financial statements.

Revenue Recognition and Earnings Manipulation

The discussion thus far has addressed the audit of accounts receivable, sales, and cash balances when the point of sale is known and therefore when, fraud aside, there is little opportunity for management to manipulate the recognition of revenue. That is, the discussion assumed that a client had met two critical revenue-recognition criteria in FASB *Statement of Financial Accounting Concepts (SFAC) No. 5,* "Recognition and Measurement in Financial Statements of Business Enterprises:"

- The amount and timing of revenue is reasonably determinable, and
- The earnings process is complete or virtually complete.

But what if the criteria hadn't been met? When the timing of revenue is *not* reasonably determinable or the earnings process is *not* complete, management may exercise discretion in the timing of revenue recognition, which can sometimes translate into a deliberate misreporting of earnings, often called **earnings manipulation**.

The SEC Responds to Earnings Manipulation: Staff Accounting Bulletin No. 104, "Revenue Recognition"

➤ earnings management

In a 1998 speech, "The Numbers Game," Arthur Levitt Jr., then SEC chairman, acknowledged the Commission's view that earnings manipulation was serious and was motivated in part by the resolve of some public companies to meet analysts' earnings forecasts:

Increasingly, I have become concerned that the motivation to meet Wall Street earnings expectations may be overriding common sense business practices. Too many corporate managers, auditors, and analysts are participants in a game of nods and winks. In the zeal to satisfy consensus earnings estimates and project a smooth earnings path, wishful thinking may be winning the day over faithful representation. As a result, I fear that we are witnessing an erosion in the quality of earnings, and therefore, the quality of financial reporting. Managing may be giving way to manipulation; integrity may be losing out to illusion.[3]

Research confirms Levitt's suspicions. For example, a 1999 Commission of Sponsoring Organizations (COSO) study of fraudulent financial reporting occurring

---

3   Arthur Levitt, Jr., "The 'Numbers Game.'" Speech at New York University Center for Law and Business, September 28, 1998.

between 1987 and 1997 found that 50 percent of the 204 sampled companies over-stated revenue, primarily by recording revenue prematurely or fictitiously.[4] Con-firming the COSO findings, a 2000 Panel on Audit Effectiveness study of 96 SEC Accounting and Auditing Enforcement Releases involving Big Five firms found that approximately 70 percent of the public companies studied had overstated revenue, again by reporting revenue prematurely or fictitiously.[5] The findings are clear: Manipulation occurs most often in revenue and revenue-related accounts (such as receivables). For example, the Panel on Audit Effectiveness study re-ported that misreporting expenses, the second most common manipulation, oc-curs about half as often as misreporting revenue.

Responding to Levitt's criticisms, the SEC in December 1999 issued *Staff Accounting Bulletin (SAB) No. 101,* "Revenue Recognition"—revised and reissued in 2003 as *SAB No. 104*—which establishes the Commission's view on recognizing revenue when a revenue transaction is not governed by an existing accounting pronouncement. For example, although existing accounting pronouncements govern revenue recognition for several types of transactions (such as *SFAS No. 50,* product financing) and in several industries (such as *SFAS No. 51,* the cable tele-vision industry), the literature still leaves considerable room for interpretation, in particular for managements motivated more by the illusion of earnings than by selling product in the normal course of business. Absent a transaction- or industry-specific accounting pronouncement, an auditor's guidance for judging whether a client should recognize revenue appears in *SFAC No. 5* and, assuming a public company, *SAB No. 104.*

SFAC No. 5 states that revenues should be recognized when an entity has:

- Substantially accomplished what it must do to be entitled to the benefits represented by the revenues.

And, "substantial accomplishment" usually occurs

- By the time product or merchandise is delivered or services are rendered to customers.

As summarized in Figure 11-12, *SAB No. 104* adds clarity to the SEC's interpreta-tion of *SFAC No. 5* by adding four criteria the staff views as essential for recogniz-ing revenue. Because policies for recognizing revenue are not generally standard-ized across industries—or even for companies within industries—companies disclose revenue recognition policies in a footnote to the financial statements. For example, Union Carbide, a major marketer of chemical and plastic products and, since 2001, a wholly owned subsidiary of Dow Chemical, discloses revenue recog-nition policies in the company's 2003 Management Discussion and Analysis (MD&A), a required part of *Form 10-K,* the annual report to the SEC, as follows:

Union Carbide

MD&A: Substantially all of the Corporation's revenues are from transactions with Dow. Sales are recognized when the revenue is realized or realizable, and has been earned, in ac-cordance with the U.S. Securities and Exchange Commission's Staff Accounting Bulletin No. 104, "Revenue Recognition in Financial Statements." Approximately 96 percent of

---

4   M. S. Beasley, J. V. Carcello, and D. R. Hermanson, *Fraudulent Financial Reporting: 1987–1997 An Analysis of U.S. Public Companies.* Committee of Sponsoring Organizations of the Treadway Commission, 1999, p. 23.

5   The Panel on Audit Effectiveness, *Report and Recommendations.* Stamford: CT, 2000, Appendix F.

FIGURE 11-12: *SEC Revenue Recognition Criteria*

Criteria	Interpretation
1. Persuasive evidence of an arrangement exists.	A final agreement was executed by personnel authorized by the customer.
2. Delivery has occurred or services have been rendered.	The customer has taken title and assumed the risks and rewards of ownership for products specified in the customer's purchase order or sales agreement.
3. The seller's price to the buyer is fixed or determinable.	The customer does not have the unilateral right to terminate or cancel the contract and receive a cash refund.
4. Collectibility is reasonably assured.	There is no reason to believe the customer is unable to pay.

Source: Adapted from *SEC Staff Accounting Bulletin No. 104*, "Revenue Recognition."

the Corporation's sales are related to sales of product, while 4 percent is related to the licensing of patents and technology. Revenue for product sales is recognized as risk and title to the product transfer to the customer, which for trade sales, usually occurs at the time shipment is made. Substantially all of the Corporation's trade sales are sold FOB ("free on board") shipping point or, with respect to countries other than the United States, an equivalent basis. Title to the product for trade sales passes when the product is delivered to the freight carrier. UCC's standard terms of delivery are included in its contracts of sale, order confirmation documents, and invoices. Freight costs and any directly related associated costs of transporting finished product are recorded as "Cost of sales."

Union Carbide's MD&A points to a subtle reality: Revenue recognition is complex, in part because arm's length negotiations between sellers and buyers contemplate a wealth of conditions intended to protect each side's interests. Most companies are faithful to policies that comply with *SFAS No. 5* and *SAB No. 104*. On the other hand, some companies are not, as discussed next.

Common Means to Manipulate Earnings

> earnings management

Figure 11-13 lists a number of means used commonly over the years to accelerate revenue and manipulate earnings. For example, companies in a variety of industries have manipulated earnings through means such as bill and hold, canceled orders, conditional sales, improper cutoff, kickbacks, preinvoicing, premature sales, side agreements, and unauthorized shipments, among others, all of which are explained briefly in Figure 11-13. In practice, the means used to manipulate earnings are sometimes both uncommon and systemic. Two examples follow: channel stuffing and capacity swaps in the telecom industry.

Channel Stuffing

To meet sales goals, suppliers sometimes offer end-of-period sales incentives designed to induce incremental demand. For example, a consumer foods supplier

FIGURE 11-13: *Common Means to Manipulate Earnings*

Bill and Hold	Recognize revenue on shipments held in third-party warehouses for future delivery to a buyer who had not initiated the bill and hold.
Cancelled Orders	Recognize revenue on cancelled or duplicate orders.
Conditional Sales	Recognize revenue before all contingencies are resolved (for example, responsibility for third-party carrier insurance).
Consignment Sales	Recognize revenue for goods shipped on consignment or on trial.
Continuing Involvement	Recognize revenue on sales for which the seller remains involved after delivery (for example, installation of software).
Improper Cutoff	Recognize revenue on shipments before the title to goods or the risks of ownership pass to the buyer.
Kickback Sales	Recognize revenue in amounts that inflate the selling price to accommodate kickbacks.
Overstated Completion	Recognize revenue in amounts that inflate the percentage of completion on construction contracts.
Partial Shipments	Recognize revenue on an order for which a significant portion of the goods ordered has not yet been shipped.
Preinvoicing	Recognize revenue on goods ordered but still in production.
Premature Shipment	Recognize revenue on goods ordered but not yet authorized by the purchaser for shipment.
Premature Sales	Recognize revenue on goods ordered but not yet shipped.
Sham Sales	Recognize revenue on falsified shipments.
Side Agreements	Recognize revenue despite agreements between the seller and buyer that forestall completion of the earnings process.
Uncertain Performance	Recognize revenue on sales for which the seller's performance is uncertain.
Uncertain Realization	Recognize revenue on sales for which collection is uncertain or unlikely.
Unauthorized Shipments	Recognize revenue on shipments not authorized by the buyer.

Sources: Adapted from: AICPA, *Practice Alert No. 95-1*, "Revenue Recognition Issues;" M. S. Beasley, J. V. Carcello, and D. R. Hermanson, *Fraudulent Financial Reporting: 1987–1997 An Analysis of U.S. Public Companies*. COSO, 1999, pp. 24–25; (**http://www.sec.gov**); and POB, *Panel on Audit Effectiveness: Report and Recommendations*. Stamford, CT: POB, 2000, p. 225.

might offer trade discounts to retail grocery stores or a pharmaceutical manufacturer might discount inventory to distributors. Sales inducements are common and, for that matter, are no different than an automobile dealership offering rebates to attract consumers. In fact, the courts have generally found that end-of-period sales inducements do not violate securities laws. For example, the First Circuit Court of Appeals concluded in *Greebel v. FTP Software, Inc.* that "(t)here is nothing inherently improper in pressing for sales to be made earlier than in the normal course," even when the practice "has the result of shifting earnings into earlier quarters."[6] And the Federal District Court for the Northern District of Illinois concluded in *Johnson v. Tellabs* that "In the business world, there certainly is nothing inherently wrong with offering incentives to customers to purchase products."[7]

➣ fraud
➣ restatement

Bausch & Lomb and Sunbeam In the extreme, end-of-period incremental volume can translate to *channel stuffing*, a potentially egregious income-enhancing practice an excerpt from *The Wall Street Journal* highlights:

Companies . . . cut deals for customers to take far more merchandise than needed and not pay for it immediately. . . . Others have promised customers unlimited rights to return the goods. By "stuffing the channel," as it is called, companies appear to be selling lots of goods, though some of those goods end up back with the company.[8]

The excerpt identifies two key elements that are common to channel stuffing but uncommon to typical end-of-period sales inducements: extended payment terms and rights of return, either of which can violate GAAP. Extended payment terms can violate the requirement in *SAB No. 104* that collectibility be reasonably assured (Figure 11-2, item 4), and rights-of-return can violate the requirement in FASB *Statement of Financial Accounting Standards No. 48*, "Revenue Recognition When Right of Return Exists," that management offset revenue with estimated returns.

End-of-period sales promotions by Baush & Lomb and by Sunbeam raised to the SEC undeniable questions about revenue recognition. For example, Bausch & Lomb introduced a program that involved distributors' rights to market Bausch & Lomb products and rights to return unsold product:

The CLD (contact lens division) launched a marketing program—the "December Program"—in which it told its distributors, in order to maintain an authorized distributorship, to purchase an unprecedented amount of . . . inventory. . . . B&L improperly recognized $22 million in revenue from this Program when, among other things, certain employees of the CLD granted unauthorized rights of return to certain distributors. . . .[9]

In turn, the SEC's case against Sunbeam demonstrates that channel stuffing borrows heavily from future-period sales and cannot be relied on repeatedly:

As Sunbeam entered 1998, channel stuffing through price discounting . . . had borrowed heavily against futures sales revenue and left the Company with no options to satisfy that

---

6   *Greebel v. FTP Software, Inc.*, 194 F. 3d 185, 203 (1st Cir. 1999).

7   *Johnson v. Tellabs, Inc.*, 262 F. Supp. 2d 937, 950 (N.D. Ill. 2003)

8   K. Brown, "Creative Accounting: Four Areas to Buff Up a Company's Picture," *The Wall Street Journal,* February 21, 2002, A1.

9   *SEC Accounting and Auditing Enforcement Release No. 987, In the Matter of Bausch & Lomb Inc.,* November 17, 1997.

debt. Reports to senior management showed customers holding as much as 80 weeks of inventory of specific products. . . . In brief, the Company was experiencing the results of a short-term approach to earnings management that had outlived its efficacy.[10]

In the cases of both Bausch & Lomb and Sunbeam, management used end-of-period sales promotions to induce end-of-period orders. However, companies have recorded sales prematurely even when sales promotions fail to induce orders. For example, facing a revenue shortfall for the fiscal year ended February 3, 2001, a vice president and a director of customer care for the Johnson & Murphy division of Genesco Inc. proposed to the division's president a plan to ship early $2.8 million in product to a high-volume customer. The customer refused the shipment, but a distribution manager, after meeting with the director of customer care, recorded the sale nevertheless. The SEC reports, "In late 2001, the Director of Customer Care told Genesco's human resources department that she could not sign her annual ethics certification as a result of her involvement in certain conduct that occurred during the fourth quarter of fiscal year 2001. She disclosed the scheme to prematurely record sales revenue."[11] An internal investigation revealed that the distribution manager had prematurely recorded revenue in five other quarters: the first three quarters of 2001 and the first two quarters of 2002.

Management's Discussion and Analysis: Bristol Myers Squibb Channel stuffing has implications for revenue recognition and for financial statement disclosure. However, channel stuffing also has implications for disclosure outside of financial statements—in particular, in Item 7, Management's Discussion & Analysis (MD&A), a required part of management's annual report to the SEC on *Form 10-K*. In 2003, the SEC included in *SAB No. 104* a fourteen-year-old quote from the SEC's *Financial Reporting Release (FRR) No. 36*, repeating a call for MD&A disclosures that all but use the term channel stuffing:

➢ restatement
➢ earnings management

The Commission stated in FRR 36 that MD&A should "give investors an opportunity to look at the registrant through the eyes of management by providing a historical and prospective analysis of the registrant's financial condition and results of operations. . . . Examples of such revenue transactions or events that the staff has asked to be disclosed and discussed in accordance with FRR 36 are: Shipments of product at the end of a reporting period that significantly reduce customer backlog and that reasonably might be expected to result in lower shipments and revenue in the next period." . . .[12]

Coincident with the SEC's call in *SAB No. 104*, Bristol Myers Squibb, following an investigation alleging guarantees and payment terms that translated to consignment sales, began in 2003 to report ranges on customers' period-end excess inventory:

The Company estimates . . . that the inventory of pharmaceutical products held by the other U.S. pharmaceuticals wholesalers was in the range of approximately $100 million in excess of or below approximately one month of supply at December 31, 2003. . . .[13]

---

10 Sunbeam Corp., *Securities Act Release No. 7976*, 74 SEC Docket 2143, 2149-50 (May 15, 2001).
11 *SEC Accounting and Auditing Enforcement Release No. 1930, In the Matter of Genesco, Inc.*, December 19, 2003.
12 *SEC SAB No. 104*, "Revenue Recognition," pp. 76–77.
13 Bristol Myers Squibb, *Form 10-K*, December 31, 2003.

Bristol Myers Squibb was the first major public company to disclose ranges of customers' excess inventory, offering readers an insight into the effect of end-of-period incremental volume.

There is abundant evidence that channel stuffing is problematic to the SEC and, for that matter, to regulators, boards of directors, and litigants. For example, in 2003 alone, the SEC filed suit against ClearOne Communications for allegations that included channel stuffing,[14] Kellogg's board passed a resolution banning channel stuffing,[15] and Campbell Soup settled what the Connecticut Treasurer's Office called "the largest settlement of a class-action lawsuit involving allegations of 'channel stuffing.'"[16] In practice, auditors mitigate the risk of channel stuffing by monitoring period-end shipping patterns, examining payment terms, and performing procedures designed to detect unusual patterns of sales returns. For example, a pattern of unusually high shipments at the end of a period followed by unusually high returns the next period would increase the risk of channel stuffing, raising questions about whether revenue should be recognized in the period that goods are shipped.

Telecom Revenue: Global Crossing

➤ fraud
➤ restatement
➤ earnings management

Decades ago, AT&T pioneered swaps between telecom competitors for the right to use undersea cable capacity—for example, a telecom company that had trans-Atlantic cable would swap capacity with a telecom that had trans-Pacific capacity. The transactions were called capacity swaps and the swap contracts carried indefeasible rights to use (IRU) a competitor's cable. Until the 1990s, capacity swaps were relatively uncommon. However, expecting that the demand to transmit Internet data across continents would require previously unimagined supplies of fiber optics, a number of companies in the 1990s raced to control undersea cable, among them Global Crossing.

Global Crossing did not record the transactions as asset swaps. Rather, management, using a method advised by their auditors, recognized revenue on the swaps immediately by drawing an analogy to FASB *Statement of Financial Accounting Standards (SFAS) No. 66*, "Accounting for Real Estate Sales." Although undersea cables are not real estate per se, Global Crossing went to FASB *Interpretation No. 43 (FIN 43)*—an interpretation of *SFAS No. 66*—which clarified that real estate includes property with integral equipment that cannot be removed and used separately absent significant costs—indeed, the very nature of undersea cable. Relying on *FIN 43*, management invoked *SFAS No. 66* to recognize revenue immediately, even though competitors like AT&T did not.[17]

Coincident with Global Crossing's swaps for capacity, cross-continent Internet traffic stabilized and cable-capacity demand dwindled, raising questions about the business purpose of Global Crossing's disclosure in 2001 of "an increase

---

14 *SEC v. ClearOne Communications, Inc., et. al.* U.S. District Court for the Fourth District of Utah, Central Division, Civil Complaint No. 2 103 CV 055 DAK.

15 See, for example, C. C. Berk, "Kellogg Board Passes Resolution to Ban 'Channel Stuffing,'" *Dow Jones News Service* (February 18, 2003).

16 See, for example, H. Brubaker, "Campbell Soup Reaches $35 Million Settlement in Class Action Suit," *The Philadelphia Inquirer* (February 7, 2003).

17 S. Romero and S. Schielel, "The Fiber Optic Fantasy Slips Away," *The New York Times,* section 3 (February 17, 2003), p. 1.

in the number of IRU agreements"[18] management had entered into. As reported in a series of articles appearing in *The Wall Street Journal*:

Experts say such transactions don't necessarily violate accounting principles. But the deals may be misleading, especially if there's no clear business purpose.[19]

and

. . . the company may have bought capacity from other carriers without yet specifying which routes it wanted, or in some cases bought unnecessary capacity on routes it had already built.[20]

In 2002, the SEC concluded formally that revenue from capacity swaps could not be recognized immediately, and several telecommunications companies restated, including Global Crossing and Qwest Communications.[21] However, the larger lesson from Global Crossing isn't so much the accounting for capacity swaps as it is the danger of justifying accounting treatments by analogy. For one thing, neither *SFAS No. 66* nor *FIN 43* was likely issued with capacity swaps in mind, making the analogy a stretch. And, for another, Global Crossing likely had no legitimate business purpose to swap capacity quite to the extent that they did. In short, never lose sight of business purpose.

Other Examples: Landfill Costs and Software Revenue

Like capacity swaps in the telecom industry, the means used to manipulate earnings are sometimes peculiar to an industry. Two examples: First, consider the case of Chambers Development, a Pittsburgh-based, solid waste-disposal company that ceased trading to became a wholly owned subsidiary of USA Waste Services (now Waste Management). GAAP allows waste-disposal companies to capitalize identifiable, quantifiable, and recoverable landfill construction costs until the landfill is ready to receive waste. However, Chambers violated GAAP to sustain profit margins that had suffered from declining landfill capacity. The SEC concluded, "Chambers had capitalized expenses to the extent necessary to meet its earnings per share requirements,"[22] a so-called "bottom-up approach" in which management first determines earnings requirements and then records amounts for revenue and expenses that meet the requirements.

> fraud
> restatement
> earnings management

Second, consider MicroStrategy, a software company that became in the 1990s the highest profile accounting fraud action the SEC took against a software developer. Although GAAP in the software industry allows companies to recognize revenue only when the earnings process is complete, the SEC accused MicroStrategy of recognizing software revenue before determining the full extent of services the company would provide to buyers. The attorney who negotiated a settlement for MicroStrategy observed, "This is a company that grew dramatically, and

---

18 Global Crossing, *Form 10-Q*, June 30, 2001.
19 D. Berman and D. Solomon, "Optical Illusion? Accounting Questions Swirl Around Pioneer in the Telecom World," *The Wall Street Journal* (February 13, 2001), p. A1.
20 D. Berman, "Global Crossing Faces SEC Probe of Accounting Practices on Leases," *The Wall Street Journal* (February 4, 2002).
21 H. Sender and D. K. Berman, "SEC Rules Against Capacity Swaps," *The Wall Street Journal* (August 21, 2002), p. B3.
22 *SEC Accounting and Auditing Enforcement Release No. 764.* Commerce Clearing House, Inc., 1996, section III F, "The 1991 Audit."

frankly its operations and growth outstripped its ability to comply with applicable accounting regulations for software revenue recognition."[23] Confirming Global Crossing, the lessons learned from Chambers and MicroStrategy are that the means to manipulate are sometimes imbedded in accounting principles specific to an industry and that, consistent with then SEC Chairman Levitt's suspicions in the 1990s, companies sometimes stretch the limits of discretion to meet the expectations of financial analysts.

The next section adds another dimension to earnings manipulation by introducing in a case study the competing incentives of management and auditors, and the roles of auditor liability and professional ethics.

Area Franchise Fees: A Case Study in Management and Auditor Incentives

Accelerating the timing of revenue recognition is crucially important to auditors for two reasons: First, management has incentives to manipulate reported earnings since, as research reveals, earnings is the most important determinant in management compensation contracts[24] and poor earnings increases both the likelihood of replacing a chief executive officer[25] and the threat of a hostile takeover.[26] Second, auditors have incentives to detect earnings manipulation, since shareholders entrust independent auditors to act as monitors over management's stewardship function and, under the *Securities Exchange Act of 1934* (Chapter 5), may bring action against an auditor for negligently overlooking inflated earnings. In response to the problems posed by earnings manipulation, the AICPA published *Audit Issues in Revenue Recognition*, an influential report that discusses the responsibilities of management, directors, and audit committees for reliable financial reporting; summarizes key guidance about whether and when revenue should be recognized; identifies problematic circumstances and transactions; and describes procedures that may help control audit risk. To demonstrate the audit implications of competing incentives and earnings manipulation, the following illustrates issues auditors confront when auditing a franchisor's accounting for area franchise fees.

Area Development Franchises

Franchise operations such as Taco Bell, Burger King, Century 21, and Radisson Inns grant local franchisees the exclusive right to market trade-name products or services within a clearly defined geographical area. In the typical franchise arrangement, both the franchisor and franchisee can accrue benefits not otherwise available to either party: The franchisor establishes control over a sales outlet without a capital investment, and the franchisee markets an established product or service without incurring the cost of development. To illustrate, consider the case of a fast food franchisor's accounting for **area franchise fees**—that is, the

23 J. Weil, "MicroStrategy, Executives Set SEC Settlement," *The Wall Street Journal* (December 15, 2000), p. A12.
24 For example, M. Jensen and K. Murphy, "CEO Incentives: It's Not How Much You Pay, It's How," *Journal of Applied Corporate Finance* (Vol. 3, No. 3, 1990), pp. 36–49.
25 For example, J. Warner, R. Watts, and K. Wruck, "Stock Prices and Top Management Changes," *Journal of Financial Economics* (Vol. 20, 1988), pp. 461–492.
26 K. Palepu, "Predicting Takeover Targets: A Methodological and Empirical Analysis," *Journal of Accounting and Economics* (Vol. 8, 1986), pp. 3–35.

up-front, lump sum fee a franchisee pays Grinder Shoppe Restaurants, Inc., to operate counter-service sandwich stores within a greater metropolitan area.

Grinder Shoppe, a publicly traded national chain, offers area development franchises, which, under the company's Uniform Franchise Offering Circular (a disclosure document required by the Federal Trade Commission), grants franchisees exclusive rights to open and operate at least two but no more than three Grinder Shoppe restaurants within five years from the inception of the agreement. The development schedule calls for Grinder Shoppe's approval of store locations, construction, and interior design. Prior to opening the first store, the franchisee attends a two-week training program. The first two weeks of all first, second, and third store operations are supervised by an on-site manager assigned by Grinder Shoppe's national office. The on-site manager returns for two-day visits after each store's first two six-month periods of operation. The area development fee is:

- Fully refundable if the franchisee cannot obtain construction and working capital financing within 90 days of signing the development agreement,
- Fifty percent refundable after the first store is opened, and
- Nonrefundable after the second store is opened.

Although Grinder Shoppe had been highly successful in the first decade of operations, the company's earnings have flattened and the stock price has declined. To rescue both earnings and the stock price, Grinder Shoppe management proposes that area franchise fees be recognized as revenue when an area franchisee obtains financing to construct the first store in an area. Management argues that, once financing is obtained, few if any area franchisees renege on the area franchise agreement.

Audit Judgment: Accounting, Liability, and Ethics

As noted in Chapter 1, *"auditors are accountants first,"* and they are because accounting and auditing are inextricably related. This suggests that, in the case of Grinder Shoppe, the auditor need first search the professional literature to identify GAAP that bear on accounting for area franchise fees. Grinder Shoppe apparently proposes that revenue be recognized when area franchisees have obtained financing—that is, the point at which area development fees are no longer fully refundable. Does GAAP concur? And if it doesn't, are there legal liability and ethical issues the auditor need address?

➤ ethics

FASB *Statement No. 45*, "Accounting for Franchise Fee Revenue," bears on Grinder Shoppe's proposed accounting. Paragraph 8 reveals that for area franchise fees:

. . . revenue ordinarily shall be recognized when all material services or conditions relating to the sale(s) have been substantially performed or satisfied by the franchisor. If the franchisor's substantial obligations under the franchise agreement relate to the area franchise and do not depend significantly on the number of individual franchises to be established, substantial performance shall be determined using the same criteria applicable to individual franchises (paragraph 5). However, if the franchisor's substantial obligations depend on the number of individual franchises established within the area, area franchise fees shall be recognized in proportion to the initial mandatory services provided. Revenue that may have to be refunded because future services are not performed shall not be recognized by the franchisor until the franchisee has no right to receive a refund.

Every sentence in paragraph 8 bears on the auditor's judgment that, in the Grinder Shoppe case, revenue should be recognized in proportion to the services management provides to area franchisees, not fully when a franchisee obtains financing. That is, in the Grinder Shoppe franchise agreement:

- *Material services are not substantially performed by the franchisor until well beyond the point that a franchisee obtains financing:* Two, two-day, on-site visits occur during and after each store's first year of operations.
- *The franchisor's obligations depend on the number of individual franchises established within the area:* The franchisee must open at least two stores, and the fee is partially refundable after the first store is opened and nonrefundable only after the second store is opened.

Clearly, management's proposal violates GAAP, specifically FASB *Statement No. 45*, leaving the client no discretion in manipulating the timing of area franchise fee revenue. If the client insists on accelerating earnings, the auditor has no alternative but to alert the client that:

- Accelerating the recognition of revenue is a departure from GAAP,
- A departure from GAAP will cause the auditor to issue a qualified or adverse opinion, depending on materiality, and an explanatory paragraph that discloses the effect of the departure on reported earnings (Chapter 3, Figure 3-7),
- The change in accounting for area franchise fees is also an inconsistency in the application of accounting principles that management cannot justify, since the change is from a generally accepted principle to a practice that is not generally accepted, and
- Research reveals that qualified opinions are associated with declines in stock prices, a risk that runs contrary to management's apparent objectives.[27]

Make no mistake about it: What the auditor must conclude is not what the client wants to hear. As a result, there is some likelihood that the client may exert influence on the auditor—for example, threaten to put next year's engagement out to bid. If the auditor considers concurring with the client to violate FASB *Statement No. 45*, the legal and ethical implications are enormous. Since Grinder Shoppe is a public company, statutory law applies and Sections 10(b) and 18 of the *Securities Exchange Act of 1934* (Chapter 5) provide shareholders with a means to recover losses resulting from false or misleading statements. In this case, shareholders could likely recover under Section 10(b) because the auditor knew that revenue had been accelerated and that FASB *Statement No. 45* had been violated, although the plaintiff's basis for action, Section 10(b) or Section 18, would be arranged in consultation with an attorney. Further, the auditor could be liable for treble damages under the Racketeer Influenced and Corrupt Organizations (RICO) Act (Chapter 5), since *Reves v. Arthur Young*, a 1993 U.S. Supreme Court case, does not provide relief from RICO when, as is the case in Grinder Shoppe, he or she participated directly with management to perpetrate the fraud.

Interestingly, the case raises at least two ethical issues: First, the auditor violates the Code of Professional Conduct, Rule 203—Accounting Principles (Chap-

---

27 For example, C. W. Chow and S. J. Rice, "Qualified Audit Opinion and Share Prices: An Investigation," *Auditing: A Journal of Practice & Theory* (Vol. 1, No. 2, Winter 1982), pp. 35–53.

ter 4), which provides that an AICPA member cannot issue an unqualified opinion if the financial statements contain a departure from an "accounting principle promulgated by bodies designated by Council." In the Grinder Shoppe case, the accounting principle violated is that "area franchise fees shall be recognized in proportion to the initial mandatory services provided" (FASB *Statement No. 45*) and the body issuing the principle is the Financial Accounting Standards Board. Violating Rule 203 can result in an administrative reprimand, such as suspension to practice before the SEC, or, worse still, revocation of a CPA's license to practice public accountancy. Second, unethical business practices impose upon an offending auditor the risk of losing the set of characteristics on which his or her reputation rests: integrity, objectivity, and credibility. What, after all, does the public rely on us for if not for our claims to credibility?

Applying Audit Sampling in Substantive Tests of Accounts Receivable

To integrate material presented in this chapter with the statistical sampling plans introduced in Chapter 9 and with the tests of revenue/receipt cycle controls introduced in Chapter 10, assume a continuing audit engagement for the Madison Corporation, a manufacturer and supplier of health care equipment whose fiscal year ends December 31. Madison is a public company and has been an industry leader for over two decades. The objective in this case is to accomplish program step 2, Figure 11-2: confirm accounts receivable balances with debtors.

Updating the Assessment of Control Risk

Assume that interim tests of controls were accomplished during September and revealed that controls over customer order, credit, shipping, billing, recording, and cash collection—Madison's major revenue/receipt activities—were effective and that undetected control deficiencies were not likely to produce aggregate error in excess of tolerable error. The auditor assesses control risk below the maximum. However, because of employee turnover since September and to assure that controls were effective during the remaining period (that is, from September to year end), the auditor:

- Updated tests of controls through December 31 by applying nonstatistical sampling to transactions recorded in October, November, and December, and
- Made inquiries of management about any significant changes to revenue/receipt cycle controls.

Consistent with the interim tests of controls, the auditor's updated tests for October through December reveal no significant inaccuracies in recorded receivables, despite Madison having replaced two key employees on October 1. No other personnel or procedures had changed since September 30. Although unaudited earnings for the first three quarters match analysts' forecasts, the auditor learns that November shipments were below management's expectations, threatening Madison's ability to meet analysts' full-year forecasted earnings, and raising the auditor's assessment of the likelihood that management may overstate fourth-quarter earnings.

Planning the Receivables Confirmation and Selecting a Sampling Plan

In this case, the auditor elects to use positive confirmations to control detection risk. In turn, the auditor selects PPS sampling for this reason: Although prior-year sampling offers no reason to expect material differences between audited and recorded amounts, the auditor has reason to control the risk of overstatement errors, since management has incentives to overstate earnings. Note carefully that, rather than an accusation that management has engaged (or will engage) in earnings manipulation, the strategy to use PPS sampling, and therefore to test for overstatement errors, is a timely precaution to control risk. Nothing more, nothing less.

Population, Logical Unit, and Anticipated Error

Accounts receivable consist of approximately 1,550 customer accounts, each represented by detailed subsidiary records totaling $1,250,000 at December 31. None of the customer accounts carries a credit balance. Because in PPS sampling the so-called *logical unit* (called the "sampling unit" in other sampling plans) is each individual dollar captured within the population, population size is 1,250,000. An aged trial balance spreadsheet is obtained from accounts receivable personnel, footed, cross-footed, traced in part to detailed subsidiary records, and agreed in total with the general ledger. Based on results from the prior-year sampling plan, the auditor estimates current-year anticipated overstatement error to be $10,000, an amount that represents less than 1 percent of recorded receivables.

Risk and Tolerable Error

To continue the sampling plan, the auditor requires estimates of tolerable error and of the risk of incorrect acceptance, which is used to determine the reliability factor for overstatement differences and the expansion factor for anticipated error. *Tolerable error*, the maximum monetary error that may exist without causing the financial statements to be misstated materially, is judged to be $90,000 by the auditor. The auditor sets the *risk of incorrect acceptance* at 0.05, a relatively low level, largely because no other procedures within the audit program in Figure 11-2 address directly whether trade receivables exist at December 31.

From Figure 9-11, page 381, *RF* (the reliability for overstatement differences) is 3.00, the intersection of the column associated with a 0.05 risk of incorrect acceptance and the row associated with zero overstatement differences. From Figure 9-12, page 382, *EF* (the expansion factor for anticipated error) is 1.6, the entry associated with a 5 percent risk of incorrect acceptance.

Sample Size

Recapping, the following variables are known or have been estimated:

- Population size (B) = 1,250,000
- Tolerable error (TE) = $90,000
- Reliability factor (RF) = 0.05
- Anticipated error (AE) = $10,000
- Expansion factor (EF) = 1.6

From this information, sample size is calculated as follows:

$$n = \frac{RF \times B}{TE - (AE \times EF)}$$

$$= \frac{3.0 \times 1{,}250{,}000}{\$90{,}000 - (\$10{,}000 \times 1.6)}$$

$$= 50$$

Thus, given the auditor's acceptable risks and tolerable error, 50 randomly selected customer accounts must be confirmed in order to acquire evidence bearing on whether the 1,550 customer accounts are fairly stated at December 31. The sampling interval is 25,000 ($1,250,000/50)

Method of Sample Selection

To select the 50 sample accounts, the auditor arrays the customer accounts alphabetically and, similar to the illustration in Chapter 9, adds a column to the spreadsheet that compiles by customer a cumulative listing of all logical units ranging from 1 to 1,250,000. A spreadsheet command imports 50 seven-digit random numbers ranging from 0000001 to 1250000 and highlights the customer account names that attach to each of the randomly selected logical units.

All confirmations are mailed in early January, and second requests are sent to nonrespondents in 10 days. For disputed balances and for nonrespondents, the auditor applies alternative procedures, which include:

1. Determining whether the account was paid subsequent to year end and, therefore, was collectible at December 31,
2. Examining copies of sales invoices to determine if and when billing occurred, and
3. Examining shipping documents to determine if and when goods were shipped.

Evaluate Sample Results

Assume that compiled confirmation responses and alternative procedures for disputed accounts and nonrespondents reveals one overstatement error: A customer's recorded account balance is $8,400 and the audited balance is $8,065, an overstatement difference of $335 that translates to a projected error of $1,000, as follows:

	(a)	(b)	(c)	(d) Tainting	(e)	(f) Projected
Error Number	Book Value	Audited Value	Difference (a) − (b)	Percentage (c) ÷ (a)	Sample Interval	Error (d) × (e)
1	$8,400	$8,065	$335	.04	25,000	$1,000

The *allowance for sampling risk* requires two separate calculations: basic precision and an incremental allowance for sampling risk. *Basic precision* is determined by multiplying the sampling interval by the reliability factor in Figure 9-11:

Sampling interval	$25,000
RF, reliability factor for 0.05 risk of incorrect acceptance	× 3.0
Basic precision	$75,000

The *incremental allowance* is determined from the projected error for the one logical unit in the illustration recorded at less than the sampling interval, as follows:

| | | Incremental Change in Reliability Factor | | | Projected |
Error Number	Projected Error	No. of Errors	Reliability Factor	Increment	Error × Increment
		0	3.00		
1	$1,000	1	4.75	1.75	$1,750

Now, the allowance for sampling risk is:

Basic precision	$75,000
Incremental allowance	1,750
Allowance for sampling risk	$76,750

From these results, the auditor would reach the following statistical conclusion:

There is a 5 percent risk (that is, the risk of incorrect acceptance) that the recorded book value, $1,250,000, is overstated by $76,750 or more.

Or, stated another way:

There is a 95 percent probability (that is, 1 – the risk of incorrect acceptance) that the recorded book value, $1,250,000, is not overstated by more than $76,750.

Since the allowance for sampling risk, $76,750, is less than tolerable error, $90,000, the results support concluding that the recorded book value in the population is not overstated by more than tolerable error at the specified risk of incorrect acceptance, 0.05, leading to the following audit conclusion:

Based on audit procedures applied, I am satisfied that Accounts Receivable, excluding the allowance for uncollectibles, is fairly stated at December 31.

Computer-Assisted Substantive Tests of Accounts Receivable

When a client's revenue/receipt cycle activities are recorded, classified, and summarized wholly or in part by computer, an auditor's substantive tests of details can be accomplished in part by computer-assisted audit techniques. Figure 11-14 lists several audit procedures and related computer-assisted techniques common to audits of accounts receivable.

To illustrate the application of computer-assisted audit techniques, assume an auditor wishes to accomplish portions of the following three substantive tests (included in Figure 11-14):

- Verify the mathematical accuracy of accounts receivable subsidiary records.
- Age receivables according to computer-stored invoice dates.
- List credit balances in accounts receivable for reclassification to accounts payable.

The auditor may either design software to accomplish these procedures or use generalized audit software supplied by outside vendors, such as the larger public accounting firms. Auditor-prepared software, in contrast, is designed for each client application and requires that the auditor accomplish all of the tasks nor-

FIGURE 11-14: *Computer-Assisted Substantive Tests: Accounts Receivable*

Audit Procedure	Computer-Assisted Substantive Test
Test mathematical accuracy.	Verify footings, cross-footings, and extensions of the accounts receivable aged trial balance and/or the subsidiary records.
Summarize data for further testing or analysis.	Age receivables according to invoice dates. List credit balances in accounts receivable for reclassification to accounts payable. Print accounts receivable confirmations.
Test accuracy of recorded data.	Trace details in subsidiary records with source documents.
Select samples.	Select samples from random number generators and aged trial balances (or subsidiary records).
Compare similar data files.	Compare aged trial balance with accounts receivable subsidiary records.

mally associated with software preparation, including developing systems flowcharts and software specifications, coding, testing, and debugging, before the software is applied in a specific audit engagement.

Figure 11-15 flowcharts the tasks necessary to accomplish the three preceding substantive tests and would be identical whether the auditor used a generalized software package or prepared tailored software. As illustrated in Figure 11-15, the computer-assisted tests require three separate files: the client's accounts receivable master file, the client's sales journal, and the auditor's software. The software would be designed to perform the following tasks for each substantive test.

Substantive Test	Computer Software Task
Verify mathematical accuracy	Foot and cross-foot the amounts recorded in each customer account within the accounts receivable master file.
	Total the balances of all customer accounts, leading to a total for all receivables.
	Display/print exceptions.
Age receivables	Trace individual customer balances on the accounts receivable master file to related sales entries in the sales journal.
	For each customer, print balances by invoice dates (that is, 0–30 days, 31–60 days, 61–90 days, 91–120 days, and over 120 days).
	Display/print aged trial balances.
List credit balances	Scan the accounts receivable master in receivables file for net credit balances.
	Display/print listing of credit balance accounts.

FIGURE 11-15:
Flowchart of Computer-Assisted Tests of Accounts Receivable

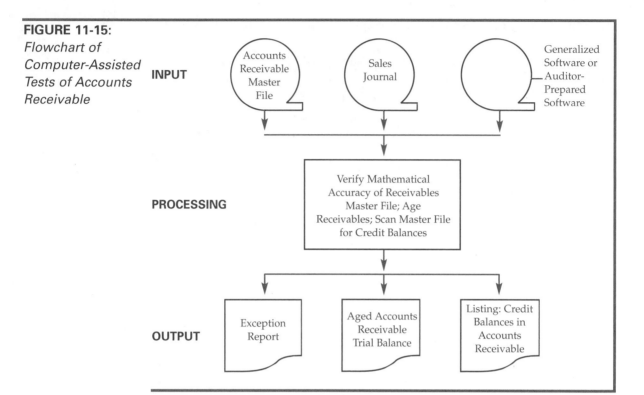

The software would be run on the client's computer, either directly by the auditor or by client personnel under the auditor's supervision. The exception report, aged trial balances, and credit balance listing—the output depicted in Figure 11-15—would be accessed by the auditor directly. The output and computer-assisted tests are then included in audit documentation and used in conjunction with other audit evidence to help form conclusions about whether receivables are fairly stated at the balance sheet date.

SUMMARY

As discussed in Chapter 10, the revenue/receipt cycle encompasses two major business functions—selling resources to customers and, subsequently, collecting cash for resources sold. In turn, these functions are reflected in three major financial statement accounts: sales, accounts receivable, and cash, each of which is discussed in this chapter in the context of substantive tests. When performing substantive tests of sales, receivables, and cash balances, an auditor's objectives are to determine that each account balance exists, represents all transactions that should be presented, represents rights of the entity, is valued appropriately, and is presented and disclosed properly in the financial statements. Importantly, the material presented in Chapter 8 on computer auditing and in Chapter 9 on audit sampling is directly applicable to substantive tests of sales, receivables, and cash, since many U.S. companies now process most all of their revenue/receipt cycle transactions by computer.

When the timing of revenue is not reasonably determinable or if the earnings process is not complete, management has some discretion in timing the amount of revenue recognized, creating opportunities to manipulate earnings. Auditors should be aware that management may have incentives to overstate earnings, since reported earnings is typically the most important variable in management compensation contracts and poor earnings performance increases both the likelihood of replacing a chief executive officer and the threat of a hostile takeover. Undetected earnings manipulation can result both in legal liability and ethical implications for the auditor.

KEY TERMS

Area franchise fees 486
Cutoff bank statements 472
Negative confirmations 464
Positive confirmations 464

Earnings manipulation 478
Kiting 477
Revenue/receipt cycle 457

REFERENCES

Auditing Standards:

AICPA, *Codification of Auditing Standards*. New York: AICPA.

SAS No. 47, "Audit Risk and Materiality in Conducting an Audit" (AU Sec. 312).

SAS No. 67, "The Confirmation Process" (AU Sec. 330).

Accounting Standards:

AICPA, *Revenue Recognition Issues*, Practice Alert No. 95-1.

FASB Statement of Financial Accounting Concepts No. 5, "Recognition and Measurement in Financial Statements of Business Enterprises."

FASB Statement of Financial Accounting Standards No. 45, "Accounting for Franchise Fee Revenue."

FASB Statement of Financial Accounting Standards No. 48, "Revenue Recognition When Right of Return Exists."

SEC Staff Accounting Bulletin No. 101, "Revenue Recognition."

Professional Reports and Speeches:

AICPA, *Audit Issues in Revenue Recognition*, 1999.

Beasley, M. S., J. V. Carcello, and D. R. Hermanson, *Fraudulent Financial Reporting: 1987–1997 An Analysis of U.S. Public Companies*. Committee of Sponsoring Organizations of the Treadway Commission, 1999.

Public Oversight Board, *Panel on Audit Effectiveness: Report and Recommendations*. Stamford, CT: POB, 2000.

Articles:

Beasley, M. S., J. V. Carcello, D. R. Hermanson, and P. D. Lapides, "Fraudulent Financial Reporting: Consideration of Industry Traits and Corporate Governance Mechanisms," *Accounting Horizons* (December 2000), pp. 441–454.

Bonner, S. E., Z. V. Palmrose, and S. M. Young, "Fraud Type and Auditor Litigation: An Analysis of SEC Accounting and Auditing Enforcement Releases," *The Accounting Review* (October 1998), pp. 503–532.

Dechow, P. M., and D. J. Skinner, "Earnings Management: Reconciling the Views of Accounting Academics, Practitioners, and Regulators," *Accounting Horizons* (June 2000), pp. 235–250.

Dechow, P. M., R. G. Sloan, and A. P. Sweeney, "Causes and Consequences of Earnings Manipulations: An Analysis of Firms Subject to Enforcement Actions by the SEC," *Contemporary Accounting Research* (Spring 1996), pp. 1–36.

Healy, P. M., and J. M. Wahlen, "A Review of the Earnings Management Literature and Its Implications for Standard Setting," *Accounting Horizons* (December 1999).

Lundelius, C. R., Jr., *Financial Reporting Fraud: A Practical Guide to Detection and Internal Control.* New York: AICPA, 2003.

Nelson, M. W., J. A. Elliott, and R. L. Tarpley, "Evidence From Auditors About Managers' and Auditors' Earnings Management Decision," *The Accounting Review* (Supplement 2002), pp. 175–202.

Nelson, M. W., J. A. Elliott, and R. L. Tarpley, "How are Earnings Managed? Examples from Auditors," *Accounting Horizons* (Supplement 2003), pp. 17–35.

Reason, T., "Accounting Fraud: Jailhouse Shock," *CFO* (September 2000), pp. 111–114.

Schipper, K., "Commentary on Earnings Management," *Accounting Horizons* (December 1989).

QUESTIONS

1. What are financial statement assertions, audit objectives, and audit procedures? How are they related?
2. What does management assert about receivables reported in financial statements?
3. How does an auditor test whether recorded accounts receivable exist?
4. Why does an auditor perform analytical procedures on receivables?
5. How does an auditor test whether recorded receivables represent bona fide rights of the client?
6. How does an auditor test the valuation of accounts receivable and sales?
7. Describe and distinguish between positive and negative confirmation requests.
8. Which financial statement assertions do receivables confirmations address?
9. Explain the purpose and nature of sales cutoff tests.
10. What is the difference between FOB shipping point and FOB point of destination?
11. How does an auditor test whether cash balances actually exist?
12. Aside from cash balances, what other information is requested by an AICPA standard form (Figure 11-8) to confirm account balance information with financial institutions?
13. Identify the internal and external documentation available to an auditor to test cutoff.
14. Explain the purpose and nature of cutoff tests of cash balances.
15. How and why does an auditor test intercompany and interbank transfers?
16. Describe some computer-assisted substantive tests an auditor might apply to accounts receivable.
17. What conditions must an entity meet before recognizing revenue for financial statement reporting purposes?
18. What key elements are common to channel stuffing?
19. What procedures would help detect channel stuffing?
20. What advantages do both franchisors and franchisees enjoy by entering into a franchise agreement, rather than conducting the entire scope of operations individually?

MULTIPLE CHOICE QUESTIONS

1. An auditor generally tests the completeness of credit sales transactions by:
   a. Confirming receivables balances with debtors.
   b. Reviewing the collectibility of receivables outstanding.
   c. Inquiring of management.
   d. Performing analytical procedures.

2. If tests of controls show that controls over shipping and billing are likely ineffective, the auditor would:
   a. Assess control risk at the minimum.
   b. Perform audit procedures at an interim date.
   c. Increase the extent of testing on receivables balances.
   d. Not rely on management's representations.

3. Which of the following might be detected by sales cutoff tests?
   a. Overstated receivables
   b. Overstated sales
   c. Kiting
   d. Misappropriated inventory

4. To test whether all sales transactions have been recorded, an auditor should test a sample drawn from an entity's file of:
   a. Receiving reports.
   b. Bills of lading.
   c. Sales orders.
   d. Sales invoices.

5. Positive accounts receivable confirmations are appropriate when:
   a. There is reason to believe that a substantial number of accounts may be in dispute.
   b. Control risk is low.
   c. Accounts receivable consists of many small balances.
   d. Confirmations are mailed during an interim period.

6. Under which of the following conditions might an auditor justify not confirming receivables balances with debtors?
   a. The auditor accepted the engagement after the balance sheet date.
   b. Prior-year confirmations revealed no errors in the receivables balance.
   c. A small number of customers comprise almost all of the receivables balance.
   d. The client is a government contractor.

7. How might an auditor proceed to address confirmations that customers do not return?
   a. Review customer purchase orders.
   b. Interview billing employees.
   c. Propose the customer balances as an audit adjustment.
   d. Review subsequent cash collections.

8. Which of the following procedures could reveal unrecorded sales at the balance sheet date?
   a. Comparing shipping documents with sales records
   b. Applying gross profit percentages to inventory shipped during the period
   c. Tracing payments received after the balance sheet date to accounts receivable records
   d. Sending accounts receivable confirmations

9. An auditor requests a cutoff bank statement primarily to:

   a. Verify the cash balance reported on the bank confirmation.
   b. Verify reconciling items on the client's bank reconciliation.
   c. Detect lapping.
   d. Detect kiting.

10. A standard bank confirmation:

    a. Requests information about indebtedness.
    b. Is sent to the bank by the client.
    c. Is signed by the client's chief executive and chief financial officers.
    d. Requests information about account numbers.

11. Assuming cash receipts from credit sales have been misappropriated, which of the following is likely to conceal the misappropriation and unlikely to be detected?

    a. Understating the sales journal
    b. Overstating the accounts receivable control account
    c. Overstating the accounts receivable subsidiary ledger
    d. Overstating the cash receipts journal

12. Which of the following cash transfers misstates cash at December 31?

    Interbank Transfers

    | | Disbursement | | Receipt | |
	Recorded in books	Paid by bank	Recorded in books	Received by bank
a.	12/31/06	01/04/07	12/31/06	12/31/06
b.	01/04/07	01/05/07	12/31/06	01/04/07
c.	12/31/06	01/05/07	12/31/06	01/04/07
d.	01/04/07	01/11/07	01/04/07	01/04/07

13. The purpose of a cutoff bank statement is to:

    a. Reconcile cash on the books with cash in the bank.
    b. Test deposits in transit and outstanding checks.
    c. Reconcile accounts payable to cash disbursements.
    d. Test subsequent cash receipts.

14. Which of the following accounting issues is most likely to raise an auditor's professional skepticism about earnings manipulation?

    a. Progress payments
    b. Allowance for doubtful accounts
    c. Sales returns
    d. Cash receipts

15. Which of the following is most likely to provide management with incentives to overstate earnings?

    a. Projected quarterly dividends
    b. Issuance of preferred stock
    c. Unbudgeted increases in materials prices
    d. A projected stock split

16. A vendor sold software to an engineering company, recorded revenue of $15,000, and included in the price end-user support for a number of hours the vendor and company have yet to determine. This is an example of:

    a. A side agreement.
    b. A consignment sale.
    c. A kickback sale.
    d. A conditional sale.

17. Under which of the following circumstances does management have some discretion in timing the recognition of revenue?

    a. The timing of revenue is not reasonably determinable and the earnings process is not complete.
    b. The amount and timing of revenue is reasonably determinable.
    c. The earnings process is complete or reasonably complete.
    d. The transaction is at arm's length.

18. Which of the following governs more in the selection of accounting principles for transactions not addressed in an FASB pronouncement?

    a. SEC *Staff Accounting Bulletin No. 104*, "Revenue Recognition"
    b. Analogous pronouncements
    c. Management's preference
    d. Business purpose

19. A public company would most likely disclose information about end-of-period incremental volume in:

    a. Management's discussion and analysis.
    b. Footnotes.
    c. The income statement.
    d. The balance sheet.

20. Global Crossing exploited capacity swaps to:

    a. Understate telecom assets.
    b. Recognize revenue prematurely.
    c. Overstate net cash flow.
    d. Defer revenue.

PROBLEMS AND DISCUSSION CASES

11-1 *Relating Errors, Frauds, Audit Procedures, and Assertions in Substantive Tests of Accounts Receivable*

Following are errors, frauds, or other circumstances that an auditor might encounter as a result of applying year-end substantive tests to accounts receivable as of December 31, 2007:

a. Sales totaling $12,500 were shipped on January 2, 2008, and recorded on December 31, 2007.
b. Balances in selected individual customer accounts do not reconcile with supporting documentation (for example, sales invoices, cash receipts).
c. Not all sales transactions are recorded.
d. The aged trial balance prepared by the client includes a customer account within the 30–60 day category that is actually 120 days old.

e. Positive confirmations were not returned by 27 of 100 mailed receivables confirmations.
f. Actual write-offs during 2007 of receivables arising from 2006 sales were greater than the December 31, 2007, allowance for doubtful accounts.

Required: For each of the preceding items indicate (1) procedures that might address the error, fraud, or circumstance and (2) the financial statement assertion addressed by each procedure.

11-2 *Receivables Confirmations*

An independent auditor is engaged to audit the financial statements of a manufacturing company that, consistent with prior years, maintains a significant balance in trade accounts receivable. The auditor is satisfied that the accounts are properly summarized and classified and that reclassifications and valuations are made in accordance with generally accepted accounting principles. The auditor is planning to use accounts receivable confirmation requests to satisfy the third standard of field work.

Required:
1. Identify and describe the two forms of accounts receivable confirmation requests commonly used in practice and indicate what factors the auditor will consider to determine which form to use.
2. What alternative procedures could the auditor use to address no replies?

11-3 *Drafting a Tailored Audit Program for Credit Sales Transactions*

You have audited the financial statements of the Heft Company, a December 31 year-end client, for several years. The interim phase of the engagement, completed on August 31, included confirming accounts receivable and indicated that internal controls over receivables are effective and therefore that control risk is below the maximum.

Credit sales are made principally to manufacturers. Of 1,500 active trade accounts receivable, about 35 percent represent 65 percent of the total dollar balance. Receivables are maintained alphabetically in five subsidiary files, and the files are controlled by one general ledger account.

Sales are posted by an operation that simultaneously updates the customer's balance (and monthly statement) and records the transaction in the sales journal. All cash receipts are in the form of customer checks that, when posted, simultaneously update the customer's ledger balance, monthly statement, and the cash receipts journal. Information for posting cash receipts is obtained from remittance advices that are returned in envelopes with the customers' checks. The bookkeeper compares the remittance advices with the list of checks that was prepared by another person when the mail was received.

Summary totals are produced monthly by the bookkeeper for posting to general ledger accounts such as Cash, Sales, and Accounts Receivable. An aged trial balance for each subsidiary is prepared monthly.

Sales returns and allowances and bad debt write-offs are summarized periodically and recorded in the general journal. Supporting documents for these journal entries are available. The usual documents arising from billing and shipping also are available.

Required: Prepare an audit program to test Heft Company's year-end trade accounts receivable. Use the substantive tests introduced within the chapter as a guide, but not as a complete answer.

(AICPA Adapted)

11-4 *Analytical Procedures, Accounts Receivable, and Sales*

Cheryl Ralston is planning analytical procedures for the December 31, 2007, financial statement audit of Singulair, Inc., a publicly traded manufacturer of small electrical appliances, including mixers, toasters, can openers, and electric blankets. The appliances are marketed to low-end retailers throughout North America. An industry trade publication estimates

Singulair's 2007 market share at 12 percent. Singulair's December 31, 2007 and 2006, balance sheets and statements of operations follow.

Singulair, Inc.
Balance Sheets
December 31, 2007 and 2006
(000 omitted)

Assets	2007	2006
Cash	$ 42,000	$ 52,500
Accounts receivable, net	325,500	175,000
Inventory	252,000	234,500
Other current assets	17,500	21,000
Noncurrent assets, net of depreciation	210,000	280,000
Total assets	$847,000	$763,000
Liabilities and Equities		
Trade accounts payable	$133,000	$143,500
Taxes payable	105,000	50,400
Noncurrent liabilities	70,000	140,000
Common stock	245,000	245,000
Retained earnings	294,000	184,100
Total liabilities and equities	$847,000	$763,000

Singulair, Inc.
Statements of Operations
Years Ended December 31, 2007 and 2006
(000 omitted)

	2007	2006
Net credit sales	$5,894,000	$4,375,000
Cost of goods sold	3,244,500	2,485,000
	$2,649,500	$1,890,000
Selling and administrative expenses	2,387,000	1,764,000
Income before taxes	$ 262,500	$ 126,000
Tax expense	105,000	50,400
Net income	$ 157,500	$ 75,600

Total industry-wide sales approximated $37.5 billion in 2007. The allowance for doubtful accounts was $24,500,000 in 2007 and $35,000,000 in 2006, and accounts receivable, net, was $200,000,000 in 2005.

Required: Using Figure 11-6, Analytical Procedures for Accounts Receivable and Sales, as a guide:
1. Perform analytical procedures you think appropriate for Singulair's December 31, 2007, audit. For example, the balance sheets and statements of operations include information that can be used to calculate the numbers of days' sales in receivables and receivables turnover and to make several informative comparisons.
2. Explain the results for each ratio or comparison. For example, an increase in receivables turnover could signal understated sales or overstated receivables, among other things.
3. Discuss substantive tests appropriate for the results explained in requirement 2. For example, an analytical procedure that signals overstated receivables could prompt an auditor to increase the extent of accounts receivable confirmations.

11-5 *Analytical Procedures and Accounts Receivable*

Martin Kline, engagement partner on RCT Manufacturing Company, a February 28, 2007, year-end client, is performing analytical procedures to better understand RCT's business and to determine where audit effort ought to be concentrated. The balance sheets and statements of operations for 2006 and 2007 follow.

RCT Manufacturing Company
Balance Sheets
February 28, 2007 and 2006

Assets	2007	2006
Cash	$ 12,000	$ 15,000
Accounts receivable, net	93,000	50,000
Inventory	72,000	67,000
Other current assets	5,000	6,000
Plant and equipment, net of depreciation	60,000	80,000
Total assets	$242,000	$218,000
Liabilities and Equities		
Accounts payable	$ 38,000	$ 41,000
Federal income tax payable	30,000	14,400
Long-term liabilities	20,000	40,000
Common stock	70,000	70,000
Retained earnings	84,000	52,600
Total liabilities and equities	$242,000	$218,000

RCT Manufacturing Company
Income Statements
Years Ended February 28, 2007 and 2006

	2007	2006
Net sales	$1,684,000	$1,250,000
Cost of goods sold	927,000	710,000
Gross margin on sales	$ 757,000	$ 540,000
Selling and administrative expenses	682,000	504,000
Income before federal income taxes	$ 75,000	$ 36,000
Income tax expense	30,000	14,400
Net income	$ 45,000	$ 21,600

Additional information:
a. Cash sales are insignificant.
b. Year-end figures are comparable to the average for each respective year.

   Required: For each year, compute accounts receivable turnover and, based on turnover, identify and discuss procedures Kline should include in the audit of accounts receivable. (AICPA Adapted)

11-6 *Sales Cutoff Tests*

During an audit of the financial statements of Houston Wholesalers, Inc., for the year ended June 30, 2007, an auditor performs several cutoff tests.

   Required:
   1. What are cutoff tests and why are they performed?
   2. The auditor wishes to test Houston's sales cutoff at June 30, 2007. Discuss procedures that should be included in the test.

11-7 *Relating Errors, Frauds, Audit Procedures, and Assertions in Substantive Tests of Cash*

Following are errors, frauds, or other circumstances that an auditor might encounter as a result of applying substantive tests to cash balances as of December 31.

a. The petty cash fund is short $75.
b. Cash in banks is overstated by $1,500.
c. Several checks were issued on December 31, but were post-dated January 2.
d. Outstanding checks per the bank reconciliation do not agree with the cash disbursements journal.
e. On December 31, the sum of $15,000 was transferred from an account in the First National Bank to an account in Tower Savings Bank.
f. The December 31 bank reconciliation contains several discrepancies.
g. On December 31, the client transferred $25,000 to a wholly owned subsidiary.

Required: Indicate a specific procedure (or procedures) that might detect each error, fraud, or circumstance and identify the assertion(s) addressed by each procedure.

11-8 *Cash Cutoff Tests*

During year-end substantive procedures for cash balances as of June 30, 2007, an auditor obtains a July 10, 2007, bank statement directly from a bank.

Required: Explain how the auditor will use the cutoff bank statement:
1. When auditing the June 30, 2007, bank reconciliation.
2. To obtain other audit information.

11-9 *Auditing a Client-Prepared Bank Reconciliation*

The following client-prepared bank reconciliation is presented to Kautz during an audit of the financial statements of Cynthia Company.

Cynthia Company
BANK RECONCILIATION
Village Bank Account 2
December 31, 2007

Balance per bank (a)		$18,375.91
Deposits in transit (b)		
12/30	$1,471.10	
12/31	2,840.69	4,311.79
Subtotal		$22,687.70
Outstanding checks (c)		
837	$6,000.00	
1941	671.80	
1966	320.00	
1984	1,855.42	
1985	3,621.22	
1987	2,576.89	
1991	4,420.88	(19,466.21)
Subtotal		$ 3,221.49
NSF check returned		
12/29 (d)		200.00
Bank charges		5.50
Error, Check No. 1932		148.10
Customer note collected by the bank		
($2,750 plus $275 interest) (e)		(3,025.00)
Balance per books (f)		$ 550.09

Required: Indicate one or more audit procedures Kautz should perform to gather evidence to support each of the items (a) through (f).

(AICPA Adapted)

11-10 *Computer-Assisted Audit Tests*

After determining that computer controls are valid, Hastings is reviewing the sales system of Rosco Corporation to determine how computer-assisted audit techniques may be used to assist in performing tests of Rosco's sales records. Rosco sells corn from one central location. All orders are received by mail or fax and indicate the preassigned customer identification number, desired quantity, proposed delivery date, method of payment, and shipping terms. Since price fluctuates daily, orders do not indicate a price. Price sheets are printed daily, and details are stored on computer. The details of orders also are maintained on computer.

Each morning the shipping clerk receives a computer printout that indicates details of customers' orders to be shipped that day. After the orders have been shipped, the shipping details are entered in the computer, which simultaneously updates the sales journal, perpetual inventory records, accounts receivable, and sales accounts. The details of all transactions, as well as daily updates, are maintained on computer and are accessible by Hastings.

Required:
1. How may Hastings use computer-assisted audit techniques to perform substantive tests of Rosco's sales records?
2. What other auditing procedures should Hastings perform in order to complete the audit of Rosco's sales records?

(AICPA Adapted)

11-11 *Identifying and Criticizing a Receivables Confirmation*

An entry-level associate in the Providence, Rhode Island, office of DeMarinis & Harrison, LLP, has drafted the following receivable confirmation for the Newman Crosby Company, a December 31, 2007, year-end client.

January 2, 2008

Newman Crosby Company
305 Columbus Avenue
Pawtucket, RI 02861

Carter, Rice, Storrs & Bement
Industrial Highway
Providence, RI 02906

Please confirm the correctness of your December 31, 2007, account balance, $45,897, directly to us. Our auditors are DeMarinis & Harrison, CPAs. This is not a request for payment.

_____

Tess Gallagher, Controller

_____ The above balance is correct.

_____ The above balance is incorrect, as noted below:

Required:
1. What type of confirmation is illustrated?
2. What is wrong with the confirmation?

11-12 *Interpreting Audit Documentation*

Following is partial evidence from an audit document.

Disbursement Date		Receipt Date	
Per Books	Per Bank	Per Books	Per Bank
12/31	01/01	01/02	12/31
12/31	01/01	12/31	12/31
01/01	01/01	12/31	12/31
12/31	01/01	12/30	12/30

Required:
1. What is the evidence attempting to detect?
2. Did it? Why or why not?

11-13 *Interpreting Audit Documentation*

Following is partial evidence from an audit document.

	Shipped	Recorded
FOB: Destination	December 31	January 02
FOB: Shipping Point	December 30	December 31
FOB: Destination	January 01	January 01
FOB: Shipping Point	December 31	January 01

Required:
1. What is the evidence attempting to detect?
2. Did it? Why or why not?

11-14 *Audit Documentation Review: Bank Reconciliation*

Following is an audit document that shows an auditor's tests of a client's bank reconciliation.

Ansonia Wire & Cable Co., Inc.   A5

Bank Reconciliation   ARE

December 31, 2007

Balance per bank, 12/31/07		$17,551,710@
Add: DIT, 12/31/07		1,578,143*
Less: O/S checks:		
No. 5775 12/24	$1,431,897&	
No. 5776 12/26	156,050&	
No. 5777 12/27	234,875&	
No. 5779 12/29	2,169,549&	
No. 5780 12/31	1,191,240&	(5,183,611)
Adjusted bank balance		$13,946,242
Balance per books, 12/31/07		$14,473,098#
Less: Check from Apex, Inc.,		
deposited 12/15,		
returned NSF on 12/18		(526,856)@
Adjusted book balance		$13,946,242

@ Agreed to 12/31/07 bank statement obtained from client/*ARE*

* Agreed to cash receipts records/*ARE*

& Agreed to cash disbursements records/*ARE*

\# Agreed to client bank reconciliation/*ARE*

Required: List the deficiencies in this document.

11-15 *Revenue Recognition, Channel Stuffing, and Guaranteed Rights of Return*

To stimulate sales, the management of Berton & Lowe, Inc., a publicly traded manufacturer of private-label food products, plans to introduce a right of return into last-week-of-the-quarter sales agreements with national distributors. Berton & Lowe's general counsel advises management that the SEC has investigated a number of companies in the consumer foods industry for channel stuffing and that the plan fits a definition of channel stuffing consistent with a number of federal litigations. For example, *In re Cableton Systems, Inc. Securities Litigation* (311 F. 3d 11, 26), the First Circuit Court of Appeals in 2002 defined channel stuffing as "inducing distributors or wholesalers to buy . . . products in excess of their projected needs by promising them that the products could be returned at any time and for any reason if they were not sold." Management understands that introducing for the first time guaranteed rights of return may condition distributors to hold-out for inducements in future quarters. Before deciding whether to implement the right-of-return inducement, management seeks your advice on accounting and disclosure.

Required:

1. How would you advise management about revenue recognition in the face of a guaranteed right of return?
2. How would you advise management about disclosure in *Forms 10-Q* and *10-K*, the quarterly and annual reports to the SEC, respectively?

11-16 *Earnings Manipulation and Area Franchise Fees*

Burger Chef Restaurants grant area franchises to operate up to two restaurants within a 100-square-mile area. The Uniform Franchise Offering Circular reveals that, following payment of the lump sum fee, Burger Chef agrees to assist in selecting franchise locations and obtaining financing, negotiate lease terms for existing structures or construction costs for a new building, and provide both initial management training and periodic on-site consultation. The area franchise fee can be refunded. To date, no area franchisees have either reneged on the franchise agreements or gone out of business. In most markets, Burger Chef ranks at least fourth in market-wide fast food revenue. The product line consists of beef, fish, and poultry sandwiches and a full-service salad bar.

Required: Identify, and explain the motive for, the key questions an auditor would address to judge when area franchise fees may be recognized as revenue.

Internet problems and discussion cases are available at http://ricchiute.swlearning.com

RESEARCH PROJECTS

1. Management Discretion and Earnings Manipulation

Earnings manipulation has long been the subject of considerable attention both in the financial press and in academic research. For example, *The Wall Street Journal*, *Forbes Magazine*, and *BusinessWeek* have all carried pieces on suspicious income and two decades ago the 1988 Supplement to the University of Chicago's *Journal of Accounting Research* was devoted exclusively to studies addressing earnings management. Interestingly, many of the earnings manipulation issues disclosed by the press have resulted in professional pronouncements intended to improve the quality of reported earnings, among them FASB *Statement No. 45*, "Accounting for Franchise Fee Revenue."

Required: Using the annual report file in an online research service (for example, LEXIS-NEXIS, the SEC's EDGAR [http://www.sec.gov]) or copies of annual reports in a library, select the annual reports of two national franchisors (for example, Burger King, Century 21, Holiday Inn, McDonald's, Radisson Inns, Taco Bell, U-Haul) and draft a report that accomplishes both of the following:

1. Compare the footnote and line-item disclosures for area development and individual site franchises.
2. Using FASB *Statement No. 45*, paragraphs 5 through 11, as a guide, list and explain the questions an auditor would ask the management of either of the franchisors to monitor whether the franchisor complied with generally accepted accounting principles.

2. Revenue Recognition and Earnings Manipulation

Not unlike a number of other articles appearing in the national press, E. MacDonald, in "Auditors Miss a Fraud and SEC Tries to Put Them Out of Business" (*The Wall Street Journal*, January 6, 2000), reports about an SEC investigation of the auditors of California Micro Devices, a computer chip maker alleged to have overstated revenue:

Within weeks, it became clear they had missed an audacious accounting fraud. An internal Cal Micro investigation uncovered "preposterous" revenue numbers "almost immediately," . . . One-third of the company's $45 million of fiscal 1994 revenue was spurious. Undetected by auditors . . . were a dozen or more accounting tricks that various employees, at various levels of management, had deployed to keep the stock buoyant. They included one particularly bold one: booking bogus sales to fake companies for products that didn't exist.

The article is a sobering warning for auditors to be mindful that clients have incentives to overstate revenue. In fact, the Panel on Audit Effectiveness goes further by recommending that auditors introduce a "forensic-type fieldwork phase" to every financial statement audit. The Panel explains:

During this phase, auditors should modify the otherwise neutral concept of professional skepticism and presume the possibility of dishonesty at various levels of management, including collusion, override of internal control and falsification of documents. The key question that auditors should ask is "Where is the entity vulnerable to financial statement fraud if management were inclined to perpetrate it?"

The *Journal's* account of Cal Micro and the Panel's recommendation suggest that detecting overstated revenue starts in the planning stage of the engagement.

   Required: Using the annual report file in an online research service (for example, LEXIS-NEXIS, the SEC's EDGAR [**http://www.sec.gov**]) or copies of annual reports in a library, select the annual report of a publicly traded company. Draft a report that accomplishes the following:

1. Compile from the annual report the company's major revenue-producing transactions. For example, the notes to General Electric's financial statements reveal that the company generates revenue from several major sources, including aircraft engines, appliances, industrial products, NBC, and plastics.
2. Using Figure 11-13, "Common Means to Manipulate Earnings," as a guide, explain how the company's management could overstate revenue to manipulate earnings.

12 Chapter

Purchases and Cash Disbursements Transactions

Major topics discussed in this chapter are:

- **The nature of the expenditure/disbursement cycle, including the flow of information through purchasing, receiving, accounts payable, and cash disbursements.**
- **An auditor's assessment of control risk and audit of internal control over financial reporting for purchases and cash disbursements transactions.**
- **The integration of computer auditing, sampling, and tests of controls within the expenditure/disbursement cycle.**
- **Assurance and consulting services related to purchases.**

Like Chapters 10 and 11 for the revenue/receipt cycle, this chapter and Chapter 13 focus on auditing the expenditure/disbursement cycle: Tests of controls are introduced here and substantive tests are introduced in Chapter 13. This chapter begins by describing the nature of the expenditure/disbursement cycle and representative internal controls over an entity's purchasing, receiving, and cash disbursements functions. In turn, the chapter discusses an auditor's consideration of internal control and uses deduction management in the consumer foods industry to illustrate how an auditor forms a preliminary opinion on internal control over financial reporting under the *Sarbanes-Oxley Act* (Section 404) and PCAOB *Auditing Standard No. 2*, "An Audit of Internal Control Over Financial Reporting." Next, the chapter presents a case illustration that integrates material introduced in Chapter 8 (information systems), Chapter 9 (sampling), and this chapter. Finally, the chapter offers examples of assurance and consulting services related to purchases and payables.

The Expenditure/Disbursement Cycle

The **expenditure/disbursement cycle** encompasses both the acquisition of goods and services ("expenditure" in the cycle's title) and the payment of cash ("disbursement") for the goods and services acquired. The cycle is related to each of the other three cycles, since it:

- Uses resources and information provided by the revenue/receipt cycle, and
- Provides resources and information for the financing and conversion cycles.

For example, the expenditure/disbursement cycle might use cash provided from the sale of inventory (revenue/receipt cycle), disburse cash to meet principal and interest payments on funds borrowed from investors in exchange for bonds (financing cycle), and disburse cash to employees who assemble inventory (conversion cycle).

Figure 12-1 summarizes the scope of the expenditure/disbursement cycle, listing the primary business functions and representative activities, journal entries, and forms. Two major business functions are associated with the cycle:

- Resources (goods and services) are acquired from vendors and employees in exchange for obligations to pay.
- Obligations to vendors and employees are paid.

FIGURE 12-1: *Scope of the Expenditure/Disbursement Cycle*

Related Business Functions	Common Activities	Common Entries	Common Forms
• Resources (goods and services) are acquired from vendors (and employees) in exchange for obligations to pay. • Obligations to vendors (and employees) are paid.	• Purchasing • Receiving • Recording • Payment (including authorizing and preparing checks)	• Purchases • Account distribution • Prepaid and accrued expenses • Adjustments • Cash disbursements	• Purchase requisitions • Purchase orders • Receiving reports • Vendors' invoices • Vouchers

Each of these business functions relates both to vendors and to employees (although employees, personnel, and payroll are discussed separately in Chapter 14).

An entity purchases inventory or supplies among other things from vendors that Purchasing department personnel select from specifications on an approved purchase requisition. A purchase order is sent to the vendor selected and, when the goods are received (and a receiving report prepared), a liability (an account payable) is recorded. The expenditure/disbursement cycle continues when the vendor's invoice arrives by fax, mail, email, or electronic data integration (EDI) and is matched with the receiving report, the purchase requisition, and the purchase order. From these paper or computer image documents, a voucher is prepared and the documents are physically attached or linked by computer, forming a voucher package, which is the basis for making a cash payment to a vendor. When payment is made, the voucher package is canceled, for example, by notation on a computer screen or by perforation on a paper voucher package.

Throughout the expenditure/disbursement cycle, journal entries are made for purchases, prepaid and accrued expenses, cash disbursements, adjustments, and account distributions. Paper or electronic documents affecting the expenditure/disbursement cycle include:

- **Purchase requisition:** A request from an employee or department supervisor that goods be purchased.
- **Purchase order**: A request issued by the Purchasing department to a vendor to purchase goods.
- **Receiving report**: A report that identifies information about goods received from a vendor.
- **Vendor's invoice**: A document that identifies goods purchased and represents formal notice about the amount and terms of payment (often called the *bill*).
- **Voucher package**: The purchase requisition, purchase order, receiving report, and invoice (often includes a summarizing document, the *voucher*).

As indicated in Chapter 10, organizational structure and control activities vary from one entity to another, although the expenditure/disbursement cycle activities identified in Figure 12-1 are relatively common. Controls within the expenditure/disbursement cycle are explained in the context of two functions common to the cycle:

- Purchasing (including ordering, receiving, and accounts payable).
- Cash disbursements.

Personnel and payroll, also related to the expenditure/disbursement cycle, are discussed in Chapter 14.

Figure 12-2 flowcharts representative purchasing and cash disbursement activities. In turn, Figure 12-3 on page 513, derived from Figure 12-2, lists common purchasing and cash disbursement activities. The following explains each major activity.

Purchasing

Purchasing involves the acquisition of goods and services from vendors. *Goods* include tangible resources, such as inventory, supplies, and equipment, and *services* include nontangible resources, like advertising, repairs and maintenance, utilities, and insurance. Goods and services may be acquired for use by, or for the benefit of, any department within an entity. Regardless of what department acquires the goods or services, though, the purchase and subsequent payment are processed through the expenditure/disbursement cycle, since the cycle serves all departments, even those like shipping and billing, which, as discussed in Chapter 10, serve the revenue/receipt cycle.

An employee of the department that requests the purchase prepares a purchase requisition, which is submitted to a supervisor for approval. Approved purchase requisitions are forwarded to Purchasing, where the request is reviewed, a vendor selected, and a purchase order prepared. A purchase order describes the goods or services requested, specifying price, quantity, shipping terms, and catalog numbers. Copies of purchase orders are sent by Purchasing to the vendor and to the requisitioning department, to Receiving, and to Accounts Payable, as depicted in Figure 12-2.

Goods ordered from vendors are delivered to the Receiving department, where the goods are compared with the purchase order and a receiving report is

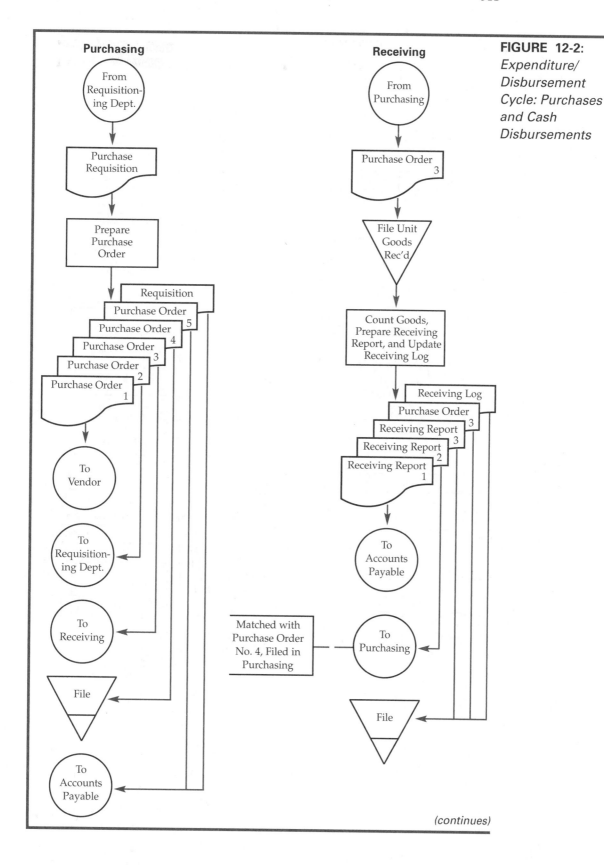

FIGURE 12-2:
*Expenditure/
Disbursement
Cycle: Purchases
and Cash
Disbursements*

(continues)

authoriZe Payment

Make Payment

FIGURE 12-2
(continued)

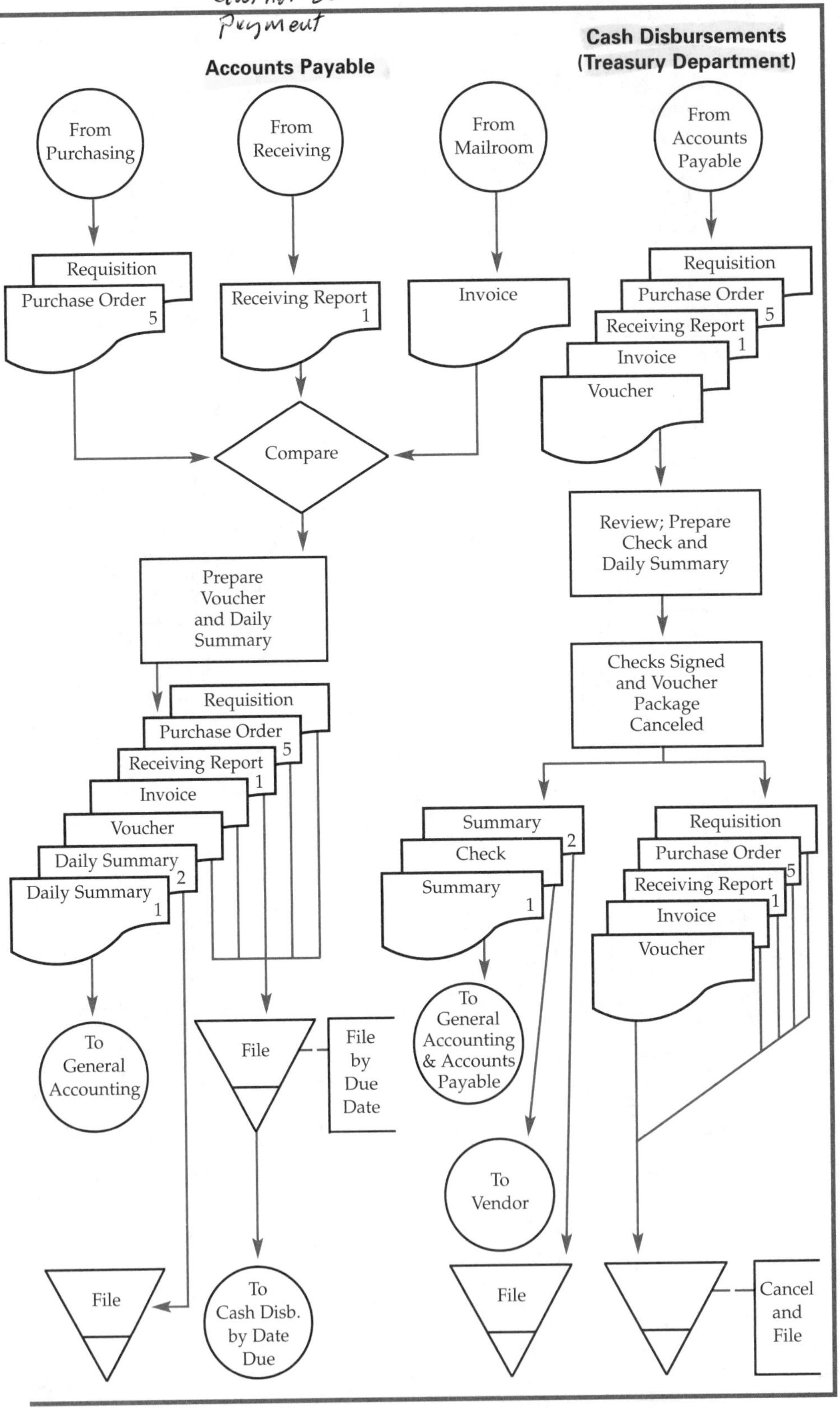

FIGURE 12-3: *Summary of Purchasing and Cash Disbursements Activities*

Purchasing
- Accept approved purchase requisitions from user departments.
- Prepare purchase order, distribute copies, and retain file copy.

Receiving
- File purchase orders until goods are received.
- Upon receipt of goods, count quantities and compare with purchase order.
- Prepare receiving report.
- Forward goods to Inventory Control.
- Forward copies of receiving report to Accounts Payable and to Purchasing; retain file copy of receiving report, purchase order, and updated receiving log.

Accounts Payable
- Compare purchase requisition, purchase order, receiving report, and vendor's invoice.
- Prepare voucher and daily summary; assemble voucher package.
- File voucher package by due date; forward to cash disbursements (Treasury department) on date due.
- Forward daily summary to General Accounting for recording; retain file copy.

Cash Disbursements (Treasury Department)
- Review voucher packages received from Accounts Payable on due date.
- Prepare checks and daily summary.
- Have checks signed by authorized signatories.
- Forward checks to vendors.
- Forward summary to General Accounting and Accounts Payable for recording; retain file copy of summary.
- Cancel and file voucher packages.

prepared. Receiving department personnel also maintain a receiving log cross-referenced to related receiving reports. A copy of the receiving report is forwarded to Purchasing and to Accounts Payable. Similar procedures are required for the purchase of services—that is, memoranda are completed indicating that the services have been rendered.

Accounts Payable personnel file receiving reports with related purchase requisitions and purchase orders pending receipt of a vendor's invoice, the bill. Some companies use a voucher system for recording and controlling payables. Typically, a voucher is prepared by Accounts Payable personnel upon receipt of a vendor's invoice. A voucher package consisting of the voucher, vendor's invoice, receiving report, purchase order, and purchase requisition is filed in an unpaid vouchers file by due date, and a copy of the daily summary of vouchers, prepared in Accounts Payable, is forwarded to General Accounting for recording in a voucher register. Column totals in the voucher register are posted to general ledger accounts.

Cash Disbursements

Cash disbursements should be authorized and executed by personnel who report to the treasurer and are independent of purchasing and recording, as illustrated in Figure 12-2. Voucher packages in the unpaid voucher file are forwarded to the Treasury department, usually prior to the date payment is due. Personnel in the Treasury department review voucher packages for accuracy and authenticity before approving vouchers for payment and submitting vouchers for check printing. For vouchers involving new or unfamiliar vendors, special precautions should be taken to assure that the transaction is bona fide, since employees are more apt to perpetrate disbursement frauds with fictitious company names than with established vendors.

To minimize opportunities for unauthorized use, blank checks should be prenumbered, and voided checks should be retained and accounted for. Unused checks should be controlled physically (preferably under lock and key), thereby limiting access to authorized personnel only. Once printed by computer, drawn checks (that is, checks completed as to payee, date, amount, and facsimile signature) and approved supporting vouchers should be reviewed by an individual not otherwise involved in either processing or recording payables. Checks drawn in amounts above specified limits may require a second, manual signature. For example, it's common to have a facsimile signature printed on all checks processed by computer, but to require a second manual signature for checks drawn for an amount above, say, $50,000. In no circumstances should checks be signed "blank" (without payee, date, and amount) or drawn to "Cash" (bearer paper that can be cashed by anyone).

Signed checks should be mailed directly to the payee without intervention by employees responsible for approving, recording, or processing the transaction. Paid voucher packages should be canceled immediately—for example, some small entities cancel voucher packages in the presence of check signers. Cancellation prevents duplicate payment and is often accomplished by perforating the voucher package or by notation on a computer screen. Canceled voucher packages, with check numbers entered on the vouchers, should be filed. A daily summary of all remittances should be prepared and forwarded to Accounts Payable for posting to the subsidiary payables ledger and to General Accounting for recording in the voucher register. In a voucher system, the voucher register replaces the cash disbursements journal.

Payments are sometimes made in advance of actually receiving the goods or services. Examples include deposits with vendors for goods ordered and prepayments for insurance, rent, and advertising. Advance payments should be made only when authorized and only with supporting documents. Accounting personnel should carefully review prepayments to determine the appropriate account classification. At the end of an accounting period, all advance payments should be reviewed by designated personnel and adjusting journal entries made to reflect expenses in the proper period.

Internal Control Objectives and Potential Errors or Frauds

The following discussion, summarized in Figure 12-4, identifies control objectives, describes examples of errors or frauds that may arise if an objective is not achieved, and offers examples of control activities that management may implement to prevent or detect errors or frauds in the expenditure/disbursement cycle. The control objectives relate generally to transaction authorization, execution, and recording, and to restricting employee access to assets.

Transaction Authorization

Effective control over an entity's purchasing activities requires that purchases be made only in accordance with general or specific authorization. All purchases

FIGURE 12-4: *Purchasing and Cash Disbursements: Objectives, Potential Errors or Frauds, and Control Activities*

Control Objectives	Types of Errors or Frauds That Could Occur If Objective Is Not Met	Control Activities Designed to Prevent or Detect Errors or Frauds
Transaction Authorization		
• Vendors should be approved prior to purchasing goods.	Purchase could be made from unauthorized vendors, potentially resulting in purchasing from related parties without senior management's knowledge or from foreign vendors in violation of import quotas.	Prepare lists of authorized vendors. Establish criteria for adding to, changing, or deleting from the vendor list.
• Types, quantities, payment, terms, and prices should be approved for all products and services.	Unnecessary goods may be ordered, potentially resulting in write-downs of unusable or unsaleable inventory. Goods may be purchased at noncompetitive prices or unfavorable terms, resulting in reduced earnings.	Maintain updated guidelines for purchase transactions (e.g., competitive bids, specific authorization for all purchases exceeding minimum dollar amounts). Establish procedures for reviewing and approving purchase prices and terms prior to purchase.
Execution		
• Received goods should be counted and inspected for quality.	Damaged or unordered goods could be accepted, potentially creating delays in receiving the goods desired.	Establish procedures for inspecting and counting goods received before releasing the carrier.
• All cash disbursements for goods and services should be based on a bona fide liability.	Cash could be disbursed to unauthorized parties, potentially resulting in fraudulent payments. Duplicate payments could be made, potentially resulting in misspent cash.	Prenumber and control vouchers and checks. Cancel voucher packages immediately upon payment. Require manual dual signatories for all checks over a prespecified amount.

(continues)

FIGURE 12-4 *(continued)*

Control Objectives	Types of Errors or Frauds That Could Occur If Objective Is Not Met	Control Activities Designed to Prevent or Detect Errors or Frauds
Recording		
• All goods and services received should be accurately and promptly reported.	Goods may be received but not reported, potentially resulting in understated inventory and liabilities.	Prenumber receiving reports, and subsequently review for prompt recording.
• Purchases and cash disbursements transactions should be recorded properly and in the proper accounting period.	Account balances may be inaccurate, potentially resulting in misstated financial statements.	Total input documents (e.g., number of documents, dollar amounts) and reconcile journals and ledgers.
		Establish processing and recording procedures.
		Establish validation procedures to verify postings (e.g., check digits).
• Purchases and cash disbursements transactions should be posted accurately to individual vendor accounts.	Summaries of detailed records may not agree with control accounts.	Batch and reconcile input totals to processed and output controls.
	Transactions may be posted to improper vendor accounts, potentially resulting in improper payments.	Promptly investigate correspondence from vendors (e.g., collection notices).
Access to Assets		
• Access to purchasing and cash disbursement records and to forms and documents should be restricted to personnel authorized by management.	Records, forms, or documents may be misused by unauthorized personnel, potentially resulting in misstated payables or diversion for personal use.	Establish physical controls over unused forms and documents.
		Segregate responsibilities for authorization, execution, and recording functions.
		Maintain listings and samples of authorized signatories.

should be initiated by user departments and approved by authorized supervisors. Goods or services should not be ordered in the absence of authorized purchase requisitions. Required authorization procedures vary with the cost or nature of the goods or services requested, but should be specified in writing.

Vendors should be approved by management before Purchasing executes an order. For example, many companies prepare lists of authorized vendors and establish criteria for adding to, changing, or deleting from the list. Otherwise, purchases could be made from vendors whose product quality is repeatedly inferior, from related parties without management's knowledge, or from foreign vendors in violation of regulated import quotas.

In addition to authorizing vendor lists, management should also establish policies for the types, quantities, payment terms, and prices of goods and services purchased. Failure to establish the types of goods and services authorized for purchase could result in reduced earnings caused by write-downs of unusable or unsalable inventory, or unnecessary purchases made for the benefit of employees or related parties. In turn, authorizing quantities, payment terms, and prices protects against excessive warehousing costs for unnecessary inventory, unfavorable payment terms, and noncompetitive prices. As a result, management should maintain current price lists and actively seek suppliers whose goods and services optimize price and quality. Where applicable, competitive bids or formal price quotations should be obtained from suppliers, particularly for purchases involving high-priced items, large quantities, or infrequently ordered items.

Transaction Execution

Goods should be inspected for quality when received, and quantities should be verified by physical count and compared with purchase orders. If not inspected, counted, and compared, a company risks production delays while returning damaged or unordered goods and awaiting delivery of the goods ordered. To avoid delays, management should require that Receiving personnel inspect and count all received goods before releasing the carrier.

After goods or services are received, a liability is incurred and, in turn, cash is disbursed. Management should institute policies to assure that cash is disbursed only for bona fide liabilities, thereby protecting against disbursements for goods not received, payment to unauthorized parties, and duplicate payments. To control against improper disbursements, management could prenumber and control vouchers and checks, require a second manual signature for checks exceeding prespecified amounts, and cancel paid voucher packages immediately upon payment.

Recording

After purchase transactions are executed, all goods and services received should be reported promptly to Accounts Payable, indicating title has passed, and to Purchasing, indicating ordered goods have been received. Otherwise, goods and services may be received and used, but not recorded, thereby understating inventory and liabilities. Many companies control the receipt of goods and services by prenumbering receiving reports, reviewing for prompt recording, and maintaining a receiving log that lists sequentially each receiving report processed.

To protect against inaccurate account balances and therefore against misstated financial statements, management should institute policies to assure that all purchases and cash disbursements are recorded properly and in the proper period.

Management could control the recording function by preparing input totals, by reconciling journals and subsidiary ledgers, and by establishing procedures for processing and recording.

However, proper recording within general ledger control accounts does not necessarily mean that transactions are posted properly to individual vendor subsidiary accounts, since summaries of detailed records may not agree with control accounts. To control against inaccurate vendor accounts, management could establish validation procedures to verify postings, and reconcile input totals to processed and output totals. In addition, authorized personnel should investigate correspondence from vendors, particularly collection notices.

Access to Assets

Management should establish procedures to safeguard assets by restricting access to purchasing and cash disbursement records and forms. Otherwise, records or forms may be misused by unauthorized personnel, potentially resulting in misstated payables or diversion of cash or other assets for personal use. Many companies control access to purchasing and cash disbursements by prenumbering and controlling forms and documents; maintaining lists and samples of authorized signatories; and segregating responsibility for authorizing, executing, and recording.

Assessing Control Risk and Auditing Internal Control Over Financial Reporting

As introduced in Chapter 6 and illustrated for the revenue/receipt cycle in Chapter 9, considering internal control involves obtaining an understanding of the system, performing tests of controls, and assessing control risk. The following addresses an auditor's consideration of internal control within the expenditure/disbursement cycle, focusing on purchasing, receiving, cash disbursements, and recording.

Obtain an Understanding

Obtaining an understanding of internal control is a means to an end—the end being an audit plan and, in the case of a public company, to report on internal controls over financial reporting—and addresses these questions: How is the system supposed to work, and what control activities has management implemented to assure that the system does indeed work? Apart from evaluating the audit committee's effectiveness and obtaining an understanding of information technology and reviewing *Sarbanes-Oxley*, Section 404, documentation (Chapter 8), an auditor obtains an understanding of internal control by:

1. Performing a *review of Section 404* or other *documentation,*
2. *Documenting* the system,
3. Performing *transaction walkthroughs,* and
4. Determining whether existing control activities are potentially reliable in assessing *control risk* below the maximum.

Review *Sarbanes-Oxley* Section 404 or Other Documentation

An auditor begins for a public company by reviewing the *Sarbanes-Oxley* Section 404 documentation management prepared to memorialize the process for assessing the effectiveness of internal control over financial reporting. The auditor develops a general understanding of the control environment; the control activities; and how the entity identifies, captures, communicates, and monitors external and internal information in a form and time frame that enables employees to discharge their assigned responsibilities. The auditor reviews the client's documentation and interviews employees in Purchasing, Receiving, Accounts Payable, and Cash Disbursements—the departments introduced earlier and illustrated in Figure 12-2. A public company's Section 404 documentation typically adds detail related to each of the columns depicted in Figure 12-2 and, for that matter, to activities not apparent from Figure 12-2. For example, Figure 12-5 illustrates an abbreviated form of the Section 404 documentation that memorializes the preparation of a month-end accrual for promotion expenses a manufacturer pays to retailers for expenses the retailer incurs to promote the manufacturer's product, called in Chapter 10 "trade promotion" or "trade spending." Notice that the documentation

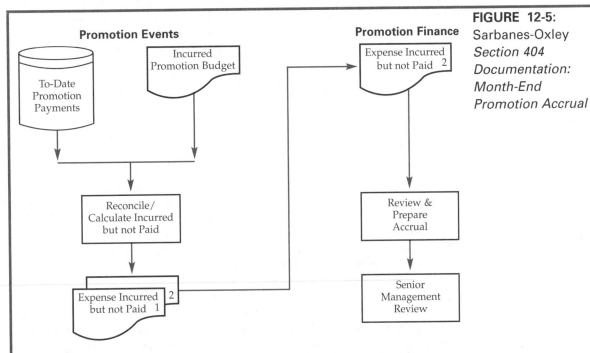

FIGURE 12-5:
Sarbanes-Oxley
*Section 404
Documentation:
Month-End
Promotion Accrual*

Month-End Promotion Accrual Process
At month end, management records a promotion accrual for promotion expenses retailers have incurred but not paid. Promotion Events reconciles retailers' incurred promotion expenses to promotion payments made to date and calculates amounts incurred but not paid. Promotion Finance reviews amounts incurred but not paid and prepares a month-end accrual that senior management reviews.

Controls
● Promotion Events reconciles promotion payments to budgeted promotion estimates.
● Promotion Finance reviews amounts incurred but not paid and prepares month-end promotion accrual.
● Senior management reviews accrual.

includes a flowchart, a brief explanation of the month-end accrual procedures, and a list of controls management implemented over financial reporting.

As explained in Chapter 10, the management of a nonpublic entity may not have documented internal control in any way near the detail that a public company would to comply with *Sarbanes-Oxley*. For a nonpublic entity, the auditor performs a preliminary review by interviewing client personnel—for example, the purchasing manager, receiving clerk, and accounts payable department manager—and reviewing accounting procedures manuals to develop a general understanding of the client's control environment; accounting system (for example, the flow of purchase and payment transactions); and how the entity identifies, captures, communicates, and monitors external and internal information in a form and time frame that enables employees to discharge their assigned responsibilities. The preliminary review determines whether investing additional audit effort—for example, documenting and performing tests of controls—is likely to support a decision to assess control risk below the maximum, thereby allowing the auditor to assess detection risk above the minimum and therefore to restrict the extent of substantive tests for the very account balances that are processed through the expenditure/disbursement cycle: Accounts Payable, Prepaid Expenses, and Accrued Liabilities. If the preliminary review reveals that existing controls are inadequate to justify assessing control risk below the maximum, then the auditor's documentation of the system is limited simply to a memorandum in the working papers that describes the reasons for not continuing to consider internal control.

System Documentation

A company's expenditure/disbursement cycle can be documented with flowcharts, questionnaires, and/or narratives. For example, Figure 12-2, discussed earlier, illustrates a flowchart for purchases and cash disbursements. In turn, Figure 12-6 illustrates a questionnaire for purchasing, receiving, accounts payable, and cash disbursements. As in Chapter 10, the questionnaire is designed to elicit a *No* response when a potential deficiency is apparent. That is, a *No* response would indicate a commonly used control is not used and therefore that, lacking compensating controls, a significant deficiency might exist. Alternatively, or in conjunction with a flowchart and/or questionnaire, an auditor could describe the system—or segments of the system—in a written narrative. For example, a narrative could be used to describe the distribution of documents and reports outside of the dominant areas of concern—that is, outside of purchasing, receiving, accounts payable, and cash disbursements.

FIGURE 12-6: *Questionnaire: Purchases and Cash Disbursements*

Question	*Answer: Yes, No, or N/A*	*Remarks*
Purchasing:		
1. Are policies and procedures for reviewing and processing purchase requisitions clearly defined?		
2. Are prenumbered purchase orders prepared for all approved purchase requisitions?		

FIGURE 12-6 *(continued)*

Question	Answer: Yes, No, or N/A	Remarks

3. Are competitive bids or price quotations obtained for purchased goods and services?
4. Are price lists maintained for repetitive transactions that do not require competitive bids or price quotations?
5. Are purchase transactions reviewed periodically by personnel independent of Purchasing?
6. Are copies of purchase orders forwarded to the requisitioning department and to Receiving and Accounts Payable?
7. Are lists of previously authorized vendors maintained by Purchasing?

Receiving:
1. Are prenumbered receiving reports prepared for all goods received?
2. Is a receiving log maintained for all receiving reports processed?
3. Are all received goods inspected, counted, and compared with copies of purchase orders?
4. Are Receiving personnel independent of Purchasing, Accounts Payable, and Cash Disbursements?

Cash Disbursement and Recording:
1. Are voucher packages reviewed before being approved for payment?
2. Are steps taken to assure that unfamiliar payees (vendors) are bona fide?
3. Are voucher packages and checks reviewed by signatories before they sign checks (or before submitting vouchers for check preparation)?
4. Are voucher packages canceled when or immediately after checks are signed?
5. Are signed checks delivered directly to the mailroom without intervention by other personnel?
6. Are Cash Disbursements personnel (for example, Treasury department) independent of Purchasing, Receiving, and Accounts Payable?
7. Is account distribution indicated on the purchase requisition by the requisitioning department?
8. Are vouchers prepared from requisitions and purchase orders received from Purchasing, from receiving reports received from Receiving, and from invoices received from the mailroom?
9. Are daily summaries of processed vouchers forwarded by Accounts Payable to General Accounting for summary entries?

Transaction Walkthroughs

To confirm his or her understanding of the system flowcharted in Figure 12-2, and to comply with responsibilities the PCAOB imposed for public company audits (Chapter 8), the auditor could select canceled voucher packages and compare the related purchase requisitions, purchase orders, receiving reports, and invoices for compliance with company policies and with documents filed in Purchasing, Receiving, and Accounts Payable. System documentation—for example, the flowchart—would be revised if transaction walkthroughs reveal that the auditor's understanding of internal control is inaccurate.

Identification of Control Activities

Following system documentation, and assuming that controls are potentially reliable in assessing control risk below the maximum, an auditor continues as follows:

- Identify the system's *control objectives*. The first column of Figure 12-4 identifies control objectives for purchases and cash disbursements transactions.
- Consider the *potential errors or frauds* that might result if specific control objectives are not met. The second column of Figure 12-4 identifies examples of potential errors or frauds.
- Determine what *control activities* management uses to prevent or detect potentially material errors or frauds. The third column of Figure 12-4 identifies examples of potential controls.
- Design *tests of controls*.

Those control activities relevant to management's financial statement assertions about accounts payable, prepaid expenses, and accrued liabilities are subjected to tests of controls, described next.

Tests of Controls: Purchasing and Cash Disbursements

In tests of controls over high-volume transactions like purchases and cash disbursements, an auditor's strategy is to expend significant audit effort testing controls, since evidence supporting the assessment of control risk below the maximum would justify restricting substantive tests of account balances at year end and would bear on the auditor's responsibility to report for a public company on management's assessment of internal control. Tests for the purchasing, receiving, and cash disbursement system flowcharted in Figure 12-2 are presented in the following sections. Later in the chapter, a case illustrates how an auditor can use sampling to accomplish tests of controls over cash collections.

Purchasing

Given the significant resources often expended for goods and services, purchases made at anything other than competitive and authorized prices can spell the difference between successful and unsuccessful enterprises. Tests of controls of an entity's purchasing activities focus on whether all purchases are properly authorized. Representative tests follow.

> **Tests of Controls: Purchasing**
> 1. Randomly select a sample of paid voucher packages.
>   a. Review each voucher package for cancellation (for example, perforation).
>   b. Review documents in each sampled voucher package for authorization.

> c. Compare details on purchase requisitions, purchase orders, receiving reports, vendors' invoices, and vouchers and verify mathematical accuracy.
> 2. For each sampled voucher package, obtain a copy of the related purchase order and requisition from Purchasing department files.
>   a. Compare purchase orders in voucher packages with copies of purchase orders in Purchasing department files.
>   b. Trace prices on purchase orders to competitive bids, formal price quotations, or other pricing sources.
>   c. Examine periodic reports by personnel independent of the Purchasing department about prices and vendor selection practices.

A paid voucher package is the primary source from which the tests of purchasing are performed. In Step 1a, the auditor tests whether paid voucher packages are canceled, thereby addressing whether duplicate payments could occur. However, the test does not assure that cancellation occurred simultaneously with (or immediately after) payment—only direct observation by the auditor could assess whether the time span between payment and cancellation is reasonable.

Step 1b addresses transaction authorization and requires that the auditor examine signatures or initials on the (1) purchase order, indicating an authorized transaction; (2) receiving report, indicating responsibility for incoming goods; and (3) voucher, indicating a cash payment was authorized. In Step 1c, the auditor tests whether all documents agree and, therefore, that goods were received and paid for at the price quoted and in the quantity ordered.

In Step 2a, the auditor compares sampled voucher packages with copies of purchase orders and requisitions filed in the Purchasing department, as shown in Figure 12-2. Here the intent is to determine if all paid vouchers resulted from authorized purchases. Steps 2b and 2c, in contrast, address whether the prices paid are competitive. That is, evidence of competitive bids or price quotations would suggest management is conscientiously attempting to safeguard assets—in particular, cash—by seeking the best prices available.

Receiving

The receipt of goods is the first step in readying inventory for conversion and in recognizing a liability. Since little can be done after the fact to determine if receiving procedures are applied appropriately, an auditor could consider visiting the Receiving department on a surprise basis, determining whether received goods are conscientiously counted and compared with purchase orders. Some additional tests follow.

> **Tests of Controls: Receiving**
> For each sampled voucher package, obtain the related copy of the receiving report from Receiving department files.
>
> 1. Compare receiving reports in voucher packages with copies of receiving reports in Receiving department files.
> 2. Review receiving reports for evidence that received goods have been inspected, counted, and compared with packing slips and purchase orders.
> 3. Trace receiving reports to entries in the receiving log.

In addition to observing the Receiving department on a surprise basis, an auditor can design tests that address whether goods received per the voucher packages used to test purchasing controls agree with Receiving department files, such as the copy of the receiving report filed in Receiving and the receiving log (a chronological listing of goods received). In Step 1, the auditor compares the receiving report in Accounts Payable with the copy filed in Receiving and tests whether the copy used by Accounts Payable to prepare a voucher is in error. Step 2 addresses the accuracy of quantities received by examining evidence that received goods are inspected, counted, and agreed with a packing slip, the vendor's list of goods shipped that is normally found on or within a shipped carton. In Step 3, the auditor tests further for discrepancies in reported quantities by comparing receiving reports to entries in the company's receiving log.

Cash Disbursement and Recording

Cash payment activities are particularly susceptible to frauds, because cash is liquid and only an unauthorized payee and forged endorsement are necessary to misappropriate funds. An auditor's tests of controls over payments to vendors focus on approvals for payment, proper journal entries and, to the extent possible, the authenticity of signatures.

The recording function for purchases and cash disbursements encompasses entries to accounts payable, requiring that an auditor determine whether details recorded within a voucher register are recorded in the proper vendor accounts and agree in total with the general ledger. Representative tests follow.

Tests of Controls: Cash Disbursement and Recording

For each sampled voucher package, obtain the canceled check.

1. Examine canceled checks for signatures and endorsements.
2. Compare details of the voucher package with the canceled check: check number, date, payee, and amount.
3. Trace voucher packages and canceled checks to postings in accounts payable and to entries in the voucher register.
   a. Review entries in the voucher register for appropriate account distribution (classification).
   b. Verify the mathematical accuracy of the voucher register for selected periods and trace totals to entries in the general ledger.
   c. Scan the voucher register for unusual items (for example, unfamiliar vendor names) and unusually large amounts, and investigate any items identified.

The tests discussed thus far address whether purchases are authorized, executed, and recorded properly. But they ignore the possibility that authorized transactions might be executed with unauthorized or fictitious vendors. Thus the tests for cash disbursement and recording focus on canceled checks, the primary evidence that vendors were paid and bona fide.

In Step 1, the auditor examines the signatures and endorsements on canceled checks, looking specifically for unusual items. For example, a manually signed check would be unusual for a company that normally processes disbursements by computer. On one hand, the check might have been for an amount exceeding limits authorized, thereby legitimately requiring manual signatures. On the other hand, the manual signature might indicate a fraud.

Step 2 compares details of the canceled check with the related voucher package, thereby assuring that the amount paid was the amount owed. In Step 3, the auditor traces the voucher package to entries in accounts payable and in the voucher register. The entries are tested for appropriate account distribution, such as expense classification for financial reporting and tax purposes, and the voucher register is tested for mathematical accuracy and unusual items.

Assess Control Risk

To complete the consideration of internal control within the expenditure/disbursement cycle, an auditor reviews system documentation and the results of tests of controls and determines whether existing controls can be relied on to:

1. Assess control risk below the maximum,
2. Assess detection risk above the minimum, and, therefore,
3. Restrict substantive tests.

The assessment of control risk is made for the financial statement assertions (Chapter 4) embodied within the expenditure/disbursement cycle's related account balances (accounts payable, prepaid expenses, and accrued liabilities), transaction classes (purchases and cash disbursements), and financial statement disclosures. In general, the assessment is based on the types of errors or frauds that could occur, necessary control activities that should prevent the errors or frauds, whether the necessary procedures exist and are followed, and any deficiencies in internal control.

To illustrate, consider in Figure 12-4 (first column) the first objective for transaction authorization,

Objective:
   • *Vendors should be approved prior to purchasing goods.*

and the first corresponding control activity (third column) for that objective:

Control activity:
   • *Prepare lists of authorized vendors.*

Step 3c of the tests of controls for Cash Disbursement and Recording tests whether the control activity for approving vendors in Figure 12-4 is operating effectively:

Test of control:
   • *Scan the voucher register for unusual items (for example, unfamiliar vendor names) and unusually large amounts, and investigate any items identified.*

Assume the auditor examines the voucher register for unfamiliar vendors and large amounts and discovers that an intolerable number of purchase transactions are made with unauthorized vendors. In this case, the auditor would conclude that control risk for the assertion *obligations* is at the maximum, because accounts payable may include liabilities for purchases not rightfully owed by the entity. For example, an employee who commits an employer's resources to purchase goods for his or her personal benefit is a liability of the employee, not the entity. Substantive tests applicable to the expenditure/disbursement cycle in general and to accounts payable in particular are introduced in Chapter 13.

Form a Preliminary Opinion on Management's Assessment of Internal Control Over Financial Reporting

Under the *Sarbanes-Oxley Act* (Section 404) and PCAOB *Auditing Standard No. 2,* "An Audit of Internal Control Over Financial Reporting," an auditor of a public company is obligated to form an opinion on management's assessment of internal control over financial reporting as of the end of the fiscal year (Chapter 8). The opinion is based partly on tests of controls, particularly those focused on financial reporting. Consider, for example, tests of controls an auditor might perform for the month-end promotion accrual process illustrated at Figure 12-5.

To control the month-end accrual for trade promotion expense incurred but not yet paid, the system illustrated at Figure 12-5 involves two departments: Promotion Events and Promotion Finance. Promotion Events reconciles to-date promotion payments with the approved and incurred promotion expenses. The difference—that is, the amount by which incurred promotion expenses exceeds payments to date—represents the liability for incurred but not paid expenses. In turn, Promotion Finance reviews the difference and prepares a month-end accrual that senior management approves. The auditor's tests translate to three critical questions:

- Does Promotion Events reconcile promotion payments to incurred promotion expenses?
- Does Promotion Finance review amounts incurred but not paid and prepare the month-end promotion accrual?
- Does senior management review the accrual?

Representative tests follow.

Tests of Controls: Month-End Promotion Accrual
1. Review reconciliation of to-date promotion payments to incurred promotion expenses; test calculation of incurred but not paid expenses.
2. Review accrual.
3. Search for post-period-end payments for evidence of unrecorded promotions.

In Step 1, the auditor reviews in detail Promotion Events' reconciliation, matching particularly the incurred promotion expenses and the to-date payments for a selection of trade promotions. For example, a manufacturer may have authorized funds to reimburse a retailer for promoting the manufacturer's product to consumers—say, for example, $5,000 to pay for media advertising or product displays. At issue is Promotion Event's reconciliation between the amount the retailer incurred and the amount the manufacturer reimbursed the retailer. The excess is the amount incurred but not paid at the end of the month—that is, the month-end accrual. In Step 2, the auditor reviews the accrual for incurred but not paid expenses across retailers on all promotions. In Step 3, the auditor searches payments made after month end for evidence of payments for promotion programs that were not recorded among the incurred promotion expenses, since unrecorded programs would understate the month-end accrual.

➢ restatement

Promotion accruals are an important part of a manufacturer's financial reporting, since FASB *Emerging Issues Task Force (EITF) No. 01-09*, "Accounting for Consideration Given by a Vendor to a Customer," requires that *total promotion expenses* be reflected as a reduction from sales, not as a cost or operating expense, thereby systematically reducing a manufacturer's reported revenue by the amount paid for promotions. In some companies, promotion expenses are staggering. For example, following enactment of *EITF No. 01-09*, DelMonte Foods, The Gillette Company, and PepsiCo restated financial statements for promotion expenses that approximated $55, $142, and $630 million.[1] More revealing, PepsiCo's restated total revenue declined from $5,330 million to $4,700 million, demonstrating that promotion expenses approximated 12 percent of total revenue. These companies had not manipulated trade promotions, but others had. Consider, for example, Aurora Foods, a producer and marketer of branded foods that include Duncan Hines, Mrs. Butterworth's, Log Cabin, and Van Kamp.

During the 1999 audit, PricewaterhouseCoopers, having discovered troubling trade promotion documents, notified the audit committee of the board of directors, which initiated a special investigation headed by Ropes & Gray, a law firm, and Deloitte & Touche. The investigators discovered that senior management had directed mid-level managers to make inadequate accruals and to misdirect the company's auditors, resulting in materially misstated trade-promotion liabilities that drove in part restated 1998 and 1999 financial statements and, for that matter, over a dozen class action complaints the company and management settled in 2001.[2] In 2001, Aurora Foods' former chief executive officer (CEO) admitted in court that he had deceived investors. While brief, the CEO's testimony was telling: "You stood silent when it was not disclosed," the U.S. District Judge asked. "I did, your honor," the former CEO replied.[3]

> fraud
> restatement
> earnings management

Although *EITF No. 01-09* addressed accounting by the *payor* of promotion expenses (for example, payments by companies like Aurora Foods), the recent press has reported accounting abuse by the *payees*—the retailers that receive manufacturers' promotion fees. Consider, for example, U.S. Foodservice, the second largest food distributor in the United States.

In 2000, Dutch Royal Ahold NV, the world's third largest retailer, acquired U.S. Foodservice, adding to U.S food industry investments that included Bi-Lo, Stop & Shop, and Giant Food. Much like grocery retailers, such as Safeway and Kroger, U.S. Foodservice entered into annual promotion contracts with food manufacturers and suppliers, including Kraft Foods, Kellogg, and General Mills. However, rather than spread anticipated promotion funds over the entire year as earned, U.S. Foodservice instead booked some of the anticipated funds as revenue immediately. Following an internal investigation, Ahold announced in early 2003 that U.S Foodservice's accounting for trade promotion drove an $880 million fraud Ahold's interim chief financial officer said was engineered by the subsidiary's chief marketing officer and executive vice president for purchasing, allegedly to increase their incentive compensation.[4] One month later, SEC Commissioner Paul S. Atkins, in an interesting twist, observed that financial fraud was not restricted to businesses controlled by U.S. companies:

> fraud
> restatement
> earnings management

Much of the attention has focused on failures of U.S. corporations, such as, of course, Enron, WorldCom, Global Crossing, and now HealthSouth. Yet, U.S. investors are not alone in experiencing recent profound failures, some of which were caused by questionable accounting practices, bad management, and poor internal controls. Names like . . . Royal Ahold . . . come to mind. . . . It is not an issue unique to the U.S. . . .[5]

1 J. Steinberg, "Accounting Changes for Sales Incentives Causes Restatements," *The CPA Journal* (June 2003), pp. 34–38.
2 *SEC Accounting and Auditing Enforcement Release No. 1361, SEC v. Aurora Foods*, January 23, 2001.
3 "Former CEO of Aurora Admits Guilt," *The Washington Post* (September 5, 2001), p. E5.
4 R. J. McCartney and B. A. Masters, "Ahold Raises Discrepancy to $880 Million," *The Washington Post* (May 9, 2003), p. E1.
5 Paul S. Atkins, "The Sarbanes-Oxley Act of 2002: Goals, Content, and Status of Implementation." Speech by the SEC Commissioner at AICPA National Conference on SEC Developments, March 25, 2003.

Evidence that controls over the month-end promotion accrual are ineffective—for example, if Steps 2 or 3 reveal that Promotion Finance or senior management, respectively, do not review the accrual—would cause the auditor to judge whether the ineffectiveness suggests a control that does not allow management to prevent or detect misstatements in the normal course of business (a deficiency?). If so, is the ineffectiveness more than remotely likely to cause a more than inconsequential misstatement (significant deficiency) or, worse, a *material* misstatement (material weakness in internal control)? As discussed in Chapter 8, a single material weakness that is not corrected completely by the last day of the fiscal year would cause the auditor to reach an adverse opinion about management's internal controls over financial reporting.

Computer Auditing and Sampling Applied to Tests of Controls Over Cash Disbursements

To illustrate the material introduced in this chapter and to integrate the material presented on computer information systems (Chapter 8) and audit sampling (Chapter 9), assume a continuing audit engagement for Gorham Corporation, a medium-size manufacturer of paper products whose fiscal year ends June 30. The specific objective in this case is to determine whether Gorham's controls over cash disbursements are effective.

Computer System: Accounts Payable, Data Entry, and Computer Processing

For the past two years, Gorham has used the accounts payable, data entry, and computer processing system flowcharted in Figure 12-7. Data entry and processing are accomplished by computer. The vouchers and batched totals are entered at workstations connected by a local area network (LAN). Consistent with the cash disbursements functions depicted in Figure 12-2, input data are sorted and edited, checks and the voucher register are printed, and all processed files are updated.

Consideration of Internal Control

The following sections discuss the review of the system, tests of controls, and control risk for Gorham Corporation's payables and disbursements.

Understanding the System

The auditor decides to document the system with both a flowchart and a questionnaire. The flowchart appears in Figure 12-7, and transaction walkthroughs indicate that the flowchart is accurate. The questionnaire consists of the nine disbursement and recording questions listed in Figure 12-6. Questions 1, 3, 5, 6, 8, and 9 result in *Yes* responses, but questions 2, 4, and 7 receive *No* responses, indicating the following deficiencies:

- No procedures exist to assure that unfamiliar payees are bona fide.
- Voucher packages are not canceled when, or immediately after, checks are signed.
- Account distribution is not indicated on the purchase requisition by the requisitioning department.

FIGURE 12-7: *Gorham Corporation: Flowchart of Accounts Payable, Data Entry, and Computer Processing*

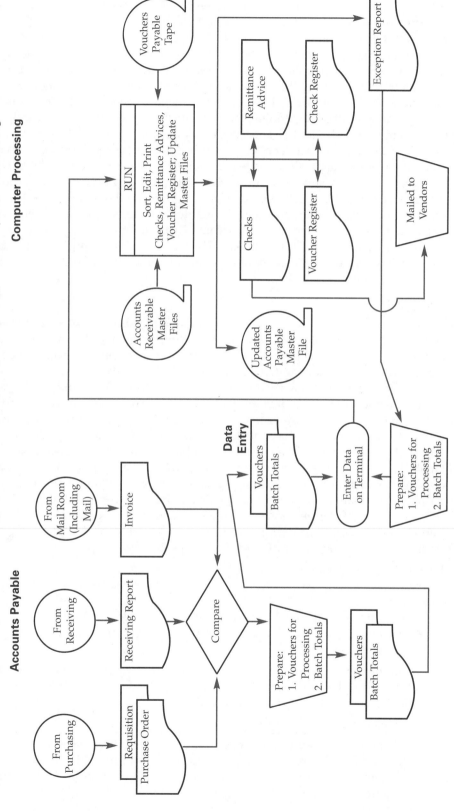

Although significant, the auditor believes no one or combination of these deficiencies is sufficient to render the system wholly ineffective. In this case, the auditor reaches this conclusion for three reasons: First, even though no steps are taken to assure that unfamiliar payees are bona fide, inspection of the check register indicates that vendors unfamiliar to the auditor accounted for less than 1 percent of the cash payments during the year. Thus payments to unfamiliar vendors are immaterial and therefore of little audit consequence. Second, although voucher packages are not canceled simultaneously when (or immediately after) checks are signed, inquiries indicate they are canceled by Accounts Payable personnel at the end of the day that the checks are prepared. To assure that cancellation does in fact occur at day's end, the auditor visited Accounts Payable unannounced at the end of two successive business days, observed the cancellation process, and noted no discrepancies or deficiencies. Because checks are prepared only once per day and cancellation occurs on the same day, the auditor concluded that the likelihood of duplicate payment is remote. Third, account distribution is not indicated by the requisitioning department but is indicated by the Accounts Payable department in consultation with the requisitioning department, which the auditor believes is a sufficient compensating control.

Tests of Controls

Because all checks are prepared by computer and payables are processed manually, the auditor elects the following strategy for testing controls. Parallel simulation, which requires that the auditor prepare software to process client-prepared input under controlled conditions (Chapter 8), will be used to test the effectiveness of controls over data entry and computer processing. To accomplish parallel simulation, the auditor prepares software that focuses on code verification and selected data conversion controls: batch totals, character validity, limit tests, and sequence tests. All of these tests relate to input controls, which are of particular concern in this case because data entry is accomplished on remote workstations (see Figure 12-7), which are susceptible to frauds if unauthorized personnel gain access to user identification numbers. Assume that parallel simulation is accomplished on Gorham's computer and that no significant exceptions are found.

Given the deficiencies noted per the questionnaire, three types of errors or frauds could occur. The first two appear at the fourth objective of Figure 12-4 (middle column), and the third at the sixth objective:

Potential Errors or Frauds:
- *Cash could be disbursed to unauthorized parties, potentially resulting in fraudulent payments.*
- *Duplicate payments could be made, potentially resulting in misspent cash.*
- *Account balances may be inaccurate, potentially resulting in misstated financial statements.*

After considering the potential errors or frauds and other evidence gathered during interim tests, the auditor drafts the following tests for cash disbursement and recording, all of which were explained earlier in the chapter.

Step	Tests of Controls
	For each sampled voucher package, obtain the canceled check.
1.	Examine canceled checks for appropriate signatures and endorsements.
2.	Compare details of the voucher package with the canceled check: check number, date, payee, and amount.

3. Trace voucher packages and canceled checks to postings in the accounts payable subsidiary ledger and to entries in the voucher register.
    a. Review entries in the voucher register for appropriate distribution (classification).
    b. Verify the accuracy of the voucher register (foot and cross-foot) for selected periods, and trace totals to entries in the general ledger.
    c. Scan the voucher register for unusual items (such as unfamiliar vendor names) and unusually large amounts, and investigate any items identified.

As discussed in Chapter 9, the auditor next determines which, if any, tests can be accomplished by sampling and whether to use statistical or nonstatistical sampling. For Gorham Corporation's cash disbursements system, Steps 1, 2, and 3a can be accomplished with sampling. Further, the auditor decides to use statistical sampling, because the system processes very large numbers of checks (that is, large population sizes). Because interim tests of controls in prior years revealed very few errors, the auditor selects sequential (stop-or-go) sampling as the statistical sampling plan. The results of the sequential sampling plan are summarized in Figure 12-8, a sequential sampling worksheet, and Figure 12-9, an analysis of deviations.

Two observations about Figure 12-8: First, note that for attribute 2 the achieved probability, 80.54 percent, is *less* than desired reliability, 95.0 percent, suggesting the auditor should increase sample size—that is, the auditor should go on with the sequential sampling plan for attribute 2. However, note that in the explanation in Figure 12-8 and the analysis of deviations in Figure 12-9, the deviation resulted from an oversight by the payee's employees. As a result, the auditor does not believe that Gorham's failure to investigate the matter is sufficiently compelling to warrant increasing sample size. Second, even though attribute 5 resulted in one deviation, the achieved probability from Figure 9-9, 91.73 percent, exceeds desired reliability, 90.0 percent. As a result, the auditor does not need to increase sample size. Steps 3b and 3c are performed by the auditor, and no exceptions are noted.

Control Risk

The auditor's assessment of control risk for Gorham Corporation's controls over cash disbursements would be based on the following quantitative and qualitative factors:

- No exceptions were noted when parallel simulation was run with actual client data.
- Achieved reliability exceeded desired reliability for four of five attributes tested, and for one attribute, the deviation observed was (1) the result of a vendor's oversight and (2) not deemed sufficiently compelling to warrant additional testing.
- The questionnaire revealed three control deficiencies.

In this case, the auditor's decision would likely be to assess control risk below the maximum for assertions related to controls over cash disbursement and recording, because parallel simulation and audit sampling indicate that the three deficiencies are not likely to produce aggregate error in excess of tolerable error.

FIGURE 12-8: *Sampling Worksheet: Cash Disbursements*

A10
RJW 5/12/07

Gorham Corporation
Sampling Worksheet—Cash Disbursements
June 30, 2007

Attribute	Desired Reliability	Tolerable Rate	Sample Size*	Number of Deviations	Achieved Probability*
1. Signatures on checks are appropriate.	.98	.04	100	0	98.31
2. Endorsements on checks are appropriate.	.95	.03	100	1+	80.54
3. Details of voucher package agree with canceled check.	.95	.05	70	0	97.24
4. Details of voucher tie to entries.	.95	.05	70	0	97.24
5. Account distribution is appropriate.	.90	.08	50	1++	91.73

*   See Figure 9-9.
\+   As noted at A11, failure to endorse was an oversight by Elston employees. Therefore, there is no need to increase sample size.
\++ See analysis of occurrences at A11.

Conclusion
Based upon procedures performed, the achieved probability exceeds desired reliability for 4 of 5 attributes, and the one deviation for attribute 2 resulted from a vendor's oversight.

FIGURE 12-9: *Analysis of Deviations: Cash Disbursements*

A11
RJW 5/12/07

Gorham Corporation
Analysis of Deviations—Cash Disbursements
June 30, 2007

Attribute	Number of Deviations	Nature of Deviations	Effect on Substantive Detailed Testing
2	1	Ck no. 3267, $5,320, Elston Corp. Check was accepted for deposit by Elston's bank, but not endorsed.	No additional audit work is necessary because of alternate procedures (i.e., review of Dun & Bradstreet reports; telephone conversation with Elston Corp. officials indicate failure to endorse was an oversight by Elston employees).
5	1	Ck no. 9861, $2,319, Davis Co. Purchase was charged to travel and entertainment expense rather than advertising expense.	No additional audit work is necessary because (1) achieved probability (91.73) exceeds desired reliability (.90) and (2) the error does not affect income, and neither expense affects overhead in inventory. (The client corrected the error.)

Other Assurance and Consulting Services

Companies purchase goods and services within the boundaries of criteria set by management, and are under no obligation to reveal purchasing patterns publicly. In contrast, state and local governmental units purchase goods and services under the constraint of public scrutiny. Governmental units, such as cities, housing authorities, port authorities, and school boards are bound by procurement laws imposed, for example, by local laws, by taxpayer referendum, or by oversight authorities such as a city council. For example, many governmental units require that purchases over a minimum dollar amount, say $10,000, be opened to competitive bids (if not public hearings) and that the sealed bids be opened at a preannounced public forum. Over the years, governmental units have often engaged public accounting firms to provide either assurance or attestation services that report on management's compliance with local procurement laws. For example, following alleged extortion charges against a New England mayor in the awarding of city contracts, the city council engaged the Boston office of a Big Four firm to report on management's compliance with city procurement laws for publicly funded construction contacts. As discussed and illustrated in Chapter 18, compliance with contractual agreements, among them government regulations, is a common attestation service guided in practice by *SAS No. 62*, "Special Reports."

In practice, purchase and payables consulting services are rather common. Two examples: First, one firm entered into an alliance with Bank of America to promote the bank's corporate MasterCard and to provide purchase consulting services to the bank's corporate card users. Targeted to Bank of America corporate users that had revenues exceeding $75 million and small purchases (typically under $350) exceeding $10 million annually, the firm evaluated the small purchase practices of the bank's corporate card users to identify potential consulting clients in need of substantially more cost-effective purchasing systems. Second, another firm reached an agreement with the national headquarters of Camp Fire Boys & Girls to surrender the financial statement audit in order instead to provide the company with full-time, on-site accounting and information systems services, including payables processing, network and personal computer support, and financial reporting. Camp Fire's national executive director reported that, although the audit fee had been less than $50,000 annually, fees for the outsourcing arrangement would total $300,000 to $400,000 annually.

Similar to Camp Fire's arrangement, many companies have outsourced work previously done internally. Outsourcing is not at all new. For example, companies first outsourced payroll to Automated Data Processing, Inc., in the 1950s and colleges began to outsource cafeteria management to Aramark Corporation in the 1960s. However, outsourcing services are far more common today. For example, a poll reported that 86 percent of some well-known companies such as American Airlines, DuPont, Exxon, Honda, and IBM outsource, and that the most frequently outsourced activities were manufacturing, transportation/distribution/warehousing, temporary services, travel, and forms management. In fact, among the Big Three U.S. automakers, General Motors outsources 30 percent of vehicle production and Ford 50 percent. The outsourcing of technology and information processing has been a boom industry, particularly for niche consultants and public accounting firms, although the benefits accruing to the purchasers of outsourced services can be clouded by some costly downsides over time, among them long-term information services contracts that, owing to cheaper technology prices, may no longer be competitive.

SUMMARY

The expenditure/disbursement cycle encompasses the acquisition of resources from vendors (and employees, Chapter 14) and subsequent payments for resources acquired. Common vendor-related activities include purchasing, receiving, recording, and cash payment. Documents evidencing appropriate transaction authorization and execution typically include purchase requisitions, purchase orders, receiving reports, vendors' invoices, and vouchers. Together these documents form a voucher package that serves as a basis for making payments to vendors.

Cash disbursements should be authorized and executed by personnel independent of the recording function, and access to unused checks and check preparation should be limited to authorized personnel. Tests of controls of an entity's purchasing activities focus on whether purchases and related disbursements are properly authorized, executed, and recorded. Substantive tests of accounts payable, prepaid expenses, and accrued liabilities, three accounts that bear on the expenditure/disbursement cycle, are introduced next, in Chapter 13.

KEY TERMS

Expenditure/disbursement cycle 508
Purchase order 510
Purchase requisition 510

Receiving report 510
Vendor's invoice 510
Voucher package 510

REFERENCES

Professional Standards:

PCAOB Auditing Standard No. 2, "An Audit of Internal Control Over Financial Reporting."
AICPA, *Codification of Statements on Auditing Standards*. New York: AICPA.

Books:

Committee of Sponsoring Organizations of the Treadway Commission (COSO), *Internal Control: Integrated Framework*. Evaluation Tools. New York: COSO, 1992.

Committee of Sponsoring Organizations of the Treadway Commission (COSO), *Internal Control: Integrated Framework*. Executive Summary. New York: COSO, 1992.

Committee of Sponsoring Organizations of the Treadway Commission (COSO), *Internal Control: Integrated Framework*. Framework. New York: COSO, 1992.

Committee of Sponsoring Organizations of the Treadway Commission (COSO), *Internal Control: Integrated Framework*. Reporting to External Parties. New York: COSO, 1992.

QUESTIONS

1. Identify the major business functions and activities common to the expenditure/disbursement cycle.
2. Describe the major documents associated with the expenditure/disbursement cycle.
3. Why should policies assure that goods and services are purchased only from approved vendors?
4. Who should authorize and execute cash disbursements?
5. How can management control against unauthorized or duplicate cash payments?
6. How and why does management restrict access to assets in the expenditure/receipt cycle?
7. How can companies approve vendors before Purchasing executes an order?
8. What is a remittance advice?
9. Proper recording within general ledger control accounts does not necessarily mean that transactions are posted accurately to individual vendor accounts. What controls can management institute to assure that detailed records agree with control accounts?

10. Why should the Receiving department be segregated from inventory control and, if possible, from shipping?
11. In the audit of a nonpublic company, how does an auditor perform a preliminary review of internal control over purchases and cash disbursements transactions?
12. Explain how an auditor could perform "transaction walkthroughs" for purchases and cash disbursements.
13. Why do auditors not usually rely on substantive tests alone when auditing accounts payable that result from credit purchase transactions?
14. What is the primary focus of an auditor's tests of controls over purchasing?
15. How does an auditor test whether purchase transactions are authorized in accordance with management's prespecified criteria?
16. Explain the primary focus of an auditor's tests of cash disbursements to vendors.
17. As a normal part of tests of controls for cash disbursements, an auditor examines signatures and endorsements on canceled checks, if they're available, looking specifically for unusual items. Give two examples of unusual items an auditor might confront.
18. What is a trade promotion accrual?
19. How does FASB *Emerging Issues Task Force No. 01-09*, "Accounting for Consideration Given by a Vendor to a Customer," bear on financial reporting?
20. Explain the key issues an auditor addresses when testing management's control over a promotion accrual.

MULTIPLE CHOICE QUESTIONS

1. Which of the following functions is not common to the expenditure/disbursement cycle?
   a. Resources are acquired from vendors in exchange for obligations to pay.
   b. Obligations to vendors are paid.
   c. Resources are held, used, or transformed.
   d. Resources are acquired from employees in exchange for obligations to pay.

2. The expenditure/disbursement cycle begins with requisitions from user departments and ends with the receipt of materials and the recognition of a liability. An auditor's primary objective in reviewing the cycle is to:
   a. Obtain an understanding of the client's prescribed policies and procedures sufficient to plan the audit.
   b. Investigate the handling and recording of unusual acquisitions.
   c. Consider the need to increase substantive tests of purchases and accounts payable.
   d. Assure that materials ordered, received, and paid for are actually on hand.

3. Which of the following is not essential for Accounts Payable to process a payment?
   a. Receiving log
   b. Receiving report
   c. Invoice
   d. Purchase order

4. Paid vouchers are canceled to:
   a. Enter evidence of payment.
   b. Affix responsibility for payment.
   c. Prevent duplicate payment.
   d. Destroy payment documents.

5. The Receiving department is responsible to:
   a. Count goods received.
   b. Prepare requisitions.
   c. Review receiving reports.
   d. Approve purchase orders.

6. Purchase orders, receiving reports, and invoices comprise:
   a. The vendor's authorization documents.
   b. Key receiving documents.
   c. Summary payment documents.
   d. A voucher package.

7. A requisition is used typically to request a:
   a. Purchase.
   b. Shipment.
   c. Payment.
   d. Journal entry.

8. Filing purchase orders until goods are received is typically done by:
   a. Purchasing.
   b. Receiving.
   c. Accounts Payable.
   d. Cash Disbursements.

9. Prenumbering receiving reports most likely relates to which of the following internal control objectives?
   a. Disbursements should be made only for bona fide liabilities.
   b. Vendors should be approved before payment.
   c. Goods received should be reported accurately.
   d. Access to purchase records should be posted accurately to vendor accounts.

10. Unnecessarily ordering goods is an error or fraud most closely related to:
    a. Authorization.
    b. Execution.
    c. Recording.
    d. Access to Assets.

11. An auditor's consideration of internal control in a financial statement audit consists of four steps. The auditor begins by identifying control procedures and continues in which of the following orders?
    a. Design tests of controls, determine control procedures management uses, consider errors or frauds that could occur.
    b. Consider errors or frauds that could occur, determine control procedures management uses, design tests of controls.
    c. Determine control procedures management uses, design tests of controls, consider errors or frauds that could occur.
    d. Consider errors or frauds that could occur, design tests of controls, determine control procedures management uses.

12. An auditor documents a system and performs transaction walkthroughs primarily to:
    a. Understand the system.
    b. Assess control risk.
    c. Form an opinion on internal control over financial reporting.
    d. Plan substantive tests.

13. When considering internal controls over purchases and disbursements, the auditor will be influenced least by:

    a. Procedures manuals.
    b. Audit work done by an entity's internal auditors.
    c. Compensating controls that offset deficiencies.
    d. Controls in other cycles.

14. Which of the following is most crucial to a Purchasing department?

    a. Authorizing the acquisition of goods
    b. Assuring the quality of goods acquired
    c. Verifying the propriety of goods acquired
    d. Reducing the cost of goods acquired

15. Which of the following control activities would most likely prevent or detect purchases from unauthorized vendors?

    a. Maintain updated guidelines for purchase transactions.
    b. Establish procedures for reviewing and approving purchase prices and terms prior to purchase.
    c. Require a second manual signature on all checks over a prespecified limit.
    d. Establish criteria for adding to, changing, or deleting from the approved vendor list.

16. An auditor's primary concern when performing tests of controls over purchasing is to determine whether:

    a. Purchases are properly authorized.
    b. Purchases are properly recorded.
    c. Purchase orders agree to purchase requisitions.
    d. Purchasing personnel are performing their assigned functions properly.

17. How can an auditor test to determine whether Receiving department procedures are applied properly?

    a. Test a sample of receiving documents.
    b. Observe receiving procedures on a surprise basis.
    c. Review procedures manuals.
    d. Interview Receiving department personnel.

18. Which of the following control activities could prevent or detect payment of goods not received?

    a. Counting goods when received
    b. Matching the purchase order, receiving report, and vendor's invoice
    c. Comparing goods received with goods requisitioned
    d. Verifying vouchers for accuracy and approval

19. An internal control questionnaire indicates that an approved receiving report accompanies every check request. To test this control, an auditor could select and examine:

    a. Receiving reports and determine that the related canceled checks are dated no earlier than the receiving reports.
    b. Receiving reports and determine that the related canceled checks are dated no later than the receiving reports.
    c. Canceled checks and determine that the related receiving reports are dated no earlier than the checks.
    d. Canceled checks and determine that the related receiving reports are dated no later than the checks.

20. Which of the following would prevent a paid disbursement from being paid a second time?
    a. Individuals responsible for signing checks should prepare vouchers.
    b. Disbursements should be approved by at least two responsible officials.
    c. The disbursement date should be within a few days of the date the voucher is presented for payment.
    d. The official signing the check should cancel the supporting documents.

PROBLEMS AND DISCUSSION CASES

12-1 *Controls Over Purchases and Cash Disbursements*

Assume you are considering a client's controls over purchases and cash disbursements. System documentation was accomplished through flowcharts and narratives and, in conjunction with a transaction walkthrough, revealed the following potential deficiencies:

a. Costs of carrying inventory have increased significantly since the prior year.
b. Purchase prices are sometimes unusually high or fluctuate significantly from month to month.
c. Purchase discounts are frequently not taken.
d. During lunch, the controller commented to you that on two occasions during the year duplicate payments had been made for a single transaction.
e. Cash disbursements records do not always reconcile with general ledger control accounts.

Required: For each potential deficiency, indicate a control or controls that management could implement to reduce the likelihood of errors or frauds.

12-2 *Errors, Fraud, and Control Activities*

During an audit of Dundee Corporation's financial statements, you become aware of the following control activities over purchasing and cash disbursements activities:

1. Purchases are made only from companies that warrant products for workmanship and related damages.
2. Competitive bids are required for all purchases in excess of $12,000.
3. A written memorandum is required for each purchase discount not taken.
4. Receiving reports are prenumbered sequentially and controlled.
5. Voucher packages are canceled immediately after payment.
6. A procedures manual is maintained for all job functions related to processing purchases and cash disbursements transactions.
7. Postings are verified by check digits.

Required: For each control activity indicate (a) a potential error or fraud that the control might prevent or detect and (b) the objective the control serves.

12-3 *Identifying Weaknesses and Inefficiencies in a Purchasing System*

Madeline Jones, Lecimore Company's Purchasing department manager, has established new policies and procedures to guide the day-to-day operations of purchasing agents and clerical staff. She is satisfied that the policies and procedures conform with management's objectives and that there are no major deficiencies either in the department's policies or in the procedures that control the department's operations. Some of the policies and procedures follow.

- All significant purchases are put out to competitive bid, although the likelihood of timely delivery and vendor reliability are considered in awarding contracts.
- Purchasing provides vendors with memoranda detailing minimum acceptable product-quality specifications.

- The Materials, rather than the Purchasing, department manager is responsible for assuring that vendors adhere to quality specifications.
- The Materials department manager prepares purchase requests based on a four-month production schedule.
- Ninety percent of a critical raw material is supplied by a single vendor. The vendor, the low bidder in each of the past few years, has a good delivery record and is quite reliable.
- As production plans change, rush and expedite orders are made directly to the Purchasing department by production managers. Materials ordered for canceled production runs are stored for future use. Although the costs for rush and expedite orders are borne exclusively by the Purchasing department, Jones considers the costs essential to the department's reputation as a contributing team player.
- Materials needed to accomplish engineering changes are ordered by the Purchasing department immediately after the Engineering department approves changes. Jones is proud of the Purchasing department's quick response. Materials on hand are not reviewed before any orders are placed.
- Partial shipments and advance shipments (that is, those received before the requested date of delivery) are accepted by the Materials manager, who notifies the Purchasing department of the receipt. The Purchasing department is responsible for following up on partial shipments. No action is taken to discourage advance shipments.

Required: Identify weaknesses and inefficiencies in Lecimore Company's purchasing policies and procedures, and make recommendations to improve each.

12-4 *Interpreting a Systems Flowchart*

The flowchart on pages 541-542 illustrates a system for executing purchases and cash disbursement transactions.

Required: Indicate what each of the letters *A* through *L* represent in the flowchart. (Do not discuss inadequacies in internal control.)

12-5 *Judging the Adequacy of Control Activities*

Dunbar Camera, Inc., manufactures high-priced motion picture cameras for the movie industry. The component-parts specifications are vital to the film-making process. Dunbar buys valuable camera lenses and large quantities of sheet metal and screws. Vendors bill screws and lenses on a unit basis, and sheet metal on the basis of weight. The receiving clerk is responsible for documenting the quality and quantity of all merchandise received. A preliminary review of internal control indicates the following procedures.

Receiving Report
1. Approved purchase orders are prenumbered and filed numerically. The copy sent to the receiving clerk is an exact duplicate of the copy sent to the vendor. The receiving clerk records the receipt of merchandise on the purchase order copy.

Sheet Metal
2. The company receives sheet metal by rail. The rail company weighs the sheet metal independently, and reports both the weight and receipt date on the bill of lading that accompanies deliveries. The receiving clerk agrees the weight on the bill of lading to the purchase order.

Screws
3. The receiving clerk opens cartons containing screws, and inspects and weighs the contents. The weight is converted to number of units by conversion charts. The receiving clerk then agrees the computed quantity to the purchase order.

PROBLEM 12-4: *Flowchart*

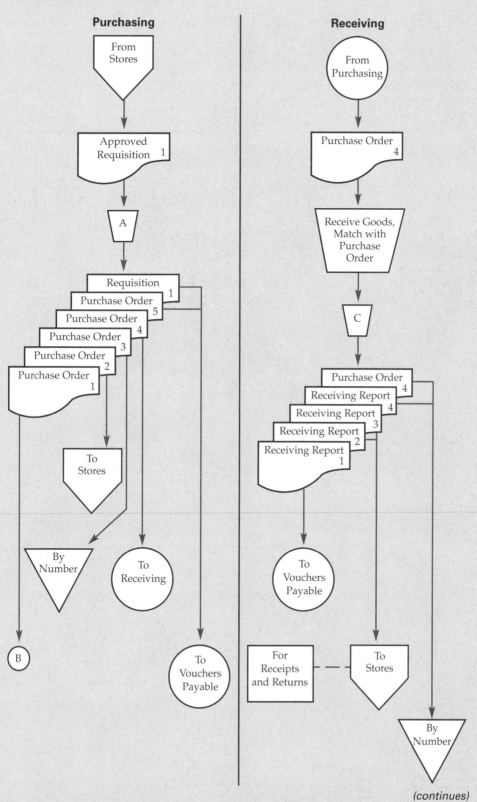

(continues)

PROBLEM 12-4 *(continued)*

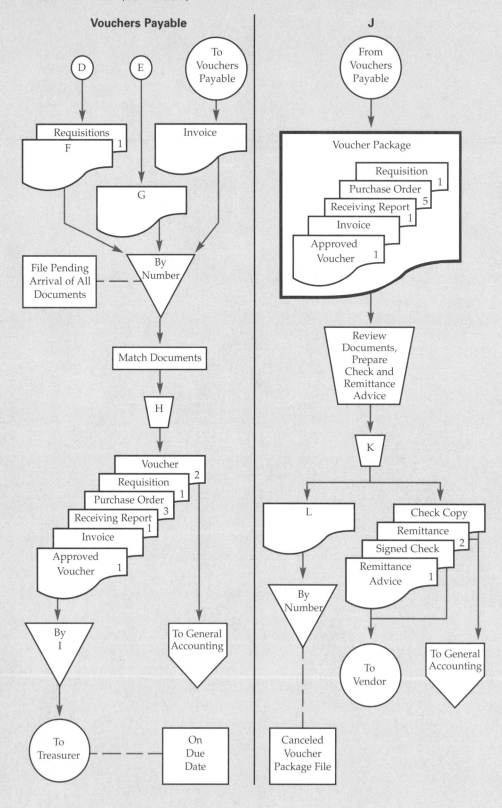

Camera Lenses

4. Each camera lens is delivered in a separate corrugated carton. Cartons are counted as they are received by the receiving clerk, who agrees the number of cartons to the purchase order.

Required:

1. Explain why the control activities for receiving reports and the receipt of sheet metal, screws, and camera lenses, respectively, are adequate or inadequate.
2. For each inadequate procedure you identify, describe misstatements that might be in the financial statements.

(AICPA Adapted)

12-6 *Identifying Procedures for Purchase Requisitions and Purchase Orders*

Long has been engaged to audit the financial statements of Maylou Corporation. To help consider controls over purchases, Long obtained the purchases flowchart below.

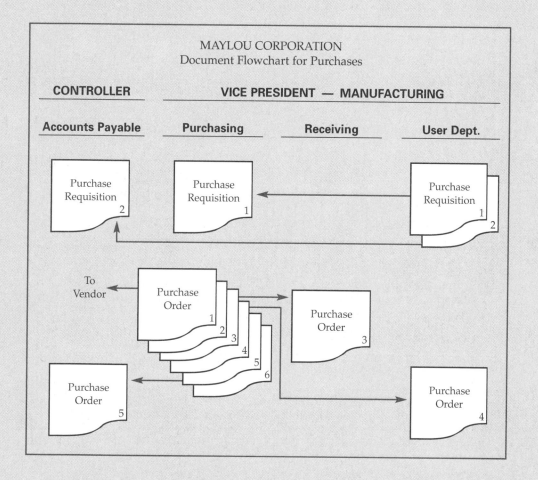

Required: Identify the procedures for purchase requisitions and purchase orders that Long would expect to find if Maylou's controls over purchases are effective. For example, purchase orders should be prepared only after first considering the quantity to order.

(AICPA Adapted)

12-7 *Recommending Improvements to a Purchase Requisition*

Properly designed documents and forms improve the likelihood that employees will adhere to prescribed policies and procedures. For example, consider a multicopy purchase order, with one copy intended for mailing to the vendor and the remaining copies distributed to the stores and to the Purchasing, Receiving, and Accounting departments. The purchase order currently used by the National Industrial Corporation appears below.

PURCHASE ORDER

SEND INVOICE ONLY TO:

297 HARDINGTEN DR., BX., NY 10461

TO _____   SHIP TO _____

_____   _____

_____   _____

DATE TO BE SHIPPED	SHIP VIA	DISC. TERMS	FREIGHT TERMS	ADV. ALLOWANCE	SPECIAL ALLOWANCE
QUANTITY		DESCRIPTION			

PURCHASE CONDITIONS

1. Supplier will be responsible for extra freight cost on partial shipment, unless prior permission is obtained.

2. Please acknowledge this order.

3. Please notify us immediately if you are unable to complete order.

4. All items must be individually packed.

Required:
1. In addition to the name of the company, what other information would an auditor recommend be included in the purchase order illustrated?
2. What control objectives are served by distributing copies of the purchase order to the stores and to the Purchasing, Receiving, and Accounting departments?

12-8 *Drafting an Internal Control Questionnaire*

Taylor has been engaged to audit the financial statements of University Books, Inc., a college bookstore serving the university community and the general public. University Books maintains a large imprest cash fund exclusively for the purpose of buying used books from students. The cash fund is active year round because the university offers a variety of courses throughout the year, many with varying starting and completion dates. Receipts are prepared for each purchase, and reimbursement vouchers are submitted periodically.

Required: Draft a questionnaire to use in documenting University Book's controls over the imprest cash fund. The questionnaire should elicit *Yes* or *No* responses.

(AICPA Adapted)

12-9 *Drafting Tests of Controls from an Internal Control Questionnaire*

Following are selected questions from internal control questionnaires relating to a company's purchasing, receiving, cash disbursements, and recording functions. A *Yes* response to a question indicates a potential strength of the system, and a *No* a potential deficiency.

a. Are prenumbered purchase orders prepared for all approved purchase requisitions?
b. Are competitive bids or price quotations obtained for purchased goods and services?
c. Are price lists maintained for repetitive transactions that do not require competitive bids or price quotations?
d. Are copies of purchase orders forwarded to the requisitioning department and to Receiving?
e. Are all goods received, inspected, counted, and compared with copies of purchase orders?
f. Are voucher packages reviewed before being approved for payment?
g. Are voucher packages and checks reviewed by signatories before signing checks?

Required: Assume that inquiries indicate the answer is *Yes* to each question. For each question, draft a test of controls that you believe would provide persuasive evidence that the answer is correct.

12-10 *Identifying the Purpose of Tests of Controls*

Following are several tests of controls introduced in the chapter.

Tests of Controls:
- Examine periodic reports by non-Purchasing department personnel regarding purchase prices and practices.
- Observe Receiving department procedures, determining whether received goods are counted and compared with quantities and descriptions on purchase orders.
- Foot the voucher register for a selected period and compare with posting in the general ledger.
- Observe voucher cancellation procedures, determining whether vouchers are canceled by or in the presence of check signers.

Required: For each test, indicate the expenditure/disbursement cycle activity tested and the purpose of the test.

12-11 *Sequential Sampling and Tests of Receiving Controls*

Harold Brodkey plans to apply sequential sampling to the receiving controls used by the Ozyck Corporation, a December 31, 2007, year-end manufacturer and supplier of home lighting fixtures. Based on a review of prior-year working papers, Brodkey assesses the following desired reliabilities and tolerable deviation rates for each of three tests of controls:

Test of Control	Risk of Assessing Control Risk Too Low	Expected Population Deviation Rate
1. Compare receiving reports in voucher packages with copies of receiving reports in Receiving department files.	.95	.06
2. Review receiving reports for evidence that received goods have been inspected, counted, and compared with packing slips and purchase orders.	.90	.05
3. Trace receiving reports to entries in the receiving log.	.85	.07

Brodkey performs the sampling plan on September 10 and finds one deviation each for tests number 2 (receiving report no. 1429 includes a receiving clerk's approval initials indicating the receiving report agrees with the packing slip and P.O., but not that the received goods were counted) and 5 (although receiving report no. 2137, Winston-Raleigh Co., reads 12,500 units, the receiving log reads 12,250 units).

Required: Prepare audit working papers to document the sequential sampling plan and the analysis of deviations.

Internet problems and discussion cases are available at http://ricchiute.swlearning.com

RESEARCH PROJECT

The Purchasing Function in a Real Entity

Few departments within a corporation, not-for-profit institution, or governmental entity can have quite as significant an influence on cost containment as Purchasing, since the purchasing function directly affects so many financial statement accounts, among them cash, advertising, insurance, inventory, supplies, and accounts payables. As a result, in many entities, the policies and procedures for purchasing are typically centralized, meaning that all purchases for all departments are processed by the Purchasing department, and quite formal, meaning the documentation supporting each purchase is standardized, explicit, and controlled. In short, much is at stake.

Required: Although access to the Purchasing department of a real-world entity can be problematic, there is much to be learned from how individual entities process purchase transactions. Contact and interview the purchasing manager for a corporation, not-for-profit institution, or governmental entity in your area and:

1. Document the purchasing procedures in a flowchart or a narrative memorandum.
2. Obtain blank copies of forms used in the purchasing function (for example, purchase requisitions, purchase orders, receiving reports) and explain each form's purpose and distribution throughout the entity.
3. What recommendations would you make to improve the entity's purchasing procedures?

Interactive quizzes are available as a student learning resource at http://ricchiute.swlearning.com

Chapter 13

Accounts Payable, Prepaids, and Accrued Liabilities

Major topics discussed in this chapter are:

- The relationship between financial statement assertions and audit procedures in the audit of payables, prepaids, and accrued liabilities.
- The relationship among audit risk; nonfinancial measures; and the nature, timing, and extent of substantive tests.
- Substantive tests applicable to assertions about accounts payable, prepaid expenses, and accrued liabilities.
- Expense recognition and earnings manipulation in accounting for capitalized advertising costs, excess reserves, and environmental liabilities.
- Audit sampling in substantive tests of accounts payable.
- Computer-assisted audit techniques applicable to accounts payable.

This chapter begins by discussing how each of the financial statement assertions introduced in Chapter 6—existence or occurrence, completeness, rights and obligations, valuation or allocation, and presentation and disclosure—is tested for audits of accounts payable, a major financial statement account within the **expenditure/disbursement cycle**, and how audit risk and nonfinancial measures bear on the nature, timing, and extent of substantive tests. The chapter then relates the assertions to substantive tests of accounts payable, prepaid expenses, and accrued liabilities. In turn, the chapter addresses audit, legal, and ethical questions auditors face when a client is confronted with liabilities for which management has some discretion in avoiding otherwise sensitive disclosures: environmental liabilities. The chapter concludes by illustrating how auditors apply nonstatistical sampling (Chapter 9) and computer-assisted audit techniques (Chapter 8) in substantive tests of accounts payable.

Financial Statement Assertions, Objectives, and Audit Procedures

Within the expenditure/disbursement cycle, purchases and accounts payable are usually the highest transaction-volume and the largest dollar-balance accounts. The cycle affects other financial statement accounts—for example, prepaid expenses and accrued liabilities, both of which are discussed in this chapter—but the volume of prepaid and accrual transactions is not often large. However, owing to the judgment demanded in accounting for accruals, auditing some accruals, particularly those involving accounting estimates such as loss contingencies, can be rather complex. Auditing accounting estimates is discussed in Chapter 17—although the reversal of excess reserves into income inappropriately, a type of earnings manipulation, is discussed in this chapter. Auditing purchases and payables is emphasized in this chapter and discussed later in the context of specific financial statement assertions. Figure 13-1 relates each assertion to specific audit procedures and summarizes the discussion that follows.

FIGURE 13-1: *Relating Financial Statement Assertions and Audit Procedures: Purchases and Accounts Payable*

Assertions	Audit Procedure
Existence or occurrence	Confirm with creditors. Test cutoff.
Completeness	Test for unrecorded liabilities. Perform analytical procedures. Test cutoff.
Rights and obligations	Confirm with creditors. Test for unrecorded liabilities.
Valuation or allocation	Verify accounts payable trial balance. Confirm with creditors. Test for unrecorded liabilities.
Presentation and disclosure	Compare statement presentation and disclosure with those required by GAAP.

Existence or Occurrence

Within the expenditure/disbursement cycle, the existence or occurrence assertion addresses whether all recorded payables exist at the balance sheet date and whether all recorded purchase transactions occurred during the period. The existence of accounts payable balances may be tested by confirming balances with creditors, although payables confirmations are used less frequently than receivables confirmations and generally are not used when the auditor suspects understatements. When confirmations are not used, the auditor can test existence by examining the documents that support recorded payables—for example, purchase orders, receiving reports, and invoices. The occurrence assertion is addressed by testing cutoff to determine whether purchases are recorded in the proper accounting period.

Completeness

The completeness assertion addresses whether all purchase transactions and payables balances that should be presented in the financial statements actually are presented. That is, were all transactions recorded? Completeness is tested by reviewing post-balance sheet date cash disbursements for payments made on previously unrecorded payables and by examining unmatched receiving reports (those filed in an unpaid vouchers file) to assure that liabilities have been recorded at the balance sheet date. In addition, analytical procedures are used to detect any unusual relationships that might suggest unrecorded liabilities, such as a significant increase in the average number of days' purchases in accounts payable. Testing cutoff also addresses completeness.

Rights and Obligations

Within the expenditure/disbursement cycle, the rights and obligations assertion addresses whether payables and other recorded liabilities are bona fide obligations of the entity. Payables obligations may be tested by confirming recorded balances with creditors and by searching for unrecorded liabilities—that is, by examining cash disbursements for the period subsequent to the balance sheet date, as explained above.

Valuation or Allocation

The valuation assertion addresses whether existing payables are reported in the financial statements at appropriate dollar amounts. The value of payables is tested by verifying the mathematical accuracy of the accounts payable aged trial balance, by confirming payables with creditors, and by testing for unrecorded liabilities.

Presentation and Disclosure

The presentation and disclosure assertion addresses whether recorded payables are properly classified, described, and disclosed in the financial statements. To test presentation and disclosure, an auditor compares a client's financial statement disclosures with those required by generally accepted accounting principles. Disclosure guidelines, such as the AICPA's annually updated *Accounting and Audit Manual* and proprietary audit-firm databases, are frequently used by practicing auditors.

Audit Risk: Nonfinancial Measures and Substantive Tests of Accounts Payable

Substantive testing of expenditure/disbursement cycle accounts involves obtaining and evaluating evidence about an entity's acquisition of resources and the obligations that often result from resource acquisitions, like accounts payable. Although cash disbursements are encompassed by the expenditure/disbursement cycle, they're not addressed in this chapter since substantive tests of cash balances were discussed and illustrated in Chapter 11 (see Figure 11-7, page 471).

Like the revenue/receipt cycle, the expenditure/disbursement cycle varies in scope from one entity to another and, therefore, so do the audit procedures applied to the cycle. Thus, the substantive tests discussed in this chapter are representative, not definitive. The nature, timing, and extent of the procedures applied in an engagement depend on the assessed levels of *control risk* (the likelihood that material error could occur and not be detected by internal control) and *inherent risk* (the susceptibility of an account balance to material error for which there is no related internal control), and the resulting level of *detection risk* (the likelihood that error could occur and not be detected by audit procedures) an auditor is willing to accept for each assertion. However, nonfinancial measures can impact an auditor's assessment of audit risk. For example, assume an auditor discovers that, relative to competitors in the industry, an audit client has failed to be the low-price provider of production materials, has experienced unfavorable price variances, and has lagged significantly in product development. Each of these discoveries would raise an auditor's professional skepticism in this way: Since uncompetitive price and lagging product development threaten profitability, management has incentives to manipulate earnings and an auditor has reason to design audit procedures that will offer persuasive evidence bearing on understated expenses.

When control and inherent risks are assessed below the maximum and detection risk above the minimum, auditors are less apt to confirm payables balances, more apt to perform substantive tests at interim dates, and more apt to restrict the extent of substantive tests applied to purchases and payables. However, the audit programs illustrated in this chapter assume that an auditor has assessed control risk and inherent risk for the assertions of *occurrence, completeness, obligations*, and *valuation* at the *maximum* for two reasons. First, assume that tests of controls over purchasing, receiving, and cash disbursement (Chapter 11) reveal that internal control deficiencies are likely to produce aggregate error in excess of tolerable error for the following control procedures:

- *Purchasing:* Purchase orders are authorized by a department manager's signature or initials.
- *Receiving:* Receiving reports are agreed to purchase orders.
- *Disbursement:* Disbursements are compared with entries in the accounts payable subsidiary ledger.

Second, assume that, owing to problematic nonfinancial measures, the auditor is skeptical about management's incentives to understate expenses.

As a result, to hold audit risk to a *minimum*, the auditor assesses the acceptable level of detection risk at the *minimum*. That is, from Chapter 2:

$$DR = \frac{AR}{IR \times CR}$$

$$\text{Minimum} = \frac{\text{Minimum}}{\text{Maximum} \times \text{Maximum}}$$

The auditor holds audit risk to a minimum by assessing the acceptable level of detection risk at the minimum, which bears directly on the nature, timing, and extent of planned substantive tests:

- *Nature:* Use more persuasive procedures (for example, test for unrecorded payables).
- *Timing:* Perform procedures at the balance sheet date.
- *Extent:* Test more extensively (for example, increase sample sizes).

A program of substantive tests for purchases and accounts payable is presented in Figure 13-2, and is keyed to—and discussed in the context of—the financial statement assertions presented in Chapter 6: existence or occurrence, completeness, rights and obligations, valuation or allocation, and presentation and disclosure. If an entity's system of internal control has changed since the auditor assessed control risk at interim, he or she should either reassess the assessed level of control risk through additional tests of controls or, in contrast, unilaterally increase the assessed level of control risk without additional tests of controls and increase the extent of substantive testing at the balance sheet date.

FIGURE 13-2: *Substantive Tests: Purchases and Accounts Payable*

Assertions	Procedures

Valuation	1. Verify mathematical accuracy of accounts payable.
	    a. Obtain an accounts payable aged trial balance from Accounts Payable department personnel.
	    b. Foot and cross-foot the trial balance.
	    c. Compare total accounts payable per the trial balance with accounts payable in the general ledger.
	    d. Trace sampled vendor accounts to voucher packages and examine supporting documents.

Existence Obligations Valuation	2. Consider the need to confirm year-end accounts payable directly with creditors.
Existence or occurrence Completeness	3. Test cutoff to determine whether purchases and payables are recorded in the proper accounting period.
Completeness Valuation Obligations	4. Test for unrecorded liabilities.
Existence or occurrence Completeness Valuation	5. Perform analytical procedures.

Presentation
  and disclosure
	6. Review financial statements to determine whether:
	    a. Accounts and notes payable and other liabilities are properly classified and described.
	    b. Disclosures are adequate.

Verify Mathematical Accuracy

The first step in addressing the valuation assertion is to verify the mathematical or clerical accuracy of recorded accounts payable. For example, to accomplish tests of mathematical accuracy, an auditor could import an aged trial balance into a spreadsheet file similar to Figure 13-3, and write commands to foot and cross-foot the trial balance and to compare and reconcile the client's trial balance total with the general ledger balance. If discrepancies are observed, or if deficiencies were detected in tests of controls, the auditor may conduct additional tests of mathematical accuracy. For example, the auditor may select a sample of accounts from the trial balance and trace each account to a voucher package in the unpaid vouchers file and to the voucher register and accounts payable subsidiary records.

Confirm Payables

Unlike the confirmation of receivables (Chapter 11), there's no presumption in the profession that an auditor is required to justify his or her opinion on financial statements when payables are not confirmed. In fact, payables are not commonly confirmed in practice, unless internal control is ineffective (and other forms of

FIGURE 13-3: *Accounts Payable Aged Trial Balance*

(Schedule prepared by client)

The Wilson Company
Accounts Payable Aged Trial Balance
December 31, 2007

Account Number	Vendor Name	Balance Dec. 31, 2007	0–30 Days	31–60 Days	Over 60 Days
0001	Adams Supply	$ 7,859.76	$ 7,859.76		
0002	Andres & Company	17,621.40	17,621.40		
0003	Art Design Inc.	784.50	784.50		
0004	Ashton Mfg.	10,005.00	9,000.00	$ 1,005.00	
0005	Attleboro Bindings	1,147.61	1,147.61		
0006	Bates Motel	123.49	123.49		
0007	Christie & Co.	1,456.90			$1,456.90
•	•	•	•	•	•
•	•	•	•	•	•
•	•	•	•	•	•
0162	Van Nuys & Co.	6,724.82	6,724.82		
0163	Wallace's	12,654.09	12,654.09		
0164	Western Electric	1,164.21	1,164.21		
0165	Yantze Inc.	550.00		550.00	
		$238,858.89	$225,282.64	$10,125.50	$3,450.75

evidence, such as detailed vendors' invoices, are unavailable) or the auditor is concerned that liabilities may be overstated.

A dominant concern in auditing *receivables* is the detection of overstatements, and confirmation is an effective procedure to verify the existence, rights, and valuation of recorded accounts receivable, since the overstated receivable would be listed on the entity's accounts receivable trial balance. In auditing *payables*, however, the risks are quite different: An auditor is usually concerned with the risk of understatement, since an understated liability (for example, an account payable) results typically in an understated expense (for example, advertising expense) and, correspondingly, in overstated income. Confirming recorded payables with vendors is not an effective means for detecting unrecorded liabilities because the *un*recorded payable obligation would not be listed on an accounts payable trial balance and, therefore, a confirmation request would not be sent.

This does not mean that auditors are never concerned with the risk of overstated liabilities, only that understatement is more common. An auditor may suspect overstatement, for example, if he or she has reason to believe that an entity motivated by tax avoidance has overstated liabilities and thus understated taxable income. Also, if an entity's income is significantly lower than in preceding years and liabilities are significantly higher, an auditor may suspect that liabilities are overstated if there is no other apparent reason for the reduction in reported income.

When the confirmation of payables is considered necessary by an auditor, balances are usually confirmed as of the balance sheet date rather than at interim.

Confirming payables balances requires direct communication with vendors, requesting that an itemized statement of account be sent directly to the auditor. Unlike positive and negative receivables confirmations, payables confirmation requests usually do not reveal the audited entity's recorded balance; rather, they request a statement reflecting the vendor's records. A sample payables confirmation request appears in Figure 13-4.

FIGURE 13-4: *Accounts Payable Confirmation*

THE WILSON COMPANY
15 Artubus Drive
Stony Brook, NY 11790

January 7, 2008

Alpine Roofing Company
305 Columbus Avenue
Pawtucket, RI 02861

Our auditors, Cheever & Yates, LLP, are auditing our financial statements for 2007. Will you please furnish them with the following information as of December 31, 2007:

- An itemized statement of amounts that we owe you.
- An itemized statement of any merchandise that you have consigned to us.
- An itemized list of any notes, acceptances, or other obligations that we owe you.

Please reply directly to our auditors. An envelope addressed to our auditors is enclosed.

Maxine Kuman
Controller
The Wilson Company

As in the case of receivables confirmations, an auditor should mail second (and perhaps even third) requests to vendors who fail to respond. For accounts that are not confirmed, an auditor could examine subsequent cash payments, vendors' invoices, and receiving documents.

Test Cutoff

Purchases cutoff tests are quite similar in nature and logic to sales cutoff tests, discussed in Chapter 11. An auditor tests purchases cutoff to determine whether purchases and the corresponding payables are recorded in the appropriate period—that is, whether purchases of goods are recorded in the period that title to the goods passed to the purchasing entity, and whether services are recorded in the period rendered. Cutoff tests relate most directly to the existence and completeness assertions.

Cutoff tests of purchase transactions involve selecting and examining a sample of purchase entries on or near year end—for example, ten days before to ten days after year end. Receiving reports are examined for each sampled purchase entry. A purchase of goods and a related payable should have been recorded in the year under audit if shipping terms are:

- *FOB shipping point* (origin) and goods were <u>shipped</u> by the seller on or before year end, or
- *FOB destination* and goods were <u>received</u> on or before the year-end date.

Transactions for services should be reflected in the year under audit if the services were received by the entity on or before the year-end date.

Another aspect of cutoff relates to prepayments and accruals. An auditor should review the entity's year-end entries relating to prepaid and accrued expenses to determine whether expenses are recognized in the appropriate accounting period. Prepayments and accruals are discussed more fully later in the chapter.

Test for Unrecorded Liabilities

As noted above, auditors often are concerned that liabilities may be understated as a result of unrecorded payables. This does not mean, however, that an auditor is never concerned with overstated liabilities, only that understatement is more common, since understating liabilities can result in overstated income. Figure 13-5 depicts the sources for testing accounts payable balances for both understatements and overstatements. Testing for understatements, or unrecorded liabilities, is discussed first.

A **search for unrecorded liabilities** is closely related to tests of cutoff and, in fact, may result in the detection of items recorded in the wrong accounting period. Similarly, cutoff tests may reveal unrecorded liabilities. However, auditors usually conduct an investigation specifically designed to detect unrecorded liabilities, and thus specifically related to the assertions of completeness, valuation, and obligations.

Four basic sources are used to search for unrecorded payables:

- A year-end accounts payable trial balance.
- The cash disbursements journal.
- Canceled (paid) voucher packages.
- The file of unmatched receiving reports (filed in an unpaid vouchers file).

Assuming a December 31 year end, an auditor would trace a sample of disbursements for January to receiving reports contained in canceled voucher packages; if goods were received or title to the goods passed on or before December 31, the accounts payable trial balance should reflect a liability. Likewise, because many accounting systems require a completed **voucher package**—purchase requisition, purchase order, receiving report, and vendor's invoice—before a payable is recorded, an auditor would examine unmatched (unprocessed) receiving reports; again, if goods were received or title passed on or before December 31, the accounts payable trial balance should reflect the liability. The search for unrecorded liabilities is completed by asking management whether they are aware of any significant payables not recorded and not detected by the above tests.

Even though payables understatement is often an overriding concern, an auditor cannot ignore the potential for overstatement, since some clients may have incentives to overstate expenses (for example, to avoid income taxes). Three basic sources are used to test for overstated payables:

- A year-end accounts payable trial balance.
- The cash disbursements journal.
- Canceled (paid) voucher packages.

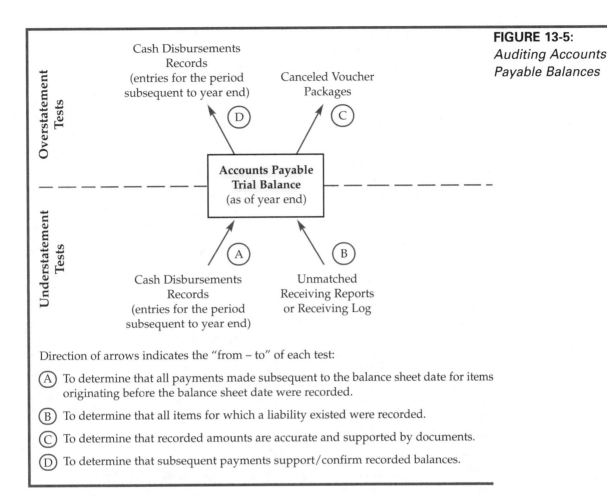

FIGURE 13-5:
Auditing Accounts Payable Balances

Direction of arrows indicates the "from – to" of each test:

(A) To determine that all payments made subsequent to the balance sheet date for items originating before the balance sheet date were recorded.

(B) To determine that all items for which a liability existed were recorded.

(C) To determine that recorded amounts are accurate and supported by documents.

(D) To determine that subsequent payments support/confirm recorded balances.

Assuming a December 31 year end, an auditor would trace sample items from the accounts payable trial balance to receiving reports and shipping terms contained in canceled voucher packages; title should have passed on or before December 31. In addition, sampled items would be traced to subsequent payments in the cash disbursements journal, assuring that the liability was paid and, therefore, that documentation for returned goods was not concealed. For example, a payable recorded on or before December 31 with payment terms of 2/10, net 30, should have been paid no later than January 10 to take advantage of the 2 percent discount and no later than January 30 if the discount were not taken. If not paid, an auditor would obtain an explanation from management; nonpayment could suggest the liability did not exist as of December 31, despite documentation to the contrary.

Perform Analytical Procedures

As in tests of receivables balances (Chapter 11), the role of year-end analytical procedures for payables is to direct attention to unusual, unreasonable, or otherwise unexplainable relationships among accounts or account components. That is, analytical procedures can be used to identify accounts that appear reasonable in relation to other accounts and therefore do *not* require additional substantive testing, or accounts that appear unusual or unreasonable and therefore *do* require additional substantive testing.

Figure 13-6 presents in detail the intuition and potential explanations for several key analytical procedures, and lists several other procedures used commonly in practice. For example, consider the number of days' purchases in payables and accounts payable turnover. If the number of days' purchases in payables was at or around 30 days, and payables therefore turned over 12 times (360 days/30 days) for four successive years, this would suggest that purchases, payables, and cash disbursements behaved similarly for the four-year period and would not signal the need for additional substantive tests of details. However, if the number of days' purchases was at or around 30 days for the three preceding years and 45 days for the current year (turnover = 360/45 = 8 times), then this unexpected variation could indicate any one or more of the following potential explanations:

- Payment problems: Management may be having difficulty making payments.
- Overstated purchases.
- Understated payables.

An auditor should investigate any unusual relationships between or among accounts and design additional substantive tests of details if warranted. For example, if management is having difficulty making payments, the auditor might first consider whether cash flow was adequate (Chapter 11 cash collections) and, if it was not, then increase the scope of testing for unrecorded liabilities (understated payables), as discussed earlier in the chapter.

Presentation and Disclosure

Item 6 of the program for substantive testing of purchases and payables requires that an auditor assess whether expenditure/disbursement cycle accounts such as payables, accrued liabilities, and related purchase and expense accounts are classified and disclosed in accordance with generally accepted accounting principles. Payables and accrued liabilities usually are classified as current if due within one year or expected to be paid either with existing current assets or by incurring additional current liabilities. Depending on materiality, liabilities such as trade accounts payable, and other items—such as advances (for example, from officers), customer credit balances, dividends payable, interest payable, and liabilities for product warranties—should be disclosed separately. For example, Coca-Cola's 2003 annual report discloses payables and accruals of $4.1 billion and $3.7 billion in 2003 and 2002, respectively, and, to distinguish accruals from payables, discloses in a footnote separate amounts for four accruals (accrued marketing, container deposits, accrued compensation, sales and payroll taxes) and for accounts payable.

Prepaid Expenses and Accrued Liabilities

For most entities, the balance in Accounts Payable summarizes a rather large volume of recurring transactions, is material and, therefore, is often the most time-consuming audit area within the expenditure/disbursement cycle. However, two other accounts in the cycle are rather important to an audit: Prepaid Expenses and Accrued Liabilities. But they are important because they result from timing

FIGURE 13-6: *Analytical Procedures for Accounts Payable and Purchases*

Analytical Procedure	Intuition/Comparisons	Potential Explanations
Number of days' purchases in payables: $$\frac{\text{Credit Purchases}}{\text{Average Accounts Payable}}$$	Computes the number of days that payables are outstanding. Compare to prior years and to industry data. Compare to credit sales terms.	*Increases* Slow payments Understated purchases Overstated payables *Decreases* Fast payments Overstated purchases Understated payables
Payable Turnover: $$\frac{360 \text{ days}}{\text{Number of days' purchases in payables}}$$	Computes the number of times payables turn over during the year. Compare to prior years and to industry data. Compare to inventory turnover. Compare to receivables turnover.	*Increases* Fast payments Understated purchases Overstated payables *Decreases* Slow payments Overstated purchases Understated payables
Compare: Accounts payable balance to Prior-year payables balance + Credit purchases − Cash disbursements	Reconstructs the ending payables balance from three sources: the prior-year balance, and additions to (credit purchases) and deletions from (cash disbursements) the prior-year balance.	*Accounts Payable Balance >* Overstated payables Understated credit purchases Overstated cash disbursements *Accounts Payable Balance <* Understated payables Overstated credit purchases Understated cash disbursements

(continues)

FIGURE 13-6 (continued)

Analytical Procedure	Intuition/Comparisons	Potential Explanations
Compare: Purchases to (Market share × Industry sales) × (1 − Ave. markup %)	Estimates sales from industry data.	*Purchases* > Overstated purchases *Purchases* < Understated purchases
Other analytical procedures Compare both purchases and payables with budgets or forecasts.		
Compare both purchases and payables with prior years.		
Compare payables divided by total current liabilities for the current and prior years.		
Compare purchases divided by payables for the current and prior years.		
Compare individual vendor payables for the current and prior years.		

differences between when cash is expended and an asset or liability is recorded, not because of volume or even materiality. In fact, the volume of transactions underlying prepaid expenses and accrued liabilities is often small, prompting auditors either to test all of the transactions and events underlying individual prepaid expense and accrued liability accounts or to rely on analytical procedures.

Prepaid Expenses

Prepaid expenses normally result because the future service potential of assets may extend beyond the period in which payment is made. Common examples include prepaid insurance, prepaid rent, prepaid advertising, and supplies. To illustrate, the following focuses on prepaid insurance, although the audit issues discussed apply to other prepaid expenses as well.

Controls

In general, an auditor is concerned with three predominant controls in the audit of prepaid insurance—control procedures over:

- The acquisition of new insurance policies,
- The disbursement of cash for premiums, and
- The recording of expense and premium disbursements.

The acquisition of new insurance coverage should be authorized by the board of directors, and the insurance company and policy selected should be approved by personnel authorized by management. As in other types of cash payments within the expenditure/disbursement cycle, the authority to disburse cash for premiums should be segregated from the responsibility to record both the disbursement and the charge to insurance expense, thereby separating the execution and recording functions. As a further control over recording, an *insurance register* should be maintained to compile detailed information about coverage, terms, and payment due dates.

Substantive Tests

Figure 13-7 illustrates an audit working paper for prepaid insurance and indicates how an auditor addresses each of the financial statement assertions. To test existence, the auditor examines current insurance policies and, as documented on the working paper, may confirm the coverage, terms, due dates, and unexpired premiums directly with insurance carriers.

AUDIT DOCUMENTATION REVIEW

Completeness is tested two ways, though neither is apt to reveal errors or frauds because the transactions in Figure 13-7 have been tested 100 percent. First, the auditor assures that total insurance coverage exceeds the replacement cost of all tangible assets. Second, cutoff testing is performed but is not documented directly on the prepaid insurance working paper. Rather, cutoff testing is addressed during substantive tests of accounts payable and the auditor's search for unrecorded liabilities, both of which were discussed earlier in the chapter.

Rights and obligations are tested by examining the insurance policies and, as in Figure 13-7, confirming the policy with insurance carriers. In turn, an auditor tests valuation by recalculating unexpired premiums through evidence obtained from the prior year's unexpired insurance and from current premiums. In addition, to address clerical accuracy, the auditor reconciles premium payments with

FIGURE 13-7: *Analysis of Prepaid Insurance*

The Wilson Company
Prepaid Insurance
December 31, 2007

D4
SEB 1/15/08

Insurer Policy Number	Coverage	Period	Premium	Year Paid	Unexpired Premium 12-31-04	Additions	Expense	Unexpired Premium 12-31-07
Provident Ins. AE-1067-48139[d]	Automobiles—collision, comprehensive, uninsured motorist; covers all autos operated	Jan. 1, 2006 Dec. 31, 2008	$9,000[e]	06	$6,000[f]	—	$3,000[g]	$3,000[a,h]
Washington Ins. PBL-462-1986-63[d]	Casualty—buildings, covers all buildings and equipment	July 1, 2007 June 30, 2012	$7,000	07	—	$7,000[i]	1,750[g]	5,250[a,h]
NY Equitable NY 743-96218[d]	Business interruption	Oct. 1, 2006 Sept. 30, 2008	$3,000[e]	06	2,625[f]	—	1,500[g]	1,125[a,h]
					$8,625	$7,000	$6,250	$9,375[h]
					c	c	b,c,j	b,c,j

Note: Total coverage exceeds the replacement cost of all insured assets.
a   Cross-footed.
b   Agreed to general ledger.
c   Footed.
d   Examined insurance policy, agreeing policy number, terms, period covered, and premium.
e   Examined premium notice in company files, and traced to prior-year working papers which indicated payment was agreed to cash disbursements records in the year paid (2004).
f   Agreed to 12-31-04 general ledger and last year's working papers.
g   Calculated.
h   Confirmed with insurance company. See insurance confirmation file.
i   Examined premium notice and traced to cash disbursements; policy is for five years, but premiums are paid two years in advance during the first four years, and the fifth year is paid one year in advance.
j   Agreed to trial balance.

cash disbursements records, and total expense and unexpired premiums with the general ledger.

Finally, the presentation and disclosure assertion is not particularly problematic except in one area: the adequacy of insurance coverage. An auditor should determine whether total insurance coverage exceeds his or her best estimate of the replacement cost for all tangible assets, insured or otherwise. If replacement cost exceeds insurance coverage, the client is partially self-insured. In this case, the excess of replacement cost over insurance should be disclosed in a note to the financial statements, though not accrued as a liability, since the conditions for accruing loss contingencies in FASB *Statement of Financial Accounting Standards No. 5*, "Accounting for Contingencies,"—that is, the loss is probable and the amount of the loss can be estimated reasonably—would not have been met.

Capitalized Costs: AOL

Companies in a number of industries have enhanced earnings by capitalizing costs that otherwise should be expensed. Take AOL, for example. In the mid-1990s, AOL, through an advertising campaign designed to expand its subscription customer base, included in promotional circulars and bundled in computer packaging disks that contained AOL startup software. In fiscal 1995 and 1996, AOL capitalized the advertising costs in an account called Deferred Membership Acquisition Costs, and amortized the costs over a 24-month period. The capitalized costs amounted in fiscal years 1995 and 1996 to $77 million and $314 million, respectively, fully 19 percent and 33 percent of total assets, respectively.

> earnings management

However, invoking AICPA Accounting Standards Executive Committee *Statement of Position (SOP) 93-7*, "Reporting on Advertising Costs," the SEC argued that a company cannot capitalize direct-solicitation advertising costs absent convincing evidence that future net revenues from the customers solicited will exceed the amount of the costs capitalized. The SEC concluded that AOL "could not meet this standard because the volatile and unstable nature of the Internet marketplace precluded reliable predictions of future net revenues."[1] In October 1996, AOL announced that all capitalized advertising costs would be written off and, in 2000, without admitting or denying guilt, consented to a cease and desist order that prevented capitalizing advertising costs and to a $3.5 million civil penalty. AOL's position on capitalized advertising costs, and the SEC's response, points to an issue quite common in audit practice: a client's liberal interpretation of a professional pronouncement. For example, *SOP 93-7*, notes that the "reliability of accounting estimates decreases as the length of the period for which such estimates are made increases . . ., the period over which the benefits of direct-response advertising are amortized often is *no longer than the greater of one year or one operating cycle*"[2] (emphasis supplied). Through 1994, AOL amortized advertising costs over one year but, beginning in 1995, increased the amortization period to two years.

Accrued Liabilities

Accrued liabilities result because some unpaid obligations for services may have been incurred before the balance sheet date. Common examples include accrued

---

1 *SEC Accounting and Auditing Enforcement Release No. 1257*, "In the Matter of America Online, Inc.," May 15, 2000.
2 *AICPA Statement of Position 93-7*, "Reporting on Advertising Costs."

property taxes, accrued payroll taxes, accrued product warranty costs, accrued rent, accrued interest, and accrued income taxes. The discussion below focuses on accrued property taxes, although the issues are common to other accrued liabilities.

Controls

In the audit of property taxes, an auditor is concerned with an entity's controls over three activities:

- Recognition of accrued taxes.
- Recording of expense for taxes owed.
- Disbursement of cash for taxes.

When an entity conducts business in several locations, particularly across the country or overseas, management should institute policies to assure that liabilities for property taxes in all relevant municipalities, states, or countries are accrued at the balance sheet date. The recording of property tax expense should be based on bills actually received or estimated from prior years (adjusted for tax rate changes), if any. As with other cash payments processed through the expenditure/disbursement cycle, responsibility for disbursing cash and for recording disbursements should be separated. If property taxes are paid in several localities, separate property tax records should be maintained to compile and control both accruals and payments.

Substantive Tests

AUDIT DOCUMENTATION REVIEW

Figure 13-8 illustrates an audit working paper for accrued property taxes and indicates how each relevant financial statement assertion is addressed. To test occurrence, obligations, and valuation, an auditor examines receipted property tax bills for the current year, if available, or, as in Figure 13-8, compares the current provision for property tax expense with prior-year payments for reasonableness. In testing reasonableness, though, the auditor should consider plant asset additions/disposals and tax rate changes, because either or both could alter the amount owed for the current year. In turn, reasonableness tests also address completeness, since unusual fluctuations in accrued property taxes from one year to the next could signal underaccruals or overaccruals.

Excess Reserves: W.R. Grace

> earnings management

In a September 1998 speech, "The Numbers Game," introduced in Chapter 1, then SEC Chairman Arthur Levitt identified five examples of what he called "hocus pocus" accounting. One, "cookie jar reserves," translates to building up excess reserve balances in high-income periods and reversing the excess to operating income in lower-income periods, thereby smoothing earnings over time and marking earnings to analysts' expectations. Soon after the speech, in a complaint alleging cookie jar reserves, the SEC filed suit against W.R. Grace, then a specialty chemical and health care business. The complaint alleged that, from 1991 through 1995, Grace recorded $20 million in excess reserves on the financial statements of a health care subsidiary, National Medical Care, a medical products supplier and kidney-dialysis and home-health services provider that produced a large portion of Grace's consolidated net income. Commenting on the complaint, the SEC's en-

FIGURE 13-8: *Analysis of Accrued Property Taxes*

		D7
		1/16/08
		SEB

The Wilson Company
Accrued Property Taxes
December 31, 2007

Balance, Dec. 31, 2006		$ 34,230[a]
Provision for property tax expense		35,000[d]
Payments:		
State of Missouri	$15,473[b]	
State of Illinois	12,696[b]	
City of St. Louis	3,210[b]	
City of Chicago	2,842[b]	(34,221)
Balance, Dec. 31, 2007		$ 35,009
		c,e

a   Agreed to general ledger and to financial statements.
b   Traced to receipted tax bill and cash disbursements records.
c   Footed.
d   Provision for property tax expense appears reasonable, since the provision reasonably approximates 2006 actual payments adjusted for plant asset additions less retirements (See E1).
e   Agreed to trial balance.

forcement director said, "Extra earnings were put into a reserve to save for a rainy day so they could use it when they wanted to goose up the numbers."[3]

Detecting managed reserves is particularly troubling in practice, since reserves can't always be tied to transactions. For example, unlike prepaid expenses, for which the amount prepaid is traceable to cash disbursements records, reserves for future liabilities—say, for example, environmental liabilities or warranty guarantees—are estimates. Auditors rely on FASB *Statement of Financial Accounting Standard No. 5*, "Accounting for Contingencies," introduced earlier, to address GAAP, and on *Statement on Auditing Standards No. 57*, "Auditing Accounting Estimates," introduced in Chapter 17, to evaluate the reasonableness of management's estimates. For example, under *SAS No. 57*, an auditor might review and test the process management used to develop an estimate, or might develop an estimate independently and mark the estimate to management's. However, the risk imbedded in a reserve depends largely on the controls management implements to constrain the process of developing a reserve. Absent management override, the risk of misstatement in recorded reserves is a function of internal control.

---

3   M. Schroeder, "SEC Accuses Grace of Fraud in Accounting," *The Wall Street Journal* (December 23, 1998), p. A16.

Expense Recognition and Earnings Manipulation

➤ earnings management

The discussion thus far has centered on issues that are challenging but, given the state of the art in accounting and auditing, fairly predictable for experienced practitioners: challenging because timing the incurrence of an expense (prepaids, accruals) or the recognition of a liability (payables) presents opportunities for management to manipulate earnings, but predictable because, although not the subject of an authoritative pronouncement, GAAP for payables, prepaids, and accruals is fairly well understood. But what about expenses and liabilities that are at once both challenging and *un*predictable? One example is excess reserves, discussed above. Another follows in the form of a case study that illustrates the competing incentives of management and auditors, and the roles of auditor liability and professional ethics, in accounting for environmental liabilities.

Environmental Liabilities: A Case Study in Management and Auditor Incentives

Environmental liabilities impose upon an auditor considerable responsibilities that are made more daunting by the thousands of pages of environmental regulations accompanying a variety of federal statutes, among them the Congressional *Comprehensive Environmental Response, Compensation, and Liability Act* (CERCLA or, more popularly, the "Superfund" legislation), the *Superfund Amendment and Reauthorization Act*, and the *Clean Air Act*. Clearly, the figure to ground relationship between industry and the environment has reversed since the industrial revolution. Rather than a natural setting on which industry intrudes selectively, the environment has become a commodity within an artificial setting of high-stakes economic and societal constraints. At the extreme, the economic interests are represented by industrial polluters to whom the commodity exists for little more than unrelenting exploitation and the promise of short-term gain. In contrast, society's interests are represented by environmental law, and what's at stake is nothing less than a legal system's triumph over chaos. In the short term the economy may prosper, in the long term society pays, and the auditor lies in middle, mindful both of management's incentives and of the compelling environmental liabilities management may leave in its wake.

Legal Liability for Industrial Pollution

Industrial polluters may be held liable for noncompliance with existing laws and regulations, for personal injury or property damage, and for the contingent liability potentially most significant to audited financial statements: the remedial cleanup responsibilities imposed by the Superfund legislation. Parties responsible for hazardous waste-site cleanup costs may include not only current site owners and operators, but also hazardous waste transporters and the owners and operators of the site at the time waste was disposed. As illustrated in the Eleventh Circuit Court of Appeals precedent-setting decision in *U.S. v. Fleet Factors Corp.* (1990), liability also can extend to secured creditors, even those that did not participate directly in dumping hazardous waste:

. . . a secured creditor will be liable if its involvement with the management of the facility is sufficiently broad *to support the inference that it could affect hazardous waste disposal discussions if it so chose* (emphasis added).

For example, involvement may be ruled sufficiently broad when a credit agreement requires that the borrower obtain the secured creditor's approval to ship products.

The liability of industrial polluters is joint and several (Chapter 5), since the federal government may recover from any one party identified by the Environmental Protection Agency (EPA) as a "**potentially responsible party**" (PRP). But the question of who dumped what and when, and therefore who exactly is a PRP, is not without controversy. For example, *The Wall Street Journal* reported that Westinghouse had disputed an EPA order to pay an estimated $14.9 million to clean an upstate New York contamination site in part because Westinghouse disputed responsibility for the contamination.

Cleanup Costs: Expense versus Capitalization and Contingent Liabilities

Once identified as a PRP for a Superfund site, an entity is then responsible to estimate the costs of cleanup. For example, in an extensive and forthcoming footnote accompanying its audited financial statements, Columbia Gas System, Inc., reported in part the following about Columbia Transmission, a subsidiary:

As a consequence of its self-assessment program, Columbia Transmission in recent years recorded projected compliance costs relating to the remediation of low levels of contamination by PCB-based lubricating oils in certain air compressors and other pollutants, including mercury. Further progress by Columbia Transmission in its self-assessment activities resulted in additional pre-tax charges of $65 million . . .

Although it's clear from the note that Columbia Gas expensed the costs of cleanup, could the costs have been capitalized? The FASB has not issued a Statement of Financial Accounting Standards about whether to expense or capitalize current costs, but the Board's Emerging Issues Task Force has issued a consensus opinion in Issue 90-8, *Capitalization of Costs to Treat Environmental Contamination*. The consensus was that costs incurred to treat environmental contamination—such as engaging consulting engineers, and removing and neutralizing toxic waste—generally should be expensed, but may be capitalized, if, for example, the costs extend the life of the property, prevent future contamination, or further ready property currently held for sale.

Contingent liabilities for future cleanup costs present at least two problems, one related to measurement and a second to recognition. The measurement problem is management's role in casting into dollars a liability based on preliminary estimates and on interpreting the EPA's definition of acceptable cleanup. Under AICPA *Statement of Position (SOP) 96-1*, "Environmental Remediation Liabilities," the recognition problem (Should a liability be recognized on the balance sheet?) is judged by criteria established in FASB *Statement of Financial Accounting Standards No. 5*, "Accounting for Contingencies": Recognize a loss contingency if the loss is probable and the amount of the loss can be estimated reasonably. In many cases, the entity will disclose the liability in a footnote rather than on the balance sheet, since cleanup cost estimates are not sufficiently reliable to justify recording a liability. For example, the Columbia Gas footnote referred to above lends insight into the difficulty of estimating costs and also discloses a reserve for future cleanup costs:

The eventual total cost of full future environmental compliance for the Columbia Gas System is impossible to estimate due to, among other things: (1) the possibility of as yet unknown contamination, (2) the possible effect of future legislation and new environmental *agency rules, (3) the possibility of future litigation, (4) the possibility of future designations as a potential responsible party by the EPA and difficulty of determining liability, if any, in proportion to other responsible parties, (5) possible insurance and rate recoveries, and (6) the effect of possible technological changes relating to future remediation. However, reserves have been established based on information currently available which resulted in a total recorded net liability of $110.9 million for the Columbia Gas System. . . . As new issues are identified, appropriate additional liabilities will be recorded.*

Management and Auditor Incentives

The management of a potentially responsible party has incentives to understate the costs of cleanup and therefore to overlook or to underestimate the magnitude of the potential liability, largely because the reported estimated costs and liabilities can affect stock prices when disclosed. For example, Arco, Exxon, and Phillips all experienced significant declines in stock prices as a result of environmental disasters. Likewise, auditors have incentives to provide themselves with a reasonable degree of assurance that material environmental liabilities are disclosed, since shareholders may bring action against an auditor for negligently overlooking unreported environmental liabilities. To demonstrate the audit implications of competing incentives, the following illustrates issues auditors confront when auditing environmental liabilities.

Ground Water Contamination

Owing mostly to a major fresh water aquifer, several square miles in the town of Grainert, Illinois, had undergone significant residential development over a fifteen-year period. Utilities were drawn from a regional power affiliate, and water from pumps located on each homeowner's property. Coexisting with the residential subdivisions was a preexisting regional storage facility built originally by an ethanol plant but operated now by the Humbolt Oil Co., Inc., a publicly traded Louisiana-based distributor of refined oil and gas products.

Following complaints from residents whose property abutted the storage facility, *The Grainert Daily Herald*, a local newspaper, published a front-page article citing speculation by local engineers that a floating oil pool may have formed atop the aquifer. A photo accompanying the article showed surface contamination one hundred yards from a chain link fence and a sign on the fence that read, "Humbolt Oil." Although the piece did not otherwise implicate Humbolt, the article's closing line read: "A spokesperson for Humbolt Oil's Grainert storage facility refused comment." After the news story broke, Humbolt's chief executive officer revealed in a private conversation with the auditor that the *Daily Herald's* account was patently false, that the EPA had recently completed an unreported investigation, that management planned to fight vigorously if the EPA issued a Superfund notice letter, and that disclosure of environmental liabilities in the financial statements was out of the question.

Audit Judgment: Accounting, Liability, and Ethics

➤ ethics

The newspaper article and conversation have more than trivial implications for Humbolt's auditors, since they raise no less than four related audit issues:

- Illegal acts,
- Audit risk,
- Current cleanup costs (if any), and
- The potential for material contingent liabilities.

Under *Statement on Auditing Standards (SAS) No. 54*, "Illegal Acts by Clients," an auditor is not responsible for designing audit procedures to detect *in*direct illegal acts (Chapter 5), among them violations of environmental laws, unless specific information, such as *The Grainert Daily Herald* article and the impending EPA report, directs his or her attention to a potential violation. Here, the auditor should make inquiries of Humbolt Oil's management about policies they've implemented to prevent ground water contamination, to assure compliance with environmental laws and regulations, and to estimate cleanup costs.

Given the considerable attention drawn to environmental disasters, including oil spills on both coasts and in the Gulf of Mexico, the AICPA issued a *Risk Alert* that suggests auditors inquire of management whether a company has been named a potentially responsible party and whether the company has a high risk of exposure to environmental liabilities. Although the auditor's conversation lent insight to both questions, both should be asked again when the EPA letter arrives, and, given the newspaper account, the auditor should, under *Statement on Auditing Standards No. 47*, "Audit Risk and Materiality in Conducting an Audit," consider assessing the inherent risk (Chapter 2) of environmental liabilities at the maximum when planning audit risk.

Consistent with the FASB's EITF Issue 90-8, *Capitalization of Costs to Treat Environmental Contamination*, discussed previously, the auditor should consider whether management has incurred current cleanup costs and whether the costs have been charged to expense in the current period. More problematic is the difficult judgment about whether disclosure is required by FASB *Statement of Financial Accounting Standards No. 5*, "Accounting for Contingencies." In this case, the EPA has neither named Humbolt a potentially responsible party nor claimed violation of federal laws or regulations, although the threat looms large. Thus, although it's unclear whether a loss is probable and, if so, whether the amount of the loss can be estimated reasonably, it is clear that no disclosure at all may be inappropriate. In addressing the issue of environmental liabilities with Humbolt Oil's management, the auditor should point out that:

- Once named a potentially responsible party, the company will be jointly and severally liable for all cleanup costs even if the prior storage-facility operator was responsible for only some of the ground water contamination;
- Although disclosure of a contingent liability under FASB *Statement No. 5* requires disclosure in the financial statements only if a loss is "probable," SEC *Financial Reporting Release No. 36* requires disclosure in Form 10-K's Management Discussion and Analysis unless management determines that the loss is *not* "reasonably likely," a lower level of probability;
- Although disclosure of environmental liabilities has been associated with stock price declines (see footnote 2), failure to comply with FASB *Statement No. 5* is a departure from GAAP; and
- A departure from GAAP will cause the auditor to issue a qualified or adverse opinion, depending on materiality, and an explanatory paragraph that discloses the effect of the departure on reported earnings (Chapter 3, Figure 3-7).

If the auditor considers concurring with the client to overlook environmental liabilities, he or she risks serious legal and ethical implications. Since Humbolt Oil is publicly traded, statutory law applies and Sections 10(b) and 18 of the *Securities Exchange Act of 1934* (Chapter 5) provide shareholders with a means to recover losses resulting from false or misleading statements. In this case, if disclosure was

➢ fraud

not made, shareholders could likely recover under Section 10(b) since publication of a newspaper account makes plain that the auditor knew, or should have known, that exposure to environmental liabilities was likely. The plaintiff's basis for action [Section 10(b) or Section 18], though, would be judged by the plaintiff in consultation with an attorney. Further, as discussed in Chapter 5, the auditor could be liable for treble damages under the *Racketeer Influenced and Corrupt Organizations Act* (RICO), since *Reves v. Arthur Young*, a 1993 U.S. Supreme Court case, does not provide relief from RICO when, as is the case in Humbolt, he or she participated directly with management to perpetrate the fraud.

The case raises at least two ethical issues. First, the auditor violates the *Code of Professional Conduct*, Rule 203—Accounting Principles (Chapter 4), which provides that an AICPA member cannot issue an unqualified opinion if the financial statements contain a departure from an "accounting principal promulgated by bodies designated by Council." In the Humbolt Oil case, the accounting principal violated is failure to disclose a contingent liability for cleanup costs, and the body issuing the principal is the FASB. Violating Rule 203 can result in an administrative reprimand, such as suspension to practice before the SEC, or revocation of a CPA's license to practice public accountancy. Second, overlooking disclosure of environmental liabilities raises serious questions about the auditor's ethical character, since siding with the client injures at least two major stakeholders: Humbolt Oil shareholders and all those who rely on Humbolt management to preserve the land they're entrusted with.

Nonstatistical Sampling in Substantive Tests of Accounts Payable

To integrate material presented in this chapter with the nonstatistical sampling applications introduced in Chapter 9, assume a continuing audit engagement for Skynob Corporation, a wholesaler of college and high school supplies whose fiscal year ends December 31. The objective in this case is to determine whether recorded accounts payable are fairly stated at December 31.

Assessment of Control Risk

Assume the consideration of internal control was accomplished as of October 31 and revealed that controls over payables were effective and, therefore, not likely to produce aggregate error in excess of tolerable error. The auditor assesses control risk below the maximum. However, these tests did reveal delays of 36 to 48 hours in recording disbursements, thereby suggesting potential year-end cutoff problems that could result in overstated payables and overstated cash at December 31, the balance sheet date. At year end, the auditor made inquiries of management, which indicated that neither the control procedures nor responsible personnel had changed since interim. Thus the auditor has no reason to perform additional tests of controls for the period November 1 to December 31, although the delay in recording disbursements would affect planned audit procedures.

Selecting a Sampling Plan

Although Skynob's cash disbursements volume is high, payables represent only 5 percent of total liabilities, an amount the auditor judges material but not highly material. Rather, long-term debt, leases, and equity are far more material to Skynob's financial statements, and, further, tests of controls suggest debt and leases may entail more risk than payables.

For the Skynob engagement, the auditor now has three important pieces of information:

- Controls over payables are effective.
- Disbursement recording is sometimes delayed, suggesting the possibility of overstated payables and overstated cash at the balance sheet date.
- Payables are material, but neither as material nor as risky as long-term debt and leaseholds.

From this information, the auditor decides to confirm a sample of accounts payable balances, since year-end balances could be overstated and, in this case, the auditor believes confirmations would be less costly than extensive cutoff tests. The auditor elects to use a nonstatistical sampling plan because there is no apparent reason to quantify audit risk.

The auditor's confirmation of Skynob Corporation's payables balances is accomplished by the nonstatistical sampling plan introduced in Chapter 9.

Population, Sampling Unit, and Determination of Sample Size

At December 31, the audit population consists of 253 vendor accounts, totaling $475,000. The accounts payable trial balance, the source for selecting accounts for confirmation, is clerically accurate and agrees in total with the general ledger. Each vendor account represents a sampling unit. To choose an appropriate sample size, the auditor must next classify the degree of audit assurance desired, choose an appropriate assurance factor, and estimate tolerable error and key-dollar items, all of which appear in the nonstatistical sampling plan in Chapter 9.

Because the auditor plans some reliance on internal control in assessing control risk below the maximum and some reliance on cutoff tests, the auditor requires a moderate degree of audit assurance (see the decision aid on page 386, Chapter 9). Because some error is anticipated, the auditor's assurance factor is 8.

The auditor decides to set tolerable error, the maximum monetary error that may exist without causing the financial statements to be misleading, at $25,000, which is a little over 5 percent of Skynob's recorded book value. The amount of key-dollar items is set at $8,000, and 28 of the 253 account balances in the population are $8,000 or more, and in total sum to $275,000.

Recapping, the following information is known:

$$
\begin{aligned}
B &= \text{Recorded book value} &&= \$475,000 \\
KD &= \text{Key-dollar items} &&= \$275,000 \\
TE &= \text{Tolerable error} &&= \$25,000 \\
AF &= \text{Assurance factor} &&= 8
\end{aligned}
$$

From these data, sample size can be calculated using the method introduced in Chapter 9.

$$
\begin{aligned}
n &= \left(\frac{B - KD}{TE}\right) \times AF \\[2mm]
&= \left(\frac{(\$475,000 - \$275,000)}{\$25,000}\right) \times 8 \\[2mm]
&= 64
\end{aligned}
$$

Ninety-two confirmations are mailed on January 3: 28 to vendors with balances of $8,000 or more (the key-dollar items) and 64 to vendors whose accounts were selected randomly from the 225 remaining accounts (that is, 253 accounts less 28 key items).

Evaluating Results

Assume confirmations are received from 24 of the key-dollar accounts and from 61 of the 64 randomly selected accounts. For nonresponding vendors, the auditor examines subsequent payments and voucher packages. The confirmations and other procedures reveal $5,975 of known error.

Known error:

Key-dollar items	$3,625 overstatement
Randomly selected items	$2,350 overstatement
	$5,975 overstatement

From this information, likely error, the auditor's estimate of total population error, is a $11,887 overstatement, calculated as follows:

Likely error:

Key-dollar error   = $ 3,625

Other error:

$$\frac{\$2,350}{\left(\frac{64}{(253-28)}\right)} = \frac{8,262}{\$11,887 \text{ overstatement}}$$

In this case, because tolerable error ($25,000) exceeds likely error ($11,887), the auditor concludes that payables are not likely misstated materially. However, the auditor could propose adjusting known error only; that is, propose an audit adjustment reducing payables by $5,975.

Computer-Assisted Substantive Tests of Accounts Payable

When an entity's accounting information system processes data by computer, some of an auditor's substantive tests of details can be accomplished by computer. Figure 13-9 lists several computer-assisted techniques for a series of audit procedures common to accounts payable. These procedures can be accomplished through software prepared by the auditor or through generalized audit software available from outside vendors.

SUMMARY

The expenditure/disbursement cycle encompasses two major business functions: acquiring resources from vendors and employees and paying obligations to vendors and employees. These business functions lead to one major balance sheet account: Accounts Payable. The functions also result in prepaid expenses and accrued liabilities. When performing substantive tests of payables, an auditor's

FIGURE 13-9: *Computer-Assisted Substantive Tests: Accounts Payable*

Audit Procedure	Computer-Assisted Substantive Tests
Test mathematical accuracy	Verify footings, cross-footings, and extensions of the accounts payable aged trial balance and/or detailed subsidiary records.
Summarize data for further testing or analysis	Age payables according to due dates.
	List debit balances in accounts payable for reclassification to accounts receivable.
	Print accounts payable confirmations.
Test accuracy of recorded data	Compare details in accounts payable trial balance with detailed subsidiary records.
	Compare details in subsidiary records with source documents (e.g., voucher packages).
Sample selection	Select accounts for testing from a random number generator and the aged accounts payable trial balance.
Compare similar data files	Compare charges/credits in detailed subsidiary records with the purchases/cash disbursements master files.

major objectives are to determine that each account exists, represents all transactions that should be presented, represents rights or obligations of the entity, is valued properly, and is presented and disclosed properly within the financial statements.

Environmental liabilities result not from transactions incurred during the period but from events such as hazardous waste disposal and ground water contamination perpetrated currently or over a period of years. Federal statutes, such as the "Superfund" legislation and the Clean Air Act, impose considerable penalties on potentially responsible parties, penalties that management has incentives to overlook, since disastrous environmental liabilities can affect both stock prices and financial position. Auditors need be aware of the risk of illegal acts from environmental contamination and the potential for material contingent liabilities.

KEY TERMS

Environmental liabilities 564
Expenditure/disbursement cycle 547
Potentially responsible party 565

Search for unrecorded liabilities 554
Voucher package 554

REFERENCES

Auditing Standards:

AICPA, *Codification of Statements on Auditing Standards*. New York: AICPA.

SAS No. 47, "Audit Risk and Materiality in Conducting an Audit" (AU Sec. 312).

SAS No. 54, "Illegal Acts by Clients" (AU Sec. 317).
SAS No. 57, "Auditing Accounting Estimates" (AU Sec. 342).

Accounting Standards:

AICPA Statement of Position (SOP) 96-1, "Environmental Remediation Liabilities."
FASB Statement No. 5, "Accounting for Contingencies."
FASB Emerging Issues Task Force (EITF), Issue 90-8, "Capitalization of Costs to Treat Environmental Contamination."
FASB Emerging Issues Task Force (EITF), Issue 93-5, "Accounting for Environmental Liabilities."

Professional Reports and Speeches:

Levitt, A., "The Numbers Game." Remarks by the SEC Chairman. New York University Center for Law and Business, September 28, 1998.

Levitt, A., "Renewing the Covenant with Investors." Remarks by the SEC Chairman. New York University Center for Law and Business, May 10, 2000. (**http://www.sec.gov**)

Public Oversight Board, *Panel on Audit Effectiveness: Report and Recommendations*. Stamford, CT: POB, 2000.

Articles:

Beets, S. D., and C. C. Souther, "Corporate Environmental Reports: The Need for Standards and an Environmental Assurance Service," *Accounting Horizons* (June 1999), pp. 129–145.

Cahill, L. B., "Issues in Environmental Auditing," *Petroleum Independent* (November 1992), p. A2.

Roussey, R. S., Jr., "Auditing Environmental Liabilities," *Auditing: A Journal of Practice & Theory* (Spring 1992), pp. 47–57.

Stevens, M. G., "New Accounting for Environmental Liabilities," *The Practical Accountant* (December 1996), pp. 47–51.

QUESTIONS

1. How can an auditor test whether all payables transactions that should be recorded are actually recorded?
2. What does management assert about payables reported in financial statements?
3. Explain how an auditor determines whether all recorded payables actually represent bona fide obligations of the entity.
4. What procedures might an auditor use in testing the valuation assertion for purchases and payables?
5. Explain an auditor's objective when testing the existence or occurrence assertion for accounts payable.
6. Under what conditions is an auditor most likely to confirm payables?
7. Why is confirmation ineffective in detecting understatement of liabilities?
8. How do pricing and product development bear on the risk of earnings manipulation?
9. How and why does an auditor test purchases cutoff?
10. What can an auditor learn from the number of days' purchases in payables?
11. How could an auditor reconstruct the expected year-end accounts payable balance?
12. Describe how an auditor searches for unrecorded liabilities.
13. Under what conditions would an auditor consider confirming accounts payable?
14. What major sources does an auditor use to test for overstated accounts payable, and how are those major sources used?

15. In testing prepaid insurance, how does an auditor address rights and obligations?
16. Can a client capitalize marketing costs that are expected to benefit future periods?
17. What is a cookie jar reserve?
18. What are the major internal controls an auditor considers when designing substantive tests of accrued property taxes?
19. What is meant by a "potentially responsible party"?
20. Under what conditions might an entity not responsible for dumping toxic waste be held responsible by the U.S. Environmental Protection Agency?

MULTIPLE CHOICE QUESTIONS

1. Which of the following procedures is most telling in addressing the existence assertion for accounts payable?

   a. Test for unrecorded liabilities.
   b. Confirm balances with creditors.
   c. Verify the accounts payable trial balance.
   d. Perform analytical procedures.

2. Assume an auditor's interim consideration of internal control in the expenditure/disbursement cycle reveals that control risk can be assessed below the maximum and detection risk above the minimum for some assertions. Which of the following is true about substantive tests applied to accounts payable?

   a. The auditor is more apt to confirm payables balances.
   b. The auditor is less apt to perform substantive tests at the balance sheet date only.
   c. The auditor is more apt to increase the extent of substantive tests.
   d. The auditor is more apt to ignore the risk of incorrect acceptance when sampling accounts payable.

3. To help hold detection risk to a minimum for assertions related to payables, an auditor might:

   a. Confirm payables at an interim date.
   b. Search for unrecorded payables.
   c. Perform analytical procedures on nonfinancial measures.
   d. Make inquiries of management.

4. Of the following, which is an accounts payable confirmation most likely to include? An itemized statement of:

   a. Invoices.
   b. Purchase orders.
   c. Shipping documents.
   d. Notes, acceptances, and other obligations.

5. Which of the following procedures would help an auditor test for overstatements of accounts payable at the balance sheet date?

   a. Trace entries in the cash disbursements records to items in the accounts payable trial balance.
   b. Agree items in the file of unmatched receiving reports to the accounts payable trial balance.
   c. Trace items in the accounts payable trial balance to documentation contained in canceled voucher packages.
   d. Coordinate cutoff tests performed for receiving and for shipping.

6. The purpose of purchase cutoff tests is to determine whether:
   a. All purchases are recorded.
   b. Vendor invoices have been paid on time.
   c. The client has title to the goods purchased.
   d. Payables are recorded in the appropriate period.

7. In testing cutoff for purchases and payables at December 31, an auditor is confronted with the following four scenarios. Which of the four most likely represents a cutoff error, requiring that the auditor propose an adjusting journal entry?
   a. Shipping terms are FOB shipping point. Goods were shipped on December 31. The purchase was recorded on December 31.
   b. Shipping terms are FOB destination. Goods were shipped on December 31. The purchase was recorded on December 31.
   c. Shipping terms are FOB shipping point. Goods were shipped on January 2. The purchase was recorded on January 4.
   d. Shipping terms are FOB destination. Goods were shipped on December 31. The purchase was recorded on January 2.

8. An auditor has estimated an amount represented by the following expression: (market share × industry sales) (1 − average markup percentage). Which of the following best characterizes what the auditor has estimated?
   a. Purchases.
   b. Purchases from industry data.
   c. Payables.
   d. Payables from industry data.

9. An auditor has estimated an amount represented by the following expression: (365) / (credit purchases / average accounts payable). Which of the following best characterizes what the auditor has estimated?
   a. Average purchases
   b. Average payables
   c. Number of days' purchases in payables
   d. Payables turnover

10. An auditor would consider confirming accounts payable if:
    a. Internal control is ineffective.
    b. There is a risk that payables may be understated.
    c. Detailed vendors' invoices are available.
    d. Management has hired new accounts payable employees.

11. In performing analytical procedures in the expenditure/disbursement cycle, an auditor detects that payables divided by current liabilities appear low in comparison with prior years. Which of the following courses of action might this unusual relationship suggest?
    a. Increase the scope of testing for unrecorded liabilities.
    b. Confirm payables balances with creditors.
    c. Decrease the scope of cutoff testing at the balance sheet date.
    d. Decrease the scope of testing for unrecorded liabilities.

12. Which of the following is not necessary to test for unrecorded liabilities?
    a. Canceled voucher packages
    b. Cash disbursements records
    c. Cash receipts records
    d. The accounts payable trial balance

13. An increase in the number of days' purchases in accounts payable could mean that:

    a. Purchases are overstated.
    b. Payables are understated.
    c. Payments to vendors are made sooner.
    d. Purchases are made more often.

14. The risk of misstatement in the amount management estimates for a reserve is directly related to the:

    a. Effectiveness of internal control.
    b. Experience of management in estimating the reserve.
    c. Extent of documentation.
    d. Tone at the top.

15. In addressing control procedures for prepaid insurance, which of the following controls would not be relevant to the auditor?

    a. Controls over purchase cutoff
    b. Controls over the acquisition of new insurance policies
    c. Controls over the disbursement of cash for insurance premiums
    d. Controls over the recording of expenses and premium disbursements

16. Which of the following procedures is an auditor least likely to perform when auditing prepaid insurance?

    a. Confirm policies with insurance carriers.
    b. Examine insurance policies.
    c. Value insured property.
    d. Agree balances to the general ledger.

17. Which of the following procedures is most relevant to testing the completeness assertion for prepaid insurance?

    a. Testing whether insurance coverage exceeds the replacement value of insured tangible property
    b. Confirming insurance policies with carriers
    c. Reconciling premium payments with cash disbursement records
    d. Agreeing total expense and unexpired premiums with the general ledger

18. In addressing control procedures for accrued property taxes, which of the following controls would not be relevant to the auditor?

    a. Controls over the recognition of accrued taxes
    b. Controls over recording expense for taxes owed
    c. Controls over the disbursement of cash for taxes
    d. Controls over fixed asset additions

19. Which of the following are likely legitimate reasons why a potentially responsible party would have difficulty estimating environmental cleanup costs?

    a. Possible as yet unknown contamination
    b. Possible future legislation
    c. Possible insurance recoveries
    d. Possible preexisting contamination

20. Under which of the following conditions would it be inappropriate for a potentially responsible party to capitalize toxic waste cleanup costs?

   a. The costs relate to a long-existing disposal site.
   b. The costs extend the life of the property.
   c. The costs prevent future contamination.
   d. The costs further ready property currently held for sale.

PROBLEMS AND DISCUSSION CASES

13-1 *Relating Errors, Frauds, Audit Procedures, and Assertions in Substantive Tests of Accounts Payable*

Following are errors, frauds, or other circumstances an auditor might encounter as a result of applying year-end substantive tests of details to accounts payable as of December 31, 2007:

   a. The aged trial balance does not agree with individual accounts payable ledger records.
   b. The auditor suspects that accounts payable may be overstated.
   c. Several shipments were received from an overseas FOB shipping point on January 2, 2008.
   d. The December 31, 2007, accounts payable balance appears low in comparison with the prior two years.
   e. The Accounts Payable department maintains a file of unmatched receiving reports, that is, receiving reports for which an invoice had not yet been received.
   f. Payables are not usually recorded until two days following the date that goods are received.

   Required: For each of the above, indicate (1) a specific detailed test or tests that might address the error, fraud, or circumstance and (2) the financial statement assertion addressed by each test.

AUDIT DOCUMENTATION REVIEW

13-2 *Confirming Accounts Payable*

Stanford Seeles, engagement partner for the audit of the Torgesen-Tate Corporation, is planning the nature, timing, and extent of audit procedures for accounts payable. Prior-year working papers reveal that confirmation requests were mailed to 100 of Torgesen-Tate's 1,000 suppliers; the sample consisted mostly of large dollar balances. Management and Seeles spent a substantial number of hours resolving rather minor differences between the confirmation replies and Torgesen-Tate's accounting records. Alternative audit procedures were used for those suppliers who did not respond to the confirmation requests.

   Required:
   1. What are the audit objectives Seeles ought to consider when planning audit procedures?
   2. Discuss circumstances that would compel Seeles to confirm payables. Is Seeles required to confirm payables?
   3. Discuss why large dollar balances might not be an efficient basis for selecting accounts to confirm. Suggest a more efficient basis.

13-3 *Designing Substantive Procedures for Accounts Payable*

Taylor is engaged to audit Rex Wholesaling for the year ended December 31, 2007. Taylor considered internal controls over purchasing, receiving, trade accounts payable, and cash disbursement and has decided not to proceed with tests of controls. Based on analytical procedures, Taylor believes that trade accounts payable may be understated at December

31. Taylor requested and obtained from management a client-prepared trade accounts payable spreadsheet listing the amount owed each vendor.

Required: Discuss additional substantive audit procedures that Taylor should apply to trade accounts payable.

13-4 *Comparing Receivables and Payables Confirmations*

There is a presumption in the profession that an auditor is required to justify his or her opinion on financial statements when *accounts receivable* (Chapter 10) are not confirmed, but not when *accounts payable* are not confirmed. In fact, as noted in Chapter 12, payables are not commonly confirmed in practice.

Required: Compare the confirmation of accounts receivable with the confirmation of accounts payable on two issues: generally accepted procedures of auditing and the form of confirmation requests.

13-5 *Purchase Cutoff*

Partly to address the existence and completeness assertions, auditors typically test purchase cutoff at the balance sheet date, thereby addressing whether purchase transactions are recorded in the proper accounting period. Your audit supervisor has asked that you perform a purchase cutoff test for the Ridgeview Corporation, a December 31, 2007, year-end client. The supervisor suggests that you test all purchase transactions over $5,000 for the period December 25, 2007 through January 5, 2008. Audit working papers compiled during the December 31 physical inventory observation indicate that the last receiving report used on December 31 was No. 13402. The following data is available for eight purchase transactions.

AUDIT DOCUMENTATION REVIEW

Receiving Report Number	Amount	Date Shipped	Date Received	Shipping Terms
13398	$13,500**	Dec. 26	Dec. 28	FOB: Origin
13399	7,560*	Dec. 27	Dec. 27	FOB: Dest.
13400	24,000*	Dec. 29	Dec. 29	FOB: Origin
13401	5,000**	Dec. 31	Dec. 31	FOB: Origin
13402	15,980*	Dec. 29	Dec. 31	FOB: Dest.
13403	9,765*	Dec. 30	Jan. 02	FOB: Dest.
13404	45,000**	Jan. 01	Jan. 03	FOB: Dest.
13405	10,855**	Dec. 31	Jan. 02	FOB: Origin

Note:

* indicates the purchase was included in December 31 payables.

** indicates the purchase was *not* included in December 31 payables.

Required: For the purchase data above, indicate whether (and why) the purchase is treated properly or improperly in December 31 accounts payable. Prepare an adjusting journal entry for the purchases treated improperly.

13-6 *The Motivation to Understate or Overstate Payables*

Auditors are often concerned that liabilities may be understated as a result of unrecorded payables. On the other hand, auditors may be concerned that liabilities are overstated as a result of payables recorded in the wrong accounting period, among other things.

Required:
1. Give several reasons why an entity may want to understate payables.
2. Give several reasons why an entity may want to overstate payables.

13-7 *Analytical Procedures, Accounts Payable, and Purchases*

Cheryl Ralston is planning analytical procedures for the December 31, 2007, financial statement audit of Singulair, Inc., a publicly traded manufacturer of small electrical appliances, including mixers, toasters, can openers, and electric blankets. The appliances are marketed to low-end retailers throughout North America. An industry trade publication estimates Singulair's 2007 market share at 12 percent. Singulair's December 31, 2007 and 2006, balance sheets and statements of operations follow.

Singulair, Inc.
Balance Sheets
December 31, 2007 and 2006
(000 omitted)

Assets	*2007*	*2006*
Cash	$ 42,000	$ 52,500
Accounts receivable, net	325,500	175,000
Inventory	252,000	234,500
Other current assets	17,500	21,000
Noncurrent assets, net of depreciation	210,000	280,000
Total assets	$847,000	$763,000
Liabilities and Equities		
Trade accounts payable	$133,000	$143,500
Taxes payable	105,000	50,400
Noncurrent liabilities	70,000	140,000
Common stock	245,000	245,000
Retained earnings	294,000	184,100
Total liabilities and equities	$847,000	$763,000

Singulair, Inc.
Statements of Operations
Years Ended December 31, 2007 and 2006
(000 omitted)

	2007	*2006*
Net credit sales	$5,894,000	$4,375,000
Cost of goods sold	3,244,500	2,485,000
	$2,649,500	$1,890,000
Selling and administrative expenses	2,387,000	1,764,000
Income before taxes	$ 262,500	$ 126,000
Tax expense	105,000	50,400
Net income	$ 157,500	$ 75,600

Total industry-wide sales approximated $37.5 billion in 2007. Singulair's average markup percentage was 11 percent in 2007 and 10.5 percent in 2006, and ending inventory and payables on December 31, 2007, were $140,500 and $125,000, respectively.

Required: Using Figure 13-6, Analytical Procedures for Accounts Payable and Purchases, as a guide:

1. Perform analytical procedures you think appropriate for Singulair's December 31, 2007, audit. For example, the balance sheets and statements of operations include information that can be used to calculate the numbers of days' purchases in payables and payables turnover and to make several informative comparisons.

2. Explain the results for each ratio or comparison. For example, an increase in payables turnover could signal understated purchases or overstated payables, among other things.
3. Discuss substantive tests appropriate for the results explained in requirement 2. For example, an analytical procedure that signals overstated payables could prompt an auditor to increase the scope of cutoff testing.

13-8 *Tests for Unrecorded Payables*

Unrecorded payables result in two potentially material misstatements in an entity's financial statements: *understated liabilities*, because the credit to payables is not recorded, and *overstated net income*, because a corresponding expense is not recorded. As a result, auditors typically perform a search for unrecorded payables during year-end substantive testing.

Required: Prepare an audit program to search for unrecorded payables.

13-9 *Unrecorded Payables*

You are in the final stages of your audit of Ozine Corporation's financial statements for the year ended December 31, 2007, when the corporation's chief executive officer, Gordon Sumner, approaches you. Sumner believes there is no point to your examining purchases transacted on or after January 1, 2008, since (a) bills pertaining to 2007 that were received too late to be included in the December voucher register were recorded as of year end by journal entry, (b) the internal auditor made tests after year end, and (c) he would furnish you with a letter certifying that there were no unrecorded liabilities.

Required:
1. Should an auditor's test for unrecorded liabilities be affected by the fact that the client made a journal entry to record 2007 bills that were received late? Discuss.
2. Should an auditor's test for unrecorded liabilities be affected by the fact that a letter is obtained in which a responsible management official certifies that to the best of his or her knowledge all liabilities have been recorded? Discuss.
3. Should an auditor's test for unrecorded liabilities be eliminated or reduced because of the internal audit tests? Discuss.
4. Assume that the corporation had no internal auditor but, owing to some government contracts, an auditor for a federal agency had spent three weeks auditing the records. How would the auditor's unrecorded liability test be affected by the work of the federal auditor?
5. What sources in addition to the 2007 voucher register should the auditor consider to locate possible unrecorded liabilities?   (AICPA Adapted)

13-10 *Liability for Loss Contingencies*

Harper has completed tests of accounts payable and other liabilities for Hawthorne Corporation, and now plans to determine whether there are any loss contingencies arising from litigation, claims, or assessments.

Required: Discuss the procedures Harper should follow to audit the existence of loss contingencies arising from litigation, claims, and assessments.   (AICPA Adapted)

13-11 *Testing an Automated Payables System*

During your audit of the financial statements of Delaney Manufacturing Company for the year ended December 31, 2007, you find that at January 1, 2007, the company had installed the following computer system for recording raw material purchases and accounts payable:

a. Vendors' invoices are sent directly to the Accounts Payable department by the Mail department.

b. All supporting documents are attached to the invoices and accumulated in the Accounts Payable department. Cash discounts are computed, and the invoices are totaled, tied to supporting documents, and entered in a local access network by an employee at a workstation.

c. At the workstation, the employee enters the payable on a template that requires data entry for the related debit distribution to departmental inventories.

d. An invoice register is compiled automatically by payable and by debit distribution from the accumulated templates. In this operation, totals are compared with the amounts recorded for the related account payable.

e. The general ledger control account is posted monthly from the totals shown in the invoice register and all other journals.

f. Accounts payable are sorted by due dates.

g. On the due dates, the payables are processed to prepare checks.

h. At the end of the month, the accounts payable in the unpaid file are compared with the general ledger control account.

Required: What audit procedures would you use to test the accounts payable balance at December 31, 2007?

13-12 *Applying GAAP to Loss Reserves*

Cotronic, Inc., a publicly traded acquirer and lessor of low-technology office equipment, reports on the balance sheet Net Investment in Direct Financing Leases approximating $3.2 billion, an amount that reflects aggregate minimum lease payments, estimated residual values, unearned income, and the allowance for uncollectible accounts. To account for potential uncollectible accounts, Cotronic estimates potential uncollectibles as 3 percent of aggregate minimum lease payments and charges the estimate to expense through the following entry: *Dr* Provision for Doubtful Accounts, *CR* Allowance for Doubtful Accounts. The accounting mimics Cotronic's accounting for uncollectible receivables on equipment sold outright to customers.

Owing to lease terms ranging from 2 to 5 years, Carol DelSanto, Cotronic's chief financial officer, proposes to you, an audit partner, that estimated losses on doubtful accounts be charged to an account called Unamortized Provision for Doubtful Accounts (*Dr* Unamortized Provision for Doubtful Accounts, *Cr* Allowance for Doubtful Accounts) and amortized to income over the life of the property leased (*Dr* Provision for Doubtful Accounts, *Cr* Unamortized Provision for Doubtful Accounts). DelSanto argues that amortizing expense over the life of the property leased better matches for the entire lease portfolio the expense for uncollectible accounts with the revenue stream for accounts collected.

Required: Do you agree with DelSanto? Explain.

13-13 *Auditing Property & Casualty Insurance*

During an audit of the financial statements of Custer-McClurg, Inc., Timothy Barnes, the engagement manager, requested and received a client-prepared property & casualty insurance spreadsheet that included information about premiums.

Required:

1. Identify the type of information, in addition to premium information, that would ordinarily be included in a property & casualty insurance schedule.

2. What audit procedures should Barnes perform to test the client-prepared property & casualty insurance schedule?

AUDIT DOCUMENTATION REVIEW

13-14 *Working Paper Review: Accounts Payable*

Following is an audit working paper that documents an auditor's work for Feldman Services, Inc.'s accounts payable aged trial balance for the year ended December 31, 2007.

(Schedule Prepared by Client)
01/12/08

Feldman Services, Inc.
Accounts Payable Aged Trial Balance

Account Number	Vendor Name	Balance 12/31/07	0–30 Days	31–60 Days	Over 60 Days
00001	Acorn Shops	$ 31,890	$ 31,890		
00002	Aftran Inc.	17,869	15,432		$ 2,437
00003	Astrid & Strugg	6,670	6,670		
00005	Balfour	12,980	11,980		
00006	Baldoni Corp.	500	500		
00007	Benton Inc.	23,930	23,930		
00008	Boylston & Way	12,403	12,403		
00009	Britton Company	10,944		$ 10,944	
00010	Cristwich Inc.	4,530		4,530	
●	●	●	●	●	●
●	●	●	●	●	●
00452	Youngstown Co.	23,907	23,907		
		$2,569,340	$2,158,320	$301,020	$110,000
		a			

a Footed.

Required: List the deficiencies in this working paper.

13-15 *Working Paper Review: Accrued Property Taxes*

Following is an audit working paper that documents an auditor's work for Sempier & Fiske, Inc.'s accrued property taxes payable for the year ended December 31, 2007. Sempier is a first-year audit client.

DD4
01/15/08

AUDIT DOCUMENTATION REVIEW

Sempier & Fiske, Inc.
December 31, 2007

Balance, 12/31/06		$75,984a
Provision for property tax expense		75,000
Payments:		
State of Indiana	$34,930b	
City of Indianapolis	17,340b	
City of Ft. Wayne	8,450b	
City of So. Bend	10,346b	(71,066)
Balance, 12/31/07		$79,918
		c

a Agreed to prior auditor's working papers.
b Traced to cash disbursements records.
c Footed.

Required: List the deficiencies in this working paper.

13-16 *Earnings Manipulation and Environmental Liabilities*

During the planning stage of an audit, the engagement partner and manager tour the assembly facilities of York Chemicals, a manufacturer and supplier of chemical solvents to auto body shops nationwide. Solvent is stored in forty-gallon drums stacked by stock number in a warehouse awaiting shipment. Fifty yards from the assembly plant, but within a chain link fence that surrounds the property, is a ditch containing damaged barrels. Oil seepage is apparent beneath the barrels and on the unpaved roadway leading to the ditch.

Required: Identify, and explain the motive for, the key questions an auditor should ask management about the ditch, damaged barrels, and seepage.

Internet problems and discussion cases are available at http://ricchiute.swlearning.com

RESEARCH PROJECT

Management Discretion and Environmental Liabilities

Since the Exxon Valdez incident brought surface contamination to the evening news, the press has been replete with references to environmental disaster, making most everyone conscious of the devastating effects of industrial pollution, toxic waste disposal, and manufacturing and transport accidents. Underscoring many of these articles and newscasts is the unmistakable implication that industry is mortgaging the future of the planet and, in particular, that audited financial statements may not adequately portray the effects of environmental liabilities. For example, the March 9, 1993, late edition of *The New York Times*, in a piece by John Holusha entitled, "Stocks May Not Reflect Cleanup Liabilities That May Come Soon," began, "The earnings of Smokestack America seem likely to face new setbacks because of future liabilities for cleaning up the environment, according to a Price Waterhouse survey. The survey which covered manufacturing companies, public utilities and extractive industries, found that 62 percent have known environmental liabilities that are both material and undisclosed."

Required: Using the newspaper and magazines file in LEXIS-NEXIS, Factiva, or newspapers and magazines in a library, select an article or series of articles about environmental matters involving a particular company in, for example, the manufacturing, utilities, or extractive industries. Using the annual report file in the LEXIS-NEXIS, SEC's EDGAR (**http://www.sec.gov**), or copies of annual reports in a library, select the annual report of the same company issued for the fiscal year that includes the date of the article. Draft a report that accomplishes the following:

1. Summarize the article, indicating key issues that would suggest the need for disclosing environmental liability in the financial statements.
2. From the key issues in requirement 1, list and explain questions an auditor would likely pose to the management of the company you've selected.
3. Determine whether the company's financial statements include disclosures you think are related to the article and, either if so or if not, explain why you believe the company is or is not among those implicated in *The New York Times*.

Interactive quizzes are available as a student learning resource at
http://ricchiute.swlearning.com

Part 4

Auditing Other Cycles and Completing an Audit

14 Chapter

Personnel and Payroll

Major topics discussed in this chapter are:

- The nature of the personnel management and payroll functions within the expenditure/disbursement cycle.
- Controls over personnel and payroll.
- The auditor's consideration of controls over personnel and payroll.
- Substantive tests applicable to payroll accounts.
- Earnings manipulation in accounting for payroll costs and post-retirement health care benefits.

The previous two chapters focused on tests of controls and substantive tests of purchases and accounts payable, both of which are processed through the expenditure/disbursement cycle. This chapter continues the discussion, focusing on tests of controls and substantive tests related to personnel and payroll. The chapter begins by reviewing the nature of the cycle, introducing activities and controls common to personnel and payroll, and explaining an auditor's consideration of controls over personnel, payroll preparation, and payroll-related cash disbursements. In turn, substantive tests of payroll account balances are introduced. Finally, the chapter addresses earnings manipulation in payroll costs and in post-retirement heath care obligations.

The Expenditure/Disbursement Cycle: Personnel and Payroll

As discussed in Chapter 12, the **expenditure/disbursement cycle** encompasses the acquisition of, and payment for, resources acquired from vendors and from employees. Figure 14-1 summarizes the scope of the cycle as it relates to personnel and payroll, and indicates the two major business functions encompassed by personnel and payroll:

- Resources (services) are acquired from employees in exchange for obligations to pay, and
- Obligations to employees are paid.

Personnel and payroll are critical to most entities for at least three reasons: First, salaries and wages are a major expenditure for most service, manufacturing, and nonprofit entities. Second, in manufacturing companies, labor is an important component in valuing inventory and, if misclassified, both inventory and cost of

FIGURE 14-1: *The Scope of the Expenditure/ Disbursement Cycle: Personnel and Payroll*

Related Business Functions	Common Activities	Common Entries	Common Forms
• Resources (services) are acquired from employees in exchange for obligations to pay. • Obligations to employees are paid.	• Prepare and update personnel records. • Prepare and record payroll. • Distribute paychecks to employees.	• Payments to employees (cash disbursements) • Account distribution • Accrued payroll	• Personnel records • Time records • Payroll register • Employee earnings records

goods sold could be misstated materially. Third, payroll typically includes several categories of employee compensation, including salaries, hourly wages, incentive compensation and bonuses, overtime, vacation pay, and employee benefits such as pensions, health care, and profit sharing.

Personnel and payroll activities include hirings and terminations, payroll preparation and recording, and the distribution of payroll checks to employees. Journal entries are made for wage and salary payments, account distribution, and end-of-period accruals. Documents include:

- **Personnel records**: Information for each employee, including date of employment, job classification, salary or hourly pay rate, promotions, payroll deductions, terminations, etc.
- **Time record**: Hours worked by an employee during a pay period.
- **Payroll register**: A record of gross pay, withholdings, deductions, and net pay for each employee for a pay period; the basis for preparing paychecks, recording payroll, and updating employee earnings records.
- **Employee earnings record**: A cumulative, year-to-date summary of total earnings, withholdings, and deductions for each employee.

Figure 14-2 flowcharts representative personnel and payroll activities and Figure 14-3, derived from Figure 14-2, summarizes briefly the flow of documents and activities common to personnel and payroll.

Personnel

Without exception, all action taken by management on behalf of an employee— including hiring, promoting, transferring, and terminating—should be approved both by department supervisors and by the Personnel department, and should be documented in an employee's *personnel records*. Typically, personnel records also document:

- Salary or wage rates.
- Payroll deductions.
- Employee signatures.
- Job classification.
- Performance evaluation.

FIGURE 14-2: *Flowchart of Expenditure/Disbursement Cycle: Personnel and Payroll*

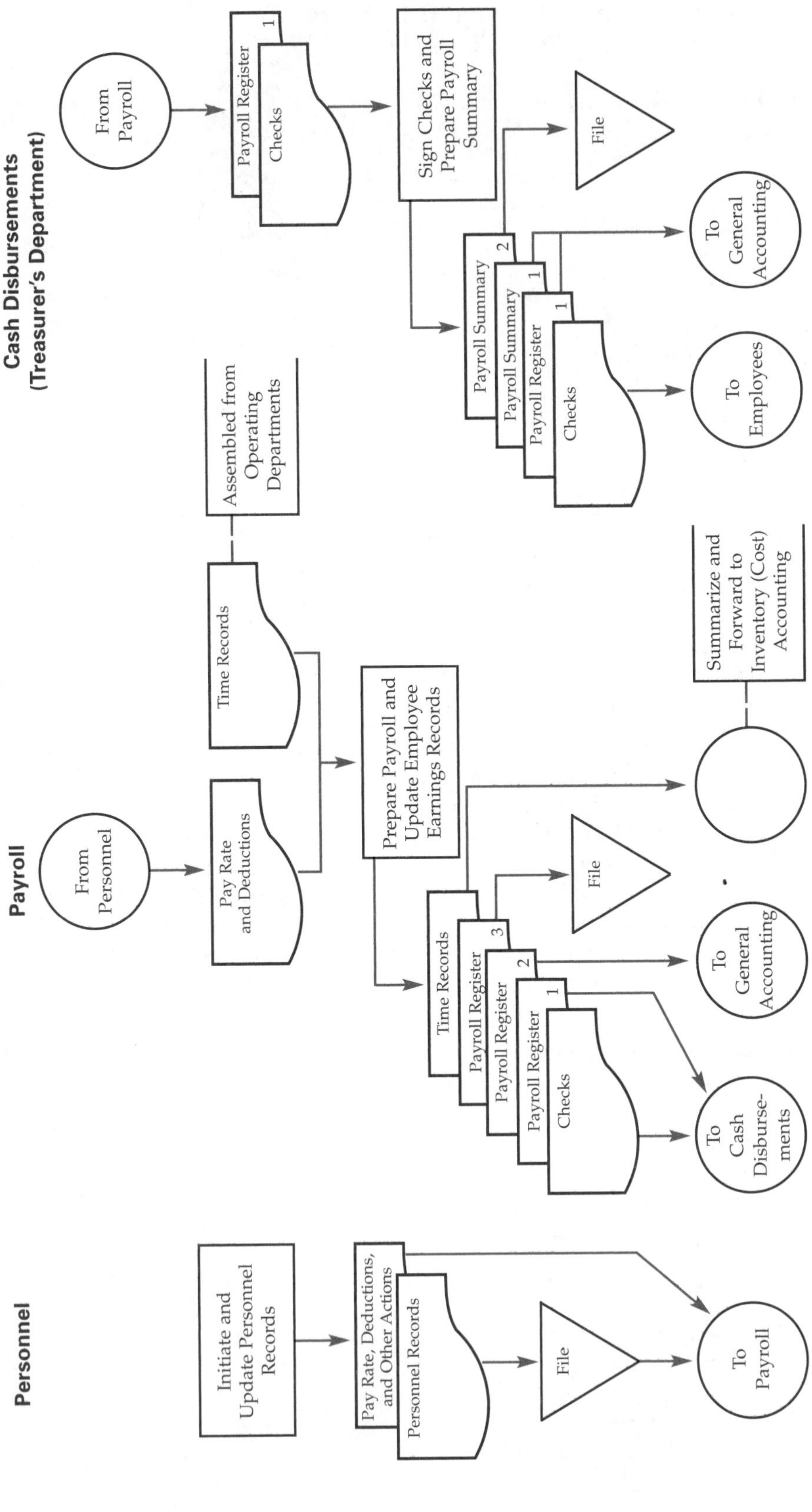

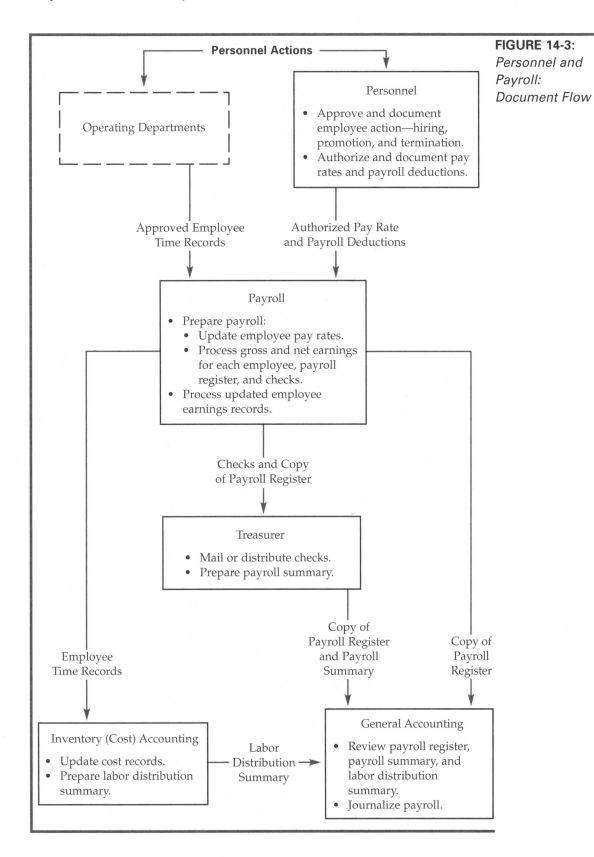

FIGURE 14-3:
Personnel and Payroll: Document Flow

To minimize the likelihood of fraud, personnel records should not be accessible to employees who are responsible for preparing, approving, or distributing payroll. For example, an employee who processes personnel records *and* prepares the payroll could destroy a salaried employee's termination records and abscond with (and forge endorsements for) subsequent paychecks.

When employees are terminated, the Personnel department should determine the nature and terms of any related termination settlement, such as lump sum cash payments and accrued vacation pay. Immediately thereafter, the Payroll department should be advised of the termination settlement and notified that further compensation has ceased.

Payroll Preparation and Distribution

Typically, the main source to prepare hourly wage employees' payroll and the payroll register is each employee's magnetic identification card: Employees "punch" in (out) at the beginning (end) of the work day on time clocks that interface directly with the company's computer, thereby creating an internally stored time record that software merges with pay rate and deduction data to compile payroll for the period. In addition, hours worked also may be accumulated in manufacturing departments for each production project, thereby creating a second time record—for example, an *accumulated departmental labor charge report*—which Inventory (Cost) Accounting uses for charging direct labor hours to work-in-process inventory.

From the information in the payroll register, facsimile-signed paychecks are printed and forwarded to the Treasury department along with a copy of the payroll register. The payroll register also is copied to General Accounting. As a control over payroll accuracy, the payroll register may be checked in detail by an employee not otherwise involved in payroll preparation. The payroll also should be reviewed for reasonableness by management. Each pay period, coincident with payroll preparation, cumulative employee earnings records are updated, providing a year-to-date summary of total earnings, taxes withheld, and deductions (for example, for federal and state income taxes, union dues, health insurance, savings, etc.).

Paychecks forwarded to the Treasury department should be compared electronically with listings in the payroll register. In small middle-market entities, signed checks should be delivered to operating department supervisors for distribution to individual employees. However, in large entities, it is preferable that signed paychecks be distributed by a person independent of both the operating department and Payroll—called a paymaster in some companies—thereby removing opportunities for department supervisors to dismiss an employee, withhold knowledge of the dismissal from Payroll, and then divert the check for his or her own use. The payroll register and the payroll summary prepared by Treasury department personnel should be copied to General Accounting.

To obtain reasonable assurance that paychecks are distributed to bona fide employees only, an employee independent of payroll preparation sometimes compares, on a test basis, endorsements on canceled payroll checks, if returned by the bank, with employee signatures maintained within personnel records. Differences could suggest errors or frauds, and should be investigated. At the end of the year, employee W-2 forms should be prepared and mailed to employees. Mailed W-2 forms that are returned by the postal service as undeliverable should be investigated, since returned W-2 forms could signal either incorrect addresses or, more serious, nonexistent employees.

A separate bank account (or accounts) should be maintained exclusively for payroll disbursements. Controls should limit access to blank checks and should assure that, if signed manually, checks are signed only by authorized officials.

Internal Control Objectives and Potential Errors or Fraud

Chapter 12 discussed control objectives for purchasing and cash disbursements. The following focuses on internal control over transaction authorization, execution, recording, and access to assets for personnel and payroll. The discussion identifies control objectives, examples of errors or frauds that may arise if objectives are not achieved, and examples of control procedures designed to prevent or detect errors or frauds. Figure 14-4 summarizes.

➤ fraud

FIGURE 14-4: *Personnel and Payroll: Objectives, Potential Errors or Frauds, and Control Procedures*

Objective	Types of Errors or Frauds That Could Occur If Objective Not Met	Control Procedures Designed to Prevent or Detect Errors or Frauds
Transaction Authorization		
• Employees should be hired according to criteria authorized by management.	Unqualified employees may be hired, potentially resulting in excessive training costs, unnecessary relocation costs, or penalties for violating equal opportunity laws.	Establish clear statements of hiring policies and procedures. Maintain updated personnel records for all employees. Verify employment applications.
• Compensation and payroll deductions should be made in accordance with management's authorization.	Employees may be paid unauthorized amounts, potentially resulting in excessive labor costs or violation of union contracts. Accruals for pensions, vacations, or bonuses may be calculated from inaccurate information, potentially resulting in misstated accruals.	Maintain updated listings of authorized pay rates and deductions. Establish procedures for reviewing and approving pay rates and deductions.
• Adjustments to payroll or personnel records should be made in accordance with management's authorization.	Unauthorized adjustments may be processed to increase an employee's pay, potentially misappropriating cash and overstating labor costs.	Establish clear statements of adjustment policies and procedures.

(continues)

FIGURE 14-4 *(continued)*

Objective	Types of Errors or Frauds That Could Occur If Objective Not Met	Control Procedures Designed to Prevent or Detect Errors or Frauds
Execution		
• Payroll and personnel procedures should be established in accordance with management's authorization.	Employees could process paychecks for terminated or fictitious employees, potentially resulting in misappropriated cash.	Establish personnel and payroll procedures manuals. Periodically verify employee reassignments and personnel action reports.
• All payroll cash disbursements should be based upon a recognized liability.	Cash may be disbursed for services not performed, potentially resulting in misappropriated cash and overstated labor costs.	Prenumber and control time records, paychecks, and adjustment forms. Require manual dual signatories for all pay over a prespecified dollar amount.
Recording		
• Amounts due to employees should be recorded at the proper amounts, be recorded in the proper period, and be properly classified.	Payroll costs, labor costs, and related liabilities (e.g., federal tax withheld) may be inaccurate, potentially resulting in misstated expenses and liabilities. Summaries of detail records (e.g., payroll register and summary of labor costs) may not agree, potentially resulting in miscalculated payroll or misapplied labor costs.	Establish and document account distribution procedures. Reconcile appropriate ledgers and journals. Establish physical barriers over unused documents and forms.
Access to Assets		
• Access to personnel and payroll records and to forms and documents should be restricted to personnel authorized by management.	Records, forms, or documents may be misused by unauthorized personnel, potentially resulting in misapplied cash or unauthorized labor costs.	Prenumber and control forms and documents. Segregate responsibilities for authorizing, executing, and recording payroll and personnel transactions. Maintain listings and samples of authorized signatories.

Transaction Authorization

Much as management should approve vendors (Chapter 12), management also should establish criteria for hiring line and staff employees. Otherwise, unqualified employees may be hired, potentially resulting in excessive training costs, unnecessary relocation costs, or penalties for violating equal opportunity laws, among other things. To control against unauthorized hiring, management should establish written hiring policies, verify all relevant information included in employment applications, and maintain updated personnel records for all employees.

Likewise, management should authorize compensation and payroll deductions, thereby protecting against excessive labor costs, violations of union contracts, and inaccurate accruals for pensions, vacations, or bonuses. Many companies control compensation and deductions by establishing procedures for reviewing and approving pay rates and deductions and by maintaining updated, authorized pay rates by job classification.

Although entry-level pay rates may be determined by authorized pay rate listings, management should authorize subsequent adjustments—for example, for promotions, transfers, and merit increases. Otherwise, unauthorized pay increases could be processed. Management could control unauthorized pay increases by establishing written policies for pay rate adjustments and communicating the policies to the Personnel department and to operating department supervisors.

Execution

In labor-intensive businesses, such as the automotive industry, labor costs can be both extensive and subject to negotiated labor contracts, suggesting the need for controls that assure accurate payrolls. Otherwise, management could violate labor contracts, or employees could process paychecks for terminated or fictitious employees. As a result, most medium- to large-sized companies usually establish personnel and payroll procedures manuals and advertise available job openings widely throughout the company.

To control against disbursements for work not performed, all cash disbursements for payroll should be based on a recognized liability. Paychecks should reflect compensation for services actually rendered, just as disbursements to vendors should be based on goods and services actually received. Management can control unauthorized payroll disbursements by requiring a second, manual signature for all unusual or excessive paycheck amounts.

Recording

All amounts owed to employees should be recorded at the proper amounts and in the proper period, and should be classified properly. Otherwise, payroll and labor costs and related liabilities such as taxes withheld may be inaccurate, potentially resulting in misstated expenses, labor costs, and liabilities. In addition, summaries of detailed records, such as payroll summaries and registers, may not agree, which could result in miscalculated payroll or misapplied labor costs. In short, accurately calculated paychecks do not necessarily result in proper account distribution or properly applied labor costs. To control against improper recording, management could establish account distribution and labor cost allocation procedures and reconcile appropriate ledgers, journals, and summaries.

Access to Assets

To control against misapplied cash and unauthorized labor costs, management should institute policies that restrict access to personnel and payroll records to authorized personnel only. For example, management could establish physical barriers over unused documents and forms (for example, safes); prenumber documents; maintain listings of authorized signatories; and segregate responsibility for authorizing, executing, and recording payroll and personnel transactions—the same controls listed in Chapter 12 for purchases and cash disbursements.

Segregation of Duties To assure adequate segregation of duties, Personnel department responsibilities should be separated from payroll preparation, and both should be separated from cash disbursements and operating departments. Otherwise, an authorization function (personnel) would be combined with an execution function (payroll), thereby increasing opportunities for unauthorized employee action and for inflated pay rates. In addition, combining payroll with operating departments, such as Production or Inventory Control, increases opportunities for unauthorized disbursements because an employee would be responsible both for reporting hours worked and for calculating gross pay.

Considering Internal Control

Chapter 12 discussed the auditor's consideration of controls over three expenditure/disbursement cycle functions: purchasing, receiving, and cash disbursement. The following focuses on an auditor's consideration of controls over the cycle's personnel and payroll activities.

Obtain an Understanding

In the initial phase of considering internal control, an auditor attempts to determine how the system is supposed to work and whether control procedures have been prescribed by management to assure that the system is functioning as planned. Obtaining an understanding of the system includes:

1. Performing a *preliminary review*,
2. *Documenting* the system,
3. Performing a *transaction walkthrough*, and
4. Determining whether existing *controls* are potentially reliable in assessing control risk below the maximum.

Preliminary Review

In a preliminary review, an auditor develops a general understanding of a client's *control environment*, the *flow of transactions and records* through the accounting system, and the *control procedures* management has implemented to prevent or detect errors or frauds. For example, an auditor could obtain an understanding by reviewing the client's personnel and payroll procedures manual and by interviewing employees in Personnel and Payroll. Assuming the preliminary review suggests that further consideration of internal control is likely to justify assessing control risk below the maximum and, thereby, restricting substantive tests of payroll balances, an auditor would proceed as follows.

System Documentation

Figure 14-2, discussed earlier, illustrates a flowchart for personnel and payroll. In turn, Figure 14-5 illustrates a questionnaire, a second method for obtaining system documentation about personnel and payroll and about the distribution of payroll checks. Alternatively, an auditor could use a narrative to describe the payroll system either in whole or in part. For example, to document payroll procedures for hourly employees, an auditor might use flowcharts and questionnaires and

FIGURE 14-5: *Questionnaire: Personnel and Payroll*

Question	Answer: Yes, No, or N/A	Remarks
Personnel and Payroll		
1. Are all employee changes—hiring, promotions, transfers, terminations—approved by operating department supervisors and by the Personnel department?		
2. Are all employee changes documented in personnel records?		
3. Are all employee changes communicated promptly to the Payroll department?		
4. Do employee personnel records include authorizations for all deductions and withholdings?		
5. Are guidelines established for determining account distribution for labor charges?		
6. Are employees who prepare or process payroll independent of hiring and terminations and excluded from distributing paychecks to employees?		
7. Is payroll approved by a responsible official independent of payroll preparation and processing?		
8. Is the preparation of employee time records supervised to assure that hours reported are accurate?		
Cash Disbursement		
1. Are paychecks distributed by personnel independent of the Personnel and Payroll departments?		
2. Is the payroll bank account reconciled monthly by an employee independent of payroll preparation, processing, and distribution?		
3. Are employees required to provide identification before receiving a paycheck?		
4. Are unclaimed paychecks returned to an employee independent of payroll preparation, processing, and distribution?		
5. Are W-2 forms compared with payroll records and mailed by employees independent of payroll preparation, processing, and distribution?		
6. Are returned W-2 forms (for example, marked "return to sender" by the U.S. Postal Service) investigated by employees who are independent of payroll?		

prepare a narrative description of the executive payroll, which typically involves fewer personnel and, therefore, fewer payroll checks.

Transaction Walkthrough

To confirm his or her understanding of the system flowcharted in Figure 14-2, the auditor could select a line item from a processed payroll register and trace the information (1) to time records summarized in the Payroll department and filed in the Inventory Accounting department and (2) to records maintained in the Personnel department. The purpose of the walkthrough, however, is not necessarily to test control procedures, but to confirm the flowchart and completed questionnaire.

Identification of Control Procedures

An auditor completes the system documentation and continues the consideration of internal control in the same manner as outlined in Chapter 12 for purchases and cash disbursements:

- Identify the system's *control objectives*. The first column of Figure 14-4 identifies control objectives for personnel and payroll.
- Consider the *potential errors or frauds* that might result if specific control objectives are not met. The second column of Figure 14-4 identifies examples of potential errors or frauds.
- Determine what *control procedures* are used by the entity to prevent or detect potentially material errors or frauds. The third column of Figure 14-4 identifies examples of potential controls.
- Design *tests of controls*.

Only those control procedures relevant to financial statement assertions are subjected to tests of controls, which are discussed next.

Tests of Controls: Personnel and Payroll

Generally, internal evidence prepared by the client is the only persuasive audit evidence available for testing payroll. As a result, auditors often rely predominantly, if not exclusively, on tests of controls rather than substantive procedures when auditing payroll. If the results of tests of controls indicate that control procedures can be relied on in assessing control risk below the maximum, substantive testing focuses on analytical procedures such as ratio analysis. Some representative tests of controls for personnel and payroll and for the distribution of payroll checks are discussed next for the system flowcharted in Figure 14-2.

Personnel and Payroll

The payroll register is an entity's continuing record of employee compensation and provides the basis for preparing, distributing, and recording periodic payroll. Representative tests of controls follow.

Tests of Controls: Personnel and Payroll

1. Obtain the payroll register for a selected period (or periods) and verify the mathematical accuracy.
2. Obtain a related payroll summary and a labor distribution summary.
   a. Verify the mathematical accuracy of payroll and labor distribution summaries and compare with totals in the payroll register.

> b. Trace totals to postings in the general ledger and in cost accounting records.
> 3. Select a random sample of employees from the payroll register and obtain the personnel file for each employee selected.
>   a. Examine files for completeness and review employee action reports for authorization.
>   b. Compare pay rates and payroll deduction information in personnel records with entries in the payroll register; for hourly employees, obtain time records and recompute gross earnings for the payroll period.
>   c. Trace sampled entries in the payroll register to postings in individual employee cumulative earnings records.
>   d. Trace selected employee names to a payroll register for a prior period and to a payroll register for a subsequent period; examine employee action reports for newly hired or terminated personnel.

As implied in Step 1, the payroll register is the starting point for an auditor's tests of personnel and payroll. In Step 2, the auditor addresses mathematical accuracy and postings by footing and cross-footing the payroll register and reconciling totals with related summary schedules and with the general ledger and inventory accounting records. Payroll accuracy and account distribution are of major concern to an auditor because of the significant impact of payroll on no less than seven financial statement accounts, including payroll expense, payroll taxes, work-in-process inventory, finished goods inventory, cost of sales, accrued payroll, and accrued payroll taxes.

In Step 3, an auditor selects a sample of entries in the payroll register as a basis for testing personnel records for completeness and proper authorization and for determining whether employee compensation accurately reflects authorized pay rates, payroll deductions, and hours worked. In addition, the auditor examines postings to individual employee cumulative earnings records, because these records provide the basis for preparing W-2 forms and for calculating payroll tax expense.

Distribution of Employee Paychecks

Tests of payments to employees focus on the existence and authenticity of employees to whom disbursements are made, rather than cash disbursements per se. Representative tests follow.

> **Tests of Controls: Distribution of Paychecks**
> 1. Obtain a sample of canceled payroll checks.
>   a. Trace details of sampled checks (payee name, date, amount, and check number) to entries in the payroll register.
>   b. Compare endorsements on checks with signatures in employee personnel records.
> 2. Take control of payroll checks just prior to distribution by department supervisors, and personally distribute checks to properly identified employees.

In Step 1a, the auditor traces details of sampled paychecks to entries in the payroll register, thereby addressing whether checks are recorded properly. Step 1b, sometimes called a "payroll payoff," focuses on the authenticity of employees by comparing endorsements on canceled checks with signatures maintained in employee personnel records. The auditor also addresses the authenticity of employees in Step 2 by personally distributing paychecks to employees during work hours. This procedure normally requires that the auditor first examine an employee identification card with photo, if available, to assure that the employee is actually who he or she purports to be.

Assess Control Risk

To complete the consideration of internal control for personnel and payroll, an auditor reviews system documentation and the results of tests of controls and determines whether existing controls are effective and can be relied on to assess control risk below the maximum, to assess detection risk above the minimum, and, therefore, to restrict substantive tests of payroll. The evaluation is based on the types of errors or frauds that could occur, control procedures that should prevent the errors or frauds, a determination of whether the necessary procedures exist and are followed, and any deficiencies in internal control.

Assuming control procedures are effective, auditors normally restrict year-end substantive tests of payroll to analytical procedures. If analytical procedures then suggest that payroll-related balances are not reasonable, an auditor would increase the extent of year-end testing by performing expanded substantive tests of details. The analytical procedures applied to payroll are discussed next.

Analytical Procedures: Payroll and Accruals

If the results of tests of controls indicate that control risk cannot be assessed below the maximum, substantive procedures would be expanded accordingly. Also, if significant changes in control procedures or their method of application occurred subsequent to testing controls, the auditor would have to either reconsider internal control—for example, through additional tests of controls—or assess control risk at the maximum without reconsidering the controls. However, as noted previously and implied in the representative year-end procedures within Figure 14-6, substantive tests of payroll usually focus primarily or exclusively on analytical procedures such as the following:

Analytical Procedure
- Compare both direct labor and payroll to budgets and to prior years.
- Compare the ratios of payroll to total expenses and payroll to sales with prior years.
- Compare the ratios of direct labor to cost of sales and direct labor to sales with prior years.
- Compare commissioned sales payroll to sales times average commission rates.
- Compare payroll to prior-year payroll adjusted for pay rate changes and the number of employees.
- Compare the ratio of payroll tax expense to payroll with prior years.
- Compare accrued payroll and accrued payroll tax expense with prior years.

For example, if total direct labor approximated 35 percent of cost of sales for the previous two years, an auditor would expect the percentage for the current year to be close to 35 percent, unless changes have occurred that would be expected to

FIGURE 14-6: *Substantive Tests: Payroll*

Assertions	*Procedures*
Obligations Valuation	1. Determine by analytical procedures the reasonableness of payroll expense and account distribution.
Obligations Valuation Completeness	2. Determine the reasonableness of accruals for wages, salaries, and related accounts.

Presentation and disclosure	3. Review financial statements to determine whether:
	  a. Payroll and related accruals are properly classified and described.
	  b. Disclosures are adequate.

alter the relationship. However, if the ratio increased significantly from expected, the auditor might consider the following alternative explanations:

- Wage rate changes.
- Employee hiring.
- Overstated direct labor.
- Understated cost of sales.

In practice, auditors usually determine the reasonableness of accruals with little detailed testing. For example, if employees are paid biweekly and one week's payroll is accrued at the end of the year, an auditor could simply determine whether the accrual is equal to approximately 50 percent of the total payroll for the most recent complete pay period. If different categories of employees are paid at different intervals, an auditor might recalculate the accrual and examine subsequent payroll disbursements.

Finally, an auditor should review financial statements to determine that payroll and related accounts are properly classified and described and that all material information is disclosed. For example, information relating to stock options or deferred compensation plans should be included in the notes to the financial statements.

Payroll, Post-Retirement Benefits, and Earnings Manipulation

Payroll is an example of a financial statement caption auditors are able to "tie down" pretty much to the dollar, since, like in the audit of cash, an entity's payroll records should mirror the bank's records for paychecks cleared and, equally comforting to auditors, employees will complain loudly if paychecks are miscalculated. In short, there's little room for management to exercise discretion in recording current and accrued payroll. However, two payroll-related issues offer some room for manipulation: capitalizing payroll costs and post-retirement benefits other than pensions.

Capitalized Payroll Costs: Safety-Kleen

Payroll is a period expense. However, motivated to enhance reported earnings, some companies over the years have capitalized payroll costs inappropriately,

➤ fraud

rather than charge payroll to the current period. Take, for example, Safety-Kleen, Inc., a publicly traded provider of industrial-waste collection and disposal services. Characterized by the SEC as a "massive accounting fraud,"[1] the chief executive and financial officers, among other executives, exploited schemes that recorded unrealized contingent-contract claims to overstate revenue and capitalized payroll costs to understate period expenses. Not unlike AOL, discussed in Chapter 13 in the context of capitalized marketing costs, Safety-Kleen capitalized payroll-related costs in financial statement accounts that summarized marketing and start-up activities.

➤ restatement

In March 2000, following discovery of the fraud, the board of directors authorized an internal investigation that drove in July 2000 $534 million in restatements to Safety-Kleen's previously reported 1997, 1998, and 1999 net incomes. However, following the restatements and relying in part on a false management representation letter (Chapter 17) management had provided the independent auditor, the SEC in 2002 filed suit against Safety-Kleen, alleging among other things that management had full knowledge the representation letter "falsely represented that: (i) the consolidated financial statements were fairly presented in conformity with GAAP; (ii) there were no material transactions, agreements or accounts that were not properly recorded; . . . and (iv) that there had been no fraud involving management or employees who had significant roles in the company's internal controls."[2] Simultaneous with filing the complaint, Safety-Kleen, without admitting or denying the Commission's allegations, consented to a final judgment permanently enjoining the company from violating securities laws. The case is instructive, largely because it makes clear that, even in accounts for which conventional wisdom suggests there's little likelihood of material fraud, management may be incented to commit fraud nevertheless.

Post-Retirement Benefits Other Than Pensions

Largely because of the uncertainty management faces in estimating *future* obligations, another personnel-related cost leaves considerable room for discretion and, therefore, requires an auditor's critical attention: **post-retirement benefits other than pensions**—in particular, obligations for the discounted present value of future health care costs.[3] A survey reported in *BusinessWeek* estimates that post-retirement health care benefits are offered by over 90 percent of the companies that employ more than 5,000, and Deloitte & Touche estimates that future health care costs will range between a staggering $100 and $500 billion. However, partly because the costs to fund post-retirement health care benefits were neither tax deductible nor, for that matter, binding obligations under prior definitions of liabilities, companies had largely ignored obligations for future health care costs in their current financial statements, electing instead to pay retirees' actual out-of-pocket health care costs as the costs were incurred, providing a penetrating example of off-balance-sheet financing and of a cash basis "pay-as-you-go" system.

---

1   *SEC Accounting and Auditing Enforcement Release No. 1690,* "In the Matter of Safety-Kleen, Inc.," December 22, 2003.
2   *SEC v. Safety-Kleen, Inc., et al., Compliant,* United States District Court for the Southern District of New York, December 12, 2002.
3   Post-retirement benefits also include life insurance, tuition assistance, and housing subsidies, among other things, all of which are important to retirees but none of which is usually as material to financial statements as the discounted present value of future health care costs.

In response, the FASB issued *Statement of Financial Accounting Standards No. 106*, "Employers' Accounting for Postretirement Benefits Other Than Pensions," a statement *The Wall Street Journal* called "one of the most significant changes to accounting ever . . . a rule on postretirement health benefits that could cut corporate profits by hundreds of billions of dollars,"[4] because, for the first time ever, the present value of future health care expenses and liabilities would be recognized in current financial statements.

Management and Auditor Incentives

Prior to *SFAS No. 106*, management was not required to report future liabilities for nonpension post-retirement benefits. As a consequence, none did. Although discretion over reporting the liability ceased with *SFAS No. 106*, management retains some discretion over the amount of the liability reported, since future health care benefits are quite unpredictable both in timing (who will become ill when?) and in amount (who of the ill will be ill with what?). Clearly, management has incentives to understate the discounted present value of future health care obligations, largely because of the effect on reported income. For example, IBM's $2.3 billion charge to first-quarter 1991 net income to adopt *SFAS No. 106* drove the company's first reported quarterly loss ever.[5] Auditors have incentives to assure that management's charge to income and reported liability are fairly presented in all material respects, since materially misstated amounts can affect current share prices and future health care payouts, and, as demonstrated in Chapter 5, auditors can be held liable for negligently failing to detect materially misstated financial statements. The following illustrates issues auditors confront when auditing an employer's accounting for post-retirement health care.

Health Care Obligations

Like pension benefits, post-retirement health care benefits are a form of deferred compensation, the costs of which should be recognized over the *attribution period*, the period from the date an employee is hired to the date he or she is fully eligible to receive benefits (usually the retirement date). An employer is ultimately liable for the *expected post-retirement benefit liability*: the discounted present value of benefits expected to be paid in the future to employees and to their beneficiaries and eligible dependents. At the balance sheet date, the employer discloses in the financial statements the *accumulated post-retirement benefit liability*, the portion of the expected obligation that employees have earned as of the balance sheet date. Equally important, the employer discloses the *expected long-term rate of return on plan assets*. For example, in 2003, Deere and Company disclosed that the expected long-term rates of return in each of the three years 2000 through 2003 were 8.5 percent. *SFAS No. 106* offers guidance on determining the expected rate of return. However, the guidance offers some discretion in interpretation, since the rate is based in part on "the rates of return *expected* to be available for reinvestment." *Expected* rates of return demand forecasts of future events, which can't be verified fully, leave room for alternative interpretation and, in extreme cases, invite manipulation. Consider the following case.

---

4   "FASB Issues Rule Change on Benefits," *The Wall Street Journal* (December 20, 1990), p. A3.
5   "IBM to Record Large Charge for New Rule," *The Wall Street Journal* (March 29, 1991), p. A3.

Ansonia Wire & Cable Company, an East Coast manufacturer and supplier of extruded copper wire products, employs over 1,000 nonunion production and clerical employees, all of whom are eligible to participate in a defined benefit post-retirement health plan. During year-end audit work, Ansonia's chief executive and chief financial officers broach post-retirement health care obligations with the auditor. Management is concerned that an excessive post-retirement liability on their year-end financial statements will:

- Endanger the success of an initial public offering of class B common stock contemplated for the following year, and
- Raise the debt-to-equity ratio, causing the potential violation of a debt covenant on an existing commercial loan.

To maintain comparability with other wire and cable companies competing in the market for initial public offerings, and to understate the amount of the post-retirement benefit obligation, management proposes that the rate used to calculate the return on plan assets be equivalent to the high rate at which Ansonia's investment portfolio is performing.

Audit Judgment: Accounting, Liability, and Ethics

➤ ethics

What management proposes runs dangerously close to deception, a clear violation of generally accepted accounting principles. If Ansonia's management insists on a high discount rate (even one that approximates the company's actual return on investment), the auditor has no alternative but to alert the client that:

- *SFAS No. 106* requires that the rate of return on plan assets be based on the expected long-term rate of return on plan assets, not a rate experienced otherwise by the reporting entity,
- Overstating the rate understates the post-retirement benefit liability, thereby understating total liabilities,
- Understating total liabilities in this case effectively deceives potential participants in the planned initial public offering and the bank whose debt covenants are apparently tied in part to the debt-to-equity ratio,
- An overstated rate of return, and the resulting understatement of liabilities, is a violation of GAAP, and
- A departure from GAAP will cause the auditor to issue a qualified or adverse opinion, depending on materiality, and an explanatory paragraph that discloses the effect of the departure on reported earnings (Chapter 3).

➤ fraud

If the auditor considers conspiring with Ansonia management to overstate the expected rate of return, he or she risks serious legal and ethical implications. Assuming the initial public offering is effected, purchasers of the securities may take action under the Securities Act of 1933, Section 11 (Chapter 5), if any part of the registration statement contained an untrue statement of a material fact, in this case an untrue statement about existing liabilities. Further, the commercial bank holding Ansonia's long-term debt could bring an action under common law (Chapter 5) for losses, if any, on Ansonia's debt repayment, alleging that the bank relied on the financial statements in presuming that reported total debt, the numerator in the debt-to-equity ratio, was not misstated and, therefore, that the resulting ratio did not violate an existing debt covenant. As discussed in Chapter 5, the auditor could be liable for treble damages under the Racketeer Influenced and Corrupt Organizations (RICO) Act, since *Reves v. Arthur Young*, a 1993 U.S. Supreme Court case, does not provide relief from RICO when, as is the case in Ansonia, he or she participated directly with management to perpetrate the fraud.

The case raises at least two ethical issues. First, the auditor violates the Code of Professional Conduct, Rule 203—Accounting Principles (Chapter 4), which provides that an AICPA member cannot issue an unqualified opinion if the financial statements contain a departure from generally accepted accounting principles. In the Ansonia case, the accounting principle violated is encompassed within an authoritative pronouncement: *SFAS No. 106*. Violating Rule 203 can result in an administrative reprimand, such as suspension to practice before the SEC or revocation of a CPA's license to practice. Second, conspiring with a client to deceive potential shareholders and commercial lenders raises serious questions about the auditor's ethical character, questions that far exceed the mere minimum standards of the AICPA's Code of Professional Conduct.

SUMMARY

In addition to purchases and cash disbursements transactions, the expenditure/ disbursement cycle also processes transactions and events related to personnel and payroll. Activities typically associated with personnel and payroll include the maintenance of personnel records and labor records, payroll preparation and account distribution, and cash disbursements to employees. Common documentation for personnel and payroll includes personnel records—the evidence supporting employee hirings, promotions, and terminations—and employee time records.

Audit tests of payroll usually focus on interim tests of controls. However, unlike most other audit areas, interim testing also includes procedures normally associated with year-end substantive tests of account balances. As a result, year-end testing of payroll often focuses on analytical procedures designed to assess the reasonableness of recorded payroll expense and accruals. If the consideration of internal control indicates control procedures are ineffective, or if analytical procedures suggest that payroll and payroll-related accounts appear unreasonable, an auditor would increase the extent of year-end testing to include substantive tests of details.

Unlike payroll expense, which can be recalculated or estimated with some degree of certainty, the discounted present value of post-retirement health care obligations require estimation, since it's not clear which employees will live to retirement, who of those who live will become ill, and, for that matter, what they'll be ill with and when. Although management must report post-retirement health care obligations, there are opportunities to understate the obligations, among them the choice of an expected rate of return.

KEY TERMS

Employee earnings record 585
Expenditure/disbursement cycle 584
Payroll register 585
Personnel records 585

Post-retirement benefits other than
  pensions 598
Time record 585

REFERENCES

Auditing Standards:

AICPA, *Codification of Statements on Auditing Standards*. New York: AICPA.

Accounting Standard:

FASB Statement of Financial Accounting Standards No. 106, "Employers' Accounting for Postretirement Benefits Other Than Pensions."

Books:

Committee of Sponsoring Organizations of the Treadway Commission (COSO), *Internal Control: Integrated Framework*. Evaluation Tools. New York: COSO, 1992.

Committee of Sponsoring Organizations of the Treadway Commission (COSO), *Internal Control: Integrated Framework*. Executive Summary. New York: COSO, 1992.

Committee of Sponsoring Organizations of the Treadway Commission (COSO), *Internal Control: Integrated Framework*. Framework. New York: COSO, 1992.

Committee of Sponsoring Organizations of the Treadway Commission (COSO), *Internal Control: Integrated Framework*. Reporting to External Parties. New York: COSO, 1992.

QUESTIONS

1. Identify the major activities associated with a company's Payroll, Personnel, and Treasury departments.
2. Explain why personnel and payroll are important to management.
3. Identify the categories of compensation that payroll typically includes.
4. What is a payroll register?
5. Why should management establish written hiring criteria?
6. What would an auditor expect to be documented in payroll records?
7. From which responsibilities should Payroll department employees be separated?
8. Why do companies maintain separate bank accounts for payroll?
9. How can management assure that payroll checks are distributed only to bona fide employees?
10. How can management mitigate the likelihood of department managers processing payroll checks for terminated employees or processing unauthorized promotions and transfers?
11. Explain why Personnel department employees should be separated from payroll preparation, and why Personnel and Payroll department employees should be separated from cash disbursements.
12. How might an auditor perform a transaction walkthrough when considering controls over personnel and payroll?
13. Auditors are usually able to tie payroll costs to the dollar. Why?
14. What might an auditor learn by comparing direct labor and payroll to budgets and to prior years?
15. What source does an auditor use as the starting point for tests of personnel and payroll activities?
16. Why are payroll preparation accuracy and appropriate account distribution of major concern to an auditor?
17. How does an auditor test whether employees whose names appear on payroll registers are bona fide, that is, actually employed by the company?
18. How can management control against paychecks being prepared for unauthorized or fictitious employees?

19. How can an auditor test the authenticity of employees to whom payroll checks are disbursed?

20. Why does the accounting for post-retirement health care obligations create so much more difficulty for accountants and auditors than the accounting for and auditing of payroll expense?

MULTIPLE CHOICE QUESTIONS

1. Which of the following statements best explains why the accuracy of payroll calculations and of payroll account distribution is critical to an auditor?

    a. Employees will complain to management if their paychecks do not reflect wages or salaries earned.
    b. Payroll is paid in cash, an account that is highly susceptible to fraud.
    c. Generally accepted auditing standards require that tests of cash and payroll be coordinated.
    d. Payroll impacts several balance sheet and income statement accounts.

2. Disagreement between amounts recorded in a payroll register and a payroll summary could suggest:

    a. Dismissed employees who remain on the payroll.
    b. Miscalculated payroll.
    c. Inaccurate job costing records.
    d. Inappropriate payroll deductions.

3. Procedures for wage-rate adjustments is an example of a control for:

    a. Transaction authorization.
    b. Transaction execution.
    c. Segregation of duties.
    d. Access to assets.

4. Which of the following is a record of gross pay, withholding, and deductions?

    a. Payroll register
    b. Time record
    c. Employee earnings record
    d. Personnel record

5. Obtaining an understanding of internal control over personnel and payroll does not include:

    a. Performing a preliminary review.
    b. Documenting the system.
    c. Performing a transaction walkthrough.
    d. A payroll payoff.

6. Tests of controls over personnel and payroll focus on the preparation, distribution, and recording of earned salaries and wages. Which of the following is the primary source from which tests of personnel and payroll are derived?

    a. Time records
    b. Labor distribution summary
    c. Employee earnings record
    d. Payroll register

7. Why does an auditor examine postings to employee cumulative earnings records?

   a. Undetected errors would accumulate across years, making subsequent payroll accounts misstated.
   b. Cumulative earnings records are the basis for preparing W-2 forms and for calculating payroll tax expense.
   c. To detect unreported employee terminations.
   d. To detect overstated wages paid to undeserving employees.

8. On a surprise basis, an auditor may elect to distribute paychecks to employees personally. What is the primary purpose of this audit procedure?

   a. To assure that no extra payroll checks are prepared and distributed.
   b. To test whether all paid employees exist.
   c. To assure that paychecks are not distributed to an employee absent on the day the auditor distributes checks.
   d. To test the procedures for distributing paychecks.

9. Considering internal control over personnel and payroll is least likely to include:

   a. Identifying control objectives.
   b. Considering potential errors or frauds that might occur.
   c. Determining control procedures management uses.
   d. Designing substantive tests.

10. Which of the following is likely an ineffective test of personnel records and a payroll register?

    a. Compare pay rates and payroll deduction information in personnel records with entries in the payroll register.
    b. Recalculate withholdings.
    c. Trace sampled entries in the payroll register to postings in employee cumulative earnings records.
    d. Examine files for completeness.

11. In determining whether control procedures are potentially reliable in assessing control risk below the maximum, an auditor performs four tasks, listed below in random order:

    (1) Design tests of controls.
    (2) Consider potential errors or frauds.
    (3) Identify control objectives.
    (4) Determine control procedures.

    In what order are these tasks performed in a financial statement audit?

    a. 1, 2, 3, 4
    b. 3, 2, 4, 1
    c. 2, 3, 4, 1
    d. 4, 3, 1, 2

12. After completing tests of controls, an auditor concludes from available evidence that control risk can be assessed below the maximum and detection risk above the minimum. Under these conditions:

    a. Substantive tests of controls can be eliminated.
    b. Substantive tests can be limited to analytical procedures.
    c. The extent of substantive tests of details can be restricted.
    d. Substantive tests of details can be performed at an interim date.

13. Which of the following financial statement assertions is of least concern to an auditor when testing payroll?

    a. Occurrence
    b. Valuation
    c. Completeness
    d. Allocation

14. To assess the reasonableness of total payroll, an auditor could:

    a. Compare the ratios of direct labor to cost of sales and direct labor to sales with prior years.
    b. Compare the ratios of payroll to total expenses and payroll to sales with prior years.
    c. Compare payroll to prior-year payroll adjusted for pay rate changes and the number of employees.
    d. Compare accrued payroll and accrued payroll tax expense with prior years.

15. How could management exploit payroll to manipulate earnings?

    a. Capitalize labor costs.
    b. Misapply payroll to inappropriate job costing centers.
    c. Delay disbursing withheld taxes to the government.
    d. Misstate W-2 forms to employees.

16. Management has incentives to overstate the discounted present value of future health care obligations because the effect is to:

    a. Understate investment performance.
    b. Understate net income.
    c. Understate assets.
    d. Understate liabilities.

17. Current generally accepted accounting principles require that the discount rate for calculating the present value of future post-retirement health care benefits be based on:

    a. The current rate of return on the reporting entity's investment portfolio.
    b. The current average rate of return on the investment portfolio of other companies operating in the reporting entity's industry.
    c. The expected long term rate of return on plan assets.
    d. The current rate of return on high-quality, fixed-income investments.

18. The transition obligation in accounting for post-retirement health care benefits is the difference between:

    a. The accumulated post-retirement obligation and the value of the assets funded to date.
    b. The accumulated post-retirement obligation and the expected post-retirement obligation.
    c. The unfunded future benefits and the value of the assets funded to date.
    d. The unfunded future benefits and the expected post-retirement obligation.

19. In the accounting for post-retirement benefits, management has discretion over:

    a. Complying with FASB *Statement of Financial Accounting Standards No. 106.*
    b. Expected rates of return.
    c. Retiree payouts.
    d. Mandatory retirements.

20. Post-retirement health care benefits are a form of:
    a. Period expenses.
    b. Long-term expenses.
    c. Compensation.
    d. Deferred compensation.

PROBLEMS AND DISCUSSION CASES

14-1 *Controls Over Personnel and Payroll*

You are considering the controls over a client's personnel and payroll activities. System documentation was accomplished with a questionnaire and a narrative memorandum and, in conjunction with a transaction walkthrough, indicated that the following potential errors or frauds may exist:

a. Several recent hirings violated equal opportunity laws.
b. A pay raise to employees in Department A was not approved by management.
c. An unauthorized, unapproved, and excessively high paycheck was cashed by a bona fide employee, but the check was for hours neither authorized nor worked.
d. Detailed payroll records sometimes do not agree with labor summaries or payroll tax accruals and go unnoticed.
e. When an employee's time record is not available, the employee obtains a new time record from an open bin outside the payroll office.

   Required: For each potential error or fraud, indicate a control procedure(s) that management could implement to prevent or detect the error or fraud.

14-2 *Identifying Deficiencies in Internal Control*

An auditor's audit working papers include the following narrative description of a segment of the Croyden, Inc., factory payroll system and the flowchart presented on pages 608–609.

**AUDIT
DOCUMENTATION
REVIEW**

Narrative Memorandum

Internal control over the Personnel department is effective and is not included in the accompanying flowchart.

   At the beginning of each work week, payroll clerk No. 1 reviews the Payroll department files to determine the employment status of factory employees, prepares time records, and distributes them as each individual arrives at work. The clerk verifies the identity of each payee before delivering signed checks to the factory supervisor. At the end of each work week, the supervisor distributes payroll checks for the preceding work week, reviews the current week's employee time records, notes the regular and overtime hours worked on a summary form, and initials the time records. The supervisor then delivers all time records and unclaimed payroll checks to payroll clerk No. 2.

   Required:
   1. What are the deficiencies in internal control?
   2. What inquiries should the auditor make to clarify whether additional deficiencies exist?

(AICPA Adapted)

14-3 *Errors, Fraud, and Control Procedures*

During your audit of Fletcher Corporation's financial statements, you become aware of the following control procedures over Fletcher's personnel and payroll activities.

   1. All substantive information in employment applications is thoroughly checked and verified before offering an employment contract.

2. Authorized pay rates are maintained in personnel files for each employee.
3. All Personnel and Payroll department procedures are clearly written in updated procedures manuals.
4. Dual signatories are required for all paychecks exceeding $1,200.
5. Procedures are established for charging direct labor hours to appropriate jobs.
6. Responsibility for authorizing, executing, and recording payroll is vested in separate personnel.

Required: For each control procedure, indicate (a) a potential error or fraud that might be prevented or detected as a result of the control procedure and (b) the control objective served by the control procedure.

14-4 *Improving Controls Over Hiring and Payroll*

Linscott Supply Company employs about 50 production workers. Based on interviews, the factory supervisor hires or rejects job applicants. New hires prepare a W-4 form (Employee's Withholding Exemption Certificate) for the supervisor, who enters an hourly pay rate in the corner of the form and then passes the form on to a payroll clerk, thereby notifying Payroll that the worker has been employed. The supervisor advises Payroll of subsequent pay rate adjustments verbally.

A supply of blank time records is kept in a box near the factory's front door entrance. Each worker takes a time record on Monday morning, writes in his or her name, and notes daily arrival and departure times in pencil on the time record. At the end of the week, workers drop the time records in a box near the door. A payroll clerk collects completed time records from the box on Monday morning. Two payroll clerks divide the records alphabetically between them, one taking A to L, and the other M to Z. Each clerk is fully responsible for his or her portion of the payroll. The clerks compute gross pay, deductions, and net pay, post the details to each employee's earnings records, and prepare and number the payroll checks. Employees are deleted from the payroll when they fail to turn in a time record.

Payroll checks are signed manually by the chief accountant and given to the supervisor. The supervisor distributes the checks to the workers and arranges to deliver checks to workers who are absent. The payroll bank account is reconciled by the chief accountant, who also prepares quarterly and annual payroll tax returns.

Required: How might Linscott Supply Company improve controls over hiring and payroll?

14-5 *Designing Compensating Controls*

Early in your audit of Kimberly Corporation, you note that the factory supervisor approves time records for hours worked and hourly rates and also distributes the payroll checks.

Required:
1. Design compensating controls you would pursue before concluding that an internal control deficiency exists.
2. If you find no compensating controls for the factory payroll, what audit procedures would test for errors or frauds?

14-6 *Why Not Substantive Tests?*

When auditing within the expenditure/disbursement cycle, auditors often rely predominantly on interim tests of controls rather than year-end substantive tests of details. In fact, in many cases year-end procedures consist primarily of updating the auditor's understanding of the system, testing payroll activities, and performing analytical procedures to test the reasonableness of reported payroll balances.

Required: Explain why an auditor might rely predominantly on tests of controls, rather than substantive tests of details, in auditing payroll.

PROBLEM 14-2: *Flowchart*

| Factory Employees | Factory Supervisor | Personnel |

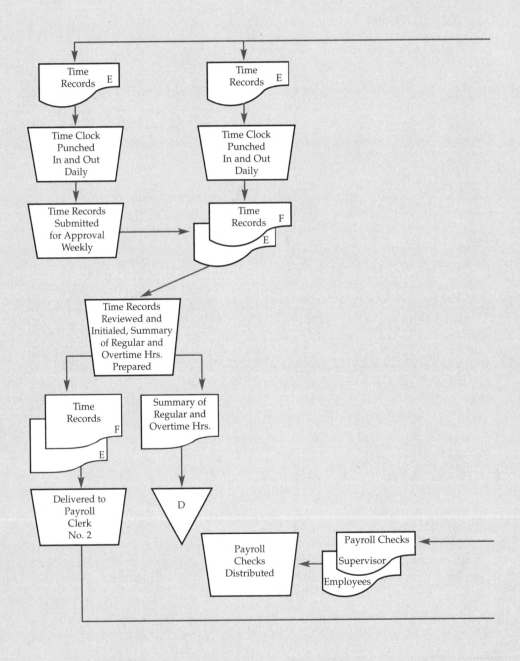

PROBLEM 14-2 *(continued)*

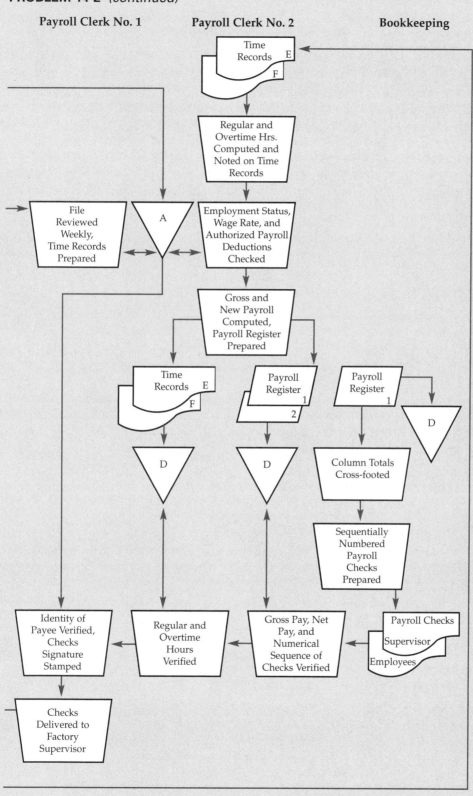

Payroll Clerk No. 1   Payroll Clerk No. 2   Bookkeeping

14-7 *Drafting Tests of Controls from an Internal Control Questionnaire*

Following are selected questions from an internal control questionnaire relating to a company's personnel and payroll functions. A Yes response indicates a potential strength of the system, and a No a potential weakness.

a. Do operating department supervisors and the Personnel department approve all employee changes (hirings, transfers, promotions, terminations)?
b. Do employee personnel records include authorizations for all deductions and withholdings?
c. Are employees who prepare payroll independent of payroll processing?
d. Does a responsible official independent of payroll preparation and processing approve the payroll?
e. Does an employee independent of payroll preparation, processing, and distribution reconcile the payroll bank account monthly?
f. Do employees independent of the Payroll department forward for investigation returned W-2 forms?

Required: Assume that inquiries indicate the answer is Yes to each question. Design tests of controls that you believe would provide persuasive evidence that control risk is below the maximum.

14-8 *Selecting Audit Procedures*

An auditor is designing an audit program for a computerized payroll and is drafting procedures for payroll preparation, labor cost distribution, and paycheck distribution.

Required: For each of the following procedures, indicate whether the proposed audit step should or should not be included in the audit program. Justify each No response.
1. Review software that computes payroll.
2. Determine whether checks are delivered to department timekeepers for distribution.
3. Review workers' compensation claims.
4. Reconcile time record hours to hours recorded on production job records.
5. Distribute checks to employees on a sample basis.
6. Obtain a certificate from the timekeeper for employees who were absent when the auditor distributed paychecks and who are to be paid later.
7. Verify documents in payroll files.
8. Review procedures for payroll check signing.

14-9 *Why a Separate Bank Account for Payroll?*

Many organizations maintain separate bank accounts for payroll, thereby segregating all payroll disbursements from general disbursements, such as payments for purchases, inventory, plant assets, and investments.

Required: Discuss why a separate bank account should be maintained for payroll and why one general bank account can be used for all other disbursements.

14-10 *Auditing Payroll*

James, who was engaged to audit the financial statements of Talbert Corporation, is about to audit payroll. Talbert uses a computer service center to process weekly payroll as follows:

Each Monday, Talbert's payroll clerk inputs data on preprinted, service center-prepared input forms that are faxed to the service center. The service center imports data from the input form to master files. Weekly payroll is then processed. The weekly payroll register and payroll checks are printed and delivered by messenger to Talbert on Thursday. Part of the sample James selected includes the input form and payroll register shown on the following two pages.

PROBLEM 14-10: *Talbert Corporation Payroll Input—Week Ending Friday, November 26, 2007*

| | Employee Data—Permanent File | | | Current Week's Payroll Data | | | | | |
| | | | | | Hours | | Special Deductions | | |
Name	Social Security	W-4	Information	Hourly Rate	Reg	OT	Bonds	Union	Other
A. Bell	999-99-9991	M-1		10.00	35	5	18.75		
B. Carr	999-99-9992	M-2		10.00	35	4			
C. Dawn	999-99-9993	S-1		10.00	35	6	18.75	4.00	
D. Ellis	999-99-9994	S-1		10.00	35	2		4.00	50.00
E. Frank	999-99-9995	M-4		10.00	35	1		4.00	
F. Gillis	999-99-9996	M-4		10.00	35			4.00	
G. Hugh	999-99-9997	M-1		7.00	35	2	18.75	4.00	
H. Jones	999-99-9998	M-2		7.00	35			4.00	25.00
I. King	999-99-9999	S-1		7.00	35	4		4.00	
New Employee									
J. Smith	999-99-9990	M-3		7.00	35				

(continues)

PROBLEM 14-10 *(continued)*

Employee	Social Security	Hours Reg	Hours OT	Payroll Reg	Payroll OT	Gross Payroll	FICA	Fed	State	Other Withheld	New Pay	Check No.
A. Bell	999-99-9991	35	5	350.00	75.00	425.00	26.05	76.00	27.40	18.75	276.80	1499
B. Carr	999-99-9992	35	4	350.00	60.00	410.00	25.13	65.00	23.60		296.27	1500
C. Dawn	999-99-9993	35	6	350.00	90.00	440.00	26.97	100.90	28.60	22.75	260.78	1501
D. Ellis	999-99-9994	35	2	350.00	30.00	380.00	23.29	80.50	21.70	54.00	200.51	1502
E. Frank	999-99-9995	35	1	350.00	15.00	365.00	22.37	43.50	15.90	4.00	279.23	1503
F. Gillis	999-99-9996	35		350.00		350.00	21.46	41.40	15.00	4.00	268.14	1504
G. Hugh	999-99-9997	35	2	245.00	21.00	266.00	16.31	34.80	10.90	22.75	181.24	1505
H. Jones	999-99-9998	35		245.00		245.00	15.02	26.40	8.70	29.00	165.88	1506
I. King	999-99-9999	35	4	245.00	42.00	287.00	17.59	49.40	12.20	4.00	203.81	1507
J. Smith	999-99-9990	35		245.00		245.00	15.02	23.00	7.80		199.18	1508
Totals		350	24	3,080.00	333.00	3,413.00	209.21	540.90	171.80	159.25	2,331.84	

Required:
1. Discuss how James could verify data on the payroll input form.
2. Discuss procedures James could follow to examine the payroll register.

(AICPA Adapted)

14-11 *Post-retirement Benefits Other Than Pensions*

Nonunion production, clerical, and middle-management employees of the Intersect Corporation participate in a post-retirement benefit plan that encompasses health care, housing subsidies, and tuition benefits for surviving dependent children. Recent newspaper accounts indicate that the employment contract covering production employees will expire soon after the balance sheet date. In discussing the disclosures necessary to comply with *SFAS No. 106*, "Employers' Accounting for Postretirement Benefits Other Than Pensions," Intersect's chief financial officer tells the auditor that, although she plans to comply with *SFAS No. 106*, she does not plan to disclose that the health care plan is unfunded.

Required:
1. Explain why you think Intersect's chief financial officer would prefer not to disclose that the health care plan is unfunded.
2. Does failing to disclose that a health care plan is unfunded violate generally accepted accounting principles?

Internet problems and discussion cases are available at http://ricchiute.swlearning.com

RESEARCH PROJECT

Management Discretion and Post-Retirement Health Care Obligations

Owing in part to unprecedented controversy, the Financial Accounting Standards Board deliberated over ten years about the accounting for post-retirement obligations other than pensions. The stakeholders on either side of the controversy included some who predicted worldwide financial doom if the obligations were reported, others who claimed that reported liabilities overlooked significant off-balance-sheet financing if not reported, and still others who were daunted by the sheer complexity of the measurement issues involved. Other accounting issues have been controversial, but no other has involved such staggering dollar amounts.

Required: Using the newspaper and magazines file in LEXIS-NEXIS or newspapers and magazines in a library, select an article about the effect on a publicly traded company's financial statements of adopting FASB *Statement of Financial Accounting Standards No. 106*, "Employers' Accounting for Postretirement Benefits Other Than Pensions." Using the annual report file in LEXIS-NEXIS, the SEC's EDGAR filing system (**http://www.sec.gov**), the company's Web site, or copies of annual reports in a library, select the annual report of the same company issued for the fiscal year referred to in the article. Draft a report that accomplishes the following:
1. Summarize the article, indicating key issues (such as management's or the financial community's reaction to the effect of the disclosure on reported income).
2. List and explain questions an auditor would likely pose to the management of the company you've selected.
3. Summarize the company's disclosures about post-retirement health care obligations from the balance sheet, the income statement (if separately disclosed), the footnote summarizing accounting policies (often note 1), and the footnote summarizing the health care obligation.

Interactive quizzes are available as a student learning resource at http://ricchiute.swlearning.com

15 Chapter

Inventory and Fixed Assets

Major topics discussed in this chapter are:

- The nature of the conversion cycle.
- An auditor's consideration of internal control over inventory and fixed assets.
- Substantive tests applicable to inventory and fixed assets.
- Applications of audit judgment to questions about management discretion in write-downs of impaired assets.
- Computer-assisted audit techniques applicable to inventory and fixed assets.
- Assurance service opportunities related to the conversion cycle.

Continuing the discussion of audit method, this chapter introduces tests of controls and substantive tests applicable to two major conversion cycle accounts: inventory and fixed assets. Internal control is discussed first, and then substantive tests of account balances. The chapter begins by summarizing the nature of the conversion cycle; introducing controls over an entity's inventory, inventory accounting, and fixed asset transactions; explaining an auditor's consideration of internal control within the conversion cycle; and suggesting assurance service opportunities. Next, the chapter explains specific substantive tests of details applicable to inventory and fixed assets. In turn, the chapter addresses accounting, legal, and ethical questions auditors face when auditing discretionary write-downs of impaired assets. Computer-assisted substantive tests (Chapter 8) relevant to inventory and fixed assets are presented at the end of the chapter. An auditor's obligations for internal control under the *Sarbanes-Oxley Act*, Section 404, "Management Assessment of Internal Controls," SEC rules (*Management's Reports on Internal Control Over Financial Reporting*), and PCAOB *Auditing Standard No. 2*, "An Audit of Internal Control Over Financial Reporting," were discussed and illustrated in chapters 8, 10, and 12.

The Conversion Cycle

The conversion cycle encompasses the production of finished products for sale, and relates directly to two other cycles: It uses resources and information provided by the expenditure/disbursement cycle and provides resources and information to the revenue/receipt cycle. For example, the conversion cycle uses raw materials purchased from vendors through the expenditure/disbursement cycle and produces finished goods that are sold to customers through the revenue/receipt cycle.

Figure 15-1 summarizes the scope of the conversion cycle, listing primary business functions and related activities, journal entries, and forms. One major business function is captured by the cycle:

- Resources are held, used, or transformed.

Although stated simply, this one business function can be quite significant, because it relates both to inventory and to fixed assets, often two of the largest dollar-value assets in capital-intensive companies.

Inventory: An Introduction

As noted in Chapter 12, when an entity purchases raw materials inventory, a purchase order is sent to the vendor, goods are received, and a liability is recorded. Assuming a perpetual inventory system, activities within the conversion cycle include recording purchases in perpetual records, processing accumulated costs through a cost accounting system, and physically controlling the inventory.

Throughout the conversion cycle, journal entries are made to process inventory costs through production, to record the cost of goods sold, and to write down obsolete or damaged inventory. Paper or computer image documents include:

- **Labor charge report**: A summary of labor costs to be applied to work-in-process inventory.
- **Materials requisition**: An operating department's formal request for materials.
- **Perpetual inventory record**: A cumulative record of quantities on hand for an item or a class of inventory.

Fixed Assets: An Introduction

Property, plant, and equipment—that is, fixed assets—are used both directly and indirectly to transform raw materials into finished products. For example, equipment might be used directly to extrude wire from copper, while a building would be used indirectly in the sense that wire extrusion equipment is housed within a manufacturing plant. As a result, fixed assets are related both to the conversion cycle and to inventory: to the conversion cycle because fixed assets transform inventory from raw materials to finished goods, and to inventory because some depreciation is applied to products as overhead.

Throughout the conversion cycle, journal entries are made to record depreciation and to apply overhead to inventory. Paper or computer image documents include:

- **Depreciation schedule**: A spreadsheet computing and summarizing depreciation.
- **Overhead application report**: A summary of overhead applied to work-in-process inventory.

The following section discusses the nature of the conversion cycle and related internal control considerations. The major activities and controls related to inventory—inventory control and inventory accounting—are discussed first, followed by fixed assets: records, additions, disposals, and depreciation.

FIGURE 15-1: *The Scope of the Conversion Cycle*

Primary Business Function	Common Activities	Common Entries	Common Forms
Resources are held, used, or transformed	**INVENTORY** • Maintaining perpetual inventory records • Recording (cost accounting) • Physically controlling inventory	• Processing inventory costs through production (raw materials, work in process, finished goods) • Cost of goods sold • Write-down of obsolete or damaged inventory	• Labor charge reports • Materials requisition forms
	FIXED ASSETS • Additions • Disposals and retirements • Recording • Depreciation allocation	• Depreciation • Overhead applied • Addition, disposals, and retirements	• Depreciation schedules • Overhead application reports

Inventory and Internal Control

Control procedures over inventory vary depending on whether the inventory is held by a nonmanufacturing or manufacturing company. In the case of a nonmanufacturing wholesaler or retailer, goods are acquired from vendors and sold to customers without alteration. Thus the conversion cycle of a nonmanufacturing entity accounts only for holding and physically controlling inventory prior to sale. But for a manufacturing company, the conversion cycle is more complex: Raw materials acquired from vendors must be transformed prior to sale, and the costs of transformation, such as direct labor and manufacturing overhead, must be accumulated and classified. The functional areas that control and record inventory are inventory control and inventory accounting, respectively.

Inventory Control

Figure 15-2 illustrates the flow of inventory within a manufacturing company. The acquisition of inventory is part of the expenditure/disbursement cycle, and the distribution of finished goods is part of the revenue/receipt cycle. The conversion cycle encompasses movement of goods through the production process.

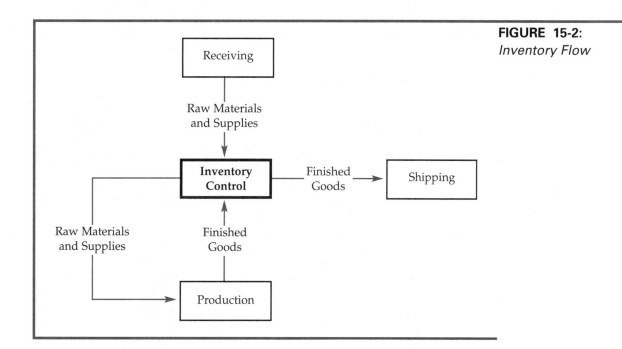

FIGURE 15-2:
Inventory Flow

A materials requisition form is prepared by production personnel to request materials and supplies for use in production. Requisitions should be approved by a supervisor and forwarded to Inventory Control. Materials and supplies should not be released by Inventory Control personnel in the absence of an approved requisition.

Raw materials and finished goods should be controlled by Inventory Control personnel not involved in purchasing, receiving, shipping, production, or recording. Access to storage areas should be limited to authorized personnel. Physical safeguards are necessary within each of the production departments to protect work in process.

Inventory Control personnel should be responsible not only for controlling transfers of inventory in and out of storage areas, but also for monitoring inventory levels and for reporting slow-moving or damaged items. Inventory levels should be monitored to assure that they are neither too high, which would result in needlessly high carrying costs, nor too low, which could risk insufficient quantities on hand. Many companies monitor inventory levels through quantitative techniques such as *economic-order-quantity* models, which optimize the relationship between carrying costs and the risk of shortages, or *just-in-time*, an inventory management method that reduces carrying costs to zero because required supplies arrive "just in time." As a means for determining whether inventory is obsolete or otherwise unusable, slow-moving or damaged items should be reported to responsible officials and, if appropriate, removed from inventory; salable items should be written down to net realizable value and sold as scrap.

Inventory Accounting

Throughout the conversion cycle, entries are made to record the movement of inventory through the production process. Inventory (cost) accounting systems vary widely due to variations in the nature and complexity of production processes. Generally, though, an inventory accounting system involves two major sets of records: perpetual inventory records and cost records.

Perpetual Inventory Records

Inventory quantities, physical locations, and selected unit cost information usually are accumulated on perpetual inventory records maintained for a variety of major inventory classifications, including supplies, raw materials, and finished goods. Work-in-process inventory also should be controlled on perpetual records, though the records may take the form of progress reports, such as job-cost summaries.

As inventory flows through the production process, perpetual records should be updated continually, thereby providing a cumulative up-to-date record of quantities, physical location, and selected unit cost information. Updated information should be generated from formal source documents, such as requisitions, invoices, production reports, and shipping documents, which themselves should be controlled through sequential prenumbering and formal indications of approval (for example, initials) or specific authorization, as discussed in Chapter 12.

In many companies, significant segments of inventory are stored off-premises in public warehouses or transferred either to dealers on consignment or to outside companies for processing. Off-premises inventory should be accounted for and controlled by the outside parties holding the goods. Periodically, a company should confirm off-premises inventory, physically count quantities at off-premises locations, and reconcile confirmed or counted quantities with internal perpetual records.

Cost Records

Perpetual inventory records are used predominantly to account for inventory quantities throughout the production process. An inventory accounting system, however, also must account for inventory costs, which may be allocated on a FIFO, LIFO, average cost, or other acceptable basis. Whatever the cost-flow approach used, an inventory accounting system should be designed to account for and control inventory costs as they flow through the accounts illustrated in Figure 15-3.

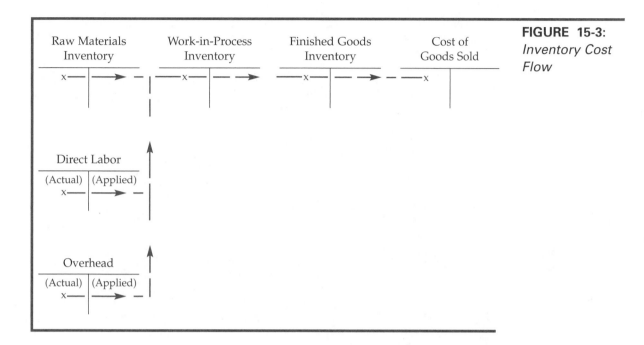

FIGURE 15-3: *Inventory Cost Flow*

Like perpetual inventory records, cost accounting records and reports should be updated continually, thereby providing an up-to-date record of accumulated costs. The updated information should be communicated to General Accounting personnel for summarizing and for recording journal entries in general ledger control accounts. If updated information is not communicated to the Accounting department, accounts such as Raw Materials, Work in Process, and Finished Goods could be misstated. For example, if units of a particular raw material are physically transferred to production, the related inventory costs (for raw materials) should be transferred from raw materials to work-in-process inventory; otherwise, raw materials inventory would be overstated and work-in-process inventory understated, although total inventory would not be misstated. Thus, cost accounting records should be updated continually and agreed to—or periodically reconciled with—general ledger control accounts. To maintain effective segregation of duties, cost accounting records should be maintained by personnel independent of perpetual records, general accounting, purchasing, production, and inventory control.

Internal Control Objectives and Potential Errors or Frauds: Inventory

The following discussion, summarized in Figure 15-4, identifies some control objectives for inventory, describes examples of errors or frauds that may arise if an objective is not achieved, and offers examples of control procedures to prevent or detect errors or frauds in inventory. The objectives relate to transaction authorization, execution, recording, and access to assets.

FIGURE 15-4: *Inventory: Control Objectives, Potential Errors or Frauds, and Control Procedures*

Control Objectives	Types of Errors or Frauds That Could Occur If Objective Is Not Met	Control Procedures Designed to Prevent or Detect Errors or Frauds
Transaction Authorization Production should be authorized in accordance with management's criteria.	Unauthorized quantities or products may be produced, potentially resulting in obsolete, excess, or otherwise unusable inventory and excess carrying costs.	Prepare statements of criteria for determining which products are to be produced and in what quantities.
Transaction Execution Procedures for using and physically transferring inventory should be established in accordance with management's authorization.	Unauthorized personnel may circumvent existing procedures, potentially resulting in stolen or misused inventory. Inventory may be misplaced, potentially resulting in unused assets.	Prepare inventory-processing manuals, including procedures for controlling inventory movement. Restrict access to inventory to authorized personnel.
Recording Inventory used or transferred should be recorded at the correct amounts, be recorded in the proper period, and be properly classified.	Inventory placed in production may not be recorded, potentially resulting in misstated inventory and cost of sales.	Establish processing and recording procedures. Prenumber and control materials release forms and production orders. Maintain logs of inventory movement into and out of storerooms and production stages. Conduct periodic inventory counts, and investigate differences between recorded and actual quantities. Limit access to inventory and blank forms.
Inventory-related adjustments (e.g., to adjust recorded inventory to physical counts; to write down obsolete or unusable inventory) should be authorized in accordance with management's criteria.	Unauthorized adjustments may be recorded to conceal physical shortages, potentially resulting in misused and misstated inventory.	Establish policies for approving and recording adjustments. Prenumber and control inventory adjustment forms.

(continues)

FIGURE 15-4 *(continued)*

Control Objectives	Types of Errors or Frauds That Could Occur If Objective Is Not Met	Control Procedures Designed to Prevent or Detect Errors or Frauds
Access to Assets		
Access to inventory should be restricted to personnel authorized by management.	Inventory could be stolen, lost, or diverted, potentially resulting in misapplied assets and misstated accounts.	Establish physical controls over inventory (e.g., fences, locks, inventory control clerks).
		Maintain insurance and fidelity bonds for personnel handling valuable inventory.
		Maintain adequate insurance coverage for assets.
		Segregate responsibility for handling inventory from inventory recording, cost accounting, and general accounting.
Access to production, cost accounting, and perpetual inventory records should be restricted to personnel authorized by management.	Inventory records could be misused, destroyed, or lost, potentially resulting in misstated and misused inventory. Establish policies for approving and recording adjustments.	Establish physical controls over unused forms and records.
		Maintain files of authorized signatures.
		Perform periodic compliance audits.

Transaction Authorization

Before goods are produced, production should be authorized according to management's criteria. That is, no goods should be produced that are not specifically authorized by management. Otherwise, unauthorized products or quantities may be produced (perhaps, for example, for the express benefit of employees, rather than the company), potentially resulting in excess or otherwise unusable inventory and in excess carrying costs. To control against unauthorized production, management could prepare written statements of criteria for determining which products to produce and in what quantities. For example, management could require that no goods be produced unless quantities on hand have declined to a predetermined amount.

Transaction Execution

In order to avoid lost or misused inventory, management should authorize procedures for using and physically transferring inventory. For example, management could prepare inventory processing manuals, including procedures for controlling inventory movement, and could restrict access to inventory to authorized personnel.

Recording

Establishing procedures for using and transferring inventory, though, does not necessarily mean that inventory transfers and use will be recorded properly. Therefore, to avoid misplaced or misstated inventory, used or transferred inventory should be recorded at the correct amounts, be recognized in the proper period, and be classified properly. To control inventory recording, management could establish processing and recording procedures, prenumber and control materials release forms and production orders, and maintain logs of inventory movement into and out of storerooms and production stages.

Throughout, but most often at the end of, an accounting period, companies make journal entries to adjust recorded inventory to physical counts or to adjust carrying value for obsolete or unusable inventory. To avoid unauthorized adjustments—for example, adjustments to conceal physical shortages—management should require that all inventory adjustments be authorized in accordance with management's criteria. For example, management could establish policies for approving and recording adjustments and, in large companies, prenumber and control inventory adjustment documents.

Access to Assets

Inventory—particularly valuable consumer products, like portable appliances—can be stolen, lost, or diverted, potentially resulting in misapplied assets and misstated accounts. As a result, access to inventory should be restricted to personnel authorized by management. In practice, a variety of techniques are available to control inventory. For example, management could establish physical control over inventory (for example, fences, locks, inventory control clerks); maintain insurance, both for inventory and for inventory personnel (that is, fidelity bonds); and segregate responsibility for handling inventory from inventory recording, cost accounting, and general accounting.

In turn, management also should restrict access to production, cost accounting, and perpetual inventory records, thereby preventing misuse, destruction, or loss of inventory or inventory records. For example, management could establish physical controls over unused forms and records, maintain files of authorized signatures, and perform periodic compliance audits to assure that employees comply with controls.

Fixed Assets and Internal Control

Some companies use a separate cycle to process the acquisition, use, and disposition of fixed assets—land, buildings, machinery, and equipment. In others, the expenditure/disbursement cycle may process fixed asset additions, the revenue/receipt cycle may process disposals, and the conversion cycle may process transactions and events relating to the use of fixed assets. The latter is assumed in the following discussion, which focuses on controls applicable to fixed assets.

Fixed Asset Records

Land, buildings, machinery, and equipment should be documented in detailed records that account separately for each individual asset. For example, each detailed record might include the purchase date, historical cost, depreciation method, estimated useful life, salvage value, and accumulated depreciation. The records should be maintained by personnel not responsible for physically controlling fixed assets.

Periodically, but no less than annually, detailed records should be reconciled with fixed asset general ledger control accounts. Also, responsible personnel independent of fixed asset recording and physical control should periodically determine that recorded assets actually exist by observing machinery and equipment and by comparing identification numbers and general descriptions with detailed records.

Fixed assets also should be insured against fire or other potential casualties. As a result, assets should be appraised periodically to determine that insurance coverage reasonably approximates replacement cost. If coverage is inadequate, an entity could risk serious losses through both business interruption and an inability to replace productive assets. Clearly, the consequences of underinsurance can be devastating.

Additions

Unlike many other purchases, individual fixed asset additions are often material, necessitating specific authorization by the board of directors or by senior management. In many entities, formal authorization is required for major repairs or improvements. Since the expenditures may be large, management should assess the desirability of replacing, rather than repairing or improving, existing assets. Authorizations should be documented in writing and be sufficiently detailed to provide employees with a basis for executing fixed asset transactions. On a related note, additions should be reported to insurance companies, and coverage increased accordingly.

Unforeseen circumstances, such as vendor price increases, could raise the purchase price of an asset above amounts originally authorized, thereby requiring additional authorization (or approval). As a result, procedures should require that actual costs be compared with amounts authorized, and cost overruns reported to senior management for authorization. An entity also should assure that authorized additions actually are received and functioning as expected.

In addition to purchasing fixed assets, an entity might hire outside contractors to construct (or modify) buildings, machinery, or equipment. Constructed additions also should be authorized, and additional controls should be implemented that allow the entity to inspect and approve both actual production and detailed cost records as construction progresses. Inspection and approval privileges and cost records allow an entity to monitor progress continually, assuring that the project will meet the specifications and cost ceilings authorized by senior management.

Disposals

Fixed asset disposals, such as sales or retirements, should be authorized by senior management. Authorizations should be documented, and copies forwarded to accounting personnel to assure that assets disposed of are subsequently removed from fixed asset accounts.

Since insurance premiums usually are determined by the appraisal value of assets carried, asset disposals should be reported to insurance companies and premiums adjusted accordingly. Disposal of assets may result in gains or losses, measured by the difference between the asset's net book value and proceeds from the disposition. Controls should be established to assure that proceeds are deposited and gains or losses are recorded.

Depreciation

Over time and through use, the future service potential of fixed assets (other than land) expires, and is recognized as depreciation expense. Depreciation expense for fixed assets used in production is assigned to work-in-process inventory as applied overhead and, as a result, flows through the conversion cycle. When finished goods are sold, depreciation expense is charged against revenue as part of the cost of sales.

Because of the significant impact depreciation expense can have on reported net income, an entity should maintain formal policies for determining depreciation methods, estimated useful lives, and salvage values. Periodically, the policies should be reviewed to determine whether they reasonably approximate actual experience. For example, if a particular type of machinery is depreciated over five years but normally lasts ten years, useful lives should be reconsidered.

Internal Control Objectives and Potential Errors or Frauds: Fixed Assets

Earlier, control objectives for transaction authorization, execution, recording, and access to assets were discussed for inventory. The following discusses control objectives for fixed assets. The discussion, summarized in Figure 15-5, identifies

FIGURE 15-5: *Fixed Assets: Control Objectives, Potential Errors or Frauds, and Control Procedures*

Control Objectives	Types of Errors or Frauds That Could Occur If Objective Is Not Met	Control Procedures Designed to Prevent or Detect Errors or Frauds
Transaction Authorization Plant additions, disposals, and retirements should be authorized in accordance with management's criteria.	Assets may be purchased or sold without management's knowledge, potentially resulting in misapplied cash and misstated fixed asset records. Assets may be disposed of at unfavorable prices, potentially resulting in lost resources.	Prepare written procedures for all additions, disposals, and retirements. Periodically compare prices received for scrap with published prices.
Transaction Execution Procedures for operating, using, and physically moving fixed assets should be established in accordance with management's authorization.	Unauthorized personnel may circumvent existing procedures, potentially resulting in stolen or misused equipment. Equipment may be misplaced, potentially resulting in unused assets.	Establish procedures for operating, using, moving, and otherwise controlling fixed assets. Restrict access to movable fixed assets.

(continues)

FIGURE 15-5 *(continued)*

Control Objectives	Types of Errors or Frauds That Could Occur If Objective Is Not Met	Control Procedures Designed to Prevent or Detect Errors or Frauds
Recording Fixed assets added, disposed, or retired should be recorded at the correct amounts, be recorded in the proper period, and be properly classified.	Fixed asset transactions may go unreported, potentially resulting in misstated balances.	Establish procedures for processing and recording fixed asset transactions. Establish procedures for identifying fixed assets eligible for disposal (e.g., sell as scrap) and retirement. Maintain detailed fixed asset records. Periodically reconcile fixed asset records with existing assets and investigate differences.
Depreciation and amortization should be calculated in accordance with management's authorization, be recorded in the proper period, and be properly classified.	Depreciation could be miscalculated or recognized on fixed assets not in service, potentially resulting in misstated depreciation expense and asset book values.	Establish policies for determining depreciation methods and for calculating depreciation on all categories of fixed assets.
Access to Assets Access to fixed assets should be restricted to personnel authorized by management.	Fixed assets (e.g., equipment) could be stolen or lost, potentially resulting in misapplied assets and misstated accounts.	Establish physical controls over unused fixed assets (e.g., garages, secured fences). Maintain adequate insurance coverage. Segregate physical custody of fixed assets from fixed asset records and general accounting.
Access to asset and depreciation records should be restricted to personnel authorized by management.	Fixed asset and depreciation records could be misused, destroyed, or lost, potentially resulting in misstated assets.	Establish physical controls over unused forms and records. Perform periodic compliance audits, reconciling recorded assets with existing assets.

control objectives, describes examples of errors or frauds that may arise if an objective is not achieved, and provides examples of controls often used by management to prevent or detect errors or frauds.

Transaction Authorization

Just as production should be authorized, fixed asset additions, disposals, and retirements should be authorized in accordance with management's criteria. Otherwise, assets such as machinery and equipment may be purchased or sold without management's knowledge, or assets may be disposed of at unfavorable prices, thereby sacrificing otherwise attainable resources. To control unauthorized transactions, management could develop written procedures for all additions, disposals, and retirements, and periodically compare scrap sale prices with published price lists.

Transaction Execution and Recording

Optimum operating capacity simply cannot be attained unless all fixed assets are accounted for, operating properly, and protected from misuse. For this reason, management should establish procedures for operating, using, physically moving, and restricting access to movable fixed assets.

To avoid unreported transactions, fixed asset additions, disposals, and retirements should be recorded at the correct amount, be recognized in the proper period, and be classified properly. Unrecorded or improperly recorded transactions could result in misstated fixed asset accounts, and therefore misstated financial statements. Management can control the recording function by establishing procedures for processing and recording fixed asset transactions and for identifying fixed assets eligible for sale or retirement. In addition, detailed fixed asset records should be maintained and periodically reconciled with existing assets.

The expiration of future service potential—depreciation and amortization—should be calculated in accordance with management's authorization and be recorded in the proper period. Otherwise, depreciation could be miscalculated or recognized on fixed assets not actually in service, either of which could result in misstated depreciation expense. As a result, management should establish policies for determining depreciation methods and for calculating depreciation on all fixed assets.

Access to Assets

To control against stolen or lost fixed assets, access should be restricted to personnel authorized by management. Likewise, access to manufacturing areas and to production sites should be restricted, thereby reducing the likelihood of misused assets and, correspondingly, misstated accounts. Management should establish physical controls over unused assets (for example, garages, secured fences), maintain adequate insurance coverage, and segregate the physical custody of fixed assets from recording and general accounting.

Just as access to fixed assets should be restricted, so should access to fixed asset records. Otherwise, fixed asset records could be altered to conceal shortages or be destroyed or lost, potentially resulting in misstated accounts. To control fixed asset records, management should establish controls over unused forms and records (for example, locked cabinets or safes) or could perform periodic compliance audits, reconciling recorded assets with existing assets.

Considering Internal Control: Inventory

As explained in Chapter 8 and illustrated for the revenue/receipt and expenditure/disbursement cycles in Chapters 10, 12, and 14, an auditor's consideration of internal control involves obtaining an understanding of the system, testing controls, and assessing control risk. The following discussion focuses on an auditor's consideration of conversion cycle controls. Controls over inventory are addressed first, followed by controls over fixed assets.

Obtain an Understanding

An auditor's objective is to obtain an understanding of a client's internal controls: How is the system supposed to work and what controls have been prescribed by management to assure that the system does work? As discussed in Chapter 8, obtaining an understanding consists of (1) performing a preliminary review, (2) documenting the system, (3) performing a transaction walkthrough, and (4) determining whether existing controls are potentially reliable in assessing control risk below the maximum.

Preliminary Review

The purpose of the preliminary review is to determine whether further consideration of the controls is likely to justify restricting substantive tests of inventory. An auditor performs the preliminary review for inventory by reading the client's procedures manuals and by interviewing client personnel who are responsible for perpetual inventory records, cost records, and inventory accounting. Assuming that existing controls appear potentially reliable in assessing control risk below the maximum, an auditor proceeds by documenting the system.

System Documentation

An entity's inventory control and inventory accounting procedures can be documented with flowcharts, questionnaires, and/or narratives, although detailed flowcharts are less common in practice, particularly for small- to medium-size companies. Figure 15-6 illustrates an internal control questionnaire for inventory,

FIGURE 15-6: *Questionnaire: Inventory*

	Performed by:_____	
	Date:_____	
Question	*Answer: Yes, No, or N/A*	*Remarks*
Physical Control		
1. Is inventory reasonably protected from physical deterioration and theft (e.g., fenced areas, restricted access storerooms)?		
2. Are materials requisition forms required to obtain materials and supplies for use in production?		
3. Are Inventory Control personnel segregated from purchasing, receiving, shipping, production, and recording functions?		*(continues)*

FIGURE 15-6 *(continued)*

Performed by:_____

Date:_____

Question	Answer: Yes, No, or N/A	Remarks

4. Are Inventory Control personnel responsible for controlling transfers in and out of storage areas?

5. Are Inventory Control or other personnel responsible for monitoring inventory levels and reporting slow-moving or damaged items?

6. Is access to inventory restricted to authorized personnel?

7. Are physical inventory counts taken at least once a year for all inventories?

8. Is insurance coverage maintained and periodically reviewed for all inventory?

Perpetual Inventory Records

1. Are perpetual inventory records continually updated on a timely basis?

2. Are perpetual records maintained by employees independent of shipping, receiving, cost accounting, production, inventory control, and general accounting?

3. Are perpetual records reconciled with general ledger control accounts on a regular basis?

4. Are source documents (e.g., invoices, requisitions, bills of lading, etc.) that are related to perpetual records prenumbered, approved, and sent to General Accounting for entry in control accounts?

5. Are periodic inventory counts reconciled with perpetual records?

Cost Records

1. Are cost records continually updated on a timely basis?

2. Are cost records maintained by employees independent of perpetual records, production, inventory control, and general accounting?

3. Are cost records reconciled with general ledger control accounts on a regular basis?

4. Are cost accountants familiar with and continually updated about production processes?

5. Are direct and indirect production costs accumulated in sufficient detail to enable accurate charges to work-in-process or finished goods inventory?

6. Are all inventory transfers reported and recorded on a timely basis?

7. Are production personnel required to explain price and volume variances?

focusing on physical control, perpetual inventory records, and cost records, three areas critical to inventory control. A *No* response to any question indicates a control procedure is not used and, therefore, that lacking compensating controls, a material error or fraud could occur. Alternatively, or in conjunction with a flowchart or questionnaire, an auditor could use a narrative memorandum, for example, to document materials transfer and recording procedures.

Transaction Walkthrough

To confirm his or her understanding of the system, the auditor could trace one or several materials transfers from raw materials to work in process, to finished goods perpetual records, and to entries and postings in cost records, inventory accounting, and general accounting. Several transfers, rather than a single transfer, are often used for a transaction walkthrough, because individual units transferred (for example, from raw materials to work in process) are not likely to be identifiable as the same units transferred from work in process to finished goods.

Identification of Control Procedures

An auditor identifies controls to be relied on in assessing control risk below the maximum and designs tests of controls using the same approach outlined in Chapter 10 for the revenue/receipt cycle and in Chapters 12 and 14 for the expenditure/disbursement cycle:

- Identify the system's *control objectives*. The first column of Figure 15-4 identifies control objectives for inventory.
- Consider the *potential errors or frauds* that might result if specific control objectives are not met. The second column of Figure 15-4 identifies examples of potential errors or frauds.
- Determine which *control procedures* are used by the entity to prevent or detect potentially material errors or frauds. The third column of Figure 15-4 identifies examples of potential controls.
- Design *tests of controls*.

Tests of controls for inventory are described next.

Tests of Controls: Inventory

Tests of controls over inventory focus on whether transfers of inventory through the production process are authorized and recorded. However, since tests of purchasing (Chapter 12) and selling (Chapter 10) may include tests of inventory records, an auditor should carefully coordinate tests to avoid duplication of effort.

Perpetual Records

Tests of controls over an entity's perpetual records focus on physical transfers of inventory to and from raw materials, work in process, and finished goods. The accuracy of recording transfers is important for at least two reasons. First, inaccurate recording of transfers could suggest that control procedures are neither complied with nor operating as planned, casting doubt on the reliability of the records. Second, inaccurate recording could suggest the possibility of double-counted inventory quantities. For example, if 100 units of raw materials inventory are transferred to work in process, perpetual records should reflect a 100-unit reduction in raw materials and a 100-unit increase in work in process. If, however, only the increase in work in process is recorded, raw materials would be overstated by 100 units, resulting in double counting. Correspondingly, if only the decrease in raw materials is recorded, work in process would be understated by 100 units. Some representative tests for perpetual records follow.

Tests of Controls: Perpetual Records

1. For sampled purchases of raw materials, compare quantities and unit costs from vendors' invoices with perpetual records, coordinating with tests of purchases in the expenditure/disbursement cycle.
2. For sampled transfers of raw materials from inventory control, trace to:
   a. Approved materials requisitions.
   b. Transfers to work-in-process perpetual records, comparing quantities and unit costs.
   c. Summary transfer entries in general ledger control accounts.
3. For sampled transfers from work in process, trace to:
   a. Transfers to finished goods perpetual records, comparing quantities and unit costs.
   b. Summary transfer entries in general ledger control accounts.
4. For sampled transfers from finished goods, trace to:
   a. Shipping documents, comparing quantities and unit costs, coordinating with tests of sales in the revenue/receipt cycle.
   b. Summary of cost of goods sold and sales entries.

In Step 1, the auditor tests whether raw materials quantities and unit costs per the perpetual inventory records reflect actual purchases made during the period. Step 2, in contrast, tests transfers from raw materials to work-in-process perpetual records, but from three different perspectives. First, in Step 2a, the auditor tests whether transfers were prompted by approved materials requisitions. That is, transfers to work in process should occur only when production personnel request raw materials for specific jobs. Second, Step 2b tests whether quantities and unit costs on materials requisitions are reflected accurately in work-in-process perpetual records. Third, in Step 2c, the auditor's focus shifts to the integrity of accounting records by tracing summary transfer entries from work-in-process perpetual records to Raw Materials and Work-in-Process Inventory, two general ledger control accounts.

In Step 3, the auditor focuses on transfers from work-in-process records to finished goods perpetual records. The logic and intent of Steps 3a and 3b are identical to Steps 2b and 2c, respectively. Step 4, the logical follow-up to Steps 2 and 3, focuses on transfers from finished goods perpetual records. Since transfers from finished goods inventory should result only from shipments, the auditor in Step 4a traces transfers out of finished goods perpetual records to shipping documents filed in the Shipping department (see Figure 10-2, pages 415–416). In Step 4b, sampled finished goods transfers are traced to cost of goods sold and to sales entries, thereby assuring that the cost of finished goods shipped is matched with realized sales revenues.

Cost Records

Although crucial to an entity's inventory accounting system, perpetual records are intended primarily as a control over the location and flow of inventory *quantities*.

Tests of controls also must be performed for the flow of inventory *costs* from raw materials to work in process, finished goods, and cost of goods sold.

Cost accounting systems differ significantly from company to company, depending on the products manufactured or processed. As a result, tests of controls also vary significantly from engagement to engagement. In many audits, though, an auditor focuses on accumulated labor and overhead charges to work-in-process inventory. Several tests follow.

Tests of Controls: Cost Records

1. Obtain summaries of charges to work-in-process inventory.
2. Test accumulated direct labor and overhead charges:
   a. For sampled direct labor charges, reconcile amounts with (1) departmental labor charge reports, coordinating with tests of labor records in the expenditure/disbursement cycle and (2) work-in-process perpetual records.
   b. For sampled overhead charges, reconcile rates with authorized standard costs, assuring that the basis for application (for example, direct labor hours) is appropriate.
3. Review the basis for determining standard overhead rates, determining that:
   a. Expenses charged to overhead are reasonable and consistent with the prior period, and
   b. Standard rates reasonably approximate actual costs.
4. Determine the disposition of overapplied and underapplied overhead.

As indicated in Step 1, tests of cost records stem from a client's summary of charges (debits) to work-in-process inventory and, as suggested by Steps 2 through 4, focus on direct labor and overhead charges.

In Step 2a, the auditor traces direct labor charges to two independent sources: departmental labor charge reports and work-in-process perpetual records (assuming labor charges are included in perpetual records, which in some companies may not be the case). Step 2b addresses whether overhead charges agree with authorized standard costs, and whether the basis for applying overhead—for example, direct labor hours, units of production, etc.—is appropriate. In turn, Step 3 further addresses standard overhead costs, but from the viewpoint of whether overhead is applied consistently with the prior period and reasonably approximates actual costs.

Step 4 addresses how a client disposes of overapplied and underapplied overhead. Under generally accepted accounting principles, normal variances between actual and standard costs—the basis for determining overapplied and underapplied overhead—should be charged to the period incurred, usually through cost of sales. In contrast, abnormal variances, such as idle facilities expense or excessive spoilage, should be allocated between ending inventory and current operations, again through cost of sales.

Assess Control Risk

An auditor reviews system documentation and the results of tests of controls to determine whether existing control procedures can be relied on to assess control risk below the maximum, assess detection risk above the minimum, and therefore to restrict substantive tests of inventory. The evaluation is based on four issues: (1) the types of errors or frauds that could occur, (2) necessary control procedures that should prevent or detect the errors or frauds, (3) whether the necessary procedures exist and are followed, and (4) any deficiencies in internal control. Substantive tests applicable to inventory are discussed later in the chapter. But first, the chapter considers internal controls over fixed assets.

Considering Internal Control: Fixed Assets

The following discusses the auditor's consideration of controls over fixed assets.

Obtain an Understanding

Compared to inventory, fixed asset transactions are considerably less numerous, and individual transactions usually involve considerably larger dollar amounts. Thus, although the steps in a review of the system are identical (preliminary review, system documentation, transaction walkthrough, and evaluation), an auditor's focus is different, since any one transaction alone could exceed the auditor's tolerable error for fixed assets.

Preliminary Review

The preliminary review is performed by reading the client's procedures manuals and by interviewing client personnel responsible for fixed asset additions, disposals and retirements, and recording. Assuming controls are potentially reliable in assessing control risk below the maximum, an auditor proceeds to system documentation.

System Documentation

Flowcharts are seldom used to document fixed asset systems, primarily because the number of transactions is not likely to justify extensive flowcharting. Rather, auditors often use internal control questionnaires similar to the one in Figure 15-7 to identify apparent deficiencies and narratives to document procedures for fixed asset additions, disposals and retirements, and recording.

Transaction Walkthrough

To confirm her or his understanding of an entity's fixed asset system, an auditor could trace an addition transaction, a disposal transaction, and a retirement transaction through the system and examine depreciation schedules for conformity with prescribed procedures. Alternatively, some auditors ignore transaction walkthrough altogether, electing instead to perform substantive tests of details on all fixed asset transactions at year end. In that case, tests of controls also would be ignored.

Identification of Control Procedures

Following system documentation, an auditor continues considering internal control exactly as outlined earlier in the chapter for inventory. Figure 15-5 identifies control objectives (column one), potential errors or frauds (column two), and control procedures (column three).

Tests of Controls: Fixed Assets

When the number of fixed asset transactions is limited, an auditor may limit— or even forego—tests of controls, electing instead to assess control risk at the

FIGURE 15-7: *Questionnaire: Fixed Assets*

Performed by:_____
Date:_____

Question	Answer: Yes, No, or N/A	Remarks

Fixed Asset Records

1. Are detailed records maintained for each class of fixed assets (e.g., land, buildings, machinery, equipment)?
2. Is responsibility for maintaining fixed asset records segregated from responsibility for physically controlling fixed assets and from general accounting?
3. Are detailed records reconciled periodically with general ledger control accounts?
4. Are procedures followed to determine whether recorded fixed assets actually exist?
5. Are access to and the use of fixed assets restricted to authorized personnel?
6. Is insurance coverage maintained and reviewed for all fixed assets?
7. Are fixed assets physically safeguarded from deterioration and theft?

Additions

1. Do procedures require authorization by the board of directors or senior management for fixed asset additions?
2. Are actual expenditures for fixed assets compared with amounts authorized?
3. Are procedures established to assure that fixed assets purchased are delivered in accordance with orders placed?
4. Are fixed asset additions promptly recorded in fixed asset records?
5. Are fixed asset additions promptly reported to General Accounting?
6. Are insurance companies notified of fixed asset additions in order to increase insurance coverage?
7. Is construction in progress—whether internally or externally contracted—authorized and periodically inspected?

Disposals and Retirements

1. Do procedures require authorization by the board of directors or senior management for fixed asset disposals and retirements?
2. Are procedures established to assure that the proceeds from fixed asset disposals are recorded properly and deposited?

(continues)

FIGURE 15-7 *(continued)*

| | Performed by:_____ |
| | Date:_____ |

Question	Answer: Yes, No, or N/A	Remarks
3. Are fixed asset disposals and retirements promptly recorded in fixed asset records?		
4. Are fixed asset disposals and retirements promptly reported to General Accounting for recording gains or losses?		
5. Are insurance companies notified of disposals and retirements to assure that insurance coverage is altered accordingly?		

Depreciation

1. Are procedures established to assure that additions are added to depreciation records and that disposals/retirements are deleted?
2. Are procedures established to assure that depreciation is recorded only for those fixed assets actually in service during the period?
3. Are procedures established for determining depreciation methods, estimated useful lives, and salvage values?

maximum, assess allowable detection risk at the minimum, and rely on substantive tests of details. However, if the number of transactions is large, an auditor may elect to perform tests of controls over an entity's recording, addition, disposal, and depreciation activities.

Fixed Asset Records

Tests of fixed asset records focus on the relationship between detailed records and the general ledger and on the existence of, and insurance coverage for, recorded assets. Some representative tests follow.

> **Tests of Controls: Fixed Asset Records**
> 1. Reconcile total fixed assets per detailed records with the general ledger and investigate any differences.
> 2. Physically inspect sampled fixed assets.
> 3. Review the adequacy of insurance coverage on recorded assets.

A company's detailed fixed asset records may take the form of a spreadsheet or a ledger and, as indicated in Step 1, should be reconciled in total with the general ledger. In Step 2, the auditor assures that the fixed assets—particularly additions for the current year—physically exist and have not been disposed of or retired. In Step 3, the auditor reviews the adequacy of fixed asset insurance coverage, since inadequate coverage may require financial statement disclosure.

Additions

An auditor's predominant concern in tests of fixed asset additions is that the related transactions are authorized and properly recorded. Several appropriate tests follow.

Tests of Controls: Additions

1. Obtain a summary of fixed asset additions from Accounting personnel.
2. Foot the summary and reconcile total additions with total additions per the general ledger.
3. Randomly select a sample of additions, and for each sampled addition:
    a. Examine authorization(s), purchase order (or contract), receiving report, vendor's invoice, and other supporting documents.
    b. Examine evidence of cash payment (for example, a canceled check) and trace to an entry in the voucher register (or other cash disbursements records).
    c. Examine evidence of an obligation for payment (for example, a note payable) and trace to subsidiary and general ledger accounts.
    d. Determine that classification as a fixed asset, rather than repairs and maintenance expense, is consistent with policy.

The company's summary of fixed asset additions, the basis for testing additions, may take the form of a spreadsheet or a detailed worksheet, among other things. Step 2 determines whether the summary is mathematically accurate and reconciles the summary with the general ledger, the source for preparing financial statements.

Step 3 addresses the substance of recorded fixed asset addition transactions. Additions can be sampled, as suggested in the program, or tested entirely, which is common when additions are not numerous. In Step 3a, the auditor examines evidence that an addition was authorized and an asset received. Evidence of authorization could appear within the board of directors' minutes, particularly for substantial additions such as buildings, or could take the form of a division manager's memorandum. Receiving reports and invoices would indicate that the additions arrived and were billed by independent vendors.

Step 3b, in contrast, determines whether the addition was paid for and was recorded properly as a cash disbursement. If a note or other obligation exists, the auditor would examine the document in Step 3c, reconciling details with the subsidiary records and the general ledger. Step 3d assures that additions are classified properly as fixed assets rather than as repairs and maintenance expense. In addition, the step assures that classification as an asset or expense is consistent with company policy. For example, in some companies, additions of less than a predetermined dollar amount, say $5,000, might be charged to expense regardless of useful life, since the burden of record keeping is not necessarily justified for immaterial amounts.

Disposals

Like additions, an auditor is concerned that fixed asset disposals are authorized and properly recorded. Some representative tests follow.

Tests of Controls: Disposals

1. Obtain a summary of fixed asset disposals and retirements from Accounting personnel.
2. Foot the summary and reconcile total disposals with total disposals per the general ledger.
3. Randomly select a sample of disposals, and for each sampled disposal:
   a. Examine authorization(s), the contract, the sales invoice, and other supporting documents.
   b. Examine the entry in the cash receipts records.
   c. Examine the note receivable, if there is one, and trace to subsidiary and general ledger accounts.
   d. Calculate any gain or loss and trace to the general ledger.

A company's summary of fixed asset disposals and retirements—for example, a spreadsheet—is obtained in Step 1, tested for mathematical accuracy in Step 2, and agreed to the general ledger. As with additions, disposals and retirements may be sampled or tested entirely.

In Step 3a, the auditor examines evidence that the transaction is authorized, for example, by reading the board of directors' minutes, and that the transaction occurred, as would be suggested by a signed contract and a sales invoice. Step 3b examines entries in the cash receipts records, thereby further supporting whether transactions occurred. If a note was received for a disposed asset, the auditor should examine the instrument and reconcile the transaction with the general ledger, as indicated in Step 3c. In Step 3d, the auditor recalculates any gain or loss from the disposal transaction, reconciling the amount with entries in the general ledger.

Depreciation

Tests of depreciation involve calculations and the review of recorded amounts, useful lives, and salvage values. Similar tests are performed for the amortization of intangible assets and the depletion of wasting assets. Several appropriate tests of depreciation follow.

Tests of Controls: Depreciation

1. Review depreciation methods by asset class and policies for useful lives and salvage values.
2. Randomly select a sample of fixed assets, and for each sampled asset:
   a. Determine whether the useful life and salvage value are consistent with policies.
   b. Recalculate depreciation expense and accumulated depreciation.

In Step 1, the auditor reviews methods and policies to assure that depreciation is calculated as planned. Step 2 tests sampled assets but also could be performed for all assets. Step 2a determines whether each asset's useful life and salvage value are consistent with company policy (Step 1), and Step 2b recalculates depreciation expense and accumulated depreciation.

Assess Control Risk

The auditor assesses control risk for fixed assets in the same manner as discussed earlier for inventory.

Financial Statement Assertions and Audit Procedures

Inventory and fixed assets are the most significant financial statement accounts processed through the conversion cycle. The following section provides an overview of how practicing auditors typically test each of the financial statement assertions introduced in Chapter 4: existence or occurrence, completeness, rights and obligations, valuation or allocation, and presentation and disclosure. Figure 15-8 summarizes the discussion by relating each assertion to specific audit procedures.

FIGURE 15-8: *Relating Assertions and Audit Procedures: Inventory and Fixed Assets*

	Audit Procedures	
Assertions	*Inventory*	*Fixed Assets*
Existence or occurrence	Observe physical inventory. Confirm off-premises inventory. Test cutoff.	Observe asset additions. Test cutoff.
Completeness	Observe physical inventory. Confirm off-premises inventory. Test cutoff. Perform analytical procedures.	Observe asset additions. Test cutoff. Perform analytical procedures.
Rights and obligations	Confirm off-premises inventory. Test cutoff. Review consignment and purchase commitments.	Test additions. Test cutoff. Examine contracts and other documentation.
Valuation or allocation	Test final priced inventory. Review physical inventory for obsolete, slow-moving, or otherwise unsalable goods.	Verify accuracy of recorded fixed assets and depreciation expense. Test additions and disposals.
Presentation and disclosure	Compare statement presentation and disclosures with those required by GAAP.	Compare statement presentation and disclosures with those required by GAAP.

Existence or Occurrence

Within the conversion cycle, the existence or occurrence assertion addresses whether all recorded inventory and fixed assets existed at the balance sheet date and whether all recorded inventory and fixed asset transactions occurred during the period.

For inventory, existence or occurrence is tested by three separate but related procedures. First and foremost, the auditor observes the client's physical count of inventory, often at the balance sheet date, thereby assuring that recorded inventory exists. Second, for off-premises inventory, the auditor confirms recorded quantities with consignees or public warehouses. Finally, inventory cutoff is tested to assure that inventory-related transactions, such as purchases and sales, are recorded in the proper accounting period.

The existence of fixed asset balances and occurrence of transactions are tested by observing additions (and perhaps some previously existing assets) and by testing cutoff, to assure that additions and disposals are recorded in the proper accounting period.

Completeness

The completeness assertion addresses whether all inventory and fixed asset transactions that should be presented in the financial statements actually are presented. That is, were all transactions recorded? To test completeness for inventory, an auditor observes the physical inventory and confirms off-premises inventory to assure that all inventory is recorded. Cutoff tests assure that the recording of year-end transactions is not postponed to the next accounting period. Analytical procedures also address completeness by testing whether recorded balances appear reasonable in relation to other accounts. Completeness for fixed assets is addressed by testing additions to assure they are all recorded, by testing cutoff, and by performing analytical procedures.

Rights and Obligations

Within the conversion cycle, the rights assertion addresses whether an entity has property rights to inventory and to fixed assets. Rights to inventory are tested by confirming off-premises inventory quantities and by testing cutoff, which assures that rights to recorded inventory exist as of the balance sheet date. In addition, auditors also test current obligations for future commitments by reviewing any outstanding consignment or purchase agreements.

For fixed assets, rights are examined by testing additions (and disposals), by testing cutoff to determine whether rights exist at the balance sheet date, and by examining contracts or other supporting documentation, such as invoices for purchased assets and cost records for internally manufactured equipment.

Valuation or Allocation

The valuation assertion addresses whether existing inventory and fixed assets are carried in the financial statements at appropriate amounts. For inventory, an auditor addresses carrying value primarily by testing the client's final priced inventory, but also by reviewing physical inventory for obsolete, slow-moving, or otherwise unsalable goods. The carrying value of fixed assets is tested by verifying the mathematical accuracy of recorded fixed assets and of the client's recorded depreciation expense. Valuation also is addressed when an auditor tests additions and disposals, since added fixed assets should be included in the current financial statements and disposed assets should not.

Presentation and Disclosure

The presentation and disclosure assertion addresses whether recorded inventory and fixed assets are properly classified, described, and disclosed in the financial statements. Presentation and disclosure are tested by comparing a client's financial statement disclosures with generally accepted accounting principles for each reported account. Disclosure guidelines, such as the AICPA's annually updated *Accounting and Audit Manual* and proprietary audit-firm databases, are used frequently by practicing auditors.

The following sections expand on this discussion by illustrating and further explaining each audit procedure. Substantive tests of inventory are discussed first, followed by tests of fixed assets.

Substantive Tests of Inventory

Substantive tests of inventory center on observing client employees count inventory (and confirming off-premises inventory not observed), testing priced inventory (for example, unit prices), testing cutoff, and performing analytical procedures. A program of substantive tests appears in Figure 15-9 and is keyed to, and discussed in the context of, the financial statement assertions presented earlier.

FIGURE 15-9: *Substantive Tests: Inventory*

Assertions	Procedures
Existence Completeness	1. Observe physical inventory.
Existence Completeness Rights	2. Confirm inventory at off-premises locations.

Valuation	3. Obtain the final priced inventory records.
	  a. Extend, foot, and cross-foot the final priced inventory.
	  b. Test unit prices.
	  c. Agree total inventory per the final priced inventory with the general ledger.

Existence or occurrence Completeness Rights	4. Test cutoff, coordinating with tests performed for sales and receivables and for purchases and payables.
Completeness	5. Perform analytical procedures.

Presentation and
  disclosure
	6. Review financial statements to determine whether:
	  a. Inventories and cost of sales are properly classified and described.
	  b. Disclosures are adequate.

Observe Physical Inventory

As discussed in Chapter 4, knowledge obtained directly by an auditor through observation can provide a highly persuasive form of evidence, and nowhere is observation more relevant than in testing inventory. Observation of a client's procedures for physically counting inventories contributes to no less than two assertions:

- *Existence.* Do inventories reported on the balance sheet physically exist?
- *Completeness.* Do inventories reported on the balance sheet include all materials, work in process, and finished goods?

Planning Inventory Counts

An auditor does not physically count inventory for a client, nor does the auditor physically participate as a counter. Rather, client personnel count and document inventory quantities, and the auditor observes the client's procedures. For periodic inventory systems, the physical counts serve as the only measure of quantities on hand; for perpetual systems, the counts serve both as a measure of quantities on hand and as a test of the perpetual records.

Inventory quantities may be counted at interim rather than at year end. From an auditor's point of view, the appropriate timing of inventory counts depends on the type of inventory system—periodic or perpetual—and the effectiveness of internal control. Interim counts are more appropriate when well-kept perpetual records are maintained, internal control (including physical control over the movement of inventory) is effective, and perpetual records and financial statement accounts can be reconciled with year-end balances. Otherwise, counts on or near the balance sheet date are more appropriate—for example, when a periodic inventory system is used, when perpetual records are not well kept, or when internal control is ineffective.

Some time in advance of the count date, an auditor should plan for the inventory observation by reviewing management's proposed inventory counting procedures and their written instructions for employees who will count the inventory. The procedures should be well planned and among other things might provide for:

- Controlling or eliminating stock movement on the count date.
- Stocking or arranging inventory in a manner convenient for counting (for example, like-sized rows, clear separations between inventory classes).
- Pretesting counting devices such as weight scales.
- Segregating stock not to be included in the count, such as inventory held on consignment from suppliers.
- Identifying off-premises stock to be included in the count, such as inventory out on consignment with customers.
- Preparing preprinted count media, such as multipart tags, count sheets, or punched cards.
- Documenting damaged or obsolete inventory.

The employees who count inventory should be given written instructions that include information such as the:

- Count date and times.
- Names of supervisors and count teams by location.
- Count media.
- Procedures for counting and documenting quantities.
- Procedures for controlling and accounting for count media before, during, and after the physical counts.

The procedures and instructions should be complete, explicit, and reasonably adequate to facilitate accurate and reliable counts.

Observing Client Inventory Counts

Prior to, or on, the inventory count date, the in-charge auditor should coordinate with audit staff members assigned to the observation, providing them with duties, detailed instructions, and copies of the client's instructions. In general, most staff members' duties will include:

- Observing count teams,
- Making and documenting test counts, and
- Noting damaged or slow-moving inventory.

An auditor observes client count teams in order to determine whether counters are adhering to the client's instructions and are counting and documenting quantities accurately. Count teams should proceed systematically, taking precautions to cover all, but not more than, their assigned areas; counting outside assigned areas could result in double-counting, thereby potentially overstating inventory.

In conjunction with observing count teams, an auditor should make and document test counts of some inventory items, agreeing quantities with count media compiled by client personnel. Test counts should be included in audit documentation and indicate all details necessary to agree quantities subsequently with the final priced inventory, as illustrated in Figure 15-10. Documented details might include count media numbers (for example, tag numbers), inventory stock numbers

FIGURE 15-10: *Inventory Test Counts*

				C19
				1/27/08
				DN

The Wilson Company
Inventory Test Counts
December 31, 2007

Inventory Ticket Number	Location & Description	Count per: Client	Count per: Audit	Difference: Over (Under)
	Warehouse A			
0462	Part A24—Copper cable	870 ft.	820 ft.[a]	50 ft.[b]
0163	Part A98—Rubber tubing	565 ft.	565 ft.[a]	—
0241	Part A99—Synthetic tubing	405 ft.	400 ft.[a]	5 ft.[b]
0328	Solder	125 lb.	125 lb.[a]	—
0612	3/8" Wire binding	600 ft.	600 ft.[a]	—
0761	3/4" Wire binding	298 ft.	295 ft.[a]	3 ft.[b]
0824	298 Engine oil	125 qts.	125 qts.[a]	—
0822	Bushings, 5/8"	625	625[a]	—
	Department A—Finishing			
0014	Plating fluid	405 gal.	410 gal.[a]	(5 gal.)[b]
0129	Electrolyte solution	75 gal.	75 gal.[a]	—
0146	Oaklite 32	127 gal.	127 gal.[a]	—

a Reconciled with client's final priced inventory (work done 1/17/08—see C20–C24).
b Difference confirmed by client recount, and inventory tag corrected.

Conclusion
Based on test counts and observations, I am satisfied that the client's count procedures were reasonable, that counts were reasonably accurate, and that neither Warehouse A nor Dept. A.—Finishing contains significant quantities of obsolete, slow-moving, or otherwise nonsalable inventory.

and descriptions, and quantities. In addition, an auditor should document any damaged or slow-moving goods, since these items may need to be adjusted to net realizable value in the accounts.

Information should be documented for goods shipped and received on the inventory count date. Assuming title passes on the count date, inventory shipments should be excluded from physical counts, and receipts should be included. Information documented for shipments and receipts on the count date is used in conjunction with other information in tests of cutoff.

Some goods on hand may represent consignments from suppliers and, therefore, are the supplier's inventory. An auditor should determine that all goods held on consignment are segregated from inventory prior to the physical counts. An auditor can further test for consignments by reviewing consignment agreements and making inquiries of client personnel.

Following completion of all inventory observation procedures, each audit staff member should prepare a memorandum summarizing his or her observations, any significant departures from the client's preplanned instructions, and a conclusion about the accuracy of client counts.

Many companies, particularly those in retail industries, count inventory throughout the fiscal year, typically at month end. For example, Rite Aid, the drug store chain introduced in Chapters 8 and 10, periodically counted inventory at selected stores, and recorded on the books amounts for inventory "shrink"—declines in inventory presumably attributed to loss or theft. For stores not selected for physical counts, management estimated shrink by marking the shrink to like-sized stores. However, in fiscal 1999, Rite Aid systematically understated the estimate for approximately 2,000 stores, resulting in an aggregate decrease in shrink—and corresponding increase in reported pretax income—in the amount of $13.8 million. In short, Rite Aid reported shrink properly for stores selected for counting, but understated the estimate of shrink for stores not counted, thereby burying the misstatement in a less easily audited accounting estimate.

Confirm Off-Premise Inventory

Inventory held off-premises by consignees or in public warehouses need not necessarily be observed by an auditor, but should be confirmed. An example of a typical off-premises inventory confirmation request appears in Figure 15-11. If inventory in public warehouses is significant in relation to current or total assets, an auditor also should make supplemental inquiries, such as:

- Discussion about the client's control procedures for the preemployment investigation of warehouse managers, and tests of related evidence.
- Review of the client's control procedures to monitor the performance of warehouse managers and to test related evidence.
- Observation of physical counts whenever practical and reasonable.
- Confirmation from lenders (on a test basis, where appropriate) about pertinent details of warehouse receipts pledged as collateral.

Test Final Priced Inventory

Physical inventory counts provide information about quantities, but not about carrying values. Thus, after completed count media are summarized, employees not otherwise responsible for inventory record keeping or control should extend the quantities by unit costs in spreadsheets, resulting in a final priced inventory

FIGURE 15-11: *Confirmation Request for Off-Premises Inventory*

The Wilson Company
15 Artubus Drive
Stony Brook, NY 11790

January 7, 2008

McGowen Warehousing
12456 Dartmouth Road
Indianapolis, IN 46298

Our auditors, Cheever & Yates, CPAs, are auditing our financial statements for 2007. Will you please furnish them with the following information regarding merchandise held in your custody for us as of December 31, 2007?

- Quantities on hand, including:
    Lot number.
    Date received.
    Description of merchandise.
- A statement about whether the quantities were determined by physical count or represent your recorded amounts only.
- A list of negotiable or non-negotiable warehouse receipts issued, if any.
- A statement of any known liens against this merchandise.
- Indication of any damaged, spoiled, or deteriorated merchandise.

A prompt reply to our auditors will be appreciated. An envelope addressed to our auditors is enclosed.

Maxine Kuman
Controller

by item number, product line, and inventory classification. To facilitate follow-up, each line item on the final priced inventory should identify the count media from which quantities were compiled. Quantities and the final priced inventory should be reconciled by client personnel with perpetual records and control accounts, respectively, and necessary adjustments should be recorded.

As part of year-end substantive procedures, an auditor obtains the client's final priced inventory and performs tests of clerical accuracy. The auditor should extend (multiply quantities by unit costs), foot, and cross-foot the priced inventory, agreeing test counts with priced quantities as illustrated in Figure 15-10 (tick mark *a*); dollar amounts to control accounts; and required adjustments to general ledger entries. Unit prices per the final priced inventory should be agreed with source documents on a sample basis, giving consideration to the cost flow methods adopted. For example, if raw materials costs are assigned to production on a first-in, first-out basis, unit costs should be agreed with the latest vendor invoices available for a period prior to the inventory count date, since the latest prices would be assigned to raw materials inventory and earlier costs would have been charged to work in process.

To test whether inventory is reported at the lower of cost or market (LOCOM), an auditor during a physical inventory observation (above) and again during tests of the final priced inventory considers in general whether inventory may be obsolete but in particular whether the carrying value of inventory approximates the estimated value of inventory. However, testing LOCOM depends in part on management's willingness to report to the auditor issues that bear on carrying value. Take, for example, Gerber Scientific, Inc., an April 30 year-end Connecticut provider of sign making, specialty graphics, and flexible apparel materials that operated primarily in four separate subsidiaries.

In February 2000, Gerber senior management, aware of a large discrepancy between the final price inventory and the general ledger balance, ordered an internal investigation of inventory that was completed by the company's internal auditors, who notified senior management in late April that inventory was overstated by $6 million. In response, management in an April 25, 2000, press release disclosed the company would record a charge of $6 million, although thereafter, in early May, internal auditors told senior management the inventory overstatement had been revised to $6.2. In a May 25, 2000, press release, senior management reported April 30, 2000, net earnings of $1.7 million, and attributed the quarter-over-quarter decline in earnings in part to the inventory charge. Unbeknown to Gerber's auditors, the company's summer budgeting process discovered that the company recorded only $4.7 million of the $6.2 million inventory charge, accounting for $1.5 million ($6.2 – $4.7 million) of Gerber's $1.7 million in 2000 earnings. Although impermissible under GAAP, management amortized the $1.5 million inventory overstatement to each of the next four fiscal quarters in equal amounts of $375,000. The SEC, in an order instituting cease-and-desist proceedings, said:

After learning of the $1.5 million error, the Company failed to correct the press release, proceeded to file its Form 10-K with material misstatements . . . and then sought to eliminate the error in a manner that contravened GAAP and hid its true impact. Gerber's actions after discovery of the $1.5 million error were knowing or reckless . . .[1]

The Gerber case makes clear that company-initiated internal investigations yield important audit evidence. However, more to the point, a company's budgeting process—often completed when auditors are not in the field—can raise questions that either refute prior reported results (for example, were the results of the internal investigation complete?) or signal future audit issues (for example, how did the inventory misstatement bear on future budget expectations?).

Test Cutoff

An auditor compiles inventory cutoff documentation during the physical inventory observation. The documentation includes shipping documents and receiving reports, and is used to test sales cutoff in conjunction with substantive tests for sales and accounts receivable (Chapter 11) and purchase cutoff in conjunction with substantive tests for purchases and accounts payable (Chapter 13).

The cutoff information, however, cannot necessarily be agreed with inventory account balances. For example, if goods are received (and title passes) on the count date, tracing related receiving reports to subsequent purchase and payable entries does not assure that the received goods were counted in inventory. Like-

---

1   *SEC Accounting and Auditing Enforcement Release No. 1987, In the Matter of Gerber Scientific, Inc.,* April 8, 2004.

wise, if goods are shipped (and title passes) on the count date, tracing related shipping documents to subsequent sales and receivables entries does not assure that the shipped goods were not counted in inventory. As a result, during the physical inventory observation, an auditor must assure that shipped and received goods are controlled to avoid both double-counting, as in the case of counting shipped goods in inventory, and undercounting, as in the case of failing to count received goods.

Perform Analytical Procedures

An auditor uses analytical procedures—for example, comparing relationships between and among accounts—to address completeness and to determine whether conclusions drawn from substantive tests of details are reasonable. For example, inventory price tests might indicate that a client's inventory is priced accurately. But an auditor would not likely conclude that the priced sample was representative if other tests indicated that quantities at year end had dropped sharply since the prior year, and yet the general ledger book value of inventory had not.

For inventory, an auditor might use any of the following analytical tests, among others:

- Compare cost of sales divided by average inventory—inventory turnover—for the current year with that for prior years, thereby testing whether turnover is reduced, suggesting slow-moving or obsolete inventory.
- Compare the number of days' sales in inventory for the current year with that for prior years, again testing turnover.
- Compare gross profit margin for the current year with that for prior years, thereby testing whether inventory might possibly be understated or overstated.
- Compare volume-adjusted manufacturing costs for the current year with those for prior years, thereby testing whether unit costs might possibly be understated or overstated.
- Compare inventory, overhead, and cost of sales to budget, thereby testing whether any or all exceeded or fell short of management's expectations.

If any of the preceding tests reveal unusual relationships, an auditor would first make inquiries of management and then design additional detailed substantive tests or extend sample sizes if necessary. For example, in the above price-testing illustration, the auditor might increase sample size, thereby performing additional price tests and attempting to control the risk of incorrect acceptance.

Although auditors routinely apply analytical procedures in financial statement audits, ratios reconstructed long after an audit failure can be instructive about clues that auditors may have missed. Consider, for example, Miniscribe,   ➤ fraud
which in the 1980s ranked second to Seagate Technology in industry-wide disk drive sales. In a dramatic announcement made public in the early 1990s, an internal investigation revealed management had "perpetrated a massive fraud" over a number of years by ignoring inventory obsolescence, creating fictitious inventory in transit, and packaging bricks and scrap to appear like disk-drive shipments.[2] For example, although companies in the ever-developing disk-drive industry

---

2   "Miniscribe Chairman Charged with Fraud in Company's Collapse," *The Wall Street Journal* (March 12, 1993), p. A10.

routinely record reserves for obsolescence, Miniscribe reserved $4.85 million in 1985 but only $2.78 million in 1986, despite an increase in sales from $114 million to $185 million.[3] Interestingly, selected ratios signaled that inventory may have been misstated. For example, Drake and Peavy report that, although inventory turnover did not signal problems, two ratios seemingly unrelated to inventory did: Miniscribe's current and quick ratios (Chapter 6), respectively, declined from 2.43 and 1.45 in the first quarter to 1.62 and 0.94 in the third quarter, fully one-half the industry average.[4] Commenting on these among other signs, a forensic accountant who testified in behalf of Miniscribe bondholders said, "The red flags at Miniscribe . . . were so numerous that only a blind man or someone in on it could miss them."[5] Ratios don't isolate misstatements, but they do point to relationships auditors can't ignore.

Review Financial Statement Disclosures

An auditor reads financial statements to assess whether inventory and cost of sales are properly classified, described, and disclosed in accordance with generally accepted accounting principles. Inventories usually are stated at the lower of cost or market, according to a cost flow assumption (for example, first-in, first-out), and may be classified as supplies, raw materials, work in process, and finished goods. Accrued losses should be disclosed for any purchase commitments made at unfavorable prices.

Substantive Tests of Fixed Assets

Fixed assets are less susceptible to frauds than some other assets, such as cash, securities, and some types of inventories. As a result, auditors often address some financial statement assertions at interim when considering internal control. For example, an auditor addresses existence when physically inspecting fixed assets in conjunction with tests of controls over records. Thus, some substantive procedures are performed at interim, and follow-up or additional tests are done at year end for the intervening period since interim. Figure 15-12 presents a program of representative year-end substantive tests for fixed assets and depreciation and is keyed to the assertions discussed earlier.

Verify Accuracy of Recorded Fixed Assets

To test the mathematical accuracy of fixed asset records, an auditor obtains a client-prepared schedule summarizing detailed asset records. The schedule should include beginning balances, additions, disposals, and ending balances by fixed asset class, as illustrated in Figure 15-13. The auditor should reconcile beginning balances per the schedule with the prior-year financial statements. The accuracy of the summary schedule is checked by footing and cross-footing and by agreeing totals with general ledger accounts. Details for selected assets are then traced to the underlying detailed records.

---

3   L. Berton, "Numbers Game: How Miniscribe Got Its Auditor's Blessing on Questionable Sales," *The Wall Street Journal* (May 14, 1992), p. A1.

4   P. D. Drake and J. W. Peavy, III, "Fundamental Analysis, Stock Prices, and the Demise of Miniscribe Corporation," *Journal of Portfolio Management* (March 1995).

5   L. Berton, "Numbers Game: How Miniscribe Got Its Auditor's Blessing on Questionable Sales," *The Wall Street Journal* (May 14, 1992), p. A1.

FIGURE 15-12: *Substantive Tests: Fixed Assets and Depreciation*

Assertions	Procedures

Valuation	1. Verify mathematical accuracy of recorded fixed assets.
	   a. Obtain a year-end summary schedule of detailed fixed asset records; foot and cross-foot the schedule.
	   b. Agree total fixed assets per the summary schedule with the general ledger.
	   c. Randomly select a sample of fixed assets from the summary schedule and trace to detailed fixed asset records.

Existence or occurrence
Completeness
Rights
Valuation
	2. Test additions and disposals since interim.
	   a. Examine supporting documentation and trace to entries in accounting records.
	   b. Observe (physically inspect) additions.

Existence or occurrence Completeness Rights	3. Test cutoff to determine whether fixed asset additions and disposals near year end are recorded in the appropriate accounting period.

Valuation	4. Verify mathematical accuracy of depreciation expense.
	   a. Obtain a summary schedule of depreciation expense organized by asset class from accounting personnel; foot and cross-foot the schedule.
	   b. Trace totals per the summary schedule to totals in the general ledger.
	   c. Randomly select a sample of fixed assets from the summary schedule and recalculate depreciation expense.

Completeness	5. Perform analytical procedures.

Presentation and disclosure	6. Review financial statements to determine whether:
	   a. Fixed assets, accumulated depreciation, and depreciation expense are properly classified and described.
	   b. Disclosures are adequate.

Test Additions and Disposals Since Interim

Additions and disposals since interim are tested in the same manner as discussed earlier under tests of controls. If relatively few fixed assets have been acquired since interim, an auditor may physically inspect all recorded additions. Otherwise, a randomly selected sample of additions should be observed.

While physically inspecting additions, an auditor also should be alert for other assets that appear to be new and, therefore, that may represent unrecorded additions. Likewise, he or she should be cognizant of areas where fixed assets may recently have been removed, suggesting the possibility of unrecorded disposals. For example, an area within a manufacturing plant may appear unusually clean and contain obvious floor markings that could suggest a machine was removed.

In addition, and closely related to the existence and rights assertions, an auditor also examines documents supporting fixed asset additions and traces the

FIGURE 15-13: *Schedule of Fixed Assets and Accumulated Depreciation*

Schedule prepared by client.

The Wilson Company
Fixed Assets and Accumulated Depreciation
December 31, 2007

E1
1-18-08
JB

Fixed Assets

	Final Bal. 12-31-06	Additions	Retirements/ Disposals	Balance 12-31-07	Adjustments/ Reclass.	Adjusted Bal. 12-31-07
Land	$ 257,650 c	$ 15,200 E2		$ 272,850		$ 272,850 b
Buildings	3,461,520 c		$90,000 E2	3,371,520		3,371,520 b
Machinery & Equipment	1,590,850 c	175,000 E2		1,765,850		1,765,850 b
Furniture & Fixtures	621,420 c			621,420	$37,400	658,820 b
Automobiles	105,000 c			105,000		105,000 b
	$6,036,440	$190,200	$90,000	$6,136,640	$37,400	$6,174,040 b
	a	a	a	a, TB	a	a

Accumulated Depreciation

	Final Bal. 12-31-06	Expense	Retirements/ Disposals	Balance 12-31-07	Adjustments/ Reclass.	Adjusted Bal. 12-31-07
Buildings	$1,461,850 c	$138,000 d	$48,000 E2	$1,551,850	$24,000	$1,575,850 b
Machinery & Equipment	825,500 c	81,500 d		907,000		907,000 b
Furniture & Fixtures	242,100 c	26,500 d		268,600		268,600 b
Automobiles	68,250 c	13,200 d		81,450		81,450 b
	$2,597,700	$259,200 d	$48,000	$2,808,900	$24,000	$2,832,900 b
	a	a	a	a, TB	a	a

a   Footed.
b   Cross-footed.
c   Agreed to 12-31-06 general ledger and financial statements.
d   Recalculated for reasonableness.
TB Agreed to trial balance.

additions to entries in the accounting records. Documentation may take several forms, depending on the nature of the asset, such as an invoice for purchased machinery or a contract for constructed buildings. Supporting documentation also addresses asset valuation, because supporting documents such as invoices, contracts, and canceled checks also represent evidence of an asset's historical cost.

Test Cutoff

Cutoff tests for fixed assets address whether additions and disposals near year end are recorded in the proper accounting period. Since acquisitions are processed through the expenditure/disbursement cycle and disposals through the revenue/receipt cycle, fixed asset cutoff can be tested in conjunction with cutoff tests for purchases and payables and for sales and receivables. Retired assets that are not sold, however, should be tested separately.

Verify Accuracy of Depreciation Expense

As part of an auditor's tests of valuation, he or she tests depreciation expense, since fixed assets are reported net of accumulated depreciation. Year-end detailed tests may not be necessary, however, if interim tests of controls indicate that control over depreciation is adequate. Rather, an auditor might test the reasonableness of depreciation instead through analytical procedures.

If an auditor decides to perform detailed substantive tests of depreciation expense at year end, a summary schedule of depreciation organized by asset class should be obtained from accounting personnel. The schedule should include beginning accumulated depreciation balances (which should be agreed with the prior-year financial statements), current year depreciation expense, reversals of accumulated depreciation for disposed assets, and ending accumulated depreciation balances, as illustrated in Figure 15-13. The auditor would test the schedule's accuracy by footing and cross-footing and by agreeing totals with general ledger accounts. Depreciation expense for selected assets should be recalculated.

On balance, the conventional wisdom is that depreciation likely causes little in the way of incremental audit risk, since the means to calculate depreciation expense are fairly straightforward. However, the case of Waste Management, Inc., ≻ restatement the world's largest supplier of solid waste disposal services, shows quite the opposite. From at least 1992 through 1996, senior management reversed depreciation entries rolled-up from field disposal locations and systematically increased the salvage values and useful lives of trucks, equipment, and containers. Aware of the reversals, Waste Management's auditors proposed adjusting journal entries that remained unrecorded. Owing to years of uncorrected misstatements for asset impairments, environmental liabilities, capitalized interest, and depreciation, among other things, Waste Management restated pretax income for fiscal years 1992 through 1996, and for the first three quarters of 1997, in the cumulative amount of $1,432 million—then the largest restatement ever. Of the restatement, $509 million related to depreciation and salvage values.

More revealing, in an unprecedented disclosure about the auditor of a Fortune 500 company, the SEC reported that the Waste Management engagement partner, in an effort to reverse the effects of previously unrecorded proposed adjusting journal entries (PAJEs):

. . . approached Waste Management and proposed a plan—in the form of a "Summary of Action Steps" ('Action Steps')—to reduce, going forward, the cumulative amount of the

PAJEs and to change, among other things, the accounting practices that gave rise to the PAJEs and to the other known and likely misstatements. For each accounting issue, the Action Steps identified the minimum steps Waste Management "must do" to correct the problem while also proposing two additional approaches—"reasonable" and "conservative"—to which the Company should aspire. The "must do" column specified the steps that the Company must do to write off the cumulative amount of the PAJEs over time— typically between five and seven years—and to change certain, but not all, of the accounting practices underlying the PAJEs and the other known and likely misstatements. The accounting issues for which the Action Steps provided "must do" corrective steps . . . (included) . . . Depreciation/Salvage Value . . .[6]

Clearly, correcting misstatements "over time" effectively violates GAAP, since the financial statements remain misstated by the misstatements that remain uncorrected and, for that matter, raises serious questions about an auditor's objectivity and independence (Chapter 4). Material uncorrected departures from GAAP drive a qualified or adverse opinion (Chapter 3), not a plan to correct the departure prospectively.

Perform Analytical Procedures

To address completeness, an auditor uses analytical procedures such as ratio and trend analysis and comparison of relationships between and among related accounts. For fixed assets, an auditor might use any of the following analytical tests, among others:

- Compare repairs and maintenance costs for the current and prior years, thereby testing whether unusually large expenses signal potentially capitalizable assets.
- Compare repairs and maintenance costs for the current year with budgeted amounts, again testing for signals of potentially capitalizable assets.
- Compare depreciation expense divided by total depreciable assets for the current and prior years, thereby testing whether depreciable assets might be miscalculated.
- Compare units of production divided by total productive assets, thereby testing whether assets may have been retired or disposed of without proper recording.

As in other analytical procedures, unusual items should be investigated by inquiries of management and then by additional substantive tests if necessary. For example, an auditor would likely recalculate depreciation if depreciation expense divided by productive assets declined significantly without a corresponding decline in total productive assets.

Review Financial Statement Disclosures

The balance sheet should be read to determine whether fixed assets and related accumulated depreciation balances are properly classified and described. When a single net book value is reported for fixed assets in a condensed balance sheet, details should be included in the notes to the financial statements. Disclosures should include depreciation methods (including any differences between meth-

---

6   *SEC Accounting and Auditing Enforcement Release No. 1405, In the Matter of Arthur Andersen LLP,* June 19, 2001.

ods for tax and financial reporting purposes), useful lives employed for major asset categories, and other significant policies, such as policies for capitalizing major repairs and reporting gains and losses.

An entity may possess significant leasehold rights, though not ownership, to property and, as a result, may be required to capitalize the related asset. For example, a lease that transfers substantially all of the benefits and risks incident to property ownership should be accounted for as (1) the acquisition of an asset and incurrence of an obligation by a lessee and (2) the sale or financing arrangement by a lessor. An auditor should examine all lease agreements, assuring that the transactions are accounted for properly under FASB *Statement of Financial Accounting Standards No. 13*, "Accounting for Leases," and other related statements and interpretations. All leased assets requiring capitalization under generally accepted accounting principles should be properly classified and described in the balance sheet, and details of lease agreements should be disclosed in notes to the financial statements.

The income statement should be reviewed to determine whether depreciation expense is properly reported. Depreciation expense included in cost of sales should be disclosed separately in the income statement or in notes to the statements.

Management Discretion and Write-Downs of Impaired Assets

For years, companies have written off the book value of fixed assets, natural resources, and intangibles disposed of voluntarily through sale or abandonment, or involuntarily through casualty or condemnation. However, only in the past two decades have companies begun with any regularity to write off **impaired assets**—assets that continue in use but that have suffered an impairment of value as a result, for example, of corporate restructuring or slumping demand for uncompetitive products. For example, although not then required by an authoritative pronouncement, IBM, coincident with a restructuring in the late 1980s, wrote off over $2 billion in software investments and other assets[7] and AT&T, driven by technological advances, wrote off over $6 billion in obsolete telephone network equipment.[8] Owing in part to the potential for earnings manipulation, the Financial Accounting Standards Board added in 1988 an "impairment" project to its technical agenda, issued in 1990 a "Discussion Memorandum," and issued in *Statement of Financial Accounting Standards (SFAS) No. 121*, "Accounting for the Impairment of Long-Lived Assets and for Long-Lived Assets to Be Disposed of," which was superceded in 2001 by *SFAS No. 144*, "Accounting for the Impairment or Disposal of Long Lived Assets." But despite *SFAS No. 144*, management continues to have some latitude on matters of measurement, among them the fair market values used to calculate the impairment loss recognized on assets written down.

Management and Auditor Incentives

The literature suggests that management could have two motives for manipulating the timing and the amount of impaired asset write-downs,[9] both of which

---

7 "IBM Announces Big Write-off, Restructuring," *The Wall Street Journal* (December 6, 1989), p. A3.
8 "AT&T Reports Loss for Quarter and All of 1988," *The Wall Street Journal* (January 27, 1989), p. C20.
9 For example, see L. J. Zucca and D. R. Campbell, "A Closer Look at Discretionary Write-downs of Impaired Assets," *Accounting Horizons* (September 1992), pp. 28–41.

relate to earnings management: "income smoothing" and "big baths." **Income smoothing** refers to a company maintaining a steady rate of earnings growth over a series of years, thereby providing no reason for the financial markets to impute unexpected risk either to the company or to the company's expected stock price. As a result, management could be motivated to recognize asset write-downs in otherwise high-income periods, thereby maintaining steady growth and, correspondingly, diluting expectations of higher than expected income the following year. A **big bath**, in contrast, refers to the practice of timing asset write-downs to occur in an abnormally *un*profitable year, signaling to the financial markets that bad times have long since passed. Interestingly, asset write-downs always result in higher reported future earnings, because future period depreciation expense is computed on lower fixed asset carrying values. Auditors have incentives to assure that the timing and amount of management's charge to current income is fairly presented in all material respects, since materially misstated amounts can affect current share prices, and, as discussed in Chapter 5, auditors can be held liable for negligently failing to detect materially misstated financial statements. The following addresses issues auditors confront when auditing discretionary write-downs of impaired assets.

Discretionary Write-Downs

Fixed assets normally are carried in the balance sheet at historical cost less accumulated depreciation—that is, book value—unless events cause the value of the asset to decline permanently and significantly below book value. Typically, the events driving asset impairment relate to market forces not predicted when the assets were acquired. For example, declining gold prices and a persistently weak gold market caused the Battle Mountain Gold Company to recognize asset impairment write-downs material to their financial statements:

Note 2: Asset Impairment

➤ restatement

. . . the Company recognized charges totaling approximately $23.3 million, net of $11 million income tax benefits . . . for the impairment in value of certain of the Company's assets. The charges included: (1) a write down of $17.6 million, net of a restated $9 million income tax benefit, of the Company's investment in the San Luis mine in Colorado to reduce the carrying value of the investment to a level which the Company believes will be recoverable under current market conditions (lower gold prices, compared with those at the time of project conception, and greater than anticipated capital expenditures resulting from a difficult start-up period led to the write down), (2) a write off of $4 million, net of a restated $2 million income tax benefit, and (3) an impairment of $1.7 million, included as other income (expenses), net, to adjust to current market the value of certain equity securities acquired upon the previous disposition of a discontinued project.

Items (1) and (3) in the footnote relate to asset impairment write-downs, and item (2) to a voluntary abandonment.

When the carrying amount of a long-lived asset is not recoverable, a company recognizes an **impairment loss**: the amount by which the carrying amount of the asset exceeds the fair value of the asset—fair value representing, for example, the undiscounted cash flows expected from the use and eventual disposal of the asset. Judging the significance of an impairment loss is largely a matter of the loss's materiality to the financial statements. Judging recoverability, however, is problematic, particularly when an auditor suspects income smoothing. Consider the following case.

Hawthorne Corporation, a publicly owned West Coast manufacturer of office products, rents a wide variety of mailing, shipping, copier, and facsimile equipment under short-term agreements, generally for periods of three to twelve months. Charges for equipment rental and maintenance contracts are billed in advance, and income is recognized when earned. Analysts have forecasted current earnings per share to be $4.80, an increase over the prior year that would maintain the company's 10 percent increase in each of the last five years. Through the close of the current fiscal year, but before year-end audit work begins, unaudited net income from operations is $1,755,000, $6.00 per share, although almost all of the net income is from mailing, shipping, and facsimile systems. At a conference with management, the chief financial officer (CFO) tells the auditors that, owing both to a retraction in the copier market and to Hawthorne's dwindling market share, the value of fixed assets used to manufacture the unprofitable line of copier products has been impaired. The CFO proposes that an impairment loss of $350,000 ($1.20 per share) be recognized currently, an amount reflecting the difference between recorded book value and fair value, measured by the CFO as the undiscounted expected future cash flows. Management argues that other competitors in the business have recognized impairment losses.

Audit Judgment: Accounting, Liability, and Ethics

Although it's not clear that Hawthorne Corporation's proposed treatment of impaired copier production assets necessarily departs from generally accepted accounting principles, there are at least two reasons to suspect earnings management. First, recognizing the impairment loss would be consistent with income smoothing, since earnings per share would fall to $4.80, an amount consistent with the company's five-year growth rate and, not coincidentally, with analysts' earnings forecasts. Second, a search of the current annual report file in LEXIS-NEXIS for the key words "asset impairment" reveals that, contrary to management's claim, no publicly traded competitors in the office products industry have recognized an asset impairment for copiers. If Hawthorne's management insists on booking an impairment loss, the auditor has no alternative but to alert the client that:

➤ ethics

- Management will need to provide persuasive evidence that the claimed decline in copier production asset values is permanent (how does management know that the copier market has retracted?).
- Lacking persuasive evidence that the impairment loss is reasonable, the auditor will conclude that the loss is materially misstated, a departure from GAAP.

A departure from GAAP will cause the auditor to issue a qualified or adverse opinion, depending on materiality, and an explanatory paragraph that discloses the effect of the departure on reported earnings (Chapter 3, Figure 3-2).

If the auditor considers concurring with management about the impairment loss without persuasive evidence that the loss is reasonable, he or she risks serious legal and ethical implications. Since Hawthorne is publicly traded, statutory law applies and Sections 10(b) and 18 of the *Securities Exchange Act of 1934* (Chapter 5) provide shareholders with a means to recover losses resulting from false or misleading statements. In this case, shareholders could likely recover under Section 10(b) since the auditor knew, or should have known, that evidence supporting the impairment loss consisted of the CFO's oral claims, one of which

➤ fraud

(competitors' impairment losses) was not accurate. However, the plaintiff's basis for action—Section 10(b) or Section 18—would be judged by the plaintiff in consultation with an attorney. Further, as discussed in Chapter 5, the auditor could be liable for treble damages under the *Racketeer Influenced and Corrupt Organizations (RICO) Act*, since *Reves v. Arthur Young*, a 1993 U.S. Supreme Court case, does not provide relief from RICO when the auditor participated directly with management to perpetrate the fraud.

The case raises at least two ethical issues. First, the auditor's conduct may violate the Code of Professional Conduct, Rule 203—Accounting Principles (Chapter 4), which provides that an AICPA member cannot issue an unqualified opinion if the financial statements contain a departure from GAAP. In the Hawthorne case, the accounting principle violated is disclosure of a suspicious impairment loss that has not necessarily been realized. Violating Rule 203 can result in an administrative reprimand, such as suspension to practice before the SEC, or revocation of a CPA's license to practice public accountancy. Second, concurring with a disclosure based entirely on a client's oral claims raises serious questions about the auditor's ethical character, particularly when the client may have ulterior motives for booking the loss (that is, income smoothing, meeting analysts' forecasts) and when available evidence disputes the client's claim.

Computer-Assisted Substantive Tests of Inventory and Fixed Assets

Although audit procedures can be performed effectively on transactions processed manually, computer systems allow an auditor to be just as effective and more reliable, because some audit tests often can be applied to entire audit populations rather than to samples, and because human processing errors are less likely. When part or all of a company's conversion cycle activities are recorded, classified, or summarized by computer, an auditor's year-end procedures can be accomplished by computer-assisted substantive and other tests of details. Figure 15-14 lists several computer-assisted techniques for a series of audit procedures common to audits of inventory and fixed assets.

To illustrate computer-assisted substantive tests, assume an auditor wishes to accomplish portions of the substantive tests for inventory:

- Verify mathematical accuracy of the final priced inventory and perpetual records.
- Compare details in the final priced inventory with perpetual records.
- Perform price tests.
- Merge physical inventory counts with perpetual inventory records.

Any or all of these procedures can be accomplished using either generalized audit software or auditor-prepared software, although in either case the auditor's methodology would be identical to the procedures flowcharted in Figure 15-15.

As illustrated in Figure 15-15, the computer-assisted tests require four data files: the perpetual inventory file, the physical inventory quantities file, the final priced inventory file, and the invoice price and terms file. The audit software would be designed to perform the following tasks for each of the above substantive tests.

FIGURE 15-14: *Computer-Assisted Audit Tests: Inventory and Fixed Assets*

Audit Procedure	Computer-Assisted Substantive Test	
	Inventory	*Fixed Assets*
Test mathematical accuracy.	Verify footings, cross-footings, and extensions of the final priced inventory and/or perpetual records.	Verify footings, cross-footings, and extensions of detailed fixed asset records. Recompute depreciation.
Summarize data.	Print listing of off-premises inventory for confirmation, and print confirmations. Array perpetual inventory records in descending order by dollar amounts to select target items for test counting. Access and print year-end receipts and shipments for agreement with cutoff information obtained during the physical inventory observation.	Print fixed asset additions for observation. Print fixed asset disposals for agreement with recorded gain or loss.
Test accuracy of recorded data.	Trace details in final priced inventory to perpetual records. Perform price tests. Trace details in perpetual records to machine-readable source documents (e.g., receiving reports, production records).	Trace details in fixed asset records to machine-readable source documents.
Make sample selection.	Select inventory items for price testing using internally stored random-number generators and perpetual records.	Select additions for testing (or observation) from internally stored random-number generators and detailed fixed asset records.
Compare similar data files.	Compare charges/credits in perpetual inventory records with the purchases/sales master files. Merge physical inventory counts with perpetual inventory records.	Agree fixed asset additions/disposals with the cash disbursements/cash receipts master files.

FIGURE 15-15:

Flowchart of Computer-Assisted Tests

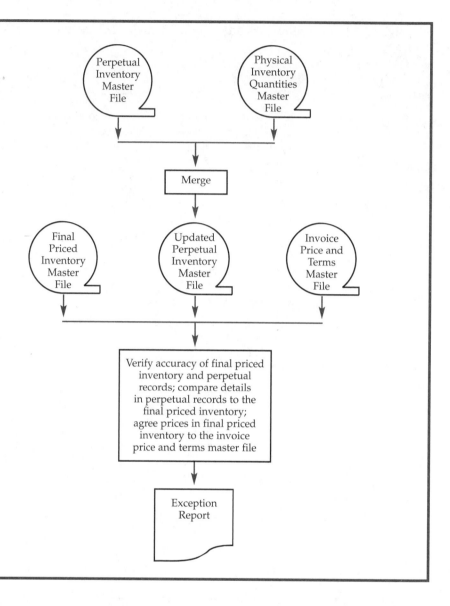

Substantive Test	Computer Software Task
Verify mathematical accuracy.	Foot, cross-foot, and test extensions for the details constituting each stock number within the perpetual inventory file.
	Foot, cross-foot, and test extensions for each line item in the final priced inventory file.
	Print exceptions.
Compare details.	Compare quantities listed in the final priced inventory master file with quantities listed in the perpetual inventory file.
	Print exceptions.

Substantive Test	*Computer Software Task*
Perform price tests.	Compare prices listed in the final priced inventory file with invoice prices contained within the invoice price and terms file.
	Print exceptions.
Merge physical counts with perpetual records.	Update quantities within the perpetual inventory file quantities counted on the physical inventory date and contained within the physical inventory quantities file.
	Print exceptions.

Auditors typically perform the tests listed previously and illustrated in Figure 15-15 on their own laptop computers, although an auditor could arrange with client computer personnel to load and run the software on the client's computer. The software could be run either directly by the auditor or by client personnel under the auditor's supervision. Computer-assisted tests would be documented within the audit documentation and used in conjunction with other audit evidence to form judgments about whether the client's inventory is fairly stated at the balance sheet date.

Assurance Services

Historical cost financial statements capture *financial* information about both inventory and fixed assets, but little about the *nonfinancial* information that also bears directly on investors', creditors', and suppliers' *information risk*. Consider, for example, the case of an institutional investor. Share prices represent the market's average estimate of the per-share discounted present value of future cash flows likely to accrue to a company. The market arrives at an average share price by interpreting financial information, for which independent auditors reduce information risk, and nonfinancial information, for which no profession reduces information risk. In the industrial age, financial information was far more important than nonfinancial information, precisely because industrial assets, such as the inventory and fixed assets reported on the balance sheet, translated into future returns. For example, return was fairly highly correlated with the historical cost of industrial assets that produced product for sale.

However, in the information age, nonfinancial information, rather than industrial era assets, produce a significant share of future returns. For example, if you were to buy a Motorola cellular phone today for, say, $100, about $15 or so would represent materials inventory cost (for example, plastic, wire) and about $85 would be the value of the nonfinancial information—the knowledge assets—Motorola used to design and assemble the phone. Motorola's share price captures financial information made reliable by audited financial statements, and nonfinancial information about knowledge assets that is replete with uncontrolled information risk. The public accounting profession has a unique opportunity to react to the market's demand for nonfinancial information that supplements industrial era financial information and lends insight into the value of knowledge assets and management's capacity to innovate. For example, one reaction is assurance services about production, back orders, and product quality—information that is already shared by some major vendors and suppliers. And a second is assurance services that answer the question, "Where does value come from?" rather than, "Where does cost go?" the question answered by GAAP-based historical cost financial statements.

SUMMARY

The conversion cycle relates to the holding, use, or transformation of resources such as inventory and fixed assets. Internal controls over inventory focus primarily on the physical safeguarding of inventory and recorded accountability. Thus, tests of controls over inventory focus on whether transfers of inventory through production are properly authorized and recorded in perpetual records and cost records. Substantive tests of inventory and cost of sales include physical inventory observation, confirmation of off-premises inventory, verification of the accuracy of final priced inventory records, cutoff tests, analytical procedures, and review of financial statement presentation and disclosures.

Controls over fixed assets and tests of the controls focus on detailed asset records and on the proper authorization and recording of asset additions and disposals. Tests of controls over depreciation involve recalculations and reviewing depreciation methods, useful lives, and salvage values. Substantive tests of fixed assets and depreciation include verifying mathematical accuracy, testing additions and disposals, testing cutoff, analytical procedures, and reviewing financial statement presentation and disclosures.

Although write-offs of fixed assets, natural resources, and intangibles are common when the assets are disposed of voluntarily or involuntarily, it has become common for companies to partially write off assets that, in the discretion of management, have suffered an impairment in value caused, for example, by slumping demand. Auditors should be cognizant of whether the impairment in value is permanent and significant, whether the timing of the write-off is necessarily coincident with management's incentives to smooth income, and whether management's estimate of recoverable value is reasonable.

KEY TERMS

Big bath 652
Depreciation schedule 615
Impaired assets 651
Impairment loss 652
Income smoothing 652

Labor charge report 615
Materials requisition 615
Overhead application report 615
Perpetual inventory record 615

REFERENCES

Professional Standards:

AICPA, *Codification of Auditing Standards*. New York: AICPA.
SAS No. 47, "Audit Risk and Materiality in Conducting an Audit."
SFAS No. 144, "Accounting for the Impairment or Disposal of Long-Lived Assets."

Books:

Committee of Sponsoring Organizations of the Treadway Commission (COSO), *Internal Control: Integrated Framework*. Evaluation Tools. New York: COSO, 1992.

Committee of Sponsoring Organizations of the Treadway Commission (COSO), *Internal Control: Integrated Framework*. Executive Summary. New York: COSO, 1992.

Committee of Sponsoring Organizations of the Treadway Commission (COSO), *Internal Control: Integrated Framework*. Framework. New York: COSO, 1992.

Committee of Sponsoring Organizations of the Treadway Commission (COSO), *Internal Control: Integrated Framework*. Reporting to External Parties. New York: COSO, 1992.

Articles:

Nurnberg, H., and N. W. Dittmar, Jr., "Auditing Considerations of FASB 121," *Journal of Accountancy* (July 1996), pp. 71–78.

Pearson, M., and L. L. Okubara, "Restructuring and Impairment of Value: A Growing Controversy," *Accounting Horizons* (March 1987), pp. 35–41.

Schuetze, W., "Disclosure and the Impairment Question," *Journal of Accountancy* (December 1987), pp. 26–32.

Stevens, M. G., "When Impaired Assets Are a Drag," *Practical Accountant* (February 1994), pp. 52–54.

Titard, P. L., and D. B. Pariser, "Impaired Assets: Meeting Users' Information Needs," *Journal of Accountancy* (December 1996), pp. 55–61.

Zucca, L. J., and D. R. Campbell, "A Closer Look at Discretionary Writedowns of Impaired Assets," *Accounting Horizons* (September 1992), pp. 30–41.

QUESTIONS

Inventory

1. Identify the major business function and activities common to the conversion cycle.
2. How does the conversion cycle of a manufacturing company differ from that of a retailer or wholesaler?
3. Describe the flow of inventory costs through the accounts of a manufacturer.
4. What is the major focus of tests of controls for perpetual records and for cost records?
5. How can management control against misplaced or misused inventory?
6. What procedure does an auditor use to determine whether recorded inventory exists?
7. For what reason does an auditor test a client's final priced inventory?
8. Identify and briefly describe the financial statement assertions that are relevant to physical inventory observations.
9. Under what conditions are interim, as opposed to year-end, physical inventory counts appropriate?
10. Explain an auditor's role during a physical inventory observation.

Fixed Assets

11. Why should fixed assets be appraised periodically?
12. Identify some control procedures for fixed asset additions and disposals.
13. Why might an auditor elect to perform only limited or no tests of controls for fixed assets?
14. What is the focus of tests of controls for fixed asset records?
15. What is the focus of tests of controls for fixed asset additions and disposals?
16. How does an auditor test the valuation of fixed assets and depreciation?
17. Describe some substantive tests applicable to fixed asset additions and disposals.

18. Why would an auditor test cutoff for fixed asset transactions?
19. Given that write-downs decrease reported net income, why would management be motivated to write down impaired assets?
20. What incentives does an auditor have to assure that the timing and amount of discretionary write-downs for impaired assets is fairly presented in all material respects?

MULTIPLE CHOICE QUESTIONS

Inventory

1. Which of the following control procedures is most likely to prevent or detect errors or frauds resulting from the production of unauthorized products or unauthorized quantities of authorized products?

    a. State criteria for determining production.
    b. Establish procedures for processing and recording production.
    c. Conduct periodic inventory counts.
    d. Limit access to inventory and to unused forms.

2. Although significant in the aggregate, a manufacturing company's parts inventory includes thousands of small dollar-value items. The company could establish control over the parts by requiring:

    a. Separation of the store-keeping function from the production and inventory record-keeping functions.
    b. Approval of parts requisitions by a company officer.
    c. Maintenance of inventory records for all parts included in the inventory.
    d. Physical counts of the parts by surprise.

3. Which of the following financial statement assertions are addressed by the physical observation of inventory counts?

    a. Existence and valuation
    b. Rights and completeness
    c. Presentation and disclosure
    d. Completeness and existence

4. A purpose of perpetual inventory records is to:

    a. Benchmark quantities of inventory counted.
    b. Benchmark the general ledger balance for inventory.
    c. Account for inventory carrying values on hand.
    d. Account for inventory quantities on hand.

5. To determine whether merchandise is included in ending inventory, an auditor could test:

    a. Open purchase orders.
    b. Purchase cutoff.
    c. Commitments made by Purchasing.
    d. Invoices received on or around year end.

6. Off-premises inventory held for a company in a public warehouse should be:

    a. Audited by independent auditors.
    b. Audited by internal auditors.
    c. Controlled by warehouse employees.
    d. Controlled by company employees.

7. From which of the following procedures would an auditor obtain evidence about the existence of inventory?

   a. Physical inventory observation
   b. Written representations from management
   c. Confirmation of inventories in a public warehouse
   d. Recomputation of the final priced inventory

8. A company's physical count of inventory revealed quantities higher than reflected in the perpetual inventory records. This could be the result of failing to record:

   a. Sales.
   b. Sales discounts.
   c. Purchases.
   d. Purchase returns.

9. Auditors usually trace the details of the test counts made during the physical inventory observation to the final priced inventory, a procedure that is done to provide evidence that items observed by the auditor at the physical inventory count date are:

   a. Owned by the client.
   b. Not obsolete.
   c. Physically present at the time the final priced inventory is prepared.
   d. Included in the final priced inventory.

10. An auditor would most likely discover slow-moving inventory through:

    a. Inquiries of sales personnel.
    b. Inquiries of production personnel.
    c. Physical observation of inventory.
    d. Review of perpetual inventory records.

Fixed Assets

11. What control objective is served by management implementing written procedures for all additions, disposals, and retirements?

    a. Procedures for operating, using, and physically moving plant assets should be established in accordance with management's criteria.
    b. Plant asset additions, disposals, and retirements should be authorized in accordance with management's criteria.
    c. Plant asset additions, disposals, and retirements should be recorded at the correct amounts, recorded in the proper period, and classified properly.
    d. Access to plant assets should be restricted to personnel authorized by management.

12. Which of the following is most likely a potential deficiency in a small company's fixed asset additions?

    a. Disbursements are not reviewed for equipment bought for less than $10,000.
    b. Equipment is purchased by the requisitioning department.
    c. Equipment is replaced when the estimated useful life expires.
    d. Proceeds from the sale of replaced equipment are recorded as other income.

13. Depreciation on assets used in manufacturing should be:

    a. Charged to applied overhead.
    b. Charged to raw materials inventory.
    c. Removed from cost of sales.
    d. Added to the assets' carrying value.

14. Depreciation expense should be recognized:

    a. Monthly.
    b. Retroactively.
    c. On fixed assets in service.
    d. On all fixed assets.

15. Which of the following explanations could reasonably explain a significant debit to accumulated depreciation?

    a. Repairs have lengthened the life of an asset significantly.
    b. Prior-year depreciation was understated.
    c. A reserve was recorded for losses on the retirement of assets.
    d. Excessive recurring losses on retired assets.

16. Which of the following financial statement assertions are addressed by testing the cutoff for plant asset additions?

    a. Existence and rights
    b. Valuation or allocation
    c. Completeness and valuation
    d. Presentation and disclosure

17. To control fixed asset additions, a company should establish control procedures that require:

    a. Capitalizing the cost of fixed asset additions that exceeds a specified dollar amount.
    b. Restricting access to fixed assets.
    c. Classifying as investments fixed asset additions that are not used in the business.
    d. Authorizing and approving major fixed asset additions.

18. Which of the following audit procedures is least likely to detect unrecorded fixed asset additions?

    a. Reviewing insurance policies
    b. Reviewing repairs and maintenance expense
    c. Reviewing property tax files
    d. Reviewing documents for fixed asset additions

19. Which of the following would not likely motivate management to time the write-off of impaired assets in the current period?

    a. Current unaudited net income is abnormally high in relation to prior years.
    b. The current rate of earnings growth is abnormally low in relation to prior years.
    c. Current unaudited, fully diluted earnings per share is abnormally high in relation to prior years.
    d. Current unaudited selling and administrative expenses are abnormally low in relation to prior years.

20. Which of the following provides management with some latitude in measuring the amount recognized in discretionary write-downs of impaired assets, even with the advent of an authoritative pronouncement?

    a. Estimated future cash flows
    b. The date to which future cash flows are discounted
    c. Fair market values
    d. Impairment loss recognized

PROBLEMS AND DISCUSSION CASES

Inventory

15-1 *Controls Over Inventory and Fixed Asset Records*

Assume you are considering internal control over a client's inventory and fixed asset records. System documentation was accomplished with a flowchart and questionnaire and, in conjunction with a transaction walkthrough, revealed the following potential deficiencies in internal control:

a. Although immaterial in relation to the financial statements taken as a whole, employees sometimes use company assets and tools to build products for home use.
b. Inventory is sometimes misplaced, resulting in potentially time-consuming production delays.
c. During an interim month, the controller observed that inventory containing precious metals was stolen.
d. Delivery trucks were sold during the year without management's knowledge.
e. Scrap sales are sometimes executed but not recorded.
f. Depreciation for the first quarter was inaccurate, although not materially misstated.
g. Cash receipts personnel were observed making notations in fixed asset records.

Required: For each potential deficiency, indicate one or more control procedures that management could implement to reduce the likelihood of errors or frauds.

15-2 *Errors, Fraud, and Control Procedures*

While auditing Trowbridge Corporation's June 30, 2007, financial statements, you become aware of the following controls or procedures over Trowbridge's inventory control and inventory accounting activities:

> fraud

1. No new products are produced without management's express written authorization.
2. Access to the warehouses is restricted to personnel named in a memorandum dated August 10, 2006.
3. Inventory movement into and out of storerooms and production sites is logged in journals maintained by Inventory Control personnel.
4. All personnel named in the August 10, 2006, memorandum (Item 2) are bonded for loss or theft.
5. Responsibility for handling inventory is segregated from inventory recording, cost accounting, and general accounting.
6. All materials release and production forms are maintained under lock and key and are distributed only to authorized personnel.

Required: For each control procedure, indicate (a) a potential error or fraud that might be prevented or detected as a result of the control procedure and (b) the control objective served by the control procedure.

15-3 *Auditing Overapplied and Underapplied Overhead*

Denise Ondeyko, CPA, is drafting an audit program to test controls over the Purdue Corporation's cost records.

Required:
1. Explain the importance of determining the disposition of overapplied and underapplied overhead. In your explanation, describe how overhead should be treated.

2. List and explain some items that should be included in overhead. What should not be included?

15-4 *Drafting Tests of Controls from an Internal Control Questionnaire*

Following are selected questions from an internal control questionnaire relating to a company's inventory control, perpetual inventory, and cost records. A *Yes* response indicates a potential strength, and a *No* response a potential weakness, of the system.

a. Is inventory reasonably protected from physical deterioration and theft?
b. Are materials requisition forms required to request materials and supplies for use in production?
c. Are physical inventory counts taken at least once per year for all inventories?
d. Are perpetual inventory records continually updated on a timely basis?
e. Are perpetual records reconciled with general ledger control accounts on a regular basis?
f. Are all inventory transfers reported and recorded on a timely basis?
g. Are production personnel required to explain price and volume variances?

Required: Assume that inquiries indicate the answer is *Yes* to each question. Draft tests of controls that you believe would provide persuasive evidence that the answer to each question, *a* through *g*, is correct.

15-5 *Designing Tests of Controls*

Alicin Nagle, an in-charge auditor, is reviewing the inventory controls for the City of Carlton's vehicle maintenance facility. Nagle has learned the following:

a. Vehicle maintenance records indicate that, even though the total number of trucks is decreasing, the number of inoperative trucks waiting for spare parts is increasing.
b. Stockroom employees have been unable to find some parts, even though the perpetual inventory system shows the parts on hand.
c. The investment in spare parts inventory has remained at about the same level in each of the last three years.
d. Many of the spare parts can be used for passenger cars.
e. A clerk in the parts warehouse office maintains the perpetual inventory records.

Required: Design tests of controls for each item listed.

15-6 *Relating Errors, Frauds, Audit Procedures, and Assertions in Substantive Tests of Inventory*

Following are errors, frauds, or other circumstances that an auditor might encounter as a result of applying year-end substantive tests of details to inventory as of December 31, 2007.

a. Perpetual inventory records for selected products are not accurate.
b. A material amount of inventory is held in several public warehouses throughout the Midwest.
c. Unit prices for selected products on the final priced inventory appear low; the client uses the first-in, first-out cost flow assumption.
d. The final priced inventory reflects quantities from the perpetual inventory records.
e. Goods were received on December 31, but not recorded until January 2, 2008.
f. The client has begun to lag behind competitors in market share; the client is in the computer industry.

Required: For each of the above items, indicate (a) a specific substantive test or tests that might address the error, fraud, or circumstance and (b) the financial statement assertion addressed by each test.

15-7 *Auditing Raw Materials Purchases*

During your audit of the financial statements of The Gary Manufacturing Company for the year ended December 31, 2007, you find that at January 1, 2007, the company had installed the following procedures for recording raw material purchases and payables.

a. Vendors' invoices are sent directly to the Accounts Payable department by the Mail department.
b. All documents supporting the invoices are accumulated in the Accounts Payable department and attached to the invoices. After being checked and cash discounts computed, the invoices are entered on computers at workstations.
c. An invoice register is prepared from data compiled on-screen.
d. The general ledger control account is posted monthly from the totals shown in the invoice register and all other journals.
e. On due dates, the accounts payable are processed to prepare checks and remittance statements.
f. At the end of the month, unpaid accounts payable are compared with the general ledger control account.

Required: List the procedures you would use to audit raw material purchases.

15-8 *Auditing Perpetual Inventory Records*

Decker is auditing the financial statements of Allright Wholesale Sales, Inc., for the year ended December 31, 2007. Allright has been in business for many years, although the company has never been audited. Decker is satisfied that ending inventory is fairly stated in all material respects and is considering alternative procedures to audit management's representations about the beginning inventory, which was not observed.

Allright sells only one product, bottled water, and maintains perpetual inventory records. In addition, Allright takes physical inventory counts monthly. Decker already has confirmed purchases with the supplier and has decided to concentrate on the reliability of perpetual inventory records and on analytical procedures to the extent that data within the prior years' unaudited records will allow.

Required: Design audit procedures, including analytical procedures, that Decker should apply to evaluate the reliability of perpetual inventory records and to audit the January 1, 2007, inventory. (AICPA Adapted)

15-9 *Drafting Employee Instructions for a Physical Inventory Observation*

In connection with his audit of the financial statements of Knutson Products Co., an assembler of home appliances, for the year ended May 31, 2007, Ray Mendez is reviewing with Knutson's controller the plans for a physical inventory at the company warehouse on May 31, 2007.

Part A. Finished appliances, unassembled parts, and supplies are stored in the warehouse, which is attached to Knutson's assembly plant. The plant will operate during the count. On May 30, the warehouse will deliver to the plant the estimated quantities of unassembled parts and supplies required for May 31 production, but there may be emergency requisitions on May 31. During the count, the warehouse will continue to receive parts and supplies and to ship finished appliances. However, appliances completed on May 31 will be held in the plant until after the physical inventory.

Part B. Warehouse employees will join with Accounting department employees in counting the inventory. The inventory takers will use a tag system.

Required: For Part A, what procedures should the company establish to assure that the inventory count includes all items that should be included and that nothing is counted twice? For Part B, what instructions should the company give to the inventory takers?

(AICPA Adapted)

15-10 *Identifying Problems in a Physical Inventory Observation*

Late in December 2007, your public accounting firm accepted an audit engagement at Fine Jewelers, Inc., a corporation that maintains a diamond wholesale store in New York City and retail jewelry stores in several Eastern cities. A buyer employed by the wholesale store purchases diamonds in the New York diamond market. The wholesale store carries a substantial inventory of diamonds that are set in rings and in other quality jewelry based on orders from the retail stores and from independent customers. The corporation values inventory by the specific identification cost method.

Required: Assume you are satisfied that Fine Jewelers, Inc., has no jewelry left by customers for repair or for sale on consignment and that no inventory owned by the corporation is in the possession of outsiders.

1. Discuss problems the auditor should anticipate confronting on the physical inventory as a result of the:
   a. Different locations of the inventories.
   b. Type of inventory.
2. a. Explain how your audit program for this inventory would differ from that used for most other inventories.
   b. Draft procedures for the audit of the corporation's diamond and diamond jewelry inventories, identifying any steps that you would apply only to the retail stores or to the wholesale store.
3. Assume that a shipment of diamond rings was in transit by messenger from the wholesale store to a retail store on the inventory date. What additional audit steps would you take to satisfy yourself as to the gems that were in transit from the wholesale store on the inventory date?

(AICPA Adapted)

15-11 *Designing Procedures for a Physical Inventory Observation*

Your audit client, Household Appliances, Inc., operates a retail store in the center of town. Lacking sufficient storage space, Household keeps undisplayed inventory in a public warehouse outside of town. The warehouse receives inventory from suppliers and, on request from your client by a shipping advice or telephone call, delivers merchandise to customers or to the retail outlet. The accounts are maintained at the retail store by a bookkeeper. Each month the warehouse sends to the bookkeeper a quantity report indicating opening balance, receipts, deliveries, and ending balance. The bookkeeper compares book quantities on hand at month end with the warehouse report and adjusts the books to agree with the report. No physical counts of the merchandise at the warehouse were made by your client during the year. You are now preparing for your audit of the current year's financial statements. Last year you issued an unqualified opinion.

Required:
1. Design audit procedures for observing the physical inventory of Household Appliances, Inc.:
   a. At the retail outlet, and
   b. At the warehouse.
2. As part of your tests, would you verify inventory quantities at the warehouse by:
   a. A warehouse confirmation? Why?
   b. Test counts of inventory at the warehouse? Why?

3. Since the bookkeeper adjusts the books to quantities shown on the warehouse report each month, what significance would you attach to the year-end adjustments if they were substantial? Discuss.

4. Assume you are unable to satisfy yourself as to the inventory. Could you issue an unqualified opinion? Why?

(AICPA Adapted)

15-12 *Identifying Causes for Inventory Discrepancies*

Ashton Tate, an in-charge auditor, has completed the year-end physical inventory observation at a large wholesaler of automotive parts. Tate reviewed management's inventory-taking instructions before the start of the physical inventory, made and recorded test counts, observed the controls over the inventory-taking process, and noted no significant exceptions. Tate's subsequent comparisons of the quantities shown on the count sheets with quantities listed on the perpetual inventory records disclosed numerous discrepancies.

Required: Other than theft, what are the likely causes of the discrepancies?

15-13 *Shortages in Physical Inventory Quantities*

After observing a physical inventory, an auditor compared the physical inventory counts with the perpetual inventory records and noted apparent shortages that were materially larger than those found at the end of the previous year.

Required:
1. Identify possible causes, other than theft, for the differences between the physical counts and the perpetual inventory records.
2. Briefly describe potential adverse effects the differences could cause.
3. Assuming that theft caused the differences, give recommendations to prevent theft.

15-14 *Inventory and Fixed Asset Disclosures*

LOC Container Corporation is preparing financial statements for the fiscal year ended April 30, 2007. Because all of LOC Container's shares are traded within state, the company does not file reports with the Securities and Exchange Commission. The company manufactures plastic, glass, and paper containers for sale to food and drink manufacturers and to distributors. LOC maintains separate control accounts for raw materials, work-in-process, and finished goods inventories for each of the three types of containers. Inventories are valued at the lower of cost or market. The company's fixed assets are classified into the following major classes: land, office buildings, furniture and fixtures, manufacturing facilities, manufacturing equipment, and leasehold improvements. All fixed assets are carried at cost. Depreciation methods vary depending on the type of asset and acquisition date. LOC plans to present the inventory and fixed assets at April 30, 2007, as follows:

Inventories	$1,659,609
Property, plant, and equipment (net of depreciation)	$3,578,475

Required: What information must LOC Container Corporation disclose about inventories and fixed assets in audited financial statements issued to shareholders?

15-15 *Audit Documentation Review: Inventory Test Counts*

Following is inventory test count documentation memorializing Donald Schwab's physical inventory observations in the Hillsdale Company's roofing materials warehouse on December 31, 2007, the date of the physical inventory (and the last day of the fiscal year), including his follow-up work tracing test counted items to the client's final priced inventory on January 11, 2008.

AUDIT DOCUMENTATION REVIEW

Hillsdale Company, Inc.   C60
Inventory Test Counts: Roofing Materials Warehouse   DS
January 11, 2008

Ticket Number	Description	Count per: Client	Count per: Audit	Difference: Over (Under)
1245	Stock No. C10568: Shake shingle	1470 ct	1430 ct*	40 ct
1324	Stock No. D56748: Tile shingle	1539 ct	1539 ct+	
1034	Stock No. E56849: Tenpenny nails	205 ft	400 ft*	(195) ft
1076	Stock No. L38271: Tar paper	125 ft	120 ft	
1089	Stock No. E56849: Edged Shake shingle	978 ct	978 ct*	
1090	Stock No. C84059: Facing glue	587 ga	578 ga+	
1099	Stock No. F57487: Carriage House shingle	798 ct	798 ct*	
0014	Stock No. G57849: Grand Manor shingle	1287 ct	1292 ct*	(5 ct)
0129	Stock No. B77473: Sun Surf shingle	647 ct	647 ct*	
0146	Stock No. S75743: Classic Revival	547 ct	547 ct*	
0324	Stock No. T47383: Dimensional shingle	569 ct	569 ct*	

+Agreed to client's corrected count sheet.
* Agreed to client's final priced inventory.

Conclusion

Based on test counts, I am satisfied that the client's count procedures were reasonable and that there are no significant quantities of otherwise nonsalable items.

Required: List the deficiencies in this document.

Fixed Assets

15-16 *Controls Over Fixed Assets*

You became aware of the following control procedures for Gatehouse & Company's fixed assets:

1. All scrapped assets are agreed with published price lists before being offered for sale and are never sold for amounts significantly below established prices.
2. Procedures for operating, using, moving, and controlling fixed assets are firmly established in periodically updated procedures manuals.
3. Procedures are established for identifying assets as potential scrap sale items, although actual sales must first be approved by division managers.
4. Physical custody over fixed assets is segregated from recording.
5. Fixed assets on the floor are reconciled periodically with fixed asset records, and vice versa.

Required: For each control procedure, indicate (a) a potential error or fraud that might be prevented as a result of the control procedure and (b) the control objective served by the control procedure.

15-17 *Drafting Tests of Controls from an Internal Control Questionnaire*

Following are selected questions from an internal control questionnaire about a company's fixed asset records, additions, disposals, retirements, and depreciation functions. A *Yes* response indicates a potential strength of the system, a *No* response a potential weakness.

1. Are procedures followed to determine whether recorded fixed assets actually exist?
2. Is insurance coverage maintained and reviewed for all fixed assets?
3. Do procedures require authorization by the board of directors or senior management for fixed asset additions?
4. Are actual expenditures for fixed assets compared with amounts authorized?

5. Are procedures established to assure that the proceeds from fixed asset disposals are recorded properly and deposited?
6. Are fixed asset disposals and retirements promptly reported to General Accounting for recording gains and losses?
7. Are procedures established to assure that additions are added to depreciation records and disposals/retirements deleted?

Required: Assume that inquiries indicate the answer is *Yes* to each question. Draft a test of controls that you believe would provide persuasive evidence that the answer to each question is correct.

15-18 *Relating Errors, Frauds, Audit Procedures, and Assertions in Substantive Tests of Fixed Assets*

Following are errors, frauds, or other circumstances that an auditor might encounter as a result of applying year-end substantive tests of details to fixed assets as of December 31, 2007.

1. During the physical inventory observation, the auditor sees machinery not present during the December 31, 2006, physical inventory.
2. Separate detailed records now are maintained for all fixed assets.
3. New equipment was installed during late December and early January.
4. Depreciation expense is lower than in 2006, and yet additions far exceeded disposals and retirements in 2007.
5. Equipment may have been disposed of, but the disposal was not recorded.

Required: For each of the above items, indicate (a) a specific substantive test or tests that might address the error, fraud, or circumstance and (b) the financial statement assertion addressed by each test.

15-19 *Auditing Manufacturing Equipment, Depreciation, and Repairs*

In connection with a recurring audit of the financial statements of the Louis Manufacturing Company for the year ended December 31, you have been assigned the audit of these accounts: Manufacturing Equipment, Accumulated Depreciation, and Repairs to Manufacturing Equipment. Your review of Louis's policies and procedures has disclosed the following:

a. The Manufacturing Equipment account includes the net invoice price plus related freight and installation costs for all of the equipment in Louis's manufacturing plant.
b. The Manufacturing Equipment and Accumulated Depreciation accounts are supported by a subsidiary ledger that shows the cost and accumulated depreciation for each piece of equipment.
c. An annual budget for capital expenditures of $1,000 or more is prepared by the budget committee and approved by the board of directors. Capital expenditures over $1,000 that are not included in this budget must be approved by the board of directors, and variations of 20 percent or more must be explained to the board. Approval by the supervisor of production is required for capital expenditures under $1,000.
d. Company employees handle installation, removal, repair, and rebuilding of the machinery. Work orders are prepared for these activities and are subject to the same budgetary control as other expenditures. Work orders are not required for internal expenditures.

Required:
1. Identify the objectives of your audit of the Manufacturing Equipment, Accumulated Depreciation, and Repairs to Manufacturing Equipment accounts.
2. Draft audit procedures for current-year additions to the Manufacturing Equipment account.

(AICPA Adapted)

15-20 *Adjustments, Reclassifications, and the Audit of Fixed Assets*

Rivers is the auditor for a manufacturing company with a balance sheet that includes the caption "Property, Plant, and Equipment." Management has asked Rivers if audit adjustments or reclassifications are required for the following material items that have been included or excluded from Property, Plant, and Equipment.

a. A tract of land was acquired during the year. The land is the future site of the client's new headquarters, which will be constructed the following year. Commissions were paid to the real estate agent used to acquire the land, and expenditures were made to relocate the previous owner's equipment. The commissions and expenditures were expensed and are excluded from Property, Plant, and Equipment.

b. Clearing costs were incurred to make the land ready for construction. The costs were included in Property, Plant, and Equipment.

c. During the land-clearing process, timber and gravel were recovered and sold. The proceeds from the sale were recorded as other income and are excluded from Property, Plant, and Equipment.

d. A group of machines was purchased under a royalty agreement that provides royalty payments based on units of production from the machines. The cost of the machines, freight costs, unloading charges, and royalty payments were capitalized and are included in Property, Plant, and Equipment.

Required:

1. Describe the general characteristics of assets, such as land, buildings, improvements, machinery, equipment, fixtures, etc., that should normally be classified as property, plant, and equipment, and identify audit objectives in connection with the audit of Property, Plant, and Equipment.

2. Indicate whether each of the items *a* to *d* requires one or more audit adjustments or reclassifications, and explain why adjustments or reclassifications are required or not required.

(AICPA Adapted)

15-21 *The Existence and Title to Land Holdings*

Terra Land Development Corporation is a closely held family business engaged in purchasing large tracts of land, subdividing the tracts, and installing paved streets and utilities. The corporation does not construct buildings for the buyers of the land and does not have any affiliated construction companies. Undeveloped land is usually leased for farming until the corporation is ready to begin development. The corporation finances land acquisitions by mortgages; the mortgages require audited financial statements. You have now begun your firm's initial audit of the financial statements for the year ended December 31, 2007. Your preliminary review of the accounts indicates that the corporation would have had a highly profitable year except that the corporate officers—all members of the family—were reimbursed for exceptionally large travel and entertainment expenses.

Required: The corporation has three tracts of land in various stages of development. List the audit procedures necessary to audit the physical existence of and title to the corporation's three land holdings.

(AICPA Adapted)

15-22 *Drafting Adjusting Journal Entries*

You are auditing the financial statements of Ute Corporation for the year ended December 31, 2007. The client has prepared the following schedules for the fixed assets and depreciation accounts. You have agreed the opening balances with the general ledger and with your prior-year audit documentation.

Ute Corporation
Analysis of Fixed Assets and
Related Allowance for Depreciation Accounts
Year Ended December 31, 2007

Description	Final 12/31/06	Additions	Retirements	Per Books 12/31/07
Land	$ 22,500	$ 15,000		$ 37,500
Buildings	120,000	175,000		295,000
Machinery and Equipment	385,000	40,400	$26,000	399,400
	$527,500	$230,400	$26,000	$731,900

Allowance for Depreciation

Description	Final 12/31/06	Additions*	Retirements	Per Books 12/31/07
Buildings	$ 60,000	$ 8,300		$ 68,300
Machinery and Equipment	173,250	39,220		212,470
	$233,250	$47,520		$280,770

*Depreciation expense for the year.

Your audit reveals the following information:
a. All equipment is depreciated on the straight-line basis (no salvage value) based on the following estimated lives: buildings, 25 years, built in 1995; all other items, 10 years. Company policy is to take one-half year's depreciation on all asset acquisitions and disposals during the year.
b. On April 1, the company entered into a ten-year lease contract for a die-casting machine with annual rentals of $5,000 payable in advance every April 1. The lease is cancelable by either party (60 days written notice is required), and there is no option to renew the lease or to buy the equipment at the end of the lease. The estimated useful life of the machine is ten years with no salvage value. The company recorded the die-casting machine in the machinery and equipment account at $40,400, the discounted present value at the date of the lease, and $2,020, applicable to the machine, has been included in depreciation expense for the year.
c. The company completed the construction of a wing on the factory building on June 30, although the useful life of the building was not extended. The lowest construction bid received was $175,000, the amount recorded in the Buildings account. Company personnel were used to construct the addition at a cost of $160,000 (materials, $75,000; labor, $55,000; and overhead, $30,000).
d. On August 18, $15,000 was paid for paving and fencing a portion of land owned by the company and used as a parking lot for employees. The expenditure was charged to the Land account.
e. The amount shown in the machinery and equipment retirement column represents cash received on September 5 upon disposal of a machine purchased in July 2006 for $48,000. The accountant recorded depreciation expense of $3,500 on this machine in 2007.
f. Crux City donated land and a building appraised at $100,000 and $400,000, respectively, to Ute Corporation for a plant. On September 1, the company began operating the plant. Because no costs were involved, no entry was made for the transaction.

Required: Prepare the adjusting journal entries that you would propose at December 31, 2007, to adjust the accounts for transactions *a* to *f*. The books have not been closed. Round computations to the nearest dollar. (AICPA Adapted)

15-23 *Drafting Audit Procedures for Depreciation*

You have been assigned to audit the fixed assets of the Johnson Corp., a manufacturer of janitorial supplies. The company maintains a detailed property ledger for all fixed assets. You prepare an audit program for the asset balances but have yet to prepare one for accumulated depreciation and depreciation expense.

Required: Draft audit procedures for accumulated depreciation and for depreciation expense.

15-24 *Audit Documentation Review: Fixed Assets and Accumulated Depreciation*

AUDIT DOCUMENTATION REVIEW

Following is a client-prepared schedule that captures fixed assets and accumulated depreciation for Rock View Corporation, and for which Molly Giles has completed audit work.

Schedule Prepared by Client
E2

Rock View Corporation
Fixed Assets and Accumulated Depreciation
December 31, 2007

Fixed Assets

	Final Balance 12-31-06	Additions	Retired/ Disposed	Balance 12-31-07	Adjust/ Reclass.	Adjusted Balance 12-31-07
Land	$ 657,908#	$24,965 E6	$110,000	$ 572,873	$21,000	$ 593,873
Buildings	989,602#	E6	46,000	943,602		943,602
Machinery/ Equipment	456,239#	55,000 &		511,239		511,239
Trucks	129,560#			129,560		129,560
	$2,233,309	$79,965	$156,000	$2,157,274	$21,000	$2,178,274

Accumulated Depreciation

	Final Balance 12-31-06	Expense	Retired/ Disposed	Balance 12-31-07	Adjust/ Reclass.	Adjusted Balance 12-31-07
Building	$345,876#	$ 78,453@		$424,329		$424,329
Machinery/ Equipment	128,452#	34,983@		163,435		163,435
Trucks	42,493#	12,873@		55,366		55,366
	$516,821	$126,309		$643,130		$643,130

\# Agreed to prior-year working papers.
& Observed new machine on plant floor.
@ Agreed to client depreciation spreadsheet.

Required: List the deficiencies in this document.

15-25 *Earnings Manipulation and Impaired Assets*

The Sonora Company mines precious metals at excavation sites throughout North and South America. Although sales of copper and gold have flattened during the year and gold sales are well below the prior year, the company remains profitable, largely because of efficient mining technologies and a major company-wide cost containment program. No new sites have been discovered in the past two years and all existing mines have been depleted by no less than 50 percent. Sonora's chief executive officer is strongly considering a discretionary write-down of selected mines, arguing that the assets' values are significantly impaired.

    Required: Identify, and explain the motive for, the key questions an auditor must ask to judge whether management's discretionary write-down of impaired assets is appropriate.

Internet problems and discussion cases are available at http://ricchiute.swlearning.com

RESEARCH PROJECT

Discretionary Write-downs of Impaired Assets

Although once unusual, write-downs of impaired assets increased markedly in the 1980s. For example, D. Fried, M. Schiff, and A. Sondhi ("Impairments and Writeoffs of Long-Lived Assets," *Management Accounting*, August 1989, pp. 48–50) report that of 702 companies studied during the period 1980–1985, write-offs increased in number from 38 to 207 and in pretax amount from $28.3 million to $117.5 million. Reports of asset write-downs are quite common today. For example, Progress Energy, in a note to the 2002 audited financial statements, reports that:

Effective January 1, 2002, the Company adopted SFAS No. 144, "Accounting for the Impairment or Disposal of Long-Lived Assets." SFAS No. 144 provides guidance for the accounting and reporting of impairment or disposal of long-lived assets. The statement supersedes SFAS No. 121, "Accounting for the Impairment of Long-Lived Assets and for Long-Lived Assets to be Disposed Of." In 2002 and 2001, the Company recorded pre-tax long-lived asset and investment impairments of approximately $388.8 million and $209.0 million, respectively. There were no impairments recorded in 2000. Estimated impairments of assets held for sale of $58.8 million is included in the 2002 amount, which relates to Railcar Ltd.

    Required: Using the newspaper and magazines file in Factiva, or newspapers and magazines in a library, select an article about the effect on a publicly traded company of a discretionary write-down of impaired assets. Using the SEC's EDGAR system (**http://www.sec.gov**) or copies of annual reports in a library, select the annual report of the same company issued for the fiscal year referred to in the article. Draft a report that accomplishes the following:

1. Summarizes the article, indicating key issues, like management's or the financial community's reaction to the effect of the disclosure on reported income.
2. Lists and explains questions an auditor would likely pose to the management of the company you've selected.
3. Summarizes the company's disclosures about asset write-downs that appear in the footnotes (that is, the footnote summarizing the write-down and the footnote summarizing accounting policies—if separately explained) and the income statement (if disclosed as a separate line item).

Interactive quizzes are available as a student learning resource at http://ricchiute.swlearning.com

16 Chapter

Investments, Debt, and Equity

Major topics discussed in this chapter are:

- The nature of the financing cycle.
- Controls over the custody, recording, valuation, acquisition, and sale of investments and over the issuance and retirement of long-term debt and equity securities.
- An auditor's consideration of internal control in the financing cycle.
- Substantive tests of investments, long-term debt, and equity balances.
- Application of audit judgment to questions about management discretion in accounting for financial instruments.
- Assurance and consulting service opportunities related to investments.

This chapter introduces tests of controls and substantive tests applicable to three major financing cycle accounts: investments, long-term debt, and equity. The chapter begins by summarizing the nature of the financing cycle and by introducing controls over the custody, recording, valuation, acquisition, and sale of investments and over the issuance and retirement of debt instruments and equity securities. In turn, an auditor's consideration of internal control in the financing cycle is introduced, and detailed substantive tests are explained. Next, the chapter addresses accounting, legal, and ethical questions auditors face when auditing financial instruments. Finally, the chapter offers examples of assurance and consulting service opportunities related to investments. An auditor's obligations for internal control under the *Sarbanes-Oxley Act*, Section 404, "Management Assessment of Internal Controls," SEC rules (*Management's Reports on Internal Control Over Financial Reporting*), and PCAOB *Auditing Standard No. 2*, "An Audit of Internal Control Over Financial Reporting," were discussed and illustrated in Chapters 8, 10, and 12.

The Financing Cycle

The financing cycle processes transactions and events that generate capital funds, and is directly related to two other cycles: It uses resources and information provided by the expenditure/disbursement cycle and provides resources and information to the revenue/receipt cycle. For example, the financing cycle might process a cash disbursement (expenditure/disbursement cycle) to retire long-term debt and process a cash receipt (revenue/receipt cycle) from the sale of capital stock.

Figure 16-1 summarizes the scope of the financing cycle, listing the cycle's primary business functions and common activities, journal entries, and forms. Two major business functions are associated with the cycle:

- Capital funds are received from investors and creditors.
- Capital funds are used for operations or temporarily invested until needed for operations.

The cycle begins with management's decisions about the optimum sources of capital funds from debt and equity financing and the optimum allocation of funds between internal operations and outside investments. In turn, the cycle encompasses the payment of dividends on capital stock and interest on debt, and the redemption of capital stock (treasury stock transactions) and the retirement of debt.

Throughout the financing cycle, journal entries are made for the issuance and retirement of debt and capital stock and the acquisition and sale of investments. Common forms and documents include:

- **Bond certificate**: A debt security document representing a stated amount of corporate debt. Bond certificates are frequently issued in denominations of $1,000.
- **Commercial paper**: A general category of commercial loan instruments, due and payable in accordance with terms described on the instrument.
- **Stock certificate**: An equity security document representing ownership of a stated number of shares of capital stock.
- **Treasury bill**: A debt instrument issued by the U.S. Treasury Department.

Internal control considerations for the three major groups of transactions underlying the financing cycle are:

- Investments in marketable securities,
- Issuance of long-term debt securities, and
- Issuance of equity securities.

Investments are discussed first, followed by debt and then equity.

Investments

Depending on cash position and operating cash requirements, an entity may invest resources in:

1. Marketable debt instruments and marketable equity securities, such as instruments representing ownership (for example, common and preferred stock), rights to acquire ownership (for example, warrants, rights, and call options), or rights to dispose of ownership (for example, put options), or
2. Government obligations, such as U.S. Treasury bills.

The financing cycle processes current and noncurrent investments, directing resources into other private- and public-sector equity and debt instruments, with the objective of optimizing financial return on idle cash. In short, the financing cycle processes transactions that convert internal resources into external investments, liquidating when necessary to convert investments into cash either for internal working capital needs or for alternative investments.

The major functions and controls related to investments are discussed in the following sections. Custody, recording, and valuation are addressed first, followed by acquisitions, sales, and income.

FIGURE 16-1: *The Scope of the Financing Cycle*

Primary Business Function		Common Activities	Common Entries	Common Forms
• Capital funds are received from investors and creditors	DEBT	• Recording • Incurrence and retirement • Interest	• Debt incurrence • Debt retirement • Interest expense	• Bond certificates • Notes
	EQUITY	• Recording • Issuance and retirement • Dividends	• Stock issuance • Stock retirement • Dividends	• Stock certificates
• Capital funds are used for operations or temporarily invested until needed for operations	INVESTMENTS	• Custody • Recording • Valuation • Acquisitions and sales • Income	• Investment acquisitions • Investment sales • Interest income • Dividend income	• Bond certificates • Commercial paper • Stock certificates • Treasury bills

Custody, Recording, and Valuation

Generally, an entity's investment securities are held in the custody of either internal officials or independent external custodians, such as stock brokerage firms. Although less common, internal custody is required by law in some towns and municipalities. If securities are maintained internally, at least two officials should be held jointly responsible, thereby minimizing the likelihood of unauthorized sales (in the absence of collusion). Securities maintained by internal parties should be counted periodically on a surprise basis by employees who do not otherwise have custody or access.

An employee independent of the custodial function should maintain detailed records for securities held, compiling information such as certificate numbers and quantities. Detailed records offer a control over securities that should be in the custody of either external custodians or internal officials. If maintained externally, securities listings should be prepared by the custodian at least monthly, mailed to the company, and reconciled with internal records.

Acquisitions, Sales, and Income

All acquisitions and sales of current and noncurrent securities should be authorized by the board of directors or an authorized investment committee. Periodically, recorded acquisition and selling prices should be compared with published price quotations, such as those in *The Wall Street Journal*, assuring that transactions were recorded at accurate prices.

Debt and equity securities yield income in the form of interest and dividends, respectively, and result in gains or losses when sold. Dividend income should be recognized when declared, interest income accrued when earned, and gains and losses recorded when the securities are sold. Periodically, recorded income, gains, and losses should be recalculated by employees not otherwise responsible for the custody, acquisition, or sale of securities.

Debt

Long-term debt, such as a bond or a commercial bank loan, is incurred to raise capital funds for internal investment, potentially yielding a rate of return greater than the cost of financing the debt. For example, an entity would issue 7 percent, ten-year bonds only if the internal rate of return is expected to be higher than 7 percent; otherwise, the debt would not be economically feasible.

Generally, debt incurrence and retirement transactions are relatively few in number, but are usually accompanied by extensive supporting documents, such as SEC filings and bond issuance authorizations from shareholders and the board of directors. The financing cycle processes debt incurrence and retirement transactions, directing resources through the revenue/receipt and expenditure/disbursement cycles, respectively. Following are specific control procedures for several of the more common debt-related financing cycle activities: recording, incurrence, retirement, and interest.

All long-term debt, such as bonds and loans, should be authorized by the board of directors. Authorizations should be expressly documented in the board's minutes, clearly indicating maximum indebtedness and the names of officers authorized to negotiate each transaction.

Typically, debt instruments such as loan agreements contain restrictive covenants that, if violated by a debtor, could result in the debt becoming due immediately. For example, a restrictive covenant might cause a loan to become due if a debtor's current ratio falls below a predetermined level, say 1 to 1. Interestingly, even if a debtor violates a restrictive covenant, the creditor is not likely to know without investigating. As a result, creditors often require that debtors submit annual reports from their auditors on compliance with contractual provisions. (This type of report is discussed in Chapter 17.)

Bonds and notes present additional control problems, since unissued instruments are held by the entity and are therefore susceptible to frauds. Unissued bonds and notes should be prenumbered consecutively and controlled by an employee who neither maintains detailed debt records nor has access to general accounting records. Periodically, an independent employee should physically inspect unissued debt instruments and account for the numerical sequence.

When retired, debt instruments should either be canceled—for example, by perforation—or be destroyed. Records should be kept for canceled instruments, and affidavits from witnesses should be kept for destroyed instruments.

All debt instruments should be accounted for in detailed records, often called *bond* or *note registers*. The registers should be maintained by an employee not otherwise responsible for the custody, incurrence, or redemption of long-term debt. Periodically, an independent employee should reconcile the registers with the general ledger. An authorized employee should calculate interest expense in accordance with the terms of each instrument, and the resulting payments should be processed through the expenditure/disbursement cycle.

Equity

Equity securities (common and preferred stock) are issued by a company in order to raise capital funds for internal investment, such as capital expansion. Like long-term debt incurrence and retirement, equity issuance and retirement transactions are generally not numerous, but are usually supported by extensive documentation, such as authorizations and SEC registration statements. The financing cycle processes equity issuance and retirement transactions, directing resources through the revenue/receipt and expenditure/disbursement cycles, respectively. Following are specific control procedures for several common activities: recording, issuance, retirement, and dividends.

All transactions relating to equity securities, including issuance, retirement, and dividend distributions, should be formally authorized by the board of directors and documented. Some transactions also may require shareholder approval in accordance with state laws or corporation bylaws. All issuances and retirements should be approved both in price and in quantity by the board of directors either specifically or generally, as in the case of authorized stock option plans.

Stock certificates should be prenumbered consecutively, signed by authorized officers when issued, and promptly canceled when surrendered for retirement. Unissued certificates should be physically safeguarded with access limited to authorized individuals. Treasury shares that have not been retired and canceled should be accounted for and controlled.

Many companies enhance control over equity securities by utilizing independent *registrars* and *transfer agents* (for example, investment bankers) to assure that securities are issued, recorded, and transferred properly. In some small companies, however, detailed equity securities records are maintained internally by employees, necessitating particularly effective internal controls, since in many cases securities can be easily converted into cash. If records are maintained internally, the custody of stock certificates, processing of stock transactions, and detailed record keeping each should be performed by separate officials or employees.

Depending on the materiality and volume of stock transactions, a company's detailed records might include a *shareholders' ledger* to account for outstanding shares and owners, a *transfer journal* to record shares transferred, and *certificate control records* to account for the numbers of issued and unissued shares. The shareholders' ledger should be up-to-date, particularly as of dividend record dates, and periodically reconciled with the transfer journal and certificate control records. The reconciliations should be performed by an employee not otherwise responsible for the records. If an entity has stock option plans or convertible securities (for example, convertible preferred stock or bonds) outstanding, adequate records of equity shares reserved for potential issuance also should be maintained. A company should maintain adequate procedures and policies to assure that all applicable SEC filing requirements are met and that stock exchange regulations and securities laws are not violated. Some of these filing requirements, regulations, and laws are discussed in Chapter 5.

Unlike interest on long-term debt that must be paid in accordance with debt instruments outstanding, dividends on capital stock are paid only if declared by the board of directors. Cash dividends to individual shareholders should be computed from record date information in the shareholders' ledger and paid from a special bank account reserved for dividend payments. The dividend bank account should be reconciled periodically by an independent employee not otherwise responsible for maintaining shareholder records or processing dividend payments. Although not usually a significant problem, unclaimed dividend checks, resulting, for example, from incorrect shareholder mailing addresses, should be returned to an independent official and controlled until resolved.

Internal Control Objectives and Potential Errors or Frauds: Investments, Debt, and Equity

The following discussion focuses on internal control over investments, debt, and equity. As in previous chapters, the discussion identifies control objectives for transaction authorization, execution, recording, and access to assets. Examples of potential errors or frauds are described, along with examples of control procedures often used to prevent or detect the errors or frauds. Figure 16-2 summarizes the discussion.

Transaction Authorization and Execution

Before trading securities on the capital markets, all investment acquisitions and sales should be authorized in accordance with management's criteria. Lacking authorization, investments could be made in violation of company policies. For example, bonds could be purchased without regard for the fact that the board of directors resolved to restrict investment in non-AAA bonds to 5 percent of the total investment portfolio. In addition, capital funds could be obtained at excessive interest rates or with overly restrictive debt covenants, resulting in uneconomical financing. To control these potential errors, management could establish policies for selecting and approving investment transactions and for obtaining capital funds, and prepare lists of authorized investments if necessary.

FIGURE 16-2: *Investments, Debt, and Equity: Objectives, Potential Errors or Frauds, and Control Procedures*

Control Objectives	Types of Errors or Frauds That Could Occur If Objective Is Not Met	Control Procedures That Should Prevent or Detect Errors or Frauds
Transaction Authorization and Execution		
Investment transactions (marketable securities, long-term debt, and equity investments) should be made in accordance with management's authorization.	Investments could be made in violation of company policies (e.g., an investment portfolio that includes more debt instruments than allowed by the board of directors), potentially resulting in more risk on investments than desired.	Establish policies for selecting and approving investment transactions. Prepare lists of authorized investments.
Sources of capital funds—debt and equity—should be authorized in accordance with management's criteria.	Capital funds could be obtained at unfavorable terms/cost or with overly restrictive covenants, potentially resulting in uneconomical financing.	Establish policies for obtaining capital funds.
Adjustments of investments (e.g., adjustment of carrying value), debt (e.g., adjustment of debt obligations after renegotiation), and equity (e.g., changes to par or stated value of stock) should be authorized in accordance with management's criteria.	Unauthorized or incorrect adjustments could be made, potentially resulting in misstated accounts and violations of loan covenants.	Establish policies for approving investment, debt, and equity adjustments. Prenumber and control adjustment forms. Require specific authorization for adjustments exceeding preestablished dollar amounts.
Recording		
Investment, debt, and equity transactions should be recorded at the correct amounts, in the proper period, and properly classified.	Detailed or subsidiary records may be inaccurate, potentially resulting in inaccurate account balances and misstated financial statements.	Establish processing and recording procedures. Review board minutes regularly for directives related to dividend, long-term debt, and treasury transactions. Prepare schedules of interest and loan payment due dates.

(continues)

FIGURE 16-2 *(continued)*

Control Objectives	Types of Errors or Frauds That Could Occur If Objective Is Not Met	Control Procedures That Should Prevent or Detect Errors or Frauds
Access to Assets Access to securities should be restricted to personnel authorized by management.	Securities may be lost, stolen, destroyed, or diverted, potentially resulting in misapplied resources and misstated accounts.	Establish physical barriers over investment securities (e.g., locked safes), or place them with independent parties, such as brokers. Carry insurance and fidelity bonds. Maintain files of authorized signatures. Segregate investment approval from accounting and from custody of securities.
Access to investment, debt-, and equity-related records and forms should be restricted to personnel authorized by management.	Records may be lost or stolen, potentially resulting in the reporting of inaccurate carrying values. Forms could be used to sell securities and divert the cash proceeds, potentially resulting in misappropriated assets and misstated financial statements.	Establish physical barriers over forms and records. Prenumber critical forms. Carry insurance and fidelity bonds. Account for all unissued, issued, and retired securities by an official independent of physically controlling securities, accounting, and cash activities.

Journal entries that adjust investment carrying values and debt obligations should be authorized in accordance with management's criteria; otherwise, unauthorized or incorrect adjustments could be made, potentially resulting in misstated accounts and violations of loan covenants. To control adjustments, management could establish processing procedures, prenumber and control adjustment forms, and require specific authorization for adjustments exceeding preestablished amounts.

Recording

If detailed or subsidiary records are inaccurate, then account balances may be inaccurate and financial statements misstated. As a result, all investment, debt, and equity transactions should be recorded at the correct amounts, in the proper period, and classified properly. Management could control against inaccurate records by establishing processing and recording procedures, regularly reviewing board minutes for financing cycle resolutions, and preparing schedules of interest and loan payment due dates.

Access to Assets

Apart from cash, few assets are more susceptible to frauds than investment securities: There is a ready market for them and, as a result, they can be converted into cash easily. Therefore, access to securities should be restricted to personnel authorized by management. Otherwise, securities may be lost or stolen, potentially resulting in misapplied resources and misstated accounts. Management can help control securities by establishing physical barriers, such as fireproof safes, although more often securities are held by independent custodians such as brokerage houses. In addition, personnel responsible for approving investments should not be responsible for recording or for maintaining custody of the securities.

To protect capital funds, access to accounting records and forms should be restricted to personnel authorized by management. If access is not restricted, records may be lost or stolen, or forms could be used to sell securities and divert the cash proceeds. Management could control access by establishing physical barriers over prenumbered forms and records and by carrying insurance and fidelity bonds. Also, officials responsible for unissued, issued, and retired securities should not be responsible also for physically controlling securities or for performing accounting and cash activities.

Considering Internal Control in the Financing Cycle

As discussed in Chapter 6, an auditor considers an entity's internal controls as a basis for assessing control risk. However, in some instances an auditor may conclude that the volume of investment, debt, and equity transactions is not sufficiently large to justify either the cost of performing tests of controls or the resulting reduction in control risk below the maximum. In these instances, the auditor would obtain an understanding of the system sufficient to plan the audit, omit tests of controls, and design substantive tests of account balances assuming allowable detection risk is at the minimum. In short, the auditor relies exclusively on substantive testing.

If an entity's investments and financing (for example, issuance of bonds, stock, etc.) are maintained by an independent custodian, such as a broker or underwriter, the auditor's review of the system will consist primarily of obtaining an understanding of how the transactions are authorized and how documentation from the custodian is recorded in the general ledger. As a result, when custodians are used, transaction execution—the purchase, sale, issuance, and retirement of securities—and access to assets are of less concern to the auditor, because they are handled by independent external parties. In contrast, if securities are maintained by internal officials, such as a corporate secretary, the auditor would be concerned with control procedures over transaction authorization, execution, recording, and access to assets, because all aspects of the entity's investment and financing transactions are handled internally, and inadequate segregation of duties could lead to fraud.

In practice, flowcharts are not often used to document an entity's investment, debt, and equity accounting systems. More often, auditors use questionnaires—for example, Figure 16-3 for investments, Figure 16-4 for debt, and Figure 16-5 for

FIGURE 16-3: *Questionnaire: Investments*

Performed by:_____

Date:_____

Question	Answer: Yes, No, or N/A	Remarks

Custody, Recording, and Valuation

1. Are securities and other negotiable instruments in the custody of an independent custodian? If not, are they adequately secured (e.g., locked in a safe)?

2. Are at least two officials responsible for internally held securities?

3. Is a detailed record of securities maintained by an official independent of officials responsible for custody?

4. Is the listing of investments periodically reconciled with investment records?

5. Are securities in the name of the client (or restrictively endorsed in the name of the client)?

6. Are independent officials responsible for reviewing and reporting changing securities' values?

7. Are adequately detailed investment records and general ledger control accounts maintained for the various investment classifications?

Acquisitions, Sales, and Income

1. Are acquisitions and sales of investment securities authorized by the board of directors or a duly authorized investment committee?

2. Are brokers, custodians, or other intermediaries authorized or designated by the board of directors?

3. Are brokers' advices promptly compared with documented acquisition and sales authorizations?

4. Is an independent check made to determine whether acquisition or sales prices are fair and objective?

5. Is investment income (e.g., interest, dividends) periodically recalculated and verified?

equity—to identify deficiencies, and narratives to document procedures for the custody, recording, valuation, acquisition, and sale of investments.

Financial Statement Assertions and Audit Procedures

Within the financing cycle, investments, long-term debt, and capital stock are typically the most material financial statement account balances. Each account is discussed next in the context of the audit procedures commonly used by auditors to address each of the financial statement assertions introduced in Chapter 6: existence or occurrence, completeness, rights and obligations, valuation or allocation,

FIGURE 16-4: *Questionnaire: Debt*

Performed by:_____
Date:_____

Question	Answer: Yes, No, or N/A	Remarks
1. Are all long-term debt and other borrowings authorized by the board of directors?		
2. Is an officer responsible for determining whether all debt covenants are complied with?		
3. Are unissued bonds and notes prenumbered consecutively and controlled by an official independent of recording?		
4. Are all retired debt instruments canceled or destroyed?		
5. Are adequately detailed bond and note registers and general ledger accounts maintained for the various debt classifications?		
6. Are interest payments and accruals periodically recalculated?		

FIGURE 16-5: *Questionnaire: Equity*

Performed by:_____
Date:_____

Question	Answer: Yes, No, or N/A	Remarks
1. Are all capital stock issuances, retirements, and dividend distributions authorized by the board of directors?		
2. Are capital stock transactions authorized by stockholder vote, where required by state law?		
3. Are unissued stock certificates prenumbered consecutively and safeguarded?		
4. Are independent registrars and transfer agents authorized by the board of directors?		
5. Are detailed capital stock records such as a stockholders' ledger, transfer journal, certificate control records, and general ledger control accounts maintained for the various capital stock classifications?		
6. Are detailed capital stock records maintained by officials independent of the custody of securities?		
7. Are treasury shares adequately controlled and accounted for?		
8. Are procedures established to assure that the entity is complying with stock exchange and securities laws?		
9. Are dividend payments and accruals periodically recalculated?		

and presentation and disclosure. Figure 16-6 relates each assertion to specific audit procedures and summarizes the discussion that follows.

Existence or Occurrence

Within the financing cycle, the existence or occurrence assertion addresses whether all recorded investments, debt, and capital stock exist at the balance sheet date and whether all recorded investment, debt, and capital stock transactions occurred during the period.

Testing the existence or occurrence assertion for investments depends on whether securities are maintained externally by an independent trustee/broker or internally by authorized personnel. If securities are maintained externally, the auditor would confirm balances with the independent trustee or broker; if held internally, the auditor would physically inspect and count all securities on hand. In turn, cutoff testing also addresses existence or occurrence by assuring that all investment transactions are recorded in the proper accounting period.

The existence or occurrence of long-term debt can be tested three ways: First, all recorded loans and other notes payable, including terms, due dates, and accrued interest, are confirmed with creditors. Second, to support the results of confirmation procedures, the auditor physically examines all bond indentures and other long-term indebtedness agreements, thereby determining whether all outstanding debt was confirmed. Third, the auditor physically inspects unissued instruments, thereby testing whether all issued securities are recorded as long-term debt. That is, long-term debt could be understated if a debt instrument were neither on hand nor recorded.

For capital stock, an auditor tests existence or occurrence by verifying recorded shareholders' equity balances. That is, the auditor would foot and cross-foot the client's schedule of changes in shareholders' equity balances, account for unissued or retired shares, and, if detailed records and stock certificates are maintained externally, confirm shares outstanding with registrars and transfer agents. In addition, the auditor would examine supporting documentation and authorizations for any stock issuances, stock dividends, and stock splits occurring during the year. Of course, if securities transactions are executed by independent registrars or transfer agents, the auditor would confirm capital stock transactions and balances directly with the registrar or agent.

Completeness

The completeness assertion addresses whether all investments, long-term debt, and capital stock that should be presented in the financial statements actually are presented. That is, were all transactions recorded?

For investments, completeness is addressed by testing cutoff, which tests whether otherwise bona fide transactions are recorded in the proper accounting period, and by analytical procedures, which help determine whether recorded investment balances are reasonable or, in contrast, appear unusual, thereby requiring inquiries of management and/or additional substantive tests.

Analytical procedures also constitute a primary test of completeness for long-term debt and capital stock, because unusual relationships—for example, widely varying ratios in comparison with prior years—may signal unrecorded or improperly recorded transactions. However, for long-term debt, the auditor also should inspect and account for unissued instruments, and for capital stock, the auditor also would verify recorded shareholders' equity balances.

FIGURE 16-6: *Relating Financial Statement Assertions and Audit Procedures: Investments, Long-Term Debt, and Capital Stock*

Assertions	Audit Procedures		
	Investments	Long-Term Debt	Capital Stock
Existence or occurrence	Confirm securities held by trustees/brokers. Physically inspect securities held internally. Test cutoff.	Confirm loans and other notes payable with creditors. Examine bond indentures and other long-term indebtedness agreements. Physically inspect unissued instruments.	Verify recorded stockholders' equity balances. Examine supporting documentation and authorizations for stock issuances, stock dividends, and stock splits.
Completeness	Test cutoff. Perform analytical procedures.	Perform analytical procedures. Physically inspect and account for unissued instruments.	Perform analytical procedures. Verify recorded stockholders' equity balances.
Rights and obligations	Confirm securities held by trustees/brokers. Physically inspect securities held internally.	Confirm loans and other notes payable with creditors. Examine bond indentures and other long-term indebtedness agreements. Confirm bond and serial note balances and interest payments directly with trustees.	Verify recorded stockholders' equity balances.
Valuation	Verify securities transactions. Confirm securities held by trustees/brokers. Check quoted securities prices.	Verify debt-related transactions. Confirm loans and other notes payable with creditors. Recalculate interest and premium/discount amortizations.	Verify recorded stockholders' equity balances.
Presentation and disclosure	Compare statement presentation and disclosures with those required by GAAP.	Compare statement presentation and disclosures with those required by GAAP.	Compare statement presentation and disclosures with those required by GAAP.

Rights and Obligations

Within the financing cycle, the rights assertion addresses whether an entity has property rights to investments, and the obligations assertion addresses whether long-term debt and capital stock represent bona fide obligations.

Rights to investments are tested by confirming securities held by external trustees/brokers and/or by physically inspecting securities on hand, depending on whether the securities are maintained internally or externally.

For long-term debt, obligations are tested by confirming loans and other notes with creditors, by examining bond indentures and other indebtedness agreements, and by confirming bond and serial note balances and interest payments with trustees. In turn, because issued capital stock is held by many shareholders, auditors typically test obligations by verifying recorded shareholders' equity balances as discussed earlier, rather than by confirming with shareholders.

Valuation

The valuation assertion addresses whether investments, debt, and capital stock balances are carried in the financial statements at appropriate dollar amounts.

For investments, valuation is addressed by verifying securities transactions and unit prices—that is, market values—at the balance sheet date and by confirming securities held by trustees. For debt, auditors test valuation by verifying debt-related transactions, by confirming loans and other notes payable with creditors, and by recalculating interest and amortizations of premiums and discounts. The carrying value of capital stock is tested by verifying recorded shareholders' equity balances, which is also a primary test of existence or occurrence, completeness, and rights and obligations.

Presentation and Disclosure

The presentation and disclosure assertion addresses whether recorded investments, debt, and capital stock are properly classified, described, and disclosed in the financial statements. As indicated in earlier chapters, presentation and disclosure are tested by comparing a client's financial statement disclosures with generally accepted accounting principles for each reported account. Disclosure guidelines, such as the AICPA's annually updated *Accounting and Audit Manual* and proprietary audit-firm databases, are often used by practicing auditors to assure that disclosures are complete.

Substantive Tests of Investments in Marketable Securities

A program of representative substantive tests applicable to investments is presented in Figure 16-7 along with the related financial statement assertions.

Verify Mathematical Accuracy and Examine Documentation

An auditor's tests of clerical accuracy relate primarily to a schedule of securities transactions that summarizes investment activity for the entire year, as illustrated in Figure 16-8. The spreadsheet schedule for securities trading activity is the

FIGURE 16-7: *Substantive Tests: Investments and Investment Revenue*

Assertions	*Procedures*
Valuation	1. Obtain a schedule of securities transactions from client personnel and verify mathematical accuracy: a. Foot and cross-foot the schedule. b. Reconcile security balances with the general ledger. 2. For sampled (or all) transactions: a. Examine board of directors' or other appropriate authorization. b. Examine broker's advice or other documentation. c. Compare price with published market quotations. d. Test calculations for dividend and interest income and accruals, for premium and discount amortizations, and for gains and losses on sales.
Existence Valuation Rights	3. Confirm securities held by trustees or physically inspect and count securities on hand.
Existence Completeness	4. Test cutoff to determine whether acquisitions, sales, and investment revenue are recorded in the proper accounting period.
Valuation	5. Review the valuation of securities.
Completeness	6. Perform analytical procedures.
Presentation and disclosure	7. Review financial statements to determine whether: a. Investments, gains and losses, and investment revenue are properly classified and described. b. Disclosures are adequate.

auditor's primary source for testing acquisitions, sales, and the recognition of dividend and interest income. Because the schedule is the primary source for testing, the auditor tests the schedule's mathematical accuracy and reconciles balances with the general ledger, thereby assuring that detailed records accurately represent the investment account's recorded general ledger balance.

In Step 2, Figure 16-7, the auditor samples or tests all investment transactions for board of directors' or other authorization (for example, an investment committee); for broker's advice; for published market quotations; and for properly calculated dividend and interest accruals, premium and discount amortizations, and gains and losses on sales. Thus, the focus of Step 2 is on whether recorded transactions are authorized and, equally important, whether they actually occurred.

Confirm or Physically Inspect Securities

For securities held off-premises by a custodian, such as a brokerage house, an auditor confirms details with the custodian and compares confirmation responses with management's records. The auditor also should determine whether the custodian is trustworthy, and therefore whether a client's investments are secure. Normally, though, this procedure is not performed when the custodian is well known and insured, such as a national or regional brokerage house.

FIGURE 16-8: *Investments: Marketable Equity Securities*

The Wilson Company
Investments: Marketable Equity Securities
December 31, 2007

D2
AP 1/10/08

Description	Date Acquired/ Sold	No. Shares	Price per Share	Balance 12/31/06	Transactions: at Cost Acquired	(Sold)	Balance 12/31/07	Realized Gain (Loss)	Divided Income	Market Value 12/31/07 Per Share	Total
Trading											
ABC Corp.—											
Common	5/20/04	700	$23	$16,100[a]			$16,100[d,j]		$ 725[f]	$25.50[g]	$17,850[h]
Albion Co.—											
Common	6/30/05	800	32	25,600[a]					1,050[f]	35.00[g]	35,000[h]
	7/15/07	200	34		$6,800[b]		32,400[d,j]				
Elston Inc.—											
Common	8/12/06	500	19	9,500[a]							
	9/30/07	300	17			$(5,700)[c]	3,800[d,j]	$(600)[e]	550[f]	16.00[g]	3,200[h]
Merton Inc.—											
Common	11/15/00	800	18	14,400[a]			14,400[d,j]		1,100	23.00[g]	18,400[h]
				$65,600[a]	$6,800	$(5,700)	$66,700[d,j]	$(600)	$3,425		$74,450[h]
				i	i		i		i		i

(continues)

FIGURE 16-8 (continued)

Description	Date Acquired/ Sold	No. Shares	Price per Share	Balance 12/31/06	Transactions: at Cost Acquired	Transactions: at Cost (Sold)	Balance 12/31/07	Realized Gain (Loss)	Divided Income	Market Value 12/31/07 Per Share	Market Value 12/31/07 Total
Available-for-sale											
Carter, Rice— Common	12/01/03	1,000	$28	$28,000ᵃ			$28,000 ᵈ·ʲ		$2,050ᶠ	33.00ᵍ	$33,000ʰ
Ling Inc.— Common	10/09/05	1,500	13	19,500ᵃ			19,500 ᵈ·ʲ			18.00ᵍ	27,000ʰ
Winston Corp.— Common	5/10/05	800	15	12,000ᵃ							
	12/30/07	800	17			$(12,000)ᶜ	—	$1,600ᵉ	875ᶠ	—	
				$59,500ᵃ		$(12,000)ᶜ	$47,500	$1,600	$2,925		$60,000
				i			i		i		i

a Traced to general ledger and prior-year working papers.
b Agreed with broker's advice, cash disbursements records, and board of directors' authorization.
c Agreed with broker's advice, cash receipts records, and board of directors' authorization.
d Traced to general ledger.
e Calculated and agreed with general ledger.
f Agreed with dividend rates in Standard & Poor and calculated; traced proceeds to cash receipts records.
g Agreed with 12/31/07 market quotations in 1/2/08 *The Wall Street Journal.*
h Calculated.
i Footed.
j Cross-footed.

For securities held internally, an auditor should inspect physically and count the securities on hand and compare the certificate numbers, quantity, and description of securities with detailed records. In addition, an auditor should determine if a client's balance sheet valuation procedures for infrequently traded securities are reasonable and reliable. Infrequently traded securities are of particular concern to the auditor, because there may not be objective, balance sheet date price quotations for the securities, thereby necessitating that the auditor consult an investee's audited financial statements and credit ratings in order to assess the reasonableness of carrying values.

Test Cutoff

Cutoff tests are performed to determine that securities transactions near the balance sheet date are recorded in the proper accounting period. Supporting documentation may be examined for all or a sample of the acquisitions and sales shortly before and after the balance sheet date. Transaction dates and amounts for each transaction reviewed should be agreed with detailed records and entries in the general ledger. The auditor should recalculate gains and losses for each sales transaction examined and agree the calculations with recorded amounts. Tests of cutoff also should be performed for investment revenue transactions near the balance sheet date, and accruals for interest revenue should be reviewed for reasonableness.

Review Valuation

An auditor tests valuation by examining documentation supporting transactions recorded and by recalculating dividend and interest income. Examining supporting documentation, however, substantiates historical cost only. Thus an auditor examines market quotations to assure that marketable equity securities are reported at the lower of aggregate cost or market, and that marketable debt securities are reported at the lower of cost or cost less permanent declines in market value.

In substantive tests of marketable securities, market values below aggregate cost and permanent declines in market value pose a significant risk, particularly when a company's investment portfolio is large relative to total assets. Consider, for example, Conseco, Inc., an Indiana-based financial services holding company that conducted all of its finance operations through a wholly owned subsidiary, Conseco Finance.

➢ restatement

Conseco Finance originated, purchased, sold, and serviced consumer and commercial loans that management pooled into groups and sold to a special purpose entity (SPE). In turn, the SPE sold bonds to the public that were backed by the principal and interest payments due from the pools. In return, Conseco Finance received two things: the proceeds of the bond sales and so-called interest-only securities that entitled Conseco Finance to receive from the pool principal and interest payments that exceeded payments the pool made to bondholders. Conseco Finance carried the interest-only securities on the balance sheet as assets but, consistent with GAAP, was required each quarter to adjust "other than temporary" declines in the securities' market value, measured as the discounted present value of future cash flows. However, management controlled the assumed discount rate, among other parameters within the discounted cash flow calculation, thereby avoiding impairment charges that would have diminished the interest-only securities' carrying value and reduced Conseco Finance's reported net income.

In March 2000, Conseco's independent auditors discovered—and notified the board of directors about—the improper present value calculations and the inflated carrying value for interest-only securities. On March 31, 2000, Conseco announced a $350 million after-tax write-down to the interest-only securities' carrying value, driving a 16 percent decline in Conseco's share price. In April 2000, Conseco and Conseco Finance filed *Forms 10-K* for 1999 that restated the first three quarters and revised the fourth quarter of 1999, driving an additional 10 percent decline in Conseco's share price.[1] The case of Conseco and Conseco Finance makes clear that the effectiveness of an audit is very much dependent on an auditor's grasp of the multiparty transactions a client enters into, GAAP for the transactions, and management's propensity to misdirect evidence an auditor uses to assess compliance with GAAP.

Perform Analytical Procedures

An auditor can use analytical procedures to test completeness and to determine whether conclusions drawn from substantive tests are reasonable. Several representative analytical procedures follow.

- Compare current-year purchase and sales transactions to those of prior years and to the entity's stated investment plans.
- Compare current-year dividends, interest, and other investment income with those of prior years.
- Calculate the percentage of accrued investment income to total investments and estimate total accrued income based on current investments.

Any unusual or unexpected relationships should be investigated further through inquiries of management and additional substantive tests of details.

Review Financial Statement Disclosures

Financial statements are read to determine that investments are classified properly and described in the balance sheet and that gains and losses and investment revenue are properly presented in the income statement. Under *Statement of Financial Accounting Standards No. 115*, "Accounting for Certain Investments in Debt and Equity Securities," debt held to maturity and debt or equity that is either held in a trading portfolio or made available for sale should be reported separately in the balance sheet. And disclosures for each classification vary: Debt held to maturity is stated in the balance sheet at cost; debt or equity in a trading portfolio or available for sale is marked to market.

Substantive Tests of Long-Term Debt

For most companies, long-term debt transactions are likely to be relatively infrequent but highly material, resulting in extensive—if not exclusive—reliance on substantive procedures. A representative program of substantive tests applicable to debt is presented in Figure 16-9 and is tied to financial statement assertions.

---

1   *SEC Accounting and Auditing Enforcement Release No. 1973, In the Matter of Conseco, Inc.,* March 10, 2004.

FIGURE 16-9: *Substantive Tests: Debt and Interest Expense*

Assertions	*Procedures*
Existence or occurrence Valuation Completeness Obligations	1. Obtain a schedule of bonds, notes payable, and other long-term indebtedness from accounting personnel and verify mathematical accuracy. a. Foot and cross-foot the schedule. b. Reconcile totals with balances in the general ledger. c. Examine documentation supporting debt-related transactions. d. If debt instruments are maintained internally, review a sample of entries in detailed bond records and physically inspect and account for unissued instruments.
Existence Obligations Valuation	2. Confirm bonds outstanding and interest payments directly with trustees, and loans and notes payable directly with creditors, coordinating with bank confirmations where appropriate (Chapter 12).
Existence or occurrence Obligations	3. Obtain bond indentures and other long-term indebtedness agreements: a. Examine documentation and board of directors' authorizations. b. Determine that proceeds are recorded properly and used as intended by the board. c. Review for compliance with restrictive covenants.
Valuation	4. Recalculate interest paid or accrued and amortizations of premiums or discounts.
Existence or occurrence Completeness	5. Perform analytical procedures.
Presentation and disclosure	6. Review financial statements to determine whether: a. Debt obligations are properly classified and described in the balance sheet and interest expense is properly reported in the income statement. b. Disclosures are adequate.

Verify Mathematical Accuracy and Examine Documentation

To test mathematical accuracy, an auditor examines a schedule that summarizes debt transactions for the year. Figure 16-10 illustrates.

The auditor foots and cross-foots the schedule, reconciling totals with balances in the general ledger, and, as illustrated in Figure 16-10, examines documentation supporting each debt-related transaction. For example, new debt would be reconciled with cash receipts records and with the board of directors' authorization, and the auditor would examine the debt instrument, determining which assets, if any, had been pledged as collateral. In turn, payments would be reconciled in amount with bonds or notes and with cash disbursements records. If debt instruments are maintained internally, an auditor would review a sample of entries

FIGURE 16-10: *Long-Term Debt, Bonds, and Related Interest*

EE1
GS
1/12/08

The Wilson Company
Long-Term Debt: Bonds, Notes Payable, and Related Interest
December 31, 2007

Description	Balance 12/31/06	Principal — Additions	Principal — Payments	Balance 12/21/07	Balance 12/31/06	Interest — Expense	Interest — Payments	Balance 12/31/07
8% bonds, due 12/31/2014; due $1,000,000 per year; 10-yr. bond; issued 1/1/02; face $1,000,000; quarterly interest.	$ 800,000 [a,j]	—	$100,000 [c]	$ 700,000 [d,e]	$20,000 [a]	$ 80,000 [f]	$ 80,000 [g]	$20,000 [d,e]
9% note to First Nat'l Bank; due 12/31/09; 3-yr. note; incurred 1/1/07; face $360,000; semiannual interest; due $60,000 every six months.		$360,000 [b,k]	120,000 [c]	240,000 [d,e]	—	32,400 [f]	—	32,400 [d,e]
10% note to Nat'l Bank; due 6/30/09; 3-yr. note; incurred 7/01/06; face $300,000; quarterly interest; due $50,000 every six months.	250,000 [a,j]	—	100,000 [c]	150,000 [d,e]	15,000 [a]	30,000 [f]	30,000 [g]	15,000 [d,e]
	$1,050,000 [a]	$360,000	$320,000	$1,090,000 [d,e]	$35,000 [a]	$142,400	$110,000	$67,400 [d,e]
	h	h	h	h	h	h	h	h

(continues)

FIGURE 16-10 (continued)

a   Traced to general ledger and prior-year working papers.
b   Examined note, agreed with cash receipts records and board of directors' authorization.
c   Agreed amount with bond/note, and agreed with cash disbursements records.
d   Traced to general ledger.
e   Cross-footed.
f   Calculated.
g   Calculated and agreed with cash disbursements records.
h   Footed.
i   Land and buildings at 1001 Dexter St. pledged as collateral.
j   Investment in Carter, Rice (see D2) pledged as collateral.
k   Land and buildings at 131 Japonica Street pledged as collateral.

in detailed bond records and physically inspect and account for unissued instruments. Otherwise—that is, if debt is handled by independent trustees—the auditor would confirm, as indicated next.

Confirm Bonds, Loans, and Notes Payable

Bonds and interest payments should be confirmed directly with trustees, thereby determining whether the debt exists, is valued properly, and represents a bona fide obligation. In turn, loans and other notes payable are confirmed directly with creditors. All returned confirmations should be examined in detail and agreed with recorded balances, and differences should be investigated.

Examine Bond Indentures and Other Long-Term Indebtedness Agreements

All long-term indebtedness agreements should be examined by the auditor to determine that transactions were executed in accordance with board of directors' authorizations, including the subsequent use of borrowed funds. If funds are not used as stipulated in indebtedness agreements, the entity may be in violation of state or federal laws, because monies would have been expended in violation of agreements with creditors. When examining debt instruments, the auditor should note all restrictive covenants and determine that the company is in compliance for the current period. For example, if a long-term note in the amount of $1,000,000 carries a debt covenant specifying that the borrower's current ratio may not fall below 3 to 2, lack of compliance at the balance sheet date could result in the creditor calling the loan immediately, thereby requiring that the auditor propose a journal entry to reclassify the principal from a long-term to a current liability.

Recalculate Interest and Amortizations

Interest paid or accrued for the year should be recalculated by the auditor and reconciled with the general ledger, as illustrated in Figure 16-10. In addition, any related interest payments should be reconciled with cash disbursements records. If outstanding bonds were issued originally at more or less than face value, the related premium or discount amortization should be recalculated by the auditor and compared with entries in the general ledger.

Interestingly, the risk of interest rate fluctuations has pointed to violations of GAAP that actually had very little to do with interest rates. A case in point is Microsoft's accounting for a reserve for interest that management said in public filings would "provide for shifts in interest rates or other economic events which may adversely impact Microsoft's return on its portfolio." However, rather than factual or statistical evidence, management relied solely on discretion to adjust the reserve, causing the SEC to conclude the "reserve was determined in a manner that did not comply with GAAP, and its balance and the adjustments thereto lacked a proper basis under GAAP."[2] The Microsoft case is instructive to auditors about reserves: While subject to discretion and estimation, management should have a basis in fact to support changes in reserve balances.

---

2   *SEC Accounting and Auditing Enforcement Release No. 1563, In the Matter of Microsoft Corporation,* June 3, 2002.

Perform Analytical Procedures

To test existence or occurrence and completeness, and to confirm the results of detailed substantive tests of details, the auditor performs analytical procedures such as ratio analysis and comparisons of relationships among related accounts or transactions. For example, analytical procedures for long-term debt could include any or all of the following tests:

- Compare current amortization amounts with prior actual amounts and current budgeted amounts.
- Compare current interest costs with prior actual costs and current budgeted costs.
- Compare current and noncurrent debt obligations with prior actual obligations and current budgeted obligations.
- Compare debt issue costs and premiums/discounts to prospectuses and other internal debt reports.

Although no one of the previous analytical procedures will necessarily detect misstatements, they could direct an auditor's attention to accounts or balances requiring additional tests of details or inquiries.

Review Financial Statement Disclosures

Financial statement classifications, descriptions, and disclosures relating to debt and interest expense should be read by the auditor. The currently maturing portion of long-term debt should generally be classified as a current liability in the absence of refinancing agreements. Disclosures should include information regarding maturities, interest rates, and other terms and conditions; assets pledged as collateral; debt conversion features; and troubled debt restructurings.

Substantive Tests of Capital Stock, Retained Earnings, and Earnings per Share

Figure 16-11 presents a program of substantive tests for capital stock, retained earnings, and earnings per share and, like the other audit programs, is tied to the assertions introduced earlier. The procedures listed in Figure 16-11 encompass all the major types of transactions that normally affect shareholders' equity. However, it is unlikely that all these transactions would occur within a single year for any given audit client. In fact, in many cases, changes in shareholders' equity are

FIGURE 16-11: *Substantive Tests: Capital Stock, Retained Earnings, and Earnings per Share*

Assertions	Procedures

Existence or occurrence
Valuation
Completeness
Obligations
	1. Verify recorded stockholders' equity balances.
	  a. Obtain a schedule of changes in stockholders' equity accounts from accounting personnel.
	  b. Foot and cross-foot the schedule, reconciling balances with the general ledger.
	<div align="right">*(continues)*</div>

FIGURE 16-11 *(continued)*

Assertions	Procedures
	c. If detailed records and stock certificates are maintained internally: (1) Examine a sample of entries in the stockholders' ledger, the transfer journal, and certificate control records. (2) Foot the stockholders' ledger and reconcile with the general ledger. (3) Account for unissued certificates, examine retired shares for evidence of cancellation, and count treasury shares on hand. d. If detailed records and stock certificates are maintained externally, confirm shares outstanding, unissued shares, and treasury shares directly with registrars and transfer agents.
Occurrence Valuation	2. Review stock issuances, stock dividends, and stock splits: a. Examine supporting documentation and authorizations. b. For issuances, compare the authorized number of shares and price per share with entries in the general ledger, and compare proceeds from issuance with cash receipts records. c. For stock dividends, compare the authorized number of shares and value per share and determine that stock dividends are recorded in accordance with GAAP. d. For stock splits, examine memorandum entries and compare with authorized number of shares and assigned value per share.
Occurrence Valuation	3. Review treasury stock transactions: a. Examine supporting documentation and authorizations. b. Compare authorized number of shares and price per share with entries in the general ledger. c. Compare disbursements for purchases and receipts for sales with cash records. d. Determine that the basis of accounting is appropriate.
Occurrence Valuation	4. Verify recorded dividends. a. Examine supporting documentation and authorization. b. Recalculate dividends and agree with entries in general ledger. c. Reconcile recorded dividends with cash records.
Valuation	5. Recalculate earnings per share.
Completeness	6. Perform analytical procedures.
Presentation and disclosure	7. Review financial statements to determine whether: a. Capital stock, retained earnings, and earnings per share are properly classified and described. b. Disclosures are adequate.

attributable solely to changes in retained earnings resulting from net earnings or losses and from dividend payments.

Verify Shareholders' Equity Balances

To address the valuation of shareholders' equity from the standpoint of mathematical accuracy, an auditor should obtain a client-prepared schedule summarizing changes in shareholders' equity accounts, including capital stock and related premium accounts for each class of stock outstanding, treasury stock accounts, and retained earnings. The schedule is footed and cross-footed by the auditor and the totals are reconciled with the general ledger, as illustrated in Figure 16-12. Other procedures for verifying shareholders' equity depend on whether equity transactions are executed through independent parties or internally, as described in Figure 16-11.

FIGURE 16-12: *Capital Stock and Additional Paid-In Capital*

J2
1/12/08
AP

The Wilson Company
Capital Stock and Additional Paid-In Capital
December 31, 2007

	Authorized	Issued & Outstanding	Amount (at Par)	Additional Paid-In Capital
Balance, Dec. 31, 2006, $5 par. Issued 6/1/07 at par (proceeds in cash)	15,000 Shs[a]	12,000 Shs[b] 2,000 Shs[c]	$60,000[b] 10,000[d]	$5,000[b] —
Balance, Dec. 31, 2007	15,000 Shs	14,000 Shs	$70,000	$5,000
		[e]	[e]	

a Agreed with corporate charter.
b Traced to general ledger and prior-year working papers.
c Agreed with board of directors' authorization.
d Agreed with cash receipts records.
e Footed.

Review Stock Issuances, Stock Dividends, and Stock Splits

If the number of shares outstanding has increased during the year as a result of stock issuances, stock dividends, or stock splits, the supporting documentation and authorizations should be examined for each transaction. For stock issuances (sales of previously unissued stock), an auditor should determine through recalculation that the general ledger entries accurately reflect the number of shares and selling price per share authorized by the board of directors. In the case of par or stated value stock, the auditor should determine that the selling price is properly allocated to capital stock and related premium accounts. Proceeds from the issuance of stock should be traced to cash receipts records.

When dividends are issued to shareholders in the form of additional shares of stock, an auditor should determine that entries in the general ledger reflect the number of shares and value per share authorized by the board of directors. The auditor also should review the assigned value per share to determine whether the value is appropriate relative to the number of shares issued.

Although stock splits have no effect on total shareholders' equity, they do increase the number of shares outstanding. An auditor should review underlying documentation and related memorandum entries to determine that stock splits were authorized and that the change in shares outstanding is recorded properly.

Review Treasury Stock Transactions

Many entities, particularly large publicly traded corporations, frequently buy and sell shares of their own stock. Shares may be acquired directly from shareholders in a stock redemption, or may be bought and sold on the open market. Treasury stock transactions may be undertaken for a variety of reasons including, for example, the acquisition of shares needed for distribution to employees under employee stock option plans. An auditor should review documentation and authorizations for treasury stock transactions and examine related entries in the general ledger and cash records. The auditor should determine that the accounting method used to record treasury stock transactions complies with generally accepted accounting principles and that general ledger entries accurately reflect the method used by the company.

Verify Recorded Dividends

Supporting documentation and authorizations should be reviewed by an auditor for all dividends declared during the year under audit. The mathematical accuracy of dividends should be verified through recalculation and comparing totals with the general ledger and cash records.

Recalculate Earnings per Share

An auditor should recalculate earnings per share to determine that all increases and decreases in shares outstanding are reflected properly in earnings per share. In some cases, entities with complex capital structures are required to report several earnings per share amounts. An auditor should review the terms of all outstanding stock rights, warrants, options, and convertible securities to determine whether reported earnings per share are consistent with generally accepted accounting principles.

Perform Analytical Procedures

Analytical procedures typically are not used for equity accounts unless the volume and breadth of transactions are extensive. When transactions are extensive, any or all of the following analytical procedures, among others, may be informative.

- For the current year, compute the return on shareholders' equity, the book value per share, and the dividend payout ratio, and compare figures with those of prior years.
- Compare current-year dividend amounts with those of prior years.

- Compute current-year balances for common and preferred stock and additional paid-in capital, and compare with balances of prior years.
- Compare current-year treasury shares with those of prior years.

Of course, the auditor would investigate any unusual or unexpected relationships.

Review Financial Statement Disclosures

An entity's financial statements should be read to determine whether all shareholders' equity balances are properly classified and described in the balance sheet and whether earnings per share are properly reported in the income statement. Notes to the financial statements should be reviewed to determine that disclosures are adequate. Frequently, disclosures relating to shareholders' equity are fairly extensive and include detailed schedules of changes in capital stock balances and retained earnings.

Introduced in Chapter 4, special-purpose-entities (SPEs) are particularly relevant to auditors when addressing financial statement disclosures about debt and equity in general and about cash flows in particular. A case in point is the complex structured transactions that Dynergy, Inc., an energy provider and trader, entered into with Citigroup, a global financial service holding company that financed the transactions.

Owing to concerns that operating cash flows were significantly below reported earnings for trading-related contracts—thereby raising the risk that investors would question the quality of earnings—Dynergy, on the advice of their independent auditor, set up Project Alpha, a complex arrangement that involved no less than two SPEs, three interconnected loans, hedging transactions, a linked tax benefit, and a long-term gas purchase agreement that was the mechanism for Alpha to repay $300 million to a syndicate of lenders.[3] Although the syndicate's loan more likely represented financing cash flows under FASB *SFAS No. 95*, "Statement of Cash Flows," management, without objection from their independent auditor, classified the $300 million as operating cash flows, thereby reducing significantly the gap between operating cash flow and earnings.[4] Although the distinction between operating and financing cash flow is sometimes cloudy, *SFAS No. 95* provides guidance: "the appropriate classification shall depend on the activity that is likely to be the predominant source of cash flow for the item."[5] In the case of Project Alpha, the predominant source of cash flow was a loan, not the sale of natural gas.

In orders instituting proceedings before the SEC, both Citigroup and Dynergy, without admitting or denying the SEC's findings, submitted offers of settlement the SEC accepted. Among other things, Citigroup paid a $9 million penalty plus $9.75 million in disgorgement and prejudgment interest, and Dynergy restated 2001 financial statements to conform with GAAP. The Dynergy case is instructive partly because it hints at the sheer complexity of commodity exchange contracts but mostly because it illustrates clearly the audit implications of linkages between reported earnings and operating cash flow.

➣ restatement

---

3   *SEC Accounting and Auditing Enforcement Release No. 1821, In the Matter of Citigroup, Inc.,* July 28, 2003.
4   *SEC Accounting and Auditing Enforcement Release No. 1631, In the Matter of Dynergy, Inc.,* September 24, 2002.
5   *FASB SFAS No. 95,* "Statement of Cash Flows," par. 24.

Management Discretion in Accounting for Financial Instruments

Dominated by historical cost accounting, traditional financial statements provide little direct information about the market value of a company. The accounting profession in general, and the Financial Accounting Standards Board (FASB) in particular, has long been handcuffed in responding to this criticism, since current value, unlike historical cost, is neither objective nor wholly verifiable. Interestingly, the objectivity and verifiability arguments make sense for many assets, but not for those assets that have a readily determinable market value, such as investments in debt and equity securities.

Prior to 1993, the authoritative literature on investments was inconsistent across industries, and the generally accepted, though contradictory, lower-of-cost-or-market rule treated differently the accounting for unrealized gains and losses on debt held for sale and on noncurrent equity securities: Reductions in value (unrealized losses) were recognized, but appreciations (unrealized gains) were not. In response, the FASB added a far-reaching financial instruments project to its agenda that has since resulted in several pronouncements, among them *Statement of Financial Accounting Standards No. 115*, "Accounting for Certain Investments in Debt and Equity Securities," which requires that debt and equity securities be accounted for in three separate portfolios: "held to maturity," "trading securities," and "available for sale." **Held-to-maturity securities** are debt and equity investments that an entity has both the positive intent and the ability to hold until maturity. **Trading securities** are debt and equity investments held for sale in the near term. **Available-for-sale securities** are debt and equity investments not classified as either held-to-maturity or trading. Note from Figure 16-13 that unrealized gains and losses on trading securities—that is, "paper" gains (and losses)—are recognized as current earnings on the income statement, but that gains and losses on held-to-maturity or available-for-sale securities are recognized only when an actual sale occurs.

FIGURE 16-13: *Investment Securities Portfolios*

Investment Portfolios	Securities Included	Unrealized Gains and Losses	Balance Sheet Disclosure
Held-to-maturity securities	Debt and equity that an entity has both the positive intent and ability to hold till maturity	Not recognized	Amortized cost: Current or noncurrent asset
Trading securities	Debt and equity held for sale in the near term	Recognized in current earnings	Fair value: Current assets
Available-for-sale securities	Debt and equity not classified as held-to-maturity or trading	Excluded from earnings; reported in shareholders' equity	Fair value: Current or noncurrent assets

Management and Auditor Incentives

The differential treatment of unrealized gains and losses across investment portfolios provides management with opportunities to manage reported earnings. Two examples: First, management could shift securities to or from a trading securities portfolio, thereby managing the recognition of unrealized gains and losses. In a period of declining (or excessively rising) earnings but rising (or declining) share prices in selected available-for-sale securities, management could boost (or reduce) earnings by reclassifying available-for-sale securities to trading securities and accounting for the resulting unrealized gains (or losses) in current earnings. Second, within the available-for-sale portfolio, management could selectively sell securities that would result in gains, and hold securities that would result in losses. In a dissent to *SFAS No. 115*, two FASB members pointed out that "an impressive amount of empirical evidence indicates that many financial institutions" had selectively sold or held securities, and that selective trading "undermines the relevance and reliability of accounting information."[6] Auditors, in turn, have incentives in general to assure that management complies with the requirements of *SFAS No. 115* and in particular to monitor management's intent, as the following case illustrates.

Accounting for Financial Instruments: A Case Study

Owing to several cost-effective design changes in its truck filter product line, Provident Corporation, a publicly traded company, dominates the automotive filter aftermarket. To meet analysts' forecasts of projected annual earnings, fourth quarter income from operations will have to exceed both the company's expectations and all prior years' fourth quarter results. The company has considerable debt and equity security holdings partitioned within trading, available-for-sale, and held-to-maturity portfolios.

Late in the fourth quarter, management hosts a meeting with the auditors, ostensibly to plan the timing of, and the company's involvement in, year-end audit work. During the meeting, Provident's chief executive officer (CEO) alerts the auditors about securities trades planned for the last month of the fiscal year. The CEO claims that, although management had the undisputed intent to hold selected debt instruments to maturity, the likelihood of failing to meet analysts' earnings projections suggests the company no longer has the ability to hold the securities. As a result, the CEO plans to transfer debt securities from the held-to-maturity portfolio into the trading securities portfolio, and to sell all available-for-sale securities for which the realized gain will exceed by 15 percent the original purchase price. The CEO believes that meeting analysts' forecasts is crucially important to Provident's shareholders. The auditor believes that the company's fourth quarter trading strategy is driven partly by shareholder expectations, and mostly by the CEO's executive compensation contract, which is tied to the magnitude of reported earnings and to Provident's share price.

Audit Judgment: Accounting, Liability, and Ethics

Provident's fourth quarter trading strategy raises three questions. First, has the CEO planned trades that either circumvent or violate generally accepted accounting

> ethics

---

6 *Statement of Financial Accounting Standards No. 115*, "Accounting for Certain Investments in Debt and Equity Securities," par. 25.

principles, specifically *SFAS No. 115*? Rather than circumvent *SFAS No. 115*, management's trading strategy actually takes advantage of earnings management opportunities provided by the pronouncement. Selectively selling appreciated available-for-sale securities while simultaneously holding depreciated securities is not precluded by *SFAS No. 115*, even though the motive clearly is to inflate earnings with recognized gains on selective securities trades. Shifting debt securities from the held-to-maturity portfolio into the trading securities portfolio allows management to recognize unrealized gains in current earnings, which is not precluded by *SFAS No. 115* either, although in this case the auditor would likely be skeptical that the CEO's argument—earnings may fall below analysts' projections—is necessarily a reason to conclude that the company is no longer able to hold debt securities to maturity. After all, the company is neither about to suffer a net loss nor in any apparent danger of bankruptcy.

Second, what is the auditor's potential legal liability? And third, what are the ethical implications to the auditor? Interestingly, the answer to both questions likely is "none." The CEO's trading strategy does not render the auditor culpable under either Section 10(b) or Section 18 of the *Securities Exchange Act of 1934*, since there is no intent by management to do any more than what a literal reading of *SFAS No. 115* would allow. There is no violation of generally accepted accounting principles, no violation of the Code of Professional Conduct, no false or misleading disclosures (Section 18), and no intent to deceive [Section 10(b)]. In fact, the CEO's behavior is actually consistent with the interests of Provident's shareholders: The wealth of the CEO (executive compensation) and the company's shareholders are both tied to Provident's share price. However, the auditor is responsible for determining whether other stakeholders, apart from Provident shareholders, were necessarily deceived. For example, the CEO may have a hidden agenda: If the switch from held-to-maturity to trading securities increases current assets (recall from Figure 16-13 that trading securities are carried as current assets at fair value rather than at amortized cost), the CEO may be masking a debt covenant violation tied to maintaining a prespecified current ratio.

Assurance and Consulting Services Related to Investments

One lesson learned from the savings and loan crisis of the 1980s was that public accounting firms had not adequately assessed the quality of bank loan portfolios in independent financial statement audits. In short, auditors had not determined whether default risk was captured in loan loss reserves. In response, some firms now offer a new service—often called *loan collateral reviews*—to provide banks with comfort about problem borrowers and misstated collateral. Most loan collateral reviews report on a borrower's collateral assets and internal control, and are performed using procedures agreed-upon (Chapter 17) by the practitioner and a bank loan officer. For example, the lead bank in a large multibank financing arrangement in the semiconductor and telecommunications industry might engage a public accounting firm to perform a quarterly loan collateral review, thereby offering more comfort to the participating banks than the lead bank's internal review might hold.

In the past several years, public accounting firms have leveraged heavily in the investment and financial services markets. Two examples: First, although the *Investment Advisors Act of 1940* has long allowed certified public accountants to offer investment advice that is incidental to their practices, few firms responded until recently. In 1996, Coopers & Lybrand, forebear of today's Pricewaterhouse-Coopers, became the last of the then Big Six public accounting firms to register with the Securities and Exchange Commission (SEC) as an investment advisor.[7] The practice, called at the time Coopers & Lybrand Financial Advisors LLC, operates out of major city offices, such as New York and Los Angeles, and offers reviews of investment managers' performance rather than buy/sell investment advice. Interestingly, the market is large and growing. For example, investments in employee benefit plans, such as retirement assets—estimated roughly at $3 trillion—is managed largely by investment managers.

Second, PricewaterhouseCooper's financial services industry practice introduced an Electronic Financial Services Consulting Group to help financial institutions develop electronic products and services.[8] The proliferation of Internet shopping and a joint electronic payment security agreement among IBM, MasterCard, Microsoft, and Visa translate into a growing market in electronic financial consulting, since downsized banks no longer have the luxury of excess employee capacity to manage technology, electronic commerce, and new product development. As with many other assurance and consulting service opportunities, technology is driving change.

However, the Securities and Exchange Commission, among others in the financial community, has questioned the advisability of a public accounting firm serving both as an *independent* auditor and as an investment or consulting advisor. For example, KPMG resigned as independent auditor for Communication Intelligence Corp., a software developer, to ward off SEC criticisms of the firm's now defunct strategic partnership in KPMG BayMark Capital, an independent investment banking venture that advised Communication Intelligence. *The Wall Street Journal* reported that ". . . in SEC filings and interviews, Communication Intelligence said the SEC was concerned that the two roles might conflict, and that KPMG's auditing responsibilities might be influenced by KPMG BayMark's efforts to find deals for Communication Intelligence."[9] As the SEC's criticism and KPMG's resignation suggests, some ventures into lucrative consulting services may leave firms with little choice but to serve a client either as a consultant *or* as independent auditor. In the case of Communication Intelligence, KPMG chose the former.

SUMMARY

The financing cycle involves an entity's business functions for generating and using capital funds and investing funds not currently needed for operations. Common activities related to equity and debt financing include the issuance and retirement of equity and debt securities, payment of dividends and interest to investors and creditors, and recording of equity and debt transactions. In turn, these

---

7   S. Hook, "Coopers Investor Unit Shows Change in Profession," *Accounting Today* (April 22–May 5, 1996), pp. 3, 37.

8   "PW Targets Remote Banking Market," *Public Accounting Report* (February 29, 1996), p. 4.

9   C. McCoy, "KPMG Quits as Software Firm's Auditor as SEC Questions Dual Relationship," *The Wall Street Journal* (August 12, 1996), p. B4.

functions lead to three major balance sheet accounts: investments, long-term debt, and capital stock, each of which is discussed in this chapter in the context of substantive tests of details. When performing substantive tests of investments, long-term debt, and capital stock, an auditor's major objectives are to determine that each account exists, represents all transactions that should be presented, represents rights and obligations of the entity, is valued properly, and is presented and disclosed properly within the financial statements.

Accounting for financial instruments, an attempt by the accounting profession to mark assets—in this case trading securities and available-for-sale securities—to market, is a major departure from historical cost, the measure that has long dominated financial accounting and reporting. Although an authoritative pronouncement guides the accounting for financial instruments, the pronouncement nevertheless provides management with opportunities to manage earnings by transferring securities among portfolios and by timing the sale of selected securities. Auditors have incentives to assure that management complies with the authoritative pronouncement on financial instruments and, in addition, to be cognizant of management's intent.

KEY TERMS

Available-for-sale securities 642
Bond certificate 615
Commercial paper 615
Held-to-maturity securities 642

Stock certificate 615
Trading securities 642
Treasury bill 615

REFERENCES

Auditing Standards:

AICPA, *Codification of Statements on Auditing Standards*. New York: AICPA.
SAS No. 47, "Audit Risk and Materiality in Conducting an Audit."

Accounting Standard:

Statement of Financial Accounting Standards No. 115, "Accounting for Certain Investments in Debt and Equity Securities."

Books:

Committee of Sponsoring Organizations of the Treadway Commission (COSO), *Internal Control: Integrated Framework*. Evaluation Tools. New York: COSO, 1992.
Committee of Sponsoring Organizations of the Treadway Commission (COSO), *Internal Control: Integrated Framework*. Executive Summary. New York: COSO, 1992.
Committee of Sponsoring Organizations of the Treadway Commission (COSO), *Internal Control: Integrated Framework*. Framework. New York: COSO, 1992.
Committee of Sponsoring Organizations of the Treadway Commission (COSO), *Internal Control: Integrated Framework*. Reporting to External Parties. New York: COSO, 1992.

QUESTIONS

1. Identify the business functions associated with the financing cycle.
2. Describe some control procedures applicable to capital stock.

3. What is a restrictive debt covenant?
4. Why should unissued bonds be prenumbered consecutively?
5. Explain how an auditor tests the existence of investments recorded within a client's financial statements.
6. How does an auditor test the valuation of investment securities?
7. Why does an auditor typically examine market quotations for a client's investments?
8. What procedures can be used to determine whether all transactions that should be recorded are recorded?
9. Briefly describe the procedures an auditor might use to test long-term debt and interest expense at year end.
10. Why do auditors frequently rely predominantly or exclusively on substantive tests in auditing shareholders' equity and long-term debt?
11. How does an auditor verify recorded shareholders' equity balances?
12. Identify the specific types of transactions relating to shareholders' equity that are tested by an auditor at year end.
13. How and why does an auditor test earnings per share?
14. How should unrealized gains and losses on investments in equity securities be accounted for?
15. Why do auditors examine long-term indebtedness agreements?
16. In auditing cash flows, how do auditors judge the distinction between an operating and financing cash flow when a source of cash carries characteristics of both?
17. Distinguish among held-to-maturity, trading, and available-for-sale securities.
18. How are unrealized gains on held-to-maturity, trading, and available-for-sale securities reported?
19. Briefly, why did the Financial Accounting Standards Board add the financial instruments project to its technical agenda?
20. What is a loan collateral review?

MULTIPLE CHOICE QUESTIONS

1. Assuming that one of management's control objectives is to restrict access to securities, which of the following would *not* be appropriate to satisfy the objective?

   a. Establish physical barriers over forms and records.
   b. Establish physical barriers over investment securities.
   c. Maintain files of authorized signatures.
   d. Segregate investment approval from custody of the securities.

2. What control objective is served by management's establishing policies for selecting and approving investment transactions?

   a. Sources of capital funds should be authorized in accordance with management's criteria.
   b. Investment transactions should be made in accordance with management's criteria.
   c. Investment transactions should be recorded at the correct amounts and in the proper accounting period.
   d. Access to securities should be restricted to authorized personnel.

3. Establishing policies to select and approve investment transactions addresses:

   a. Transaction authorization.
   b. Transaction execution.
   c. Transaction recording.
   d. Access to assets.

4. Failure to restrict access to debt records and forms could result in:
   a. Loan covenant violations.
   b. Misapplied resources.
   c. Uneconomical financing.
   d. Misappropriated assets.

5. Management could help assure that bond and equity transactions are recorded and classified properly by:
   a. Reviewing board minutes.
   b. Prenumbering and controlling adjustment documents.
   c. Preparing lists of authorized investments.
   d. Maintaining files of authorized signatures.

6. Management could help assure that subsidiary investment records agree to the general ledger by:
   a. Establishing physical barriers over investment securities.
   b. Accounting for unissued, issued, and retired securities.
   c. Requiring specific authorization for investment decisions.
   d. Establishing processing and recording procedures.

7. Why is it less common for auditors to perform extensive tests of controls over investments, debt, and equity?
   a. It is customary to assess control risk at the maximum for these accounts.
   b. Physical custody of securities is often vested in outside trustees.
   c. The volume of transactions is not often large enough to justify the cost of tests of controls.
   d. These transactions are not supported by extensive documentation.

8. Which of the following is likely a key question following an auditor discovering that investment securities are not held in the custody of an independent custodian?
   a. Are the securities protected from misappropriation or theft?
   b. Was the acquisition of the securities authorized?
   c. Are brokers approved by the board of directors?
   d. Is investment income verified?

9. Which financial statement assertions are served by testing cutoff over investment transactions?
   a. Existence and completeness
   b. Rights and valuation
   c. Existence and rights
   d. Presentation and disclosure

10. Which financial statement assertion is served by confirming bonds, notes, and interest payments directly with trustees?
    a. Completeness
    b. Valuation
    c. Rights
    d. Presentation and disclosure

11. How can an auditor test the assertion of completeness for capital stock?
    a. Compare disclosures with GAAP.
    b. Test supporting documentation for stock issuances, stock dividends, and stock splits.
    c. Confirm transactions with independent trustees.
    d. Perform analytical procedures.

12. Verifying stockholders' equity balances addresses:

    a. Existence.
    b. Rights.
    c. Obligations.
    d. Presentation.

13. In the audit of investments, long-term debt, or capital stock, which of the following procedures does not address rights or obligations?

    a. Test cutoff.
    b. Inspect securities.
    c. Confirm loans with creditors.
    d. Examine long-term indebtedness agreements.

14. In the audit of marketable equity securities, which of the following procedures is an auditor likely to perform for equities acquired?

    a. Examine management's investment policies.
    b. Examine brokers' advices.
    c. Confirm with companies issuing securities.
    d. Examine dividend rates.

15. How could held-to-maturity securities be disclosed on the balance sheet?

    a. As current assets, at amortized cost
    b. As current assets, at fair value
    c. As noncurrent assets, at fair value
    d. As current assets, at unamortized cost

16. Which of the following are debt and equity investments that an entity has both the positive intent and the ability to hold until maturity?

    a. Trading securities
    b. Call options
    c. Available-for-sale securities
    d. Held-to-maturity securities

17. For which of the following portfolios are unrealized gains and losses not recognized?

    a. Trading securities
    b. Call options
    c. Available-for-sale securities
    d. Held-to-maturity securities

18. Which of the following would not likely motivate management to selectively sell available-for-sale securities?

    a. Market share declined 5 percent this year.
    b. A new product has not been well received.
    c. Like each of the prior five years, current-year earnings are likely to increase by 10 percent.
    d. Management compensation is tied to earnings.

19. Which portfolio of debt and equity securities is reported always as a current asset in the balance sheet?

    a. Treasury shares
    b. Held-to-maturity securities
    c. Available-for-sale securities
    d. Trading securities

20. Which of the following did auditors most likely ignore in the bank-loan portfolios that led to the savings and loan crisis of the 1980s?

   a. Default risk
   b. Management training
   c. Collateral
   d. Leverage

PROBLEMS AND DISCUSSION CASES

16-1 *Errors, Fraud, and Control Procedures*

In your audit of Whitestable Company's December 31, 2007, financial statements, you become aware of the following controls or procedures over investments, debt, and equity.

1. On June 15, 2007, the board of directors established criteria for selecting debt and equity investments.
2. Policies have been established for selecting debt or equity financing.
3. On a monthly basis, interest and loan payment amounts are prepared or updated.
4. All internally held securities are maintained under lock and key in a fireproof vault within the treasurer's office.
5. All unissued securities are maintained and periodically checked by personnel independent of cash activities.

   Required: For each control procedure, indicate (a) a potential error or fraud that might be prevented or detected as a result of the control procedure and (a) what control objective is served by the control procedure.

16-2 *Drafting Tests of Controls from an Internal Control Questionnaire: Investment Transactions*

Following are selected questions from an internal control questionnaire for a company's investment transactions. The questions relate to the custody, recording, and valuation of investments, and to acquisitions, sales, and income. A *Yes* response to any question indicates a potential strength of the system, and a *No* response a potential weakness.

1. Is a detailed record of securities maintained by an official who is independent of officials responsible for custody?
2. Is the listing of investments periodically reconciled with investment records?
3. Are securities in the name of the entity (or restrictively endorsed in the name of the entity)?
4. Are acquisitions and sales of investment securities authorized by the board of directors or by an authorized investment committee?
5. Are brokers' advices promptly compared with documented acquisition and sales authorizations?
6. Is an independent check made to determine whether acquisition or sale prices are fair and objective?
7. Is investment income periodically recalculated and verified?

   Required: Assume that inquiries indicate no apparent weaknesses in internal control. Draft a test of controls you believe would provide persuasive evidence that no deficiencies exist.

16-3 *Relating Errors, Frauds, Audit Procedures, and Assertions in Substantive Tests of Investments*

Following are errors, frauds, or other circumstances that an auditor might encounter as a result of applying audit tests to investments as of the balance sheet date.

1. The client does not maintain detailed records for investments.
2. All debt securities are maintained in a locked, fireproof vault in the treasurer's office.
3. All equity securities are held by independent brokers.
4. The client traded heavily in marketable securities near the end of the year.
5. The market value of selected equity securities fluctuated widely throughout the year.

Required: For each, indicate (a) a specific substantive test or tests that might address the error, fraud, or circumstance and (b) the financial statement assertion addressed by each test.

16-4 *Planning the Audit of Marketable Securities*

In an audit of the financial statements of Belasco Chemicals, Inc., Karen Mack is deciding whether to inspect marketable securities on the balance sheet date, May 31, 2007, or at some other date. The marketable securities held by Belasco include negotiable bearer bonds, which are kept in a safe in the treasurer's office, and miscellaneous stocks and bonds, which are kept in a safe-deposit box at The Merchants Bank. Both the negotiable bearer bonds and the miscellaneous stocks and bonds are material to Belasco's financial statements.

Required:
1. What are the factors that Mack should consider when deciding whether to inspect securities on May 31, 2007, as opposed to other dates?
2. Assume that Mack plans to have a member of her staff inspect securities at Belasco's offices and at The Merchants Bank on May 31, 2007. What instructions should she give to the staff member about inspecting and including evidence in the working papers?
3. Assume Mack believes that sending a staff member to Belasco's offices and to The Merchants Bank on May 31, 2007, is impractical. What alternative procedures might she use to assure herself that the company physically possesses marketable securities on May 31, 2007, if the securities are inspected (a) May 28, 2007? (b) June 5, 2007?

(AICPA Adapted)

16-5 *Auditing an Investment Portfolio*

As a result of highly profitable operations over a number of years, Eastern Manufacturing Corporation accumulated a substantial investment portfolio. In auditing the financial statements for the year ended December 31, 2007, the following information came to the auditor's attention:

a. Continuing manufacturing operations resulted in an operating loss for the year.
b. In 2007, the corporation placed the securities in their investment portfolio with a financial institution that serves as custodian of the securities. Formerly the securities were kept in a safe-deposit box at a local bank.
c. On December 22, 2007, the corporation sold and then repurchased on the same day a number of securities that had appreciated greatly in value. Management stated that the purpose of the sale and repurchase was to establish a higher cost and book value for the securities and to avoid reporting a loss for the year.

Required:
1. List the objectives of the auditor's tests of the investment account.
2. Under what conditions would the auditor accept a confirmation of the securities from the custodian rather than personally inspecting and counting the securities?
3. What disclosure, if any, of the sale and repurchase of securities would the auditor recommend for the financial statements? What impact, if any, would the sale and repurchase have on the auditor's opinion on the financial statements if the client accepts the auditor's disclosure recommendations? Discuss.

(AICPA Adapted)

**AUDIT
DOCUMENTATION
REVIEW**

16-6 *Audit Documentation Review*

An audit client prepared the schedule on the following two pages. After completing the procedures listed at the bottom of the schedule, an audit assistant initialed, dated, and indexed the working paper.

Required: List the deficiencies in this working paper.

16-7 *Auditing Secured Notes and Equity Securities*

You have been engaged to audit the financial statements of the Elliott Company for the year ended December 31, 2007. You audited the December 31, 2006, financial statements. Following is the December 31, 2007, trial balance.

	Dr. (Cr.)
Cash	$ 128,000
Interest receivable	47,450
Dividends receivable	1,750
14 percent secured note receivable	730,000
Investments at cost: Bowen common stock	322,000
Investments at equity: Woods common stock	284,000
Land	185,000
Accounts payable	(31,000)
Interest payable	(6,500)
16 percent secured note payable to bank	(275,000)
Common stock	(480,000)
Paid-in capital in excess of par	(800,000)
Retained earnings	(100,500)
Dividend revenue	(3,750)
Interest revenue	(47,450)
Equity in earnings of investments carried at equity	(40,000)
Interest expense	26,000
General and administrative expense	60,000

You have obtained the following data:

a. The 14 percent note receivable is due from Tysinger Corporation and is secured by a first mortgage on land sold to Tysinger by Elliott on December 21, 2006. The note was to have been paid in 20 equal quarterly payments beginning March 31, 2006, plus interest. Tysinger, however, is in very poor financial condition and has not made any principal or interest payments to date.

b. The Bowen common stock was purchased for cash on September 21, 2006, in the market where the stock is traded actively. The stock is used as security for the note payable and is held by the bank. Elliott's investment in Bowen represents approximately 1 percent of Bowen's total outstanding shares.

c. Elliott's investment in Woods represents 40 percent of the outstanding common stock that is actively traded. Woods is audited by another auditor and has a December 31 year end.

d. Elliott neither purchased nor sold any equity investments during the year other than what is noted above.

Required: For the following account balances, discuss (a) the types of evidence you should obtain and (b) the audit procedures you should perform.

1. 14 percent secured note receivable
2. Bowen common stock
3. Woods common stock
4. Dividend revenue

(AICPA Adapted)

PROBLEM 16-6: *Audit Documentation Review*

Williston & May
Marketable Securities
December 31, 2007

Description of Security											Dividend & Interest		
Corp. Bonds	%	Year Due	Serial No.	Face Value of Bonds	Gen. Ledger 1/1	Purch. in 2007	Sold in 2007	Cost	Gen. Ledger 12/31	12/31 Market	Pay Date(s)	Amount Rec.	Accruals 12/31
A	6	2011	21-7	$ 10,000	$ 9,400[a]				$ 9,400	$ 9,100	1/15	$ 300[b,d]	$ 275
D	4	2012	73-0	30,000	27,500[a]				27,500	26,220	7/15	300[b,d]	
G	9	2013	16-4	5,000	4,000[a]				4,000	5,080	12/1	1,200[b,d]	100
R[c]	5	2014	08-2	70,000	66,000[a]		$57,000[b,c]	$66,000			8/1	450[b,d]	188
S[c]	10	2015	07-4	100,000		$100,000[c,e]			100,000	101,250	7/1	5,000[b,d]	5,000
					$106,900	$100,000	$57,000	$66,000	$140,900	$141,650		$7,250	$5,563
					a, f	f	f	f	f, g	f			
Stocks													
P 1,000 shs.—Common			1044		$ 7,500[a]				$ 7,500	$ 7,600	3/1	$ 750[b,d]	$250
											6/1	750[b,d]	
											9/1	750[b,d]	
											12/1	750[b,d]	
U 50 shs.—Common			8530		9,700[a]				9,700	9,800	2/1	800[b,d]	667
											8/1	800[b,d]	
					$17,200				$17,200	$17,400		$4,600	$917
					a, f				f, g	f			f

(continues)

PROBLEM 16-6 *(continued)*

a   Beginning balances reconciled with 2006 working papers.

b   Traced to cash receipts.

c   Minutes examined (purchase and sales approved by the board of directors).

d   Reconciled with 1099.

e   Confirmed by tracing to broker's advice.

f   Total footed.

g   Reconciled with general ledger.

16-8 *Auditing Noncurrent Investments*

Harold Brodkey is engaged in the audit of Longview Corporation's financial statements for the year ended December 31, 2007, and is about to begin auditing noncurrent investment securities. Longview's records indicate the company owns various bearer bonds, as well as 25 percent of the outstanding common stock of Industrial National Inc. Brodkey is satisfied with evidence supporting the presumption that Longview exercises significant influence over Industrial National. The various securities are at two locations:

- Recently acquired securities are in the company's safe in the custody of the treasurer.
- All other securities are in the company's bank safe-deposit box.

All the securities in Longview's portfolio are actively traded in a broad market.

Required:

1. Assuming that control procedures for securities may be relied on in assessing control risk below the maximum, what are the objectives of the audit of these noncurrent investment securities?
2. What audit procedures should Brodkey perform to audit Longview's noncurrent investment securities?

16-9 *Drafting Tests of Controls from an Internal Control Questionnaire: Debt and Equity Transactions*

Following are selected questions from an internal control questionnaire relating to a company's debt and equity transactions. A *Yes* response to any question indicates a potential strength of the system, and a *No* response indicates a potential weakness.

a. Are all long-term debt and other borrowings authorized by the board of directors?
b. Is an officer responsible for determining whether all debt covenants are complied with?
c. Are unissued bonds and notes prenumbered consecutively and controlled by an official independent of recording?
d. Are interest payments and accruals recalculated periodically?
e. Are unissued stock certificates prenumbered consecutively and safeguarded?
f. Are treasury shares adequately controlled and accounted for?
g. Are dividend payments and accruals recalculated periodically?

Required: Assume that inquiries indicate no apparent deficiencies in internal control. Draft tests of controls that you believe would provide persuasive evidence that no deficiencies exist.

16-10 *Relating Errors, Frauds, Audit Procedures, and Assertions in Substantive Tests of Long-Term Debt*

Following are errors, frauds, or other circumstances that an auditor might encounter as a result of applying audit tests to long-term debt as of the balance sheet date.

1. Detailed long-term debt records may not be accurate.
2. All debt instruments are held by banks.
3. There is no documentation supporting a bond indenture.
4. Proceeds from the bond issuance have been expended.
5. Various debt instruments required interest payments on the last day of all but two months.

Required: For each, indicate (a) a specific substantive test or tests that might address the error, fraud, or circumstance and (b) the financial statement assertion addressed by each test.

16-11 *Internal Controls Over Investments, Debt, and Capital Stock*

Ronald Ondeyko, CPA, is considering LaSalle Company's internal controls over investments, long-term debt, and capital stock. System documentation was accomplished with a questionnaire and a narrative memorandum and, in conjunction with a transaction walk-through, revealed the following potential deficiencies in internal control.

a. The historical cost of all long-term debt exceeds company policies for debt-to-equity ratios.
b. The company entered into a long-term debt agreement requiring a 2 to 1 current ratio at year end, yet the current ratio when the agreement was signed was approximately 1.5 to 1.
c. Internally held securities have been misplaced occasionally, though in all cases the securities were recovered.
d. In an open letter to the board of directors, a group of shareholders criticized the company for investing in a domestic corporation alleged to have violated human rights in a foreign country.
e. Signatures on investment authorizations vary from the chairman of the board's investment committee to the treasurer and controller.

Required: For each potential deficiency, indicate a control procedure or procedures that management could implement to reduce the likelihood of errors or frauds.

16-12 *Auditing Debt Covenants*

The following covenants are extracted from the indenture of a bond issue. Although the bond due date is 2018, failure to comply with any covenant automatically advances the due date of the loan to the date of noncompliance.

a. The debtor company shall maintain a working capital ratio of 2 to 1 at all times, and, in any fiscal year following a failure to maintain said ratio, the company shall restrict compensation of officers to a total of $250,000. Officers for this purpose shall include chairman of the board of directors, president, all vice presidents, secretary, and treasurer.
b. The debtor company shall keep all property that is security for this debt insured against loss by fire to the extent of 100 percent of actual value. Policies of insurance constituting this protection shall be filed with the trustee.
c. The debtor company shall pay all taxes legally assessed against property that is security for this debt within the time provided by law for payment without penalty, and shall deposit receipted tax bills or equally acceptable evidence of payment with the trustee.
d. A sinking fund shall be deposited with the trustee by semiannual payments of $300,000, from which the trustee shall, at his or her discretion, purchase bonds of this issue.

Required:
1. Draft audit procedures for each covenant.
2. Comment on any disclosures you think necessary.

(AICPA Adapted)

16-13 *Auditing Long-Term Debt*

You were engaged to audit the financial statements of Ronlyn Corporation for the year ended June 30, 2007. On May 1, 2007, the corporation borrowed $500,000 from Second National Bank to finance plant expansion. The agreement provided for annual payments of principal and interest over five years. The existing plant was pledged as security for the loan. Due to unexpected difficulties in acquiring the new building site, plant expansion had not begun at June 30, 2007. To make use of the borrowed funds, management decided to invest in stocks and bonds, and on May 16, 2007, the $500,000 was invested in securities.

Required:
1. What are the audit objectives in the audit of long-term debt?
2. Prepare an audit program for the audit of the long-term note agreement between Ronlyn and Second National Bank.
3. How could you verify the security position of Ronlyn at June 30, 2007?
4. In your audit of investments, how would you:
    a. Verify the dividend or interest income recorded?
    b. Determine market value?
    c. Establish the authority for security purchases?

(AICPA Adapted)

16-14 *Relating Errors, Frauds, Audit Procedures, and Assertions in Substantive Tests of Capital Stock*

The following are errors, frauds, or other circumstances that an auditor might encounter as a result of applying audit tests to capital stock as of December 31, the balance sheet date.

1. Shareholders' equity accounts are not accurate.
2. Stock dividends were issued during the year.
3. Treasury stock was purchased in December.
4. Dividends were declared and paid before the end of the year.
5. The client's common stock is traded actively on a national stock exchange.

Required: For each, indicate (a) a specific substantive test or tests that might address the error, fraud, or circumstance and (b) the financial statement assertion addressed by each test.

16-15 *Auditing Shareholders' Equity*

On May 1, 2007, you were engaged by a committee of shareholders to perform a special audit as of December 31, 2006, of the shareholders' equity of Major Corporation, whose stock is actively traded on a stock exchange. The shareholders who engaged you believe that information in the shareholders' equity section of the published annual report for the year ended December 31, 2006, is incorrect. If your conclusions confirm their suspicions, they intend to use the report in a proxy fight. Management agrees to permit your audit but refuses to permit any direct confirmation with shareholders. To secure cooperation in the audit, the committee of shareholders has agreed to this limitation, and you have been instructed to limit your audit accordingly. You also have been instructed to exclude the audit of revenue and expense accounts for the year.

Required:
1. Prepare an audit program to audit shareholders' equity, assuming no scope limitations.
2. Describe any special auditing procedures you would undertake given the limitations and other special circumstances you confront in the Major Corporation engagement.
3. Discuss the content of your report for the special engagement, including comments on the opinion that you would issue.

(AICPA Adapted)

16-16 *Auditing Shareholders' Equity*

You are engaged in an audit of the financial statements of Pate Corporation for the year ended December 31, 2007. The financial statements and records of Pate Corporation have not been audited by another auditor in prior years. The shareholders' equity section of Pate Corporation's balance sheet at December 31, 2007, is as follows:

Shareholders' equity:

Capital stock—10,000 shares of $10 par value authorized; 5,000 shares issued and outstanding	$ 50,000
Capital contributed in excess of par value	32,580
Retained earnings	47,320
Total shareholders' equity	$129,900

Founded in 2000, Pate Corporation has ten shareholders and serves as its own registrar and transfer agent. There are no capital stock subscription contracts in effect.

Required:
1. Prepare a program to audit the three accounts constituting the Pate Corporation's shareholders' equity section.
2. Why do auditors audit retained earnings?

(AICPA Adapted)

16-17 *Discrepancies Between Authorized and Outstanding Shares*

Eaton Company was incorporated July 10, 2007, with authorized capital as follows:

a. Common stock, Class A, 20,000 shares, par value $25 per share.
b. Common stock, Class B, 100,000 shares, par value $5 per share.

The capital stock account in the general ledger is credited with only one item in the year 2007, capital stock sold for cash, at par, as follows:

a. Class A, 12,000 shares.
b. Class B, 60,000 shares.

The sum of open certificate stubs in the stock certificate books at December 31, 2007, indicates that 82,000 shares of stock were outstanding.

Required:
1. Explain the discrepancy.
2. What procedures would you perform to determine the cause of the discrepancy?

(AICPA Adapted)

16-18 *Earnings Manipulation and Financial Instruments*

Signet Corporation management is transferring securities across their held-to-maturity, trading, and available-for-sale portfolios. Within the industry, management has the reputation of being aggressive, both in operating the business and in securities trading. In prior years, income from investments has exceeded 10 percent of reported earnings.

Required: Identify, and explain the motive for, the key questions an auditor must ask to judge whether management's accounting for financial instruments is appropriate.

Internet problems and discussion cases are available at http://ricchiute.swlearning.com

RESEARCH PROJECT

Management Discretion in Accounting for Financial Instruments

In September 1990, the chairman of the Securities and Exchange Commission criticized carrying investments at amortized cost and argued that, in the banking and savings and loan industries, "serious consideration must be given to reporting all investment securities at market value." Following several years of inconsistent accounting practices across industries and calls to mark selected assets to market, the Financial Accounting Standards Board issued *Statement of Financial Accounting Standards No. 115*, "Accounting for Certain Investments in Debt and Equity Securities," which responds largely to the issue of consistency, partly to the issue of market value, and, in the process, leaves some room for management discretion in managing earnings.

Required: Using the newspaper and magazines file in LEXIS-NEXIS, or newspapers and magazines in a library, select an article about a publicly traded company's accounting for financial instruments. Using the SEC's EDGAR (**http://www.sec.gov**) or copies of annual reports in a library, select the annual report of the same company issued for the fiscal year referred to in the article. Draft a report that accomplishes the following:

1. Summarizes the article, indicating key issues, like management's or the financial community's reaction to the effect of disclosures on reported income.
2. Lists and explains questions an auditor would likely pose to the management of the company you've selected.
3. Summarizes the company's disclosures about financial instruments that appear in the footnotes (for example, the footnote summarizing accounting policies, usually Note 1).

Interactive quizzes are available as a student learning resource at
http://ricchiute.swlearning.com

17 Chapter

Completing an Audit

Major topics discussed in this chapter are:

- Substantive tests of revenue and expense accounts.
- Procedures for auditing accounting estimates, including loss contingencies and fair value.
- The review for related-party transactions.
- Inquiries of a client's legal counsel.
- The role and content of a management representation letter.
- The process of forming an opinion.
- The responsibility for communicating with audit committees.
- The subsequent discovery of facts existing at the date of a report.
- The consideration of omitted procedures after the report date.

Completing an engagement poses for an auditor a number of important questions, none of which have been addressed completely thus far but all of which bear directly on the auditor's report: What risks are imposed by related parties? Are management's assertions dependent on estimates or on legal interpretations? Which of management's oral representations should we ask for in writing? How shall we go about forming an opinion on management's assertions? What should we say to directors or trustees that we might not say in our report? And what risks do we take after issuing a report for facts we learn about our client or work? This chapter addresses these among other questions an auditor confronts when completing an engagement.

The chapter begins by distinguishing between, and illustrating, tests of details and analytical procedures commonly used to test revenue and expense accounts. Next, the chapter addresses procedures for auditing accounting estimates, including fair value, and for "wrapping up" an engagement: reviewing for related-party transactions, reviewing for events that occur subsequent to the balance sheet date, making inquiries of a client's lawyer, and obtaining a management representation letter. In turn, the chapter discusses how and why an auditor performs overall analytical procedures, reviews audit documentation in detail, and arranges for an independent technical review of audit documentation by an audit partner not otherwise assigned to the engagement—each of which is an integral part of the auditor's process of formulating an opinion on an entity's financial statements taken as a whole. Finally, the chapter discusses requirements for an auditor to communicate with the audit committee, and two issues related to the period after the auditor issues an audit report: the subsequent discovery of facts existing at the report date, and the consideration of procedures omitted unknowingly during the engagement.

Substantive Tests of Revenue and Expense Accounts

A financial statement audit encompasses all the basic financial statements, not just the balance sheet. Yet the discussion of substantive procedures in Chapters 10 through 16 focused primarily on balance sheet accounts, and only secondarily on income statement accounts. Although focusing on the balance sheet is not uncommon in practice, auditors also perform substantive tests of revenue and expense accounts, because an audit report extends not only to the balance sheet, but also to the income statement. However, equally important, some financial statement users are compelled equally if not more by results of operations, which are measured by the income statement, than by financial position, which is measured by the balance sheet. For example, consider the effect of reported earnings and revenue on share prices. Commenting on *earnings* management, Arthur Levitt, former SEC chair, said in 1998 that, "I recently read of one major U.S. company that failed to meet its so-called 'numbers' by one penny, and lost more than six percent of its stock value in one day."[1] On the other hand, underscoring the impact of *revenue* on share price, Zach Investment Research, a Chicago-based research firm, correlated reported sales and earnings to stock price movement before and after public announcements for 700 companies from September 3 to October 13, 2000, and found that revenue "surprises"—that is, revenues lower or higher than Wall Street's consensus forecasts—were more likely to trigger share price reactions than earnings surprises.[2] A case in point is Motorola, which in the third quarter of 2000 met consensus earnings expectations, but missed management's $10 billion revenue target by $500,000, triggering a three-day, 22 percent stock price decline. Clearly, the market reacts to news about earnings and revenue well before audited financial statements are made public and at levels that underscore management's incentives to avoid surprises.

Not all of the financial statement assertions introduced in Chapter 6 are necessarily relevant to revenue and expense accounts. Rather, the most relevant assertions are occurrence, valuation and allocation, completeness, and presentation and disclosure, and each can be tested either by direct tests of details or by analytical procedures, or both. The following discusses and illustrates each type of test.

Tests of Details

Choosing Between Tests of Details and Analytical Procedures

Extensive tests of details, rather than analytical procedures, are appropriate when:

- Control risk is at the maximum.
- Transaction volume is low.
- Analytical procedures reveal unusual or unexpected results.
- An account requires special attention.

Analytical procedures applied during the final stages of an audit usually are intended as tests of the reasonableness of an account balance or disclosure. But their value to an auditor depends on the effectiveness of an entity's internal controls, since poorly designed or ineffective controls could result in misstated accounts and, therefore, in relationships—for example, ratios or trends—that are neither

---

1 Arthur Levitt, Jr., "The 'Numbers Game.'" Speech at New York University Center for Law and Business, September 28, 1998.
2 N. Tait, "Zack Monitors Results 'Surprises,'" *Financial Times* (October 23, 2000), p. 20.

reasonable nor reliable. Thus, when *control risk is at the maximum*, an auditor should apply direct tests of details, rather than risk being misled by analytical procedures that produce unreliable measures.

Although analytical procedures are appropriate regardless of transaction volume, very low-volume accounts are better tested by direct tests of details, since all of the recorded transactions can likely be tested, thereby minimizing uncertainty about whether an account is presented fairly. In fact, analytical procedures are not particularly informative for *low-volume accounts* because the information content of minor account balance fluctuations is often trivial.

As indicated throughout the book, tests of details are particularly appropriate when analytical procedures reveal *unusual or unexpected results*. For example, declining receivables balances coupled with steady collections and rising sales could signal overstated sales and would prompt an auditor to design detailed tests of recorded sales.

Some income statement accounts require *special attention*, thereby rendering analytical procedures inappropriate. For example, charitable contributions must be listed in detail on income tax returns, and executive compensation must be disclosed separately in Securities and Exchange Commission filings. Thus, for these among other accounts, auditors typically opt for direct tests of details rather than rely exclusively on analytical procedures.

The Nature and Extent of Tests of Details

The nature and extent of direct tests of details for revenue and expense accounts will vary depending on the circumstances, but in all cases the auditor must address the financial statement assertions listed earlier. For example, an auditor might address occurrence—that is, determine whether recorded revenue and expense transactions actually occurred—by comparing recorded revenue with underlying documents such as deposits and contracts, as illustrated in the analysis of other income in Figure 17-1, or by physically examining evidence of expenditures such as advertising copy in a local newspaper, as illustrated in Figure 17-2. Typically, valuation is tested by extending, footing, and cross-footing detail schedules prepared by the client to support recorded revenues and expenses and reconciling totals with balances in the general ledger. In addition, an auditor might trace recorded amounts for a sample of transactions to supporting documents, such as deposit slips and bank statement clearings. An auditor can test completeness by performing tests of cutoff for transactions occurring near the balance sheet date.

The occurrence, valuation, and completeness of revenue that has been earned but not yet received, or expenses incurred but not yet paid, could be tested by recalculations that match incurred costs with earned revenue in accordance with the accounting concept of matching.

Analytical Procedures

In lieu of—or in addition to—tests of details, an auditor can test the reasonableness of recorded revenue and expense balances by **analytical procedures** that focus on relationships over time, between accounts, or with industry norms. Relationships over time provide evidence about the fluctuation of account balances from one period to the next. For example, an auditor might compare the balances of current-year revenue and expense accounts with balances for the prior year, ob-

FIGURE 17-1: *Direct Tests of Details: Other Income*

BB6
1/10/08
AP

The Wilson Company
Analysis of Other Income
December 31, 2007

Date	Received From	Description	Amount
April 30	Weil & White, Inc. Los Angeles, California	Royalty Income: Annual royalty due by April 30 of each year for Weil & White's use of Wilson patents on centrifuge machines. Royalty based on Weil & White production through March 31.	$7,430[a]
December 31	Sansibar & Company Chicago, Illinois	Rent Income: Initial month's rent for property at 6204 Mitchell Street, Chicago, rented for 12 months to Sansibar.	850[b]
			$8,280
			c

a   Reconciled with royalty report (see workpaper BB9), with royalty contract, and
    with cash receipts journal.
b   Reconciled with rent agreement and with cash receipts journal; agreement expires
    November 30, 2008.
c   Footed and reconciled with general ledger.

taining explanations from management for unusual fluctuations. In turn, relationships between accounts provide evidence about whether the balance of one account is reasonable in relation to another account or to the same account for the preceding year.

An example of analytical procedures for payroll appears in the audit program in Figure 14-6, page 597, and the related discussion. Note that the payroll tests emphasize analytical procedures and, therefore, assume that controls over payroll are reliable and that transaction volume is relatively high—otherwise, direct tests of details would have been more appropriate.

Auditing Accounting Estimates: Loss Contingencies and Fair Value

Most transactions can be tested readily because the audit population is known with certainty, supporting evidence generally exists, and there are no uncertainties about the existence of an asset, liability, income, or expense. However, auditors

FIGURE 17-2: *Direct Tests of Details: Advertising Expense*

BB12
AP 1/13/08

The Wilson Company
Analysis of Advertising Expense
December 31, 2007

Date	Payee	Description	Amount
March 30	Wire & Cable Monthly Chicago, Illinois	Full-page advertisement for cable-extruding machinery.	$ 950[a]
May 15	Chemical Weekly New York, New York	Half-page advertisement for recently introduced chemical centrifuge machinery. Ad ran for six weekly issues, beginning June 1.	1,500[b]
August 10	St. Louis Post-Dispatch St. Louis, Missouri	Full-page color ad in Sunday Supplement (newspaper) advertising Wilson's support and involvement in youth job-training program.	400[a]
			$2,850
			c

a　Examined ad copy and invoice; traced to cash disbursements journal.
b　Examined ad copy and contract; traced to cash disbursements journal.
c　Footed and reconciled with general ledger.

also must apply audit procedures to **accounting estimates**, which are financial statement elements, items, or accounts that management approximates to disclose in the accounting period that gave rise to the estimate's economic substance. Examples include:

- Airline passenger revenue.
- Warranty claims.
- Uncollectible accounts receivables.
- Obsolete inventory.
- Depreciation and amortization.
- Income tax and accrued property taxes.
- Pension costs.
- Subscription income.
- Percentage of completion income on construction contracts.
- Loss contingencies.

Accounting estimates are necessary because the valuation of some accounts—or the measurement of some others—may be <u>uncertain</u> pending the outcome of future events, or because data about past events cannot be accumulated on a timely, cost-effective basis. Although management is responsible to make accounting estimates, auditors are responsible under *SAS No. 57*, "Auditing Accounting Estimates," to evaluate the reasonableness of management's estimates.

Evaluating Accounting Estimates

Accounting estimates are more susceptible to material misstatement than factual data, partly because they involve uncertainty and subjectivity, and partly because controls over estimates are more difficult for management to establish than controls over factual data. An auditor's objectives in evaluating accounting estimates are to:

- Provide reasonable assurance that management developed all material estimates, and
- Assure that the estimates are reasonable and are presented in the financial statements in accordance with GAAP.

The risk of material misstatement for accounting estimates will vary depending on the controls established by management, the complexity and subjectivity of the estimation process, the availability and reliability of relevant evidence, and the nature and uncertainty of assumptions made by management. In evaluating the reasonableness of accounting estimates, an auditor should obtain an understanding of how management developed the estimate and then, based on his or her understanding, consider:

- Reviewing and testing the process used by management,
- Developing an independent estimate for comparison, and
- Reviewing transactions or events that occurred subsequent to the balance sheet date.

The Panel on Audit Effectiveness

The Panel on Audit Effectiveness (Chapter 2) pointed to several problems unique to the audit of accounting estimates. For example, the activity in an estimated reserve account—say, for example, a loss contingency—may be driven more by management's intentions (for example, management's plan to fight a patent infringement suit vigorously) than by verifiable arm's length transactions. As discussed more fully below, loss contingencies among other accounting estimates are guided by *Statement of Financial Accounting Standards No. 5*, "Accounting for Contingencies." However, as the Panel notes, the pronouncement "offers little clarification as to when management's intent can result in a liability having been created . . . it may be difficult to distinguish between the appropriate accrual of a loss contingency based on GAAP and an inappropriate accrual of future expenses."[3] In their review of 126 SEC registrants audited by the eight largest accounting firms, the Panel found that firms audited estimates most effectively when the task was assigned early to senior members of the engagement team, such as partners and specialists, a finding that is consistent with firms consciously assigning complex audit tasks to staff with the requisite training and experience.

Loss Contingencies

One of the accounting estimates listed above, a **loss contingency**, is defined in *SFAS No. 5*, "Accounting for Contingencies," as ". . . an existing condition,

---

3   The Panel on Audit Effectiveness, *Report and Recommendations*. Stamford, CT: POB, 2000, p. 51.

situation, or set of circumstances involving uncertainty as to possible gain or loss to an enterprise that will ultimately be resolved when one or more future events occur or fail to occur." When completing an engagement, auditors are particularly concerned with the existence of unrecorded loss contingencies, because failure to recognize a material loss contingency will result in overstated income and understated liabilities and, therefore, in materially misstated financial statements. As a result, one common procedure performed toward the end of an engagement is to review for potential contingent liabilities. Examples of loss contingencies include:

- Pending or threatened litigation for patent infringements, product warranties, or product defects.
- Guarantees of third-party obligations.
- Discounted notes receivable or factored accounts receivable.
- Disputed income tax deductions.

Loss contingencies should be recognized and a liability recorded in the financial statements if:

1. A liability *probably* had been incurred at the balance sheet date, and
2. The amount of the loss can be *reasonably estimated*.

However, if the loss is either probable or estimable—that is, either (1) or (2) but not both—or if there is a *reasonable possibility* that a liability may have been incurred, then the financial statements should include a footnote explaining the nature of the contingency and an estimate of the possible loss, or range of loss, or a statement that an estimate cannot be made.

Searching for Loss Contingencies

Searching for potential loss contingencies requires that auditors exercise not only keen judgment but some creativity, since the existence of contingent liabilities is not always readily apparent. For example, a client may not have evidence on hand that a customer had filed a product liability suit. At a minimum, auditors usually perform the following procedures to search for unrecorded loss contingencies:

- Ask management about the possibility of unrecorded contingencies.
- Read minutes of the board of directors' and shareholders' meetings.
- Read contracts, loan agreements, lease agreements, and similar documents.
- Review reports prepared by agents of the Internal Revenue Service and other taxing authorities.
- Analyze legal expenses for the year and examine documentation (for example, invoices) from attorneys that may suggest litigation is pending or in progress.
- Review current-year audit documentation for indications of potential contingencies.

Importantly, auditors also are responsible for loss contingencies that occur or are discovered after the balance sheet date, because they could be material subsequent events, discussed later in the chapter.

Auditing Fair Value

Loss contingencies translate to liabilities on the balance sheet. But what about accounting estimates that appear as assets of the balance sheet, particularly those that demand approximations of fair value? FASB *Statement of Financial Accounting Concepts No. 7*, "Using Cash Flow Information and Present Value in Accounting Measurements," defines the fair value of an asset (liability) as "the amount at which the asset (or liability) could be bought (or incurred) or sold (or settled) in a current transaction between willing parties . . ." To estimate the amount at which an asset could be bought, management relies preferably on a market price observed in an arm's length exchange of a similar asset. Absent a market price, management resorts to the best information available, such as a specialist's valuation or the present value of future cash flows. However, available information can be fraught with imprecision if the information depends on assumptions, even those management makes in good faith. For example, the present value of future cash flows depends in part on the discount rate management assumes—the lower (higher) the discount rate, the higher (lower) the carrying value. Management's assumptions can have a material effect on the carrying value of an asset, raising a risk less likely when an observable market price exists.

To guide practitioners auditing fair value, the Auditing Standards Board in 2003 issued *SAS No. 101*, "Auditing Fair Value Measurements and Disclosures." Management, not the auditor, is responsible to measure and disclose the fair values in financial statements. The auditor, in contrast, is responsible to understand how management determined fair value and the controls that prevent management from arriving at estimates that are unreasonable. On occasion, the auditor may judge that the nature of the fair value estimate demands a specialist—for example, an equity specialist to value a complex derivative transaction—although he or she remains obligated to judge whether the specialist understands the context of the auditor's due diligence obligation, since the estimate will appear publicly in financial statements that anyone might see, rather than privately in a document that few might see. In most cases, though, management does not engage a specialist, leaving the auditor with the responsibility to test management's fair value measurements and disclosures.

Not unlike tests of accounting estimates under *SAS No. 57*, "Auditing Accounting Estimates," discussed above, an auditor should obtain an understanding of how management developed the estimate and then, based on his or her understanding, consider:

- Reviewing and testing the process used by management,
- Developing an independent estimate for comparison, and
- Reviewing transactions or events that occurred subsequent to the balance sheet date.

Regardless of whether the auditor tests management's process, develops an estimate, or reviews subsequent transactions, he or she focuses on the *reasonableness* of management's fair value estimate and, more often than not, reasonableness depends on management's *assumptions*. For example, consider again the discount rate management assumes to calculate the present value of future cash flows. To be reasonable, the discount rate should be consistent with the rates reported by competitors in the industry, rates available in the market, and rates used for other estimates in the current year and for similar assets in prior years. In short, the assumptions should be reasonable in their own right (make sense for this asset?) and reasonable relative to other assumptions (make sense for the financial statements taken as a whole?).

Completing an Audit

After completing the audit procedures introduced in Chapters 10 through 16 and in this chapter, an auditor performs additional procedures designed to "wrap up" the engagement and to generate additional evidence that may affect either the conclusions reached for individual accounts or the auditor's report. These procedures are to:

- Review for related-party transactions.
- Review for subsequent events.
- Make inquiries of a client's legal counsel.
- Obtain a management representation letter.
- Form an opinion.

However, an auditor's responsibility for audited financial statements does not end either on the report date or when an audit report is physically communicated to the client. Rather, an auditor continues to be responsible to:

- Communicate with the audit committee, including fraudulent financial reporting,
- Discover facts existing at the date of the auditor's report, and
- Consider omitted procedures after the report date.

These procedures and responsibilities are discussed separately next.

Related-Party Transactions

In most cases, parties to a transaction are unrelated and independent, thereby increasing the likelihood that the transaction is a bargained exchange negotiated at "arm's length." However, the parties to some transactions are not independent. Rather, the parties are related and may include, for example, affiliates, directors, principal owners, managers and their immediate family members, and others in a position to influence or to be influenced. The significance of a **related-party transaction** is this: Disclosing the legal form of the transaction may not accurately reflect its economic substance. For example, failing to disclose that the CEO of a major pharmaceutical supplier sits on the board of a publicly traded profit-making hospital would bear on the quality of the hospital's earnings if the CEO granted end-of-the-year discounts to enhance the hospital's earnings per share. *Statement on Auditing Standards No. 45*, "Omnibus Statement on Auditing Standards: 1983" (AU Sec. 334), addresses related-party transactions.

In practice, related parties are common. For example, in a survey of the public filings of 400 major companies, *The Wall Street Journal* found that 200 of the companies reported business deals with related parties.[4] A relationship between or among related parties does not necessarily mean a transaction is not at arm's length. However, an auditor should be aware that the likelihood of a related-party transaction not being at arm's length increases when management has incentives to manipulate earnings. For example, the likelihood would increase if management demonstrates an unusual urgency to maintain a favorable earnings trend in the hope of supporting the company's stock price, if management makes an overly optimistic earnings forecast at the beginning of the year, if the entity de-

---

4   J. R. Emshwiller, "Business Ties: Many Companies Report Transactions with Top Officers," *The Wall Street Journal* (December 29, 2003), p. A1.

pends wholly or primarily on a single or relatively few products for the ongoing success of the business, if the entity operates in a declining industry characterized by a large number of business failures, if there is significant pending litigation (especially litigation between shareholders and management), or if senior management operates a company as a conduit for personal gain. Any of these situations could be sufficient motivation for a client to engage in a related-party transaction that is not at arm's length. For example, on personal gain, consider the case of Adelphia Communications, once the sixth largest cable television provider in the United States.

In a complaint that centered largely on related-party transactions, the SEC alleged that the founder of Adelphia, John J. Rigas, his sons, and other senior executives—all of whom were defendants in the complaint—engaged in "blatant self-dealing," the effect of which was "one of the most extensive financial frauds ever to take place at a company."[5] The SEC alleged that, among other things, defendants shifted approximately $2.3 billion in bank debt from the balance sheet to the books of unconsolidated affiliates and misdirected company funds to purchase vacation properties, New York City apartments, and Adelphia shares in Rigas family members' names. On March 27, 2002, in a fourth-quarter 2001 earnings release, Adelphia reported the off-balance sheet financing, driving Adelphia's stock price down significantly and, in time, management to file for bankruptcy protection. At trial, the SEC's chief witness, Adelphia's former vice president for finance, offered dramatic testimony that went to the heart of how fraud occurs: "I lied in person to investors when I met them. I lied in the company's filings. I lied in the company's press releases."[6] Testimony at trial is not often that forthcoming.

> fraud

Certain relationships, such as family-owner, parent-subsidiary, or investor-investee are obvious to an auditor, and any material transactions between these parties should be investigated. However, to determine the existence of less obvious related parties, the auditor needs to follow specific procedures. For example, apart from evaluating management's procedures for identifying related parties, the auditor could review filings with the SEC and other regulatory agencies for the names of related parties and for other businesses in which the entity's officers and directors occupy directorship or management positions, determine the names of all pensions and trusts established for the benefit of employees and the names of their officers and trustees, review the shareholder listings of closely held companies to identify principal shareholders, and review material investment transactions to determine whether the nature and extent of investments during the period create related parties.

Once related parties have been identified, the auditor then examines any material transactions management entered into with these parties. But how does the auditor distinguish related-party transactions from others, particularly those that are unrecorded and/or not at arm's length? The following procedures provide guidance for identifying these transactions:

- Make known to the audit team the names of related parties.
- Review the minutes of meetings of the board of directors and executive or operating committees for information about material transactions authorized or discussed at their meetings.

---

5   *SEC v. Adelphia Communications, John J. Rigas, et al., Complaint*, July 24, 2002.
6   P. Grant, "Lying was Easy for Star Witness in Adelphia Case," *The Wall Street Journal* (May 19, 2004), p. C1.

- Review proxy material filed with the SEC for information about material transactions with related parties.
- Review conflict-of-interests statements obtained by the entity from management.
- Review the extent and nature of business transacted with major customers, suppliers, borrowers, and lenders for indications of previously undisclosed relationships.
- Review invoices from law firms for indications of the existence of related parties or related-party transactions.
- Review confirmations of loans receivable and payable for indications of guarantees.

After identifying related-party transactions, an auditor should apply the audit procedures necessary to assess the purpose, nature, and extent of the transactions and their effect on the financial statements. In general, the procedures should extend beyond simply making inquiries of management and might include obtaining an understanding of the business purpose of the transactions, examining documentation such as invoices or contracts, and determining whether the transactions were approved by the board of directors. The accounting considerations and required disclosures for related-party transactions are discussed in FASB *Statement of Financial Accounting Standards No. 57*, "Related Party Disclosures."

Subsequent Events Review

An auditor is primarily concerned with the balance sheet as of a particular date, such as December 31, and related statements of earnings, retained earnings, and cash flows for a particular period, such as January 1 through December 31. However, events sometimes occur or become known subsequent to the balance sheet date and before issuance of the audit report—the **subsequent period**—that have an effect on financial statement disclosures. An independent auditor's responsibility for subsequent events and related audit procedures is addressed in AU Sections 560 and 561 of the AICPA's *Codification of Auditing Standards*.

Subsequent events are classified into two major types:

- Type I Events: Subsequent events that reveal or confirm conditions *existing at or before* the balance sheet date and require *adjustment* to the financial statements.
- Type II Events: Subsequent events that reveal conditions *arising after* the balance sheet date and require *disclosure* in, but not adjustment to, the financial statements.

Type I Events

Type I subsequent events relate to conditions existing at or before the balance sheet date that affect estimates inherent in the process of preparing financial statements. Accordingly, the financial statements should be adjusted for any material changes in estimates. Examples include:

- Collection of receivables or settlement of liabilities in amounts substantially different from amounts recorded at the balance sheet date.
- Realization of a loss on the sale of investments, inventories, or properties held for sale when the subsequent sale merely confirms a previously existing unrecognized loss.

- Discontinuance, at an estimated loss, of operations of a subsidiary where the contributing circumstances unfolded over a period of time prior to the balance sheet date.

Some Type I subsequent events require only a reclassification of amounts, rather than adjustment, and therefore do not affect recorded net income or loss. A common example is reclassifying long-term liabilities to short-term when an expected refinancing arrangement did not occur before the liabilities became due.

Type II Events

Type II subsequent events relate to conditions that <u>did not exist at or before the balance sheet date</u>, yet are disclosed because they may be of such significance that the financial statements would be misleading if the events are not disclosed. Normally, financial statements are supplemented with pro forma information giving retroactive effect to Type II events. Examples include:

- Business combinations.
- Issuance of new notes, bonds, or other indebtedness.
- Changes in capital structure.
- Declaration of unusual cash or stock dividends or omission of a regular dividend.
- Damage from fire, flood, or other casualty.

Borderline Cases

In some cases, it's not altogether clear whether an event should be classified as Type I or Type II. For example, the sale or abandonment of significant manufacturing facilities typically results from careful management studies that, if not documented, are at least substantially contemplated over a somewhat lengthy period of time. Even if not contemplated, certainly the conditions leading to the motive for sale or abandonment (for example, significant losses over several periods) would have arisen prior to the balance sheet date. Thus, in the case of a sale or abandonment, an argument could be made for either Type I or Type II treatment: Type I because conditions giving rise to the event probably occurred before year end, and Type II because the economic impact of the event did not occur until after year end.

A related question is the decision about whether adjustment or disclosure is really necessary at all. For example, declaring a regular quarterly dividend after year end may not be considered worthy of disclosure if the entity has paid dividends for several years. That is, if a dividend is normally paid, disclosure may not be informative. On the other hand, a first-time dividend declared after year end certainly would represent useful information and should be disclosed.

Procedures in the Subsequent Period

During the subsequent period, an auditor performs the majority of, if not all, year-end substantive tests but is also responsible to detect and, if warranted, disclose material subsequent events. Some year-end substantive procedures, such as cutoff testing, partly address subsequent events, but are insufficient to discharge an auditor's responsibility for detecting and disclosing subsequent events. As a result, auditors typically perform the following procedures at or near the completion of field work.

- Read the latest available interim financial statements and compare them with the financial statements being reported on.
- Inquire of management:
  - Whether interim statements have been prepared on the same basis as the statements being audited;
  - Whether any substantial contingent liabilities or commitments existed at the date of the balance sheet;
  - Whether there was any significant change in the capital stock, long-term debt, or working capital to the date of inquiry;
  - Whether there were any significant changes in estimates for amounts included or disclosed in the financial statements; and
  - Whether any unusual adjustments were made during the period from the balance sheet date to the date of inquiry.
- Read the available minutes of meetings of shareholders, directors, and appropriate committees, such as the finance committee.
- Assemble pertinent findings resulting from inquiries of legal counsel (discussed later in the chapter) and other auditing procedures for litigation, claims, and assessments.
- Obtain a letter of representation from management (discussed later in the chapter) as of the date of the auditor's report.

In addition, the auditor would make any additional inquiries or design and perform additional procedures to address any questions or uncertainties arising from the above procedures. Disclosures would be handled as follows.

Disclosure

Type I subsequent events require adjustment to financial statements, but need not be disclosed in notes to the financial statements. In contrast, Type II events should be disclosed fully in any of the following alternative forms:

- Explanatory note.
- Parenthetical explanation.
- Reference in the financial statements to pro forma information.
- If warranted, a qualified opinion, adverse opinion, or disclaimer of opinion.

To illustrate an *explanatory note*, assume The Wilson Company incurred a contingent liability on February 5, 2007, and the auditor's report is dated February 7, 2007. The information could be disclosed in an explanatory note as follows:

Note 12: Contingent liabilities.

On February 5, 2007, management was advised by the U.S. Attorney located in New York City that a federal grand jury in New York had indicted the company on charges of conspiracy and fraud in the 2006 sale of the company's common stock to First Source Investment Company. Management has not had sufficient time to evaluate the effect this indictment will have on the company; however, management believes that the fine, if any, that could be levied against the company if found guilty of the actions charged, would not exceed $350,000.

Parenthetical explanations present a brief comment next to the accounts affected in the financial statements. For example, liquidation of a material note payable after the balance sheet date could be disclosed in parentheses aside Notes Payable on the balance sheet.

Pro forma information—that is, disclosing what the financial statements would have looked like if the event had occurred on or before the balance sheet date—may be appropriate if a Type II event is so material that historical financial statements alone would be misleading. Pro forma statements, however, can be misleading if certain events are included in the pro forma statements and other significant events are not.

Issuing a *qualified or adverse opinion or disclaiming* an opinion is typically done only as a last resort, when all other efforts to persuade the client to use alternative disclosure methods have failed. The wording of these reports was discussed in Chapter 3.

Inquiry of Client's Legal Counsel

Occasionally, an economic event can impact an entity's financial position more heavily than a transaction, a prominent example being loss contingencies, discussed earlier. A loss contingency that arises from litigation, claims, and assessments, though, is not only a disclosure matter, but also a legal matter, since the probability and amount of loss is determined by arbitration, administrative proceeding, or the courts. Thus determining the existence of a loss contingency is often a legal question, requiring that an auditor communicate directly with a client's attorney about liabilities arising from litigation, claims, and assessments.

Because of their own potential legal exposure for disclosing inaccurate or confidential information, attorneys are cautious about furnishing auditors with letters divulging legal matters, sometimes called **legal letters**, particularly matters involving **unasserted claims**—that is, claims for which a plaintiff may have a legal right but has not yet taken action. For example, an attorney may be aware that a client has infringed on another company's patent and therefore that a suit could be brought by the injured party. Consider the attorney's precarious position: If the attorney divulges the unasserted claim to the auditor, and the claim is then disclosed in the audited financial statements, the disclosure may well result in a claim being asserted against the client.

Following extensive correspondence between the AICPA and the American Bar Association about the attorney's position and the auditor's needs, the Auditing Standards Board issued *SAS No. 12*, "Inquiry of a Client's Lawyer Concerning Litigation, Claims, and Assessments." *SAS No. 12* requires that a list of legal issues be prepared by the client's management, rather than the client's attorney, and then sent to the attorney, requesting information about (1) pending or threatened litigation, claims, and assessments and (2) unasserted claims and assessments.

As illustrated in Figure 17-3, the attorney is requested to furnish the following information for all pending or threatened litigation, claims, and assessments, and to comment on differences between the attorney's and management's views:

- A description of the nature of the matter, progress to date, and action the client intends to take.
- An evaluation of the likelihood of an unfavorable outcome and an estimate, if one can be made, of the amount or range of potential loss.
- A statement that management's list of pending or threatened claims is complete, or identification of any omissions.

As also illustrated in Figure 17-3, for unasserted claims, an attorney is requested to identify any differences between management's and his or her views. Thus, *SAS No. 12* requires that an attorney respond to management's representations

FIGURE 17-3: *Inquiry Letter to Legal Counsel*

THE WILSON COMPANY
15 Artubus Drive
Stony Brook, NY 11790

February 14, 2008

John O'Hara
Attorney at Law
126 East 57th Street
New York, New York 10025

Dear Mr. O'Hara:

In connection with an audit of our financial statements at December 31, 2007, and for the period then ended, management has prepared and furnished to our auditors, Cheever and Yates, CPAs, a description and evaluation of certain contingencies, including those set forth below, involving matters with respect to which you have been engaged and to which you have devoted substantive attention on behalf of The Wilson Company in the form of legal consultation or representation. These contingencies are regarded by management as material for this purpose. Your response should include matters that existed at December 31, 2007, and during the period from that date to the date of your response.

Pending or Threatened Litigation

[In this section, management would list all pending or threatened litigation, including the following information for each: (1) the nature of the litigation, (2) the progress of the case, (3) the way management is responding or intends to respond, and (4) an evaluation of the likelihood of an unfavorable outcome and an estimate, if one can be made, of the amount or range of potential loss.]

Please furnish to our auditors such explanation, if any, that you consider necessary to supplement the foregoing information, including an explanation of those matters about which your views may differ from those stated and an indication of the omission of any pending or threatened litigation, claims, and assessments or a statement that the list of such matters is complete.

Unasserted Claims and Assessments

[In this section, management would list all probable unasserted claims and assessments, including the following for each: (1) the nature of the matter, (2) the way management intends to respond if the claim is asserted, and (3) an evaluation of the likelihood of an unfavorable outcome and an estimate, if one can be made, of the amount or range of potential loss.]

Please furnish to our auditors such explanation, if any, that you consider necessary to supplement the foregoing information, including an explanation of those matters as to which your views may differ from those stated.

We understand that whenever, in the course of performing legal services for us with respect to a matter recognized to involve an unasserted possible claim that may call for financial statement disclosure, you have formed a professional conclusion that we should disclose or consider disclosure concerning such possible claim or assessment, as a matter of professional responsibility to us, you will so advise us and will consult with us concerning the question of such disclosure and the applicable requirements

FIGURE 17-3 *(continued)*

of *Statement of Financial Accounting Standards No. 5.* Please specifically confirm to our auditors that our understanding is correct.

Please specifically identify the nature of and reasons for any limitation on your response.

> Very truly yours,
> The Wilson Company
>
> _____
>
> Raymond Carver
> President

about pending or threatened litigation and unasserted claims (but does not require that the attorney prepare a list). If an attorney fails to respond or responds insufficiently, a significant uncertainty may exist about the recording and disclosure of loss contingencies, requiring that an auditor modify the audit report, as discussed in Chapter 3.

Obtain a Management Representation Letter

Throughout an engagement, an auditor obtains numerous representations from management, some written and some oral. For example, management represents in writing that recorded transactions actually occurred (for example, in journal entries and contracts) and represents orally to the auditor that there are no material undisclosed subsequent events that would require adjustment to, or disclosure in, the financial statements. To add persuasiveness to management's representations, *SAS No. 85,* "Management Representations," requires that an auditor obtain a **management representation letter** that is addressed to the auditor, dated as of the audit report date, and signed by members of management with overall financial and operating responsibility, usually the chief executive officer and the chief financial officer. Representation letters complement, but do not supplant, auditing procedures. For example, in a representation letter, management casts to writing their oral representation that there are no subsequent events, but the written representation does not alleviate the auditor's responsibility to search for material Type I and Type II subsequent events.

The representations included in management's letter will vary depending on the circumstances, but ordinarily address four key areas:

Financial statements:
- Management acknowledges responsibility for the financial statements.
- Management believes that the financial statements are presented fairly in conformity with GAAP.

Completeness of information made available to the auditor:
- Management made available all financial records, all minutes of shareholders' and directors' meetings, and all communications from regulatory agencies about noncompliance.
- Management recorded, and made available to the auditor, all transactions.

Recognitions, measurement, and disclosure:
- Management disclosed, if necessary, and made available to the auditor, information about management or employee fraud, plans affecting the carrying value or classification of assets or liabilities, related-party transactions, guarantees or losses for which the entity is contingently liable, violations of laws or regulations, unasserted claims, title to assets, and compliance with contractual agreements.

Subsequent events and disclosure:
- Management disclosed, if necessary, and made available to the auditor, information about subsequent events.

A sample representation letter appears in Figure 17-4. Management's refusal to furnish a written letter would preclude an auditor from issuing an unqualified opinion, regardless of the results of the audit otherwise.

FIGURE 17-4: *Management Representation Letter*

THE WILSON COMPANY
15 Artubus Drive
Stony Brook, NY 11790

February 14, 2008

Cheever & Yates, LLP
345 Park Avenue
New York, New York 10154

Dear Mr. Cheever:

We are providing this letter in connection with your audit of the financial statements of The Wilson Company as of December 31, 2007 and for the period January 1, 2007 to December 31, 2007 for the purpose of expressing an opinion as to whether the financial statements present fairly the financial position, results of operations, and cash flows of The Wilson Company in conformity with generally accepted accounting principles. We confirm that we are responsible for the fair presentation in the financial statements of financial position, results of operations, and cash flows in conformity with generally accepted accounting principles.

Certain representations in this letter are described as being limited to matters that are material. Items are considered material, regardless of size, if they involve an omission or misstatement of accounting information that, in the light of surrounding circumstances, makes it probable that the judgment of a reasonable person relying on the information would be changed or influenced by the omission or misstatement.

We confirm to the best of our knowledge and belief, as of February 14, 2008, the following representations made to you during your audit.

- The financial statements referred to above are fairly presented in conformity with generally accepted accounting principles.
- The effects of any uncorrected misstatements aggregated by the auditor during the current engagement and pertaining to the latest period presented are immaterial, both individually and in aggregate, to the financial statements taken as a whole.
- We have made available to you all financial records and related data; minutes of the meetings of stockholders, directors, and committees of directors; or summaries of actions of recent meetings for which minutes have not yet been prepared.

(continues)

FIGURE 17-4 *(continued)*

- There have been no communications from regulatory agencies concerning non-compliance with or deficiencies in financial reporting practices.
- There are no material transactions that have not been properly recorded in the accounting records underlying the financial statements.
- There has been no fraud involving management or employees who have significant roles in internal control or fraud involving others that could have a material effect on the financial statements.
- The following have been properly recorded or disclosed in the financial statements: Related-party transactions, including sales, purchases, loans, transfers, leasing arrangement, and guarantees, and amounts receivable from or payable to related parties; guarantees, whether written or oral, under which the company is contingently liable; all significant estimates and material concentrations known to management that are to be disclosed in accordance with the AICPA's *Statement of Position 94-6*, "Disclosure of Certain Significant Risks and Uncertainties."
- There are no violations or possible violations of laws or regulations whose effects should be considered for disclosure in the financial statements or as a basis for recording a loss contingency, nor unasserted claims or assessments that our lawyers have advised us are probable of assertion and must be disclosed in accordance with *Financial Accounting Standards Board Statement No. 5*, "Accounting for Contingencies."
- The company has satisfactory title to all owned assets, and there are no liens or encumbrances on such assets nor has any asset been pledged as collateral.
- We have complied with all aspects of contractual agreements that would have a material effect on the financial statements in the event of noncompliance.
- To the best of our knowledge and belief, no events have occurred subsequent to the balance sheet date and through the date of this letter that would require adjustment to or disclosure in the aforementioned financial statements.

Raymond Carver, President

Maxine Kuman, Controller

Sometimes, in practice, audit evidence contradicts management's representations. For example, contrary to management's written representation that there are no material unrecorded transactions, an auditor's tests of cash disbursements and the file of unmatched receiving reports may reveal material unrecorded liabilities (Chapter 13). Clearly, management may have misrepresented unrecorded transactions unintentionally and innocently. However, if not, an auditor should consider whether he or she can rely on other of management's representations. Repeated, intentional misrepresentations could drive an auditor to resign from an engagement, since he or she could not assess reliably the risk that the financial statements may be misstated materially.

Other times, in practice, management simply misrepresents transactions or events both to the auditor and to the public. For example, consider American Bank Note Holographics (ABNH), a mass producer of secure holograms. In connection with an initial public offering in 1998, ABNH made materially false statements

➤ fraud

about recognizing revenue on bill and hold sales, on unshipped holograms, and on work in progress, among other things, in 1996, 1997, and first-quarter 1998 financial statements. For example, to help substantiate bill and hold sales to its independent auditor, ABNH obtained from a subcontractor's security firm a false affidavit attesting that security personnel had witnessed ABNH employees retrieve inventory at the subcontractor's facility as of December 31, 1997. ABNH's representation letter was silent about the misstatements. In an order instituting proceedings against ABNH, the SEC concluded the representation letter "falsely stated that: (1) '[t]here has been no fraud involving management or employees who have significant roles in internal controls;' (2) '[t]here are no transactions that have been improperly recorded in the accounting records underlying the financial statements;' (3) '[w]e have fully disclosed to you all sales terms including all rights of return;' and (4) 'receivables at December 31, 1997 . . . do not include any amounts for goods shipped on consignment or approval.'"[7] Clearly, auditors view written representation letters as important audit evidence and, to that end, the SEC finds *mis*representations actionable.

Forming an Opinion

In a public accounting firm, an audit partner, sometimes called the *engagement partner*, is responsible for reaching an overall opinion on an entity's financial position, results of operations, and cash flows, but only after:

- Performing an overall review of the financial statements through analytical procedures,
- Reviewing audit working papers, and
- Obtaining a review of the audit documentation by an audit partner not assigned to the engagement.

Each is discussed next.

Analytical Procedures as an Overall Review

SAS No. 56, "Analytical Procedures," requires that an auditor apply analytical procedures when completing an engagement to test whether the relationship among recorded account balances appears reasonable, the intent being to identify issues that might otherwise have gone undetected during detailed testing. For example, unlike detailed tests, analytical procedures applied to the relationship between recorded sales and accounts receivable would not offer evidence that the accounts are misstated, but if sales were to decrease in the current period by 50 percent, an auditor might reasonably expect receivables to decrease by a comparable percent. If receivables did not decrease, the auditor might consider several potential explanations, among them:

- The allowance for doubtful accounts might be understated.
- Accounts receivable might be overstated.
- Sales might be understated.

---

7   *SEC Accounting and Auditing Enforcement Release No. 1422,* "In the Matter of American Bank Note Holographics, Inc.," July 18, 2001.

If the relationship between account balances appears unreasonable, as in this illustration, the auditor should make inquiries of management and then (1) evaluate the reasonableness of management's replies in relation to the auditor's knowledge of the client's business and information obtained during the audit and (2) consider the need to corroborate management's replies through additional procedures, such as further substantive tests of sales, receivables, and/or the allowance for doubtful accounts.

Audit Documentation Review

AUDIT DOCUMENTATION REVIEW

After documenting audit procedures for an individual financial statement account, an auditor drafts his or her conclusion about the account in the audit working papers. The conclusion should state whether, in the auditor's judgment, the account is presented fairly, the account is not presented fairly, or evidence is insufficient or inadequate to reach a conclusion. For example, a conclusion that an account is presented fairly might be worded:

Based upon audit procedures performed, I am satisfied that Accounts Receivable is presented fairly in all material respects at December 31, 2007.

A conclusion should be included on the lead schedule for each major financial statement account audited. Thereafter, typically on or about the last day of field work, the audit partner may review the entire set of audit documentation in detail, review by interview, review by presentation, or perform an overriding review (Chapter 7), the intent being to determine whether the audit documentation demonstrates and documents compliance with auditing standards and with the firm's quality control and performance standards. Figure 17-5 illustrates a partner's review checklist, categorizing the procedures between those related to the mechanical accuracy of the audit documentation and those related to audit scope.

The audit partner reaches an overall opinion on the financial statements taken as a whole by considering the propriety of all audit conclusions documented within the working papers. If the conclusions indicate the accounts and disclosures are presented fairly in all material respects, the partner would issue an unqualified opinion on the financial statements taken as a whole. Otherwise (or if a conclusion is not reached for a specific account) the partner would consider the need to issue a qualified opinion, an adverse opinion, or a disclaimer of opinion, all of which were discussed in detail and illustrated in Chapter 3.

Obtain an Independent Technical Review

Before an audit report is communicated to a client, an audit partner or partners not otherwise assigned to the engagement (sometimes called a *concurring partner*) should review the audit documentation (sometimes called a *cold review*), determining whether auditing standards were followed and whether the audit documentation supports the conclusions and opinion reached. In some firms, the concurring partner reads the audit documentation in detail. In other firms, the concurring partner's approach is to read key evidence, such as the management representation letter, attorneys' letters, memoranda summarizing important problem areas or sensitive disclosure, and staff-prepared questionnaires on the completeness of working papers. The review is the final step in the process of reviewing audit documentation and, therefore, is the final check before an audit report is released.

FIGURE 17-5: *Audit Documentation Review Checklist*

Mechanical Accuracy
- Trace supporting balances on individual schedules to lead schedules.
- Trace lead schedule balances to working trial balances.
- Trace trial balance amounts to the financial statements.
- Review compliance with restrictive loan covenants.
- Review indexing of working paper.
- Review cross-referencing within the working papers.
- Test significant calculations in the working papers, for example:
  - Accruals for interest income and expense.
  - Accruals for state, local, and federal income taxes.
  - Accruals for pension and profit-sharing plans.
  - Depreciation.
  - Inventory price testing.
  - Lease calculations.
  - Earnings per share.
- Determine that all audit documentation is complete, properly headed, and dated.

Audit Scope
- Determine that the consideration of internal control is adequate and that the scope of year-end substantive tests of details is justified given the level of control risk.
- Determine that audit programs were appropriate for the circumstances.
- Determine that audit procedures adequately addressed the audit assertions of existence or occurrence, completeness, rights and obligations, valuation or allocation, and presentation and disclosure.
- Determine that the scope and results of the accounts receivable confirmations were reasonable.
- Determine that the physical inventory observation procedures were adequate.
- Determine that management representation letters are accurate, complete, and signed by management.
- Determine that legal letters are appropriate and signed.
- Determine that related-party transactions are disclosed as necessary.
- Review all proposed adjusting journal entries.
- Determine that the audited financial statements are properly presented in accordance with generally accepted accounting principles.
- Determine that the opinion expressed in the audit report (unqualified, qualified, adverse, or disclaimer of opinion) is justified by evidence documented within the working papers.
- Determine that all exceptions and review notes within the audit documentation have been cleared.

Communication with Audit Committees

Throughout an engagement, auditors acquire and communicate to the board of directors' audit committee information that does not necessarily require disclosure in the financial statements, but that may be helpful to the committee in discharging their responsibility for overseeing the entity's financial reporting function. The communication typically occurs in a face-to-face meeting between the audit committee and the independent auditor in which the auditor communicates findings from a prepared script and the committee poses questions unknown in advance to the auditor.

Auditor Communications to the Audit Committee

Consistent with the responsibility assumed by an audit committee as the sole intermediary between the independent auditor and the full board of directors, *SAS No. 61*, "Communication with Audit Committees," requires that auditors communicate to the audit committee information that may assist the committee in overseeing the financial reporting and disclosure process for which management is responsible. Figure 17-6 lists a number of the matters that *SAS No. 61* requires the auditor to communicate—for example, consider "significant audit adjustments."

FIGURE 17-6: *Common Auditor Communications to the Audit Committee*

- The auditor's responsibility under generally accepted auditing standards.
  Examples:
  - Reasonable, but not absolute assurance.
  - Materiality and audit risk.
- Significant accounting policies.
  Examples:
  - Revenue recognition policies.
  - Newly adopted authoritative accounting pronouncements.
- Management's judgments and accounting estimates.
  Examples:
  - Amounts or disclosures determined by estimates and judgments.
  - Disclosures judged immaterial.
- Significant audit adjustments.
  Examples:
  - Unintentional errors.
  - Intentional frauds or illegal acts.
- Other information in documents containing audited financial statements (for example, annual reports to shareholders).
  Examples:
  - Management's discussion and analysis (MD&A)
  - CEO's letter to shareholders.
- Disagreements with management.
  Examples:
  - Nature, timing, and extent of audit procedures.
  - GAAP.
- Difficulties encountered in performing the audit.
  Examples:
  - Unreasonable delays caused by management.
  - Failure to complete client-prepared schedules or spreadsheets.
- Management's consultation with other accountants about accounting and auditing matters.
  Example:
  - Second opinions solicited by management.
- Major issues discussed with management prior to retaining the auditor for the next audit.
  Example:
  - Conversations in which management linked disclosure preferences to auditor retention.

Recall from Chapter 7 that *SAS No. 88*, "Audit Adjustments," imposes on the auditor a responsibility in the planning stage of the engagement to include in the engagement letter a statement that management understands its responsibility to record material proposed adjusting journal entries. At year end, management confirms in a representation letter that unrecorded adjusting journal entries are immaterial, both individually and in the aggregate (see the second bulleted line item in the representation letter at Figure 17-4), and the auditor informs the audit committee about management's representation.

Although *SAS No. 61* requires communication with the audit committee only, some auditors also communicate some of the same matters with others in the entity who may benefit, such as internal auditors, the chief financial officer, or the chief executive officer.

Audit Committee Questions Posed to the Auditor

As discussed in Chapter 7, *SAS No. 89*, "Audit Committee Communications," requires that an auditor discuss with the audit committee the *quality, not just the acceptability,* of management's accounting principles and earnings. For example, an auditor might discuss with the audit committee side agreements that not only drove adjusting journal entries but, equally important, call into question how management's revenue recognition policies bear on the quality of earnings (Chapters 7 and 11). However, despite the auditor's responsibility to communicate fully, proactive audit committees often probe further by asking questions similar to the quality-of-earnings questions posed in Figure 17-7. For example, among other things, audit committees often ask about asset impairments, restructuring reserves, alternative methods of accounting, controversial or uncommon transactions, accounting changes, the deferral of costs, and the accrual of liabilities. The questions are neither pejorative nor disrespectful. Rather, the questions speak to the board of director's responsibility to protect the interests of shareholders.

Subsequent Discovery of Facts Existing at Report Date

After an audit report has been issued, an auditor is under no obligation to make any further inquiries or to perform additional audit procedures. Sometimes, however, new information may surface that bears on one or more of management's assertions and that would have affected either the audited financial statements or the audit report had the information come to the auditor's attention on or before the report date. For example, the auditor may become aware that technological advances have rendered inventory obsolete, suggesting that the carrying value of inventory is overstated, thereby affecting management's valuation assertion. Regardless of whether the new information could have (or should have) been known as of the report date, the auditor is responsible to discuss the matter with appropriate levels of management, including the board of directors, and to take additional action if:

- The information is reliable,
- The facts existed at the report date,
- The audit report would have been affected if the information had been known, and
- Persons are currently relying or are likely to rely on the financial statements and would attach importance to the information.

FIGURE 17-7: *Common Audit Committee Questions: The Quality of Earnings*

- In what major areas are the amounts and disclosures subject largely to estimates and judgment?
  Examples:
  - Revenue recognition.
  - Asset valuation and impairment.
  - Restructuring reserves.
  - Contingencies.
- In what areas were accounting policies problematic to select?
  Examples:
  - Transactions not governed by authoritative accounting pronouncements.
  - Transactions that offer alternative methods of accounting.
  - Controversial or uncommon transactions.
  - Distinguishing a transaction as core versus noncore.
- In what areas were the transactions or events new to the entity or controversial?
  Examples:
  - Significant reserves.
  - Changes in accounting principles or estimates.
  - Large or unusual deferral of costs or accrual of liabilities.
  - Prior-period adjustments.
- In what areas did the auditor confront management-imposed problems?
  Examples:
  - Uncorrected prior-period weaknesses in internal control.
  - Unavailable or uncooperative client personnel.
  - Inadequate schedules or spreadsheets prepared by client personnel.
  - Unavailable audit evidence.

The additional action taken by an auditor would depend on whether the client makes appropriate disclosure of the newly discovered information, as discussed next. However, in either case—whether the client makes, or refuses to make, additional disclosures—the auditor's overriding concern is to assure that current and potential financial statement users no longer rely on the original audit report.

Client Makes Disclosure

When a client agrees to disclose, the method and form of disclosure will depend on the circumstances. For example, if the effect of the newly discovered information can be determined promptly, disclosure would consist of revised financial statements and a revised audit report. The reasons for revision should be described in a note to the financial statements and referred to in the auditor's report. Further, the revised statements and report should be communicated to all persons known (or likely) to be relying on them. However, if the effect of the newly discovered information cannot be determined without a prolonged investigation, the issuance of revised statements and a revised report would necessarily be delayed. In this case, appropriate disclosure would consist of the client notifying all persons known or likely to be relying on the original statements that the report should no longer be relied on, and that revised financial statements and a revised audit report are forthcoming.

Client Refuses Disclosure

In contrast, if the client refuses to disclose, the auditor should notify each member of the board of directors and, barring legal advice to the contrary, should formally notify management, each regulatory agency having jurisdiction over the client, and each person known to be relying on the financial statements that the original audit report can no longer be relied on. For publicly traded clients, notification to each person known to be relying on the report is an ominous, time-consuming task. As a result, notification to the regulatory agencies will usually be the only practical method for the auditor to provide.

Consideration of Omitted Procedures after the Report Date

The previous section dealt with the subsequent discovery of *facts* existing at the report date. But what if a public accounting firm's peer review (Chapter 4) or internal quality control inspection reveals that a client's previously issued financial statements are fairly stated but that one or more necessary *auditing procedures* were omitted during the audit engagement? *SAS No. 46*, "Consideration of Omitted Procedures after the Report Date," addresses this question.

As with the subsequent discovery of facts, an auditor is under no obligation either to perform audit procedures after the report is issued or to conduct a retrospective review of previously completed audit work. However, because of potential legal liability for due diligence (Chapter 5), an auditor should consider consulting an attorney and, with the attorney's advice and assistance, determine a course of action.

In most cases, the auditor will assess the importance of the omitted procedures to the financial statements taken as a whole by reviewing the completed working papers, discussing the circumstances with assigned audit staff and, from this information, reevaluating overall audit scope. That is, was the extent of the auditing procedures applied adequate even in the absence of the procedures omitted? For example, an auditor might conclude that confirming loans and other long-term notes payable was adequate to partially address the assertions of existence, obligations, and valuation, even though the audit documentation reveals that bond indentures and other long-term indebtedness agreements were not examined. However, if the auditor believes that a previously issued report is no longer supported absent the procedures, and that persons are either relying or likely to rely on the report, he or she should promptly undertake to apply the omitted procedures. If the auditor concludes by performing omitted procedures that the previously issued report is no longer supported, he or she should assure that current and potential financial statement users no longer place reliance on the previously issued report—for example, by following procedures discussed earlier for the subsequent discovery of facts existing at the report date.

SUMMARY

This chapter, which concludes the discussion of detailed procedures, addressed substantive tests of revenue and expense accounts and introduced procedures necessary to complete a financial statement audit. In general, substantive tests of revenue and expense accounts take the form of detailed tests or reasonableness tests (analytical procedures), both of which can provide complete or partial support for the financial statement assertions of occurrence, valuation or allocation, completeness, and presentation and disclosure.

When completing an engagement, an auditor must review both for material subsequent events and for contingent liabilities. Each requires considerable judgment because, unlike many other audit areas, neither is recorded in the financial statements. An auditor also makes inquiries of a client's legal counsel about pending or threatened litigation and unasserted claims, and he or she obtains a representation letter from management about assertions made during the engagement.

To form an overall opinion on the financial statements taken as a whole, auditors review the entire set of audit documentation and perform overall analytical procedures. In turn, before an audit report is issued, an independent review should be performed by an audit partner not otherwise assigned to the engagement. The purpose of the independent review is to provide assurance that members of the audit team, most of whom have been involved in the details of the engagement, have not overlooked an issue central to either the audited financial statements or the audit report.

Even after communicating with the audit committee and after an audit report is issued, the auditor maintains responsibility for the subsequent discovery of facts existing at the date of the auditor's report and for considering the omission of procedures during the engagement, both of which are critical to an auditor's potential legal liability.

KEY TERMS

Accounting estimates 724	Subsequent events 730
Analytical procedures 722	Subsequent period 730
Legal letters 733	Type I subsequent events 730
Loss contingency 725	Type II subsequent events 731
Management representation letter 735	Unasserted claims 733
Related-party transaction 728	

REFERENCES

Professional Standards:

AICPA, *Codification of Auditing Standards*. New York: AICPA (AU Sec. 333, 334, 337, 342, 380, 390, 560, 561).

SAS No. 12, "Inquiry of a Client's Lawyer Concerning Litigation, Claims, and Assessments" (AU Sec. 337).

SAS No. 45, "Omnibus Statement on Auditing Standards: 1983" (AU Sec. 334).

SAS No. 46, "Consideration of Omitted Procedures After the Report Date" (AU Sec. 390).

SAS No. 57, "Auditing Accounting Estimates" (AU Sec. 342).

SAS No. 61, "Communication with Audit Committees" (AU Sec. 380).

SAS No. 85, "Management Representations" (AU Sec. 333).

SAS No. 88, "Audit Adjustments" (AU Sec. 324, 420).

SAS No. 89, "Audit Committee Communications" (AU Sec. 380).

SAS No. 101, "Auditing Fair Value Measurements and Disclosures."

Professional Reports:

Blue Ribbon Committee on Improving the Effectiveness of Corporate Audit Committees, *Report and Recommendations*. New York Stock Exchange and the National Association of Securities Dealers, 1999.

Public Oversight Board, *Panel on Audit Effectiveness: Report and Recommendations*. Stamford, CT: POB, 2000.

Articles:

Blocher, E., and G. F. Patterson, Jr., "The Use of Analytical Procedures," *Journal of Accountancy* (February 1996), pp. 53–55.

Gibson, K. M., and J. S. Gerson, "Talking with the Auditor," *Journal of Accountancy* (March 1998), pp. 63–65.

Gibson, K. M., and S. M. McEachern, "The Once and Future Auditors," *Journal of Accountancy* (February 1998), pp. 63–66.

Gibson, K. M., K. Pany, and S. H. Smith, "Do We Understand Each Other?" *Journal of Accountancy* (January 1998), pp. 53–59.

QUESTIONS

1. Identify and briefly discuss the two types of substantive tests an auditor performs for revenue and expense accounts.
2. Why does an auditor perform substantive tests of revenue and expense accounts?
3. Under what circumstances would an auditor rely on substantive tests of details rather than analytical procedures?
4. What is the purpose of analytical procedures applied in the final stages of an audit?
5. Why are accounting estimates susceptible to material misstatement?
6. What is a loss contingency?
7. How does an auditor search for an unrecorded loss contingency?
8. What is an auditor's responsibility when auditing fair value?
9. What are related-party transactions and why are they significant to an auditor?
10. How does an auditor search for related-party transactions?
11. Subsequent events occur after the last day of an entity's fiscal year and on or before the report date. Why would an auditor be concerned about transactions and events occurring in the subsequent period?
12. What is the difference between Type I and Type II subsequent events? Identify the alternative types of disclosure appropriate for Type II subsequent events.
13. What is the purpose of a management representation letter?
14. What information should an auditor request from a client's legal counsel in a letter of audit inquiry?
15. What is the relationship between audit conclusions reached for individual financial statement accounts and an auditor's overall opinion on financial statements taken as a whole?
16. In general, what procedures does an auditor apply during the subsequent period to identify significant subsequent events?
17. Under what conditions would an auditor take action for the subsequent discovery of facts existing at the report date?
18. How should an auditor proceed if a client refuses to disclose the subsequent discovery of facts existing at the report date?
19. What is an unasserted claim?
20. How should an auditor proceed in the event he or she becomes aware after the report date that audit procedures were omitted during the engagement?

MULTIPLE CHOICE QUESTIONS

1. Tests of details, rather than analytical procedures, are appropriate when:

   a. Control risk is below the maximum.
   b. Transaction volume for the account or class of transactions is high.
   c. Analytical procedures reveal unexpected results.
   d. The account does not require special attention.

2. Among the tests of details to audit royalty income, an auditor would likely:

   a. Compare amounts received to industry competitors.
   b. Examine royalty contracts.
   c. Trace to cash disbursement records.
   d. Review minutes of board of director meetings

3. Among the tests of details to audit advertising expense, an auditor would likely:

   a. Examine advertising copy.
   b. Review advertising industry data.
   c. Trace to cash receipts records.
   d. Compare to alternative advertising media.

4. Comparing current- and prior-year revenues and expenses and investigating all changes exceeding 10 percent would most likely reveal that:

   a. Management's capitalization policy for small tools changed in the current year.
   b. Declining economic conditions caused an inadequate provision for uncollectible receivables.
   c. Fourth-quarter payroll taxes were not paid.
   d. Higher current rates have not been recognized in property tax accruals.

5. Under *Statement on Auditing Standards No. 57*, "Auditing Accounting Estimates," an auditor is responsible for:

   a. Making accounting estimates.
   b. Evaluating the reasonableness of management's estimates.
   c. Auditing transactions in the subsequent period that lend insight into estimates recorded at the balance sheet date.
   d. Including accounting estimates within the letter of audit inquiry sent to all attorneys of record.

6. Which of the following would not likely be a related-party transaction?

   a. Sales to another corporation with a similar name.
   b. Purchases from an entity controlled by the purchasing entity's majority shareholder.
   c. Loan from an entity to a major shareholder.
   d. Sale of land to an entity by a director's spouse.

7. Subsequent events occur after the:

   a. Balance sheet date.
   b. Date of the auditor's report.
   c. Balance sheet date but on or before the date of the auditor's report.
   d. Date of the auditor's report but on or before the date of a registration statement.

8. The following events occurred after the end of the fiscal year but before the auditor issued a report. Which event would not require disclosure in the financial statements?

   a. Sale of a bond or issuance of capital stock.
   b. Loss of plant or inventories from a fire or flood.
   c. A major decline in the trade price of the corporation's common shares.
   d. Settlement of litigation when the event giving rise to the claim took place after the balance sheet date.

   (AICPA Adapted)

9. Of the following, which would likely be classified as a Type II subsequent event?

   a. Collection of receivables in amounts substantially different from amounts recorded at the balance sheet date.
   b. Realization of a loss of the sale of an investment when the subsequent sale confirms a previously existing unrecognized loss.
   c. Discontinuance, at an estimated loss, of operations of a subsidiary where the contributing circumstances developed prior to year end.
   d. A business combination accounted for as a purchase.

10. Although an attorney's letter reveals no significant disagreements with the management's assessment of contingent liabilities, the attorney resigns shortly thereafter, suggesting:

   a. The auditor must begin anew the audit of contingent liabilities.
   b. Undisclosed unasserted claims.
   c. The attorney was unable to conclude about the significance of litigation, claims, and assessments.
   d. An adverse opinion is necessary.

11. A letter of inquiry to a client's attorney:

   a. Absolves management from responsibility for disclosing asserted claims to an auditor.
   b. Is signed by the independent auditor.
   c. Is restricted to loss contingencies.
   d. Inquires about unasserted claims.

12. The date of a management representation letter coincides with the:

   a. Date of the auditor's report.
   b. Balance sheet date.
   c. Date of the latest subsequent event referred to in notes to the financial statements.
   d. Date of the engagement letter.

13. A management representation letter would not likely address:

   a. The financial statements.
   b. Violations of laws and regulations.
   c. Difficulties encountered in completing the audit.
   d. The completeness of financial records.

14. Management's refusal to sign a representation letter would likely result in:

   a. A qualified opinion.
   b. A violation of the *Sarbanes-Oxley Act.*
   c. An unqualified opinion with an emphasis on the matter.
   d. Incremental audit fees.

15. A final independent review of the audit documentation is normally done by:

    a. The engagement partner.
    b. The chief technical partner of the office conducting the audit.
    c. A partner not otherwise assigned to the engagement.
    d. The engagement manager.

16. Audit documentation review would not likely include:

    a. Reviewing compliance with loan covenants.
    b. Recalculating depreciation.
    c. Reviewing proposed adjusting journal entries.
    d. Determining whether exceptions were cleared.

17. Under *Statement on Auditing Standards No. 61*, "Communication with Audit Commit-tees," which of the following would an auditor typically communicate to the audit committee?

    a. Difficulties encountered in performing the audit
    b. Turnover in the staff assigned to the audit
    c. Matters included within an attorney's letter
    d. The contents of the management representation letter

18. In addition to the audit committee, auditors sometimes communicate matters to others, although not likely to the:

    a. Internal auditor.
    b. General counsel.
    c. Investor relations director.
    d. Press.

19. Assuming a client refuses to disclose the subsequent discovery of facts existing at the report date, the auditor might notify:

    a. Creditors.
    b. Institutional shareholders.
    c. Regulatory authorities.
    d. Suppliers.

20. Assuming an auditor discovers omitted procedures after the report date, he or she should:

    a. Perform the procedures.
    b. Notify regulatory authorities.
    c. Reevaluate audit scope.
    d. Rescind the audit report.

PROBLEMS AND DISCUSSION CASES

17-1 *Why Coordinate Tests of Balance Sheet and Income Statement Accounts?*

In a properly planned financial statement audit, auditors typically coordinate tests of balance sheet and income statement accounts. For example, in practice auditors often coordinate tests of accounts receivables and sales, and of accounts payable and purchases.

Required: Discuss reasons for coordinating the tests of balance sheet and income statement accounts, illustrating by examples.

AUDIT DOCUMENTATION REVIEW

17-2 *Independent Audit Documentation Review*

Nicole Lutes, a partner in a regional public accounting firm, is conducting the independent technical review—the "cold" review—of audit documentation for the December 31, 2007, year-end audit of Singer Corporation. In 2004, two years before Lutes was admitted to the partnership, she was the audit manager on the Singer engagement. One of the working papers, a schedule of ratios and an analysis of account balance changes from 2006 to 2007, reveals that advertising expense, stated at $150,000 on December 31, 2006, increased to $180,000 in 2007, an increase of $30,000, or 20 percent. Sales and cost of goods sold in both years were relatively stable. Lutes reviews a schedule, "Analysis of Advertising Expense," which reveals that for $20,000 of the 2007 advertising expense balance, the audit staff examined advertising copy and invoices and traced payments to the cash disbursements records. Interim tests of controls indicated that control procedures over advertising transactions are not particularly reliable. The audit documentation provides no explanation of the $30,000 increase in advertising.

Required:
1. Explain the purpose of an independent technical review of working papers.
2. Is Lutes a reasonable choice to perform the 2007 independent technical review given that she was the manager on the 2004 Singer Corporation engagement? Explain.
3. In your judgment, were the nature and scope of the audit of advertising expense reasonable? Explain.

17-3 *Related-Party Transactions*

In any audit engagement, an auditor is concerned that financial statements reflect properly the economic substance of material related-party transactions. To achieve this objective, auditors attempt to determine the existence of related parties and the nature of transactions entered into between the audit client and the related parties. During the course of an audit engagement, you have identified two potential related-party transactions. The first involves a significant shareholder who has borrowed cash to purchase a new home. The second is an affiliated company that has agreed to supply your audit client with raw materials.

Required: Describe how each of the two potential related-party transactions should be structured so that the legal form of the transaction accurately reflects the economic substance. Include the items an auditor would review to assure that the transaction is made at "arm's length."

17-4 *Drafting a Related-Parties Footnote*

Subsidiaries of First of America, a major commercial bank, have made loans to First of America directors and executive officers. The loans totaled $56,965,000 at December 31, 2007 (3.6 percent of total shareholders' equity), and $42,405,000 at December 31, 2006. During 2007, $39,201,000 in new loans were made, and repayments and other reductions totaled $24,641,000. Management believes that the loans do not affect materially the financial condition of First of America, that the loans are consistent with sound business practice in the banking industry, and that the loans do not impose more than the normal risk of collectibility. There is every reason to believe the loans were made at nonpreferential terms and rates, and no reason to believe the loans were made to immediate members of the directors' families or violated either corporate policy or applicable laws and regulations.

Required: Draft a related-parties footnote for First of America's December 31, 2007, financial statements.

17-5 *Responsibility for Subsequent Events*

Michael is auditing the financial statements of Diannah Corporation as of and for the period ended September 30, 2007. Michael plans to complete field work and sign the auditor's report on November 15, 2007. Michael's audit work is designed primarily to obtain evidence that will provide a reasonable degree of assurance that Diannah Corporation's September 30, 2007, financial statements present fairly the financial position, results of operations, and cash flows in accordance with generally accepted accounting principles. Michael is concerned, however, about events and transactions of Diannah Corporation that occur after September 30, 2007, since Michael does not have the same degree of assurance for these events as for those that occurred in the period ending September 30, 2007.

Required: Define what is commonly referred to in auditing as a "subsequent event" and describe the two general types of subsequent events that require consideration by the management of Diannah Corporation and evaluation by Michael.   (AICPA Adapted)

17-6 *Identifying Subsequent Events*

Although an auditor reaches an opinion on financial statements as of the last day of a client's fiscal year—for example, December 31—the auditor is also responsible for material transactions or events occurring through the last day of field work that provide additional evidence about financial statement disclosures as of the balance sheet date.

Required: Describe the procedures an auditor should apply at or near the completion of field work to identify material subsequent transactions or events.

17-7 *Disclosing Subsequent Events*

Jason Hirsch, engagement partner for the December 31, 2007, Flowmeter, Inc., financial statement audit, is aware that events and transactions that took place after December 31, 2007 (but before he issues his report dated February 28, 2008), may affect the company's financial statements. The following material events or transactions have come to Hirsch's attention.

1. On January 3, 2008, Flowmeter, Inc., received a shipment of raw materials from Canada. The materials had been ordered in October 2007, and shipped FOB shipping point in November 2007.
2. On January 15, 2007, the company settled and paid a personal injury claim of a former employee as the result of an accident that occurred in March 2006. The company had not previously recorded a liability for the claim.
3. On January 25, 2008, the company agreed to purchase for cash the outstanding stock of Porter Electrical Co. The acquisition is likely to double the sales volume of Flowmeter, Inc.
4. On February 1, 2008, a plant owned by Flowmeter, Inc., was damaged by a flood, resulting in an uninsured loss of inventory.
5. On February 5, 2008, Flowmeter, Inc., issued and sold to the general public $2,000,000 in convertible bonds.

Required: For each of the events or transactions, discuss audit procedures that should have brought the item to the auditor's attention, and the form of (and reasons for) disclosure in the financial statements.   (AICPA Adapted)

17-8 *Detecting and Distinguishing Between Type I and Type II Events*

Windek is nearing completion of an audit of the financial statements of Jubilee, Inc., for the year ended December 31, 2007. Windek currently is concerned that subsequent events may require adjustment to or disclosure in the financial statements.

Required:
1. Briefly explain what is meant by a "subsequent event."
2. How do those subsequent events that require financial statement adjustment differ from those that require financial statement disclosure?
3. What are the procedures that should be performed in order to identify subsequent events?   (AICPA Adapted)

17-9 *Detecting Loss Contingencies*

An independent auditor has completed substantive tests of balance sheet and income statement accounts, and now plans to begin procedures designed to determine whether there are any loss contingencies arising from litigation, claims, or assessments. Thus far, the auditor has inquired of (and discussed with) management the policies and procedures they have adopted for identifying, evaluating, and accounting for litigation, claims, and assessments.

   Required: What procedures should the auditor follow to detect loss contingencies arising from litigation, claims, and assessments?

17-10 *Responsibilities for Management Representation Letters*

Statement on Auditing Standards No. 85, "Management Representations," requires that an independent auditor obtain a written representation letter from management, and precludes the auditor from issuing an unqualified opinion if management—in particular, the chief executive officer—refuses to sign the letter.

   Required:
   1. What are the objectives of obtaining a management representation letter?
   2. Who should prepare and sign the letter?
   3. When should a representation letter be obtained?
   4. Why should a representation letter be prepared for each year in which an audit is performed?

17-11 *Drafting a Management Representation Letter*

L. B. Feldman is completing the June 30, 2007, audit of Carter, Rice, Storrs & Bement, a manufacturer and supplier of paper products. The company has operated successfully since 1948 when it was founded by Charles Carter, still the chief executive officer. The last day of field work is August 2, 2007. During the engagement, Feldman received numerous oral representations, but is particularly concerned with representations relating to:

   - Potential irregularities involving management and employees.
   - Related-party transactions.
   - Compensating balances involving restrictions on cash balances.
   - Possible violations of state law.
   - Loss contingencies.
   - Potential unasserted claims or assessments.

Feldman has no evidence to suggest that any of the items listed is necessarily a problem in the engagement, but she is concerned that the client may not sign a management representation letter because of the potential legal implications if some of the items listed were to occur without management's knowledge.

   Required:
   1. Draft a management representation letter, including the proper date, addressee, and signatory. The letter should cover only the items listed.
   2. How should Feldman proceed if management fails to sign the representation letter?

17-12 *What to Include in a Management Representation Letter*

During the audit of the financial statements of Amis Manufacturing, Inc., the company's president, R. Alderman, and E. K. Luddy, the auditor, reviewed matters that were supposed to be included in a written representation letter. Upon receiving the following client representation letter, Luddy contacted Alderman to state that the letter was incomplete.

To: E. K. Luddy, CPA

We are providing this letter in connection with your audit of the financial statements of Amis Manufacturing, Inc., as of December 31, 2007, and for the period January 1, 2007 to

December 31, 2007, for the purpose of expressing an opinion as to whether the financial statements present fairly the financial position, results of operations, and cash flows of Amis Manufacturing, Inc., in conformity with generally accepted accounting principles. We confirm that we are responsible for the fair presentation in the financial statements of financial position, results of operations, and cash flows in conformity with generally accepted accounting principles.

Certain representations in this letter are described as being limited to matters that are material. Items are considered material, regardless of size, if they involve an omission or misstatement of accounting information that, in the light of surrounding circumstances, makes it probable that the judgment of a reasonable person relying on the information would be changed or influenced by the omission or misstatement.

We confirm, to the best of our knowledge and belief, that there were no:

- Plans or intentions that may materially affect the carrying value or classification of assets and liabilities.
- Communications from regulatory agencies concerning noncompliance with, or deficiencies in, financial reporting practices.
- Agreements to repurchase assets previously sold.
- Violations or possible violations of laws or regulations whose effects should be considered for disclosure in the financial statements or as a basis for recording a loss contingency.
- Unasserted claims or assessments that our lawyer has advised are probable of assertion and must be disclosed in accordance with *Statement of Financial Accounting Standards No. 5.*
- Capital stock repurchase options or agreements or capital stock reserved for options, warrants, conversions, or other requirements.
- Compensating balance or other arrangements involving restrictions on cash balances.

R. Alderman, President
Amis Manufacturing, Inc.

March 14, 2008

Required: Identify the other matters that Alderman's representation letter should confirm.   (AICPA Adapted)

Internet problems and discussion cases are available at http://ricchiute.swlearning.com

RESEARCH PROJECTS

1. Annual Reports and the Audit Process

Throughout an engagement, the independent auditor makes observations, documents evidence, confirms transactions, tests accounting data, compares recorded amounts, and makes many inquiries, all with a discerning eye toward the engagement's two major end products: audited financial statements and the auditor's report, both of which are printed within a corporation's annual report to shareholders. In short, the engagement proceeds forward to a discernible end. But much like a crime scene lends leads to a crime, so too does the annual report lend insight to the audit process. Much can be learned about audit practice from little more than management's annual report.

Required: Select an annual report for a publicly traded corporation and, from disclosures contained within the auditor's report, management's statement of responsibility for the financial statements, and the audited financial statements, draft a report that responds to each of the following:

1. For those expense captions identified explicitly on the income statement, which would likely have been audited by tests of details and which would likely have been subjected to analytical procedures only? Why?
2. Explain the accounting and disclosure issues likely underlying each reported accounting estimate and loss contingency.
3. Explain the disclosures, if any, made for related-party transactions. What likely motivated the transaction?
4. Explain the disclosures, if any, made for subsequent events, distinguishing between those that were Type I events and those that were Type II events.
5. Identify the transactions or events, if any, that likely were included in a legal letter. Explain information the auditor would have required from a lawyer to disclose the transactions or events adequately.
6. What disclosures included within the financial statements were likely included in management's representation letter?

2. Is This a Subsequent Event?

The daily financial press is replete with newsworthy releases that bear on the financial operations of publicly traded corporations. Not coincidentally, some of the releases translate to significant subsequent event disclosures in corporate financial statements since, after leaving the field, an auditor's first clue to a subsequent event often comes from news clippings.

Required: Using financial statements in EDGAR (**http://www.sec.gov**), the AICPA's *Accounting Trends and Techniques*, or copies of annual reports in a library, select the report for a publicly traded corporation that disclosed a material subsequent event. Using the newspaper file in LEXIS-NEXIS or recent copies of *The Wall Street Journal*, select an article you believe may translate to a material subsequent event for a publicly traded corporation. Draft a report that accomplishes the following:

1. For the annual report selected, explain the intuition underlying the subsequent event and whether the event is a Type I or Type II subsequent event.
2. For the article selected:
   a. Explain why you believe the article may translate to a Type I or Type II subsequent event.
   b. Draft the subsequent event footnote using as a guide the language in the disclosures you discuss in requirement 1 among other disclosures you may locate in LEXIS-NEXIS, *Accounting Trends and Techniques*, or the library.

Interactive quizzes are available as a student learning resource at
http://ricchiute.swlearning.com

Part 5

Other Assurance and Attestation Services, Compliance and Internal Auditing

Other Assurance and Attestation Services

Major topics discussed in this chapter are:

- **The AICPA Special Committee on Assurance Services' (the Elliott Committee) recommendations for assurance service opportunities.**
- **Assurance services for:**
  - **Electronic commerce.**
  - **Health care providers.**
- **Attestation services for:**
  - **Compilations and reviews of financial statements.**
  - **Interim financial information.**
  - **Comprehensive basis of accounting other than GAAP.**
  - **Specified elements, accounts, or items of a financial statement: GAAS and agreed-upon procedures.**
  - **Compliance with contractual requirements.**
  - **Letters for underwriters.**
  - **Financial forecasts and projections.**
  - **Personal financial statements.**
  - **Applications of accounting principles.**

Prior chapters introduced assurance services offered by Consumers Union (Chapters 1, 3) and public accounting firms (Chapters 1–3, 8, 10, 12, 15, 17). In addition, prior chapters illustrated a number of attestation services offered by public accounting firms—including services by PricewaterhouseCoopers for Wilson Sporting Goods' Ultra golf ball assertions (Chapters 1, 2), PricewaterhouseCoopers for Stanley H. Kaplan's SAT improvement assertions (Chapter 1) and the Deloitte & Touche/Gradient Technologies partnered service on Internet security (Chapter 8), among others. This chapter outlines recommendations of the AICPA Special Committee on Assurance Services (the Elliott Committee), introduces industry-specific assurance services offered by the public accounting profession for electronic commerce and for health care providers, and illustrates several common attestation services for which the profession has issued professional guidance.

Recall from Chapter 1 the distinction between assurance and attestation services: Assurance services improve (or report on) the quality of information; in contrast, attestation services are a type of assurance service in which the attestor—typically, a public accounting firm—offers assurance about subject matter that is the responsibility of another party. However, as the collected experience of practitioners in new markets increases, the distinction is likely to be less important. In fact, another equally useful way to think about assurance and attestation services in the public accounting profession is this: While attestation services have long been offered (for example, the AICPA's eleven attestation standards date back to 1986), assurance services are rather new.

Assurance Services

Professional Growth Through New Assurance Services, an interim report of the AICPA Special Committee on Assurance Services (the Elliott Committee), observes that the power to decide information content has shifted from the producers of information (for example, public companies) to the consumers of information (such as investors, creditors, and managers, among other informed decision makers), and that information technology enables dramatic change both in what decision makers demand and in what practitioners provide. What's more, although certified public accountants hold a regulated monopoly in the market for financial statement audit services, other professionals such as niche consultants will likely compete to provide nonregulated, consumer-driven assurance services. Public accounting firms have compelling economic incentives to enter—rather than ignore—the assurance services market, since the growth of individual firms may depend crucially on which firms succeed when the market clears. Does this mean that audited financial statements have no value? No, it means that in the information age, audited financial statements are only one part of the information mix that decision makers seek. It's no coincidence that the "auditing" departments of many public accounting firms are now called "assurance" departments.

The well-respected services of Consumers Union and Underwriters Laboratories aside, what new industry-specific value-added assurance services are likely to be demanded from public accounting firms? Figure 18-1 outlines six assurance services common in practice today. *Electronic commerce* services assure the authenticity and security of electronic transactions and communication, including digital-bank electronic payment cards, encryption systems, wide area computer

FIGURE 18-1: *AICPA Recommended Assurance Service Opportunities*

Electronic Commerce
Assuring the authenticity and security of electronic transactions and communication.

Health Care Performance
Assuring the effectiveness of health care organizations and reporting on systems and controls.

Risk Assessment
Assuring the quality of information about the likelihood and magnitude of adverse events.

Information Systems Reliability
Assuring information integrity and controls.

Business Performance
Assuring the relevance and reliability of performance measures.

Elder Care
Assuring the financial transactions and care of the elderly.

networks, and electronic systems software. *Health care performance* services assure the quality—and the outcomes—of services offered by health care organizations, including reports on information systems and controls. *Risk assessment* assurances report on the likelihood and magnitude of risks that entities bear (for example, in environmental practices). *Information systems reliability* services—arguably the most similar to the portfolio of professional services offered by public accounting firms in the past (see Chapter 8)—assure the integrity of information and controls. *Business performance* services assure the relevance and reliability of performance measures such as product market share, product warranty and quality guarantees, and benchmarking against leading competitors. Finally, *elder care* services assure the financial transactions of the elderly and monitor, for example, home health care contracts and nursing home services. The following two sections of the chapter offer illustrations for two of these services: electronic commerce and health care performance.

Electronic Commerce Assurances: WebTrust and SysTrust

Introduced in Chapter 8, electronic commerce and Internet technology have revolutionized the way that information is exchanged and business is transacted. The industrial age has given way to the information age and, correspondingly, to electronic commerce. For example, in the 1980s, large companies such as General Motors and Sears required that trading partners use *electronic data integration* (EDI, Chapter 6) to order and bill, marking the first evidence of electronic commerce actually ruling out paper transactions. EDI standards, developed in 1988 by the American National Standards Institute and called *ANSI X12*, allow trading partners to communicate in common electronic formats that accomplish an assortment of tasks without paper, including order entry, invoicing, claims filing, just-in-time inventory management, and rapid response to customer order patterns.

In the 1990s, electronic commerce penetrated larger markets, becoming available both to small companies and to retail customers in the form of electronic shopping, banking, entertainment, education, and financial networks on the Internet. Virtually any business transaction can be executed electronically and settled in digital cash, essentially eliminating the need for paper documents. However, the anonymity of electronic commerce also increases the risk of unauthorized surveillance and transmission failures, opening a new market for *data integrity* (for example, do processing systems alter transactions?) and *data security* (for example, do processing systems preclude unauthorized disclosure?) assurance services the profession is well positioned to offer. For example, in a data security assurance service, a practitioner offers assurances that:

- Parties to a transaction are authentic, and
- Transactions and documents are protected.

However, like the attestation and audit service engagements introduced earlier in the text, a practitioner needs a set of *criteria* against which to measure authenticity and protection. For example, in an attestation service for internal control (Chapter 8), the measurement criteria appear in the Committee on Sponsoring Organization's (COSO) 1992 report, *Internal Control: Integrated Framework*, which provides evaluation tools for the control environment, risk assessment, control activities, information and communication, and monitoring. In contrast, to date there are no generally accepted data-security measurement criteria, suggesting that the profession could either develop—or partner with other professions to develop— say, *Data-Security Standards in Telecommunications*.

Although characterized by the AICPA as an attest service, the profession in 1999 mandated criteria in the market for data integrity services: the *WebTrust*[1] seal of assurance, a business-to-consumer (as opposed to business-to-business) assurance service partnered jointly by the American Institute of CPAs (AICPA) and the Canadian Institute of Chartered Accountants (CICA). Called CPA WebTrust in the United States (and CA WebTrust in Canada), the service offers consumers comfort about the business practices, transaction integrity, and information protection of companies that market products over the Internet. The WebTrust seal of assurance—literally an icon on an electronic commerce provider's Web site—symbolizes to customers that a CPA (or CA in Canada) has issued an unqualified opinion that the provider has abided by all three of the WebTrust principles:

WebTrust Principle	*The Company:*
● Business Practices:	Discloses, and executes transactions in accordance with, its business practices for electronic commerce.
● Transaction Integrity:	Maintains effective controls to provide reasonable assurance that customers' electronic transactions are completed and billed as agreed.
● Information Protection:	Maintains effective controls to provide reasonable assurance that private customer information is protected.

An example of a CPA WebTrust unqualified opinion appears in Figure 18-2.

In 2000, the profession rolled out *SysTrust*,[2] a data security service that speaks to the reliability of a company's information system. Also partnered jointly by the AICPA and CICA, SysTrust offers management comfort about the availability, security, integrity, and maintainability of a company's information system. The SysTrust seal of assurance symbolizes that a CPA has issued an unqualified opinion and that the company has abided by all four of the SysTrust principles:

SysTrust Principle	*The Company's System:*
● Availability:	Is available for operation and use at times set forth in service agreements.
● Security:	Is protected against unauthorized physical and logical access.
● Integrity:	Is complete, accurate, timely, and authorized.
● Maintainability:	Can be updated when required in a manner that continues to provide for system availability, security, and integrity.

In practice, WebTrust and SysTrust work in tandem to assure seamless data integrity and data security reliability within and between businesses. For example, consider three downstream processing companies in the oil industry: Company A explores for crude oil, Company B refines oil, and Company C markets oil-product additives. Assuming all three purchase WebTrust and SysTrust services, all three would rely internally on SysTrust for data reliability and Companies B and C would rely on the WebTrust seals held by Companies A and B, respectively, for data integrity.

---

1 For a more complete discussion of WebTrust, see **http://www.aicpa.org**.
2 For a more complete discussion of SysTrust, see **http://www.aicpa.org**.

FIGURE 18-2: *Independent Assurer's Report on WebTrust Assurance Services*

We have examined the assertion by management of L. Altman, Inc., regarding disclosure of its electronic commerce business practices on its Web site and the effectiveness of its controls over transaction integrity and information protection for electronic commerce (**http://www.laltman.com**) during the period August 1, 2007 through October 31, 2007.

These electronic commerce disclosures and controls are the responsibility of L. Altman, Inc., management. Our responsibility is to express an opinion on management's assertions with regards to the AICPA/CICA WebTrust criteria based on our examination.

Our examination was conducted in accordance with attestation standards established by the American Institute of Certified Public Accountants and, accordingly, included:

(1) obtaining an understanding of L. Altman's electronic commerce business practices and its controls over the processing of electronic commerce transactions and the protection of related private customer information, (2) selectively testing transactions executed in accordance with disclosed business practices, (3) testing and evaluating the operating effectiveness of the controls, and (4) performing such other procedures as we considered necessary in the circumstances. We believe that our examination provides a reasonable basis for our opinion.

Because of inherent limitations in controls, errors or fraud may occur and not be detected. Furthermore, the projection of any conclusions, based on our findings, to future periods is subject to the risk that (1) changes made to the system or controls, (2) changes in processing requirements, or (3) changes required because of the passage of time may alter the validity of such conclusions.

In our opinion, during the period August 1, 2007 through October 31, 2007, L. Altman, Inc., in all material respects:

- Disclosed its business practices for electronic commerce transactions and executed those transactions in accordance with its disclosed business practices,
- Maintained effective controls to provide reasonable assurance that customers' transactions using electronic commerce were completed and billed as agreed, and
- Maintained effective controls to provide reasonable assurance that private customer information obtained as a result of electronic commerce was protected from uses not related to L. Altman's business based on the AICPA/CICA WebTrust criteria.

The CPA WebTrust seal of assurance on L. Altman's Web site for electronic commerce constitutes a symbolic representation of the contents of this report and it is not intended, nor should it be construed, to update this report or provide any additional assurance.

This report does not include any representation as to the quality of L. Altman's goods or services nor their suitability for any customer's intended purpose.

Assuming measurement criteria are available and data security risk drives sufficient demand, the profession could offer assurances on digital electronic bank payment cards ("smart cards"), on EDI security, on Internet commerce software and transactions, and on digital authorization and signature verification, among a host of other things. Interestingly, some practitioners within the profession already offer some of these services. For example, Deloitte & Touche and Thurston Group, Inc., a private merchant bank in Chicago, entered into a joint venture, called NetDox, Inc. NetDox uses Internet capability and encryption technology to transmit electronically legal briefs, insurance forms, financial documents, and other confidential information that had been delivered by overnight mail to avoid data surveillance and to ensure confirmation of receipt.[3] NetDox bundles transmission software with email services that enable subscribers to route electronic documents through NetDox and that enables NetDox to track delivery, retain an electronic thumbprint of the transmission, and assure the security of the transmission. Joint ventures, such as NetDox, offer public accounting firms an important means to overcome competition and to enjoy economies of scale. For example, barriers to the profession's entry into the data security assurance service market could likely come from several formidable sources, among them competition from major electronic service providers such as Microsoft.

Health Care Assurances and Core Competencies

Interestingly, public accounting firms of all sizes—from Big Four to local firms—are designing and marketing creative assurance services, and some are offering value-added services in conjunction with financial statement audits. Three examples follow from the health care industry.

First, owing to accusations about three doctors' irregular research and billing practices, the University of California at San Diego engaged KPMG to lend assurance about the quality of the university's fertility research program.[4] Among other things, the firm investigated whistle-blowers' allegations of false insurance claims, unjustifiable billings for physicians in training, and whether viable embryos were used illegally in clinical research. The university could have relied on an internal investigation, but leveraged instead on the credibility of a Big Four firm to win back public confidence.

Second, Moss Adams, a prominent West Coast firm, offers a variety of benchmarking assurances to health care providers throughout the country.[5] For example, Moss Adams compiles financial and productivity data and then benchmarks the relative performance of physicians' groups for health maintenance organizations. Interestingly, Moss Adams enjoys a presence in other industry-specific assurance markets as well—for example, performance measurement in the apparel, forest products, and financial institutions industries—making them an important example of a regional firm that demonstrates leadership in new product development.

Third, have you ever had need for a health care provider: a hospital, a specialist, managed care? How did you—how does anybody—select among them? Most rely on word of mouth or on published reports of local data, such as *The Cleveland Area Hospital Quality Outcome Measurements and Patient Satisfaction Report*. Others have the benefit of large employers who rate the quality of employee health care. For example, Marriott, PepsiCo, and Xerox demand and rate outcome data from health maintenance organizations (HMOs); GTE prepares an elaborate report card from employee medical records and physician interviews; and USAir compiles and compares employee and national treatment data.[6] What is clear is that there

3   D. Bank, "Deloitte & Touche Auditors to Account for E-Mail Delivery with NetDox Inc." *The Wall Street Journal* (January 30, 1997), p. B2.

4   L. Berton, "Accountants Expand Scope of Audit Work," *The Wall Street Journal* (June 17, 1996), pp. B1, B8.

5   G. Cheney, "Regional Firm Hits National Market with New Assurance Services," *Accounting Today* (January 6–19, 1997), pp. 3, 9.

6   *Business Week* (April 8, 1996), p. 74.

is a need, and a demand, for health care provider assurances, since over $3 trillion is spent annually on health care in the United States.

Two decades ago, certified public accountants came to the table armed with a well-defined set of competencies, among them knowledge of generally accepted accounting principles and generally accepted auditing standards, a facility in the ways of evaluating evidence, a deft sense of how to manage risk, and tact in engaging and retaining clients. The next two decades will require this *plus* a much broader set of core competencies that make clear the CPA's capability to contribute value. Adapted from the report of the Special Committee on Assurance Services' Subcommittee on Competencies, Figure 18-3 lists some core competencies for the twenty-first century. Although some of the competencies are attained in preprofessional curricula, the bulk are attained from nothing short of a concentrated commitment to lifelong learning.

FIGURE 18-3: *Core Competencies for Assurance Services*

Administrative Capability
An understanding of practice economics, financial management, staffing and staff development, managing financial return on professional engagements.

Analytical Skills
Search and research skills, systems analysis and review, analytic models to support professional judgment, recognizing and understanding anomalies, knowing what should be there and sensing what is not.

Business Advisory Skills
Applying technical knowledge to insightful recommendations, seeing solutions to complex problems, taking intellectual risks to create ideas that help clients achieve their objectives.

Communication Skills
Express ideas clearly and unambiguously, collaborate on decision-making teams, lead discussion, inspire confidence.

Intellectual Capability
Challenge conventional thinking, imagination, diagnostic thinking.

Marketing and Selling
Develop credentials in a market or industry, draft compelling service proposals, offer value, close.

Model Building and Technology
Understand methods and databases to measure performance and outcomes unambiguously, master relevant technologies.

People Development
Offer coaching and feedback, allocate tasks to capable staff, project positive role model for subordinates and peers.

Relationship Management
Understand client needs, leverage relationships through coordination and interaction, establish and maintain credibility with key decision makers.

Capacity for Work
Strong work ethic, calm in the face of demanding pressure.

Attestation Services

Following are several common attestation services for which the profession has issued professional guidance, including *Statements on Standards for Attestation Services* and *Statements on Auditing Standards*.

Compilations and Reviews of Unaudited Financial Statements

What assurances can a practitioner offer about unaudited financial statements? Actually, the level of assurance has changed over the years. Prior to the 1980s, despite guidance in the now superseded *Statement on Auditing Procedure No. 38*, "Unaudited Financial Statements," and an AICPA *Guide for Engagements to Prepare Unaudited Financial Statements*, services for unaudited statements confused users and practitioners. Some users, such as small lending institutions, believed that practitioners must have applied "some" procedures to prepare unaudited statements: maybe not enough to issue an opinion, but certainly enough to offer minimum assurances. And some practitioners were uncertain about the extent of procedures to apply: Should they apply any at all, and what could they say about what they had done?

The confusion led to two problems: First, some small companies were denied access to the commercial-capital market, since the companies were unable to afford the audits that lending institutions demanded. Second, some users placed more reliance on the unaudited statements than practitioners intended, resulting in a considerable number of legal liability cases, among them *1136 Tenants' Corp. v. Max Rothenberg & Co.* (Chapter 5). In response, the AICPA held meetings with the American Bankers Association, prompting two new financial statement services: a *review* of financial statements (introduced in Chapter 1), which provides less assurance than an audit; and a *compilation* of financial statements, which provides no assurance at all (and, therefore, is not an attestation service). The *Accounting and Review Services Committee's* (Chapter 1) *Statements on Standards for Accounting and Review Services* (SSARS), particularly *SSARS No. 1*, provide guidance for performing compilation and review services for nonpublic companies.

In a **review engagement**, an attestation service performed under the AICPA's attestation standards (Chapter 2), the independent accountant performs analytical procedures, makes inquiries of management, and issues a report that provides *negative assurance*, using language that states the accountant is "not aware of any material modifications that should be made to the financial statements in order for them to be in conformity with GAAP." Note the subtle difference between an audit report and a review report: An audit report (Chapter 3) gives *positive assurance* (". . . the financial statements present fairly . . . in conformity with GAAP"), whereas a review report gives only *negative assurance* (". . . not aware of . . . modifications that should be made"). Because review engagements require less work (that is, analytical procedures and inquiries, rather than audit procedures), reviews are less costly and are usually requested by small, owner-managed companies. For example, when evaluating commercial loan applications, banks will often rely on the negative assurance provided by a review report, rather than demand that an applicant produce the positive assurance of a far more expensive audit report, a demand they made freely prior to *SSARS No. 1*.

In a **compilation engagement**, the accountant compiles financial statements from management's unaudited and unreviewed accounts, and issues a report that provides literally no assurance. The service merely compiles financial statements in proper form, but is useful to rather small owner-managed companies that elect to outsource the preparation of financial statements rather than to employ accounting personnel internally. Specifically, a compilation report states that the accountant "has not audited or reviewed the financial statements and, accordingly, does not express an opinion or any form of assurance." Compilation services are less costly than reviews and are often selected by small companies that have neither the expertise to prepare financial statements nor the need for assurances.

Like a financial statement audit, a practitioner needs to be independent to perform a review engagement, but need not be to perform a compilation. Each service is discussed more fully next.

Compilation of Financial Statements

A **compilation of financial statements** consists of "presenting in the form of financial statements information that is the representation of management *without undertaking to express any assurance* on the statements."[7] In a compilation engagement, an accountant compiles unaudited financial statements but offers no assurances about whether the statements are presented in conformity with GAAP. Even though compilations require no audit procedures and no expression of assurance, *SSARS No. 1*, "Compilation and Review of Financial Statements," recognizes that, because of potential liability, an accountant might feel uncomfortable compiling financial statements unless he or she also performs other accounting services for the client, such as general ledger bookkeeping.

When engaged to compile financial statements, an accountant develops:

- Knowledge about accounting principles and practices in the entity's industry, and
- An understanding of the entity's transactions, accounting records, and the qualifications of accounting personnel.

Although an accountant is not required to perform any audit procedures, he or she may become aware of errors, omissions, or other deficiencies in information that management supplies. For example, a remarkably high gross margin may suggest a company did not record the companion cost of sales entry for each recorded sale, thereby requiring that the accountant obtain additional information. If the client refuses to provide necessary information, the accountant should withdraw from the engagement.

Compiled financial statements are accompanied by an accountant's report dated as of the day the compilation was completed. The report describes the scope of the accountant's work, includes a statement about the nature and limitations of a compilation, and states explicitly that an audit was not performed and an opinion is not expressed. A standard compilation report follows.

Accountant's Compilation Report

The accompanying balance sheet of Tolman Company is of December 31, 2007, and the related statements of income, retained earnings, and cash flows for the year then ended have been compiled by us.

A compilation is limited to presenting in the form of financial statements information that is the representation of management (owners). We have not au-

---

7   Accounting and Review Services Committee, *Statement on Standards for Accounting and Review Services No. 1*, "Compilation and Review of Financial Statements." New York: AICPA, 1978, par. 4.

dited or reviewed the accompanying financial statements and, accordingly, do not express an opinion or any other form of assurance on them.

Source: SSARS No. 1.

Each page of the compiled financial statements should include a reference such as "See Accountant's Compilation Report." If not independent of a client, an accountant may still compile statements, although the last paragraph of the report should read, "We are not independent with respect to X Company."

Even though a compilation does not require determining whether financial statements conform with GAAP, an accountant may nevertheless become aware of material departures. For example, a client may have capitalized research and development costs even though FASB *Statement of Financial Accounting Standards No. 2,* "Accounting for Research and Development Costs," requires they be charged as period expenses. If a client does not revise the statements to conform with GAAP, the accountant considers revising the standard compilation report. To illustrate, assume Fallon Company's financial statements disclose land at appraised value rather than cost. The second paragraph should be expanded and a new paragraph added to the standard compilation report as follows:

Independent Accountant's Compilation Report: Departure from GAAP
. . . However, we did become aware of a departure from generally accepted accounting principles that is described in the following paragraph.

As disclosed in note 2 to the financial statements, generally accepted accounting principles require that land be stated at cost. Management has informed us that Fallon Company has stated its land at appraised value and that, if GAAP had been followed, the land account and stockholders' equity would have been decreased by $_____.

Source: SSARS No. 1.

Review of Financial Statements

A **review of financial statements** consists of "performing inquiry and analytical procedures that provide the accountant with a reasonable basis for expressing negative assurance that there are no material modifications that should be made to the statements in order for them to be in conformity with GAAP or, if applicable, with another comprehensive basis of accounting."[8] Thus, on the basis of inquiry and analytical procedures, an accountant expresses negative assurance: more assurance than a compilation report, but less than an audit report. Owing to the potential for legal liability, an accountant might feel uncomfortable reviewing financial statements unless he or she also performs a compilation or another accounting service for a review client.

Ordinarily, an accountant's analytical procedures and inquiries consist of the following.

- Analytical procedures that may identify unusual matters, such as:
  - Comparing current with comparable prior-period financial statements,
  - Comparing financial statements with budgets and forecasts, and

---

8 Accounting and Review Services Committee, *Statement on Standards for Accounting and Review Services No. 1,* "Compilation and Review of Financial Statements." New York: AICPA, 1978, par. 4.

- Studying relationships between financial statement elements expected to conform with predictable patterns (for example, Sales and Accounts Receivable).
- Inquiries about the entity's accounting principles and practices, and about procedures for recording, classifying, summarizing, and disclosing transactions in the financial statements.
- Inquiries about actions taken at meetings of shareholders and the board of directors.
- Considering whether the financial statements appear to conform with GAAP.
- Obtaining reports from other accountants engaged to audit or review a subsidiary's financial statements.
- Inquiries of persons responsible for financial and accounting matters concerning:
  - Whether the financial statements have been prepared in accordance with GAAP,
  - Changes in the entity's business or accounting principles,
  - Questions that arose when performing inquiry and analytical procedures, and
  - Subsequent events that have a material effect on the financial statements.

As with compilations, reviewed financial statements should be accompanied by an accountant's report dated as of the day the review was completed. The report should state that a review was performed in accordance with AICPA standards and that the financial statements are the representations of management. The nature of a review should be described, and the report should expressly state that the scope of a review is substantially less than an audit. A standard review report follows.

Independent Accountant's Review Report

We have reviewed the accompanying balance sheet of Goff Company as of December 31, 2007, and the related statements of income, retained earnings, and cash flows for the year then ended, in accordance with Statements on Standards for Accounting and Review Services issued by the American Institute of Certified Public Accountants. All information included in these financial statements is the representation of management of Goff Company.

A review consists principally of inquiries of company personnel and analytical procedures applied to financial data. It is substantially less in scope than an audit in accordance with generally accepted auditing standards, the objective of which is the expression of an opinion regarding the financial statements taken as a whole. Accordingly, we do not express such an opinion.

Based on our review, we are not aware of any material modifications that should be made to the accompanying financial statements in order for them to be in conformity with generally accepted accounting principles.

Source: SSARS No. 1 and SSARS No. 7.

Each page of the reviewed financial statements should include a reference such as "See Accountant's Review Report."

A review does not provide a basis for determining whether financial statements conform with GAAP. But when an accountant becomes aware of material departures from GAAP, the financial statements are revised or the report modified. The following illustrates a modified review report assuming a departure from GAAP.

Independent Accountant's Review Report: Departure from GAAP

(First two paragraphs unchanged)

Based on our review, with the exception of the matter described in the following paragraph, we are not aware of any material modifications . . .

As disclosed in note X to the financial statements, generally accepted accounting principles require that inventory cost consist of material, labor, and overhead. Management has informed us that the inventory of finished goods and work in process is stated in the accompanying financial statements at material and labor cost only, and that the effects of this departure from generally accepted accounting principles on financial position, results of operations, and changes in financial position have not been determined.

Source: SSARS No. 1.

Interim Financial Statements

Prior to 2000, reviews by independent accountants of a public company's financial statements were voluntary.[9] However, beginning in 2000, the SEC's *Final Rules: Audit Committee Disclosure* require that a public company's quarterly financial statements (*Form 10-Q*) be reviewed, in part because ". . . earnings management could be deterred by imposing more discipline of the process of preparing interim financial information . . ."[10] *SAS No. 100*, "Interim Financial Information," provides guidance on interim review procedures and on reporting, but allows a practitioner to express negative assurance only, not an opinion, on interim financial information. That is, the accountant states whether he or she is *aware of any material modifications necessary to conform the information with GAAP*, not whether the statements actually do conform with GAAP, since the limited inquiries and analytical procedures prescribed by *SAS No. 100* are not adequate to form an opinion on the quarterly financial statements.

Interim Review Procedures

Compared to annual financial statement audits, practitioners typically have far less time available to assemble **interim financial statements**. As a result, costs, expenses, deferrals, and accruals are often estimated to a greater extent in interim than in annual financial statements.

A review of interim financial information under *SAS No. 100* consists primarily of analytical procedures and inquiries that include:

- Analytical procedures that may identify unusual matters, including:
  - Comparing interim financial information with the immediate preceding interim period and with corresponding prior periods;

---

9   Based on data from 238 companies that voluntarily purchased 10-Q quarterly reviews and 133 companies that had 10-K reviews, one study found that voluntary purchasers tended to be larger (total assets), have more business segments, spend more on internal auditing, and have more shares owned by officers and directors. (M. Ettridge, D. Simon, D. Smith, and M. Stone, "Why Do Companies Purchase Timely Quarterly Reviews?" *Journal of Accounting and Economics* (September 1995).

10 Securities and Exchange Commission, *Final Rule: Audit Committee Disclosure.* Washington, D.C.: SEC, 1999.

- Considering plausible relationships between both financial data (for example, sales to cost of sales) and nonfinancial data (for example, payroll expense to number of employees);
  - Comparing recorded amounts, or ratios calculated from recorded amounts, to budgets, forecasts, and industry gross margin information; and
  - Comparing disaggregated revenue information—for example, by segment or product line—with comparable prior periods.
- Inquiries about internal control, including significant changes.
- Reading the minutes of shareholders' and directors' meetings to identify actions that may affect the interim financial information.
- Considering whether the interim financial information conforms with GAAP.
- Obtaining reports from other accountants engaged to review a subsidiary's financial information.
- Inquiries of personnel responsible for financial and accounting matters concerning:
  - Whether the interim financial information has been prepared in accordance with GAAP,
  - Changes in business activities and accounting principles,
  - Matters about which questions have arisen, and
  - Events subsequent to the date of interim financial information that would have a material effect on the information.
- Obtaining written representations from management.

Note that these procedures are substantially less in scope, and require far less work, than an audit: The auditor's effort is limited to analytical procedures and inquiries, rather than to search and verification procedures.

Reporting on a Separate Interim Period

An accountant's report accompanies reviewed interim financial information and includes a statement that the review was made in accordance with AICPA standards. The report identifies the interim financial information reviewed, describes the nature of procedures performed, and states that the scope of a review is substantially less than an audit. Interestingly, the three paragraphs of the interim review report communicate a similar message in substantially similar language to that of a *SSARS No. 1* review report, illustrated earlier, but note carefully that the interim review procedures contemplated by *SAS No. 100* actually impose somewhat more extensive requirements on the independent accountant than does a *SSARS No. 1* review. For example, unlike *SSARS No. 1*, *SAS No. 100* requires inquiries about an entity's internal controls and analytical procedures that compare recorded amounts (or ratios calculated from recorded amounts) to expectations the accountant develops. A review report KPMG issued for PepsiCo, Inc., follows.

Independent Accountant's Report on Interim Financial Information

The Board of Directors

PepsiCo, Inc.

We have reviewed the accompanying Condensed Consolidated Balance Sheet of PepsiCo, Inc. and Subsidiaries as of September 6, 2003 and the related Condensed Consolidated Statements of Income and Comprehensive Income for the twelve and thirty-six weeks ended September 6, 2003 and September 7, 2002 and the Condensed Consolidated Statement of Cash Flows for the thirty-six weeks ended September 6, 2003 and September 7, 2002. These condensed consolidated financial statements are the responsibility of PepsiCo, Inc.'s management.

We conducted our review in accordance with standards established by the American Institute of Certified Public Accountants. A review of interim financial information consists principally of applying analytical procedures and making inquiries of persons responsible for financial and accounting matters. It is substantially less in scope than an audit conducted in accordance with auditing standards generally accepted in the United States of America, the objective of which is the expression of an opinion regarding the financial statements taken as a whole. Accordingly, we do not express such an opinion.

Based on our review, we are not aware of any material modifications that should be made to the condensed consolidated financial statements referred to above for them to be in conformity with accounting principles generally accepted in the United States of America.

As discussed in *Basis of Presentation and Our Divisions* in the Notes to the Condensed Consolidated Financial Statements, PepsiCo, Inc. changed the reporting calendar from months to fiscal periods for certain of its businesses. Prior year quarterly results have been restated for this change.

We have previously audited, in accordance with auditing standards generally accepted in the United States of America, the Consolidated Balance Sheet of PepsiCo, Inc. and Subsidiaries as of December 28, 2002, and the related Consolidated Statements of Income, Common Shareholders' Equity and Cash Flows for the year then ended not presented herein; and in our report dated February 6, 2003, we expressed an unqualified opinion on those consolidated financial statements. In our opinion, the information set forth in the accompanying Condensed Consolidated Balance Sheet as of December 28, 2002, is fairly presented, in all material respects, in relation to the Consolidated Balance Sheet from which it has been derived.

KPMG LLP
New York, New York

October 7, 2003

As in compilations and reviews under *SSARS No. 1*, a review of interim financial information may reveal a material departure from GAAP, even though no audit procedures are performed. If a client does not revise the interim financial information, the accountant should consider revising the standard review report, describing the nature of the departure, and the effect on interim information. For example, assume a client excludes certain lease obligations from assets and liabilities that should be capitalized in accordance with FASB *Statement No. 13*, "Accounting for Leases." Modifications to the standard review report follow.

**Independent Accountant's Report on Interim
Financial Information: Departure from GAAP**

(First two paragraphs unchanged)

Based on information furnished to us by management, we believe that the Company has excluded from property and debt in the accompanying balance sheet certain lease obligations that should be capitalized to conform with accounting principles generally accepted in the United States. This information indicates that if lease obligations were capitalized at September 30, 2007, property would be increased by $\_\_\_\_\_$, long-term debt by $\_\_\_\_\_$, and net income and earnings per share would be increased (decreased) by $\_\_\_\_\_$, $\_\_\_\_\_$, $\_\_\_\_\_$, and $\_\_\_\_\_$, respectively, for the three-month and nine-month periods then ended.

Based on our review, with the exception of the matter described in the preceding paragraph, we are not aware of any material modifications . . .

Source: SAS No. 100.

Interim Information Accompanying Audited Statements

SAS No. 100 also addresses the effect on a standard audit report when unaudited interim financial information accompanies audited financial statements. SEC *Regulation S-K, Item 302(a)* requires that quarterly sales, income, and earnings per share data be presented as supplementary information outside the audited financial statements or in an unaudited note to the statements. An independent auditor should review the interim information in accordance with the procedures outlined earlier. However, a separate report is not issued, and a standard audit report need not refer to the quarterly information, unless the information is either omitted or not reviewed, in which case the audit report should be modified (called "exception reporting").

Comprehensive Bases of Accounting Other Than GAAP

For some entities, financial statements prepared in accordance with GAAP may be less telling than statements prepared on another comprehensive basis of accounting. For example, not-for-profit philanthropic organizations may be better served by the cash basis of accounting, and utility rate-making commissions may consider themselves better served when state-regulated utilities prepare financial statements in conformity with the commission's prescribed chart of accounts. *SAS No. 62*, "Special Reports" (AU Sec. 623), identifies four generally accepted, comprehensive bases of accounting:

- Cash receipts and disbursements basis of accounting.
- A basis of accounting used to comply with a regulatory agency's requirements.
- A basis of accounting used to file income tax returns.
- A set of criteria having substantial support (for example, price-level adjusted financial statements).

These are the *only* four generally accepted comprehensive bases of accounting. Stated another way, any other bases of accounting, among them bases designed to portray a wholly unrealistic financial position, should be interpreted by an auditor as a departure from GAAP, thereby requiring that the auditor issue a qualified opinion or, if materiality warrants, an adverse opinion (Chapter 3).

If an entity's financial statements are presented on a generally accepted comprehensive basis other than GAAP, an accountant's report should include:

- A title that includes the word *independent*, and
- Separate paragraphs stating the:
  - Statements were audited and are management's responsibility,
  - Audit complied with GAAS,
  - Comprehensive basis of accounting, and

- Auditor's opinion on whether the financial statements conform to the comprehensive basis of accounting.

A report on cash basis financial statements follows.

OCBOA (handwritten)

**Independent Auditor's Report on
Cash Basis Financial Statements**

No I/S or Balance Sheet (handwritten, in margin)

1 (handwritten) We have audited the statements of assets and liabilities arising from cash transactions of Slater Company as of December 31, 2007, and the related statement of revenue collected and expenses paid for the year then ended. These financial statements are the responsibility of the company's management. Our responsibility is to express an opinion on these statements based on our audit.

2 (handwritten) We conducted our audit in accordance with generally accepted auditing standards. Those standards require that we plan and perform the audit to obtain reasonable assurance about whether the financial statements are free of material misstatement. An audit includes examining, on a test basis, evidence supporting the amounts and disclosures in the financial statements. An audit also includes assessing the accounting principles used and significant estimates made by management, as well as evaluating the overall financial statement presentation. We believe that our audits provide a reasonable basis for our opinion.

3 (handwritten) As described in note 1, these financial statements were prepared on the basis of cash receipts and disbursements, which is a comprehensive basis of accounting other than generally accepted accounting principles.

4 (handwritten) In our opinion, the financial statements referred to above present fairly, in all material respects, the assets and liabilities arising from cash transactions of Slater Company as of December 31, 2007, and the revenue collected and expenses paid during the year then ended, on the basis of accounting described in note 1.

Source: SAS No. 62.

Specified Elements, Accounts, or Items of a Financial Statement and Nonfinancial Statement Assertions

An independent accountant may be engaged to attest to specified financial statement elements, accounts, or items within an entity's financial statements, as opposed to an entire set of financial statements taken as a whole. Generally, these engagements either:

- Apply *generally accepted auditing standards* and express an *opinion*, or
- Apply *agreed-upon procedures* and express *limited assurance*.

GAAS

Compliance with contractual agreements sometimes requires that an entity provide an opinion, rather than a review or compilation report, on a specified financial statement item, such as gross sales. For example, a retailer's lease agreement with a shopping mall may tie rental payments to gross sales (for example, 2 percent of sales), thereby requiring that the retailer engage an independent auditor to report on gross sales only, rather than financial position, results of operations, and cash flows, as in a typical financial statement audit. When an independent accountant is engaged to express an opinion on specified financial statement items, the report should describe the scope of the engagement; identify the elements, accounts, or items audited; and state the auditor's opinion. The following illustrates a restricted-use report (*SAS No. 87*, "Restricting the Use of an Auditor's Report") expressing an unqualified opinion on gross sales.

> **Independent Auditor's Report on Gross Sales for the Purpose of Computing Rental Payments**
>
> We have audited the accompanying schedule of gross sales (as defined in the lease agreement dated March 4, 2007, between Fain & Company, as lessor, and Anderson Little Stores Corporation, as lessee) of Anderson Little Stores Corporation at its North Main Street store, Pawtucket, Rhode Island, for the year ended December 31, 2007. This schedule is the responsibility of Anderson Little Stores Corporation's management. Our responsibility is to express an opinion on the schedule based on our audit.
>
> We conducted our audit in accordance with generally accepted auditing standards. Those standards require that we plan and perform the audit to obtain reasonable assurance about whether the schedule of gross sales is free of material misstatement. An audit includes examining, on a test basis, evidence supporting the amounts and disclosures in the schedule. An audit also includes assessing the accounting principles used and significant estimates made by management, as well as evaluating the overall schedule presentation. We believe that our audit provides a reasonable basis for our opinion.
>
> In our opinion, the schedule of gross sales referred to above presents fairly, in all material respects, the gross sales of Anderson Little Stores Corporation at its North Main Street store, Pawtucket, Rhode Island, for the year ended December 31, 2007, in conformity with the basis specified in the lease agreement referred to above.
>
> This report is intended solely for the information and use of the boards of directors and managements of Anderson Little Stores Corporation and Fain & Company and is not intended to be and should not be used by anyone other than these specified parties.
>
> *Source: SAS No. 62 as amended by SAS No. 87.*

Agreed-Upon Procedures

In contrast, an independent accountant may be engaged to apply agreed-upon procedures—that is, procedures that are insufficient to express an opinion either on the item or, for that matter, on the financial statements from which the item was taken. For example, the *Federal Depository Insurance Corporation (FDIC) Improvement Act of 1991*, a response to the savings and loan industry debacle of the 1980s, requires insured depository institutions to have independent accountants perform agreed-upon procedures that test a bank's compliance with the FDIC's "safety and soundness" laws and regulations. The FDIC laws and regulations relate primarily to loans made to insiders and to dividend requirements. The agreed-upon procedures were developed jointly by representatives of both the AICPA and the banking profession. However, in most other agreed-upon procedures engagements, the procedures are engagement-specific and are drafted by the independent accountant and by what the profession calls the "specified users" (the client and other beneficiaries of the accountant's report).

Under *SSAE No. 10*, "Attestation Standards: Revision and Recodification," agreed-upon procedures can be applied to management's written or unwritten assertions. For example, management may have made a written assertion that "all investment securities owned by Hendriken Corporation during 2007 were traded on exchanges specified in the company's investment policy," or that "employee evaluations included in personnel files as of September 30, 2007, are dated within the time frame prescribed by the company and the United Auto Workers, Local 317." In contrast, management may have made an unwritten assertion that a municipality's property and equipment records are recorded properly in an enterprise fund under a modified accrual basis of accounting.

Practitioners provide *limited*, but not *negative*, assurance in both engagements. *Limited assurance* means the accountant makes a direct positive statement—for example, "We found no difference," or "We found no exceptions." In contrast, *negative assurance* means the accountant makes a negative statement—for example, "We are not aware . . .," or "Nothing came to our attention. . . ." In practice, negative assurance is reserved for review-level engagements. A limited-assurance report on agreed-upon procedures includes:

- A title that includes the word *independent*.
- The names of the specified users and a statement that the users agreed to the procedures.
- Reference to the assertion and to the character of the engagement.
- Reference to standards established by the AICPA.
- A statement that the sufficiency of the procedures is solely the responsibility of the specified users and a disclaimer of responsibility for the sufficiency of the procedures.
- A list of the procedures performed and the findings.
- A statement that the accountant was not engaged to perform an audit, a disclaimer of opinion on the effectiveness of internal control, and a statement restricting the use of the report.

An illustration of a restricted-use report follows.

Independent Accountant's Report
on Agreed-Upon Procedures

We have performed the procedures described below, which were agreed-upon by the Trustee of LaSalle Company, solely to assist you in evaluating the accompanying Schedule of Claims of Creditors to determine the validity of the claims of LaSalle Company as of May 31, 2007. This agreed-upon procedures engagement was performed in accordance with standards established by the American Institute of Certified Public Accountants. The sufficiency of these procedures is solely the responsibility of the Trustee of LaSalle Company. Consequently, we make no representations regarding the sufficiency of the procedures described below either for the purpose for which this report has been requested or for any other purpose. The procedures and associated findings are as follows:

1. Compare the total of the trial balance of accounts payable at May 31, 2007, prepared by LaSalle Company, to the balance in the related general ledger account.

The total of the accounts payable trial balance agreed with the balance in the related general ledger account.

2. Compare the amounts for claims received from creditors (as shown in claim documents provided by LaSalle Company) to the respective amounts shown

in the trial balance of accounts payable. Using the data included in the claims documents and in LaSalle Company's accounts payable detail records, reconcile any differences found to the accounts payable trial balance.

All differences noted are presented in column 3 of the Schedule. Except for those amounts shown in column 4 of the Schedule, all differences were reconciled.

3. Examine the documentation submitted by creditors in support of the amounts claimed and compare to the following documentation in LaSalle Company's files: invoices, receiving reports, and other evidence of receipt of goods or services.

No exceptions were found as a result of these comparisons.

We were not engaged to, and did not, perform an audit, the objective of which would be the expression of an opinion on the specified elements, accounts, or items. Accordingly, we do not express such as opinion. Had we performed additional procedures, other matters might have come to our attention that would have been reported to you.

This report is intended solely for the use of the Trustee of LaSalle Company and is not intended to be and should not be used by anyone other than those specified parties who have agreed to the procedures and taken responsibility for the sufficiency of the procedures for their purposes.

Source: SAS No. 75 and SAS No. 87.

Reports on Compliance with Contractual Agreements or Regulatory Requirements

An audit client also may engage an auditor to attest to management's compliance with contractual agreements such as bond indentures, loan agreements, or government grant-reporting requirements. An engagement to report on compliance with contractual agreements usually arises when an audit client has borrowed funds and entered into a contractual arrangement that imposes a requirement on the borrower to make payments into a sinking fund, to maintain a minimum current ratio, or to restrict dividend payments to shareholders. An auditor's reporting obligation under *SAS No. 62,* "Special Reports" (AU Sec. 623), is to provide assurance either in a separate report or in a paragraph within the standard audit report, although the auditor should not express assurance unless the financial statements have been audited. A separate restricted-use report on compliance with a contractual agreement follows.

Independent Auditor's Report on Compliance with a Contractual Agreement

We have audited, in accordance with generally accepted auditing standards, the balance sheet of Potter Company as of December 31, 2007, and the related statements of income, retained earnings, and cash flows for the year then ended, and have issued our report thereon dated February 16, 2008.

In connection with our audit, nothing came to our attention that caused us to believe that the Company failed to comply with the terms, covenants, provisions, or conditions of sections 12 to 17, inclusive, of the Indenture dated July 21, 2005, with Citizens Bank insofar as they relate to accounting matters. However, our audit was not directed primarily toward obtaining knowledge of such noncompliance.

This report is intended solely for the information and use of the boards of directors and managements of Potter Company and Citizens Bank and is not intended to be and should not be used by anyone other than the specified parties.

Source: SAS No. 62 and SAS No. 87.

Letters for Underwriters

Less than five months after AT&T announced their decision to split into three separate companies, securities in Lucent Technologies—comprised of Bell Laboratories and AT&T's telecommunications equipment segment—were sold on the New York Stock Exchange in the then largest initial public offering of securities in U.S. history, $3.1 billion. Consistent with the *Securities Act of 1933*, AT&T first filed a registration statement (Chapter 5) with the SEC before offering Lucent securities for sale to the public. As is typical, an investment bank and other financial institutions served as AT&T's underwriters by purchasing some of the securities for investment or resale and by selling the bulk of the securities to the public. (An underwriter is an intermediary between an offering entity and the investing public and, as a result, is a primary party to the registration process.)

The *Securities Act of 1933* holds an underwriter responsible for performing a "reasonable investigation" of all financial and accounting data before participating in the filing. To fulfill their responsibility to investigate financial and accounting matters they are not experts in, underwriters for the Lucent Technologies offering engaged PricewaterhouseCoopers,[11] AT&T's independent auditors, to prepare what is often called a **comfort letter** in accordance with *SAS No. 72*, "Letters for Underwriters and Certain Other Requesting Parties." In general, the letter reports:

- An *opinion* on whether the latest audited financial statements comply with the Act's accounting requirements, and
- *Negative assurance* on unaudited interim financial information for the period between the date of the latest audited financial statements and the date of the registration statement.

Under *SAS No. 86*, "Amendment to SAS No. 72," an accountant is generally precluded from commenting in a comfort letter about *nonfinancial* data reported in management's discussion and analysis that accompanies the registration statement. For example, the accountant generally would not comment about backlog information, number of employees, or square footage devoted to production facilities. Unaudited interim *financial* information is subjected to the inquiries and analytical procedures prescribed by *SAS No. 71*, "Interim Financial Information," introduced earlier in the chapter.

Comfort letters vary in content depending on an underwriter's needs. For example, an underwriter's needs will vary for foreign offerings, including Eurodollar and other off-shore offerings, or for acquisition transactions, including exchanges of stock rather than stock-for-cash offerings. The purpose of the accountant's comfort letter is to provide assurance to the underwriter, not to the

---

11 "C&L Reaps Profits from Largest-Ever IPO," *Public Accounting Report* (March 31, 1996), p. 3.

SEC. As a result, the letter is not filed with the SEC as part of the registration statement. Rather, the letter is held by the underwriter and produced only as a defense against claims by securities purchasers. Because of the variety and, in particular, the length of comfort letters prepared in practice, a sample letter is not illustrated here. However, an appendix to *SAS No. 72* includes seventeen letters covering a wide range of circumstances, among them Example A, a typical letter.

Financial Forecasts and Projections

Most all of the reports issued by independent accountants and auditors attest to financial information compiled from transactions and events that occurred in the past. Reports on forecasts and projections, in contrast, are a break from tradition: Attestations are made about transactions and events that not only haven't yet happened but that may never happen at all. This change in direction—attesting to the past versus the future—does not preclude an independent accountant from assisting an entity in preparing published forecasts and projections. But an accountant should never allow an entity to use his or her name in a manner that may lead users to believe the accountant vouches for the achievability of a financial forecast or projection. The Auditing Standards Board's *Statement on Standards for Attestation Engagements (SSAE) No. 10*, Chapter 3, entitled "Financial Forecasts and Projections," defines a *financial forecast* and a *financial projection*, and sets forth standards and guidance for engagements to compile, examine, or apply agreed-upon procedures to prospective financial statements.

Forecasts and Projections

Financial forecasts and projections are referred to as **prospective financial statements**. A **financial forecast** is a prospective financial statement that presents an entity's expected financial position, results of operations, and cash flows. Unlike audited, compiled, or reviewed financial statements, all of which are based on past transactions and events, forecasts are based on expected transactions and events, and reflect assumptions the reporting entity expects to exist and the course of action management expects to take. A financial forecast may be expressed in single monetary amounts or as a range of amounts.

In contrast, a **financial projection** is also a prospective financial statement that presents an entity's expected financial position, results of operations, and cash flows, but is based on one or more hypothetical assumptions. For example, a financial projection may be prepared to evaluate one or more hypothetical courses of action—that is, "What would happen if . . . ?" Like a forecast, a financial projection may contain a range of monetary amounts.

Compilation of Prospective Financial Statements

A compilation of prospective financial statements involves:

- Assembling prospective financial statements based on management's assumptions, and
- Performing compilation procedures, including comparing the prospective financial statements with the summaries of significant assumptions and accounting policies.

The summary of significant assumptions is essential to a reader's understanding of the prospective financial statements. An accountant should not compile prospective financial statements that omit the summary of assumptions or, in the case of a financial projection, that fail to disclose the hypothetical assumptions.

To illustrate a compilation report on prospective financial statements, assume that Curtis Corporation engages an independent accountant to prepare projected financial statements that will be used in negotiating a plant expansion loan from the Industrial National Bank. A compilation report follows.

Accountant's Compilation Report on a Financial Projection

We have compiled the accompanying projected balance sheet, statements of income, retained earnings, and cash flows of Curtis Corporation as of December 31, 2007, and for the year then ended, in accordance with standards established by the American Institute of Certified Public Accountants.

The accompanying projection and this report were prepared for the Industrial National Bank for the purpose of negotiating a plant expansion loan and should not be used for any other purpose.

A compilation is limited to presenting in the form of a projection information that is the representation of management and does not include evaluation of the support for the assumptions underlying the projection. We have not audited the projection and, accordingly, do not express an opinion or any other form of assurance on the accompanying statements or assumptions. Furthermore, even if the loan is granted and the physical plant is expanded, there will usually be differences between the projected and actual results, because events and circumstances frequently do not occur as expected, and those differences may be material. We have no responsibility to update this report for events and circumstances occurring after the date of this report.

Note in this case that there was only one hypothetical assumption: that the loan was granted.

Examination of Prospective Financial Statements

In an examination of prospective financial statements, an independent accountant expresses an opinion. But unlike an opinion on audited financial statements, which provides assurance about whether the statements conform with GAAP, an opinion on prospective financial statements provides assurance on whether (1) the prospective financial statements conform with AICPA guidelines, that is *SSAE No. 10*, "Attestation Standards: Revision and Recodification," and (2) the assumptions provide a reasonable basis for a forecast or projection. The following illustrates a standard report on the examination of a financial forecast.

**Independent Accountant's Report on
an Examination of a Financial Forecast**

We have examined the accompanying forecasted balance sheet, statements of income, retained earnings, and cash flows of McCabe Company as of December 31, 2007, and for the year then ended. These forecasted financial statements are the responsibility of the company's management. Our responsibility is to express an opinion on these forecasted financial statements based on our examination made in accordance with standards for an examination of a forecast established by the American Institute of Certified Public Accountants.

Our examination was conducted in accordance with attestation standards established by the American Institute of Certified Public Accountants and, accordingly, included examining, on a test basis, evidence supporting the accompanying forecasted balance sheet, statements of income, retained earnings, and cash flows and performing such other procedures as we considered necessary in the circumstances. We believe that our examination provides a reasonable basis for our opinion.

In our opinion, the accompanying forecasted balance sheet, statements of income, retained earnings, and cash flows of McCabe Company as of December 31, 2007, and for the year then ended are presented in conformity with guidelines for presentation of a forecast established by the American Institute of Certified Public Accountants, and the underlying assumptions provide a reasonable basis for management's forecast. However, there usually will be differences between the forecasted and actual results, because events and circumstances frequently do not occur as expected, and those differences may be material. We have no responsibility to update this report for events and circumstances occurring after the date of this report.

Source: Adapted from SSAE No. 10

Like the compilation report on a financial projection illustrated earlier, the above report alerts readers that assumptions may not mirror future events and circumstances, and that the accountant is under no obligation to update the report if future information casts doubt on earlier assumptions.

Applying Agreed-Upon Procedures to Prospective Financial Statements

Accountants are sometimes engaged to apply agreed-upon procedures to prospective financial statements for the express benefit of a specified third party, such as a commercial bank. However, these engagements may be accepted only if (1) the specified users have participated in establishing the nature and scope of the engagement and take responsibility for the procedures performed, (2) the report is distributed only to the specified users, and (3) the statements include a summary of significant assumptions. The agreed-upon procedures may be limited or extensive, but responsibility for their adequacy rests with the user.

A report on the results of applying agreed-upon procedures should:

- Indicate the prospective financial statements covered.
- Indicate that use of the report is limited to the specified user.
- Describe the procedures performed.
- Disclaim an opinion on the statements and assumptions if the procedures are less than those usually performed in an audit.
- State the accountant's findings.
- State that the prospective results may not be achieved.
- State that the accountant assumes no responsibility to update the report.

Personal Financial Statements

Much like businesses, individuals or families also may require audited financial statements, though for different reasons. For example, a political candidate may elect to disclose publicly his or her personal financial position, or an individual may need personal statements to acquire bank credit when organizing a business.

Interestingly, **personal financial statements** differ markedly from financial statements prepared in accordance with GAAP. For example, assets are reported at estimated current values in personal financial statements, thereby requiring that the accountant attest to current value, a more challenging task than attesting to historical cost.

The AICPA's *Statement of Position 82-1*, "Accounting and Financial Reporting for Personal Financial Statements," and *Personal Financial Statements Guide* provide guidance to auditors and accountants for audit and nonaudit engagements on personal financial statements. The *Guide* illustrates an unqualified report on the personal financial statements of a married couple.

Independent Auditor's Report
on Personal Financial Statements

We have audited the statement of financial condition of Mr. and Mrs. Robert V. Bracken as of December 31, 2007, and the related statement of changes in net worth for the year then ended. These statements are the responsibility of Mr. and Mrs. Bracken. Our responsibility is to express an opinion on these statements based on our audit.

In our opinion, the financial statements referred to above present fairly, in all material respects, the financial position of Mr. and Mrs. Robert V. Bracken as of December 31, 2007, and the changes in their net worth for the year then ended, in conformity with generally accepted accounting principles.

Reports on the Application of Accounting Principles

Occasionally, an accountant will report to a nonclient about the application of accounting principles. For example, entities sometimes engage an independent accountant (called the "reporting accountant") to report on the application of an accounting principle proposed by the entity's independent auditor (called the "continuing accountant")—that is, a second opinion. *SAS No. 50*, "Reports on the Application of Accounting Principles," amended by *SAS No. 97*, "Amendment to *SAS No. 50*," provides guidance when an auditor reports on the application of an accounting principle. A sample report follows. Note carefully from the language in the report that the accountant reports on an actual—a *specific*—transaction. *SAS No. 97* prohibits an accountant from reporting on a hypothetical transaction.

Independent Accountants' Report
on the Application of Accounting Principles

We have been engaged to report on the appropriate application of accounting principles generally accepted in the United States to the specific transaction described below. This report is being issued to Prospect Company for assistance in evaluating accounting principles for the described specific transaction. Our engagement has been conducted in accordance with standards established by the American Institute of Certified Public Accountants.

The facts, circumstances, and assumptions relevant to the specific transaction as provided to us by management of Prospect Company are as follows:

[Text describing facts, circumstances, and assumptions.]

[Text discussing accounting principles.]

The ultimate responsibility for the decision on the appropriate application of accounting principles generally accepted in the United States for an actual transaction rests with the preparers of financial statements, who should consult with their continuing accountants. Our judgment of the appropriate application of accounting principles generally accepted in the United States for the described specific transaction is based solely on the facts provided to us as described above; should these facts and circumstances differ, our conclusion may change.

Source: SAS No. 97.

Because the request for a second opinion may have been motivated by a disagreement between the client and the continuing accountant, the reporting accountant should consult with the continuing accountant to assure that all relevant facts are revealed. In short, if there are disagreements, the continuing accountant should be privy to both sides of the story.

SUMMARY

Although an emerging rather than a mature product line, assurance services are offered currently by several public accounting firms and are encouraged by the prominent work and recommendations of the AICPA Special Committee on Assurance Services (the Elliott Committee). Importantly, the potential for assurance services is far more vast than the electronic commerce and health care assurances illustrated in this chapter. As Jim Naus, former managing partner of Crowe Chizek has said, "The methods that accountants use to check data and information can be spread to almost any field and can provide valuable information for a wide range of clients."[12]

More mature, but also promising, attestation services have long been offered by the profession and guided by the Auditing Standards Board's attestation standards (Chapter 2). For example, attestation services are offered commonly for compilations and reviews of financial statements, interim financial information, comprehensive bases of accounting other than GAAP, agreed-upon procedures, compliance with contractual requirements, letters for underwriters, financial forecasts and projections, personal financial statements, and applications of accounting principles.

KEY TERMS

Comfort letter 775

Compilation engagement 763

Compilation of financial statements 764

Financial forecast 776

Financial projection 776

Interim financial statements 767

Personal financial statements 776

Prospective financial statements 776

Review engagement 763

Review of financial statements 765

---

12 L. Berton, "Accountants Expand Scope of Audit Work," *The Wall Street Journal* (June 17,1996), p. B8.

REFERENCES

Statements on Auditing Standards (SAS):

AICPA, *Codification of Auditing Standards*. New York: AICPA.

SAS No. 50, "Reports on the Application of Accounting Principles" (AU Sec. 625).

SAS No. 62, "Special Reports" (AU Sec. 623).

SAS No. 72, "Letters for Underwriters and Certain Other Requesting Parties" (AU Sec. 634).

SAS No. 75, "Engagements to Apply Agreed-Upon Procedures to Specified Elements, Accounts or Items of a Financial Statement" (AU Sec. 622).

SAS No. 76, "Amendments to *SAS No. 72*, Letters for Underwriters and Certain Other Requesting Parties" (AU Sec. 622).

SAS No. 86, "Amendments to SAS No. 72, Letters for Underwriters and Certain Other Requesting Parties" (AU Sec. 634).

SAS No. 87, "Restricting the Use of an Auditor's Report" (AU Sec. 532).

SAS No. 97, "Amendment to *SAS No. 50*, 'Reports on the Application of Accounting Principles'" (AU Sec. 625).

SAS No. 100, "Interim Financial Information" (AU Sec. 722).

Statements on Standards for Accounting and Review Services (SSARS):

AICPA, *Codification of Statements on Standards for Accounting and Review Services*. New York: AICPA.

SSARS No. 1, "Compilation and Review of Financial Statements."

SSARS No. 7, "Omnibus Statement on Standards for Accounting and Review Services—1992."

Statements on Standards for Attestation Engagements (SSAE):

SSAE No. 10, "Attestation Standards: Revision and Recodification."

Professional Report:

AICPA Special Committee on Assurance Services (The Elliott Committee), *Professional Growth Through New Assurance Services*. New York: AICPA, 1995.

Web Site:

AICPA, Assurance Services: **http://www.aicpa.org**.

Articles, Books:

Beets, S. D., and C. C. Souther, "Corporate Environmental Reports: The Need for Standards and an Environmental Assurance Service," *Accounting Horizons* (June 1999), pp. 129–145.

Boritz, J. E., and D. Cockburn, "1998 Audit Symposium Panel Discussion on Assurance Services," *Auditing: A Journal of Practice & Theory* (1998, Supplement), pp. 133–151.

Brackney, K. S., and G. L. Helms, "A Survey of Attestation Practices," *Auditing: A Journal of Practice & Theory* (Fall 1996), pp. 85–98.

Chan, S., M. Govindan, J. Y. Picard, G. S. Takach, and B. Wright, *EDI Control, Management, and Audit Issues*. New York: AICPA, 1995.

Cheney, G., "Regional Firms Hits National Market with New Assurance Services," *Accounting Today* (January 6–19, 1997).

Cheney, G., "Creating the Firms of the 21st Century," *Accounting Today* (December 16, 1996–January 5, 1997), pp. 1, 70.

Elliott, R. K., "Assurance Services and the Audit Heritage," *Auditing: A Journal of Practice & Theory* (1998, Supplement), pp. 1–7.

Elliott, R. K., "The Future of Assurance Services: Implications for Academia," *Accounting Horizons* (December 1995), pp. 118–127.

Elliott, R. K., "AICPA Assurance Services Committee: What is the Future of Auditing," *Journal of Corporate Accounting and Finance* (Winter 1994–95), pp. 87–97.

Elliott, R. K., "Confronting the Future: Choices for the Attest Function," *Accounting Horizons* (September 1994), pp. 106–124.

Elliott, R. K., "The Future of Audits," *Journal of Accountancy* (September 1994), pp. 74–82.

Elliott, R. K., "The Third Wave Breaks on the Shores of Accounting," *Accounting Horizons* (June 1992), pp. 62–85.

Elliott, R. K., and D. M. Pallais, "To Market, To Market We Go," *Journal of Accountancy* (September 1997), pp. 81–86.

Elliott, R. K., and D. M. Pallais, "Build on Your Firm's Strengths," *Journal of Accountancy* (August 1997), pp. 53–58.

Elliott, R. K., and D. M. Pallais, "First Know Your Market," *Journal of Accountancy* (July 1997), pp. 56–63.

Elliott, R. K., and D. M. Pallais, "Are You Ready for Assurance Services?" *Journal of Accountancy* (June 1997), pp. 47–51.

Elliott, R.K., "Assurance Services and the Audit Heritage," *Auditing: A Journal of Practice & Theory* (1998, Supplement), pp. 1–7.

Elliott, R. K., "Twenty-First Century Assurance," *Auditing: A Journal of Practice & Theory* (March 2002), pp. 139–146.

Korento, R. K., "In CPAs, We Trust," *Journal of Accountancy* (December 1997), pp. 62–64.

Koreto, R. J., "A WebTrust Experience," *Journal of Accountancy* (October 1998), pp. 99–102.

Mancino, J. M., and D. M. Guy, "Reviews of Financial Statements: SAS 71 vs. SSARS," *Journal of Accountancy* (March 1993), pp. 61–67.

Mancino, J. M., and C. E. Landes, "A New Look at the Attestation Standards," *Journal of Accountancy* (July 2001), pp. 41–45.

Melancon, B. C., "A Path for the Future," *Journal of Accountancy* (February 1998), pp. 82–86.

Pacini, C., and D. Sinason, "The Law and CPA WebTrust," *Journal of Accountancy* (February 1999), pp. 20–24.

Pacini, C., S. E. Ludwig, W. Hillison, D. Sinason, and L. Higgins, "SysTrust and Third-Party Risk," *Journal of Accountancy* (August 2000), pp. 73–78.

Ratcliffe, T. A., "OCBOA Financial Statements," *Journal of Accountancy* (October 2003), pp. 71–75.

Uzumeri, M. V., and R. H. Tabor, "Emerging Management Metastandards: Opportunities for Expanded Attest Services," *Accounting Horizons* (March 1997), pp. 54–66.

Williamson, A. L., "The Mirror Standards," *Journal of Accountancy* (December 1995), pp. 87–91.

Woloskey, H. W., "Choosing ElderCare Assurance Services," *The Practical Accountant* (January 1998), pp. 33–37.

QUESTIONS

1. Compare and contrast assurance and attestation services.
2. What are electronic commerce assurance services?
3. What are health care performance services?
4. What are information systems reliability services?
5. What are elder care services?
6. Explain the *WebTrust* transaction-integrity principle.
7. What are *SysTrust* services?
8. Discuss why entry into the assurance services market is important to public accounting firms.
9. Explain what is meant by a compilation and by a review of financial statements.
10. Explain the difference between an audit report and a review report.
11. Describe the purpose and give examples of analytical procedures performed in a review of financial statements.

12. In what situations might an independent accountant review interim financial information?

13. Why are costs, expenses, deferrals, and accruals often estimated to a greater extent in interim than in annual financial statements?

14. What is a "comprehensive basis of accounting other than GAAP"?

15. To what does an auditor's opinion relate when an entity's financial statements are prepared on a comprehensive basis of accounting other than GAAP?

16. Explain the purpose of letters for underwriters.

17. What does an accountant typically include in a letter for underwriters?

18. Explain the difference between a financial forecast and a financial projection.

19. What does a report on personal financial statements typically address?

20. Under what conditions might an independent accountant report on the application of accounting principles?

MULTIPLE CHOICE QUESTIONS

1. Assuring the relevance of a company's internal measures is a(n):
   a. Business performance service.
   b. Benchmarking service.
   c. Risk assessment service.
   d. Information systems service.

2. Maintaining controls to provide reasonable assurance that customers' transactions are completed as agreed is the intent of *WebTrust*:
   a. Business practices principle.
   b. Transaction integrity principle.
   c. Information protection principle.
   d. Internal control principle.

3. In a data integrity assurance service, an accountant assures that:
   a. Encryption technology is secure.
   b. Cash is not diverted.
   c. The parties to a transaction are authentic.
   d. Credit card information is protected.

4. Which of the following is not likely a core competency for assurance services?
   a. Business advisory skills.
   b. Model building and technology.
   c. Relationship management.
   d. Enterprise resource skills.

5. Which of the following would not be considered an attest engagement under *SSAE No. 10*, "Attestation Standards: Revision and Recodification"?
   a. A compilation of financial statements
   b. A letter for an underwriter
   c. A report on the application of an accounting principle
   d. A report on financial statements that are prepared on a comprehensive basis of accounting other than GAAP

6. In a review engagement, the independent accountant's procedures include:
   a. Examining bank reconciliations.
   b. Confirming accounts receivable with debtors.
   c. Reading the financial statements to consider whether they appear to conform with GAAP.
   d. Obtaining a letter of audit inquiry from all attorneys of record.

7. Which of the following is correct about the AICPA's attestation standards?

   a. The attestation standards supersede generally accepted auditing standards.
   b. The attestation standards supersede generally accepted auditing standards only for financial statement audits of publicly traded corporations.
   c. The attestation standards apply to all attest engagements.
   d. The attestation standards derive their authority from general acceptance among practitioners.

8. Which of the following procedures is not appropriate to a review of interim financial information?

   a. Confirm cash balances with all banks and depositories.
   b. Make inquiries concerning the accounting system and any significant changes in the internal control structure.
   c. Perform analytical procedures to identify and provide a basis for inquiry about relationships and individual items that appear unusual.
   d. Read the minutes of meetings of stockholders, boards of directors, and committees of the board.

9. When reporting on a separate interim period, an accountant's report would:

   a. State that a review was made in accordance with AICPA standards.
   b. Refer to generally accepted auditing standards.
   c. Refer to the consistent application of generally accepted accounting principles.
   d. Explain the accountant's responsibility for annual financial statements.

10. Which of the following is not a comprehensive basis of accounting other than GAAP?

    a. Cash receipts and disbursements
    b. Mark to market
    c. Price level adjusted financial statements
    d. A regulatory agency's requirements

11. In an attestation engagement, negative assurance means that the accountant:

    a. Found no exceptions.
    b. Is not aware of exceptions.
    c. Is not independent.
    d. Disclaims an opinion.

12. When engaged to express an opinion on one or more specified elements, accounts, or items of a financial statement, an auditor:

    a. May not describe auditing procedures applied.
    b. Should advise that professional standards preclude anything other than a piecemeal opinion.
    c. May assume that the first standard of reporting about generally accepted accounting principles does not apply.
    d. Should perform the engagement only if the specified elements, accounts, or items constitute a major portion of the financial statements.

13. *Statement on Auditing Standards No. 62*, "Special Reports," is explicit about what is meant by a comprehensive basis of accounting other than GAAP. Of the following, which is not a comprehensive basis of accounting according to *SAS No. 62*?

    a. Cash receipts and disbursements basis of accounting
    b. A basis of accounting used to comply with a regulatory agency's requirements
    c. Historical cost adjusted for the current value tangible assets
    d. A basis of accounting used to file income tax returns

14. Which of the following would not be appropriate to a report on an engagement to apply agreed-upon procedures to specified financial statement items?
    a. Indicate the intended distribution of the report.
    b. Provide an opinion on the specified elements, accounts, or item.
    c. Enumerate the procedures performed.
    d. State that the report relates only to the elements, accounts, or items specified.

15. In a comfort letter, an accountant:
    a. Includes an opinion on whether interim financial statements comply with federal requirements.
    b. Concludes on nonfinancial information.
    c. Provides assurance to the SEC that financial statements comply with GAAP.
    d. Complies with generally accepted auditing standards.

16. What is meant by a financial forecast under *Statement on Standards for Accountants' Services on Prospective Financial Information*, "Financial Forecasts and Projections"?
    a. A prospective financial statement that predicts an entity's expected financial position, results of operations, and cash flows
    b. A prospective financial statement that presents an entity's expected financial position, results of operations, and cash flows
    c. A prospective financial statement that presents an entity's expected financial position, results of operations, and cash flows based on one or more hypothetical assumptions
    d. A prospective financial statement that predicts an entity's expected financial position, results of operations, and cash flows based on one or more hypothetical assumptions

17. A compilation of prospective financial statements does not:
    a. Consider assumptions specified by management.
    b. Include inquiries of management.
    c. Opine on financial statements.
    d. Comply with AICPA standards.

18. Which of the following is not appropriate for the accountant's report on the results of applying agreed-upon procedures to prospective financial statements?
    a. State the accountant's opinion on the results of applying the agreed-upon procedures.
    b. Indicate the prospective financial statements reported on.
    c. Indicate that the use of the report is limited to the specified user.
    d. Indicate that the prospective results may not be achieved.

19. In an engagement to report on personal financial statements, the accountant:
    a. Compiles financial statements.
    b. Reviews financial statements.
    c. Reports on assets that are carried at estimated current values.
    d. Reports on assets that are carried at historical costs.

20. Under *Statement on Auditing Standards No. 50*, "Reports on the Application of Accounting Principles," an independent accountant may give a second opinion on matters relating to a financial statement audit performed by another independent accountant. Which of the following is not appropriate to the accountant's report?
    a. Indicate that the ultimate responsibility for deciding on the appropriate accounting principles rests with the continuing accountant.
    b. State the facts, circumstances, and assumptions relevant to the transaction.
    c. State that the engagement has been conducted in accordance with standards established by the AICPA.
    d. State that the accountant's judgment of the appropriate application of accounting principles is based solely on the facts provided by the client.

PROBLEMS AND DISCUSSION CASES

18-1 *Proposing on an Assurance Service Engagement*

VAN Technologies, a value-added network service provider, links subscribing electronic data integration (EDI) networks, receives network transmissions from trading partners, translates transmissions into an ANSI X12 format, and functions as an electronic post office by transmitting and acknowledging orders electronically. Owing to widespread reports of data security problems in EDI networks, several subscribers have approached management, questioning VAN's controls over hacker attacks, transmission failures, identification authentication, and infiltration of confidential data files. In response, management asks an engagement partner in Settles & Weick LLP to propose on offering assurances that would quiet subscribers' fears.

Required:

1. Is the engagement an assurance service engagement or an attestation service engagement? Explain.
2. Discuss the barriers the engagement partner should consider before proposing on the engagement.

18-2 *Compilation of Financial Statements*

A compilation of financial statements involves presenting management's assertions in the form of financial statements without expressing any degree of assurance. Nevertheless, even though no assurance is expressed, an independent accountant must comply with the provisions of *SSARS No. 1*, "Compilation and Review of Financial Statements."

Required:

1. Identify the type of knowledge and understanding that an independent accountant should obtain in a compilation engagement.
2. How does an accountant inform users of the nature and limitations of a compilation?
3. What actions should an independent accountant take when he or she becomes aware of a material departure from GAAP in financial statements compiled?

18-3 *Review of Financial Statements*

Christopher Rossi, CPA, has been engaged by the Barrington Company, a nonpublicly held manufacturer of children's toys, to review Barrington's December 31, 2007, financial statements. Rossi accepts the engagement, and performs inquiry and analytical procedures sufficient to provide a reasonable basis for expressing negative assurance that no material modifications are necessary to conform the statements with generally accepted accounting principles. While making inquiries of Barrington's chief financial officer, Rossi discovers that land is carried at appraised value rather than historical cost and that the company refuses to adjust the December 31, 2007, statements. All inquiries and analytical procedures are completed on January 28, 2008.

Required: Prepare the review report Rossi would present to Barrington's board of directors, assuming the effect on financial statements of carrying land at appraised value has not been determined by management.

18-4 *Interim Financial Statements*

Chad Summe, who has audited the financial statements of the Ft. Mitchell Group, Inc., a publicly held company, for the year ended December 31, 2007, has been asked to perform a limited review of the unaudited interim financial statements of the Group for the quarter ending March 31, 2008. The engagement letter states that a limited review does not provide a basis for expressing an opinion.

Required:

1. Explain why Summe's limited review will not provide a basis for expressing an opinion.
2. What are the review procedures that Summe should perform, and what is the purpose of each procedure?

(AICPA Adapted)

18-5 *Minimizing Misunderstandings About Unaudited Financial Statements*

The limitations on a practitioner's professional responsibilities when associated with unaudited financial statements are often misunderstood, although the risk of misunderstanding can be reduced substantially by carefully following professional pronouncements and by taking other appropriate measures.

Required: The following describes situations a practitioner may encounter in his or her association with unaudited financial statements. Briefly discuss the extent of the practitioner's responsibilities and, if appropriate, the actions he or she should take to minimize any misunderstandings.

1. A group of investors who own a farm managed by an independent agent engage an independent accountant to prepare quarterly unaudited financial statements. The accountant prepared the financial statements from information supplied by the independent agent. Subsequently, the investors find that the statements were inaccurate because the agent embezzled funds. The investors refuse to pay the accountant's fee and blame the accountant for allowing the embezzlement to go undetected, contending that representations from the independent agent should not have been relied on.

2. In comparing the trial balance with the general ledger, an accountant finds an account labeled "Audit Fees" in which the client has accumulated the accountant's quarterly billings for accounting services, including the preparation of quarterly unaudited financial statements.

3. To determine appropriate account classification, an accountant reviewed a number of the client's invoices. The accountant noted in the audit documentation that some invoices were missing, but felt they did not affect the unaudited financial statements and thus did nothing further. The client subsequently discovered that invoices were missing and contended that the accountant should not have ignored the missing invoices when preparing the financial statements and had a responsibility to at least inform the client that they were missing.

4. An accountant is engaged to review the financial statements prepared by a client's controller. During the review, the accountant learns of several items that by generally accepted accounting principles would require adjustment to the statements and notes. The controller agrees to make the recommended adjustments but refuses to add the notes because the statements are unaudited.　　　　　(AICPA Adapted)

18-6 *Comprehensive Bases of Accounting Other Than GAAP*

Rose & Co., LLP, has completed the audit of the financial statements of Bale & Booster, a partnership, for the year ended December 31, 2007. The financial statements were prepared on the income tax (cash) basis and include footnotes indicating that the partnership was involved in continuing litigation for alleged infringement of a competitor's patent. Damages, if any, resulting from the litigation could not be estimated as of the last day of field work. Prior-year financial statements were not presented.

Required: Draft an audit report.

18-7 *An Opinion Based on Agreed-Upon Procedures*

Management often calls for an independent auditor's assistance. For example, an audit client's management might request that their auditor apply agreed-upon procedures to some but not all of the financial statement accounts of a company that management considers a serious candidate for acquisition. Assume that Uclean Corporation, an audit client, has requested that your firm perform agreed-upon procedures at Ajax Corporation. At the completion of the engagement, an audit assistant prepared the following report for your review:

We have applied certain agreed-upon procedures, as discussed below, to accounting records of Ajax Corporation, as of December 31, 2007, solely to assist Uclean Corporation in connection with the proposed acquisition of Ajax Corporation.

We have examined the cash in bank and accounts receivable of Ajax Corporation as of December 31, 2007, in accordance with generally accepted auditing standards and, accordingly, included such tests of the accounting records and such other auditing procedures as we considered necessary in the circumstances.

In our opinion, the cash and receivables referred to above are presented fairly, in all material respects, as of December 31, 2007, in conformity with generally accepted accounting principles. We therefore recommend that Uclean Corporation acquire Ajax Corporation pursuant to the proposed agreement.

Required: Comment on the proposed report, describing those assertions that are:
1. Incorrect or should otherwise be deleted.
2. Missing and should be inserted. (AICPA Adapted)

18-8 *Describing Findings in an Agreed-Upon Procedures Engagement*

Agreed-upon procedures engagements on financial statement elements, accounts, or items of a financial statement and on nonfinancial statement assertions require that the independent accountant describe both the procedures and the findings in his or her report. Following are two agreed-upon procedures—one for cash and another for invoices—and two alternative means of reporting findings for each procedure.

Agreed-Upon Procedure: Cash
Trace all outstanding checks appearing on a bank reconciliation as of a certain date to checks cleared in the bank statement on the subsequent month.

Description of Findings A
All outstanding checks appearing on the bank reconciliation were cleared in the subsequent month's bank statement.

Description of Findings B
Nothing came to my attention as a result of applying the procedure.

Agreed-Upon Procedure: Invoices
Compare the amounts of the invoices included in the over ninety days column shown in an identified schedule of aged accounts receivable of a specific customer as of a certain date to the amount and invoice date shown on the outstanding invoice, and determine whether the amounts agree and whether the invoice dates precede the date indicated on the schedule by more than ninety days.

Description of Findings A
All outstanding invoice amounts agreed with the amounts shown on the schedule in the over ninety days column, and the dates shown on such invoices preceded the date indicated on the schedule by more than ninety days.

Description of Findings B
The outstanding invoice amounts agreed within an approximation of the amounts shown on the schedule in the over ninety days column, and nothing came to our attention that the dates shown on the invoices preceded the date indicated on the schedule by more than ninety days.

Required: For each agreed-upon procedure, explain which description of findings, *A* or *B*, is appropriate, and why.

18-9 *Financial Statement versus Nonfinancial Statement Assertions in Agreed-Upon Procedures Engagements*

Understanding whether agreed-upon procedures relate to a specified element, account, or item of a financial statement or to a nonfinancial statement assertion is important because the professional pronouncements for each differs: *SAS No. 75*, "Engagements to Apply Agreed-Upon Procedures to Specified Elements, Accounts or Items of a Financial Statement"; and *SSAE No. 4*, "Agreed-Upon Procedures Engagements." Following are a series of items for which an independent accountant might apply agreed-upon procedures.

a. The cash accounts included in an entity's general ledger maintained for the purpose of preparing financial statements represented as being in accordance with generally accepted accounting principles.
b. A schedule of accounts receivable on an entity that reflects the accounts receivable presented in conformity with generally accepted accounting principles.
c. An entity maintained an effective internal control over financial reporting based on established criteria.
d. The accounts included in the caption property and equipment identified in a statement of assets, liabilities, and capital presented on an income tax basis.
e. An entity complied with requirements of specified laws, regulations, rules, contracts, and grants.
f. Investment securities were traded on approved exchanges.
g. The gross income component of a statement of operations presented in accordance with the rules of a regulatory agency.
h. Statistical production data complied with policy.

Required: Indicate whether each item is a specified element, account, or item of a financial statement or a nonfinancial statement assertion.

18-10 *Personal Financial Statements*

Roger Francoeur, a candidate for town council, is campaigning on a platform of open government and fiscal responsibility. During his campaign, Francoeur requests that you prepare personal financial statements, fully disclosing his financial position for the twelve-month period ended June 30, 2007. Unfamiliar with the nature of personal financial statements, Francoeur asks that you explain the major similarities and differences between the financial statements and audit reports that are issued for personal and corporate financial statements.

Required: Describe the major similarities and differences alluded to by Francoeur, indicating the rationale underlying each difference. Ignore differences related to the titles of financial statements.

18-11 *Inappropriate Behavior in a Nonattest Engagement*

Brown received a telephone call from Calhoun, the sole owner and manager of a small company, asking Brown to prepare financial statements for the company. Calhoun told Brown that the statements were needed in two weeks but was vague when Brown asked about the intended use of the statements. Brown was convinced that Calhoun thought Brown's work would constitute an audit. To avoid confusion, Brown decided not to explain to Calhoun that the engagement would be to prepare the financial statements only. Brown understood that a substantial fee would be paid if the work was completed in two weeks, accepted the engagement, and started work at once.

Brown discovered an accrued expense account labeled "Professional Fees" and learned that the balance in the account represented an accrual for the cost of Brown's services. Brown suggested to Calhoun's bookkeeper that the account name be changed to "Fees for Limited Audit Engagement." Brown also reviewed several invoices to determine whether accounts were being classified properly. Some invoices were missing. Brown listed in the audit documentation the missing invoice numbers with a note indicating that they should be followed up during the next engagement. Brown also discovered that fixed assets were carried at estimated current replacement costs. Based on available records, Brown prepared a balance sheet, income statement, and statement of shareholder's equity. In addition, Brown drafted the notes but decided that any mention of the replacement costs would only mislead the readers. Brown suggested to Calhoun that readers of the financial statements would be better informed if they received a separate letter from Calhoun explaining the meaning and effect of the estimated replacement costs of the fixed assets. Brown mailed the financial statements with the following note from Calhoun included on each page:

The accompanying financial statements are submitted to you without complete audit verification.

Required: Identify the inappropriate actions of Brown and indicate what Brown should have done to avoid each inappropriate action.

(AICPA Adapted)

Internet problems and discussion cases are available at http://ricchiute.swlearning.com

RESEARCH PROJECTS

1. Assurance Services and Retail Electronic Commerce

Woolford Marketing, an Internet marketing organization, estimates that by the year 2005, no less than one billion subscribers will access Internet browser services to purchase goods and services electronically. Like today, most subscribers are expected to use a single, primary transaction media: credit cards. Given that most people willingly pay annual credit card fees averaging, say, $50, there's reason to believe the same people would be willing to pay, say, $5 annually to purchase assurances against invasion of privacy and harassment from unwanted solicitors, translating to a $5.0 billion assurance service market (1 billion subscribers × $5) for data-security assurances alone. For perspective, consider that currently Fortune 500 companies pay less to public accounting firms for financial statement audits. There is every reason to believe that information technology could create considerable demand for data-security assurances, but no reason to doubt that demand could create ferocious competition from assurance service providers far removed from the public accounting profession.

Required: Using a Web portal, such as Netscape's *Navigator* or Microsoft's *Explorer*, link to a Web site that offers retail, business, entertainment, or education purchases and draft a report that describes the Web site's offerings and identifies assurances you think consumers (or the Web site manager) would be willing to purchase (or supply). For example, what assurances would *you* want about credit card number security and freedom from unwanted solicitation?

2. The Motivation for Professional Standards

This chapter referenced a number of *Statements on Auditing Standards (SASs)*, *Statements on Standards for Accounting and Review Services (SSARSs)*, and *Statements on Standards for Attestation Engagements (SSAEs)*, since all of the attestation services introduced in the chapter are guided by professional pronouncements. Like many professional standards in public accounting, the issues that drove some of the pronouncements addressed in this chapter were somewhat controversial—in fact, they likely would not have reached the Auditing Standards Board's technical agenda otherwise. For example, *SSARS No. 1*, "Compilation and Review of Financial Statements," resulted largely because the price of an audit, the only attest service independent accountants were empowered to perform on financial statements, raised the cost of capital beyond the means of many small owner-managed companies. The review services introduced in *SSARS No. 1* offered lending institutions the negative assurance they needed, and provided a cost-effective attestation alternative for players in the commercial-capital market.

Required: Select any *SAS*, *SSARS*, or *SSAE* referenced at the end of any chapter in this text, and draft a report that identifies the stakeholders and the issue(s) that likely drove the pronouncement. Sources include *In Our Opinion*, a publication of the Auditing Standards Board; the Board's letter to the profession included in exposure drafts for *SASs*, *SSARSs*, or *SSAEs*; the financial press (for example, *The Wall Street Journal*, *BusinessWeek*); the professional literature (for example, *Journal of Accountancy*, *The CPA Journal*, *Accounting Today*); and magazines published by state societies of CPAs, such as *The Michigan CPA*.

3. The Work of Robert K. Elliott

Robert K. Elliott, KPMG partner and chair of the AICPA's Special Committee on Assurance Services (the Elliott Committee), has been quite influential in awakening the profession to the obsolescence of financial statement audits and to the need for innovative value-added assurance services. In the following series of insightful and accessible articles, he has highlighted the role of information technology in the creation of post-industrial wealth, and framed the scope of potential assurance services to replace financial statement audits as a dominant revenue source for major public accounting firms.

- Elliott, R. K., "The Third Wave Breaks on the Shores of Accounting," *Accounting Horizons* (June 1992), pp. 62–85.
- _____, "The Future of Audits," *Journal of Accountancy* (September 1994), pp. 74–82.
  - _____, "Confronting the Future: Choices for the Attest Function," *Accounting Horizons* (September 1994), pp. 106–124.
  - _____, "AICPA Assurance Services Committee: What is the Future of Auditing," *Journal of Corporate Accounting and Finance* (Winter 1994–95), pp. 87–97.
  - _____, "The Future of Assurance Services: Implications for Academia," *Accounting Horizons* (December 1995), pp. 118–127.
  - _____, "Assurance Services and the Audit Heritage," *Auditing: A Journal of Practice & Theory* (1998, Supplement), pp. 1–7.

The work of the Elliott Committee has been influential in paving the way for new assurance services.

Required:
1. From the articles listed, explain:
   a. The role of information technology on the reporting entity and on financial report users.
   b. Why financial statement audits may become obsolete and the demand for new assurances services will increase.
   c. The likely content of assurance standards.
2. Identify and summarize articles from the business and accounting press (for example, *The Wall Street Journal*, *Accounting Today*) or from the accounting literature (for example, *Journal of Accountancy*, *The CPA Journal*) that contradict Elliott. For example: R. Telberg, "CPAs Cautioned on Assurance Services," *Accounting Today* (January 22–February 11, 1996), pp. 1, 34.

Interactive quizzes are available as a student learning resource at http://ricchiute.swlearning.com

Glossary

A

Accounting and Review Services Committee (ARSC) the senior technical committee of the AICPA responsible for promulgating pronouncements on accounting and review services.

accounting estimates financial statement elements, items, or accounts that have been approximated by management.

accounting system methods and records established by management to record and report transactions and events and to maintain accountability for assets and liabilities.

adjusting entries (audit adjustments) journal entries proposed by the independent auditor that conform management's financial statements to generally accepted accounting principles.

adverse opinion a communication within an attestation report or an audit report indicating, respectively, that management's assertion is *not presented fairly* in conformity with established criteria, or that management's financial statements do *not present fairly* the financial position, results of operations, and cash flows in conformity with generally accepted accounting principles.

agreed-upon procedures engagement an attest service in which the independent accountant is engaged to report on an item using procedures the contracting parties agree to.

AICPA Code of Professional Conduct the principles, rules of conduct, interpretations, and rulings governing an AICPA member's ethical responsibilities to the public, to clients, and to colleagues in the profession.

allowance for sampling risk the auditor's allowance for the risk that a sample may contain disproportionately more or less monetary misstatement than exists within the population.

American Institute of Certified Public Accountants (AICPA) the national, voluntary membership organization of certified public accountants.

applications controls controls implemented by management over a computer system's applications.

analytical procedures evaluations of financial information made by a study of plausible relationships among financial and nonfinancial data.

application software interacts with operating software to perform specific tasks, like word processing or airline reservations.

area franchise fee the up-front, lump sum fee a franchisee pays a franchisor for the exclusive right to market the franchisor's product or service.

assurance three-party contracts that improve the quality of information.

attestation a communicated statement of opinion, based upon convincing evidence, by an independent, competent, authoritative person concerning the degree of correspondence in all material respects of accounting information communicated by an entity with established criteria.

attestation (attest) engagement a professional services engagement in which a practitioner issues a written communication that expresses a conclusion about subject matter that is the responsibility of another party.

attestation report a letter communicating the assertion attested to, management's and the attestor's responsibilities, what an attestation engagement entails, and the attestor's opinion.

attestation risk the probability that an attestor may unknowingly fail to appropriately modify a conclusion on an assertion that is materially misstated.

attestation (attest) standards eleven general, field work, and reporting standards for attestation engagements.

attribute a characteristic of a control procedure.

attribute estimation sampling a statistical sampling plan for tests of controls that reaches conclusions about a rate of deviation from a prescribed control procedure.

attributes sampling plan an audit sampling plan designed to test the rate of deviation from a prescribed control procedure.

audit committee a committee of an entity's board of directors that serves as an intermediary between the independent auditor and the full board.

audit documentation the principal record of auditing procedures applied, evidence obtained, and conclusions reached.

audit adjustments see adjusting entries.

audit evidence the underlying accounting data and corroborating information used by auditors to test management's financial statement assertions.

audit hooks a computer-assisted audit technique in which an auditor reserves exits in a client's application software to insert at will commands for audit processing.

auditing a systematic process of objectively obtaining and evaluating evidence regarding assertions about economic actions and events to ascertain the degree of correspondence between those assertions and established criteria and to communicate the results to interested users.

Auditing Standards auditing pronouncements issued by the Public Company Accounting Oversight Board. Under the authority of Section 103 of the *Sarbanes-Oxley Act of 2002*, PCAOB Rule 3100, "Compliance with Auditing and Related Professional Practice Standards," requires that registered public accounting firms comply with professional practice standards the PCAOB establishes.

Auditing Standards Board (ASB) the senior technical committee of the AICPA responsible since 1978 to promulgate auditing standards and procedures for nonpublic entities.

Auditing Standards Executive Committee (AudSEC) the senior technical committee of the AICPA responsible to promulgate auditing standards and procedures during the years 1972–1978.

audit population all the items constituting an account balance or class of transactions.

audit procedures detailed methods or techniques used by an independent auditor, such as observation, documentation, confirmation, mechanical tests of accounting data, comparisons, and inquiries, to discharge his or her responsibilities under generally accepted auditing standards.

audit program a detailed list of audit procedures to be performed for a particular aspect of a financial statement audit.

audit report a letter communicating what was audited, management's and the auditor's responsibilities, what an audit entails, and the auditor's opinion.

audit risk the probability that an auditor may unknowingly fail to appropriately modify an opinion on financial statements that are materially misstated.

audit services assurance services that improve the quality of financial statements.

audit trail records and documents that support executed transactions.

available for sale securities debt and equity securities not classified as held-to-maturity securities or trading securities.

balanced scorecard Measures of an entity's financial, customer, internal business, and internal learning activities.

base case system evaluation (BCSE) A computer-assisted audit technique in which an auditor prepares test data to test every possible condition a client's software will confront.

benchmarking the process of measuring products, services, and practices against competitors and other leading entities.

big bath refers to the practice of a company timing asset write-downs to occur in an abnormally *un*profitable year, signaling to the financial markets that bad times have long since passed.

bill of lading a Uniform Commercial Code shipping document.

bond certificate a document (debt security) representing a stated amount of debt owed by an entity.

breach of contract violation of the terms of a contract.

business risk the probability that a practitioner may incur damages despite issuing an appropriate report.

Certified Public Accountants (CPAs) individuals who have passed the Uniform CPA Examination and have satisfied all the education and experience requirements of their respective state boards of accountancy.

client strategy template a model to identify a client's growth strategy, financial goal, operating priorities, potential adverse influences, markets, competitors, business units, strategic alliances/joint ventures, products, and customers.

collusion a fraud perpetrated by two or more employees, each of whose job responsibilities is necessary to complete the fraud. (Collusion is controlled by adequate segregation of duties.)

comfort letter in an initial public offering of securities, a written communication from the independent accountant to an underwriter about procedures the accountant performed on the unaudited financial statements and schedules accompanying a client's registration statement.

commercial paper a general category of commercial loan instruments, due and payable in accordance with terms described on the instrument.

Committee on Auditing Procedure (CAP) the senior technical committee of the AICPA responsible for promulgating auditing standards and procedures during the years 1939–1972.

common law law evolving from precedent-setting court cases; based on the doctrine of stare decisis: principles of law that are established in precedent-setting cases are handed down to succeeding cases within the jurisdiction.

compilation of financial statements (compilation engagement) a nonattest service in which the accountant prepares financial statements from a client's unaudited and unreviewed accounts and issues a report that provides no assurance, using language that states the accountant "has not audited or reviewed the financial statements and, accordingly, does not express an opinion or any form of assurance."

completeness an assertion within financial statements that all transactions and accounts that should be presented in the financial statements are included.

compliance audit an audit designed to assess whether a not-for-profit entity's financial statements are presented fairly in accordance with generally accepted accounting principles and whether the entity has complied with applicable laws and regulations. Compliance audits are performed either by independent auditors or by governmental auditors.

consulting services two-party contracts that recommend uses for information.

contingencies an existing condition, situation, or set of circumstances involving uncertainty as to possible gain or loss that will ultimately be resolved when one or more future events occur or fail to occur (for example, pending litigation for a patent infringement suit).

contingent monetary effects in responding to detected illegal acts, payments such as fines, penalties, and damages that, in some circumstances, such as violations of the *Foreign Corrupt Practices Act*, may be quite substantial.

control activities (procedures) policies and procedures established by management in addition to the control environment and the accounting system to provide reasonable assurance that specific objectives are achieved.

control environment management's and the board of directors' attitude toward, awareness of, and corrective actions concerning internal control.

control risk the risk that error could occur and not be prevented or detected by the internal controls.

conversion cycle the policies and procedures encompassing the production of finished products for sale.

covered person in the SEC's auditor independence rules, a member of a publicly traded company's audit engagement team, a partner or manager who supplies the company at least 10 hours of nonaudit services, and any partner employed in the lead engagement partner's office.

credit memoranda documents indicating that a customer's account will be credited for goods returned by the customer.

customer order a written (or unwritten, in the case of a telephone order) request from a customer to purchase goods.

customer remittance advice a document that accompanies a sales invoice and is intended to be returned with a customer's cash remittance (payment) for handling and recording.

cutoff bank statement a seven- to ten-day bank statement for a period usually beginning the first day after the balance sheet date (for example, January 1). A cutoff bank statement is used to verify deposits-in-transit and outstanding checks appearing on the year-end bank reconciliation.

database management (DBM) system in computer systems, an integrated collection of stored data that can be ac-

cessed for processing wholly or in part, by authorized access codes.

depreciation schedule a worksheet computing and summarizing depreciation.

detection risk the risk that error could occur and not be detected by the auditor's procedures.

deviation in a control procedure, the absence of an attribute.

difference estimation a classical variables sampling plan designed to estimate the amount of monetary misstatement in a population—called the difference estimate—from the difference between recorded and audited amounts observed in a sample.

disclaimer of opinion a one-paragraph letter communicating that an attestor or an auditor, respectively, does not express an opinion on management's assertion or on management's financial statements.

discovery sampling a sampling plan designed to calculate the sample size required to achieve a desired probability of observing at least one deviation in a sample if the population deviation rate equals or exceeds a specified critical rate of deviation.

documentation see "audit documentation."

dual-purpose tests auditing procedures designed to provide evidence about both control risk and likely monetary error.

earnings manipulation management's altering of reported earnings (either upward to inflate earnings or downward to deflate earnings); typically occurs when the accounting for a transaction or event allows management some discretion over the timing or the amount of earnings to be reported.

economy and efficiency audit a governmental audit under the GAO's *Government Auditing Standards*; an economy and efficiency audit includes determining (1) whether the entity is acquiring, protecting, and using its resources economically and efficiently; (2) the causes of inefficiencies or uneconomical practices; and (3) whether the entity has complied with laws and regulations concerning matters of economy and efficiency.

embedded audit modules a computer-assisted audit technique in which an auditor places generalized audit software within a client's application software for the purpose of selecting data for subsequent testing, such as the selection and printing of accounts receivable confirmations.

employee earnings record a record maintained for each employee that provides a cumulative, year-to-date summary of total earnings, withholdings, and deductions.

end-user computing computer information systems in which management empowers end users to develop task-specific application software.

engagement letter a written agreement between an independent auditor and an audit client that describes the terms of the audit engagement and the role of the auditor.

environmental liability an actual or contingent liability arising from the violation by an entity of environmental laws and regulations, such as the Congressional Comprehensive Environmental Response, Compensation, and Liability Act of 1980 ("CERCLA" or, more popularly, the "Superfund" legislation); the Superfund Amendment and Reauthorization Act of 1986; and the Clean Air Act of 1990.

errors unintentional mistakes or omissions of amounts or of disclosures in financial statements.

ethics rulings issued by the AICPA's professional ethics division and intended to summarize the applicability of Rules of Conduct and Interpretations to specific situations.

evidential matter the accounting data that underlie financial statements (for example, journals, ledgers) and the corroborating information that underlies accounting data (for example, contracts, canceled checks).

existence or occurrence an assertion within financial statements that all recorded assets, liabilities, and equities exist at a given date, and all recorded transactions occurred during a given period.

expenditure/disbursement cycle the policies and procedures encompassing the acquisition and purchase of goods and services.

financial audits in governmental auditing, determining whether financial reports and related items, such as elements, accounts, or funds are fairly presented, whether financial information is presented in accordance with established or stated criteria, and whether the entity has adhered to specific financial compliance requirements.

financial forecast a prospective financial statement that presents an entity's expected financial position, results of operations, and cash flows.

financial projection a prospective financial statement that presents an entity's expected financial position, results of operations, and cash flows, and is based on one or more assumptions.

financial statement assertions explicit and implicit representations embodied within financial statements and related to existence or occurrence, completeness, rights and obligations, valuation or allocation, and presentation and disclosure.

financial statement audit an audit of an entity's four basic financial statements—balance sheet (statement of financial position), income statement, statement of cash flows, and (if applicable) statement of retained earnings—the purpose of which is to form an opinion on whether the statements present fairly in all material respects the entity's financial position, results of operations, and cash flows in conformity with generally accepted accounting principles.

financing cycle the policies and procedures encompassing the acquisition of capital funds.

flowchart interrelated symbols that diagram the flow of transactions and events through an accounting system.

Foreign Corrupt Practices Act (FCPA) federal statutory law preventing payments or gifts to foreign governments or officials and requiring compliance with record keeping and internal-control provisions.

foreseeable third parties under common law, third parties who have a reasonable need to rely on financial statements but, because they're the furthest removed from a contractual agreement for audit services, generally enjoy the least favorable position in auditor liability cases.

foreseen third parties under common law, third parties not specifically identified by name to the auditor as beneficiaries of an entity's audited financial statements, but whose general identity and purpose for relying on the audited statements are known by the auditor.

fraud an intentional misrepresentation of a material fact that includes *fraudulent financial reporting* (an intentional misstatement or omission of amounts or disclosures in financial statements) and *misappropriation of assets* (theft of an entity's assets).

general controls controls implemented by management over a computer system's organization and operation, software development, hardware, accessibility, and data.

generally accepted accounting principles (GAAP) the consensus at any point in time about which resources and obligations should be recorded as assets and liabilities, which changes in assets and liabilities should be recorded, when changes should be recorded, how assets and liabilities and changes in them should be measured, and what should be disclosed in financial statements.

generally accepted auditing standards (GAAS) ten authoritative statements that represent the guidelines and measures of quality for the financial statement audit of a nonpublic company.

general standards the first three of the ten generally accepted auditing standards, they require adequate technical training and proficiency, an independence in mental attitude, and due professional care.

general use reports auditor reports not restricted for use to specified parties, such as reports on audited financial statements.

governmental auditors auditors employed by governmental entities. Employers include state legislative audit departments and the U.S. General Accounting Office (GAO).

government auditing standards standards for the audit of governmental entities, contained in GAO, *Governmental Auditing Standards* (sometimes called "generally accepted governmental auditing standards" [GAGAS]).

gross negligence a lack of even minimum care in performing professional services; for example, a reckless departure from generally accepted auditing standards.

held-to-maturity securities debt an entity has the positive intent and ability to hold to maturity.

illegal acts violations of laws or governmental regulations.

impaired assets assets an entity continues to use but that have suffered a decline in value as a result, for example, of corporate restructuring or of slumping demand for uncompetitive products.

impairment loss in accounting for the discretionary write-down of impaired assets, the amount by which the asset's carrying amount exceeds the asset's fair value.

income smoothing refers to a company's maintaining a steady rate of earnings growth over a series of years, thereby providing no reason for the financial markets to impute unexpected risk in the company or in expected stock prices.

independent auditors certified public accountants within public accounting firms who perform independent financial statement audits.

information technology automated means to originate, process, store, and communicate information, such as recording devices, communication systems, computer systems, and other electronic devices.

inherent risk the susceptibility of an account balance to error, assuming there are no related control procedures.

integrated test data a computer-assisted audit technique in which fictitious test data are integrated with actual client data without the computer department's knowledge, thus allowing the auditor to compare the client's output with the results expected by the auditor.

interim attestation standards adopted temporarily by the Public Company Accounting Oversight Board and consisting of the Auditing Standards Board's *Statements on Standards for Attestation Engagements.*

interim financial statements financial statements reflecting financial position, results of operations, and cash flows for a period less than a fiscal year (for example, quarterly financial statements).

interim professional auditing standards adopted temporarily by the Public Company Accounting Oversight Board and consisting of the Auditing Standards Board's Statements on Auditing Standards.

interim professional practice standards adopted temporarily by the Public Company Accounting Oversight Board and consisting of *Interim Professional Auditing Standards* and *Interim Attestation Standards.*

internal auditors employees of an entity whose job is to conduct operational audits among other audit activities for the entity. Internal audit reports are not made available to the public.

internal control a process, effected by an entity's board of directors, management, and other personnel, designed to provide reasonable assurance that the entity achieves objectives about the effectiveness and efficiency of operations, the reliability of financial reporting, and compliance with applicable laws and regulations.

internal control deficiency controls that, either in design or operation, do not allow management or employees to prevent or detect misstatements in the normal course of business (see significant deficiency and material weakness in internal control).

internal control over financial reporting a process designed by, or under the supervision of, the principal executive and principal financial officers, and effected by an entity's board of directors, management, and other personnel, to provide reasonable assurance regarding the reliability of financial reporting and the preparation of financial statements for external purposes in accordance with GAAP.

Interpretations of the Rules of Conduct issued by the AICPA's professional ethics division and intended to interpret the scope and applicability of the Rules of Conduct.

introductory paragraph the first paragraph of an attestation or audit report, intended to communicate the assertion attested to or the financial statements audited, that the assertion or statements are management's responsibility, and that the attestor/auditor is responsible only for the opinion communicated, not for the assertion or financial statements.

joint and several liability in legal liability, a plaintiff in an action against an auditor can potentially recover all damages from the auditor alone, even though the auditor's report may have contributed only partially to the plaintiff's loss.

kiting an intentional fraud that conceals cash shortages by (1) transferring funds from one bank to another, and (2) recording the receipt on or before the balance sheet date and the disbursement after the balance sheet date.

lapping an intentional fraud that conceals cash shortages resulting from delays in recording cash collections.

legal (lawyer's) letter a written representation to the independent auditor from a client's lawyer about the entity's pending and threatened litigation, claims, and assessments.

limited liability partnership (LLP) or **limited liability company (LLC)** a form of organization that provides a CPA firm with the benefits of taxation as a partnership, thereby avoiding double taxation (that is, corporate taxes to the professional corporation and individual taxes to the shareholders), and limited liability, thereby providing relief from vicarious liability.

local area network (LAN) linked microcomputers that access data files and software from a central file server and that direct print jobs from a central print server.

loss contingency an existing condition, situation, or set of circumstances involving uncertainty as to possible gain or loss to an enterprise that will ultimately be resolved when one or more future events occur or fail to occur.

management (client) representation letter written representations from management to the independent auditor about assertions made by management (for example, management has made available to the auditor all financial records) and about management's responsibility for the financial statements.

materiality the magnitude of an omission or misstatement that would have changed or influenced the judgment of a reasonable person relying on an assertion.

materials requisition a formal request for materials by an operating department.

material weakness in internal control a significant deficiency that, alone or in combination with other deficiencies, is *more than remotely likely* to cause *a material misstatement* that will not be prevented or detected (see internal control deficiency and significant deficiency in internal control).

narrative memorandum a written description of a particular phase or phases of an accounting system.

negative confirmation a written confirmation requesting that a customer respond directly to the auditor only if the account receivable balance is incorrect according to the customer's accounts payable records.

nonsampling risk all aspects of audit risk not attributable to sampling.

nonstatistical sampling plan an audit sampling plan that does not apply the laws of probability.

operating software a group of computer programs that monitor and control all input, processing, and output in a computer system.

operational audit an audit performed by an entity's internal auditors (or by independent auditors) to assess the efficiency and effectiveness of management's operating procedures.

opinion paragraph a paragraph within an attestation or audit report intended to communicate the attestor's or the auditor's opinion on whether management's assertion is reliable or on whether management's financial statements present fairly in all material respects the financial position, results of operations, and cash flows in conformity with generally accepted accounting principles.

ordinary negligence a lack of reasonable care in performing professional services; for example, violating one of the generally accepted auditing standards.

overhead application report a summary of overhead applied to work-in-process inventory.

parallel simulation a computer-assisted audit technique in which an auditor prepares software to process client-prepared input on the client's or the auditor's computer.

payroll register a record prepared each pay period, listing all employees and indicating the gross pay, withholdings, deductions, and net pay for each employee during the period.

peer (quality) review an independent outside review of a public accounting firm's quality control procedures performed by CPAs not otherwise employed by the reviewed firm.

perpetual inventory record a cumulative record of quantities on hand for a particular item or class of inventory.

personal financial statements financial statements that present the financial position of an individual or family.

personnel records documents maintained for each employee by the Personnel Department that provide a permanent record of all essential information pertaining to the employee, including date of employment, job classification, salary or hourly pay rate, promotions, payroll deductions, terminations, etc.

population all of the items within a class of transactions or account balance.

positive confirmation a written confirmation requesting that a customer respond directly to the auditor about whether the account receivable balance is correct or incorrect according to the customer's accounts payable records.

post-retirement benefits other than pensions an entity's obligations to retirees for health care, life insurance, tuition assistance, and housing subsidies, among other things.

potentially responsible party in environmental law, a party, usually an alleged industrial polluter, identified by the U.S. Environmental Protection Agency (EPA) as potentially responsible to cleanup hazardous waste.

predecessor auditor in a change of auditors, the independent auditor being replaced.

presentation and disclosure an assertion within financial statements stating that all components of the statements are properly classified, described, and disclosed.

primary beneficiaries under common law, third parties specifically identified by name to the auditor as beneficiaries of an entity's audited financial statements.

principal auditor one among two or more auditors in a multisite (that is, more than one location) or multi-entity (for example, parent and subsidiaries) audit that is responsible for reporting on financial statements. The decision as to which auditor is the principal auditor is based on the revenues and assets audited by each auditor, the extent of each auditor's knowledge of the overall financial statements, and the significance of the sites or entities audited by each auditor in relation to the combined entity's activities taken as a whole.

principles of the AICPA's Code of Professional Conduct positively worded goals in the form of declarative statements about an AICPA member's responsibilities as professionals; obligation to the public interest; sense of integrity, objectivity, and independence; and observance of professional and technical standards.

privity a relationship between parties to a contract; for example, the parties named to a professional services contract are "in privity."

probability-proportional-to-size sampling a sampling plan based in attributes sampling theory.

program audit a governmental audit under the GAO's Government Auditing Standards that includes determining (1) the extent to which the desired results or benefits established by the legislature or other authorizing body are being achieved; (2) the effectiveness of organizations, programs, activities, or functions; and (3) whether the entity has complied with laws and regulations applicable to the program.

proportionate liability in legal liability, a plaintiff in an action against an auditor can potentially recover only the portion of awarded damages that are attributed to the auditor's proportionate share of responsibility.

prospective financial statements financial statements that present an entity's expected—or expected under one or more assumptions—financial position, results of operations, and cash flows.

Public Company Accounting Oversight Board (PCAOB) established by the Sarbanes-Oxley Act "to oversee the audit of public companies that are subject to the securities laws, and related matters, in order to protect the interests of investors and further the public interest in the preparation of informative, accurate, and independent audit reports for companies the securities of which are sold to, and held by and for, public investors."

purchase order a written request to a vendor to purchase goods.

purchase requisition a written request to supervisory personnel from an employee or department requesting that goods be purchased.

qualified opinion a communication within an attestation report of an audit report indicating that *except for the effects of a matter*, respectively, management's assertion is presented fairly in all material respects in conformity with established criteria, or management's financial statements present fairly in all material respects the financial position, results of operations, and cash flows in conformity with generally accepted accounting principles.

quality control internal policies and procedures designed to assure consistent performance and achievement within an individual public accounting firm.

questionnaire in the independent auditor's consideration of internal control, a series of questions designed to detect deficiencies in an entity's control procedures.

Racketeer Influenced Corrupt Organizations (RICO) Act passed as part of the *Organized Crime Control Act of 1970*, this federal statutory law prevents the movement of organized crime into legitimate business.

ratio estimation a classical variables sampling plan designed to estimate the amount of monetary misstatement in a population—called the ratio estimate—from the ratio between recorded and audited amounts observed in the sample.

rebuttable presumption in audit documentation, absent documentation that audit work was performed, there is a presumption that the work was not performed, although an auditor could rebut the presumption with persuasive evidence.

receiving report a document containing information about goods received.

reclassification entries journal entries made within the independent auditor's audit documentation to reclassify a client's account classifications for financial statement reporting purposes.

registration statement a statement filed with the SEC, usually on Form S-1, to offer securities for sale to the public under the Securities Act of 1933.

related-party transaction a transaction that, because it is between an entity and another party related to the entity (for example, a principal owner, a director, a manager, or his/her immediate family), increases substantially the risk that the transaction is not at arm's length.

remittance advice see customer remittance advice.

restricted use reports auditor reports intended only for specified parties, such as reports communicating reportable conditions and material weaknesses in internal control.

reviewability standard audit documentation should be sufficient to enable an experienced auditor to understand *who* performed *what* work *when*, and *why* the work led to the significant judgments and conclusions documented.

revenue/receipt cycle the policies and procedures encompassing the sale of goods or services to customers and the collection of cash.

review of financial statements (review engagement) an attest service in which the independent accountant performs analytical procedures, makes inquiries of client personnel, and issues a report that provides limited (sometimes called negative) assurance, using language that states the accountant is "not aware of any material modifications that should be made to the financial statements in order for them to be in conformity with GAAP."

rights and obligations an assertion within financial statements that all assets are the rights of the entity and liabilities are the obligations of the entity at a given date.

risk the probability that management's assertions may contain material omissions or misstatements.

risk of assessing control risk too high the risk that a sample deviation rate supports assessing control risk at the maximum when, unknown to the auditor, the true deviation rate in the population supports assessing control risk below the maximum.

risk of assessing control risk too low the risk that a sample deviation rate supports assessing control risk below the maximum when, unknown to the auditor, the true deviation rate in the population supports assessing control risk at the maximum.

risk of incorrect acceptance the risk that a sample supports the conclusion that a recorded account balance is not materially misstated when, unknown to the auditor, the account is materially misstated.

risk of incorrect rejection the risk that a sample supports the conclusion that a recorded account balance is materially misstated when, unknown to the auditor, the account is not materially misstated.

Rules of Conduct eleven rules of the Code of Professional Conduct that are enforceable against AICPA members for all professional services, including financial statement auditing. The Rules are about independence, integrity and objectivity, general standards, compliance with standards, accounting principles, confidential client information, contingent fees, acts discreditable to the profession, advertising, and the form and name of an accounting practice.

sales invoice a document containing information about goods sold and representing formal notice to a customer about the amount and terms of payment.

sales order a document describing goods ordered by a customer, including all relevant information about price, quantity, and payment terms.

sample deviation rate the auditor's estimate of the true but unknown population deviation rate.

sampling applying procedures to less than 100 percent of the items that constitute an audit population.

sampling plan the procedures a practitioner uses to accomplish an audit sampling application.

sampling risk the risk that the conclusions drawn from testing a sample might be different if the entire population were tested—that is, a sample might not be representative in the sense that the sample may contain disproportionately more or fewer control deviations or monetary differences than exist in the population.

sampling unit any of the individual items constituting a population.

scope paragraph a paragraph within an audit report (usually the second) intended (1) to communicate that the audit was conducted in accordance with generally accepted auditing standards and (2) what an audit entails.

search for unrecorded liabilities a substantive audit test designed to determine whether an audit client's liabilities are understated.

Securities Act of 1933 federal statutory law regulating the initial public offering and sale of securities.

Securities and Exchange Commission (SEC) an agency of the U.S. government created by Congress in 1934 to regulate the registration and exchange of securities under the *Securities Act of 1933* and the *Securities Exchange Act of 1934*.

Securities Exchange Act of 1934 federal statutory law regulating the trading of previously issued securities.

segregation of duties the separation of employee responsibilities to prevent any one employee, acting alone, from committing and concealing frauds.

sequential (stop or go) sampling a statistical sampling plan for tests of controls in which the sample is selected in steps, with each step conditional on the results of the previous step.

shipping document a document containing information about goods shipped and representing a contract between the seller and carrier (for example, a trucking company).

significant deficiency in internal control a deficiency that, alone or in combination with other deficiencies, adversely affects the ability to initiate, record, process, or report reliably in accordance with GAAP and, more to the point, is *more than remotely likely* to cause a *more than inconsequential misstatement* that will not be prevented or detected (see internal control deficiency and material weakness in internal control).

Single Audit Act enacted by Congress in 1984, the Act was intended to improve the financial management of state and local governments receiving federal funds, establish uniform audit requirements for federal grant recipients, promote efficient and effective use of audit resources, and ensure that federal departments and agencies rely on one audit only: the single audit.

standard audit report a letter communicating what was audited, management's and the auditor's responsibilities, what an audit entails, and an unqualified opinion.

standard deviation a measure of the variation or dispersion among the items in a population.

standards of field work the fourth, fifth, and sixth of the ten generally accepted auditing standards, they require adequate planning and supervision, consideration of an entity's internal controls, and that the auditor gathers sufficient competent evidential matter.

standards of reporting the last four of the ten generally accepted auditing standards, they require that an entity's financial statements conform to generally accepted accounting principles, consistent application of accounting principles, informative disclosures, and that the auditor express an opinion on the financial statements taken as a whole.

Statements on Auditing Procedures (SAPs) auditing pronouncements issued by the Committee on Auditing Procedure from 1939–1972; fifty-four SAPs were issued and some remain effective today, codified within the AICPA's Codification of Statements on Auditing Standards.

Statements on Auditing Standards (SASs) auditing pronouncements issued from 1972–1978 by the Auditing Standards Executive Committee, and, since 1978, by the Auditing Standards Board; the statements interpret generally accepted auditing standards.

Statements on Standards for Accounting and Review Services (SSARSs) accounting and review services pronouncements issued by the Accounting and Review Services Committee.

Statements on Standards for Attestation Engagements (SSAEs) attestation engagement standards issued by the Auditing Standards Board.

statistical sampling plan an audit sampling plan that applies the laws of probability to select a sample and to evaluate the results of testing the sample.

statutory law law in written statutes enacted by Congress and by elected state legislatures.

stock certificate a document (equity security) representing ownership of a stated number of shares of capital stock.

subsequent events events (or transactions) occurring during the subsequent period (defined next) that lend hindsight to amounts and information disclosed in financial statements as of the balance sheet date.

subsequent period in subsequent events, the period after the balance sheet date and on or before the last day of field work.

substantive tests tests of details and analytical procedures performed to detect material misstatements in an account balance, transaction class, or financial statement disclosure.

successor auditor in a change of auditors, the newly appointed independent auditor.

systems control audit review files (SCARFs) logs that collect transaction information for review subsequently by the auditor.

telecommunications the transmission of alphanumeric, voice, video, facsimile and other data by wire, fiber optics, microwave, laser, or other means of transmission.

test data a computer-assisted audit technique in which the auditor processes data planted with errors that test the ability of a client's software to detect them.

tests of controls tests directed toward the design or operation of an internal control policy or procedure to assess its effectiveness in preventing or detecting material misstatements in a financial statement assertion.

tests of details substantive tests intended to detect material misstatements in the financial statements.

time record a record of hours worked by an employee during a particular pay period.

tolerable error the maximum monetary error that may exist in an account balance without causing the financial statements to be misstated materially.

tolerable rate of deviation the maximum population rate of deviation from a prescribed control procedure that an auditor will tolerate without modifying the assessed level of control risk.

tort a wrongful act, other than breach of contract, that results in injury to another person.

trading securities debt and equity securities held for sale in the near term.

transaction cycle a vehicle through which similar repetitive transactions are processed by an entity's accounting system; examples include the revenue/receipt cycle, the expenditure/disbursement cycle, the financing cycle, and the conversion cycle.

transaction tagging a computer-assisted audit technique in which a transaction record is "tagged" and then "traced" through critical control points in an information system.

treasury bill a debt instrument issued by the U.S. Treasury Department.

type I subsequent events subsequent events that reveal or confirm conditions existing at or before the balance sheet date and that require adjustment to the financial statements.

type II subsequent events subsequent events that reveal conditions arising after the balance sheet date and that require disclosure in, but not adjustment to, the financial statements.

unasserted claims claims for which a plaintiff may have a legal right but has not yet begun proceedings.

unqualified opinion a communication within an attestation or audit report indicating, respectively, that management's assertion is presented fairly in all material respects in conformity with established criteria, or that management's financial statements are presented fairly in all material respects the financial position, results of operations, and cash flows in conformity with generally accepted accounting principles.

valuation or allocation an assertion within financial statements that all assets, liabilities, equities, revenues, and expenses have been included in the statements at appropriate amounts.

variables sampling plan an audit sampling plan designed to test whether a recorded account balance is misstated materially.

vendor's invoice a document containing information about goods purchased, representing formal notice to a purchaser about the terms and due date of payment.

voucher package a set of documents (usually the purchase requisition, purchase order, receiving report, and invoice) relating to a purchase transaction.

Index

D

E

N